London
2012

CW01649791

IEZE
ART
FAIR

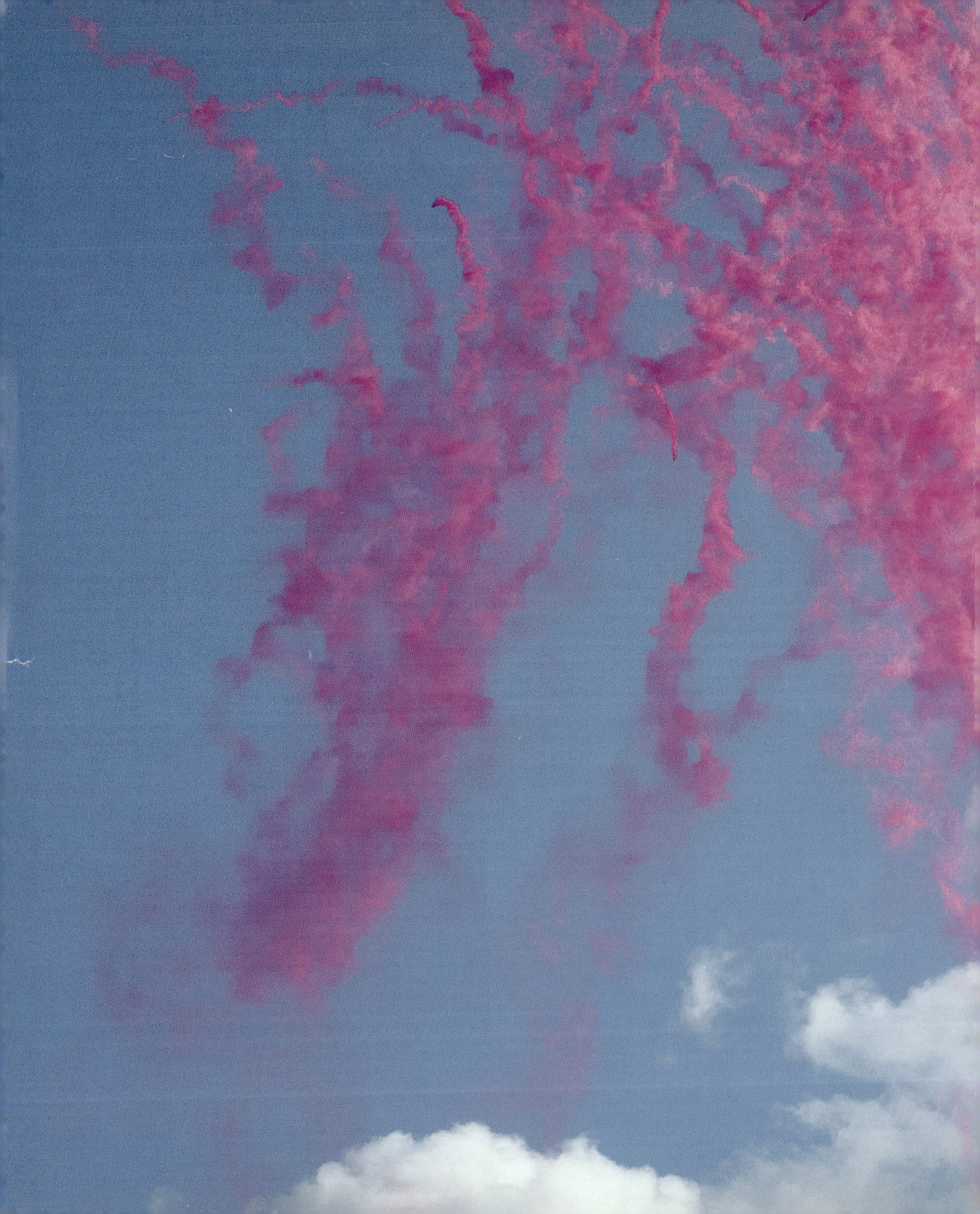

London
2012

# FRIEZE ART FAIR

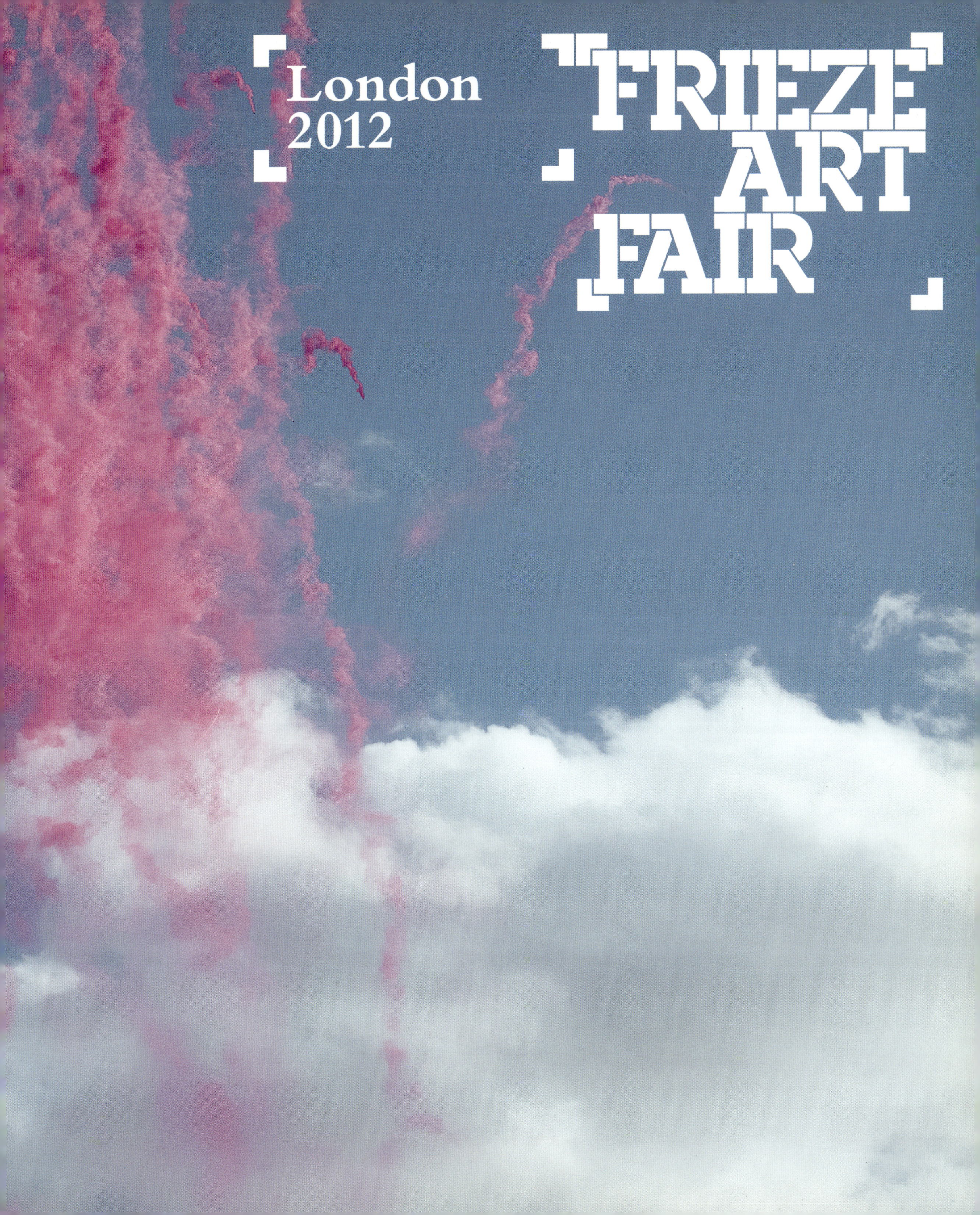

Frieze Art Fair wishes to acknowledge the generous support of the following companies and organizations:

**Main Sponsor**
**Deutsche Bank**

**Media Partners**

FT
FINANCIAL TIMES

**Sponsors and partners**

COS

CHAMPAGNE POMMERY REIMS-FRANCE

BMW

HYATT REGENCY LONDON THE CHURCHILL

Simmons & Simmons

ArtFund

THE ROYAL PARKS

# Contents

# Participating Galleries

303 Gallery
Galería Juana de Aizpuru
Galería Helga de Alvear
Andersen's Contemporary
The Approach
Laura Bartlett Gallery
Galerie Catherine Bastide
Galerie Guido W. Baudach
Marianne Boesky Gallery
Tanya Bonakdar Gallery
Bortolami
BQ
The Breeder
Broadway 1602
Gavin Brown's enterprise
Buchholz
Cabinet
Campoli Presti
Canada
Galerie Gisela Capitain
Sadie Coles HQ
Contemporary Fine Arts
Pilar Corrias Gallery
Corvi-Mora
Galerie Chantal Crousel
Thomas Dane Gallery
Massimo De Carlo
Elizabeth Dee
Allied Editions
Galerie Eigen + Art
galerie frank elbaz
Konrad Fischer Galerie
Foksal Gallery Foundation
Galeria Fortes Vilaça
Marc Foxx
Carl Freedman Gallery
Stephen Friedman Gallery
Frith Street Gallery
Gagosian Gallery
Annet Gelink Gallery
A Gentil Carioca
Gerhardsen Gerner
Greene Naftali
greengrassi
Galerie Karin Guenther
Jack Hanley Gallery
Hauser & Wirth
Herald St
Hotel
Ingleby Gallery
International Art Objects Galleries
Taka Ishii Gallery
Alison Jacques Gallery
Galerie Martin Janda
Johnen Galerie
Annely Juda Fine Art
Casey Kaplan
Georg Kargl Fine Arts
Galleri Magnus Karlsson
Paul Kasmin Gallery
Kerlin Gallery
Anton Kern Gallery
Galerie Peter Kilchmann
Tina Kim Gallery
David Kordansky Gallery
Tomio Koyama Gallery
Andrew Kreps Gallery
Galerie Krinzinger
Kukje Gallery
kurimanzutto
Yvon Lambert
Lehmann Maupin Gallery
Lisson Gallery
Long March Space
Kate MacGarry
Mai 36 Galerie
Giò Marconi
Matthew Marks Gallery
Mary Mary
Galerie Meyer Kainer
Meyer Riegger
Victoria Miro
Stuart Shave/Modern Art
The Modern Institute
Murray Guy
Galleria Franco Noero
Galleria Lorcan O'Neill
Pace
Maureen Paley
Galerie Perrotin
Galerie Francesca Pia

Galerija Gregor Podnar
Galerie Eva Presenhuber
Project 88
Rampa
Galleria Raucci/Santamaria
Almine Rech Gallery
Regina Gallery
Anthony Reynolds Gallery
Galerie Thaddaeus Ropac
Andrea Rosen Gallery
Salon 94
Aurel Scheibler
Esther Schipper
Galerie Rüdiger Schöttle
Micky Schubert
Sfeir-Semler
Sies + Höke
Galeria Filomena Soares
Sommer Contemporary Art
Reena Spaulings Fine Art
Sprüth Magers Berlin London
Standard (Oslo)
Stevenson
Galeria Luisa Strina
Galerie Micheline Szwajcer
T293
Timothy Taylor Gallery
Team Gallery
The Third Line
Vermelho
Vilma Gold
Vitamin Creative Space
Waddington Custot Galleries
Wallspace
Galerie Barbara Weiss
Fons Welters
Michael Werner
White Cube
Wien Lukatsch
Max Wigram Gallery
Wilkinson
Alex Zachary Peter Currie
Zeno X Gallery
David Zwirner

## Focus

Algus Greenspon
Altman Siegel
Ancient & Modern
Jessica Bradley
Casas Riegner
Chatterjee & Lal
Chert
dépendance
Elastic Gallery
Fonti
Hollybush Gardens
Karma International
Kimmerich
Andreiana Mihail Gallery
MOT International
Office Baroque Gallery
One And J. Gallery
Galeria Plan B
RaebervonStenglin
Raster

## Frame

47 Canal
Arcade
The Box
Bureau
Carlos/Ishikawa
La Central
Galerie Crèvecoeur
Experimenter
Galerie Cinzia Friedlaender
François Ghebaly Gallery
Kisterem
Ignacio Liprandi Arte Contemporáneo
Maisterravalbuena
Mendes Wood
Galerie Mor Charpentier
mother's tankstation
Take Ninagawa
NON
Ramiken Crucible
Société
SVIT

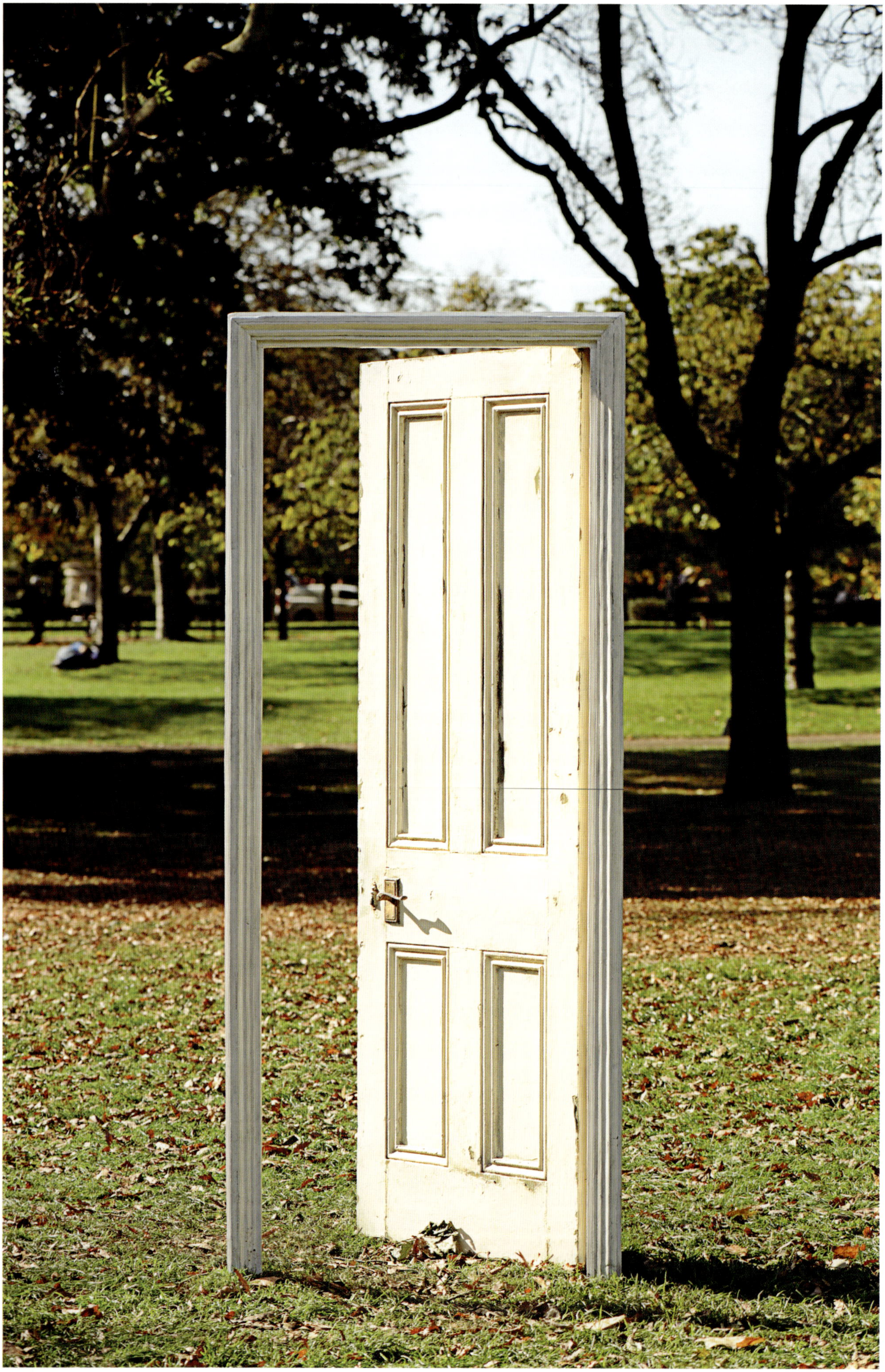

Gavin Turk
*Ajar*
2011
Painted bronze
220 × 91 × 15 cm
Installation view at
The Sculpture Park
Frieze Art Fair 2011
Shown by Galerie
Krinzinger and Aurel
Scheibler

# Foreword

We are delighted to welcome you to Frieze London. This edition is the tenth, and includes exhibitors from 34 countries, making it the most international edition of the fair to date.

To coincide with this year's fair we are launching Frieze Masters, a sister fair situated a short walk away in Regent's Park. Frieze Masters exhibits art ranging from late-20th-century works to Old Masters and ancient art. Our aim is both to show historical art from a contemporary perspective, and to locate contemporary art within a historical lineage. Together the two fairs enable visitors to experience the broadest array of art from across the world.

This year also marks the tenth anniversary of the Outset/Frieze Art Fair Fund to Benefit the Tate Collection, which since its inception has raised over £1 million to buy 86 works from the fair for the national collection.

Berlin-based artist Cécile B. Evans is the recipient of the fair's Emdash Award 2012. The award is presented to an emerging artist who lives outside of the UK, and its beneficiary is asked to produce a site-specific project for Frieze London. We are grateful to the Emdash Foundation for sponsoring both the award and Frieze Projects, the fair's acclaimed programme of specially commissioned artist projects. This is curated by Sarah McCrory, and participants include Thomas Bayrle, Aslı Çavuşoğlu, *DIS* magazine, Grizedale Arts & Yangjiang Group and Joanna Rajkowska.

McCrory has also commissioned artists Bertrand Dezoteux, Patricia Esquivias, Jimmy Merris, John Smith and Wu Tsang & Nana Oforiatta-Ayim to produce new works for Frieze Film. These are screened in the fair's auditorium and on Channel 4 during the week of Frieze London. The editors of *frieze* curate Frieze Talks, and this year's programme includes lectures, discussions and interviews with figures such as artist Tino Sehgal, filmmaker John Waters, and novelist and critic Lynne Tillman. The selector of this year's sculpture park is Clare Lilley, Director of Programme at Yorkshire Sculpture Park.

We are very grateful for the continued support of Deutsche Bank, the main sponsor of Frieze London for nine consecutive years and the main sponsor of Frieze New York and Frieze Masters in 2012. We are also pleased to continue our relationship with our media partner, the *Financial Times*.

We do hope you enjoy both art fairs in London.

Amanda Sharp and Matthew Slotover
Directors, Frieze Art Fair

# Sponsor's Foreword

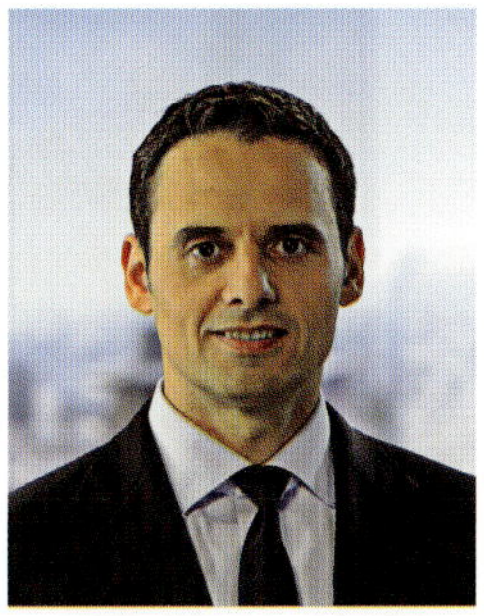

At Deutsche Bank we believe that creativity is fundamental to culture, business and society at large. We understand the power of new ideas in shaping the future, and it is an honour for the Bank to sponsor Frieze London for the ninth consecutive year.

Deutsche shares a joint commitment with the organisers to find new ways to engage with the art of our time and foster a more globally inclusive art world. This year we extended our relationship with Frieze across the globe by sponsoring the successful debut of Frieze New York, which took place in May.

Launched in London this October and also sponsored by the Bank is Frieze Masters, an exciting new fair that breaks down barriers with the past and demonstrates how old and new works presented together can expand our horizons for art for the future.

Since the 1970s, Deutsche Bank's art collection has given a platform to living artists across 928 of its offices worldwide. In tribute to the art world's great talent, last year we renamed 60 floors in our Frankfurt headquarters after internationally acclaimed artists represented in our collection.

Deutsche Bank's commitment to contemporary art is about encouraging, engaging and inspiring. We are involved in many projects that engage with the local communities where we work and nurture talent through our programmes such as the Deutsche Bank Awards for Creative Enterprises and Artist of the Year. Over the years, Deutsche has supported the careers of many artists, including Thomas Bayrle and Zheng Guogu of the Yangjiang Group, who are both part of the Frieze Projects programme this year.

We welcome you to Frieze London and hope you enjoy discovering new perspectives during your visit.

Michele Faissola

Global Head of Asset
& Wealth Management
Deutsche Bank AG

**Main Sponsor**
**Deutsche Bank**

# Outset/Frieze Art Fair Fund to Benefit the Tate Collection

We are very proud to announce the tenth anniversary of the successful collaboration between Outset, Frieze Art Fair and Tate.

Outset Contemporary Art Fund was founded in 2003 as a philanthropic organization dedicated to supporting new art. The annual fund at Frieze London was launched at the first edition of the fair in 2003 to enable Tate to acquire important works for the national collection.

Over the past ten years the fund has made an impressive contribution to the Tate collection. Over £1 million has been spent and 86 works by 56 artists have been collected, including major pieces by significant international practitioners including Olafur Eliasson, Andrea Fraser, Thomas Hirschhorn, Roman Ondák and Melanie Smith.

For the tenth anniversary of the fair and the fund, the selection panel will include Franklin Sirmans (Chief Curator of Contemporary Art, Los Angeles County Museum of Art) and Mami Kataoka (Chief Curator, Mori Art Museum, Tokyo), as well as Ann Gallagher (Head of Collections, British Art, Tate), Frances Morris (Head of Collections, International Art, Tate), Tanya Barson (Curator, International Art, Tate) and Clarrie Wallis (Curator, Contemporary British Art, Tate). The fund is organized and financed by Outset and enjoys the continuing support of Le Méridien Hotels & Resorts. We are very grateful to all the participants for their generosity and vision.

Sir Nicholas Serota, Director, Tate
Amanda Sharp and Matthew Slotover, Directors, Frieze Art Fair
Candida Gertler, Director, Outset Contemporary Art Fund

1
Artur Zmijewski
*Democracies* (2009)
20-channel video
2 hrs. 26 min.
Shown by Galerie Peter Kilchmann in 2009

2
Andreas Slominski
*Moulin Rouge* (1998/2002)
Wood, metal and tar
377 × 162 × 163 cm
Shown by Galerie Neu in 2007

3
David Shrigley
*Untitled (Elephant chooses to stand on your car)* (2004)
Ink and poster pen on paper
56 × 42 cm
Shown by Stephen Friedman Gallery in 2006
Courtesy of Tate

4
Daria Martin
*Closeup Gallery* (2003)
16mm film, 10 min.
Shown by Hotel in 2005
Courtesy of Maureen Paley

5
Hurvin Anderson
*Jersey* (2008)
Oil on canvas
250 × 208 cm
Shown by Thomas Dane Gallery in 2008
Courtesy of Tate

6
Olafur Eliasson
*Yellow versus purple* (2003)
Mixed media
75 × 75 × 1 cm
Shown by Tanya Bonakdar Gallery in 2003
Courtesy of Tate

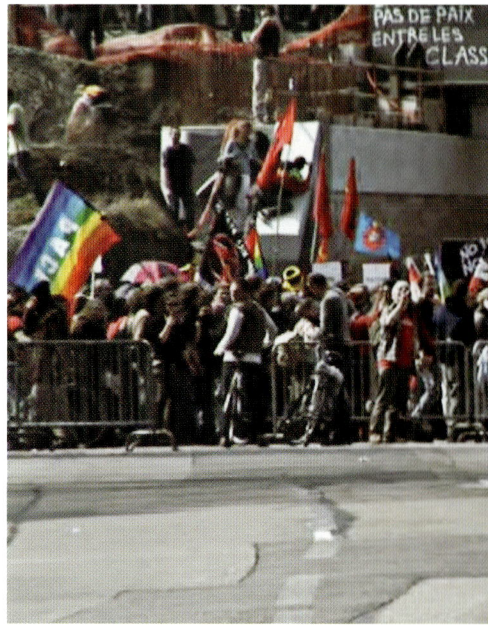


1

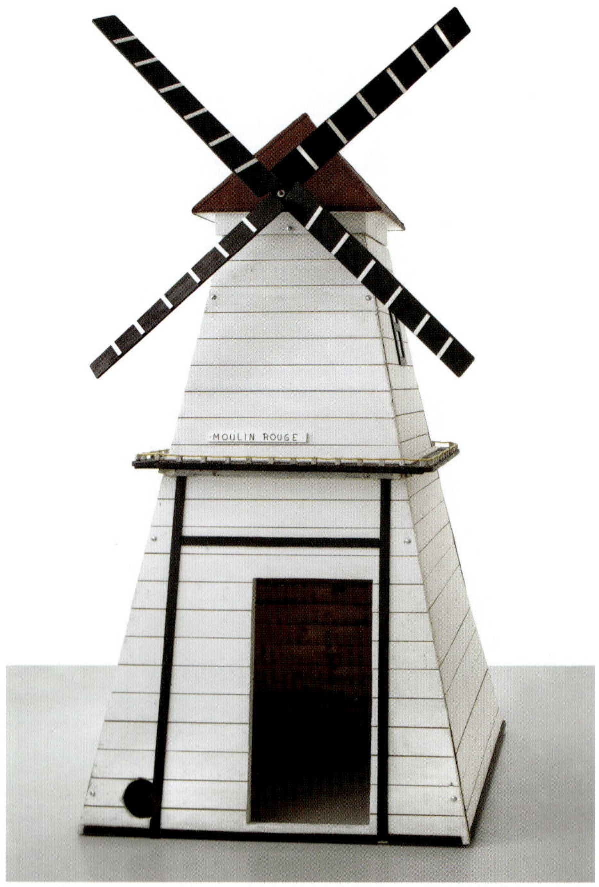


2

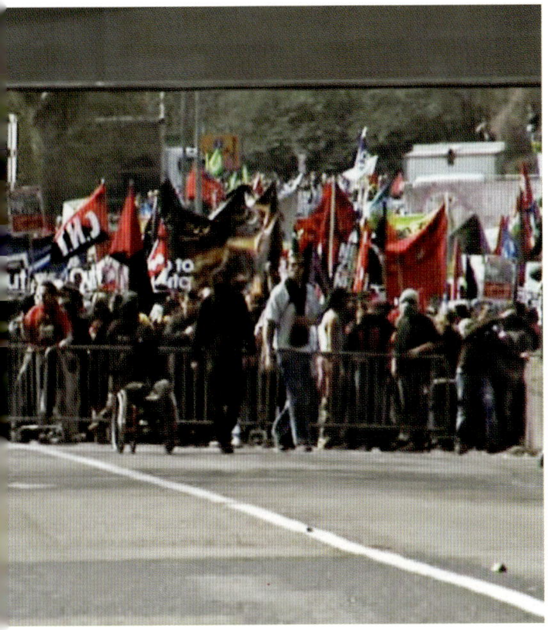

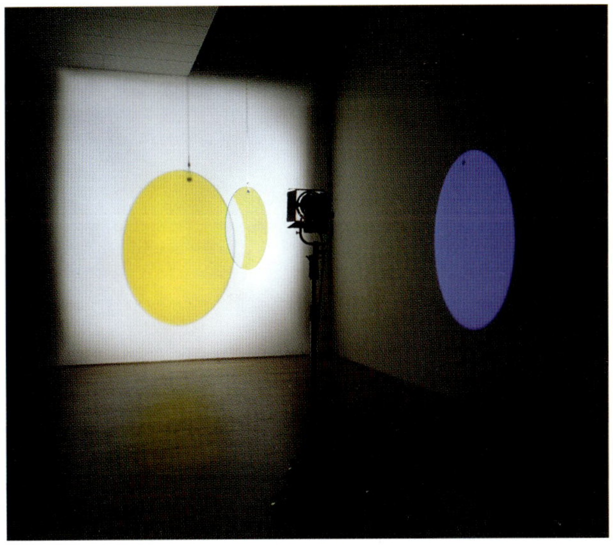

6

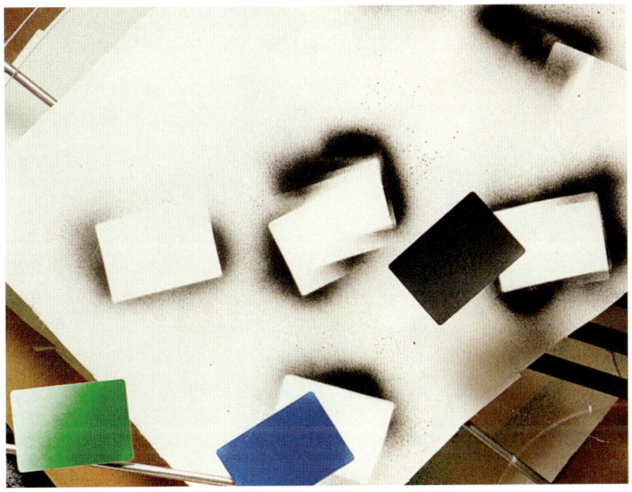

4

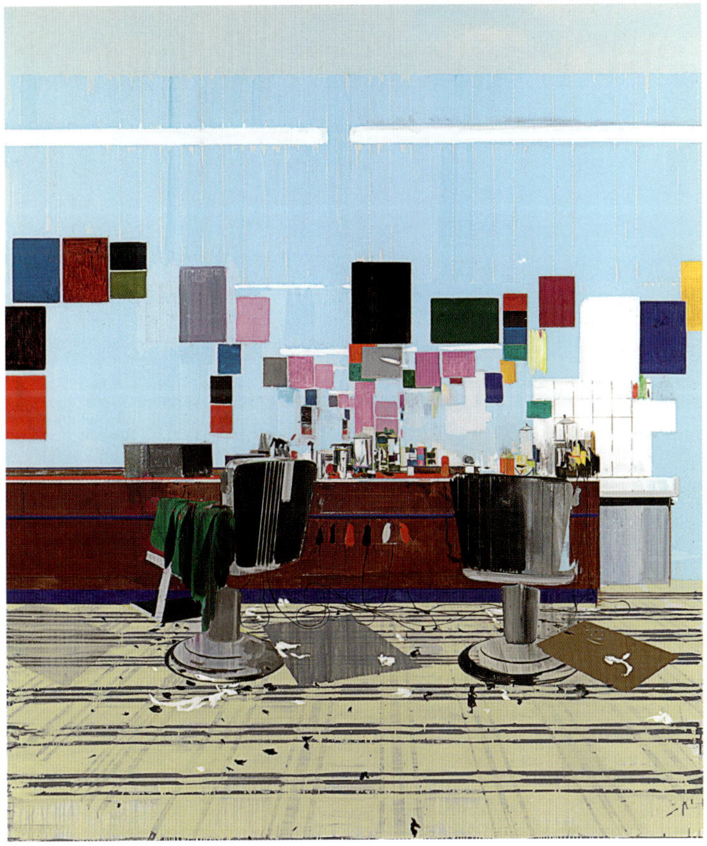

5

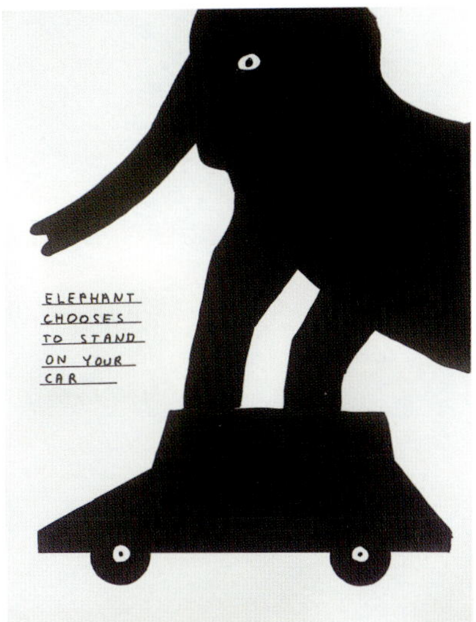


3

# Frieze Projects

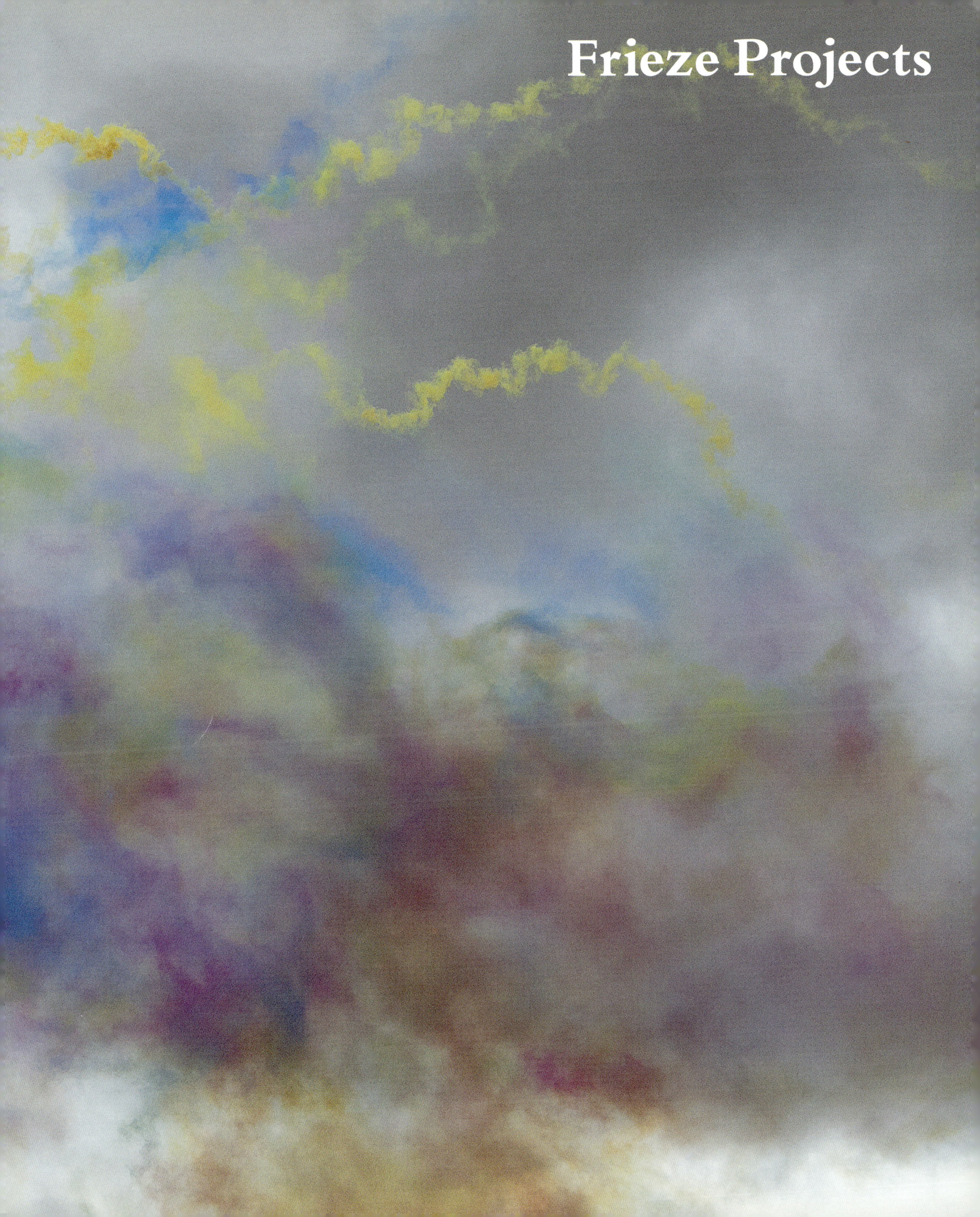

# Introduction

It's the tenth year of Frieze Art Fair and the tenth year of Frieze Projects. Initiated in 2003 as a unique way to complement and collaborate with (and at times oppose and disturb) the main body of the fair, the projects, film and talks programme is now a much-replicated format, accompanying a number of international art fairs. This year six projects by a diverse range of artists engage with a number of different disciplines, including design, online publishing, food production, popular television and the interpretation of art. The connection between the projects lies not in a single dominant theme but in the artists' appropriation of alternative disciplines to explore their ideas.

The work of Thomas Bayrle reflects his early life as a weaver in a south German mill. His introspective examinations of the intricate intersections and patterns of threads in fabric became metaphors for how he saw the world at large. In subsequent designs, popular culture icons and motifs, from animals and political figures to naked bodies and well-known products, are integrated to compose larger images. In some works the same motif is repeated in such a pattern as to construct its own shape on a larger scale. In other cases the arrangement of motifs is more oblique or humorous: hundreds of wheelbarrows form the face of Orson Welles; a portrait of Norman Mailer is produced from pencils; a horse's head is made up of trains; and a bull is composed of bears. In Bayrle's earlier work the artist's absurdist observations were embedded within an apparent method of mass production; in 1967 he created silkscreen prints for plastic raincoats that were stocked in department stores. Bayrle's interventions in the fair—including a carpeted and wallpapered entrance corridor—uses the same brightly coloured patterns he produced for those coats.

Joanna Rajkowska's journey to this project has not been easy. Rajkowska is an artist who takes on belief systems not in an attempt to change them but in order to examine their illogical attitudes and absurdities. Often her projects fail to come to fruition in the way they were first intended, but in this failure they expose social structures and often the close-minded or conformist attitudes of local communities. In a climate where the production of public art works within communities is embedded within the rhetoric of engagement, Rajkowska's refreshing approach is to challenge presumptions about how relationships between public art and audiences should work, and why—often at her own expense.

Rajkowska has also recently been struggling with personal adversity—her daughter has been ill with retinoblastoma, a form of eye cancer. Facing such a trauma has led to a shift in Rajkowska's relationship with her work. One can generalize that the art world is typically an atheistic world, which often struggles to engage with spirituality or religious undertones within art works. In the case of Rajkowska's project *Forcing a Miracle*, in which a field of incense is burnt during the fair, the artist explores without apology the power of spiritual belief.

Based in the countryside of the English Lake District, Grizedale Arts challenges the current status quo of socially engaged practice with a unique approach towards working with local and international communities. It functions as a smallholding as well as a contemporary arts organization, and the production of food has been a major part of its activities for some time. Following their recent collaboration with Eastside Projects in Birmingham, Grizedale Arts and the Yangjiang Group from Beijing work together on a project at Frieze London. Inspired loosely by a Roman

Frieze Projects is supported by

EMDASH FOUNDATION

Frieze Foundation is supported by

ARTS COUNCIL ENGLAND
LOTTERY FUNDED

Frieze Film is presented in partnership with

amphitheatre, Yangjiang Group have produced a wooden structure (including a vomitorium) that provides a view of a series of dinners, performances, talks and events. The programme includes a performance by the Yangjiang Group themselves, a dinner made with culled wildlife, and talks by experts in food history and culture. The relationship between food and art is a long and beloved one, and this project seeks to investigate and manipulate these attitudes by a multitude of means.

Aslı Çavuşoğlu spends the week of the fair as a scriptwriter for a fictional television crime show, a programme being produced with a cast and crew but not filmed. Each day the narrative she writes is enacted, with gaps to allow improvisation of some important elements of the show, from the choice of murder weapons—produced by an on-site prop team—to the positioning and direction of the actors. The weapon used for each murder is a work of art, its form influenced by a number of films and television programmes Çavuşoğlu has researched. The artist aims to create a scenario where discussions arise around themes of reality, intention and motive, drawing subtle parallels between the decision-making of a TV production crew, the solving of crime and the process of making art. As philosopher Gilles Deleuze notes in his essay 'The Philosophy of Crime Novels', the detective (and the criminal) 'pledge allegiance to justice and the truth and the powers of deduction and induction', traits sometimes associated with the practice of artists.

*DIS* is a collective of individuals hailing from a number of different backgrounds, including design, fashion, photography and technology, who produce an online magazine as a platform for exploring our contemporary condition. They often use visual and written language related to business, their *modus operandi* influenced by marketing, advertising and product placement. There is something refreshingly subversive about corporate communication being embraced rather than parodied. *DIS* responds to Frieze London with a photo shoot in and around the galleries, challenging the autonomous nature of each aspect of the fair and constructing situations that compete with the art works for our attention.

The winner of the second Emdash Award is Belgian-American artist Cécile B. Evans. Evans creates an audio guide for the fair composed not, as is convention, by art experts but by a number of contributors from other disciplines—well known in their own fields—who comment on the works within the fair. Frieze London has a large audience of art enthusiasts from the general public, as well as visitors from the professional art world. Evans' project is a reminder of how personal the interpretation of art is, and that no understanding of art can ever be wrong. Rather than a kind of institutional critique, Evans' audio guide is more generous, connecting visitors to the works in and around the fair through emotive, personal descriptions. A moving hologram figure accompanies the audio guide, standing in the fair as a figure of authority and balancing the guide's emphasis on free and open interpretation.

Frieze Foundation has once again commissioned new film and video works for the fair by emerging and established artists. The artists are Bertrand Dezoteux, Patricia Esquivias, Jimmy Merris, John Smith and Wu Tsang & Nana Oforiatta-Ayim. They represent a wide range of film-based practices, their works for Frieze Film all loosely dealing with ideas of history and memory, be it personal or collective. The way that narratives are constructed around individuals, buildings, objects and places is a theme that runs through the programme, whether it is via imagined journeys, fictitious events or romantic relationships. These works also exist as three-minute versions, screened on Channel 4 during the week of the fair.

For the fourth year Frieze Talks is programmed by *frieze* editors Dan Fox, Jörg Heiser and Jennifer Higgie. This year's talks include a conversation between artist Sturtevant and film director and artist John Waters, and panel discussions on resistance and art, criticism and its distractions, and new forms of sculpture. The programme's keynote speakers are the influential artist, novelist and critic Brian O'Doherty and the novelist and critic Lynne Tillman.

We are grateful to the Emdash Foundation for their generous support of the Frieze Projects programme. We would also like to thank our long-standing partners: Gasworks, which hosts the residency of the Emdash Award-winner Cécile B. Evans; and Channel 4, which continues to support artists' film by broadcasting Frieze Film on primetime television. Three new partners also deserve our sincere thanks, as their support and expertise has enabled three particular Frieze Projects this year: Thomas Bayrle was kindly supported by Maharam, Aslı Çavuşoğlu by Delfina Foundation, and Bertrand Dezoteux by Autodesk.

Sarah McCrory
Curator, Frieze Projects

# Thomas Bayrle

## Thomas Bayrle's patterned works for the public spaces of Frieze London take their inspiration from the artist's 1960s silkscreens for raincoats

**Thomas Bayrle** (b. 1937) is a German artist based in Frankfurt/Main, where he was a professor at the Städelschule (1975–2005). His recent solo exhibitions include those at Air de Paris, Paris (2012), Base Progetti per l'Arte, Florence (2010), Musée d'Art Moderne et Contemporain, Geneva (2009), and MACBA, Barcelona (2009). Bayrle participated in the 53rd and 50th Venice Biennales (2009 and 2003), and Documenta 6 and 3 (1977 and 1964). Bayrle's project for Frieze London has been supported by Maharam.

**Sarah McCrory** We asked you to put your stamp on the entrance corridor and a number of the open spaces at the fair. The designs you're using originally date back to 1967. I wonder if you could explain how they came about.

**Thomas Bayrle** After I completed my training as a weaver, two women I knew, Lukowski and Ohanian, who ran their own small fashion company, approached me about designing some plastic raincoats. I accepted the job, regarding it partly as a commercial venture and partly as an artistic project. The patterns on the coats evolved from pictograms of everyday household objects I had seen in cheap magazines—shoes, chairs, cups. After I designed the coats, I used the same patterns to create wallpapers, and I even produced some paintings. I rather liked the fact that the usual process—in which someone makes a painting, then the design is replicated on wallpaper, and then the pattern appears on a garment—was completely inverted. In keeping with the political sensibilities of the time, we wanted the coats to be cheap, popular and mass-produced. I had access to a silkscreening company, so on Sundays I was able to use the equipment there to print the three motifs on the plastic myself. Priced at only 25 marks each, the first edition of 700 coats sold out in no time; unfortunately we didn't get the chance to make any more because the fashion house folded.

**McCrory** Your work has amazing levels of intricacy and detail, which I assume stems from your training as a weaver. Yet the subject matter of your motifs seems clearly rooted in popular culture.

**Bayrle** Yes, weaving is very much at the heart of my work, but it's also bound in with my perspective on Western society. The process of weaving—which on the looms of the time I trained was actually quite hard, physical labour—reminds me of the rhythmic pattern of breathing in and out. A piece of woven cloth is also like a city to me, like streets and houses all contained within one square metre of fabric. I see our entire society as flat, patterned fabric; I've always thought in horizontal rather than vertical terms.

**McCrory** The images that you're using could be seen to be quite Pop, and, of course, there's lots of writing that associates you with the European Pop

*Coat*
1967
Silkscreen on plastic
101 × 127 × 6 cm
In cooperation with
Lukowski & Ohanian
Courtesy of Galerie
Barbara Weiss

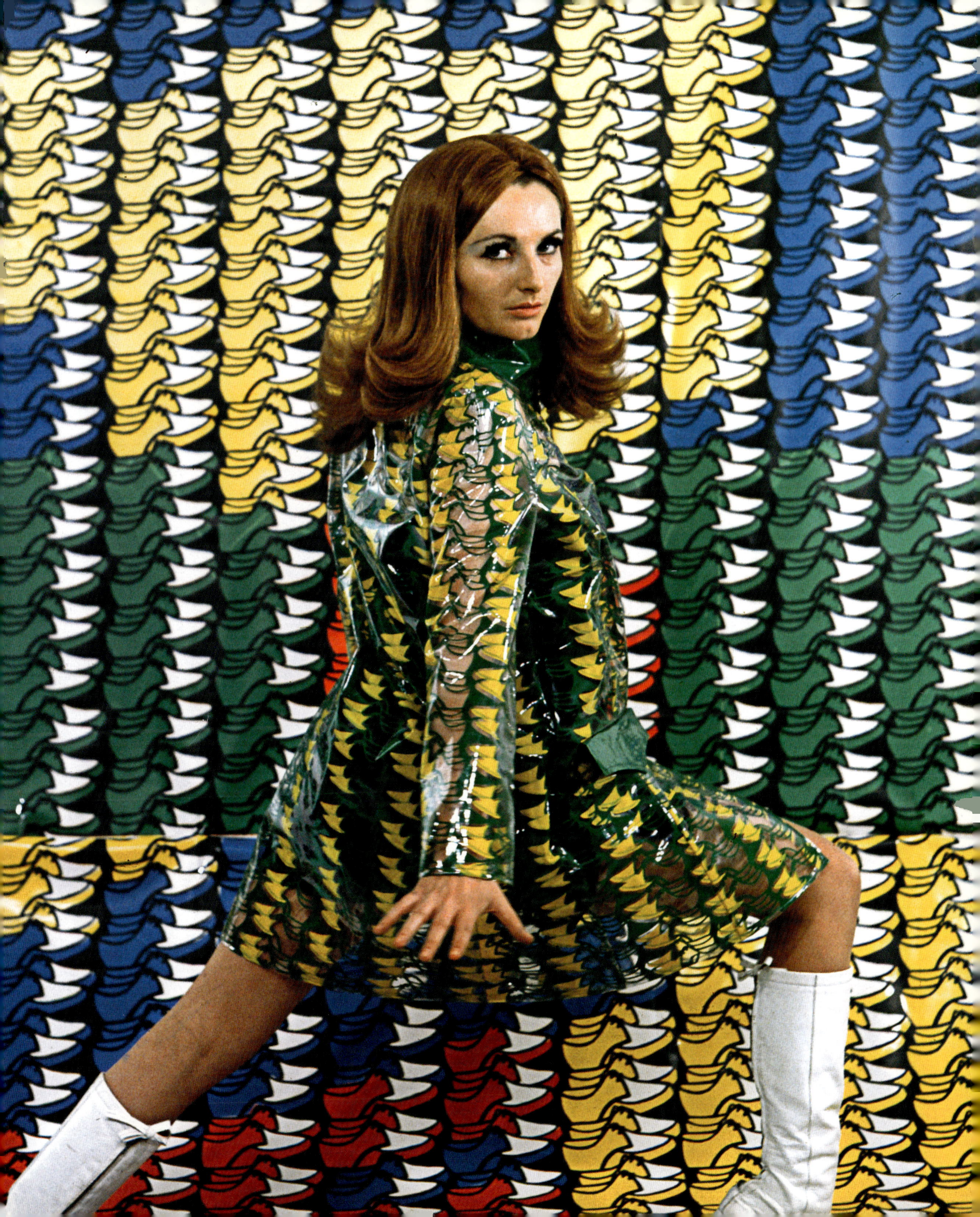

movement. Do you agree with that interpretation of your work?

**Bayrle** To be honest, I never thought about Pop at the time. It was more that I was fascinated by mass production and mass consumption, by the concept of a constructed society created by workers operating machines. Of course, as we know, mass production has brought us numerous problems, but also a lot of pleasure. I wasn't criticizing it 100 percent: I was always somewhere in the middle. People tend to want to pigeonhole you, but for me it's always been 50/50 because that halfway point is the melting pot where things come together. Given how fragile our society is, how things can oscillate wildly from one minute to the next, it seems a sensible precaution to just stay in the middle. Some might say that it's boring, but I never wanted to push back the boundaries.

**McCrory** Your position as an artist must have also been affected by the fact that you were working in factories at the time. Most Pop artists were approaching the subject from an external perspective, whereas you were working as a commercial producer.

**Bayrle** Nowadays almost the entire weaving industry is based in India, but at that point Europe still led the way. When I started my training as a weaver at around the age of 18, I was not thinking about it in political terms; I just wanted to learn about weaving patterns, about quality, about what a fabric can express. During the course of working there, however, I started to become aware of social problems. At that time, for instance, a woman in the factory would earn 1.75 marks an hour for running 20 machines, and if she only operated 19 or 18 machines, then her wage was reduced. It was certainly tough—although I'm actually very thankful today for having had that experience as things are starting to get tougher again. Of course, this kind of social reality has been a constant since the start of industrialization in Western Europe, but it seems we often forget we are a part of it. It's like sitting in the car while criticizing it for not being environmentally friendly. It's crucial we remember that we are not just on the outside looking in.

**McCrory** In Britain the class structure continues to have a bearing on society. Does the same apply in Germany?

**Bayrle** I think the old class system is still present in Germany, cleverly hidden, and it's just that we've been distracted by the drug of capitalism. Millions of people are living in poverty—in particular elderly people and single mothers with young children—so, to my mind, it's clear that we will need to face issues of class again, although every time we do it's treated as a new problem.

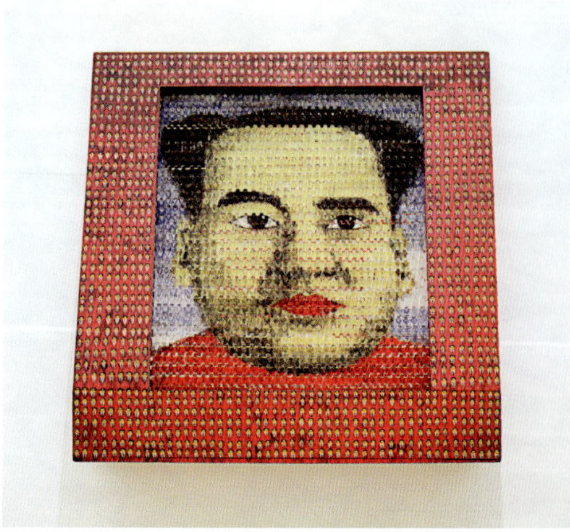

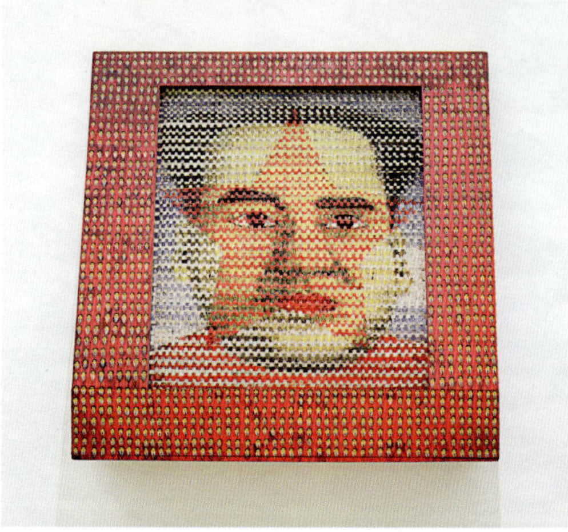

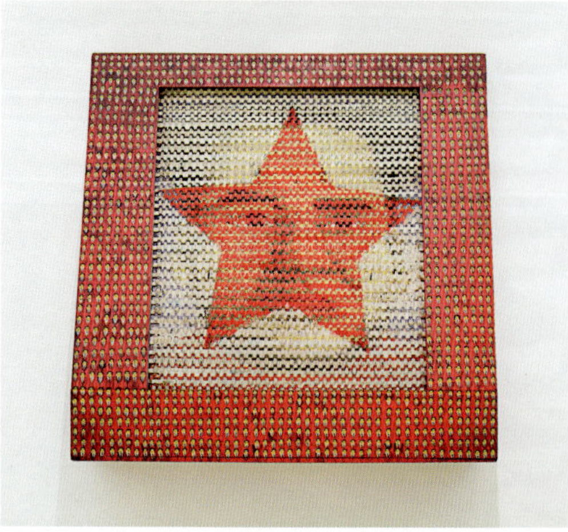

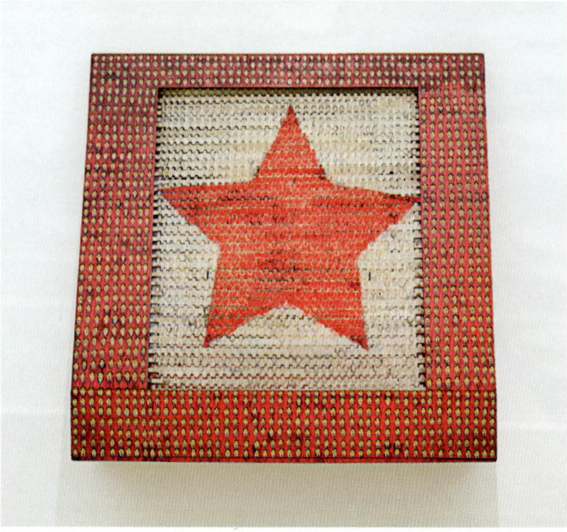

Opposite:
*Mao*
1966
Oil on wood
148 × 145 × 32 cm
Courtesy of Museum für Moderne Kunst, Frankfurt/Main

Below:
*$*
1980
Cardboard, pencil and plastic cars
84 × 64 × 8 cm
Private Collection

## 'A piece of woven cloth is like a city to me, like streets and houses all contained within one square metre of fabric.'

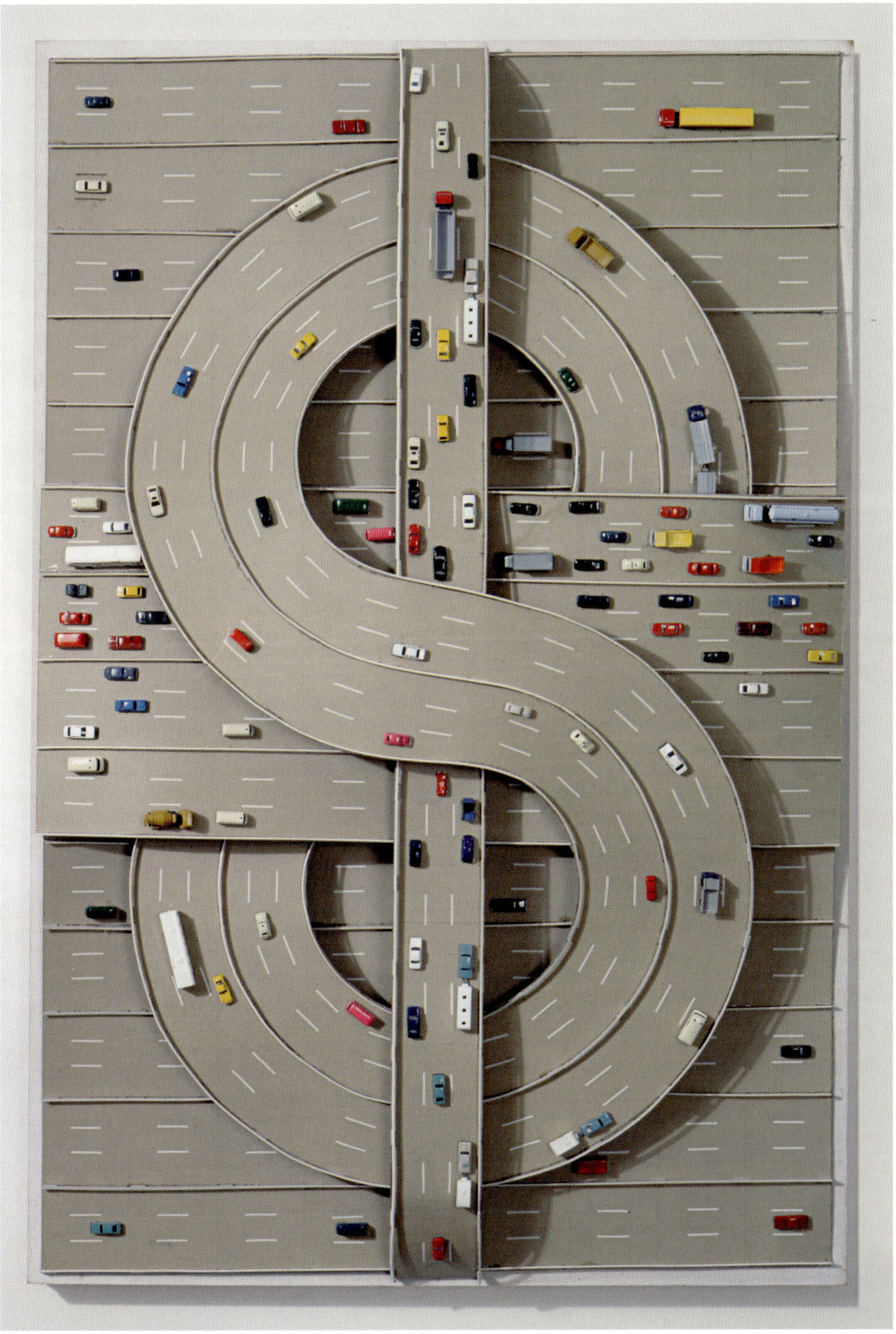

**McCrory** Do you see your work as engaging with these social problems?

**Bayrle** Whenever I design something, my aim is that it could teach something to a schoolchild. So all my work has a certain moral purpose to it. You can promote a cause in your practice up to a certain point by working alongside activist groups, but then, as an artist, there comes a moment when you cannot follow that work through completely. I have worked with many groups—the Maoists, for instance—but in the end they usually become too bureaucratic in their approach and want to involve you in all kinds of events that are not even good for their cause, although they can't see it and just blindly push forwards.

**McCrory** Which is invariably to their detriment.

**Bayrle** Ultimately, I suppose, I'm just a man in the middle of everything: weaving, manufacturing production, society. I don't have an overview of anything, not even in relation to my art. I have always worked on the details because I know that wholeness is also in the detail. That is a crucial element of my practice. Also, my work must have humour, because without humour, this world is unbearable.

# Aslı Çavuşoğlu

Influenced by Agatha Christie adaptations, Aslı Çavuşoğlu collaborates with a cast and crew on a fictional crime caper at Frieze London, in which the murder weapon is always a work of art

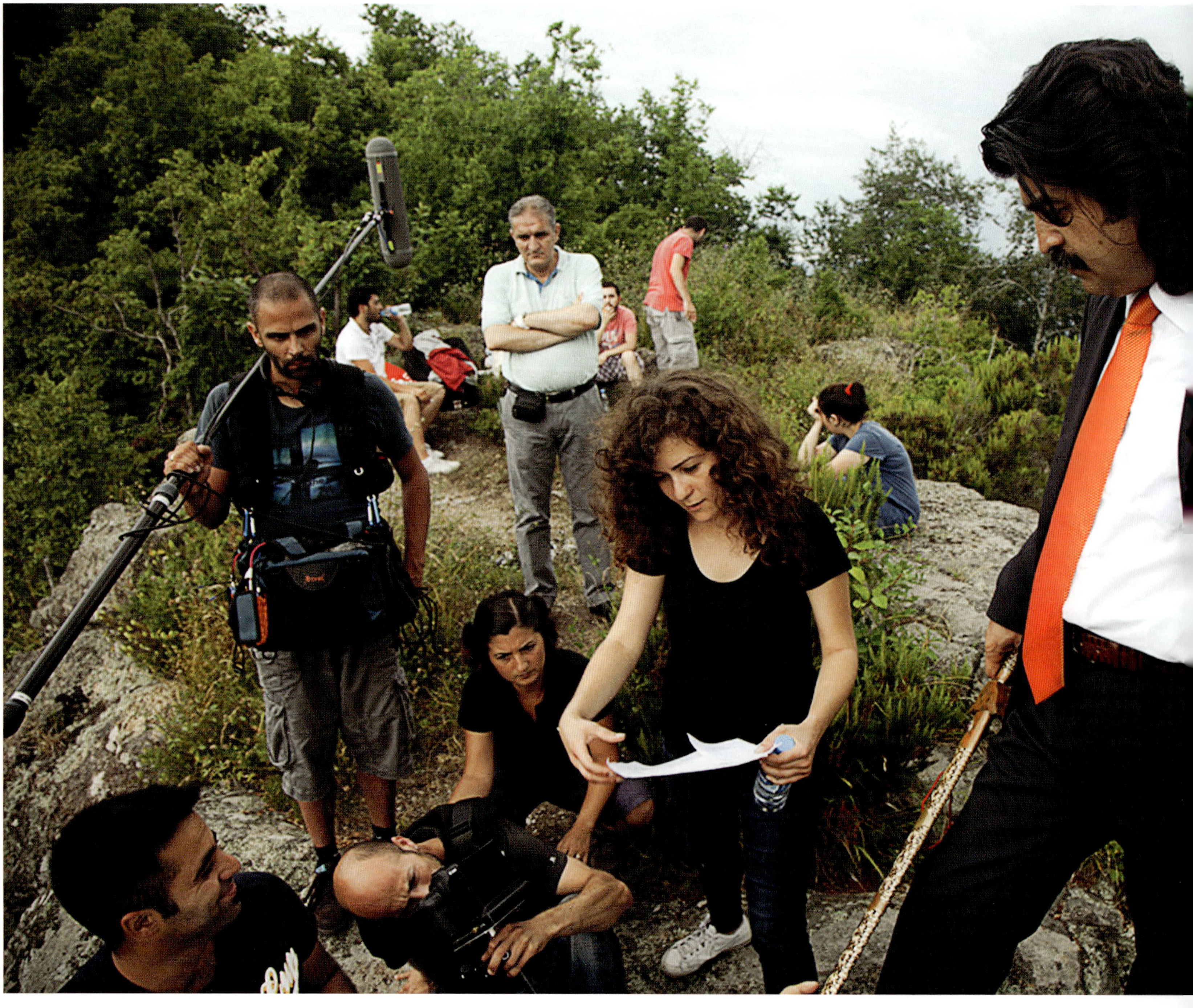

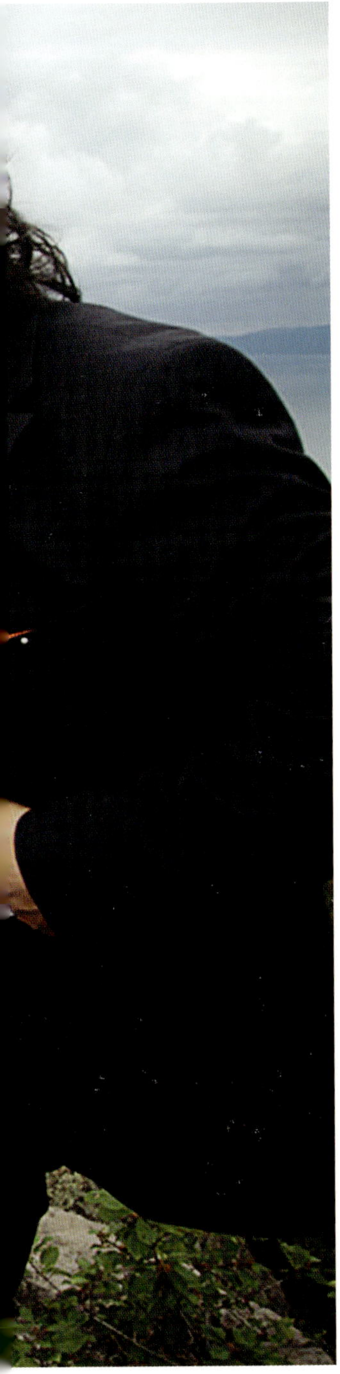

Aslı Çavuşoğlu (centre) with cast and crew during the production of her film *In Diverse Estimations Little Moscow* (2011)

**Aslı Çavuşoğlu** (b. 1982) is a Turkish artist based in Istanbul. She has participated in recent group exhibitions that include: the 11th Baltic Triennial of International Art, Tallinn (2011); Performa 11, New York (2011); 'Transient Spaces: The Tourist Syndrome', Neue Gesellschaft für Bildende Kunst, Berlin (2010); 'Fantasy & Island', FRAC Corse, Corsica (2010); and 'This Place You See Has No Size At All', Kadist Art Foundation, Paris (2009).

**Sarah McCrory** Where did the idea for your Frieze London project originally come from?

**Aslı Çavuşoğlu** I'm a huge fan of crime novels and television crime series—even if I've already seen an episode, I'll still happily watch it again. I started to ask myself what it is I enjoy about them, and I think I like how the detective devotes all of his or her mental energy to discovering the truth. For instance, if we think about Hercule Poirot, the famous Belgian detective from Agatha Christie's novels, he is driven to find out who the perpetrator is not because he's getting paid by a client or because he's working with the police department, but simply because he wants to know the truth. I also came across an article by Gilles Deleuze ['The Philosophy of Crime Novels', 1966] in which he compares the uncovering of the truth in detective novels to the philosophical process, whereby the philosopher is trying to find the truth simply because he wants to find it. Thinking back to the ancient Greek tragedies, even Oedipus could be considered to be a detective.

**McCrory** Do you think that methodology can also be applied to artistic practice?

**Çavuşoğlu** Absolutely. I find the whole concept of uncovering truth fascinating.

**McCrory** Your idea is to create a crime fiction performance at Frieze London that works on two levels: not only will it be a crime story based on a script you're going to write, but there will also be a further level of deception in that, although it will appear the story is being filmed, it will actually only be a performance of filming. What's the motivation behind your decision not to film it?

**Çavuşoğlu** Nowadays old-fashioned sleuths are rarely found in television crime dramas: it's usually a forensic pathologist who works as the detective and devotes himself to finding the truth through the use of science. Despite this premise, these shows are full of pseudo-scientific techniques that don't exist in real life. I really wanted to explore this concept of the detective trying to discover the truth through fake science, and I thought a performance would be a great way of creating a platform for debate. I really like the dynamic of the film crew—in which the producer, director and actors are always engaging with each other, discussing everything in great detail—and I also wanted to bring in some art critics, writers and genuine scientific advisers to probe the idea further.

**McCrory** I know that you're also keen to get the audience involved in the performance, to comment on or alter the narrative.

**Çavuşoğlu** Yes, my idea is to have a different pre-written script prepared for each day, which will only be about three pages long. We will then create numerous variations of that one scene, the constant element in each being that a work of art will be used as the murder weapon.

**McCrory** Why did you decide to make the weapon an art object?

**Çavuşoğlu** I've always been interested in how art is represented in television shows by pretend art. Take a scene set in a gallery: someone will be given the task of creating fake art works to give the audience the impression that the action's taking place in a real exhibition.

**McCrory** It strikes me that the creative process of the film crew in your project parallels the working practice of the artist. It's almost as though the crew represents the artist's thought process.

**Çavuşoğlu** Yes and, in a way, that's why I don't want to film the performance,

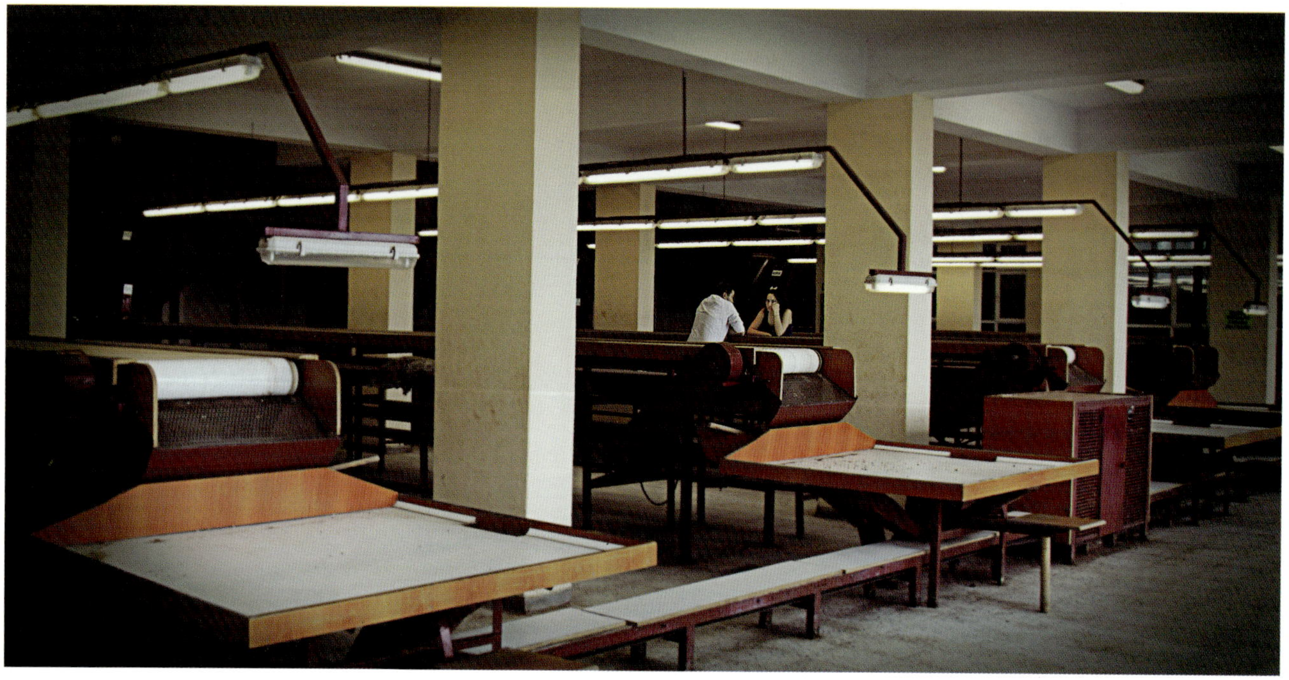

Left:
*In Diverse Estimations*
*Little Moscow*
2011
Single-channel video
HD Blu-ray with 5.1
Dolby Digital audio
12 min. 45 sec.
Commissioned by
BORUSAN A.Ş.
Courtesy of Gallery
NON

Below:
*She Who Is Salt-White*
2012
Performance
25 min.
Commissioned by
ENPAP (European
Network of Public Art
Producers)
Courtesy of Gallery
NON

because that would control it too much, and then I wouldn't really encounter any surprises. I want the audience to participate in the discussions about things, such as how the murder weapon should be used, or how much blood there would be if you hit someone on the head.

**McCrory** You've decided that the props you use in the performance will later be sold as art objects, so a fake sculpture that may be used to stab someone in the play will then be returned to the status of art work.

**Çavuşoğlu** I'm interested in how an object—in this case, a prop from a TV series—transforms into an art object by being claimed as such, speculated as such. I would like to create a black market in which the producer would sell two to three props each day for a little amount of money in order to raise funds for the production. I want to make a reference to how the film industry really works, to how the producer is always trying to scrimp and save to raise money for the next project. In fact, I see them as having quite a lot in common with institutional curators, who always seem to have to cut corners to save money.

**McCrory** What's really interesting about this project is that there are so many different voices—the audience, the producer, the film crew, the actors—and that there will be a certain level of controlled chaos. It will be interesting to see how your voice as the artist is heard, or not heard, within that process.

**Çavuşoğlu** I'll be functioning as moderator, producer, director and scriptwriter for the project, so of course I'll have a degree of control over things. I just want the process to be flexible and open.

**McCrory** I think the dynamic between the participants will be fascinating. It's a process the audience rarely gets to see. Will the professional actors have worked with the crew before?

**Çavuşoğlu** Ideally, yes. Otherwise, it might be like watching an episode of *Big Brother*, with ten people who don't know each other fighting. I'd also prefer to use actors who have already been in crime dramas if possible, although actors are usually fairly easy-going because they are so used to working with different people.

**McCrory** Will you allow the actors to have any involvement in the script at all?

**Çavuşoğlu** I'll definitely give them the freedom to improvise, because the intention is to create all these different variations. There's a Turkish filmmaker, Nuri Bilge Ceylan, who shoots hundreds of hours of film and gets the actors to do the same lines again and again in a multitude of ways—crying, laughing, smiling, etc.—and then he just cuts it in the editing room, and the actors don't have any idea what the film is going to be like. I really like that approach.

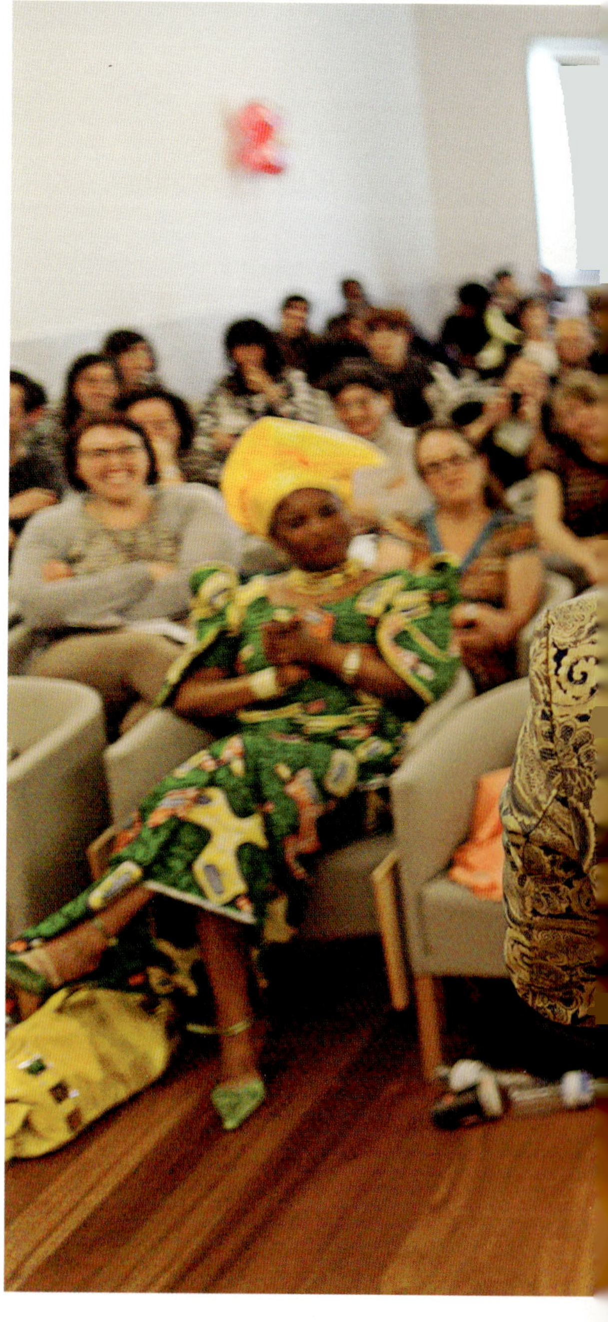

‘Deleuze compares the uncovering of the truth in detective novels to the philosophical process. Thinking back to the ancient Greek tragedies, even Oedipus could be considered to be a detective.’

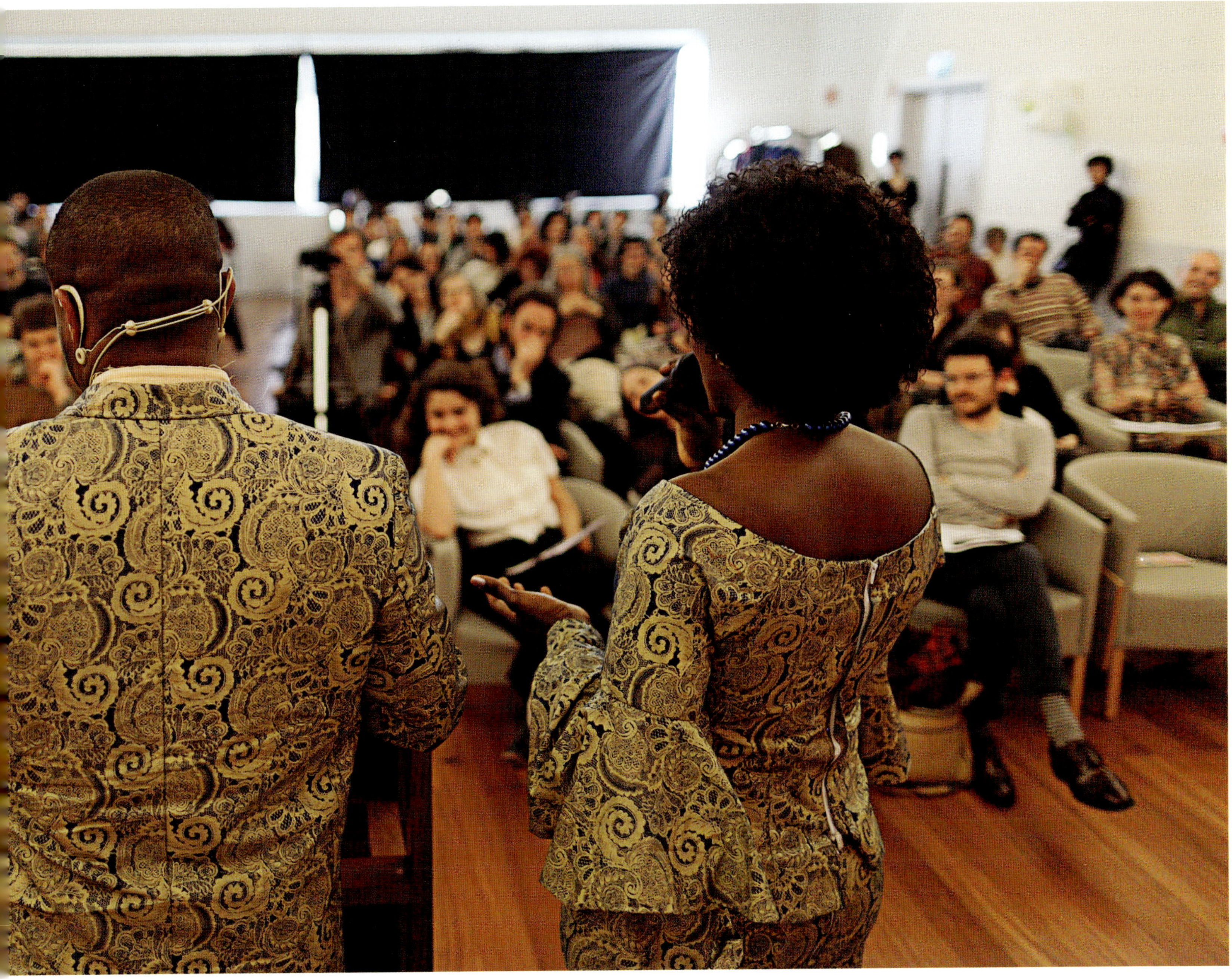

# *DIS* magazine

## The team at *DIS* shoot a distorted documentation of the fair as part of the Frieze Projects programme, playing with our perceptions of art objects and their presentation

***DIS*** is a multimedia magazine whose online platform DISmagazine.com was launched in 2010. It is produced in New York by a core team of Lauren Boyle, Solomon Chase, Marco Roso, Nick Scholl and David Toro. Recent projects include: 'The Art School Issue' (2012), in collaboration with institutions such as Cooper Union, New York; 'DIS_RT', MoMA PS1, New York (2011); and 'DIS HQ', a residency in collaboration with Lizzie Fitch at Invisible-Exports, New York (2011).

**Sarah McCrory** What is *DIS* magazine?

***DIS*** *DIS* is a post-Internet lifestyle magazine about art, fashion and commerce. It creates images, text and video for an online platform. The magazine has a default aesthetic: mass-market apparel and stock photography models bask under even lighting with a degree of unease. *DIS* tries to dismantle the traditional antagonisms of youth and counterculture. It pictures a world in which there is no 'alternative'.

**McCrory** How would you define your approach to both the making and the framing of the magazine's content? What are the main issues that you address in features and shoots?

***DIS*** We explore the banality and novelty of products and image-making, playing with ambiguity and marketing ideas as if they were products themselves. We're probably most concerned with questioning notions of taste and value systems, which we try either to break down or to *re*-present in their most heightened configuration. We try to avoid conforming to our own taste. There's been a creative and consumer vertigo induced by all the focus on the so-called 'high' and 'low' cultures. We're not interested in high or low; we're interested in the middle. That's where the fertile ground is.

**McCrory** You exist online, but is the Internet important in terms of the content of your material, or is it simply a method of delivering that content?

***DIS*** It's very important that it's both. While print journals aspire to the status of a collector's item, online-only magazines like *DIS* can be fast and loose. We thrive on the immediacy of the Internet; everything is editable and extensible. In this time-scarce culture the Internet is the only place to engage people.

**McCrory** For Frieze Projects, I am treating you—the collective body that is *DIS*—as an artists' project, which is how I have always viewed your publication. Given that you come from varied backgrounds, does that kind of categorization interest you?

***DIS*** *DIS* is a group of individuals that operate as an entity. We're not preoccupied with pursuing art careers, but art relates to what we do. We use and play with some of the same codes and concerns as art, adopting them, discarding them, side-stepping them. It's a salad bar as a production model.

We're also focused on exhibiting through forms of media that are not specific to art, such as the Internet. We're more interested

From the series 'Art School Trends'
Photograph
2012
Courtesy of *DIS* magazine

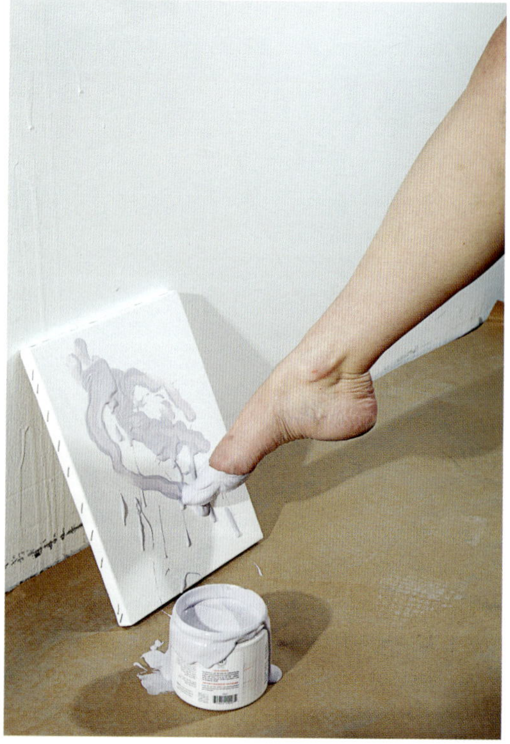

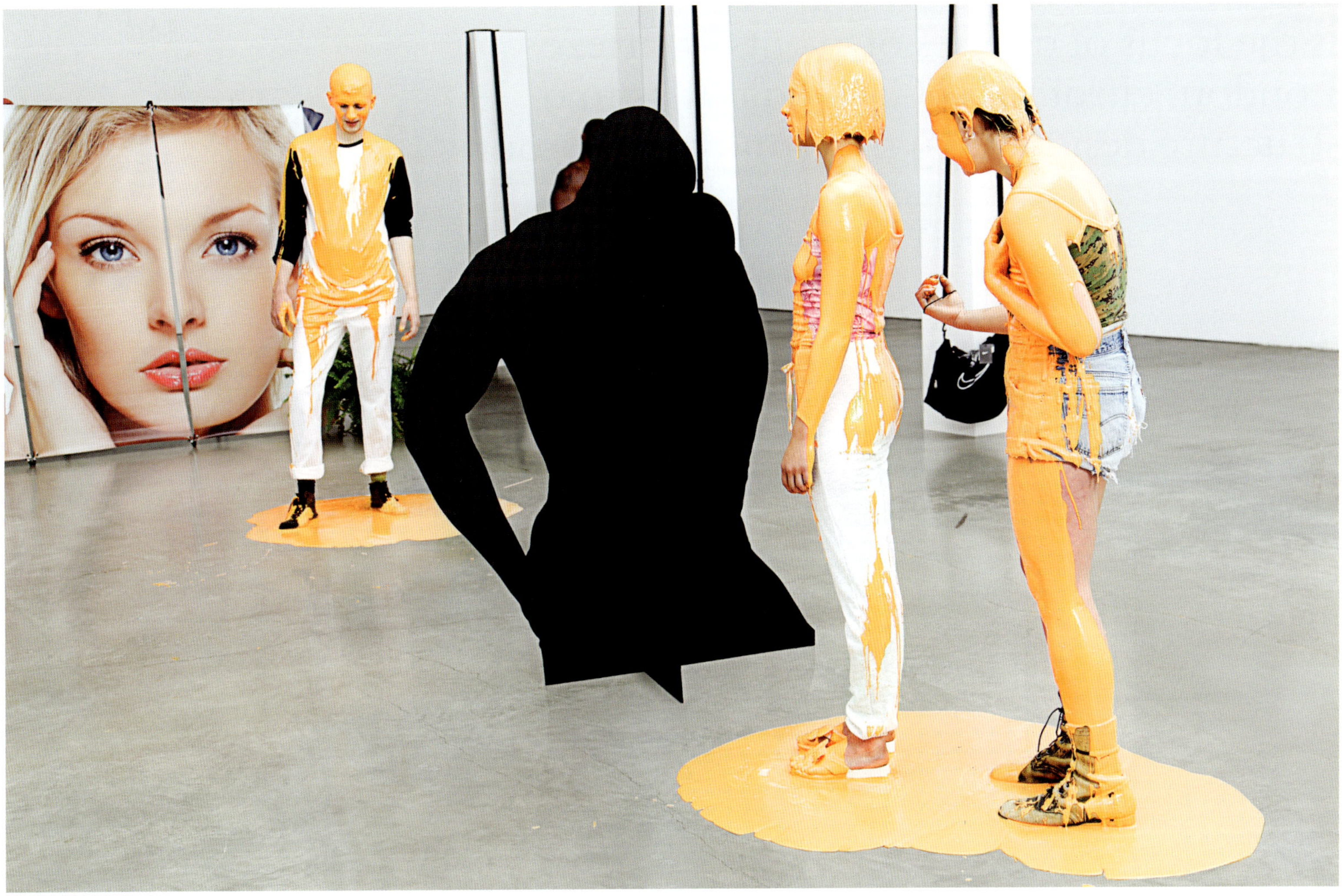

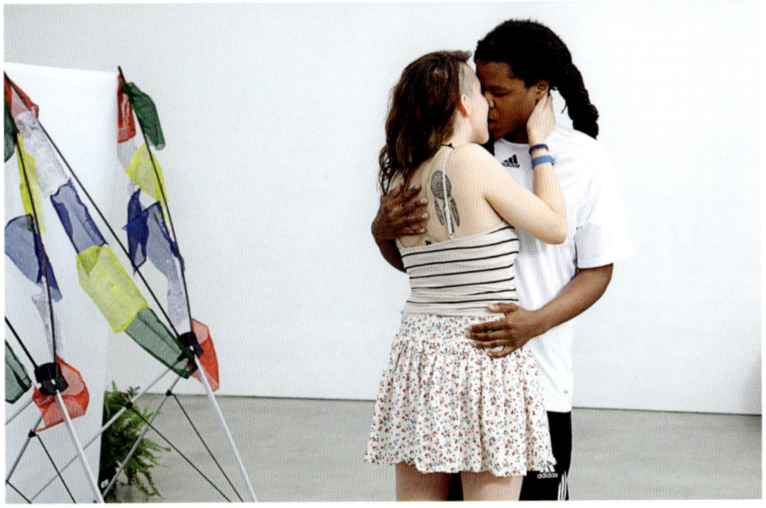

Top and above:
From the series
'Competing Images'
Photographs
2012
Courtesy of *DIS*
magazine

in igniting conversations, influencing trends and entertaining our audience than being artists. As a magazine, we have the freedom to evolve with culture and to try to make sense of it.

**McCrory** Your project involves shooting and writing a feature article at Frieze London. How will it respond to the context of the fair?

***DIS*** We're interested in new ways of documenting art. We'll be creating images in which situations we manufacture and the art works compete for the viewer's attention in the same way that galleries, exhibitions, artists and art all compete for attention at Frieze itself. The material for our project is the existing fair structures, and, in the works we will produce from this material, the art objects will always relate specifically to the image-ecology of society.

# Grizedale Arts & Yangjiang Group

Food's close relationship to community is the focus of a series of events at Frieze London, curated by Grizedale Arts in a structure designed by the Yangjiang Group

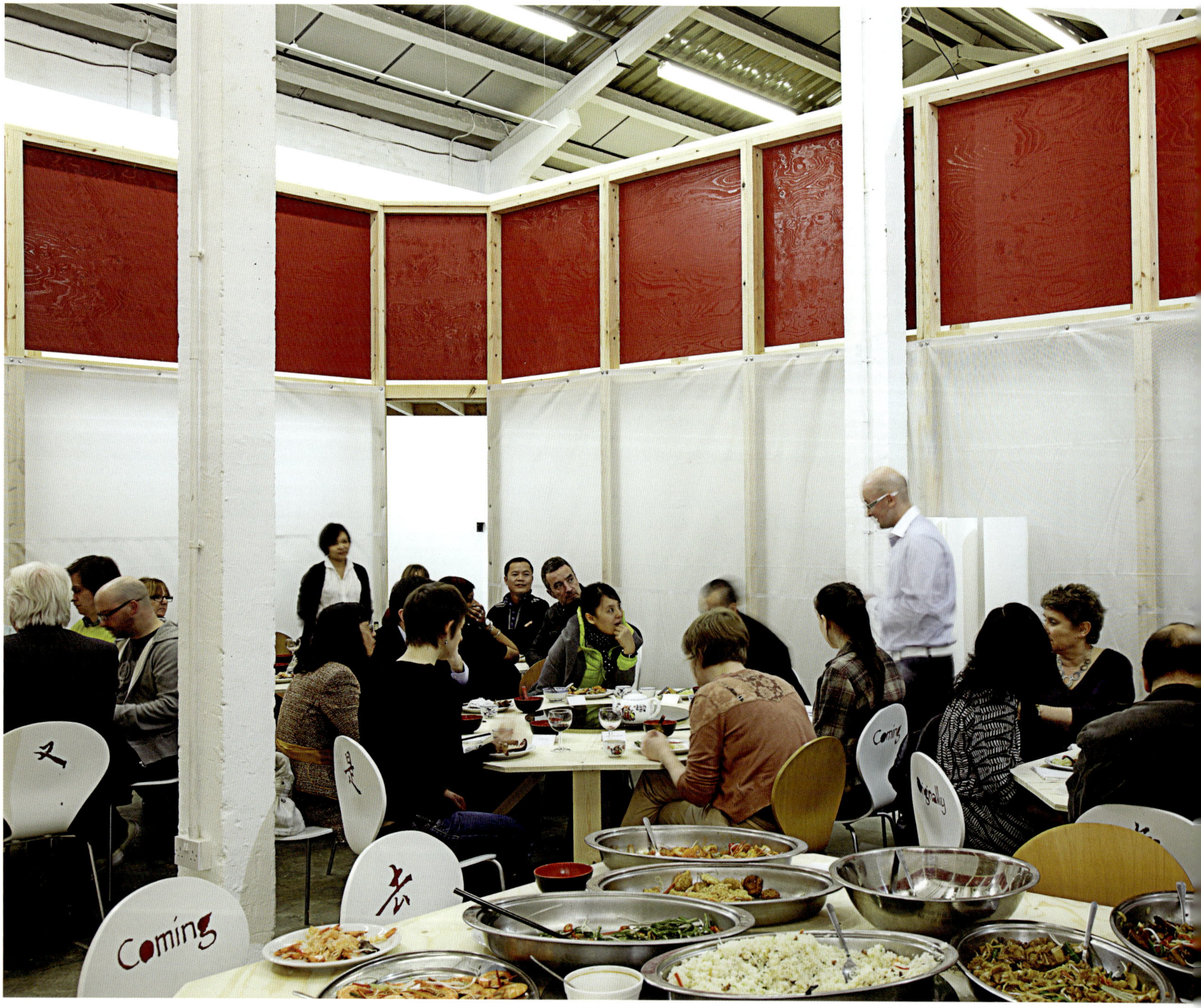

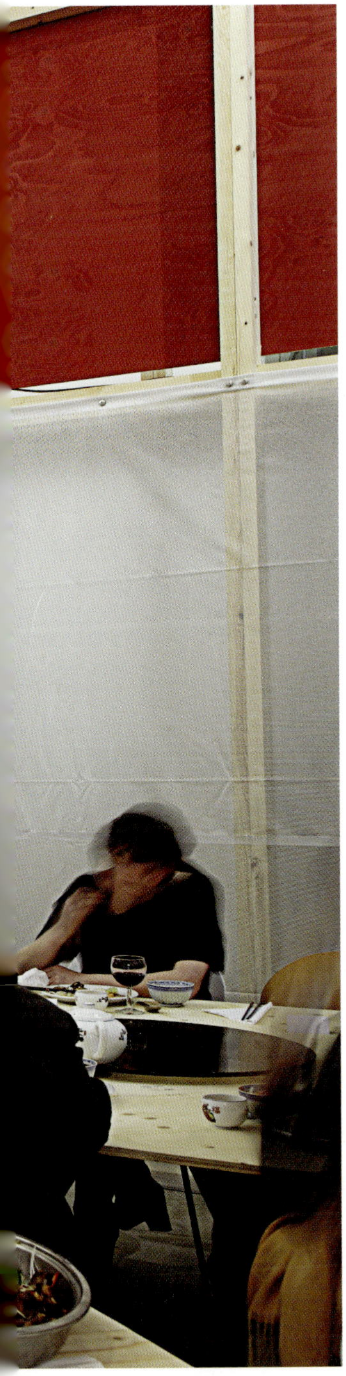

Left and below:
Yangjiang Group
From 'After Dinner Shu Fa at Cricket Pavilion' 2012
Exhibition views at Eastside Projects
Performative installation and event series
Courtesy of Eastside Projects

**Adam Sutherland** and **Alistair Hudson** direct Grizedale Arts, a curatorial project located in Coniston in the English Lake District, founded in 1968 as The Grizedale Society. As well as its residency programme based around the working farm of Lawson Park, Grizedale Arts has presented international projects such as 'The Mechanics Institute' at the 29th Bienal de Sao Paulo (2010) and 'Romantic Detachment', MoMA PS1, New York (2004). The organization collaborates at Frieze London with the Yangjiang Group, an artist collective founded in 2002 in Yangjiang, China. Its members are Chen Zaiyan, Sun Qinglin and Zheng Guogu.

**Sarah McCrory** Grizedale Arts is collaborating with the Yangjiang Group on a bespoke structure within the Frieze London tent. Within the structure there will be performances, discussions and retail all related to food—you're also collaborating on this with many other people, including food producers. It's a community of individuals working on a common subject within a shared space. This is typical of many of your projects: why do you choose to work in this way?

**Alistair Hudson** The circumstances Grizedale Arts is involved in—in social situations in our own village or on projects around the world—are too complex for a traditional art approach. For our projects to be effective they need a civic-style approach.

We are currently building a cricket pavilion with our local village, Coniston. This project with the village community is a sort of social development project. It will demonstrate how art, design and architecture can enrich life, the ambition being to get people in the village to think about how they live, how they might want to live and what they can change and improve. There is always such an aim in our projects.

We view all our projects as part of one larger, cumulative endeavour, not as finite

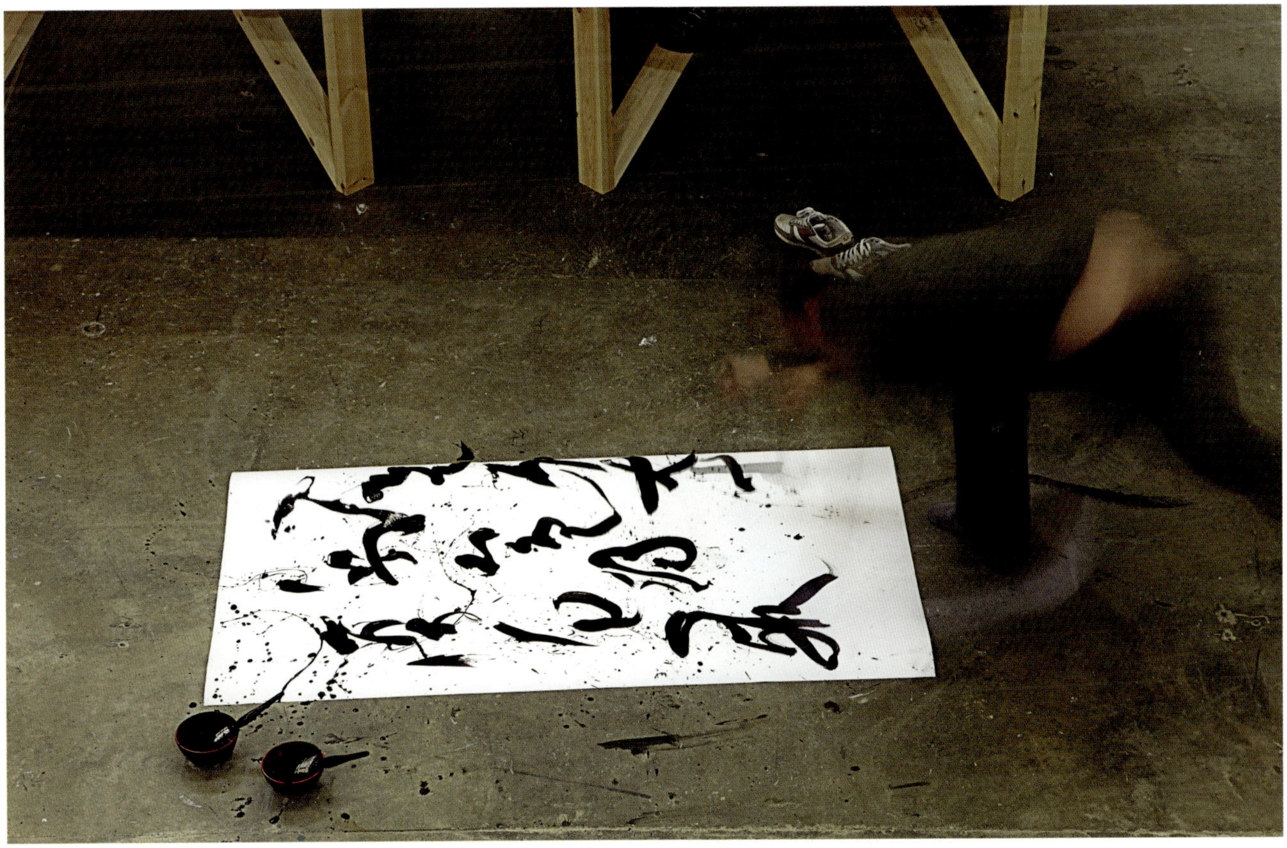

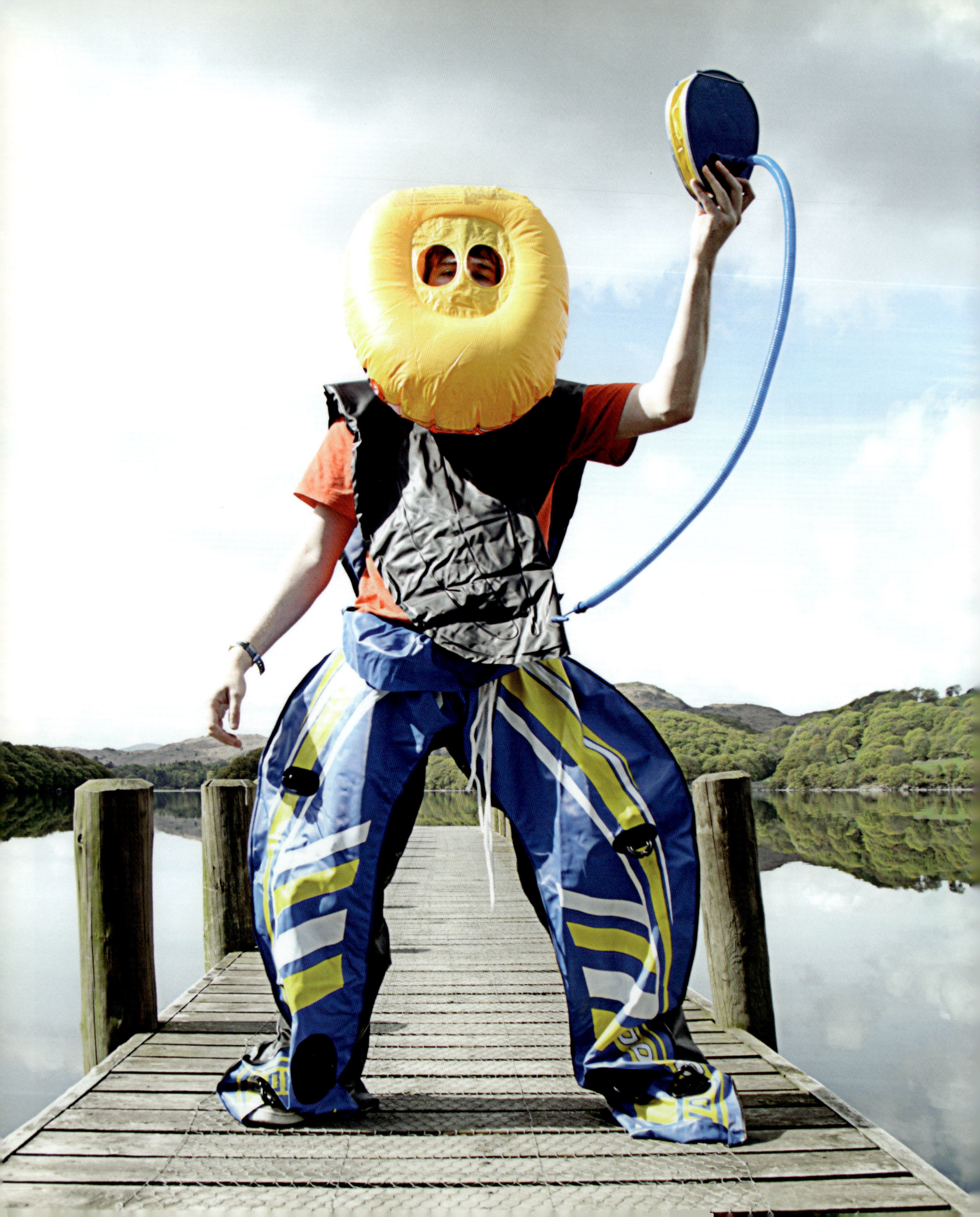

entities. Consistency is therefore a key part of our process, across both our local and international projects. We use food—the production, cooking and presentation of food—as a cornerstone to communicate many of our ideas, so the Frieze project illustrates what we are trying to do in general with our projects at the moment.

**McCrory** Your attitude to artists is quite unusual. You seem to think of them as tools.

**Sutherland** The origins of the organization include artist residencies, but constant residencies quickly saturate a place with relatively pointless art projects. For the last ten years we have been much more directional in our approach, pushing artists to do things in our non-art environment that are valued and useful to the local place and people.

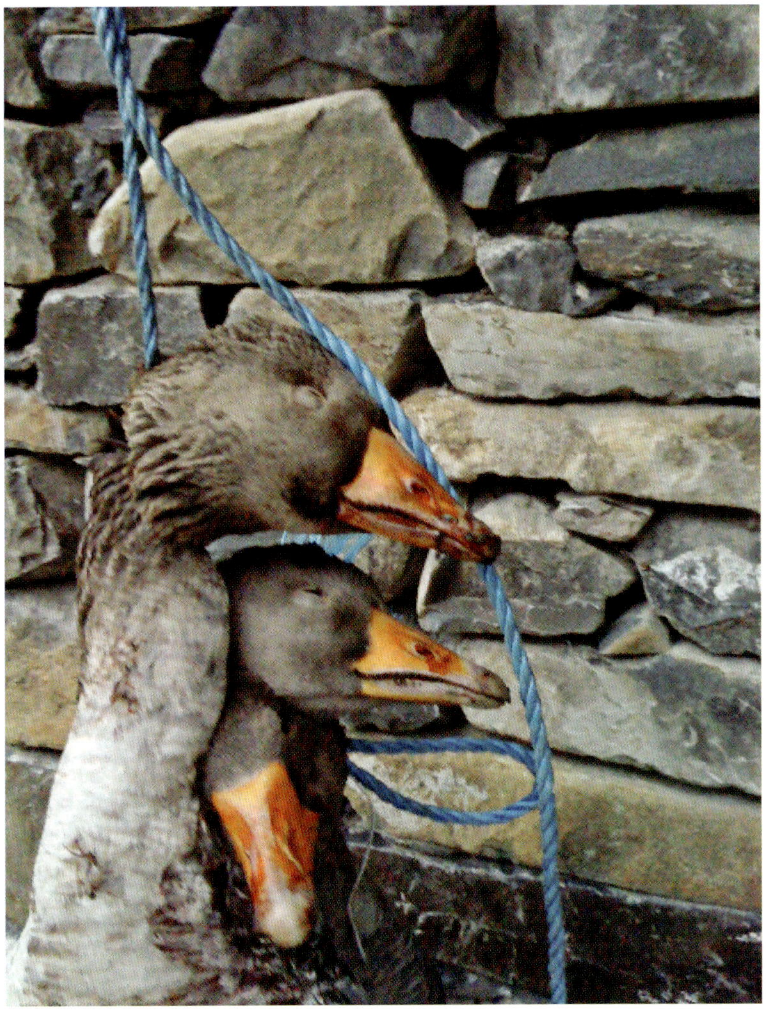

Opposite:
Bedwyr Williams
*The Dinghy King*
2004
Performance
Courtesy of Grizedale Arts

Right:
Culled Canada Geese, which were served at the AGM dinner for the Coniston Garden Club
Photography by Grizedale Arts
Courtesy of the National Trust

We are constantly asked to take on new projects in the village and the valley, to help rework and reinvigorate existing activities and buildings.

Our big project at the moment is restoring Coniston's old Mechanics Institute, which was originally conceived and initiated by John Ruskin. This has been intentionally a largely voluntary project that has involved our whole programme of artists working with the locals. We have made a new library, a shop, a reading room, a kitchen—basic facilities that are important to normal life, all involving the input of the artists, and all in everyday use and valued by the people that use them. Art is realized in living, creative solutions.

We want to rethink the role of the artist, or perhaps reform the role. This is a practical response to the place in which we are based, working in a community as citizens. The artist should be an embedded member of the community, like the grocer or butcher, or, perhaps more relevantly, the vicar. This idea really revisits the traditional role of the artist, particularly prevalent before the 1850s, as someone in the service of the greater good rather than a snooty critic of it. It's a hard about-face for artists to make, but it increasingly makes sense.

**McCrory** The way you work is quite provocative—you like to cause trouble in order to get reactions from people. Yet in Coniston you're actually rather loved these days.

**Sutherland** Yes, and it's really worrying! Actually it's great: what a nice feeling to be wanted and valued after a lifetime of provocation, mistrust and derision. I think now maybe the wider community values us, but the arts community mistrusts and derides us—ho hum!

**Hudson** I suppose the organization has always been provocative in one way or another, from its early days through to the projects in the Noughties through to now, when I think our provocation is now to the art world. The idea that art or artists should be useful really gets some people's goat, but there is definitely a growing consensus that art should be valued in terms of its function. A context like Frieze is very pertinent because its constituency understands art well, whereas when the objects and strategies of the art industry find their way to the general public, most people struggle to know how to read them—and subsequently many public institutions devote a great deal of energy to 'interpretation' and 'participation'. The success of our recent work has been based on the fact that people can value the projects' objectives without recourse to external or transposed value systems.

**McCrory** The artists you work with range from internationally renowned figures to local artists. How do you make your selection?

**Sutherland** It comes down to finding people who are going to think of things that you're not going to think of yourself—people who can surprise you. We've tried coming at it from lots of different angles, and currently we're working with very young artists and volunteers, trying to help them develop their practice in conjunction with Grizedale Arts' focus on place. In the past, when we worked with big-name artists, we sometimes found their practice was too well established to accommodate our organization's aims. I think some artists think it might taint their work, divorce them from their market, smear them with worthy paste that won't ever fully wash off.

Now that we've become so embedded in the local community in Coniston, it's much harder for us to just turn up out of the blue with a project that some artist has concocted, maybe a piece of work more relevant to their gallery output, and for us to desperately try to persuade people of its value. The process of interpretation often then looks like pretty crass propaganda, and it's often associated now with regeneration or some other economic model. The message is: 'You don't need to understand the art—but it will bring more tourists here, that's the benefit.'

**Hudson** Over the years, much of the feedback we have had from the local community essentially boiled down to: 'What's in it for us?' When the farmers have had to talk to six artists in a row about the politics of sheep farming and commoners' rights and all the things that research-based practitioners are interested in, then you start to realize that this is not the way it should work. It may sound terribly touchy-feely, but a lot of what we do now is developed more as a series of relationships than as a series of projects. It's the relationships that then generate effective, purposeful tools.

**McCrory** What are the main challenges of operating outside the more traditional art-world parameters?

**Hudson** If you present an exhibition in a museum or a gallery, the value of the work is never in question because it's sanctioned by the organization. If you're creating something that falls outside those parameters—something that doesn't look the way it's expected to—people have to decide its worth based on genuine value systems. That's the interesting challenge of running something like Grizedale Arts: for it to work, people in the community invest their time, energy or money, and then they have to then get something out of it. In terms of current discussions about how contemporary art should be financially supported, it's very interesting to develop a way of working which is not dependent on sanctions from above, but from the intrinsic value of projects. Food is a good analogy for this approach to art, as above all food is dependent on the quality of the product and its effects, including social effects.

**Sutherland** The appreciation of food is very much a part of the art-world scene, but rarely does anyone really make any interesting work on the subject. Similarly other cornerstones of culture—like gardening—receive little serious attention. It's a bit like art has cut itself adrift from much of this material. There is a bubble in which art is seen as an end in itself. Our ideal is that art is mode of communication, not a job or an end in itself. The Grizedale Arts programme attempts to push artists back into actual society—and in our case that means a small tourism-dominated village, wrought by all the same pains of incoherence and chaos that the rest of us suffer from.

Grizedale Arts staff
Maria Benjamin,
Adam Sutherland and
Alistair Hudson
The Paddy Fields,
Lawson Park, Coniston

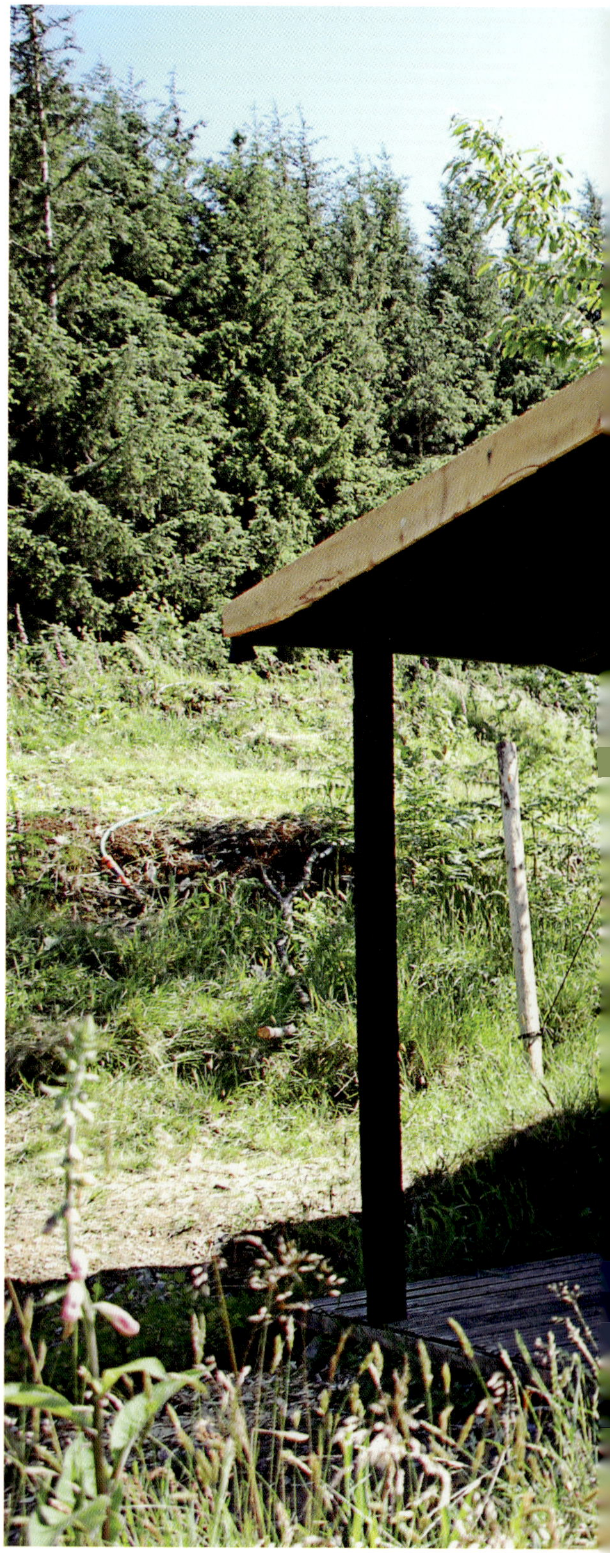

'The idea that art or artists should be useful really gets some people's goat, but there is definitely a growing consensus that art should be valued in terms of its function.'

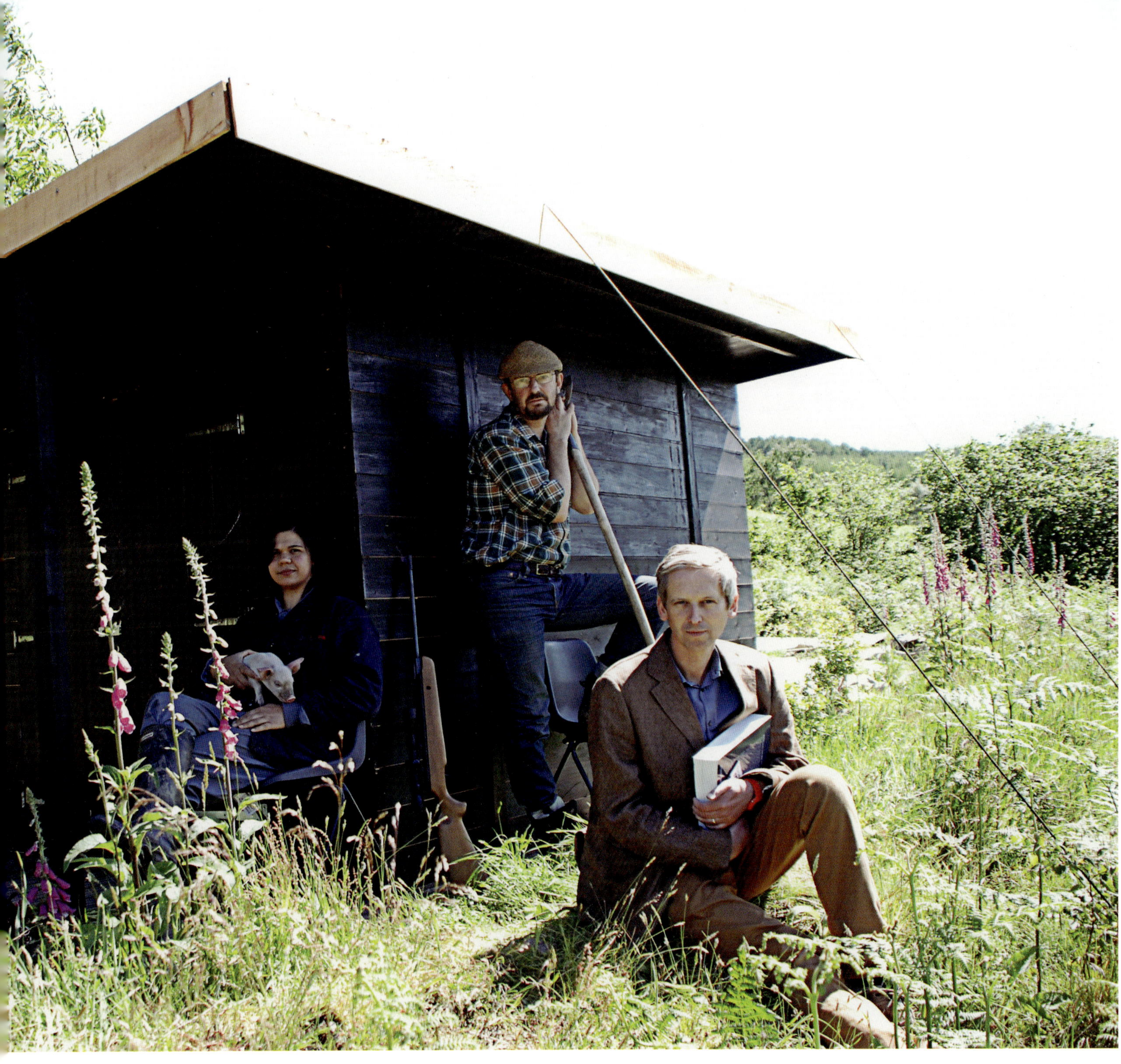

# Joanna Rajkowska

Joanna Rajkowska's wide-ranging projects produce transformative experiences for her audiences. At Frieze London the artist borrows from religious ritual by burning a field of incense in Regent's Park

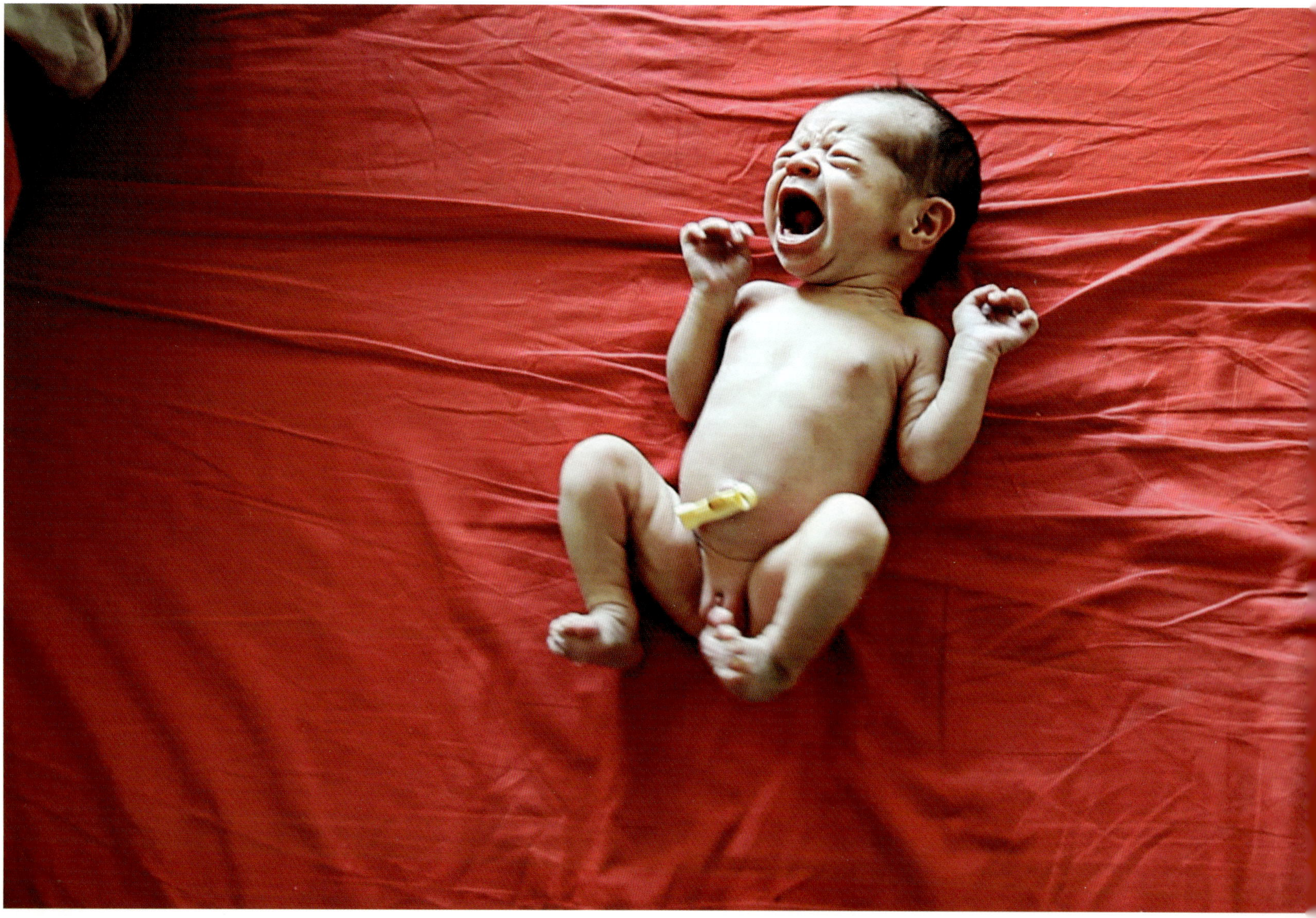

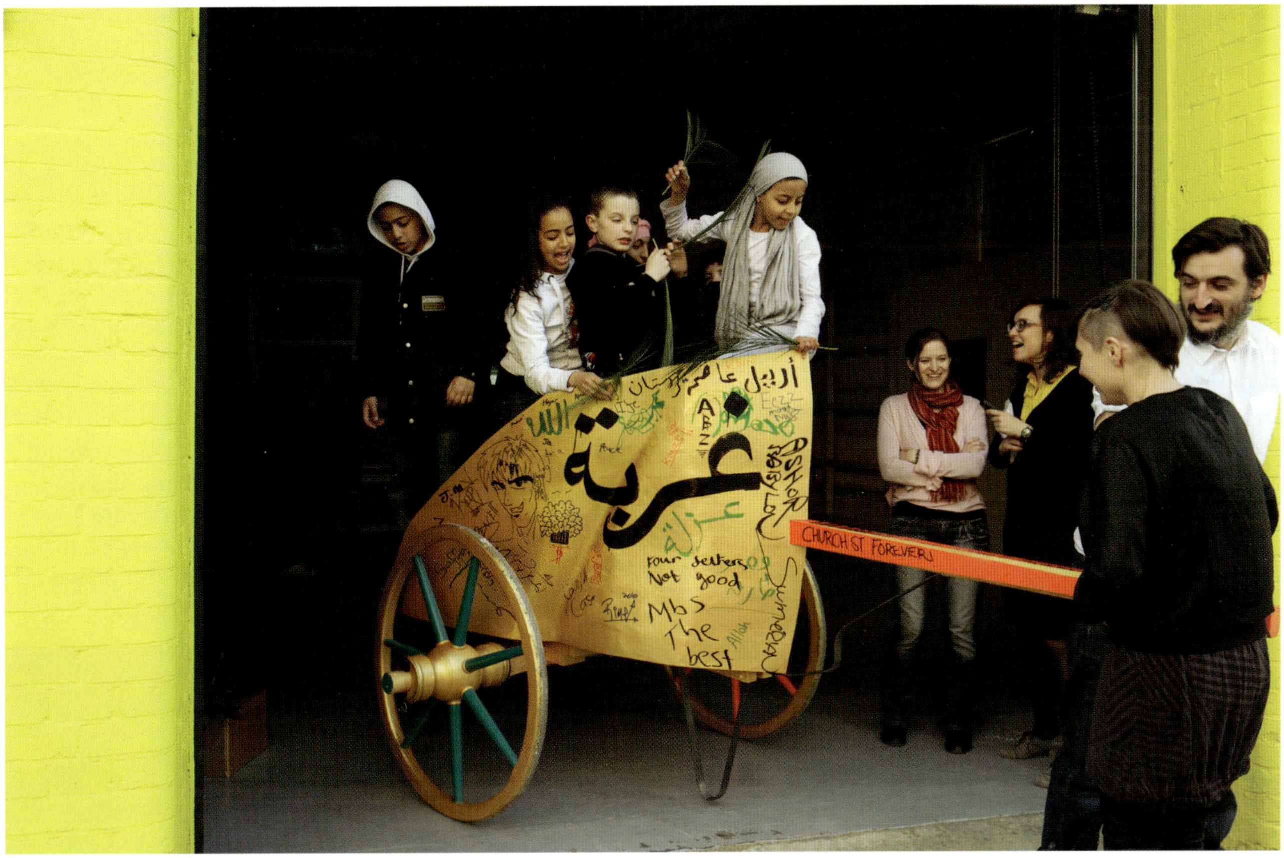


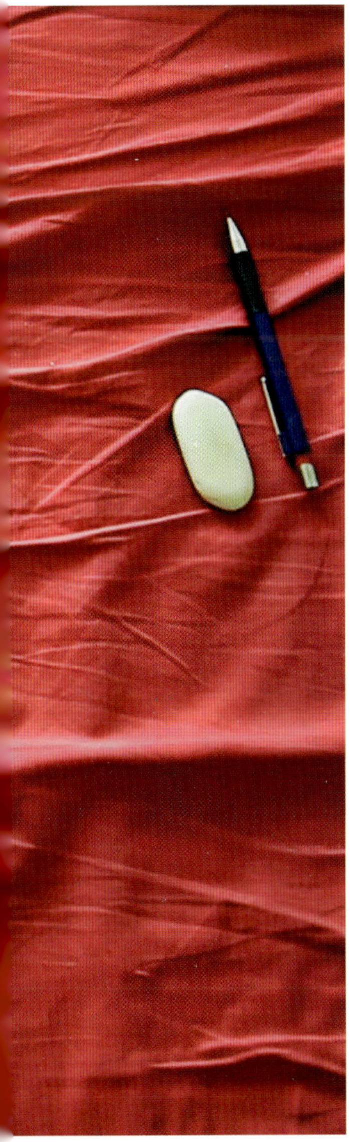

Above:
From the project *Chariot*
2010
Wood, paint and graffiti
1.5 × 1.2 × 1 m
Photography by Andrew Dixon
Courtesy of Zak-Branicka Gallery

Left:
*Red Rage*
From the project *Born in Berlin*
2012
Photograph
5 × 9 cm
Photography by Andrew Dixon
Courtesy of Zak-Branicka Gallery

**Joanna Rajkowska** (b. 1968) is a Polish artist based in London. In 2012 she featured in the group exhibition 'Forget Fear' at the 7th Berlin Biennale and presented solo exhibitions in the city that included 'Born in Berlin: A Letter to Rosa', Zak-Branicka Gallery, and 'Swamptown', Polish Institute. Her public projects in 2012 included *The Light of the Lodge* for the Copenhagen Art Festival and *The Peterborough Child* for Citizen Power Peterborough, a joint venture between Peterborough City Council and the Royal Society of Arts, London.

**Sarah McCrory** For your project at Frieze London, you transform an area of Regent's Park close to the fair into a field of smoking incense. How did you develop this idea?

**Joanna Rajkowska** I knew from the outset that I didn't want to create an object. I wanted to find a way to reflect that omnipresent sense of anticipation that hangs over art fairs: people always seem to be waiting anxiously for something to happen, for someone to come and exchange something with them. It's not only about the money—it's more than just pure trade—it's also about the things that will surprise them, that will prove they are there for a reason, and that that reason is valid.

From the start, I had this feeling that I wanted to use the tent and the surrounding area in some way; I wanted to activate it, to make it breathe. Shortly afterwards, I discovered that my baby daughter Rosa was very ill with cancer, and that gave the project a new significance—something much more profound. The sensation of waiting for something consolidated into the feeling that I was waiting for a miracle, for someone to come and tell me what I wanted to hear more than anything in the world: that Rosa would be completely cured.

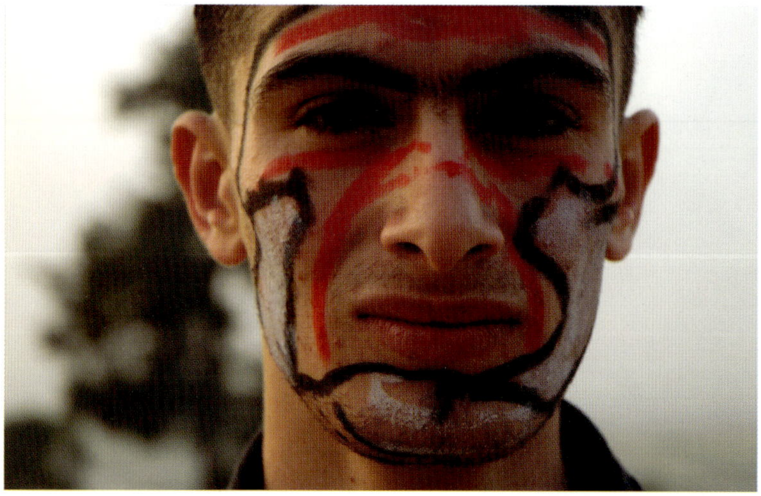

profound physical pleasure and not from, let's say, any political consensus. Witnessing that scenario was an incredible experience. I thought: if I'm ever able to induce a moment of singularity like that again—to allow someone to be completely themselves in a particular place in a particular moment—then I will have created one of these extremely rare instances of intensified experience, intensified presence, that art can sometimes generate.

When I thought about all the people that would be coming to the fair from around the world, it struck me that this was a cultural situation in which it would be possible to direct human behaviour, to shape it almost. My hope for this project is that visitors will sit or stand on the grass

**McCrory** I find your referencing of spirituality interesting because it has a complex relationship to contemporary art. Not only does the title of your work, *Forcing a Miracle*, employ a religious term, but the piece itself involves the burning of incense, which is done across many religions. Incense has a very distinct aroma—even people who aren't religious can relate to it immediately. Is this element of spirituality a new development in your practice?

**Rajkowska** To be honest, I see it as a continuation of my previous work. I remember once observing a group of people sitting in Grzybowski Square in Warsaw, which is on the border of the Jewish ghetto, gathered around the pond [Rajkowska's work *Oxygenator*, 2007]. They were watching an ozone cloud form above the surface of the water: it was bubbling up in a damp fog and escaping into the air. The people in the square were completely mesmerized: they didn't speak to one another; they just stood or sat and watched in silence. It was fascinating to see how they became completely in tune with themselves. They didn't have to communicate with anyone else: they could just watch and breathe and become perfectly conscious of their own bodies.

At the same time, the same people created a surprisingly coherent little community. The cohesion came from breathing, from

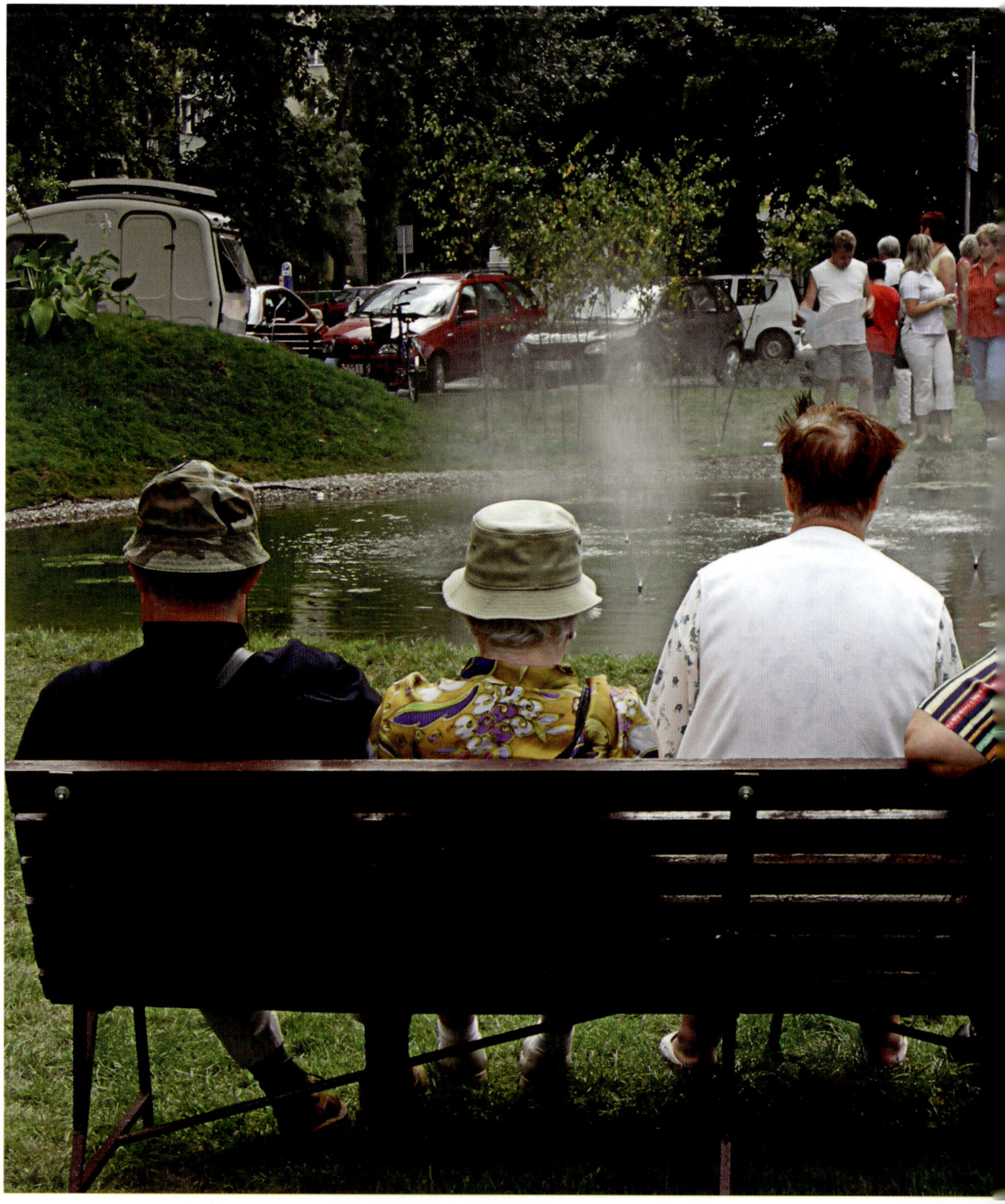

Opposite:
*Camping Jenin*
2008
Workshop at Freedom Theatre in the refugee camp in Jenin, Palestinian Authority
Photography by Leslie Dreyer
Courtesy of Zak-Branicka Gallery

Below:
From the project *Oxygenator*
2007
Grzybowski Square, Warsaw
Photography by Joanna Rajkowska
Courtesy of Zak-Branicka Gallery

‘My hope for this project is that visitors will sit or stand on the grass and just watch the incense burn and see the smoke rise—and, in that moment, become completely at one with themselves.’

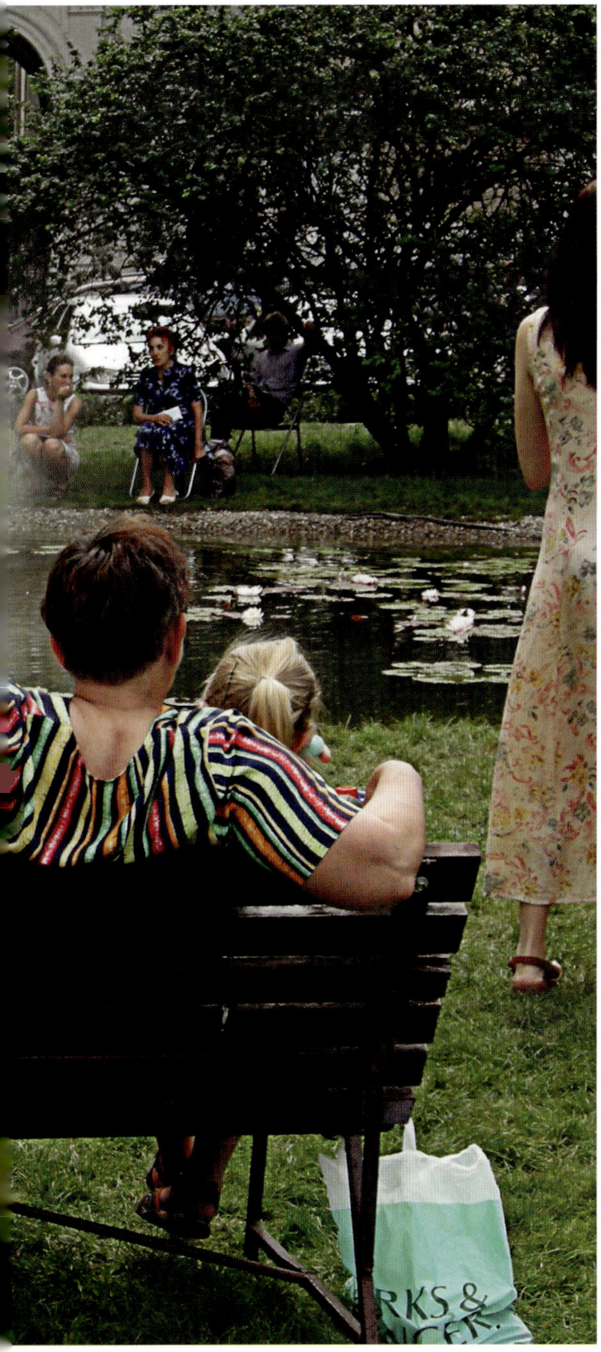

and just watch the incense burn and see the smoke rise—and, in that moment, become completely at one with themselves.

**McCrory** Art fairs tend to be contrived and controlled experiences, and visitors have certain expectations of them. What I find exciting about your project is that, experientially, it will remove people physically and mentally from the fair. It's interesting that, although you're going to set up the scenario, ultimately you won't have much control over how people respond.

**Rajkowska** That's one of the major elements of my practice: I consciously refuse to have control over my projects because I think that if you're craving control over the audience you aren't giving them any credit. You have to leave everything open so people can choose to feel one way or another. You don't have to set the direction; you're not running a kindergarten.

Another major aspect of *Forcing a Miracle* is to go beyond social rituals and put people in a situation where they don't know what to do with themselves. The fair is a highly ritualized situation—every gesture belongs to a certain expected choreography. And then you have smoke, which blurs expectations and which you can sniff and hide behind.

**McCrory** Land art, which your project references, has tended to be a male-dominated sphere, and the gestures it involves—hole-digging, earth-moving—are all predominately masculine. You have less of a domineering relationship to the land. By putting incense into the ground, it's almost like you're allowing the earth to breathe, opening it up.

**Rajkowska** I've been making public art works for over ten years now, and I realized quite early on that the appropriate point of departure for my work was a feeling of helplessness—which is to say it's not about what I can do, but rather about what I can't. Land art doesn't have to be about using heavy machinery or major construction sites: you can create a very powerful effect with a minimal intervention—a fata morgana.

Ultimately, what I like about Land art is that it overwhelms you and makes you feel really small. That's exactly how I feel myself when I embark on a new public art project. I have to deal with this uncontrollable organism of the city I'm going to be working in, but I can't ever really grasp it—it's beyond my comprehension. And when the work is finally unveiled, it seems to carry more meaning than you can understand. But you can feel it, and other people can feel it too.

That's what I love about public art. With this project I wanted the ground not only to breathe; I wanted it to burn. When you have a child that in her devilish innocence and joy is losing her eyesight, you burn—you literally burn your tissues from inside. I wanted to re-enact it in soil. I wanted London to burn and cry with me.

**McCrory** There is a great sensitivity within your practice, since, as you've already mentioned, you're not looking to force a reaction from people. Of course, that then leaves your work open to failure. How do you feel about that?

**Rajkowska** It depends, because sometimes the failures are fantastic and sometimes they're really embarrassing. I generally love failures as they are so genuine and naked. And they make me laugh at myself.

# Emdash Award: Cécile B. Evans

## Cécile B. Evans has devised an audio guide for Frieze London, comprising contributions from figures outside the art world

**Cécile B. Evans** (b. 1983), a Belgian-American artist based in Berlin, is the recipient of the Emdash Award 2012, which allows an emerging artist living outside the UK to realize a site-specific project for Frieze London. Evans has participated in recent group exhibitions that include 'Gaze & Lust: Sexuality in Contemporary Art', Bergen Kunstmuseum (2012), and the 1st Berlin Kreuzberg Biennale (2010). She is artist-in-residence at CCA Andratx, Majorca, from November 2012.

**Sarah McCrory** What was the catalyst for your Emdash Award proposal for Frieze London?

**Cécile B. Evans** I was invited by the curator Rebecca Lamarche-Vadel to present a performance for 'A Skeleton in the Closet', an exhibition she was organizing at the Heidelberger Kunstverein last year. The performance [*Lecture*, 2011] took the form of a PowerPoint presentation that explained the show to the audience based on my experiences of searching on Google and discovering various Internet rabbit holes. I found the whole process completely satisfying. After the performance in Heidelberg, several people came up to me and thanked me for helping them to understand the art works from another perspective.

Later in the year, I performed the work for a second time at 'ReMap 3' in Athens, where the crowd was totally different and absolutely understood the medium I was working with. After that performance, someone pointed out that what I was doing wasn't really fair to the artists whose work I was analysing. I took this criticism very seriously, but ultimately I felt that artists can only really control how their work is presented up to a point. One of the great things about how exhibitions work nowadays is that there comes a moment when the intentions of the curator and the artist don't really matter any more, because the audience experiences the art indirectly through the accounts of others—in the media or on blogs. We are all more aware than ever of what is going on in the world today, even if we don't have direct physical access to it.

*Lecture* served as the point of departure for my project for Frieze, and the concept was cemented while I was on an artist's residency in Lithuania, when I spent a lot of time watching British television panel shows. I really enjoyed the format of these shows, in which people you would normally never see in the same room are brought together to form an 'expert panel'—even though their authority is completely nonsensical—and when they are asked questions by the host the aim is not to get the answer right, but to riff off each other to come up with witty ripostes.

**McCrory** How did this interest in panel shows inform your idea to create an audio guide to Frieze London?

**Evans** The audio guide was an idea I had been toying with for a while. I like how a simple electronic device can somehow become this absent 'voice of truth' no matter what it's actually saying. My aim is to build up a 'dream team' of diverse contributors to the guide, like a panel show. Unlike a genuine show, of course, my panel will never exist in reality; instead, the guide will be pieced together from the different contributions to create an entirely new narrative—just as they do on reality television shows.

**McCrory** And that gives you quite a lot of control, because you can edit the guide in nuanced ways to alter how people respond to the works at the fair.

**Evans** To avoid falling into the trap of turning the guide into my own interpretation of the art, I am choosing contributors who work in fields that aren't directly related to my own. The subjective element comes from my formulation of a series of questions that force the contributors to relay their personal, emotional experiences of the works.

**McCrory** It's quite a generous gesture on your part, because there are no art specialists participating.

**Evans** I have been considering whether to include an art historian as a host for my non-art panel. It would break it up a bit, and they could share anecdotes and tit-bits about the galleries. I'm very aware of how

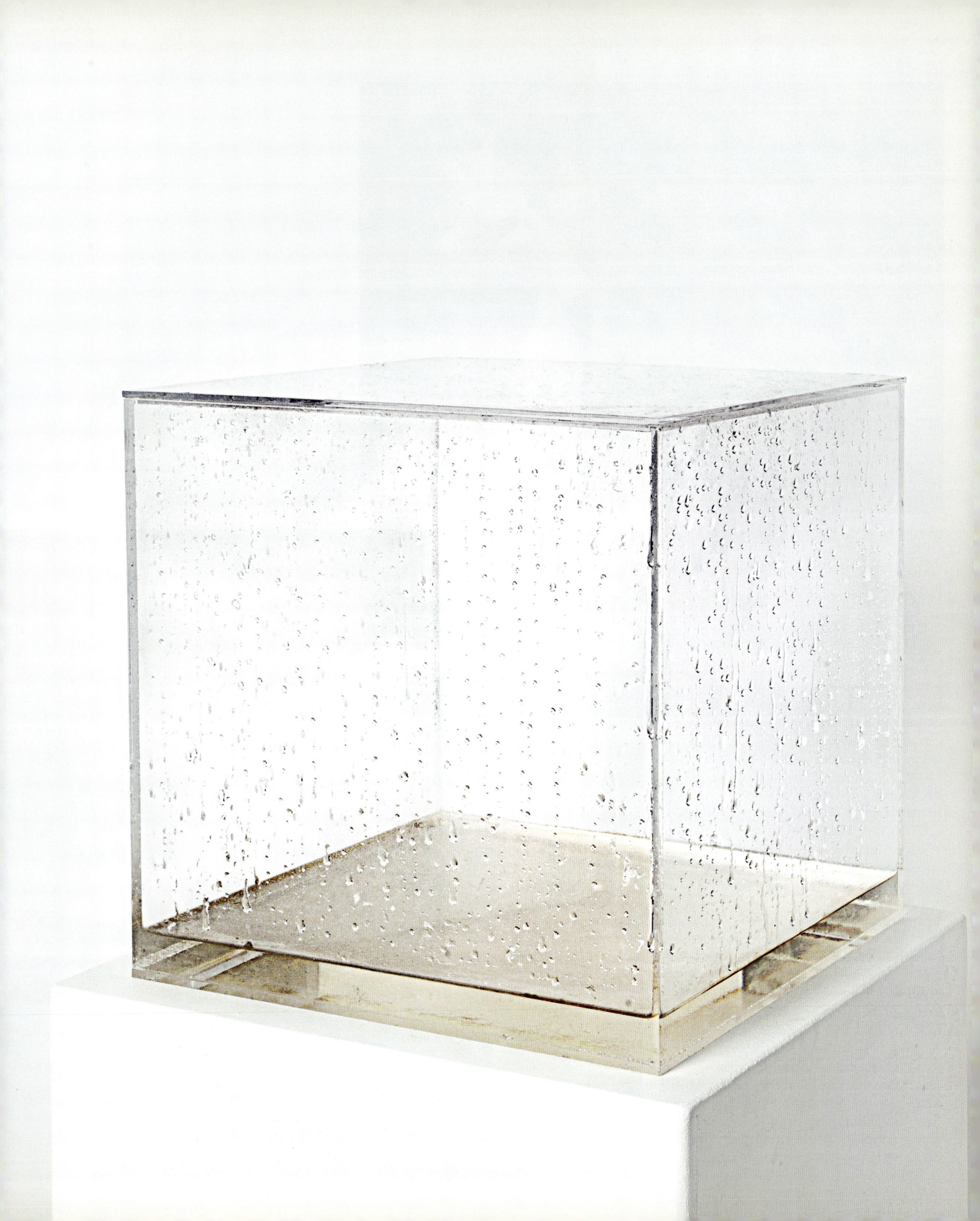

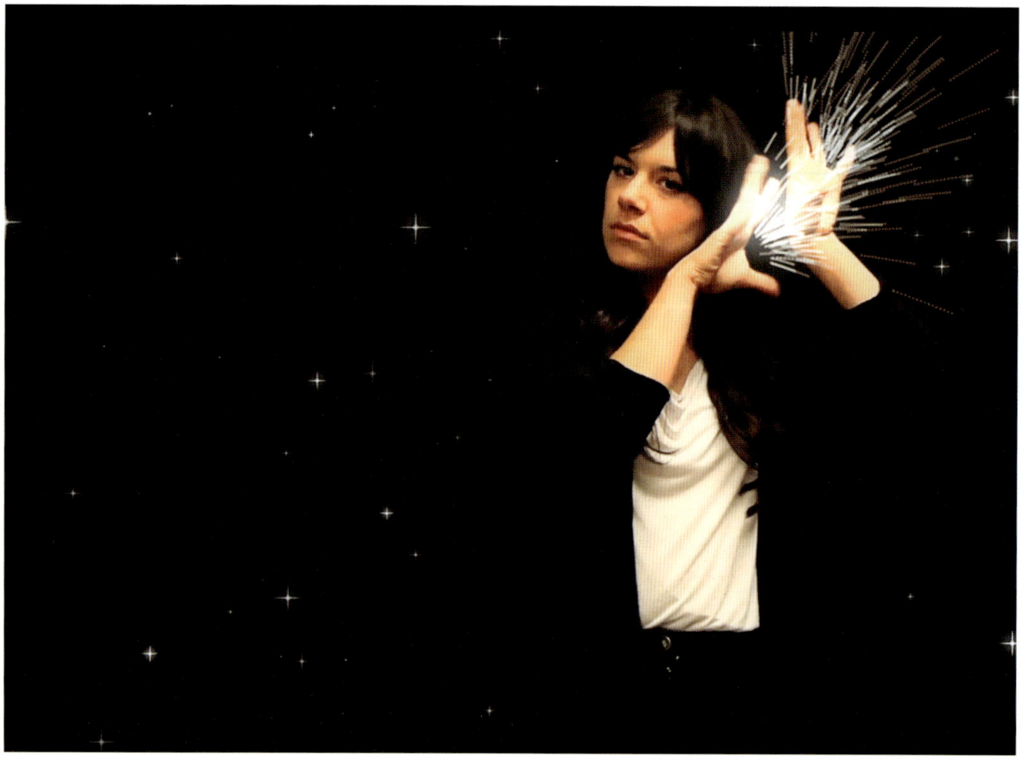

Previous page:
*Crying About Crying About*
2011
Plexiglass, acrylic and corn syrup
25 × 25 × 25 cm

Left:
*Straight Up*
2011
HD video
7 min.

Below:
*Countdown*
2012
HD video
5 min. 46 sec.

Opposite:
*Please*
2010
Corn syrup, coconut milk and pineapple juice on paper
82.5 × 63 cm

easily this work could be read as a form of mockery—in terms of it being a send-up either of the panellists or the art world—but my intention is precisely the opposite: to break down these kinds of barriers. One of the things I like best about Frieze is that it's an event for the general public, so the majority of people listening to my audio guide will not necessarily be from an art background.

**McCrory** I find the most interesting interpretations often come from people who are not talking about their own field of expertise, as their comments are not encased in jargon or skewed by insider information.

**Evans** That's so true. If you ask an artist to explain their work, they'll often default to defining it in terms of the things they're trying to eschew, such as material, intellectual or referential values. When I studied theatre, one essay that really had an impact on me was Antonin Artaud's 'No More Masterpieces' [1938], in which he observed that if you're watching a work of Shakespeare and you don't like it or you don't get it, it's not your fault: it's Shakespeare's fault or it's the director's fault. While it may not apply in every instance, it's something I always try to keep in mind in relation to my work.

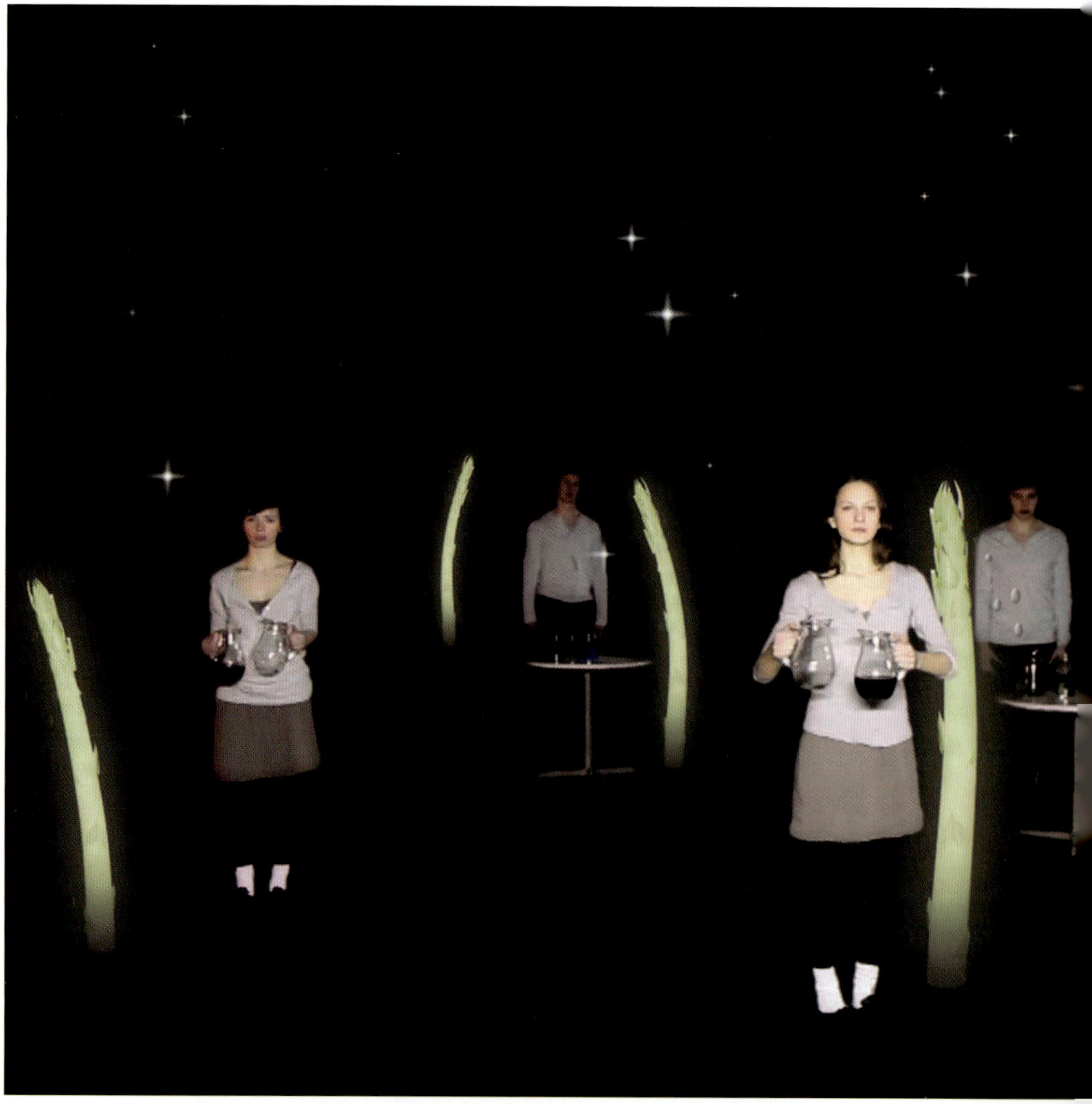

‘I like impossible tasks; I enjoy taking on something unlimited, getting a bit lost and then arriving at physical endpoints that are hopefully grounded in a sense of universality.’

**McCrory** How does the audio guide fit into the trajectory of your practice so far?

**Evans** The key point of departure in my work has always been the notion of emotional value, both in terms of the industries that seek to generate emotions—such as the movie business—and in relation to the science that’s used to explain feelings. I’ve employed rulers that are used to measure tear production [*You May Keep One of Your Children,* 2011], for example, and I’ve worked with the some structural elements from science fiction films [*Straight Up,* 2011], as well as with neuroscientists who have explained where love is located physically in the brain [*Romantic Love (from Back to Front),* 2011].

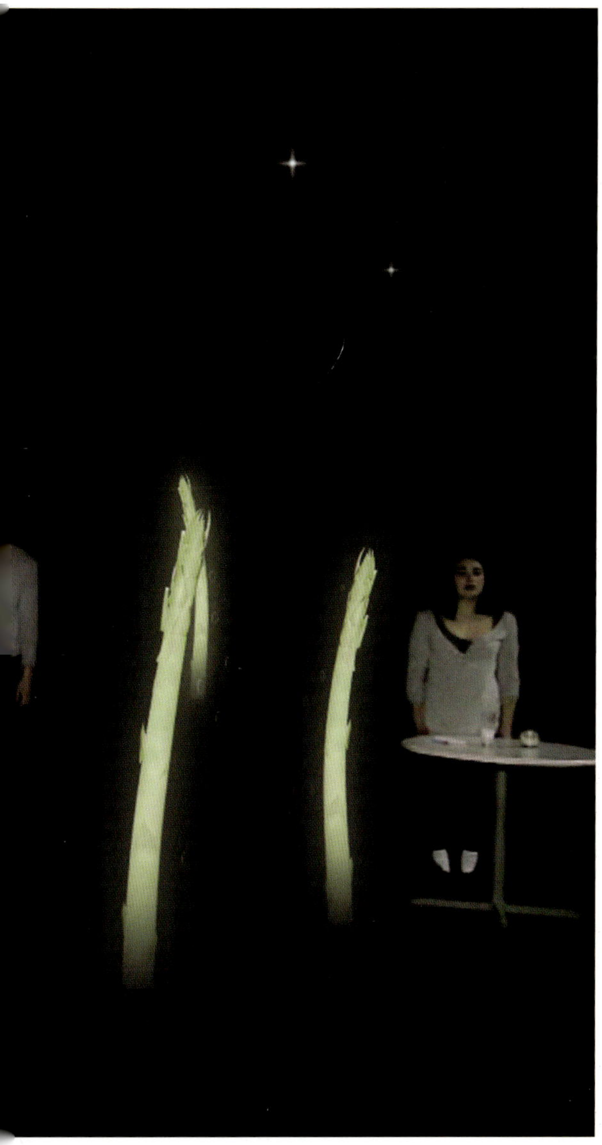

**McCrory** You strike me as something of a romantic—trying to comprehend things that are impossible to explain.

**Evans** I like impossible tasks; I enjoy taking on something unlimited, getting a bit lost and then arriving at physical endpoints that are hopefully grounded in a sense of universality. But I can’t say I’m looking for an answer, just playing with the data at a certain moment.

**McCrory** In your work for Frieze, you’re also hoping to include a new form of hologram, known as a ‘telepresence’.

**Evans** Yes, these are the virtual assistants that have been springing up in airports recently making pre-recorded announcements. The technology is really quite straightforward—it’s a person-shaped piece of Perspex onto which is back-projected an image accompanied by audio. It’s amazing to watch how seriously people take them, their suspension of disbelief, even though airports are among the first places we generally tend to rail against authority. I suppose it’s instinctual: if a guard tells you to take your shoes off and he’s made of Perspex, you do it!

**McCrory** It’s authoritative Perspex!

**Evans** Exactly! I wonder whether one of the reasons we’re so prepared to accept them is because they’re akin to something we might have seen in an old sci-fi film. I remember watching the mid-1980s television show *Jem and the Holograms* when I was a kid, which was about an all-girl rock group that used hologram technology. I recall thinking at the time: ‘Wow, this is the future! One day, I’ll be standing next to Jem!’ And now that really is happening, but not in quite the way that I thought it would! I love how wonderfully simple yet simultaneously mind-blowing these telepresences are; standing next to one is an experiential moment that feels really rare.

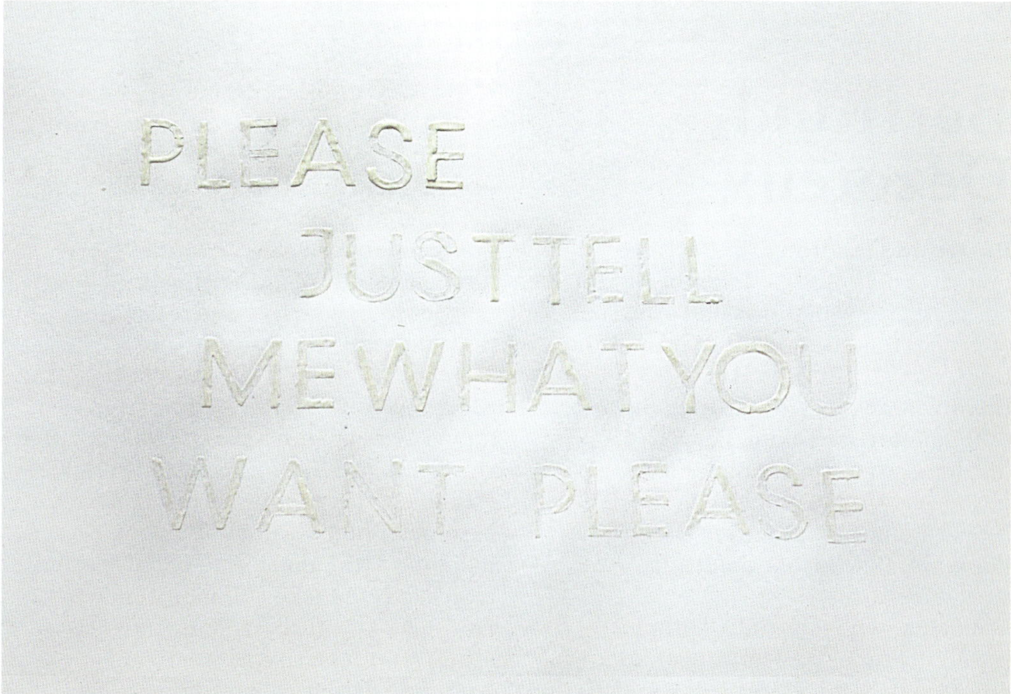

# Frieze Film

Sam Thorne introduces five artists who have produced new films for Frieze London, screened in the auditorium and on Channel 4 during the week of the fair

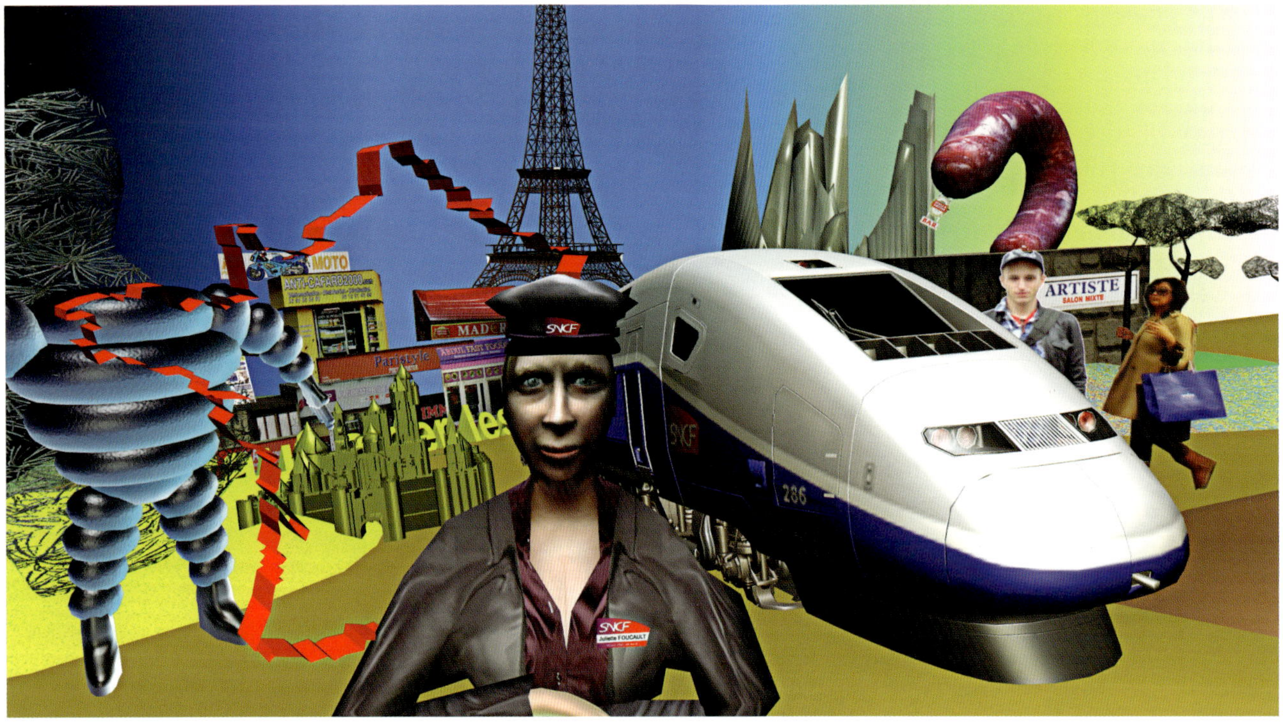


*The History of France in 3D*
2012
CGI animation
15 min.
Production in partnership with FRAC Aquitaine, Bordeaux

## Bertrand Dezoteux

**Bertrand Dezoteux** (b. 1982) is a French artist based in Bayonne. Dezoteux has presented solo shows and projects at venues that include FRAC Aquitaine, Bordeaux (2012), Sala Rekalde, Bilbao (2012), Le Carré, Bayonne (2011), Palais de Tokyo, Paris (2010), and Espace Croisé, Roubaix (2007). His recent group exhibitions include 'Low Mountains' at the Dar Bellarj Foundation, Marrakech (2012).

Dezoteux, who has studied graphic novels in France as well as traditional painting in South Korea, uses modelling software to make animations. *Le Corso* (2008) is an attempt to construct a rural video from an animal's point of view, and takes the form of an amateur documentary following a herd of galloping mammals—seemingly an ambiguous amalgam of goats and deer—who learn how to live and function in the human world.

More recently, *Txerri* (2012) follows two aggressive and mischievous CGI pigs that cause mayhem around a Basque village—Dezoteux's home town. They chase children, hump shrubbery, knock over pot plants and run along with a real severed pig's head. Made in collaboration with Dezoteux's brother Arnaud, *Sly's Drivers* (2011) features a silver Lycra-clad rendering of Sylvester Stallone, who drives an articulated lorry across a desert basin. This spoof advert for a fictional driving reality TV programme culminates with Sly dancing along with a crowd of synchronized stickmen, the final strap-line—in the style of overblown ad copy—proclaiming: 'The future F1 champion will be an American.'

For Frieze Film, Dezoteux has produced what he describes as a 'collage of elements' in which: 'The action takes place on a faraway planet, where small continents are drifting. They coagulate and form an island that compacts the history of France. All the ages, from the dinosaurs to recent times, coexist here on the same territory.' Dezoteux continues, in his words, 'to observe, as an amateur anthropologist, the behaviours of the *homo digitalis*'.

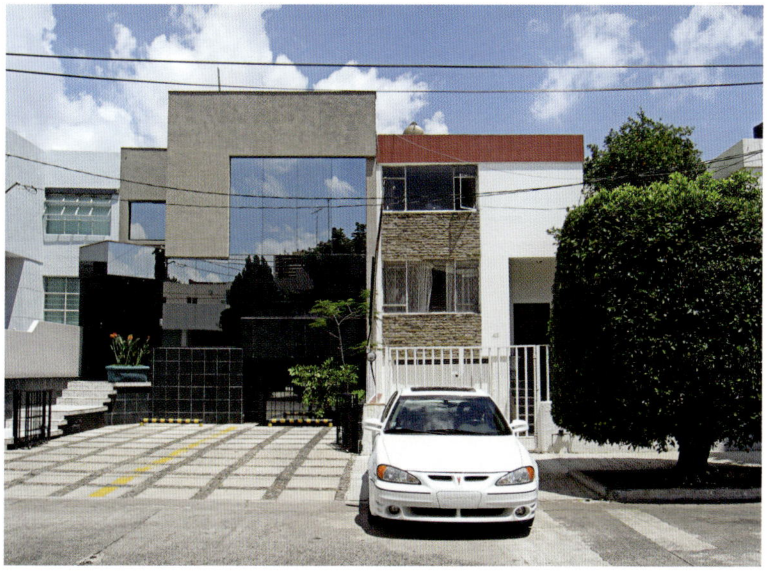

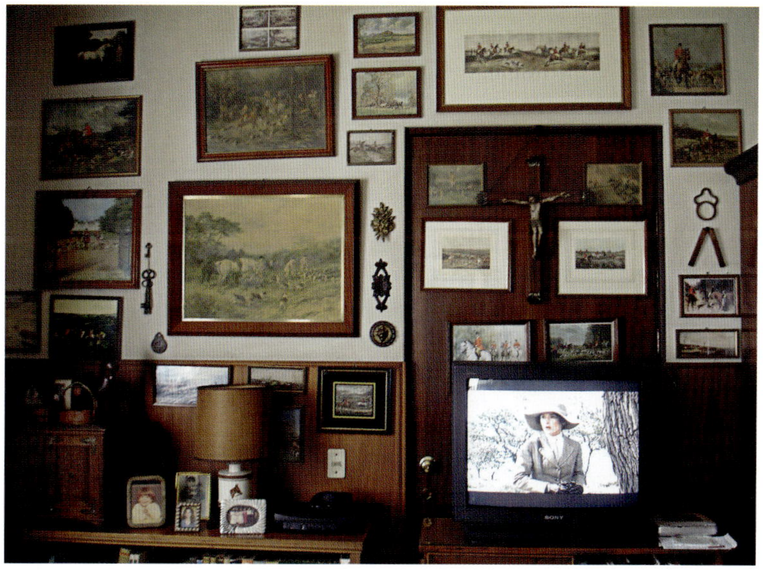

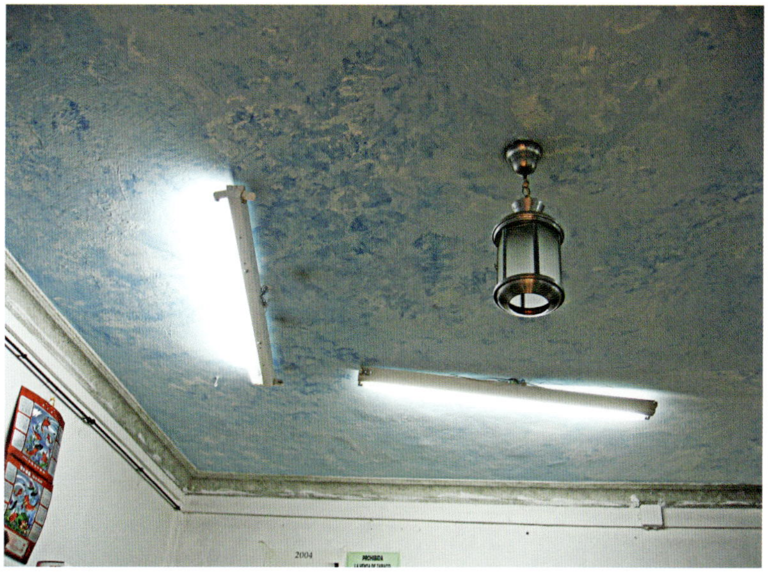

*Reads Like the Paper*
*Group 4*
2010
Single-channel video
17 min. 35 sec.
Courtesy of Murray Guy

# Patricia Esquivias

**Patricia Esquivias** (b. 1979) is a Venezuelan artist based in Madrid. Her recent solo exhibitions and projects include those at the Hammer Museum, Los Angeles (2011), Museo Nacional Centro de Arte Reina Sofía, Madrid (2009), and Midway Center for Contemporary Art, Minneapolis (2009). Her work has featured in group exhibitions such as 'LifeStories', Museum of Contemporay Art, Detroit (2011), and 'Younger than Jesus', New Museum, New York (2009).

Esquivias' series of videos 'Reads Like the Paper' (2006–ongoing) comprises a series of diaristic presentations, stories and seemingly on-the-fly observations. The artist is never fully visible, although her hands sometimes are, pointing to pictures or miming people—characters holding hands or, as she says, 'spinning on their tiptoes'. Her sing-song, almost sleepy voice tells stories that are all the more affecting for their brevity and waywardness. In one, for example, Esquivias recounts having heard Berlin's 1986 hit 'Take My Breath Away' playing on several car radios in an ice cream parlour parking lot, over which loomed a military mural. This leads her to wonder about all of 'those breaths being taken away now'. In another,as the opening sequence of the film *True Romance* (1993) plays on her laptop, the artist remembers how a brief stay in California made her reassess her ideas about homeless people.

For the new work that she has produced for Frieze Film, Esquivias considers a specific building in Madrid that she wants to read like a book: 'I would like to pick it up and take it with me and sit and find out its stories. More that that, I wish that somebody would sit beside me and tell me the stories. But how do I find this person?'

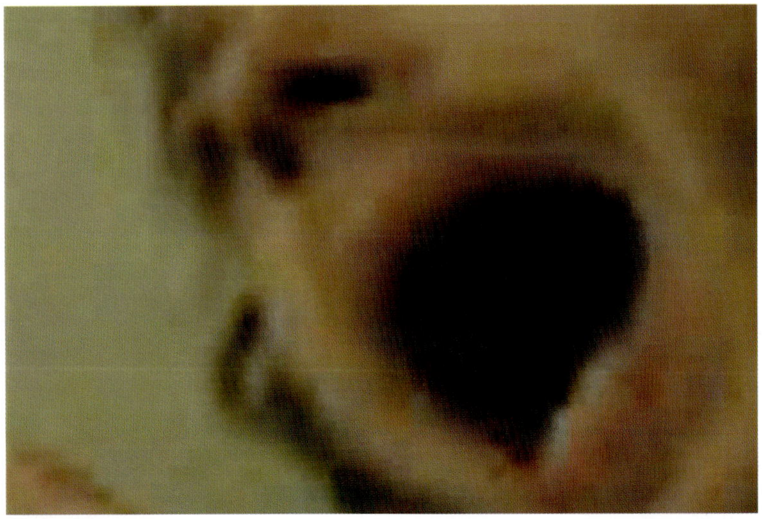

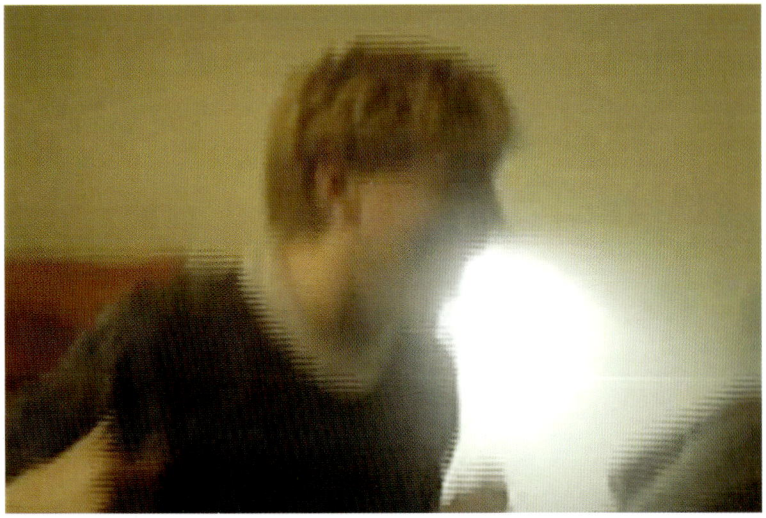

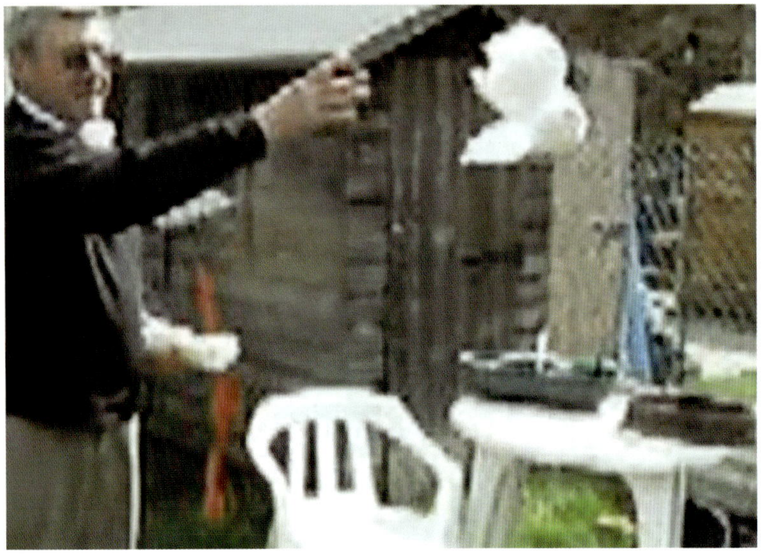

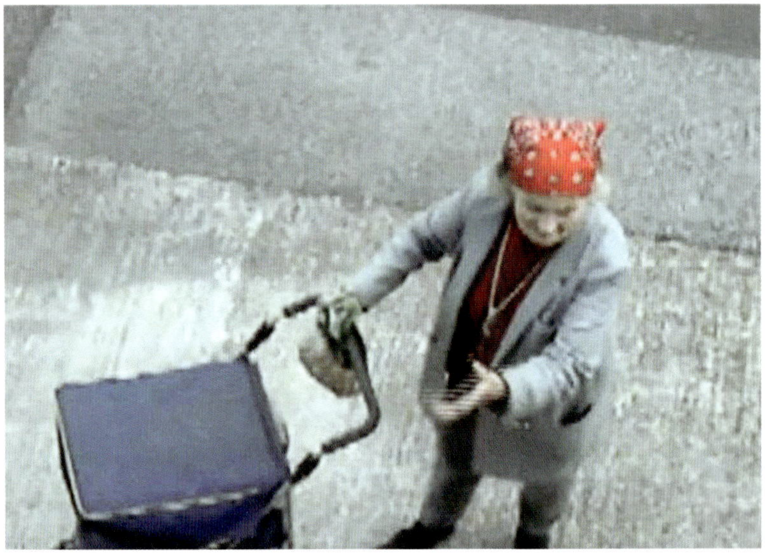

From the series 'Portraits of Domestic Bliss'
Top right and left: *(s)*
Bottom left: *(b)*
Bottom right: *(p)*
2010–12
Digital video
Durations variable

# Jimmy Merris

**Jimmy Merris** (b. 1983) is a British artist based in London. His recent solo exhibitions in the city include: 'Deep Joy on Home Soil', Studio Voltaire (2012); 'Economics 101' (with Terry Dennett), SPACE (2011); and 'Finding Your Feet in the Times of the Worried Man', Seventeen Gallery (2011).

Merris' sweetly antic short videos are concerned with economy, in the sense of brevity and limited means, but also in a way that touches upon broader socio-economic issues. In terms of process, they are staunchly lo-fi productions, patched together from snatches of distorted music, home videos, email exchanges and amateur performances. Friends, neighbours and even the artist's landlord feature as collaborators in these works, which are usually not much longer than a music video, more often the length of a YouTube clip. Unemployment and the economic downturn are frequent themes, as is implied by the titles of two 2011 works: *FOR SALE* and *Finding Your Feet in the Times of the Worried Man*.

Merris is also actively involved with Studio Downturn, a small studio complex in south London, where facilities include Jobcentre Blues (an online collection of money-related songs) and Downturn Press (a 'printing press' where techniques include dropping patties out of a first-floor window and running over paper with second-hand cars). Despite these self-consciously modest means, Merris' work is unerringly positive. 'Portraits of Domestic Bliss' (2010–12), for example, is a series of very short videos of quasi-epiphanies—a glowing computer screen, a house party—while for the performance *Happiness is Just around the Corner* (2011), the artist hugs a friend for the duration of the titular song. Building a fragile kind of optimism out of the barest of materials, Merris finds freedom (financial or otherwise) in friends, collaboration and clowning around.

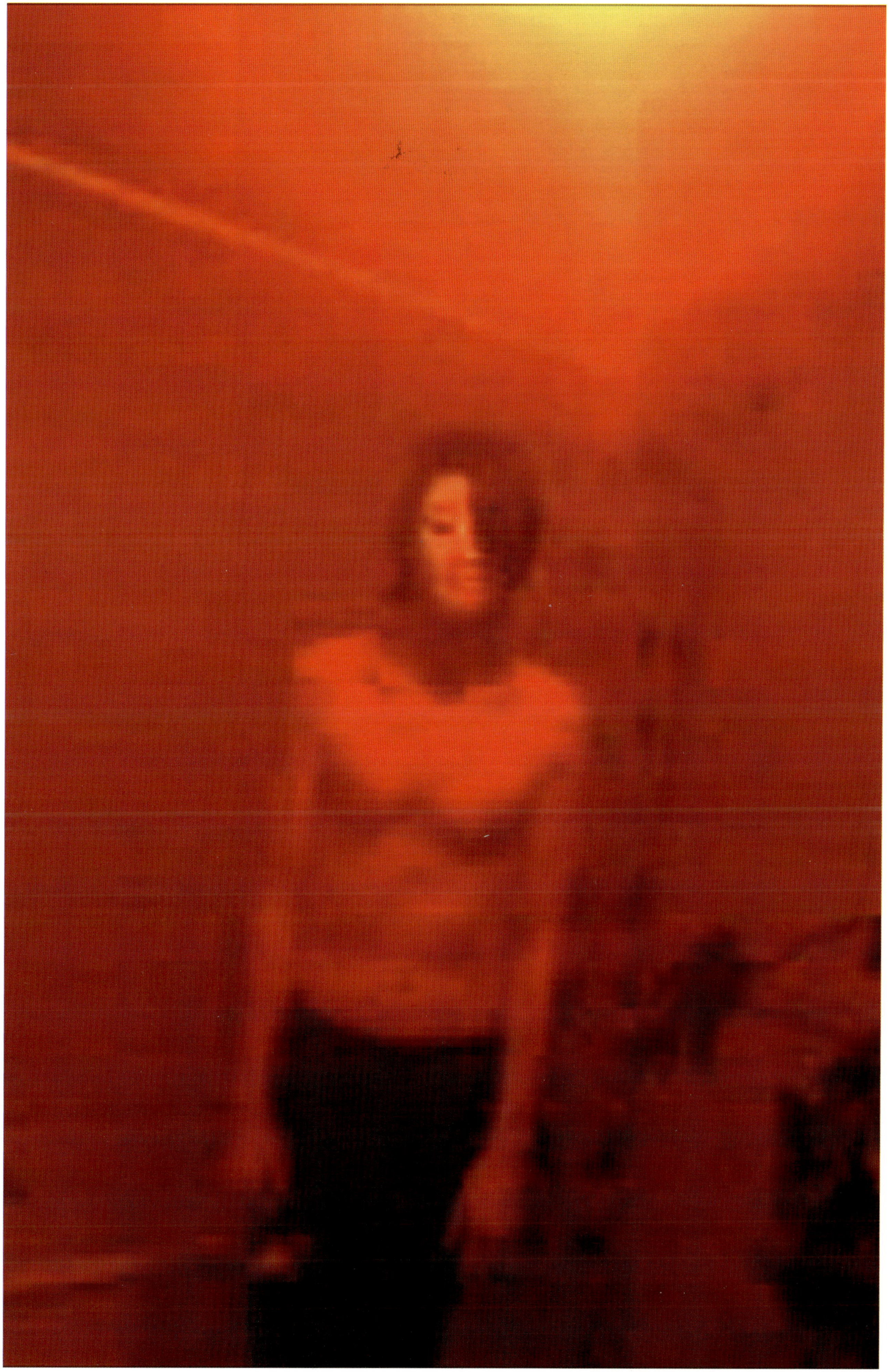

*the joyous free-for-all*
(detail)
2012
Digital video
2 min. 7 sec.

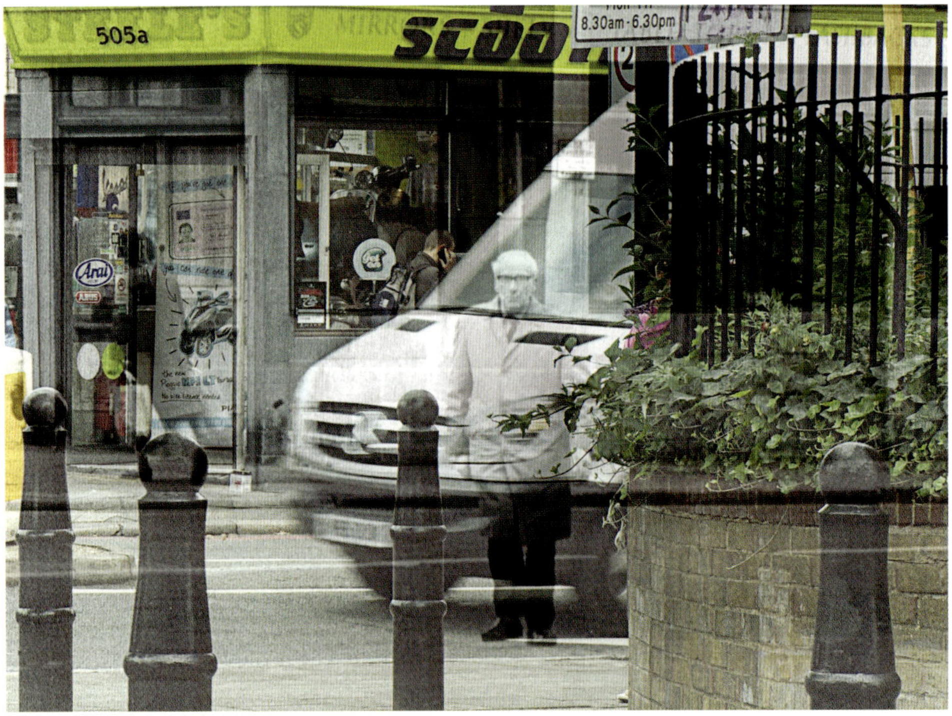


*The Man Phoning Mum*
2011
HD video
12 min.

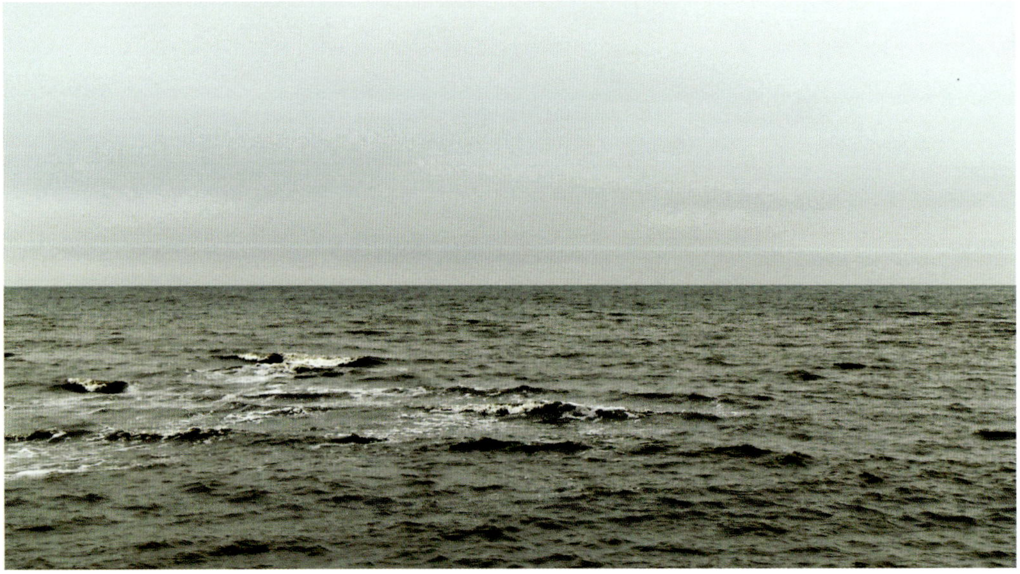

*Horizon (Five Pounds a Belgian)*
2012
HD video installation at Turner Contemporary, Margate
18 min. 35 sec.
(seamless loop)

# John Smith

**John Smith** (b. 1952) is a British artist based in London. Recent solo projects include those at Ferens Art Gallery, Hull (2012), Turner Contemporary, Margate (2012), Kestnergesellschaft, Hanover (2012), Weserburg Museum of Modern Art, Bremen (2012), and PEER, London (2011). His recent group exhibitions include 'Image Counter Image', Haus der Kunst, Munich (2012), and 'Has the Film Already Started?', Tate Britain, London (2011).

Smith's work is usually witty but deadly serious, frequently anecdotal yet also theory-driven. His early 16mm film *The Girl Chewing Gum* (1976), made while he was still a student, is consistent with the Structuralist films of the time in the way it foregrounds the technical aspects of its own production, but the way it plays out is closer to Monty Python. Filmed for a continuous ten minutes on an east London street corner, chance events are recast as a carefully scripted scene, as Smith's voice can be seemingly heard from behind the camera, appearing to 'direct' what are actually random events: 'Put the cigarette in your mouth! Good.'

In more recent works, the artist often focuses his camera on the mundane and the domestic, although broader societal pressures continue to be acutely registered. In 'Hotel Diaries' (2001–7), for example, Smith films a series of short improvised monologues in a number of hotel rooms, late-night doubts and worries meandering but always returning to the ongoing conflicts in the Middle East. His anecdotes interweave with comments about TV news coverage of the 'War on Terror', with the hotel room used as something like a found film set.

As critic Martin Herbert has written of the artist's practice: 'Representation, Smith's work implies, is at once a haven of quiet deceits and our surest stopgap against an infinite forgetting.'

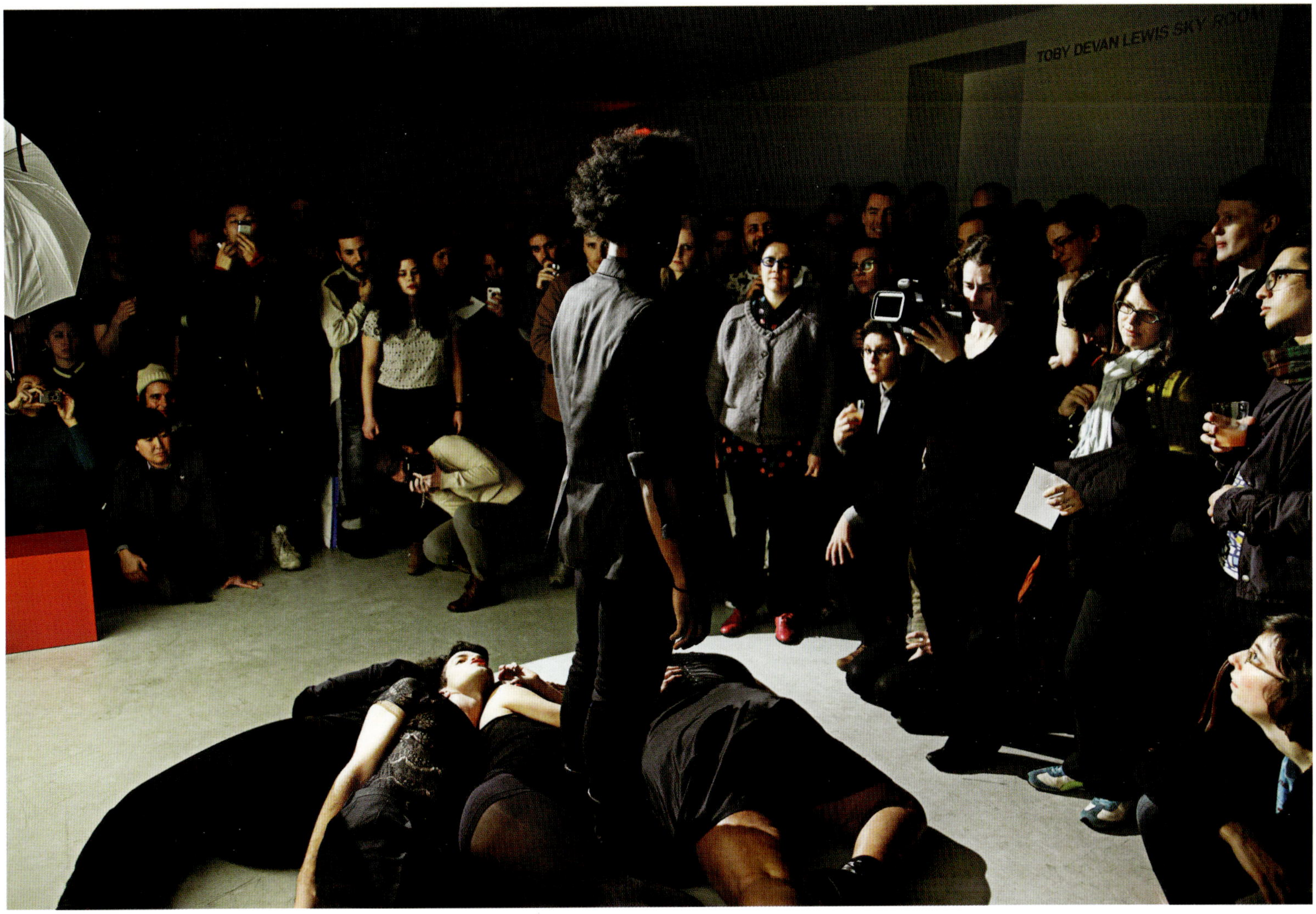


*Full Body Quotation*
2011
Performance
Exhibition view at
'Performa 11' at New
Museum, New York

# Wu Tsang

**Wu Tsang** (b. 1982) is an American artist based in Los Angeles. He has participated in recent group exhibitions that include the Whitney Biennial, Whitney Museum of American Art, New York (2012), and 'The Ungovernables: The 2012 New Museum Triennial', New Museum, New York (2012). For Frieze Film, he presents a work in collaboration with Senegal-based writer, filmmaker and cultural historian **Nana Oforiatta-Ayim**.

Wu Tsang occupies various roles—filmmaker, artist, performer, activist—although all of his work is concerned with the difficulties of accurately representing a community. In 2008 he began to co-host Wildness (with DJs NGUZUNGUZU and Total Freedom), a popular weekly performance night at the Silver Platter in Los Angeles, a small bar that has for 50 years provided a meeting place for the Latin American LGBT community. It was, as Tsang has said, 'a fun party that evolved into a more explicitly political platform'. He later co-founded a free legal clinic next door, providing legal assistance with name-changes, criminal expungement, housing, domestic violence and immigration for the transgender community. His 2012 film *Wildness* includes documentary footage of this period, such as interviews with the bar's patrons and owners, but it is also emphatically fictionalized, narrated by both the artist and (in Spanish) the invented voice of the Silver Platter itself.

Aside from this explicitly socially engaged work, Tsang is also working on an ongoing film and performance project titled *Full Body Quotation*. This is based on a technique involving performers, equipped with hidden ear-pieces, lip-synching to dialogue from carefully chosen sources. The earliest of these pieces, *The Shape of a Right Statement I* (2008), restages a YouTube clip by autism rights activist Amanda Baggs. Tsang 're-speaks' her monologue, as he stares into the camera, eyes welling with tears. As with all of the works from this series, the film gives the sense not of speaking for the subject so much as of being spoken *through*.

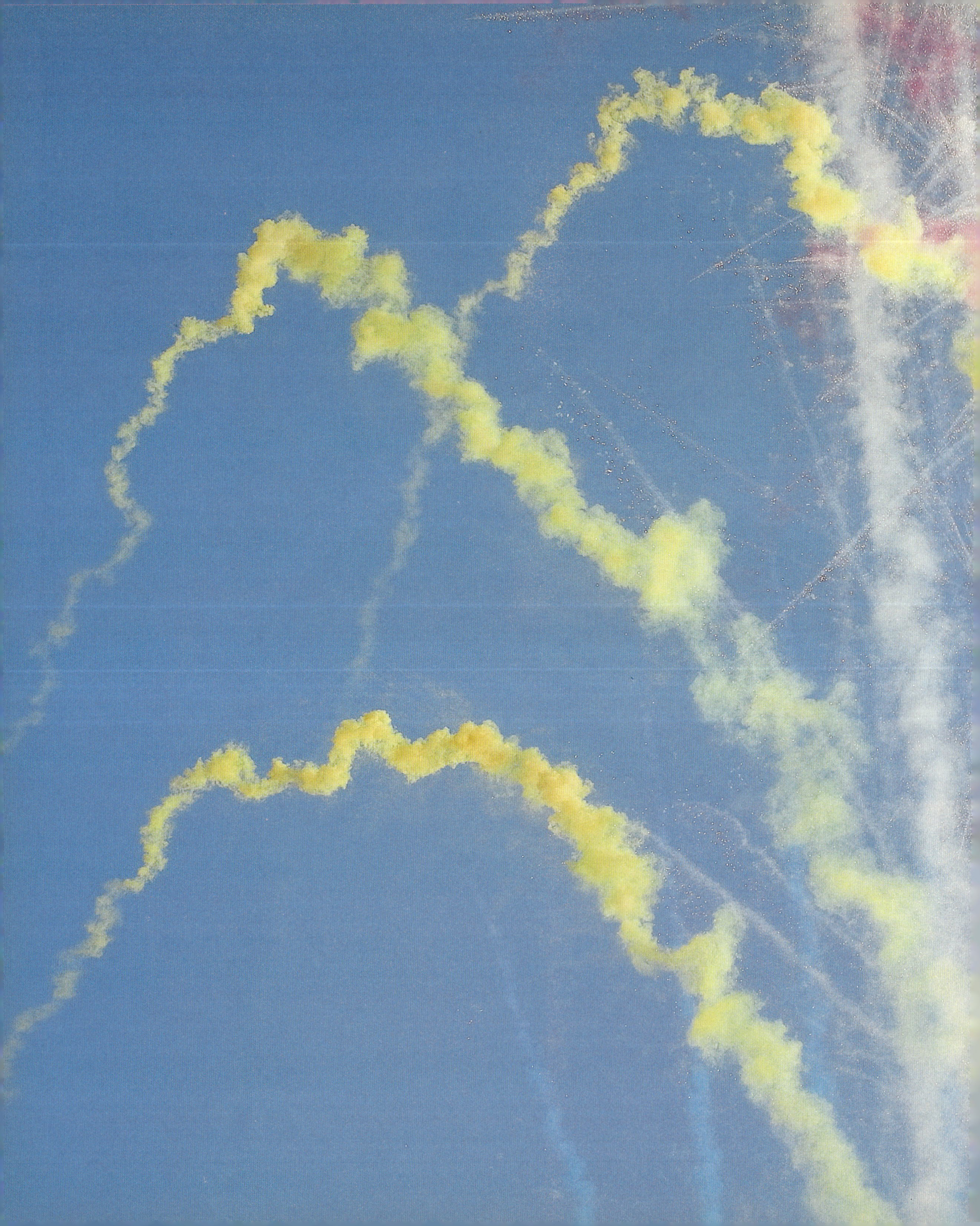

# Artists

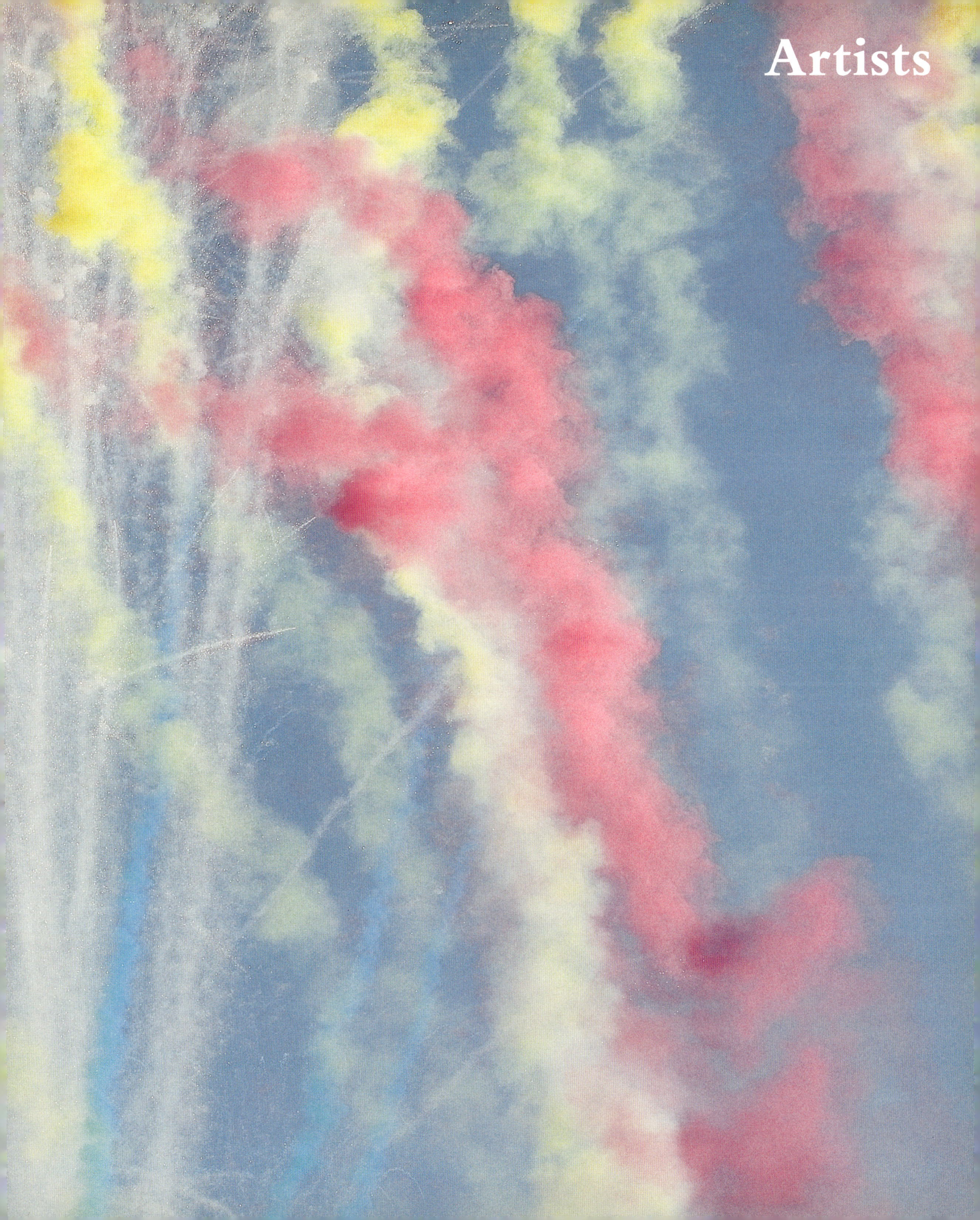

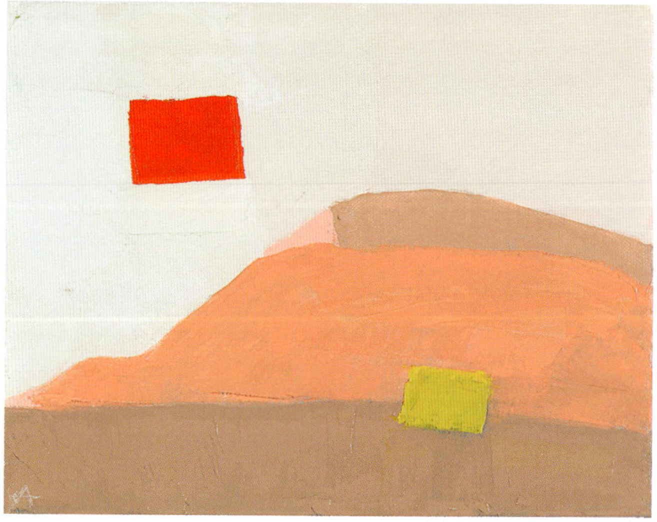
1

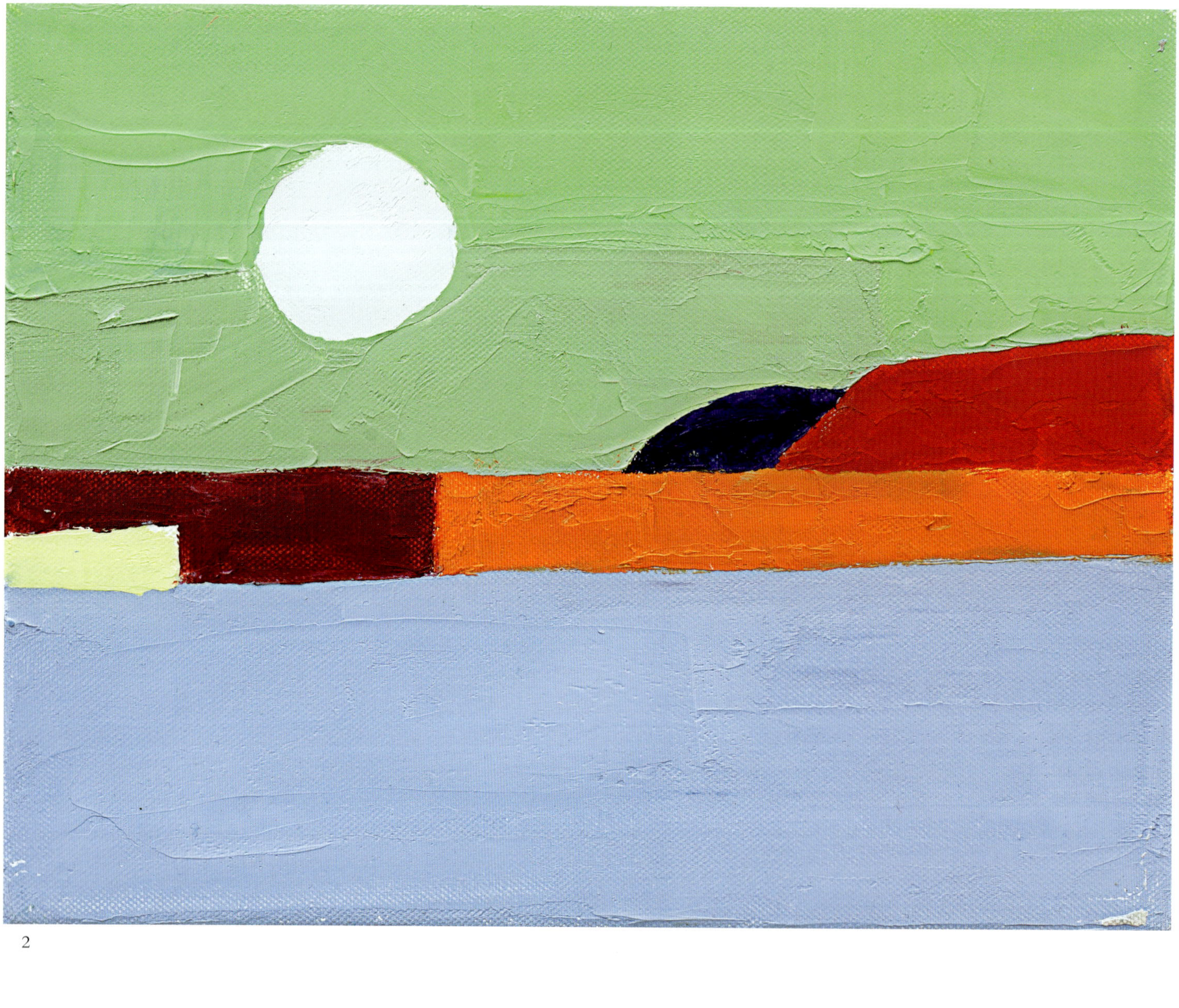
2

# Etel Adnan

Etel Adnan has spent her nomadic life exploring different paths of artistic expression, including painting, poetry, prose, journalism and writing for the theatre. Her passage from Beirut to Paris to the US and back, as well as her linguistic journeys through French, Arabic, English, Turkish and Greek, strongly influenced her desire to paint. Drawn to visual art, Adnan chose the language of abstraction, but her work is anything but hermetic. Patchwork landscapes emerge out of flat, sharply demarcated swaths of vivid paint. A contrasting element, usually a red square or rectangle posing as the sun, directs the eye, centres the composition and evenly illuminates the unmixed pigments. VSR

**Shown by**
Sfeir-Semler G7

**Biography**
Born 1925
Lives in Paris

Lebanese-born Adnan has been the subject of solo presentations at Sfeir-Semler, Beirut (2010), and Bonnafont Gallery, San Francisco (2009). She participated in Documenta 13, Kassel (2012), and her work features in public collections that include: the British Museum, London; the Centre Pompidou, Paris; Institut du Monde Arabe, Paris; and the National Museum for Women in the Arts, Washington DC.

1
*Untitled*
2010
Oil on canvas
24 × 30 cm
Courtesy of Sfeir-Semler

2
*Unitled*
2010
Oil on canvas
24 × 30 cm
Courtesy of Sfeir-Semler

3
*Untitled*
1995–2000
Oil on canvas
46 × 55 cm
Courtesy of Sfeir-Semler

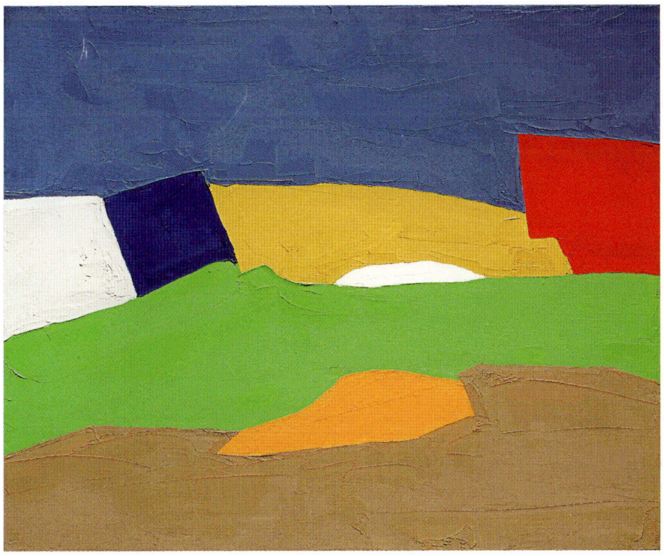

3

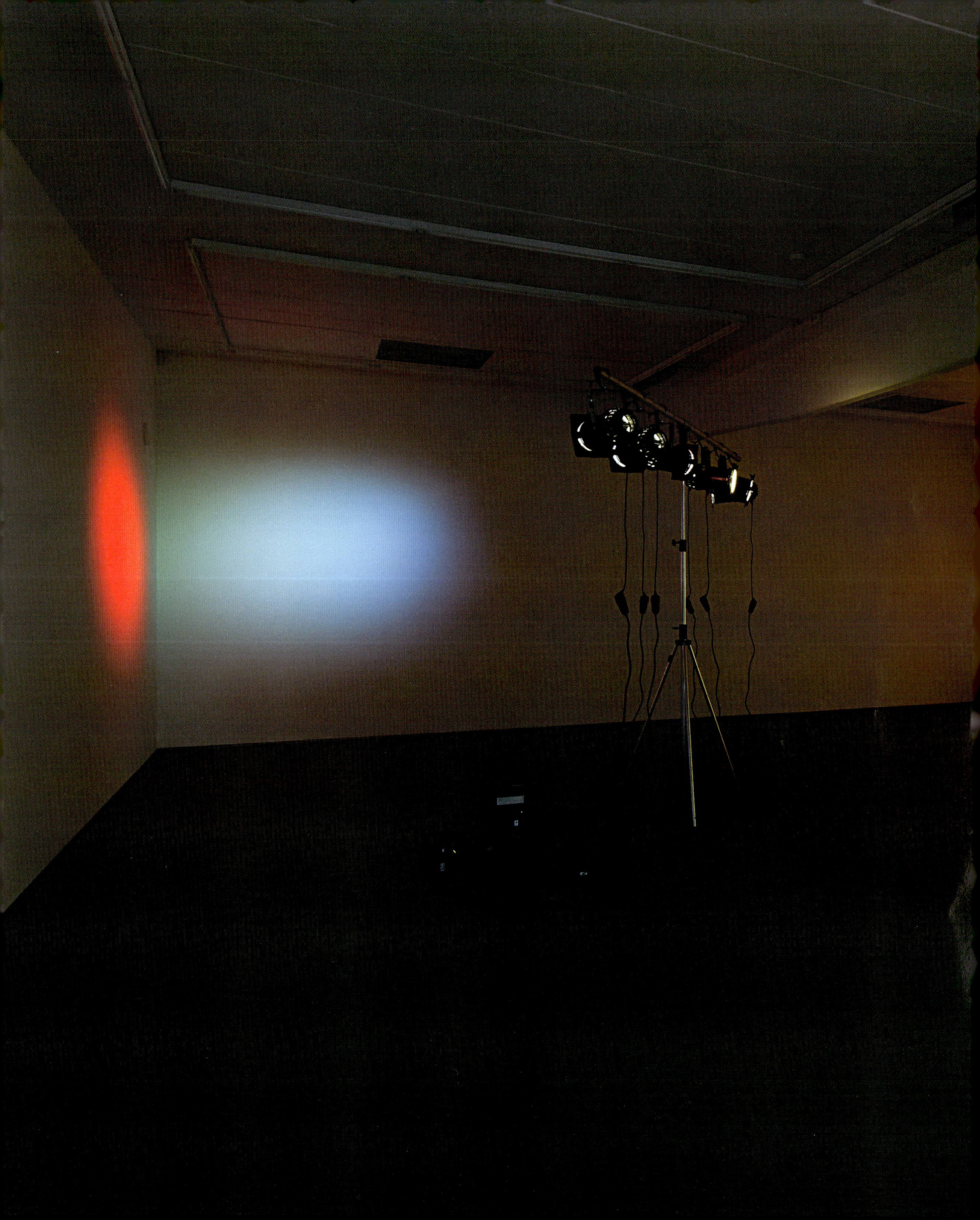

**Shown by**
Elastic Gallery S5

**Biography**
Born 1963
Lives in Stockholm

Recent solo exhibitions of Glasgow-born artist Allen include those at Die Raum, Berlin (2012), Elastic, Malmo (2011), RSTR4, Munich (2010), and Vienna Secession (2008). He has participated in group exhibitions such as 'I Wish This Was a Song: Music in Contemporary Art', Museum of Contemporary Art, Oslo (2012), which travels to Hamburger Kunsthalle in 2013, and 'Chasing Napoleon', Palais de Tokyo, Paris (2009).

*Calder Brown*
2011
Computer, lights and DMX box
300 × 200 × 150 cm
20 min.
Courtesy of Elastic Gallery

# Focus
# Dave Allen

Musical performance is at the heart of Dave Allen's installations and audio works, from his early four-channel video installation *Live Version* (1993) to more recent collaborations with avant-garde musicians Chris Corsano and Zeena Parkins (2011). The tension between amateur and professional is a consistent thread in his work, whether in his handwritten transcriptions of rock anthems *Stairway to Heaven/Highway to Hell* (1997) or in his performance installation of electric guitar feedback, later released as a 12-inch record, *It Swung Back And Forth, Back And Forth Until Forever. Then It Stopped And It Howled Endlessly* (2009). Lately he conjured the empty stage with the succinct installation *Calder Brown* (2011), using computer, lighting rig and DMX box to generate ambience and expectation in an otherwise empty gallery. SL

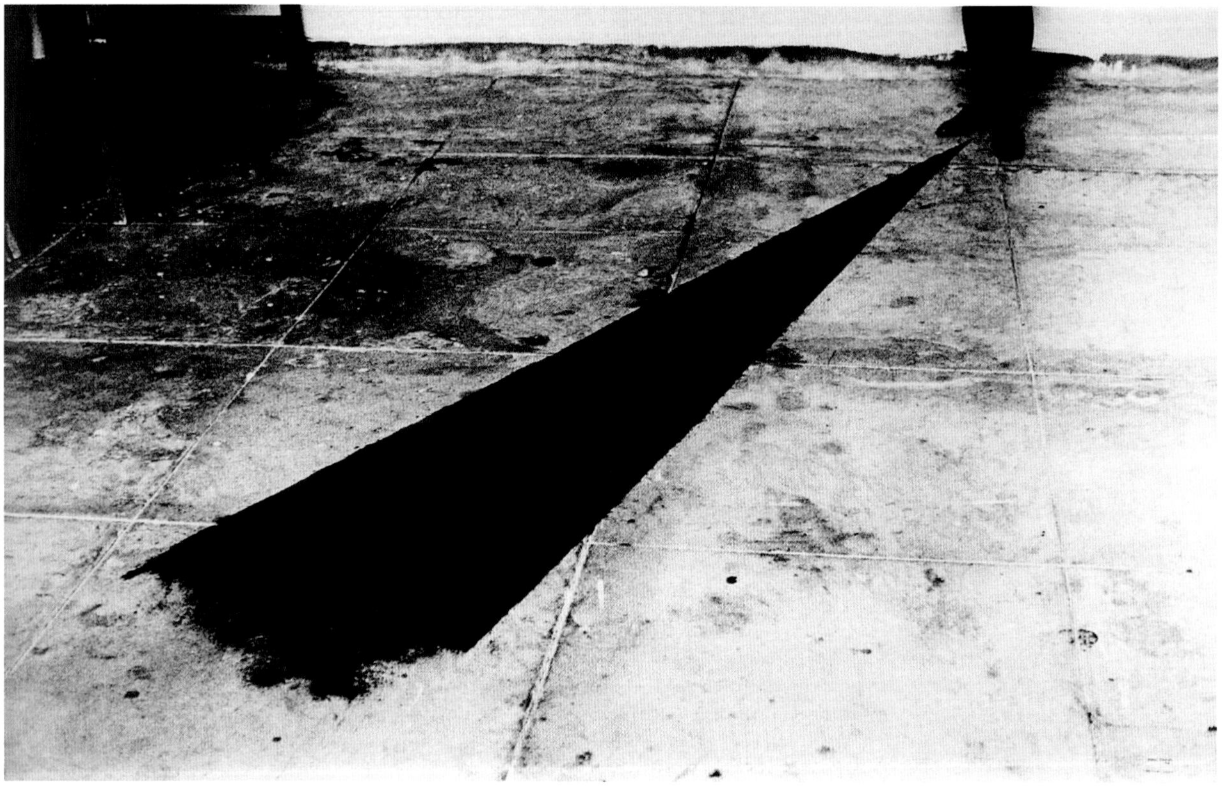

1

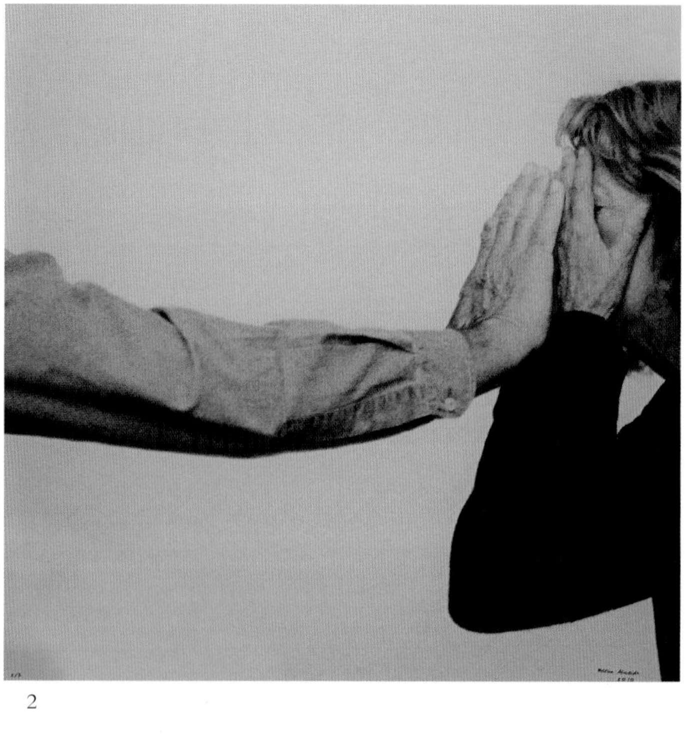

2

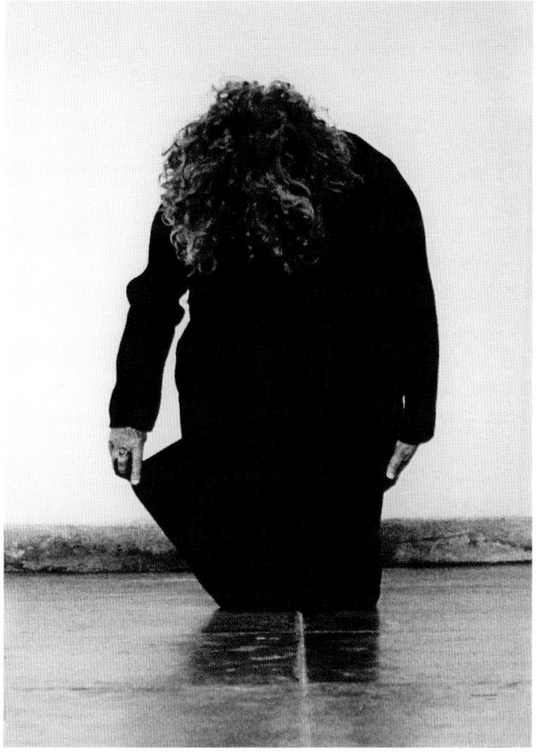

4

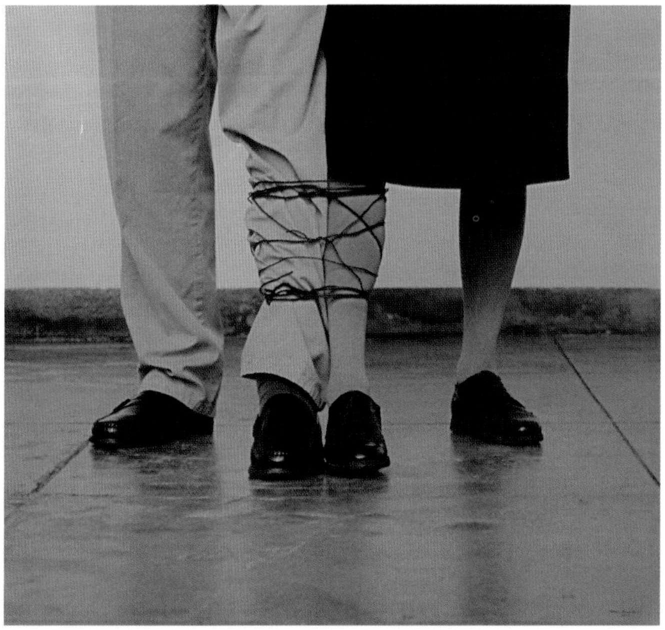

3

**Shown by**
Galería Helga de Alvear
A7
Galeria Filomena Soares
H9

**Biography**
Born 1934
Lives in Lisbon

Lisbon-born Almeida has been the subject of solo exhibition at venues such as John Hansard Gallery, Southampton (2010), Kettle's Yard, Cambridge (2009), Fundação Calouste Gulbenkian, Lisbon (2006, 1987 and 1983), Centro Cultural de Belém, Lisbon (2004), and Fundação Serralves, Porto (1995). She represented Portugal in the 51st Venice Biennale (2005). Her work features in the group exhibition 'A Bigger Splash: Painting after Performance' at Tate Modern, London, from November 2012 to April 2013.

1
*Entrada Negra*
(Black Entry)
1995
Photograph
117 × 190 cm
Courtesy of Galeria Filomena Soares

2
*Untitled*
2010
Photograph with blue acrylic paint
77 × 77 cm
Courtesy of Galeria Filomena Soares

3
*Untiled*
2010
Photograph
125 × 135 cm
Courtesy of Galeria Filomena Soares

4
*Eu estou aqui*
(I am Here)
2005
Photograph
125 × 90 cm
Courtesy of Galeria Filomena Soares

# Helena Almeida

Helena Almeida's practice over the past half-century has transitioned from exploring the physicality of mark-making in drawings and paintings to a literal investigation of corporeality in performative self-portraits, which, uniquely, she would then draw on. If the through-line remains the exploration of both the pathos and the bathos of the feminine form, such is the Portuguese artist's tonal range that peers from Lygia Clark to John Baldessari, Eleanor Antin and Adrian Piper are evoked. See *A Casa* (The House, 1980), in which Almeida and the lineation she writ herself with are occluded by swaths of blue paint, or *Dentro de mim* (Inside Me, 2000), in which the artist holds a mirror fragment that follows the line of her body—and reflects what lies beyond. QL

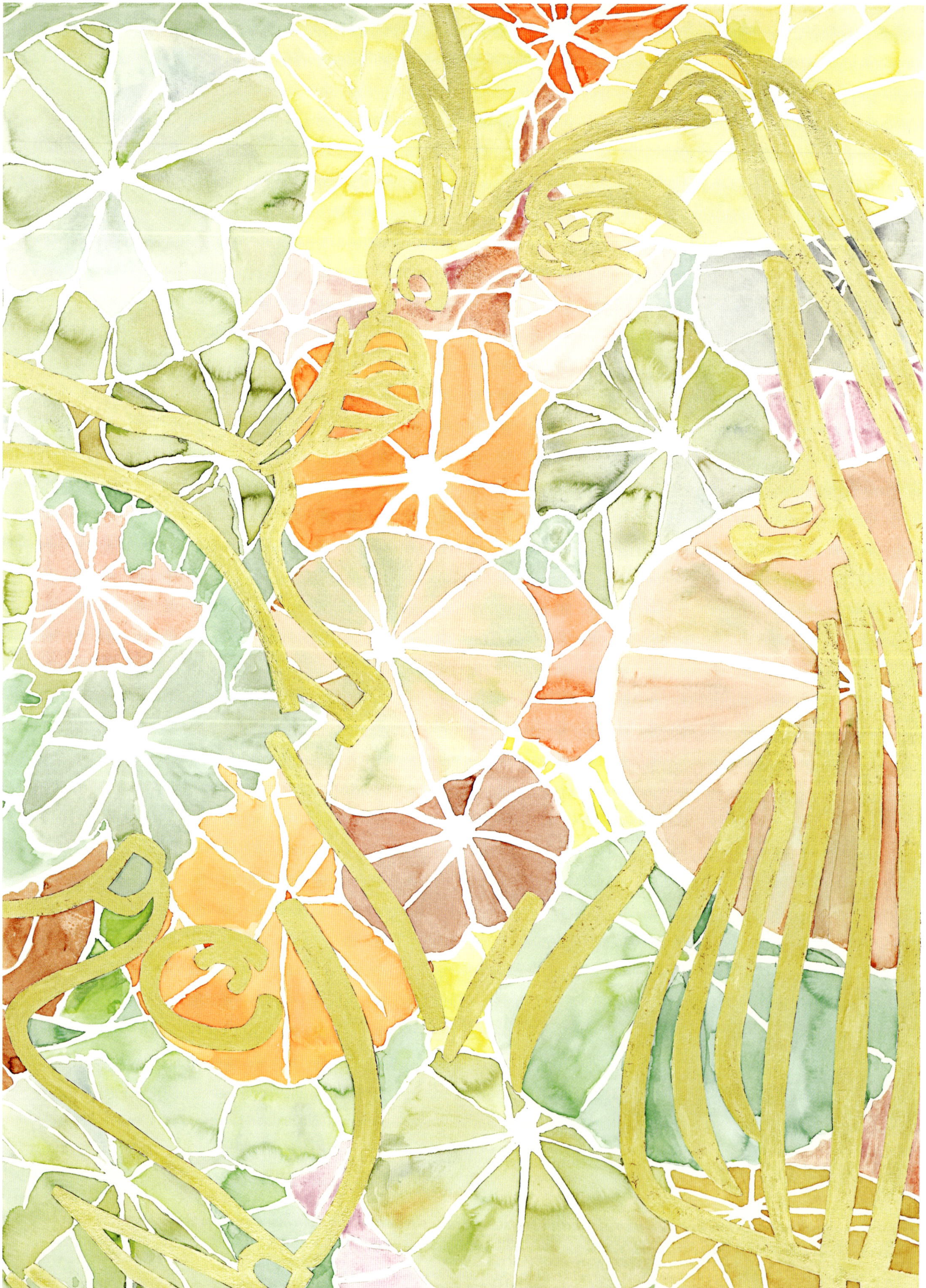

# Ghada Amer & Reza Farkhondeh

**Shown by**
Tina Kim Gallery C13

**Biography**
Live in New York

Egyptian-born Amer and Iranian-born Farkhondeh have collaborated on solo exhibitions at galleries that include Goodman Gallery, Johannesburg (2011), Galeria Filomena Soares, Lisbon (2010), Pace Prints, New York (2009), Singapore Tyler Print Institute (2008) and Stedelijk Museum, 's-Hertogenbosch (2006). In 2012 they have been artists-in-residence at OCAD University's Faculty of Arts, Toronto.

*Taste of Forever*
2012
Watercolour and gold leaf on paper
154 × 106 cm
Courtesy of Tina Kim Gallery

Ghada Amer is known for her embroidered erotica, where stitched patterns and trailing threads serve as decorative screens that only partially conceal self-pleasuring female nudes. Her collaboration with Reza Farkhondeh began informally, with Farkhondeh providing lush foliage backgrounds to Amer's over-drawing and -stitching, both in bright pastels. As the relationship became formalized (often through international residencies at printmaking studios), Farkhondeh's flora and fauna rose to the surface, mirroring the increasing proximity of the artists themselves. Farkhondeh's leafy blots are more than merely an added layer: they pressure Amer's calculated juxtapositions of tropes such as 'the feminine', 'the decorative' and 'the Eastern'. Although Amer has described her use of Farkhondeh's images as 'appropriation', in *Taste of Forever* (2012) it's Farkhondeh's flora that threaten to take over. SNS

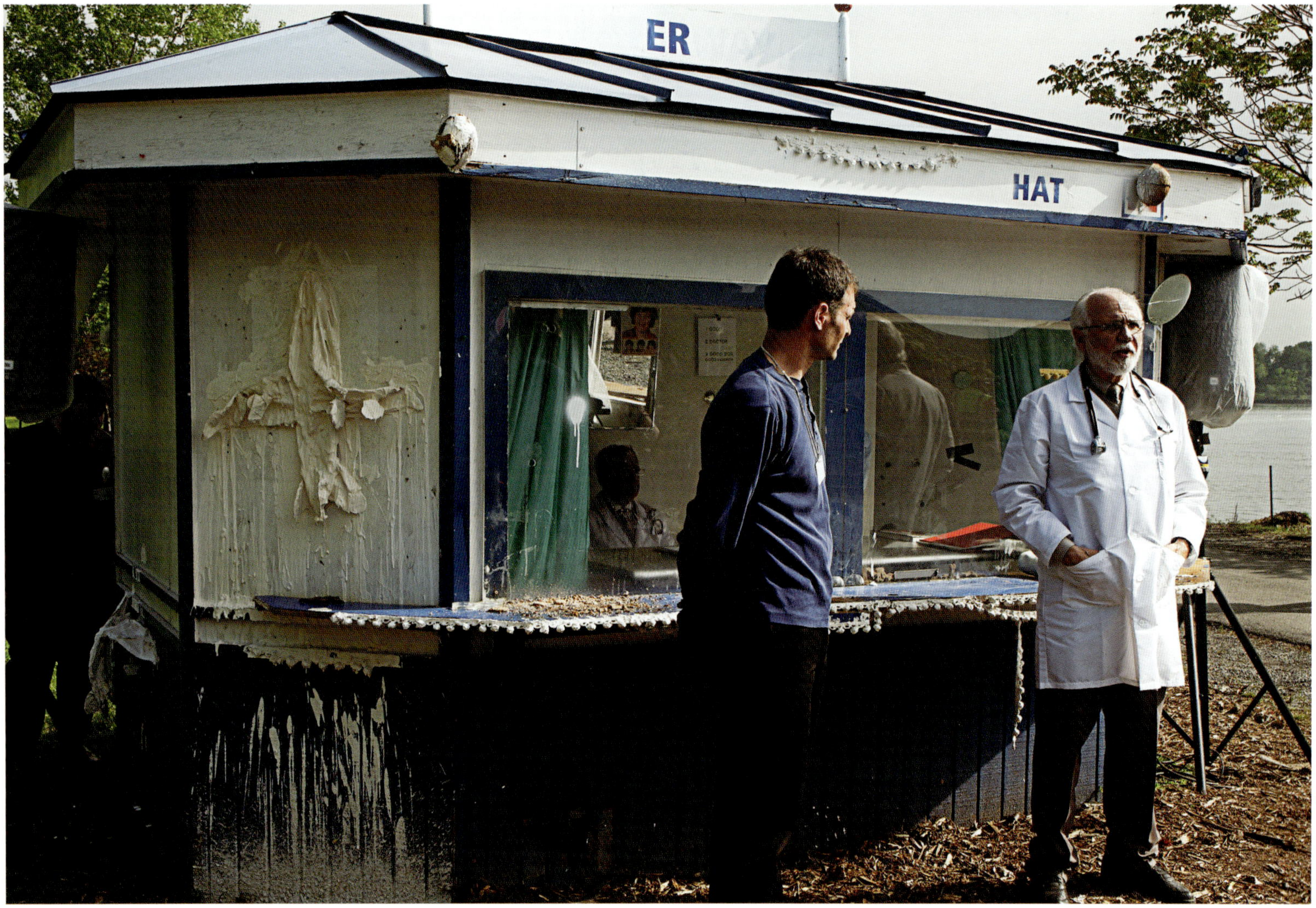

1

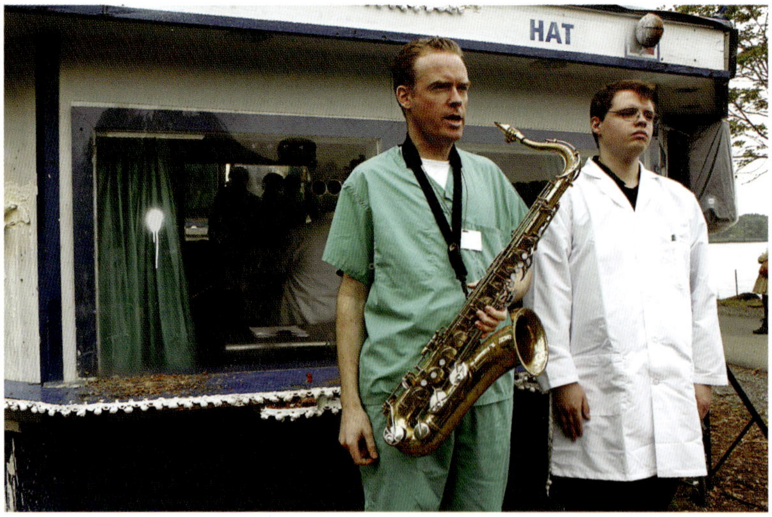

2

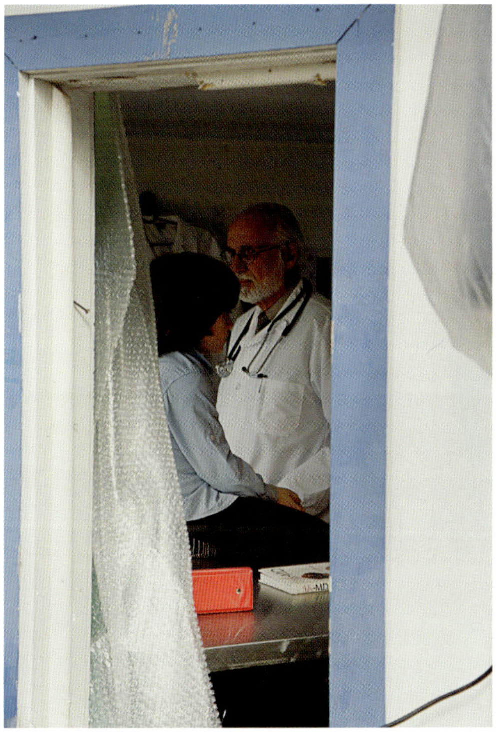

4

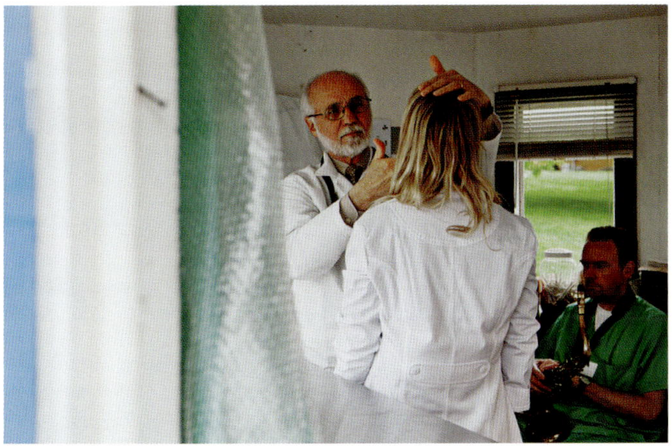

3

# Uri Aran

**Shown by**
Gavin Brown's enterprise B11
mother's tankstation R15

**Biography**
Born 1977
Lives in New York

Jerusalem-born artist Aran has presented solo shows at Gavin Brown's enterprise, New York (2012), mother's tankstation, Dublin (2010), and Rivington Arms, New York (2008). Recent group exhibitions include 'March', Sadie Coles, London (2012), 'Screening Room: Cologne', Kölnischer Kunstverein (2011), and 'Commercial Break' at the 54th Venice Biennale (2011). His forthcoming solo show at Kunsthalle Zurich takes place from January until April 2013.

1, 2, 3, 4
*Untitled (Ticket Shack)*
2012
Performance
20 min.
Courtesy of Gavin Brown's enterprise

Uri Aran's videos, sculptures, drawings and performances suspend themselves between sense and senselessness. In an untitled 2008 video a British actor is asked repeatedly to praise Mikhail Baryshnikov's dancing: the dancer, the actor finally says, 'leaves me in a state of uncertainty'. Aran invites the same response: he'll collage images of dogs and people, connecting them with drawn lines that hesitantly but inconclusively suggest hermetic logic, or confidently pop a gouged, whitewash-smeared coconut in a striped coffee cup (*Dogs and Cats*, 2008). As evidenced by *Untitled (Ticket Shack)* (2012) for Frieze Projects in New York—Randall Island's ticket shack turned into a seemingly functioning medical clinic—underlying this is a questioning of the automatic acceptance of authority; Aran, in pushing us around, asks us to push back. MH

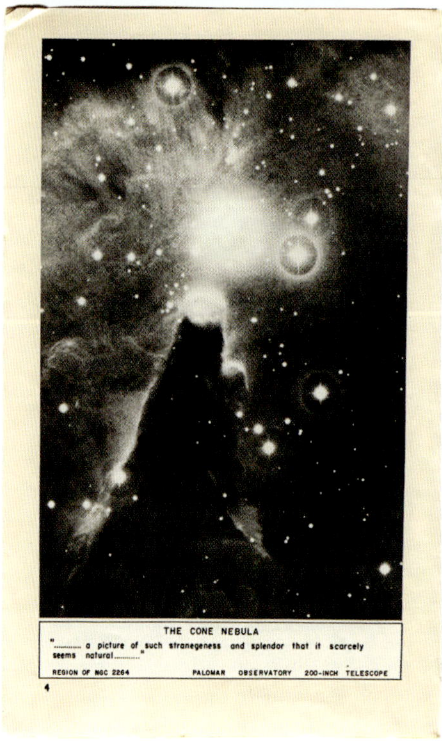
THE CONE NEBULA
"............ a picture of such straneгeness and splendor that it scarcely seems natural............"
REGION OF NGC 2264
PALOMAR OBSERVATORY 200-INCH TELESCOPE
4

1

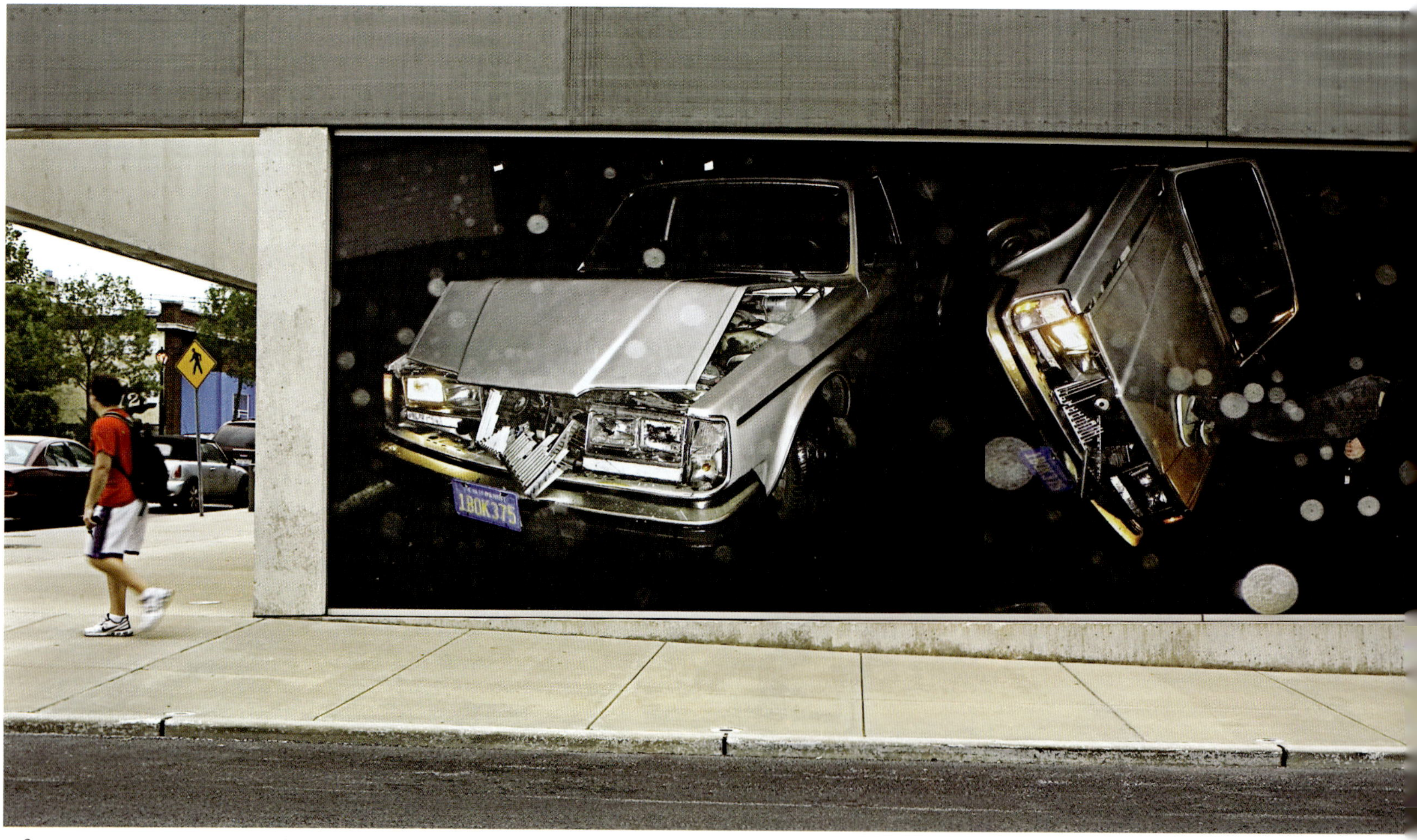
180K375

2

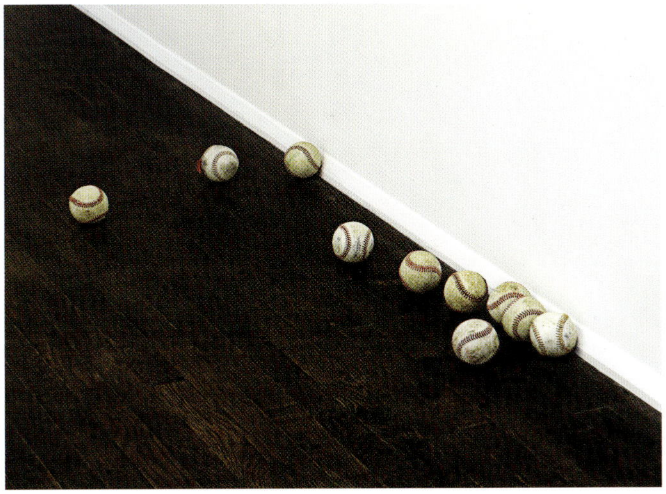

3

**Shown by**
Cabinet E3
Alex Zachary Peter Currie E20

**Biography**
Lives in Berkeley and New York

In 2012 US-based artist Bacher featured in New York exhibitions that included a solo presentation at Alex Zachary Peter Currie and group shows such as the Whitney Biennial, Whitney Museum of American Art, and 'Spies in the House of Art: Photography, Film and Video' at the Metropolitan Museum of Art, New York. She has been the subject of solo exhibitions at venues such as Kunsterein München, Munich (2009), MoMA PS1, New York (2009), and Contemporary Art Museum St Louis (2008).

1
*The Celestial Handbook*
(detail)
2011
85 framed offset book pages
Each 23 × 15 cm
Courtesy of Alex Zachary Peter Currie

2
*Crash*
2008
Inkjet print on adhesive plastic
3.5 × 10 m
Installation view at Contemporary Art Museum St Louis
Courtesy of Alex Zachary Peter Currie

3
*Baseballs*
(detail)
2009
50 used baseballs
Dimensions variable
Courtesy of Alex Zachary Peter Currie

# Lutz Bacher

Active since the 1970s, Lutz Bacher established her own elusiveness early on, responding to a demand for an interview with a collaged, photocopied sequence of imaginary questions and answers about her responses to imagery of Lee Harvey Oswald (*The Lee Harvey Oswald Interview*, 1976). The 'interview' catalogued the (impossible) process of trying to view a photograph entirely freely from one's existing preconceptions. Bacher (the name's a pseudonym) continues to trouble particular formats or media and the ways we consume them. Her photo-based work, videos and installations all give due credit to the static and short-circuits that, in her own words, 'break the flow' of every medium, suggesting that critique is far more complicated than merely denying or embracing clear sources of authority or subversion. SNS

1

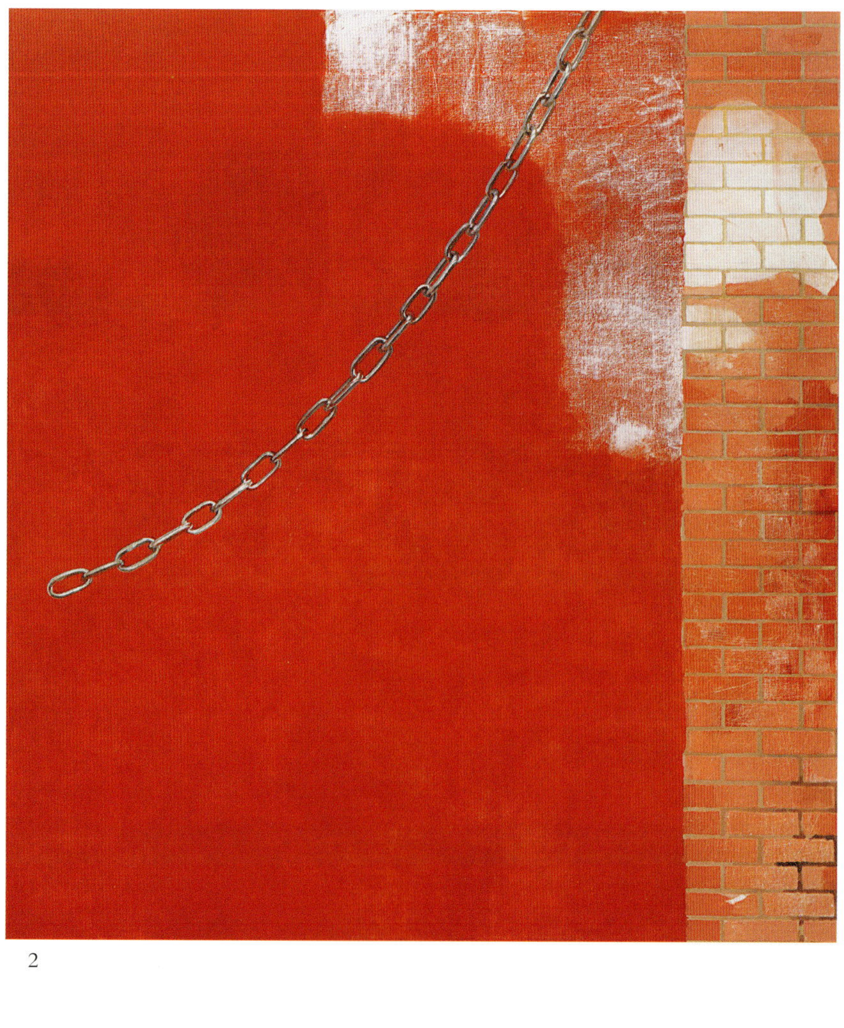

2

**Shown by**
Galerie Barbara Weiss
G1

**Biography**
Born 1964
Lives in Berlin

German-born Baer has presented solo shows at venues that include Galerie Barbara Weiss, Berlin (2012 and 2009), Richard Telles Fine Art, Los Angeles (2011 and 2008), Kunsthalle Munster (2006), Pinakothek der Moderne, Munich (2006), and Bonnefantenmuseum, Maastricht (2005). Recent group exhibitions include the touring show 'The Potosí Principle' (2010–11), whose venues included Museo Nacional Centro de Arte Reina Sofía, Madrid.

1
*Untitled*
2011–12
Oil and acrylic on canvas
180 × 135 cm
Courtesy of Galerie Barbara Weiss

2
*Rote Wand 4*
(Red Wall 4)
2012
Oil on canvas
190 × 169 cm
Courtesy of Galerie Barbara Weiss

3
*Rear Painting*
2012
Acrylic on canvas
80 × 66 cm
Courtesy of Galerie Barbara Weiss

3

# Monika Baer

Monika Baer's bold, large-scale paintings explore surface and texture. Her recent works suggest the canvas is a tool not only of display but also of concealment. A flat plane of red acrylic paint covers the surface of *Rote Wand 4* (Red Wall 4, 2012), leaving only a small portion of brickwork exposed—the subject of the work's title. *Rear Painting* (2012) boasts a nearly black canvas, punctuated by three coloured keyhole-like symbols that await unlocking. In nullifying the paintings' surface in flat swaths of colour, Baer suggests something lies beyond the canvas and a secret content exists beneath the paint. In engaging the viewer in these pictorial games, she toys with fictive narratives and imaginative outcomes. SC

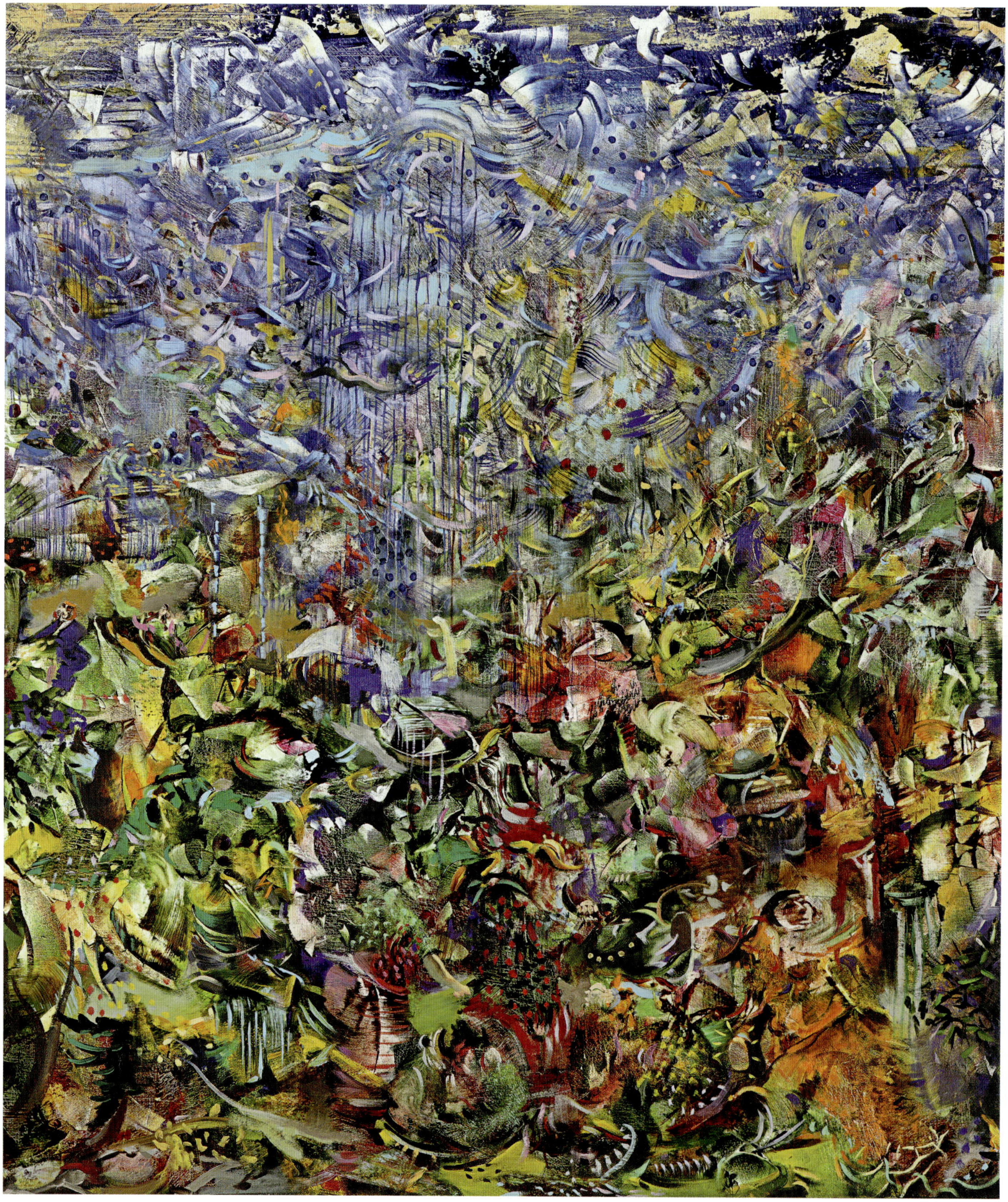

1

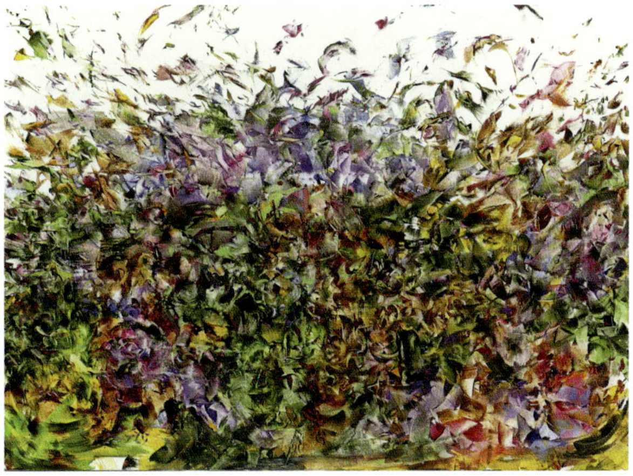

3

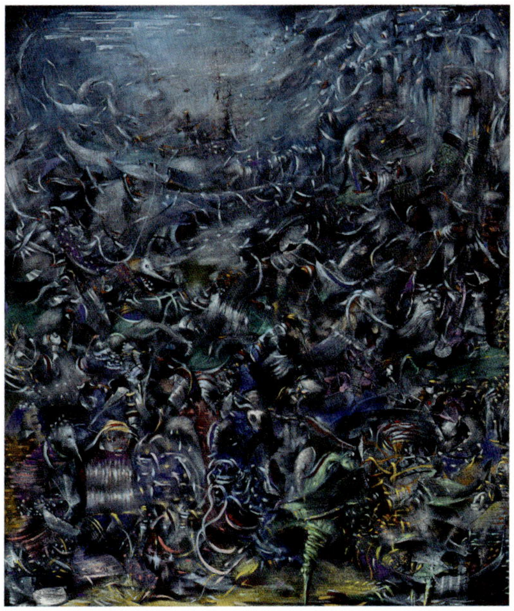

2

**Shown by**
Galerie Thaddaeus Ropac F4

**Biography**
Born 1976
Lives in New York

Iranian-born Banisadr has exhibited work in solo shows at Galerie Thaddaeus Ropac, both in Salzburg (2012) and in Paris (2010), as well as Leslie Tonkonow Artworks + Projects, New York (2011 and 2008). In 2010 he received the New York Foundation for the Arts Fellowship in Painting. Recent group exhibitions include 'XXSmall', Gemeentemuseum, The Hague (2011), and 'Unveiled: New Art from the Middle East', Saatchi Gallery, London (2009).

1
*Rock the Casbah 2*
2011
Oil on linen
91 × 76 cm
Courtesy of Galerie Thaddaeus Ropac

2
*Melencolia 1*
2012
Oil on linen
91 × 76 cm
Courtesy of Galerie Thaddaeus Ropac

3
*Stardust*
2011
Oil on linen
137 × 183 cm
Courtesy of Galerie Thaddaeus Ropac

# Ali Banisadr

Ali Banisadr's explosive canvases invoke multiple cultures and traditions. They make reference to Persian miniature painting, the work of Hieronymus Bosch and Pieter Bruegel, the brushwork of Willem de Kooning and the frenzied information overload of the 21st century. His large-scale, panoramic canvases overflow with colour, activity and detail, often affording a God's-eye view of earthly chaos and destruction. Banisadr's work has its foundation in his own experiences in Iran as child, during the eight-year Iran–Iraq war. But these powerful canvases depicting systems of collapse are equally relevant to our time of financial crisis and social upheaval. KK

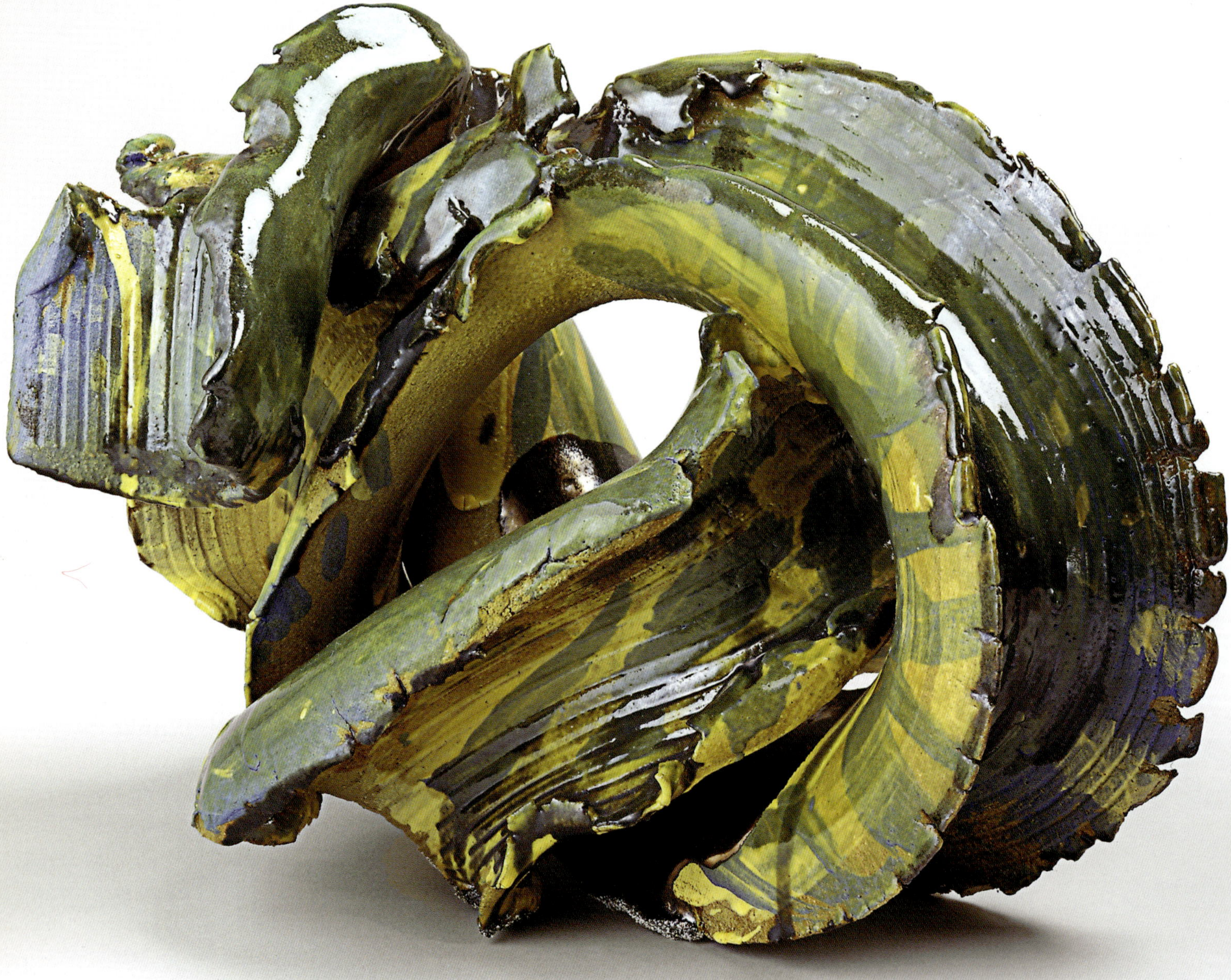

# Lynda Benglis

**Shown by**
Thomas Dane Gallery
F13

**Biography**
Born 1941
Lives in New York

Louisiana-born Benglis was the subject of survey show at the Van Abbemuseum, Eindhoven, in 2009 that travelled over the next two years to international venues such as the Irish Museum of Modern Art, Dublin, and the New Museum, New York. Her work features in public collections that include: the Museum of Contemporary Art, Los Angeles; San Francisco Museum of Modern Art; Whitney Museum of American Art, New York; MoMA, New York; and the Tate collection, UK.

*Untitled (Mean Green)*
1992–4
Ceramic
28 × 38 × 36 cm
Courtesy of Thomas Dane Gallery

Through process, movement and colour Lynda Benglis has been expanding the possibilities of abstraction for decades. Her use of materials such as beeswax, bronze, rubber and latex is erotic and richly allusive. Polyurethane foam has spilt like lava, glittery mesh knots have evoked flesh, and pleated metal wall pieces have resembled ruffled sea creatures or crumpled Grecian gowns. Benglis has said that she 'wanted to stretch the image, to have the image confront the viewer'—a goal that also animates the organic forms of her glazed, textured ceramics from recent decades. A violent olive and yellow tangle, *Untitled (Mean Green)* (1992–4), records her wrangling of rough-edged strips of clay, while its tense energy suggests an eviscerated but still living—and perhaps mythical—snake. KMJ

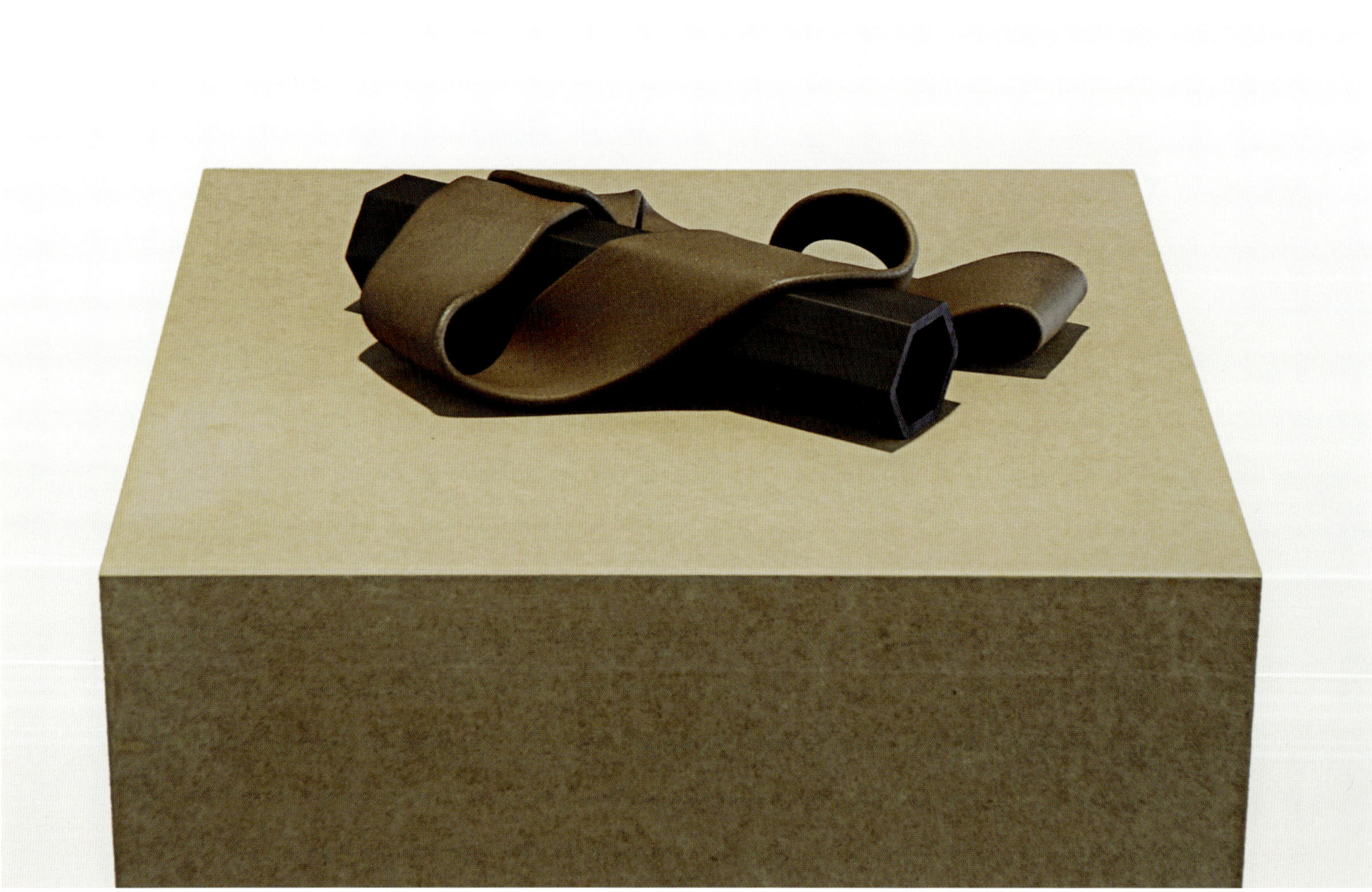

1

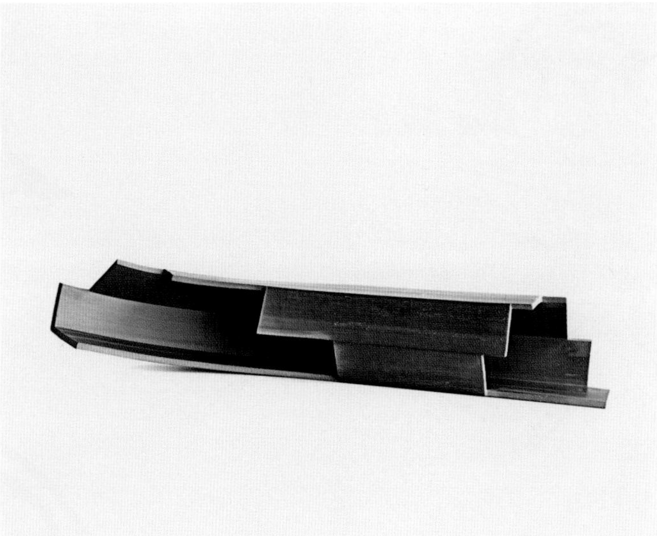
2

**Shown by**
Sadie Coles HQ C11
Andrew Kreps Gallery C5

**Biography**
Born 1976
Lives in New York

American artist Benson has presented solo shows at Artpace, San Antonio (2011), Taxter and Spengemann, New York (2011 and 2005), Overduin and Kite, Los Angeles (2011), Sadie Coles HQ, London (2009 and 2008), Miami Art Museum (2001) and Miami-Dade Community College (2001). His work has been featured in group exhibitions such as 'American Exuberance', Rubell Family Collection, Miami (2011), and 'Uncertain States of America' (2005–7), whose venues included the Serpentine Gallery, London.

1
*Extrusion V (Single Ribbon, Hex Tube)*
2011
Ceramic and MDF
91 × 46 × 46 cm
Courtesy of Andrew Kreps Gallery

2
*Untitled Extrusion*
2012
Ceramic
23 × 61 × 23 cm
Courtesy of Andrew Kreps Gallery

# Frank Benson

Frank Benson's *Human Statue (Jessie)* (2011), like its masculine precursor *Human Statue* (2006–9), uses emphatically digital methods to fuse one of the oldest representational traditions with one of the newest. Photographs of dancer/musician Jessie Gold were turned into a virtual model subsequently cast in bronze; with her flat, obscuring sunglasses and sharp mimicry of flesh, she looks pulled from a post-human *Blade Runner* society. See this as heralding the mooted Singularity if you like, but Benson seems more fascinated by fusing the sculptural with the technocratic. A work like the ceramic *Extrusion V (Single Ribbon, Hex Tube)* (2011), with its brown 'ribbon' draped softly over a hexagonal tube, at once hymns 21st-century fabrication wizardry and, in its obscure suavity, feels displaced from a moment we're yet to reach. MH

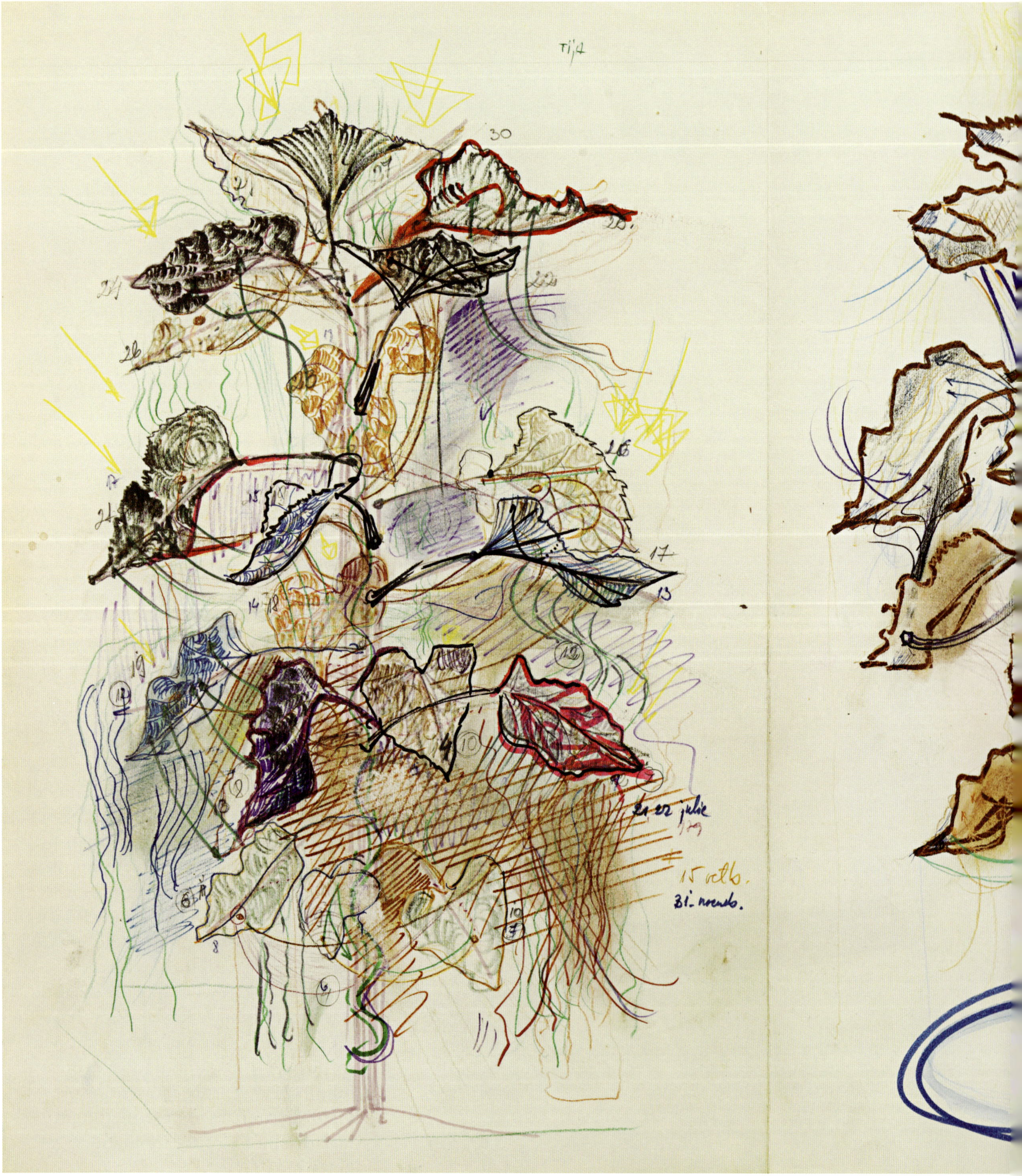

21 22 julie
15 octb.
31 noemb.

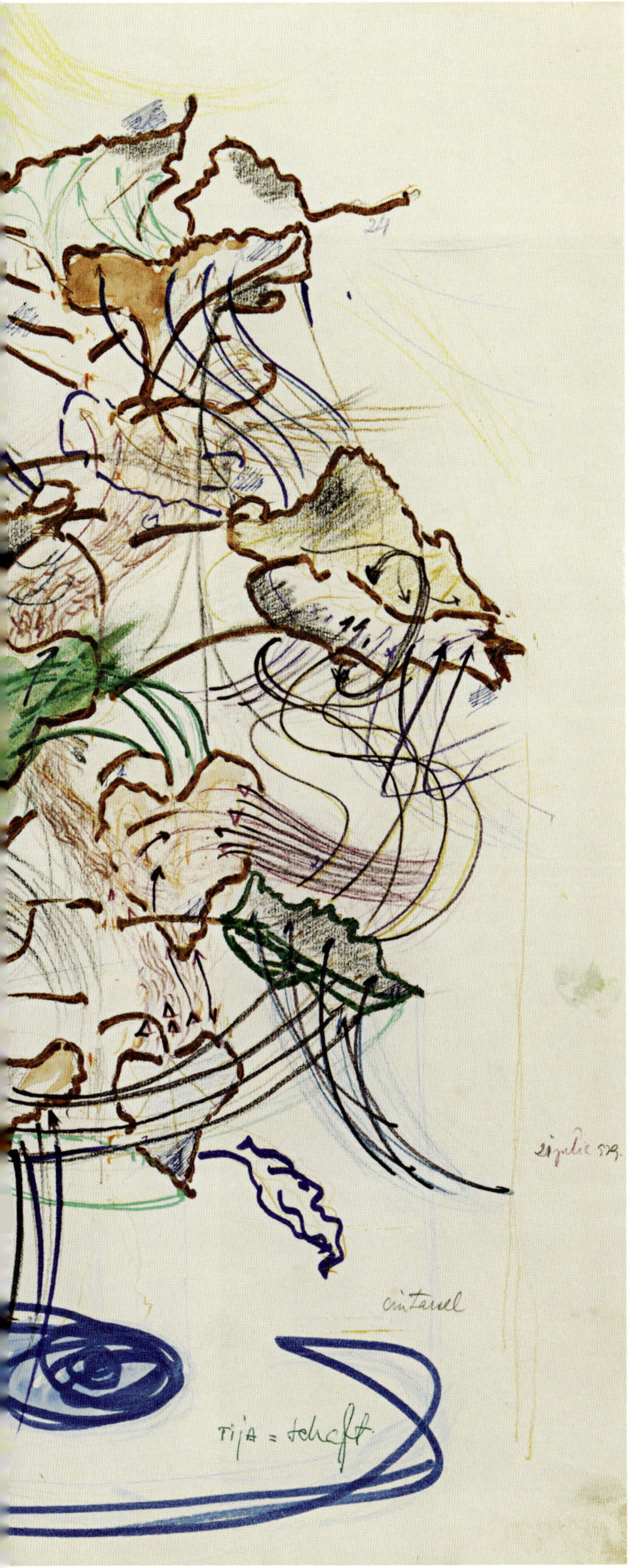

**Shown by**
Johnen Galerie D1

**Biography**
Born 1930
Lives in Timisoara

Romanian-born artist Bertalan has been the subject of exhibitions that include 'De Natura Rerum' (On the Nature of Things), Johnen Galerie, Berlin (2012), and 'Drumuri la răscruce' (Crossroads), Galeria ArTe, Bucharest (2005), as well as solo presentations at Muzeul de Artă, Timisoara (2001), performance festival Zona 3, Timisoara (1999), and Galerie am Weissenhof, Heilbronn, Germany (1990).

*Sunflowers*
1979
Red chalk, pencil and felt-tip pen on paper
54 × 69 cm
Courtesy of Johnen Galerie

# Stefan Bertalan

A founding member of the Sigma Group in Timisoara in 1963, Stefan Bertalan was initially indebted to Kandinsky and Klee: his abstract drawings of that era explicitly invoke and reanimate the spirit of the avant-gardes of the early 20th century. In the late 1960s Bertalan essayed a more kinetic style, producing three-dimensional networks of thread that still functioned as wall-mounted works. His work subsequently expanded to include text and performance, frequently with an ecological slant. The later drawings have a burgeoning vegetal strangeness about them, conjuring a perverse Eden as a means of escape from present ideological realities. BD

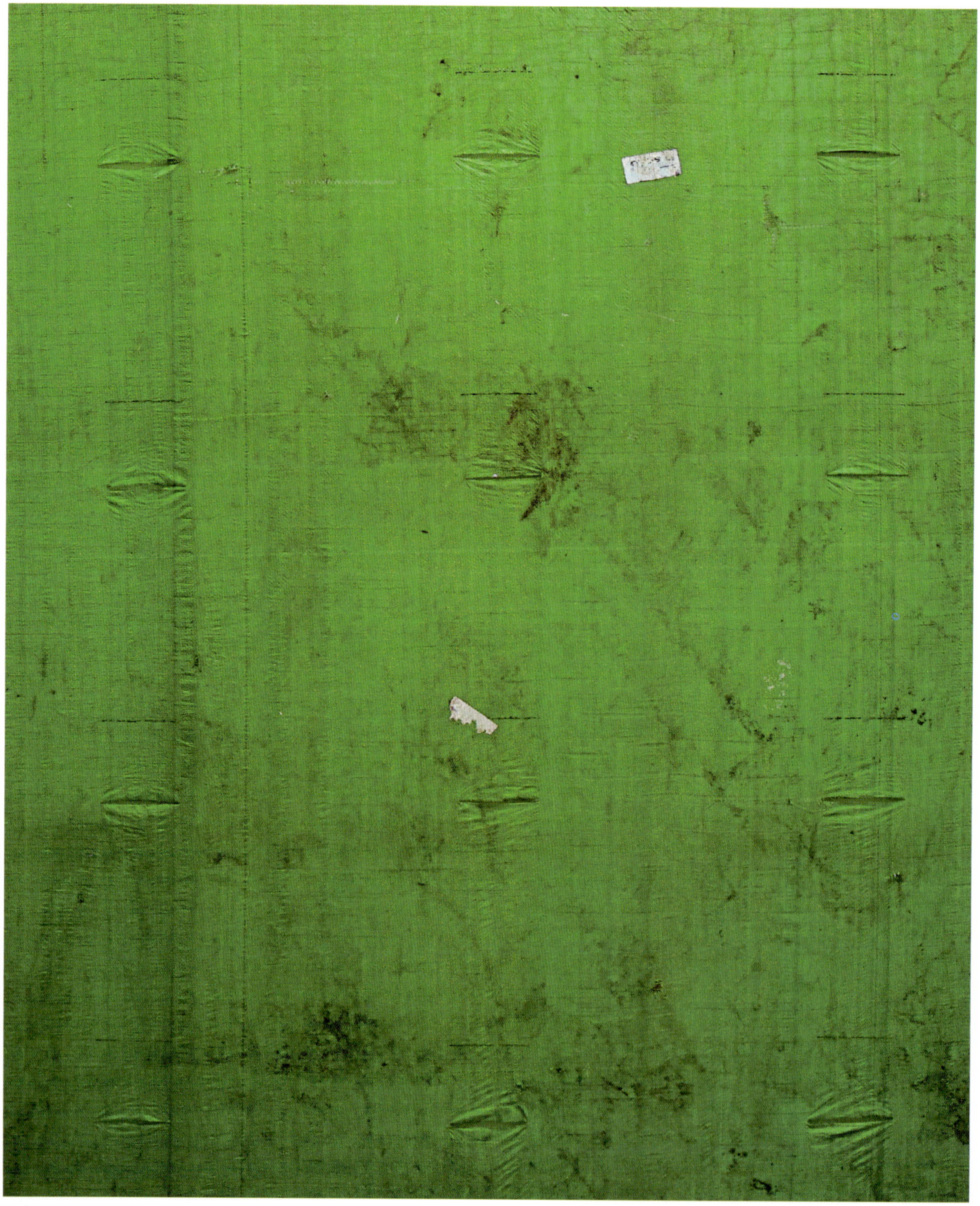

1

2

**Shown by**
Office Baroque Gallery
S8

**Biography**
Born 1985
Lives in New York

San Francisco-born artist Bobrow, a graduate of the Parsons School of Design, New York, presented the solo show 'No Sleep in the Exit Row' at Office Baroque, Antwerp (2012), and has participated in group exhibitions at venues including the Clearing Gallery, Miami (2012), Brand New Gallery, Milan (2012), and New York's Martos Gallery (2011), Andrea Rosen Gallery (2011) and Art Production Fund (2009).

1
*B.I.G.*
2011
Tarpaulin
248 × 200 cm
Courtesy of Office Baroque

2
*Bleecker St.*
2011
Tarpaulin
271 × 121 cm
Courtesy of Office Baroque

# Focus
# Aaron Bobrow

Aaron Bobrow's scruffy yet radiant monochromes allude to cool Modernist abstraction, but they also evoke speed and heat: motor oil and tanning lotion are among his materials, and the works' surfaces often bear the traces of industrial use. Bobrow acquires bright plastic tarpaulins by various means—including bartering for them or purchasing them over the Internet—and then stretches them in lieu of canvas. *The Chastity of Luis Barragán* (2011), a flame-coloured vertical monochrome, echoes the light and natural materials in the Mexican architect's designs, while the emerald-green *B.I.G.* (2011) is nicked, soiled and marred by bits of tape. Given their gritty energy, it's hardly surprising that some of the tarps were once used to cover cars or motorcycles. KMJ

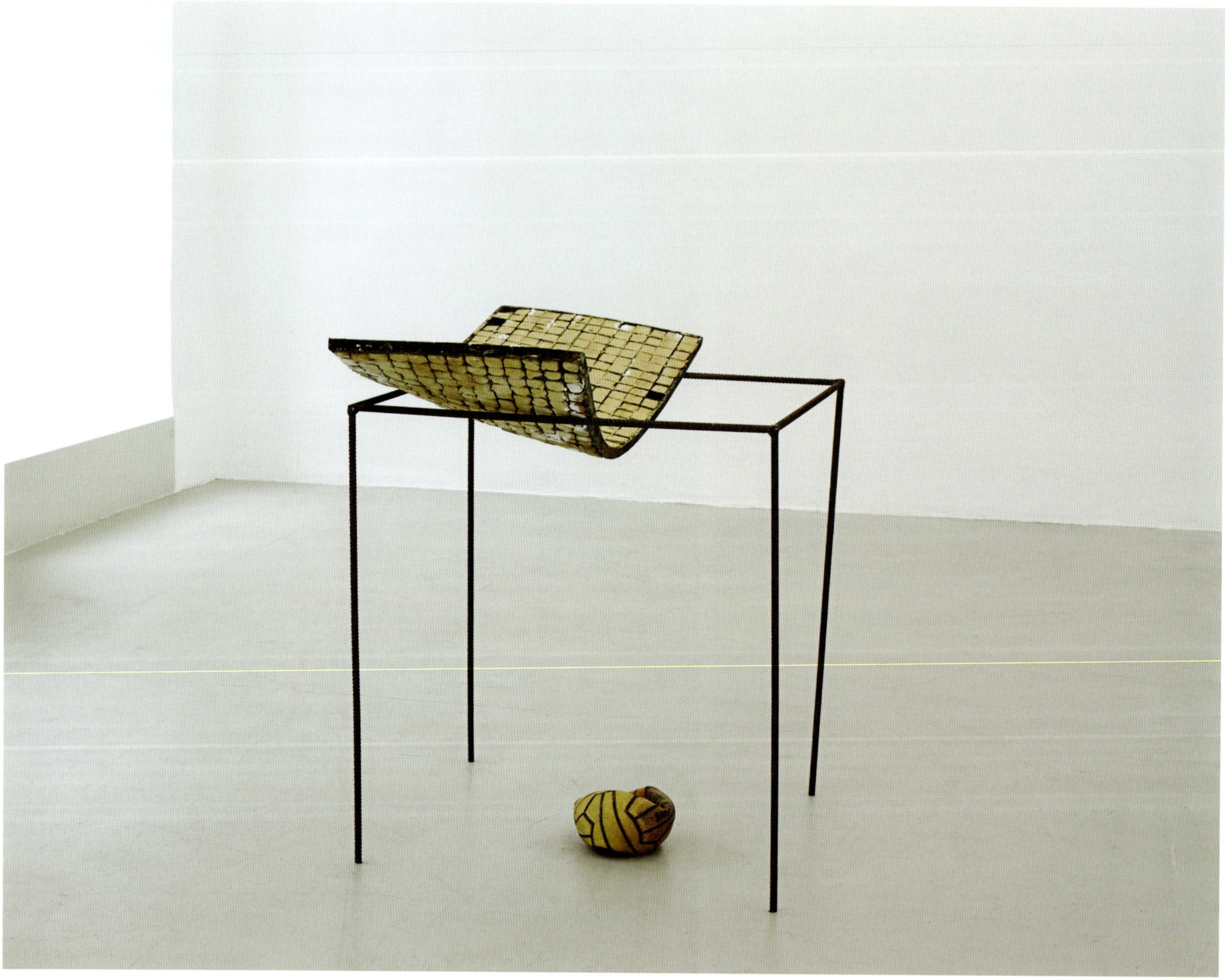

1

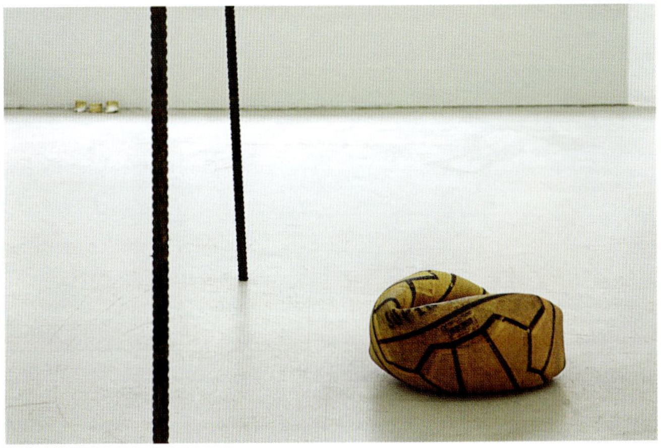

2

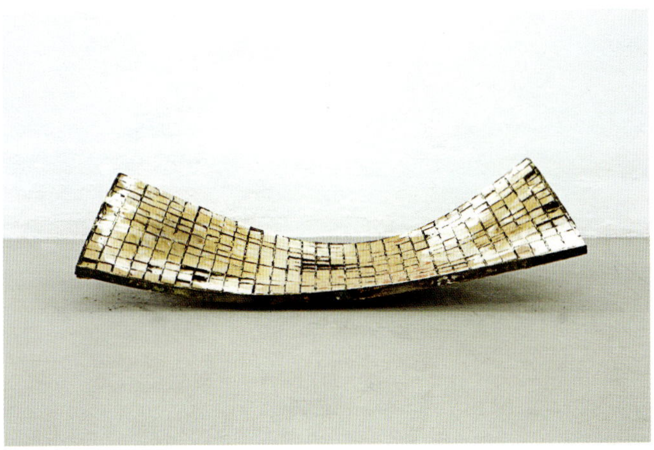

3

**Shown by**
Meyer Riegger D14

**Biography**
Born 1976
Lives in Paris

Frankfurt-born Bock has presented solo shows at venues that include Musée des Beaux-Arts de Valence (2012), Culturgest, Lisbon (2012), Meyer Riegger, Karlsruhe (2011), and Kunstmuseum Stuttgart (2010). She recently participated in the West China Art International Biennale, Yinchuan (2012), and the 11th Biennale de Lyon (2011). In 2013 she has a solo exhibition at the Museum of Contemporary Art Detroit.

1, 2, 3
*Naples Street*
(details)
2011
Four-part installation
Ceramic, steel and football
Dimensions variable
Courtesy of Meyer Riegger

# Katinka Bock

In Katinka Bock's precise and poetic sculptural works, the familiar art-historical themes of material and space become newly strange. See her exacting use over the past decade of sandstone, clay, chalk and metal, and the potent, elemental constellations in which she places them. Her works often find power in the threshold states they proffer: enacting an unstable balance, they preview the transitions that define us. See 'Die blaue Stunde' (The Blue Hour), her 2011 solo at Meyer Riegger, Karlsruhe, for which a thread dusted with blue chalk traced the gallery's street elevation. Or the two clay figures in *Trio* (2009/2011) leaning brokenly in a corner, the remnants of an unfired group that the artist fatalistically installed in public. As such, her works enact another balancing act: beautiful yet dark indeed. QL

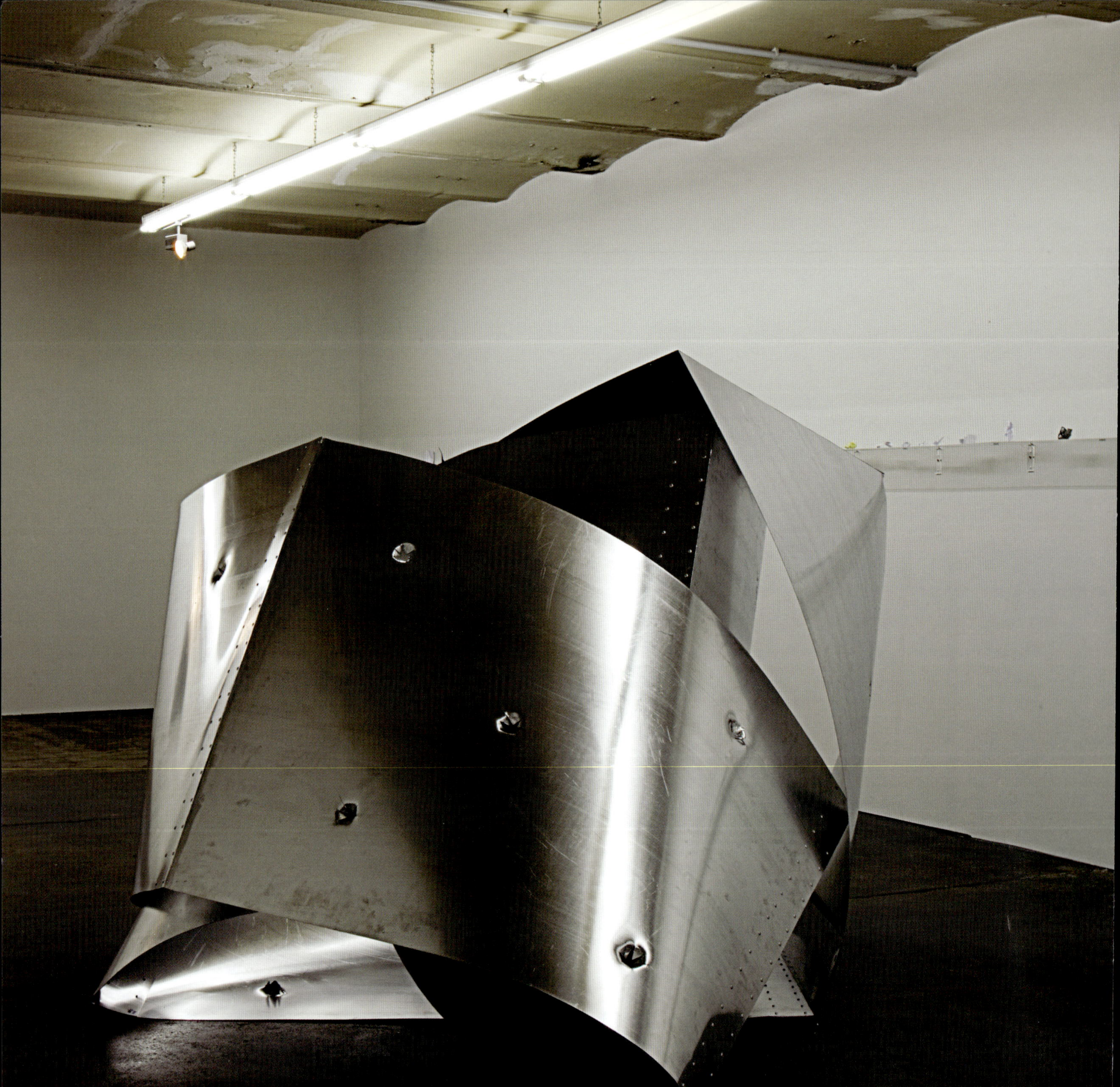

# Focus
# Rudolf Bone

**Shown by**
Galeria Plan B S12

**Biography**
Born 1951
Lives in Oradea

Romanian artist Bone has presented solo exhibitions recently at venues including Galeria Plan B, Berlin (2010), and Konstant Gallery, Oradea (2009). His group exhibitions include 'Just Another Brick in the Wall', Barbara Seiler Gallery, Zurich (2011–12), and 'Experiment and Community: Atelier 35 of Oradea, 1981–1995', MODEM, Debrecen (2011). He shows in 'Line and Erasure', with Dan Perjovschi, at Kunstverein Ludwigsburg until October 2012.

*Die*
2010
Aluminium sheet
Dimensions variable
Courtesy of Galeria Plan B

After a 15-year hiatus, sculptor and performance artist Rudolf Bone returned in 2008 with his potent mix of ritual, poetry and politics. His recent practice revisits some of his influential work from Romania in the 1980s, when he worked with collaborators such as Dan Perjovschi, as well as finding a new sense of engagement with his violent but intimate constructions. The oversized aluminium sheet sculpture *Die* (2010) has the numbers crudely punctured into each side, its original cube shape destroyed by a performance of the artist 'rolling' the die. The game of chance leaves the flimsy metal warped and tattered; we can peer into the large, empty frame, its finite possibilities cracked open and dispersed into the ether. CFW

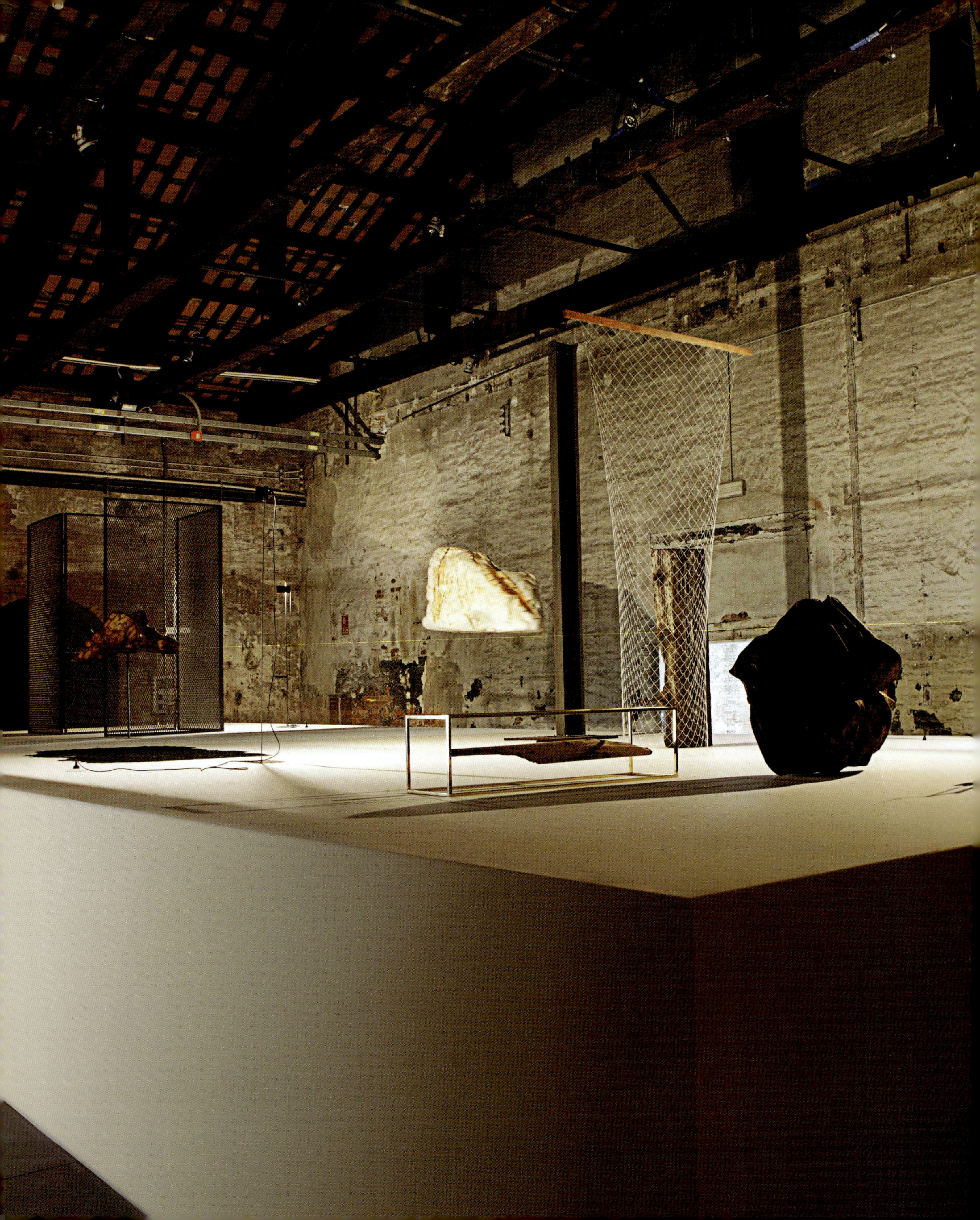

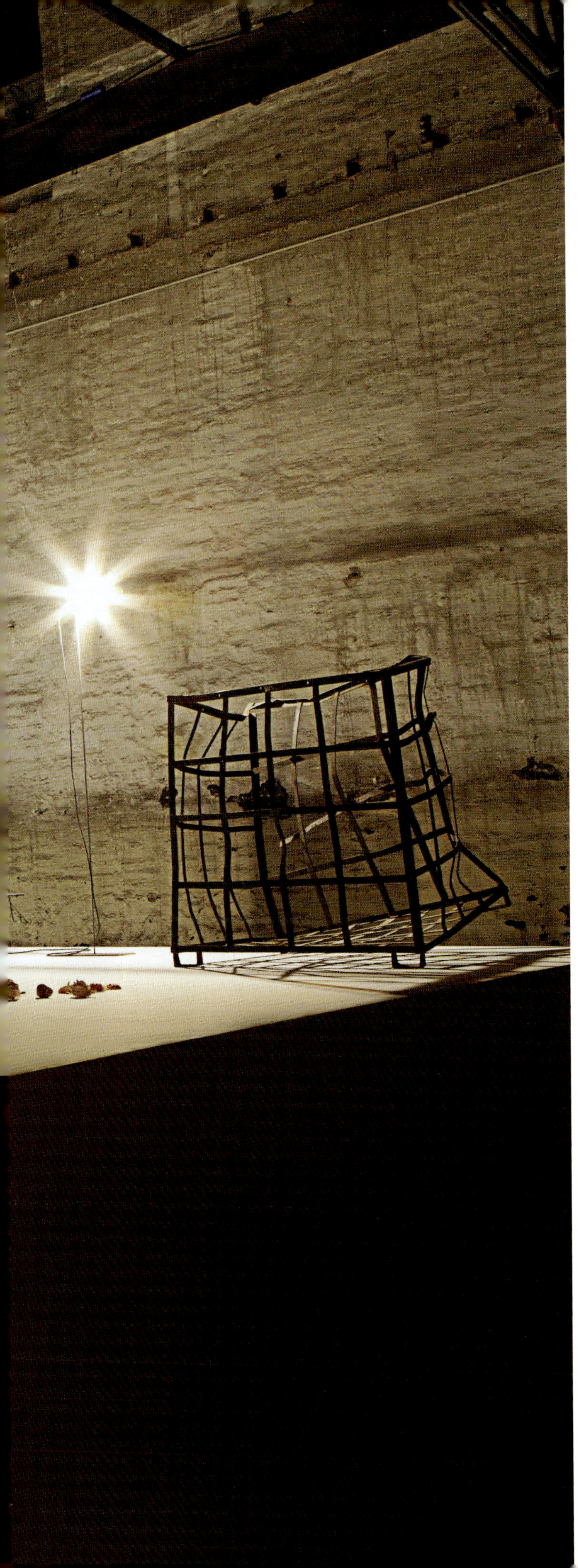

# Carol Bove

**Shown by**
Hotel F5
David Zwirner G9

**Biography**
Born 1971
Lives in New York

Geneva-born Bove was recently the subject of a solo exhibition at Palais de Tokyo, Paris (2010), in conjunction with her receipt of the Prix Lafayette 2009. She participated in Documenta 13, Kassel, and has had solo presentations at venues including the Horticultural Society of New York (2009), Kunsthalle Zurich (2004) and the Institute of Contemporary Art, Boston (2004). Her work is part of public collections that include MoMA, New York, and Yale University Art Gallery, New Haven.

*The Foamy Saliva of a Horse*
2011
Mixed media
4.5 × 15 × 5.5 m
Courtesy of Maccarone and David Zwirner

Travelling fluidly through time and space, Carol Bove's installations and assemblages of flotsam and jetsam including driftwood and shells revisit 1960s and 1970s counterculture, places from the California Bay Area to New York's industrial fringes, and 20th-century art from Constructivism to the work of Bruce Conner and Wallace Berman. Her trademark displays of books-as-objects on wall-mounted shelves summon unsettlingly contradictory voices from the Age of Aquarius; peacock feathers arrayed on linen in works like *Untitled* (2012) evoke flamboyant 1960s fashions and bohemian mystical trappings, but also opaque elegance. *The Foamy Saliva of a Horse* (2011), a tableau of items on a stage-like platform, some caged or suspended, resurrects the potent incongruities of Surrealism, which Bove has called 'the shadow of modernism'. KMJ

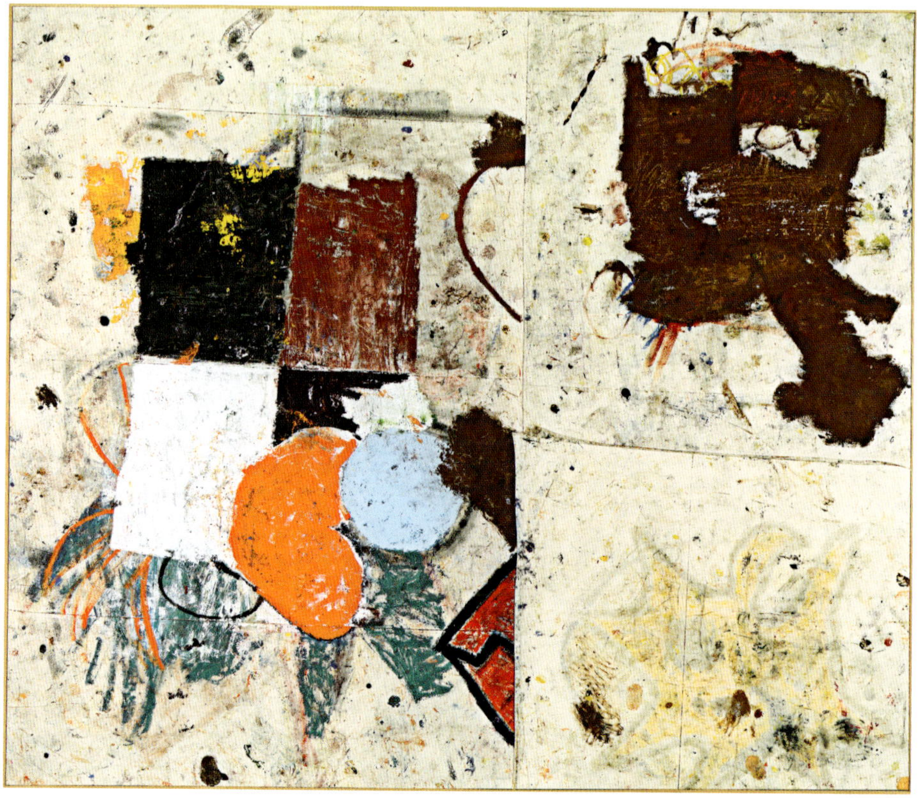
1

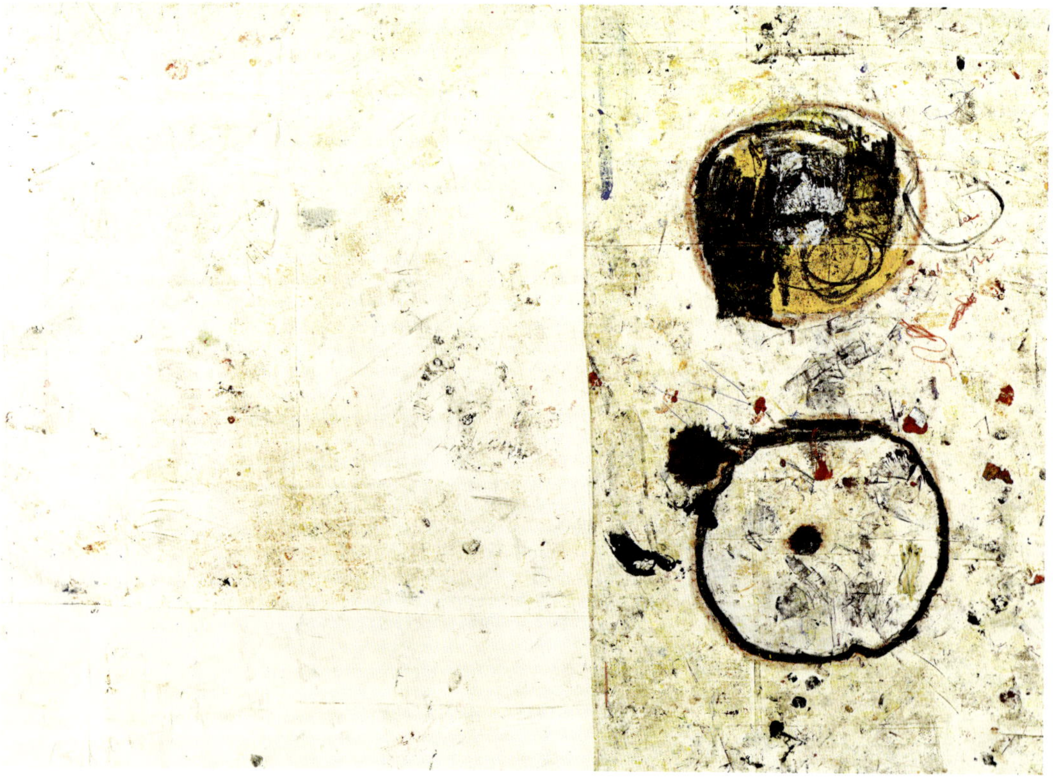
2

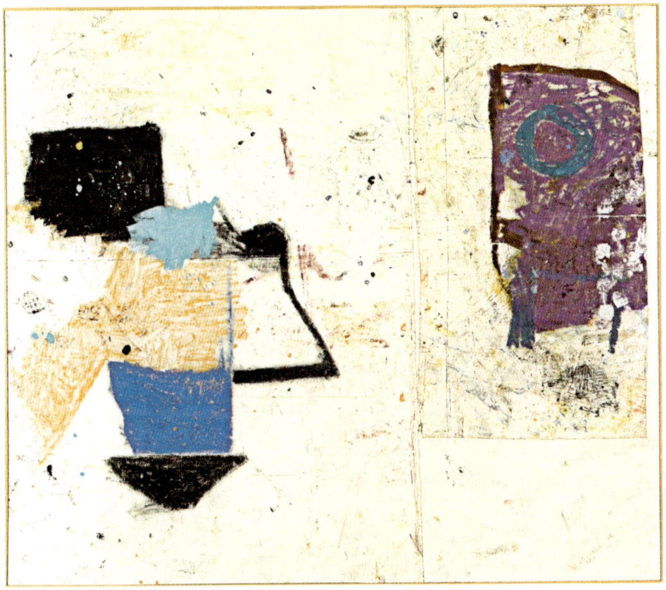

3

**Shown by**
Gavin Brown's enterprise B11
Canada G15
Galerie Eva Presenhuber C3
Almine Rech Gallery D18

**Biography**
Born 1975
Lives in New York

American-born artist Bradley has presented solo exhibitions at venues that include Galerie Eva Presenhuber, Zurich (2012), Gavin Brown's enterprise, New York (2011), Almine Rech Gallery, Paris (2011), and Peres Projects, Berlin (2008). He participated in the festival Le Printemps de Septembre, Toulouse (2011), and the Whitney Biennial, Whitney Museum of American Art (2008). Other group exhibitions include 'Pure Freude', Nationalmuseum, Berlin (2011), and 'Abstract America', Saatchi Gallery, London (2009).

1
*Bukkah Beah*
2012
Oil on canvas
295 × 341
Courtesy of Galerie Eva Presenhuber

2
*No – No*
2012
Oil on canvas
254 × 345
Courtesy of Galerie Eva Presenhuber

3
*Missus*
2012
Oil on canvas
284 × 320
Courtesy of Galerie Eva Presenhuber

# Joe Bradley

Joe Bradley's recent paintings recall Primitive art and Abstract Expressionism in equal measure. His earthy canvases often feature freehand, wonky shapes and blocks of colour. The surface of *Missus* (2012) contains bold patches of blue, black and purple that form a dominant dialogue over the canvas' more subtle pastel markings. His journey across the canvas of *No – No* (2012) sees its surface divided into two sections, one containing circular shapes on a mucky background, the other remaining relatively untouched. Bradley's works explore the process of painting in its primal form—his paintings appears as if blow-ups of smaller private experiments on paper, out-sized in confident gestures that reveal his honesty in exploring the non-restrictive potential of painting. SC

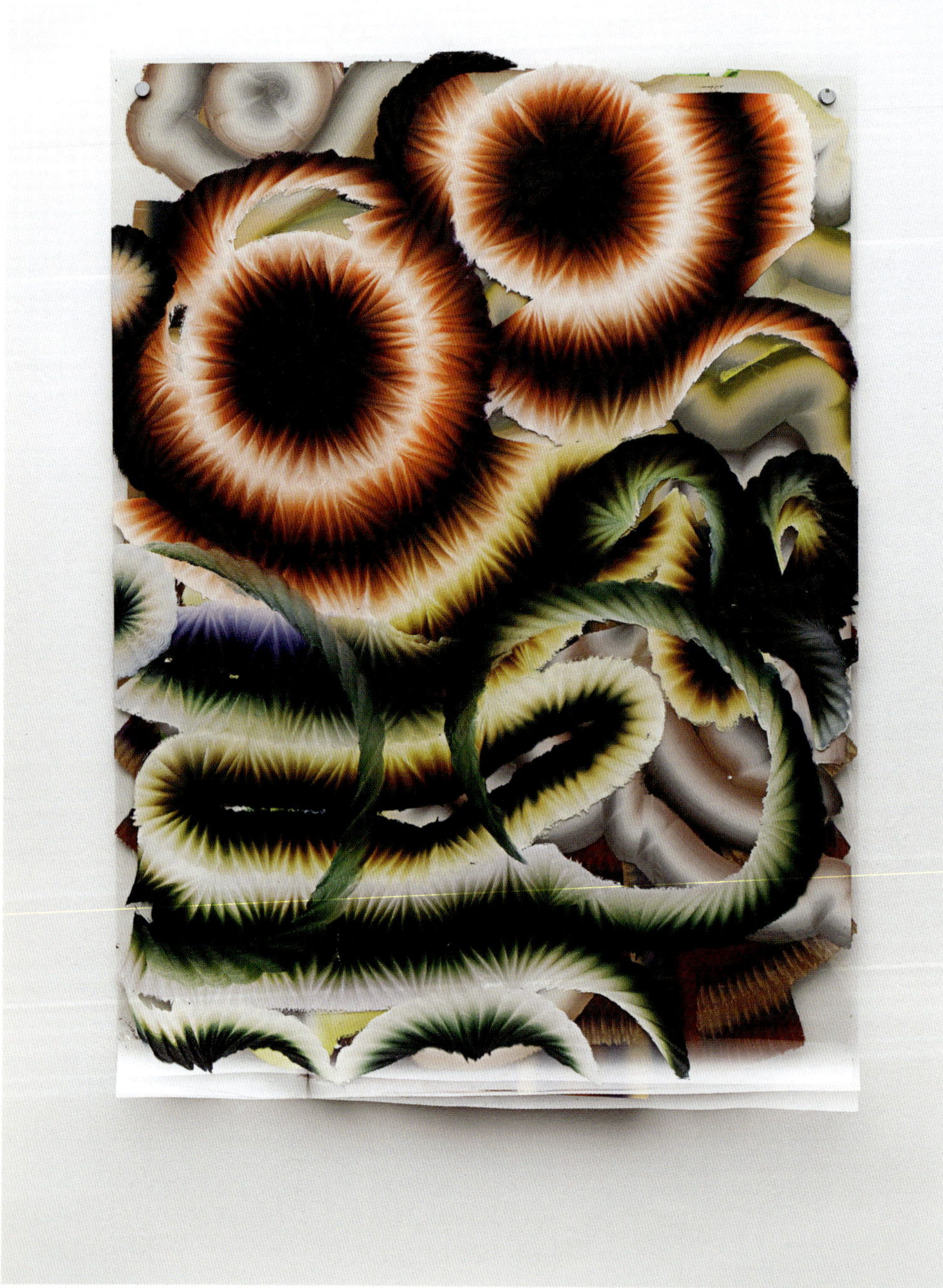
1

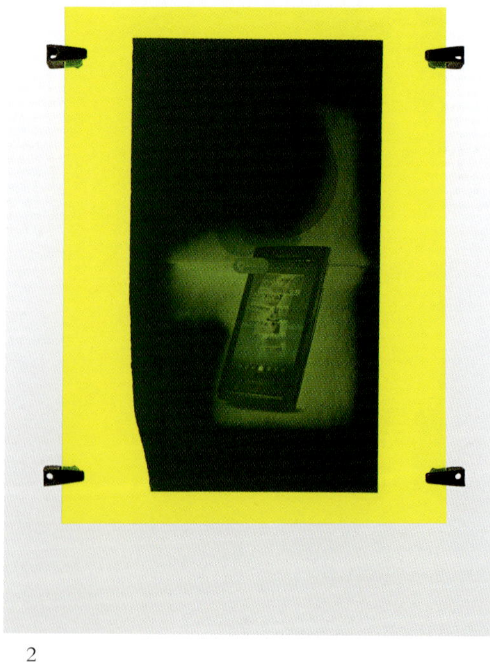
2

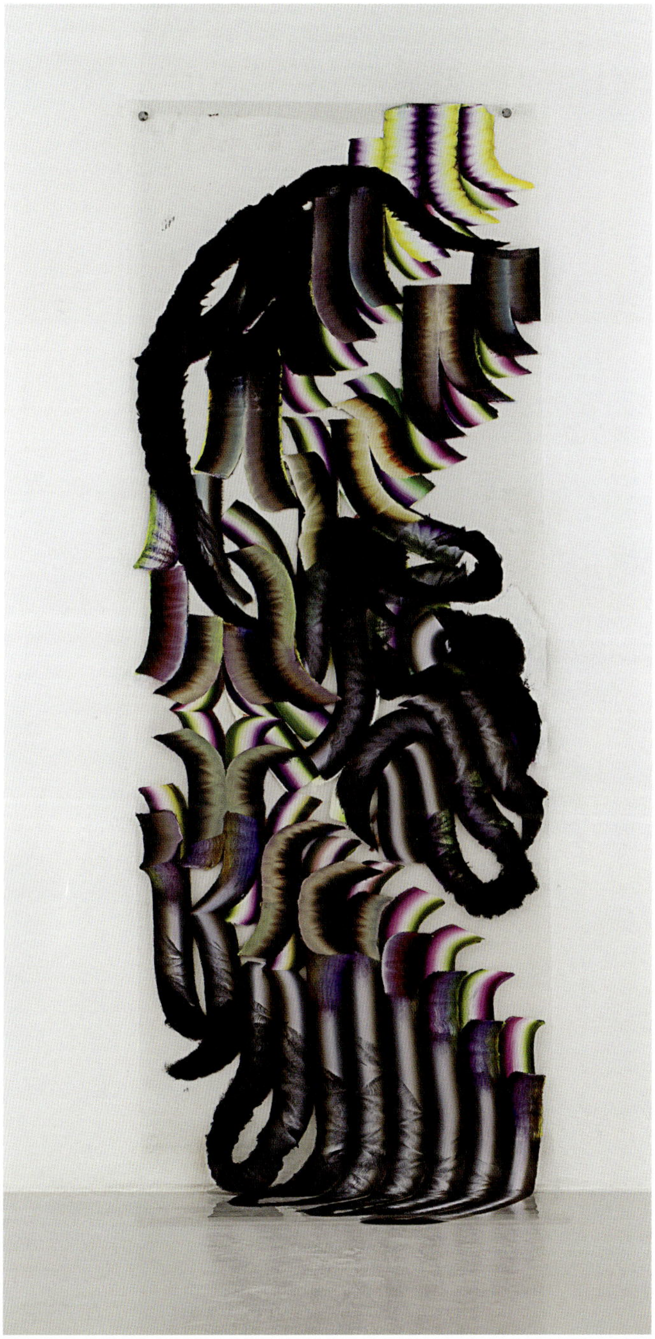

3

**Shown by**
Gavin Brown's enterprise
B11
Giò Marconi E4

**Biography**
Lives in New York

Hamburg-born Brätsch has recently been featured in two-person shows 'Glow Rod Tanning with…' at Giò Marconi, Milan (2012), with Martin Gamper, and 'Vorahnung (United Brothers and Sisters)', Kunsthalle Zurich (2011), with Adele Röder. She participated in the 54th Venice Biennale (2011) and the 8th Gwangju Biennale (2010), as well as group exhibitions such as 'Greater New York', MoMA PS1, New York (2010), and 'modernmodern', Chelsea Art Museum, New York (2009).

1
*Interchangeable Painting à la carte*
From the series 'Glow Rod Tanning'
2012
Oil on Mylar
175 × 123 cm
Courtesy of Giò Marconi

2
*Untitled*
2011
Spray-painted *New York Times* advertisement, Plexiglas and clamps
64 × 50 × 8.5 cm
Courtesy of Giò Marconi

3
*Blacky Blocked Radiants Sunbathed*
From the series 'Glow Rod Tanning'
2012
Oil on mylar
391 × 123 cm
Courtesy of Giò Marconi

# Kerstin Brätsch

Kerstin Brätsch collaborates with the living, namely Adele Röder, with whom she founded Das Institut, an 'import/export agency' specializing in the manipulation and exchange of information. But she also flirts with ghosts: that's what she calls the new renditions of paintings previously made on paper, which she copies onto crisp, unframed, draped or affixed swaths of Mylar (e.g., *Blacky Blocked Radiants Sunbathed*, 2012). *Interchangeable Painting à la carte* (2012) may be formed out of swirling vortexes of abstract motifs layered on top of each other, but it also resembles bags of bright candy left to melt and flatten in the sun. Brätsch advocates the mobility and mutability of painting, the marriage of the analogue and the digital, and the transgression of the blurry boundary between painting and design. VSR

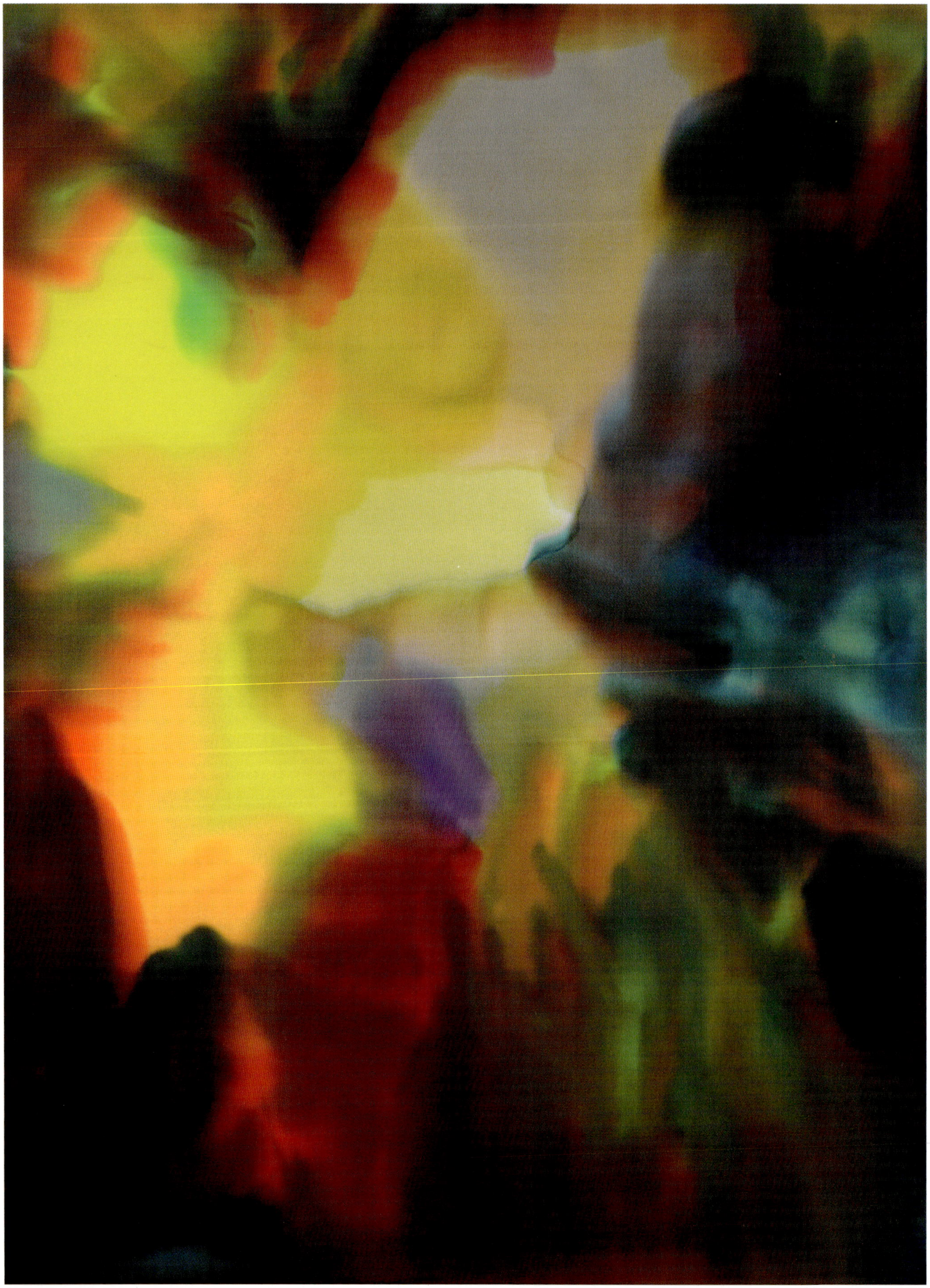

1

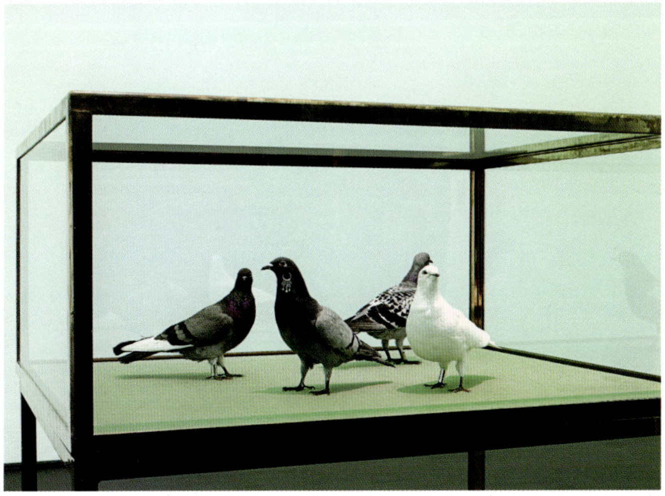

2

**Shown by**
BQ G11
Esther Schipper A3

**Biography**
Born 1968
Lives in Cologne

Berlin-born artist Braun has presented solo exhibitions at galleries that include BQ, Berlin (2012), Galleria S.A.L.E.S., Rome (2011), Kunstverein Braunschweig (2010), Kunstmuseum Liechtenstein, Vaduz (2009), and Museum Ludwig, Cologne (2008). His work was featured in the recent group exhibition 'Made in Germany Zwei: International Art in Germany' at Sprengel Museum, Hanover (2012). Braun is the subject of a solo show at the Arnolfini, Bristol, until January 2013.

1
*Untitled*
2011
Fabric dye on silk
182 × 131 cm
Courtesy of BQ

2
*Untitled*
2008
Stuffed pigeons and silver jewellery in vitrine (copper, glass, wood and fabric)
92 × 120 × 106 cm
Courtesy of BQ

# Matti Braun

Interested in what he calls 'cultural misunderstandings', Matti Braun has drawn upon ethnographical and folkloric traditions to produce ceramics, batiks, mouth-blown glass objects, a wall made of reflective mosaics (*Bali*, 1998), and a snowstorm made with polystyrene (*Edo*, 1999). His immersive room installations include *S.R.* (2003), for which he turned the main hall of the Kunstverein Freiburg into a dark pool, traversable by tree-trunk stepping stones. Braun's inspiration was the Indian filmmaker Satyajit Ray, whose unrealized screenplay 'The Alien' also informed Braun's cross-disciplinary dance, theatre and musical projects *The Alien* (2005) and *Laban the Alien* (2006). More recently, Braun flooded a gallery with ultraviolet light and laid a screed floor as a backdrop to his new untitled psychedelic paintings, rendered in fabric dye on raw silk. SL

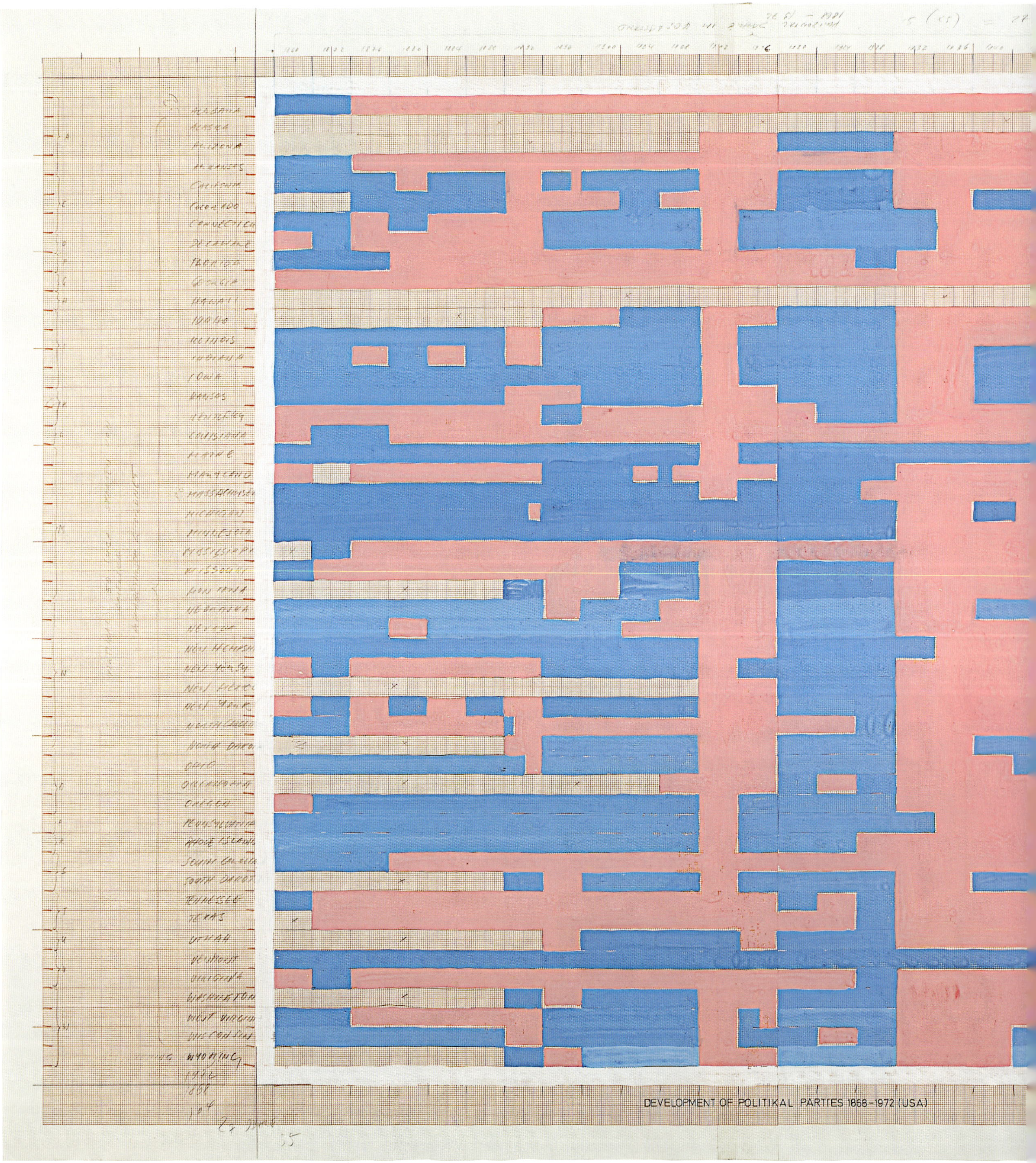
DEVELOPMENT OF POLITIKAL PARTIES 1868-1972 (USA)

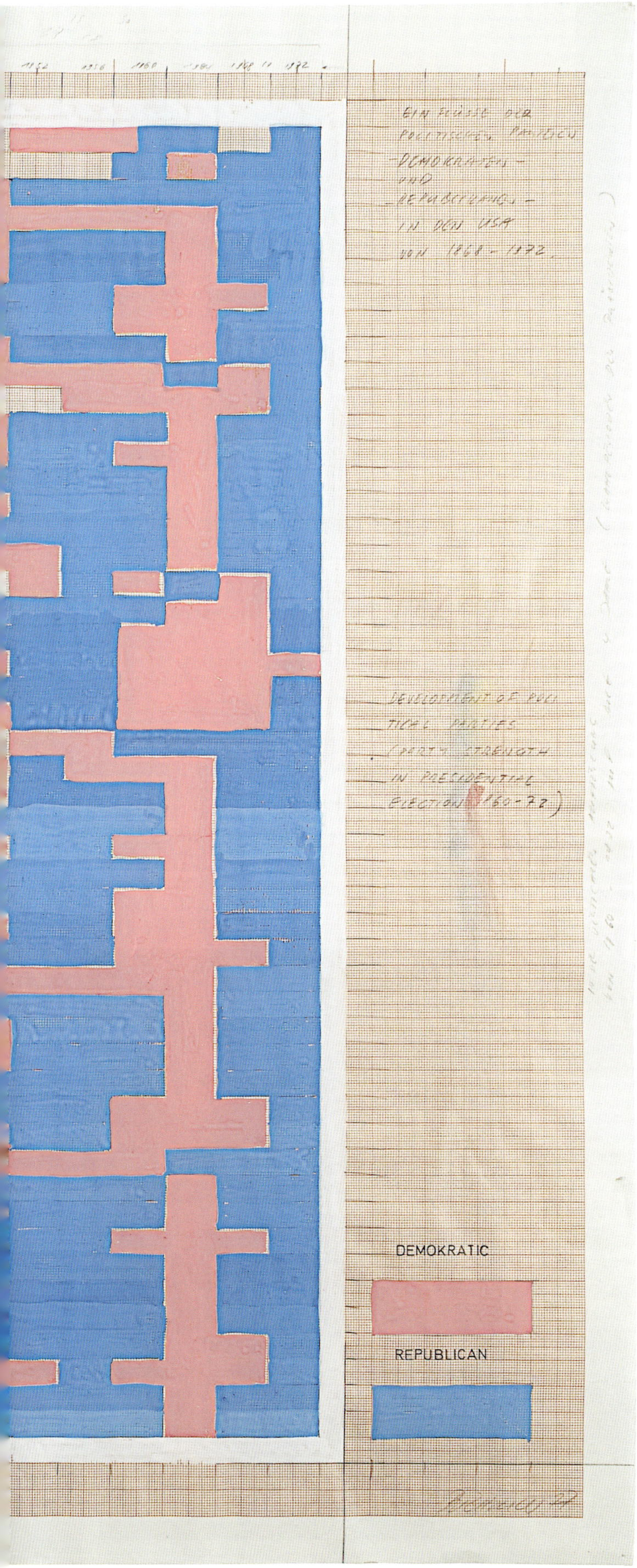


# KP Brehmer

**Shown by**
Vilma Gold B2

**Biography**
Born 1938
Died 1997

Berlin-born Brehmer has been the subject of recent survey exhibitions at institutions including Centro Andaluz de Arte Contemporáneo, Seville (2011), Hamburger Kunsthalle, Hamburg (1998), and Kunsthalle Fridericianum, Kassel (1998). His work has featured in recent group shows that include the 11th Istanbul Biennial (2009) and 'German Angst', Neuer Berliner Kunstverein, Berlin (2008), and is part of public collections such as MoMA, New York, and Berlinische Galerie, Berlin.

*Development of Political Parties 1868–1972 (USA)*
1977
Mixed media on graph paper
59 × 80 cm
Courtesy of Vilma Gold

A leading light in the German art movement Capitalist Realism, KP Brehmer devoted himself to exposing and inverting those ambient models of representation—cartography, thermography, typography etc.—by which capitalism directs and distorts meaning. For *Trivialgrafik* (1968) Brehmer remade the postage stamp as wallpaper, pillows and prints, inserting the heads of Hitler and Lenin; the stamp project *Druckmuster Ideale Rose* (1969) features variously tinted roses accompanied by directive tags: for example, 'life' for orange, 'sea' for blue. In *Development of Political Parties 1868–1972 (USA)* (1977) the colour codes (red for Republican, blue for Democrat) are nearly reversed, and the alienated graphing procedure generates an abstraction resembling early computer graphics: one of many glitches Brehmer inserted into the matrix of his day, which remains that of ours. MH

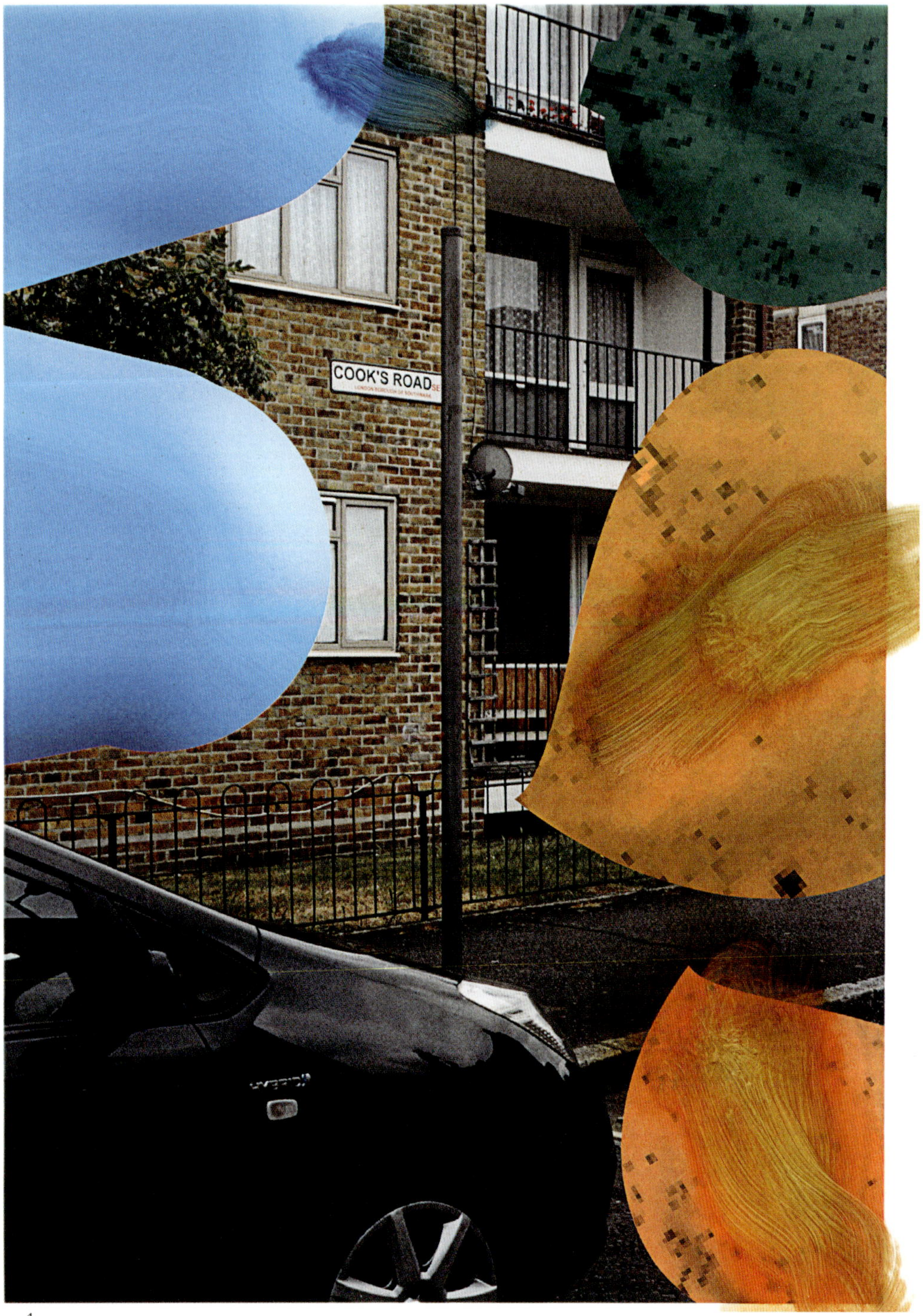

1

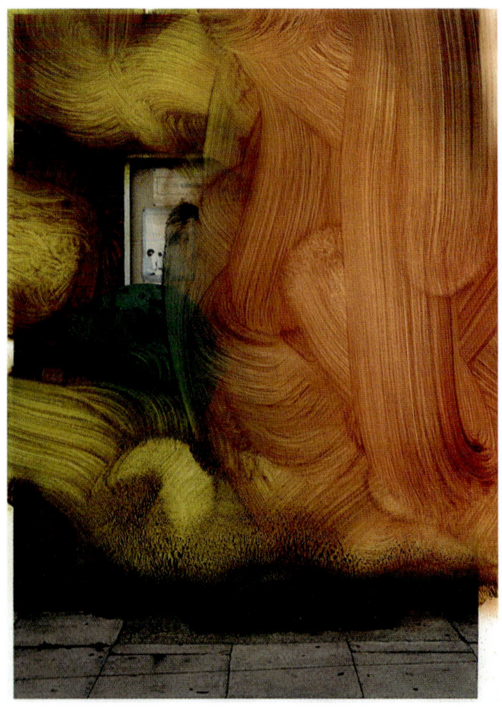
2

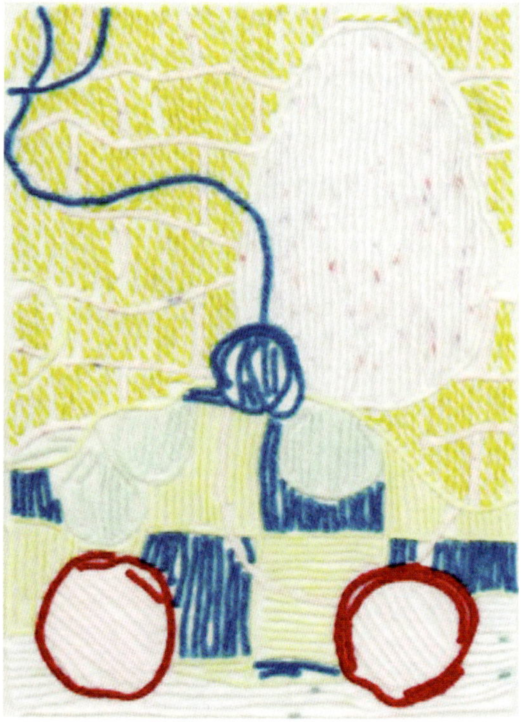

3

**Shown by**
Galerie Karin Guenther
H6
Hotel F5
Galerie Meyer Kainer F2

**Biography**
Born 1966
Lives in Berlin and London

German-born artist Breuer has been the subject of solo presentations at galleries including Cubitt Gallery, London (2010), and KW Institute for Contemporary Art, Berlin (2009), and Galerie Meerrettich im Glaspavillon an der Volksbühne, Berlin (2006). In 2012 he was presented alongside Anita Leisz at Renwick Gallery, New York, by the Viennese exhibition space Pro Choice. In 2013 he will be the subject of a solo show at Hotel, London.

1
*Learning Leads to Earning*
2011
Toner on colour copy
30 × 21 cm
Courtesy of Hotel and Galerie Meyer Kainer

2
*Untitled*
2011
Toner on colour copy
30 × 21 cm
Courtesy of Hotel and Gallery Meyer Kainer

3
*Police Car*
2012
Nylon and acrylic wool on PVC
30 × 21 cm
Courtesy of Hotel and Renwick Gallery

# Wolfgang Breuer

While Wolfgang Breuer's sculptures, installations and pictures scavenge material and images from city streets, his work is invariably depopulated and engages found objects on formal terms that seem, at first glance, to reveal more about colour, scale and design (or bad design) than about socio-political issues. For his exhibition 'News from Rome' at Cubitt Gallery, London (2010), he covered the walls with blue security grills, juxtaposing them with racks holding joyous red exercise balls. In recent images such as *Learning Leads to Earning* (2011), Breuer encroaches on photocopied pictures of hybrid cars with luscious smears of toner and collaged leaves. But he realizes that aesthetics and social behaviour are inextricably linked, each reflecting the problems and possibilities within the other. JG

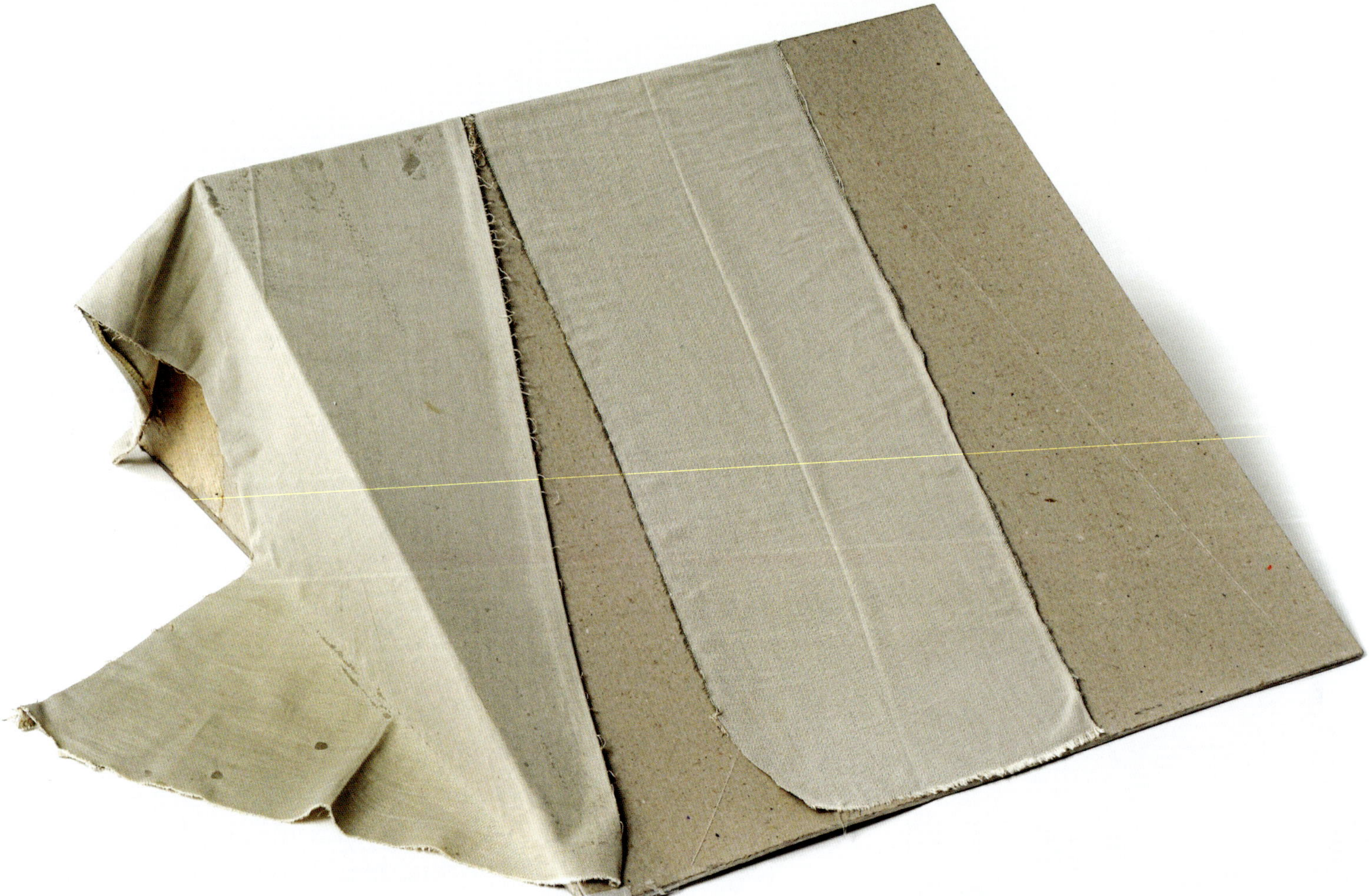

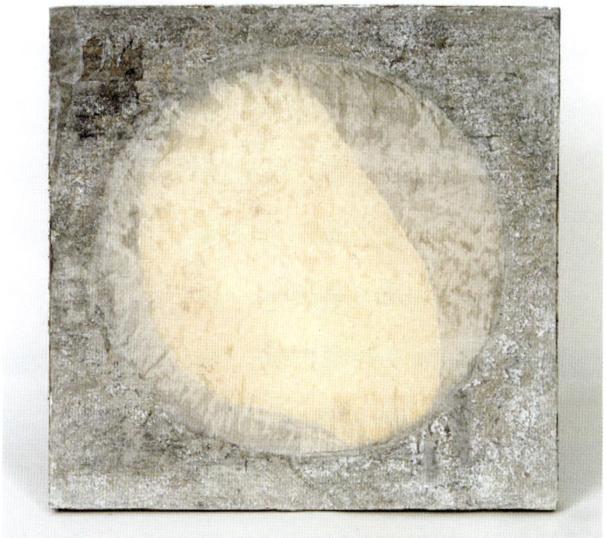

2

**Shown by**
Johnen Galerie D1
Raster S19

**Biography**
Born 1976
Lives in Warsaw

Polish artist Budny has been presented in solo shows at galleries including Kunstmuseum Stuttgart (2011), South London Gallery (2010) and Dvir Gallery, Tel Aviv (2009). His work has been featured in group exhibitions such as 'New Order', Art Stations Foundation, Poznan (2011), 'Polish', Künstlerhaus Bethanien, Berlin (2010), and 'Warsaw under Construction', Museum of Modern Art, Warsaw (2009).

1
*Untitled (Block of Ice)*
From the series 'Zywica'
2012
Cardboard, lacquer, foil, cotton fabric and ink
73 × 56 × 24 cm
Courtesy of Raster

2
*Zywica (Gold)*
2012
Cardboard, paper, acrylic paint, gold, wax and lacquer
53 × 53 × 3 cm
Courtesy of Raster

# Focus Michał Budny

Michał Budny's installations form a delicate weave between the monumental and the mundane, finding a precise vocabulary through abstract, minimal objects and sculptures. He takes abstraction at face value, at times turning urban housing spaces or musical instruments into resolute, well-crafted entities that reflect and respond to their surroundings. But the provisional nature of his materials of choice—paper, wax and Scotch Tape—reveals that process as a series of disappearing traces, their impressions of a space becoming a passing memory. His work *Untitled (Block of Ice)* (2012) in his exhibition 'Zywica' (Resin) at Raster, Warsaw (2012), was a small cardboard incline, draped at an angle with strips of beige cloth, appearing as both an architectural model and a mournfully poetic relic from a silent past. CFW

**Shown by**
Marianne Boesky Gallery E5

**Biography**
Born 1943
Lives in Fossombrone, Italy

Recent solo exhibitions of the Bologna-born Calzolari have been presented at venues such as Marianne Boesky Gallery, New York (in collaboration with Pace Gallery, New York) (2012), Ca' Pesaro, Venice (2011), Galleria Il Ponte Contemporanea, Rome (2007), and Musée d'Art Moderne et d'Art Contemporain, Nice (2003). Calzolari's work is featured in public collections including Museo Nacional Centro de Arte Reina Sofía, Madrid, and Castello di Rivoli, Turin.

*Untitled*
1988
Burnt wood, copper, frozen structure, refrigerator motor and leaden pond
340 × 200 × 60 cm
Courtesy of Marianne Boesky Gallery

# Pier Paolo Calzolari

A key figure in the Arte Povera movement, the sculptor Pier Paolo Calzolari has made work since the 1960s that employs a wide range of often organic materials (including fire, water, salt, neon, copper, moss, tobacco, feathers and eggs) to explore time, transfiguration and the fusion of art and life. His fascination with frost, a substance he identifies as embodying the only 'true white' available to the artist, may be seen in sculptures such as *Untitled* (1998), where a humming refrigeration unit combines with blocks of burnt wood, a sheet-lead 'pond' and atmospheric moisture in a meditation on cyclical loss and regeneration. Not so much static objects as dynamic systems, such works, as Calzolari has said, 'give of themselves endlessly'. TM

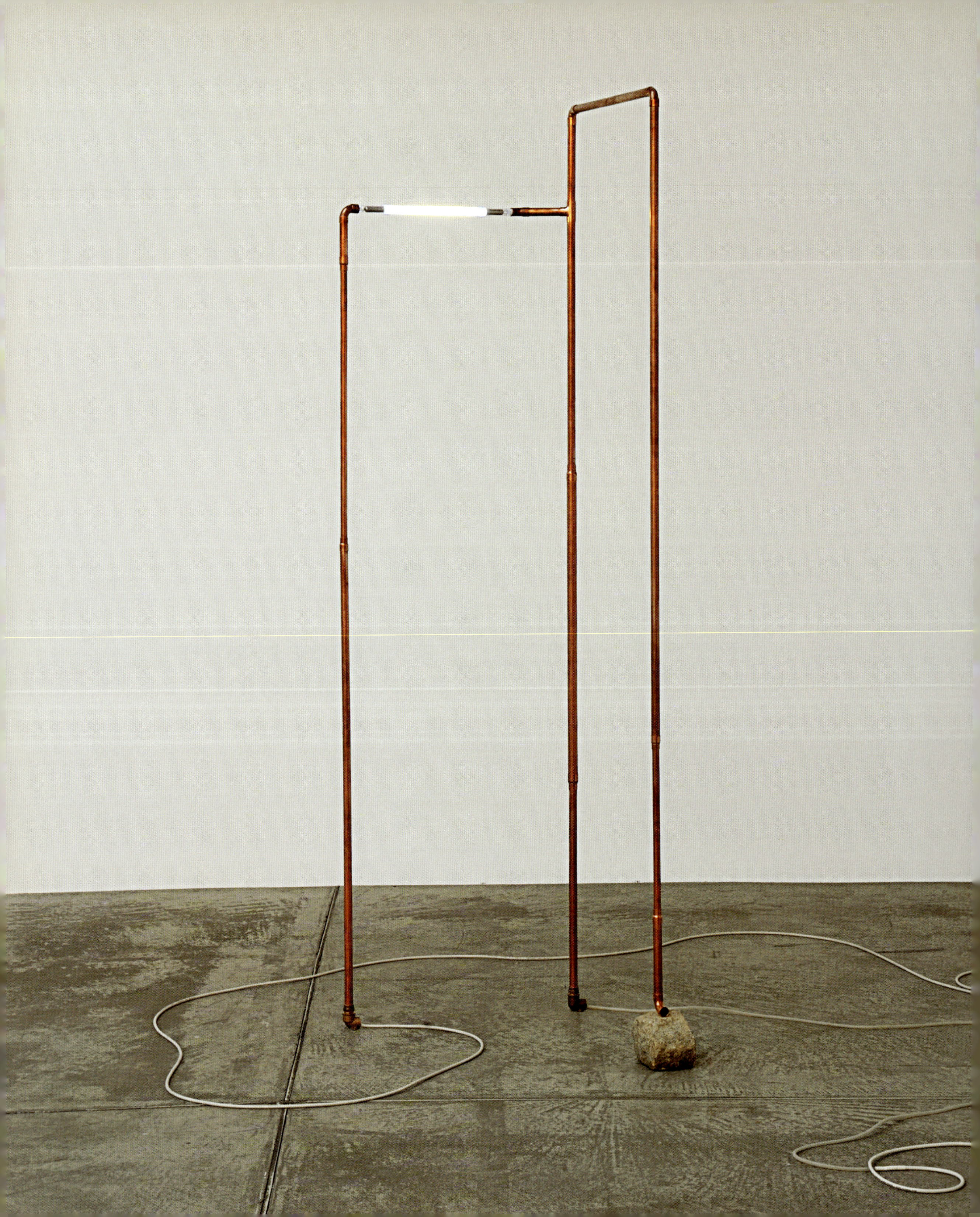

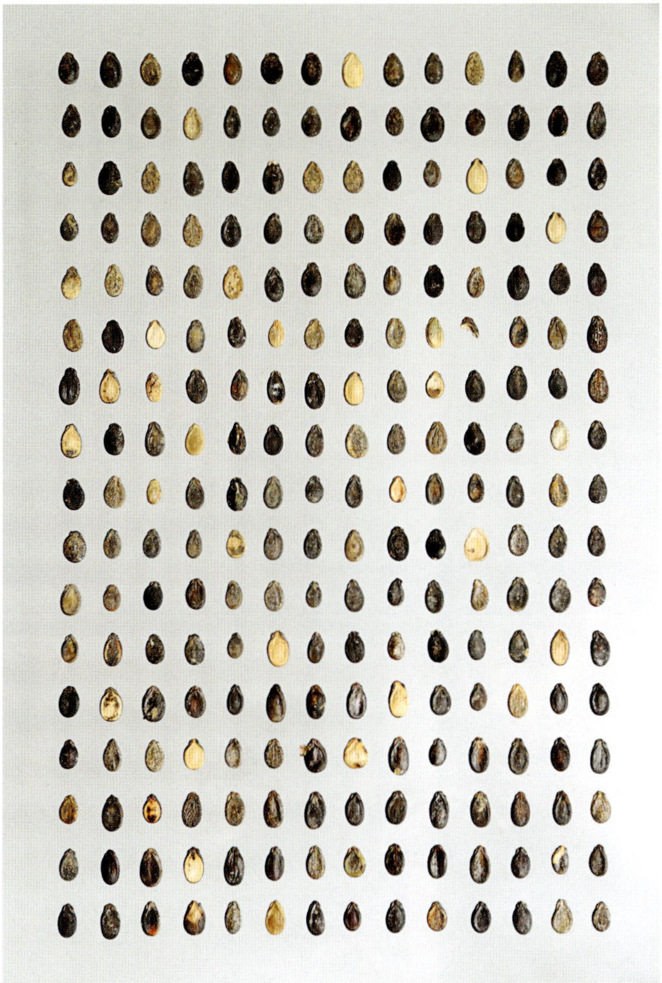

2

**Shown by**
Konrad Fischer Galerie C6
mother's tankstation R15
Wien Lukatsch F16

**Biography**
Born 1979
Lives in Berlin

Swedish-born Canell recently presented solo shows at Cubitt Gallery, London (2012), and Kunsthalle Fridericianum, Kassel (2011). Previous one-person exhibitions were held at venues such as Konrad Fischer Galerie, Berlin (2011), MUMOK, Vienna (2010), and Kunstverein Hamburg (2009). She has participated in biennials including the 18th Biennale of Sydney (2012), the 6th Liverpool Biennial (2010), the 7th Gwangju Biennale (2008) and Manifesta 7, Trentino (2008).

1
*Slight Bend of the Elbow*
2012
Copper, neon, stone, cable and 1,000 volts
180 × 70 × 60 cm
Courtesy of Private Collection, New York

2
*Impulse Slight*
(detail)
2011
Watermelon seeds, glass, log, tape and copper, Dimensions variable
Courtesy of Konrad Fischer Galerie

# Nina Canell

Nina Canell's installations and precarious assemblages of objects are suggestive of prototypes. Recalling Duchamp's quasi-scientific enquiries as well as Fischli/Weiss' iconic film *The Way Things Go* (1987), her jerry-rigged systems incorporate electrical and gaseous elements—neon in the case of *Slight Bend of the Elbow* (2012)—as well as an array of scavenged objects. Recent work *Of Air* (2012), made with Canell's frequent collaborator Robin Watkins, includes what is claimed to be 3,800 ml of air from the study of the Russian inventor of the Periodic Table, Dmitri Mendeleev, while *Words Fallen* (2012) comprises tiny grey chips of what is described as coagulated air. Canell endeavours to make art from the overlooked, atmospheric and ineffable. ST

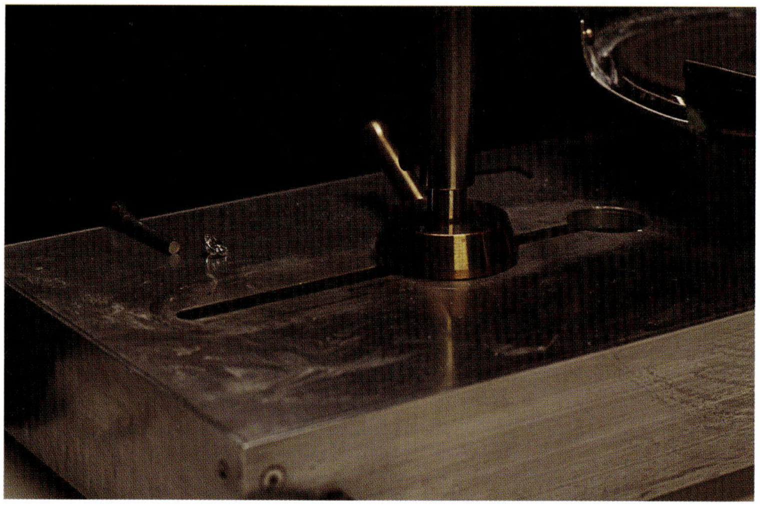

1

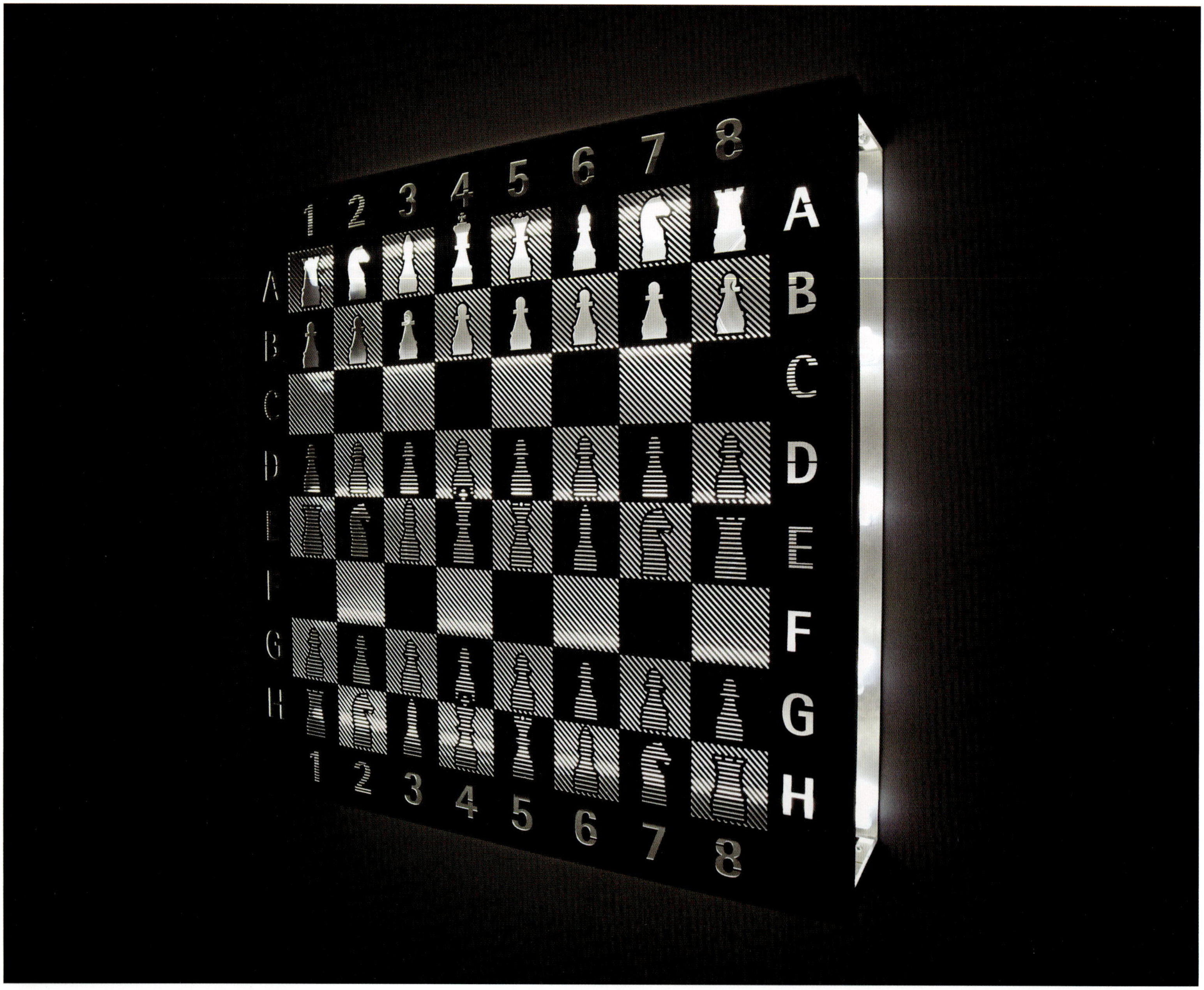


2

**Shown by**
Rampa E18

**Biography**
Born 1968
Lives in London

Bulgarian-born Çavuşoğlu has presented solo shows at venues such as The Pavilion Downtown Dubai (2011), Rampa, Istanbul (2011), Ludwig Forum für Internationale Kunst, Aachen (2009), Haunch of Venison, London (2009 and 2004), Kunstverein Freiburg (2008) and Dundee Contemporary Arts (2004). Recent group exhibitions include the 1st Kyiv Biennale, Kiev (2012), 'Migrasophia', Maraya Art Centre, Sharjah (2012), 'Zwölf im Zwölften', TANAS, Berlin (2011), and 'Pop-Up', Fundació La Caixa, Barcelona (2011).

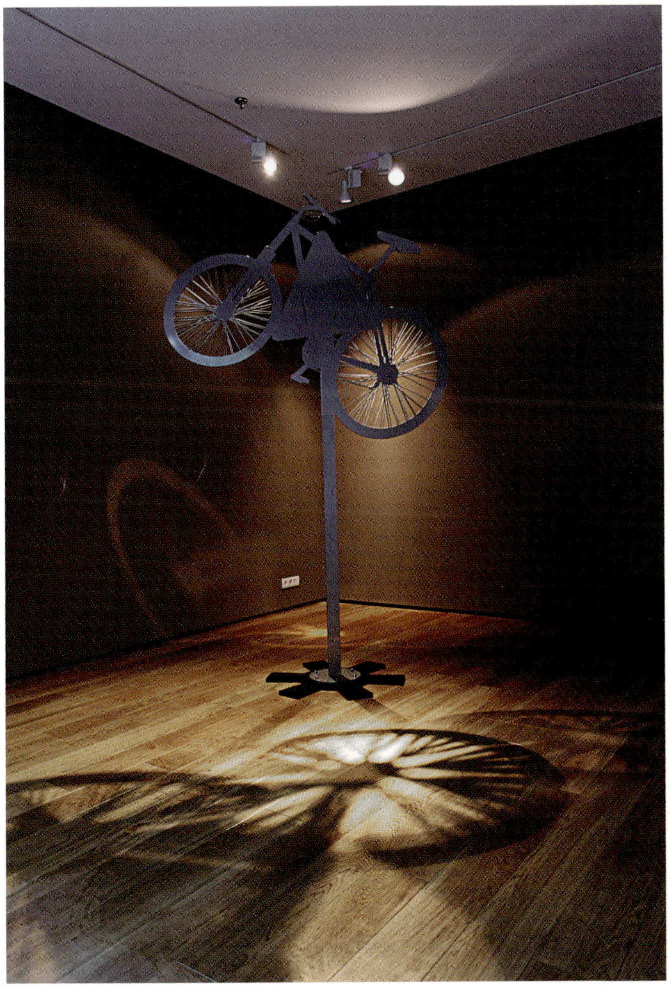
3

1
*Crystal & Flame*
2010
Five-channel synchronized HD video
Duration variable
Courtesy of Rampa and Film and Video Umbrella

2
*Double Attack*
2011
Mirror-polished stainless steel, neon lights and transformer
99 × 99 × 17 cm
Courtesy of Rampa

3
*Mountain Bike*
2011
Aluminium, steel and chrome powder coating
285 × 165 × 80 cm
Courtesy of Rampa

# Ergin Çavuşoğlu

Ergin Çavuşoğlu's films, installations and sculptures unfold in the liminal spaces between states—whether national, material or psychological. His five-channel video installation *Crystal & Flame* (2010) draws on writer Italo Calvino's analogy of fire and crystallization as the competing forces shaping the contemporary city. Çavuşoğlu's narratives never allow for resolution. Instead, as with *Crystal & Flame*'s scenes of actors rehearsing, or the drifting footage of an airport in *Point of Departure* (2006), they are always on the point of becoming. Object-based works such as *Double Attack* (2011), a steel chessboard with extra ranks of pieces in the no man's land between black and white, illustrate how, for Çavuşoğlu, the game is always wide open. JG

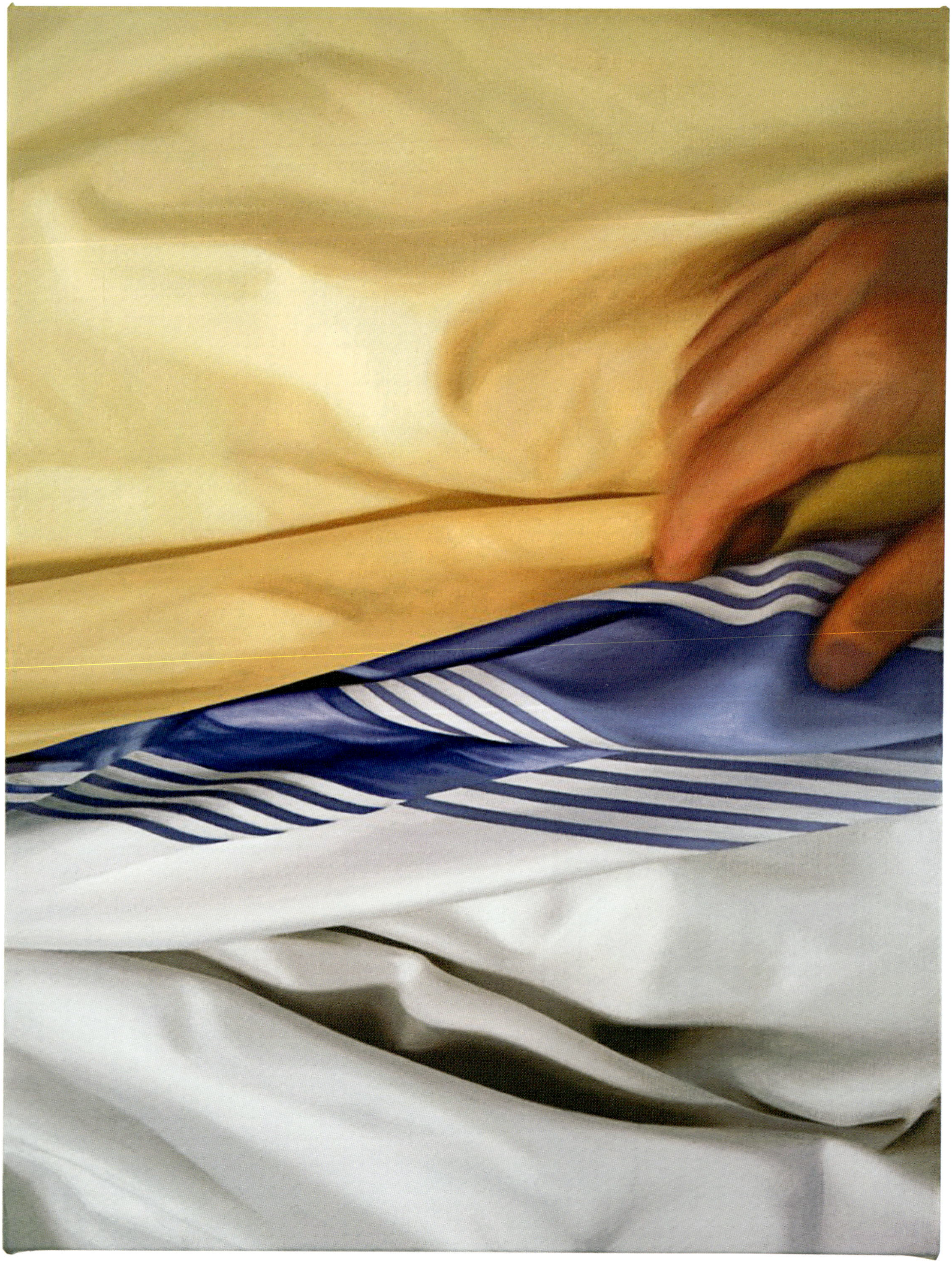

# Focus
# Mathew Cerletty

**Shown by**
Algus Greenspon S20
Office Baroque Gallery S8

**Biography**
Born 1980
Lives in New York

American artist Cerletty has presented solo shows at galleries including Algus Greenspon, New York (2011), and Office Baroque Gallery, Antwerp (2008). His work has been featured in group exhibitions including 'Cover Version LP', Brooklyn Academy of Music, New York (2011), 'Private Public Paintings', MuZee, Ostend (2010), 'It's All American', New Jersey Museum of Contemporary Art, Conventional Hall, Ashbury Park (2010), and 'The Coke Factory', Ritter/Zamet, London (2010).

*Hand in Bed*
2011
Oil on linen
43 × 34 cm
Courtesy of Algus Greenspon

Something often seems slightly off-kilter or out of reach in Mathew Cerletty's radiant and meticulous paintings—nothing is quite what it appears. *Hand in Bed* (2011), which depicts silky bed-sheet folds echoing Baroque religious art, makes one search to understand what one is seeing: soft-focus fingers reaching into the frame to touch the fabric seem caught in movement, suggesting a furtive snapshot as much as an evocation of sanctity or luxury. Cerletty's earlier hyper-realistic portraits of figures before patterned backgrounds were psychologically arresting while recalling fashion adverts and the writing of Bret Easton Ellis; his renderings of banal subjects such as a North Face logo are similarly multilayered, as is his witty expedition into the hermetic world of home furnishing catalogues in *Ikea* (2010). KMJ

# INDEX

# Alejandro Cesarco

Alejandro Cesarco creates text-based works concerned with the act of reading and, by extension, with association and conjecture. He is perhaps best known for his indices—each a list of citations both general and particular, and an index to an unwritten work. From these indices, readers are invited to imagine the implied work. Cesarco is particularly good at illustrating the way sources, influences and quotations can be knitted together to provide a portrait of a person, archetype or state of mind. In *Index (An Orphan)* (2012), philosophers Julia Kristeva and Henri Bergson sit alongside 'little green bike', the oft-cited alongside the particular and subjective. KK

**Shown by**
Ignacio Liprandi Arte Contemporáneo R18
Murray Guy F18

**Biography**
Born 1975
Lives in New York

Montevideo-born Cesarco has presented solo exhibitions and projects at venues that include MuMOK, Vienna (2012), ar/ge kunst, Bolzano (2011–12), Museo Rufino Tamayo, Mexico City (2011), and Tate Modern, London (2010). He represented Uruguay with Magela Ferrero at the 54th Venice Biennale (2011) and has been included in group shows such as 'Found in Translation', Deutsche Guggenheim, Berlin (2012), and '9 Screens', MoMA, New York (2010). His work is on show at the 30th Bienal de Sao Paulo until December 2012.

1
*Index (An Orphan)*
(detail)
2012
6 c-type prints
Each 71 × 61 cm
Courtesy of Murray Guy

2
*Methodology*
2011
HD video
7 min.
Courtesy of Murray Guy

3
*If in Time*
2012
HD video
9 min. 40 sec.
Courtesy of Murray Guy

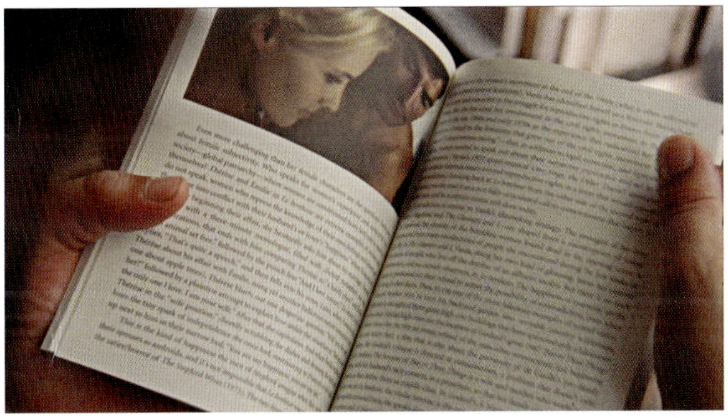

3

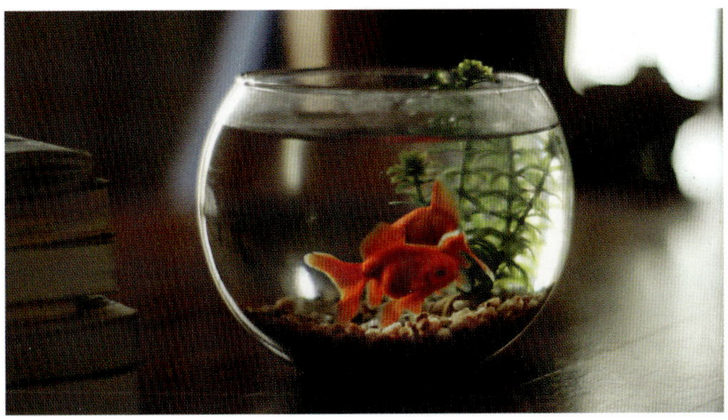

2

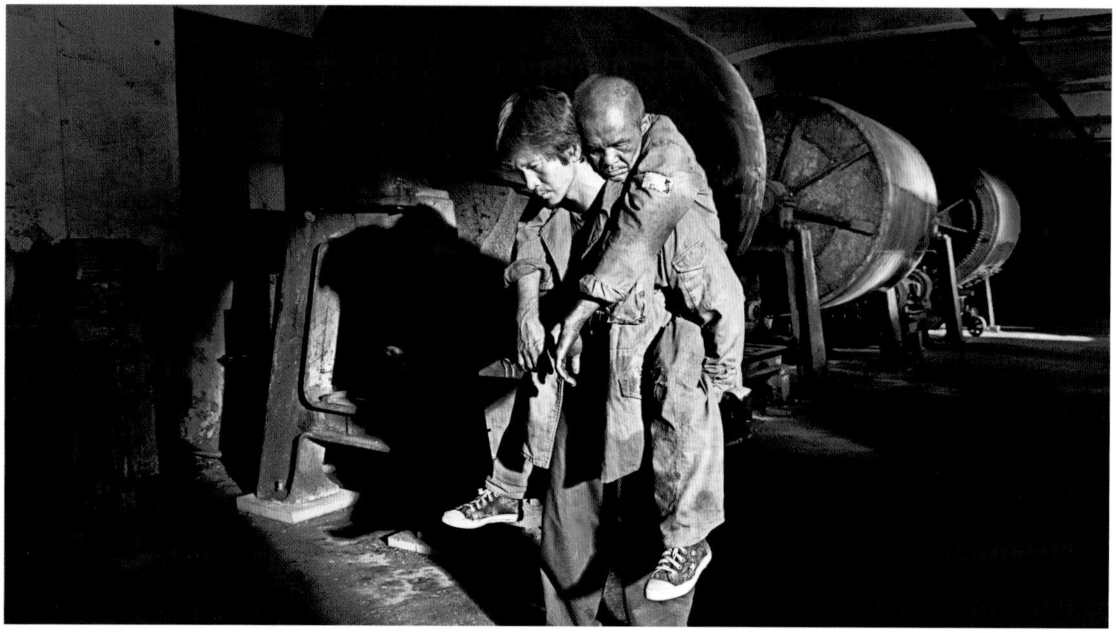

1

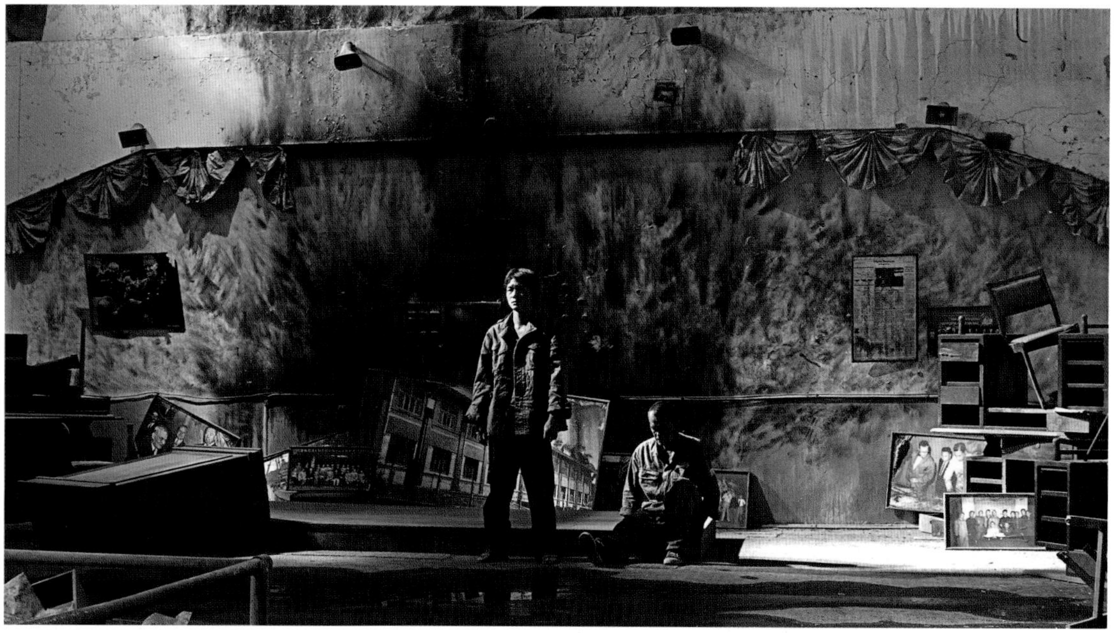

2

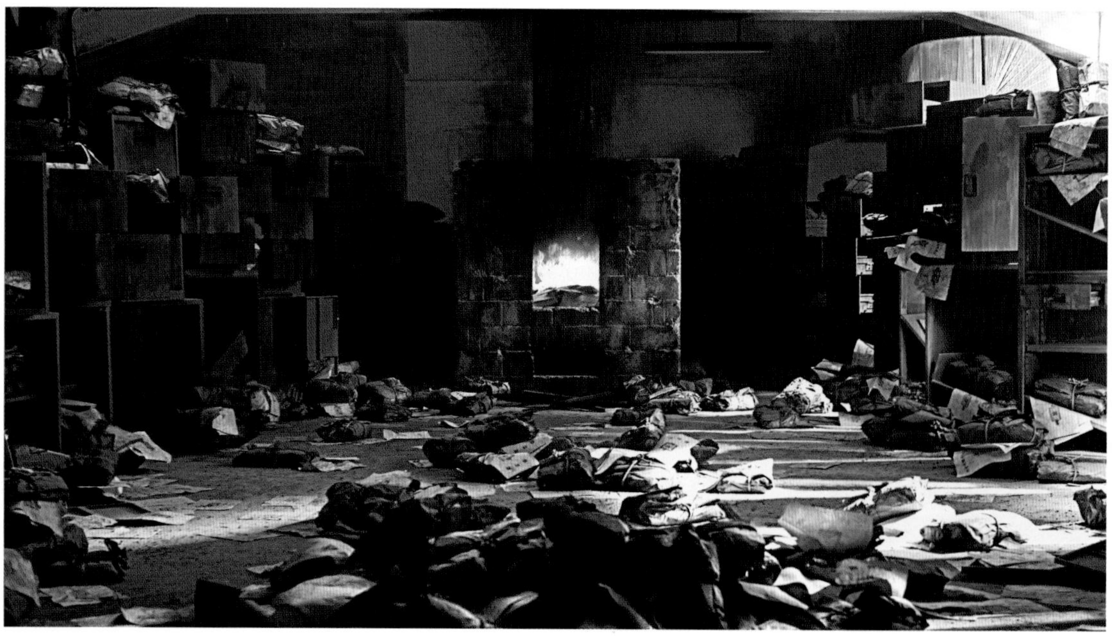

3

**Shown by**
Long March Space B7

**Biography**
Born 1960
Lives in Taipei

Taiwanese artist Chen has held solo exhibitions at public institutions such as Taipei Fine Arts Museum (2010), REDCAT, Los Angeles (2010), and Museo Nacional Centro de Arte Reina Sofía, Madrid (2008). He received the Taiwan National Culture and Arts Foundation's National Award for Arts in 2009 and the Special Prize at the 3rd Gwangju Biennale (2000). He has participated in international biennials that include the 53rd Venice Biennale (2009) and 10th Istanbul Biennial (2007).

# Chen Chieh-Jen

Chen Chieh-Jen's works problematize the history of Taiwan, from its experience of martial law and the Cold War to globalization and democracy. *Empire's Borders I* (2008–9) and *Empire's Borders II – Western Enterprises, Inc.* (2010) address Taiwan's role at the nexus of two 'empires'— the US and China. Inspired by his difficulties acquiring a visa to the US, *Empire's Borders I* explores issues of humiliation and isolation through interviews with both Chinese immigrants entering Taiwan and Taiwanese émigrés seeking entry to the US. *Empire's Borders II – Western Enterprises, Inc.* concerns the Anti-Communist National Salvation Army, a guerrilla force established with the assistance of the paramilitary arm of the CIA, of which Chen's father was a member. ND

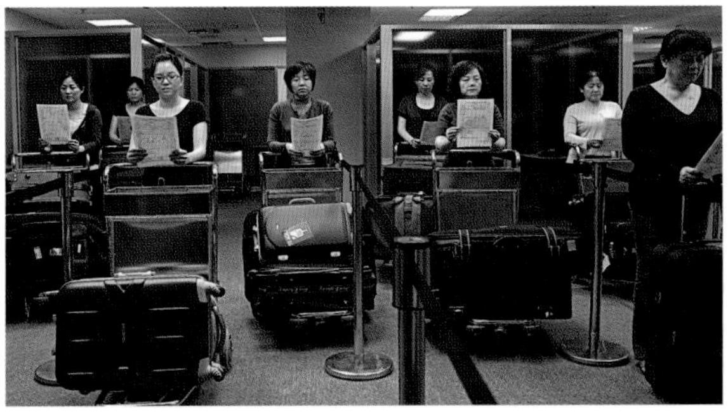

6

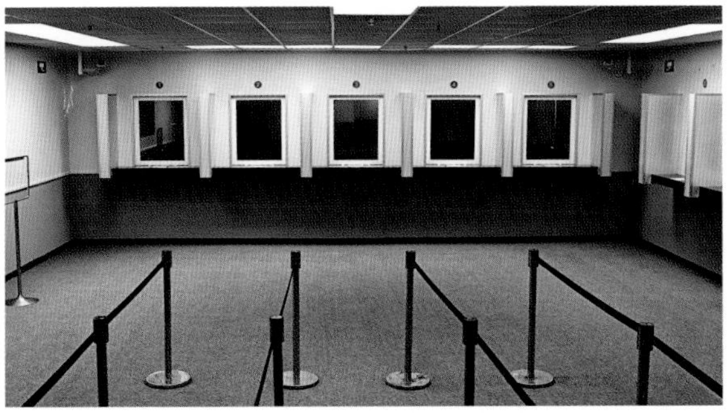

5

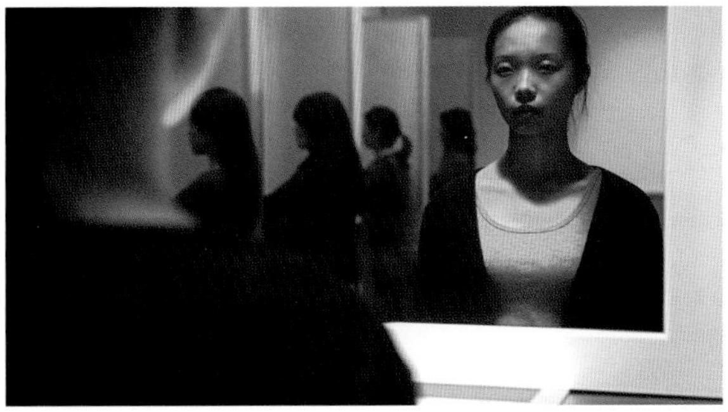

4

1, 2, 3
*Empire's Borders II – Western Enterprises, Inc.*
2010
Three-channel video installation
35 mm film transferred to Blu-ray Disc
70 min. single-channel video plus 5 min. double-channel video
Courtesy of Long March Space

4, 5, 6
*Empire's Borders I*
2008–9
35 mm film transferred to DVD
27 min.
Courtesy of Long March Space

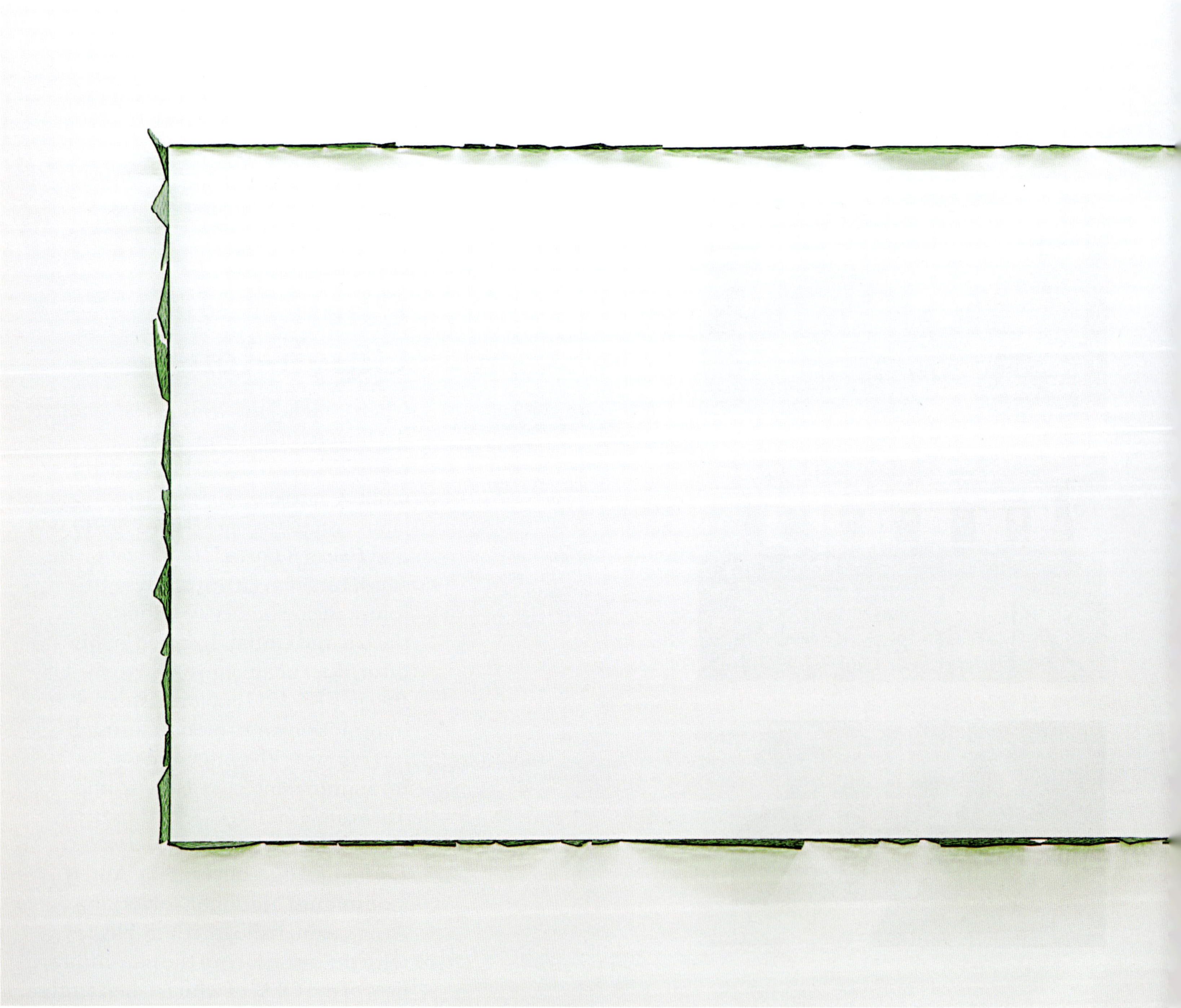

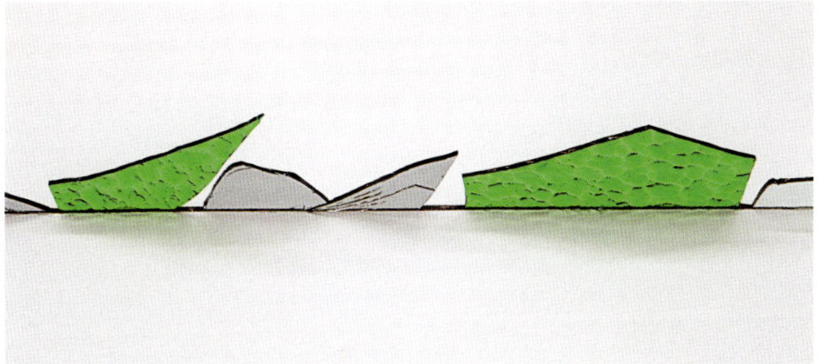

2

**Shown by**
Vermelho H3

**Biography**
Born 1979
Lives in Sao Paulo

Brazilian artist Cidade has presented solo exhibitions at galleries that include Vermelho, Sao Paulo (2012, 2010 and 2008), Fundação Serralves, Porto (2009), and Centro Cultural Sao Paulo (2008). He recently participated in the group exhibition 'You and Eye' at the 11th Havana Biennial (2012). His work is featured in public collections such as Museu de Arte Moderna, Sao Paulo, and the Tate collection, UK.

1
*Adição por subtração*
(Addition by Subtraction)
2012
Glass
150 × 300 × 10 cm
Courtesy of Vermelho

2
*Adição por subtração*
(Addition by Subtraction)
(detail)
2012
Glass
150 × 300 × 10 cm
Courtesy of Vermelho

# Marcelo Cidade

More than just an urban forager, former street artist Marcelo Cidade turns his objects and observations towards unravelling the metaphorical and physical implications of access and denial. Using familiar materials from building sites and skips to make sculptures and installations, Cidade makes apparent the paradoxical politics inherent in the city and the gallery. His work *Adição por subtração* (Addition by Subtraction, 2012) uses shards of green and clear glass embedded in the wall to outline a rectangular space. Turning into a frame the glass used to line the tops of walls to protect private property, Cidade denies us the view of the suggested paradise inside, the image just beyond our grasp. CFW

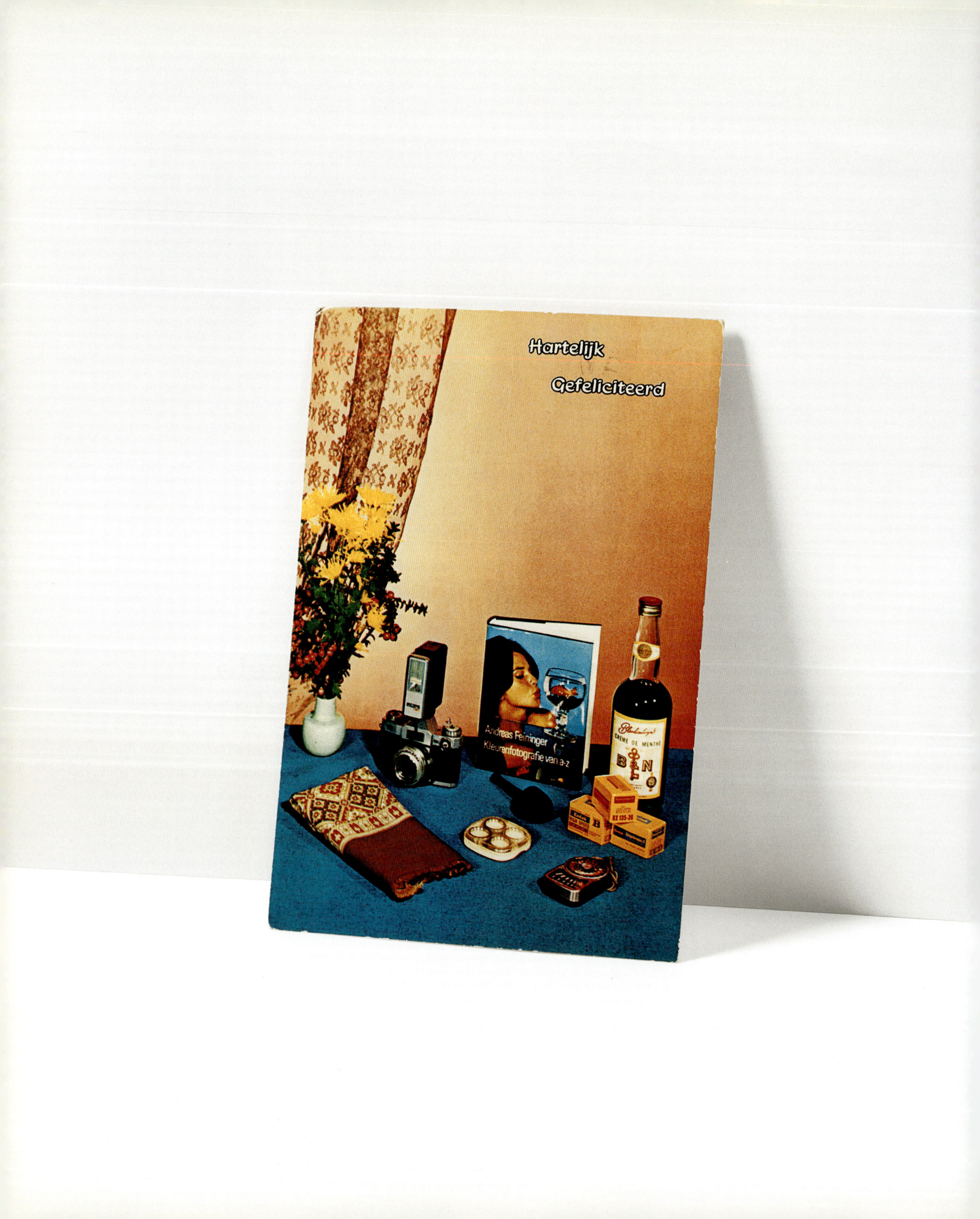
Hartelijk
Gefeliciteerd
Andreas Feininger
Kleurenfotografie van a-z
CREME DE MENTHE

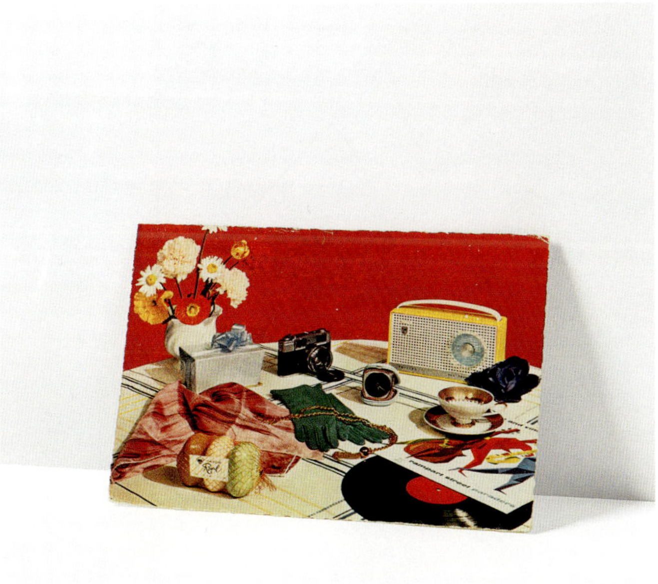

2

**Shown by**
Corvi-Mora E7
Marc Foxx B8
Anton Kern Gallery A4

**Biography**
Born 1970
Lives in New York

California-born Collier has staged solo shows at venues including Anton Kern Gallery, New York (2012, 2010 and 2008), Corvi-Mora, London (2011, 2007 and 2005), Nottingham Contemporary (2011) and Bonner Kunstverein, Bonn (2008). She participates in the group exhibition 'New Photography 2012' at MoMA, New York, until January 2013, and from April 2013 her work is included in 'The Polaroid Years' at the Frances Lehman Loeb Art Center, Poughkeepsie.

1
*Dutch Still Life #4 (Postcard)*
2012
C-type print
73 × 59 cm
Courtesy of Anton Kern Gallery

2
*Dutch Still Life #6 (Postcard)*
2012
C-type print
59 × 73 cm
Courtesy of Anton Kern Gallery

# Anne Collier

From a cool remove, as though placing artefacts under glass while wearing white cotton gloves, Anne Collier photographs vintage pop-cultural objects incorporating charged photographic images: Ingrid Bergman sobs on a record sleeve; scantily clad women pose in camera ads; suns set in banal inspirational posters. Within a pristine studio setting she reframes with mournful wit the emotional and psychological content of finds like poignantly labelled self-help cassette tapes. Cameras proliferate—for example, in bright postcards depicting gendered still lifes, such as *Dutch Still Life #1 (Postcard)* (2012), in which a camera is grouped with manly aftershave and cigarettes—as do eyes and women. Collier's work has an oblique personal undercurrent, which she has called 'the idea of a kind of deflected self-portraiture'. KMJ

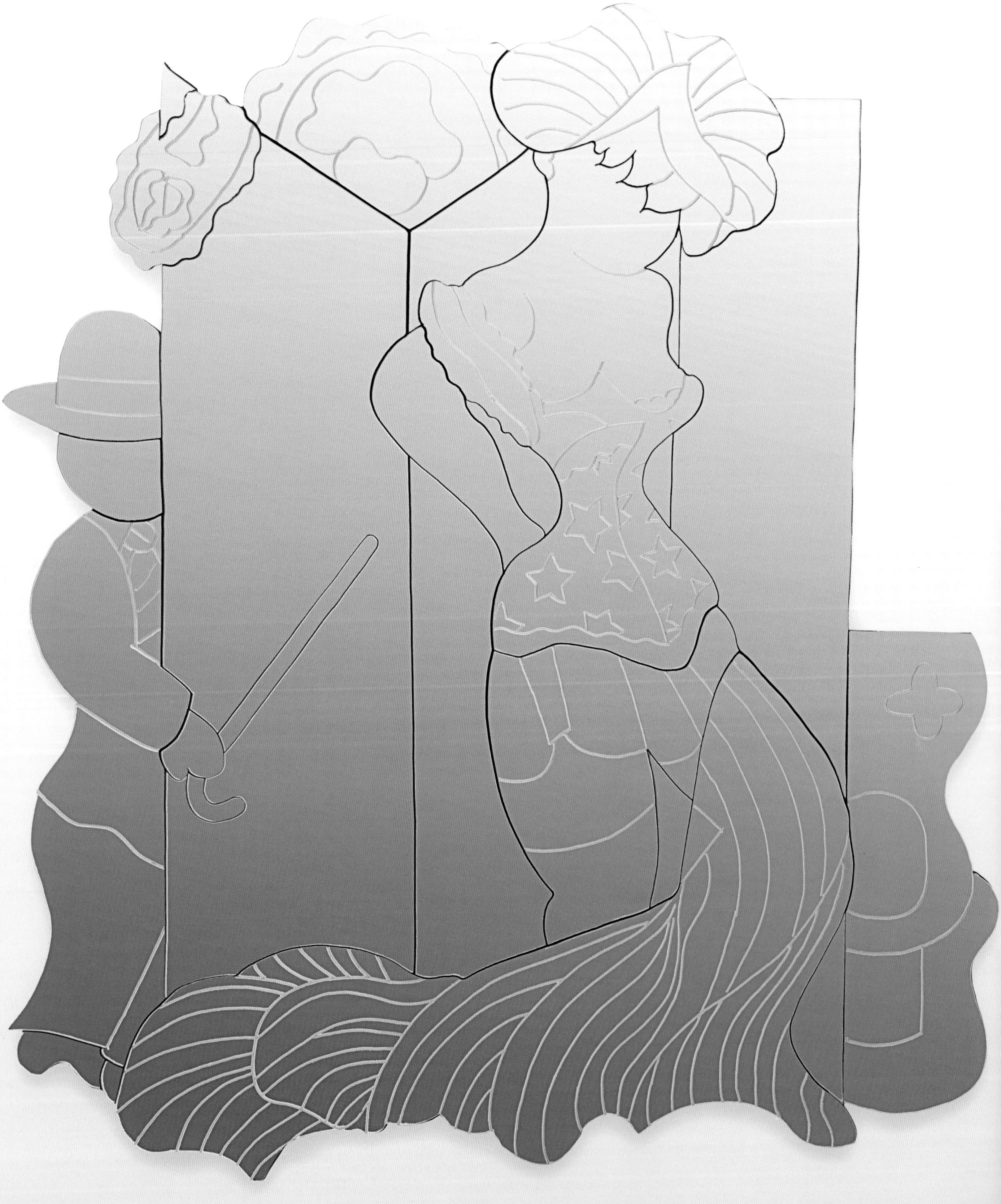

# William N. Copley

**Shown by**
Paul Kasmin Gallery F10

**Biography**
Born 1919
Died 1996

New York-born Copley has been the subject of survey exhibitions at venues such as Museum Frieder Burda, Baden Baden (2012), and Musée d'Art Moderne et Contemporain, Geneva (2004). A travelling retrospective of his work (1980–81) was presented at institutions such as Centre Pompidou, Paris. In 2010 Paul Kasmin Gallery, New York, presented a recreation of 'CPLY: X-Rated', the artist's 1974 exhibition originally displayed at the New York Cultural Center.

*Untitled*
1981–2011
Mirrored acrylic
168 × 170 × 4 cm
Courtesy of Paul Kasmin Gallery and Copley LLC

William N. Copley amassed a remarkable collection of Dadaist and Surrealist art. Unlike most collectors, however, he was also an accomplished artist. Influenced by Henri Matisse, Pierre Bonnard and René Magritte, he developed in the 1950s a bold style of sensuous, colourful figuration that anticipated subsequent developments in Pop art. CPLY (as he renamed himself) shocked many contemporary viewers with a brazen series of paintings titled 'X-Rated' (1972–4), showing concupiscent couples in flagrante. Even when his subject matter was less risqué, CPLY's taste for clashing patterns in pictures—on fabrics and wallpapers, for instance—allowed his protagonists to fizz sexily against their backgrounds. JG

1

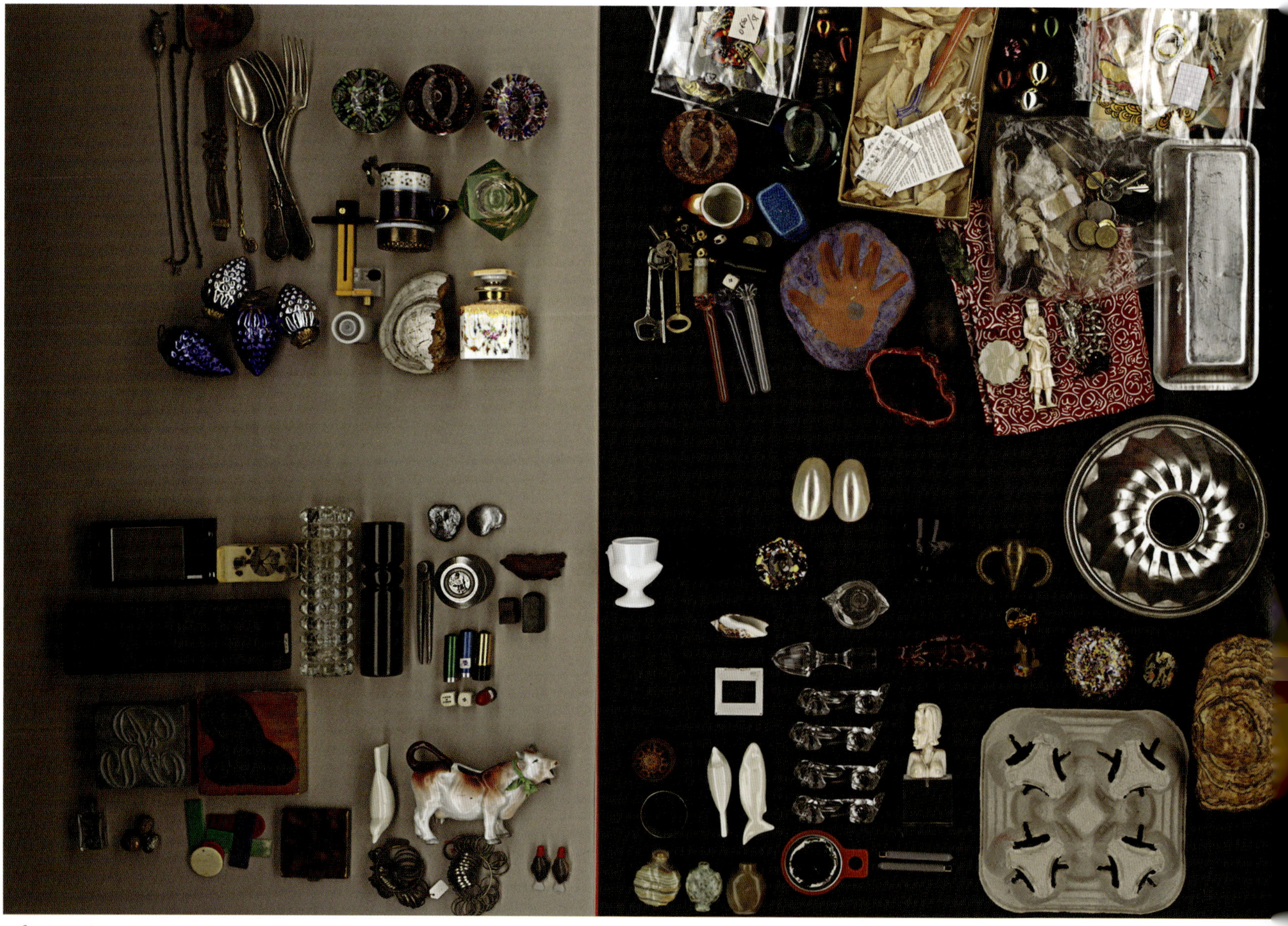

2

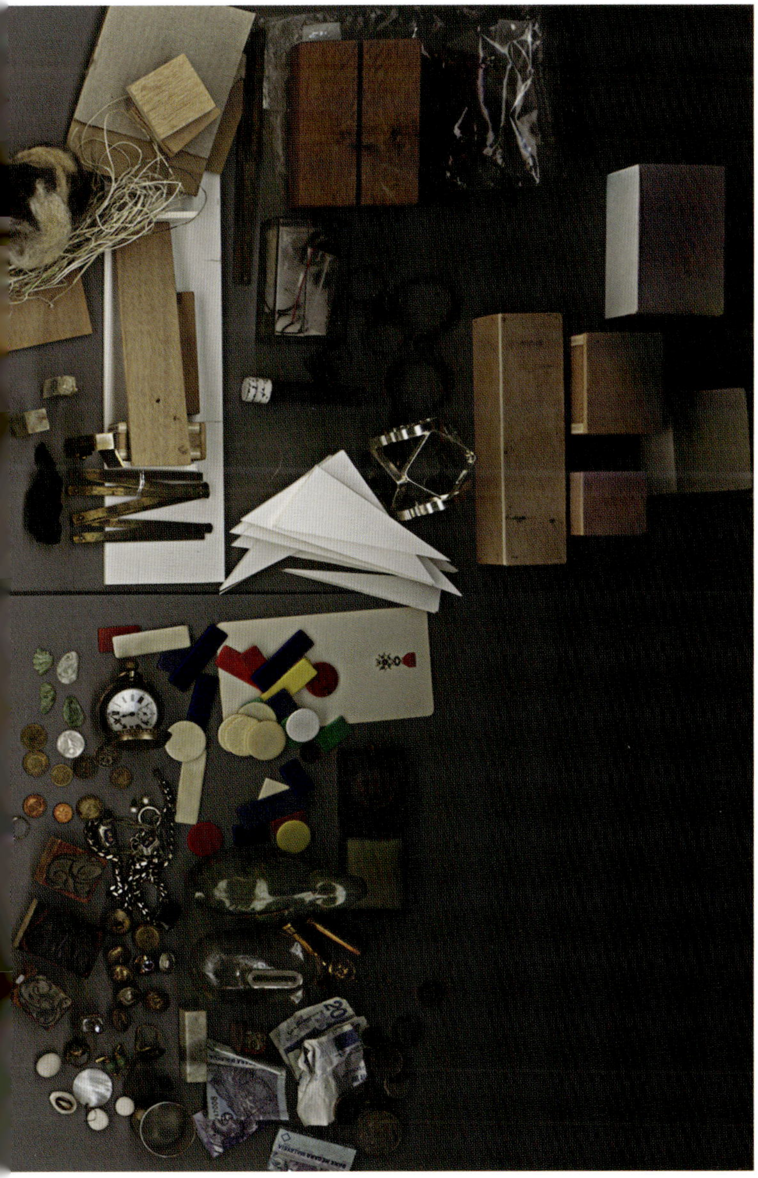

**Shown by**
Galerie Francesca Pia G1

**Biography**
Born 1974
Lives in Paris

French-born Cornaro has presented solo shows recently at venues that include Le Magasin, Grenoble (2012), FRAC Aquitaine, Bordeaux (2012), Centre d'Art Contemporain de Troyes (2010) and Kunstverein Dusseldorf (2009). Her work is part of collections such as Centre Pompidou, Paris, and Musée d'Art Moderne de la Ville de Paris. In 2013 Cornaro will be the subject of a solo exhibition at Kunsthalle Bern.

1
*Reproduction*
2010
Spray paint on wall
Dimensions variable
Courtesy of Galerie Francesca Pia

2
*Moulage sur le vif (vide poche)*
(Life Casts [Catch All])
2011
Pigment and print on rag paper
91 × 191 cm
Courtesy of Galerie Francesca Pia

# Isabelle Cornaro

Decorous yet defiantly indefinable landscapes, stages, miniatures and *mises-en-scène* might be said to characterize Isabella Cornaro's discursive yet highly constructed mixed-media practice, which plumbs the nature of objects and their cultural representations and fetishizations. Yet despite employing an endless bag of historical referents (Oskar Fischinger, Bernard Palissy, Nicolas Poussin), the artist's themes remain remarkably consistent. Take the Super-8 film *Vanité vive* (Live Vanity, 2001), in which Cornaro's hand is seen precisely placing objects on a wooden table. Or the 2011 'Photogramme' series, for which she cast table-tops laden with cursive-like tools in aluminium. Displayed like cuneiform-written tablets on plinths, the topographical monochromes simultaneously suggested décor and literature, object and painting. QL

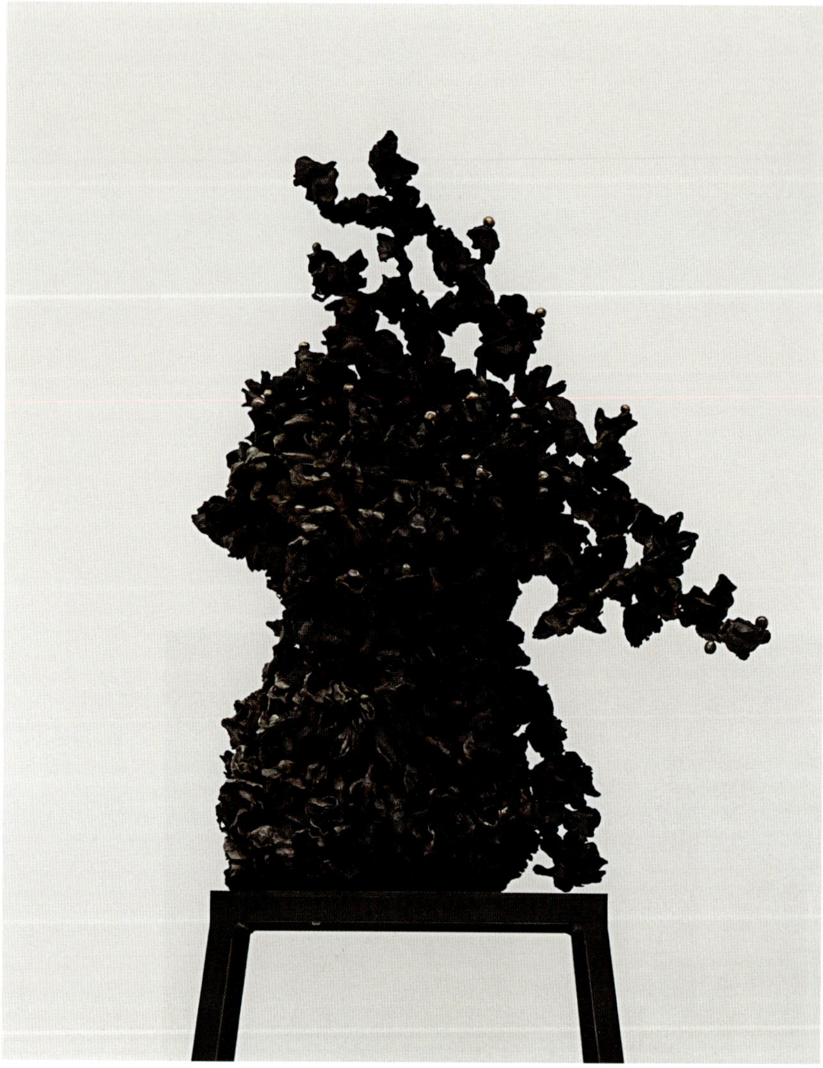

1

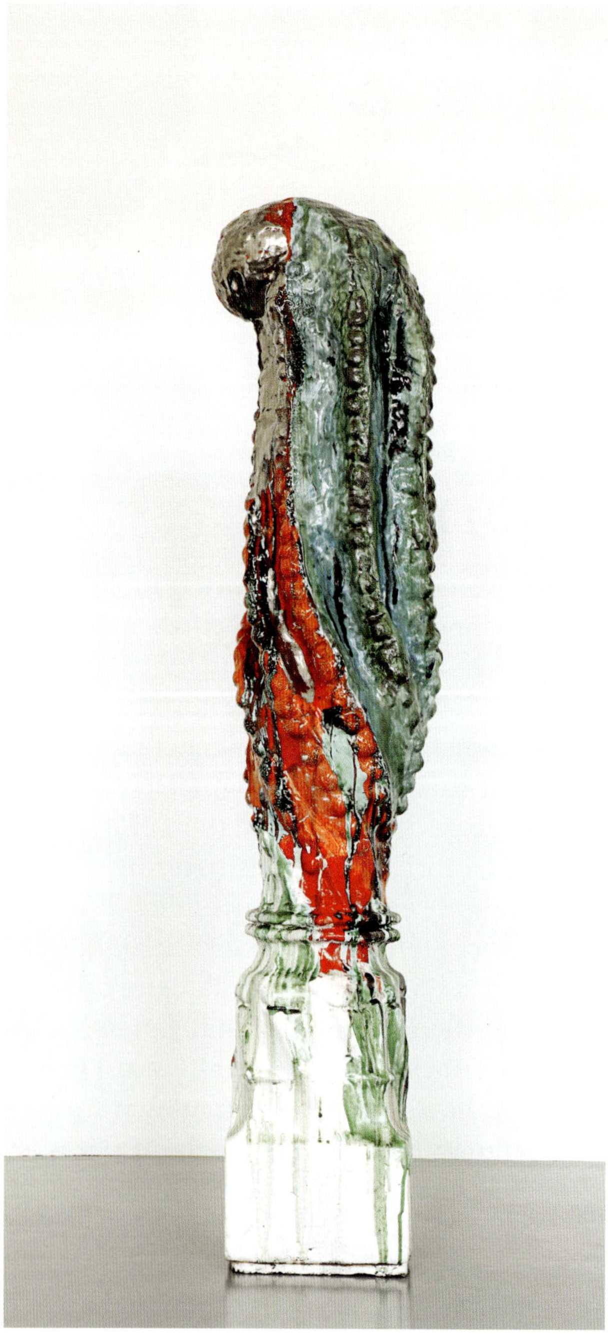

2

# Johan Creten

Johan Creten works across a range of materials and traditional techniques that are little seen in today's art world. These include stoneware and patinated bronze, as well as oozing, biomorphic enamels and glazes. His sculptures are also formally diverse, with a personal iconography that stretches from columns, delicate figurines and shrouded human figures to monumental birds and Marcel Broodthaers-referencing renderings of mussel shells (such as the series 'Odore di Femmina' ['Scent of a Woman'], 2010–ongoing). Many of these pieces fuse classical themes with contemporary politics, as is suggested by the title of *Oiseau, Guantánamo* (Bird, Guantánamo, 2011). As critic Alfredo Triff has noted, Creten's work mixes *fin-de-siècle* aesthetics with the science fiction of Arthur C. Clarke to dramatic, surprising effect. ST

**Shown by**
Galerie Perrotin F3
Almine Rech Gallery D18

**Biography**
Born 1963
Lives in Paris

Belgian-born Creten has held solo shows at insitutions such as Dhondt-Dhaenens Museum, Deurle, Belgium (2011), Musée Archéolique Henri-Prades, Lattes (2008), Stedelijk Museum de Lakenhal, Leiden (2007), and Bass Museum of Art, Miami (2003). Recent group exhibitions include 'Animal Beauty', Galeries Nationales du Grand Palais, Paris (2012). In 2013 Creten will be the subject of a solo exhibition at Galerie Perrotin, Paris.

1
*Odore di Femmina Torso – Walking the Wind*
(Scent of a Woman – Walking the Wind)
2011–12
Bronze
90 × 60 × 42 cm
Courtesy of Galerie Perrotin

2
*The Revolutionary Columns – When the Column Became a Serpent*
2009–12
Stoneware, enamel and platinum lustre
155 × 35 × 39 cm
Courtesy of Galerie Perrotin

3
*Fire-works II*
2011-12
Glazed stoneware with platinum and gold lustre
104 × 73 × 26 cm
Courtesy of Galerie Perrotin

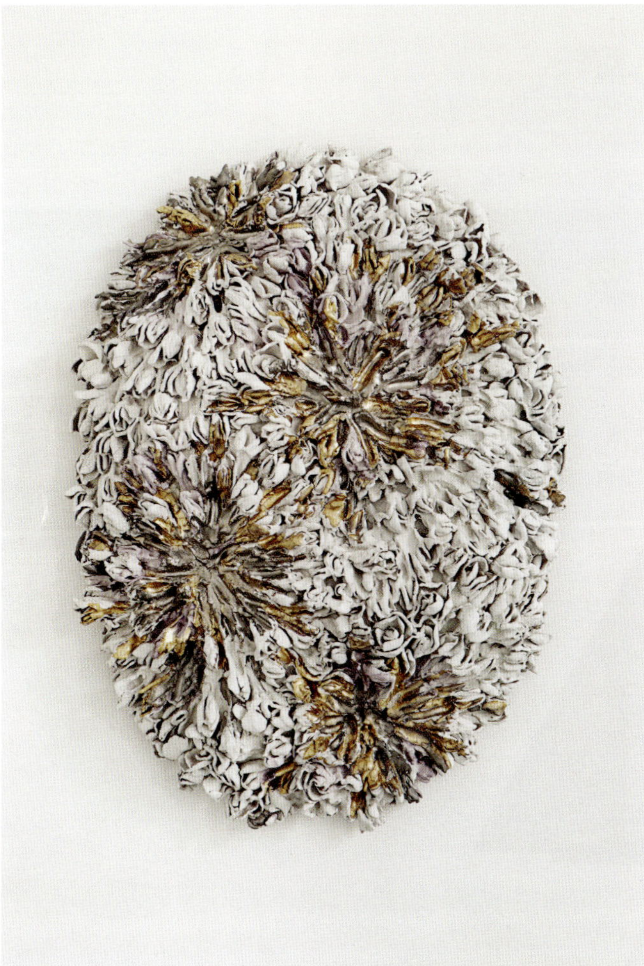

3

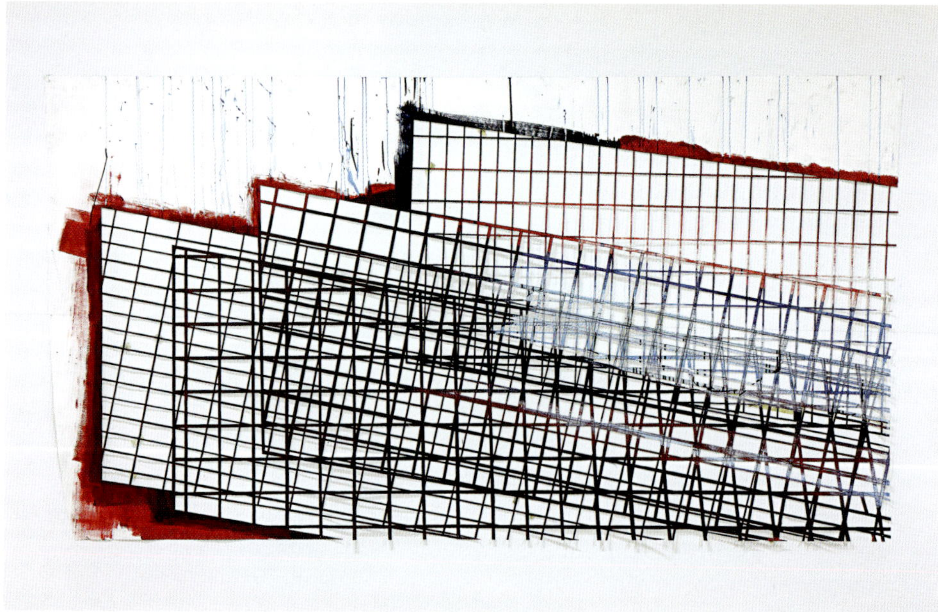
1

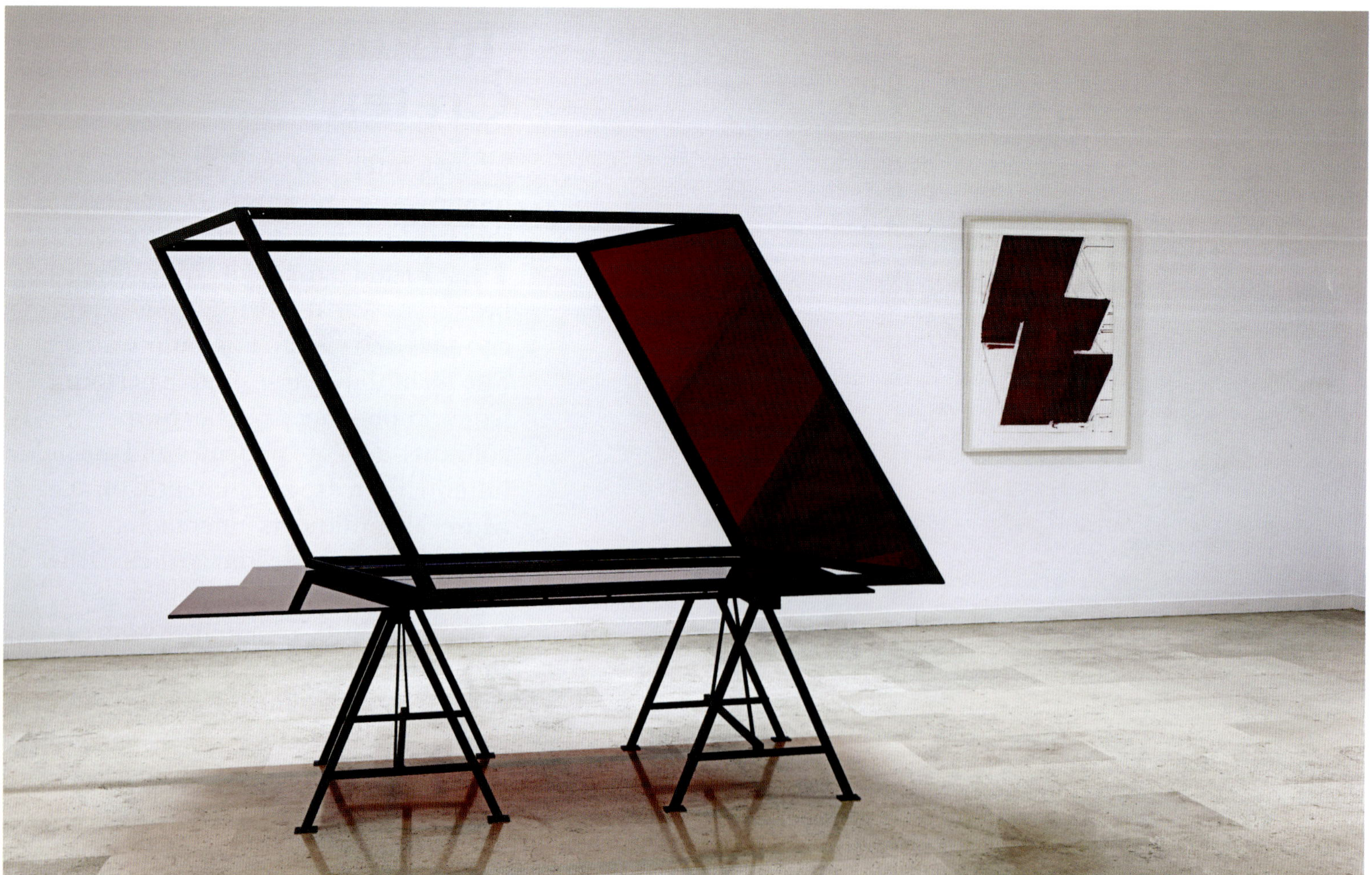
2

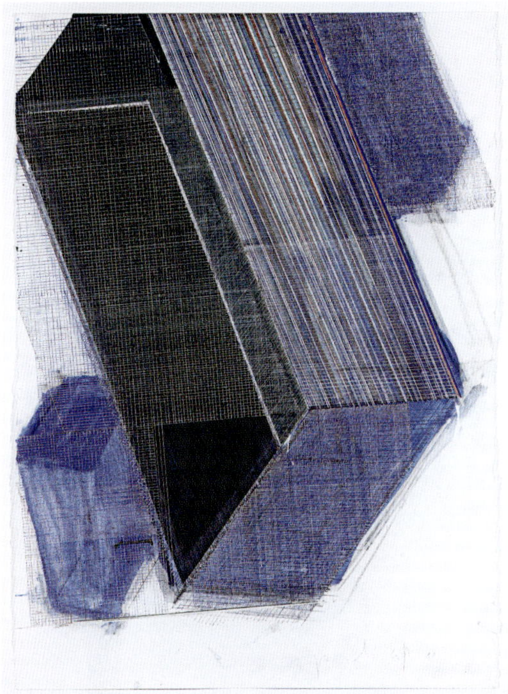
3

**Shown by**
Galería Helga de Alvear
A7
Galeria Filomena Soares
H9

**Biography**
Born 1957
Lives in Lisbon

Porto-born artist Croft has shown solo exhibitions in Lisbon at Chiado 8 Arte Contemporânea (2011), as part of the P28 Contentores project under the city's 25 April Bridge (2011), at Pavilhão Centro de Portugal (2008) and at Museu Calouste Gulbenkian (2007). His work is part of the permanent collections of international institutions including: Museu de Arte Moderna, Rio de Janeiro; Fundació La Caixa, Barcelona; and Museo Nacional Centro de Arte Reina Sofía, Madrid.

1
*Untitled*
2012
Mixed media on paper
151 × 274 cm
Courtesy of Galería Helga de Alvear

2
*Untitled*
2012
Iron and crystal with coloured film
173 × 225 × 121 cm
Installation view
Courtesy of Galería Helga de Alvear

3
*Untitled*
2012
Mixed media on paper
100 × 76 cm
Courtesy of Galería Helga de Alvear

# José Pedro Croft

If one was staging a wordless, atemporal play about the new normality of crisis, José Pedro Croft's recent sculptures might seem like worthy props, and his works on paper plausible programme notes. Despite what appears to be a solidly Modernist concern with sculptures and paintings on floors and walls, his structures' bare scenography and precarious angles seem to agree with contemporary political economists who propose that it is stasis that is in fact the exceptional state. *Untitled* (2012) is a precipitously skewed steel trapezoid, one facet glazed in oxblood-coloured film, which is placed atop two trestles. It seems like an inherently collapse-prone set-up, which, like a squared Penrose triangle, is always toppling into perspectival desperation. MA

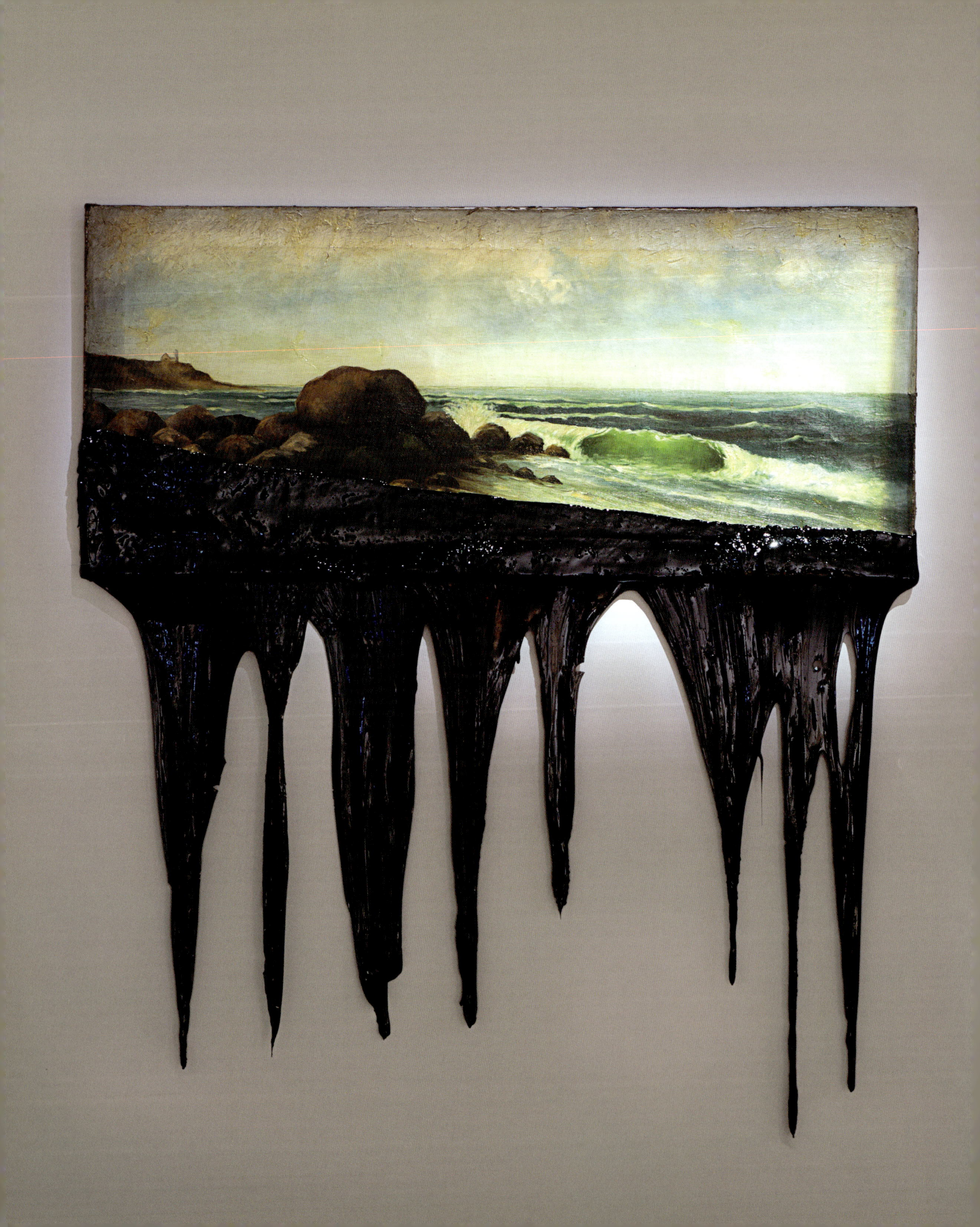

# Minerva Cuevas

**Shown by**
kurimanzutto D3

**Biography**
Born 1975
Lives in Mexico City

Mexican artist Cuevas has presented solo projects and shows at venues including Museo de la Ciudad de México (2012), Cornerhouse, Manchester (2012), Whitechapel Gallery, London (2009), Van Abbemuseum, Eindhoven (2008), and Kunsthalle Basel (2007). Her work has been featured internationally in festivals and group exhibitions such as the 6th Liverpool Biennial (2010) and the 6th Berlin Biennale (2010).

*Seascape*
From the series 'Hydrocarbons'
2012
Oil on compressed wood board covered in chapopote
102 × 93 cm
Courtesy of kurimanzutto

In 2009 Minerva Cuevas designed a coin that she called the S.COOP, had it produced by the Mexican mint and circulated the new tender at Petticoat Lane Market in London—the currency could be exchanged for ice cream at a specially designed parlour. Cuevas' monetary intervention was no mere abstract comment on the then precarious state of global currencies—the project related directly to the history of early-20th-century co-operatives and was thus of a piece with the artist's habitual address to socio-political history. The misuse of pesticides, the history of technocratic control of societies, the machinations of global food companies—all of these have been the subjects of Cuevas' varied but always *engagé* practice. BD

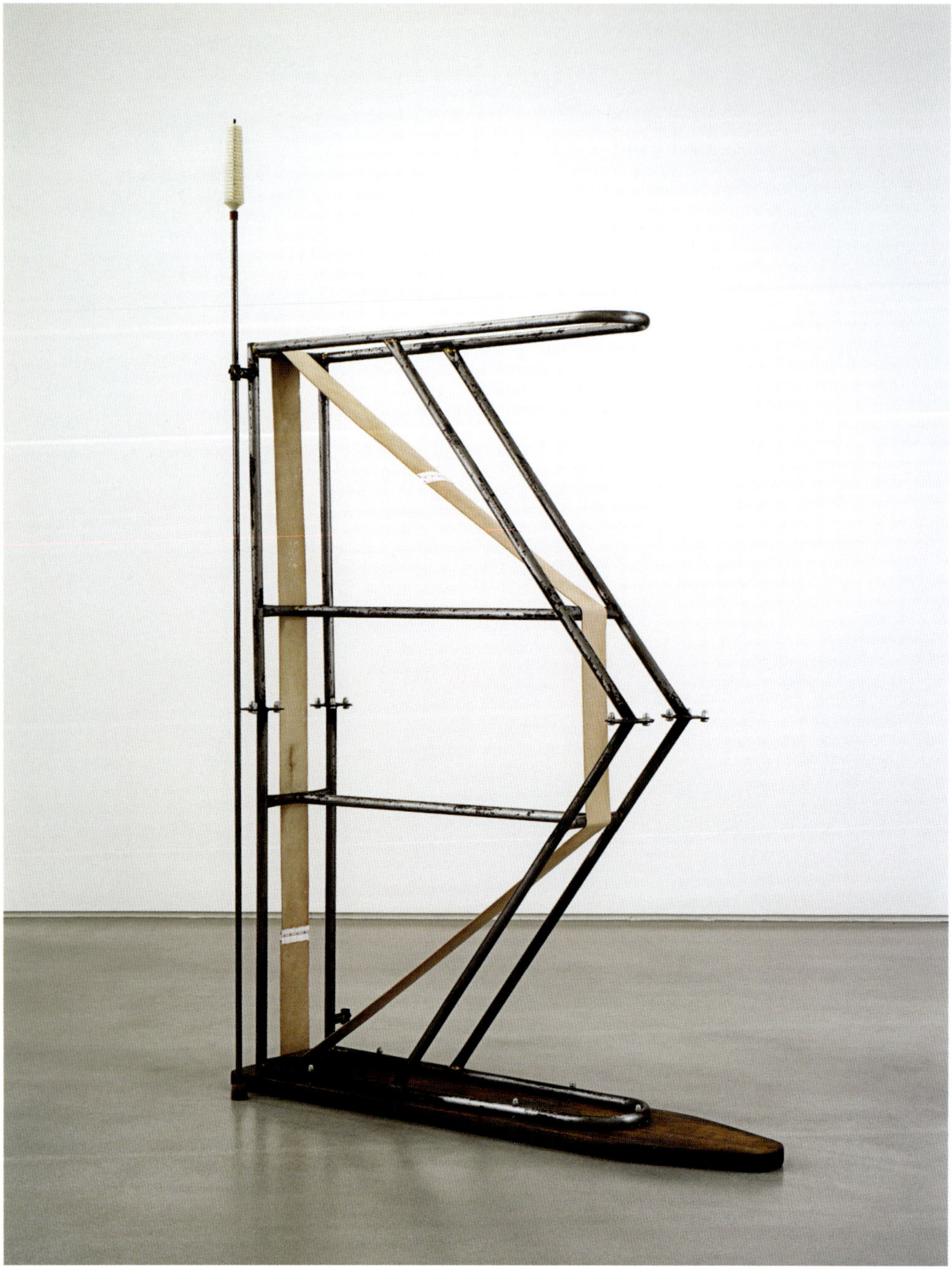

1

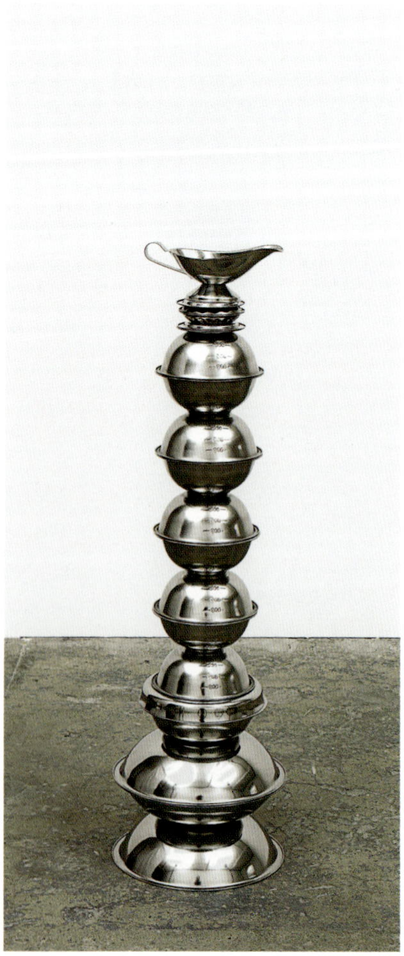

2

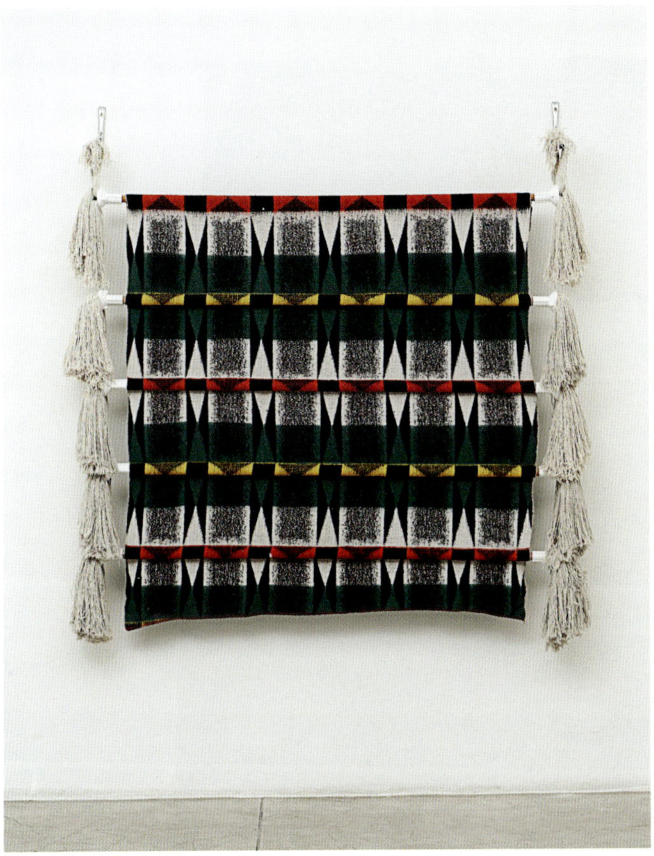

3

**Shown by**
Thomas Dane Gallery F13
Galeria Luisa Strina F6

**Biography**
Born 1969
Lives in London

Rio de Janeiro-born Da Cunha has presented solo exhibitions at galleries such as CRG Gallery, New York (2012), Galeria Luisa Strina, Sao Paulo (2011), Camden Arts Centre, London (2009), CCA Wattis Institute for Contemporary Arts, San Francisco (2007), and Neuer Aachener Kunstverein, Aachen (2007). Recent group shows include 'Richard of York Gave Battle in Vain', Whitechapel Gallery, London (2011), and 'Making is Thinking', Witte de With, Rotterdam (2011). His work is on show at the 30th Bienal de Sao Paulo until December 2012.

1
*Horse III*
2012
Ironing boards, bottle brush, curtain railing, cork, leather belt and metal fittings
222 × 40 × 140 cm
Courtesy of Galeria Luisa Strina and CRG Gallery

2
*Platinum (Column XVI)*
2010
Household metal utensils
110 × 30 × 30 cm
Courtesy of Galeria Luisa Strina

3
*Navajo I*
2011
Mop heads, wool, blanket and hooks
180 × 170 × 24 cm
Courtesy of Galeria Luisa Strina

# Alexandre da Cunha

Alexandre da Cunha relishes the unlikely match of the rubbish-digging of the skilful forager with the noble aims and intricate aesthetic of High Art, where mop heads become Baroque drapes and used skateboards become decorative fans. Da Cunha uses industrially manufactured materials found around the house to skip lightly between the histories of Duchamp's ready-made, Modernist art and architecture and a contemporary sensibility of use-values. *Horse III* (2012) is an assemblage of metal curtain railing with an ironing board as its base, bound by a leather strap from a conveyor belt. The materials' previous lives dissolve into a new, whimsical and puzzling architecture that is at once childish, futuristic and realistic. CFW

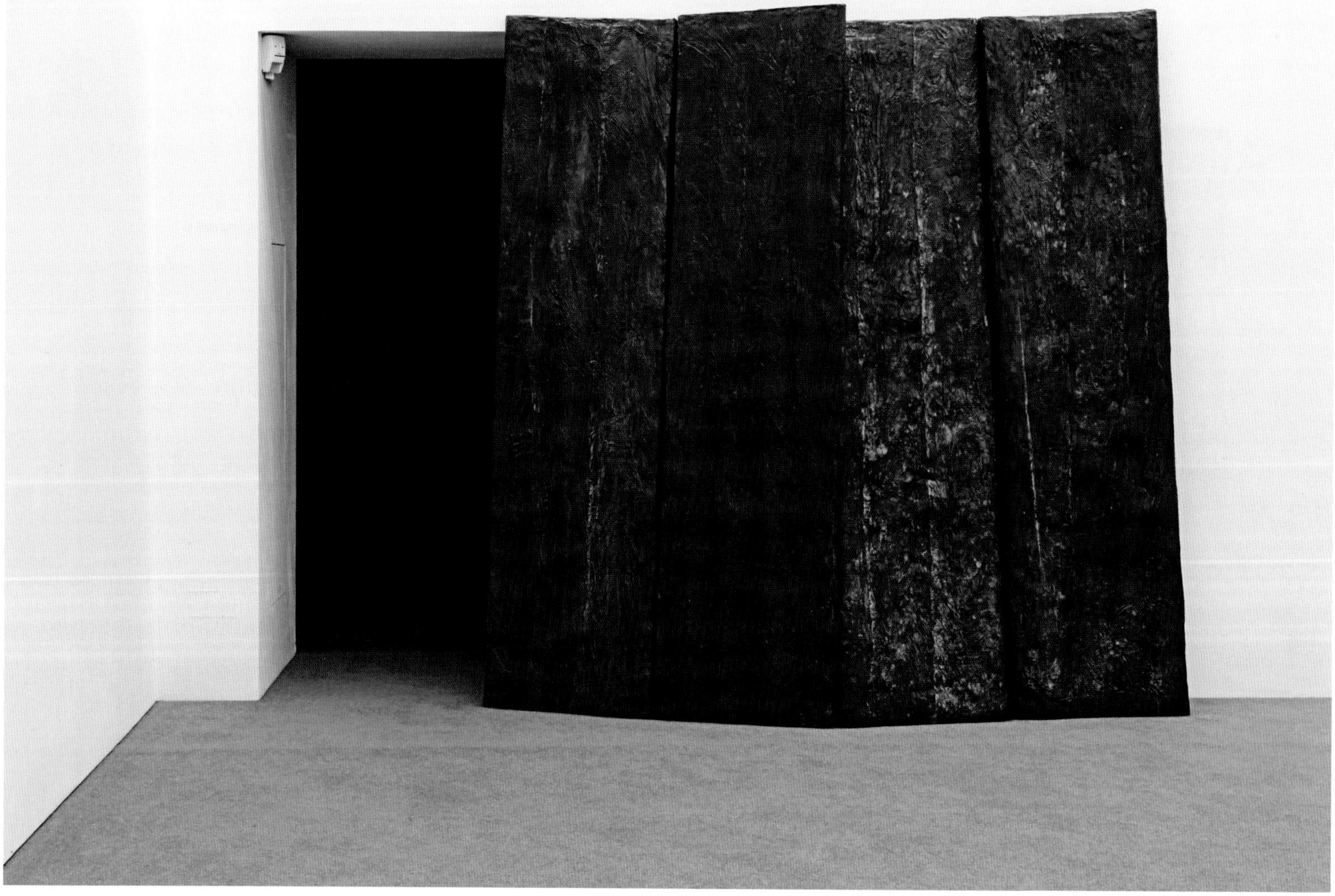

1

# Michael Dean

**Shown by**
Herald St D10

**Biography**
Born 1977
Lives in London

British artist Dean has recently presented solo projects and exhibitions at galleries such as the Henry Moore Institute, Leeds (2012), Herald St, London (2011), Kunstverein Freiburg (2011), MAK, Vienna (2011), Nomas Foundation, Rome (2010), and Laing Art Gallery, Newcastle (2010). In 2012 he participated in the artist-in-residence programme of the Lenikus Collection, Vienna, and in group shows including 'The Dan Cox Library for the Unfinished Concept of Thingly Time' at Cubitt Gallery, London.

1
*home (working title)*
2012
Concrete
255 × 255 × 4 cm
Courtesy of Herald St

2
*analogue series (head)*
2012
Concrete
18 × 18 × 18 cm
Courtesy of Herald St

Using a diverse array of media, encompassing sculpture, photography, performance, poetry and publications, Michael Dean's practice has at its crux his relationship to words and the relationship between that and the objects he creates. Taking a single word as a starting-point, concrete sculptures shaped to form abstracted typefaces respond to the dimensions of the surrounding space and each other, while publications based on the works' formative concepts accompany each of his exhibitions. The artist's consideration of the meeting point and relational distance between objects and concepts was exemplified in his recent exhibition at the Henry Moore Institute, Leeds, with the work *analogue series (head)* (2012): the round white concrete sculpture was balanced on top of the publication *(Untitled) supports the structure of the face* (2012), which itself was placed on the thick carpet installed for the exhibition. PT

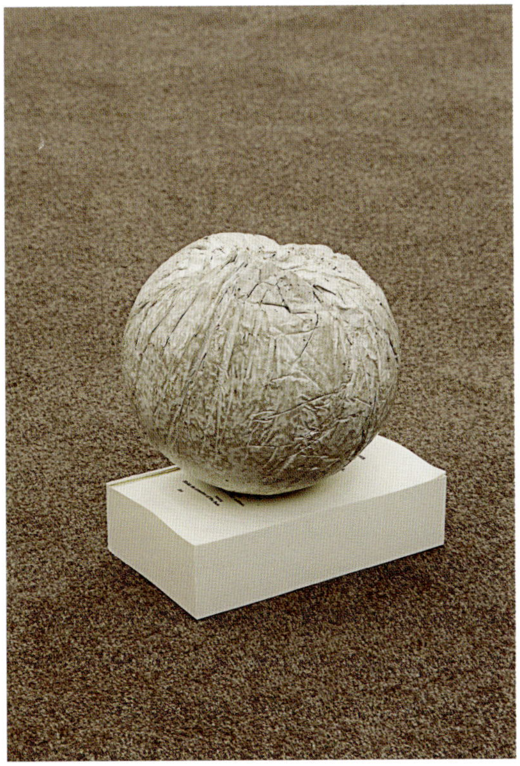

2

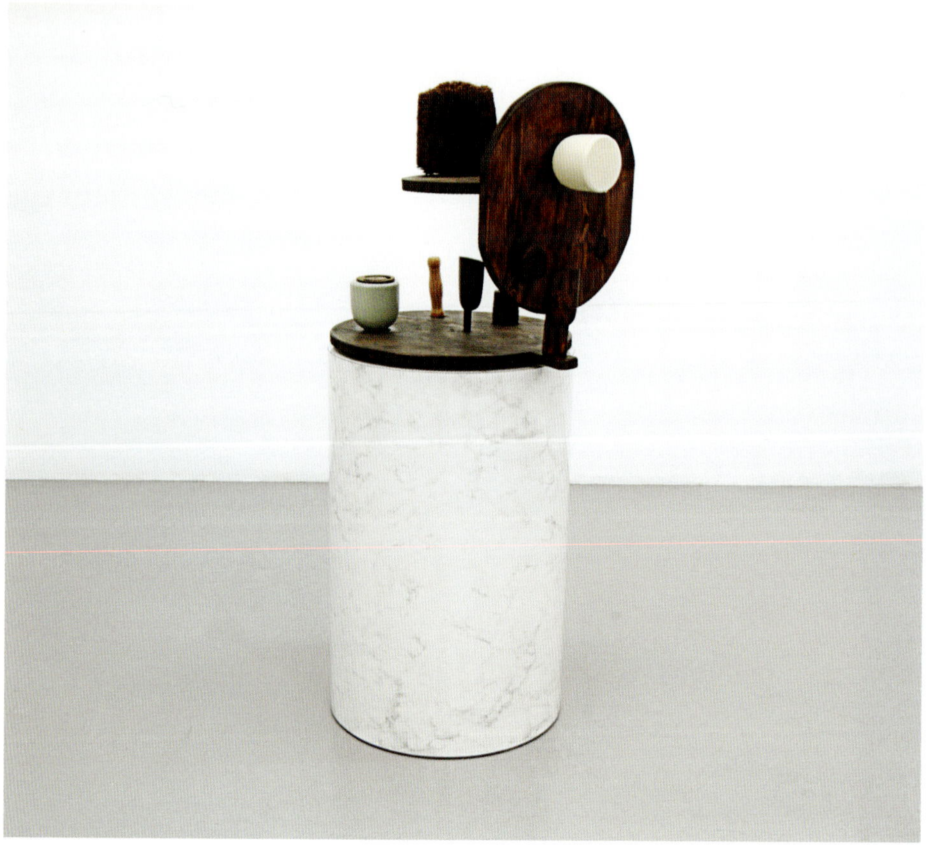
1

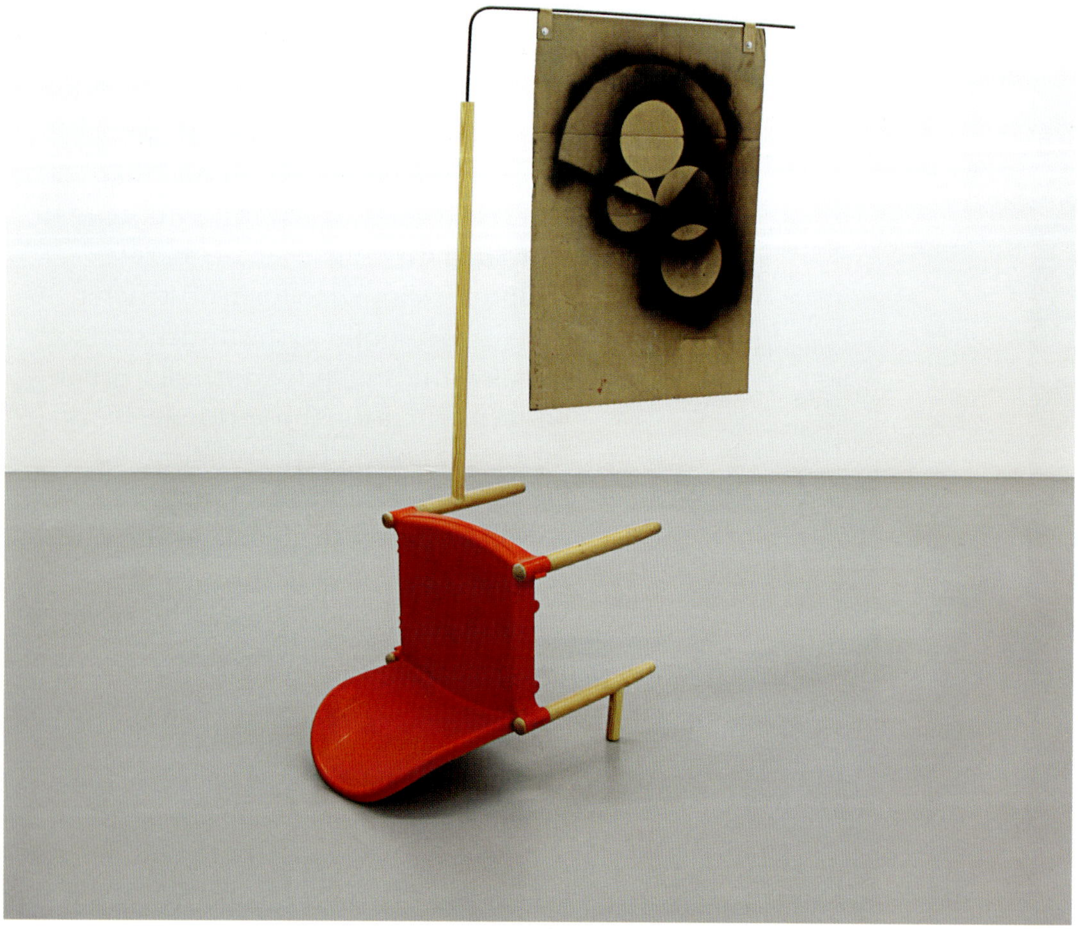
2

# Koenraad Dedobbeleer

Preoccupied with what it means to install a particular object in a particular place at a particular time, Koenraad Dedobbeleer approaches the exhibition as a site of apparition, where he presents groups of sculptures that, while they stress their familial bond through repeated forms, also point to other works by the artist that remain off-stage, or which are so far unmade. Resembling domestic furnishings and fittings put to new and unknowable uses, Dedobbeleer's sculptures bear titles that read like (deliberately stuffy) philosophical justifications or judgements: for example, *Simply a Logical Consequence* (2011) or *Neglected All Theoretical Aspects Considerably* (2012). This is art that asks us—with sly humour—to consider not only what is there, but also what is not. TM

**Shown by**
Georg Kargl Fine Arts D16
Mai 36 Galerie D9
Galerie Micheline Szwajcer B3

**Biography**
Born 1975
Lives in Brussels

Belgian-born Dedobbeleer has presented solo shows at venues such as Mai 36 Galerie, Zurich (2012), Kunstmuseum St Gallen (2012), ProjecteSD, Barcelona (2011), and Galerie Micheline Szwajcer, Antwerp (2010). He received Krefeld's Mies van der Rohe Award in 2009, and the city's Museum Haus Esters subsequently held an exhibition of his work. Dedobbeleer's recent group exhibitions include 'Tegenlicht' ('Backlight') at SMAK, Ghent (2010).

1
*Neglected All Theoretical Aspects Considerably*
2012
Varnish, lacquer and wood
133 × 64 × 50 cm
Courtesy of Galerie Micheline Szwajcer

2
*Simply a Logical Consequence*
2011
Plastic, wood, metal, cardboad and spraypaint
183 × 101 × 86 cm
Courtesy of Galerie Micheline Szwajcer

3
*Necessarily Involves Wandering*
2011
Wood, metal and plaster
101 × 81 × 11 cm
Courtesy of Galerie Micheline Szwajcer

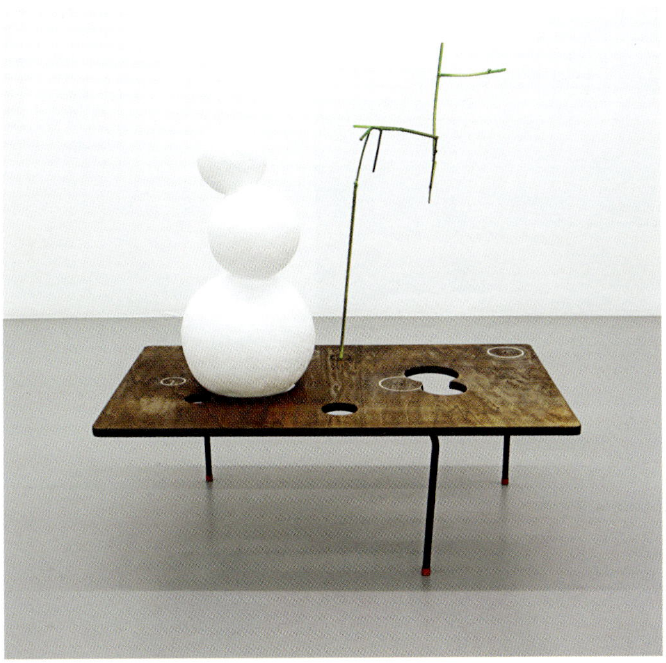

3

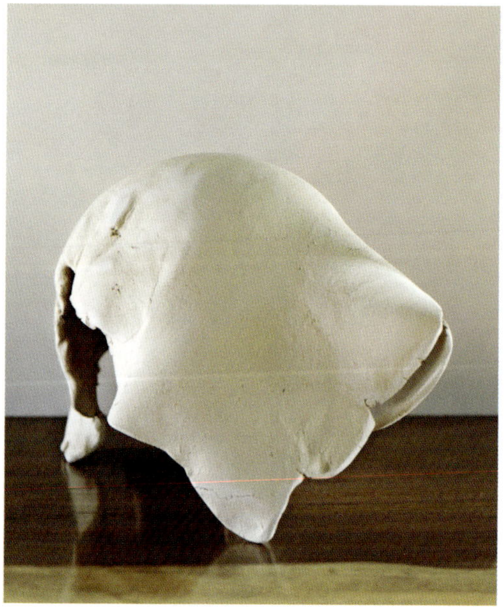

1

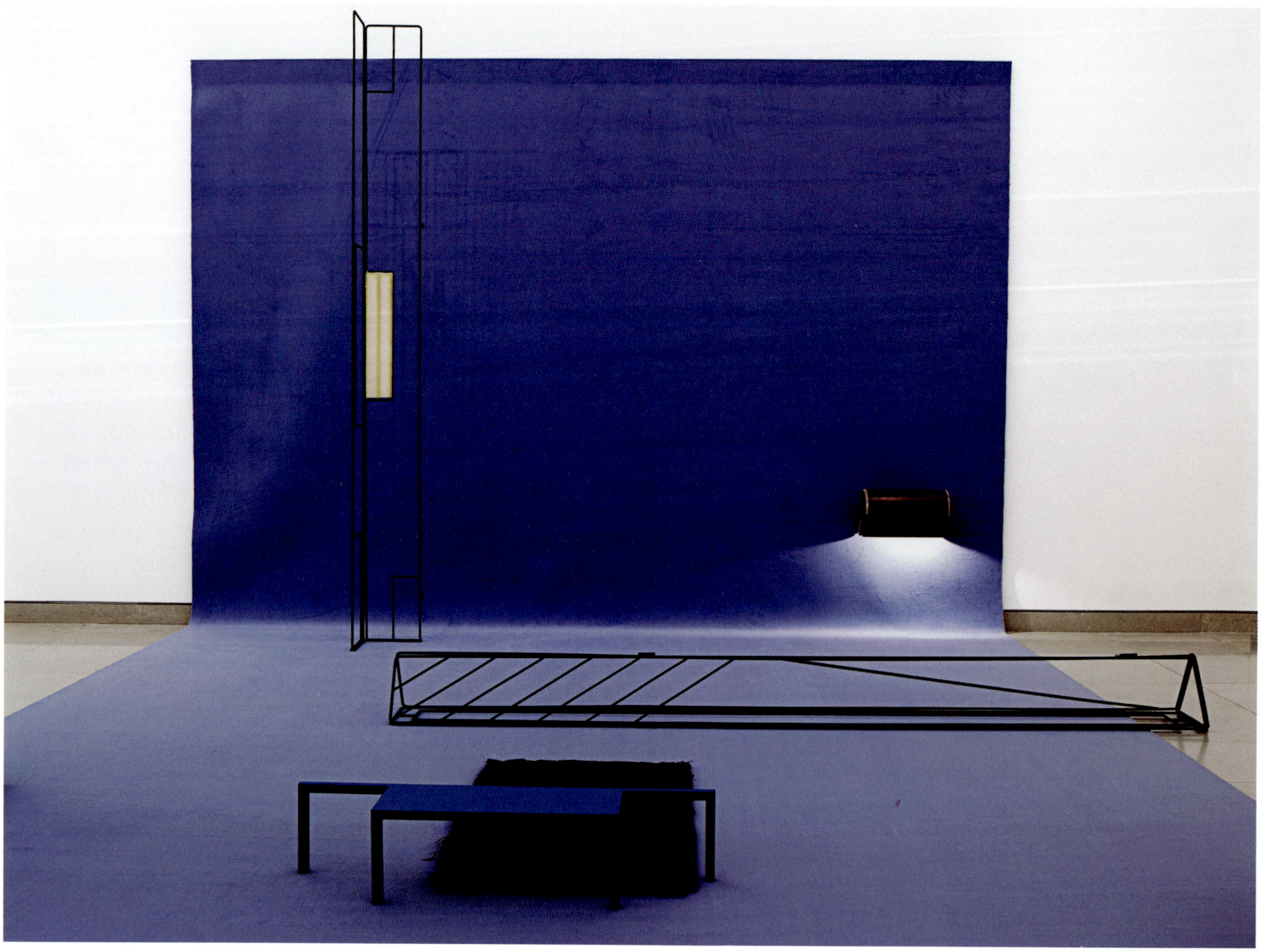

2

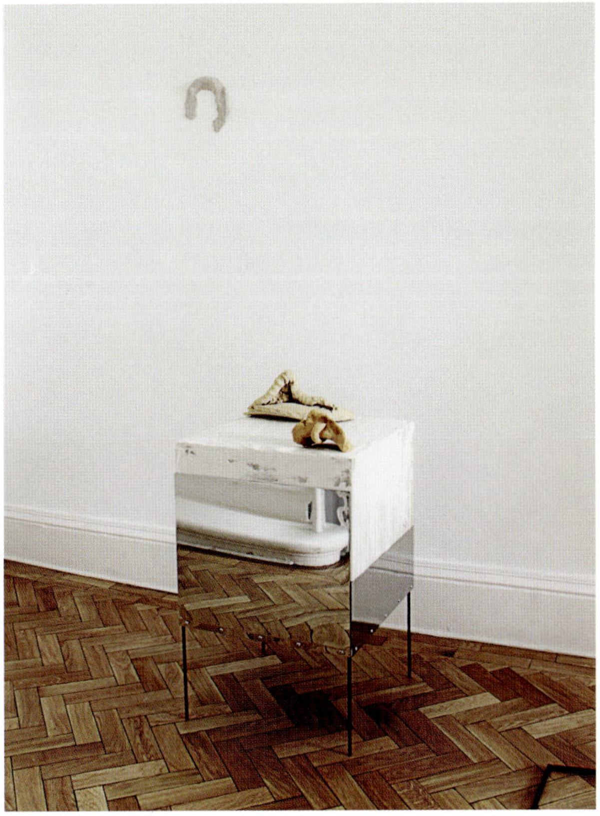
3

**Shown by**
Micky Schubert E19
Sprüth Magers Berlin London D6

**Biography**
Born 1971
Lives in Berlin

Georgian-born Djordjadze has held solo exhibitions at venues such Sprüth Magers London (2012), Malmo Konsthall (2012), Common Guild, Glasgow (2011), Contemporary Art Museum St Louis (2011), Foksal Gallery Foundation, Warsaw (2010), Kunsthalle Basel (2009) and Studio Voltaire, London (2007). Recent group exhibitions include 'Sculptural Matter', Australian Centre for Contemporary Art, Melbourne (2012), 'New Sculpture?', Zacheta National Gallery of Art, Warsaw (2012), and 'Melanchotopia', Witte de With, Rotterdam (2011). She also participated in Documenta 13, Kassel (2012).

1
*All Men Are Equal but Some Men Are More Equal, Than Others. (Orwell)*
2008
Papier mâché
18 × 31 × 15 cm
Courtesy of Sprüth Magers Berlin London

2
*Untitled*
2011
Mixed media
3.5 × 8 × 7 m
Courtesy of Sprüth Magers Berlin London

3
*Other Echoes Inhabit the Void*
2011
Foam, plaster, paint, papier mâché, stainless steel (mirrored) and steel
92 × 49 × 50 cm
Courtesy of Sprüth Magers Berlin London

# Thea Djordjadze

Thea Djordjadze's vestigial objects and elegiac installations conjure gauzy memories and half-remembered histories. An emblematic title is *Other Echoes Inhabit the Void* (2011). As she has said: 'Sometimes a story that was important to me becomes [...] lost or forgotten (I am really into forgetting), and then a new narrative emerges.' In a quiet way, her work is formally diverse, incorporating handcrafted objects in clay, papier mâché and plaster as well as furniture-like structures, truncated staircases, antique rugs and—most recently—elegant steel and wood armatures holding blocks of foam. Djordjadze's work often feels excavated, a reminder of something past while also gesturing to a provisional sort of future. ST

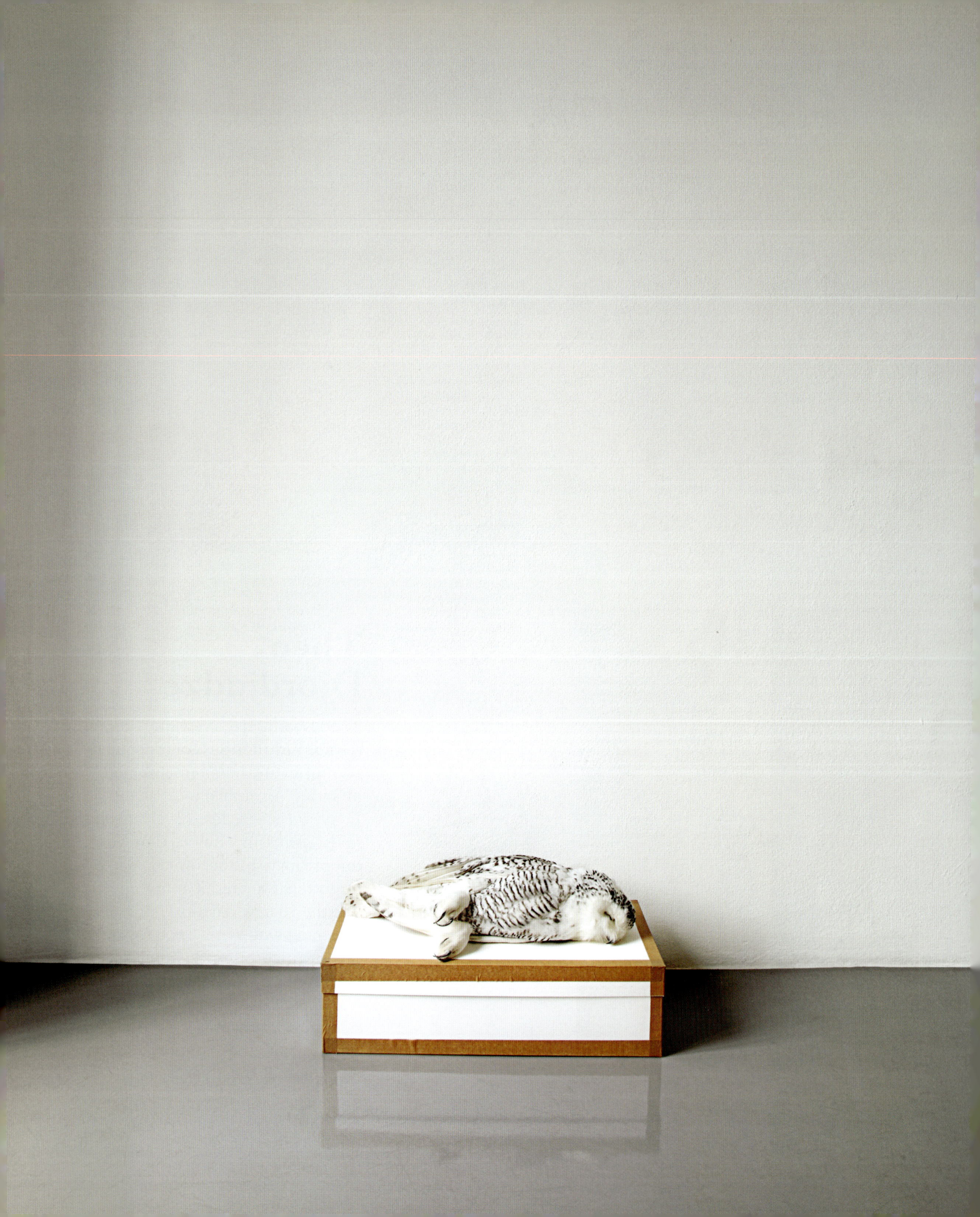

**Shown by**
Casey Kaplan B4
Yvon Lambert C2
Galleria Franco Noero A2

**Biography**
Born 1969
Lives in Berlin

Pennsylvania-born Dodge has recently presented solo shows at venues such as Galleria Franco Noero, Turin (2012), Andersen's Contemporary, Copenhagen (2011), and Kunstverein Dusseldorf, Germany (2009). In 2012 he participated in 'The Language of Less (Then and Now)' at the Museum of Contemporary Art, Chicago, and from March 2013 he presents a solo exhibition at Lentos Kunstmuseum, Linz. His work features in collections that include the Solomon R. Guggenheim Museum, New York, and Moderna Museet, Stockholm.

1
*Rose Tourmaline Inside of an Owl*
2011
Courtesy of Galleria Franco Noero

2
*Two Candles in a Doorway*
2012
Two candles hanging across from each other in a doorway
Courtesy of Galleria Franco Noero

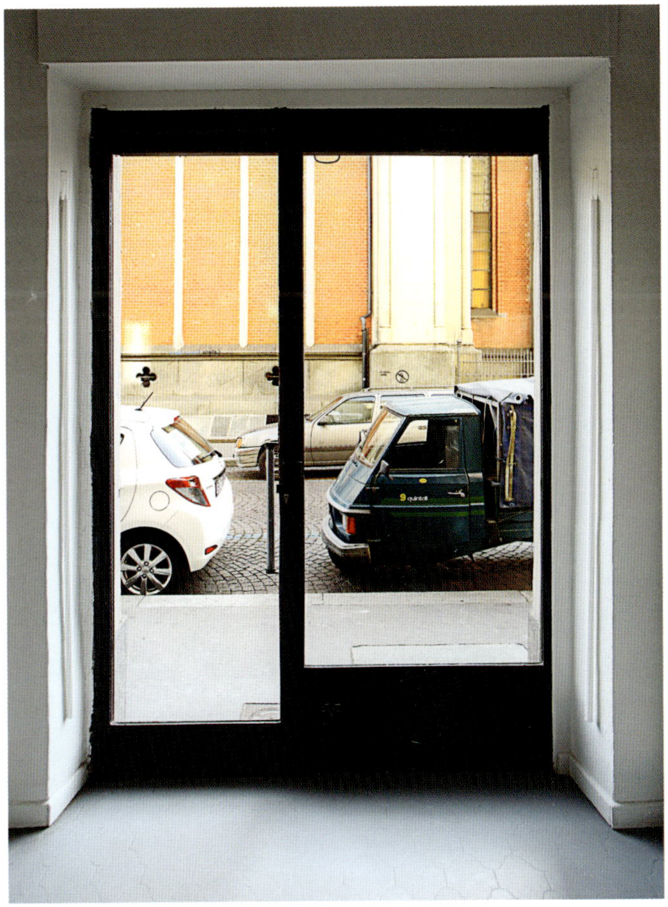
2

# Jason Dodge

A used object is not the same as a found object. Jason Dodge transforms carefully selected objects (the term 'found' has rarely, historically, been accurate) into art works through use. *The Ornithologists Are Sleeping* (2012) consists of pillows slept on only by birdwatchers. We have only the artist's word that the action took place; it is impossible, similarly, to ascertain the veracity of *Rose Tourmaline Inside of an Owl* (2011), except, of course, by buying the stuffed owl and slicing it open. Elsewhere, as in *Two Candles in a Doorway* (2012), the use has yet to take place. Dodge's work is as much about faith in magic, in transformation and transcendence, as it is about faith in art itself. JG

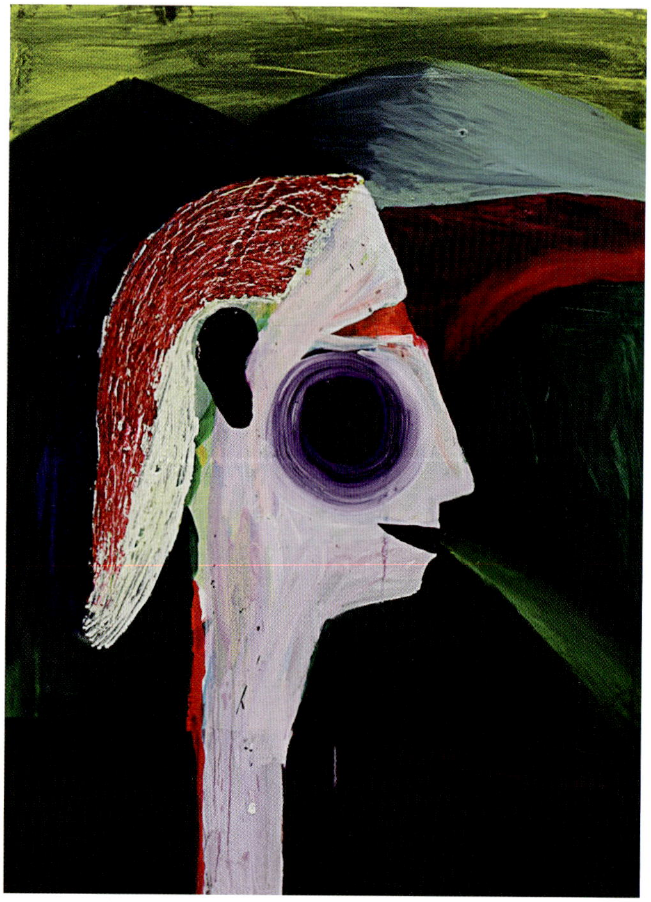

1

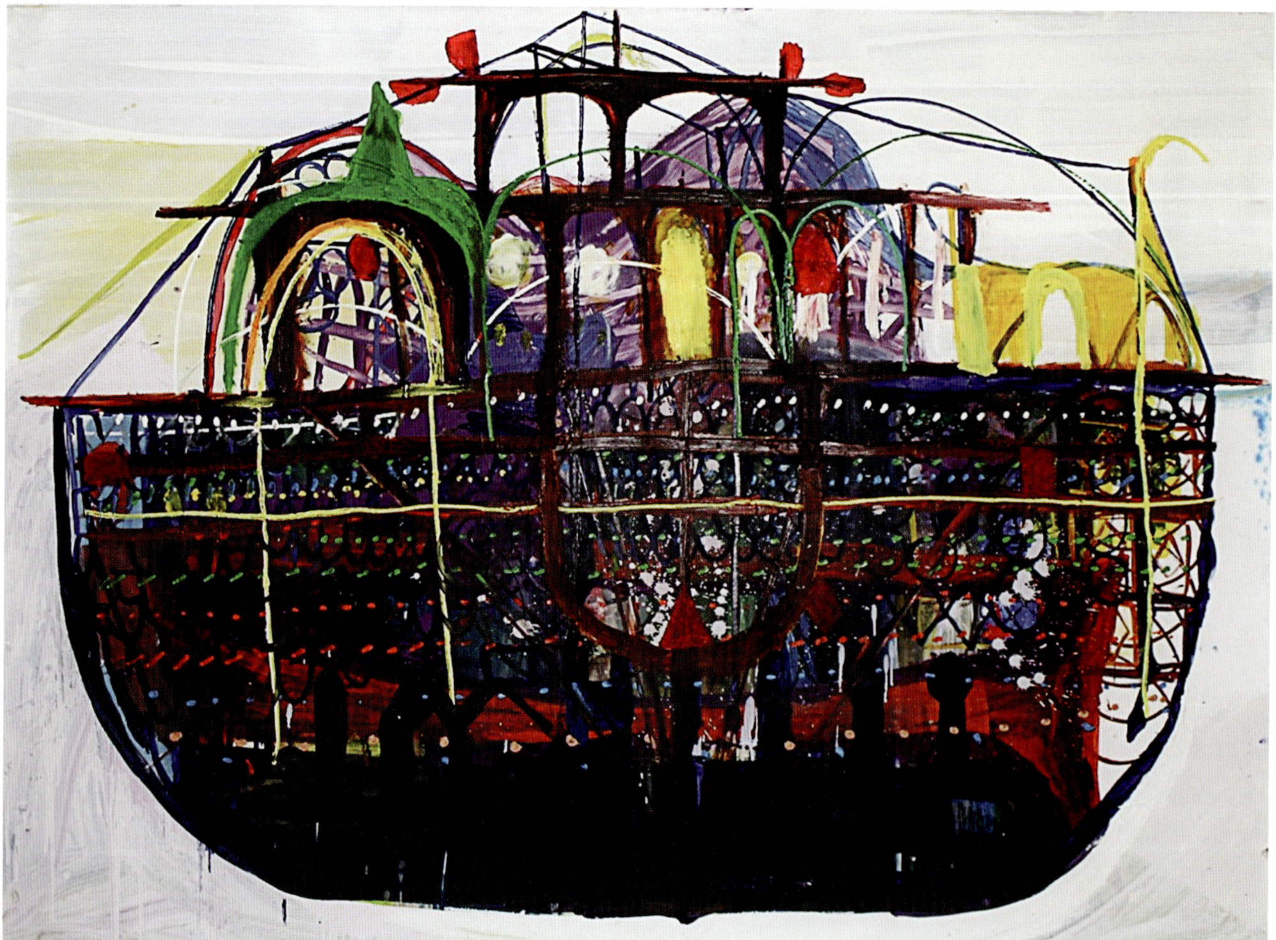

2

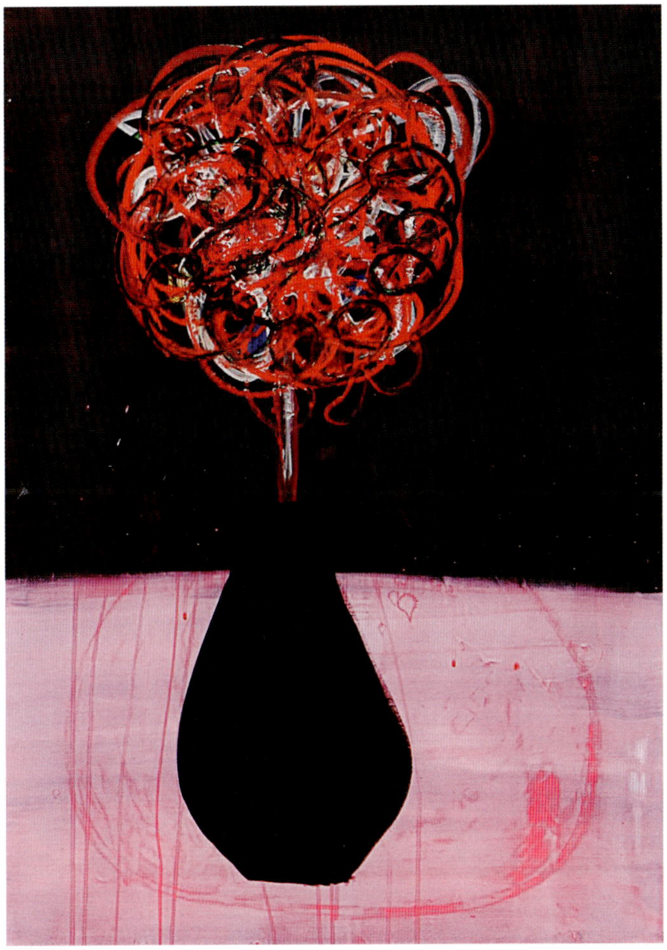

3

**Shown by**
Ancient & Modern S10

**Biography**
Born 1960
Lives in Berlin

German artist Dornfeld has presented solo exhibitions at galleries such as Soy Capitàn, Berlin (2012), Galería Casado Santapau, Madrid (2011), and Blanket Gallery, Vancouver (2010). Group exhibitions include 'Hallo Hepp', Kunstverein Heppenheim (2011), 'Herbei ein Licht!', Lismore Castle Arts, Ireland (2011), and 'Brand New You're Retro', Galerie Andreas Huber, Vienna (2010). His work is the subject of an exhibition at Galerie Waldburger, Brussels, from November 2012 until January 2013.

1
*Untitled (Profile and Mountains)*
2011
Acrylic and oil on MDF
120 × 85 cm
Courtesy of Ancient & Modern

2
*Untitled (The Ship)*
2007
Oil on canvas
150 × 200 cm
Courtesy of Ancient & Modern

3
*Untitled (Flowers on Magenta)*
2012
Acrylic and oil on canvas
100 × 70 cm
Courtesy of Ancient & Modern

# Focus
# Matthias Dornfeld

The abstracted flowers, vases, figures and landscapes that populate Matthias Dornfeld's vividly coloured paintings show a stylistic simplicity that belies a complex game of art-historical call-and-response. Utilizing common situations, subjects and compositional forms, Primitivist figures and still-life arrangements, his gestural, naïf painting technique conjures a mythological art world of suspended historical time. *Untitled (Flowers on Magenta)* (2012) is an example of one of the artist's recurrent motifs: thickly squeezed squiggles of red, white and black paint form a vivid cloud of flowers over a two-tone pink and black colour wash exemplary in its efficient economic composition and equally memorable style. PT

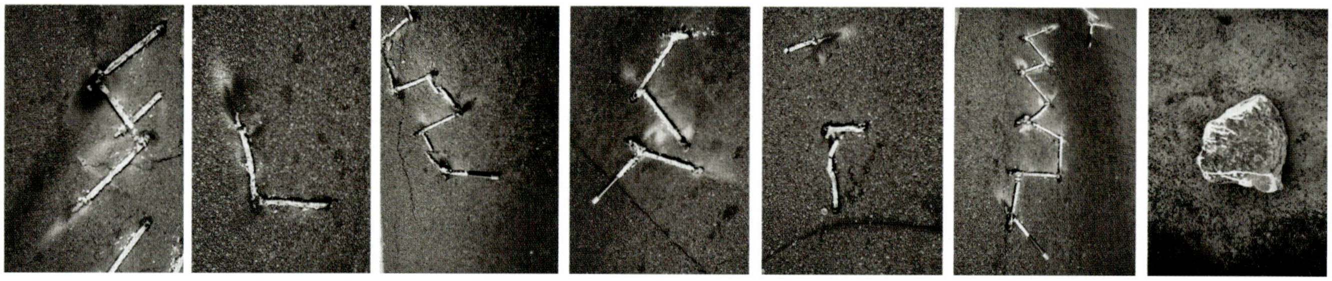

1

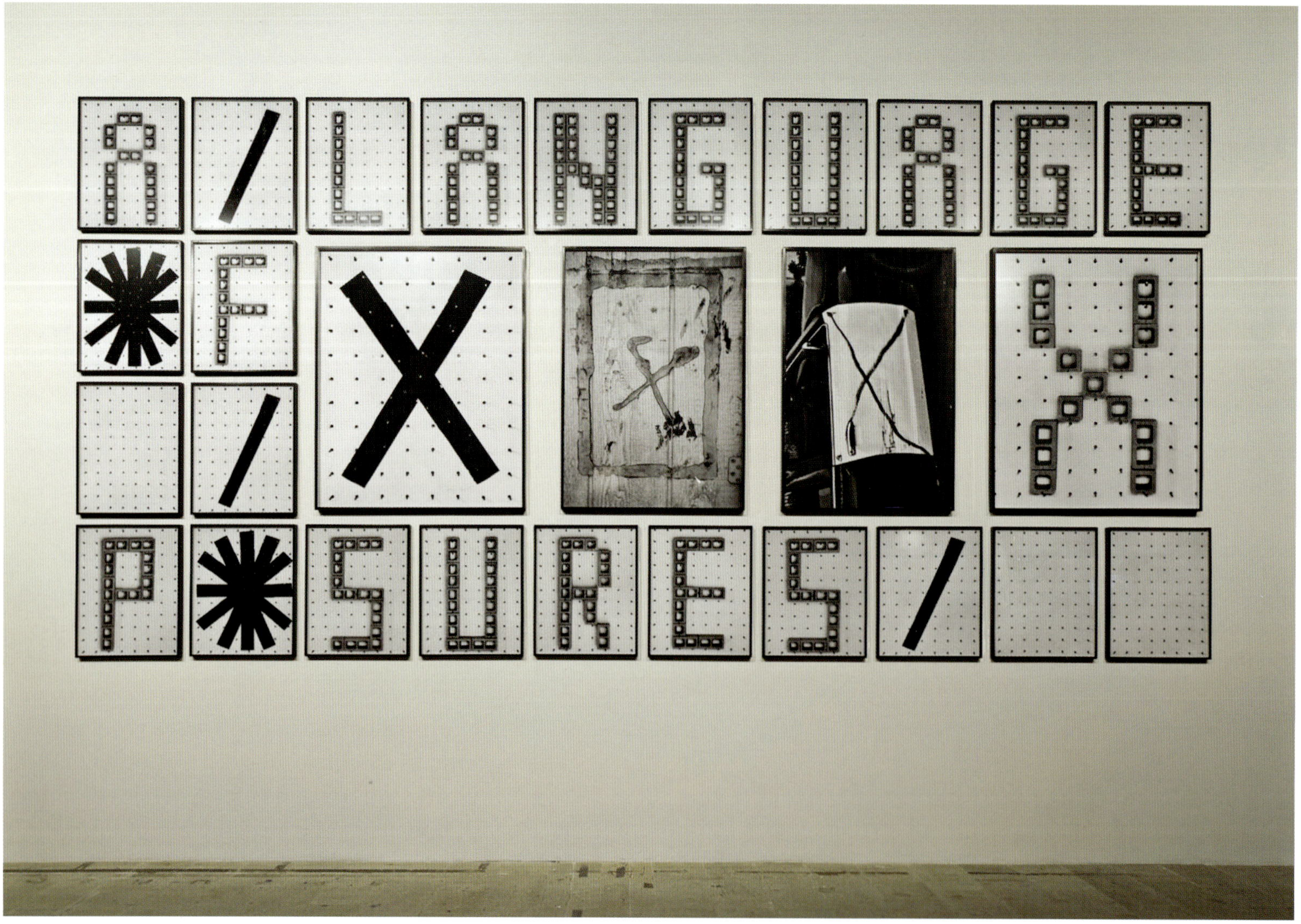


2

# Shannon Ebner

**Shown by**
Altman Siegel S9
Sadie Coles HQ C11
Wallspace E19

**Biography**
Born 1971
Lives in Los Angeles

American artist Ebner's recent solo presentations include an Artist Web Project initiated by the Dia Art Foundation, New York (2012), and exhibitions at the Hammer Museum, Los Angeles (2011), and MoMA PS1, New York (2007). She participated in the 54th Venice Biennale (2011) and the 6th Berlin Biennale (2010). Her work is part of collections such as the Stedelijk Museum, Amsterdam, and the Whitney Museum of American Art, New York. In 2013 she will present a solo exhibition at Wallspace, New York.

1
*Incendiary Distress Signals*
2011
Chromogenic prints
Each 80 × 53 cm
Courtesy of Wallspace

2
*From The Electric Comma Series (A.L.N G.U.E.*. F.X.P.S.R.)*
2011
Chromogenic prints
346 × 719 cm
Courtesy of Wallspace

3
*Ampersand*
2009
Chromogenic print
160 × 122 cm
Courtesy of Wallspace

Shannon Ebner's black and white photographs highlight language's incompleteness and uncertainty by suspending it in unsettling material form, with the click of a shutter. Concrete poetry acquires an aggressive, pixelated solidity when she documents cinderblock letters hung on pegboard and arranges the photographs in grids. Images of large cardboard letters and symbols in desolate landscapes—such as a frail-looking but deadpan ampersand propped up in scrubby terrain in *Ampersand* (2009)—echo traditional landscape photography. With their crackling aura of trauma, others could be crime-scene photos, as in the seven prints *Incendiary Distress Signals* (2011), which capture the remains of burnt-out emergency flares smouldering on shadowy asphalt like writing that has been twisted beyond recognition or verges on erasure. KMJ

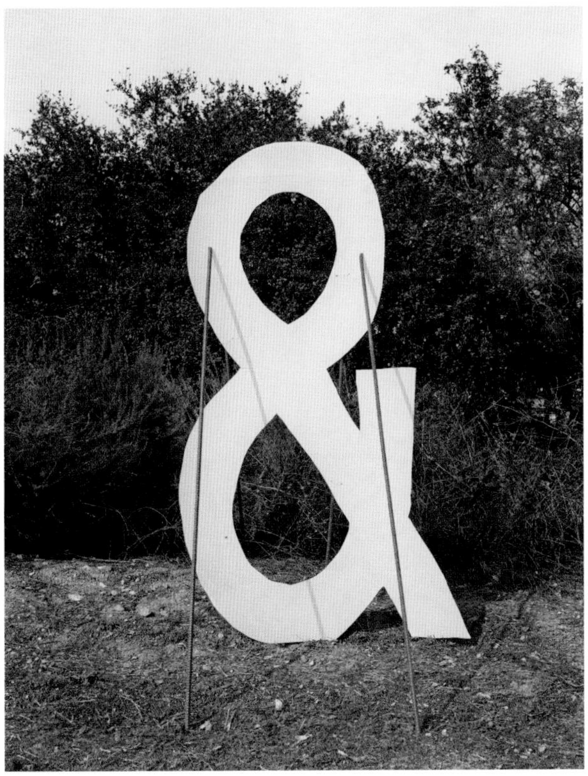

3

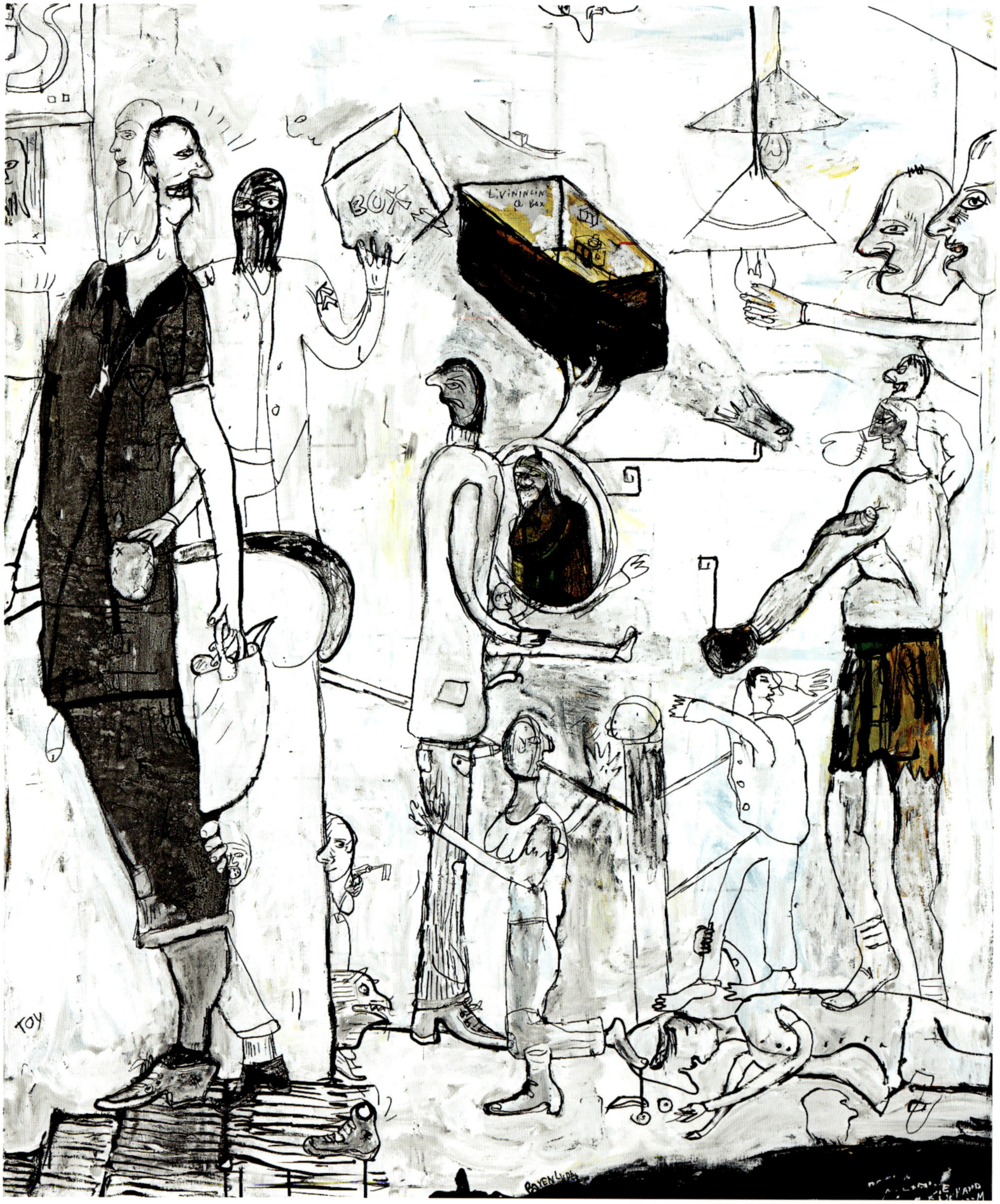


1

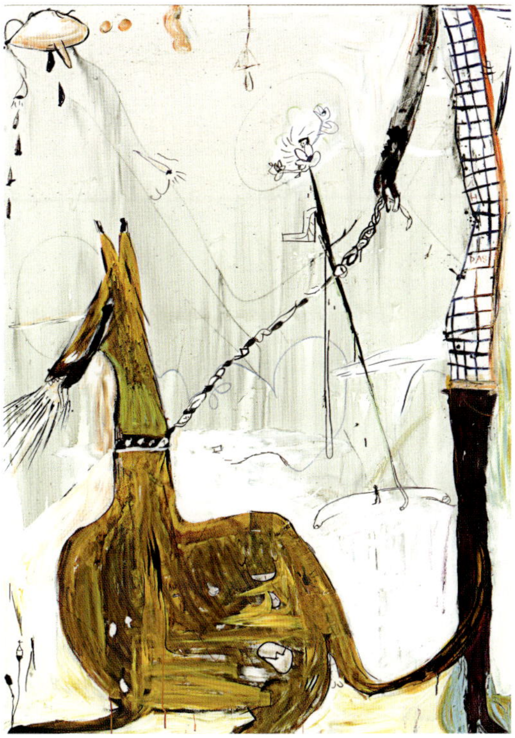

3

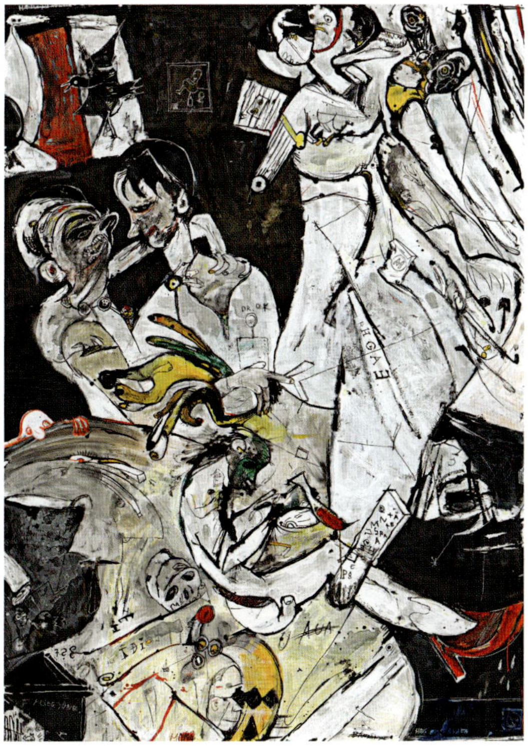

2

**Shown by**
Contemporary Fine Arts
C12

**Biography**
Born 1977
Lives in Berlin

German-born artist Eichner has been the subject of solo shows at galleries including Contemporary Fine Arts, Berlin (2012 and 2010), and Galerie am Stadtmuseum, Dusseldorf (2008). His work has been featured in group exhibitions including those staged at Anhaltische Gemäldegalerie, Dessau (2011), VW (VeneKlasen/Werner), Berlin (2010), Museum Abtei Liesborn, Wadersloh (2009), and Sichuan University Museum, Chengdu (2008).

1
*Living in a Box*
2010
Gouache, acrylic and ink on canvas
170 × 140 cm
Courtesy of
Contemporary Fine Arts

2
*Im Bett mit Dr. Ok*
(In Bed with Dr. Ok)
2011
Gouache, acrylic and ink on canvas
200 × 140 cm
Courtesy of
Contemporary Fine Arts

3
*Gelber Hund*
(Yellow Dog)
2010
Gouache, acrylic and ink on canvas
200 × 140 cm
Courtesy of
Contemporary Fine Arts

# Marcel Eichner

In trying to capture them in words, Marcel Eichner's canvases seem to be better lured by adjectives than by nouns. Although they are often peopled with what look like humans, and occasionally dogs or birds, and can be structured around a kind of notation of an interior (table, window, bulb, door), his equivocal scenarios appear primarily concerned with their scope for atmospheric attributes and jarring modifications—they are irritated, ticklish, suspicious or distraught, perhaps. *Living in a Box* (2010) seems scratched out or inked in, rather than actually painted. Cramped by illogical perspective, it features disproportionately spindly figures that trample and gesticulate around what appears to be a boxing ring, while a maquette of a room bearing the painting's title is held aloft as a kind of trophy of introspection. MA

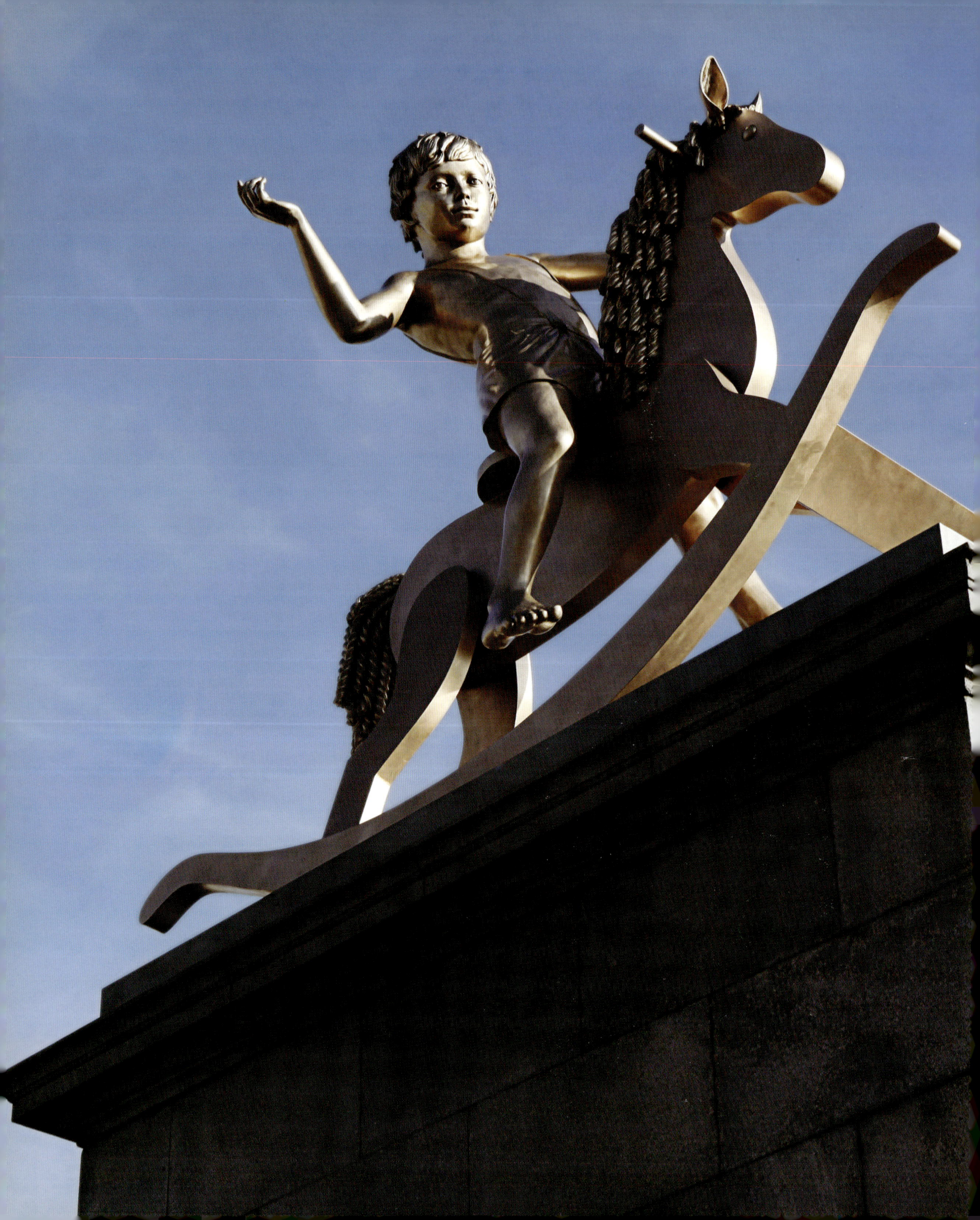

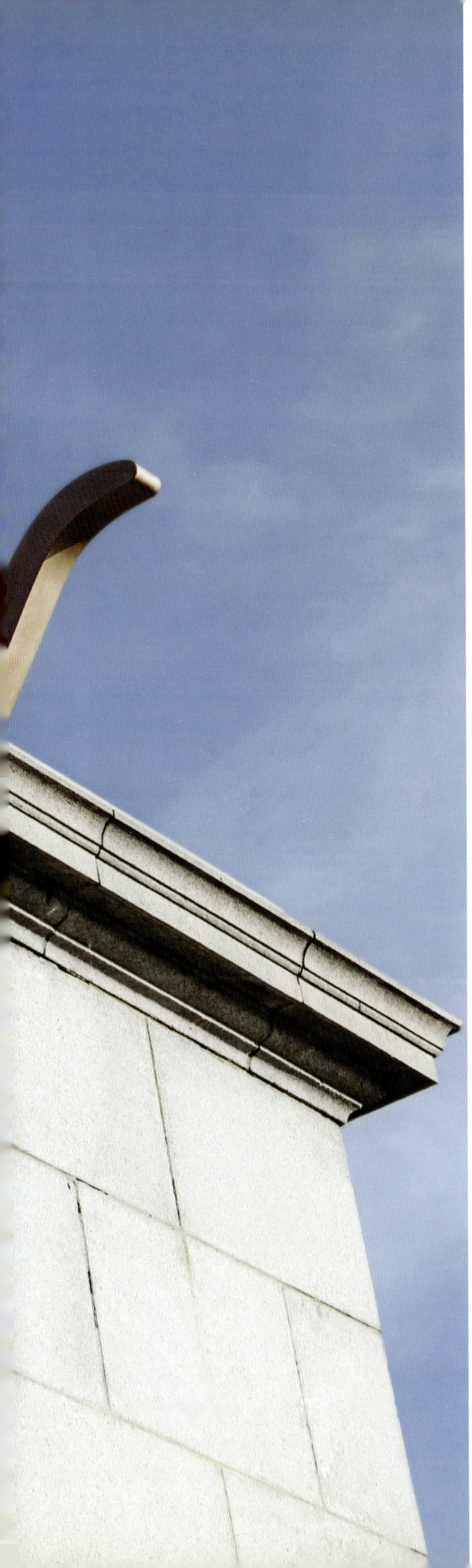

**Shown by**
Galería Helga de Alvear A7
Massimo De Carlo D8
Taka Ishii Gallery B5
Victoria Miro D2
Galerie Perrotin F3

**Biography**
Born 1961/1969
Live in London and Berlin

Danish-born Elmgreen and Norwegian-born Dragset have presented solo exhibitions and projects at venues that include Boijmans Van Beuningen, Rotterdam (2011), Centre Pompidou, Paris (2009), Serpentine Gallery, London (2006), Tate Modern, London (2004), and Statens Museum for Kunst, Copenhagen (2001). They curated the Danish and Nordic Pavilions at the 53rd Venice Biennale (2009) and participate in the 7th Liverpool Biennial, on view until November 2012. Their current exhibition at Victoria Miro, London, runs until November 2012.

*Powerless Structures Fig. 101*
2012
Bronze
4 × 4 × 1.5 m
Courtesy of Victoria Miro

# Michael Elmgreen & Ingar Dragset

Since they met in 1994, Michael Elmgreen and Ingar Dragset have collaborated on sculptures and installations that undermine institutional, sexual and economic power structures. Sometimes they do this by replicating them in fastidious detail—as with *Prada Marfa* (2005), a fully stocked Prada store in the Texas desert—then rendering them unusable (the store is permanently locked). Elsewhere they create uncannily realistic mannequins, as with their works depicting the dead collector Mr B., who floated face down in a swimming pool in *The Collectors* (2009) and was laid out in a morgue in *Untitled* (2011). Currently, for Trafalgar Square's fourth plinth, they confront an existing statue of King George IV with a bronze sculpture of a boy on a rocking horse (*Powerless Structures, Fig. 101*, 2012). JG

1

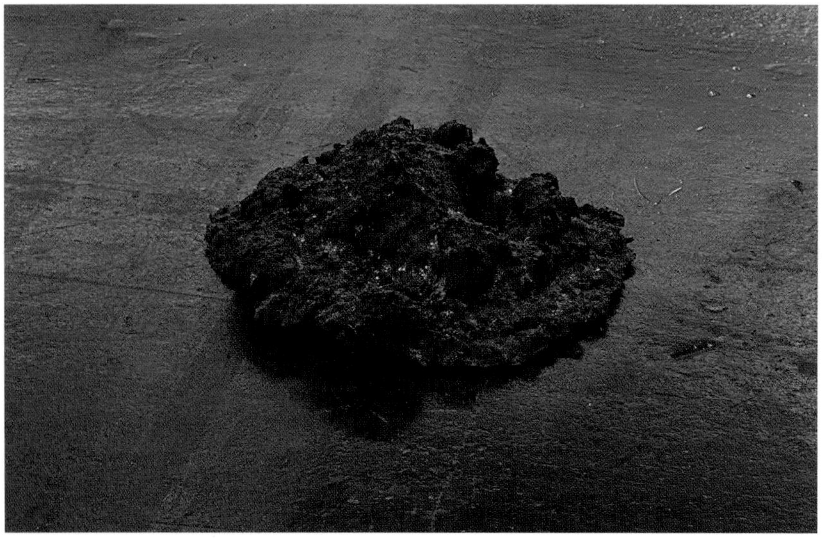
2

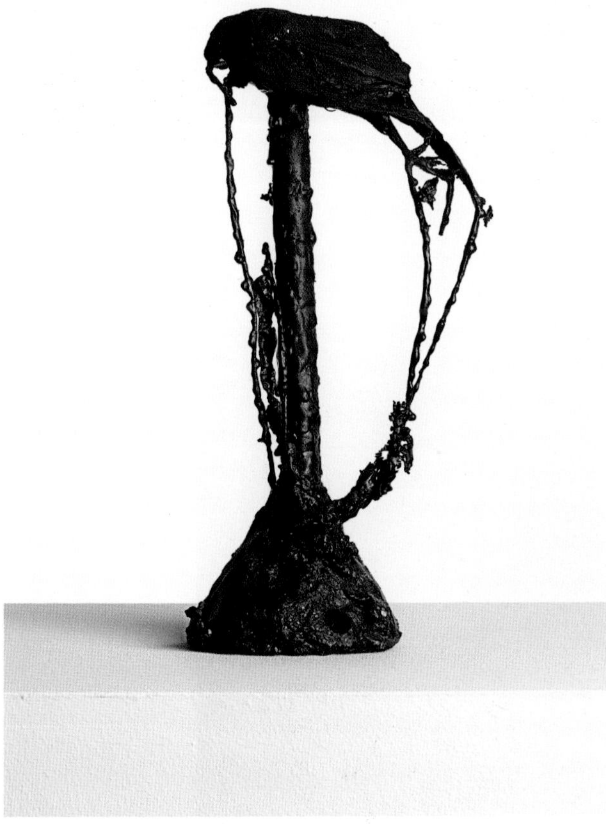

3

# Andreas Eriksson

Drawing on the landscape of his home deep in the Swedish countryside, Andreas Eriksson's atmospheric paintings, photographs and sculptures are on intimate terms with the mute traces of experience, in what might be smudges on a passage of domestic plasterwork in his canvas *In Between Windows 5* (2011) or the miniature earthworks of his bronze *Sorkhög 10* (Molehill 10, 2011). Intensely focused, and often tending towards the abstract, his works are about paying close attention to the way our perceptions shape our understanding of the world and our place in it. For all his interest in the ephemeral, however, Eriksson is at base a realist. As he has written: 'there are no optical effects in a painting: it is a painting.' TM

**Shown by**
Stephen Friedman Gallery D4

**Biography**
Born 1975
Lives in Medelplana, Sweden

Swedish artist Eriksson has been the subject of solo shows at venues including Stephen Friedman Gallery, London (2012), Galleri Riis, Stockholm (2011), Sommer & Kohl, Berlin (2011 and 2009), and MUMOK, Vienna (2008). Eriksson was presented in the Nordic Pavilion at the 54th Venice Biennale (2011). He was awarded the Baloise Art Prize in 2007 and his work is part of permanent collection such as the Louisiana Museum of Modern Art, Humlebæk, Denmark, and Moderna Museet, Stockholm.

1
*In Between Windows 5*
2011
Oil on canvas
119 × 98 cm
Courtesy of Stephen Friedman Gallery, Galleri Riis and Sommer & Kohl

2
*Sorkhög 10*
(Molehill 10)
2011
Bronze
11 × 36 × 34 cm
Courtesy of Stephen Friedman Gallery, Galleri Riis and Sommer & Kohl

3
*Content is a Glimpse 22*
2008
Bronze
25 × 13 × 8 cm
Courtesy of Stephen Friedman Gallery, Galleri Riis and Sommer & Kohl

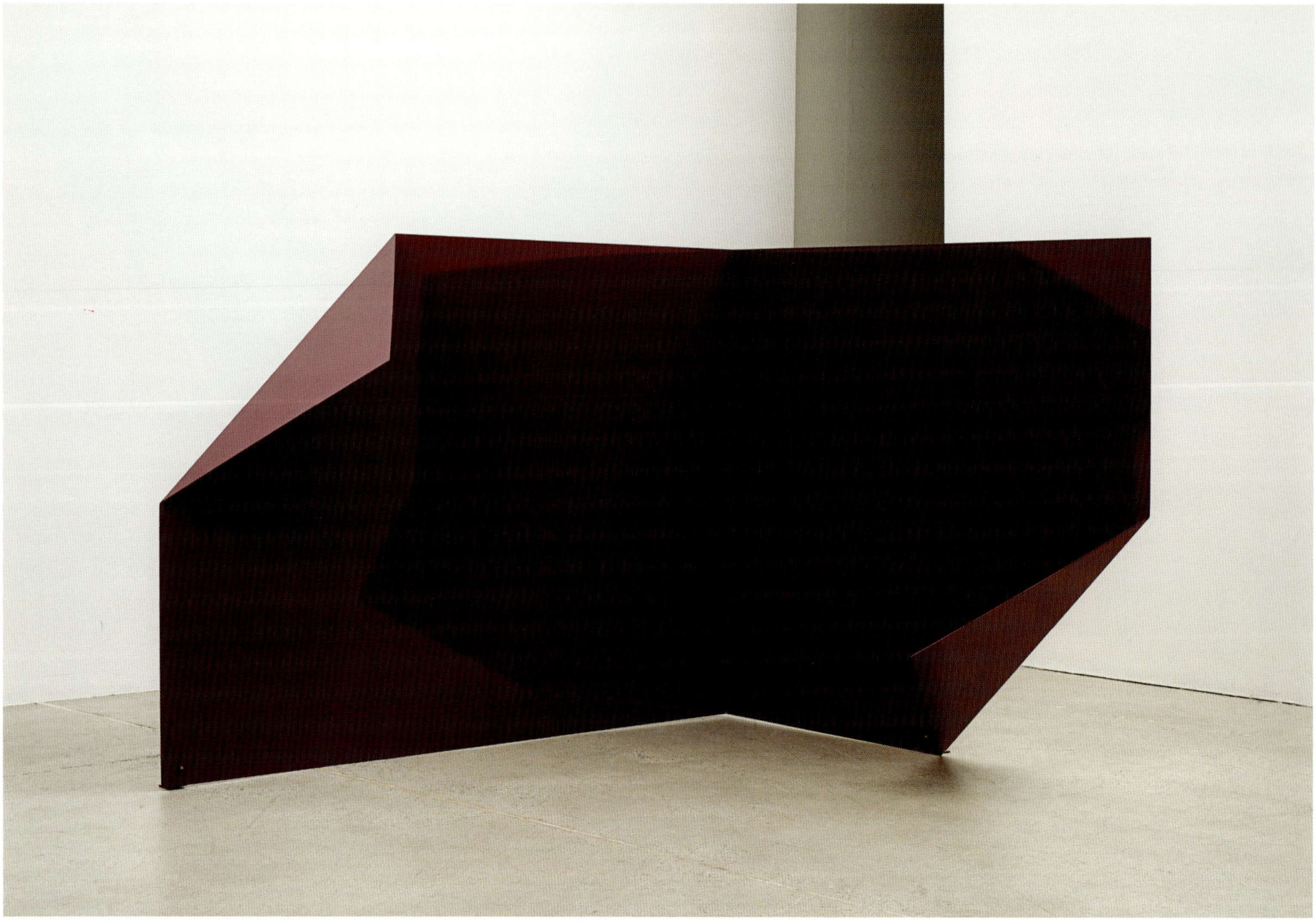
1

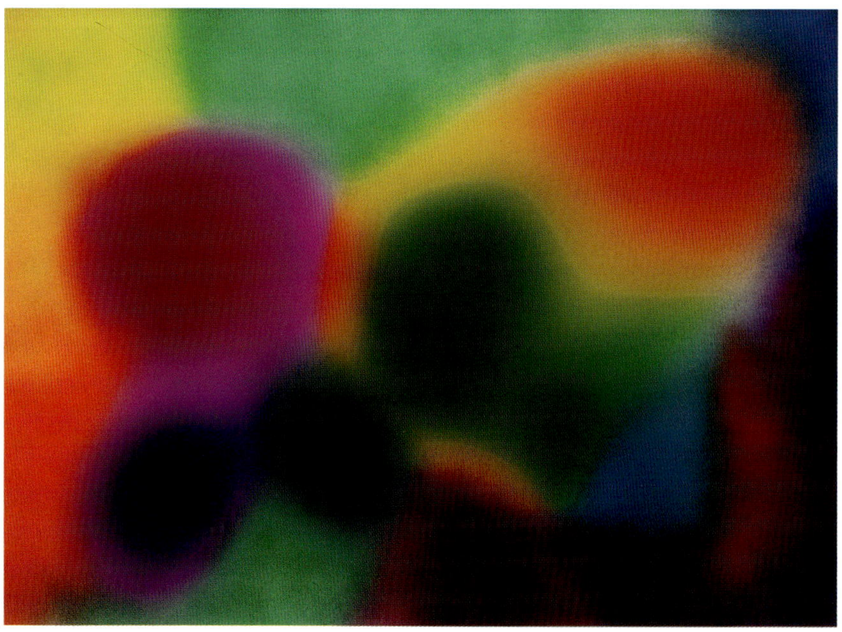
2

4

3

**Shown by**
International Art Objects Galleries G16

**Biography**
Born 1984
Lives in Los Angeles

American artist Falls received an MFA from the International Center for Photography at Bard College, Annandale-on-Hudson, New York, in 2010, the same year he was awarded the Tierney Fellowship for emerging artists in the field of photography. He has since presented solo exhibitions at galleries that include International Art Objects Galleries, Los Angeles (2012), and West Street Gallery, New York (2011). He has participated in group exhibitions at venues such as Pedro Cera Gallery, Lisbon (2012), and the Center for Photography, Woodstock, New York (2010).

1
*Untitled Sculpture (Burgundy 1)*
2012
Powder-coated aluminium and powder-coated stainless steel
122 × 137 × 167 cm
Courtesy of International Art Objects Galleries

2
*Untitled (PP3)*
2011
Acrylic on c-type print
76 × 101 cm
Courtesy of International Art Objects Galleries

3
*Untitled Roll Fade (Slate)*
2011
Artist paper
70 × 53 cm
Courtesy of International Art Objects Galleries

4
*Untitled (Magenta)*
2011
Artist paper
67 × 55 cm
Courtesy of International Art Objects Galleries

# Sam Falls

Sam Falls deconstructs photographs by slowing them down. He makes camera-less pictures such as *Untitled (Magenta)* (2011) by rolling up sheets of coloured paper and allowing them to fade under the bright Californian sun. Once the sheets are flattened, their resulting images are, in a sense, photographs of their former three-dimensional selves. *Untitled Sculpture (Burgundy 1)* (2012) is made from bent aluminium, coated on one side with non-UV-resistant paint; when sited outdoors, as the artist intends, it will selectively discolour to make fixed shadows determined by its particular location. Though invariably abstract, Fall's work has a distinct relationship to landscape photography, filtered through rigorous, process-based Conceptualism and historical Minimalism. JG

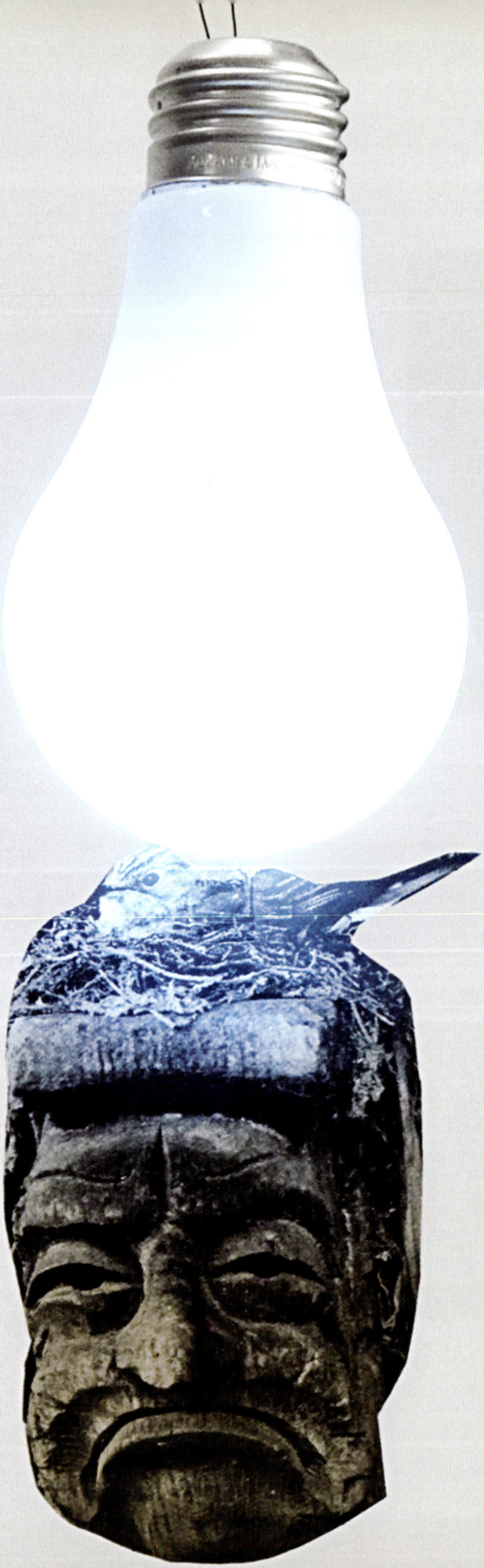

# Geoffrey Farmer

**Shown by**
Casey Kaplan B4

**Biography**
Born 1967
Lives in Vancouver

Canadian artist Farmer has presented solo exhibitions at REDCAT, Los Angeles (2011), Casey Kaplan, New York (2011), The Banff Centre, Banff, Alberta (2010), and Musée d'Art Contemporain de Montréal (2008). Farmer participated in Documenta 13, Kassel (2012), and will be the subject of a solo show at Vancouver Art Gallery in 2013.

*The Greeter*
(detail)
2011
Printed material, wood, metal, paint, tape, foam, boot and computer-programmed LEDs
245 × 60 × 50 cm
Courtesy of Casey Kaplan

Geoffrey Farmer enacts a kind of voodoo in his work, breathing strange new life into the inanimate and the found. In *The Greeter (2011)* a shrivelled totemic head is illuminated by the light of a prosaic light bulb. Farmer's large-scale installations are often organized into a processional form, giving a sense of theatricality to his works. *The Surgeon and the Photographer (2009)*, for example, features no fewer than 365 puppet figures, one for each day of the week. Accessing the spirit world through the emphatically material, Farmer works in a variety of media: sculpture, video, installation, sound. In all these he assembles fragments, working in terms of bricolage and creating juxtapositions that are genuinely uncanny: while his creations evoke instant recognition, they remain essentially strange. KK

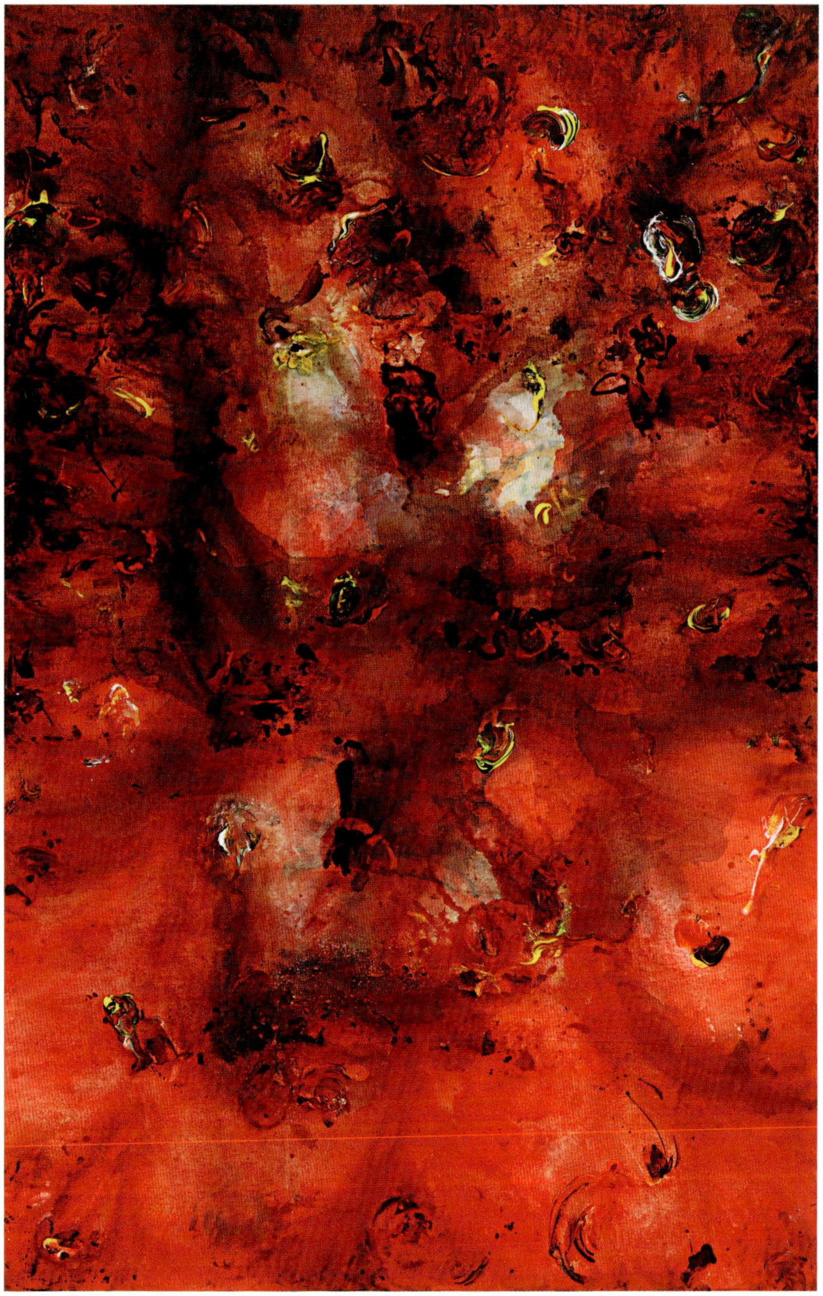

1

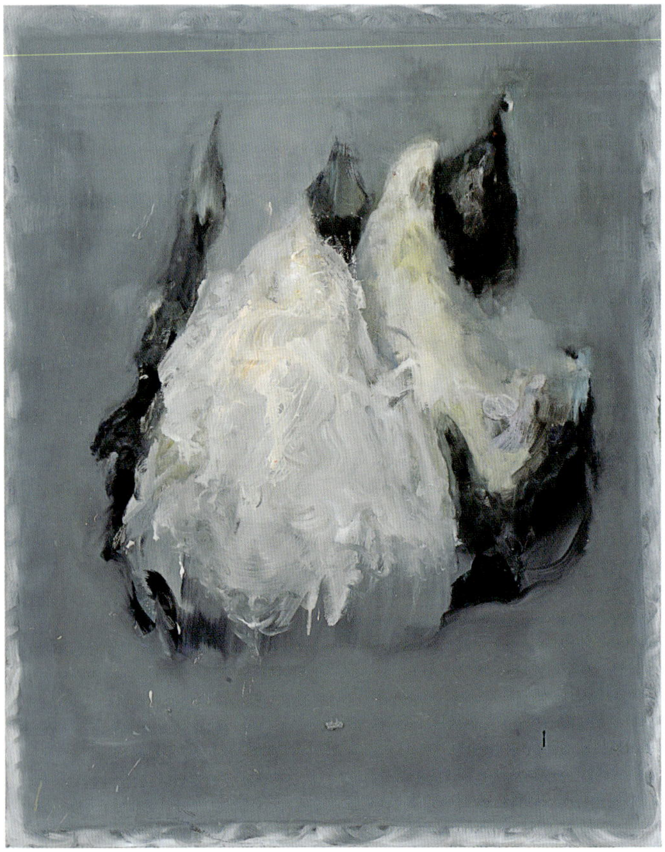

2

**Shown by**
Galerie Peter Kilchmann
E2

**Biography**
Born 1959
Lives in Berlin

Swiss-born Favre, since 2006 Professor of Painting at Universität der Künste, Berlin, has presented solo shows at galleries that include Jocelyn Wolff Gallery, Paris (2012), Galerie Barbara Thumm, Berlin (2011), Kunstmuseum Luzern, Lucerne (2009), and Carré d'Art, Musée d'Art Contemporain de Nîmes (2009). She recently exhibited as part of a show of nominees for the Marcel Duchamp Prize at Château de Tours, Tours (2012), and in other group exhibitions such as 'I Am a Berliner', Tel Aviv Museum of Art (2012).

1
*Balls and Tunnels*
2011
Ink on canvas
300 × 190 cm
Courtesy of Galerie Peter Kilchmann

2
*Ghost (No. 16)*
2011
Oil on canvas
130 × 100 cm
Courtesy of Galerie Peter Kilchmann

3
*Lapine Univers*
2011
Oil on paper
207 × 147 cm
Courtesy of Galerie Peter Kilchmann

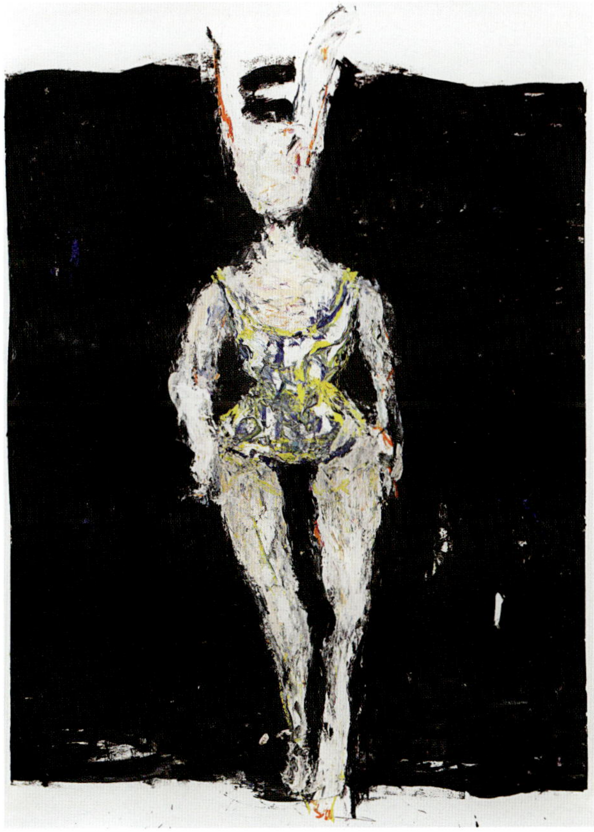

3

# Valérie Favre

The spectral, macabre fantasy world of Valérie Favre's paintings is populated by jocularly lonesome mutants, rabbit-headed acrobats and dead clowns. In vivid but dark colours with assured, strong brushstrokes, her characters move with definite but ambiguous purpose. While predominantly figurative, her abstract work retains the same sense of suspense; *Ghost (No. 16)* (2011) is hesitantly figurative, an uncertain white shape hovering on a blue-grey background, as if just out of focus but still palpable. Death and mystery lie at the heart of her work, but less a funeral march than a devious midnight celebration. CFW

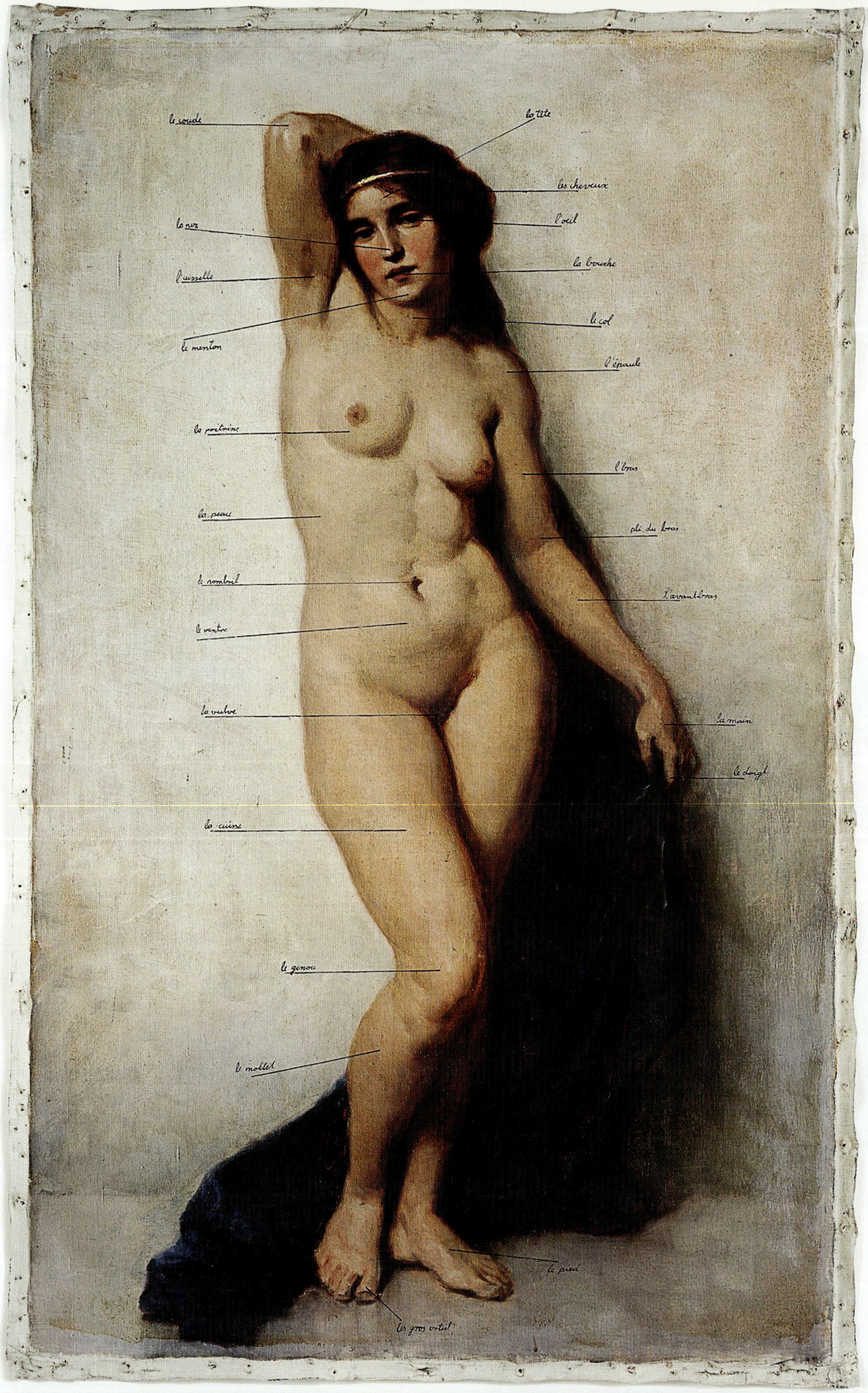
le coude
la tête
les cheveux
le nez
l'oeil
la bouche
l'aisselle
le col
le menton
l'épaule
la poitrine
l'bras
la peau
pli du bras
le nombril
l'avantbras
le ventre
la vulve
la main
le doigt
la cuisse
le genou
le mollet
le pied
les gros orteil

# Hans-Peter Feldmann

**Shown by**
303 Gallery C9
Konrad Fischer Galerie C6
Johnen Galerie D1
Galerie Francesca Pia G1
Galerie Micheline Szwajcer B3
Wien Lukatsch F16

**Biography**
Born 1941
Lives in Dusseldorf

German artist Feldmann has recently been the subject of solo exhibitions at public institutions including the Serpentine Gallery, London (2012), the Solomon R. Guggenheim Museum, New York (2011), and Museo Nacional Centro de Arte Reina Sofía, Madrid (2010). He was awarded the Hugo Boss Prize in 2010. One of his key works, *Die Toten* ('The Dead', 1967–93), is on view at the Hamburger Bahnhof, Museum für Gegenwart, Berlin, until January 2013.

*Nude with Words*
Undated
Inkjet print on canvas
125 × 75 cm
Courtesy of 303 Gallery

In 1946, aged five, Hans-Peter Feldmann began collecting pictures from books and magazines. He still does so, though many additional procedures have coalesced into his subsequent art practice, from the 108-image *Photographs Taken from Hotel Room Windows While Travelling* (1975–99) to photo-archives of sunset or lips, collections of shoes, found seascape paintings and his neat display of the $100,000-dollar winnings that he received for the Hugo Boss Prize in 2010. Feldmann's is a somewhat cracked typology, however, his Conceptualism grained with implicit backstories, as in *All the Clothes of a Woman* (1970), or admissions that collecting is not possessing, as in 2004's *Pictures of Car Radios Taken While Good Music Was Playing*. For all that his art gestures towards consolation through order, at its core is tragicomic incompleteness. MH

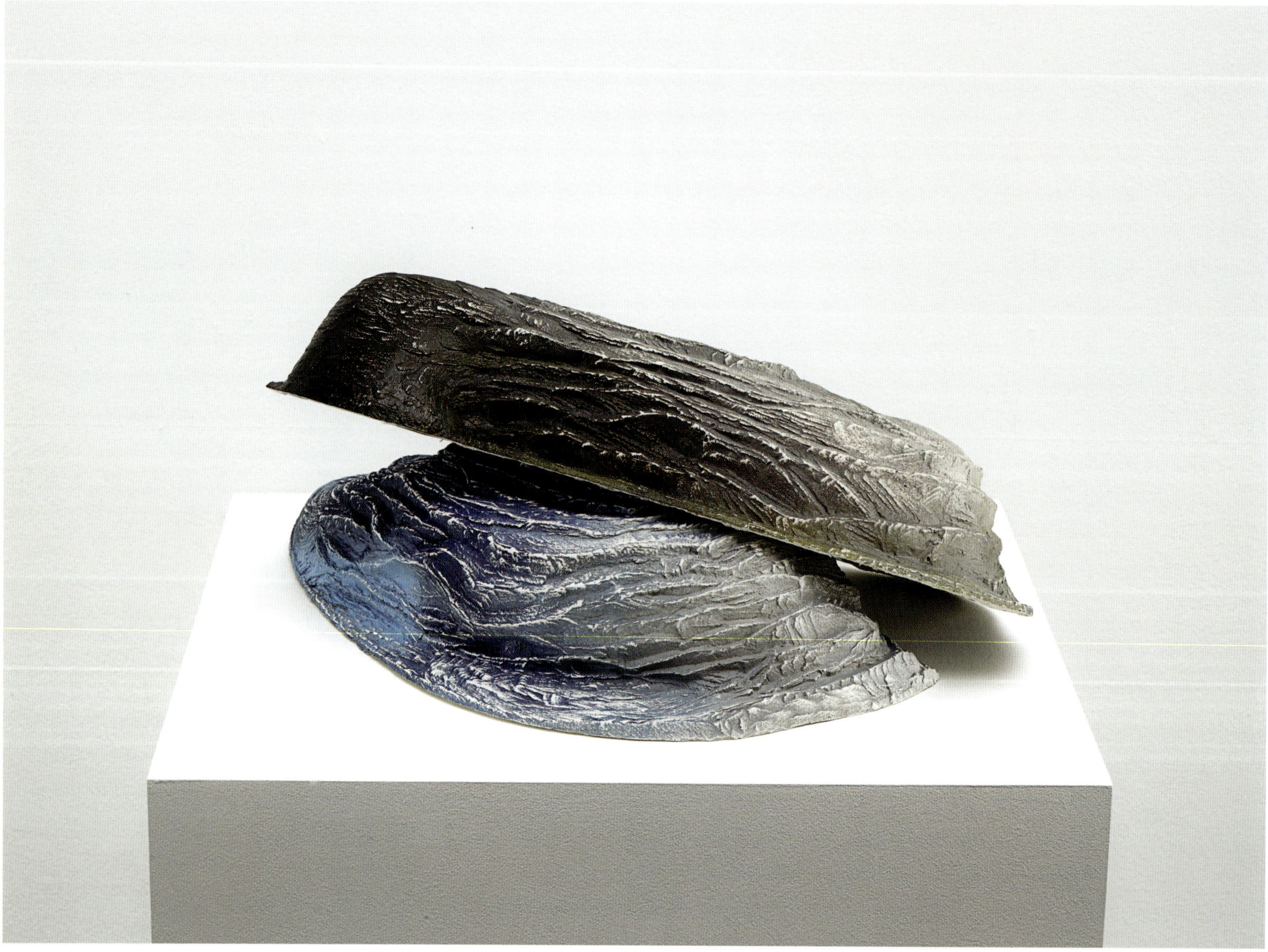

1

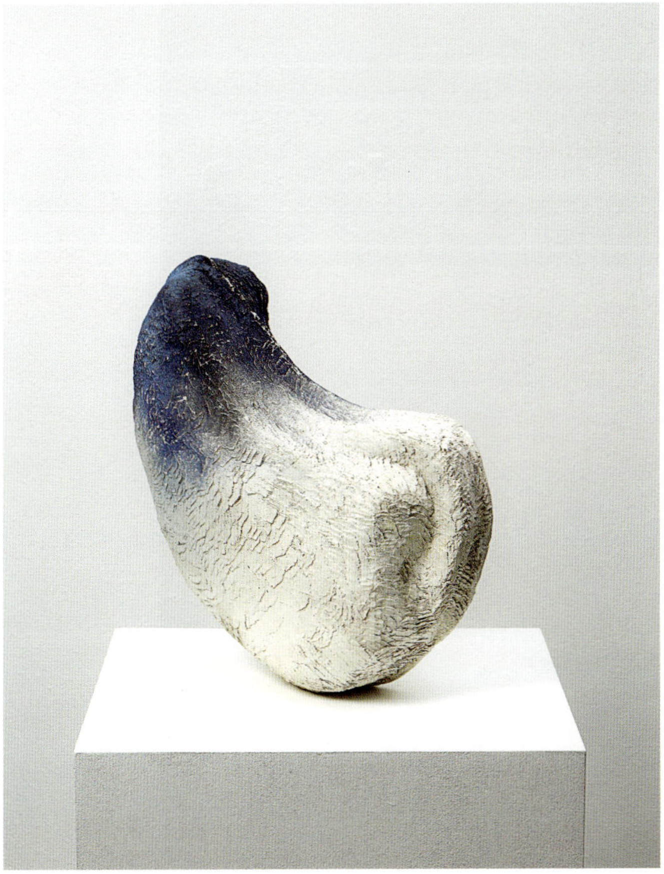

2

**Shown by**
Carl Freedman Gallery
A8

**Biography**
Born 1977
Lives in London

London-born Flood-Paddock has presented solo exhibitions at venues such as Grimm Gallery, Amsterdam (2012), Carl Freedman Gallery, London (2011), and the Hayward Gallery, London (2010). Her current solo show at the Tate Britain, London, part of the 'Art Now' programme, runs until January 2013. She was nominated for the Dazed and Confused Emerging Artist Award in 2010, the same year that her short film *Island, A Regime* was commissioned for Frieze Art Fair. Her work as artist-in-residence at Wysing Arts Centre in Cambridgeshire is on view from November 2012.

1
*London Oyster Shells*
2012
Jesmonite and paint
21 × 28 × 42 cm
Courtesy of Carl Freedman Gallery

2
*Oyster Standing*
2012
Jesmonite and paint
46 × 35 × 17 cm
Courtesy of Carl Freedman Gallery

# Jess Flood-Paddock

Jess Flood-Paddock's sculptures and installations have often comprised scaled-up versions of images that she has encountered in films, print and online. *Truman* (2010), for example, is a backdrop of a blue sky taken from a sequence in *The Truman Show* (1998), while *Sacrifice* (2010), an Aztec statue approximated using wood and photocopies, was based on something the artist found in a back-issue of *National Geographic*. More recent works such as *London Oyster Shells* (2012) have been on a smaller scale, although they feel similarly transient. Pieces like *Oyster X London Plane* (2012), for example, comprise unexpected materials such as bark, while incorporating the quasi-hidden imprints of human body parts. Flood-Paddock makes objects that seem always in flux, sculptures that ask us how images become physical form, and how this might be changing in the digital age. ST

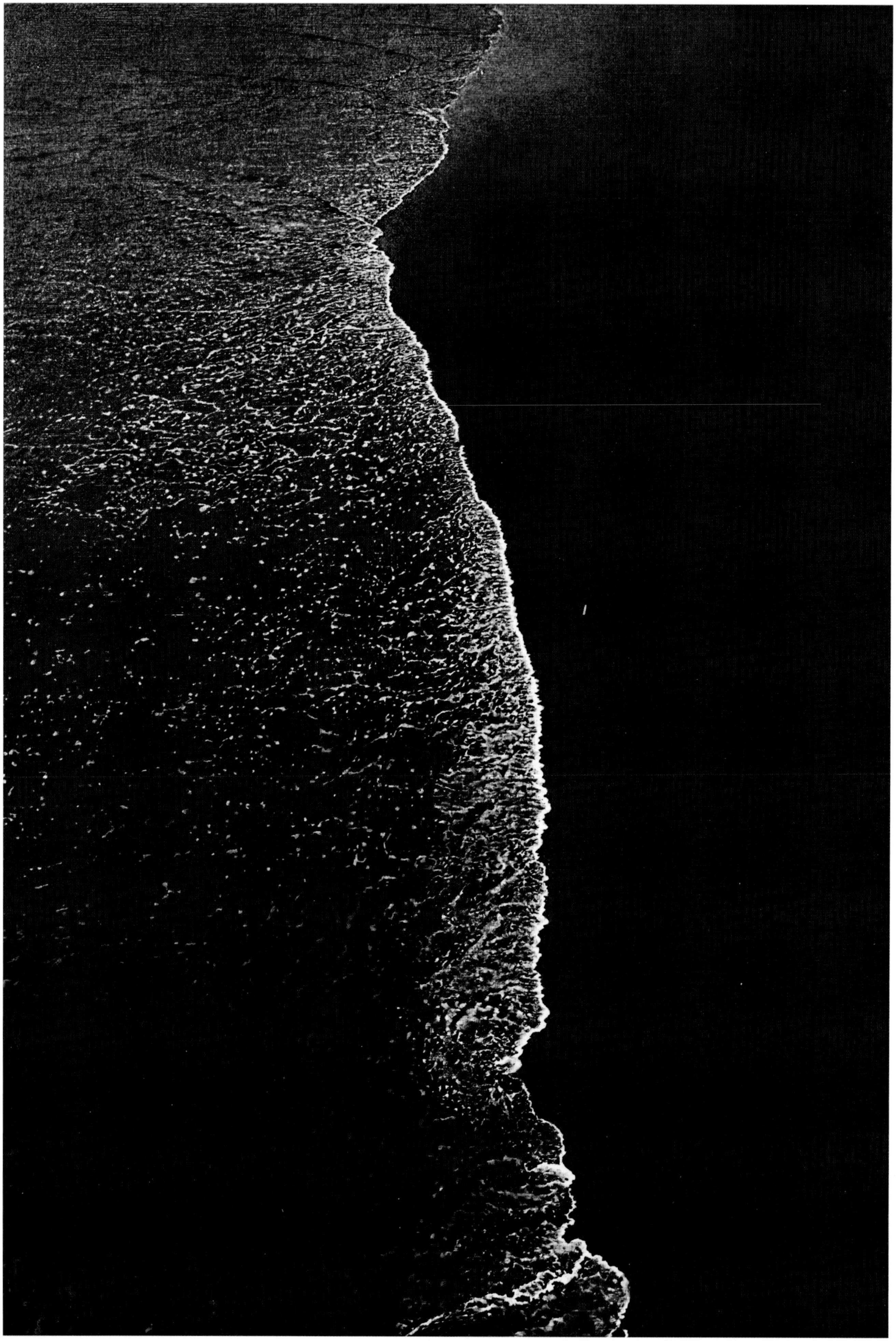

1

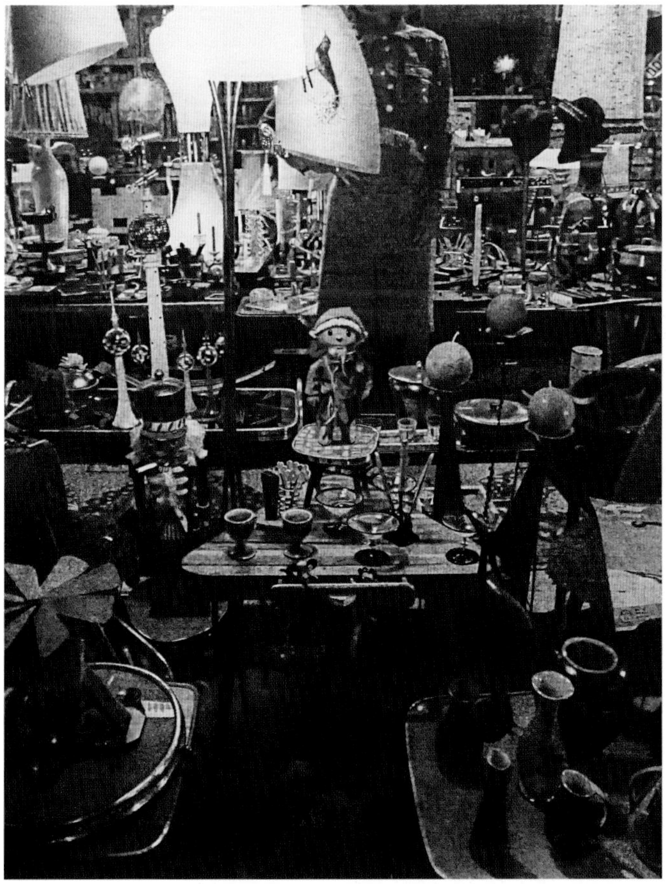

2

**Shown by**
Ingleby Gallery G19

**Biography**
Born 1970
Lives in Saltburn-by-the-Sea, Yorkshire

British artist Forster has presented solo shows at venues that include the Flag Foundation, New York (2012), Middlesbrough Institute of Modern Art (2011), Ingleby Gallery, Edinburgh (2008), and MOT International, London (2008). Recent group exhibitions include 'Slow Looking: Contemporary Drawing' at Tate Britain, London (2012). His work is part of collections such as the Whitworth Art Gallery, Manchester, and the UK's Government Art Collection.

1
*Incoming seas' edge on fourteen consecutive occasions, random time intervals. Saltburn-by-the Sea, Jan 5 2010; 11.30am-11.37am*
2010
Graphite and acrylic on card
One of 14 parts in sequence
45 × 30 cm
Courtesy Ingleby Gallery

2
*Sandman, Berlin*
2012
Graphite and acrylic on board
39 × 29 cm
Courtesy Ingleby Gallery

# Richard Forster

Richard Forster titled a recent exhibition of his painstaking pencil drawings 'Fast & Slow Time' (2011), a phrase borrowed from a book about the accelerative effects of the information age. The theme of the book contrasted revealingly with Forster's choice of pre-digital subjects: sequential photographs of receding waves on a sandy seashore, and film stills of the construction of a 1920s Bauhaus-designed housing block in Dessau. The kind of labour involved in these intense, minutely accurate drawings seems at odds with both the toil of building work and with time wasted gazing at the sea; however, Forster's sustained meditation on history (and the ways we picture it) is itself a formidable endeavour. JG

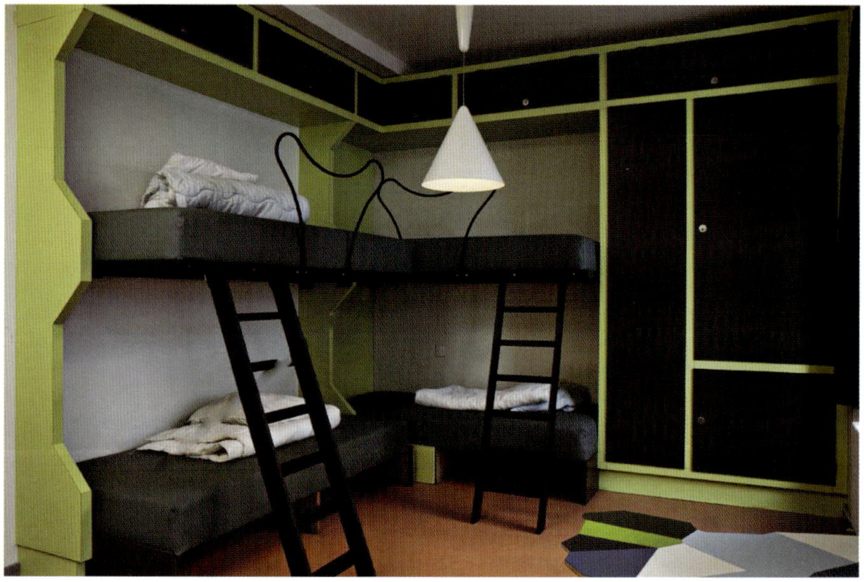
1

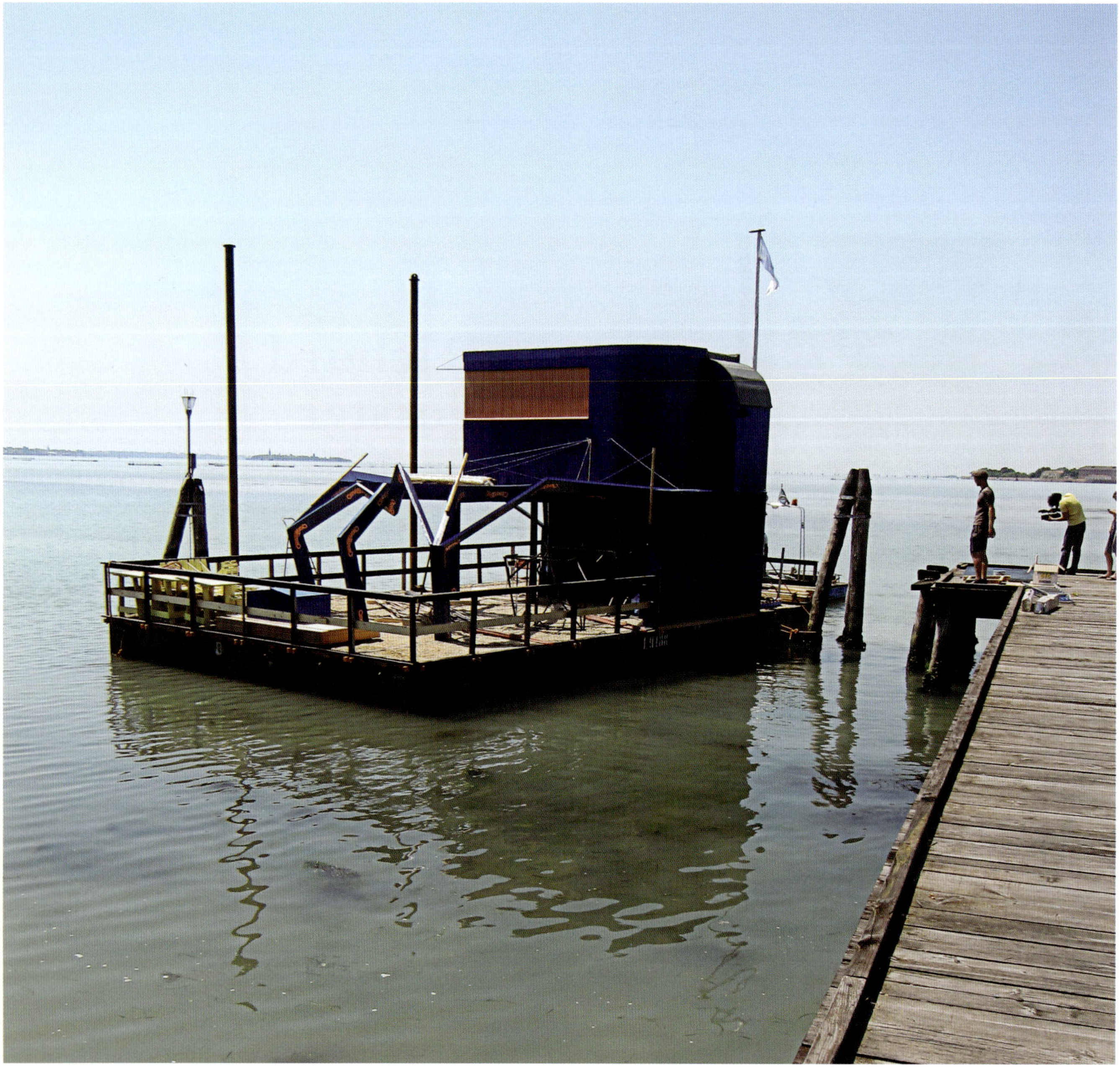
2

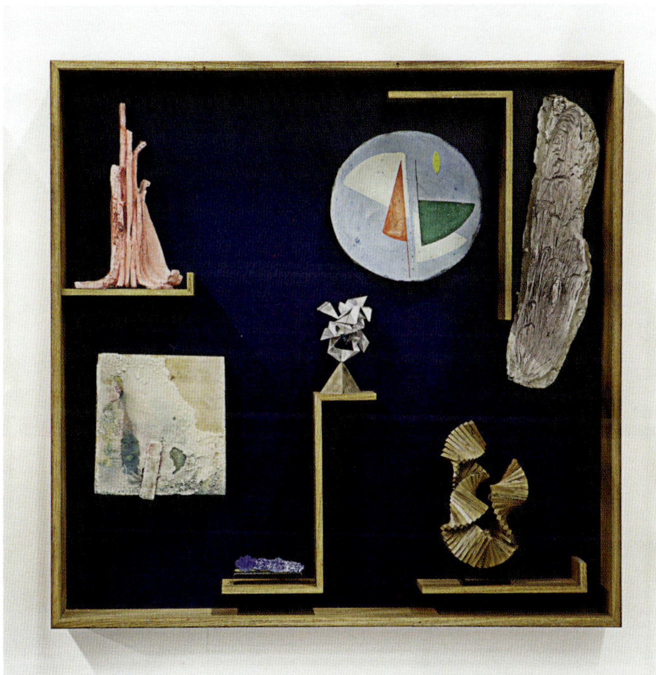

3

**Shown by**
Andersen's
Contemporary H4
Max Wigram Gallery
E13

**Biography**
Born 1971
Lives in Copenhagen

FOS is the Danish artist Thomas Poulsen. His solo projects and exhibitions include those at Statens Museum for Kunst, Copenhagen (2011), GAK, Bremen (2008), the Danish Embassy, London (2006), and Vigeland Museum, Oslo (2003). His work is included in the collections of the Statens Museum for Kunst and the Arken Museum for Modern Art, Ishoj, Denmark. FOS is the subject of a solo presentation at Max Wigram Gallery, London, in October 2012.

1
*Mændenes Hjem*
(Home for the Men)
2006
Collaboration with Kenneth Balfelt
Interior view of centre for homeless men, Copenhagen
Courtesy of Max Wigram Gallery

2
*Osloo*
2011
Floating pavilion at the 54th Venice Biennale
Courtesy of Max Wigram Gallery

3
*One Language Traveller 9*
2012
Clay, acrylic, wood and glass
122 × 122 × 20 cm
Courtesy of Max Wigram Gallery

# FOS

Since the late 1990s FOS (Thomas Poulsen) has been examining the social function of art in society, through installations, sculptures, music and performance. Notable projects include his redesign of a Copenhagen drop-in centre for homeless men, *Mændenes Hjem* (Home for the Men, 2006), and *Osloo* (2011), a floating pavilion moored in Venice during the biennale, with a bar, free daily events and a radio station. FOS developed his 'social design' hybrid of sculpture, design and architecture further still in his recent installation *One Language Traveller* (2011), a series of interconnecting environments, platforms, frames and tents representing approaches to knowledge, thought and experience, which the artist describes as 'a journey from nothing to something which in the end becomes a "language"'. SL

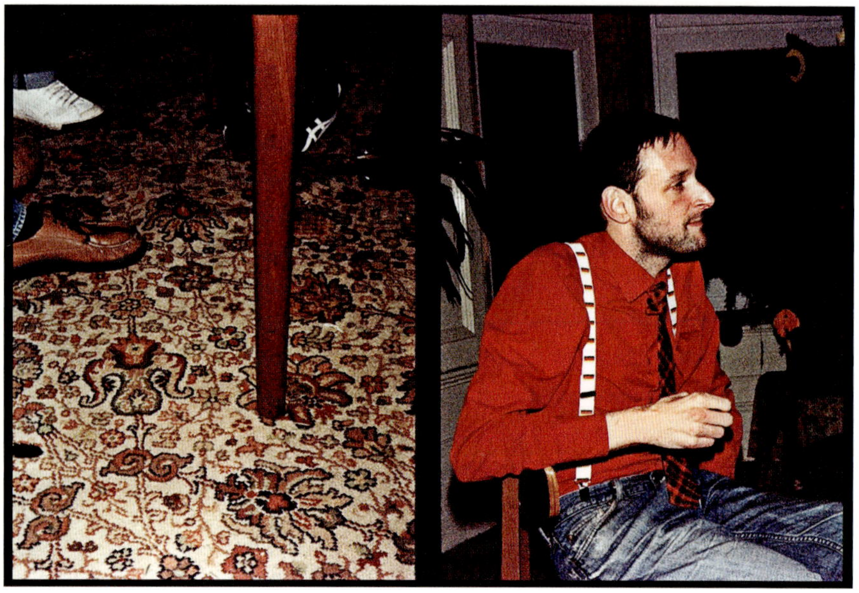

1

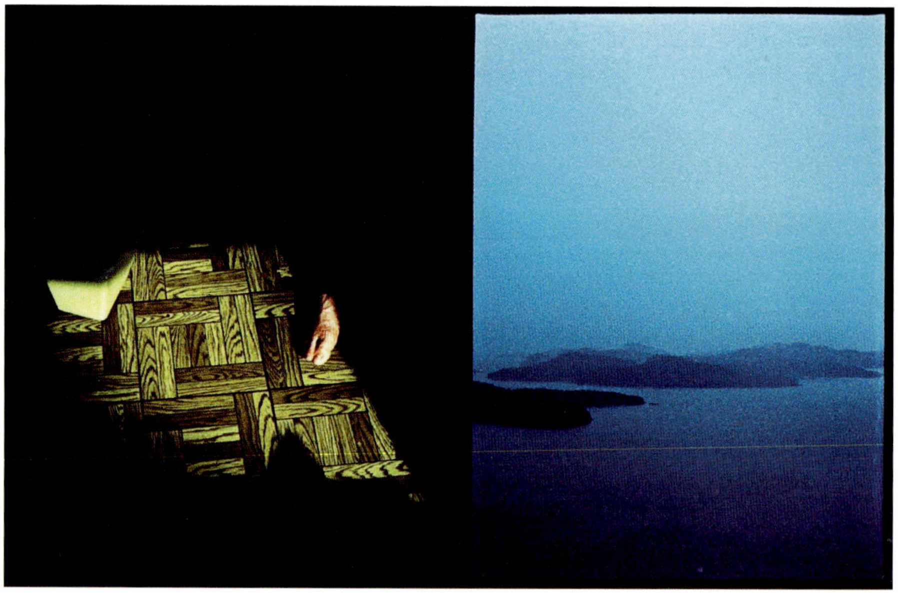

2

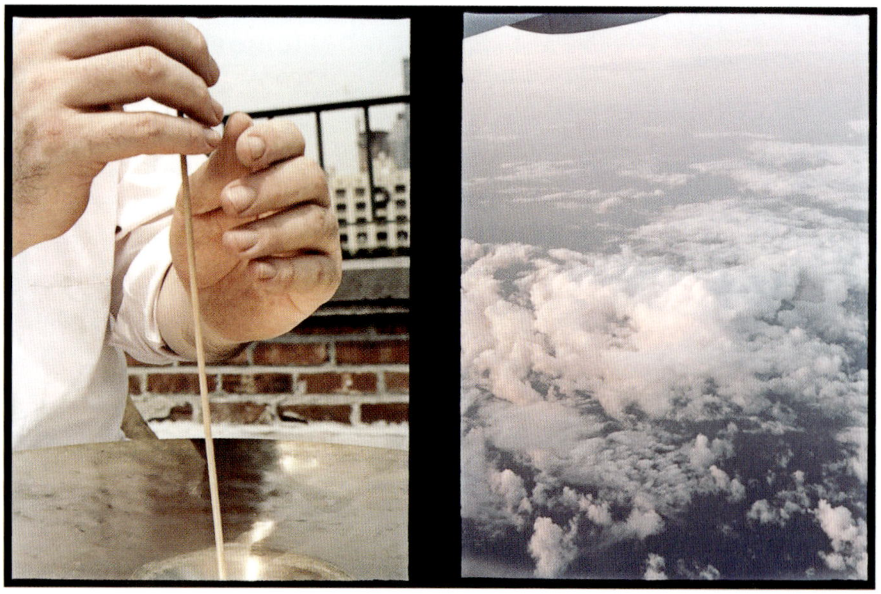

3

**Shown by**
Galerie Gisela Capitain
C10
The Modern Institute
B12

**Biography**
Born 1978
Lives in Glasgow

As one of the four nominees for the Turner Prize 2012, Scottish-born Fowler exhibits at Tate Britain, London, until January 2013. His film *The Poor Stockinger, the Luddite Cropper and the Deluded Followers of Joanna Southcott* (2012) is on view at The Hepworth, Wakefield, until mid-October 2012, before travelling to Wolverhampton Art Gallery. Other solo exhibitions have included shows at Bielefelder Kunstverein, Bielefeld (2011), and Serpentine Gallery, London (2009). He received the Paul Hamlyn Award in 2010 and the Derek Jarman Award in 2008.

1
*Alasdair, Hogmanay, Clouston Street*
2009
C-type print
65 × 65 cm
(when framed)
Courtesy of The Modern Institute

2
*Cross Laminate (Galliano Island)*
2009
C-type print
65 × 65 cm
(when framed)
Courtesy of The Modern Institute

3
*Sean and Cymbal; Congeal'd Air (NYC)*
2009
C-type print
65 × 65 cm
(when framed)
Courtesy of The Modern Institute

# Luke Fowler

Luke Fowler's films have focused largely on marginalized individuals, including the Maoist composer Cornelius Cardew, a troubled hermit named Bogman Palmjaguar and the renegade psychiatrist R.D. Laing, the latter examined in a triology of works that culminated with the feature *All Divided Selves* (2011). In contrast, his 16mm *A Grammar for Listening (Parts 1–3)* (2009) saw him collaborate with three sound artists in a trio of works that explore the relationship between sound and its filmed representation. Here field recordings capturing everything from the crackle of burning walnuts to the clanking of the Clyde shipyards to the thrum of human thought are synched with footage of the sites where the recordings took place, in a sophisticated and at times very beautiful marrying of the legacies of *musique concrète* and 1960s experimental film. TM

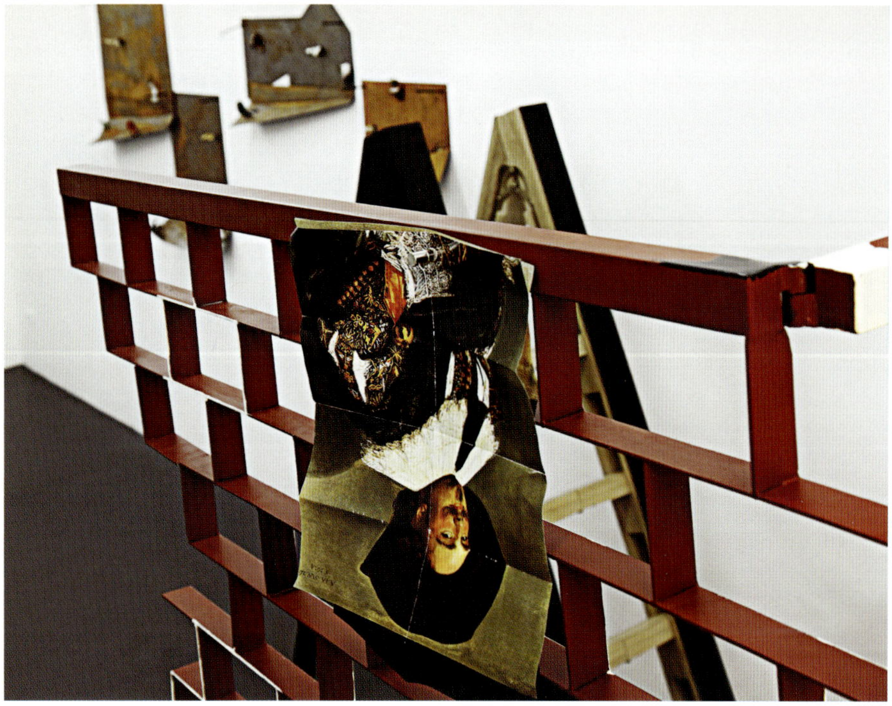

1

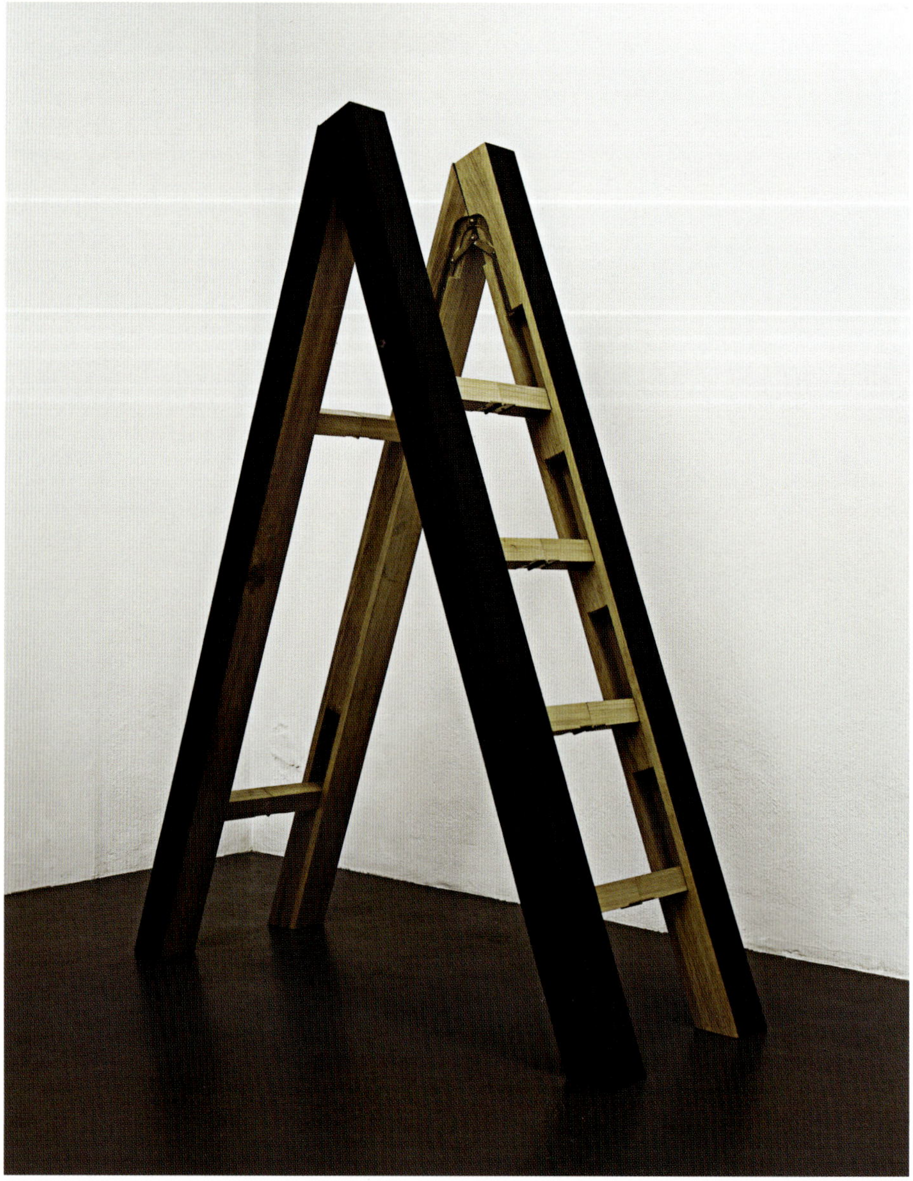

2

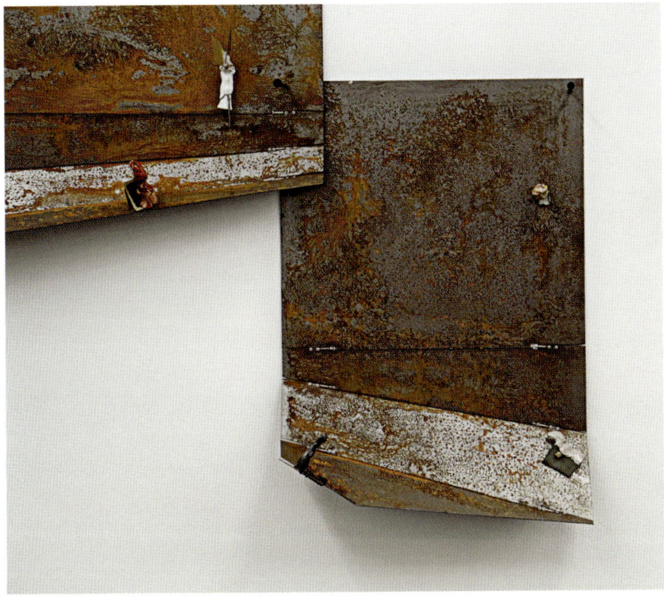

3

**Shown by**
Chert S7

**Biography**
Born 1985
Lives in Berlin

London-born Fudakowski has presented solo exhibitions recently at Chert, Tokyo (2011), Chert, Berlin (2011), Zak/Branicka Gallery, Berlin (2009), and Artpol, Krakow (2008). She has been featured in group exhibitions that include 'New Sculpture?', Zacheta National Gallery of Art, Warsaw (2012), 'Petrosphere', ReMap3, Athens (2011), and 'Based in Berlin', Atelierhaus Monbijou Park, Berlin (2011).

1
*Nothing Is Easy*
(detail)
2011
Steel and paint
92 × 360 × 12 cm
Courtesy of Chert

2
*Too Heavy for a Joke*
2011
Oak, brass and steel
188 × 144 × 51 cm
Courtesy of Chert

3
*Crazy and Sporadic, though Essentially Isolated, Acts of Violence (4)*
(detail)
2011
Steel, air-dried clay, gloss paint and magnets
67 × 47 × 19 cm
Courtesy of Chert

# Focus
# Kasia Fudakowski

Kasia Fudakowski has said her paintings, sculptures and installations are concerned with 'the scale of human emotions presented from the flippant, transient, borderline meaninglessness to the deep and clawing'. Her work often combines dull and glossy surfaces, and draws forth latent absurd or erotic connotations, as in the veneer cabinet with cartoon eyes that was part of the installation *Grand Stands* (2010), or the hoof-like element of the sculpture called *Knackered is for Horses* (2009). Lately Fudakowski has continued to reframe the properties of prosaic materials such as wood, steel and paint as puzzling conceptual objects, such as the custom-built ladder *Too Heavy for a Joke* (2011) or three ornamental gate/grate structures that critique vernacular architecture entitled *For How Much Longer Must We Improvise?* (2011). SL

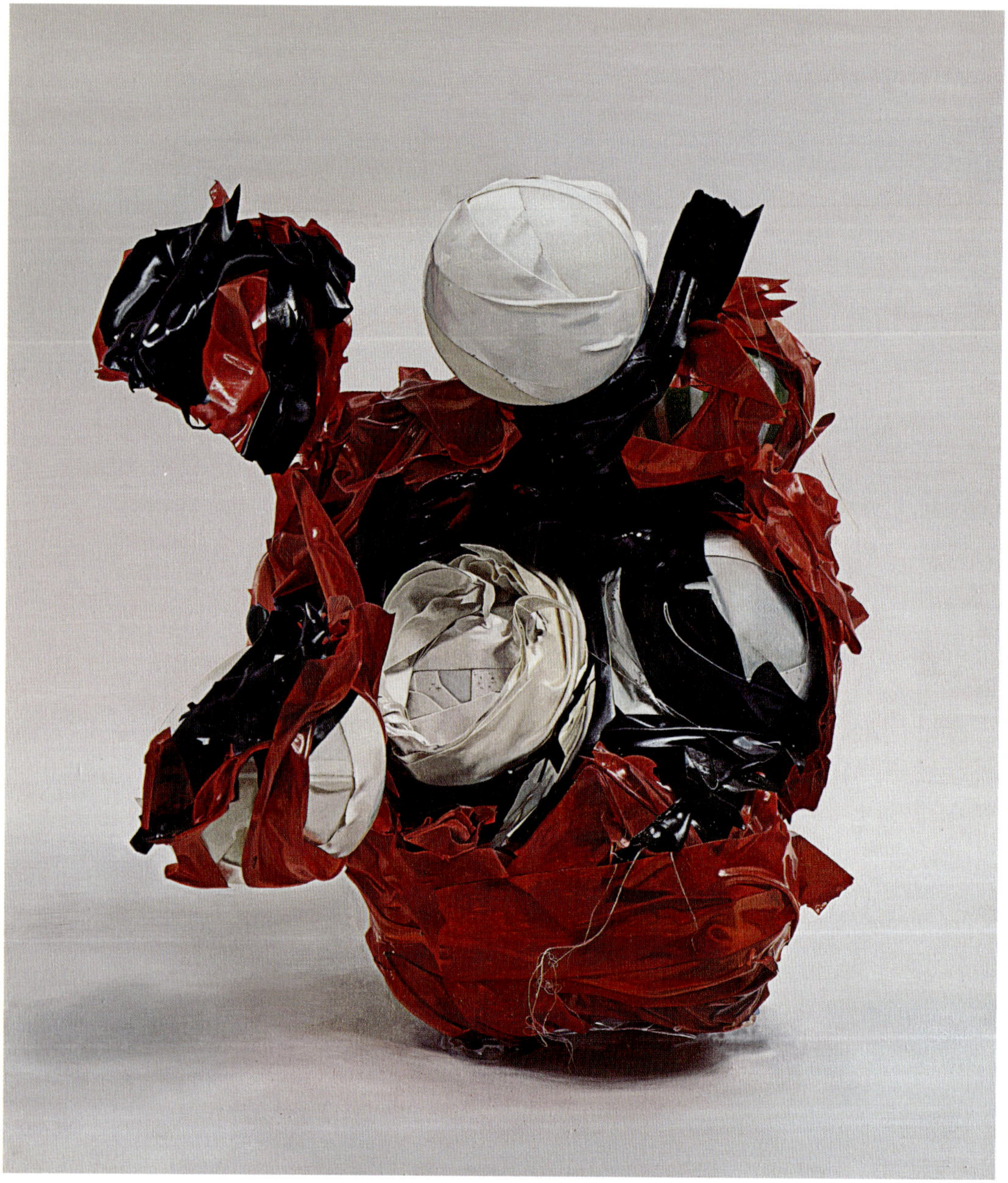

1

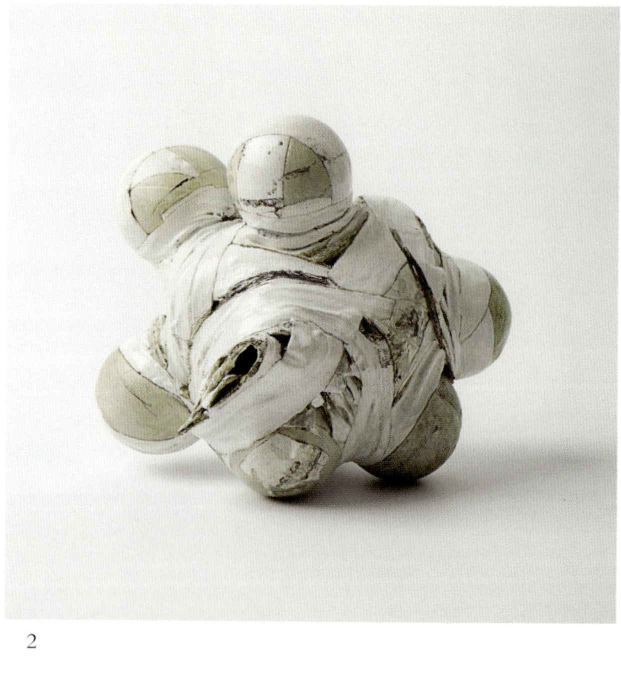

2

**Shown by**
Aurel Scheibler H1

**Biography**
Born 1967
Lives in London

Recent solo exhibitions by the British-born Gall include those at Aurel Scheibler, Berlin (2012 and 2009), David Nolan Gallery, New York (2012 and 2010), ScheiblerMitte, Berlin (2008), and Hales Gallery, London (2005). His work has been featured in group shows such as 'Sagacity', Forman's Smokehouse Gallery, London (2011), 'Undone', Henry Moore Institute, Leeds (2010–11), 'Obsession', University of Leeds (2009), and the recent exhibition 'London Twelve' at City Gallery, Prague (2012).

1
*Spirit of the Age*
2011
Oil on linen
117 × 99 cm
Courtesy of Aurel Scheibler

2
*Remnant*
2010
Acrylic on bronze
12 × 14 cm
Courtesy of Aurel Scheibler

3
*Never Say Die*
2008
Oil on linen
244 × 220 cm
Courtesy of Aurel Scheibler

# Neil Gall

Neil Gall's recent paintings and drawings are based on lumpy mini-tableaux which the artist assembles from table-tennis balls bound together by electrical tape, wire or fists of multicoloured Plasticine. These uncanny forms are illuminated, photographed and precisely accreted on canvas, linen or paper, being massively enlarged through this transcription process to discomfortingly monumental effect. *Spirit of the Age* (2011) documents a welt of matt white spheres that are almost entirely suffocated by their shiny wrapping of red and black adhesive plastic. An improvised fetish artefact whose anthropomorphic 'head' is trussed as if bandaged or blindfolded? Bringing to mind the technique of the detritus-model still lifes of his near-contemporary, the Italian painter Pierpaolo Campanini, Gall's Photorealist compositions in this vein court a more synthetic, still stickier form of Surrealism. MA

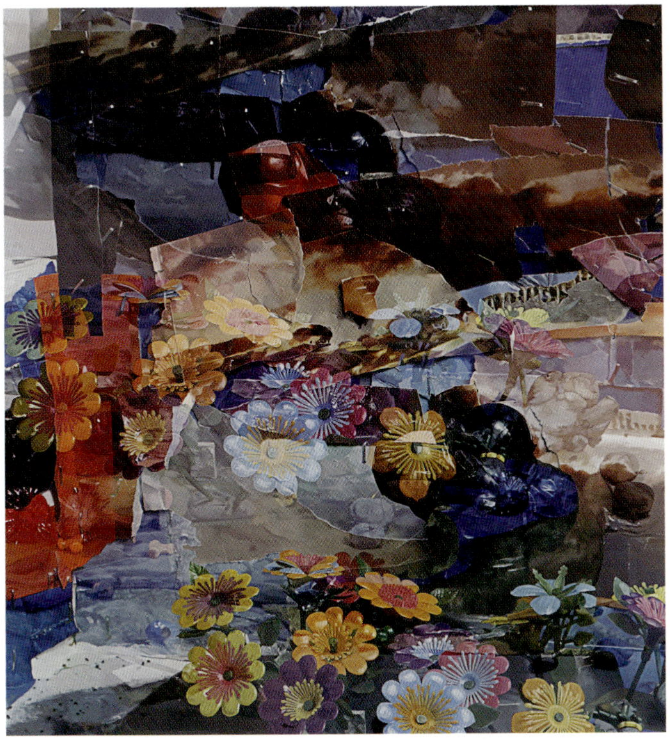

3

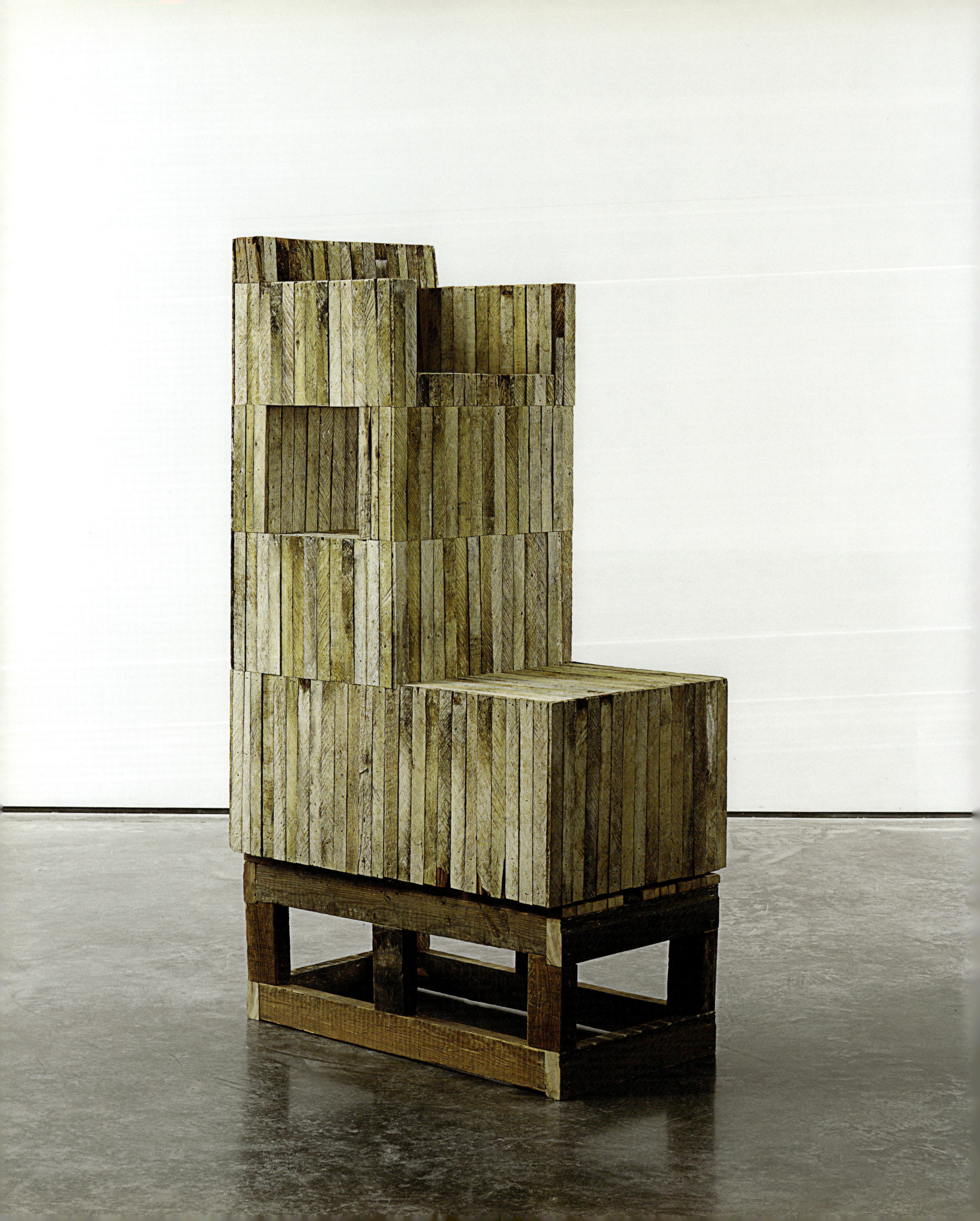

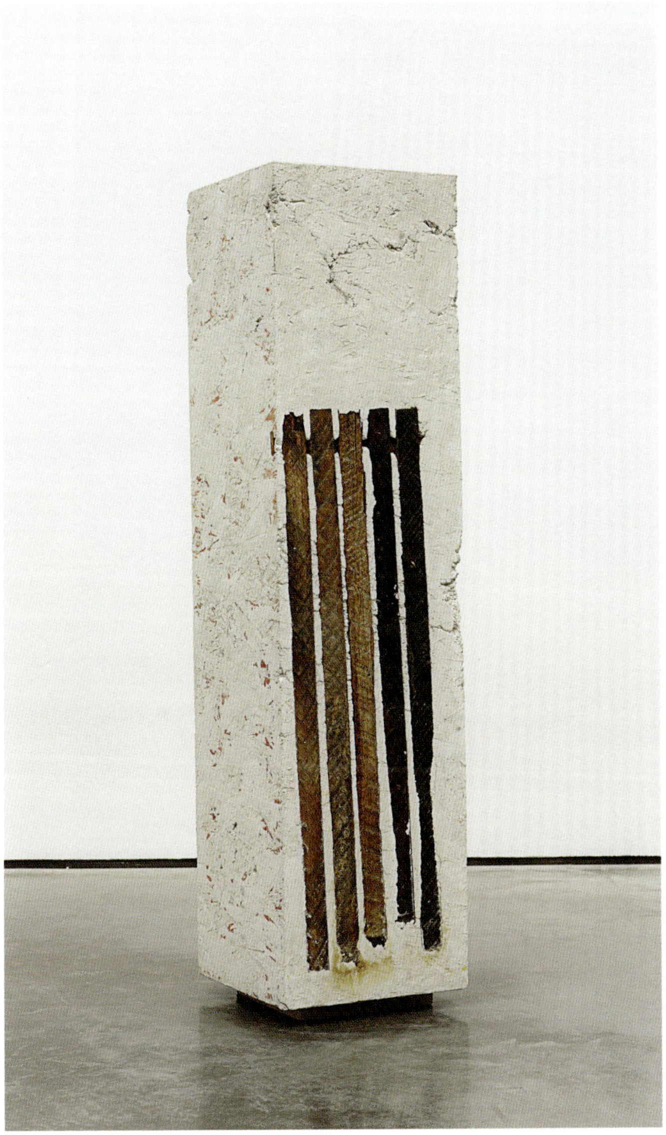

2

**Shown by**
White Cube F7

**Biography**
Born 1973
Lives in Chicago

Chicago-born Gates has been the subject of solo exhibitions at venues such as White Cube Bermondsey, London (2012), Los Angeles Museum for Contemporary Art (2011), Seattle Art Museum (2011), Milwaukee Art Museum (2010) and Museum of Contemporary Art, Chicago (2009). He participated in Documenta 13, Kassel (2012), and collaborated with academics, artists and street musicians on the project 'Cosmology of Yard' at the Whitney Biennial, Whitney Museum of American Art, New York (2010).

1
*Standing Throne 4*
2012
Wood lathe and plywood
178 × 58 × 97 cm
Courtesy of White Cube

2
*Stack 6901.23*
2011
White concrete, pulverized glass and lathe
125 × 30 × 30 cm
Courtesy of White Cube

# Theaster Gates

Theaster Gates works at the intersection of art and urban planning, frequently rescuing eloquent remnants from African-American homes or intervening in the fabric of the city to highlight and imaginatively skew aspects of black urban history. His *Dorchester Project* (2009) involved buying three abandoned buildings in Chicago and turning them into archives for relics from a local bookshop, record store and the University of Chicago art department. Sculptural series such as 'Soul Food Starter Kit' (2012) and 'Shoe Shine with Old Growth Pedestal' (2012) repurpose found materials to invoke aspects of daily life at the juncture of memory and cliché. 'Space is my monument', says Gates. 'Buildings are the carriers of people's stories. They contain, enable and rarely forget.' BD

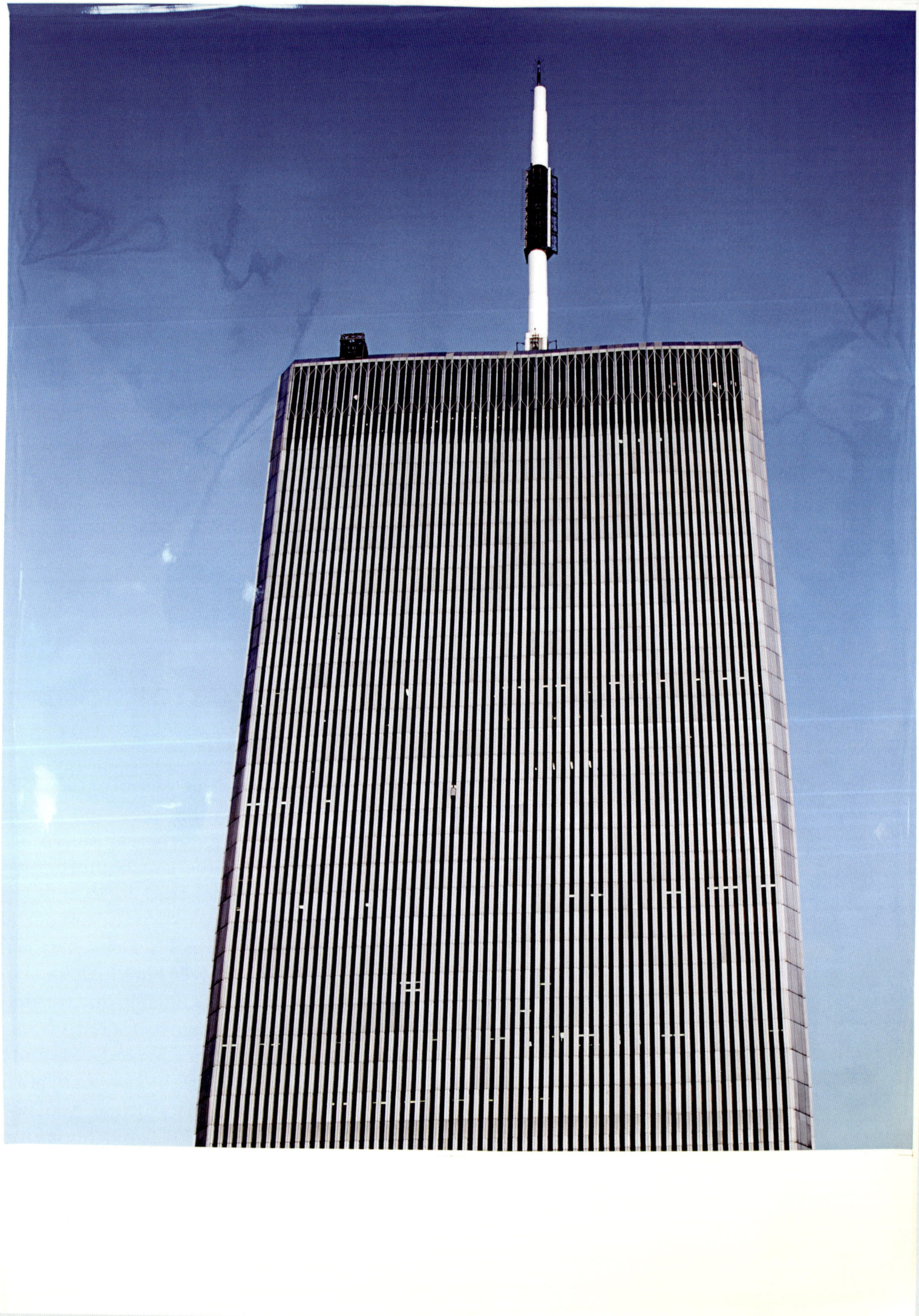

**Shown by**
Massimo De Carlo D8
Greene Naftali B10
Tomio Koyama Gallery B1
Galerie Meyer Kainer F2
Galerie Perrotin F3

**Biography**
Born 1970/1971/1967/1967
Live in Vienna

Gelitin comprises four artists: Wolfgang Gantner, Ali Janka, Florian Reither and Tobias Urban. They have presented exhibitions and performances at venues that include Austrian Cultural Forum, New York (2011), Musée d'Art Moderne de la Ville de Paris (2008), Kunsthalle St Gallen (2002) and MoMA PS1, New York (1998). Gelitin participated in the 54th, 52nd and 49th Venice Biennales (2011, 2007 and 2001), and recently featured in the group show 'Collaborations & Interventions' at CCA Andratx, Majorca (2012).

# Gelitin

Self-styled exhibitionists Gelitin create sculptural performances and installations. Their participation in 'Illuminations' at the 54th Venice Biennale (2011) saw a wood-fired furnace drip molten glass, while a variety of live performances took place on the grass outside the biennale's Arsenale. For their exhibition 'Blind Sculptures' at Greene Naftali, New York (2010), the blindfolded collaborators constructed a sculptural mash-up in front of a live audience; the resulting 'sculptures' would later be cleaved from the performance's mass of amalgamated constructions and exhibited as stand-alone works. In orchestrating their environments, Gelitin produce works under their own set of liberated contexts, while presenting the viewer with an alternative mode of engaging with their work. SC

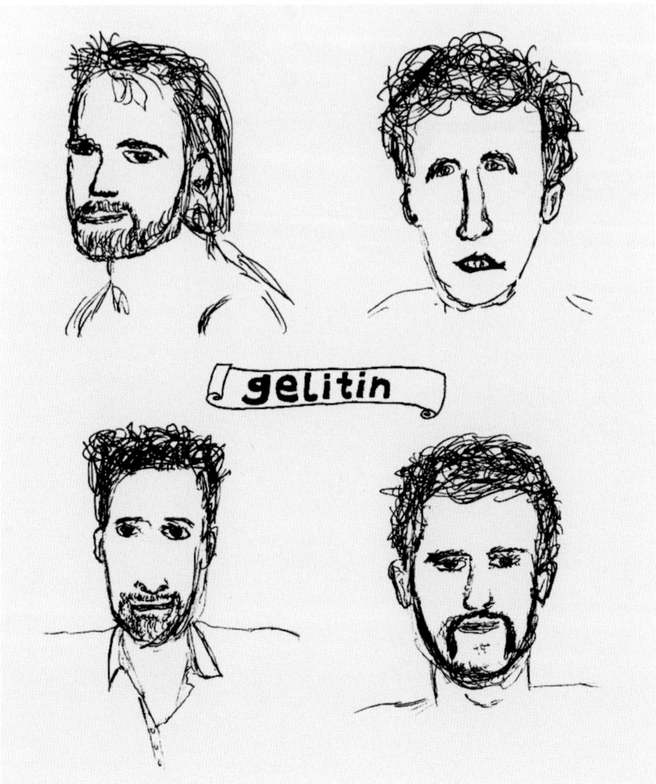

2

1
*B-Thing*
2001
C-type print
189 × 126 cm
Courtesy of Greene Naftali

2
*Untitled*
2003
Pencil on paper
30 × 21 cm
Courtesy of Greene Naftali

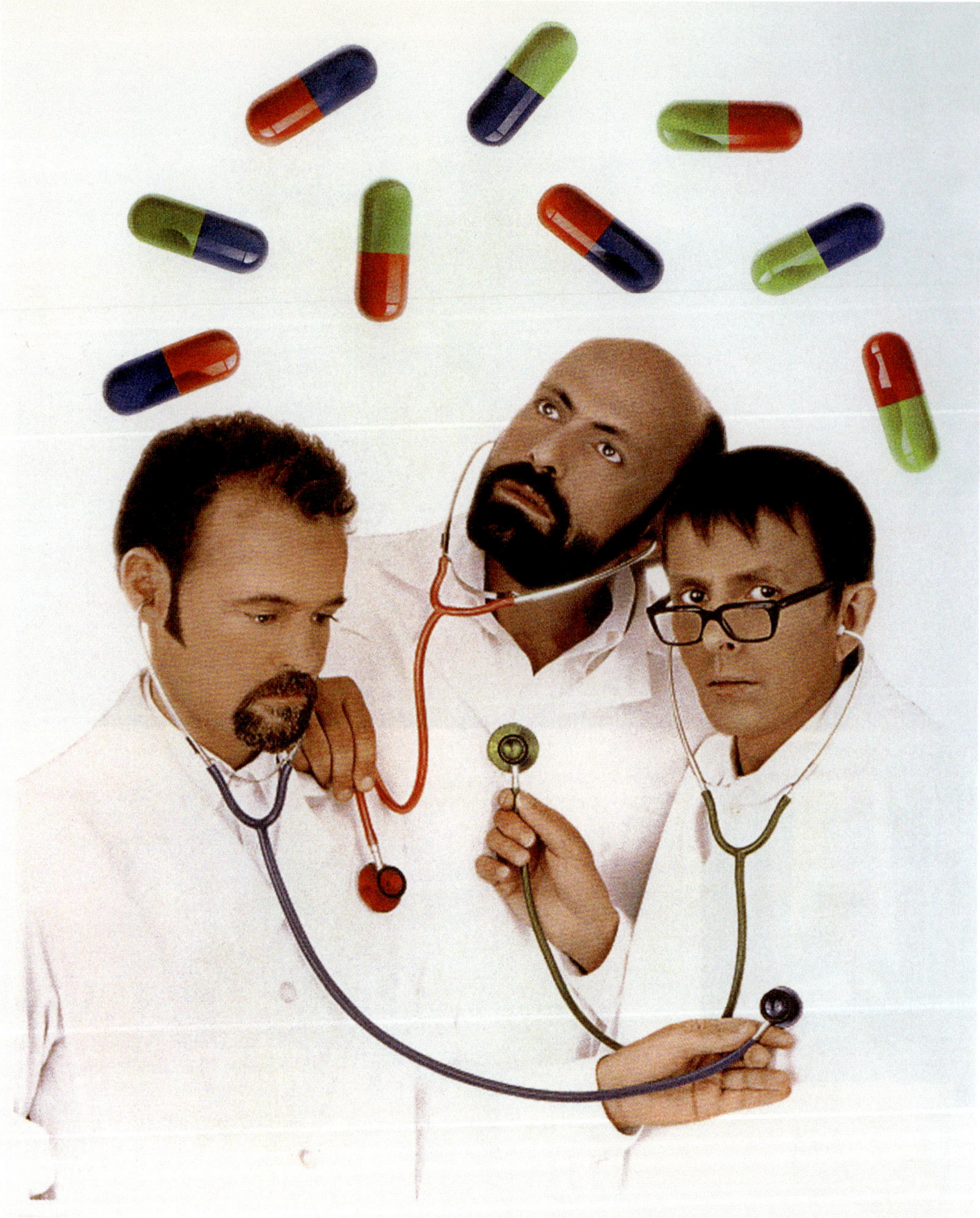

1

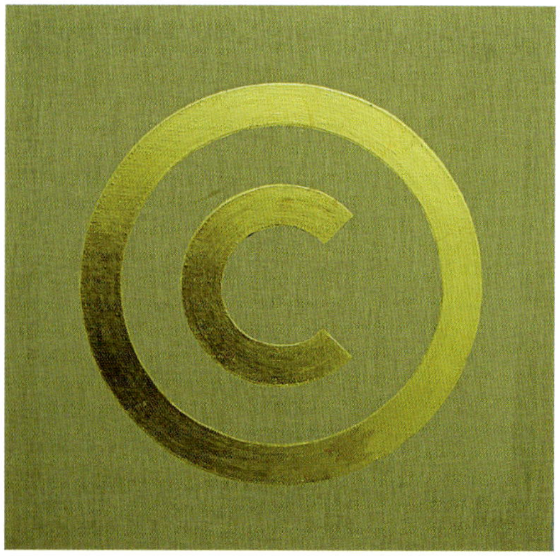

2

# General Idea

During the 1970s the collective General Idea generated an alternative art scene that surreally flouted the norms of serious cultural production. Early theatrical events, such as beauty pageants and international canasta competitions played via telephone, suspended reality from its shirt tails, while their publication *File* flagrantly aped the orthodoxy of *Life* magazine and their mascot, a coiffured poodle, grotesqued received notions of glamour. Later work, while still laced with wit, grappled with very present realities. Predicated on the ideas that the image operates as a virus and the artist as pharmacist, the sculpture *AIDS* (1989) brings Robert Indiana's *Love* (1970) down to earth with a thud. SOR

**Shown by**
Mai 36 Galerie D9
Esther Schipper A3

**Biography**
Active 1969–94

Canadian artists Felix Partz, Jorge Zontal and AA Bronson worked together as General Idea for 25 years, before the death of Partz and Zontal in 1994. Bronson continues to practise as an artist under his own name. Survey exhibitions of General Idea's work have been presented in the last decade at institutions including Musée d'Art Moderne de la Ville de Paris (2012), Art Gallery of Ontario (2012), Kunsthalle Zurich (2006), and München Kunstverein, Munich (2005).

1
*Playing Doctor*
1992
Lacquer on vinyl
225 × 150 cm
Courtesy of Esther Schipper

2
*Copyright (Blue) #3*
1987
Gold leaf on ultramarine ground on linen
53 × 53 cm
Courtesy of Esther Schipper

3
*AIDS*
1989
Lacquered metal
201 × 202 × 101 cm
Courtesy of Esther Schipper

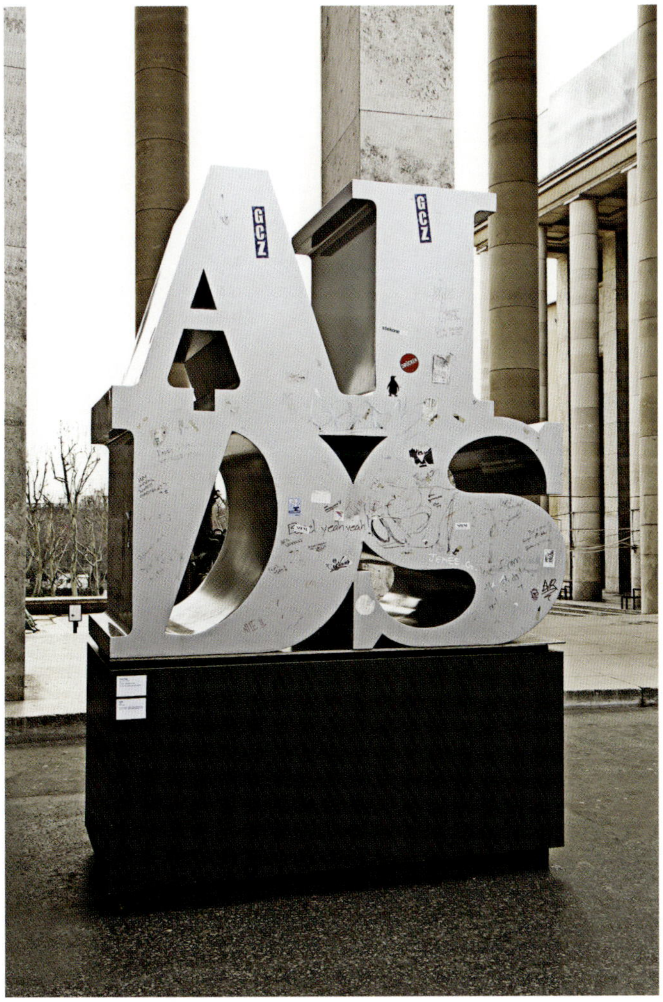


3

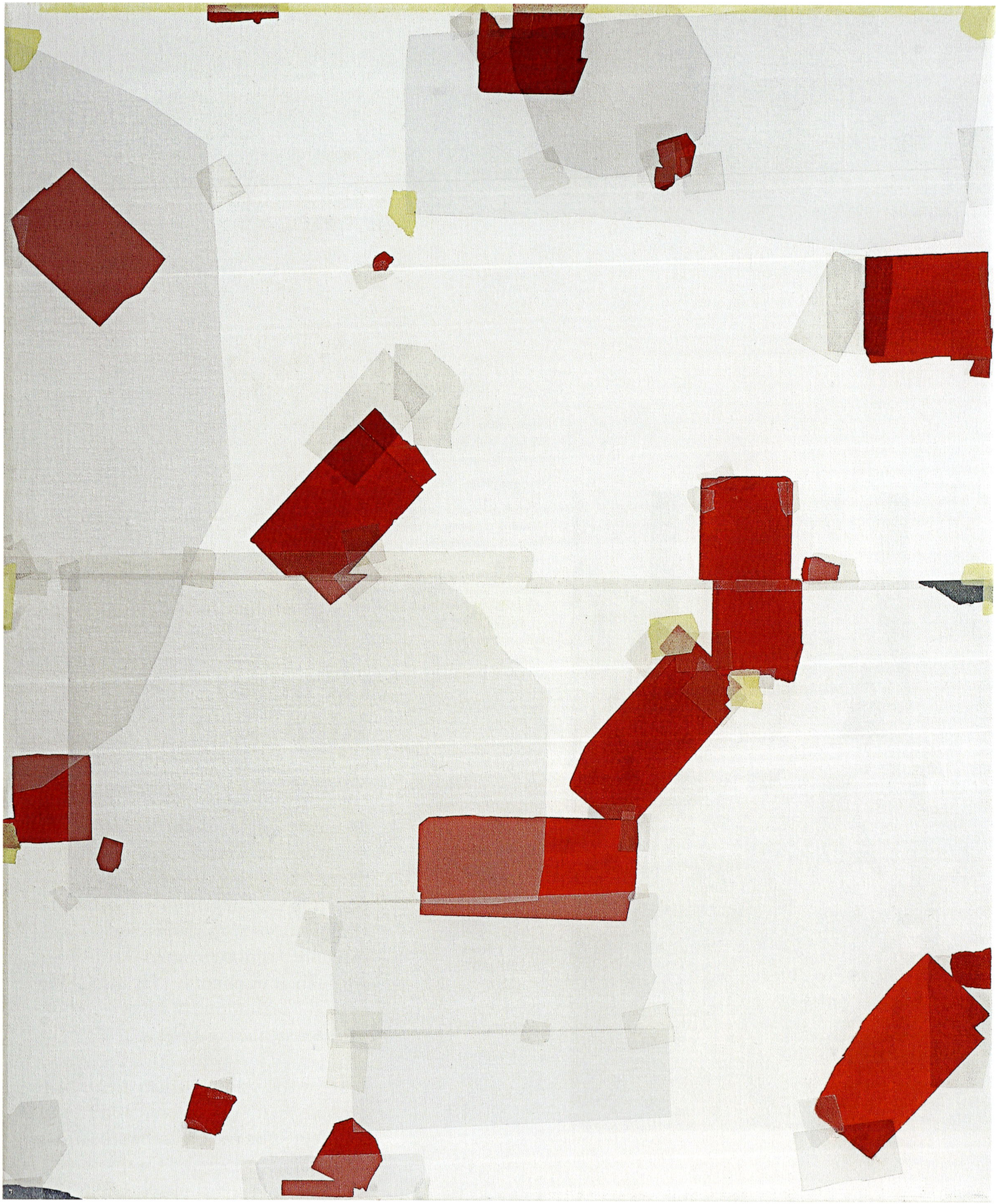

**Shown by**
Zeno X Gallery A1

**Biography**
Born 1958
Lives in Antwerp

Utrecht-born Goudzwaard has presented solo exhibitions at galleries including Cardi Black Box, Milan (2012), Stedelijk Museum, Schiedam (2011), Zeno X Gallery, Antwerp (2010 and 2007), Museum voor Moderne Kunst, Arnhem (2010), Culturgest, Lisbon (2006), and SMAK, Ghent (2005). In 2012 he was featured in group shows such as 'From a Painter's Perspective', Arti et Amicitiae, Amsterdam, and 'Roma Publications: Provisional Space', Castillo Corrales, Paris.

*Temporary Order*
2012
Oil on canvas
60 × 50 cm
Courtesy of Zeno X Gallery

# Kees Goudzwaard

Kees Goudzwaard's painting *Temporary Order* (2012) typifies the artist's deliberate, repetitive approach to re-presentation. Goodzwaard composes geometric collages of cut paper, foil or acetate quadrilaterals, which he then reproduces in oil paint on canvas before he destroys the collage. Strips and overlays of colour are rendered as carefully as the bits of tape holding the papers and films to the original plane. The result is a surface replete with tension and mysterious depth. Eschewing photographic realism, Goudzwaard engages with the history of *trompe-l'oeil* painting, but with the consummate twist of taking that aesthetic to the unexpected realm of realistic abstractions. VSR

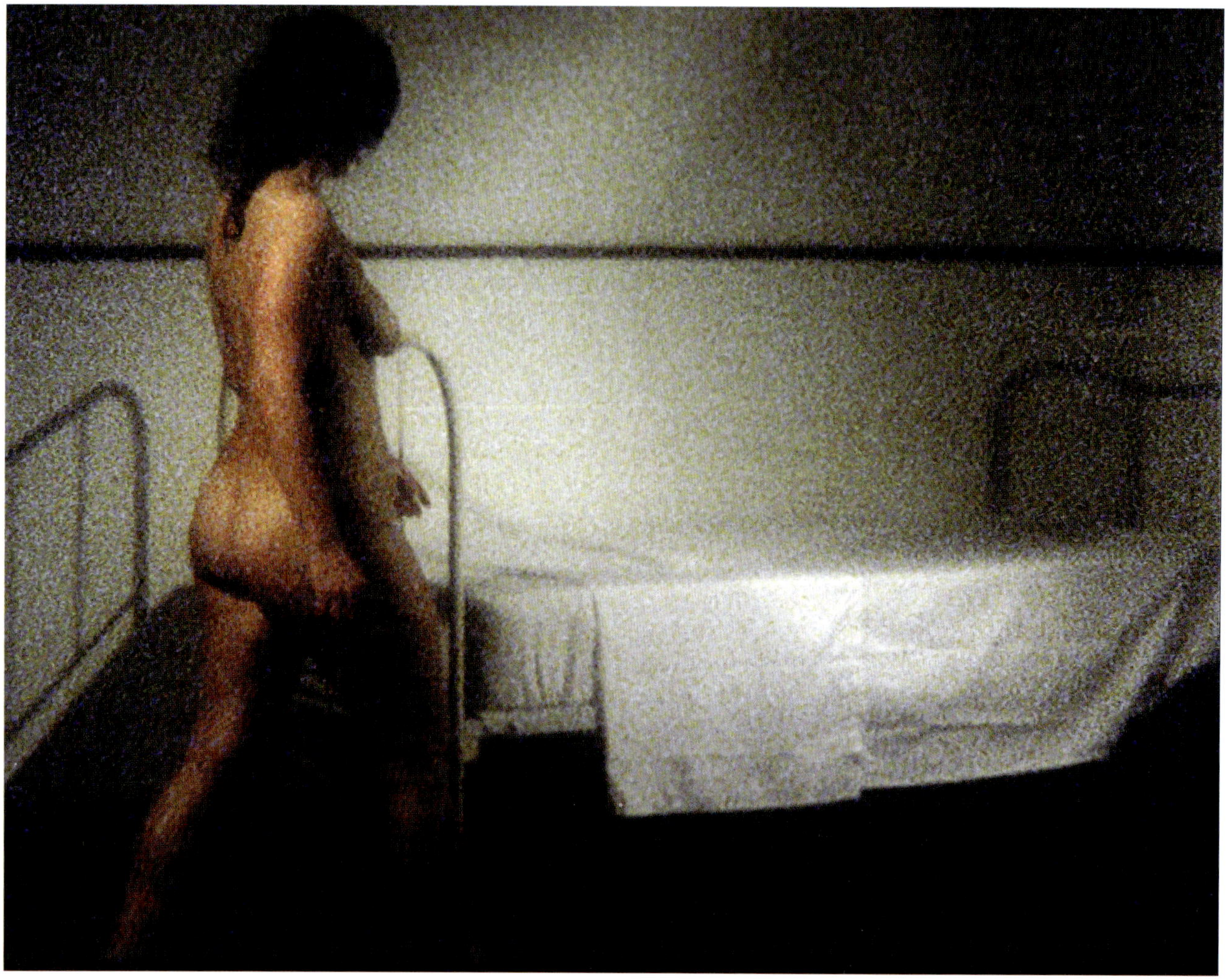

1

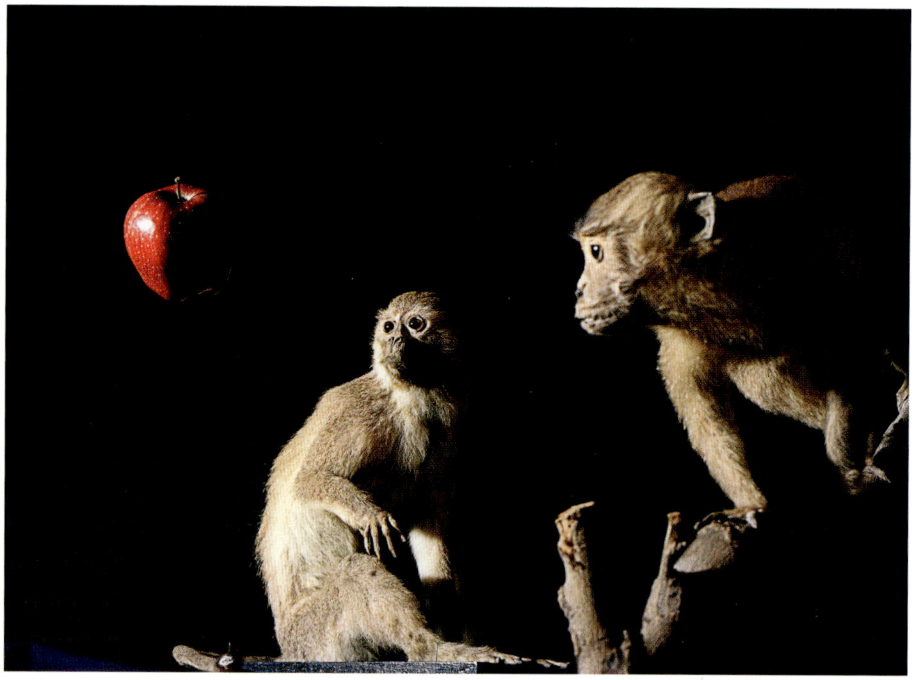

2

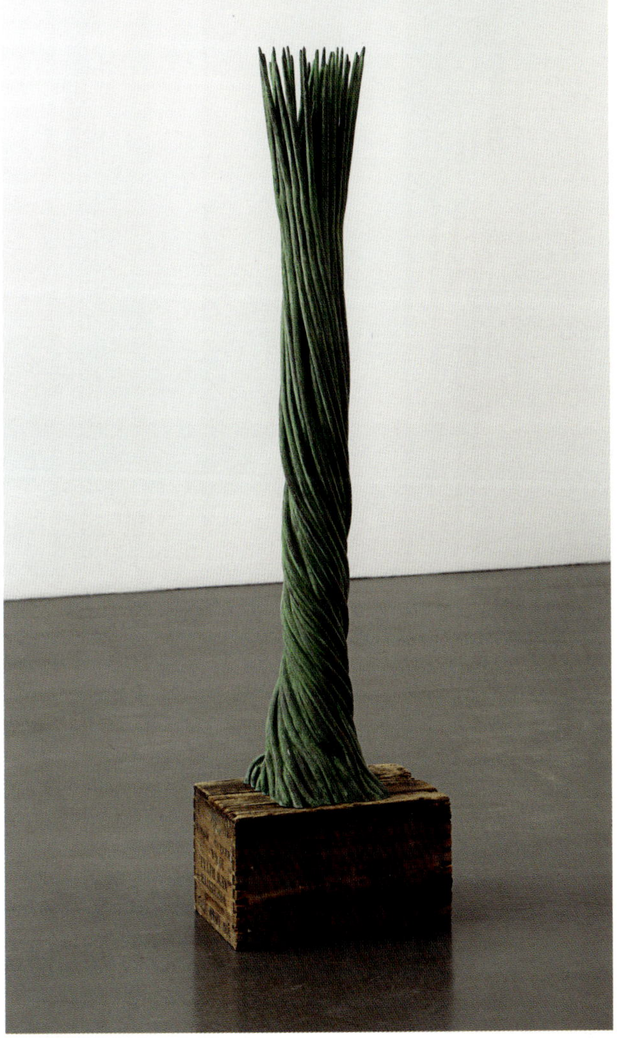

3

**Shown by**
Galeria Fortes Vilaça E8
Sies + Höke F21

**Biography**
Born 1979/1977
Live in Lisbon

Portuguese collaborators Gusmão and Paiva have presented exhibitions at venues that include Kunstnernes Hus, Oslo (2012), Kunsthalle Dusseldorf (2011), Museo Marino Marini, Florence (2011), Ikon Gallery, Birmingham (2010), CCA Wattis Institute for Contemporary Arts, San Francisco (2008), and Museu do Chiado, Lisbon (2005). They represented their country at the 53rd Venice Biennale (2009) and participated in Manifesta 7 in Trentino (2008).

1
*Getting into Bed*
2011
16mm film
2 min. 47 sec.
Courtesy of Sies + Höke

2
*Newton's Monkey, Darwin's Apple*
2011
Chromogenic print
120 × 160 cm
Courtesy of Sies + Höke

3
*Spaghetti Tornado*
2011
Patinated bronze and wooden box
120 × 22 × 22 cm
Courtesy of Sies + Höke

# João Maria Gusmão & Pedro Paiva

The 16mm silent films and photographs of João Maria Gusmão and Pedro Paiva remind us that cameras, originally developed and used by scientists, have long permitted insight into magical corners of the world otherwise unavailable to the human eye. Their film *Those Animals that, at a Distance, Resemble Flies* (2012) captures in slow motion the beating of a bee's wings. Gusmão and Paiva's work harks back to a time in which scientific, philosophical and artistic strands of intellectual endeavour were inseparable. Even an action as supposedly simple as *Getting into Bed* (2011) is an opportunity for a filmic meditation on perception and dreamy metaphor. JG

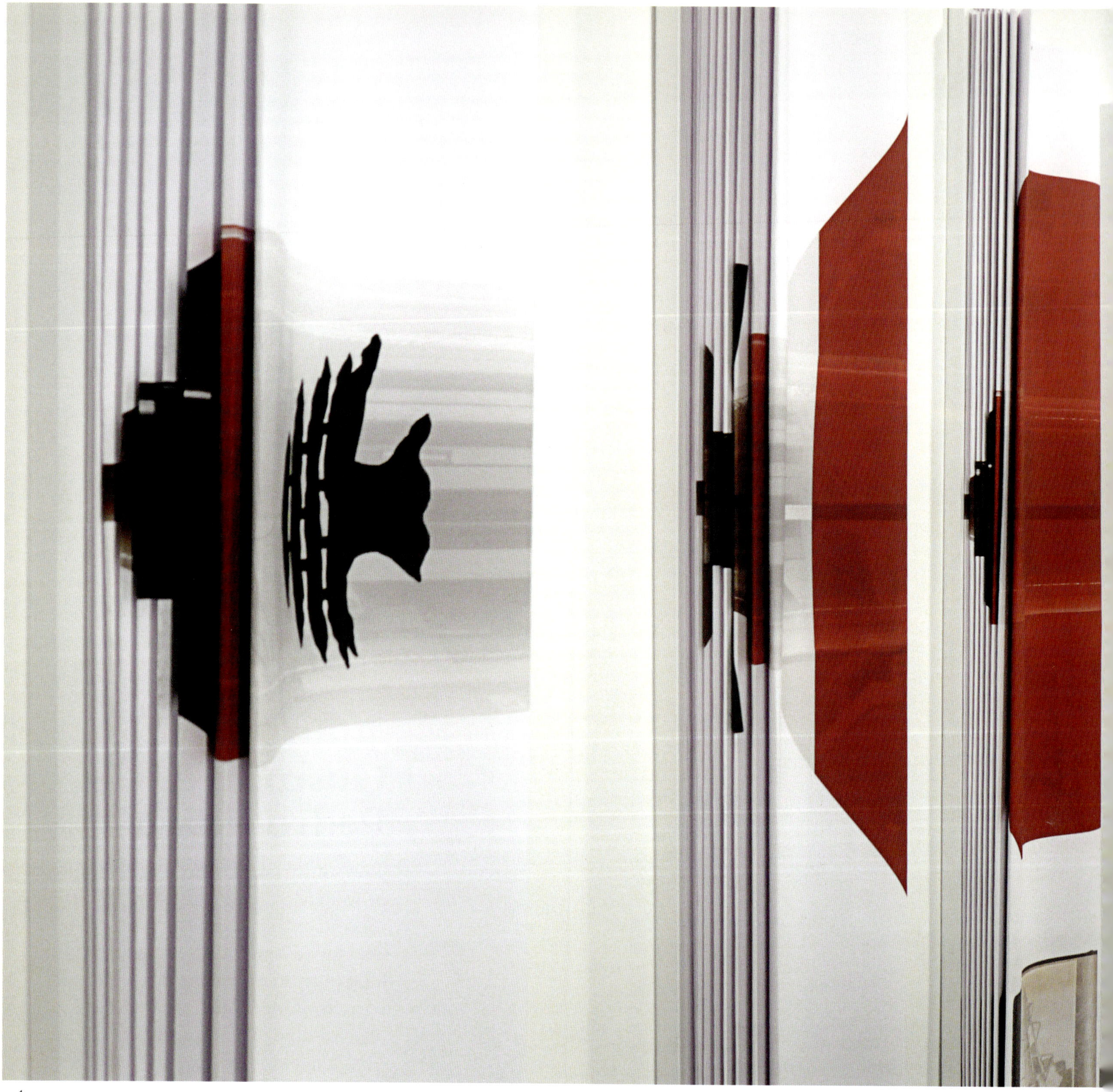

1

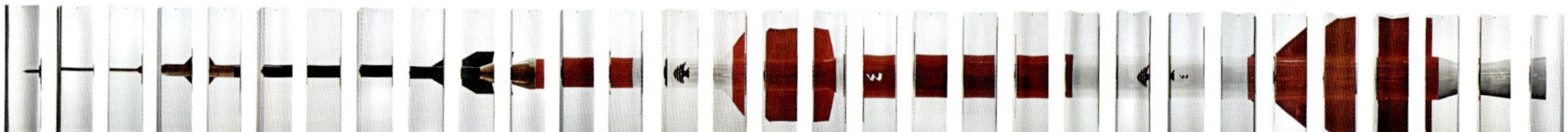

2

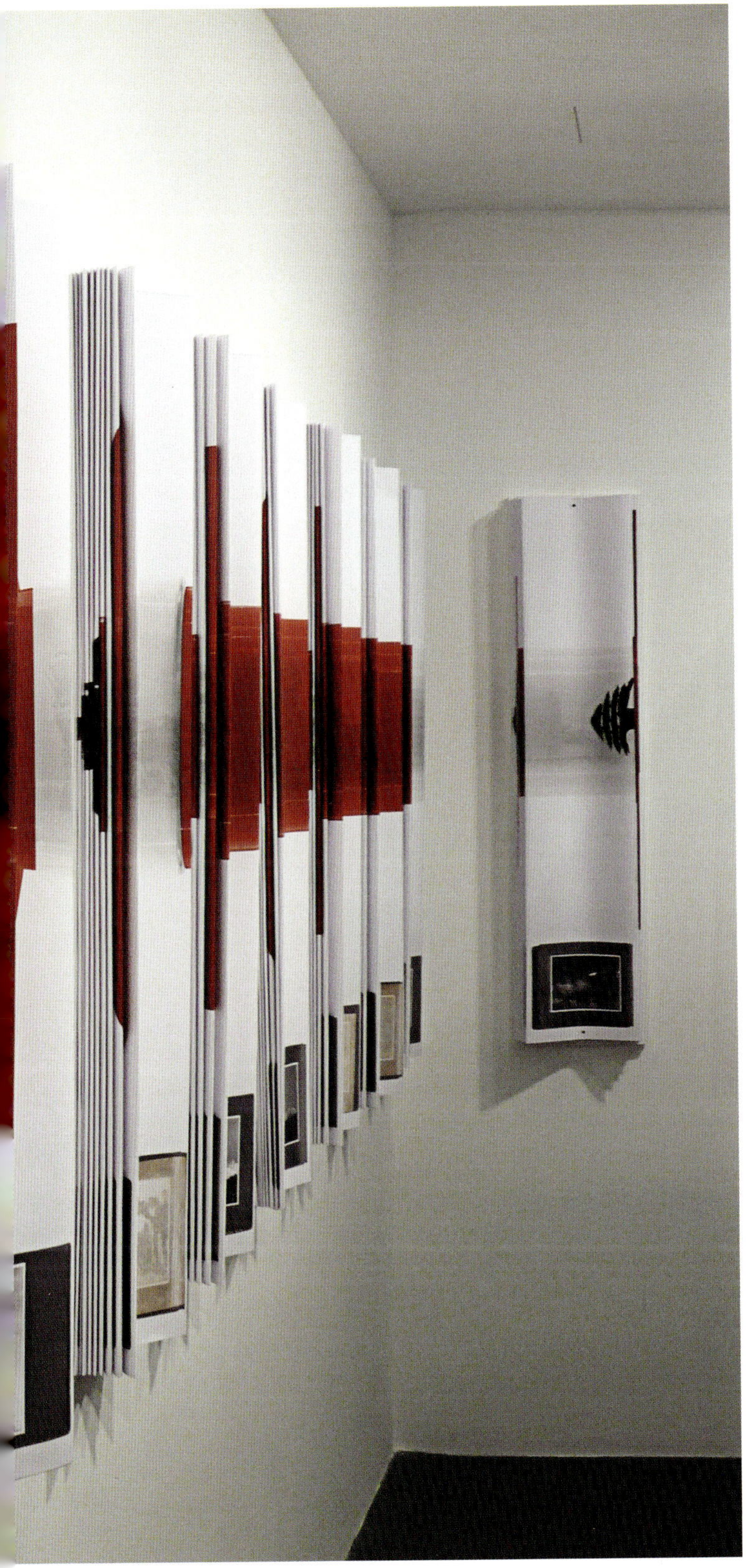

**Shown by**
The Third Line H10

**Biography**
Born 1969
Live in Beirut

Lebanese artists Hadjithomas and Joreige have been the subject of solo shows at venues including The Third Line, Dubai (2012), Beirut Exhibition Centre, Lebanon (2012), Gasworks, London (2010), Centre de la Photographie de Genève, Geneva (2009), and Musée d'Art Moderne de la Ville de Paris (2008–9). Their work featured in the 11th Biennale de Lyon (2011) and the Sharjah Biennial (2009), and is part of collections that include Centre Pompidou, Paris.

1
*The President's Album*
(detail)
2011
32 digital prints, folded and mounted on wood
120 × 800 × 10 cm
Courtesy of The Third Line

2
*The President's Album*
2011
32 digital prints, folded and mounted on wood
120 × 800 × 10 cm
Courtesy of The Third Line

# Joana Hadjithomas & Khalil Joreige

Joana Hadjithomas and Khalil Joreige use found footage and photographs to probe Lebanon's past while raising questions about collective mnemonic practices and post-conflict amnesia, the links between Cold War models of 'Arab modernity' and today's global order, the archive and the document. *The President's Album* (2011) comprises 32 copies of a monumental photograph, doubled over into rolling folds. Each part of the eight-metre-long sequence reveals one fragment of a photograph showing the 1963 launch of Cedar IV, a rocket created as part of an early Lebanese space programme. Here, as in their broader body of work begun in the early 2000s, the collaborative duo emphasize that this is less a nostalgic grasping at the past than it is an attempt, in the words of Hadjithomas, to 're-enact the process in the present'. SNS

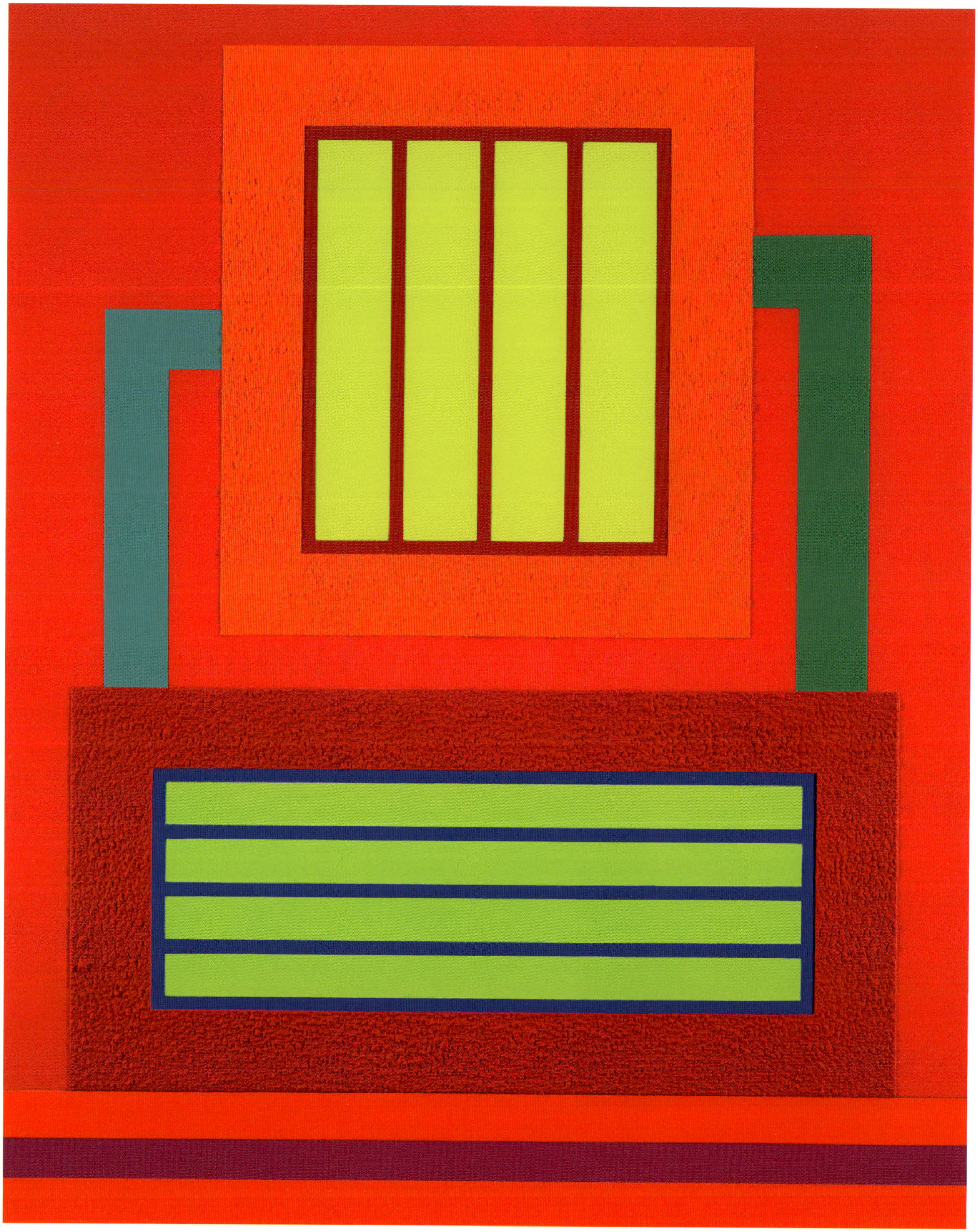

1

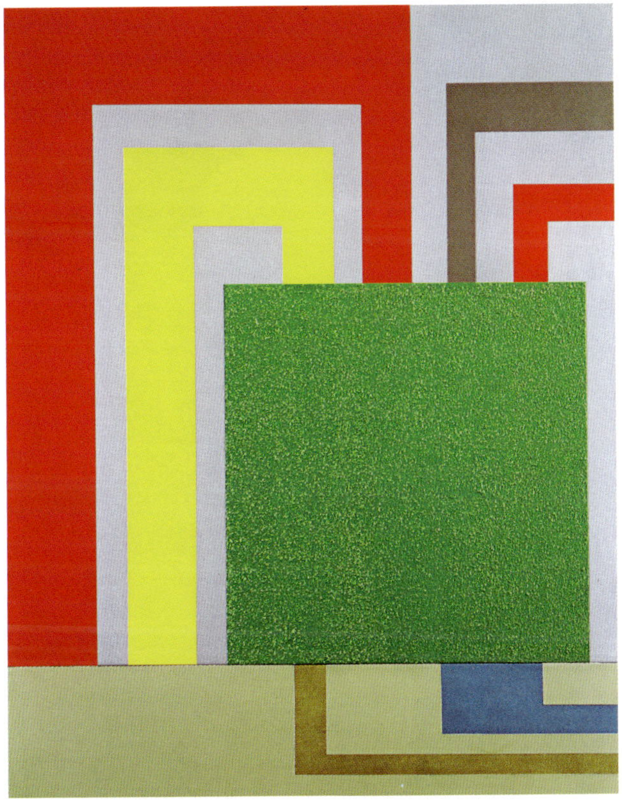

2

**Shown by**
Waddington Custot
Galleries G12

**Biography**
Born 1953
Lives in New York

New York-born Halley has presented solo exhibitions at institutions including Museum Folkwang, Essen (1998), MoMA, New York (1997), Museo Nacional Centro de Arte Reina Sofía, Madrid (1992), and the Institute of Contemporary Arts, London (1989). He recently presented site-specific installations at Disjecta Interdisciplinary Art Center, Portland (2012), and the 54th Venice Biennale (2011). His work is part of collections including: MoMA, New York; the Tate collection, UK; and Solomon R. Guggenheim Museum, New York.

1
*Delusion*
2012
Acrylic and Roll-a-Tex on canvas
174 × 137 cm
Courtesy of Waddington Custot Galleries

2
*Quick Place*
2004
Acrylic, pearlescent and metallic acrylic and Roll-a-Tex on canvas
183 × 141 cm
Courtesy of Waddington Custot Galleries

# Peter Halley

For three decades Peter Halley's geometric canvases have rigorously, radiantly compounded worldly content and autonomous abstraction. His boxy forms and duct-like lines—devoted to the right angle, flawlessly blocked with hot-to-fluorescent and variably textured colour—he calls 'cells', 'conduits', 'prisons' and 'windows', speaking to both the geometricized urban experience and, relatedly, societal structures of control. A knowingly rationalized, modular method (Halley has compared it to an architect's practice), it's one that scrambles codes; a painting like *Delusion* (2012), all glowing container frames and chromatic conduits, clarifies that aesthetic potency and mordant irony aren't mutually exclusive either. Recent generations, raptly corrupting the aseptic spaces of Modernism, owe Halley a manifest debt. MH

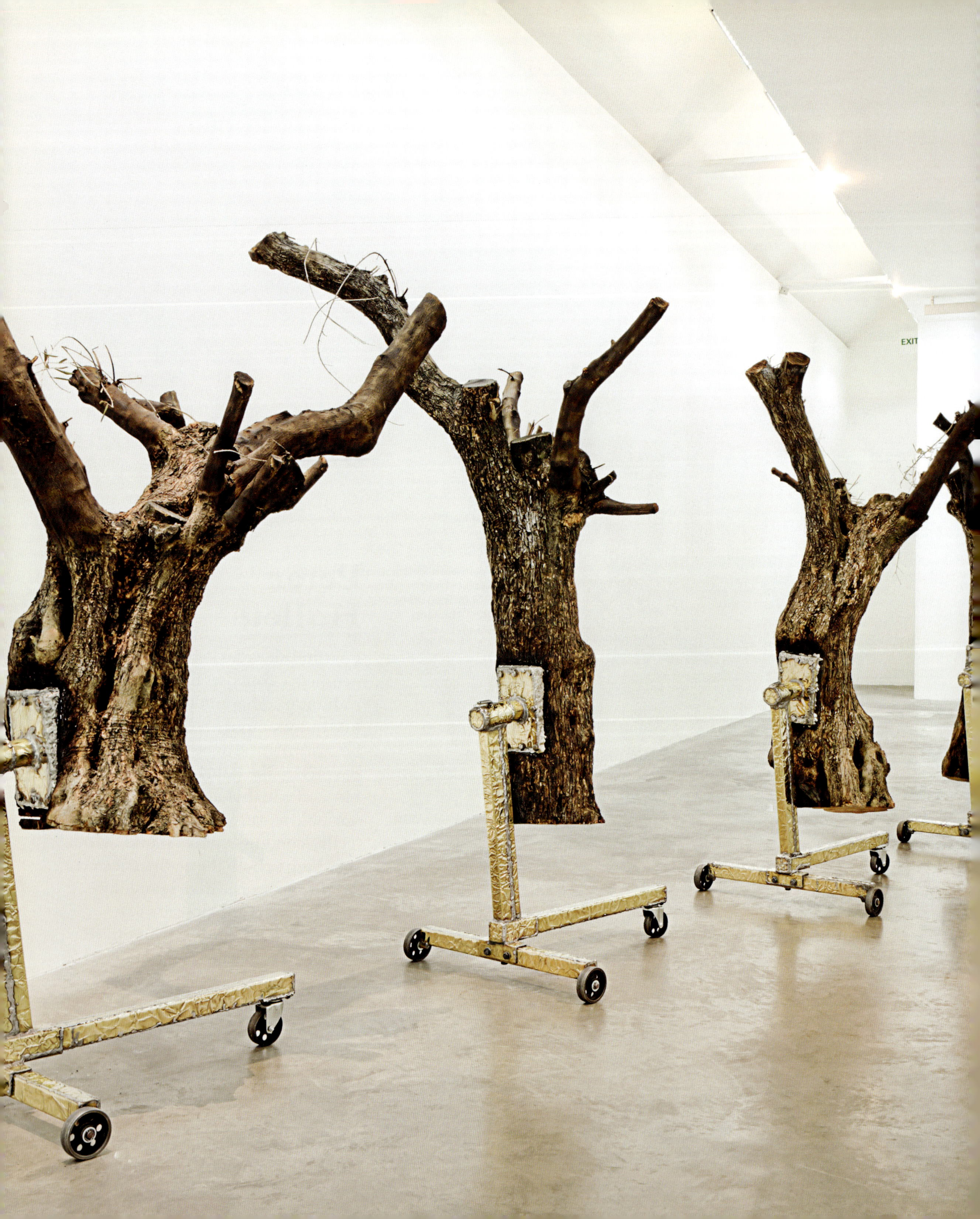
EXIT

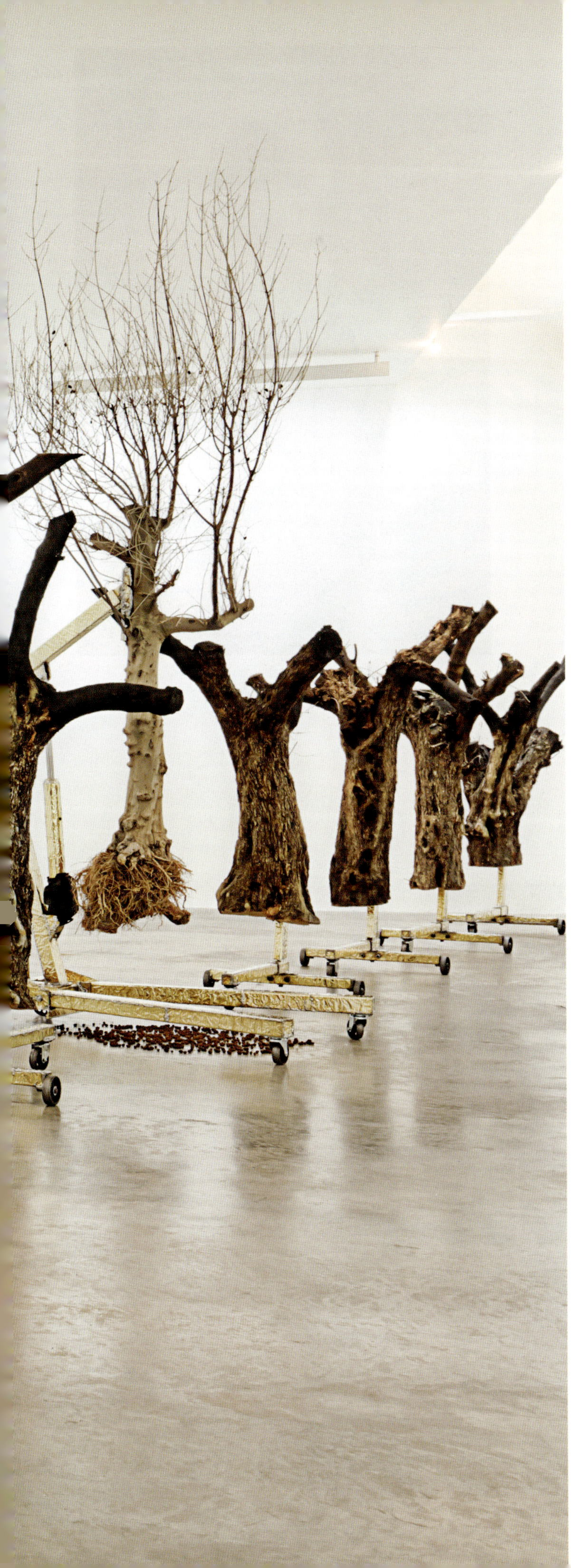

**Shown by**
Tanya Bonakdar Gallery
A5
Kerlin Gallery E17

**Biography**
Born 1963
Lives in London

Belfast-born Hapaska has presented solo shows at galleries such as Andréhn-Schiptjenko, Stockholm (2012), Kerlin Gallery, Dublin (2011 and 2003–4), Tanya Bonakdar Gallery, New York (2010, 2007 and 2002), Glasgow Sculpture Studios (2009), Camden Arts Centre, London (2007), and the Institute of Contemporary Arts, London (1995). She received the Paul Hamlyn Award 2003, represented Ireland at the 49th Venice Biennale (2001) and participated in Documenta 10, Kassel (1997).

*A Great Miracle Needs to Happen There*
2011
Olive trees, lead-free solder, brass, steel and cast iron (9 elements)
Dimensions variable
Courtesy of Kerlin Gallery

# Siobhán Hapaska

Siobhán Hapaska's practice considers the collision of technology and ritual, as evidenced by early works such as the life-size wax *St Christopher* (1995), with legs amputated at the knee, or *Delirious* (1996), a gleaming fibreglass futuristic being trapped in medieval-style stocks. *A Great Miracle Needs to Happen There* (2011) is a vast Chanukah menorah composed of eight scorched and limbless olive trees clamped in place by industrial engine stands, surrounding an intact olive tree with root ball. The persistence of articles of faith in the face of technological advance recurs in *Footings* (2011), 25 cubes cast from concrete test moulds (used in foundations of high-rise buildings), each with a well of olive oil and a flaming votive taper. SL

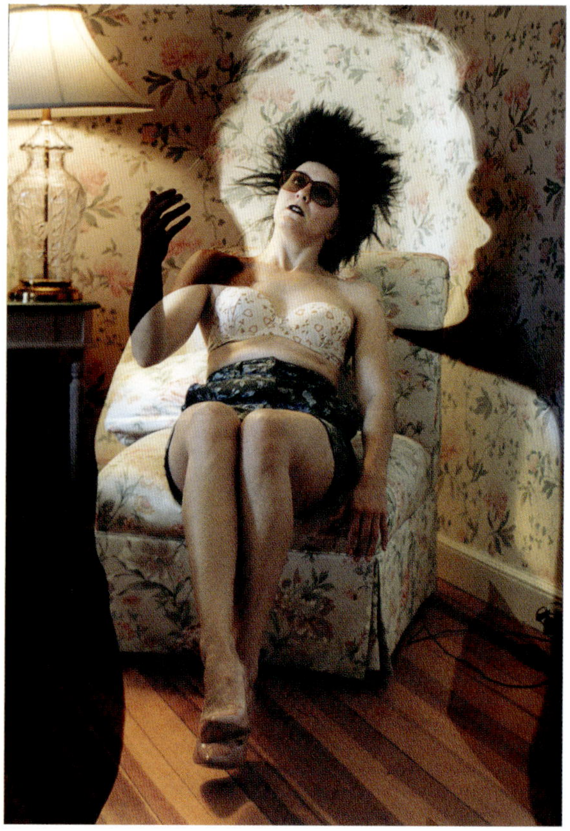

1

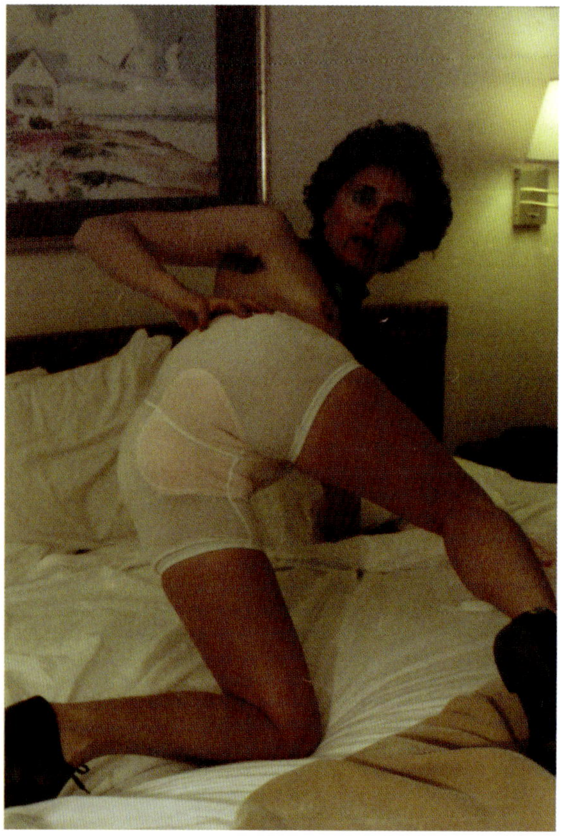

2

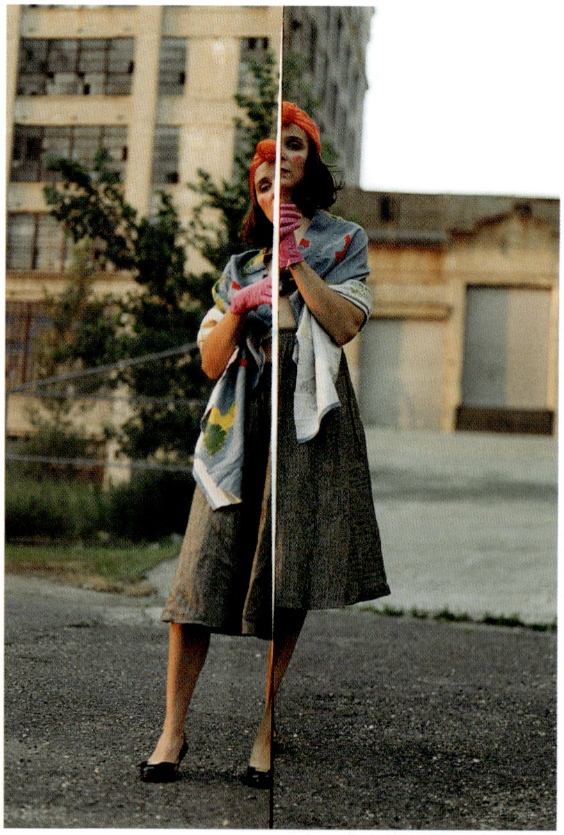

3

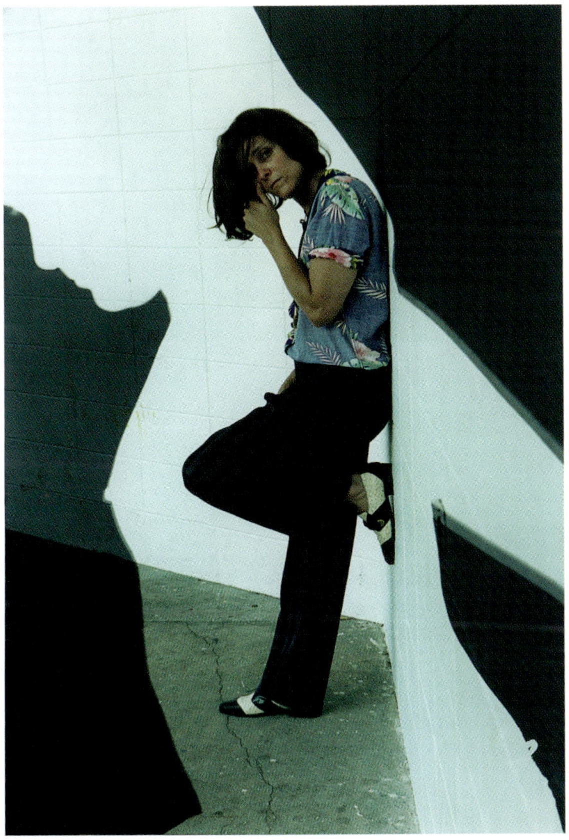

4

**Shown by**
Reena Spaulings B6

**Biography**
Born 1977
Lives in New York

Texas-born Hardy has shown solo exhibitions at Galerie Sonja Junkers, Munich (2010), Broome Social Club/ Hard Hat, Geneva (2010), and Reena Spaulings Fine Art, New York (2009). She has presented performances at venues that include the Serpentine Gallery, London (2008), and Tate Modern, London (2007), and her work has recently featured in group shows such as 'Greater New York', MoMA PS1, New York (2010), and 'Reflections on the Electric Mirror: New Feminist Video', Brooklyn Museum, New York (2009–10).

1, 2, 3, 4
*31, 6, 25, 17*
From the series 'Positions'
2009–10
C-type prints
Each 76 × 51 cm
Courtesy of Reena Spaulings

# K8 Hardy

LTTR describes itself as 'a feminist genderqueer artist collective with a flexible project oriented practice'. K8 Hardy, one of its founding members, still holds true to that tenet of flexibility. She has presented collaborative performances with musicians such as *Bare Life* (2007), a choreographic response to Giorgio Agamben. She has designed clothes and staged a fashion show with a catwalk designed by Oscar Tuazon (*Untitled Runway Show*, 2012). Hardy insists that, despite her interest in second-wave Feminism, neither her work nor the ideas she's energized by are polemical. In her 'Positions Series' (2009–ongoing), photographs of herself occupying diverse gender roles are more about clearing space and finding new freedoms than about deconstructing already threadbare ideas of identity. JG

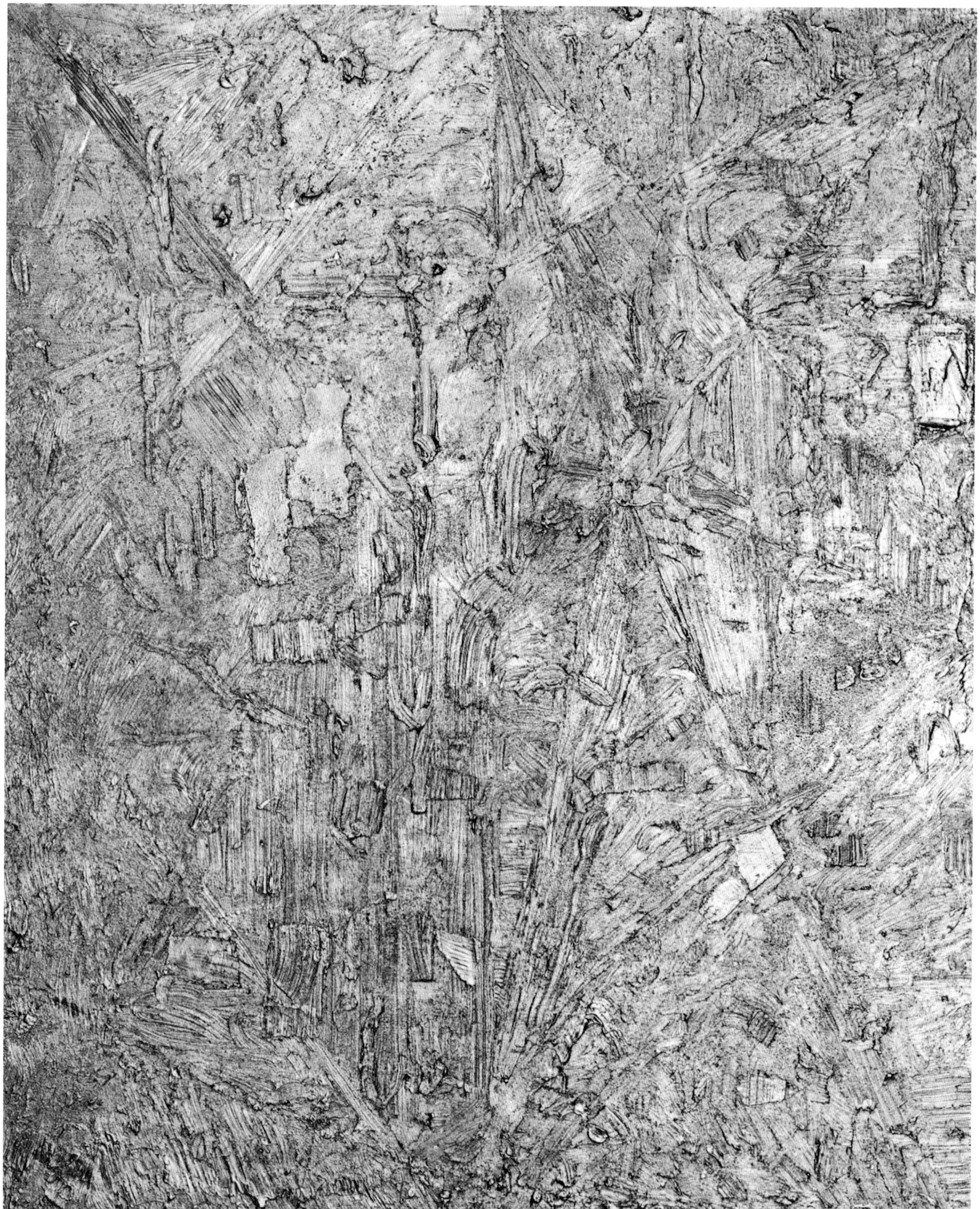

1

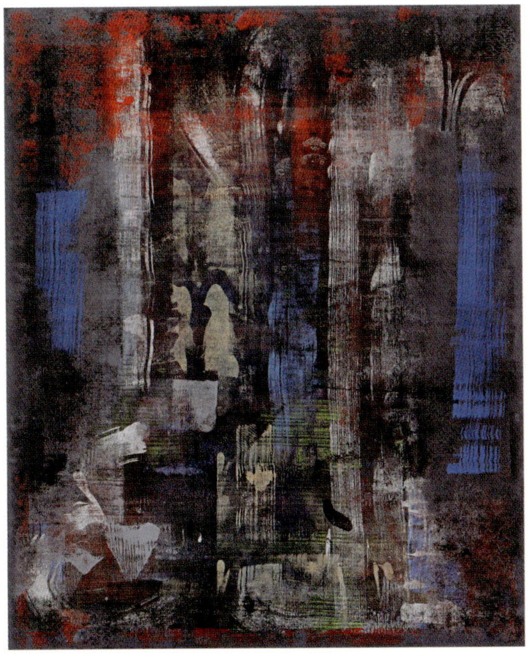

3

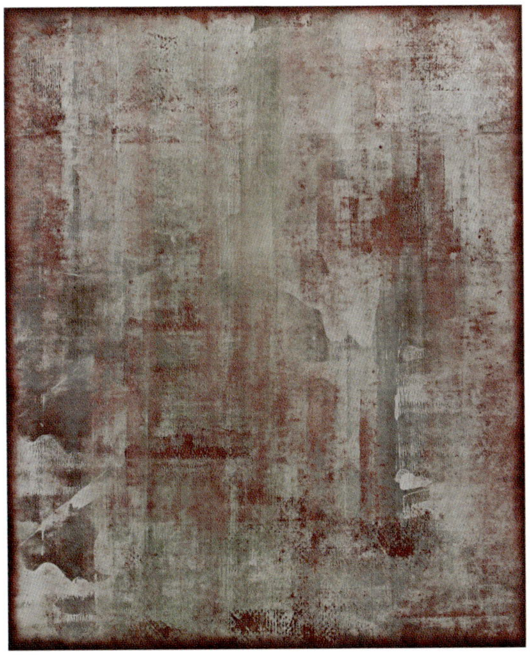

2

**Shown by**
T293 E16

**Biography**
Born 1984
Lives in Chicago

Minneapolis-born Henderson has presented solo shows at venues that include T293, Naples (2011), Museum of Contemporary Art, Chicago (2011), and Golden Gallery, Chicago (2011). His group exhibitions in 2012 include 'Richard Artschwager/Gaylen Gerber/John Henderson', Golden Gallery, New York, 'Phantom Limb: Approaches to Painting Today', Museum of Contemporary Art, Chicago, 'The Mystery Trend', Wallspace, New York, and 'Idea is the Object', D'Amelio Gallery, New York.

1
*Cast*
2012
Brass
102 × 82 × 4 cm
Courtesy of T293

2
*Untitled Painting*
2011
Oil on canvas
51 × 41 cm
Courtesy of T293

3
*Untitled Painting*
2012
Oil on canvas
51 × 41 cm
Courtesy of T293

# John Henderson

John Henderson's work critiques painting, referring to the canon of 20th-century painting, and Abstract Expressionism in particular. Henderson uses his studio as the backdrop for a series of performances that deconstruct the theatricality associated with Abstract Expressionism as a movement. In *Cleanings* (2010) he vigorously mopped his studio; the work made reference to Janine Antoni's *Loving Care* (1992), which in turn critiqued the cult of personality around Jackson Pollock. Henderson has also created a series of *trompe-l'oeil* casts, which look like and have the dimensions of paintings (each titled *Cast*). Henderson's actual canvases self-consciously appropriate the visual iconography of canonical painting, but they also reveal Henderson's own inventive skills as a painter. KK

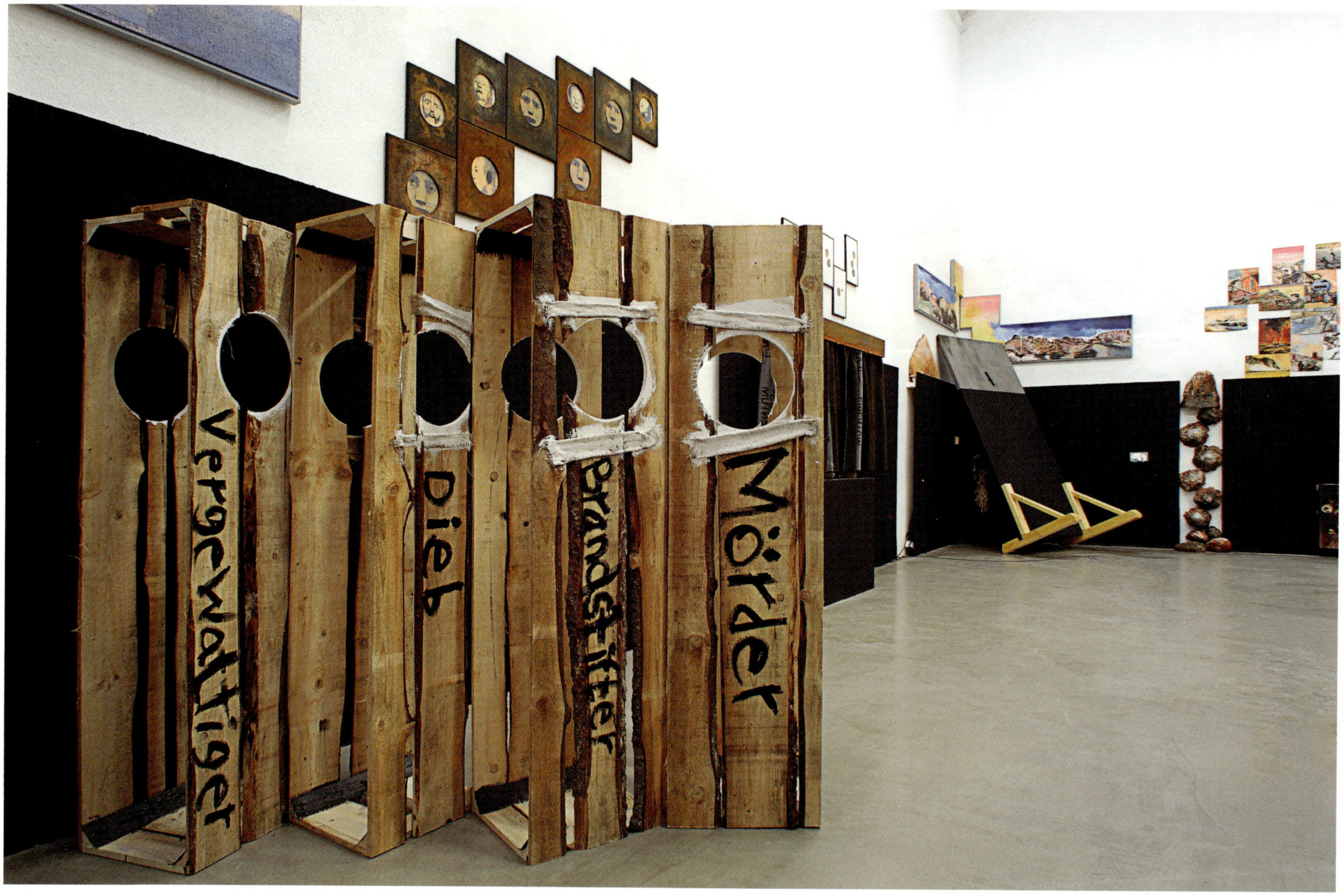


1

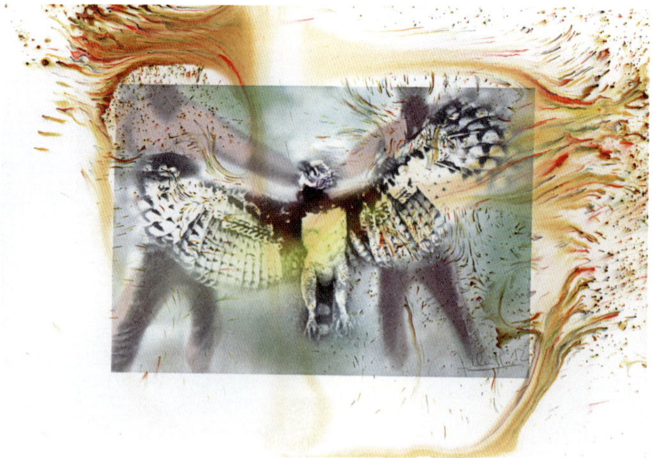

2

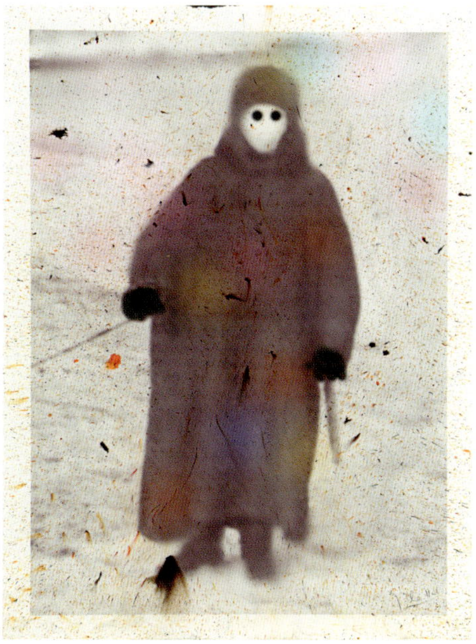

4

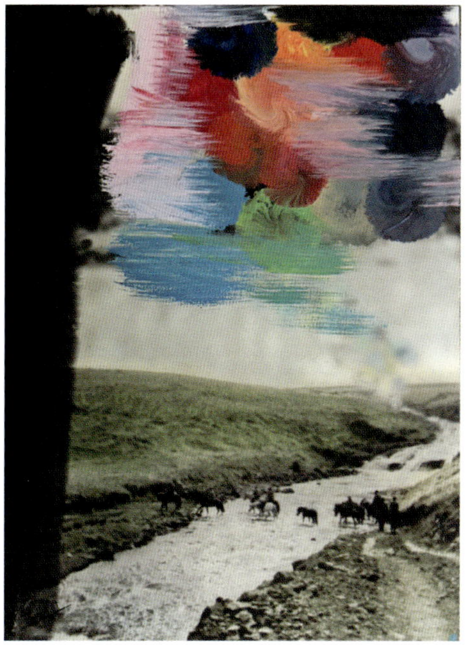

3

**Shown by**
Galerie Eigen + Art G4

**Biography**
Born 1965
Lives in Leipzig

German-born Herold has been the subject of solo exhibitions at venues that include Galerie Eigen + Art, Berlin (2011), Mecklenburgisches Staatstheater, Schwerin (2009), and the National Museum of Afghanistan, Kabul (2006). He received the City of Wolfsburg Art Award in 2005. Recent group exhibitions include 'German Now,' Seongnam Arts Centre, South Korea (2012). 'Arkhaiologia', Centre Pasquart, Biel (2011), and the 14th Vilnius Painting Triennial, Contemporary Art Center, Vilnius (2010).

1
'The Documentary Archaeologist in the Land of Accelerated Folklore'
2009
Exhibition view
Courtesy of Galerie Eigen + Art

2
*Adler*
(Eagle)
2012
Copy on photographic paper revised with stain
21 × 30 cm
Courtesy of Galerie Eigen + Art

3
*Wolkenbrüche*
(Cloudbursts)
From the series 'Island'
2011
Digital photograph on paper revised with watercolour, stain and Chinese ink
60 x 42 cm
Courtesy of Galerie Eigen + Art

4
*Führer*
(Guide)
From the series 'Island'
2011
Digital photograph on paper revised with watercolour, stain and Chinese ink
46 × 34 cm
Courtesy of Galerie Eigen + Art

# Jörg Herold

'For my recent series, I went on a journey to Iceland.' So begins a recent statement by Jörg Herold, its solemn cadences of the archaic explorer at once conjuring and wittily denigrating the artist's work as a self-proclaimed 'documentary archaeologist'. Take the aforementioned 'Island' series (2011): if Herold's copies of ethnographic photographs gesturally over-painted with a virtual rainbow of hues evoke the hand-tinted postcards of yore, they are also considerably less prosaic. And this seems to be the point. His past travels to South-East Asia and the Caucasus have borne bodies of work (painting, installation, film) only nominally scientific. Instead, Herold uses the performance of the Western observer to plumb the darkest (and brightest) recesses of origination, place, memory, authority and longing. QL

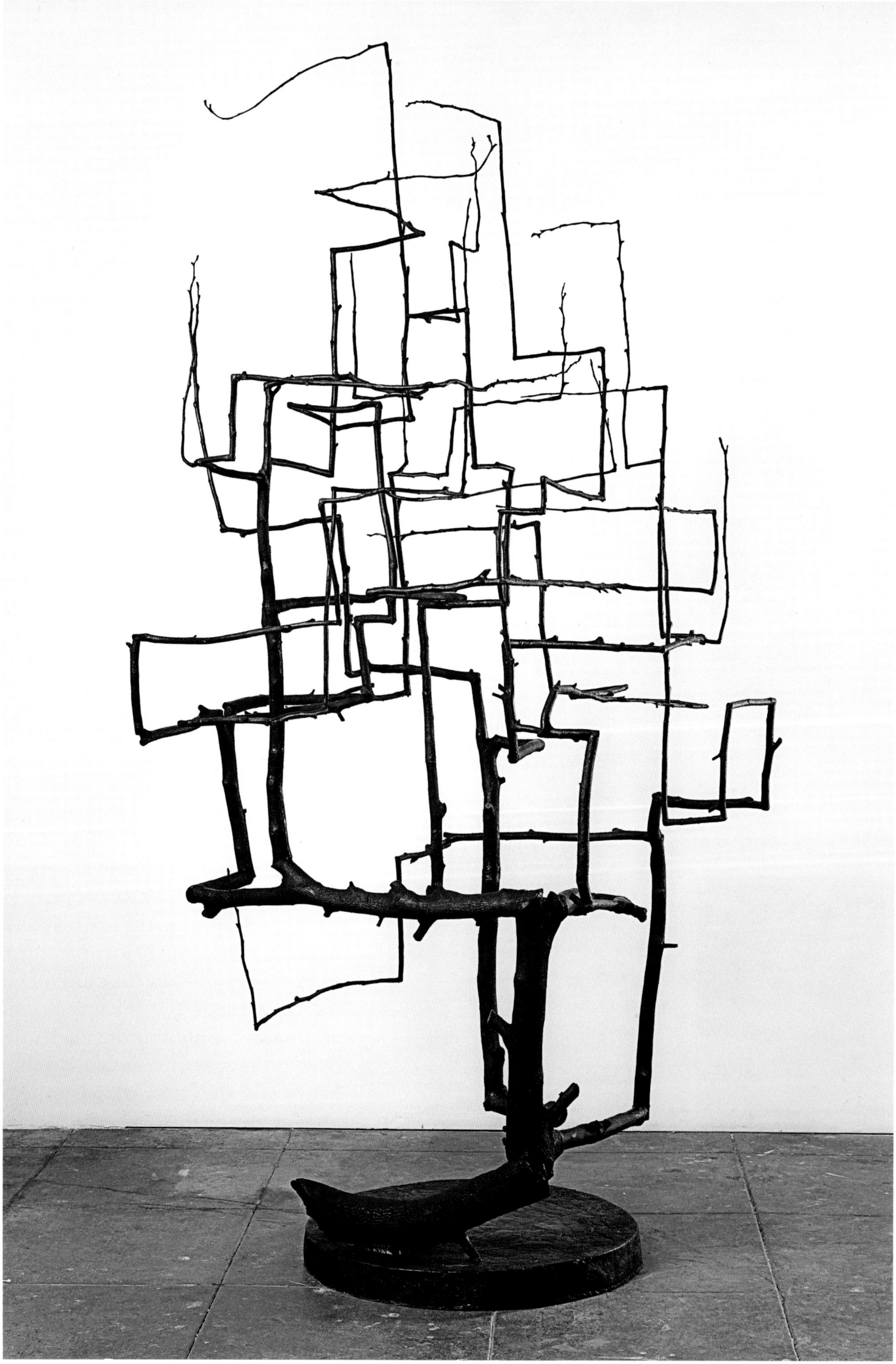

1

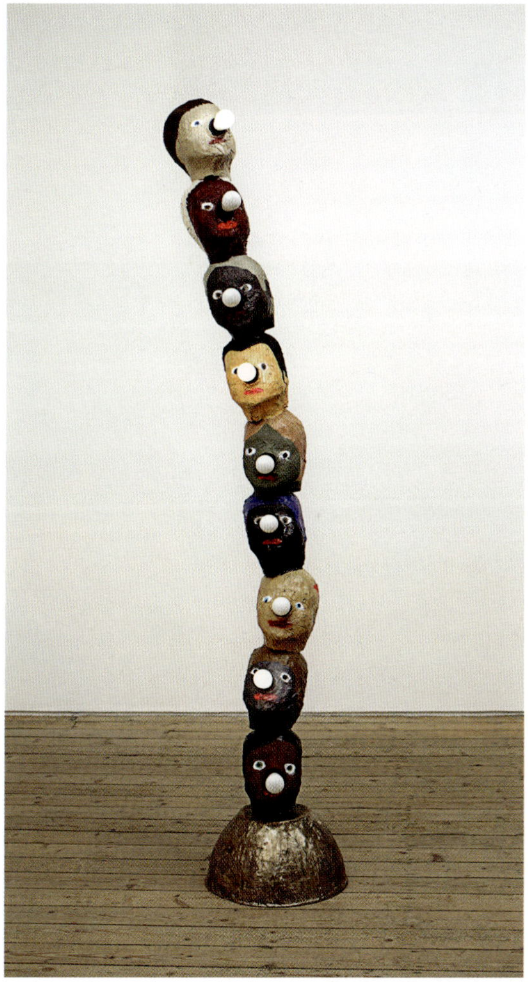

2

# Evan Holloway

**Shown by**
The Approach E21
Galleria Raucci/
Santamaria G3

**Biography**
Born 1967
Lives in Los Angeles

California-born artist Holloway has presented solo shows at galleries such as Xavier Hufkens, Brussels (2012), and The Approach, London (2009). He has contributed to group exhibitions including 'The Artist's Museum', Museum of Contemporary Art, Los Angeles (2011), and 'Moby Dick', CCA Wattis Institute for Contemporary Arts, San Francisco (2009). His work is included in the collections of the Smithsonian Hirshhorn Museum and Sculpture Garden, Washington DC, and the Whitney Museum of American Art, New York.

1
*Modified Branch*
2012
Bronze and dark patina
277 × 132 × 105 cm
Courtesy of The Approach and Xavier Hufkens

2
*Bending Stack*
2010
Bronze, paint, light bulbs and fixtures, wiring and lighting controller
157 × 30 × 30 cm
Courtesy of The Approach

Evan Holloway's sculptures present us with apparently off-the cuff imagery and 'stuff', and require that we negotiate their meaning with care and attention. His crafted composite objects entwine art-historical references with a critical view of networked consumerist society—the aim being to establish an 'analogue counter-revolution', in his words, in which physicality is valued above a digitized, virtual existence. *Modified Branch* (2012), for example, seems to demonstrate the algorithms at play in natural growth forms, while also recalling Piet Mondrian's paintings pre-*Broadway Boogie-Woogie* (1942–3). The column of heads, meanwhile, animated by flashing light bulbs for noses in *Bending Stack* (2010) may reference Minimalist vertical forms but they also challenge the impulse to elevate that which is useful, sensible or stylish. SOR

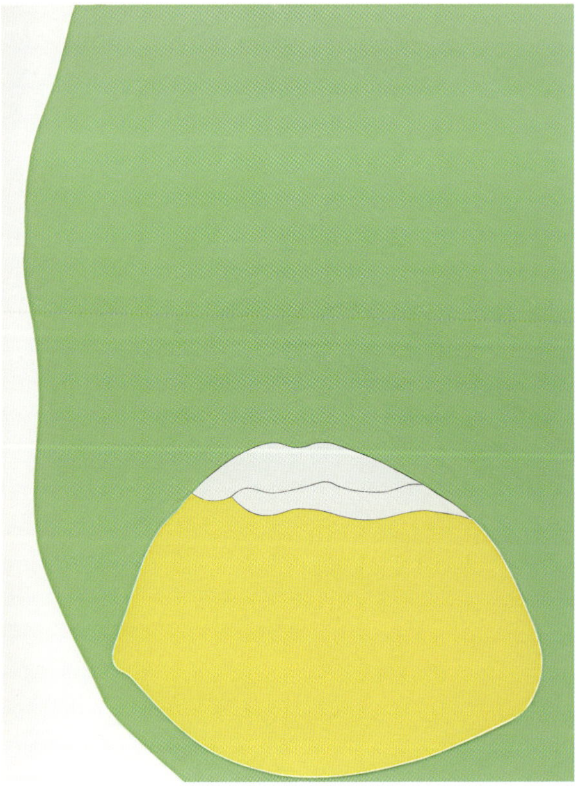

2

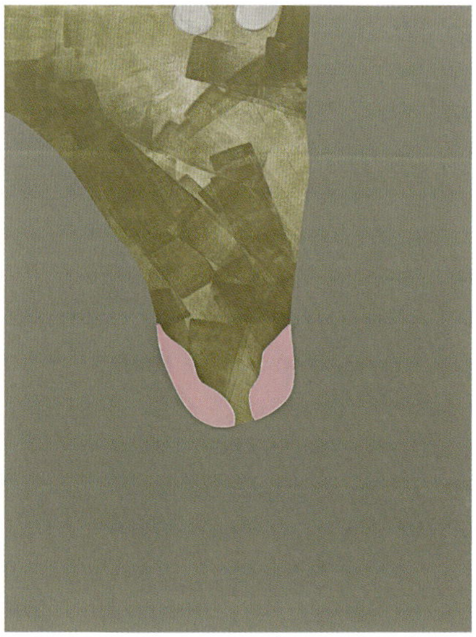

1

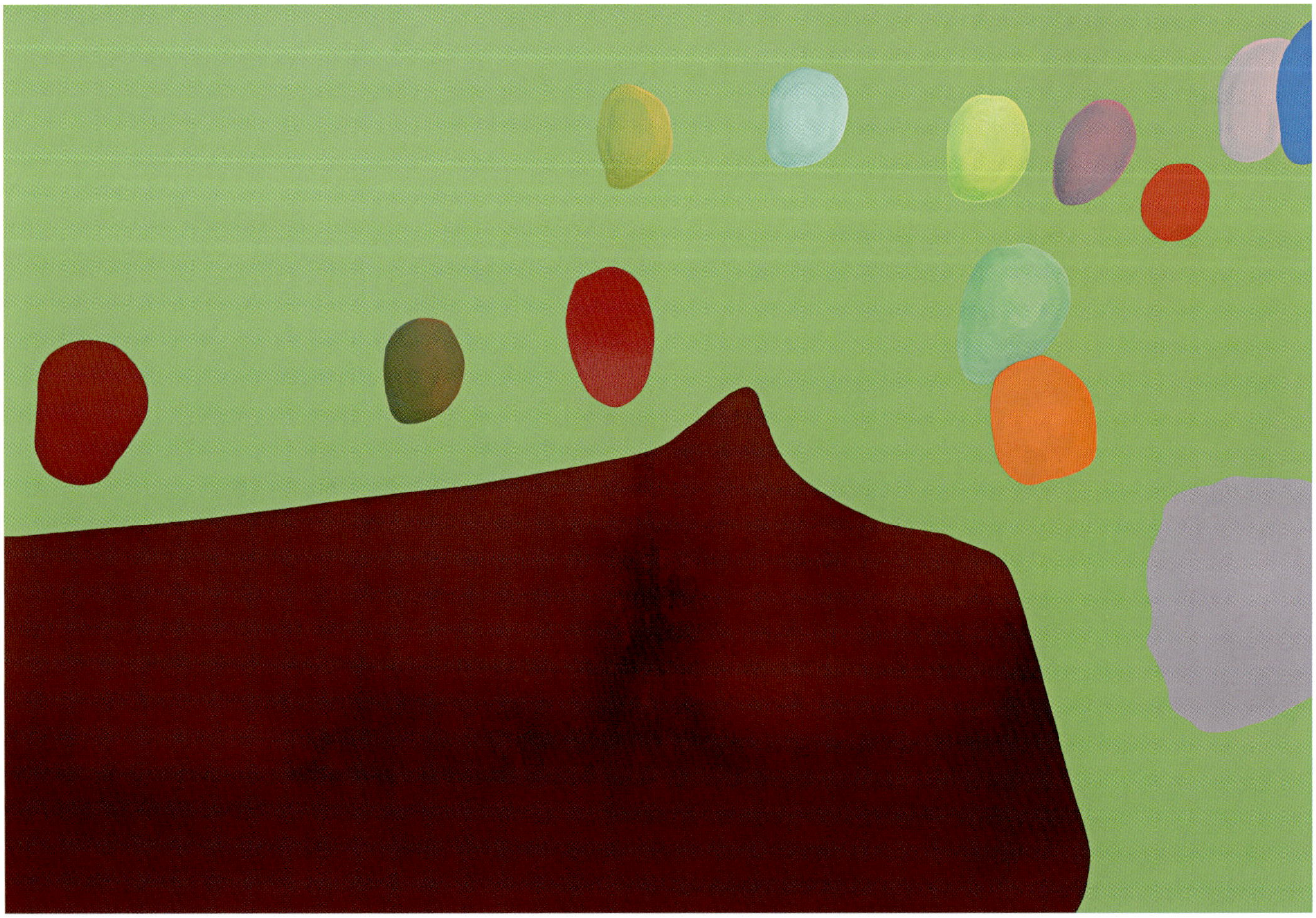

3

4

**Shown by**
Matthew Marks Gallery C7
Galleria Lorcan O'Neill G13
Sprüth Magers Berlin London D6
White Cube F7

**Biography**
Born 1962
Lives in London and New York

British artist Hume is the subject of a touring survey show, 'Flashback', on view at Aberdeen Art Gallery until January 2013, following Leeds Art Gallery, Wolverhampton Art Gallery and Hastings' Jerwood Gallery in 2012. His other public gallery solo exhibitions include those as Pinchuk Art Centre, Kiev (2012), Modern Art Oxford (2008), Kunsthaus Bregenz (2004), the Irish Museum of Modern Art, Dublin (2003), and Whitechapel Gallery, London (1999). He represented Britain at the 48th Venice Biennale (1999).

1
*Anxiety and the Horse. The Horse*
2011
Enamel on aluminium
152 × 112 cm
Courtesy of Matthew Marks Gallery

2
*Anxiety and the Horse. Angela Merkel*
2011
Enamel on aluminium
152 × 112 cm
Courtesy of Matthew Marks Gallery

3
*Anxiety and the Horse.* ♀
2011
Enamel on canvas
275 × 392 cm
Courtesy of Matthew Marks Gallery

4
*Anxiety and the Horse. Yes We Can*
2011
Enamel on aluminium
135 × 98 cm
Courtesy of Matthew Marks Gallery

# Gary Hume

Gary Hume's restless mien has carried him, since the late 1980s, from the incontestable conceptual clarity of his 'Door Paintings' (1988–ongoing)—based on hospital entryways, placing geometric art on life support—through several species of figuration and, lately, back to abstraction. Constant, however, has been his transfiguring use of workaday enamel paint and schematic outlines, interweaving of tenors and fantastic aptitude for colour. Hume's recent septet of abstract or near-abstract paintings, 'Anxiety and the Horse' (2011), was planned, he says, to reflect recent sociopolitical history. So Angela Merkel and Barack Obama are in here, though spectrally, alongside an ambiguously goggle-eyed, schematic horse, but the paintings went their own smartly consternating way: hence the title, whose cocktailing of the jittery, mysterious and matter-of-fact is, indeed, quintessentially Hume. MH

1

**Shown by**
Canada G15
Almine Rech Gallery
D18

**Biography**
Born 1963
Lives in Greenfield, MA

California-born Jane has been the subject of solo shows at venues such as Canada, New York (2012), Almine Rech Gallery, Paris (2010), and Jack Hanley, Los Angeles (2007). She featured with B. Wurtz in a two-person show at Pacific Northwest College of Art, Portland (2012). Group exhibitions include 'Collaborations and Interventions', CCA Andratx, Majorca (2012), 'New Shadow Old Legs', Eleven Rivington, New York (2011), and 'Psycho Painting', Carlson Gallery, London (2010).

1
*Snow Globe for Roman Opalka (1)*
2011
Oil on panel
104 × 112 cm
Courtesy of Canada

2
*Nox Rex #26, Hypnos*
2012
Oil on panel
40 × 51 cm
Courtesy of Canada

# Xylor Jane

The whiff of the technological Sublime in Xylor Jane's paintings—coming through in dizzying grids of digits and Jane's uniquely mathematical Pointillism—is tempered by a much more human, earthly quality. Close up, her steely technique of placing dots of paint in regimented rows softens into an evocation of patient handicrafts such as needlepoint or quilting, especially when one notices the occasional imperfections. The rainbow palette of *Nox Rex #26, Hypnos* (2012) recalls a broken liquid crystal display, the endless 1s, 8s and 0s alluding to a malfunctioning computer spewing reams of code. Numerical systems lead the artist towards thoughts of mortality as well as a degree of perfection that is only attainable in virtual realms. JG

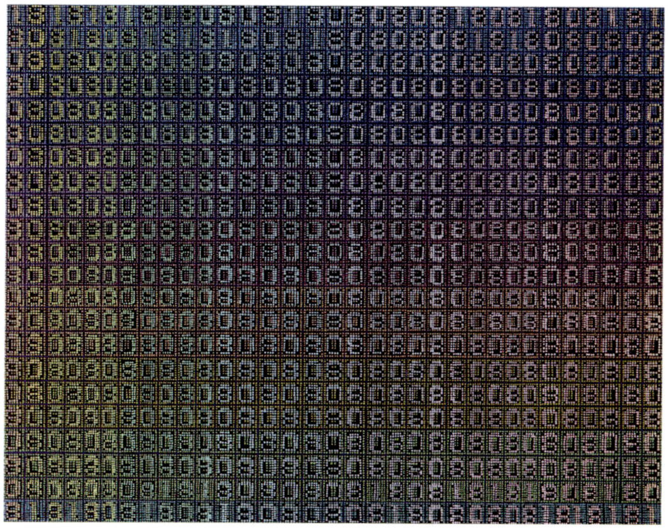

2

**Shown by**
Galerie Guido W. Baudach A10
Massimo De Carlo D8
Hauser & Wirth C8
David Kordansky Gallery C14

**Biography**
Born 1977
Lives in New York

Solo exhibitions by Chicago-born Johnson include those at Miami Art Museum (2012), South London Gallery (2012), Museum of Contemporary Art, Chicago (2012 and 2002), Sculpture Center, Long Island City, New York (2009), Kunstmuseum Magdeburg, Germany (2008), and Indianapolis Museum of Contemporary Art (2005). He was a participant in the 54th Venice Biennale (2011) and in 2012 received the David C. Driskell Prize from the High Museum of Art, Atlanta.

*Cosmic Slop 'Bring Joy'*
2012
Black soap and wax
2434× 305 × 4 cm
Courtesy of Hauser & Wirth

# Rashid Johnson

Rashid Johnson's work has been composed of photographs, steel, brass, wood, wax, soap and various found objects: books, records, live plants and CB radios. As likely to be inspired by George Clinton as by Joseph Cornell, by Carl Andre as by Eldridge Cleaver, Johnson's formally disparate but thematically coherent *oeuvre* addresses African-American history via the imbrications of science, alchemy, politics and performance. He has created a fictional society of black intellectuals (photographed wreathed in mystic fog or smoke) for *The New Negro Escapist Social and Athletic Club* (2010). The boxing promoter Don King was the starting point for his 2012 show 'Rumble', at Hauser & Wirth in New York, which included Johnson's film *The New Black Yoga* (2011), inspired by the artist's own attempt to master the physical discipline. BD

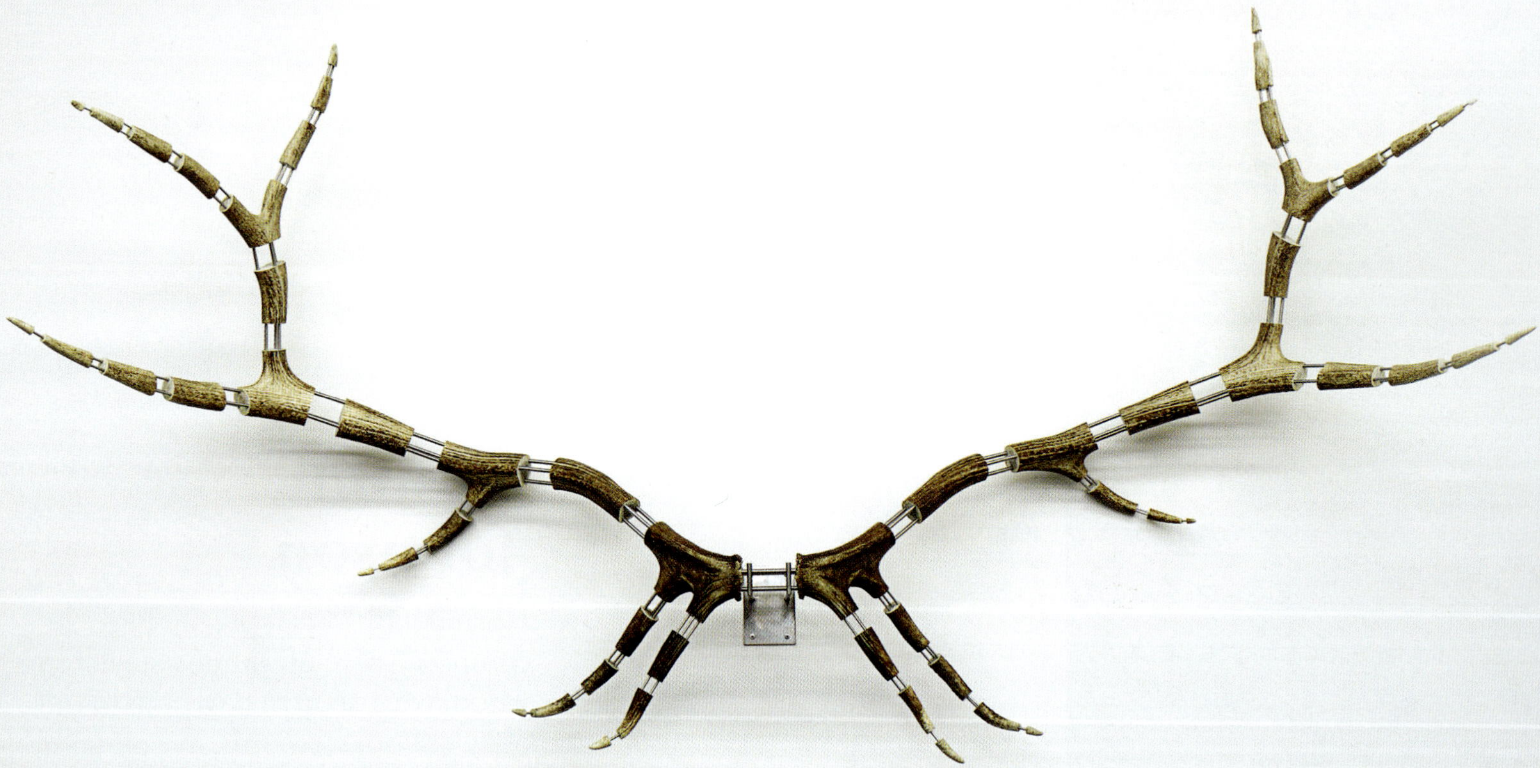

**Shown by**
Kukje Gallery C13

**Biography**
Born 1966
Lives in New York

American-born artist Joo has recently presented solo exhibitions at Blain Southern, London (2012), Galleria Marabini, Bologna (2010), Anton Kern Gallery (2009), PKM Gallery, Seoul (2008), and Asia Society, New York (2005). Joo collaborated with Damien Hirst on 'Have You Ever Really Looked at the Sun?' at Haunch of Venison, Berlin, in 2010. He represented South Korea at the 49th Venice Biennale (2001) and, with co-recipient Song Dong, received the Grand Prize at the 6th Gwangju Biennale (2006). His work is on show at the 8th Gwangju Biennale until November 2012.

*Improved Rack*
2012
Antlers and stainless steel
148 × 71 × 264 cm
Courtesy of Kukje Gallery

# Michael Joo

Michael Joo's work often involves animals and nature, and examines the way in which 'nature' as a category is itself constructed through history, culture, ideology and technology. *Stubbs (Absorbed)* (2009) is an extended riff on a zebra painting by George Stubbs (*A Zebra*, 1763). Rendered in the three dimensions of a sculpture, Joo's work refers, in addition to art history, to both artifice and technology (the sculpture is placed before a screen that depicts an anachronistic 'nature' backdrop, which makes one think of zoos and nature documentaries). *In Improved Rack* (2012) Joo presents a formidable pair of antlers, segments of which have been replaced by stainless steel. The work encapsulates the relationship between science and art,as well as our overriding narratives of evolution and natural history. KK

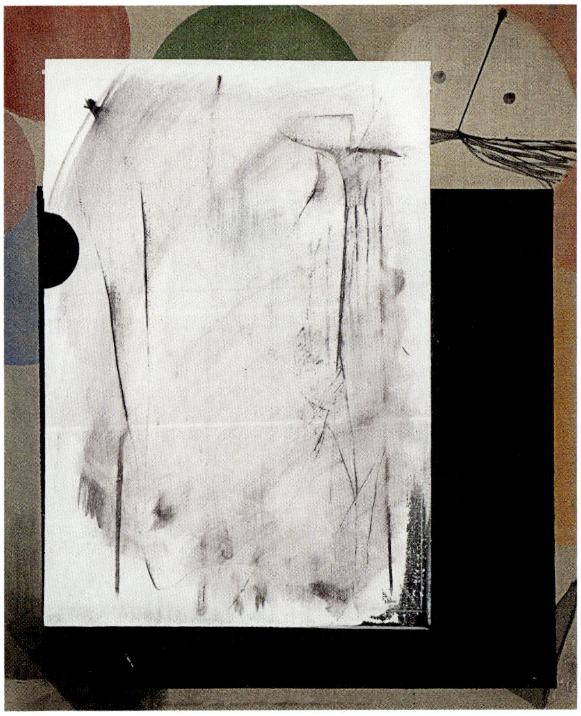
1

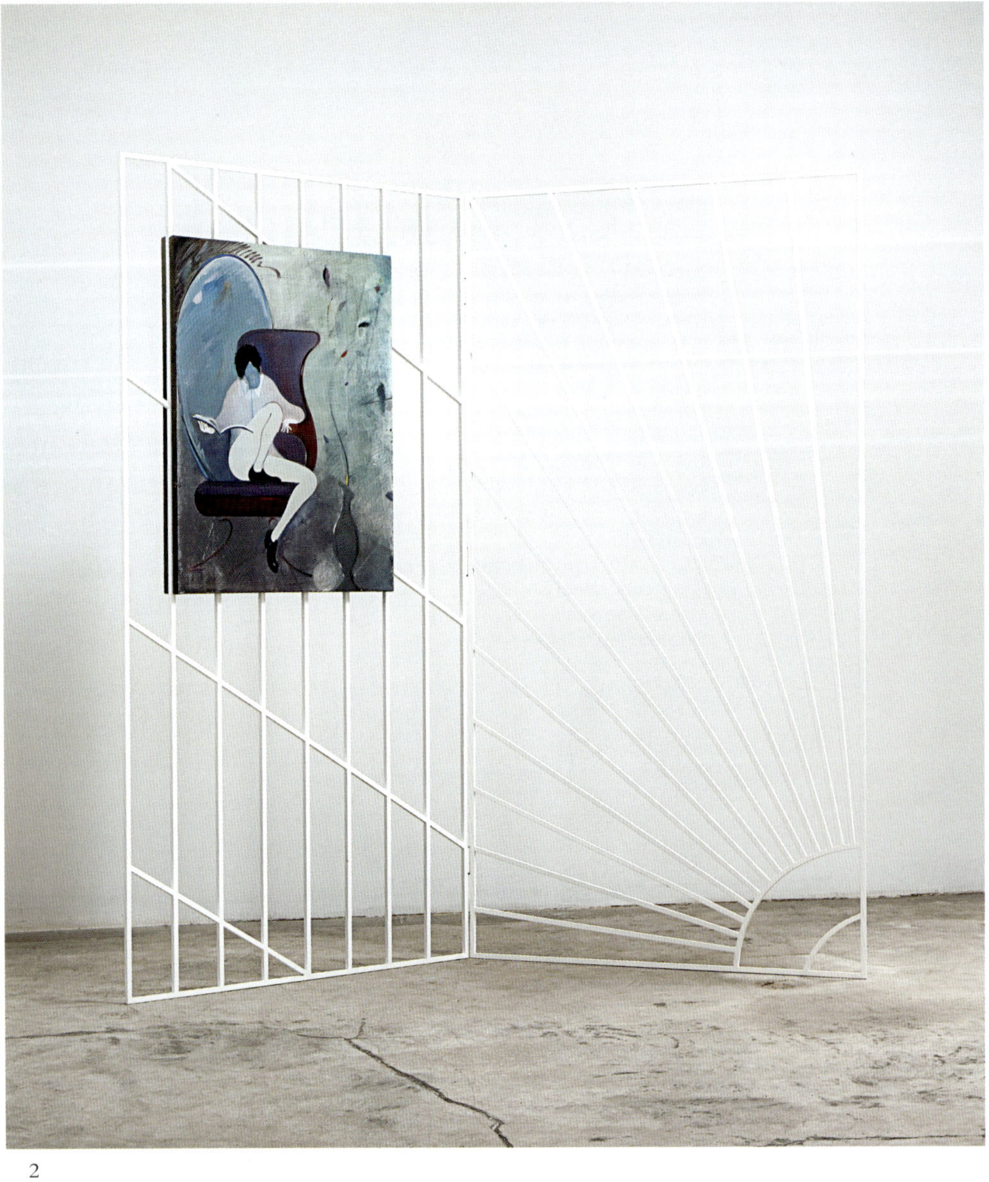
2

**Shown by**
Marc Foxx B8

**Biography**
Born 1982
Lives in Los Angeles

Russian artist Kantarovsky received an MFA from the University of California in 2010. He has recently presented solo exhibitions 'Blue Notebook No. 10' at Marc Foxx, Los Angeles (2012), and 'Mutualisms' at AMT Gallery, Milan (2009). He has participated in group exhibitions including 'Phases', Wallspace, New York (2012), 'Los Angeles Initiative', Honor Fraser, Los Angeles (2011), and 'Lost and Found', New Museum, New York (2009).

1
*Notnow*
2011
Gesso, oil, ink and watercolour on linen
76 × 61 cm
Courtesy of Marc Foxx

2
*Untitled*
2011
Powder-coated steel and two oil-on-linen paintings
203 × 116 × 25 cm
Courtesy of Marc Foxx

3
*The Third Librarian*
2012
Alkyd enamel, pigment and resin on powder-coated steel
153 × 41 × 16 cm
Courtesy of Marc Foxx

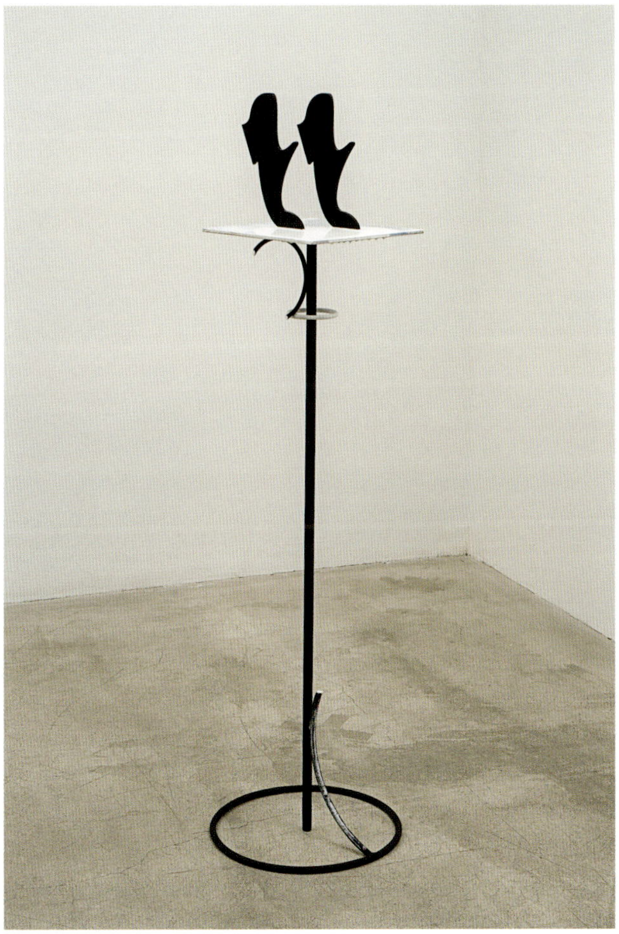

3

# Sanya Kantarovsky

The slim figures that appear in Sanya Kantarovsky's paintings and sculptures have an elegant comic quality, with tiptoe shoes, sinuous hands and waved hair reminiscent of Jacques Tati posters, old *New Yorker* covers and 1930s Soviet illustrations. Kantarovsky's painted characters are members of the intelligentsia, whether the conductor whose sheet music has escaped the stand in *Sinfonia #2* or the tribute to Soviet writer Daniil Kharms found in *The Man in the Black Coat* (both 2012), in which two black-clad officials flank the pipe-smoking blue-pyjama-wearing author. Kantarovsky sometimes mounts his canvases and cut out forms on wrought-iron screens and curlicued free-standing sculptures, lending lightness to his themes of self-absorption, creative ennui and the desire to escape. SL

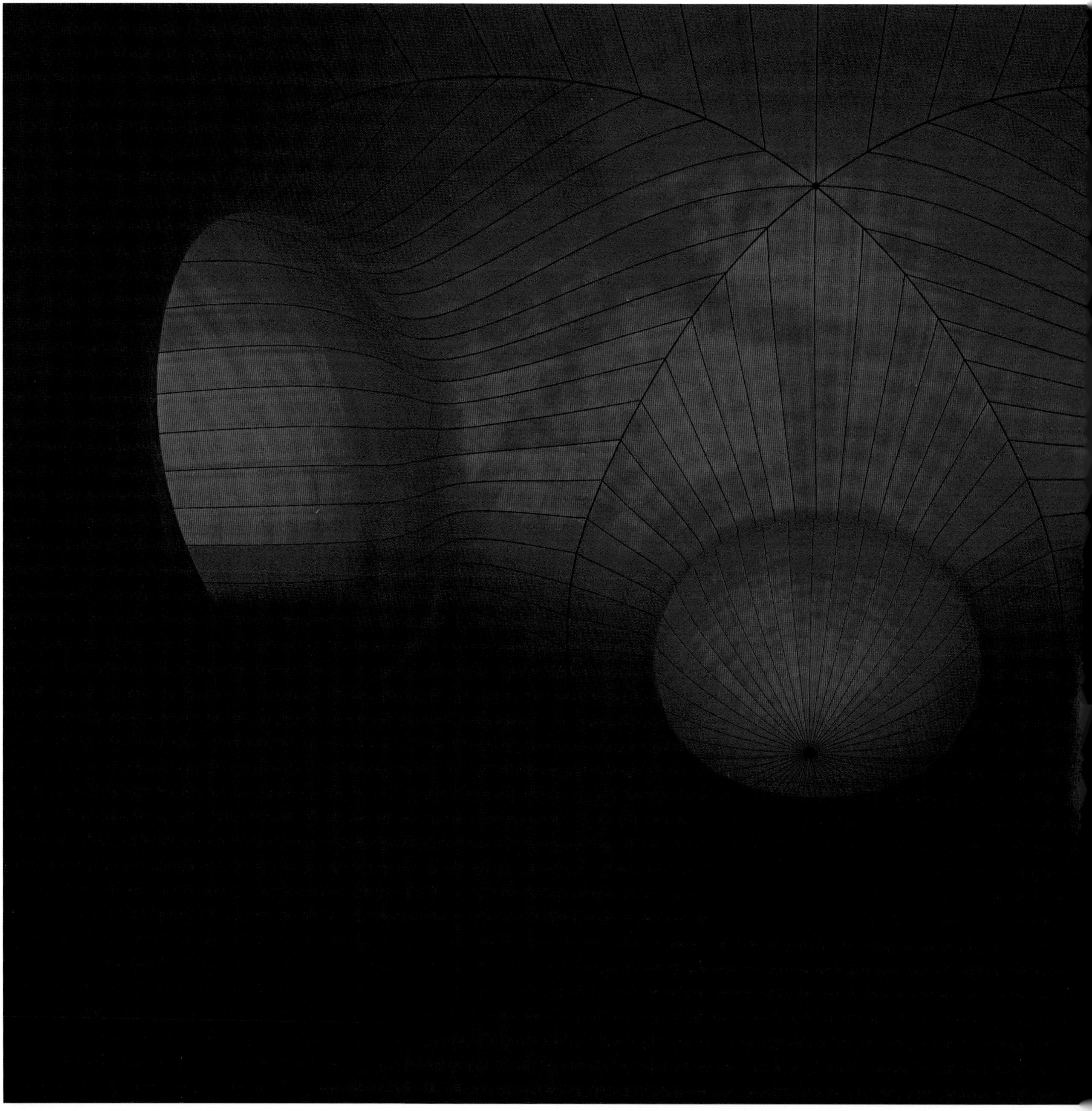

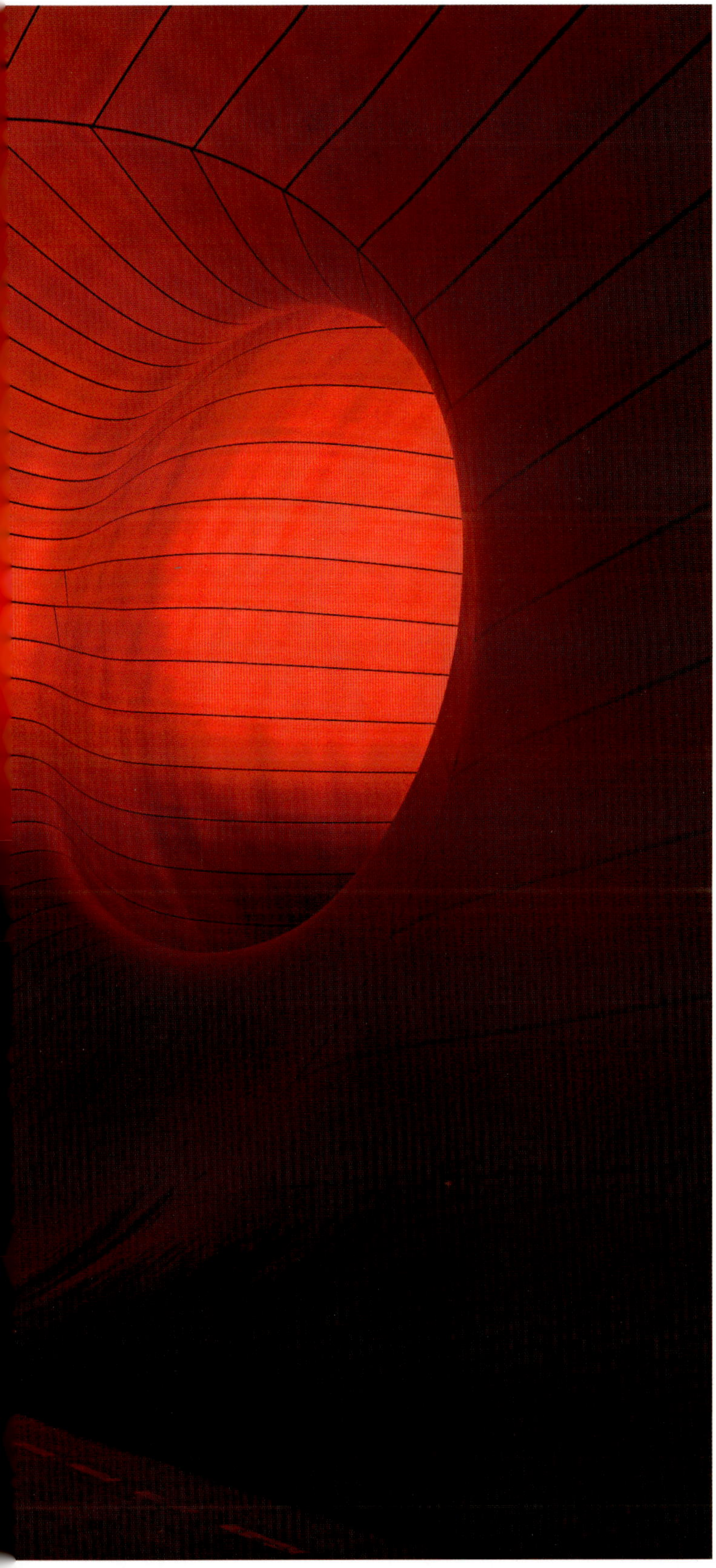

# Anish Kapoor

**Shown by**
Kukje Gallery C13
Lisson Gallery B9

**Biography**
Born 1954
Lives in London

Bombay-born British artist Kapoor, winner of the Turner Prize in 1991, has presented solo exhibitions in the last decade at institutions including Galeries Nationales du Grand Palais, Paris (2011), National Gallery of Modern Art, Delhi (2010), Royal Academy of Arts, London (2009), and Tate Modern (2002–3). Kapoor represented Britain in the 44th Venice Biennale (1990), for which he received the Premio Duemila. His work is part of collections that include: MoMA, New York; The Art Institute of Chicago; and Museo Nacional Centro de Arte Reina Sofía, Madrid.

*Leviathan*
2011
PVC
33.5 × 100 × 72 m
Courtesy of Lisson Gallery, Monumenta 2011 and the French Ministry for Culture and Communication

For more than 30 years Anish Kapoor has been producing sculptures that, whether biomorphic, minimalist, architecturally scaled or kinetic, constitute a wide-ranging investigation into presence and form. The results are frequently mesmerizing and, from deep-hued waxes and resins to mirror-polished convex and concave forms, materials remain central. Recent years have seen many of Kapoor's works become permanent fixtures in public spaces around the world, and he has also produced several monumental collaborations with the engineer Cecil Balmond, such as *Marsyas* (2002), in Tate Modern's Turbine Hall, and, most recently, *ArcelorMittal Orbit* (2012), in London's Olympic Park. As the artist himself has noted, his works often posit a binary relationship—between being and non-being, for example, or heaviness and intangibility—that turns on the question of what he has called the 'invisible object'. ST

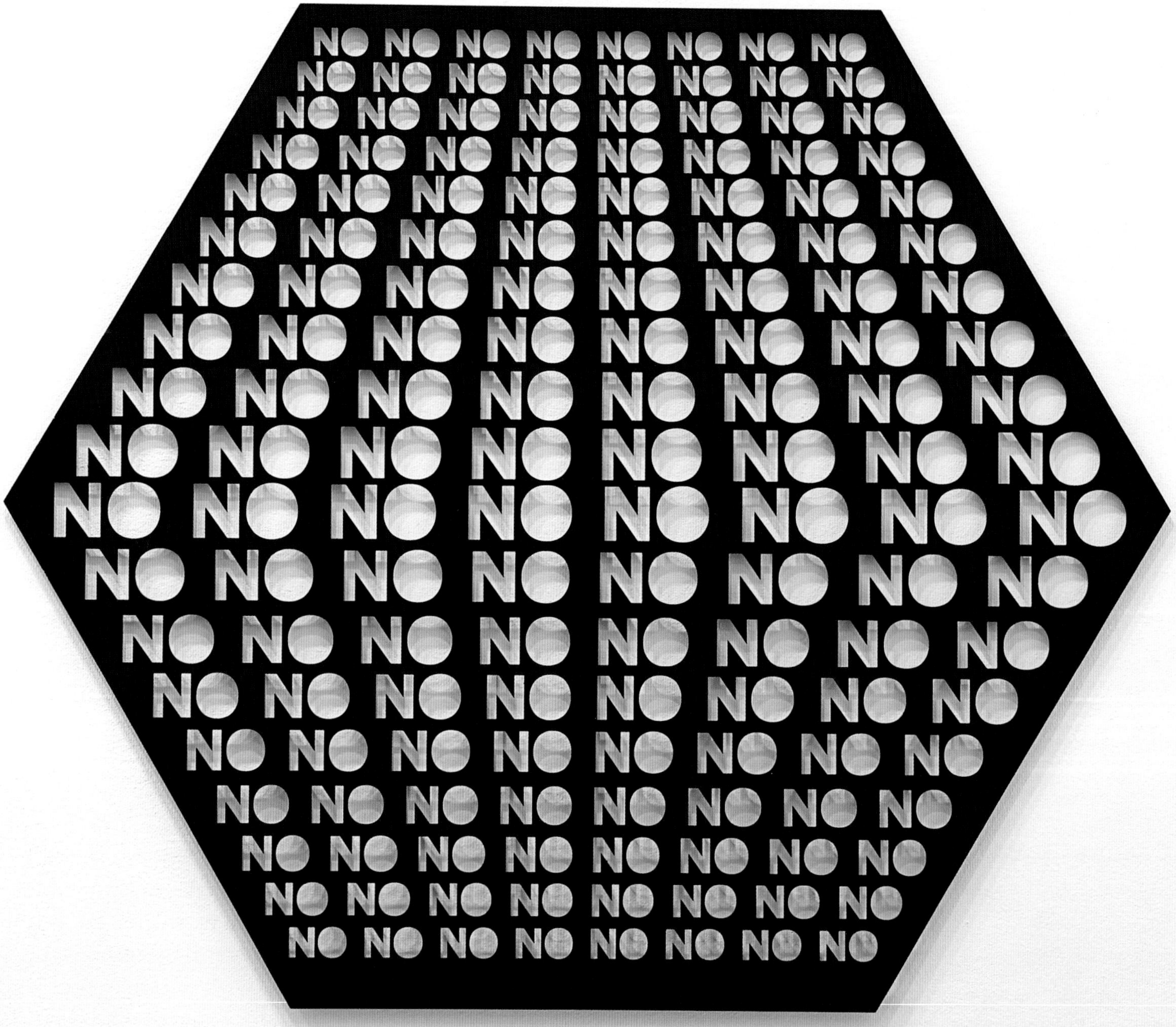
NO NO NO NO NO NO NO NO
NO NO NO NO NO NO NO NO
NO NO NO NO NO NO NO NO
NO NO NO NO NO NO NO NO
NO NO NO NO NO NO NO NO
NO NO NO NO NO NO NO NO
NO NO NO NO NO NO NO NO
NO NO NO NO NO NO NO NO
NO NO NO NO NO NO NO NO
NO NO NO NO NO NO NO NO
NO NO NO NO NO NO NO NO
NO NO NO NO NO NO NO NO
NO NO NO NO NO NO NO NO
NO NO NO NO NO NO NO NO
NO NO NO NO NO NO NO NO
NO NO NO NO NO NO NO NO
NO NO NO NO NO NO NO NO
NO NO NO NO NO NO NO NO
NO NO NO NO NO NO NO NO

# Focus
# Matt Keegan

**Shown by**
Altman Siegel S9

**Biography**
Born 1976
Lives in New York

American artist Keegan has recently presented solo exhibitions at venues including Altman Siegel, San Francisco (2011), and D'Amelio Terras, New York (2011). He has participated in group exhibitions including: 'Found in Translation', Deutsche Guggenheim, Berlin (2012), 'Circulate,' FOAM, Amsterdam (2011), 'Exposure', The Art Institute of Chicago (2011), 'The Air We Breathe', San Francisco Museum of Modern Art (2011), and 'Haunted: Contemporary Photography/Video/Performance', Guggenheim Museum Bilbao (2010).

*No No No*
2011
Laser-cut steel
87 × 87 × 5 cm
Courtesy of Altman Siegel Gallery

Encompassing publications, photography, video, painting and sculpture, the disparate media utilized by Matt Keegan are in keeping with the multiple subjects, approaches and concerns that form his collagist visual practice. Text found from signage, well-worn phrases, calendars and newspapers align his conceptual approach to personalized photographic subject matter, and graphic design notation informs his exhibitions; *No No No* (2011) shows a steel hexagon with the repeated title laser-cut in ascending and descending sizes. Assembling meaning through these myriad references and forms, Keegan creates constellations that examine legibility and illegibility in art practice and wider visual culture. PT

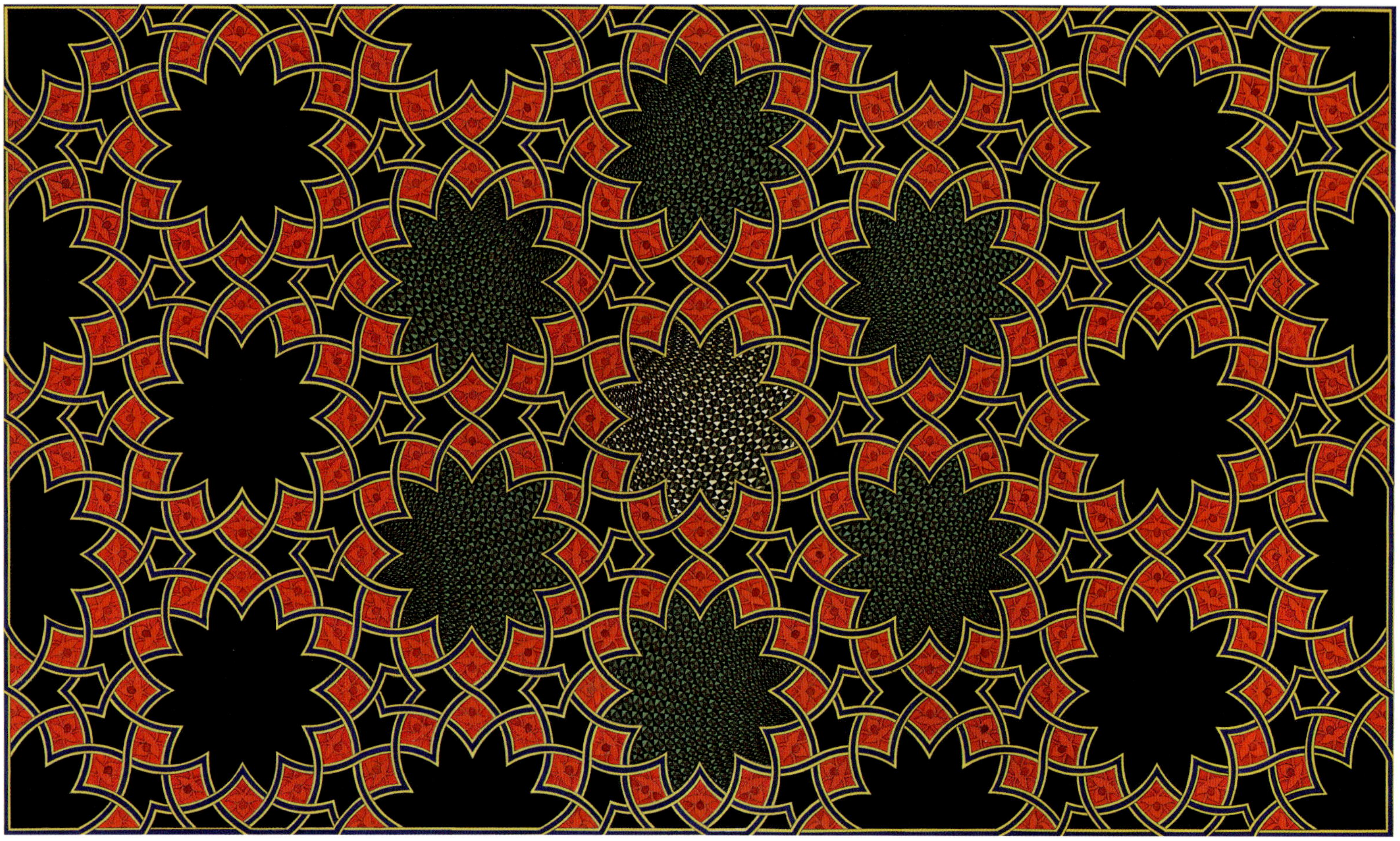
1

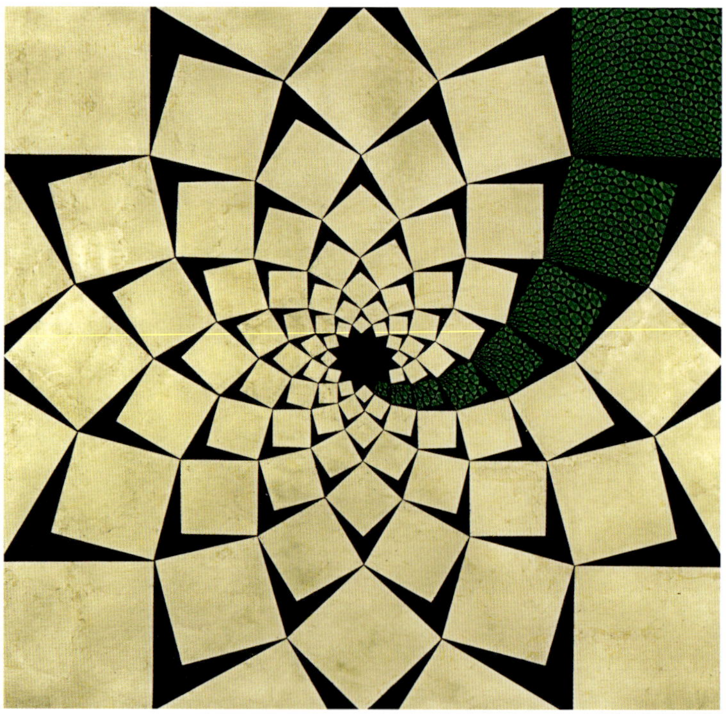
2

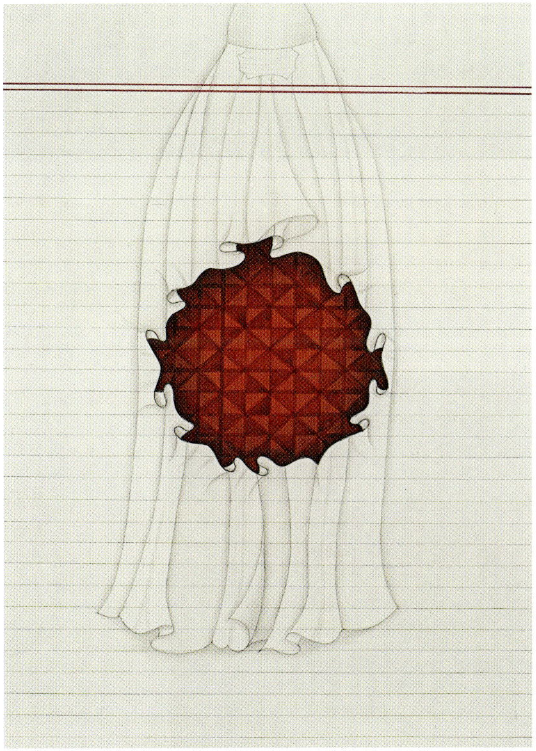

3

**Shown by**
Corvi-Mora E7

**Biography**
Born 1972
Lives in Lahore

Pakistani artist Khalid has presented solo exhibition at galleries including Corvi-Mora, London (2012), Chawkandi Art, Karachi (2010), and Pump House Gallery, London (2010). Khalid was The People's Choice winner of the Jameel Prize 2011, the touring exhibition of which has been shown at venues such as Institut du Monde Arabe, Paris (2012), and the Victoria and Albert Museum, London (2011). Her work was featured in the 10th Sharjah Biennial (2011).

1
*Pattern To Follow*
2009
Gouache and gold leaf on wasli paper
99 × 165 cm
Courtesy of Corvi-Mora

2
*Pattern To Follow*
2009
Gouache and gold leaf on wasli paper
85 × 83 cm
Courtesy of Corvi-Mora

3
*Truth*
2006
Opaque watercolour on wasli paper
45 × 36 cm
Courtesy of Corvi-Mora

# Aisha Khalid

How to occupy a centuries-old tradition as a contemporary artist, walking the line between timeliness for today and allegiance to the past? Trained in miniature painting in Lahore, Aisha Khalid engages directly with this storied mode of production while also eroding and updating it. It is not only the narrative traditions of 16th-century Mughal miniatures and Islamic geometric design that are worked over, but also the mainstream iconography that has come to signify 'the post-9/11 world' (veils, trappings of military intervention). In *Truth* (2006) Khalid hand-rules the hair-thin lines of a school composition notebook; elsewhere she's created an entire volume of such illustrated pages, invoking the imposed hierarchies of Urdu/English-language instruction in Pakistan to address global themes of standardized education and national heritage. SNS

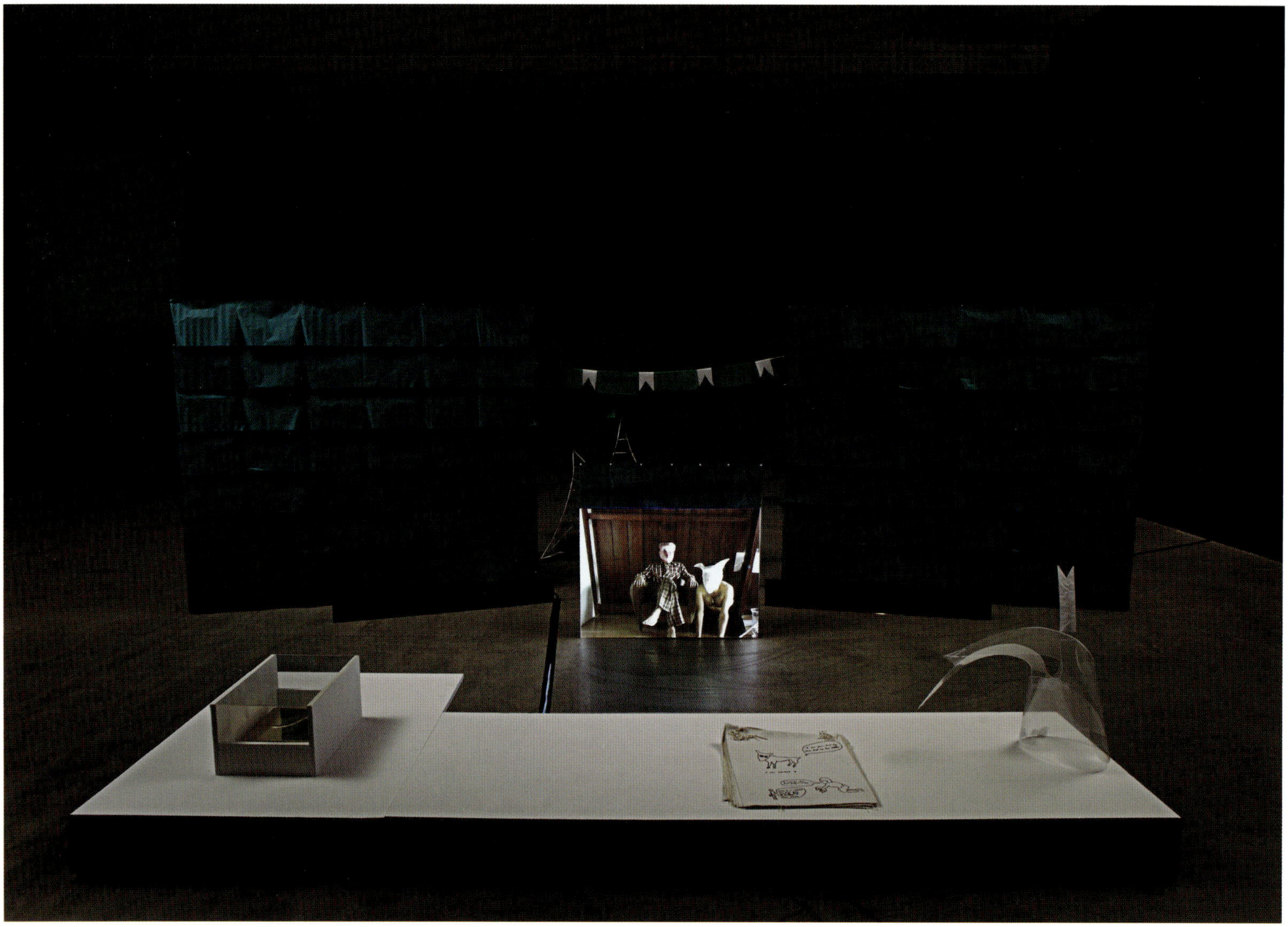

1

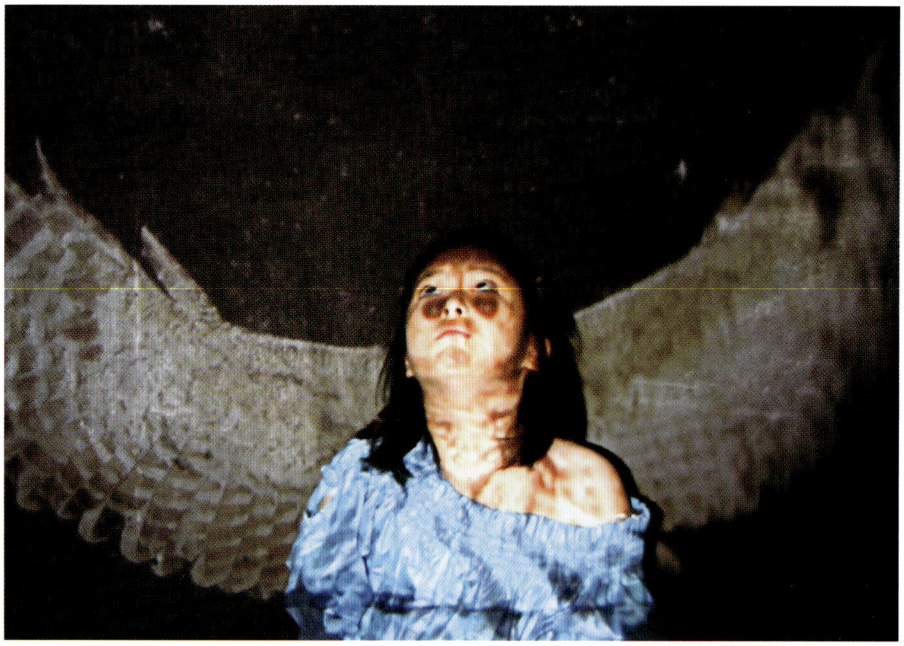

2

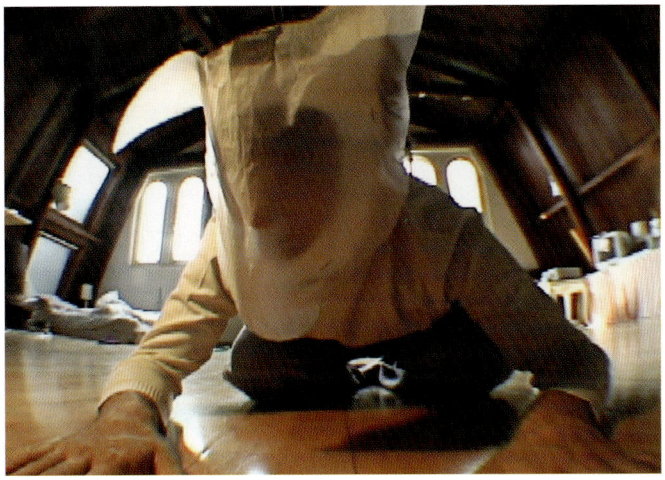

3

**Shown by**
Wilkinson G6

**Biography**
Born 1975
Lives in New York

South Korean-born Kim has recently shown solo exhibitions at Tate Modern, London (2012), Kunsthalle Basel (2011), Queens Museum, New York (2011), Haus der Kunst, Munich (2010), and Witte de With, Rotterdam (2008). Kim has presented performance at venues that include Kunstverein Ruyschstraat 4-III, Amsterdam (2011), and the New Museum, New York (2010).

1
*Dog Video Installation*
2008
Mixed media
Dimensions variable
Courtesy of Wilkinson

2
*Washing Brain and Corn*
2010
Video
16 min. 22 sec.
Courtesy of Wilkinson

3
*Dog Video*
2006
Video
7 min.
Courtesy of Wilkinson

# Sung Hwan Kim

Sung Hwan Kim's performance and video work might not seem to relate at all to his background in engineering and architecture, and yet he considers storytelling a form of logic equivalent to mathematics, since both employ structure, hierarchy and symbolic values. Kim's subject matter is tangible but never dogmatic; narratives are neither linear nor whole, but comprise poetic fragments held within elliptical architectural episodes. *Dog Video* (2006), for instance, delves into human–pet power relations from a personal, transcultural and art-historical perspective through the comparison of physical gestures, while *Washing Brain and Corn* (2010) relates, through curious imagery and evocative phrases in lyrical discordance, the story of a South Korean boy murdered by North Korean spies. SOR

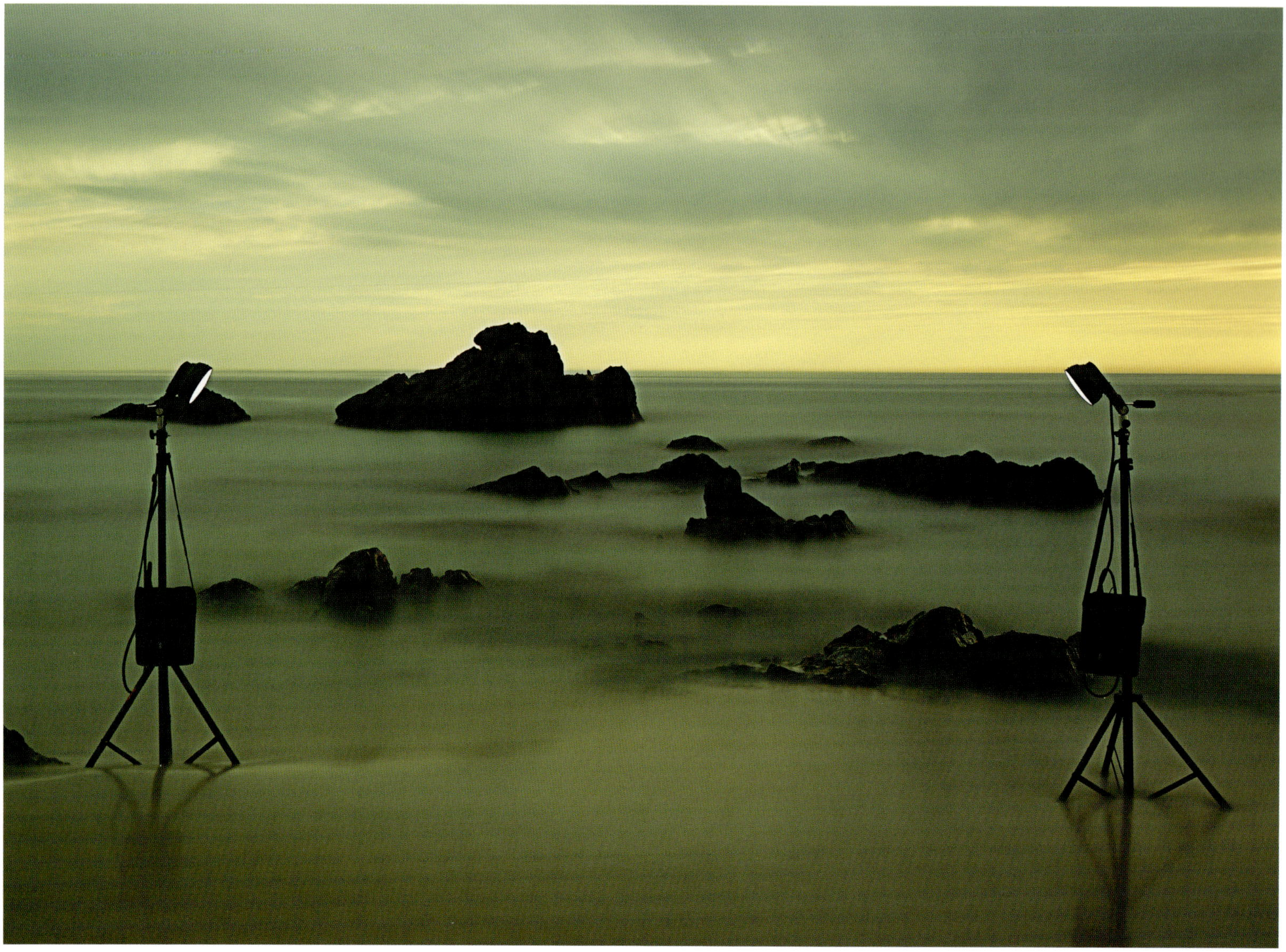

1

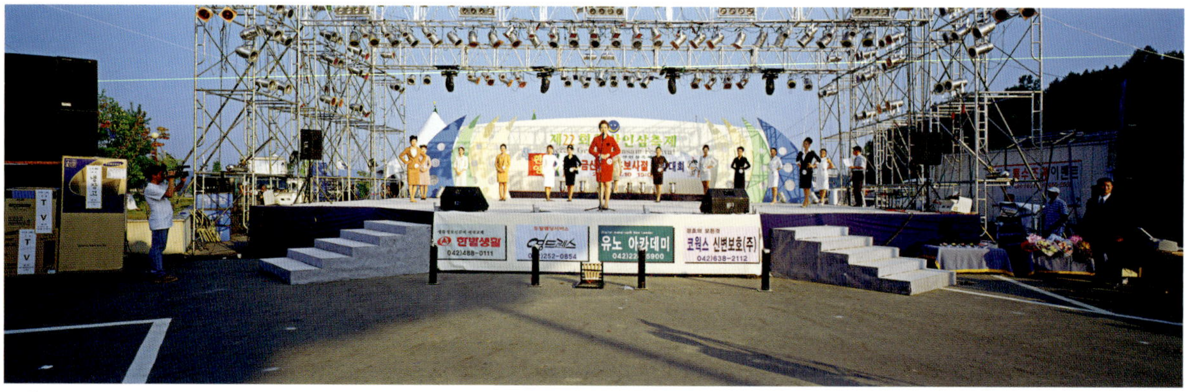


2

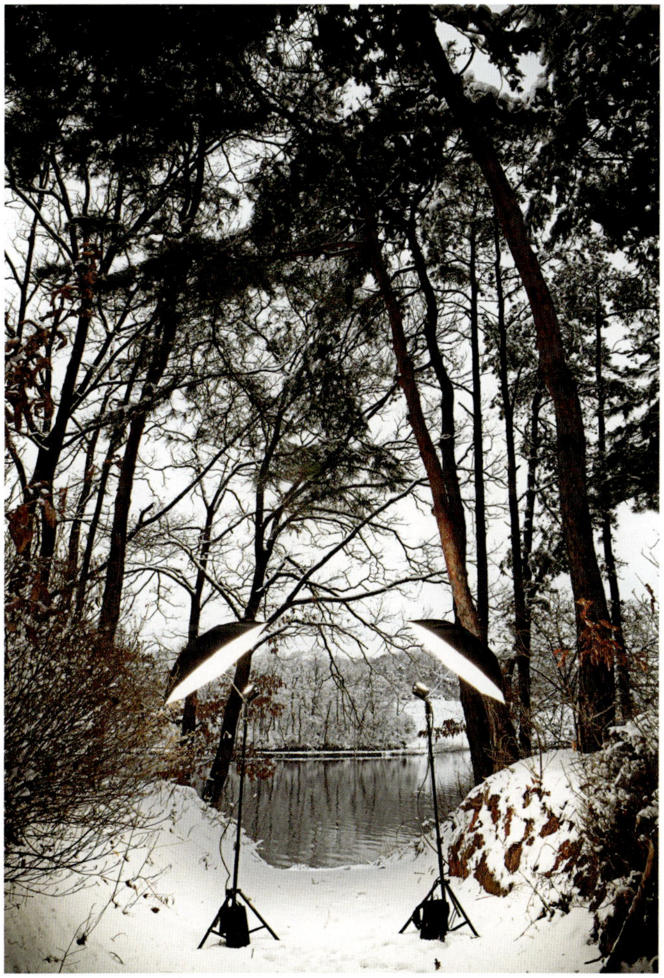

3

**Shown by**
One and J. Gallery S13

**Biography**
Born 1971
Lives in Seoul

Korean artist Kim was recently awarded the Rotary Angelo Colombo Special Prize at the 4th Biennale Giovani Monza (2011) and was artist-in-residence at the Mongin Art Centre, Seoul (2008–10). He has held solo exhibitions at venues that include One and J. Gallery, Seoul (2010), Arko Art Centre, Seoul (2007), and Künstlerhaus Bethanien, Berlin (2007). He has participated in numerous group exhibitions including 'Memoryscape', Arko Art Centre, Seoul (2010), and 'Chaotic Harmony' at the Museum of Fine Arts, Houston (2009).

1
*Sunken Rocks*
2010
Lightjet print
130 × 168 cm
Courtesy of One and J. Gallery

2
*312-800*
From the series 'The Tedious Landscape II'
2002
Digital c-type print
50 × 110 cm
Courtesy of One and J. Gallery

3
*A Snowy Path*
2010
Lightjet print
170 × 120 cm
Courtesy of One and J. Gallery

# Focus
# Kim Yunho

Kim Yunho's 'The Tedious Landscape II' (2002) show a series of beauty pageants, the countless crownings of Azalea Queens, Apple Maidens and Pepper Girls that occur throughout rural South Korea to promote local products. Such pageants seem poignantly Lilliputian in the face of world-scale markets, and it is precisely this impulse to define regional specificities in a globalizing world that drives Kim's work. The expanding world of the artist himself is mapped out in projects such as a *faux* train timetable for art fairs and videos that flash split-second images of local souvenirs. But is the 'global' really more homogenizing than the 'regional'? Kim presses the point via the Korean landscape tradition, re-shooting the tiny handful of sites where hundreds of newly married couples line up to have their portraits taken. SNS

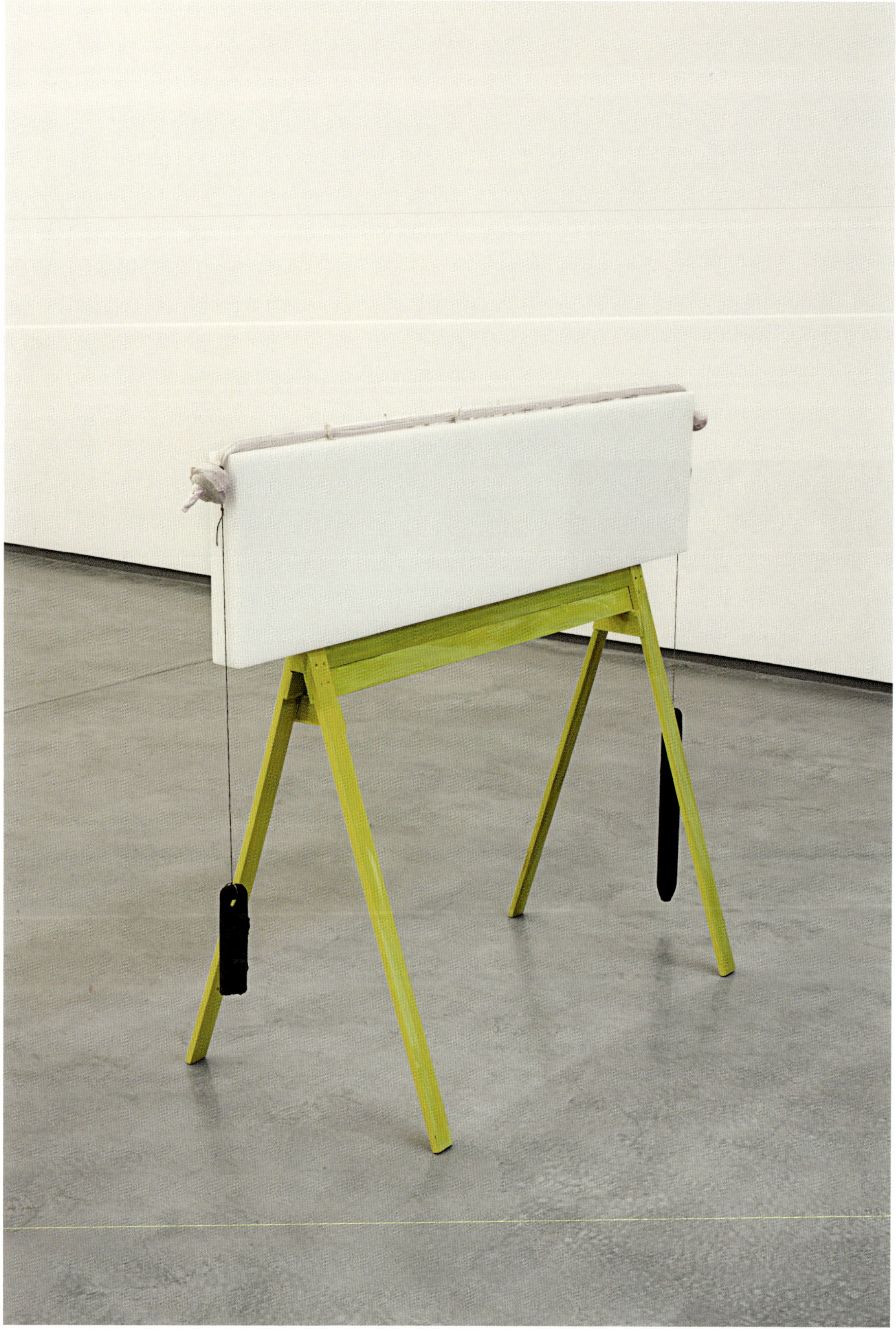

1

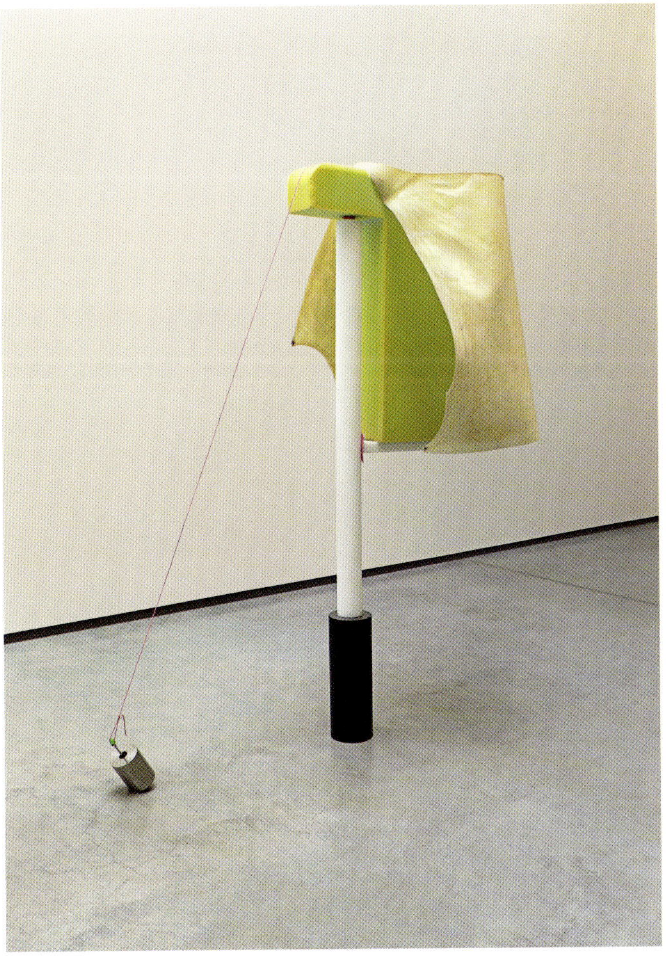

2

**Shown by**
Team Gallery E15

**Biography**
Born 1962
Lives in New York

American artist Knight has had solo shows during the last decade at galleries that include Team Gallery, New York (2012, 2007, 2005 and 2003), Display Centre for Contemporary Art, Prague (2004), D Lyx Gallery, Malmo (2004), and Sculpture Center, Long Island City, New York (2004). Knight's group exhibitions include 'Building Structures', MoMA PS1, New York (2002).

1
*Cord*
2011
Wood, polyethylene, silicone, string and iron
109 × 53 × 130 cm
Courtesy of Team Gallery

2
*Workout*
2012
Iron, rawhide, foam, polyurethane, twine and weight
140 × 49 × 115 cm
Courtesy of Team Gallery

# Ross Knight

Human in their scale and in their very corporeal concerns, Ross Knight's sculptures bring together objects familiar from the building site and hardware shop in assemblages that thrum with both art-historical allusions (among them the work of David Smith and Anthony Caro) and sexual innuendo. In his *Workout* (2012), what might be a yellow plastic phallus peeks out of a pair of cowhide chaps. Attached to the plastic is a length of red thread resembling an emergency cord or a Kabbalah bracelet, pulled taut by an iron weight, as though in an advanced-level S&M scene. Material and amatory deviance combine, here, with considerable sculptural and comic aplomb, in a work that is unafraid to explore the unintended campness of macho Modernist object-making. TM

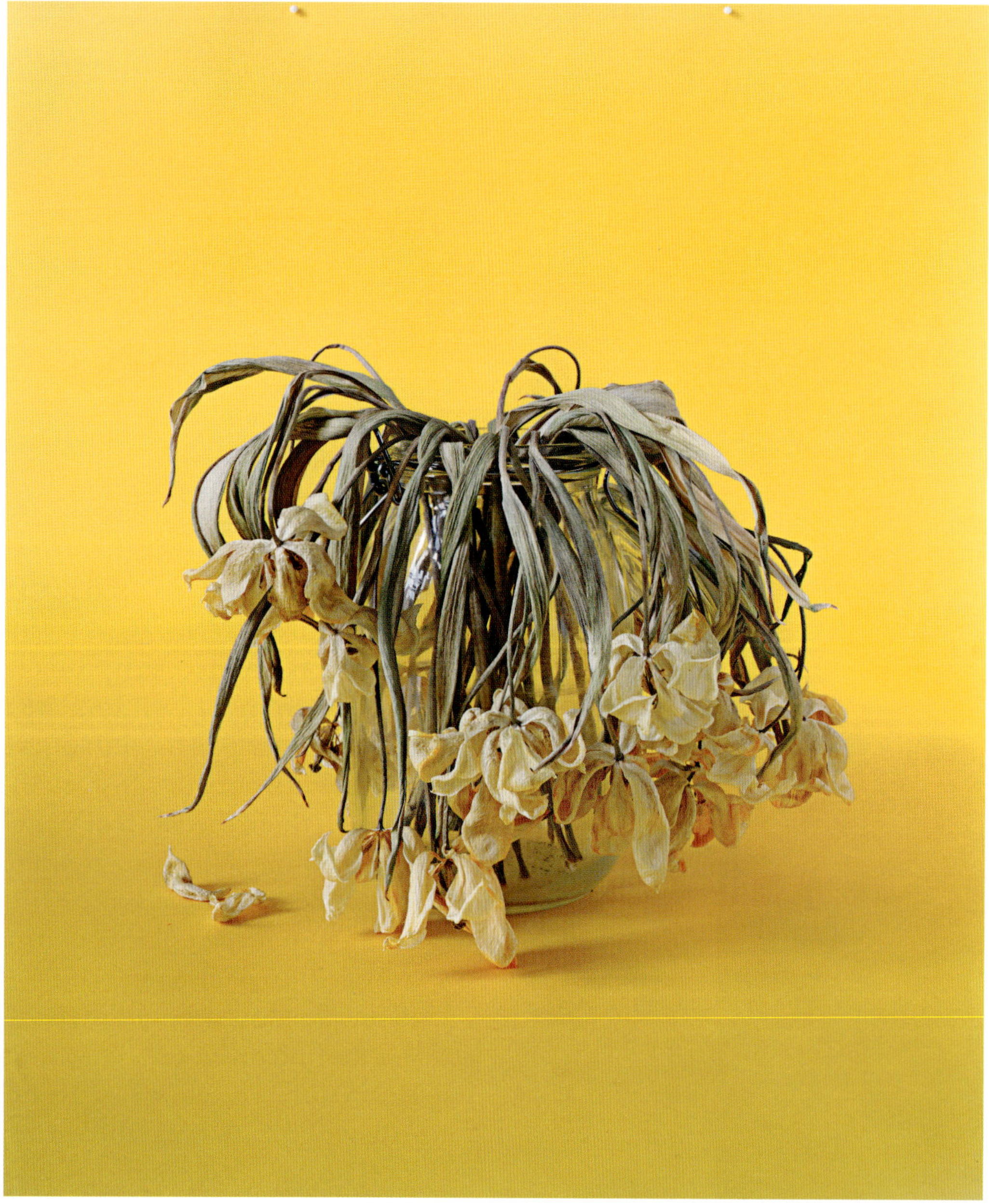

# Focus
# Susanne Kriemann

**Shown by**
RaebervonStenglin S18

**Biography**
Born 1972
Lives in Berlin

German-born Kriemann has presented solo exhibitions at venues that include Kunstverein Braunschweig (2012), Kunsthalle Winterthur (2011), Künstlerhaus Stuttgart (2009), and Stedelijk Museum Bureau, Amsterdam (2009). She received the GASAG Kunstpreis 2010, and her work has been featured in recent group shows such as 'Beyond Imagination', Stedelijk Museum, Amsterdam (2012), 'Track', SMAK, Ghent (2012), and 'Dreams of Power, Power of Dreams', Zamek Cultural Centre, Poznan (2011).

*Silent Crazy Jungle Under Glass (Yellow I & II)*
2011
Diptych: lightjet print on pearl paper
Each 145 × 120 cm
Courtesy of RaebervonStenglin

Susanne Kriemann may seem like a connoisseur of ruins, an enthusiast of the decay of the modern for its own melancholy sake, but her work, which takes the form of photographs, installations, research and found texts, is really more elaborately concerned with the historical involutions of photography, architecture and politics. At the Berlin Biennale in 2008 her installation *12 650 000* explored the city's sole hulking concrete remnant of Hitler's projected Germania. *One Time One Million* (2009) juxtaposed images of migratory birds, social housing in Sweden and the history of the Hasselblad camera. In 2012, with *Het Licht* (The Light), she pursued the afterlife of architectural Modernism in an investigation of a former left-wing newspaper office, torn down for student housing. TM

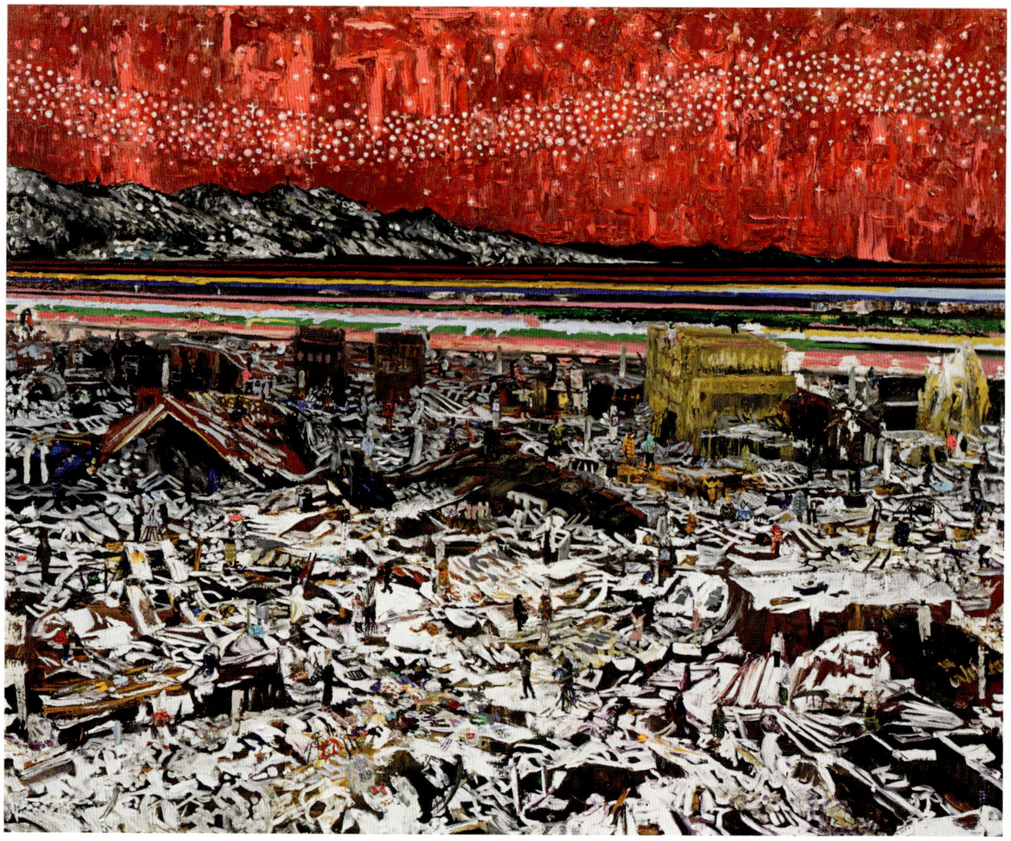
1

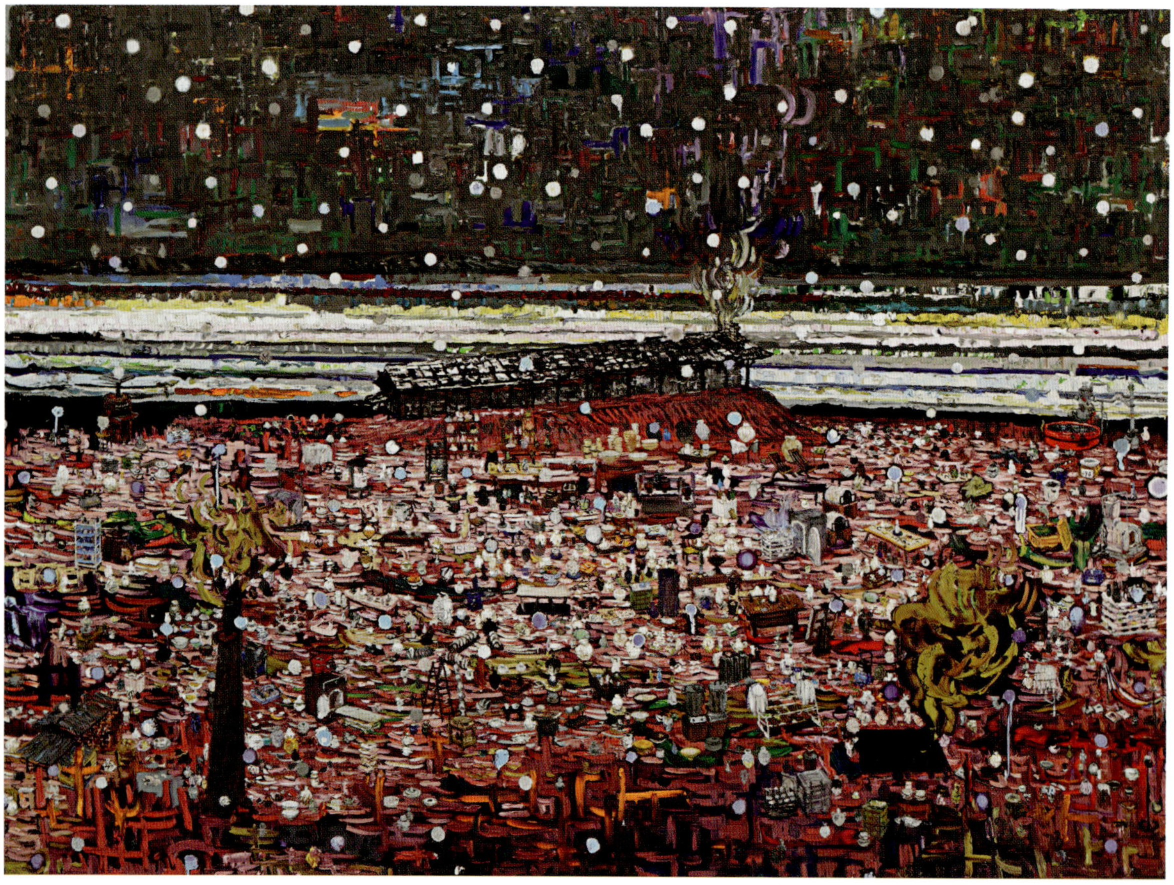
2

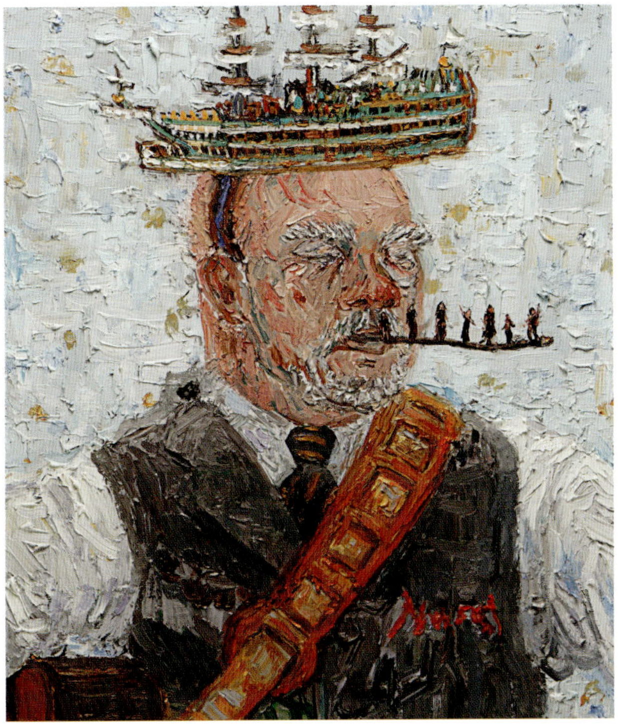

3

**Shown by**
Tomio Koyama Gallery
B1

**Biography**
Born 1978
Lives in Kanagawa

Recent solo exhibitions by Japanese-born Kuwakubo include those at Daiwa Anglo-Japanese Foundation, London (2012), Gallery Hyundai, Gangnam Space, Seoul (2010), Tokyo Wonder Site, Shibuya (2010 and 2005), and Tomio Koyama Gallery, Tokyo (2008 and 2005). In 2012 he received the VOCA (Vision Of Contemporary Art) Encouragement Prize, in conjunction with the group exhibition presented at Ueno Royal Museum, Tokyo.

1
*The Old Pomegranate Colour Clothes She Used to Wear*
2011
Oil on canvas
162 × 194 cm
Courtesy of Tomio Koyama Gallery

2
*Vessel*
2010
Oil on canvas
194 × 259 cm
Courtesy of Tomio Koyama Gallery

3
*Guitar Player at the Port*
2010
Oil on canvas
53 × 46 cm
Courtesy of Tomio Koyama Gallery

# Toru Kuwakubo

Toru Kuwakubo's paintings depict landscapes in Impressionist-style daubs of oily colour. Minute details are often overlaid on his large canvases, populating their choppy textured surfaces with figures and buildings. *The Old Pomegranate Colour Clothes She Used to Wear* (2011) catches a havocked townscape and its inhabitants under a red sky, while *Vessel* (2010) sees hundreds of pots, bowls and other containers laid out over a sprawling expanse. Kuwakubo also turns to portraiture in works such as *Guitar Player at the Port* (2010), where a miniature ship sits precariously on top of a man's head, and a plank protruding from his mouth holds miniature people. Often absurd, and uniquely detailed, his paintings reward further investigation. SC

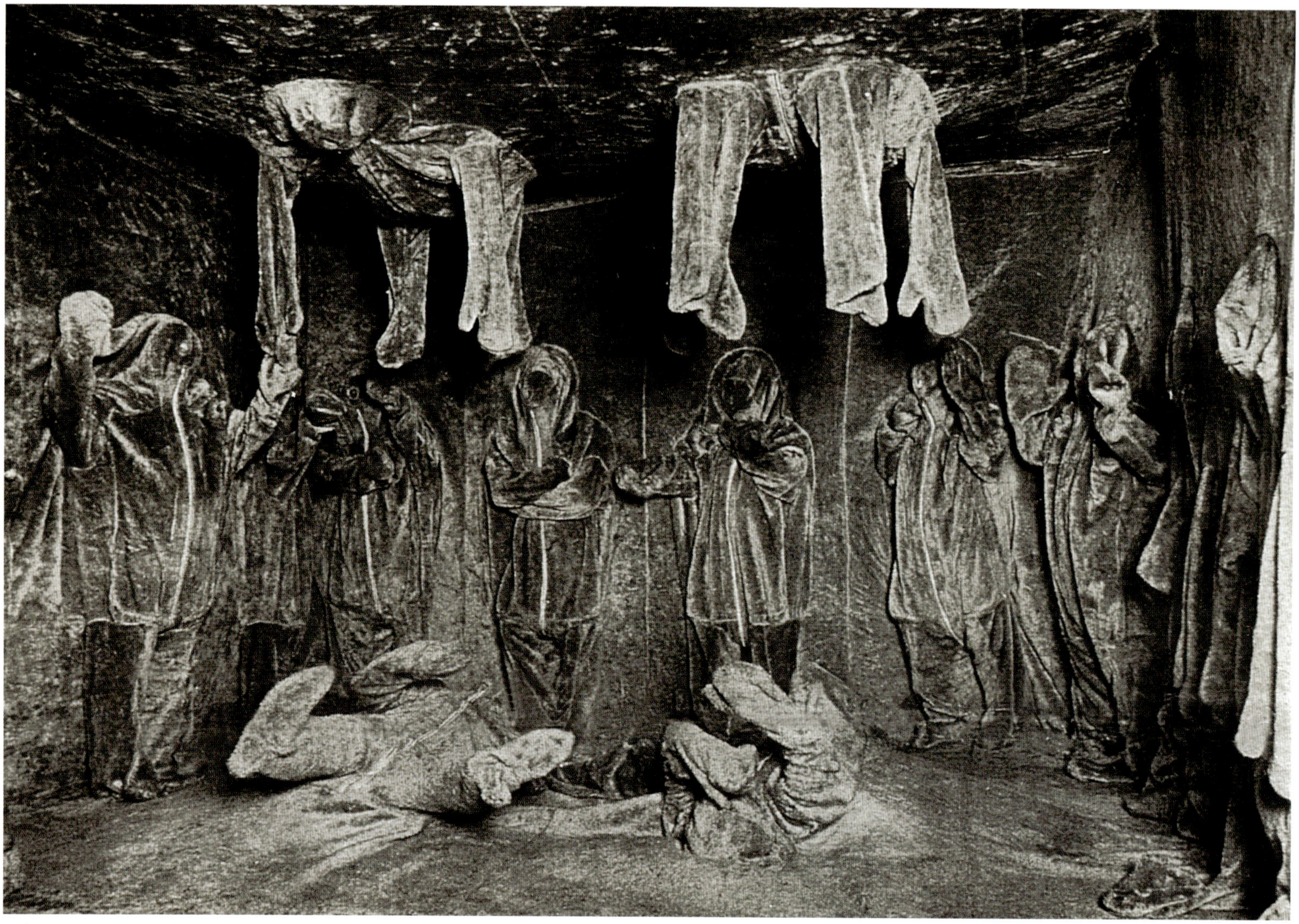

1

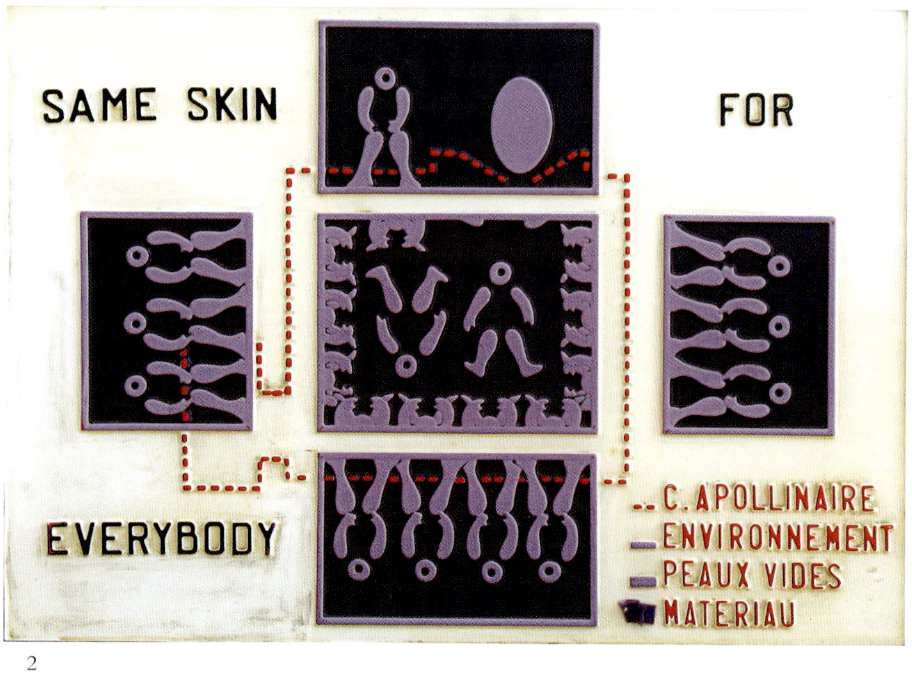
SAME SKIN
FOR
EVERYBODY
C. APOLLINAIRE
ENVIRONNEMENT
PEAUX VIDES
MATERIAU

2

**Shown by**
Broadway 1602 E14

**Biography**
Born 1937
Lives in New York

French-born Nicola L. has presented solo shows and projects in the last decade at venues such as Galerie Patricia Dorfman, Paris (2006), Brooklyn Museum, New York (2005), and Centro de Arte La Casona, Havana (2002). Her group shows include 'elles@centrepompidou', Centre Pompidou, Paris (2009–10), 'The Death of the Audience', the Vienna Secession (2009), 'The Body is the Landscape', Donation Mario Prassinos, St-Remy de Provence (2005), and 'Love, Work, Exist – Artists and Communities post-1968', Musée d'Art Moderne et Contemporain, Geneva (2004).

1
*The Fur Room*
1970
Acrylic fur
3.5 × 3.5 × 3 m
Courtesy of Broadway 1602

2
*The Fur Room*
1970
10 × 15 cm
Sketchboard for installation
Courtesy of Broadway 1602

3
*Red Foot*
1967–8
Vinyl
55 × 175 × 60 cm
Courtesy of Broadway 1602

# Nicola L.

Nicola L.'s outsize leatherette *Red Foot* (1967–8) kick-started a tumble of sculptural and performative works that have placed bodies and body parts in incongruous situations. At times these are imbued with a new practical use that inverts polite norms; at others effectiveness is eradicated through absurd means. At one end of this spectrum, sculptural heads serve as bookshelves or fish tanks, eyes as lamps; and the sculptural form of a snail-shell becomes a wardrobe, a chandelier or a birdcage. Less practical, but more politically charged, *The Fur Room* (1970)—one of a series of communalizing garments for over a dozen wearers—forms what Nicola L. describes as the 'same skin for everyone'. SOR

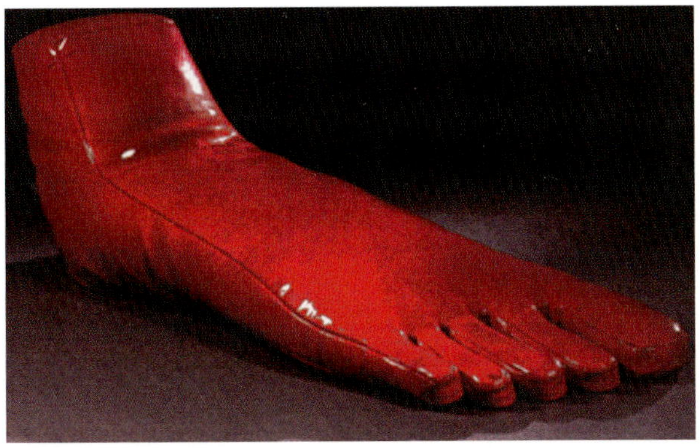

3

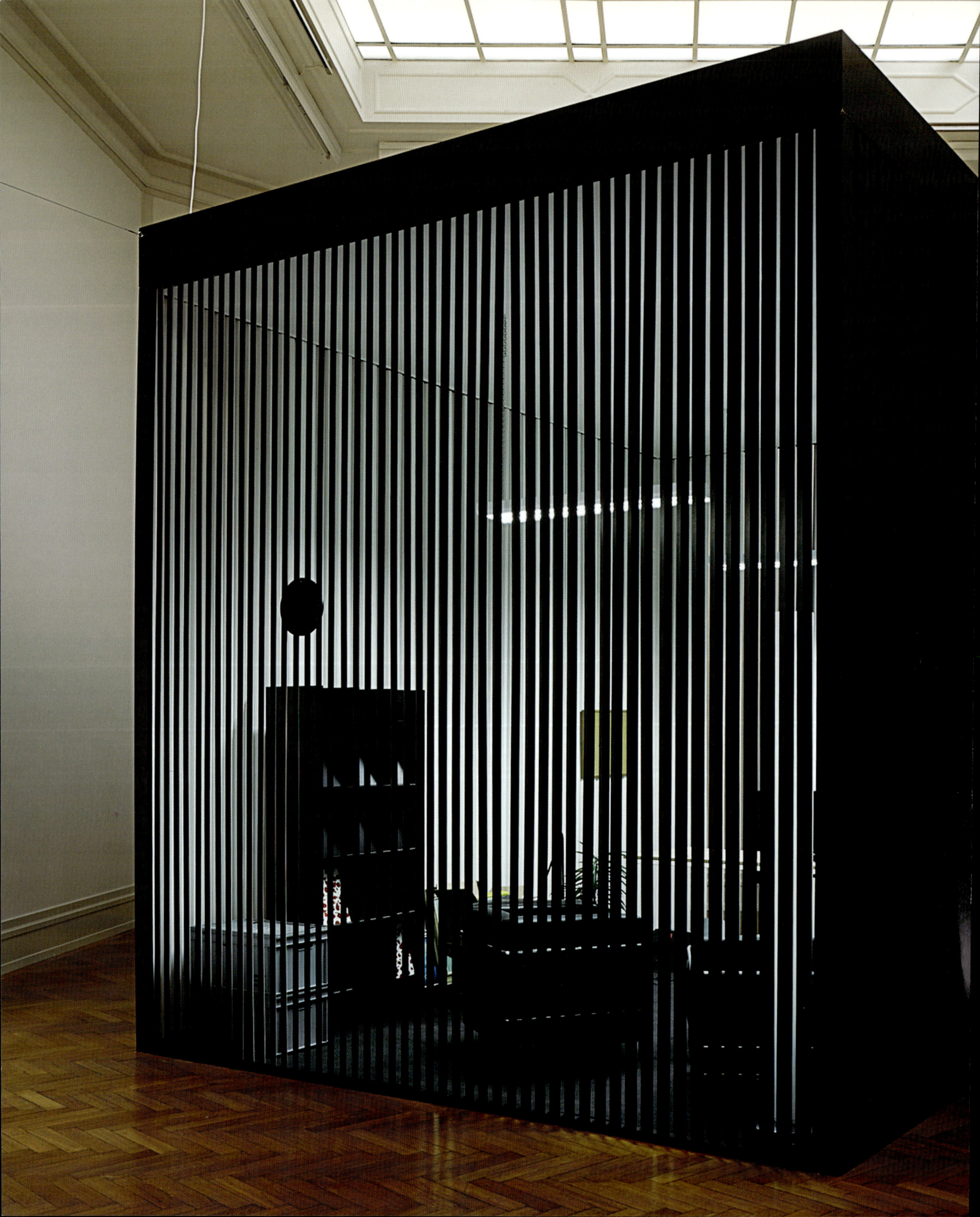

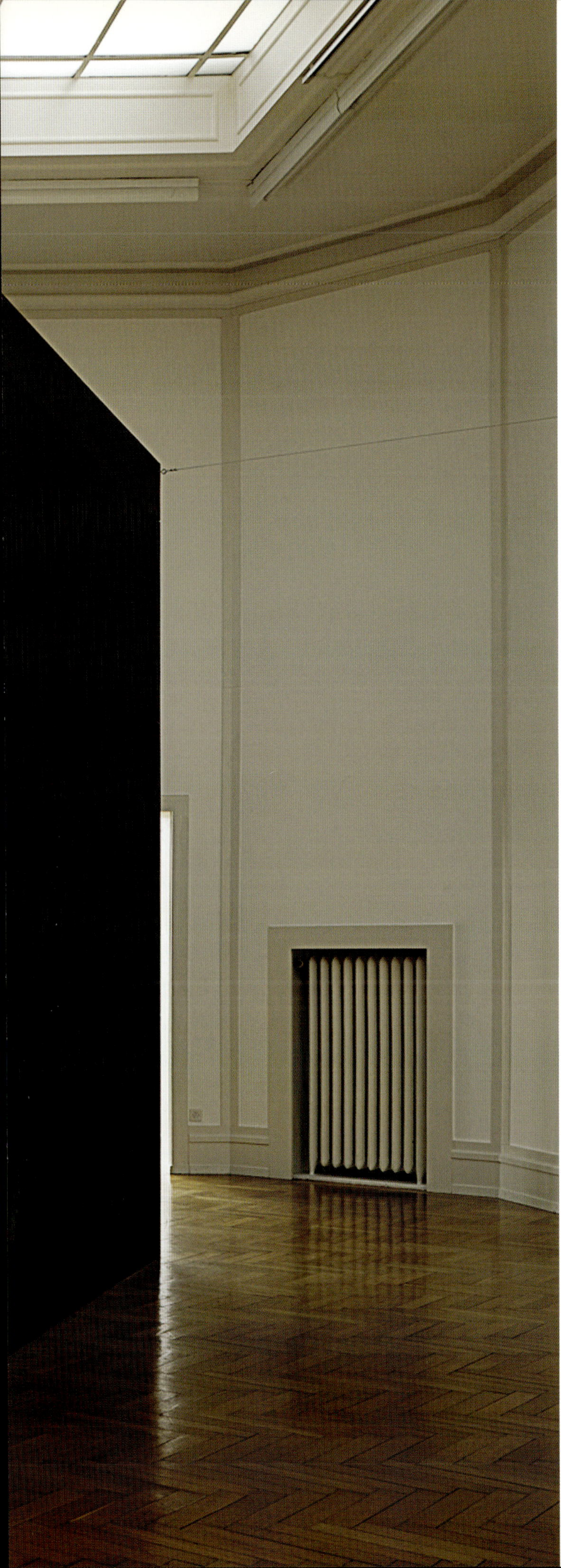

**Shown by**
Fons Welters G18

**Biography**
Born 1972
Lives in Shanghai and Amsterdam

Amsterdam-born Lester has presented solo shows at venues that include Museum Boijmans Van Beuningen, Rotterdam (2011), Rodeo Gallery, Istanbul (2010), Gallery Fons Welters (2008) and Bloomberg Space, London (2007). Recent group exhibitions include 'TV Commune', Nam June Paik Art Center, Yongin-si Gyeonggi-do, South Korea (2011–12), and participation in Documenta 13, Kassel (2012), the 29th Bienal de Sao Paulo (2010) and the 3rd Performa Biennial, New York (2009).

*Night of the 24th (The Crisis)*
2009
Wood, MDF and props
3.5 × 3.5 × 4.5 m
Courtesy of Fons Welters

# Gabriel Lester

Gabriel Lester's art is cinematographic, even when it does not involve film or video. Although he studied cinema, and sometimes makes semi-narrative films—such as *The Big One* (2011), in which characters participate in a fantastical lottery draw—much of his work is sculptural or installation-based, often alluding to narratives in mid-flow. For *Melancholia in Arcadia* (2011) Lester fabricated hardened lace curtains that in photographs appear to be blowing in the wind but which, experienced in real time, are deathly still. The office scene in *Night of the 24th (The Crisis)* (2009) is glimpsed through latticed walls; as with the curving concrete tunnel *Transition* (2012), viewers frame their own tracking shots as they move past the work. JG

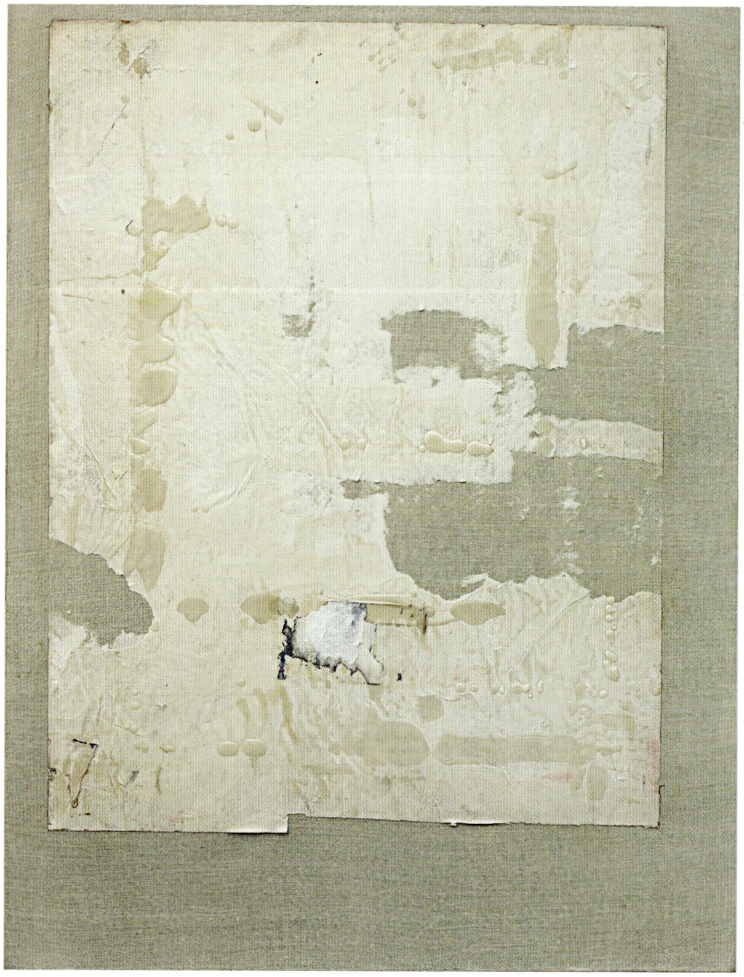

1

2

3

**Shown by**
Almine Rech Gallery
D18

**Biography**
Born 1985
Lives in New York

New York-born Lindman has shown solo exhibitions at Ribordy Contemporary, Geneva (2012), Hannah Barry Gallery, London (2011), Golden Age, Chicago (2011), West Street Gallery, New York (2010), and House Music V&A, New York (2009). His work has featured in group shows recently such as the three-person exhibition 'Traces', ACME, Los Angeles (2012), and 'Golden Age: Reference Work', Museum of Contemporary Art, Chicago (2011).

1
*White Green Painting*
2012
Found surface (resin and paper), rabbit-skin glue and fabrics
122 × 91 cm
Courtesy of Almine Rech Gallery

2
*Parrhesia*
2012
Oil and perspex on canvas and hardware
104 × 74 cm
Courtesy of Almine Rech Gallery

3
*The Best Sauce is Hunger*
2012
Oil on canvas
104 × 74 cm
Courtesy of Almine Rech Gallery

# Erik Lindman

Erik Lindman has described his mixed-media paintings as 'indirect objects', the process of their production one of 'editing'. The linguistic analogies are significant: they get at the thorny question of how to occupy the 'language' of studio painting, knowing full well that it's impossible to escape its in-built biases and dispositions. Lindman's paintings are low on colour and legible form, but his titles are often tempting leads that conjure a previously unseen landscape or the seed of a narrative—*Happier than the Morning Sun* (2012), *Jokes* (2010–11), *The Best Sauce is Hunger* (2012). Each one walks the viewer through a new variation of a shared question—how, exactly, do we go about viewing painting today, when we supposedly know everything about it? SNS

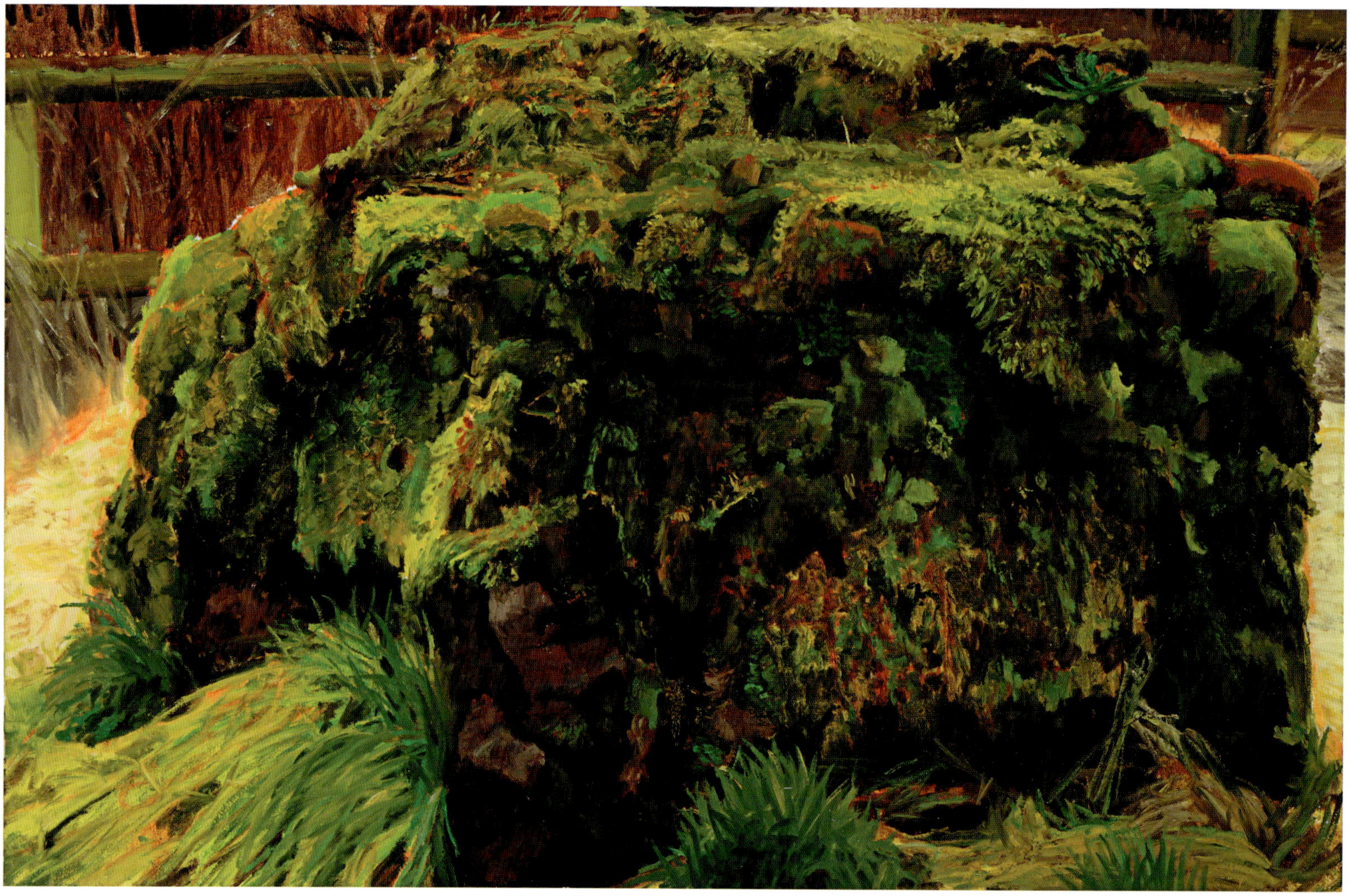

# Simon Ling

**Shown by**
greengrassi D17

**Biography**
Born 1968
Lives in London

British painter Ling has been the subject of five solo exhibitions at greengrassi, London, since 2001. His work has been featured in group exhibitions that include 'Head Wig (Portrait of an Exhibition)', Camden Arts Centre, London (2009), 'Art Now: Beating the Bounds', Tate Britain, London (2009), 'Jean-Luc Blanc: Opera Rock', CAPC Musée d'Art Contemporain de Bordeaux (2009), and 'Clouds of Witness', Islington Museum, London (2005).

*Untitled*
2011
Oil on canvas
122 × 183 cm
Courtesy of greengrassi

Simon Ling paints landscapes that seem utterly broken, eviscerated and torn apart. The bodily analogies are not incidental; a 2008 exhibition dominated by representations of tree stumps and collapsed masonry was titled 'Nail Through Finger'. Usually eschewing an orientating horizon line, Ling focuses on overlooked corners of suburban wilderness, cataloguing dense fields of information carefully and dispassionately. Ling begins most of his paintings *en plein air*; works such as *Untitled* (2011), however, acquire a hallucinatory vivacity when finished back in the studio. Unlike earlier paintings, the moss- and creeper-covered heap in *Untitled* is evidence not so much of human violence as of a natural—though no less cruel—form of entropy. JG

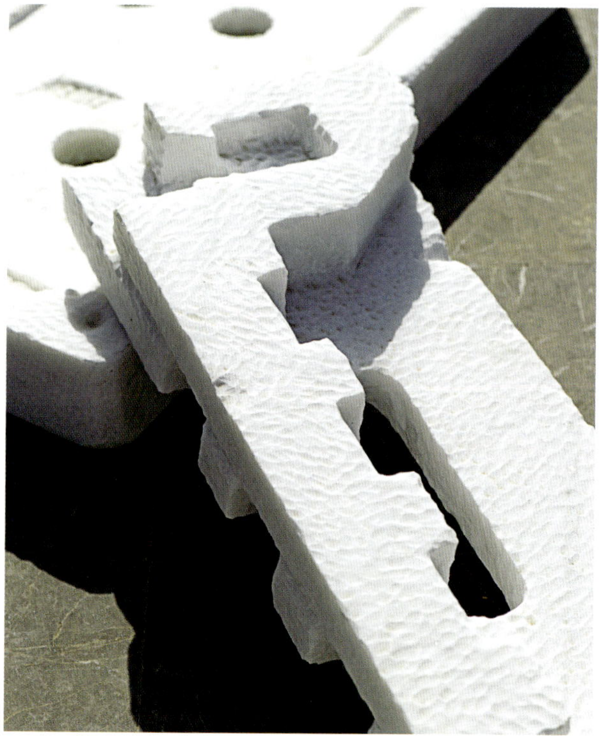

1

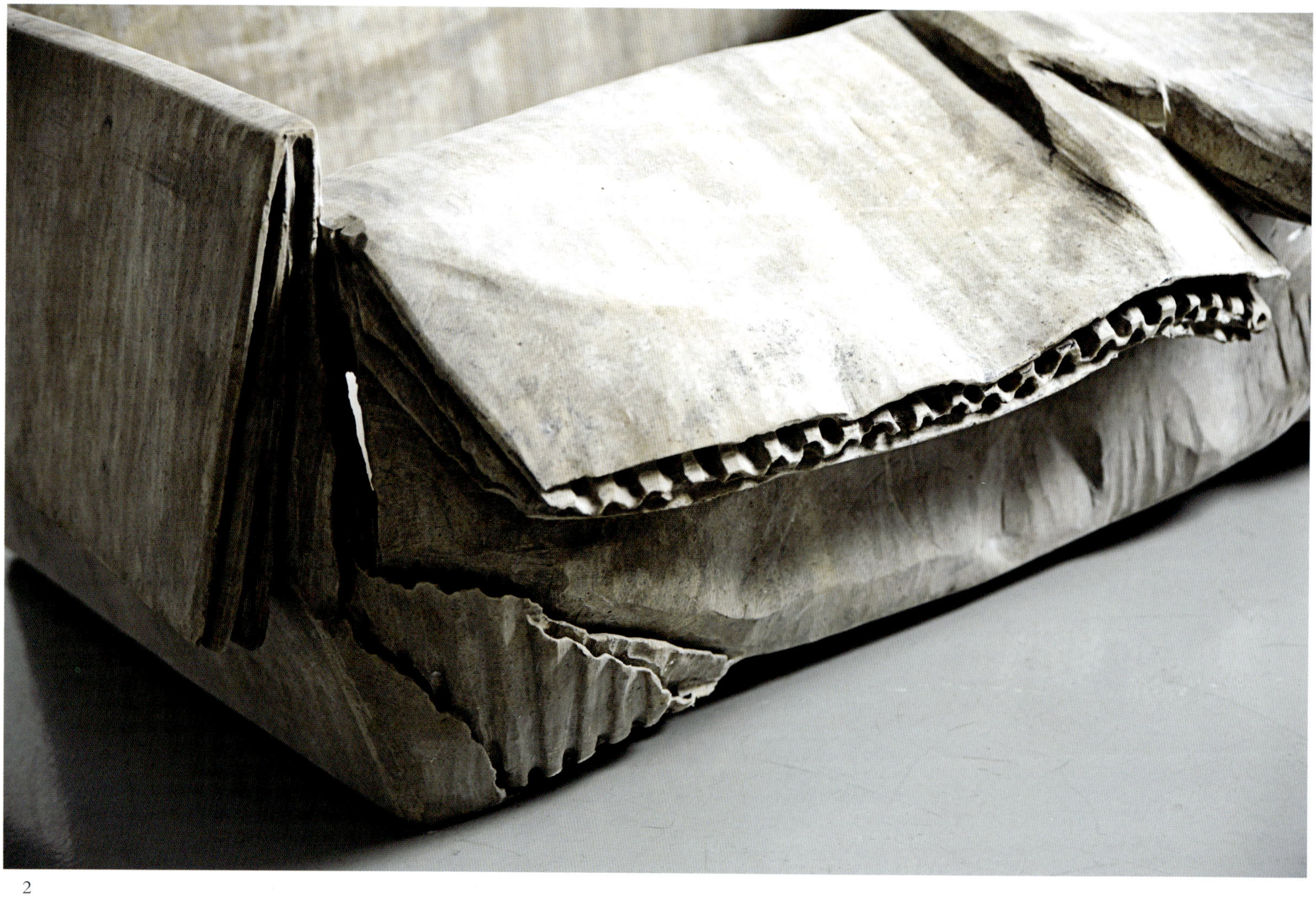

2

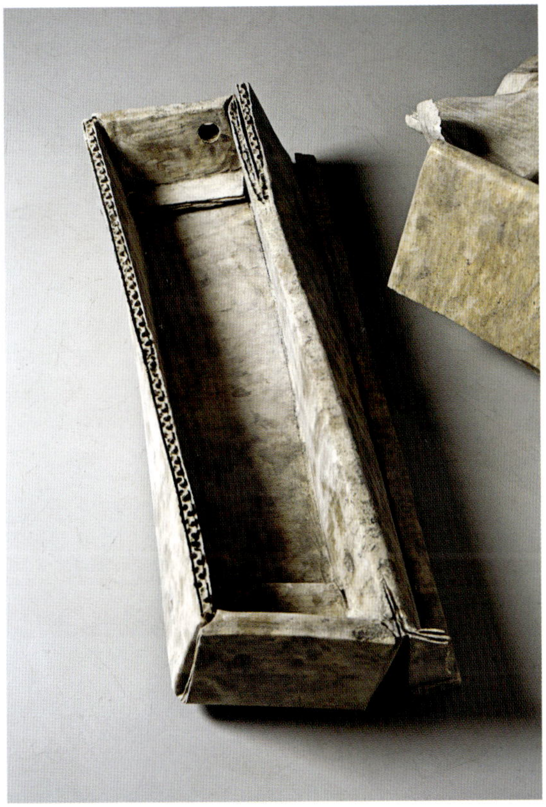

3

**Shown by**
The Breeder F14

**Biography**
Born 1970
Lives in Athens

Greek artist Lolis has been the subject of solo exhibitions at venues including Münchner Künstlerhaus, Munich (2011). He was a recipient of the Edgardo Mannucci International Sculpture Award in 2008. His work was featured in the 3rd Athens Biennale (2011) and in group exhibitions at galleries and institutions such as the Skironio Museum, Athens (2010), and Melina Mercouri Cultural Centre, Athens (2009).

1
*Untitled*
(detail)
2012
Dionysian marble
135 × 92 × 15 cm
Courtesy of The Breeder

2
*Untitled*
(detail)
2012
Moroccan marble
70 × 57 × 30 cm
Courtesy of The Breeder

3
*Untitled*
(detail)
2012
Moroccan marble
77 × 30 × 17 cm
Courtesy of The Breeder

# Andreas Lolis

Andreas Lolis' choice of subject and materials contrasts the current economic crisis and widespread anti-austerity protests in Greece with the exalted sculptural traditions of Greco-Roman art. His *trompe-l'oeil* works made for the 3rd Athens Biennale (2011) were inspired by the repercussions of the Greek debt crisis as it unfolded in the city streets. Lolis said, 'When I saw people on the terraces sleeping in cartons [cardboard boxes], it only came to me as a natural thing to co-exist with this situation—not to record it.' The ephemeral becomes monumental in his series of sculptures such as *Untitled* (2012), which appear to be made from discarded corrugated cardboard and polystyrene packaging but are carved meticulously from Moroccan and Dionysian marble. SL

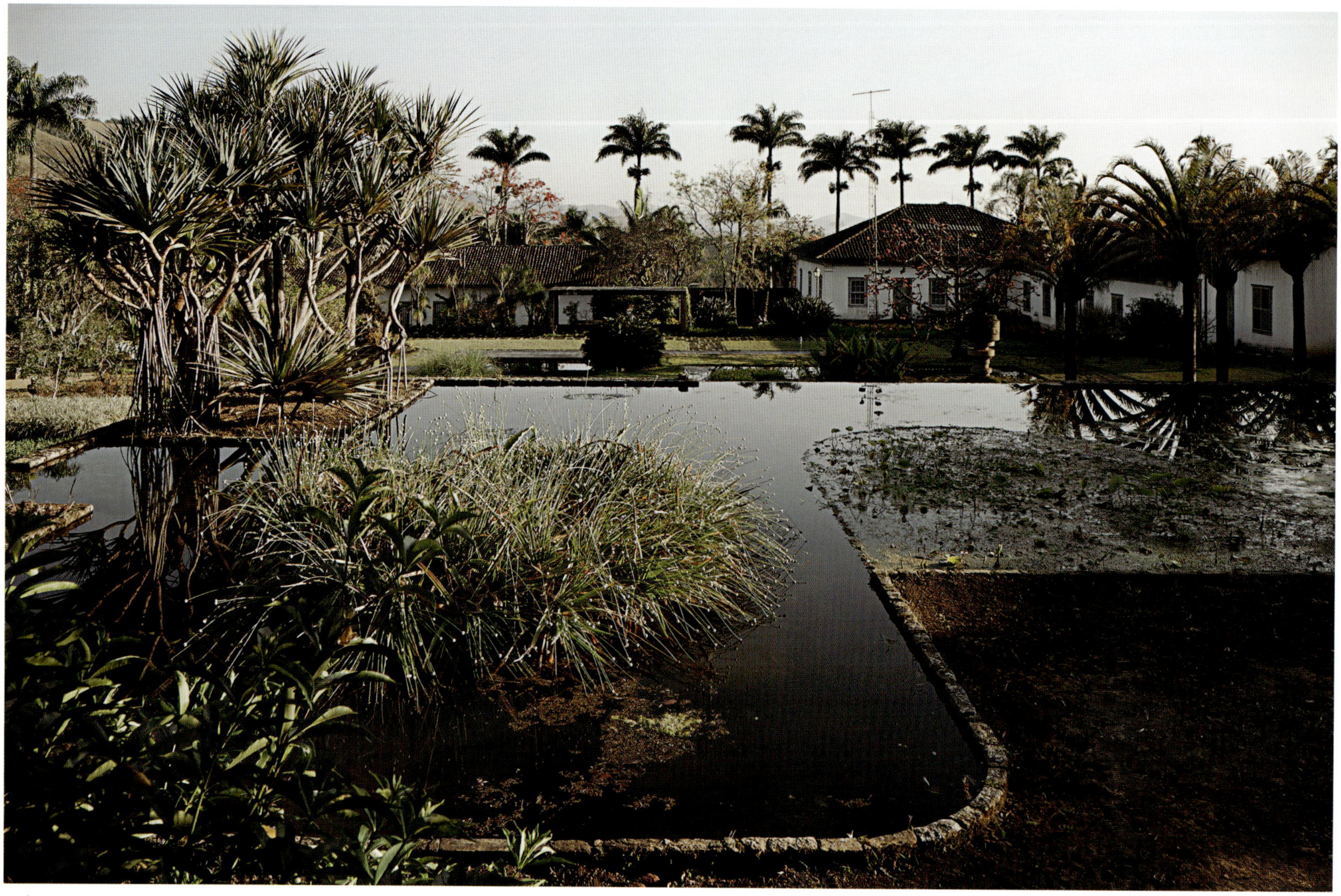

1

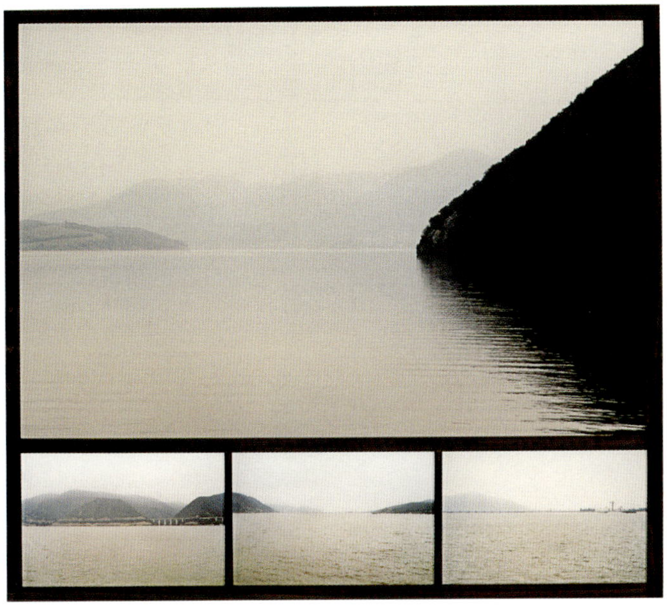

3

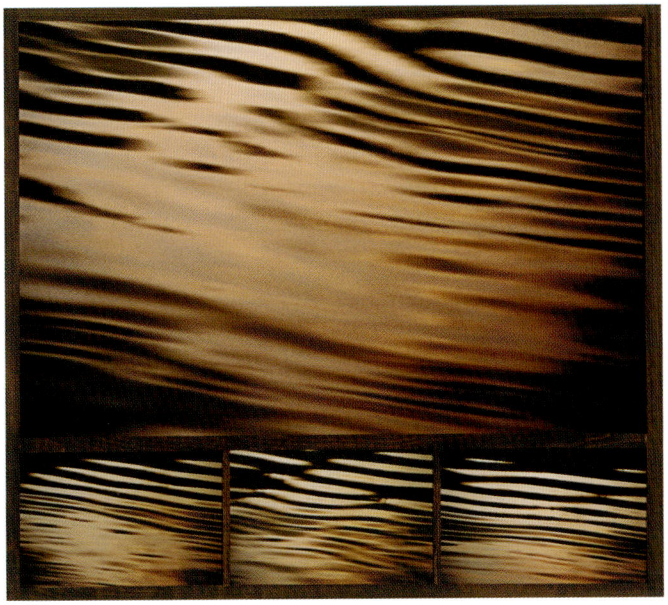

2

**Shown by**
Georg Kargl Fine Arts
D16

**Biography**
Born 1958
Lives in Vienna

Brazilian-born Lombardi has shown solo exhibitions at the Vienna Secession (2011), Centro Cultural de España, Montevideo (2006), Forum Maison Hermès, Tokyo (2005), Georg Kargl Fine Arts, Vienna (2002), Komatsu Art Space, Tokyo (1997), MUMOK, Vienna (1995), the 23rd Bienal de Sao Paulo (1996), and Palais Liechtenstein, Vienna (1995). Recent group shows include 'Cities on the River' (2010–11), an exhibition that travelled to institutions in Gyor, Bratislava and Vienna.

1
*Untitled (Jardim, Fazenda Vargem Grande #1)*
2011
C-type print
100 × 150 cm
Courtesy of Georg Kargl Fine Arts

2
*Given #22*
2000–02
C-type print
143 × 157 cm
Courtesy of Georg Kargl Fine Arts

3
*Given #25*
2000–02
C-type print
143 × 157 cm
Courtesy of Georg Kargl Fine Arts

# Inés Lombardi

Inés Lombardi primarily uses photography as a conceptual tool to collapse time. The photograph *Untitled (Jardim, Fazenda Vargem Grande #1)* (2011), from her exhibition 'Past Present – Close and Distant' (2011) at the Vienna Secession, looked closely at how gardens designed by landscape artist Roberto Burle Marx related to new and existing architecture. The series from which it was taken examined the designed spaces that shape nature, but also the way these spaces are always mediated. A pixelated video close-up reduced an image of the gardens to pure blocks of colour, appearing like one of Burle Marx's tile murals as well as providing the basis for the backdrop colours for the walls on which the photographs were hung. How we see the past, Lombardi suggests, holds the key to how we experience the present. CFW

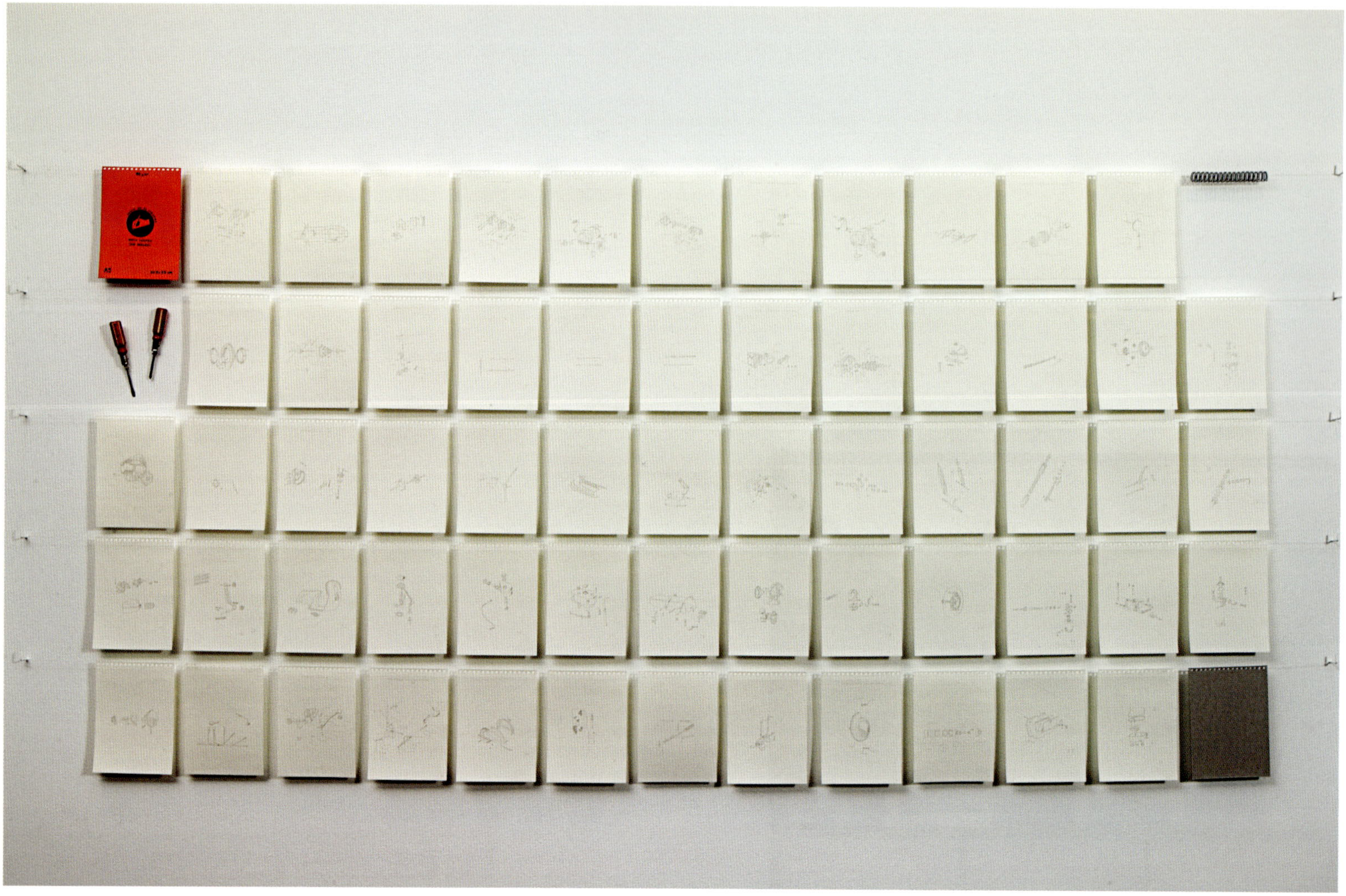

1

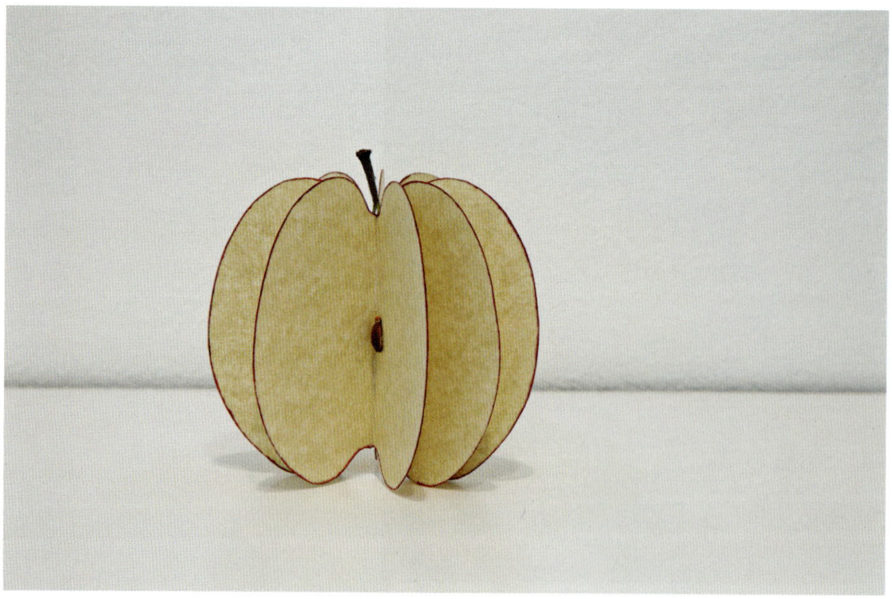

2

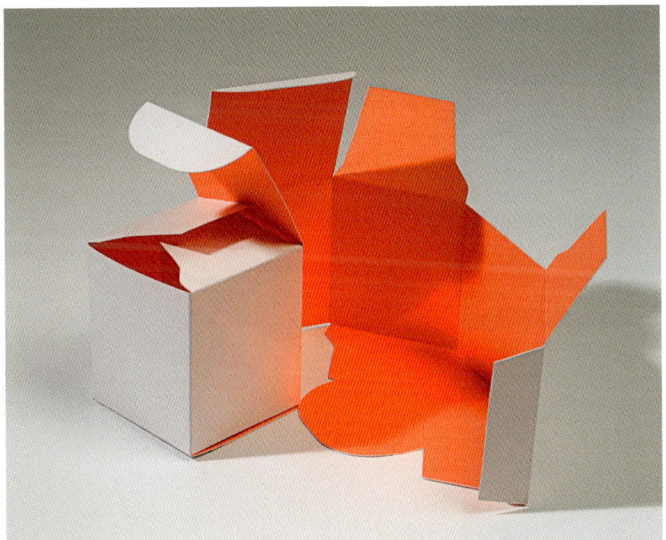

3

**Shown by**
Casas Riegner S16
Galeria Luisa Strina F6

**Biography**
Born 1978
Lives in Bogota

Colombian artist López has presented solo shows at galleries including Casas Riegner, Bogota (2012, 2007 and 2006), Gasworks, London (2010)—where he took part in a residency programme—and MUSAC, Leon (2009). He has participated in the 29th Bienal de Sao Paulo (2010) and group exhibitions such as 'Let's Talk about Houses', Museu do Chiado, Lisbon (2010), and 'Moby Dick', CCA Wattis Institute for Contemporary Arts, San Francisco (2009).

1
*Motorcycle Parts*
2008
Series of 61 drawings in pencil on paper
Each 21 × 15 cm
Courtesy of Casas Riegner

2
*Made to Measure*
2010
Paper, ink, apple seed and stem
7 × 7 × 7 cm
Courtesy of Casas Riegner

3
*The Hug*
2008
Paper
7 × 10 × 8 cm
Courtesy of Casas Riegner

# Focus
# Mateo López

Mateo López understands drawing as an expanded and explorative tool, a 'draughtsman's contract' which delights in the ordinariness of things and a confusion between two and three dimensions. An exhibition in 2006, for example, saw him create precise paper facsimiles of every object in his studio. The artist travelled for a week through Colombia on a scooter for *Motorcycle Diary* (2007), with a portable kit including an updated version of the 19th-century optical drawing device the camera lucida. Guided by whimsy throughout his passage through landscapes and unfamiliar towns, López later displayed the results of his peripatetic studio in the 61 drawings of *Motorcycle Parts* (2008), as well as *Anecdotal Topography* (2007), which gathered illustrations, diaries, maps and photographs alongside the parked scooter. MA

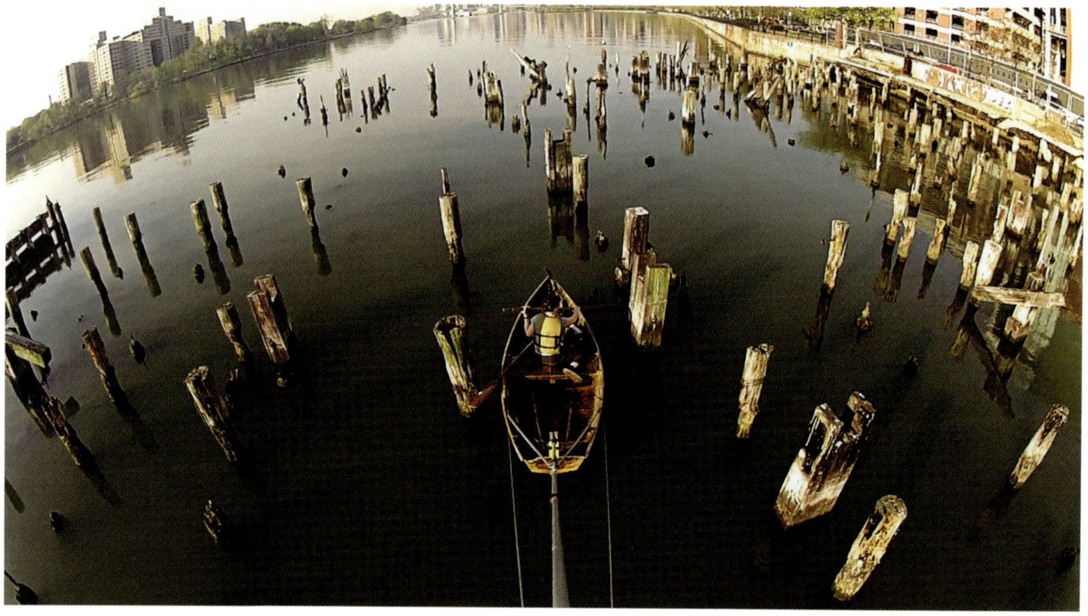

1

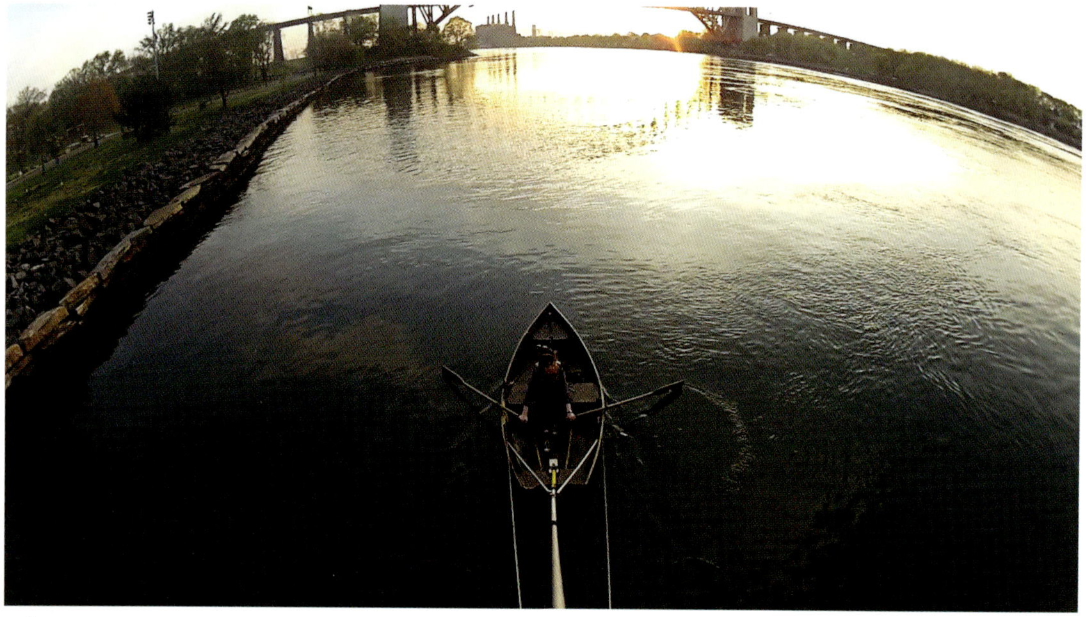

2

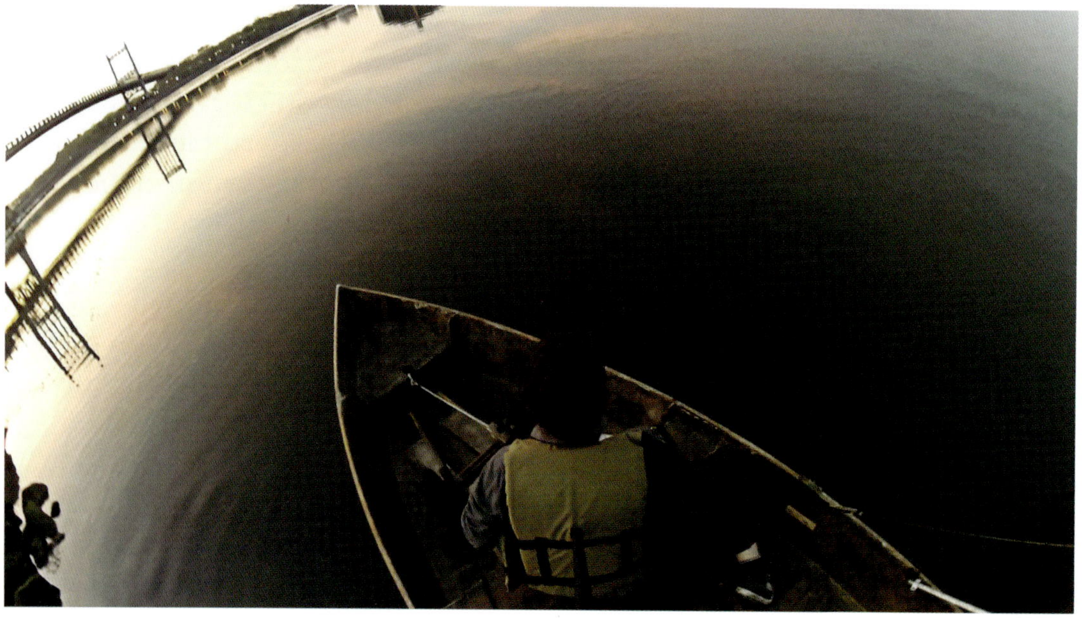

3

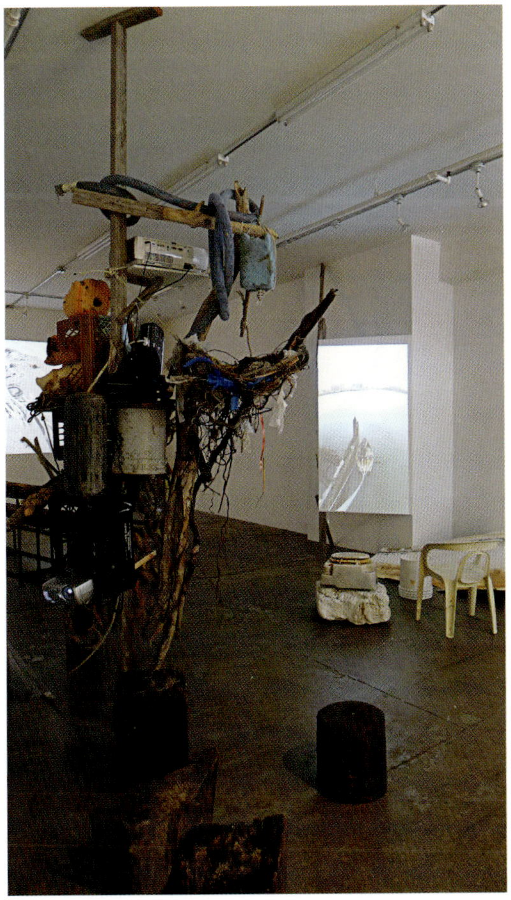

4

# Marie Lorenz

**Shown by**
Jack Hanley Gallery A9

**Biography**
Born 1973
Lives in New York

Californian-born artist Lorenz has presented solo projects and performances at venues that include Jack Hanley Gallery, New York (2012), Locust Projects, Miami (2011), the Hessel Museum of Art at Bard College, Annandale-on-Hudson, New York (2010), and the Glass Pavilion, Berlin (2008). She has been featured in recent group exhibitions such as 'Drawings Related to Performance Works', 92YTribeca, New York (2011), and 'Water Water Every Where', BRIC Rotunda Gallery, New York (2011). *The Tide and Current Taxi*, her performance and water taxi service around New York, has been ongoing since 2005.

1, 2, 3
*Hell Gate – Bronx Kill – Harlem River*
2012
HD video
16 min.
Courtesy of Jack Hanley Gallery

4
*Archipelago (Mastview)*
2012
Video installation with projection pole
Dimensions variable
20 min.
Courtesy of Jack Hanley Gallery

Marie Lorenz explores the terrain of the city, an urban wilderness she might navigate in a home-made boat or document with the aid of a video camera. In her project *Archipelago* (2012), which includes the video *Hell Gate – Bronx Kill – Harlem River*, Lorenz travels the waterways of New York City, providing new views of one of the most recorded cities in the world. Lorenz does more than merely find a new way of looking at a familiar location; instead, she taps into a long-established narrative about the intrepid urban traveller, from the 19th-century *flâneur* to Gordon Matta-Clark. Ideas about life as art, about motion, solitude and contemplation, are referenced in Lorenz' uncannily mesmerizing videos—as are Emersonian notions of self-reliance, courage and American individualism. KK

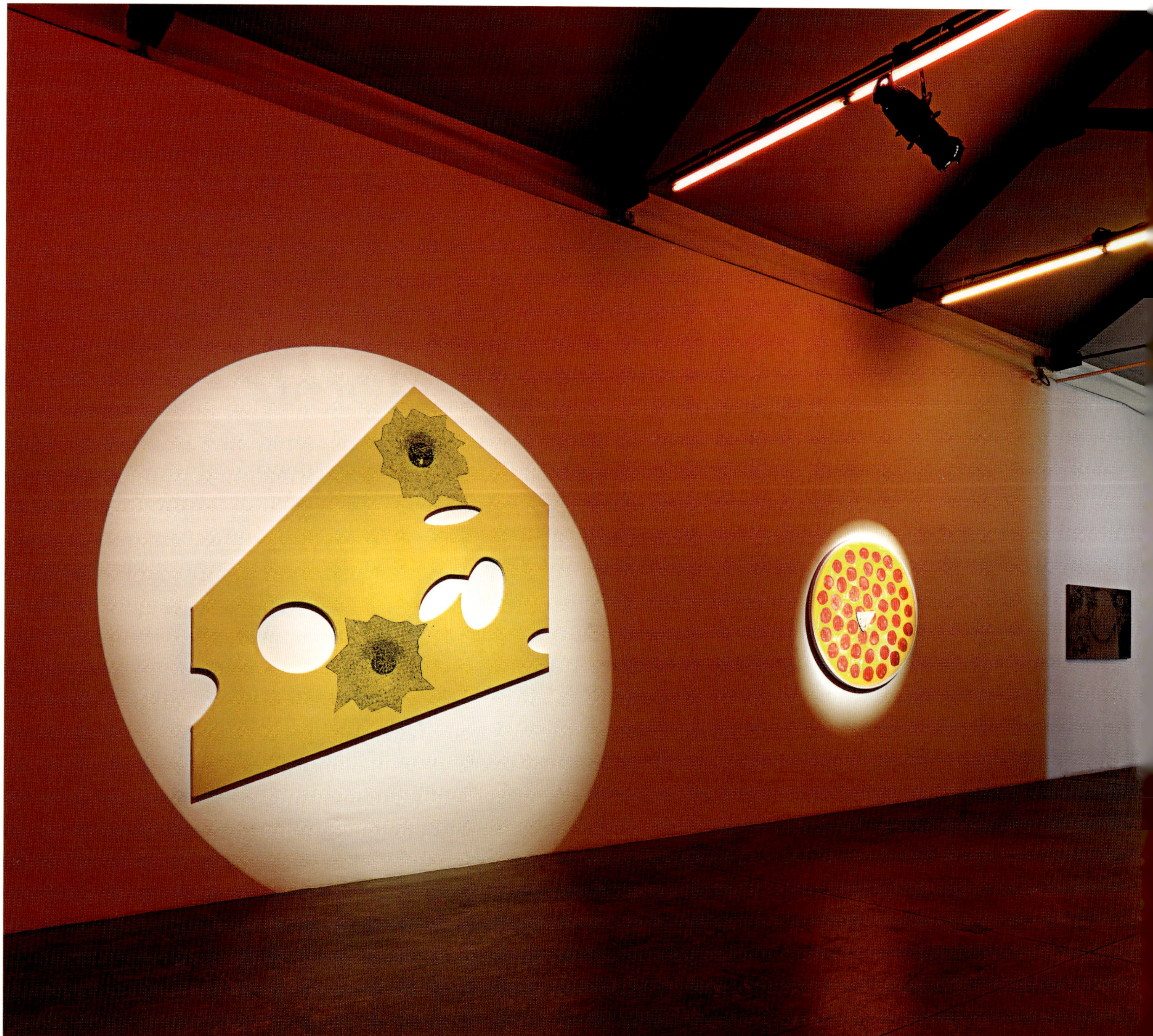

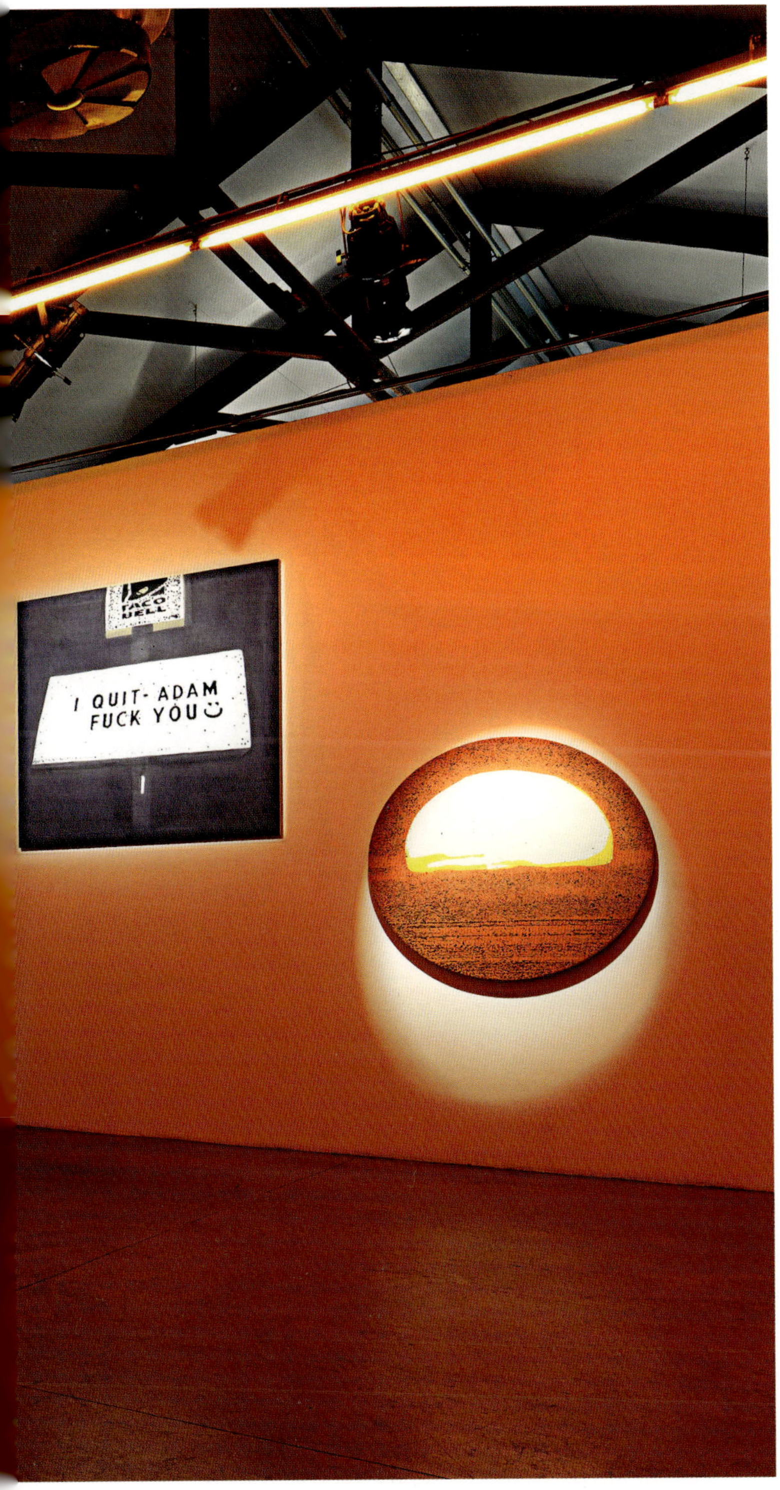


**Shown by**
Massimo De Carlo D8

**Biography**
Born 1979
Lives in New York

Las-Vegas born Lowman has shown solo exhibitions recently at venues that include Carlson Gallery, London (2012), Massimo De Carlo, Milan (2012), the American Academy in Rome (2011), and Astrup Fearnley Museum, Oslo (2009). His work has been presented in group shows such as 'George Herms: Xenophilia (Love of the Unknown)', Museum of Contemporary Art, Los Angeles (2011), 'The Last Newspaper', New Museum, New York (2010), and 'Haunted: Contemporary Photography/Video/Performance', Solomon R. Guggenheim Museum, New York (2010).

'Swiss Cheese and The Doors: A One Night Stand'
2012
Exhibition view
Courtesy of Massimo De Carlo

# Nate Lowman

Jean-Luc Godard famously said that all you need for a film is a girl and a gun. Nate Lowman makes art out of the dead-end aftermath after the credits roll: banal, smiley faces and Benday-dot bullet holes. Originally inspired by an O. J. Simpson suicide note, the smileys pop up with maniacal frequency. Ranging from deliriously slick to mournfully grungy, Lowman's downbeat Americana has also included tow-truck parts, giant air-fresheners, photos of surgically enhanced celebrities, and sugar and dirt on canvas. A recent show featured both constellations of paintings and works spot-lit on glowing orange walls: an image of Swiss cheese perforated by screen-printed bullet holes resembling dull stars, a pepperoni pizza tondo and another nearly filled by a resplendently trite setting sun. KMJ

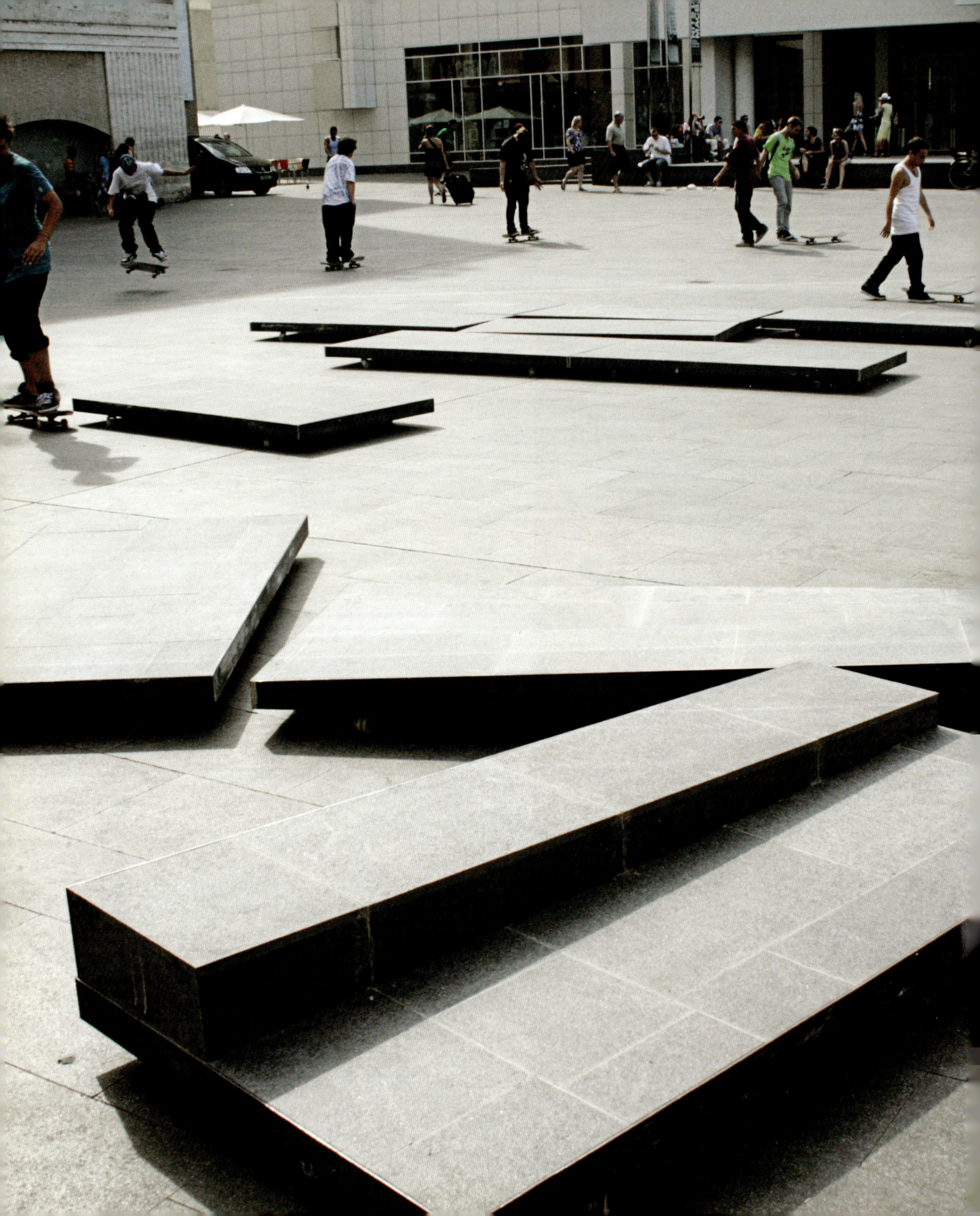

**Shown by**
A Gentil Carioca G17
Galeria Luisa Strina F6

**Biography**
Born 1971
Lives in Rio de Janeiro

Brazilian-born Lucas has been the subject of recent solo shows at KW Institute for Contemporary Art, Berlin (2010)—as the recipient of the Ernst Schering Foundation Art Award—and Gasworks, London (2007), where she was part of the artist residency programme. She participated in the 53rd Venice Biennale (2009) and 16th Biennale of Sydney (2008). Her work is included in public collections such as MACBA, Barcelona, and Museu de Arte Moderna, Rio de Janeiro.

1
*Prototipo para un suelo resbaladizo*
(Prototype for a Sliding Ground)
2009
Granite slabs mounted on wheeled metal modules
Dimensions variable
Courtesy of A Gentil Carioca

2
*Gentileza*
(Kindness)
2005
Architectural intervention
Dimensions variable
Courtesy of A Gentil Carioca

# Renata Lucas

Our external environment is arguably an ambiguous but decisive mirror to our internal state. The spatial disruptions, inversions and replications set up by Renata Lucas provide the settings to alter our ways of experiencing our surroundings, and through that our ways of sensing and communicating. Her *Prototipo para un suelo resbaladizo* (Proposition for a Sliding Ground, 2009) was a set of granite slabs and steps mounted on wheels, let loose in a public square in Barcelona for pedestrians, skateboarders or parkour practitioners to use as they saw fit. Whether filling Oscar Niemeyer's mirrored Pampulha casino with layers of scaffolding or tearing down a wall to merge a gallery space with the neighbour next door, Lucas promotes confusion and disorientation as a way of finding a productive potential. CFW

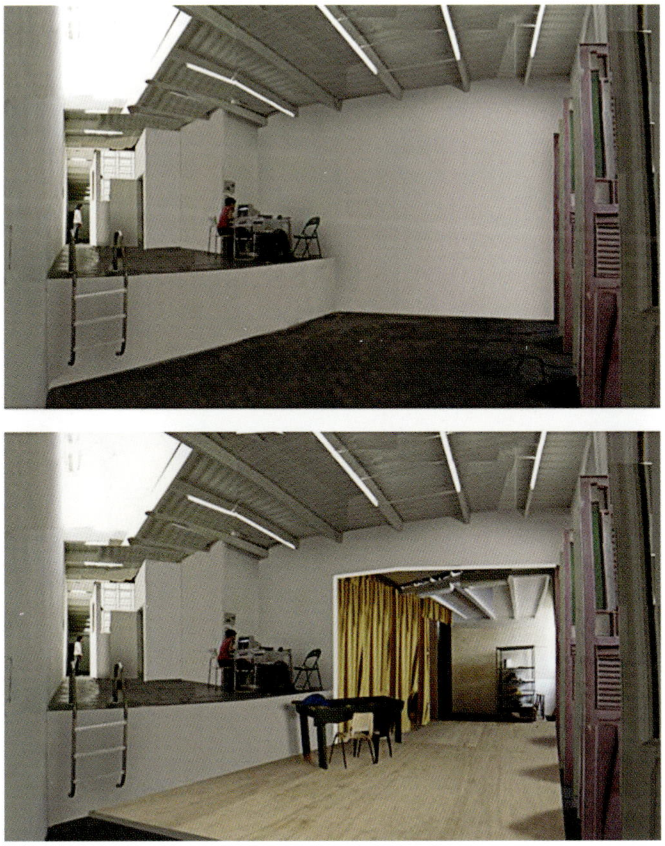

2

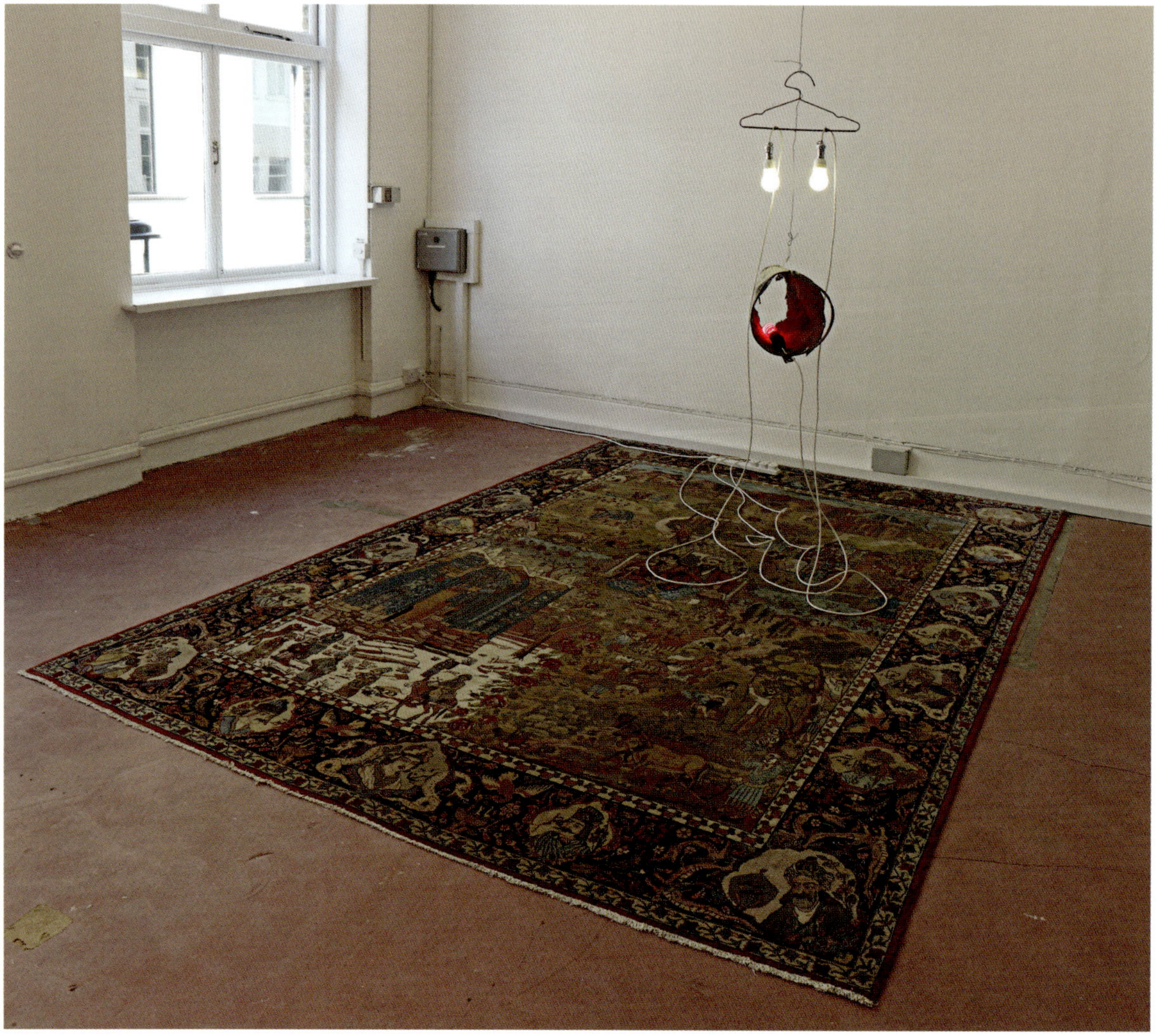
1

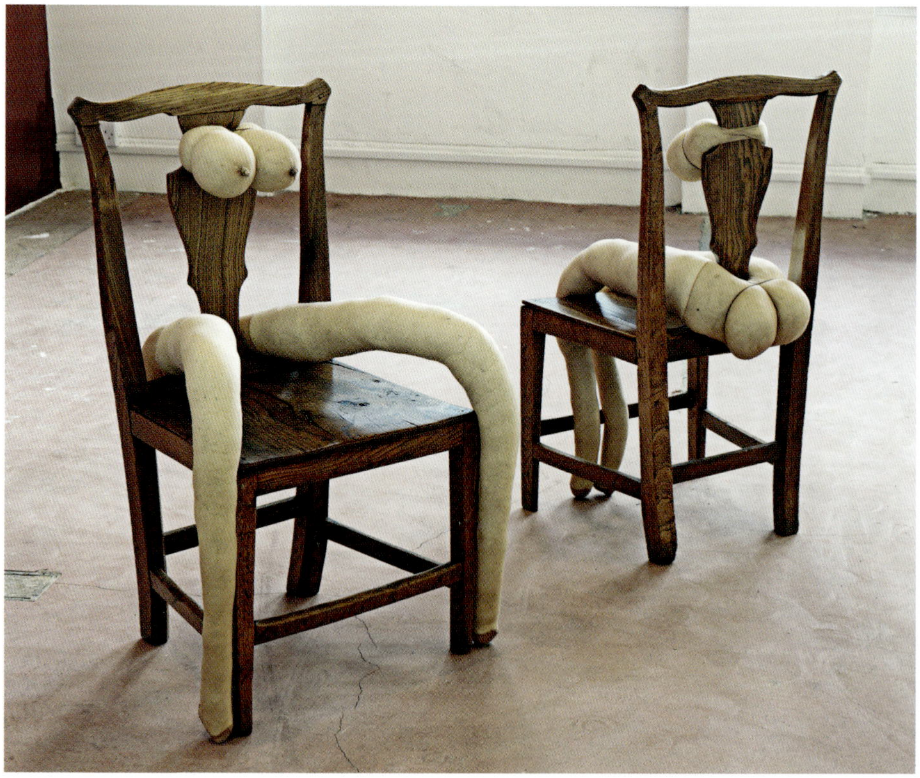
2

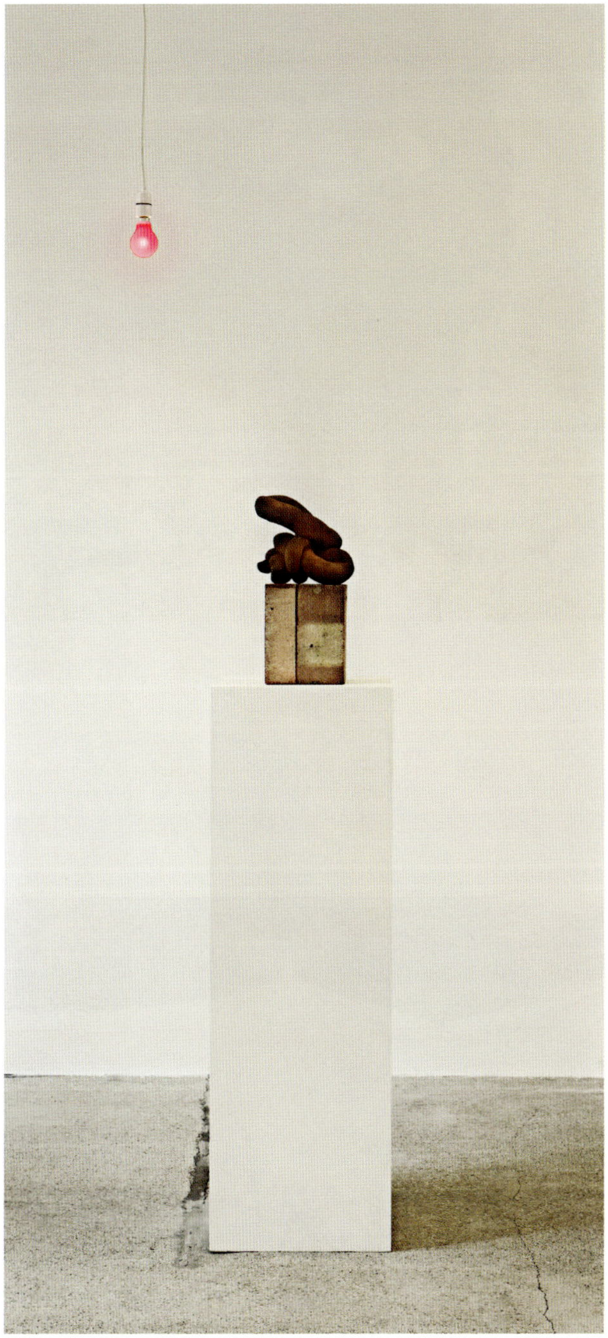

3

**Shown by**
Sadie Coles HQ C11

**Biography**
Born 1962
Lives in Suffolk

English artist Lucas has presented recent solo exhibitions at venues that include Situation, Sadie Coles (2012), the Henry Moore Institute, Leeds (2012), and Museum of Cycladic Art, Athens (2010). She has been the subject of survey exhibitions at Tate Liverpool (2005) and Tate Britain (2004), and she participated in the 50th Venice Biennale (2003). Her work is part of public collections including: Thyssen-Bornemisza Art Contemporary, Vienna; MoMA, New York; and the Tate collection, UK.

1
*Magic Mary*
2012
Metal bucket, wire, clothes hanger, light bulbs and cable
185 × 245 × 327 cm
Courtesy of Sadie Coles HQ

2
*Make Love*
2012
Diptych of two chairs, tights, kapok, linen string and wire
95 × 135 × 58 cm
Courtesy of Sadie Coles HQ

3
*Hard Nud*
2012
Cast iron with four bricks
41 × 17 × 21 cm
Courtesy of Sadie Coles HQ

# Sarah Lucas

Stereotypically, the public face of British sexuality is bawdy and puerile. Sarah Lucas' sculptures, on the other hand, present sex as domestic banality suffused with surreal improbability, which is perhaps disturbing, but possibly more accurate. While *Magic Mary* (2012) revels in fabulously vulgar humour, it also troublingly reconstructs the misogynist's tendency to reduce female anatomy to the 'essential' elements, here invoked by a broken bucket and a pair of light bulbs. *Make Love* (2012), meanwhile, with its coupling of soft and hard materials, manifests some of the more experiential dualities of sex: the fragility of flesh and the robustness of animal intent; mindless lust and conscious self-display; and the clinching embrace of lyricism and humour. SOR

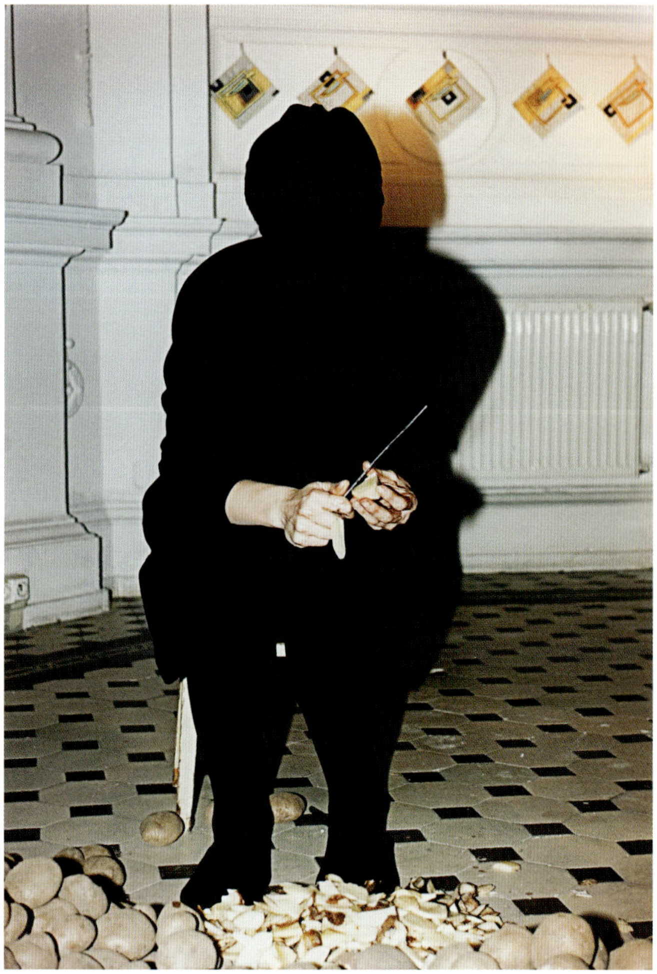

1

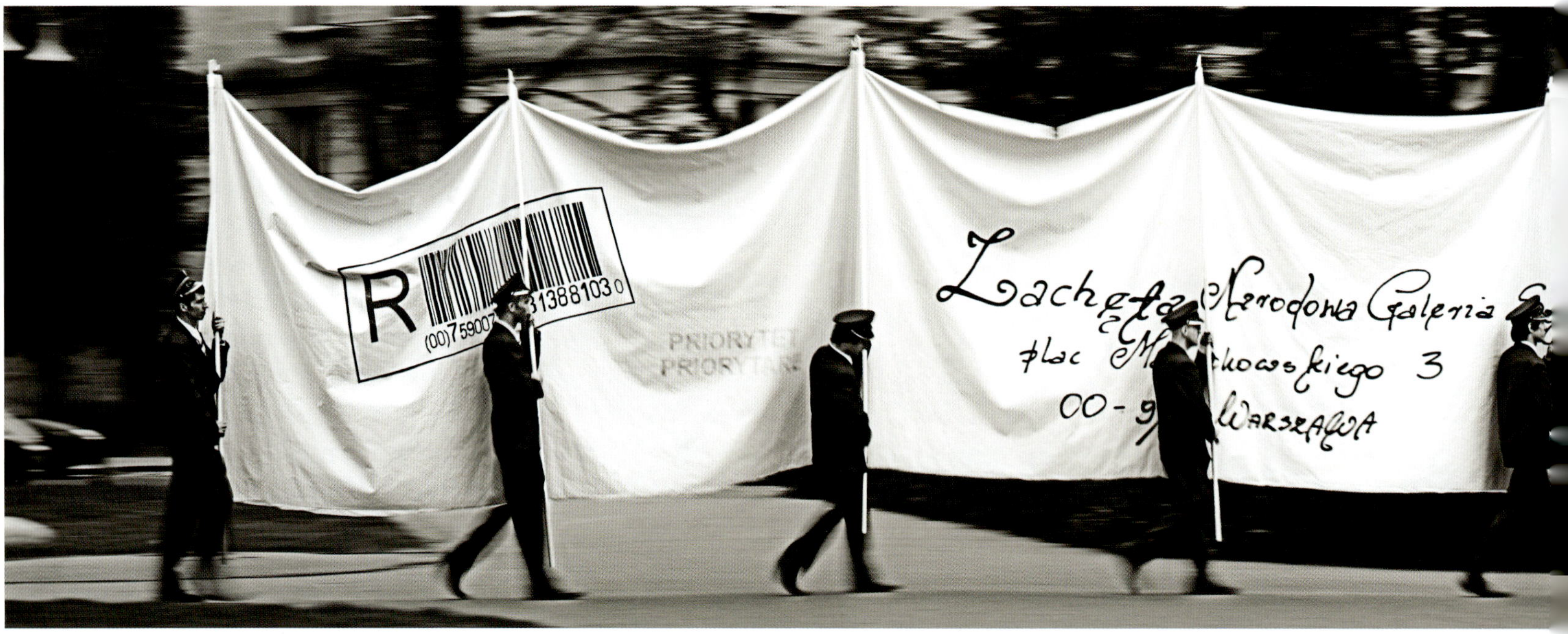


2

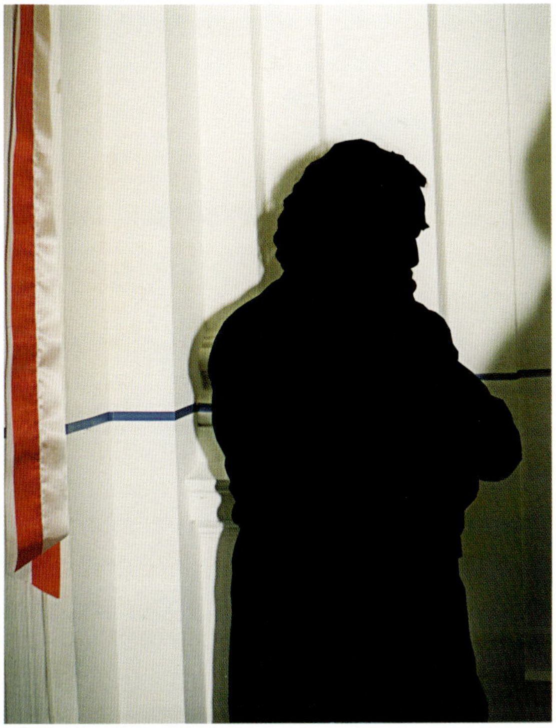

3

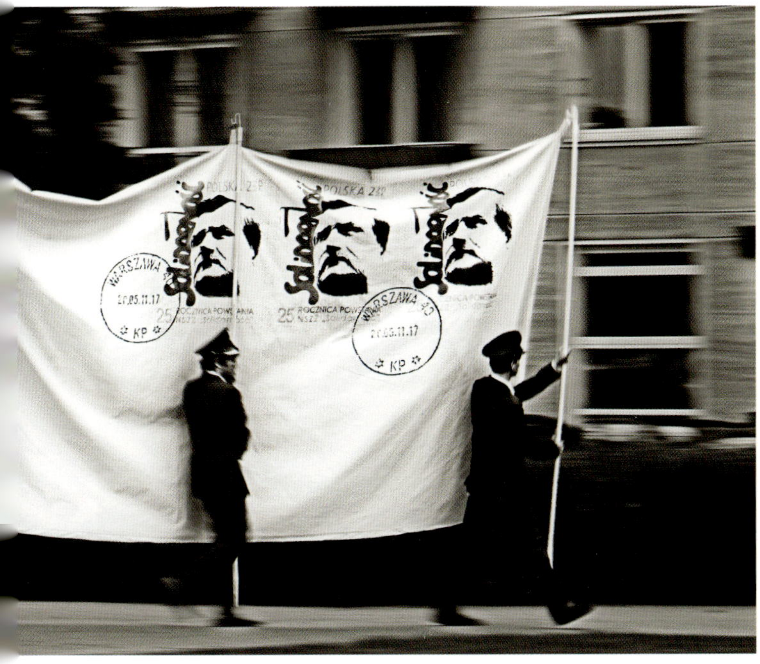

**Shown by**
Andrew Kreps Gallery C5
Kate MacGarry E11
Galerie Rüdiger Schöttle H2

**Biography**
Born 1967
Lives in London

Warsaw-born Macuga, a nominee for the Turner Prize in 2008, has presented solo shows and projects at venues that include Zacheta National Gallery of Art, Warsaw (2011), Walker Art Center, Minneapolis (2011), Whitechapel Gallery, London (2009), Kunsthalle Basel (2009) and Tate Britain (2007). She recently participated in Documenta 13, Kassel (2012), and group exhibitions including 'Newspeak: British Art Now, Part One', Saatchi Gallery, London (2010).

1
*Anti-Collage (Julita Wojcik)*
2011
Silkscreen on photograph
180 × 125 cm
Courtesy of Galerie Rüdiger Schöttle

2
*The Letter*
2011
Tapestry
3.5 × 11.5 m
Courtesy of Galerie Rüdiger Schöttle

3
*Anti-Collage (Harald Szeemann)*
2011
Silkscreen on photograph
150 × 105 cm
Courtesy of Galerie Rüdiger Schöttle

# Goshka Macuga

Goshka Macuga's is an art of reanimation, activating the potential dormant in works of art, architectural spaces and events that she blasts (as Walter Benjamin put it) out of the continuum of history. The best-known instance in recent years has been her presentation in 2009, at the Whitechapel Gallery in London, of the 1955 *Guernica* tapestry—the version of Picasso's painting that had famously been covered up at the UN in 2003 when Colin Powell spoke in favour of the invasion of Iraq. In other words, Macuga's intricate researches into 20th-century art, architecture and design come freighted with political import: for her exhibition at Zacheta National Gallery of Art, Warsaw, in 2011, she exposed the fraught history of censorship at the institution itself. BD

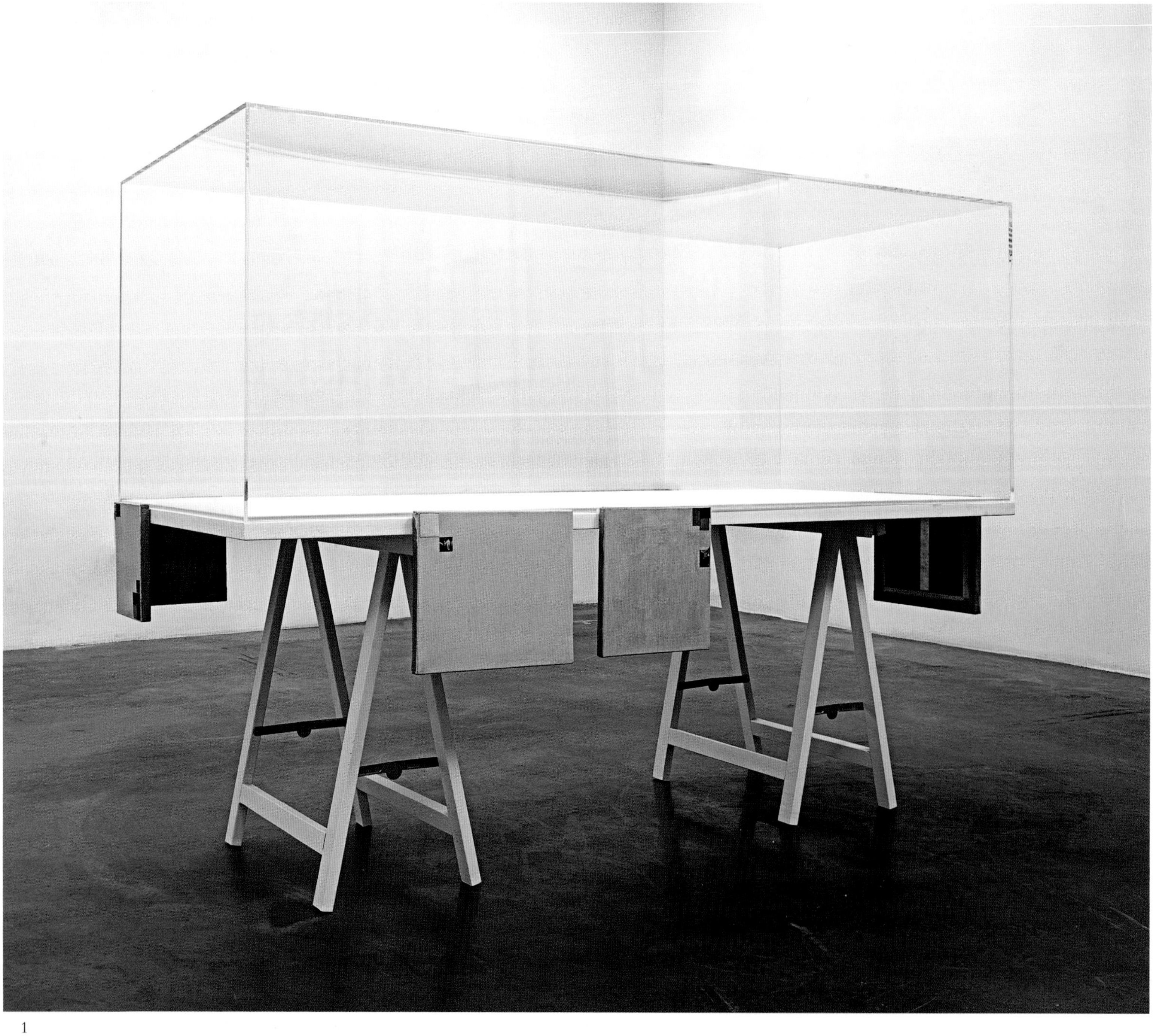

1

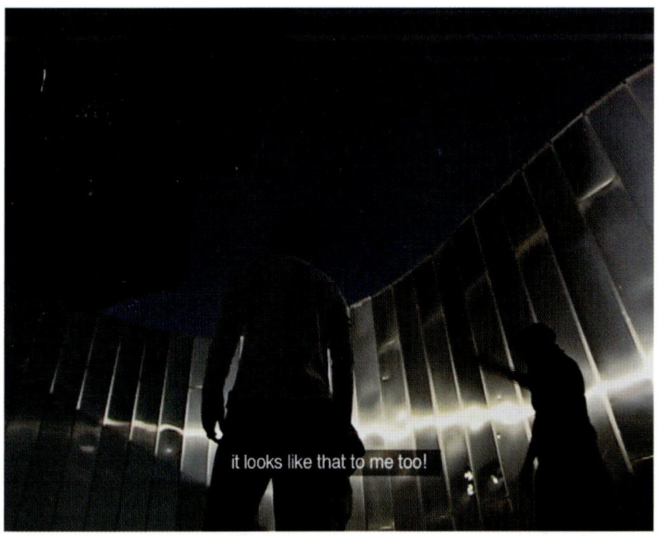


2

**Shown by**
Annet Gelink Gallery
H7
Georg Kargl Fine Arts
D16
Sprüth Magers Berlin
London D6

**Biography**
Born 1967
Lives in Zagreb

Recent solo exhibitions by Croatian artist Maljkovic include those at the Vienna Secession (2011), Museum of Contemporary Art, Zagreb (2011), Annet Gelink Gallery, Amsterdam (2010), and Museo Nacional Centro de Arte Reina Sofía, Madrid (2009). In 2010 Maljkovic received the Croatian Association of Artists Award. He is the subject of an exhibition at Van Abbemuseum, Eindhoven, until January 2013, before it travels to Baltic, Gateshead.

1
*Sources in the Air*
2011
Wooden table on trestles, Plexiglas cover and five works on canvas
157 × 200 × 75 cm
Courtesy of Annet Gelink Gallery

2
*Scene for New Heritage*
2004
DVD
4 min. 33 sec.
Courtesy of Annet Gelink Gallery

# David Maljkovic

David Maljkovic's films, collages, drawings and sculptural installations are concerned with the legacy of Croatia's Communist heritage and the architectonic grammar of Balkan Modernism. Emerging in Zagreb in the late 1990s, he became more known internationally following his 2003–4 residency in Amsterdam's Rijksakademie, and in particular for the video narrative *Scene for a New Heritage* (2004)—the first of what would become a lo-fi, high-concept trilogy—in which a group of Croatian time travellers encounter the hilltop Petrova Gora memorial. More recently, *Sources in the Air* (2011) seemed to suggest an ongoing concern for such displacement and decontextualization—an empty transparent vitrine was accompanied by five works on canvas mounted, as if in protest, on the exterior. MA

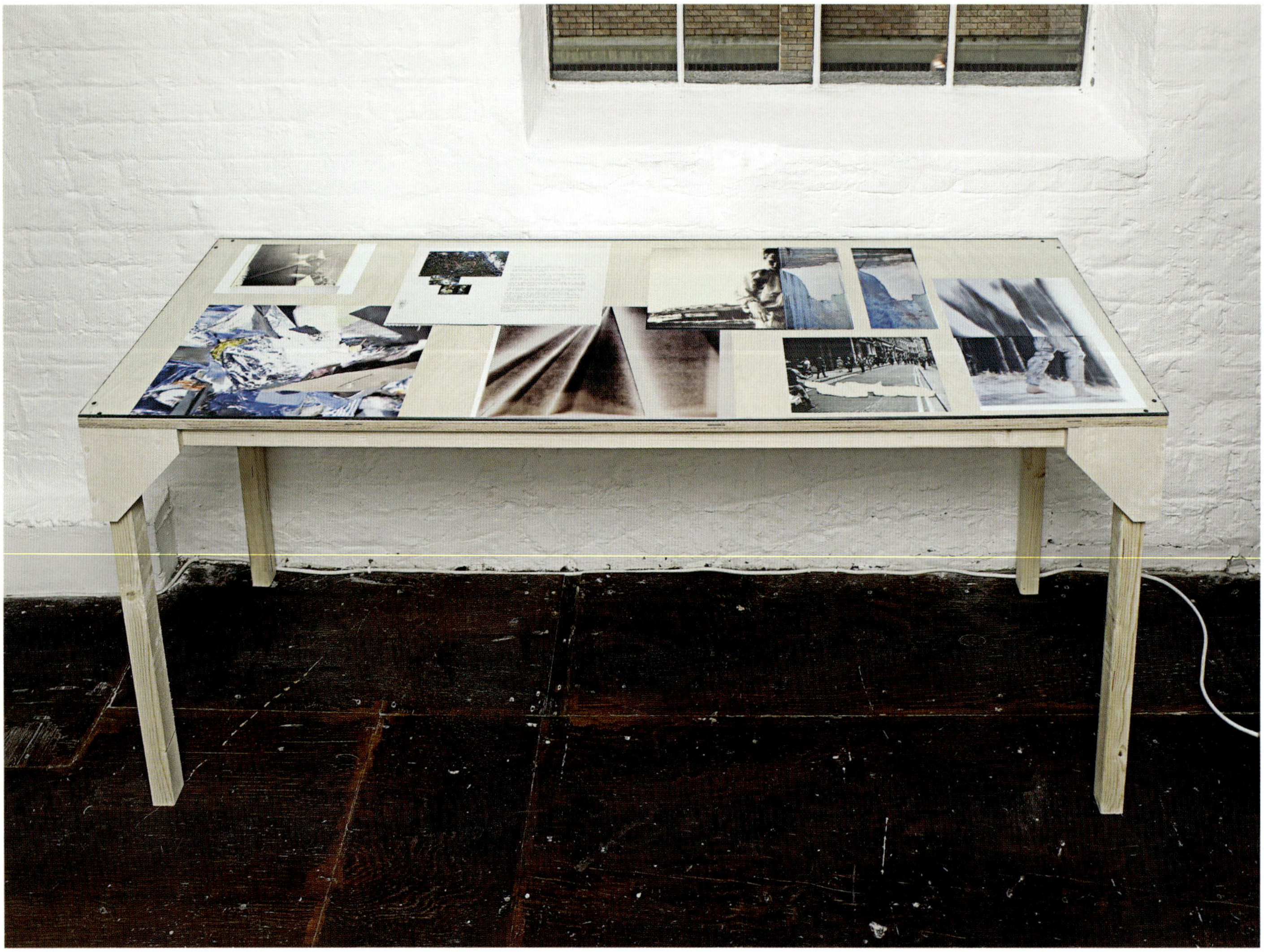

1

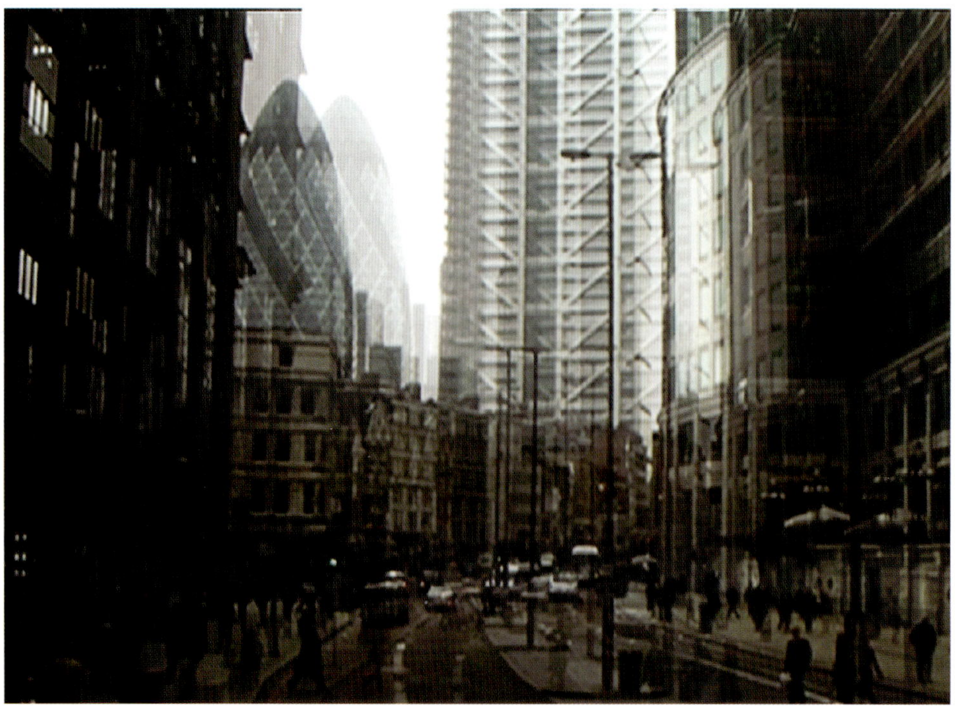

2

# Focus
# Eline McGeorge

Eline McGeorge's practice encompasses collage, photomontage, moving image and sculpture. Mixing images of the human figure with abstract tonal compositions, she constructs landscape-like vistas and uncanny connections between disparate elements. The sculptural *A World of Our Own* (2012) sees a combination of images set under glass—a pair of legs is placed side by side with an abstract monochromatic fade, and together with a collaged street scene they form a new pictorial narrative. Decontextualizing recognizable images, McGeorge weaves intricate archival medleys—*Folded and Interlaced Deren Stills* (2012) consists of cut and folded inkjet stills taken from a Maya Deren film. Utilizing existing sources, McGeorge builds on historical narratives to form a new pictorial language built on alien sources and forgotten fragments. SC

**Shown by**
Hollybush Gardens S15

**Biography**
Born 1970
Lives in London

Norwegian artist McGeorge has been the subject of several solo shows at Hollybush Gardens, London (2012, 2009, 2007 and 2005), as well as Gallery Kirkhoff, Copenhagen (2008), and Fotogalleriet, Oslo (2007). She recently participated in the programme 'Forum Expanded' at the 62st International Berlin Film Festival (2012) and was featured in group exhibitions including 'Fine Lines', Limerick City Gallery of Art (2011), and '27 Senses', Chisenhale Gallery, London (2010).

1
*A World of Our Own*
2012
Table with inkjet prints and glass top
80 × 55 × 193 cm
Courtesy of Hollybush Gardens

2
*A World of Our Own*
2012
HD video
4 min. 37 sec.
Courtesy of Hollybush Gardens

3
*Folded and Interlaced Deren Stills (A World of Our Own)*
2012
Woven inkjet prints on archival paper
49 × 44 cm
Courtesy of Hollybush Gardens

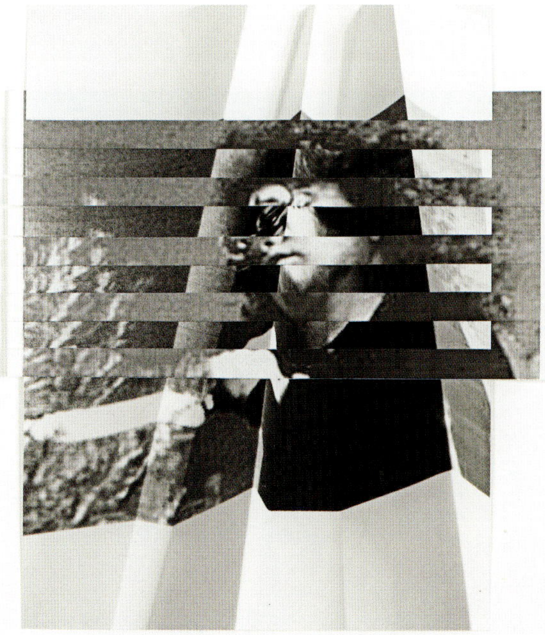

3

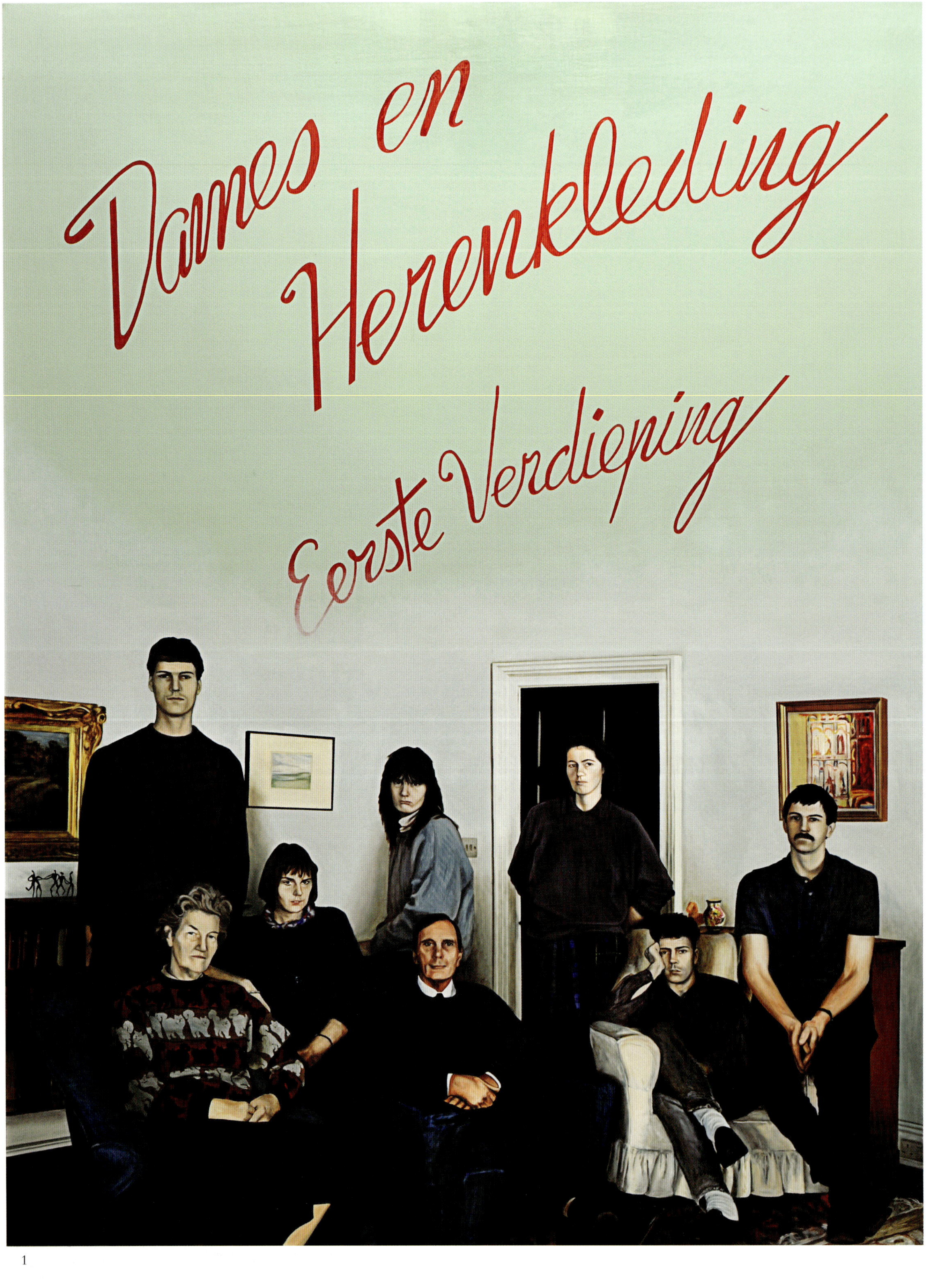
Dames en
Herenkleding
Eerste Verdieping

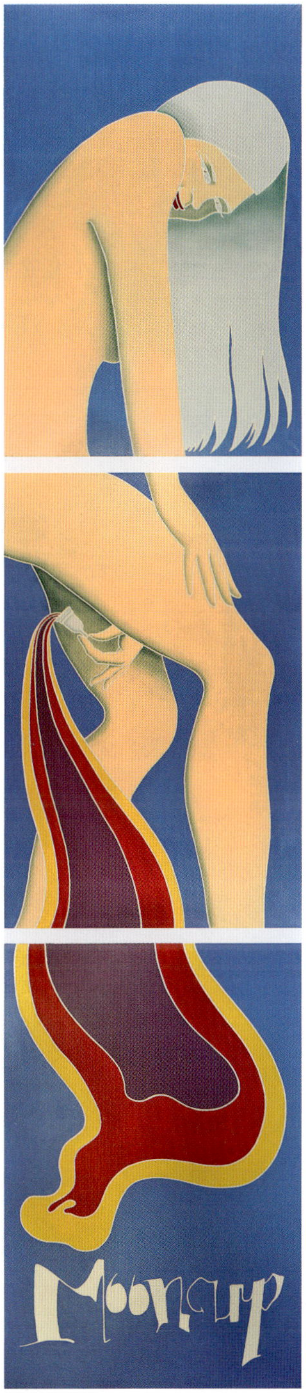

2

**Shown by**
Buchholz C4
Cabinet E3

**Biography**
Born 1977
Lives in Brussels

Glasgow-born McKenzie has presented solo exhibitions and projects at venues such as Galerie Buchholz, Cologne (2010), Cabinet, London (2010), Museum Ludwig, Cologne (2009), and MoMA, New York (2008). Group exhibitions include 'Town Gown Conflict', Kunsthalle Zurich (2011), 'The Associates', Dundee Contemporary Arts (2009), and 'Painting in Tongues', Museum of Contemporary Art, Los Angeles (2006).

1
*Dames en Herenkleding*
2012
Acrylic on canvas
380 × 280 cm
Courtesy of Cabinet

2
*Mooncup*
2012
Acrylic on canvas
Triptych
Each part 400 × 260 cm
Courtesy of Cabinet

# Lucy McKenzie

Lucy McKenzie, so Michael Bracewell recently suggested in *frieze*, could be 'the most significant artist to emerge since Damien Hirst'. Certainly the fleet-footed, frequently collaborative, cross-media practice she's hallmarked, away from primary art hubs—in Glasgow, Warsaw, Brussels—looks increasingly prescient. And seemingly changeable: consider the distance from early paintings of posters for pop concerts in the former Soviet bloc (e.g., *Depeche Mode Night*, 1999) to her 2011 collaborative installation and book as part of 'original interiors company' Atelier, a solvent of fine and applied arts that combined references to Scotland's fashion and textile history in the 1980s with McKenzie's graceful drawings of dandyish cats. Consistent, though, is her braiding together of New and Old Romanticism, the world of three decades ago to the larger European past, under the sign of fleeting Utopianism. MH

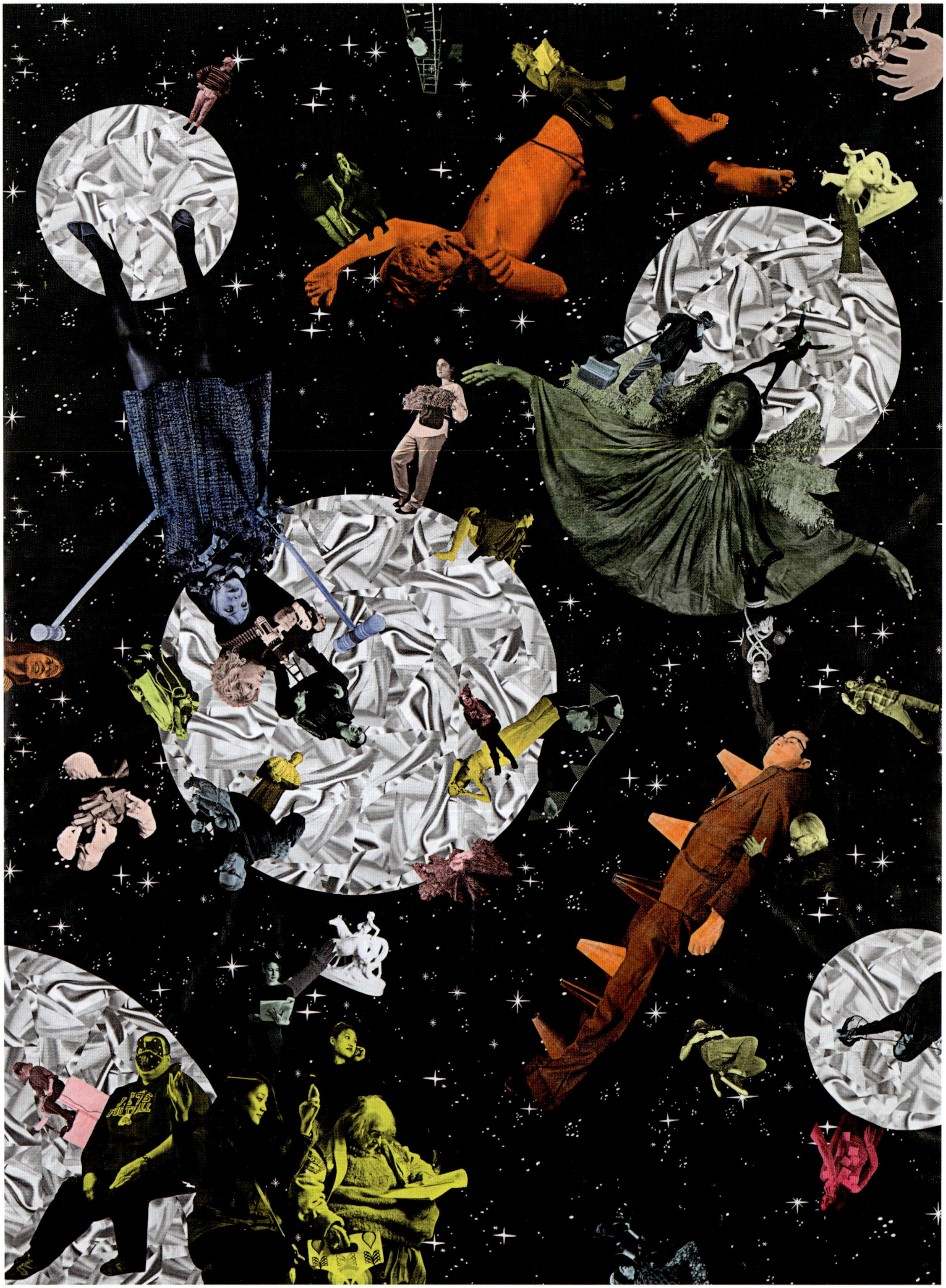

# Ryan McNamara

**Shown by**
Elizabeth Dee E22

**Biography**
Born 1979
Lives in New York

American artist McNamara has presented performances and exhibitions at galleries including Elizabeth Dee, New York (2012 and 2010), Watermill Performance Center, Water Mill, New York (2011), and the Whitney Museum of American Art, New York (2010). McNamara has participated in group shows such as 'Greater New York', MoMA PS1, New York (2010), and the 2nd Athens Biennale (2009).

*To be titled (Stars)*
2012
Canvas backdrop, performance stills and glue
315 × 226 cm
Courtesy of Elizabeth Dee

Ryan McNamara enjoys testing the role of the audience in performances. In *II* (2011), visitors were confronted with the artist and another performer buried up to their necks in the ground, singing a series of duets; in exhibition 'Greater New York' (2010) they witnessed the intimacy of McNamara taking dance lessons in the public spaces of MoMA PS1. For *Still* (2012), McNamara invited the audience to perform for the first three weeks of his debut solo gallery show. The actions of over 1,000 participants resulted in photographs staged with an array of lights, backdrops, props, costumes and wigs. He published these photographs on the gallery website while simultaneously altering and découpaging them onto props and backdrops from the performances, exhibiting these new works for the remainder of the exhibition. SL

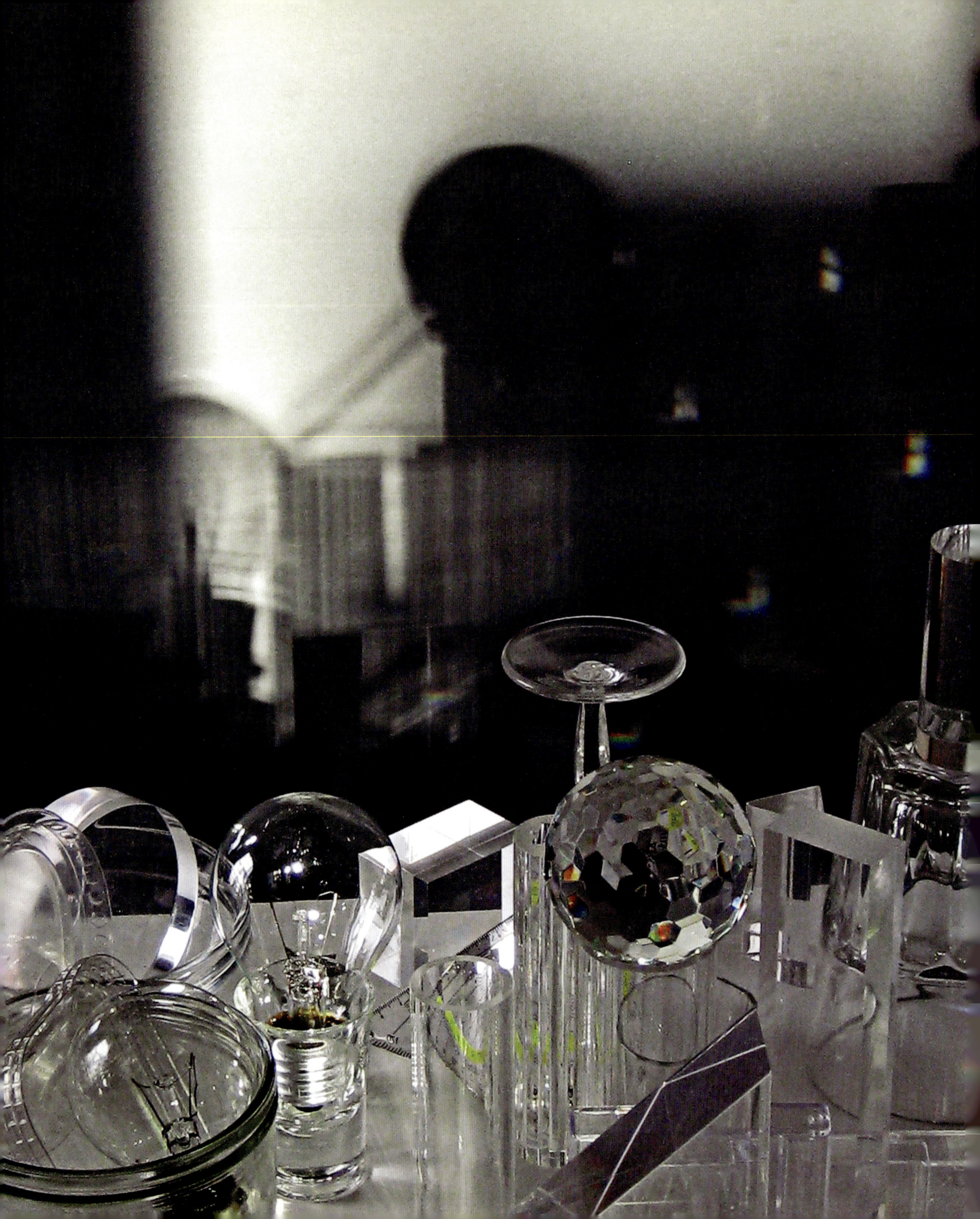

# Michaela Melián

**Shown by**
Galerie Karin Guenther
H6

**Biography**
Born 1956
Lives in Munich

German-born Melián has shown solo exhibitions in recent years at Galerie Karin Guenther, Hamburg (2012), Lentos Kunstmuseum, Linz (2009), Goethe Institut, New York (2009), Cubitt Gallery, London (2008), and Städtische Galerie Nordhorn (2011), in conjuction with her receipt of Kunstpreis der Stadt Nordhorn. Her group exhibitions in 2012 include 'The Sound of Downloading Makes Me Want to Upload', Sprengel Museum, Hanover.

*Lunapark*
2011
(detail)
Mixed-media installation
100 × 200 × 50 cm
Courtesy of Galerie Karin Guenther

Michaela Melián might be said to work like an eccentric historian cast out of the ideologically rigid academy. The artist and musician's installations, which can bring together drawing, sculpture, photography, film, music and text, often begin with a uniquely singular historical subject that reflects the cultural and political turmoil of its age. For instance, *Life as a Woman, Hedy Lamarr* (2001), explores the titular film siren, who also happened to patent 'frequency hopping', a technology used to encode radio communication during World War II and which is now used in mobile phones. More recently, Melián's research has led her to explore the National Socialist history of Munich in *Memory Loops* (2010), an audio series of voice collages, and the French inventor of the first automatic loom in her installation *House of Jacquard* (2011). QL

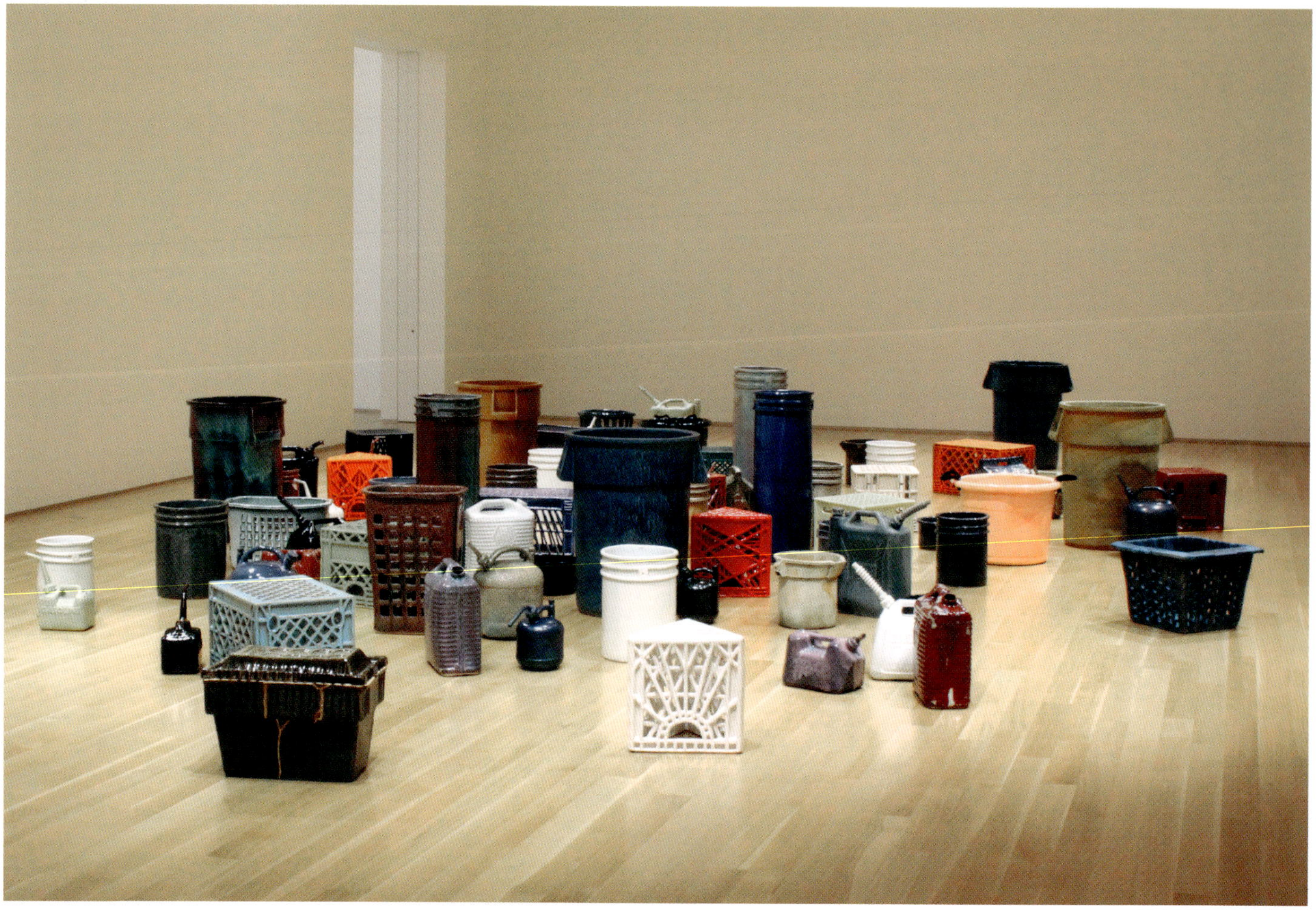

1

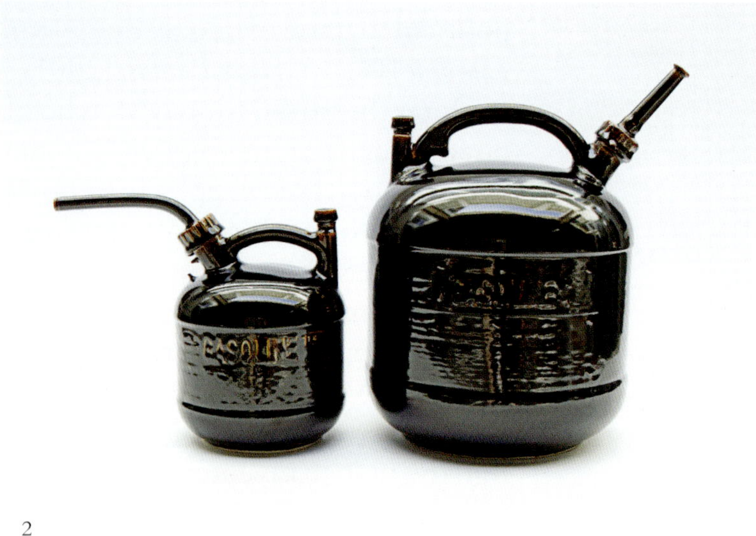

2

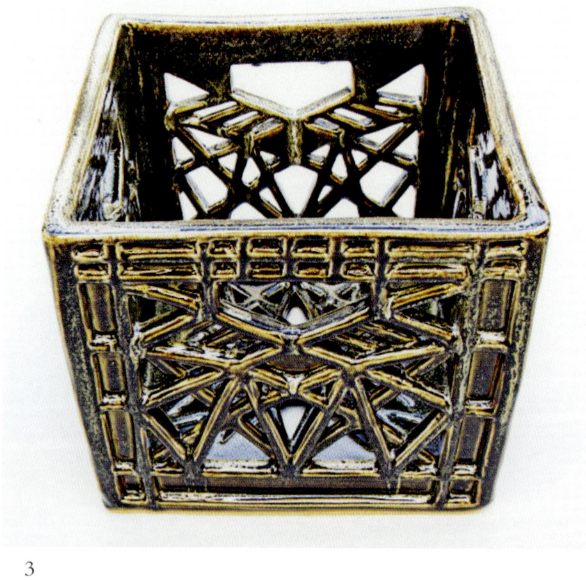

3

# Matthias Merkel Hess

**Shown by**
Salon 94 B14

**Biography**
Born 1978
Lives in Los Angeles

American-born Merkel Hess has been the subject of solo shows at ACME, Los Angeles (2011), Mary Moody Gallery, West Texas A&M University, Amarillo (2011), IKO IKO, Los Angeles (2011), Las Cienegas Projects, Los Angeles (2010), and 18th Street Arts Center, Santa Monica (2010). His group exhibitions in 2012 have included the Venice Beach Biennial, Los Angeles, and 'SUM' at the Nerman Museum of Contemporary Art, Overland Park, Kansas.

1
*Bucketry*
2012
Porcelain and ceramic
Installation view at ACME, Los Angeles
Dimensions variable
Courtesy of ACME

2
*Eagle 1 Gallon Gas Can (black/brown glaze)*
2012
Porcelain
30 × 18 × 18 cm
&
*Eagle 5 Gallon Gas Can*
2012
Porcelain
41 × 30 × 30 cm
Courtesy of Salon 94

3
*Milk Crate (Square, Black/Brown and Straw Yellow with Spots)*
2012
Porcelain
33 × 33 × 30 cm
Courtesy of Salon 94

4
*5 Gallon Water Carrier*
2012
Porcelain
43 × 30 × 15 cm
Courtesy of Salon 94

For centuries pottery has been used for vessels that carry not only goods and liquids but also specific meanings—what art historians call 'conceptual content'. When Matthias Merkel Hess refashions mass-produced vessels such as plastic bins or petrol cans in glazed ceramic, he is folding the functional role of his medium into its symbolic tradition. Merkel Hess is particularly fond of objects that are already outdated, some of them design classics such as the ubiquitous Rubbermaid Brute 40-gallon rubbish bin, which he has remade in various vibrant blue and pink glazes. His collective term for pieces such as *5 Gallon Water Carrier* (2012) is 'Bucketry'; their new function, he states, is 'to be looked at and talked about'. JG

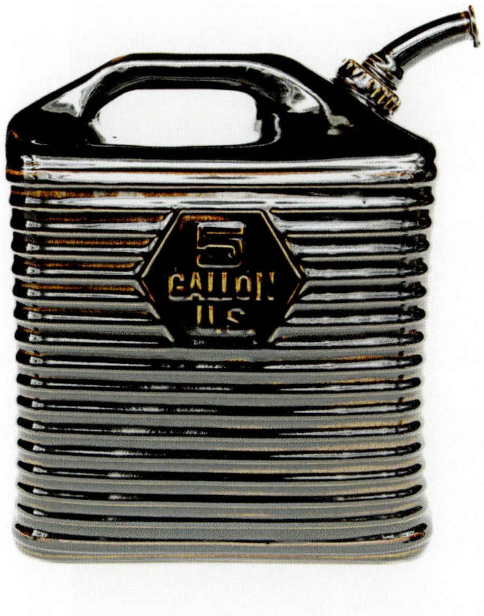

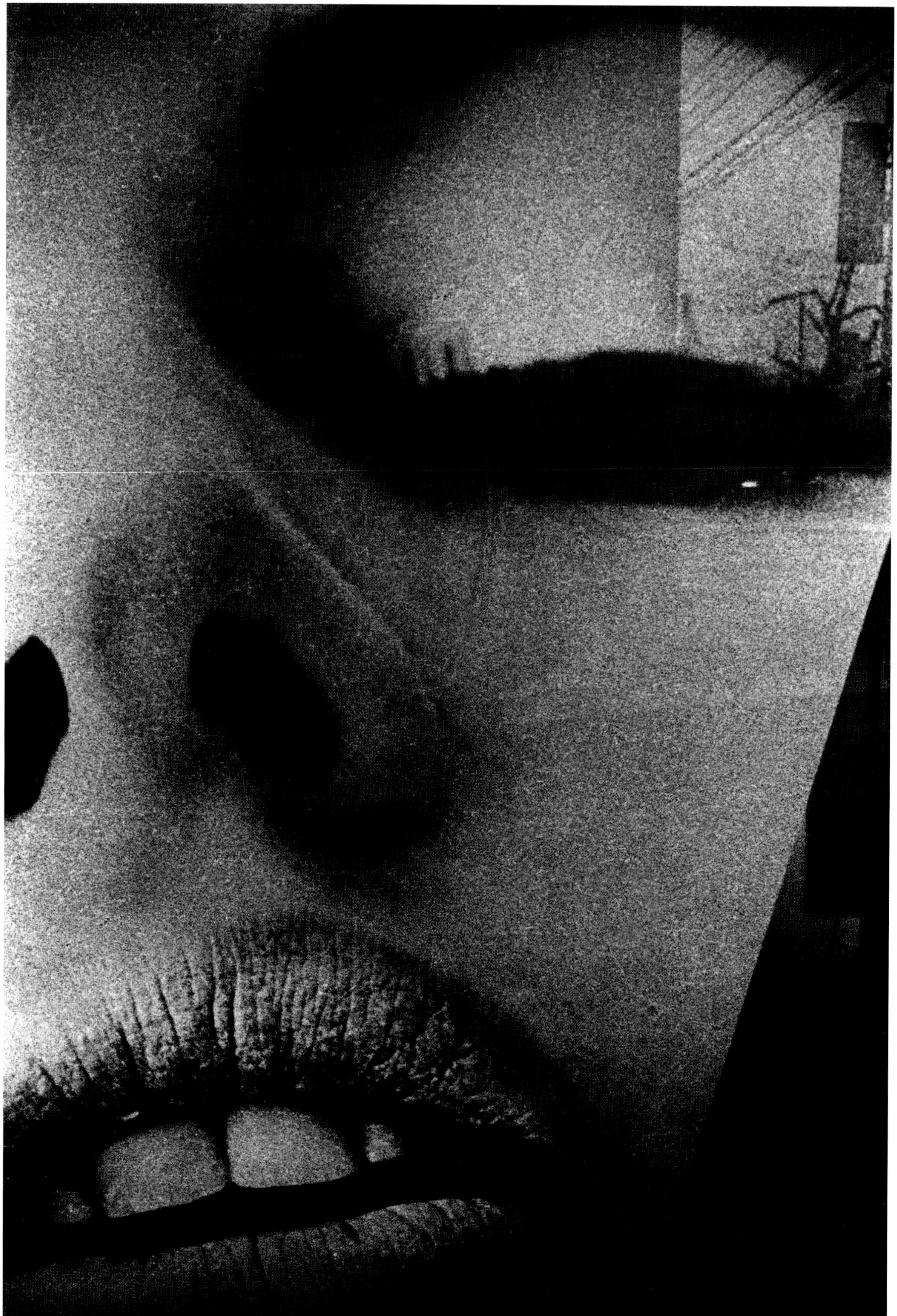

# Daido Moriyama

**Shown by**
Taka Ishii Gallery B5

**Biography**
Born 1938
Lives in Tokyo

In 2012 the Osaka-born Moriyama received an Infinity Award for Lifetime Achievement from the International Center of Photography, New York. He has recently been the subject of exhibitions at institutions such as the Los Angeles County Museum of Art (2012), Philadelphia Museum of Art (2009) and Tokyo Metropolitan Museum of Photography (2008). Until January 2013 an exhibition at Tate Modern, London, explores the works of Moriyama and photographer William Klein.

*Eros or Something Other than Eros*
1969
Print
150 × 100 cm
Courtesy of Taka Ishii Gallery

Daido Moriyama first came to prominence in the mid-1960s with his grainy black and white photographs of Japanese urban life, such as *Eros or Something Other than Eros* (1969). His images' extreme high contrast and skewed angles suggest a spontaneity, authenticity and gritty energy that complement Moriyama's best-known subject: Tokyo's Shinjuku ward during the 1960s and '70s, a period of political and social upheaval. While the east side of the area featured the Kabukicho red-light district and the ramshackle bars of Golden Gai, the west side sprouted skyscrapers and company headquarters. Moriyama remains fascinated by its oddities and contradictions: a male actor with papier-mâché breasts, a barefoot woman walking through debris, a glamorous advertisement amid a desolate cityscape. ND

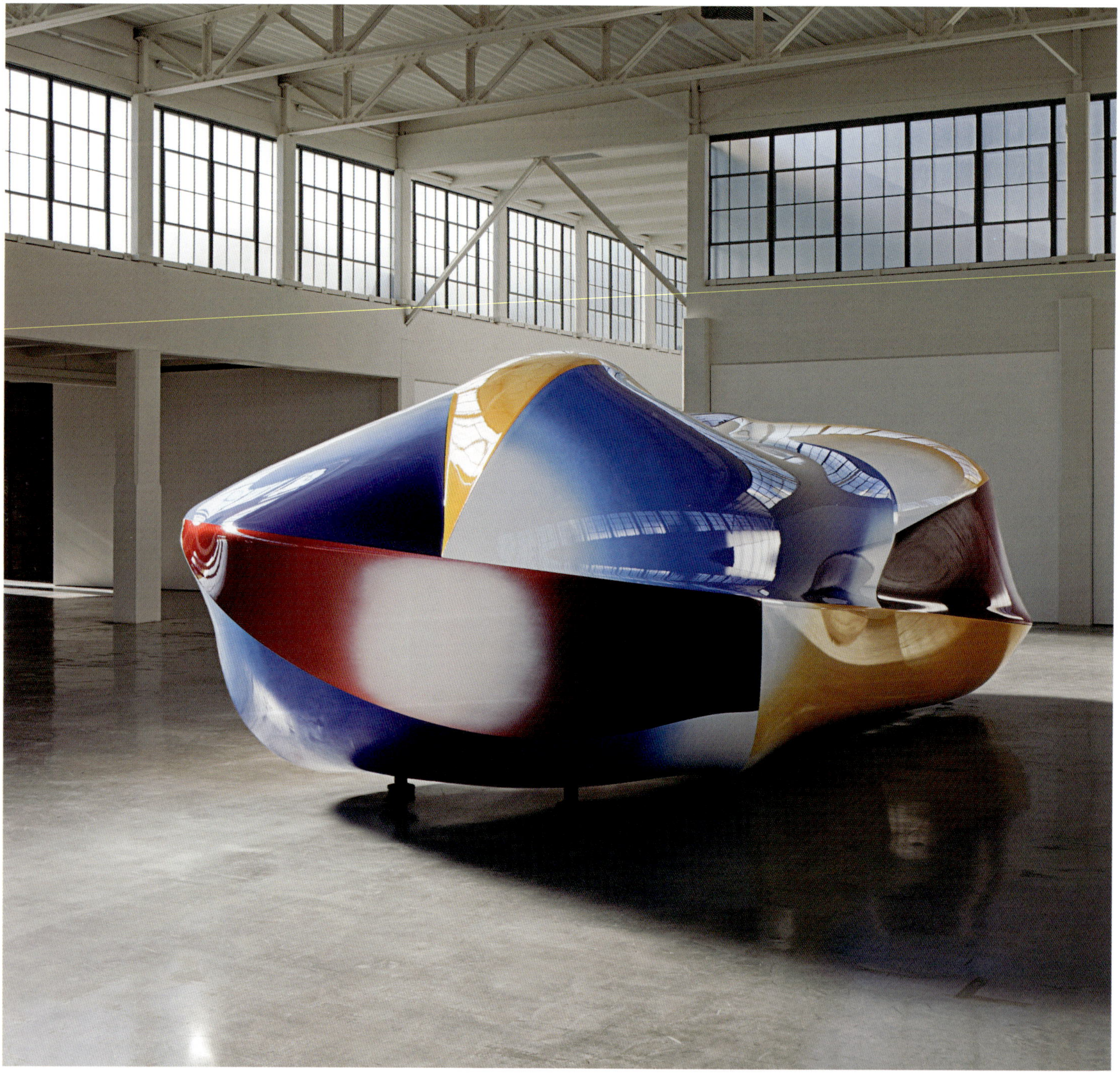

1

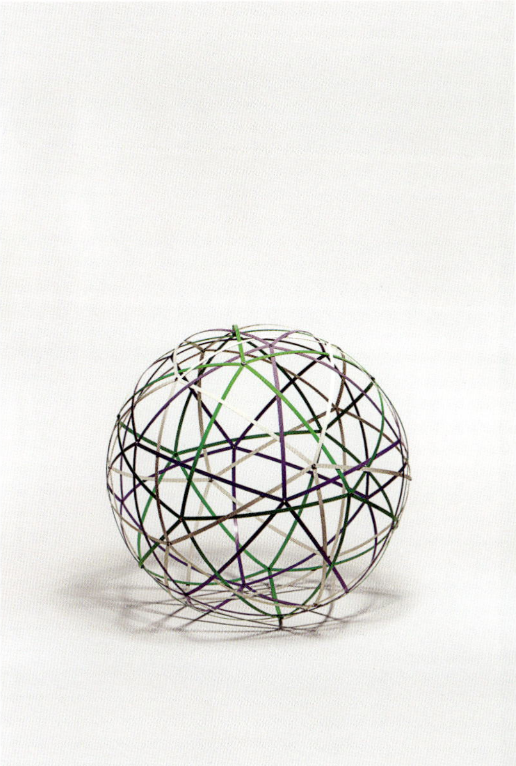

3

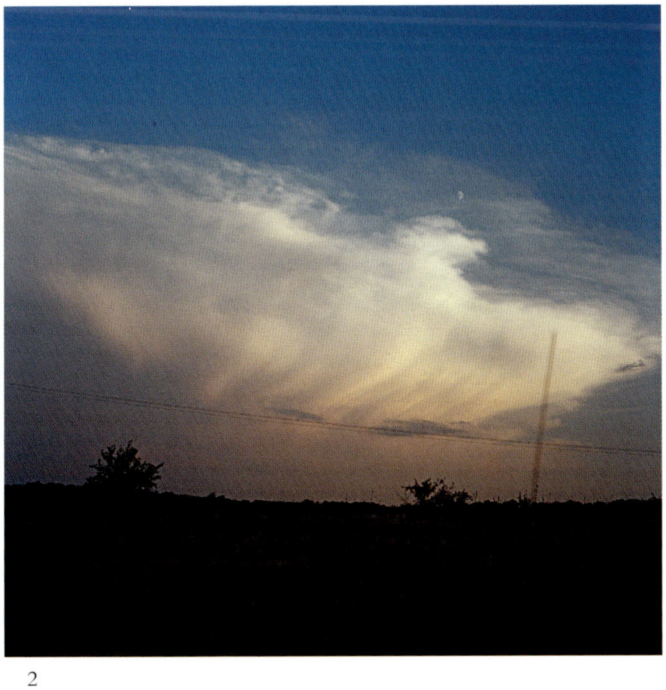

2

**Shown by**
Galerie Chantal Crousel
D11
Thomas Dane Gallery
F13

**Biography**
Born 1955
Lives in Paris

Reims-born Moulène has been the subject of solo exhibitions at Modern Art Oxford, (2012), Musée d'Art Contemporain, Nimes (2009), Centre d'Art Passerelle, Brest (2008), Culturgest, Lisbon (2007), and Jeu de Paume, Paris (2005). His work is the subject of an exhibition at Dia:Beacon, New York, until December 2012, which is accompanied by the presentation of a project at the Dan Flavin Art Institute, Bridgehampton.

1
*Body, Guyancourt, October 2011*
2011
Aluminium, basalt fibre, pigment and resin
2.5 × 8.5 × 3.5 m
Exhibition view at Dia:Beacon, New York
Produced by Renault Automobiles
Courtesy of Galerie Chantal Crousel

2
*Fénautrigues Cloud, Lot, Fr., Winter 2003*
2012
Photograph
129 × 135 cm
Courtesy of Galerie Chantal Crousell

3
*Model for Quelque chose de généralisé*
2011
Polyurethane and steel
78 × 78 × 78 cm
Galerie Chantal Crousel

# Jean-Luc Moulène

Jean-Luc Moulène become known in the late 1980s for his explorations in photography, yet his elusive work spans what he has called 'post-photography objectivation', as well as drawing and printing. He fluidly bridges the capturing of pictures and the production of things—making mental images concrete and often fusing work with documentation. For his 2005 show at the Louvre, he chose 24 small, overlooked curios from the collection to photograph individually and present as large prints atop plinths. *Body, Guyancourt, October 2011* (2011), meanwhile, is an object that appears to be a glistening abstract maquette. Over eight metres long, the surface of its sinuous form is like a polished skin of primary-coloured gradients—a huge De Stijl pebble, or a malleable prototype for an advanced boat. MA

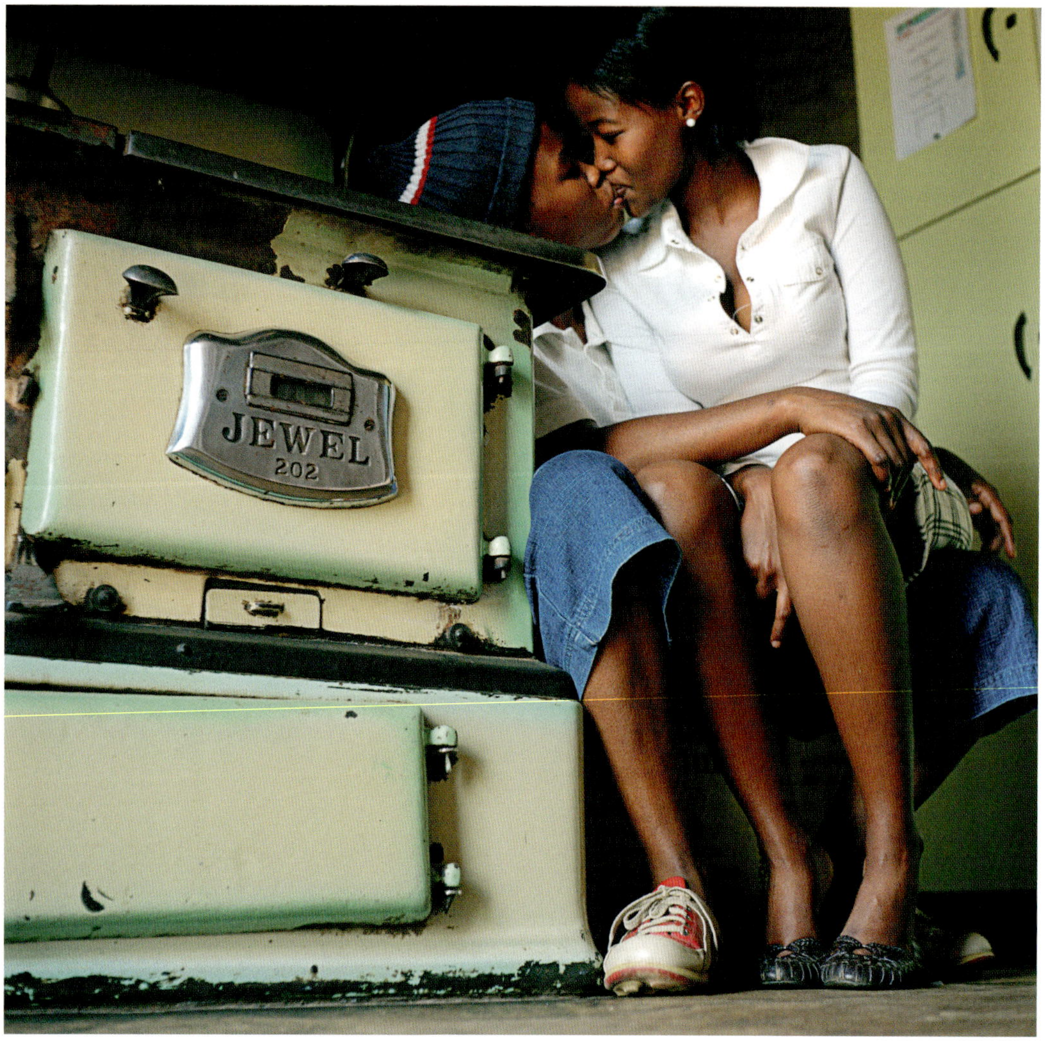


1

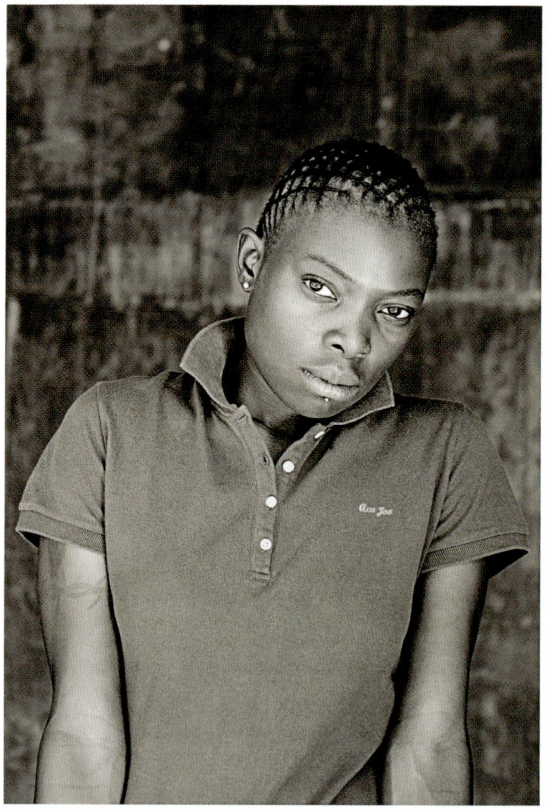

2

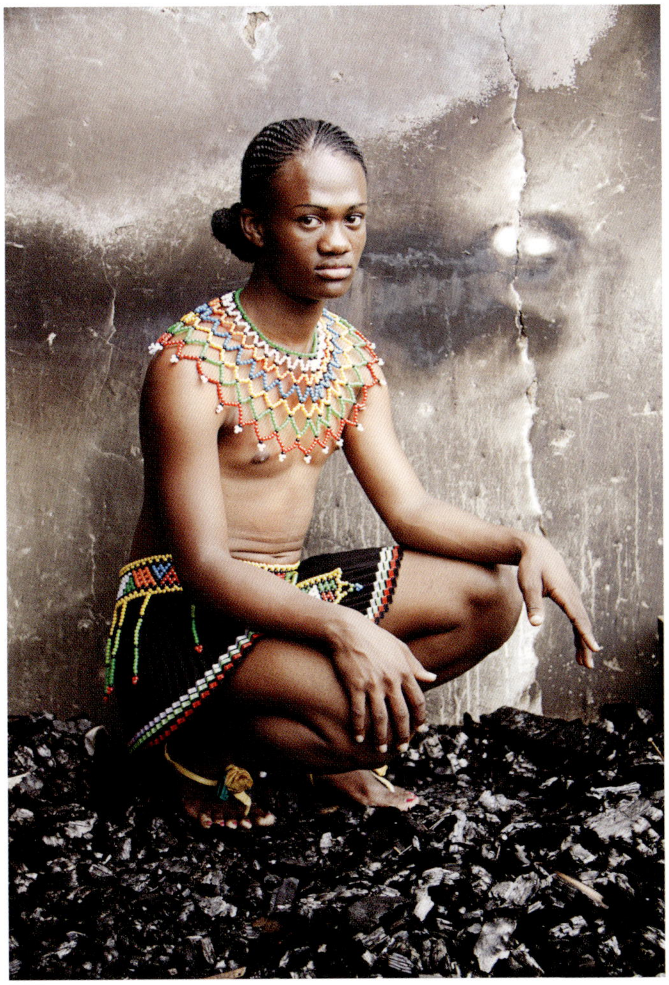

3

**Shown by**
Stevenson F17

**Biography**
Born 1972
Lives in Cape Town

Durban-born Muholi has recently presented solo shows at venues including Casa Africa, Las Palmas, Gran Canaria (2011), Stevenson, Johannesburg (2011), CCA, Lagos (2009), and Kunsthalle Vienna (2006). She recently participated in Documenta 13, Kassel (2012), and group exhibitions that include 'Face of Our Time', University of Michigan Museum of Art, Ann Arbor (2012), and 'Figures and Fictions', Victoria and Albert Museum, London (2011).

1
*Katlego Mashiloane and Nosipho Lavuta, Ext. 2, Lakeside, Johannesburg, 2007*
Lambda print
87 × 87 cm
Courtesy of Stevenson

2
*Musa Ngubane, Constitution Hill, Johannesburg, 2010*
Silver gelatin print
87 × 61 cm
Courtesy of Stevenson

3
*Ms Le Sishi I Glebelands, Durban, Jan. 2010*
C-type print
87 × 61 cm
Courtesy of Stevenson

# Zanele Muholi

The artist and activist Zanele Muholi's photographs focus, as she has written, 'on being queer in South Africa and beyond. This is the realm in which I deal with my identity, as a citizen of my country and of the world.' Simply composed, and shot in black and white and colour, her portrait images of South African LGBTI individuals bear testament to lives lived in a hostile, homophobic environment, while shots such as *Katlego Mashiloane and Nosipho Lavuta, Ext. 2, Lakeside, Johannesburg* (2007) are tender depictions of a love that thrives in the midst of hate. Photography, here, is deeply implicated in a politics of presence, and the camera becomes an instrument of both empowerment and resistance. TM

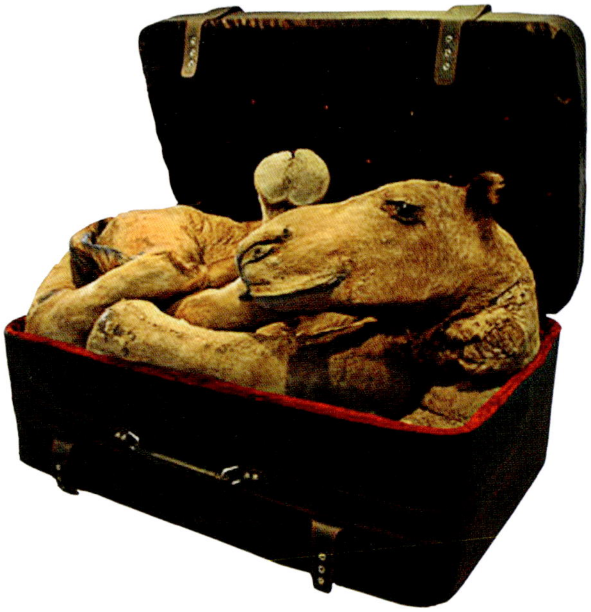

1

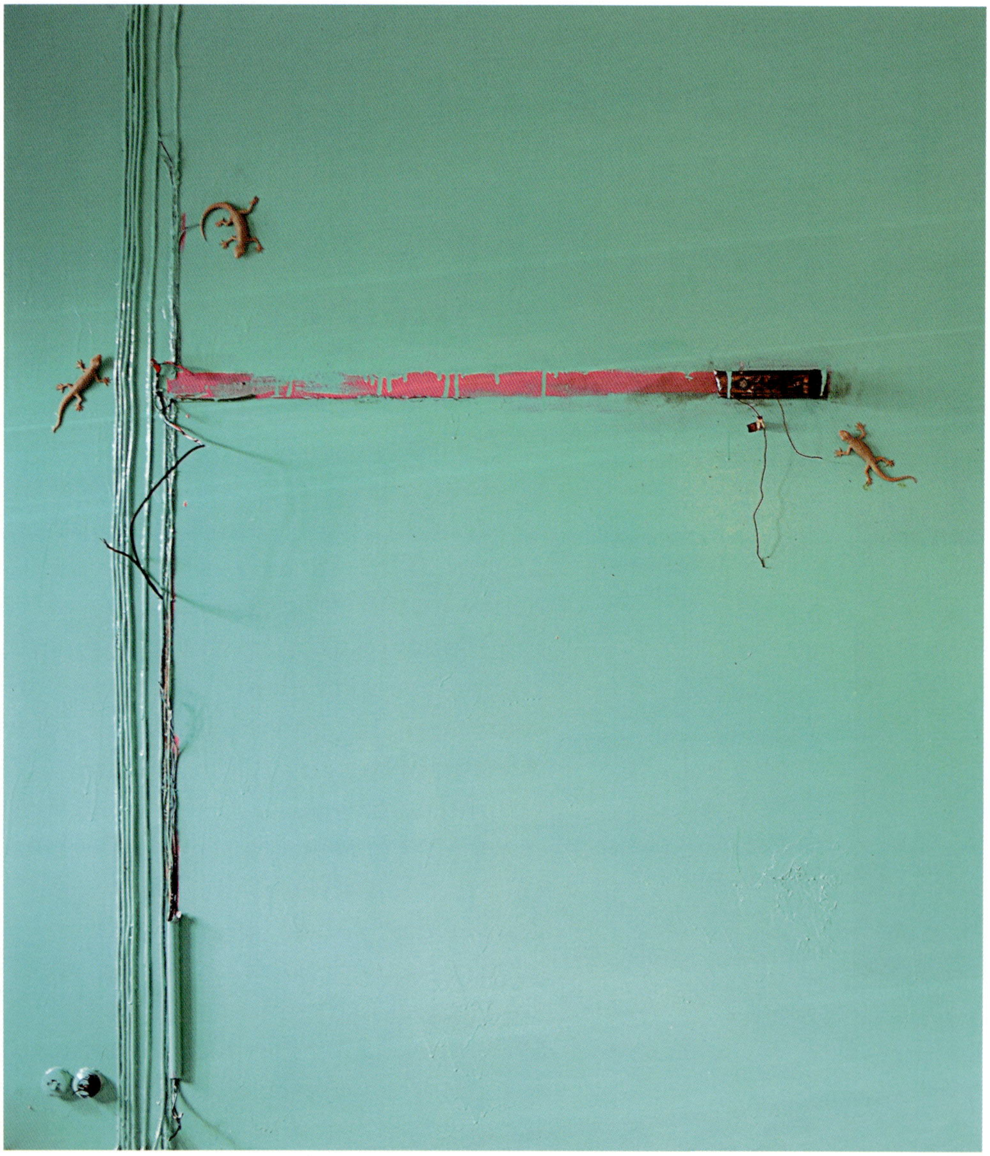

2

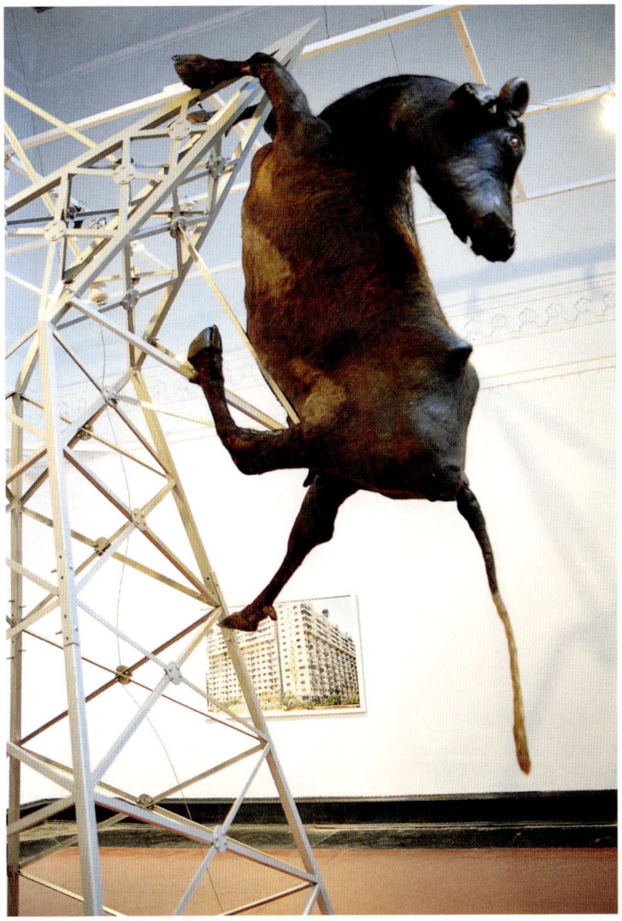

3

**Shown by**
Project 88 F15

**Biography**
Born 1970
Lives in Lahore

Karachi-born Mulji has recently shown solo exhibitions at venues that include Project 88, Mumbai (2011), Rohtas Gallery, Lahore (2011), and Elementa Gallery, Dubai (2009). Her work has been featured in group shows such as 'The Rising Tide', Mohatta Palace Museum, Karachi (2010), 'Where Three Dreams Cross' (2010), on view at Whitechapel Gallery, London, before travelling to Fotomuseum Winterthur, and 'Farewell to Post Colonialism' at the 3rd Guangzhou Triennial (2008).

1
*Arabian Delight*
2008
Rexine suitcase, taxidermied camel, metal rods, cotton wool and fabric
105 × 155 × 145 cm
Courtesy of Project 88

2
*Ode to a Tubelight*
2011
Enamel and mixed media on canvas
213 × 183 cm
Courtesy of Project 88

3
*Heavenly Heights*
2009
Taxidermied buffalo, metal rods, powder coated steel, cotton wool, ceramic and cable
434 × 188 × 300 cm
Courtesy of Project 88

# Huma Mulji

Huma Mulji says her sculptures, paintings and photographs frame the 'absurdities and conflicts of living in an urban society in transition'. Works such as *Arabian Delight* (2008), a taxidermied camel stuffed awkwardly into a battered suitcase, highlight the ways in which Pakistan has been subject to a process of Arabization. The ongoing effects of urbanization find expression in other works using stuffed animals, such as *Heavenly Heights* (2009), in which a buffalo hangs from a pylon, or *Ode to a Tubelight* (2011), a canvas depicting a wall with a lighting fixture ripped out. The missing light reveals the pink colour that the wall was once painted, while a gathering of three heat-seeking geckos emphasizes the absence of the light. SL

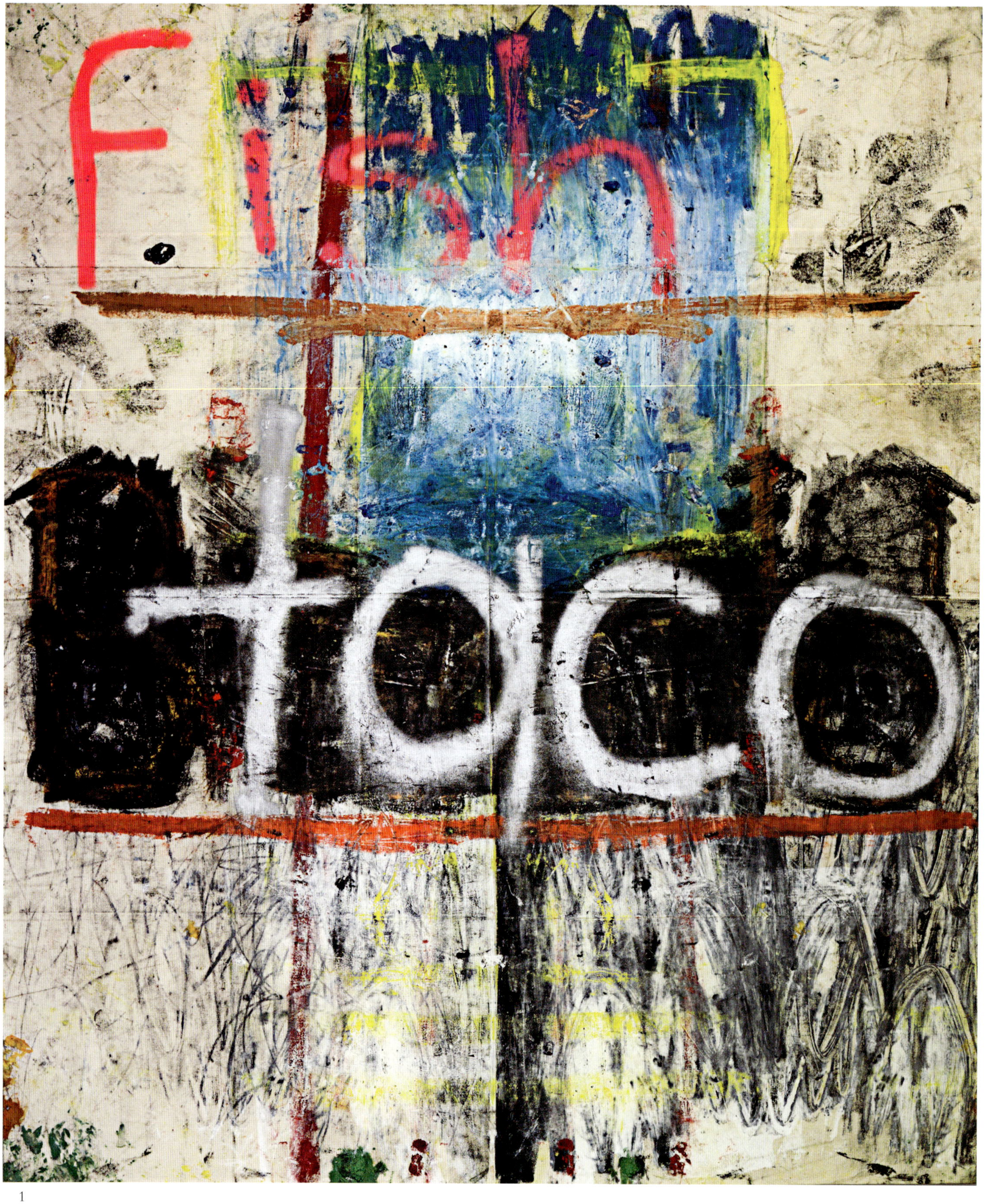


1

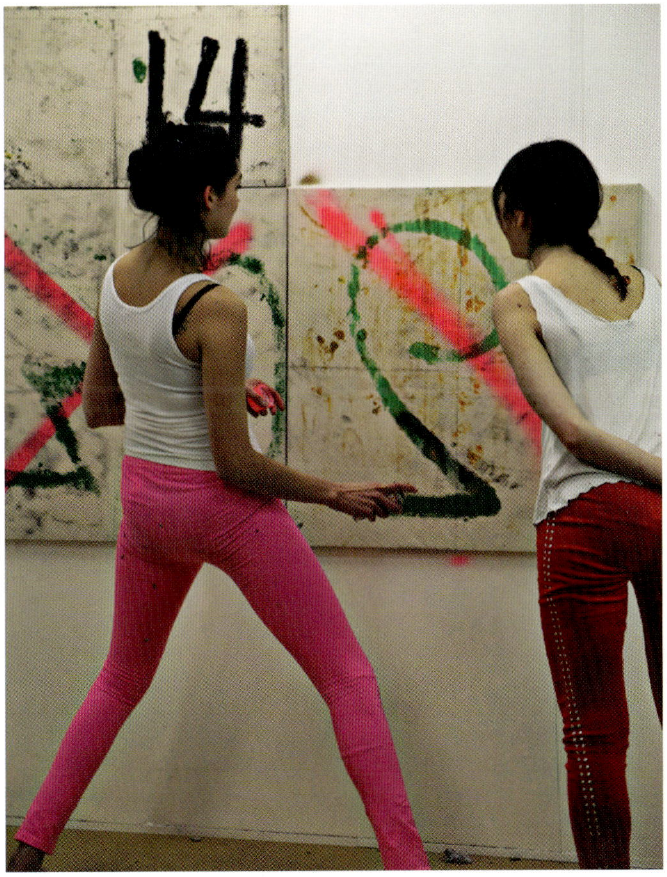


2

**Shown by**
Carlos/Ishikawa R7
Stuart Shave/Modern Art D12

**Biography**
Born 1986
Lives in London

Colombian-born Murillo, who received an MA from London's Royal College of Art in 2012, has presented recent performances at venues that include the Serpentine Gallery, London (2012), and 'To the Moon via the Beach', the Ampitheatre, Arles (2012). Other recent exhibitions and projects include those at Carlos/Ishikawa, London (2011), Hotel, London (2011), and Cole Contemporary, London (2011). In 2013 he will have solo presentations at Stuart Shave/Modern Art, London, and Isabella Bortolozzi, Berlin.

1
*Fish Taco*
2012
Spray paint, oilstick, oil and dirt on canvas
203 × 168 cm
Courtesy of Stuart Shave/Modern Art

2
Performance detail
2012
Courtesy of Stuart Shave/Modern Art and Carlos Ishikawa

# Oscar Murillo

Trained as a painter, Oscar Murillo's practice encompasses performance and installation, performative actions and socially collaborative events such as organizing a bingo night and a yoga session, in recent works *animals die from eating too much – bingo!* and *animals die from eating too much – yoga* (both 2011). The site-specificity of the work informs both its performative nature and its reception. The architecture, space and tools available—be they spray paints, oil sticks or dirt, in paintings such as *Fish Taco* (2012)—as well as the people he collaborates with in his performances produce an element of creative spontaneity that is allowed to remain uncontrolled and unresolved. PT

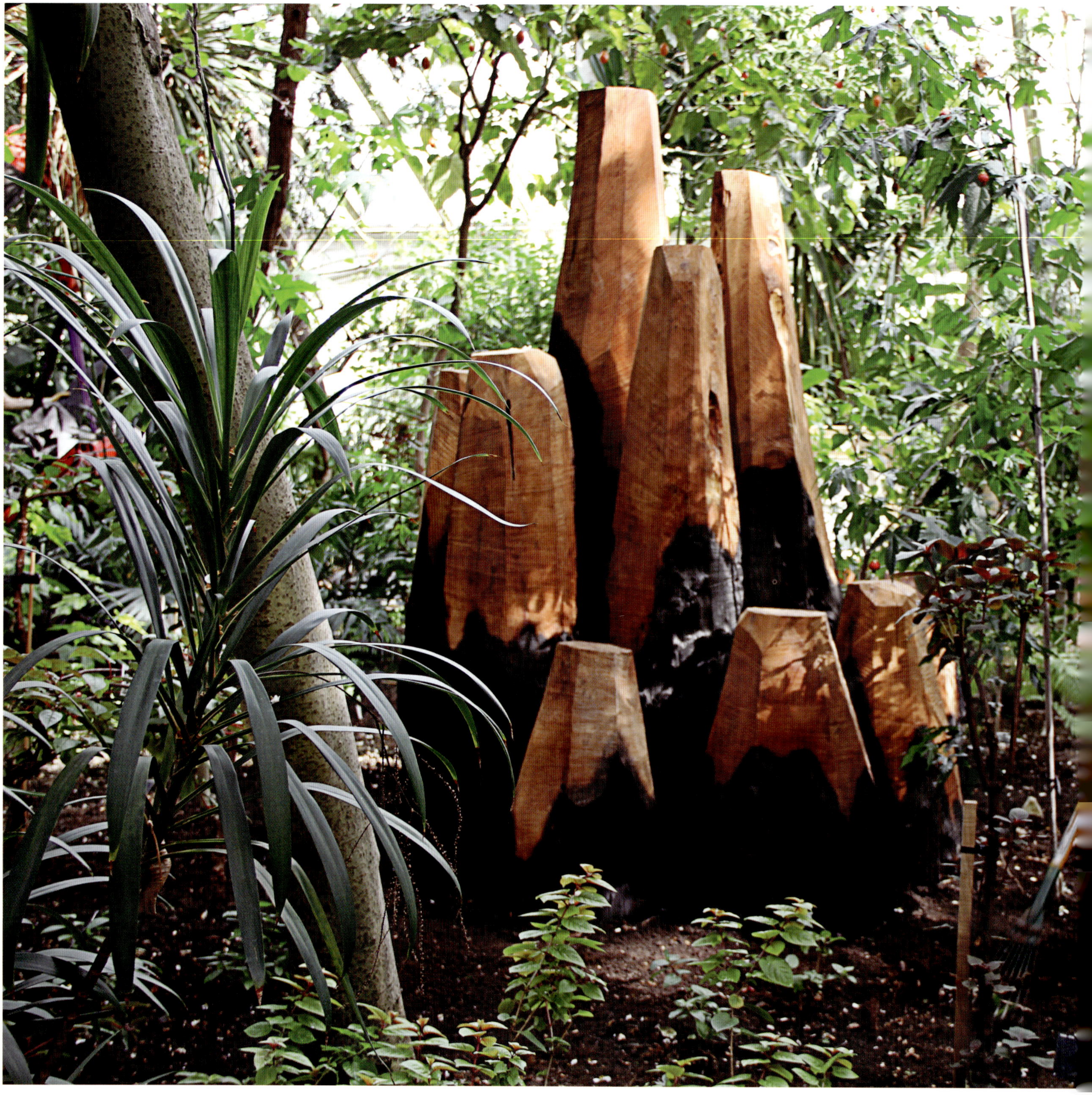

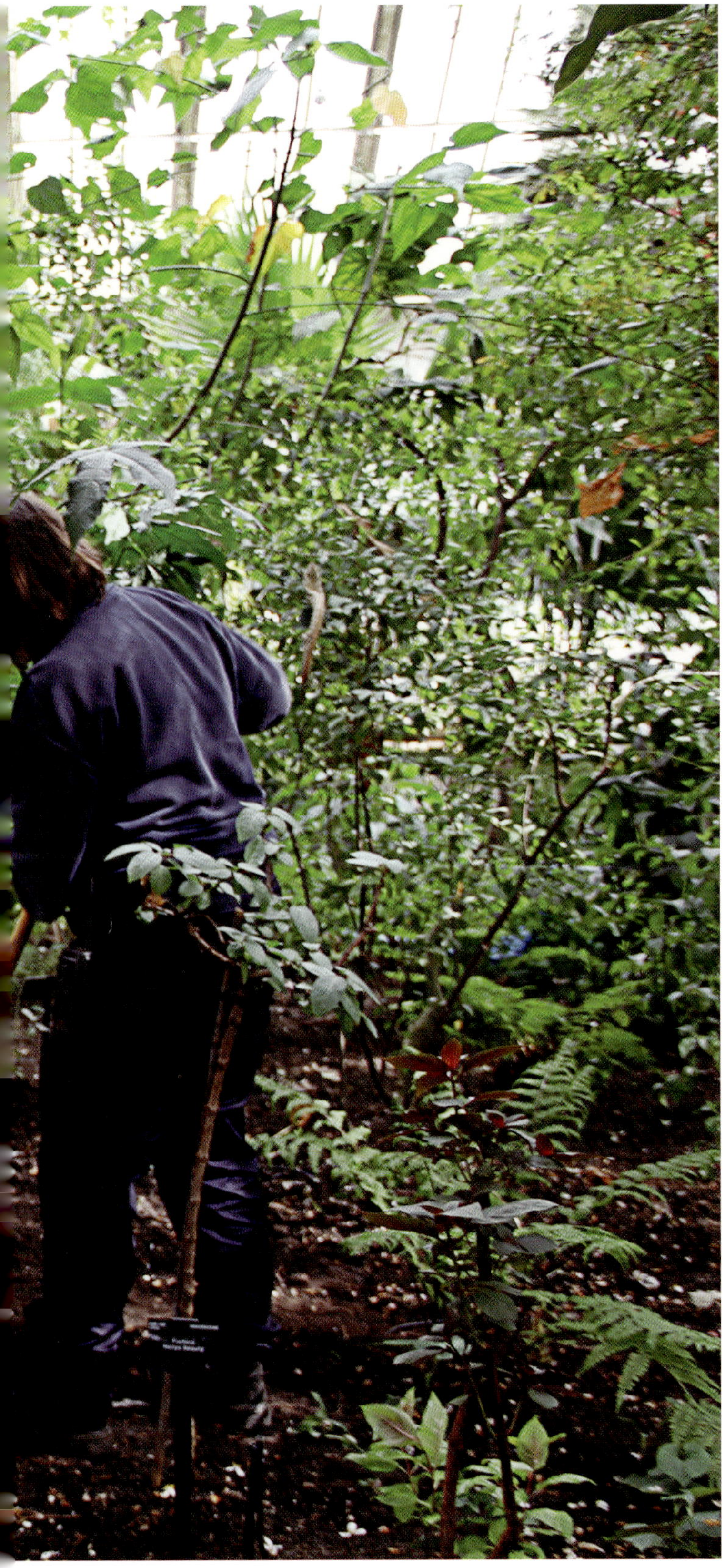

**Shown by**
Annely Juda Fine Art F9
Kukje Gallery C13

**Biography**
Born 1945
Lives in Blaenau Ffestiniog, Wales

British artist Nash has held solo exhibitions at public institutions that include Kunsthalle Mannheim (2009), Tate St Ives (2004), MuHKA, Antwerp (1996), Museum of Contemporary Art, San Diego (1995), and the Scottish National Gallery of Modern Art, Edinburgh (1990). A member of London's Royal Academy of Arts since 1999, his work is part of collections such as the Tate collection, UK, and the Metropolitan Museum of Art, New York. His exhibition at the Royal Botanic Gardens, Kew, is on view until March 2013.

*Red and Black Dome*
2007
12 pieces of partly charred yew
2.5 × 2 × 2 m
Installation view at the Temperate House, Royal Botanic Gardens, Kew
Courtesy of Annely Juda Fine Art

# David Nash

Since the late 1960s David Nash has used chainsaws, axes and fire to transform found pieces of wood—often in the form of whole trees felled by storms, lightning or disease—into sculptures that display a deep knowledge of his chosen material and the way it changes over time. Comparing his intensely physical practice to an act of 'quarrying', he has harnessed natural forces in works such as *Wooden Boulder* (1978), a large sphere that he introduced into a Welsh river that took 16 years to roll into the sea. To coincide with his exhibition at Kew's Royal Botanic Gardens this year, Nash produced a series of sculptures from its dead or dying trees, continuing his exploration of the point where nature and culture (and, significantly, happenstance and intention) meet and meld. TM

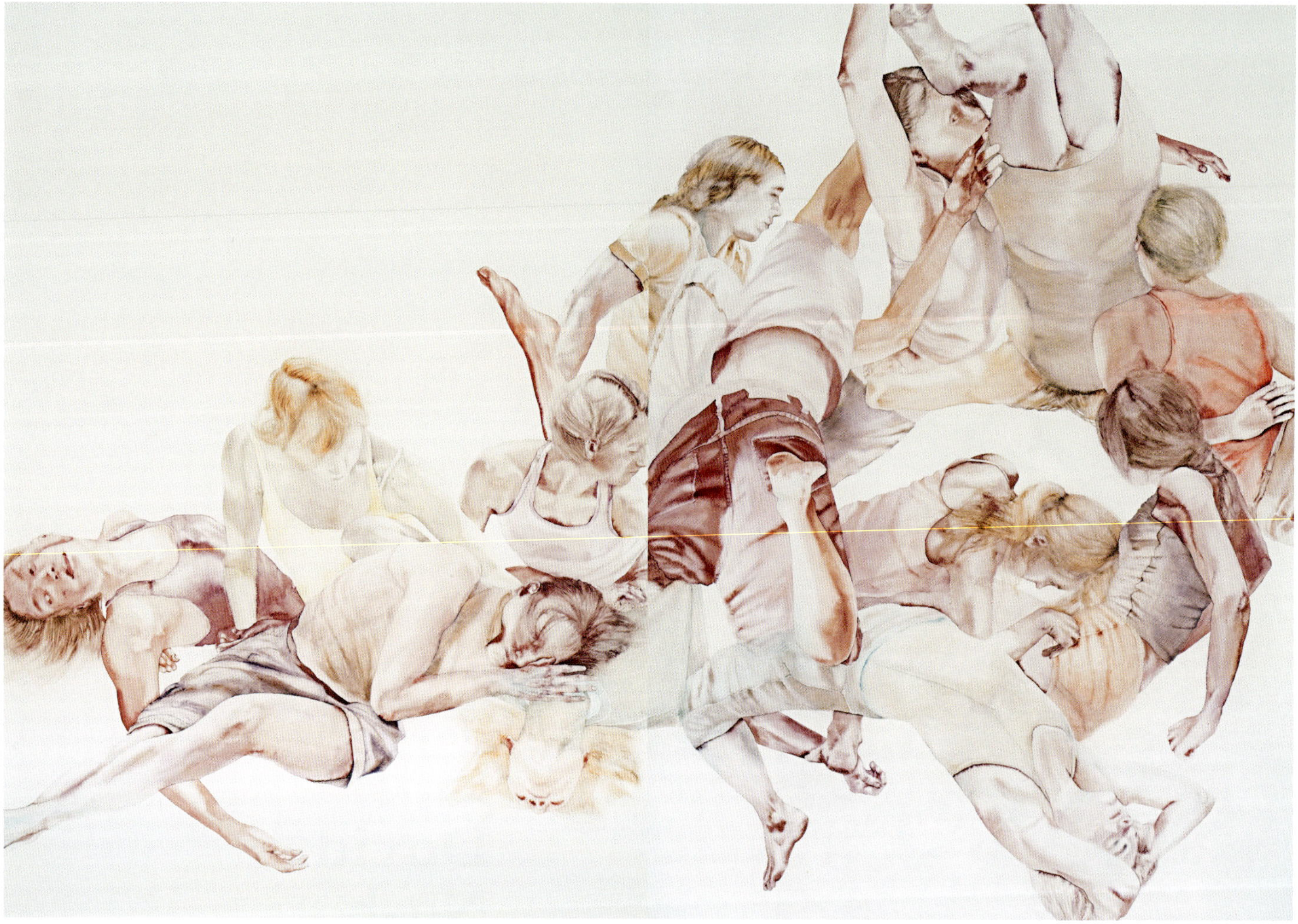

1

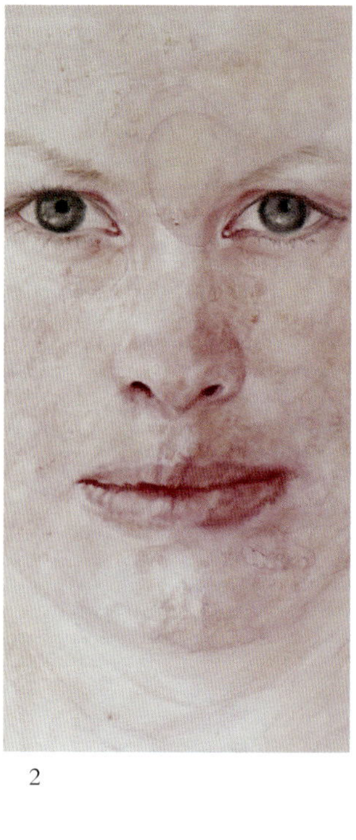

2

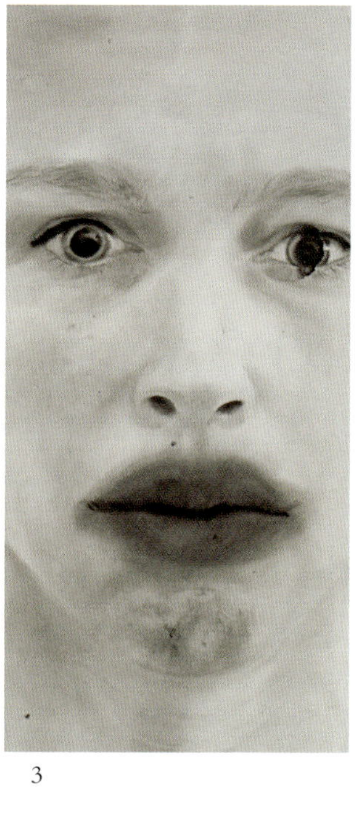

3

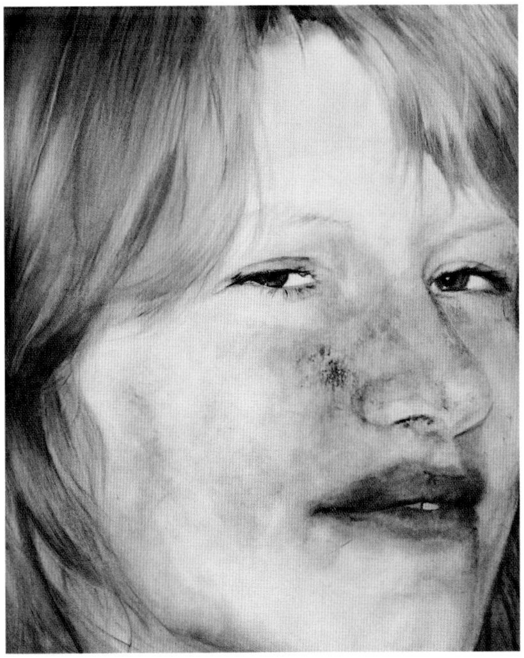

4

**Shown by**
Galleri Magnus Karlsson
E1

**Biography**
Born 1980
Lives in Stockholm

Swedish-born Nordin has shown recent exhibitions at venues such as The Studio, London (2012), Färgfabriken, Stockholm (2011), and Galleri Magnus Karlsson, Stockholm (2010) (with Niklas Eneblom and Ulf Lundin). Her group exhibitions include 'Ice Man', Arario Gallery, Cheonan, South Korea (2012), and 'She's in the Picture', Centrum för Fotografi, Stockholm (2011). Nordin's work is part of collections such as the Gothenburg Museum of Art and the Nordic Watercolour Museum, Skärhamn, Sweden.

1
*Group Piece*
2010
Watercolour on paper
178 × 245 cm
Courtesy of Galleri Magnus Karlsson

2
*Pink Noise Series*
2011
Watercolour on paper
150 × 69 cm
Courtesy of Galleri Magnus Karlsson

3
*Pink Noise Series*
2011
Watercolour on paper
150 × 69 cm
Courtesy of Galleri Magnus Karlsson

4
*Pink Noise Series*
2011
Watercolour on paper
115 × 91 cm
Courtesy of Galleri Magnus Karlsson

# Maria Nordin

Fashion photography, Body art of the 1970s and the quiet contemplation of a loved one's face provide Maria Nordin with a range of attitudes towards the human body. 'Pink Noise Series' (2011–12) comprises large watercolours of closely cropped faces, where skin and paint approach a textural equivalence. In works such as *Group Piece* (2010) clusters of figures are choreographed in close relation, performing a proximity that is generally chased out of everyday public life. The intent of the original photograph is lost to the blank white backdrop, and this ambiguity reaches a peak in the animation *Behind the Laughing Veil* (2011), where a woman laughs vivaciously at something out of sight. SOR

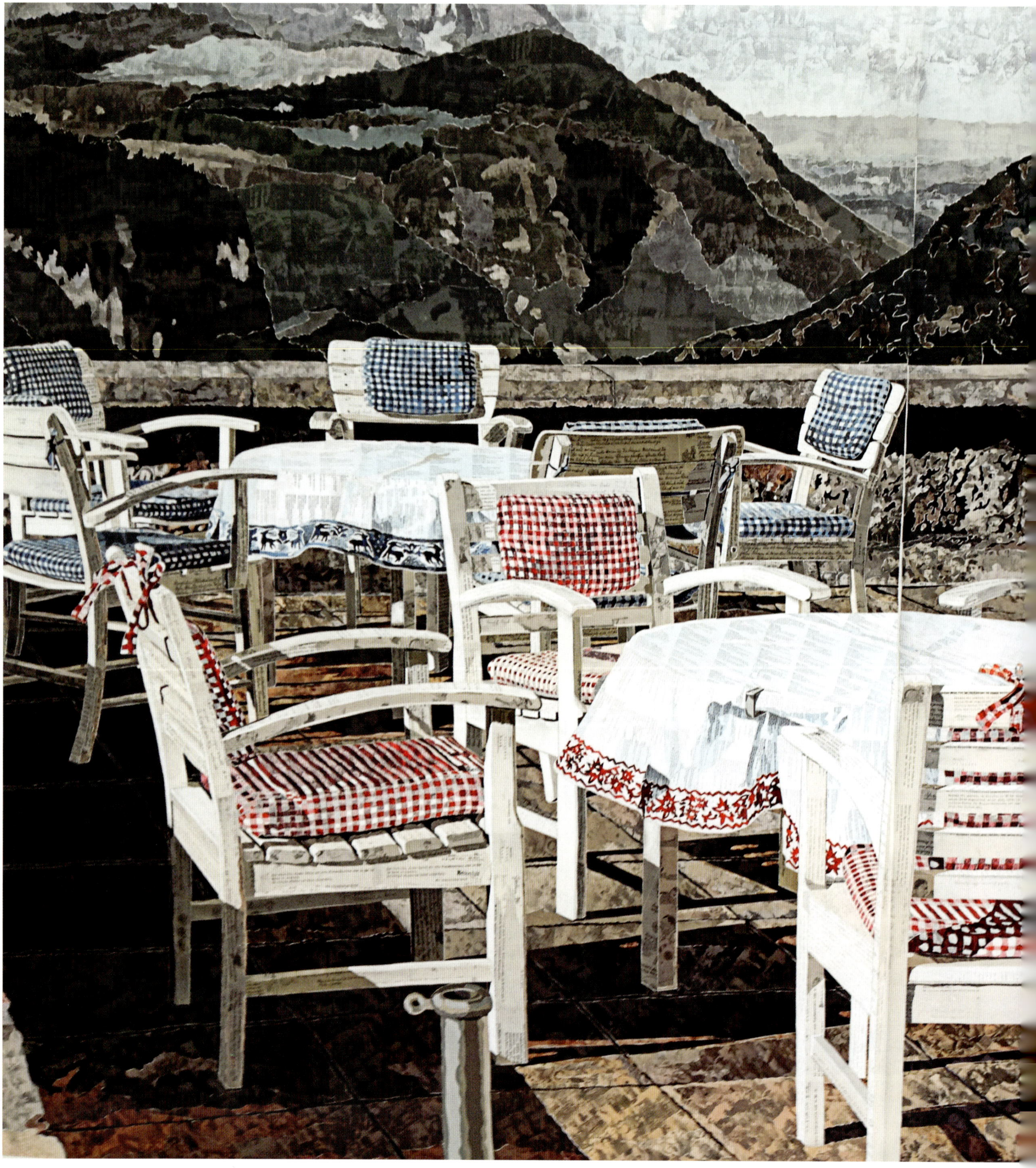

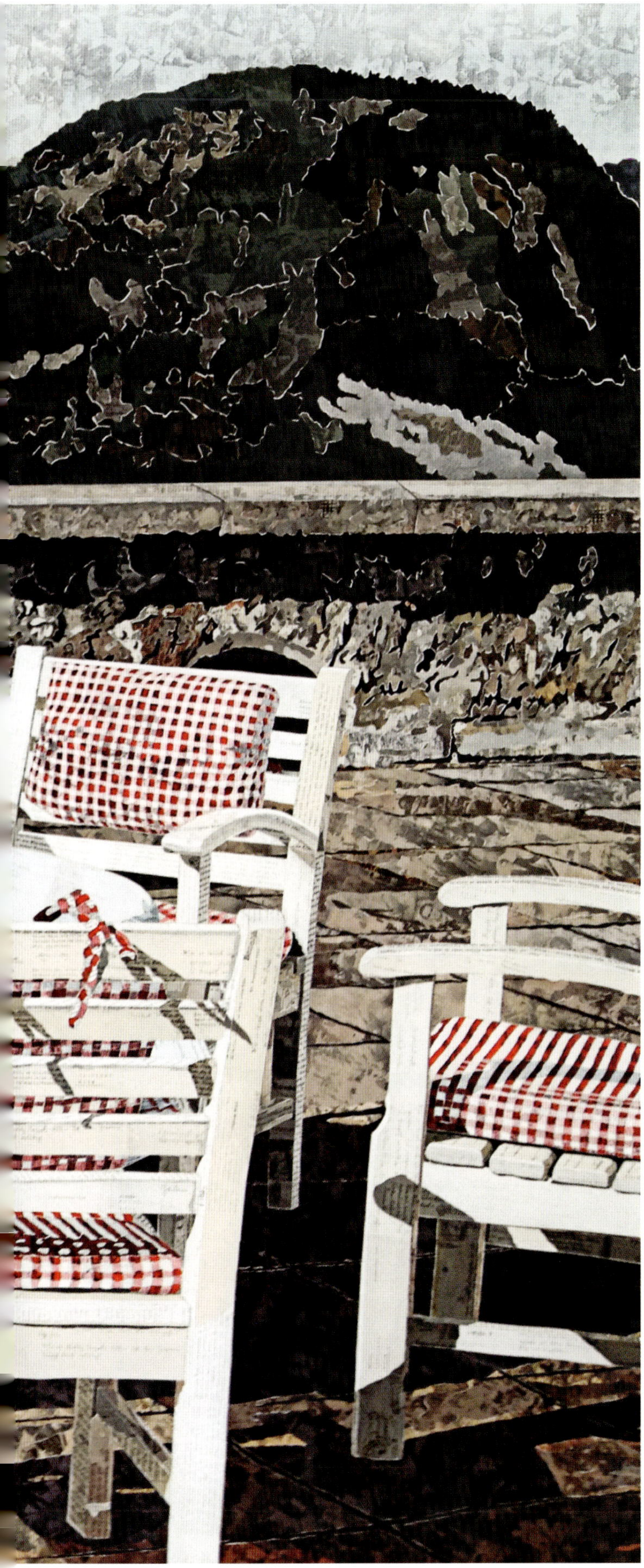

**Shown by**
Galerie Gisela Capitain C10
Anton Kern Gallery A4

**Biography**
Born 1953
Lives in Cologne

Cologne-born artist Odenbach has recently been the subject of solo exhibitions at the Freud Museum, London (2011), Kunsthalle Bremen (2008) and Hamburger Bahnhof, Museum für Gegenwart, Berlin (2006). His work is included in permanent collections such as: MoMA, New York; Kunstmuseum Bonn; the National Gallery of Canada, Ottawa; and Centre Pompidou, Paris. His solo show at Gallery Gisela Capitain, Cologne, opens in October 2012.

*Familienfeier*
(Family Celebration)
(detail)
2011–12
Collage
215 × 290 cm
Courtesy of Galerie Gisela Capitain

# Marcel Odenbach

A pioneer of German video art since the 1970s, Marcel Odenbach has long anatomized selfhood's construction, often suggesting—via archive materials—the weighty imprint of cultural and national narratives. In *Nobody is There Anymore, Where He Wanted to Be* (1989–90), trooping Nazis and a chant of 'a single German homeland' ominously counterpointed footage of a pre-reunification parade in East Berlin; later, working in Ghana, Odenbach critiqued inherited European misconceptions of Africa. Recently he has emphasized collage, a medium valorizing informational snippets. *Probeliegen* (Test it Out, 2011), depicting Sigmund Freud's psychoanalytic couch, only resembles a painting—it's a virtuoso tessellation of photographs and reveals, as you study it, fragmentary episodes from 19th- and 20th-century German and Jewish history. Where identity lies, Odenbach astringently suggests, brutal baseness is never far away. MH

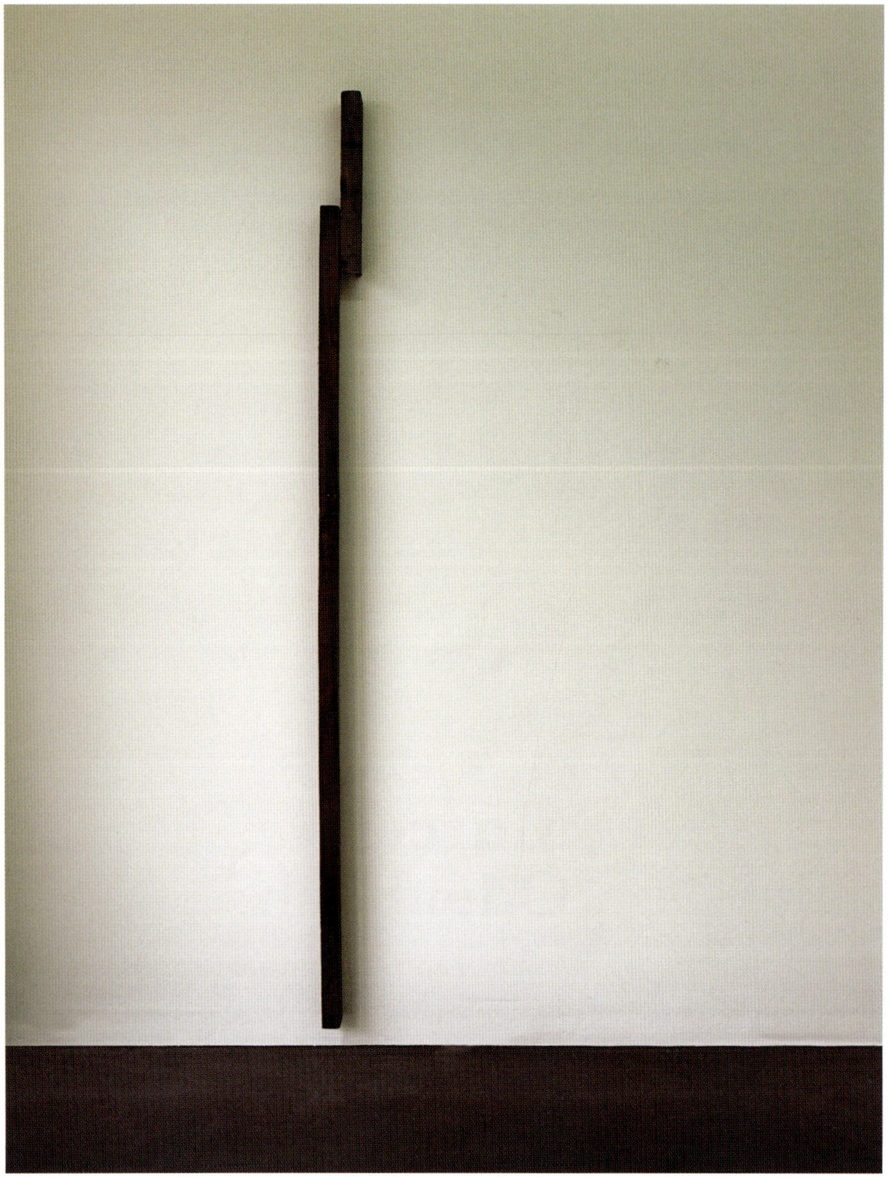

1

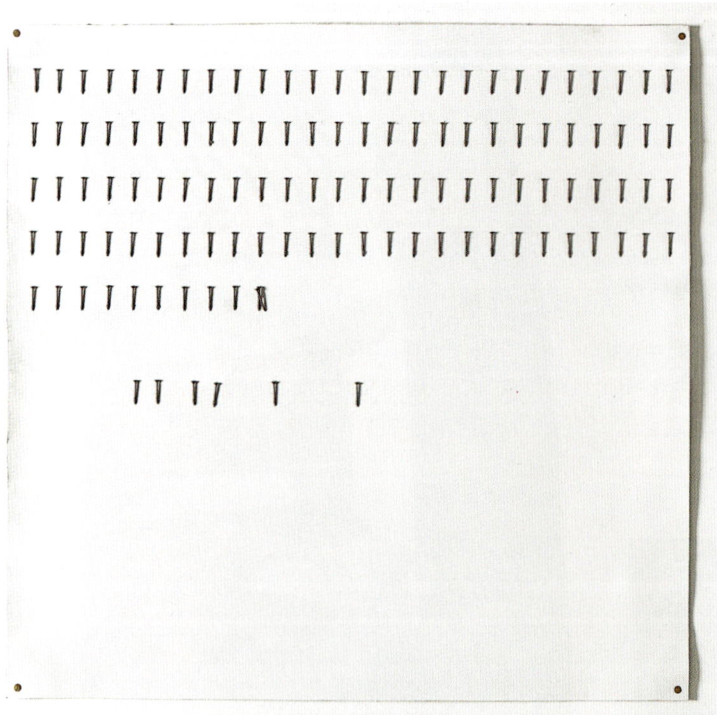

2

# Henrik Olesen

The mathematician and computing pioneer Alan Turing was driven to suicide by his prosecution for homosexuality and consequent hormone treatment. Henrik Olesen's installation *Some Illustrations to the Life of Alan Turing* (2008) treats his life as a process of physical transformation: Turing imagined our becoming digital, then had his body 'replaced' by science. Olesen's work has frequently explored such queer prehistories, not so much unearthed by his art as reimagined: in *Some Gay–Lesbian Artists and/or Artists Relevant to Homo-Social Culture* (2007) he reworked the history of homosexuality with the rigour of art historian Aby Warburg. Recent untitled works with canvas, nails and screws essay an abstract equivalent to a more recent history, approximating the repetition of techno music. BD

**Shown by**
Andersen's Contemporary H4
Buchholz C4
Cabinet E3
dépendance S11
Galleria Franco Noero A2
Reena Spaulings Fine Art B6

**Biography**
Born 1967
Lives in Berlin

Danish-born Olesen has presented solo shows and projects at venues that include Museum Ludwig, Cologne (2012), Kunstmuseum Basel (2011), MoMA, New York (2011), Studio Voltaire, London (2008), Migros Museum, Zurich (2007), Vienna Secession (2004), Sprengel Museum, Hanover (2003), and Kunstverein Braunschweig (2001). Group exhibitions in 2012 have included 'Ghosts in the Machine', New Museum, New York, 'In the Space of the Beholder', Pinakothek der Moderne, Munich, and 'Never Odd Or Even', Museum of Contemporary Art, Roskilde.

1
*Portrait of my Mother III*
2010
Used pine
205 × 8 × 6 cm
Courtesy of Buchholz

2
*Untitled*
2012
Canvas, screws, nails and glue
80 × 80 cm
Courtesy of Buchholz

3
*A.T.*
2012
Computer collage on paper
49 × 33 cm
Courtesy of Buchholz

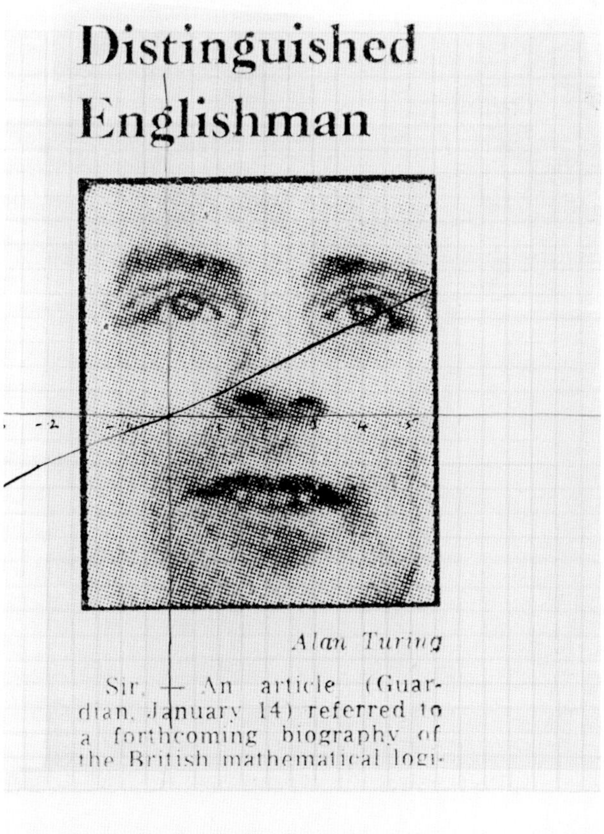


3

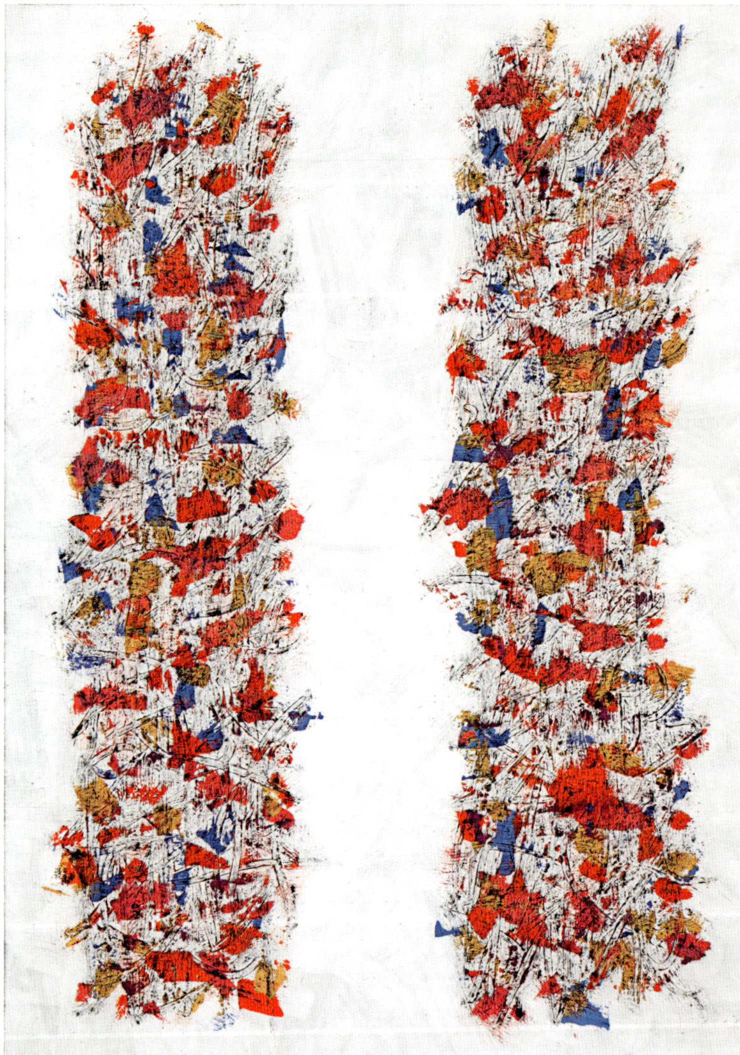

1

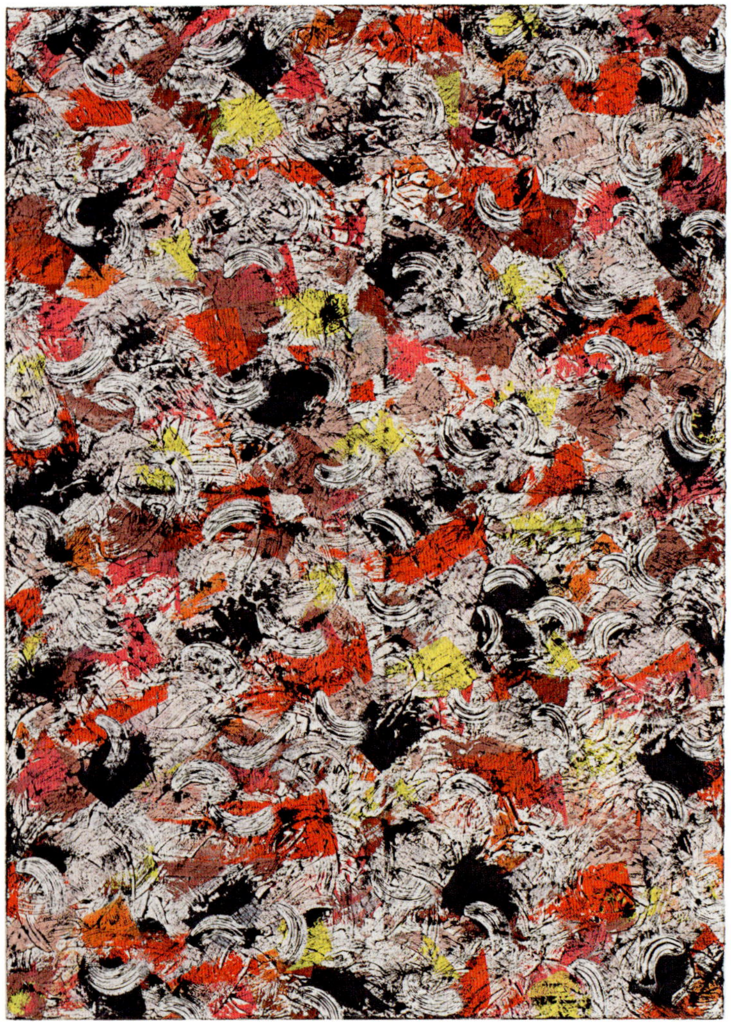

2

# Alex Olson

**Shown by**
Laura Bartlett Gallery
G14

**Biography**
Born 1978
Lives in Los Angeles

American artist Olson presented solo shows in 2012 at Lisa Cooley, New York, and Shane Campbell Gallery, Chicago. She was awarded a Steep Rock Arts Association residency in 2011 and has contributed to group exhibitions including 'Made in LA 2012', Hammer Museum, Los Angeles, and 'Emerge Selections 2011', Museum of Contemporary Art, Chicago. Her work is part of permanent collections including the Los Angeles County Museum of Art and the Museum of Contemporary Art, Chicago.

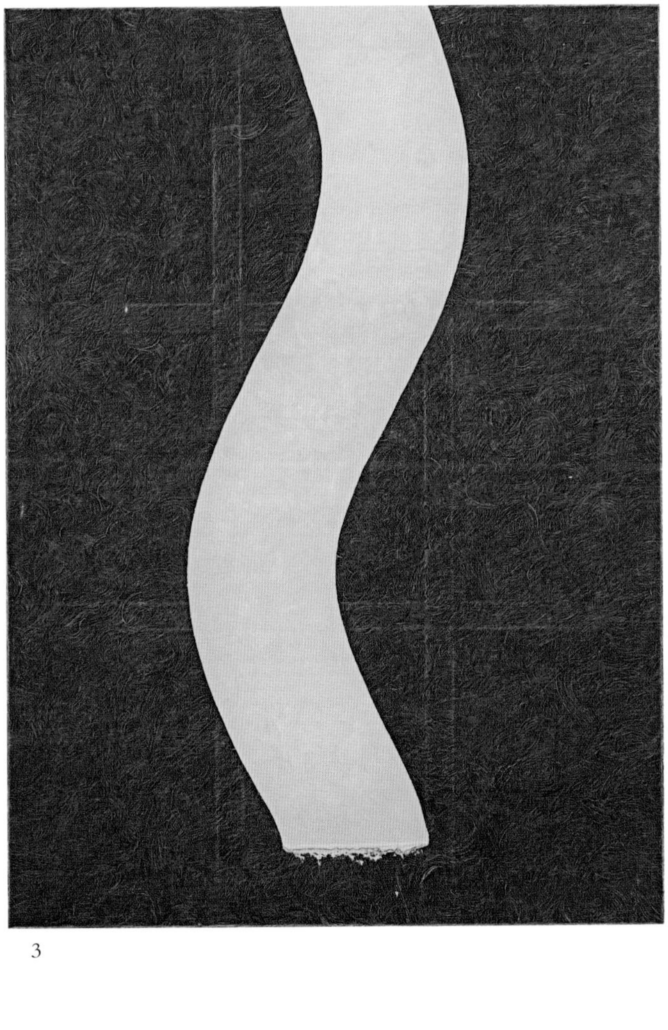
3

1
*Exchange*
2012
Oil on linen
155 × 110 cm
Courtesy of Laura Bartlett Gallery, Lisa Cooley and Shane Campbell Gallery

2
*Architect*
2011
Oil on canvas
104 × 74 cm
Courtesy of Laura Bartlett Gallery, Lisa Cooley and Shane Campbell Gallery

3
*Ship*
2012
Oil on linen
130 × 92 cm
Courtesy of Laura Bartlett Gallery, Lisa Cooley and Shane Campbell Gallery

In Alex Olson's abstract canvases, different breeds of brushstroke cohabit as uncertain stablemates. In some, such as *Ship* or *Iterations* (both 2012), bold sweeps of white dominate the frame while subtler, curled brushstrokes patiently fill up what might be mistaken for the background. In Olson's works there is really no such thing as background—her works are egalitarian surfaces where painterly incidents are arrayed as options, not as spatial narratives. *Exchange* (2012) and *Architect* (2011) almost resemble boldy patterned fabric, so evenly are Olson's marks dispersed. The paintings become more complicated when one registers the ghostly dry-brushed and half-erased marks that expose traces of the canvases' wooden supports and the paintings' previous incarnations. JG

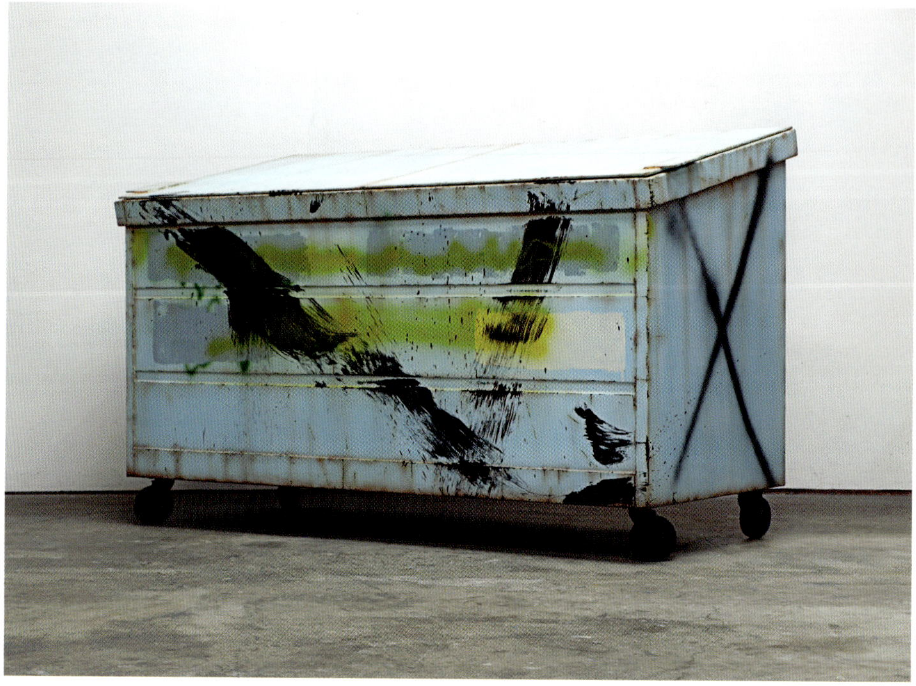

1

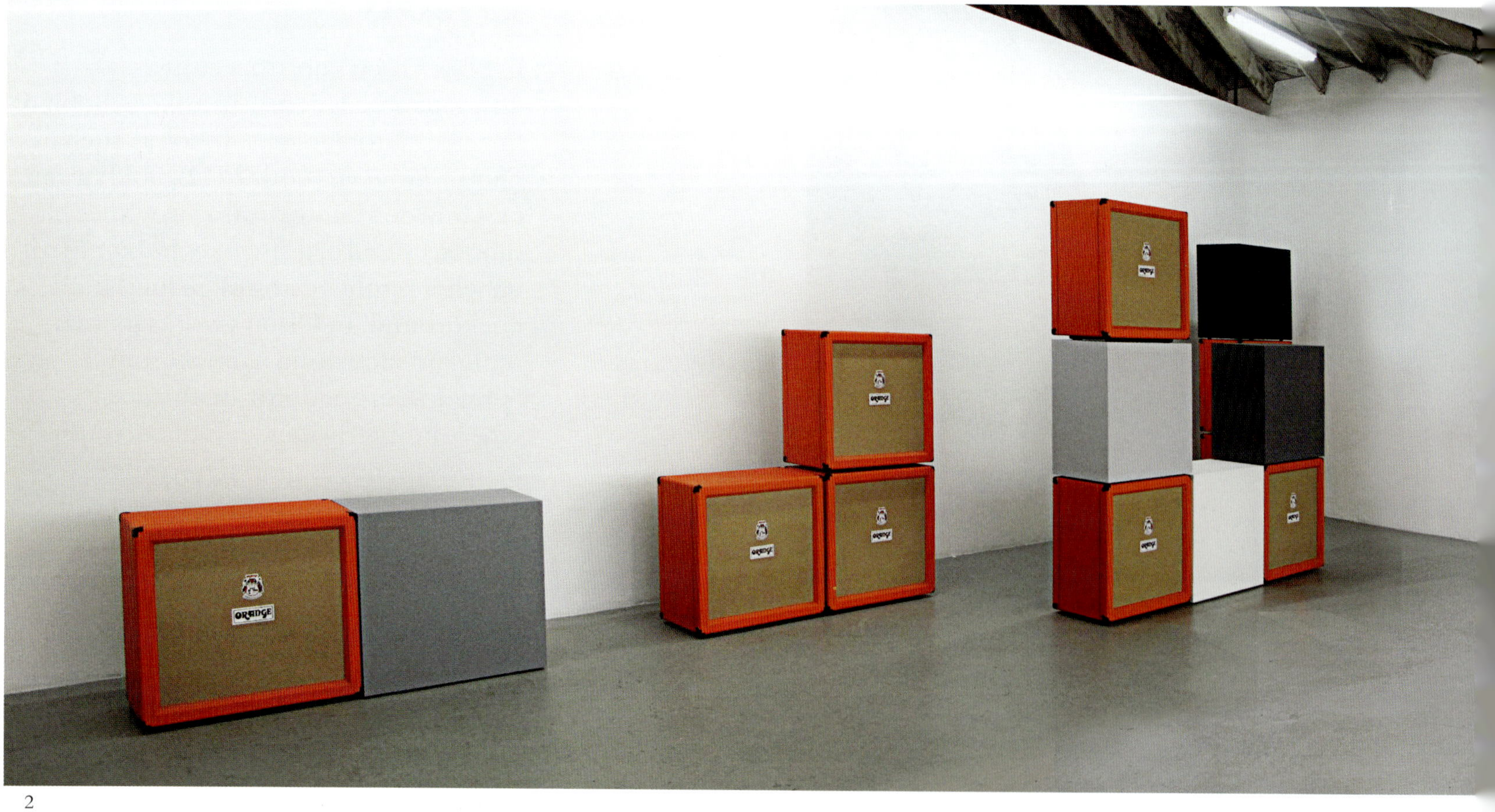


2

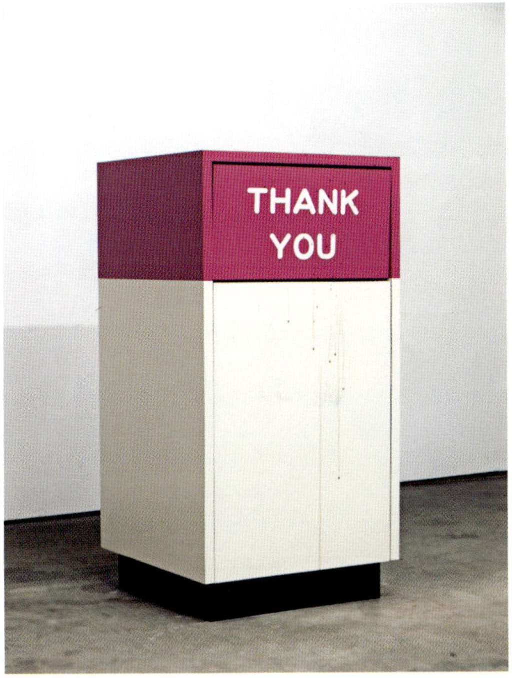


3

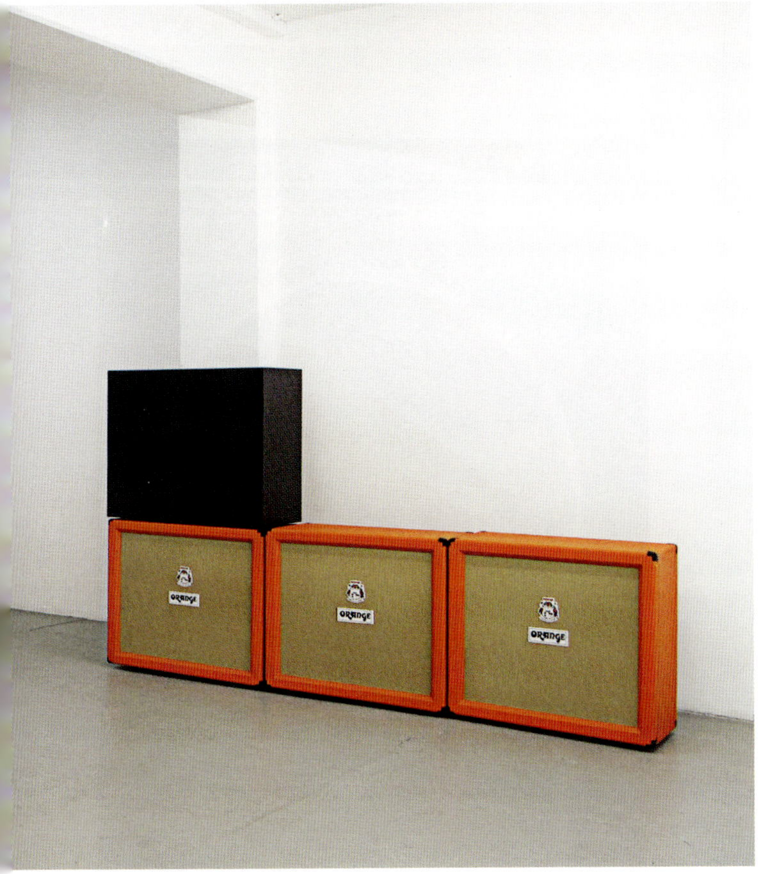

**Shown by**
galerie frank elbaz H8

**Biography**
Born 1967
Lives in Los Angeles

Japanese-born Oshiro has shown solo exhibitions at venues including Las Cienegas Project, Los Angeles (2011), galerie frank elbaz, Paris (2010), Tokyo Institute of Technology (2007) and Las Vegas Art Museum (2007). His recent group exhibitions include 'Lifelike', Walker Art Center, Minneapolis (2012), and 'The Artist's Museum', Museum of Contemporary Art, Los Angeles (2011).

1
*Dumpster (Blue with Black Swoosh)*
2012
Acrylic on stretched canvas and caster wheels
120 × 193 × 90 cm
Courtesy of galerie frank elbaz

2
*Orange Speaker Cabinets and Gray Scale Boxes (18 Parts)*
2009
Acrylic and Bondo on stretched canvas
Dimensions variable
Courtesy of galerie frank elbaz

3
*Trash Bin #17 (Magenta and Beige/Cola Drips)*
2010
Acrylic on stretched canvas
102 × 51 × 52 cm
Courtesy of private collection

# Kaz Oshiro

The TV, the refrigerator and the washing machine: the holy trinity of postwar consumerism was widely exported by the US in the wake of World War II, snapped up by buyers worldwide. The ghost of these objects—then symbols of economic success, now evocative of a contemporary culture of American wastefulness—haunts the work of Kaz Oshiro, a long-time US resident born in Okinawa. Using canvas, wooden frames, acrylic and Bondo (a vehicle repair material), the constitutive materials of easel painting are transformed into boxy *trompe-l'oeil* sculptures. The scrapes, scratches and drips accrued by rubbish bins, speakers, file cabinets and washer-dryers are Oshiro's entry point to a history of modern painting: 'I see myself as a still-life painter trying to become an abstract painter.' SNS

E

EYE

EEYEE

EEEYEEE

EEEEYEEEE

EEEEEYEEEEE

You see the light of a torch and your body feels the heat of the flame, but his body is burning. He enlightens you with the fire of his burning eyeballs. (2011-12-16)

1

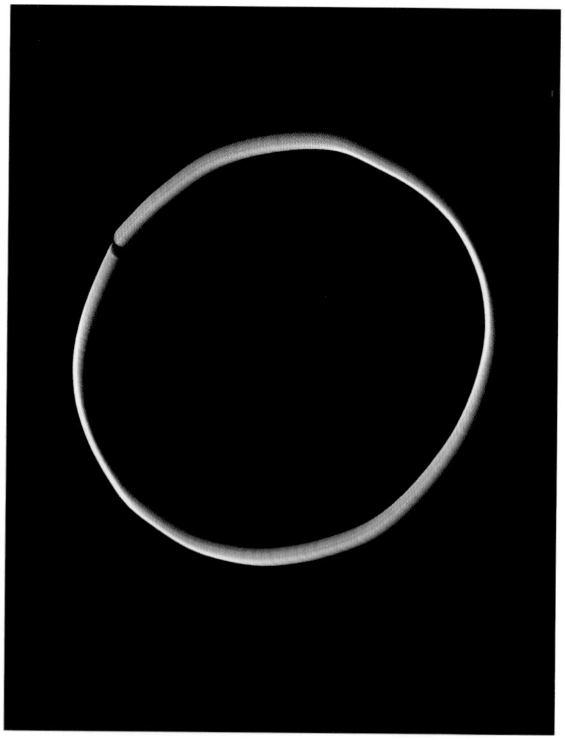

2

# Pak Sheung-Chuen

**Shown by**
Vitamin Creative Space
E6

**Biography**
Born 1977
Lives in Hong Kong

Chinese-born Pak has presented solo shows recently at the Hong Kong Museum of Art (2010), Guangdong Museum of Art, Guangzhou (2010), and Vitamin Creative Space, Guangzhou (2009). He participated in the 7th Taipei Biennial (2010), 53rd Venice Biennale (2009), 3rd Yokohama Triennial (2008) and 3rd Guangzhou Triennial (2008), as well as group shows such as the touring exhibition 'China Power Station', whose venues included Astrup Fearnley Museum of Modern Art, Oslo (2007).

1
*Daily Practice*
(detail)
2012
Mixed media
Dimensions variable
Courtesy of Vitamin Creative Space

2
*Using the Light of the Waning Moon to Draw a Full Moon*
2007
Photograph
120 × 90 cm
Courtesy of Vitamin Creative Space

3
*Measuring the Size of the Sea Storing in a Library*
2008
Books from collection of Ottendorfer Public Library
Dimensions variable
Courtesy of Vitamin Creative Space

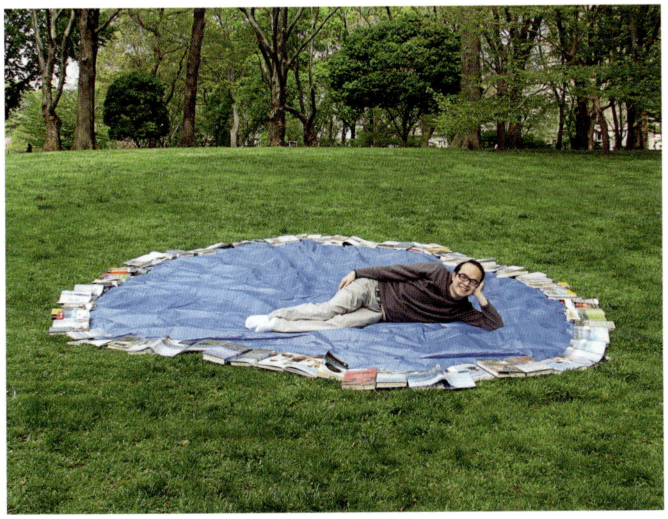
3

Playful and humorous, Pak's Conceptual and performance art excavates poignant truths in overlooked, everyday places. He has collected bags of potato crisps that contain air from different countries, waited outside an apartment block for all its residents to go to sleep, spent ten days collecting his breaths in transparent plastic bags until they filled the apartment he was renting, and waited in a museum lobby inviting visitors to take him home. In *Measuring the Size of the Sea Storing in a Library* (2008) he borrowed all the books in a Manhattan public library featuring an image of the sea on the cover. Placing them side by side and lining up their horizon lines, Pak created 'one' interminable ocean. ND

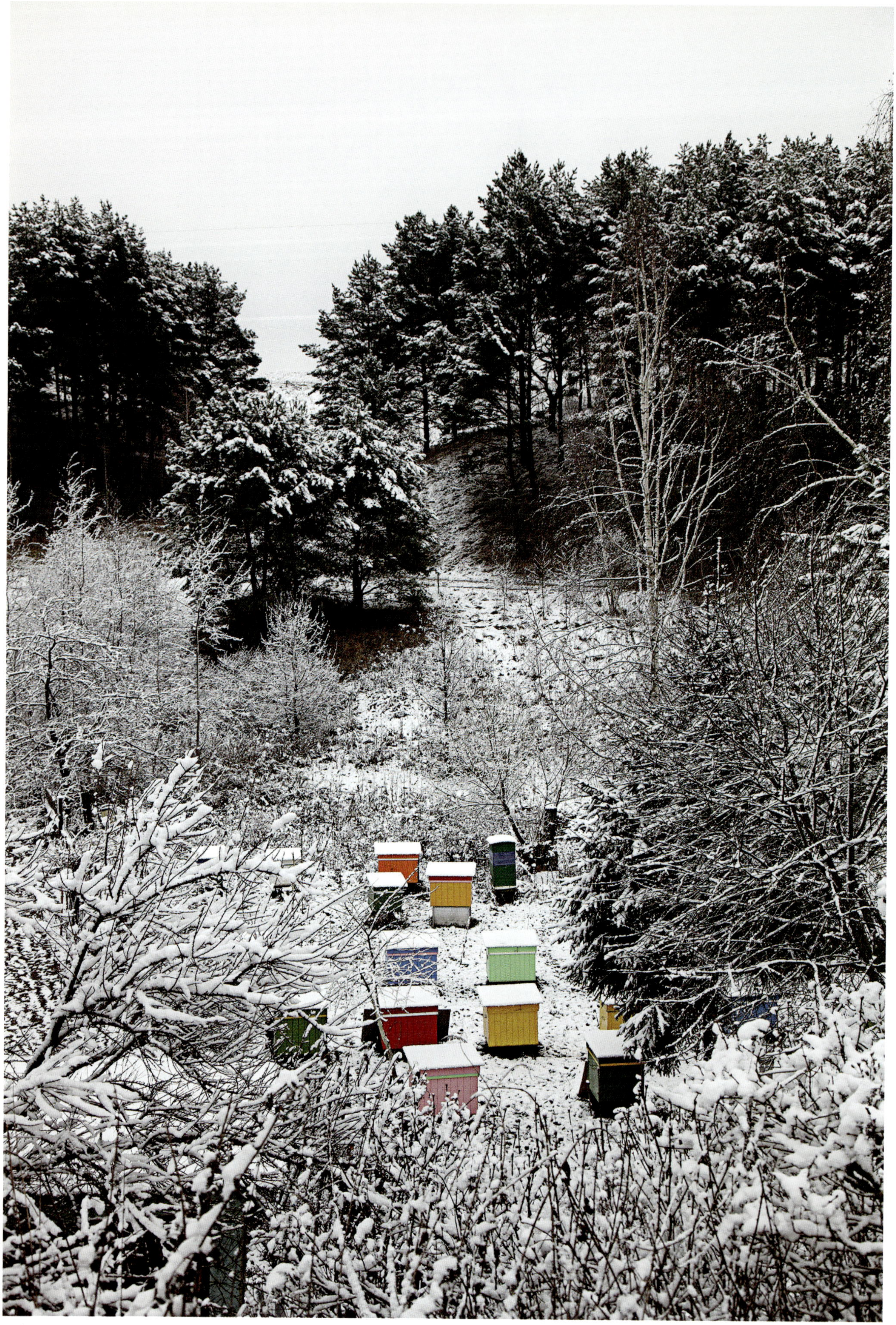

# Tim Parchikov

A cluster of brightly coloured wooden beehives are capped by snow as they stand guard in a monochrome forest (*Las Colmenas (Islavskoe)*, 2010). It is night and a woman hurries down a street strewn with rubbish, the orange glow of the streetlights reflecting off the rain-soaked pavement (*Untitled [Naples]*, 2009). Two scenes from the portfolios of photographer and filmmaker Tim Parchikov that give a sense of the mood and staging of his works as they frequently exploit the dramatic effects of enhanced saturation and contrast. His series 'Venice' (2005–11) bravely tackled what might seem like a treacherously clichéd subject for an artist—an authentic Venetian aesthetic. Often producing shots already trapped by cinematic *chiaroscuro*—think Nicolas Roeg's film *Don't Look Now* (1973)—Parchikov must have finally doubted if Venice really existed in front of the lens. MA

**Shown by**
Galería Juana de Aizpuru G5

**Biography**
Born 1983
Lives in Moscow and Paris

Moscow-born Parchikov has presented his exhibition of recent works 'Suspense' at venues including Centro Andaluz de la Fotografía, Almeria (2011), Museo di Roma in Trastevere (2011) and the Moscow Museum of Modern Art (2010). He has participated in group exhibitions at galleries including Istanbul Modern (2010) and Château d'Eau, Toulouse (2010).

1
*Las Colmenas (Islavskoe)*
2010
C-type print
180 × 120 cm
Courtesy of Galería Juana de Aizpuru

2
*Untitled (Venice, Guidecca)*
2007
C-type print
120 × 180 cm
Courtesy of Galería Juana de Aizpuru

3
*Untitled (Naples)*
2009
C-type print
120 × 180 cm
Courtesy of Galería Juana de Aizpuru

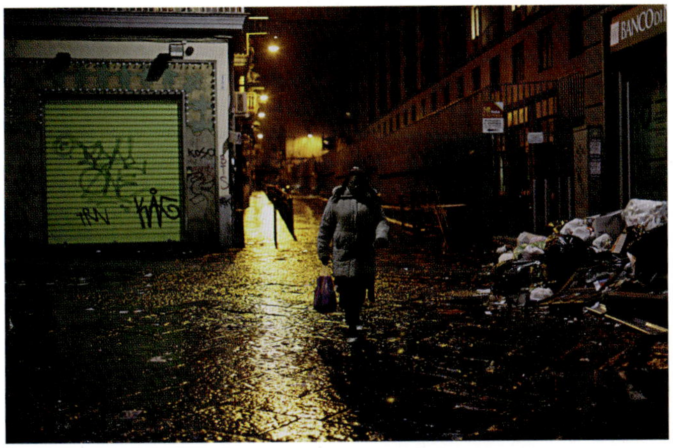


3

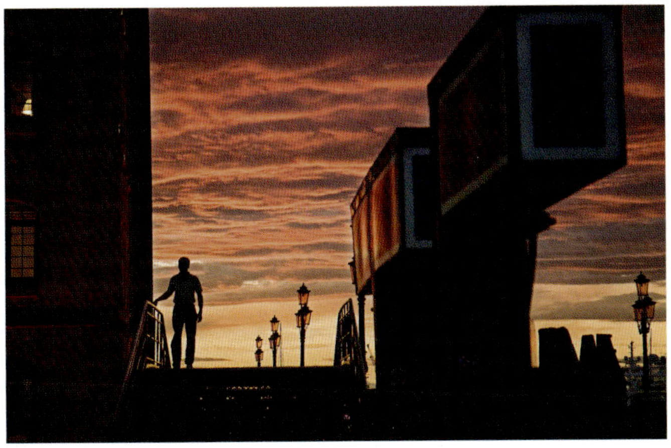

2

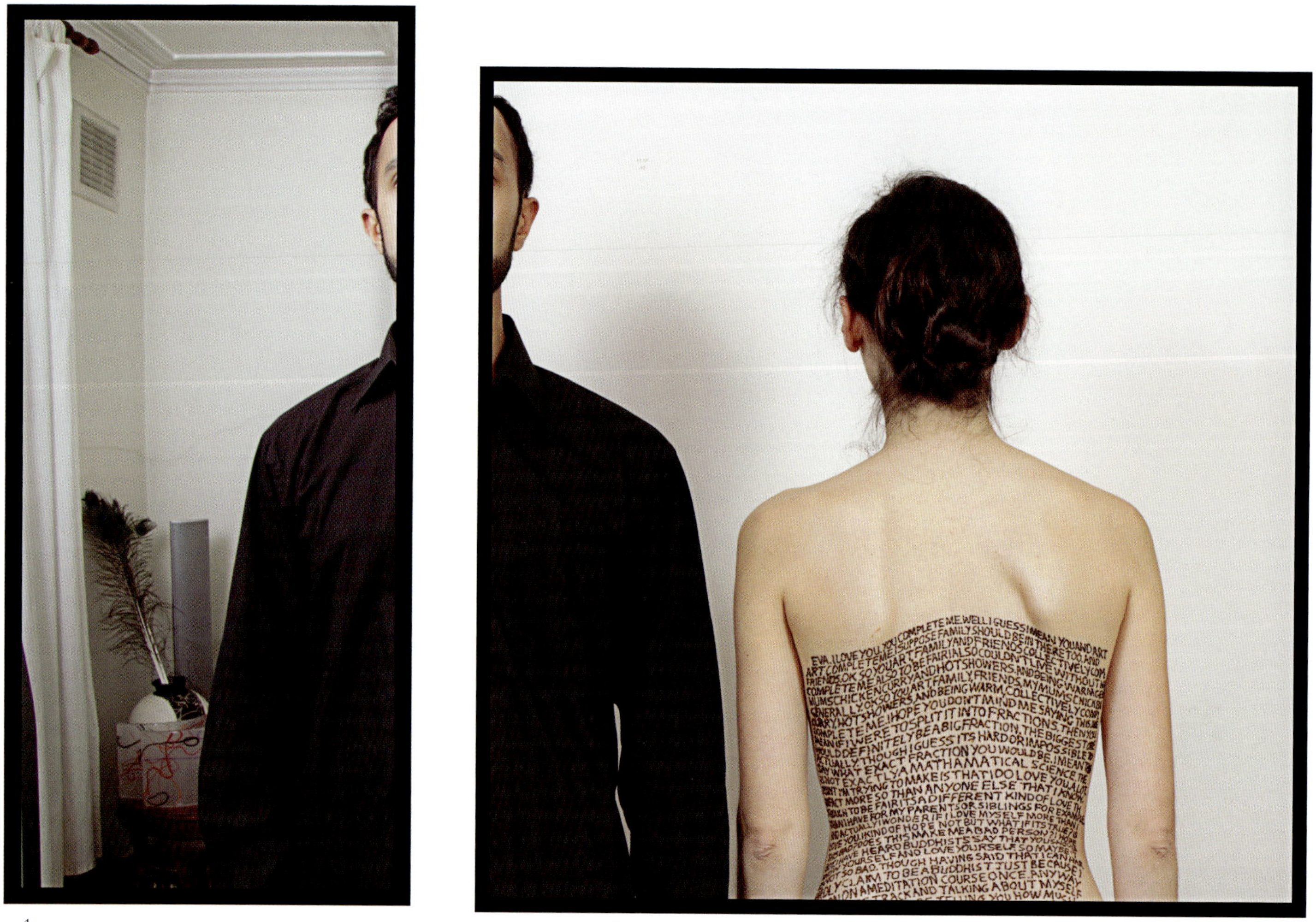
EVA, I LOVE YOU. YOU COMPLETE ME. WELL I GUESS I MEAN YOU AND ART
ART COMPLETE ME I SUPPOSE FAMILY SHOULD BE IN THERE TOO, AND
FRIENDS. OK SO YOU ART FAMILY AND FRIENDS COLLECTIVELY COM
COMPLETE ME ALSO TO BE FAIR I ALSO COULDN'T LIVE WITHOUT
MUMS CHICKEN CURRY AND HOT SHOWERS AND BEING WARM
GENERALLY. OK SO YOU ART FAMILY, FRIENDS, MY MUMS CHICKEN
CURRY, HOT SHOWERS AND BEING WARM, COLLECTIVELY COMP
COMPLETE ME. I HOPE YOU DON'T MIND ME SAYING THIS
MEAN IF I WERE TO SPLIT IT INTO FRACTIONS, THEN YOU
WOULD DEFINITELY BE A BIG FRACTION. THE BIGGEST
ACTUALLY. THOUGH I GUESS ITS HARD OR IMPOSSIBLE
SAY WHAT EXACT FRACTION YOU WOULD BE. I MEAN
IS NOT EXACTLY A MATHAMATICAL SCIENCE. THE
POINT I'M TRYING TO MAKE IS THAT I DO LOVE YOU A LOT
MORE SO THAN ANYONE ELSE THAT I KNOW
THOUGH TO BE FAIR ITS A DIFFERENT KIND OF LOVE TH
I HAVE FOR MY PARENTS OR SIBLINGS FOR EXAMPLE
ACTUALLY I WONDER IF I LOVE MYSELF MORE THAN I
LOVE YOU. I KIND OF HOPE NOT BUT WHAT IF ITS TRUE?
DOES THIS MAKE ME A BAD PERSON? I HOPE
HAVE HEARD BUDDHISTS SAY THAT YOU SHOULD
YOURSELF AND LOVE YOURSELF SO MAYBE
NOT SO BAD. THOUGH HAVING SAID THAT I CAN
CLAIM TO BE A BUDDHIST JUST BECAUSE I
ON A MEDITATION COURSE ONCE. ANYWAY
TRACK AND TALKING ABOUT MYSELF

1

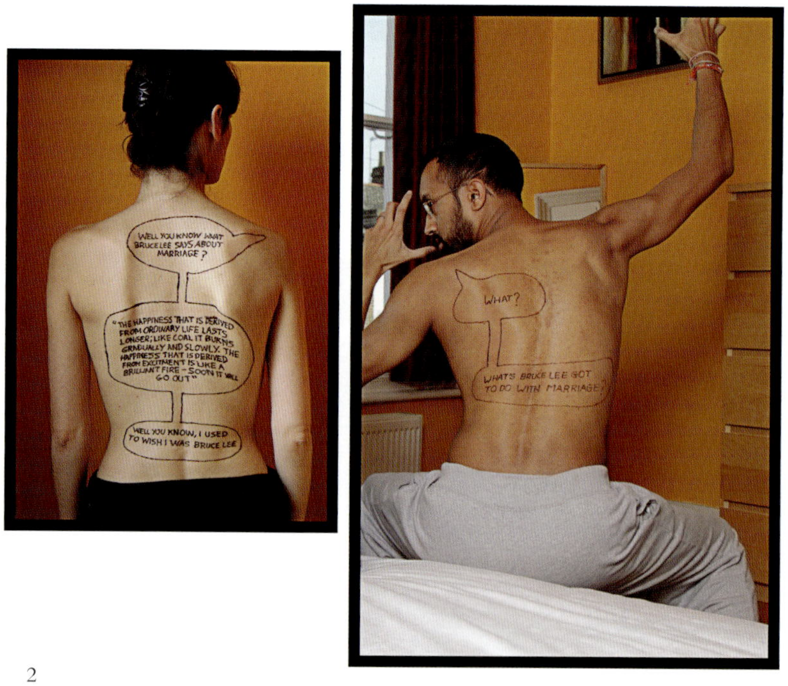
WELL YOU KNOW WHAT BRUCE LEE SAYS ABOUT MARRIAGE?
"THE HAPPINESS THAT IS DERIVED FROM ORDINARY LIFE LASTS LONGER; LIKE COAL IT BURNS GRADUALLY AND SLOWLY. THE HAPPINESS THAT IS DERIVED FROM EXCITMENT IS LIKE A BRILLIANT FIRE - SOON IT WILL GO OUT"
WELL YOU KNOW, I USED TO WISH I WAS BRUCE LEE
WHAT?
WHAT'S BRUCE LEE GOT TO DO WITH MARRIAGE?

2

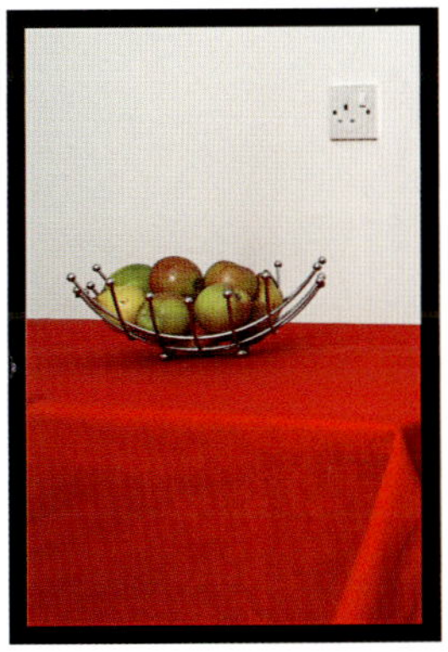

3

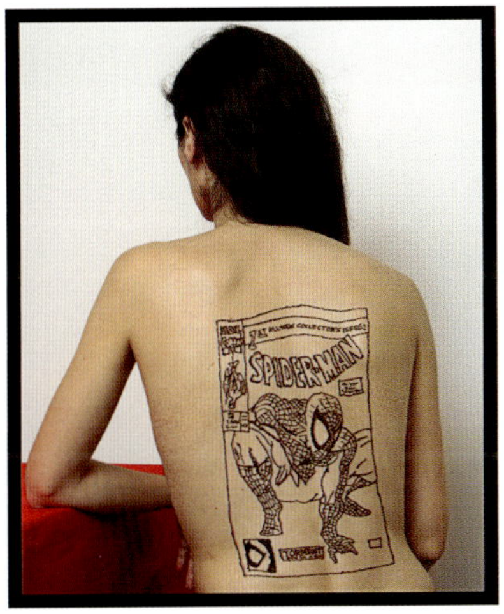

**Shown by**
Chatterjee & Lal S1

**Biography**
Born 1980
Lives in London

British-born artist Patel has been the subject of recent solo shows at galleries including Chatterjee & Lal, Mumbai (2012), and New Art Exchange, Nottingham (2012 and 2009). He has performed live at venues that include Tate Modern, London (2012), and on the suburban streets of the Minto neighbourhood as part of the Sydney Festival (2011). He presents *Be Like Water* at the Royal Opera House, London, on 27 and 28 November 2012.

1
*9*
From the series 'Mehndi'
2011
Digital photograph on archival paper
76 × 108 cm
Courtesy of Chatterjee & Lal

2
*14*
From the series 'Mehndi'
2012
Digital photograph on archival paper
81 × 98 cm
Courtesy of Chatterjee & Lal

3
*11*
From the series 'Mehndi'
2011
Digital photograph on archival paper
79 × 86 cm
Courtesy of Chatterjee & Lal

# Focus
# Hetain Patel

The body is where cultural and individual identity converge, and so for Hetain Patel traditional Indian rituals are a tool with which to understand the transcultural, British-Indian subject. While Patel does not claim to find distinct 'meaning' in his durational and often collaborative performances, which might involve dance or patterning the skin with pigment, a dialogue between sensory and associational inference triggers particular cultural memories and assumptions. In the recent photographic series 'Mehndi' (2011–12) Patel explores the shift in his family's ethnicity brought about by marriage to his French-Spanish wife, the text and comic book imagery drawn onto the couple's back accruing into an exchange that references personal and collective experience. SOR

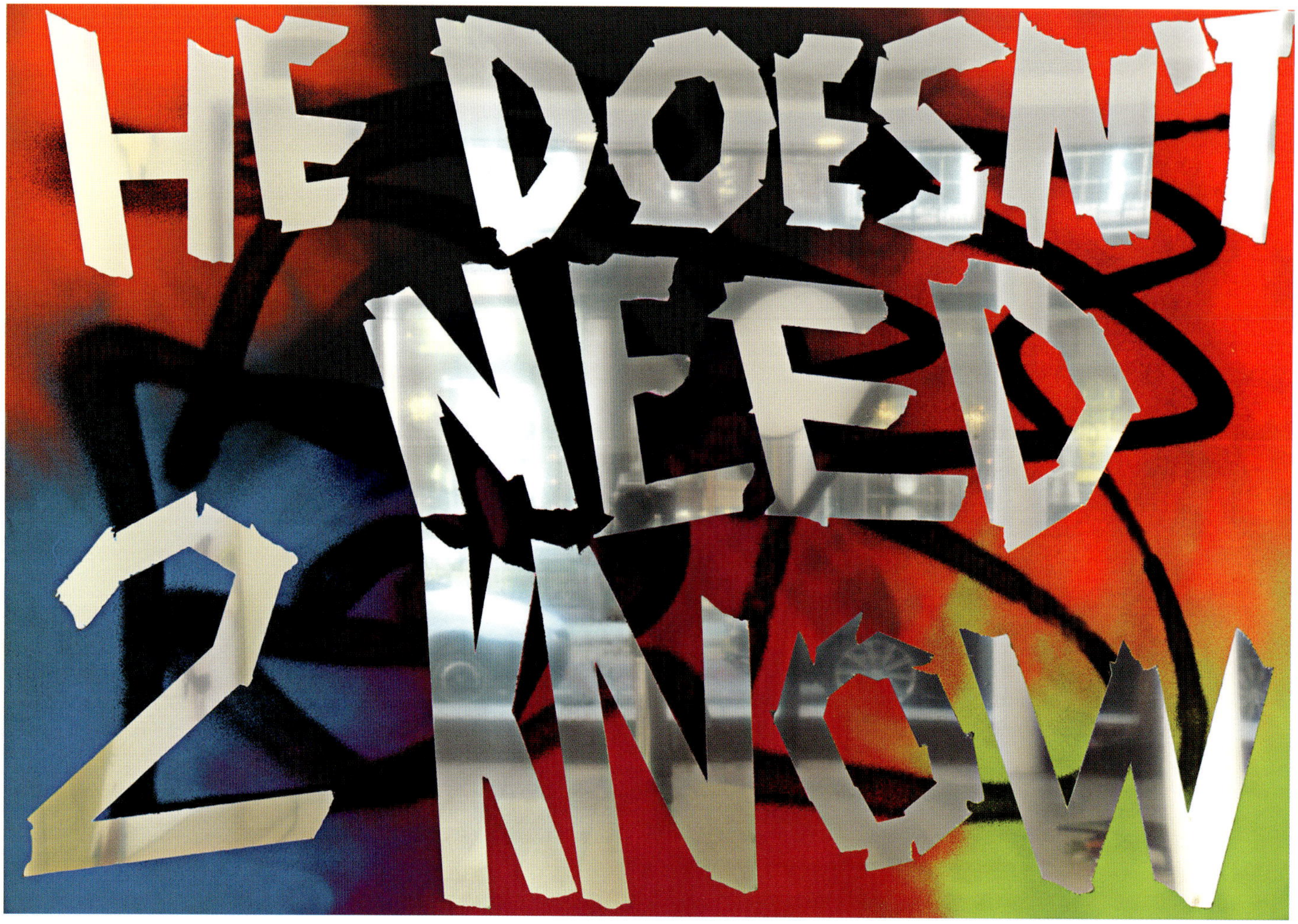


1

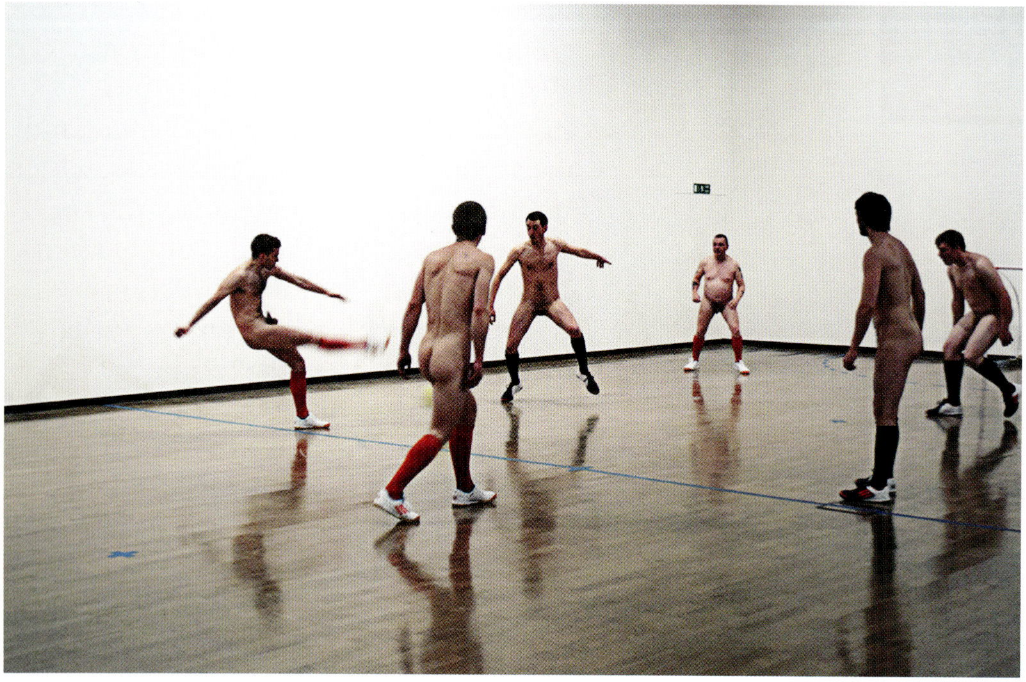

2

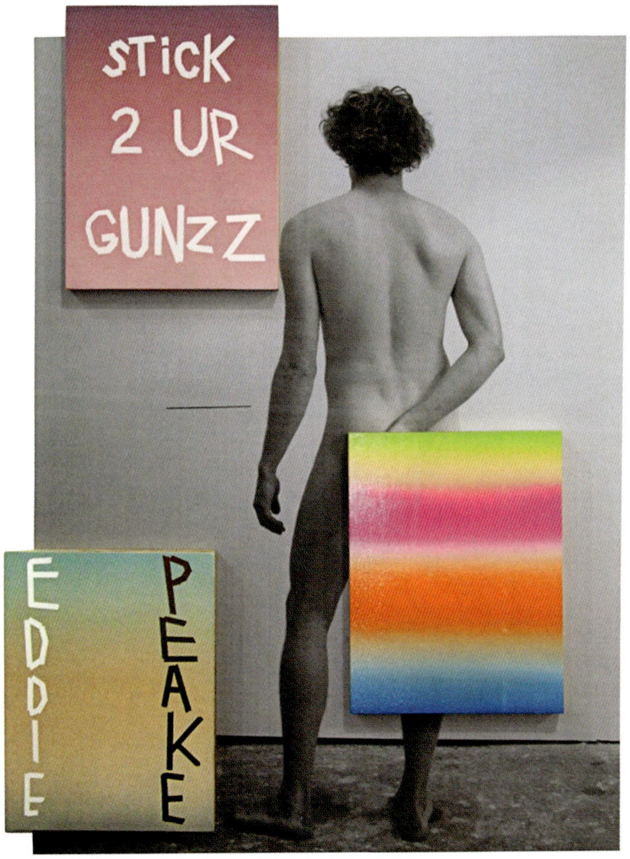


3

**Shown by**
Galleria Lorcan O'Neill
G13

**Biography**
Born 1981
Lives in London

British artist Peake, currently completing a postgraduate degree at the Royal Academy Schools, London, has presented performances in 2012 at London venues that include Tate Modern, the Royal Academy of Arts and Chisenhale Gallery. His solo exhibitions include those shown at Cell Project Space, London (2012), Mihai Nicodim Gallery, Los Angeles (2011), and Galleria Lorcan O'Neill, Rome (2012 and 2010).

1
*He Doesn't Need 2 Know*
2012
Paint on polished stainless steel
100 × 140 cm
Courtesy of Galleria Lorcan O'Neill

2
*Touch*
2012
Performance
Dimensions variable
Courtesy of Galleria Lorcan O'Neill

3
*Stick 2 Ur Gunzz*
2011
Photograph and three paintings (oil on board)
122 × 87 × 3 cm
Courtesy of Galleria Lorcan O'Neill

# Eddie Peake

Eddie Peake's work has recently included a naked game of five-a-side football (*Touch*, 2012) and synchronized dance (*DEM*, 2012). Emblazoned across his neon spray-painted canvases and mirror pieces, and rendered in an acidic palette, are angular slogans that thrust forward (but also undercut) the persona of a cocky young male artist: 'Eddie Peake Thing'; 'Putting the Don in LDN'; 'He Doesn't Need 2 Know'. Peake's work is also frequently collaborative: aside from curating several group shows, he has worked with various London-based artists and collectives. Though antic in realization, his practice's continual focus is on identity—how it can be performed and exaggerated, chopped and changed. ST

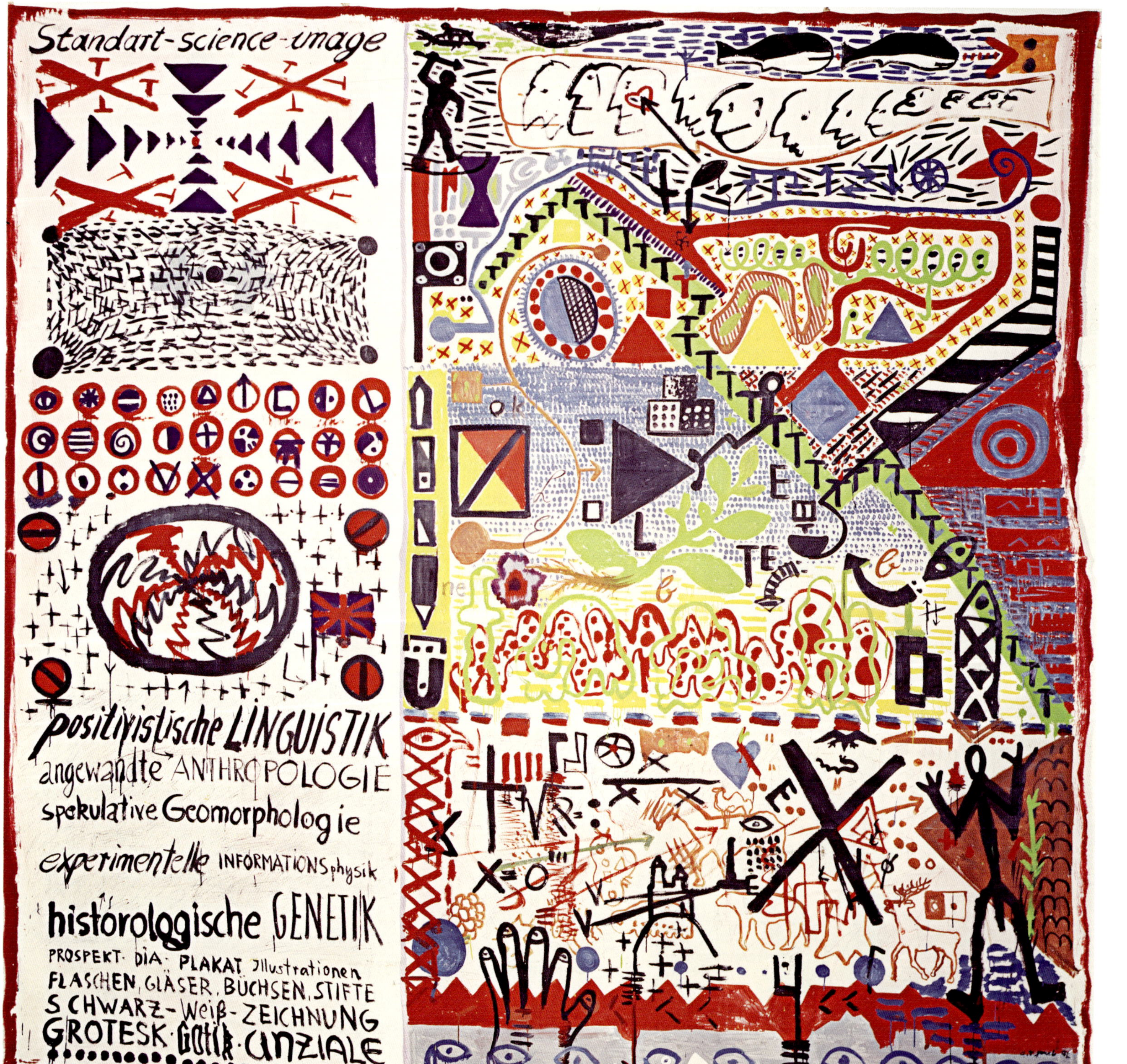

Standart-science-image
positivistische LINGUISTIK
angewandte ANTHROPOLOGIE
spekulative Geomorphologie
experimentelle INFORMATIONSphysik
historologische GENETIK
PROSPEKT · DIA · PLAKAT Jllustrationen
FLASCHEN, GLÄSER, BÜCHSEN, STIFTE
SCHWARZ-Weiß-ZEICHNUNG
GROTESK · Gotik · UNZIALE

# A.R. Penck

**Shown by**
Michael Werner F8

**Biography**
Born 1939
Lives in Dublin and Dusseldorf

Dresden-born Penck has been the subject of numerous survey exhibitions at institutions that include Museum Ludwig, Cologne (2010–11), Schirn Kunsthalle, Frankfurt (2007–8), Hiroshima City Museum of Contemporary Art (1997), Irish Museum of Modern Art, Dublin (1991), Kunstmuseum Bonn (1982) and Kunsthalle Bern (1975–6). His work is part of public collections such as: the Tate collection, UK; Museum of Contemporary Art, Los Angeles; and Centre Pompidou, Paris.

*Standart-science-image*
1973
Dispersion on canvas
283 × 280 cm
Courtesy of Michael Werner Gallery

Since the 1960s A.R. Penck has maintained an extraordinarily diverse and prolific practice. While he is perhaps best known as a painter and sculptor, Penck has also been active as a filmmaker, writer and jazz musician. His paintings often comprise graphically arresting constellations of standardized stick-man figures, animals and signs derived from the sciences, floating on planes of colour. These pictographic forms convey a sense of intensity that saw Penck come to be associated with German Neo-Expressionist painters such as Georg Baselitz, Markus Lüpertz and Jörg Immendorff (the last of whom he has collaborated with). Penck's unique language of signs continues, over a diverse set of media, to put forward and to question theories of information and communication, sense and nonsense. ST

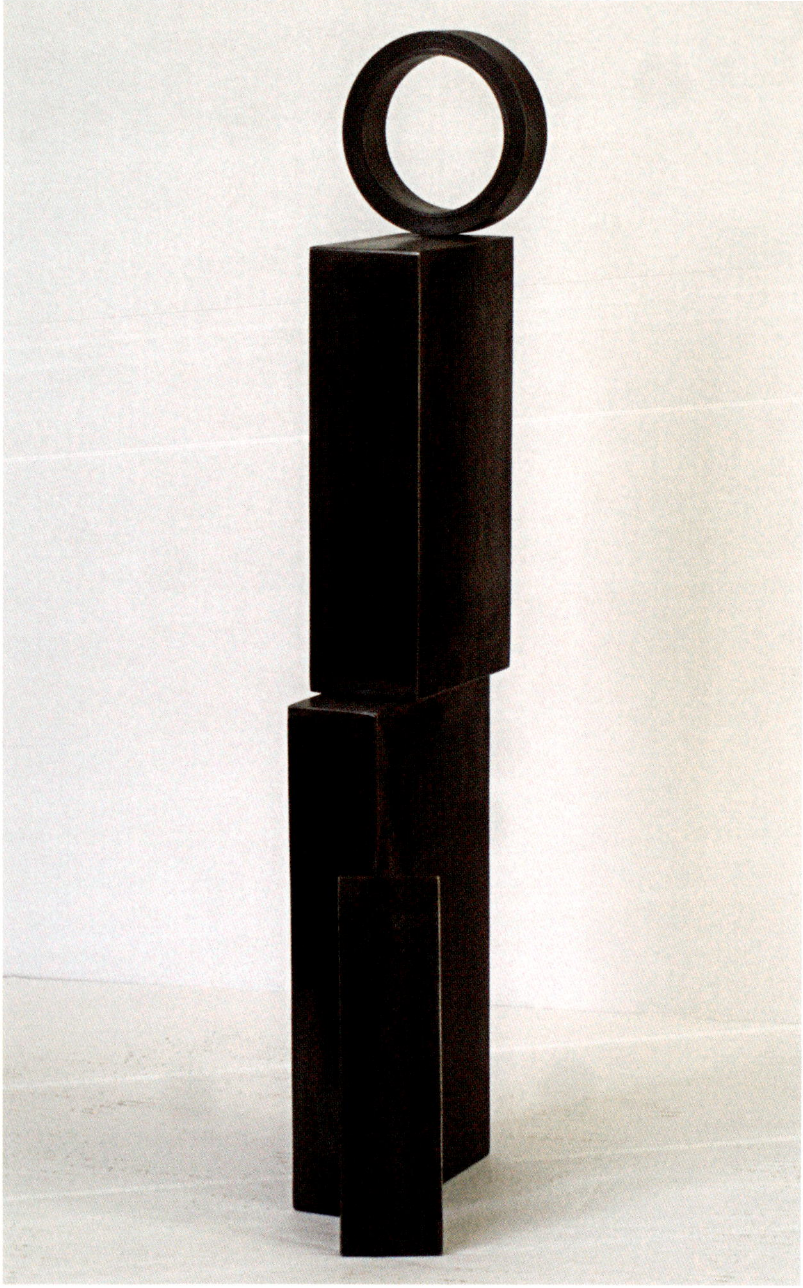

1

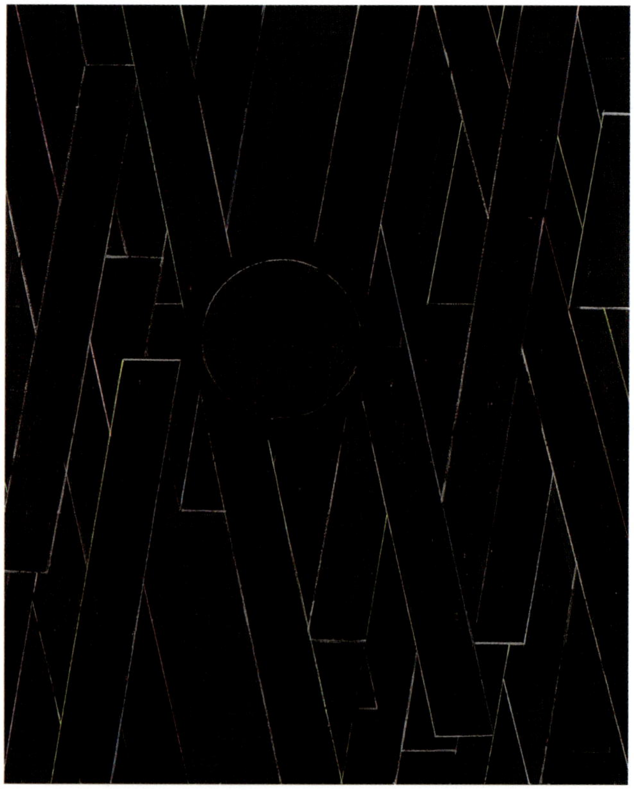

2

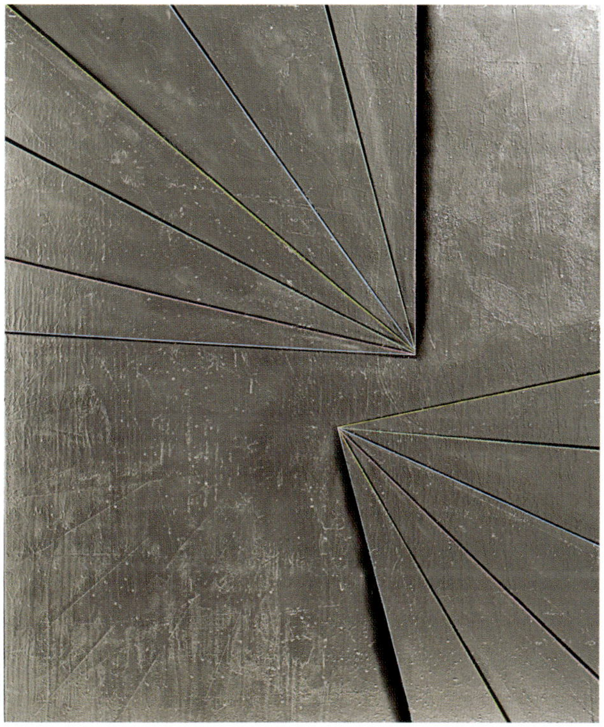

3

**Shown by**
Bortolami F11
Almine Rech Gallery
D18

**Biography**
Born 1971
Lives in London

London-born Peri has exhibited solo exhibitions and projects at galleries such as Almine Rech Gallery, Paris (2011), Bortolami, New York (2010), Tate Britain, London (2007), and Kunsthalle Basel (2006). Recent group exhibitions include 'Slow Looking: Contemporary Drawing', Tate Britain, London (2012), 'Magical Consciousness', Arnolfini, Bristol (2011), and 'Newspeak: British Art Now, Part One', Saatchi Gallery, London (2010).

1
*Seated Man*
2009
Steel
57 × 20 × 13 cm
Courtesy of Bortolami

2
*Heliomachy*
2009
Mixed media on canvas
152 × 122 cm
Courtesy of Bortolami

3
*Vision Remembered Forever*
2009
Mixed media on canvas
137 × 112 cm
Courtesy of Bortolami

# Peter Peri

Peter Peri has described the subject of his work as 'the fetishization of dissolution within modernity'. His poised sculptural works, such as *Seated Man* (2009), and striated monochromes, such as *Vision Remembered Forever* (2009), delineate a period of Modernism bounded by, say, the small canvases of Paul Klee and the blue-collar Minimalism of David Smith. While he treats the sombre lineage of the avant-garde lightly, mock-seriously alluded to in titles such as *We the Children of the 20th Century* (2011), there is often an almost sinister undertone to his work's occult-tinged geometries. A painting from 2005, *The Call*, is tellingly named after an H.P. Lovecraft story ending in what Peri calls a 'monstrous, unfathomable fourth-dimensional city'. ST

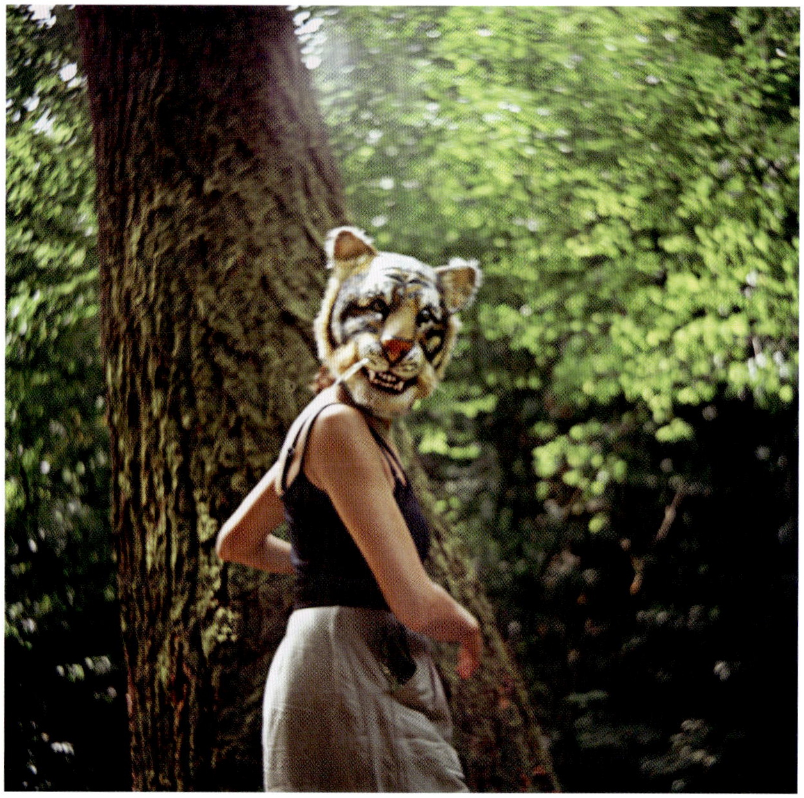

1

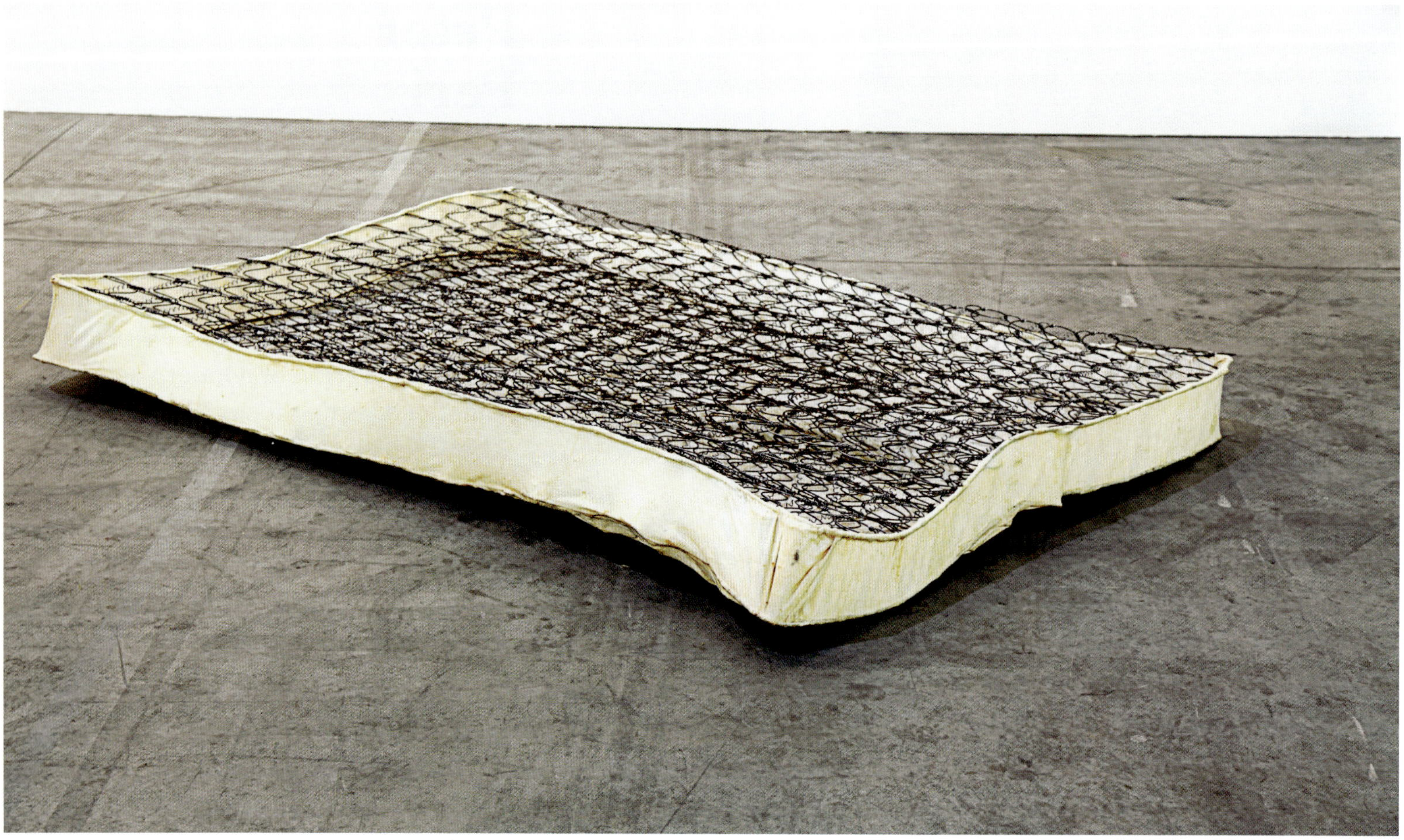

2

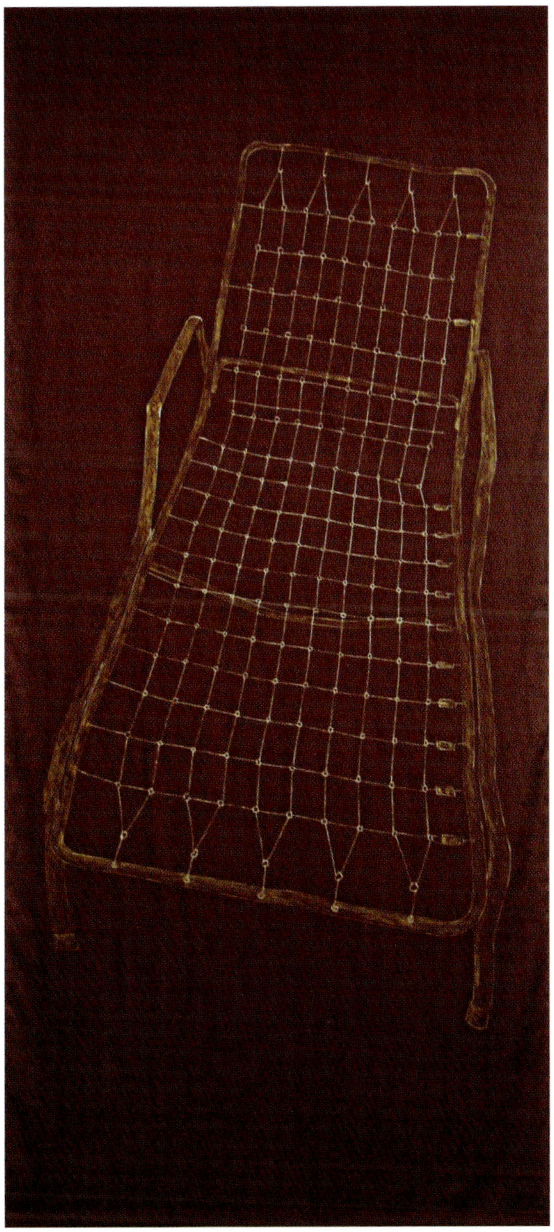

3

**Shown by**
Fonti S6

**Biography**
Born 1965
Lives in Naples

Italian artist Piscitelli has recently presented solo exhibitions in venues that include Kayne Griffin Corcoran, Santa Monica (2012), Cubitt Gallery, London (2011), and Fondazione Giuliani, Rome (2011). She has participated in the 54th Venice Biennale (2011) and in group shows such as 'Italian Video Today: Social and Individual Identity', Crane Arts, Philadelphia (2011), and 'Strange Comfort (Afforded by the Profession)', Kunsthalle Basel (2010).

1
*Tigre Valle dei Mulini*
(She Tiger in the Valley of the Windmills)
2002
Lambda print mounted on aluminium
90 × 90 cm
Courtesy of Galleria Fonti

2
*Momentanee permanenze*
(Temporary Permanences)
2011
Mattresses and latex
30 × 220 × 180 cm
Courtesy of Galleria Fonti

3
*Untitled_01*
2010
Bleach on cloth
292 × 132 cm
Courtesy of Galleria Fonti

# Focus
# Giulia Piscitelli

There is a spectral casualness to Giulia Piscitelli's mixed-media practice that might be deduced from an untitled 2010 textile work in which bleach was used to trace the familiar geometry of a cheap, outdoor recliner. With its look of the photogram, the same mix of the profane and the profound can be found elsewhere in the artist's *oeuvre*. *IDEM* (2010), for example, comprises a chandelier-like mobile made out of enormous agave leaves, while *Spica* (2011) titles a series of 11 differently coloured silk scrolls featuring pieces of wheat outlined in bleach and acid. If her early colour photographs were less prosaic, with their plain, amused look at her native Naples, Piscitelli's winning mode of turning the natural and elemental into something both disarmingly affecting and a bit terrifying resounds throughout. QL

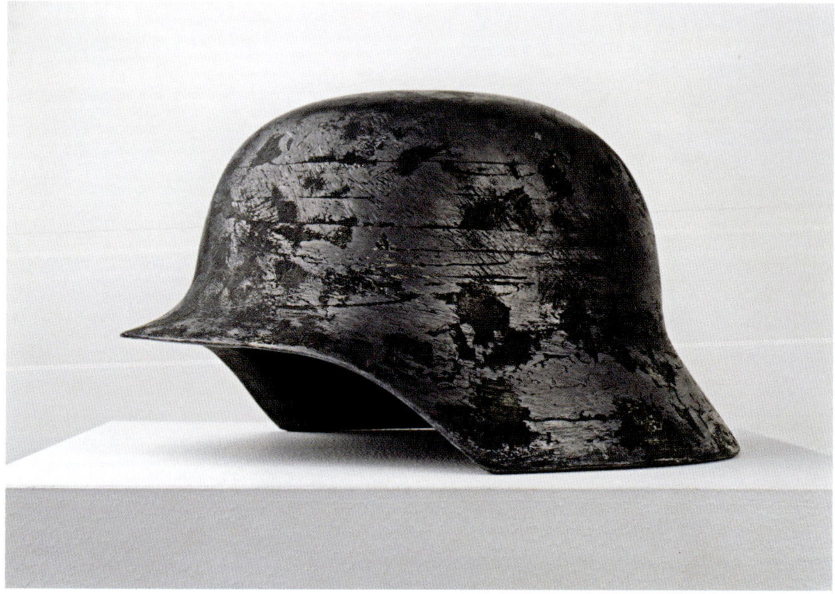
1

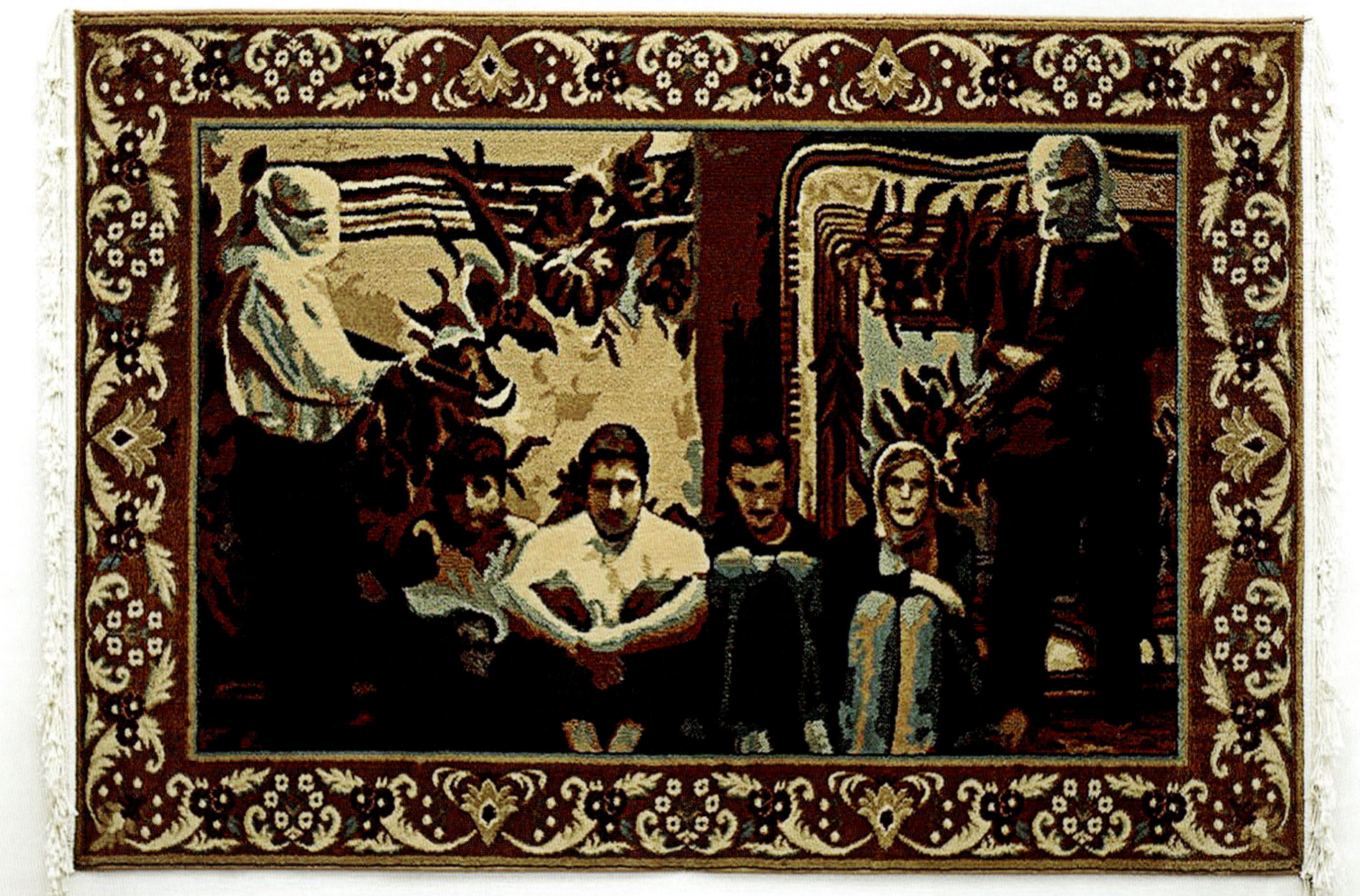
2

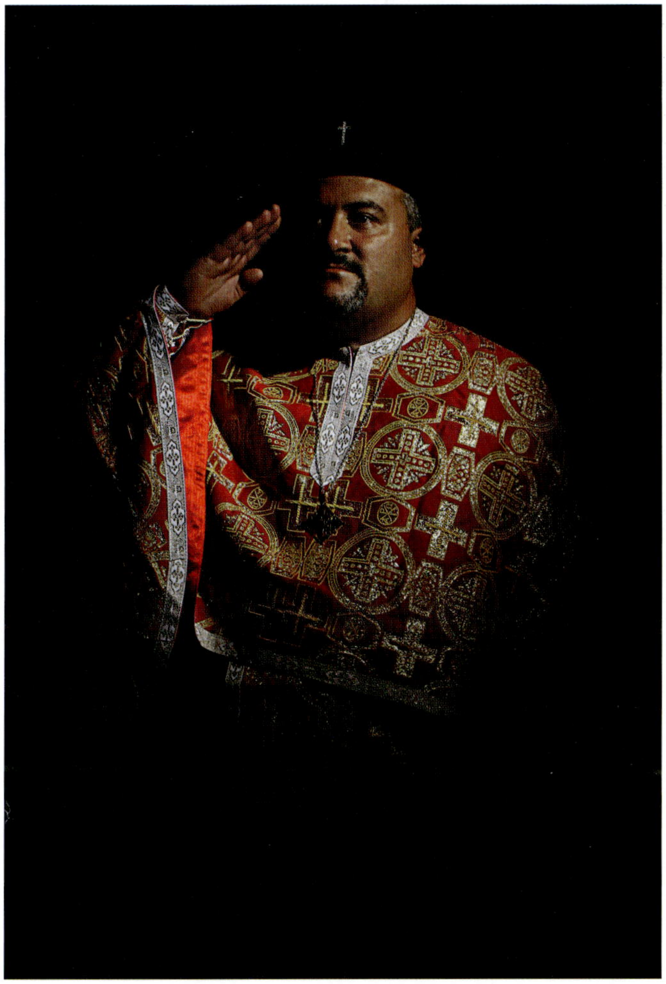

3

**Shown by**
Andreiana Mihail Gallery S3
Galeria Plan B S12

**Biography**
Born 1980
Lives in Tirgu Mures

Romanian artist Pogăcean presented a solo exhibition at Andreiana Mihail Gallery, Bucharest, in 2012. His work has been featured in group exhibitions at venues that include Műcsarnok Kunsthalle, Budapest (2012), Wilkinson Gallery, London (2009), Zacheta National Gallery of Art, Warsaw (2008), Netherlands Media Art institute, Amsterdam (2007), and National Museum of Contemporary Art, Bucharest (2004). He represented Romania at the 52nd Venice Biennale (2007).

1
*Lead*
2006
Cast lead
30 × 28 × 30 cm
Courtesy of Andreiana Mihail Gallery

2
*The Abduction from the Seraglio*
2005
Woollen carpet
110 × 160 cm
Courtesy of Andreiana Mihail Gallery

3
*Untitled*
2007
Photograph
45 × 30 cm
Courtesy of Andreiana Mihail Gallery

# Focus
# Cristi Pogăcean

Like the sceptical St Thomas pushing his finger into Christ's wound, Cristi Pogăcean invades existing forms in order to test their veracity. Unlike the apostle, however, he is rarely convinced. Caravaggio's famous painting *The Incredulity of St Thomas* (c. 1601) is itself the subject of Pogăcean's animated video *Caranime* (2002) but also resonates in sculptures such as *Obelisk* (2007), in which the artist poked holes into a monumental obelisk, transforming it into an ornamental bird house, and *Lead* (2006), in which he cast a German military helmet in heavy metal. For Pogăcean, the open wounds caused by entrenched political dogmas are to be probed fearlessly and without shame. JG

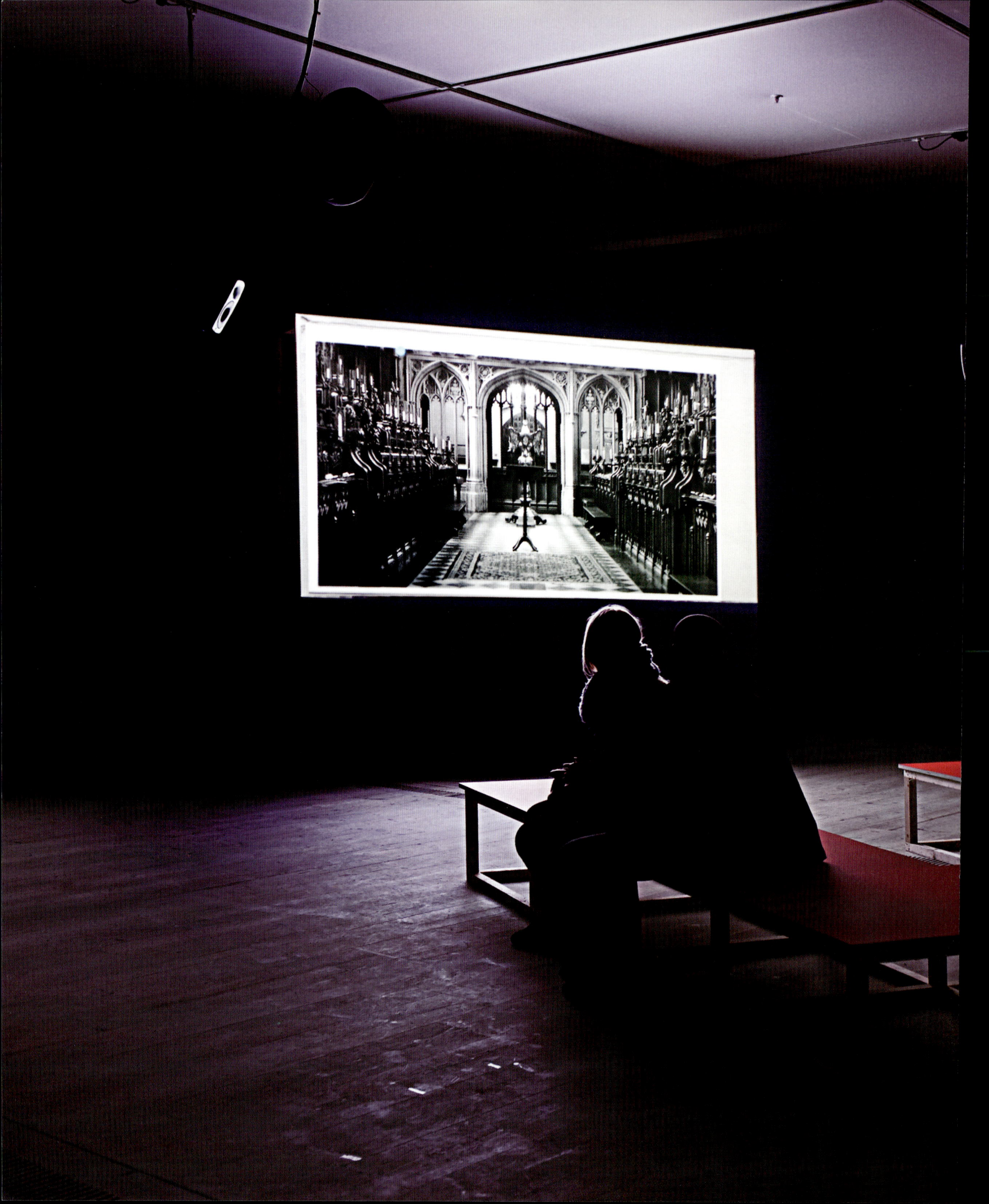

# Focus
# Elizabeth Price

**Shown by**
MOT International S2

**Biography**
Born 1966
Lives in London

British artist Price, a nominee for the Turner Prize 2012, has staged solo shows and screenings at venues such as Baltic, Gateshead (2012), Bloomberg Space, London (2012), New Museum, New York (2011), and Whitechapel Gallery, London (2010). She was included in 'British Art Show 7: In the Days of the Comet', which toured venues in the UK in 2010 and 2011.

*Choir*
2012
HD video
15 min.
Installation view at Baltic, Gateshead
Courtesy of MOT International

Although trained as a sculptor, Elizabeth Price has been making films since 2005, and each one elaborates on her central preoccupations of eroticized archives and the politics of architectural space. They take the form of tours led by on-screen guides, the narration flashing up as motion graphics. But these narrative voices actually come from a number of wildly disparate sources, including Theodor Adorno (as in *User Group Disco*, 2009) and luxury car brochures (*West Hinder*, 2012); over the course of the videos they become increasingly schizoid, sinister or didactic. Price's strategy is one of densely patterned accumulation, and her archeological critiques of Modernism and modernity pay meticulous attention to the coercive potential of classification systems. ST

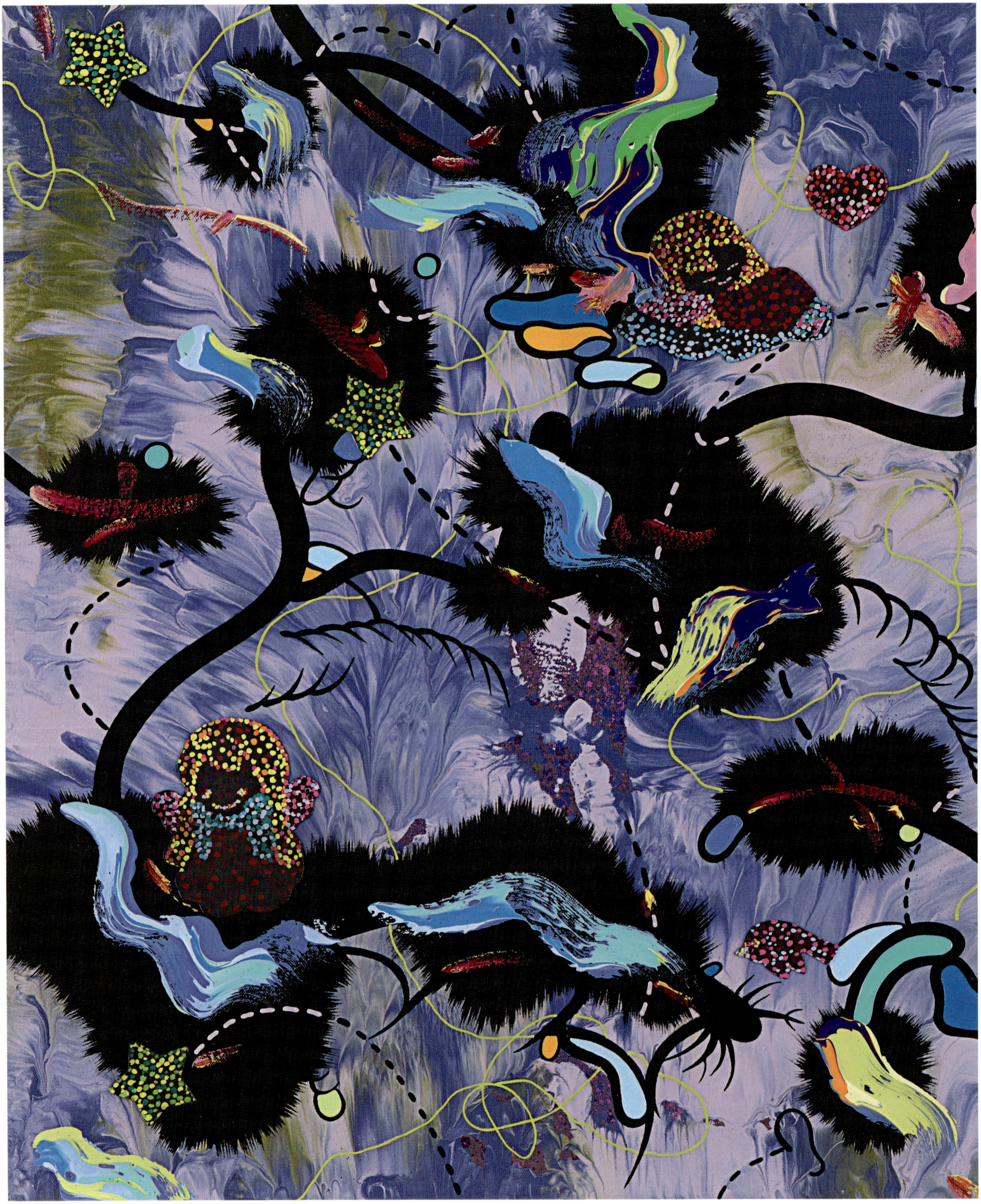

**Shown by**
Pace G8
Timothy Taylor Gallery B13

**Biography**
Born 1963
Lives in London

Hong Kong-born Rae has been the subject of solo exhibitions over the last decade at public institutions including the The New Art Gallery, Walsall (2012), Leeds Art Gallery (2012), and Musée d'Art Contemporain de Nîmes (2002–3). Professor of Painting at the Royal Academy Schools, London, and nominated for the Turner Prize in 1991, Rae has work included in collections such as the Tate collection, UK, and the Astrup Fearnley Museum of Modern Art, Oslo.

1
*Do not disturb – the tiny grass is dreaming*
2011
Oil, acrylic and gouache on canvas
61 × 50 cm
Courtesy of Timothy Taylor Gallery

2
*Curse of the Golden Flower*
2009
Oil, acrylic and gouache on canvas
132 × 112 cm
Courtesy of Timothy Taylor Gallery

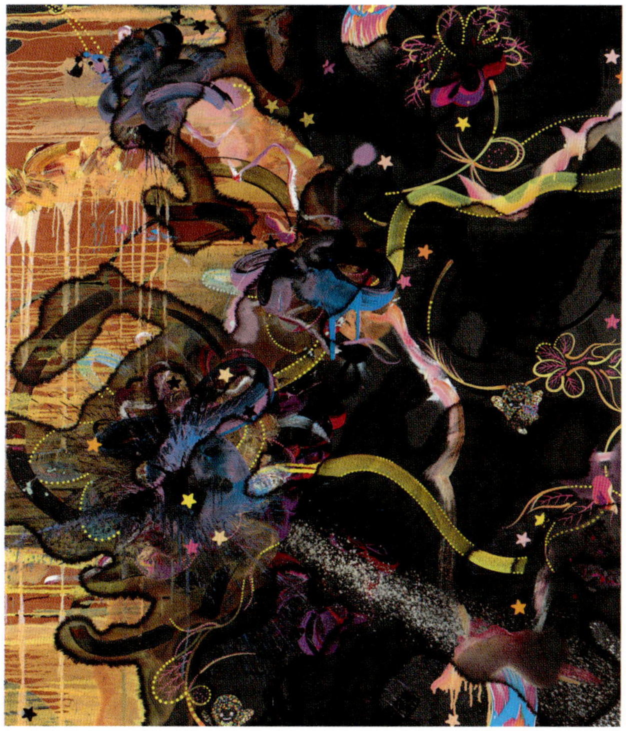

2

# Fiona Rae

It is tempting to describe Fiona Rae's paintings in terms of interrelated dualities: planes and drips, figurative and abstract, conceptual and emotive, high and low, graphic and gestural, control and improvisation. But what this rather cosy image of opposites living together in push-me, pull-you harmony misses is how complex a painting such as *Do not disturb – the tiny grass is dreaming* (2011) actually is. It references the major art-historical category of 'abstraction', while also singling out non-specific particularities from popular culture, such as cartoons, and low-end schlock, like greetings cards and clipart. From one painting to the next, abundance occurs at visual and symbolic levels, its density translating into irreverent theatrics with a shifting vocabulary. SOR

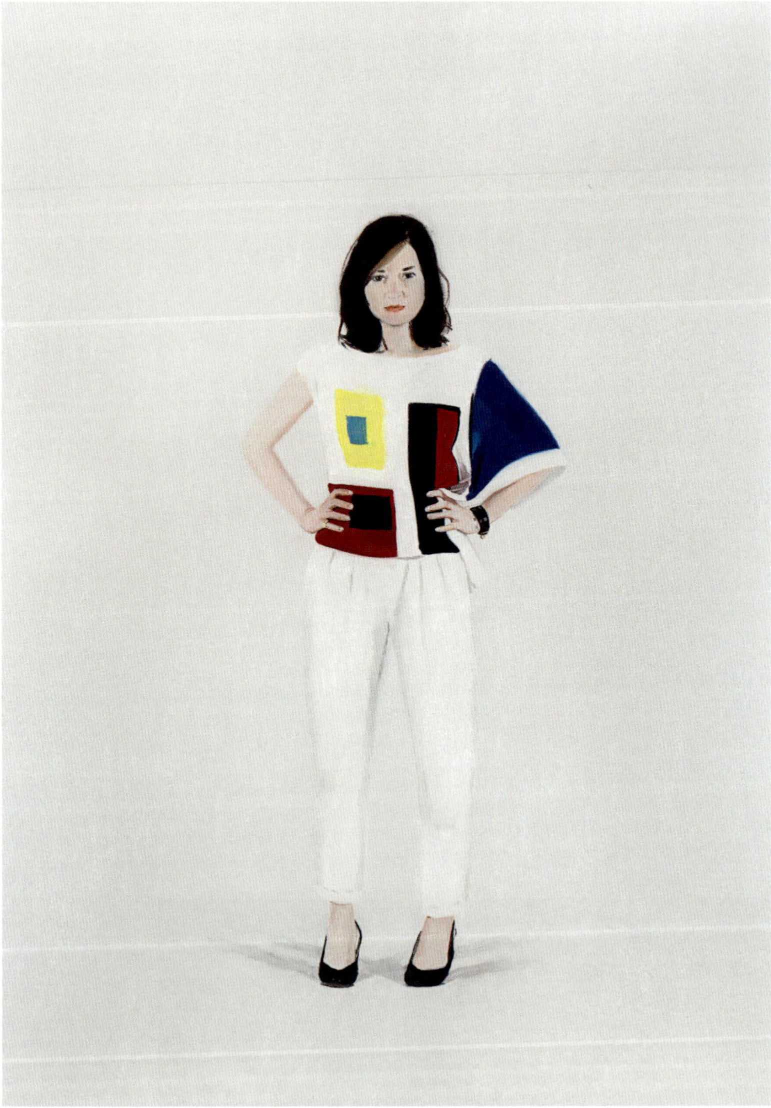

1

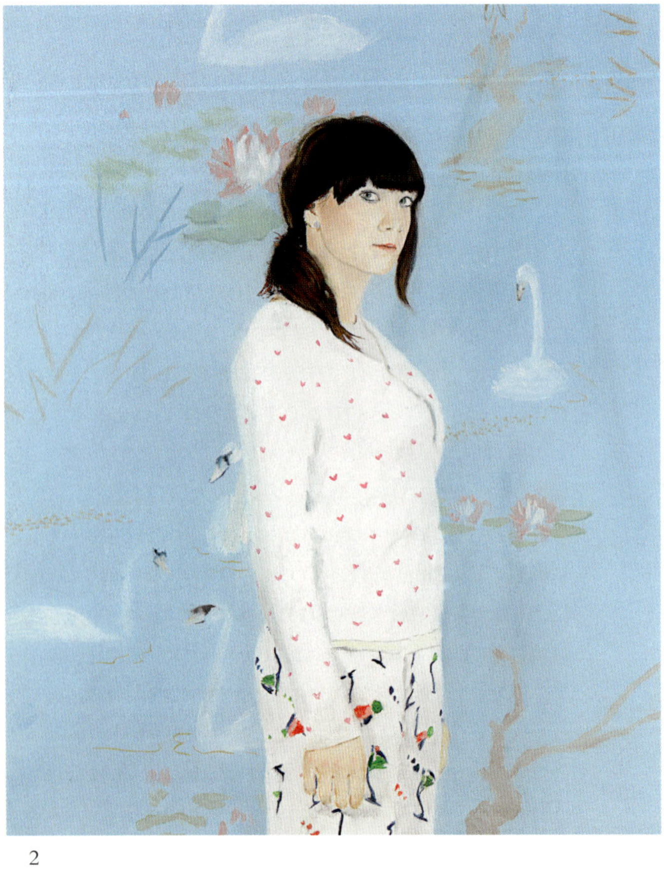

2

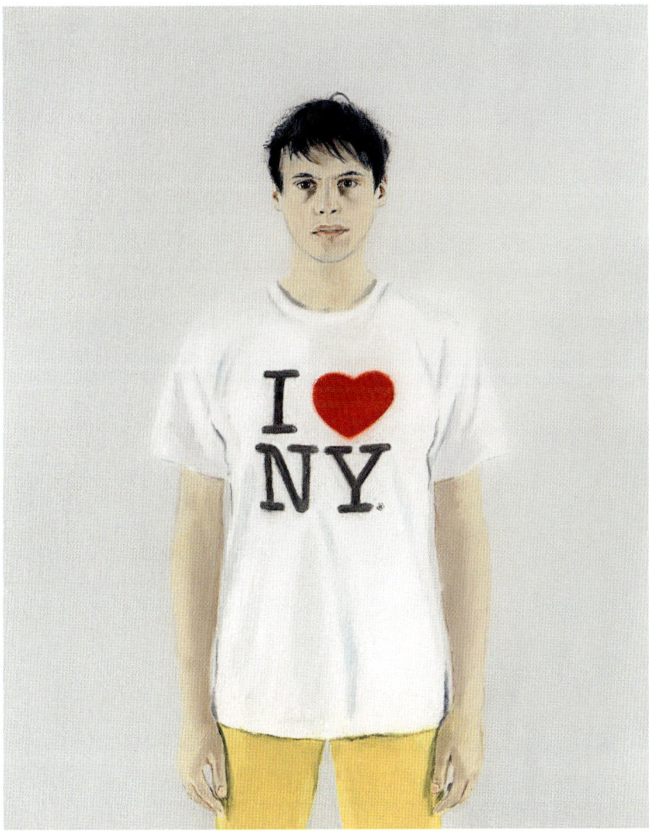


3

**Shown by**
Alison Jacques Gallery
D15

**Biography**
Born 1971
Lives in London

Bahamas-born Raho has presented solo exhibitions at galleries than include Alison Jacques Gallery, London (2012 and 2005), Effearte Gallery, Milan (2009), and Galerie Nikolaus Ruzicska, Salzburg (2008 and 2006). In 2005 he was commissioned by the National Portrait Gallery, London, to paint the portrait of Dame Judi Dench. Raho's work is part of collections such as: MoMA, New York; Berardo Collection, Sintra, Portugal; and Seattle Museum of Art.

1
*Lizzy*
2011
Oil on canvas
246 × 170 cm
Courtesy of Alison Jacques Gallery

2
*Nicki*
2012
Oil on canvas
95 × 75 cm
Courtesy of Alison Jacques Gallery

3
*Adham*
2011
Oil on canvas
95 × 75 cm
Courtesy of Alison Jacques Gallery

# Alessandro Raho

Alessandro Raho depicts his subjects, often friends, straight on and centred in spare, evenly lit spaces. The sole figure in *Adham* (2011), for instance, looks directly at the viewer with an unflinching gaze; the image is devoid of context or pretension. Raho works from photographs and admits taking inspiration from Richard Avedon, whose portraits—such as his famous 1957 photograph of Marilyn Monroe—exhibit the same bold frontality and casual honesty. Although associated with the 'Young British Artists', having graduated from Goldsmiths College in 1994 and exhibited alongside Damien Hirst and Tracey Emin in the 1995 exhibition 'Brilliant! New Art from London' at the Walker Art Center, Minneapolis, Raho evinces a quieter sensibility. ND

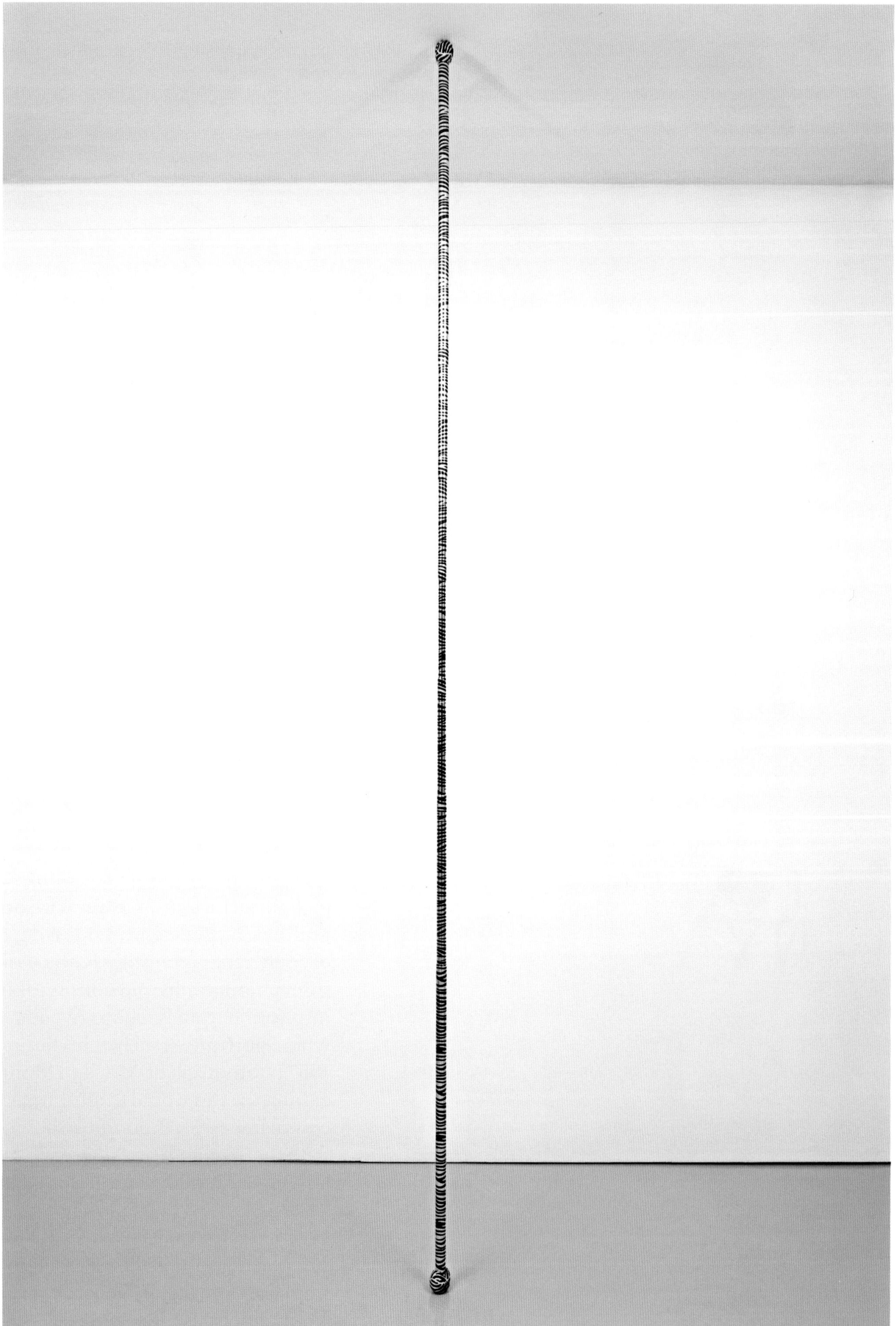

1

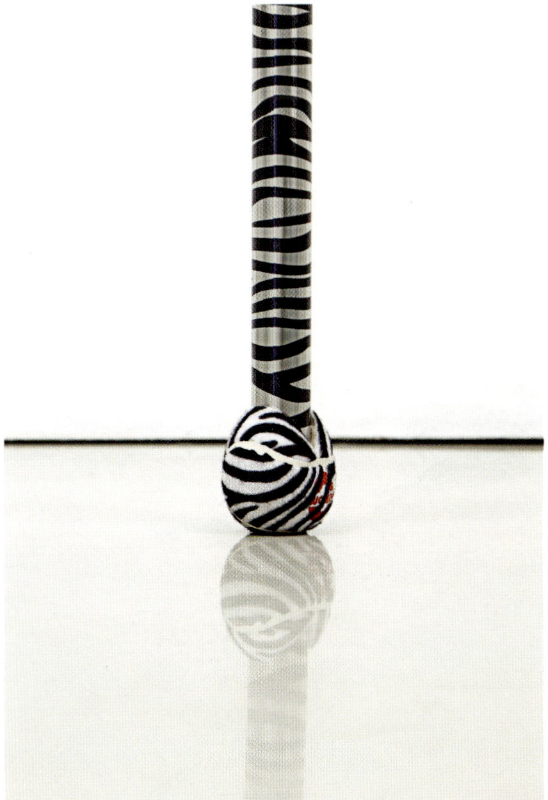

2

**Shown by**
Standard (Oslo) B15

**Biography**
Born 1981
Lives in Los Angeles

American artist Rantanen has presented solo shows at venues such as Standard (Oslo) (2012), Dan Graham Gallery, Los Angeles (2010), and Jancar Jones Gallery (2010 and 2008). His group exhibitions include 'I Think and That Is All I Am,' Thomas Duncan Gallery, Los Angeles (2012), '3,348 Hours of Sunshine,' Clifton Benevento, New York (2010), 'Space is a Place', Portland Institute for Contemporary Art (2007), and 'Elusive Quality' at the 3rd Liverpool Biennial (2004).

1
*Telescopic Pole (Walkerball/Zebra)*
2012
Anodized sandblasted aluminium and walkerballs
Dimensions variable
Courtesy of Standard (Oslo)

2
*Telescopic Pole (Walkerball/Zebra)*
(detail)
2012
Anodized sandblasted aluminium and walkerballs
Dimensions variable
Courtesy of Standard (Oslo)

# Chadwick Rantanen

Chadwick Rantanen's wry, Minimalist sculptures borrow from the design palette of practical, medical applications. Telescopic aluminium poles with attached 'walker glide' balls—functional design tools used on the end of mobility aids for the elderly—are extended to fit the floor-to-ceiling of the gallery space. Ostensibly support structures, these works act as spatial measures highlighting the very space they occupy. Their range of colours and camouflage patterns, as in *Telescopic Pole (Walkerball/Zebra)* (2012), similar to those common in sports shoe and clothing design, highlight the stripping of military functionality to one of purely aesthetic design. The discreetness of the camouflage only highlights further the disparity between the original design function and this repurposing. PT

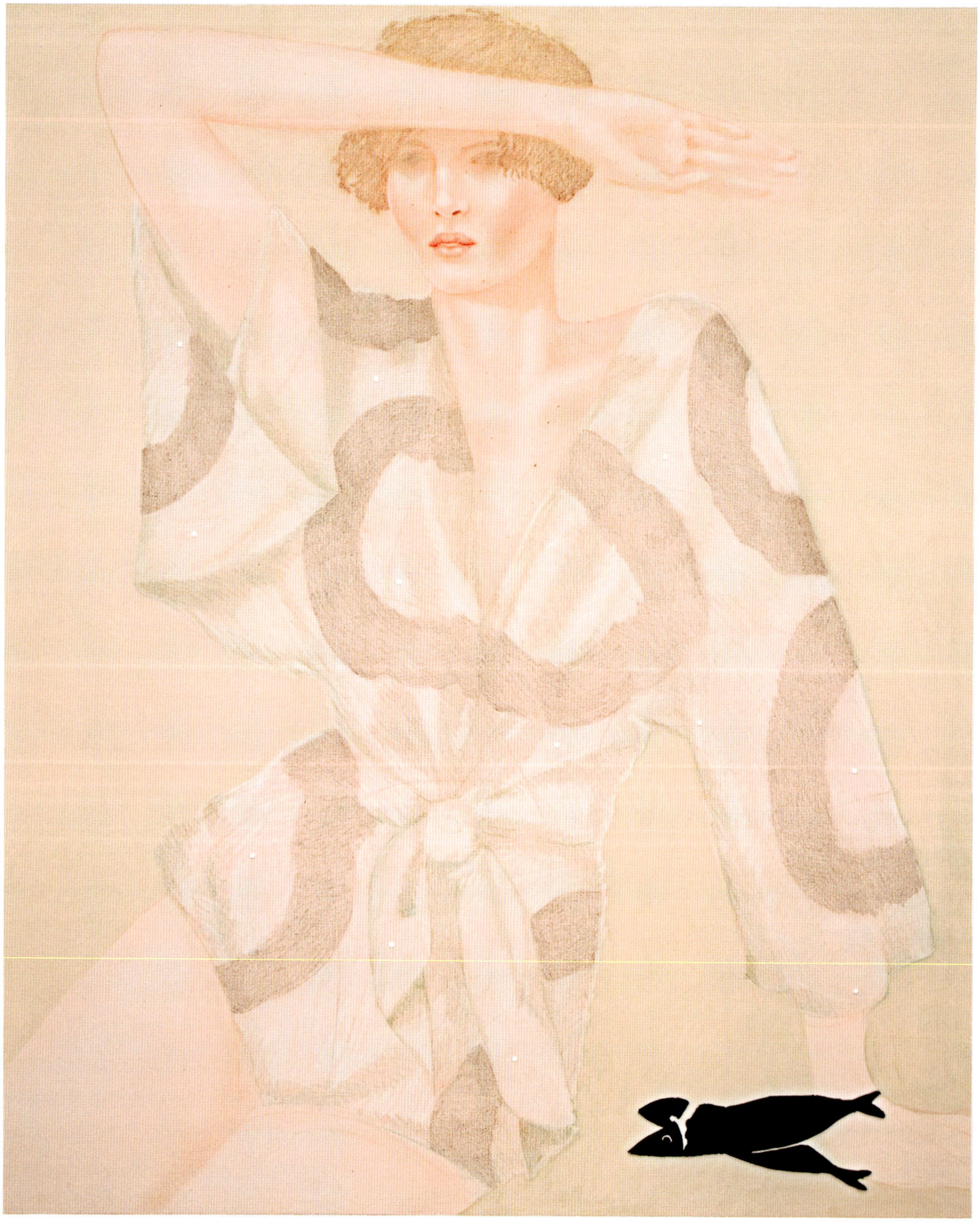

1

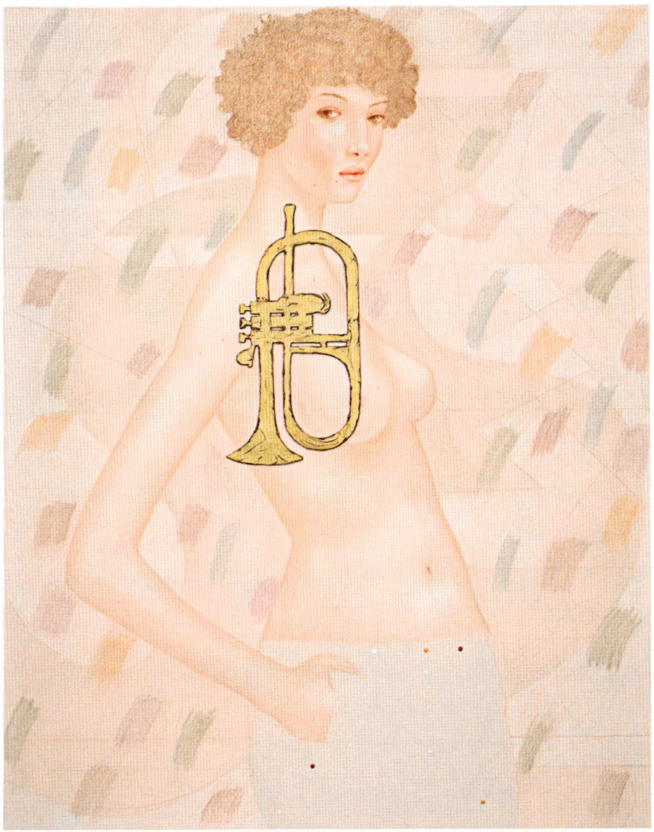

2

**Shown by**
Mary Mary F19

**Biography**
Born 1976
Lives in New York

Texas-born artist Reid, who in 2008 received an MFA from the Maryland Institute College of Art, Baltimore, has presented solo exhibitions at Lisa Cooley, New York (2012, 2010 and 2008), A Palazzo, Brescia (2012), and Mary Mary, Glasgow (2011). His work has been featured in recent group shows that include 'Beholder', Talbot Rice Gallery, Edinburgh (2011), 'Keno Twins 5', Barriera, Turin (2011), and 'Moonlighting', Hosfelt Gallery, New York (2010).

1
*Black Fish*
2012
Caran d'Ache, tinted gesso and acrylic on canvas
152 × 122 cm
Courtesy of Mary Mary and Lisa Cooley Gallery

2
*Geometry of Feelings*
2012
Caran d'Ache, tinted gesso and acrylic on canvas
152 × 122 cm
Courtesy of Mary Mary and Lisa Cooley Gallery

# Alan Reid

Androgynous, privileged-looking, aloof and disconcertingly asexual even when scantily clad, the figures Alan Reid depicts evoke Pompeiian frescoes, fascist neoclassicism and lingerie or perfume advertisements dating from the 1970s to the present. Reid renders these pastel-hued, pale-skinned, elegantly long-limbed figures with wispy coloured pencil on canvas. But there's always more: a contrasting, often abstract layer in the foreground, sometimes involving scraps scavenged from wood shops, such as brightly polychromed dowels. The dark fish in *Black Fish* (2012) suggest a jarring remove from a woman in a kimono shading her eyes, while in *Geometry of Feelings* (2012) the image of a bright trumpet is superimposed on the peach-toned topless woman—as if emotion were situated between slippery dream and starker reality. KMJ

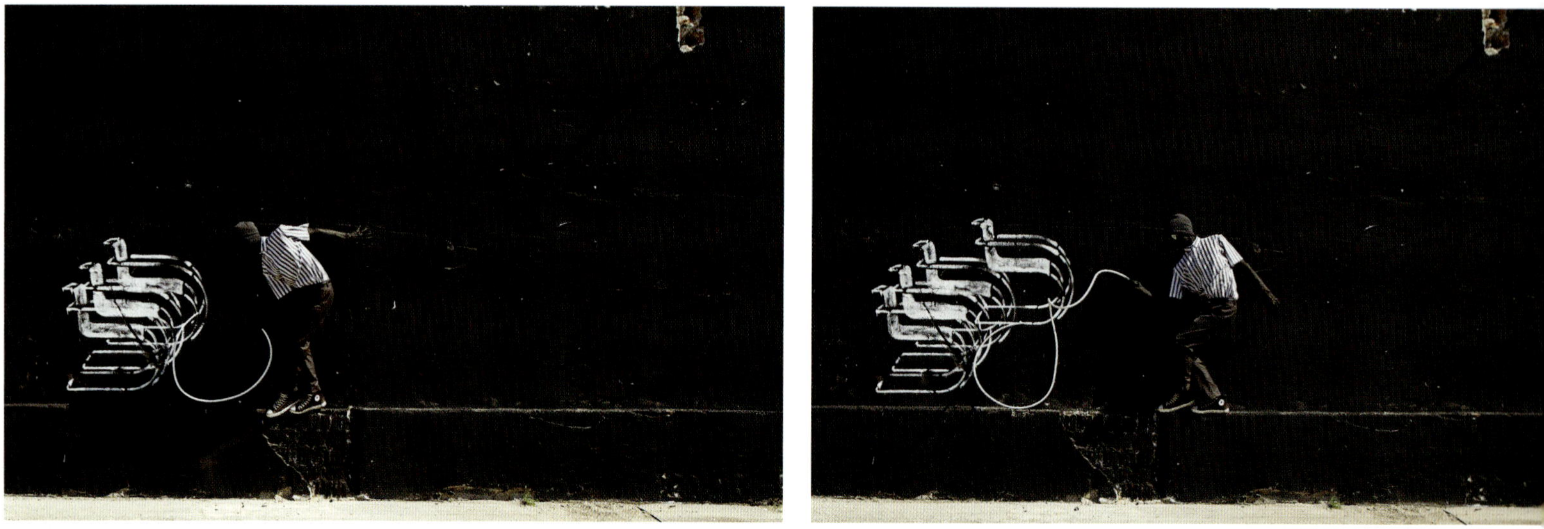

1

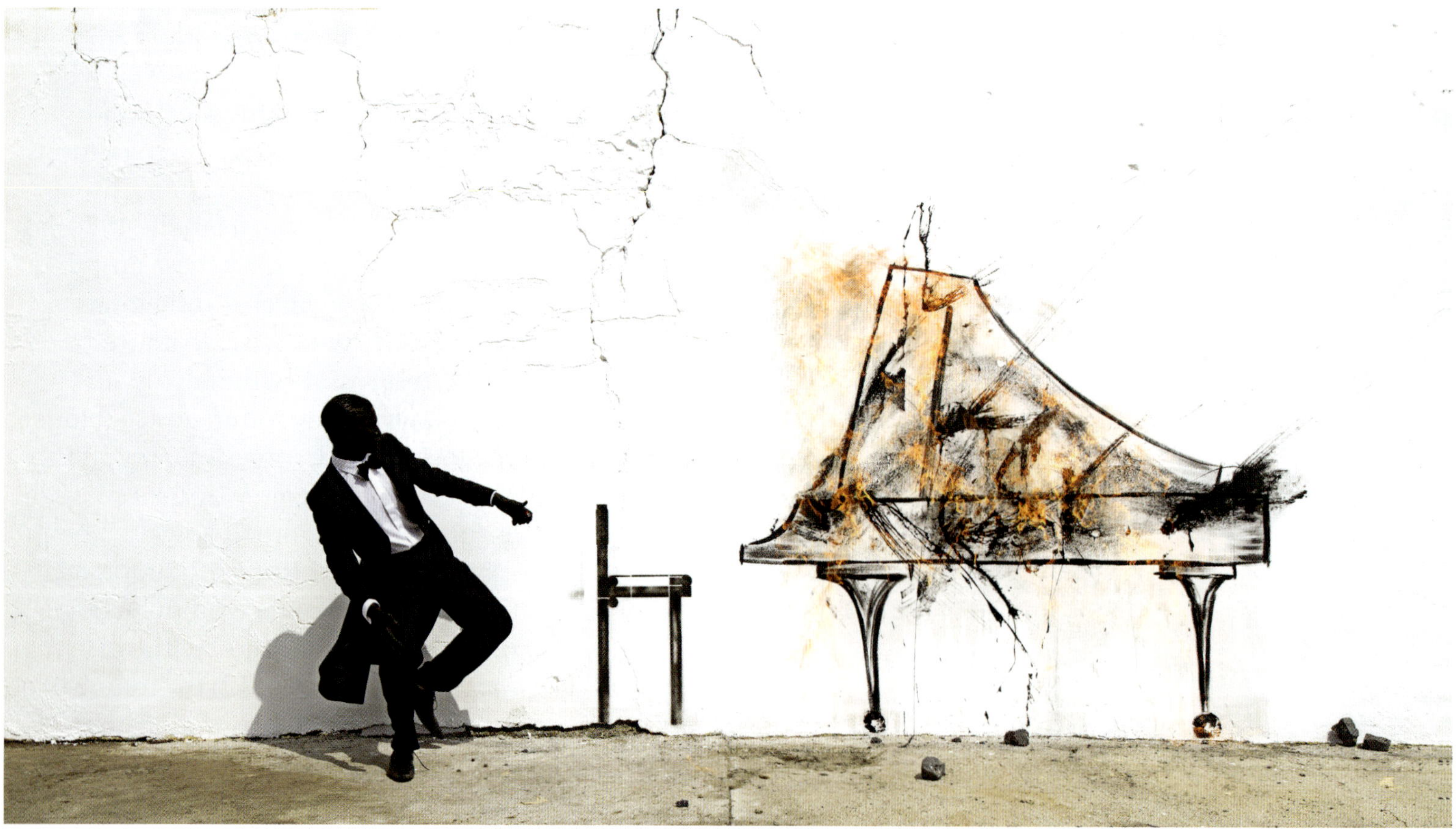

2

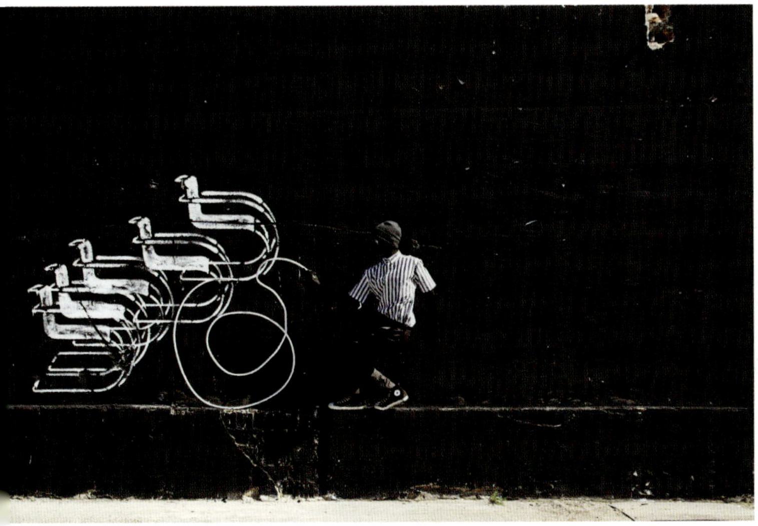

**Shown by**
Lehmann Maupin Gallery F12
White Cube F7

**Biography**
Born 1976
Lives in Berlin

Cape Town-born Rhode has presented solo shows at venues that include Los Angeles County Museum of Art (2010), The Wexner Center for the Arts, Columbus, Ohio (2009), Hayward Gallery, London (2008), and Haus der Kunst, Munich (2007). He participated in the 18th Biennale of Sydney (2012) and recent group exhibitions include 'Staging Action: Performance in Photography since 1960' at MoMA, New York (2011).

1
*Bent Mies*
2011
(detail)
12 photographs
Each 40 × 60 cm (framed)
Courtesy of Lehmann Maupin Gallery

2
*Piano Chair*
2011
Digital animation
3 min. 50 sec.
Courtesy of Lehmann Maupin Gallery

# Robin Rhode

The immediacy of drawing on a wall is, for Robin Rhode, a powerful tool for addressing the dislocations of youth and post-colonial cultures. His sequential photographic storyboards feature drawings of objects that denote leisure or a lofty quality of life, with which his alter ego then performs an illusory interaction. In *Broken Glass (Shiraz)* (2012) the doppelgänger, dressed stealthily in black and armed with a crowbar, assails a wineglass, that emblem of middle-class affluence, while the piano in the digital animation *Piano Chair* (2011) appears to catch fire. Rhode's sculptural installations—a bike made out of soap, for instance—indulge in the 'uselessness' of art as a wry means to scrutinize socio-economic disparities. SOR

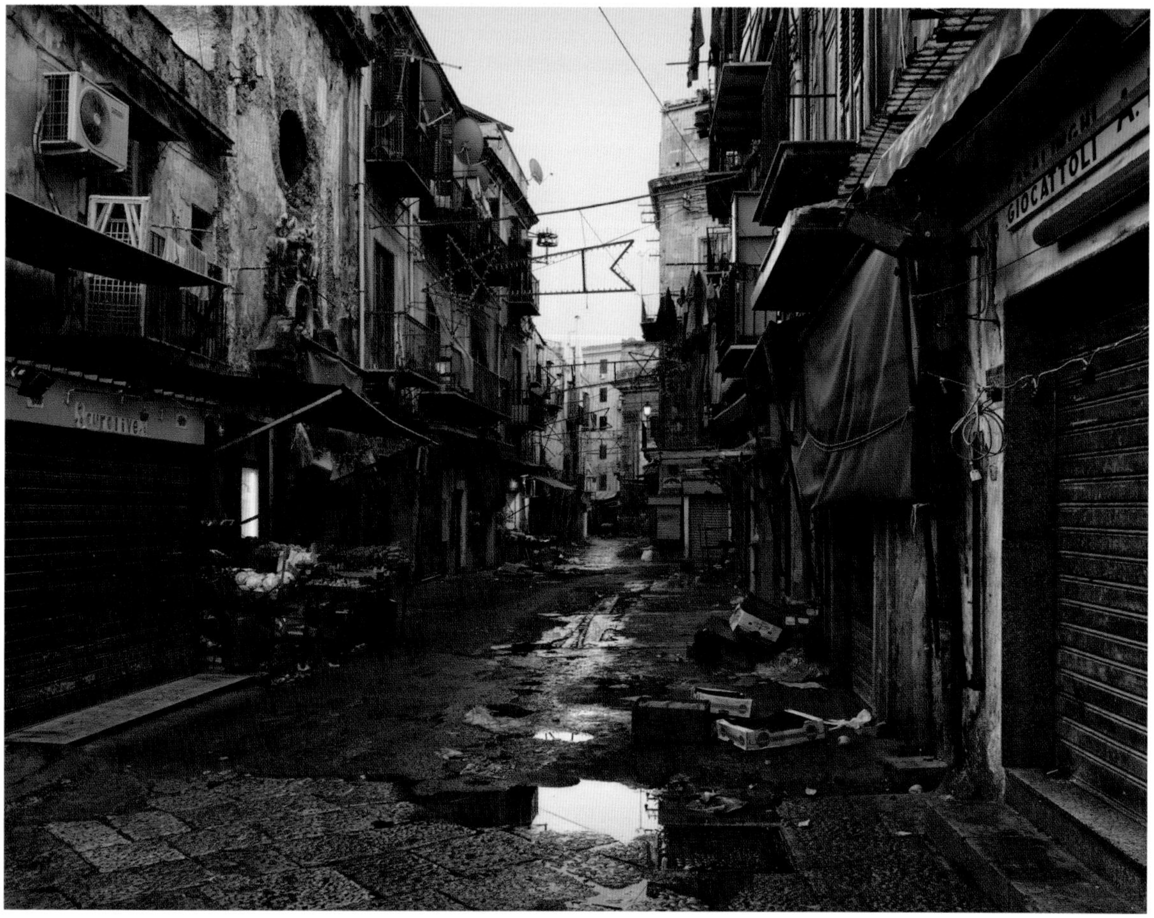


1

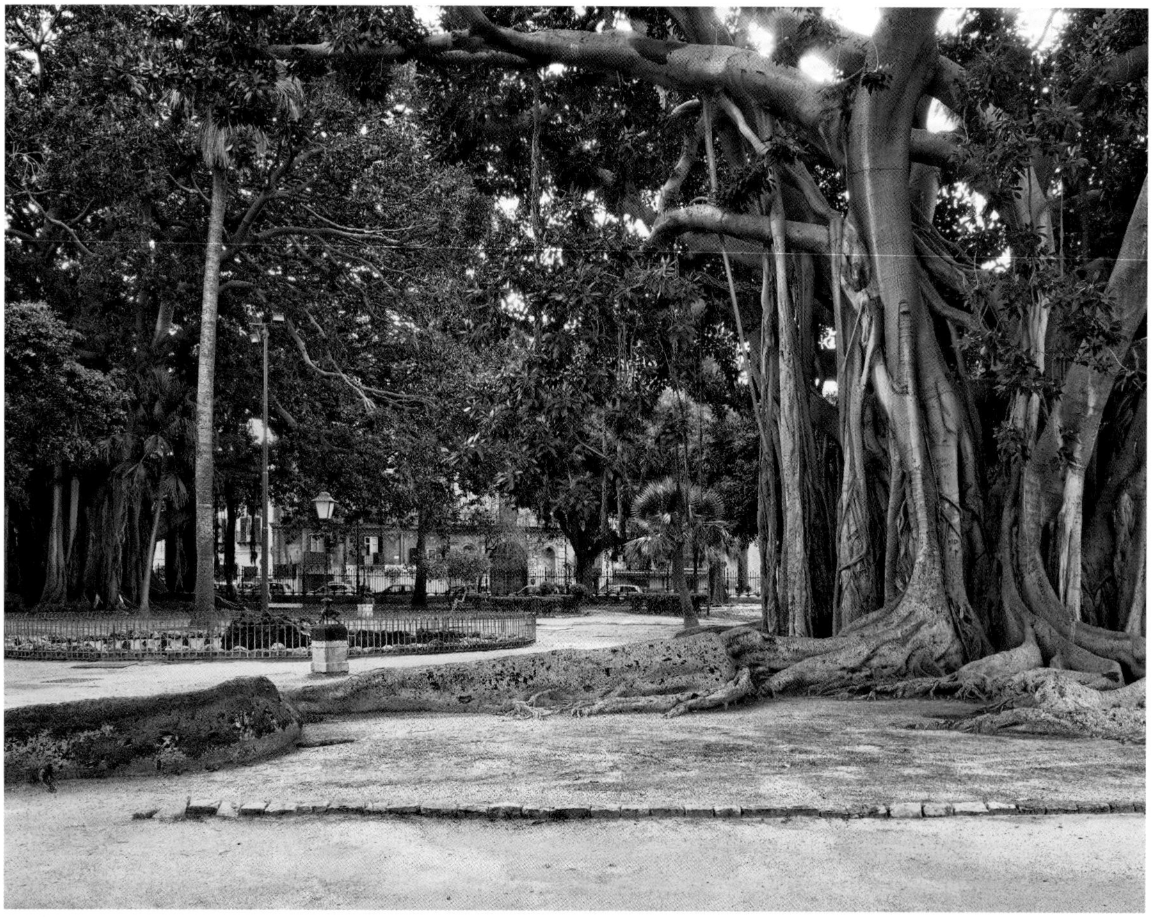

2

# John Riddy

**Shown by**
Frith Street Gallery C1

**Biography**
Born 1959
Lives in London

Solo exhibitions by British-born Riddy have been shown at venues such as Frith Street Gallery, London (2009), Foto Kunst Stadtforum, Innsbruck (2007), Victoria and Albert Museum, London (2007), and Camden Arts Centre, London (2000). Recent group shows include 'The Romantics – British Landscape: Photography after the Picturesque', Tate Britain, London (2010), and 'Utopia', Museu Colecção Berardo, Lisbon (2008).

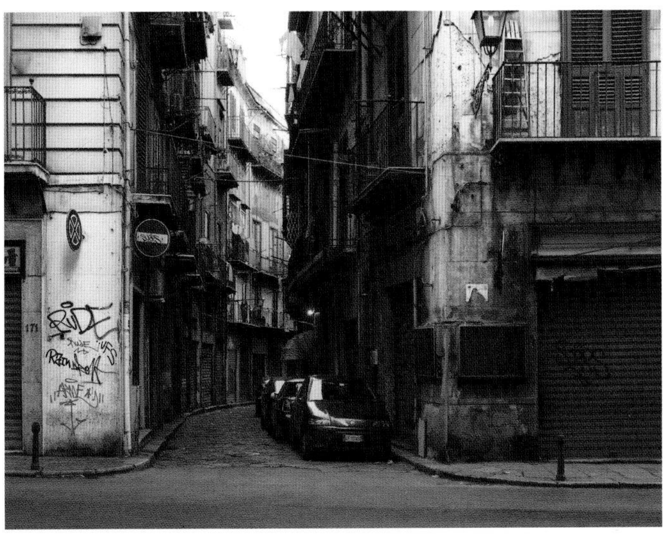

3

1
*Palermo (Carmine)*
2012
Archival pigment print
74 × 93 cm
Courtesy of Frith Street Gallery

2
*Palermo (Piazza Marina)*
2012
Archival pigment print
74 × 93 cm
Courtesy of Frith Street Gallery

3
*Palermo (Via Della Loggia)*
2012
Archival pigment print
74 × 93 cm
Courtesy of Frith Street Gallery

'The world is more interesting than my reasons for describing it.' Thus John Riddy, whose photographs evince an extreme attentiveness to space and surface, colour and texture, monumental presence and vertiginous gaps or voids. Riddy began his career photographing other artists' sculptures, and his unpeopled urban vistas retain a certain sculptural stillness. For his 2009 show 'Low Relief' at Frith Street, Riddy photographed a London composed of intricate surfaces like stage flats: historic exteriors, stray expanses of brick and Modernist estates refined to elegant flatness. It is testament to the subtle drama that Riddy can wring from flatness that his recent photographs of Palermo streets are almost shocking just by virtue of the intricate perspectives opened in their scratted façades. BD

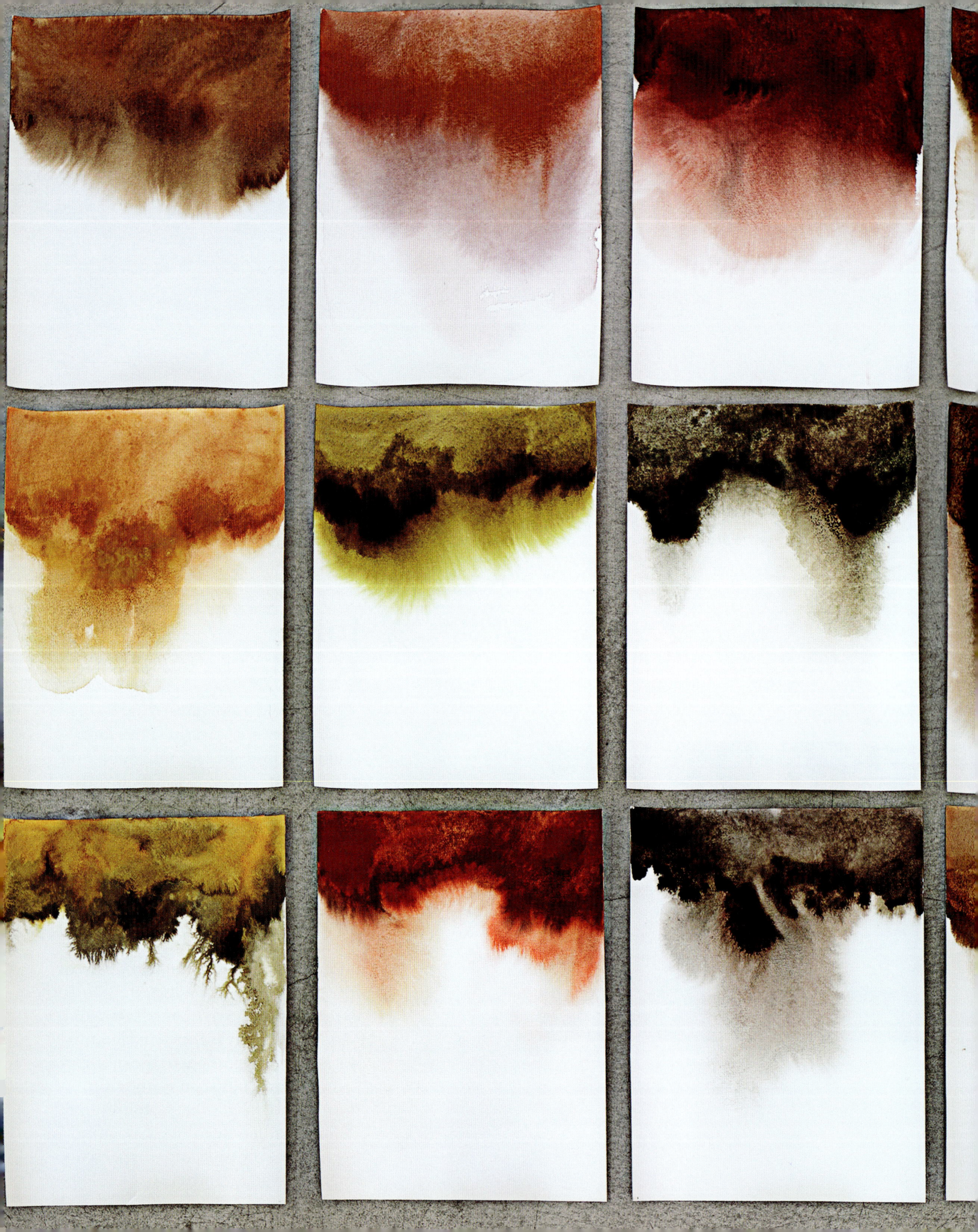

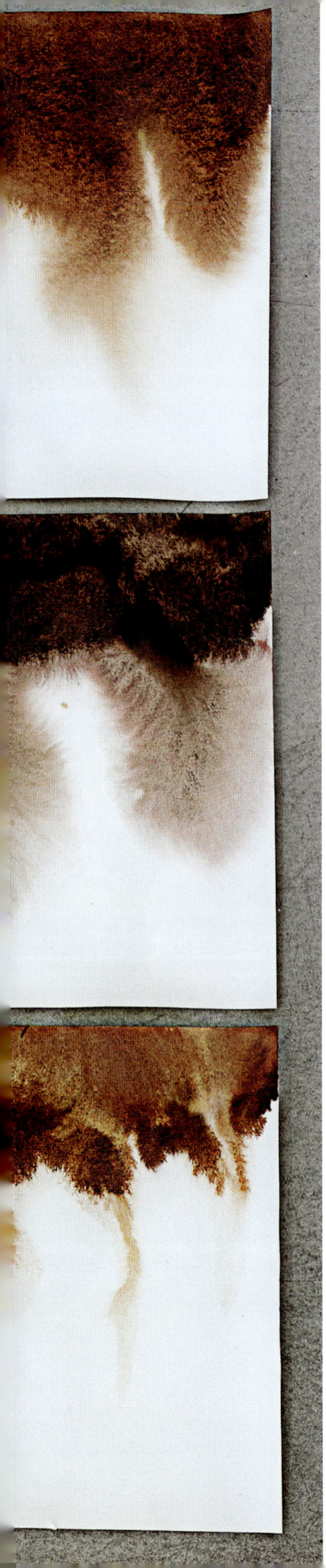

# Thiago Rocha Pitta

**Shown by**
Andersen's Contemporary H4
A Gentil Carioca G17

**Biography**
Born 1980
Lives in Sao Paulo

Brazilian artist Rocha Pitta has presented solo shows at venues including Andersen's Contemporary, Copenhagen (2012), and Escola de Artes Visuais, Parque Lage, Rio de Janeiro (2010). His work is part of permanent collections that include: the Solomon R. Guggenheim Museum, New York; MoMA, New York; and the Mori Art Museum, Tokyo. Rocha Pitta participates in the 30th Bienal de Sao Paulo until December 2012.

*Unsedimented Maps*
2012
12 sheets of gouache on paper
Each 43 × 33 cm
Courtesy of Andersen's Contemporary

The photographs, installations, sculptures and film works of Thiago Rocha Pitta address the theme of the Sublime via the landscapes of J.M.W. Turner and the writings of Joseph Conrad. The relationship between man and the sea has often been expressed in Rocha Pitta's art, as in his film *Homage to William Turner* (2004), which recorded the slow burning of a boat in the Bay of Guanabara. He dramatized the passage of time in *Youth* (2006) by placing a metal boat filled with water and salt on burning coal. An expanded conception of time informs his recent work *Monument to the Continental Drift* (2012), three fabric sails petrified with cement, and *Unsedimented Maps* (2012), a grid of 12 works on paper recalling geological processes through earthy washes of gouache. SL

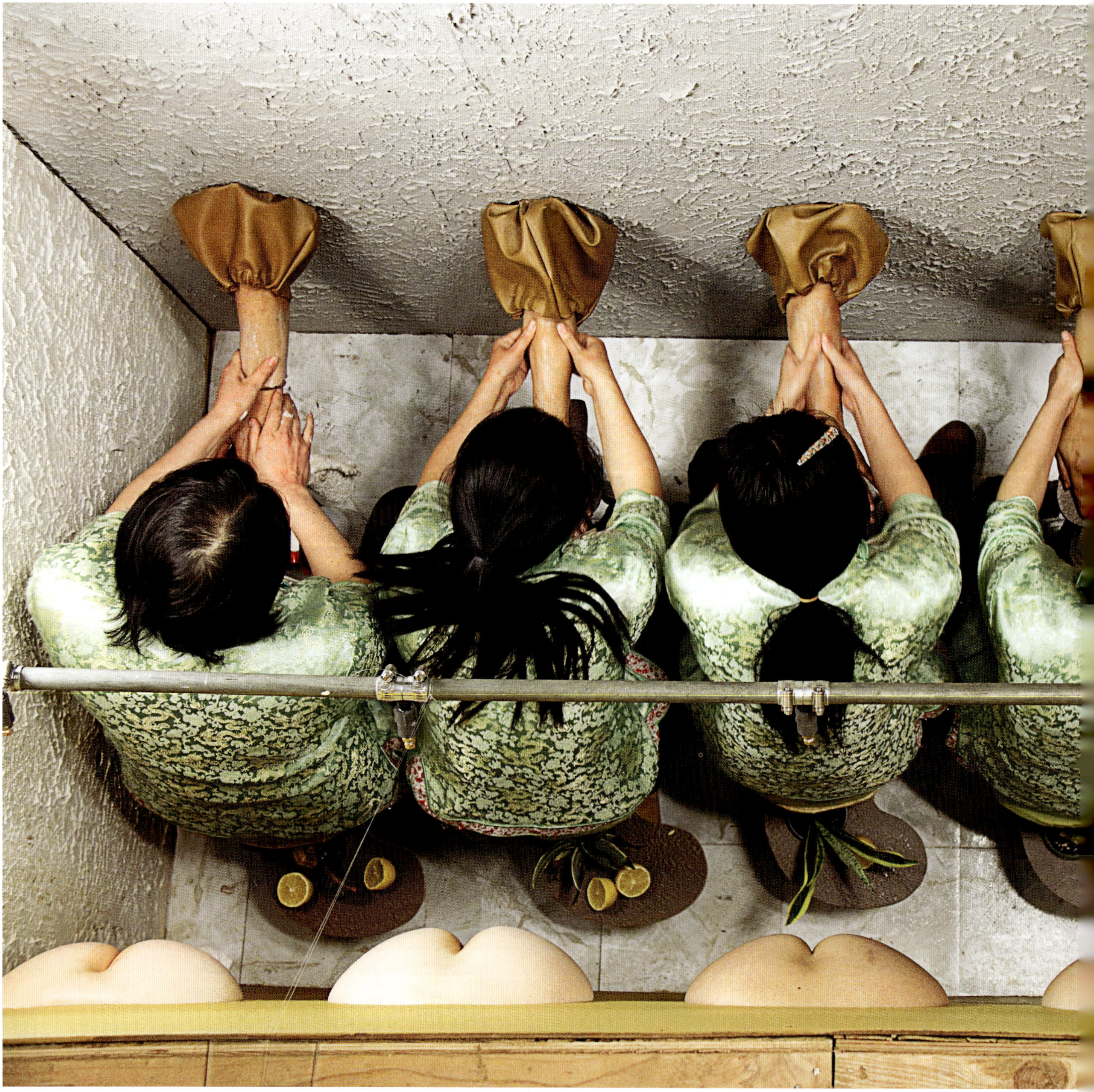

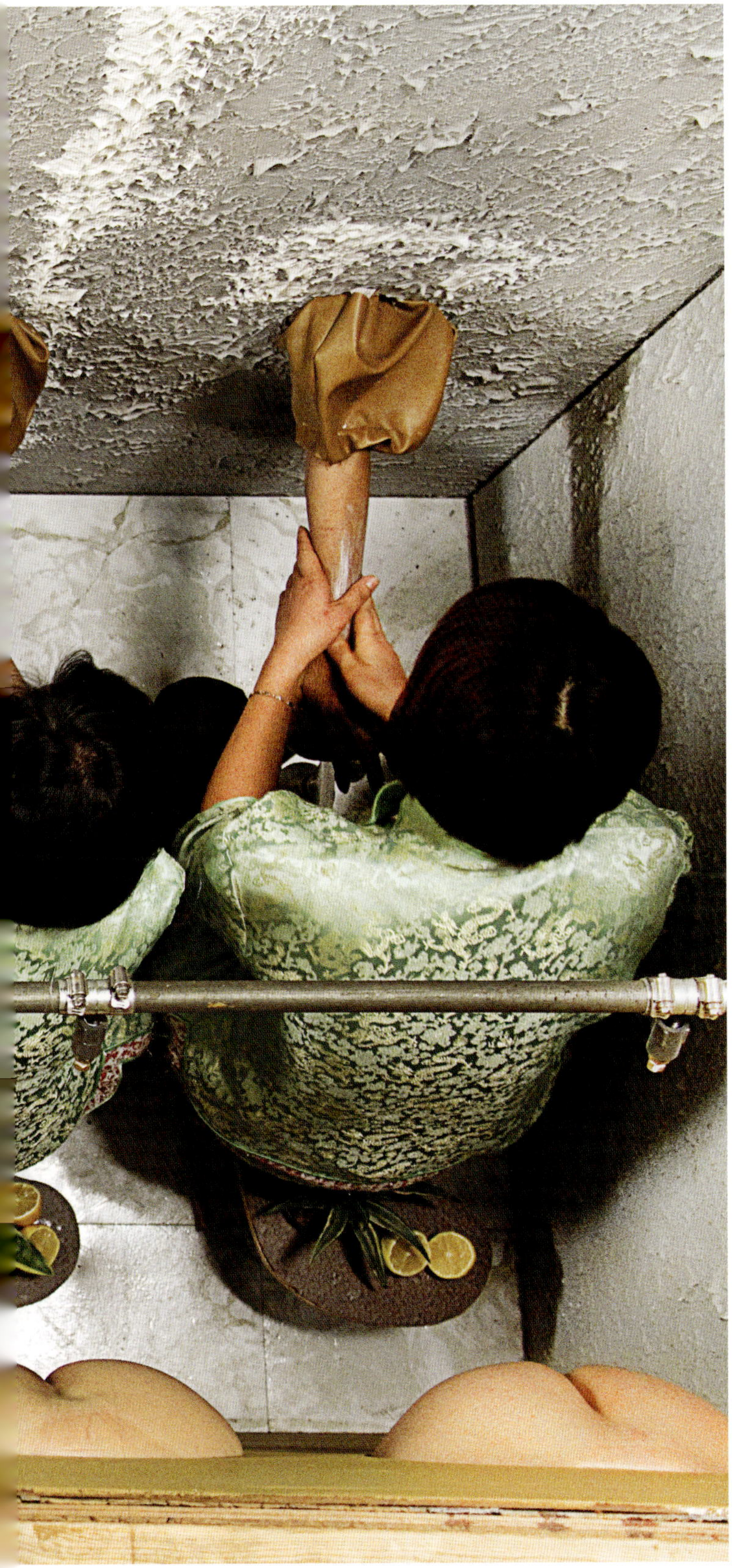

**Shown by**
Andrea Rosen Gallery
A6

**Biography**
Born 1976
Lives in New York

Buenos Aires-born Rottenberg has shown solo and project exhibitions at galleries such as Nottingham Contemporary (2012), San Francisco Museum of Modern Art (2010), KW Institute for Contemporary Art, Berlin (2006), and MoMA PS1, New York (2004). Recent group shows include 'Commercial Break', at the 54th Venice Biennale (2011), 'Once upon a Time', Guggenheim Berlin (2011), and the Whitney Biennial, Whitney Museum of American Art, New York (2008).

*Squeeze*
2010
Single-channel video installation
20 min.
Courtesy of Andrea Rosen Gallery and Nicole Klagsbrun Gallery

# Mika Rottenberg

Mika Rottenberg's videos trace the fabrication of a strange array of 'products' by a cast of female workers. Their workspaces, of Rottenberg's making, are usually factories-cum-spas where the sweat of the labourers' brows quite literally produces the end-result: perspiration is used to create 'moist tissue wipes' in one work and is marketed as 'chakra juice' in another. In *Squeeze* (2010) the factory and women's bodies alike are sites where global economies collide, as workers manufacture an ambiguous mashed cosmetic from raw materials that are somehow channelled directly from far-flung sources in Africa and India. Rottenberg's bodily poetics of production links the light grotesquerie of materials such as clay, fingernails and dough with the larger extravagances of today's hungry markets. SNS

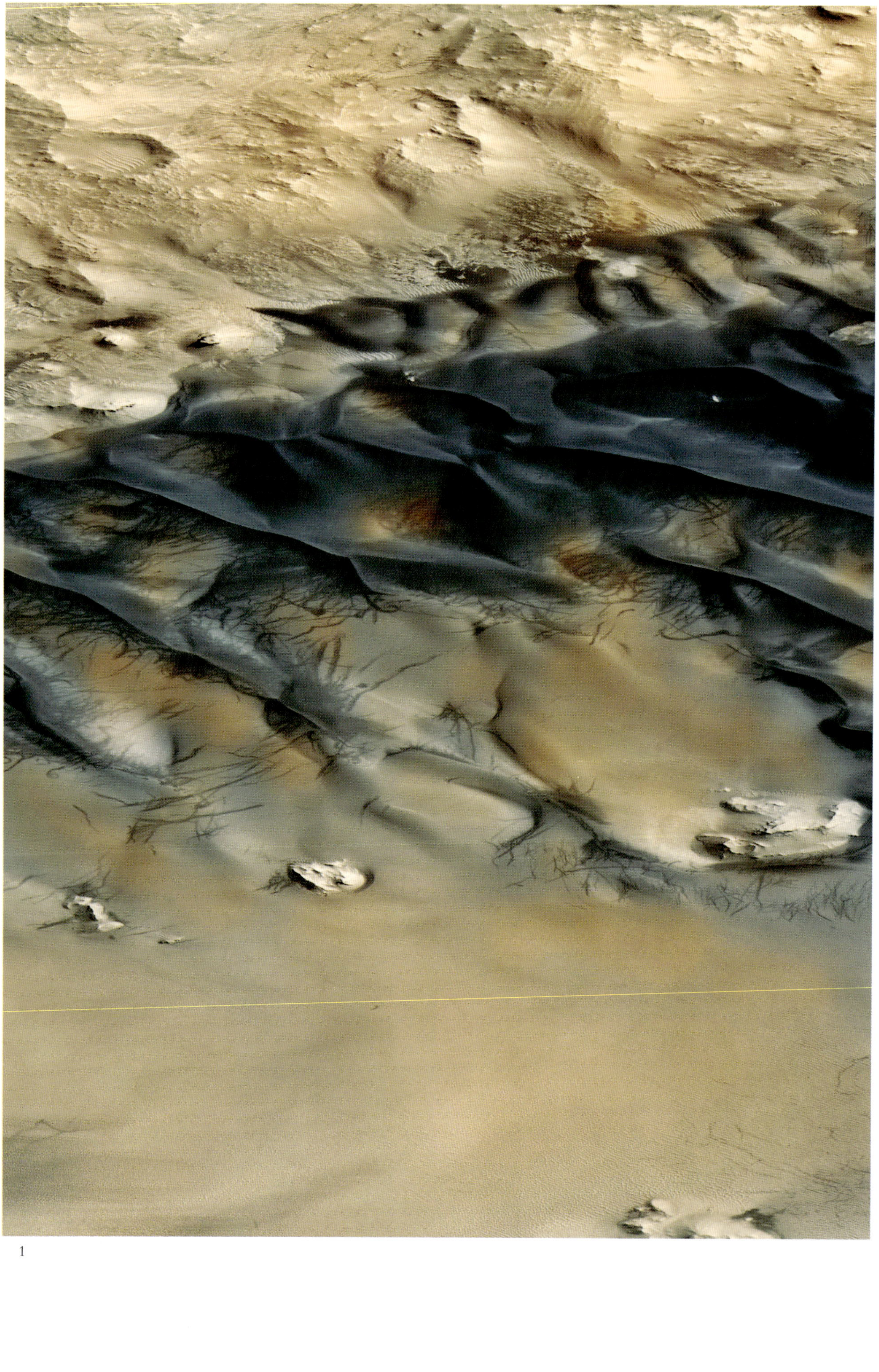

1

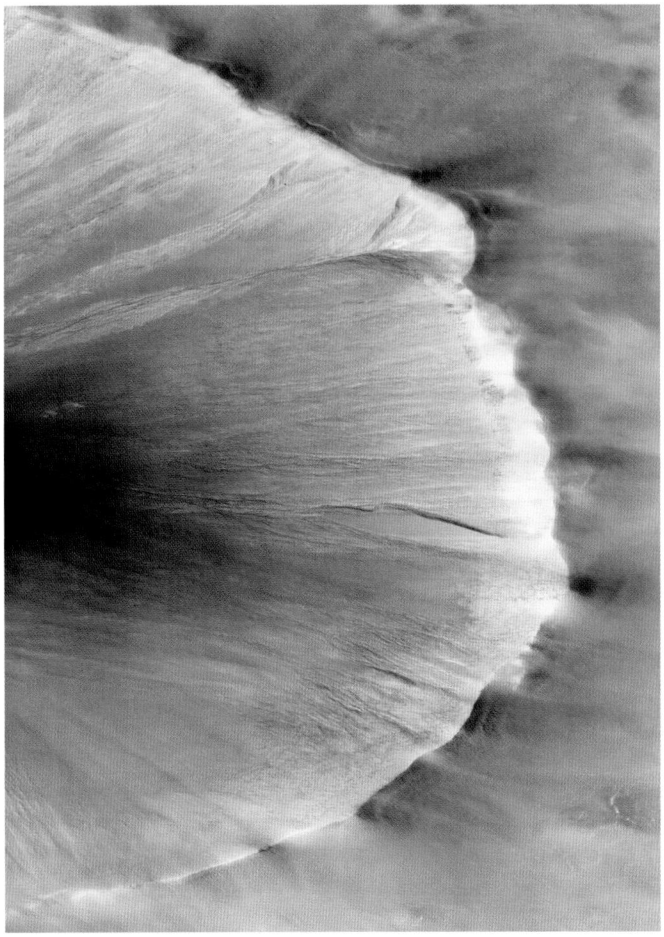

**Shown by**
Konrad Fischer Galerie C6
Gagosian Gallery D7
Johnen Galerie D1
Mai 36 Galerie D9
Galerie Rüdiger Schöttle H2
David Zwirner G9

**Biography**
Born 1958
Lives in Dusseldorf

Over the past decade German artist Ruff has shown solo exhibitions at public institutions such as Haus der Kunst, Munich (2012), Museum of Contemporary Art, Chicago (2011), Kunsthalle Vienna (2009), Moderna Museet, Stockholm (2007), Tate Liverpool (2003), and the Irish Museum of Modern Art, Dublin (2002). Ruff represented Germany at the 46th Venice Biennale (1995), and his work features in collections that include: the Solomon R. Guggenheim Museum, New York; Hamburger Bahnhof, Museum für Gegenwart, Berlin; and MoMA, New York.

1
*ma.r.s.15*
2011
C-type print with Diasec face
255 × 185 cm
Courtesy of Mai 36 Galerie

2
*m.a.r.s.19*
2011
C-type print with Diasec face
255 × 185 cm
Courtesy of Mai 36 Galerie

# Thomas Ruff

Thomas Ruff has said that 'the reality in front of the camera is reality of the first degree, the image of the reality in front of the camera is reality of the second degree, and after that, there are all possible finer degrees and falsifications.' Having produced images (or rather images of images) using blurred screen grabs from Internet porn, a war reporter's night-vision lens and abstracted motifs from *manga* comics, he has recently turned his attention to satellite photographs of Mars published on the NASA website. Digitally coloured and rotated by Ruff, these images offer a vision of human flight over the Red Planet's surface and suggest that photography is as much about imagining the future as about representing the present. TM

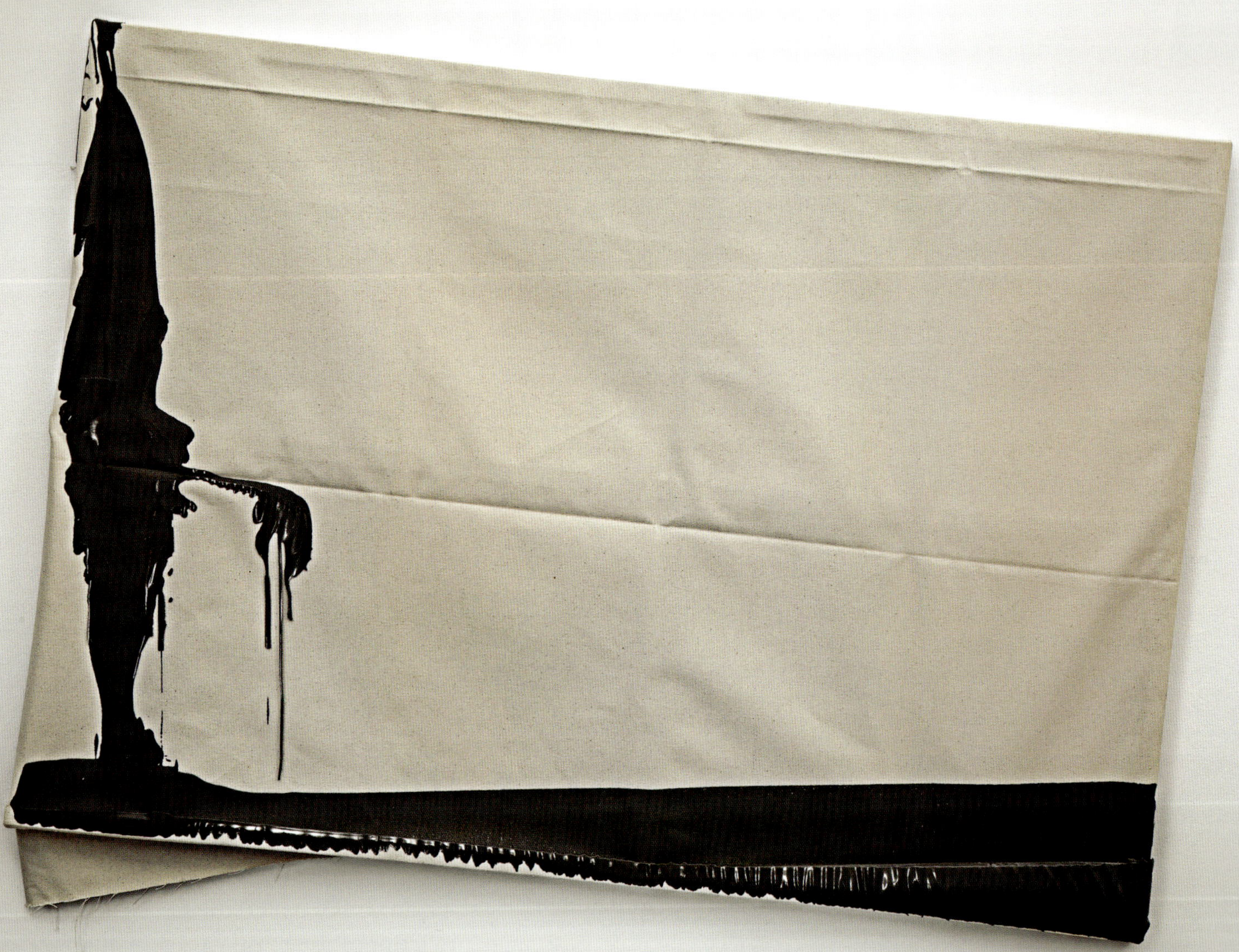

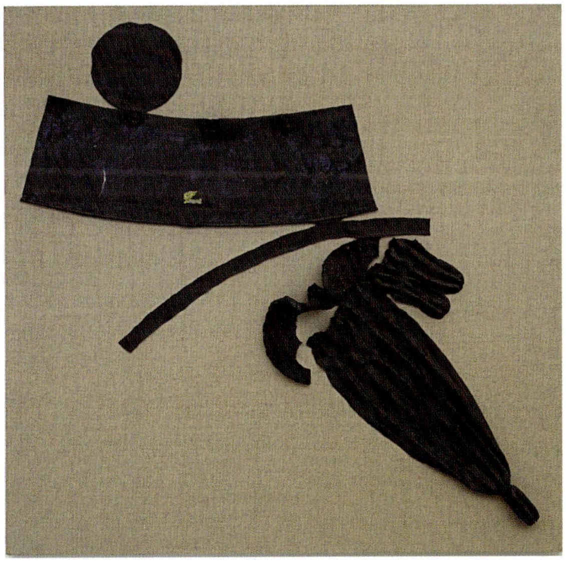

2

**Shown by**
Tanya Bonakdar Gallery
A5

**Biography**
Born 1980
Lives in Los Angeles

Argentinian artist Saban has recently held solo exhibitions at galleries that include Tanya Bonakdar Gallery, New York (2012), Praz-Delavallade, Paris (2011) and 11x7 Galeria de Arte, Buenos Aires (2011). In 2010 she was a recipient of the Santa Monica Artist Fellowship. She has also participated in group exhibitions including 'Across the Pacific', 313 Gallery, Seoul (2012), 'Made in LA 2012', Hammer Museum, Los Angeles, and 'American Exuberance', Rubell Family Collection, Miami (2011).

1
*Decant (Gray): Cascade with Two Horizons*
2011
Encaustic paint on canvas
109 × 140 cm
Courtesy of Tanya Bonakdar Gallery

2
*Representation of a Cactus*
2011
Acrylic on linen
102 × 101 cm
Courtesy of Tanya Bonakdar Gallery

# Analia Saban

Analia Saban has described her own attitude to painting as 'naïve'. That's not false modesty: she came to the medium via video and installation, and began by separating it into its constituent parts, as if it was an entirely new phenomenon that she needed to understand. Of course, Saban's knowledge of Modernist art history shines through in canvases such as *Decant (Gray): Cascade with Two Horizons* (2011), which cheekily winks at Morris Louis, Lucio Fontana and Robert Ryman. But her innocence—and her willingness to ask how even the most familiar objects work (as with *Representation of a Cactus*, 2011)—remains fundamental to her painterly investigations. JG

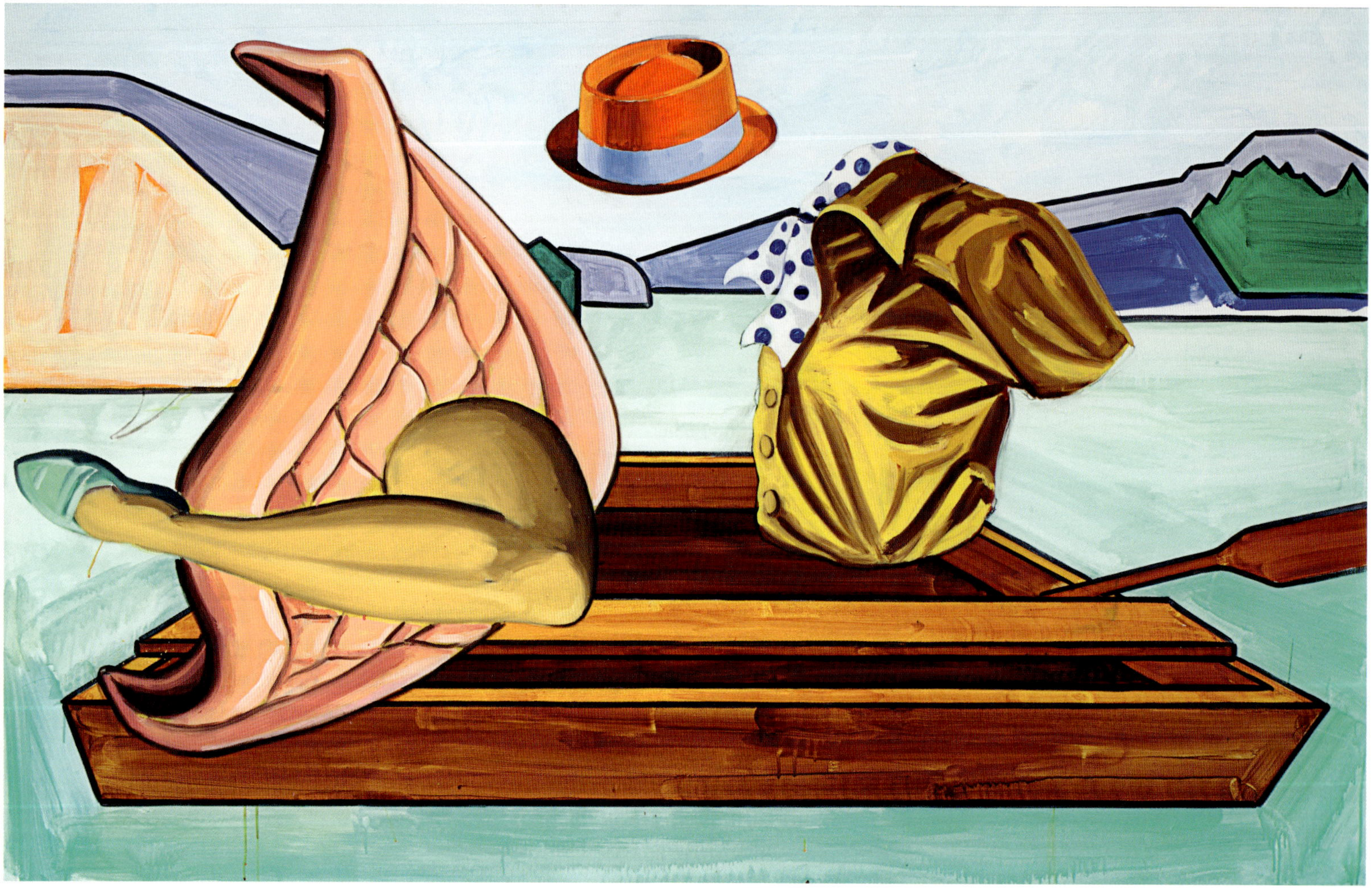

1

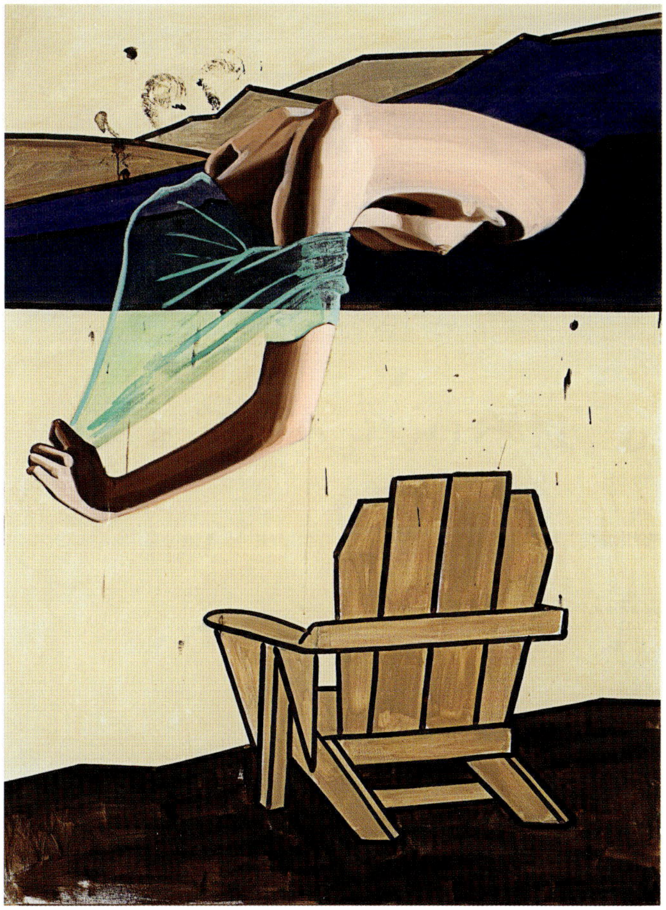

2

**Shown by**
Gerhardsen Gerner F20
Maureen Paley D5
Galerie Thaddaeus Ropac F4

**Biography**
Born 1952
Lives in New York

Oklahoma-born Salle was the subject of a major retrospective at the Stedelijk Museum, Amsterdam, in 1999, which travelled to venues across Europe, as well as survey shows at institutions including the Whitney Museum of American Art, New York (1986), and Museum Boijmans Van Beuningen, Rotterdam (1983). His work is part of public collections that include the Solomon R. Guggenheim Museum, New York; the Tate collection, UK; and MACBA, Barcelona.

1
*Green Raft*
2011
Oil and acrylic on linen
135 × 209 cm
Courtesy of Gerhardsen Gerner and Mary Boone Gallery

2
*Lookout*
2010
Oil and acrylic on linen
191 × 138 cm
Courtesy of Gerhardsen Gerner and Mary Boone Gallery

# David Salle

The canvases of David Salle fuse figuration with pop-culture iconography in surreal compositions. *Green Raft* (2011) sees a woman's shirt, a blanket, a bowler hat and a disembodied leg float in mid-air above a boat on a lake. Like many of Salle's works, the painting suggests a Postmodern salad of disparate elements brought together to form a new open-ended visual lexicon. *Lookout* (2010) features an Adirondack chair—a recurring motif in recent paintings—below a disrobing woman's torso. Here, as in many of his works, Salle combines depictions of the female form with objects from contemporary culture, referencing the traditions of painting and today's pursuits in equal measure. SC

0810 300 427

Etwas unwichtiges
(~~komplett~~ irrelevantes).

~~Banales~~ als banal
nicht einmal !

Etwas nicht einmal
~~[illegible]~~.

nicht einmal interessant
– für niemanden

nicht einmal so uninteres=
sant, daß es ~~schon~~ un=
verschämt ~~ist~~ sein kann

~~Oder~~ ~~dann~~ ~~doch~~ eher des
genaue Gegenteil davon,
oder gleich beides ~~oder~~
oder nicht ~~[illegible]~~

2

**Shown by**
Galerie Meyer Kainer F2

**Biography**
Born 1968
Lives in Vienna

Austrian artist Sandner has presented solo exhibitions at venues that include American Contemporary, New York (2011), Andreas Grimm Gallery, Munich (2011 and 2009), Galerie Grita Insam, Vienna (2010, 2007 and 2003), Tiroler Landesmuseum, Innsbruck (2008), and the Vienna Secession (2006). Group exhibitions include 'Third Thoughts', CCA Andratx, Majorca (2010), and 'Unreal: Altered Perspectives in Painting', Saatchi Gallery, London (2008).

1
*Untitled*
2012
Acrylic on canvas
280 × 200 cm
Courtesy of Galerie Meyer Kainer

2
*Untitled*
2010
Acrylic on canvas
200 × 310 cm
Courtesy of Galerie Meyer Kainer

# Stefan Sandner

Stefan Sandner's work revolves around quotations, whether shaped canvases *à la* Kenneth Noland or Frank Stella, such as *Untitled* (2010), or quotations of the more graphic kind, specifically through his enlarged painted reproductions of other people's handwritten notes and graffiti. *Cobain* (2004) was a diptych of paintings based on the posthumously published diaries of the Nirvana front man, but Sandner's eye is also caught on less exalted sources, as in *Untitled* (2004–5), based on a note taped to discarded rubbish next to his studio, which read 'Zeug ist am Verschwinden' ('Stuff is disappearing'), or *Untitled* (2012), a painting consecrating scrawled notes in English and German and a hurriedly noted telephone number. SL

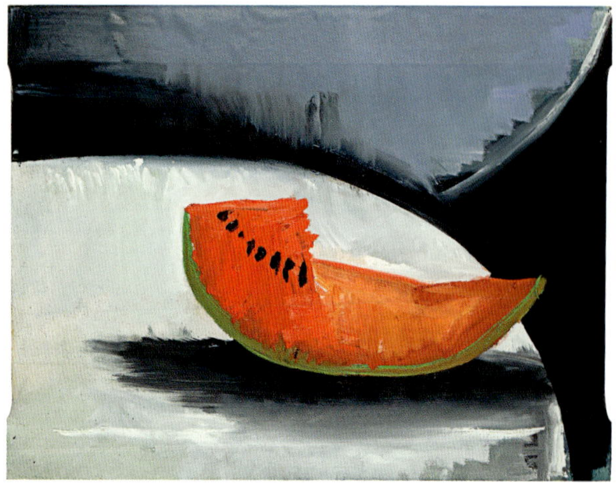
1

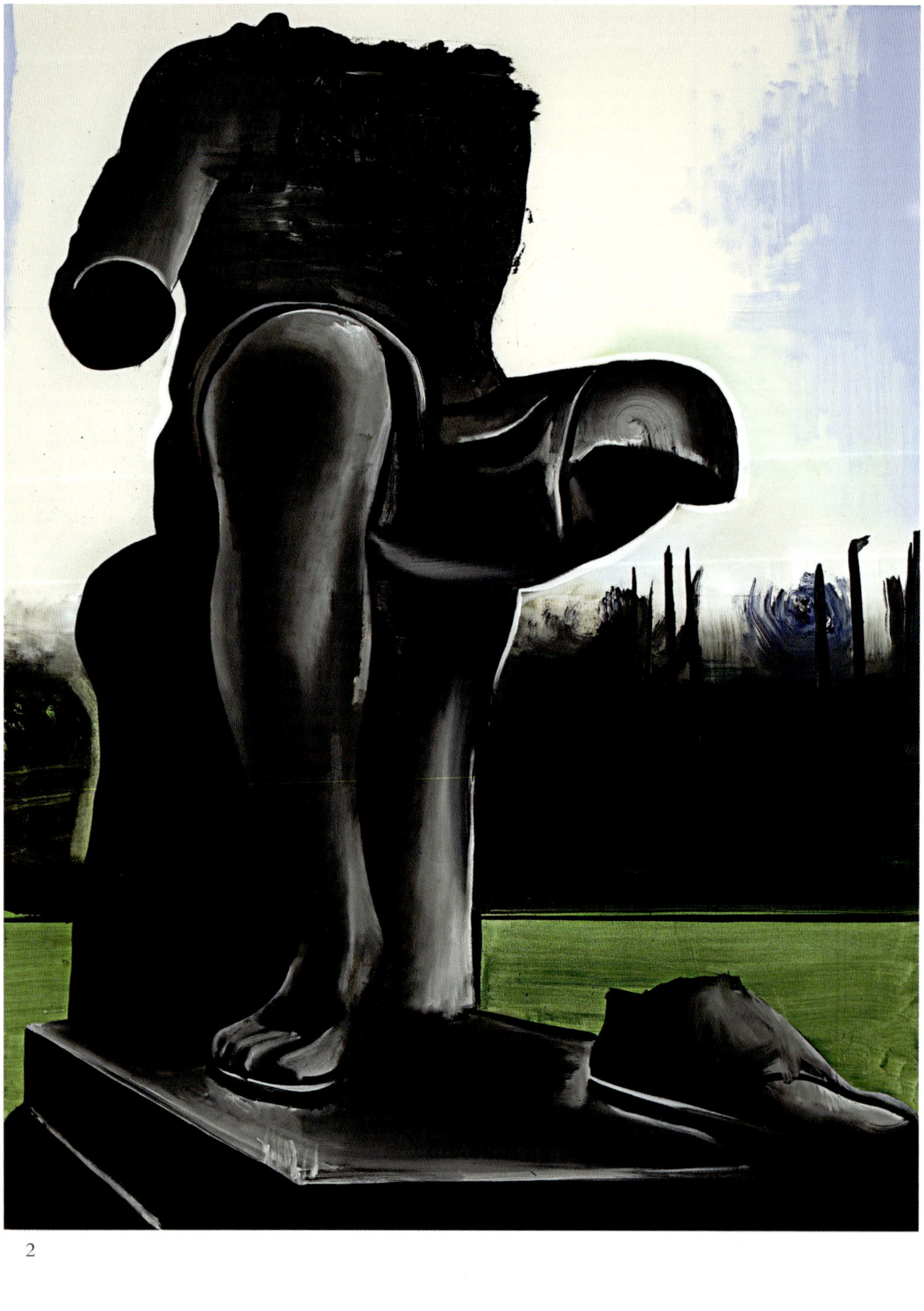
2

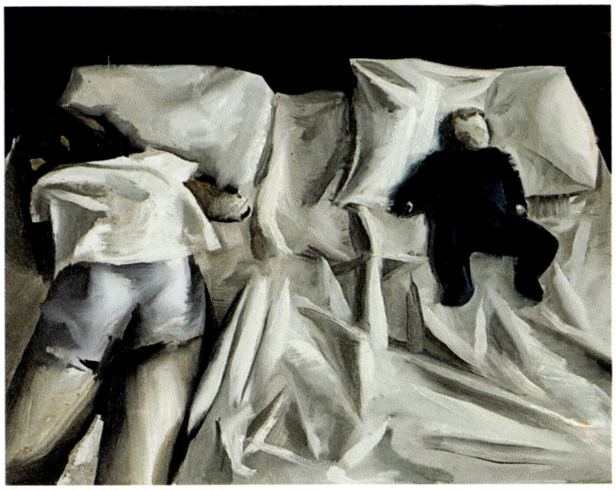

3

**Shown by**
Sadie Coles HQ C11
Foksal Gallery Foundation E9
Hauser & Wirth C8
Johnen Galerie D1
Anton Kern Gallery A4
Raster S19
Sommer Contemporary Art E10

**Biography**
Born 1972
Lives in Krakow

Polish-born artist Sasnal has presented solo exhibitions at venues that include Foksal Gallery Foundation, Warsaw (2012), Whitechapel Gallery, London (2011), Centro de Arte Contemporáneo, Malaga (2009), and Zacheta National Gallery of Art, Warsaw (2007). His work has featured in recent group exhibitions such 'Paintings between the Lines', CCA Wattis Institute for Contemporary Arts, San Francisco (2011), and 'Space: About a Dream', Kunsthalle Wien, Vienna (2011).

1
*Untitled*
2011
Oil on canvas
46 × 59 cm
Courtesy of Foksal Gallery Foundation

2
*Untitled*
2012
Oil on canvas
160 × 120 cm
Courtesy of Foksal Gallery Foundation

3
*Kacper and Rita*
2011
Oil on canvas
40 × 50 cm
Courtesy of Foksal Gallery Foundation

# Wilhelm Sasnal

'I feel unusually susceptible to pictures', Wilhelm Sasnal has said. He means photographs: their cropping aside, the gleam, saturation and flattened feel of his paintings emphasize lens-based origins. Sasnal exalts his chosen images by recasting them in quick, precise, nonchalantly luscious brushstrokes—thereby modelling the defensive navigation of an unmanageable pictorial excess, arguing for slowing and focus and, as in his parallel filmmaking practice, allowing detached events to accrue collective, ambiguously melancholy weight. Sasnal's son in bed with his blank-faced baby sister (*Kacper and Rita*, 2011), a half-eaten, boat-like watermelon slice, irradiated orange (*Untitled*, 2011), a broken monumental statue, dryly elegiac (*Untitled*, 2012): each a nudge towards subjective storytelling, each a small act of protection. MH

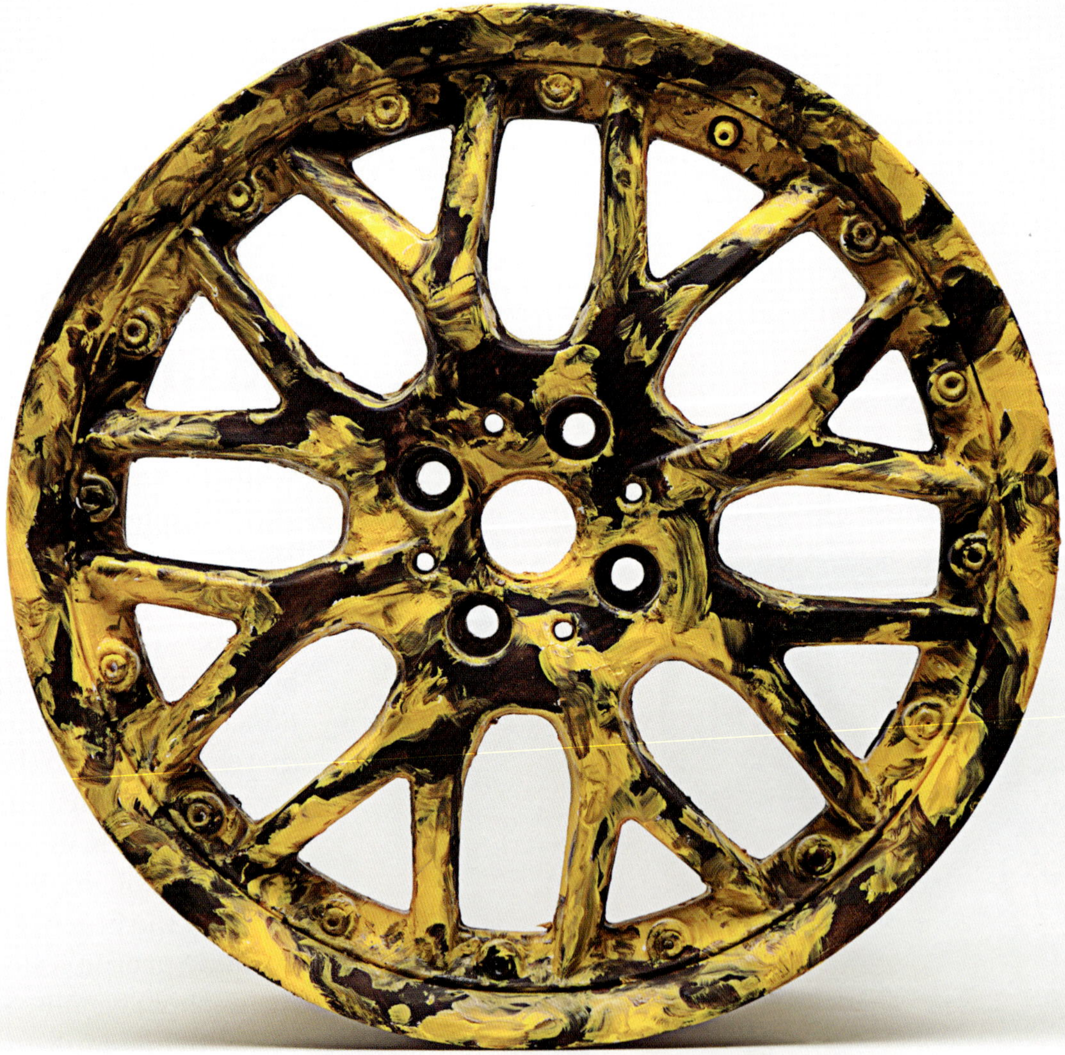

**Shown by**
Karma International S14

**Biography**
Born 1984
Lives in Berlin

Swiss-born artist Sauter presented solo exhibitions in 2011 at: Karma International, Zurich; Johan Berggren Gallery, Malmo; and New Jerseyy, Basel. Group exhibitions in which his work has been featured include 'Based in Berlin', KW Institute of Contemporary Art, Berlin (2011), 'Corso Multisala', Kunsthal Charlottenborg, Copenhagen (2011), and 'Now More than Ever', Istituto Svizzero, Milan (2010).

*Honey Extraction*
2011
Oil on aluminium
47 × 47 × 20 cm
Courtesy of Karma International

# Focus
# Thomas Sauter

The idea and action of pattern-making take on blandly painterly connotations in Thomas Sauter's paintings and objects, which treat abstraction and décor in equally irreverent ways. At his solo show in 2011 at Karma International, Zurich, elliptically titled 'Yesterday Is History, Tomorrow Is a Mystery, and Today Is a Gift', patterns both tightly detailed and as diffuse as clouds covered the series of canvases lining the gallery, as well as a series of garden tools leaning casually against the walls. Here the prongs of garden rakes and hoes were adorned with Impressionist dabs of colour, in a decidedly lighter approximation of Yayoi Kusama's polka-dot and phallus fever. Whether the decorous banality of Sauter's surfaces is underlined or contested by his deft and joyous handling of colour remains, as he sees fit, up in the air. QL

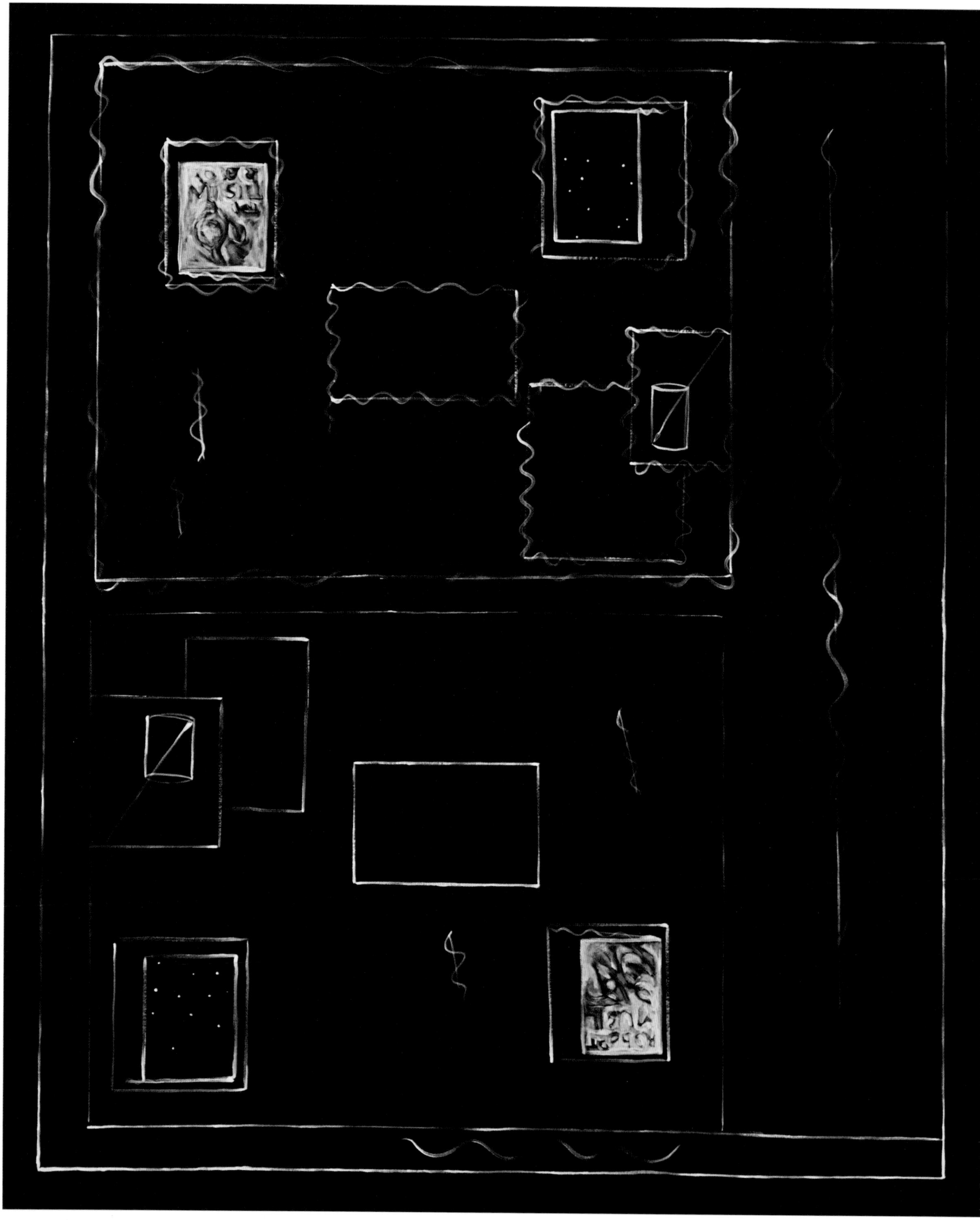

# Gerda Scheepers

**Shown by**
Mary Mary F19
Micky Schubert E19
Sprüth Magers Berlin London D6

**Biography**
Born 1979
Lives in Berlin

South African-born Scheepers has recently been the subject of solo shows at venues including Kunstverein Nürnberg, Nuremberg (2012), Micky Schubert, Berlin (2011), Tomorrow Gallery, Toronto (2011), and Mary Mary, Glasgow (2010). Group exhibitions include 'The Yarn Beam and the Revolving Stage', Galerie Thomas Flor, Dusseldorf (2011), and 'Dwelling', Marianne Boesky Gallery, New York (2011).

*Untitled*
2011
Acrylic on textile
190 × 155 cm
Courtesy of Micky Schubert

A negotiation between intimate and undetermined space occurs in Gerda Scheepers' collages, paintings and sculptures, such as 'Method and Milieu Drawings' (2009). This series of low-key semi-abstract paintings of interiors reconciles the rational quality of plans with a more expressive rendering of space. Scheepers works with a minimal vocabulary of forms: drawings of interiors seen from above, rendered in tones of white and grey on black fabric, such as *Untitled* (2011), and sculptural arrangements of objects reminiscent of stage sets, animated by the use of acid yellow and royal blue. Her work is activated by her methods of display: small plinths, painted panels on props and furniture-like constructions that reside in the space between memory, form and functionality. SL

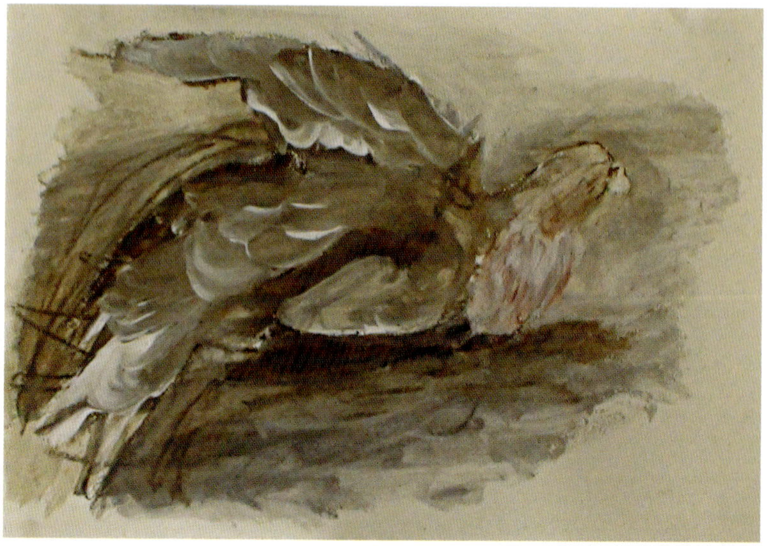

1

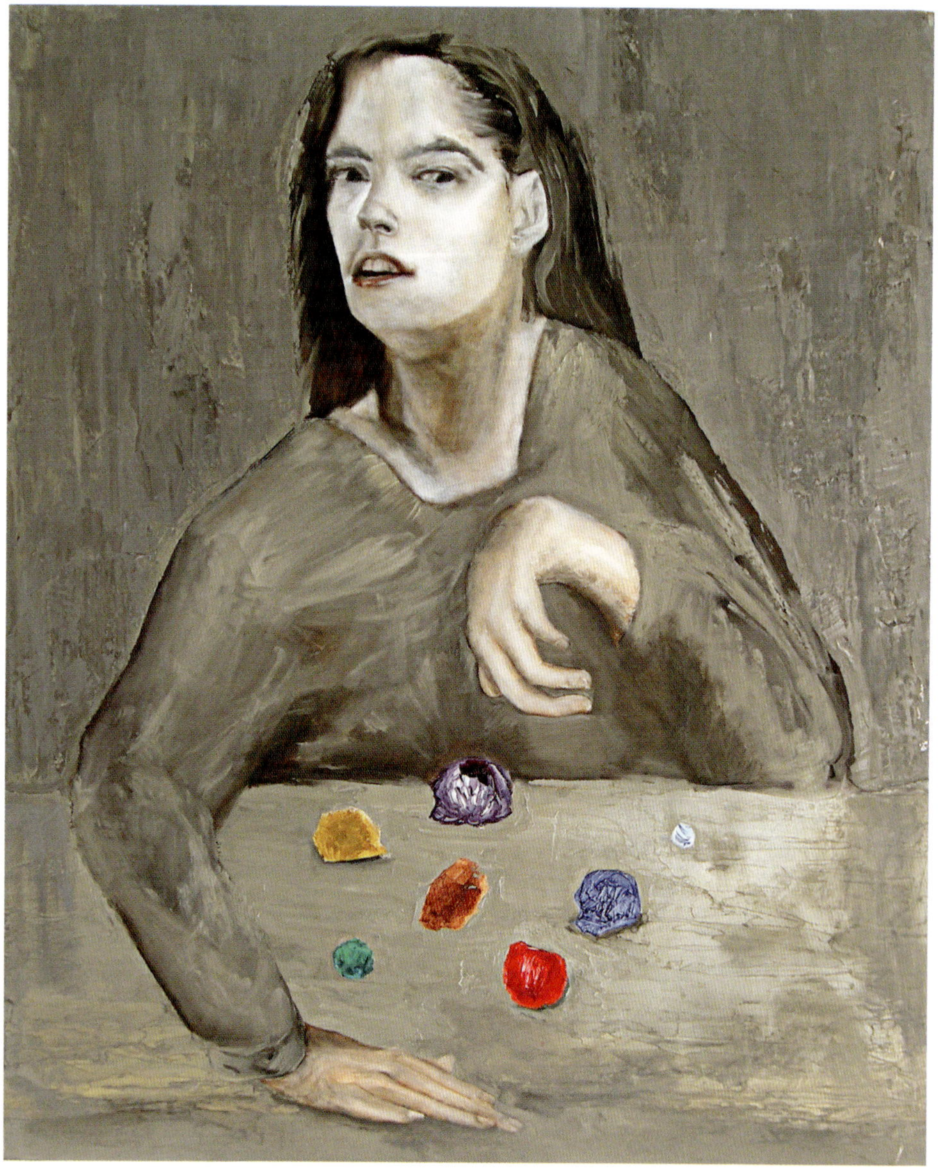

2

**Shown by**
Sommer Contemporary Art E10

**Biography**
Born 1979
Lives in Tel Aviv

Israeli artist Schlosser has held solo exhibitions at galleries and museums such as the Jerusalem Artists House (2009), Tel Aviv Museum (2008), and Sommer Contemporary Art, Tel Aviv (2007 and 2005). She received the Osnat Mozes Young Artist Painting Prize in 2009 and the Rappaport Prize for a Young Israeli Painter in 2007. Her work is part of the collection of the Haifa Museum of Art.

1
*Migratory Birds on Flight from Right to Left*
2012
Oil on canvas
46 × 61 cm
Courtesy of Sommer Contemporary Art

2
*Precious Stones*
2006
Oil on canvas
80 × 65 cm
Courtesy of Sommer Contemporary Art

3
*Stone with Two Hands*
2009
Oil on canvas
90 × 80 cm
Courtesy of Sommer Contemporary Art

# Netally Schlosser

Mysterious figures populate Netally Schlosser's paintings, as if caught in the act while performing unknown mystical acts. The earthy tones of her canvases often depict women in snapshot-like tableaux. *Precious Stones* (2006) sees the painting's protagonist hovering over a selection of coloured jewels, which punctuate the neutral canvas with vibrant colour. Similarly, *Stone with Two Hands* (2009) depicts a woman poised with an apparently floating stone in her palm, unaware of the viewer's gaze. Schlosser's recent works, including *Migratory Birds on Flight from Right to Left* (2012) and *Migratory Birds (1)* (2012), capture the temporal nature of her subject matter. By fixing 'moments' in paint, she offers the viewer a privileged perspective on ephemeral gestures and inconspicuous actions. SC

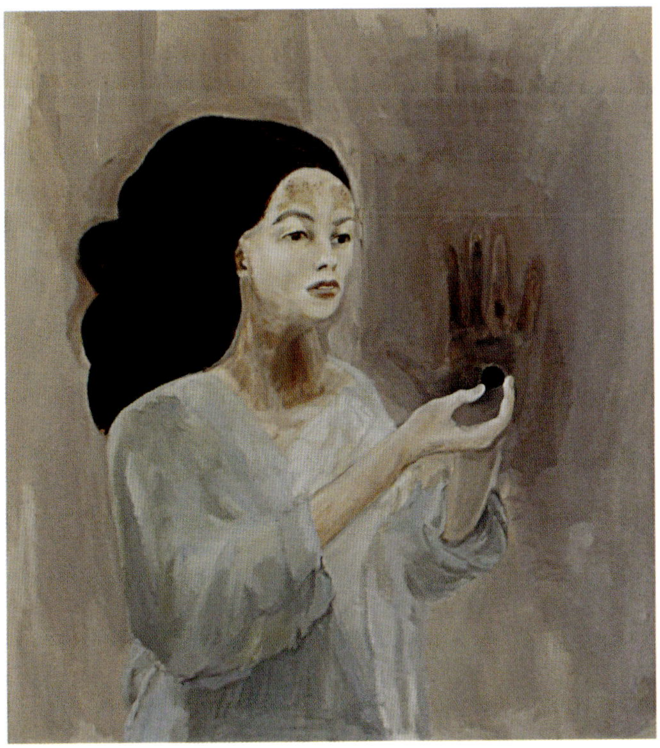
3

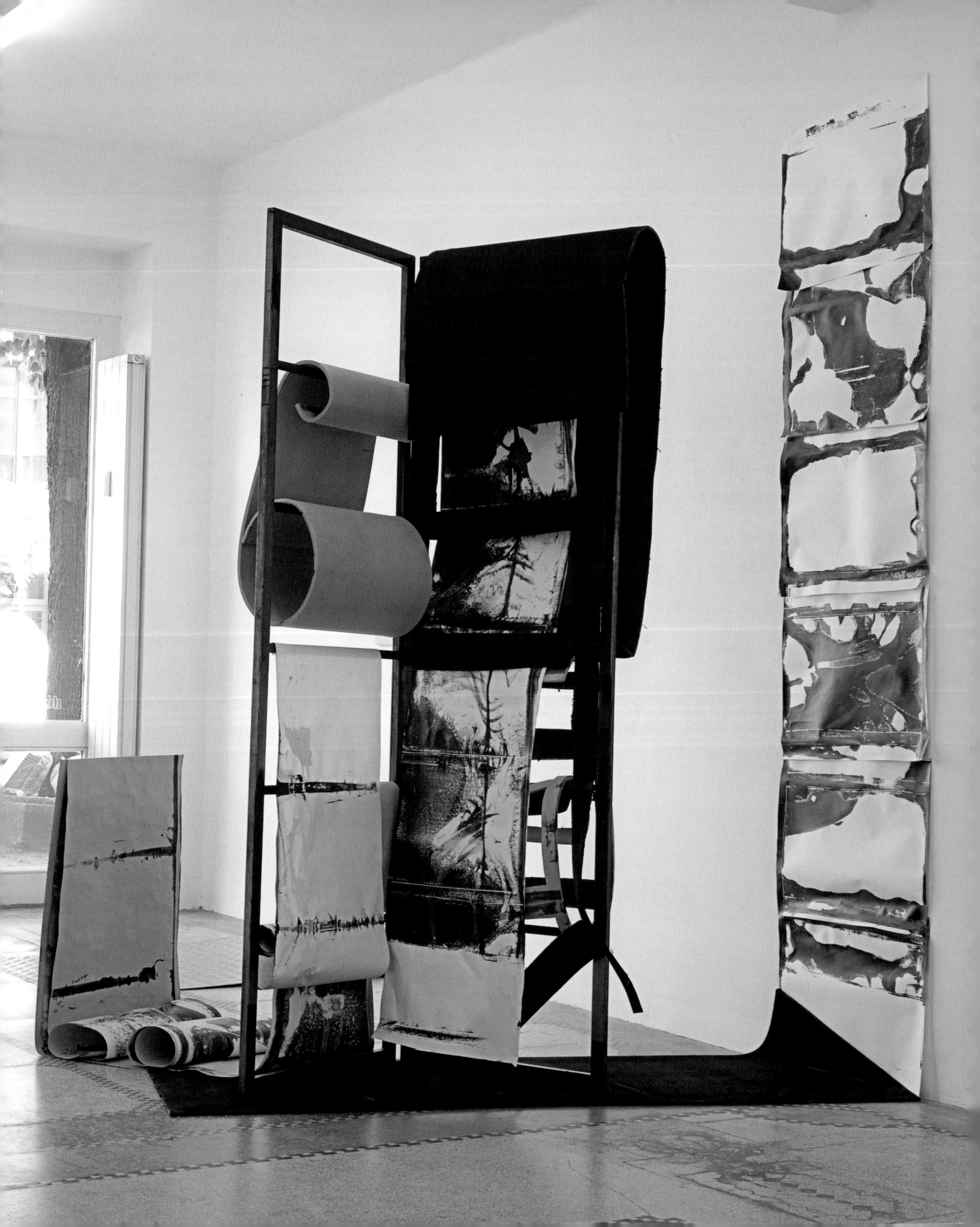

# Focus
# Nora Schultz

**Shown by**
Campoli Presti F5
dépendance S11
Reena Spaulings Fine Art B6

**Biography**
Born 1975
Lives in Berlin

Frankfurt-born Schultz has been the subject of solo shows at venues such as Portikus, Frankfurt (2012), Bloomberg Space, London (2011), and Fondazione Galleria Civica, Centro di Ricerca sulla Contemporaneità, Trento (2010). In 2010 she presented her work with Nicolas Byrne as part of a two-person exhibition at dépendance, Brussels. Group exhibitions in 2012 include 'Ecstatic Alphabets', MoMA, New York, and 'Hints and Gleams', Galerie Isabella Bortolozzi, Berlin.

*Discovery of the Primitive*
2011
Steel, camping mats, polyethylene foam, paper and ink
3 × 2 × 2 m
Courtesy of dépendance

Typically made from found industrial materials, Nora Schultz' sculptures have an intuitive, almost off-hand feel that belies their formal clarity and referential density. Much concerned with the genesis of pictorial representation, her work *Discovery of the Primitive* (2011)—a ladder-like steel frame hung with foam camping mats and rolls of over-inked paper—resembles a printing press, if such a device were used to produce not identical, legible images but utterly unrepeatable globular abstractions. If there is a tension, here, between accident and design, it is one that speaks to wider issues of how art comes into being, and what might be gained by abandoning the idea of a 'finished' work and focusing instead on the infinite unrest of process. TM

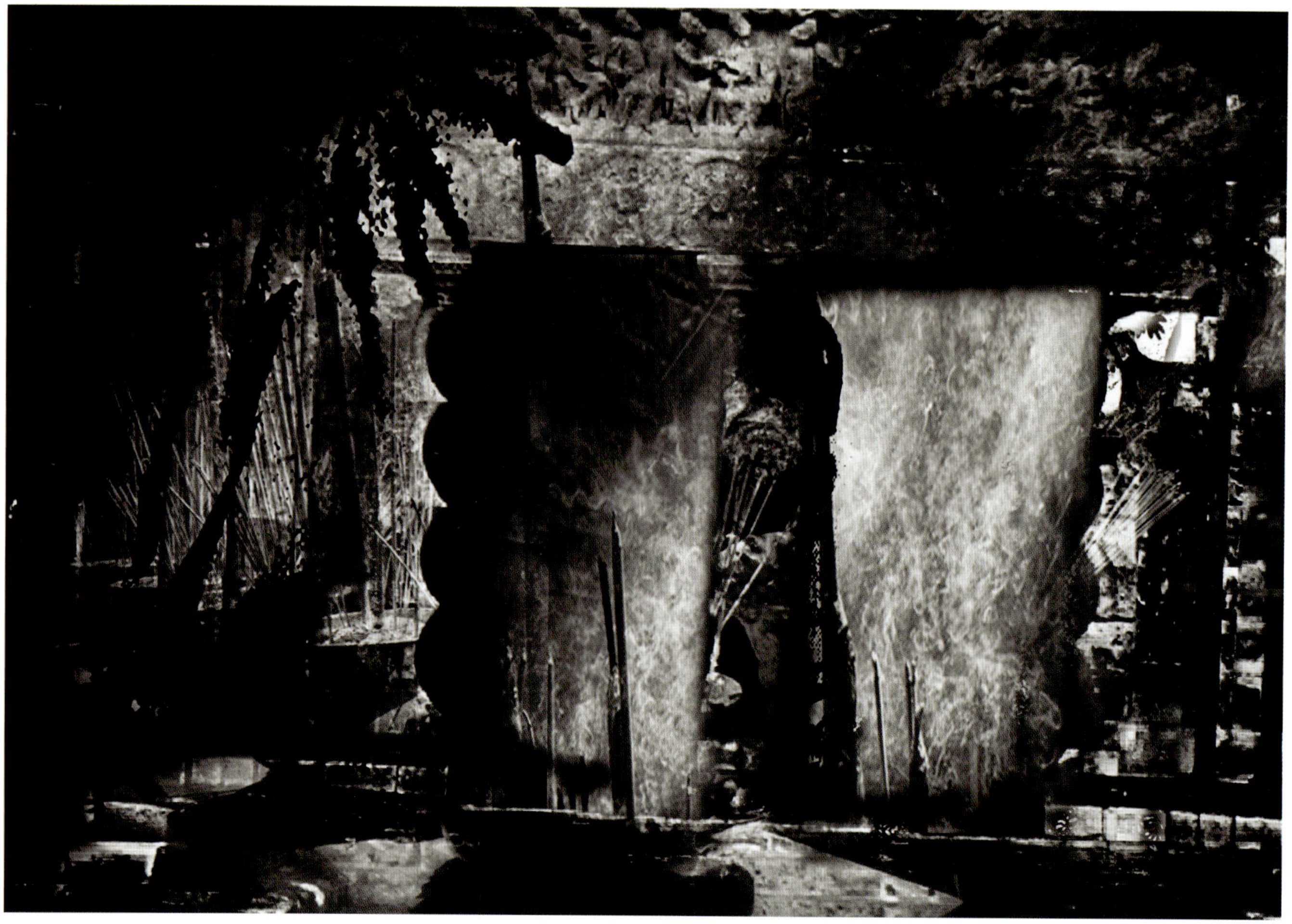

1

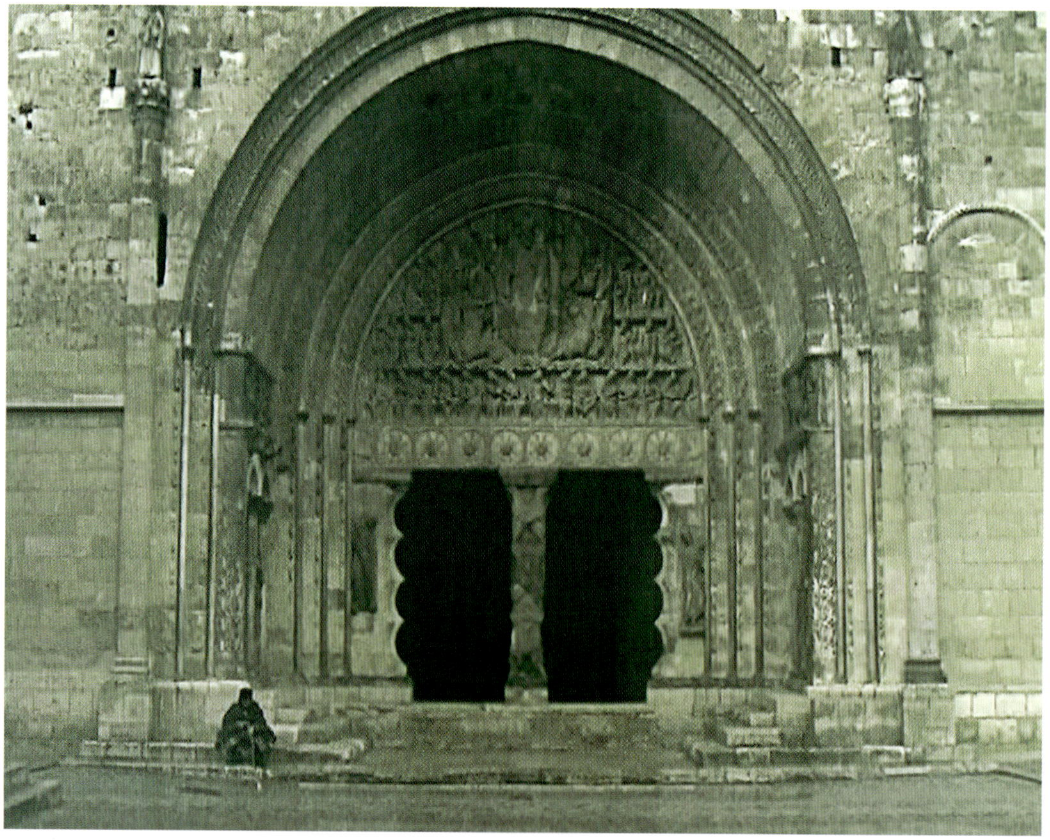

2

**Shown by**
Galerie Guido W. Baudach A10
SVIT R9
Vilma Gold B2

**Biography**
Born 1974
Lives in Berlin

German-born artist Selg has presented recent solo shows at galleries that include Galerie Guido W. Baudach, Berlin (2011), SVIT, Prague (2010), and Vilma Gold, London (2010). He is the founder and director of publisher Possible Press, Berlin, and his work has featured in group exhibitions including 'Gesamtkunstwerk: New Art from Germany', Saatchi Gallery, London (2011), and the Loften International Art Festival, Norway (2011).

1
*Remembrance*
2010
Piezo print on paper
60 × 84 cm
Courtesy of Galerie Guido W. Baudach

2
*Habima Fuchs*
2010
DVD
5 min. 19 sec.
Courtesy of Galerie Guido W. Baudach

3
*Flowers of Ruwenzori*
2011
Wood, palm leaf, straw, fabric and metal
73 × 16 × 16 cm
Galerie Guido W. Baudach

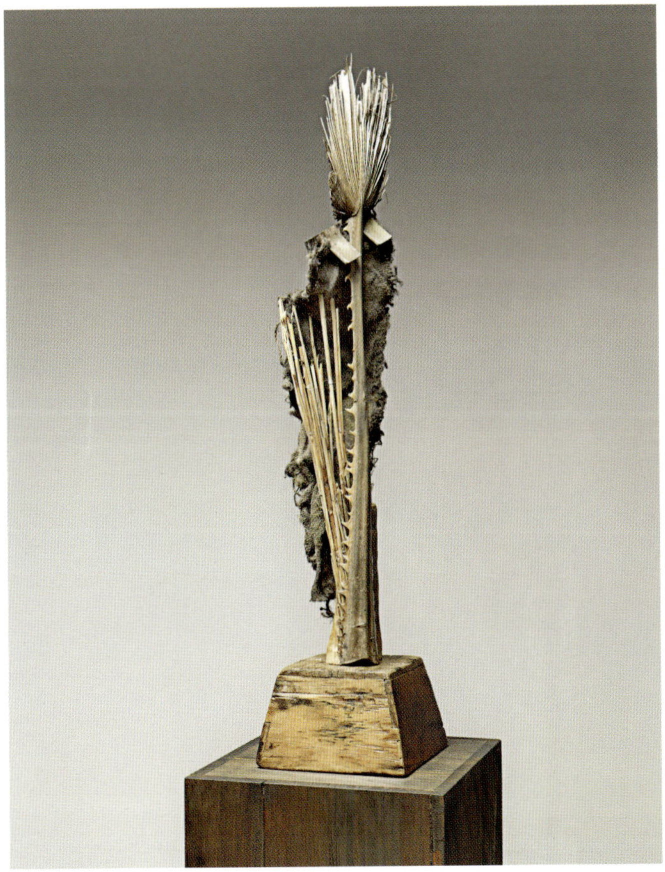

3

# Markus Selg

When Markus Selg chose to live for a while in the backwoods of the Czech Republic, it wasn't to reduce the range of his wildly omnivorous art practice. He subscribes to the notion of living life as a *Gesamtkunstwerk*—a total work of art that embraces as many forms as possible—which he achieves by synthesizing Germanic myths, folk tales, religious narratives, classical music and art history in sculptures, films, digital images and atmospheric, theatrical installations. His film *Habima Fuchs* (2010) shows artist Astrid Sourkova absorbed in her work on the steps of a church; like Selg's witchy, mysterious assemblages of natural materials, such as *Flowers of Ruwenzori* (2011), the film outlines a singular vision of artistic self-determination. JG

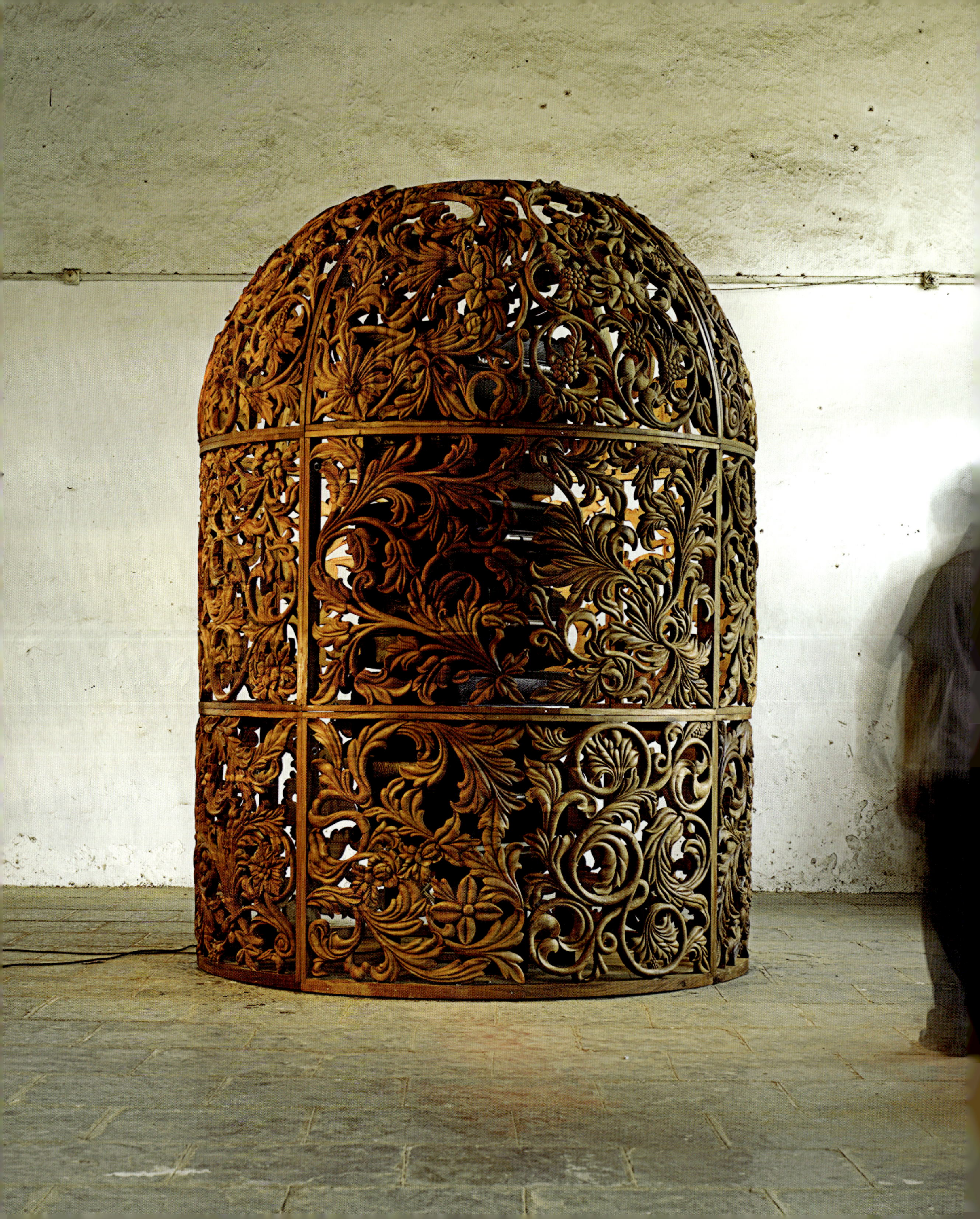

# Sudarshan Shetty

**Shown by**
Galerie Krinzinger D13

**Biography**
Born 1961
Lives in Mumbai

Indian-born Shetty has presented solo shows and projects at galleries that include Galerie Krinzinger, Vienna (2012 and 2008), Galleryske, Bangalore (2011, 2009, 2006 and 2005), Dr Bhau Daji Lad Museum, Mumbai (2010), and Fukuoka Asian Art Museum, Japan (2001). Recent group exhibitions include 'Contemplating the Void', Solomon R. Guggenheim Museum, New York (2010), and 'Dark Materials', GSK Contemporary, Royal Academy of Arts, London (2008)

*From Here to There and Back Again*
2009
Carved wood and suitcases
3 × 2 × 2 m
Courtesy of Galerie Krinzinger

Sudarshan Shetty creates enigmatic sculptural installations, often with kinetic elements—a dog skeleton upturned and moving on a wooden bed, a brass phallus swinging like a pendulum into the opening of a steel house, a cast aluminium television set oozing fake blood. Although Shetty's work explores themes such as love and loss, he uses participation and playfulness to break down the barriers between art and life. *The House of Shades* (2010) presents a kiosk lined with revolving rows of sunglasses, reversing the conventions of display and leaving the viewer feeling viewed. Shetty's interest in the convergence of different traditions is evident in *From Here to There and Back Again* (2009), a gazebo elaborately hand-carved by Indian craftsmen surrounding a stack of six black suitcases; the work serves as a description of the Vedic concept that there are six internal 'enemies' of the soul. ND

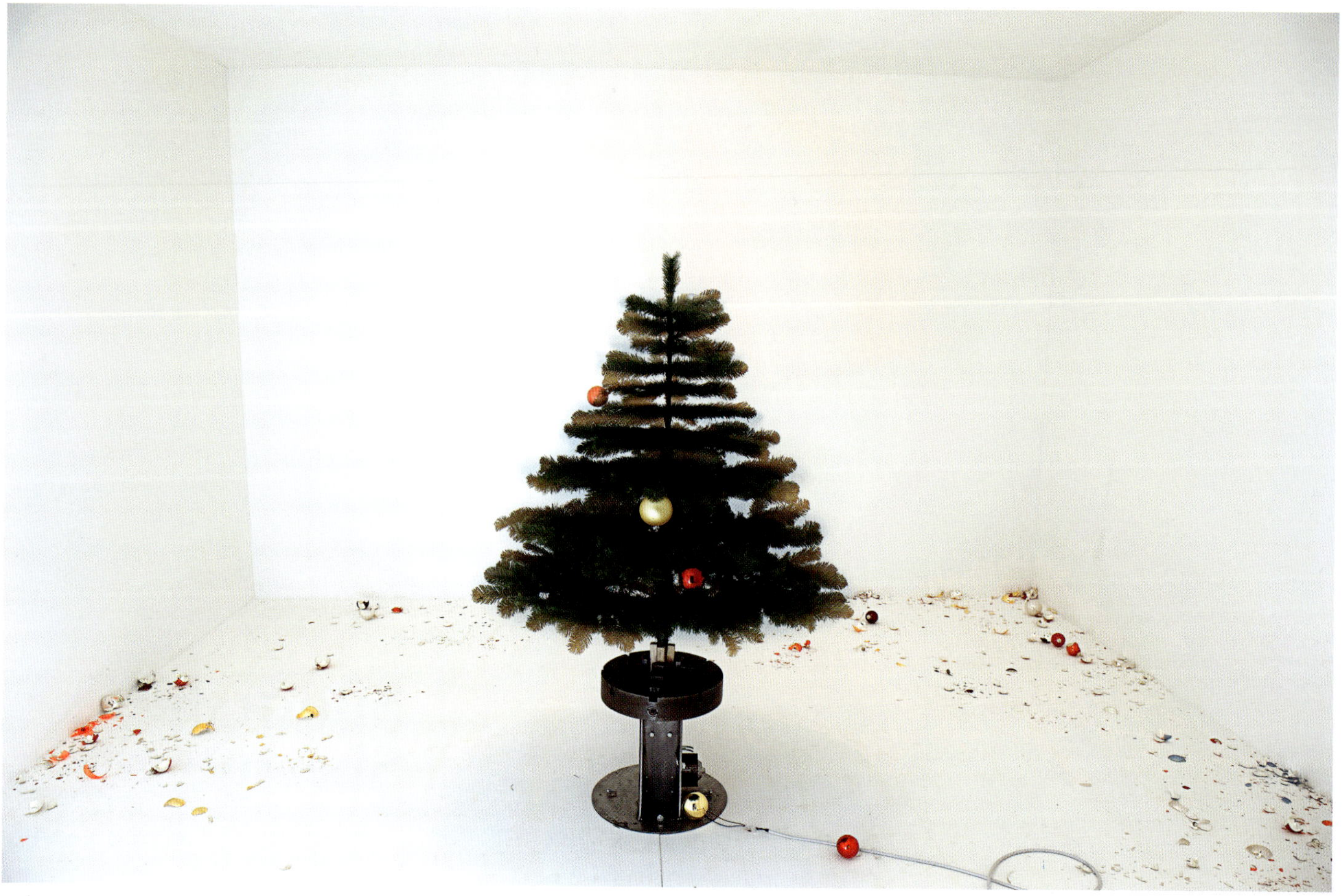

1

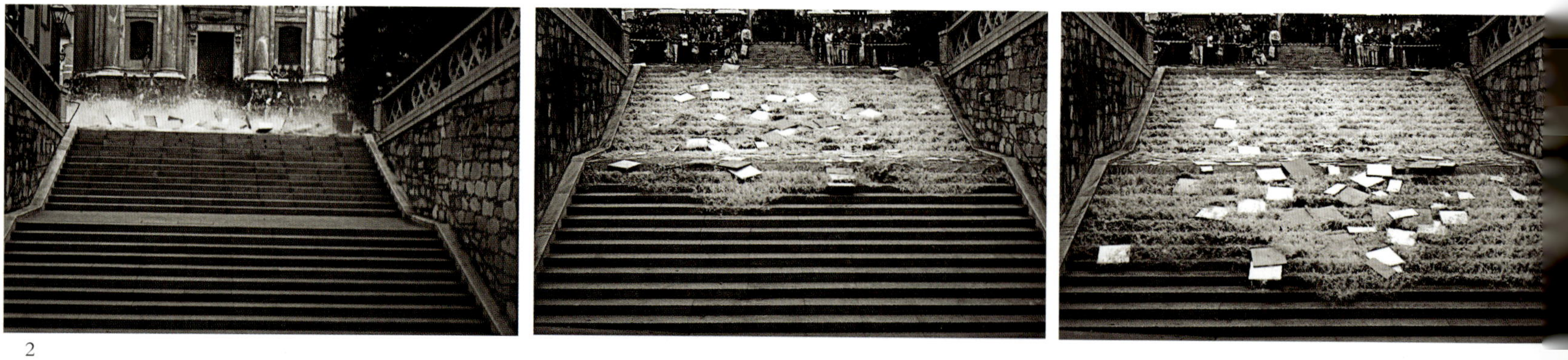

2

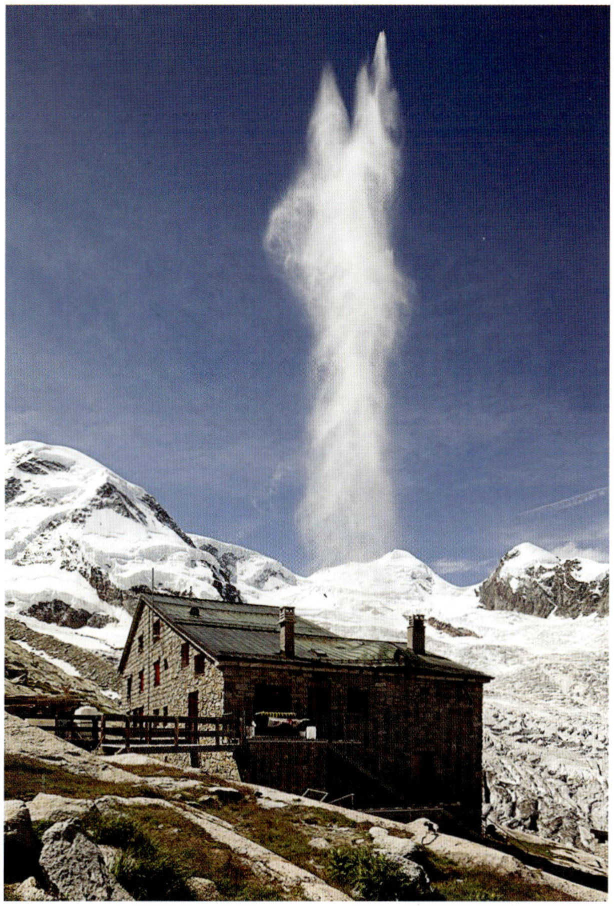

3

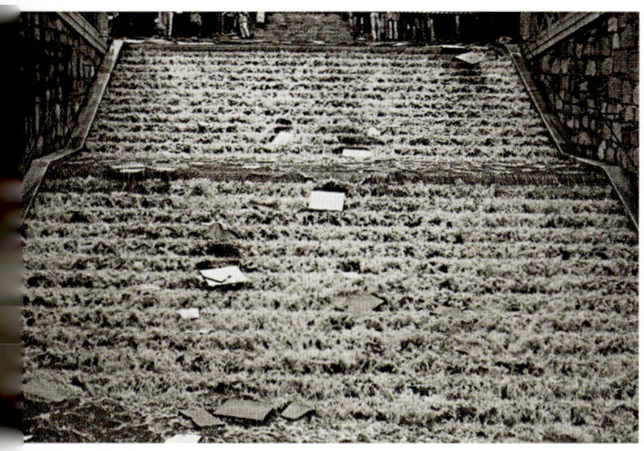

**Shown by**
Hauser & Wirth C8
Galerie Martin Janda G10
Galerie Barbara Weiss G1

**Biography**
Born 1938
Lives in St Gallen

Swiss artist Signer has recently presented solo shows at venues such as HAB Gallery, Nantes (2012), Sala de Arte Público Siqueiros, Mexico City (2011), the Swiss Institute, New York (2010), and Palais de Tokyo, Paris (2008). He has participated in group exhibitions that include 'The New Décor', Hayward Gallery, London (2010), and 'The Quick and the Dead', Walker Art Center, Minneapolis (2009). His forthcoming solo exhibition at Galerie Martin Janda, Vienna, runs from November 2012 until January 2013.

1
*Zimmer mit Weihnachtsbaum*
(Room with Christmas Tree)
2010
Installation
Dimensions variable
Courtesy of Galerie Martin Janda

2
*Aktion mit 48 Kisten, Graz*
(Action with 48 Boxes, Graz)
1993
4 photographs
Each 30 × 45 cm
Courtesy of Galerie Martin Janda

3
*Monte Rosa*
2011
Photograph
59 × 39 cm
Courtesy of Galerie Martin Janda

# Roman Signer

'Laughing is useless. ... There is no reason to laugh in the moment. I laugh after actually.' Thus Roman Signer, whose 'momentary sculptures'—known to his audience mostly as photographs, films and videos—are of a piece with the truth of slapstick: authentic comedy is a matter of deadpan attention to detail, not antic or haphazard japery. In *Cap with Rocke*t (1983) a firework whips a knitted hat from the artist's head; in *Stool – Kurhaus Weissbad* (1992) a four-legged stool is blasted out of a window. There are explosions and spectacles aplenty in Signer's work—bursts of flame and smoke, water spurting from boots and crashing cars—but a quality of sculptural stillness too, and wry precision. BD

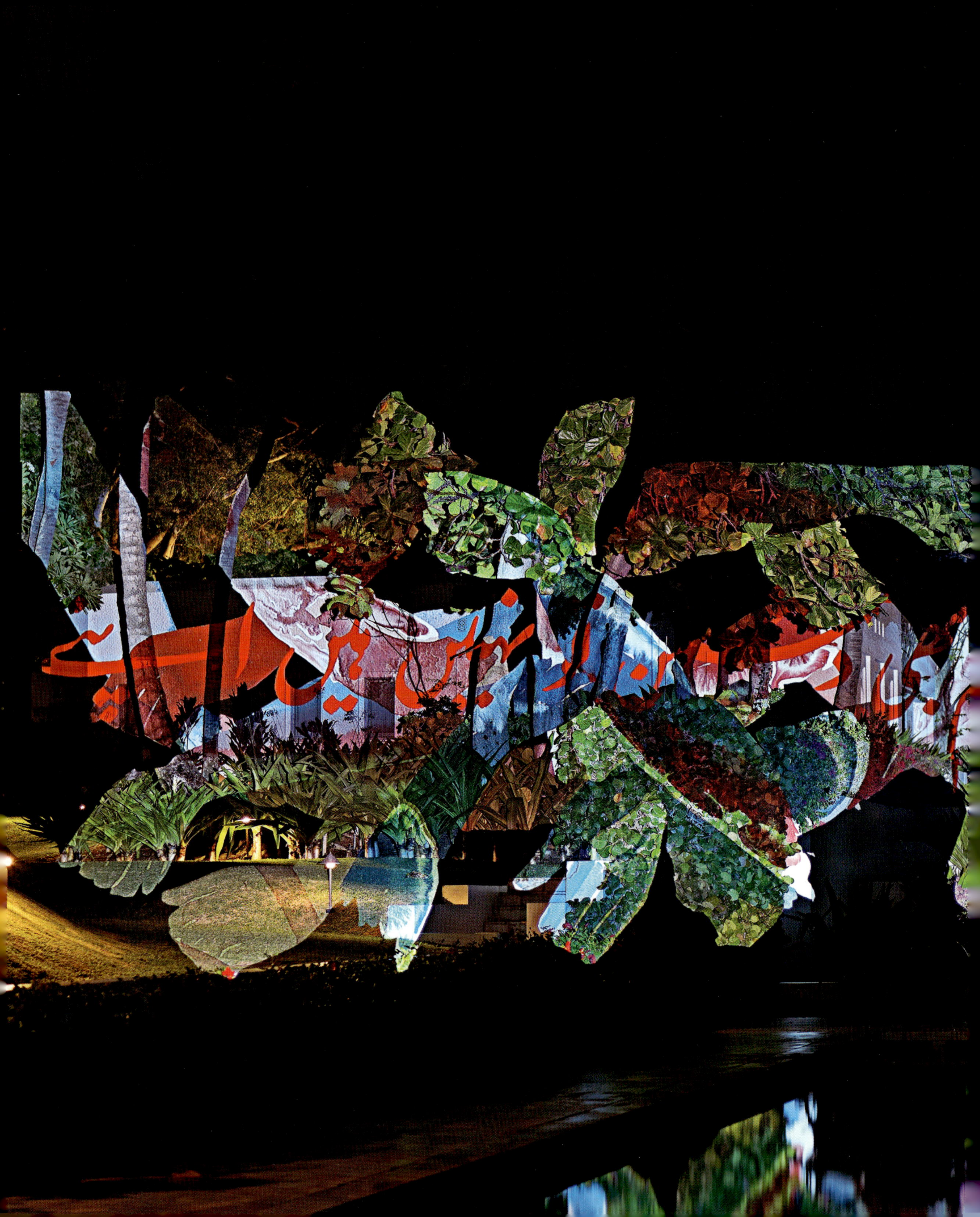

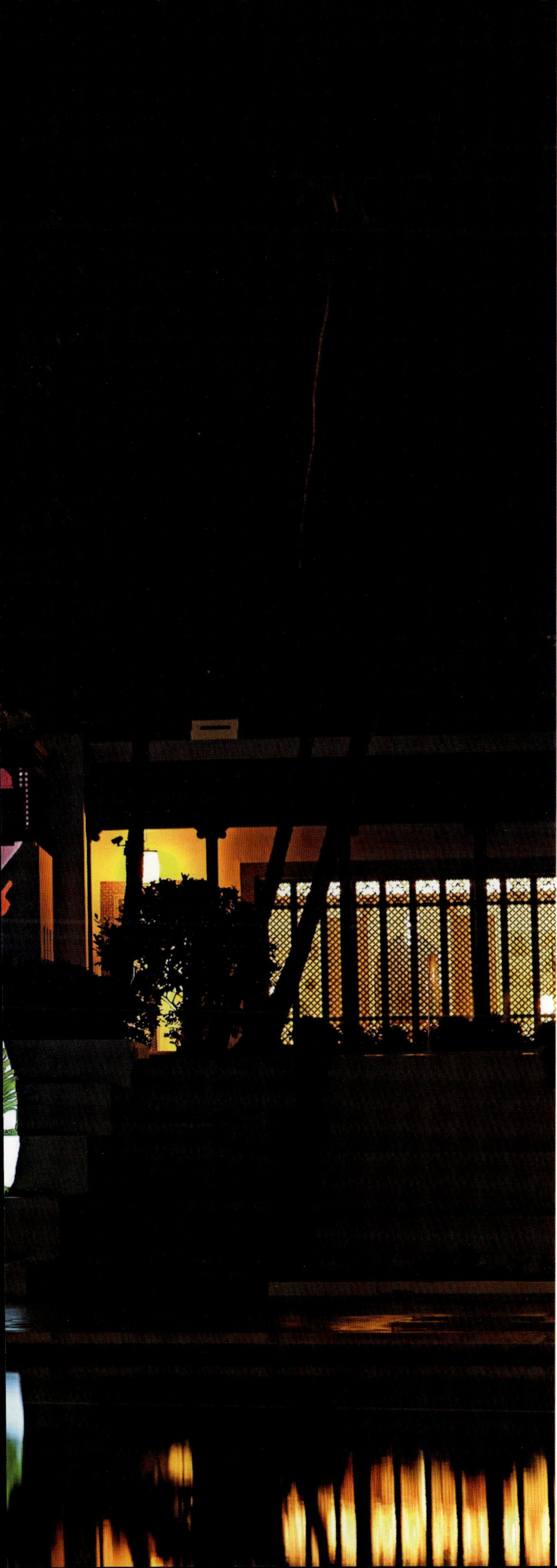

**Shown by**
Pilar Corrias Gallery H5

**Biography**
Born 1969
Lives in New York

Pakistani-born artist Sikander has been the subject of solo exhibitions at institutions such as the San Francisco Art Institute (2011), Museum of Contemporary Art, Tokyo (2010), and Museum of Contemporary Art, Sydney (2007). She participated in the 54th Venice Biennale (2011) and won the SCMP Art Futures Award at the Hong Kong International Art Fair in 2010. Her work is part of collections including MoMA, New York, and the Museum of Contemporary Art, Los Angeles. Until January 2013 her work is featured as part of 'Doris Duke's Shangri La: Architecture, Landscape and Islamic Art', Museum of Arts and Design, New York.

From the series 'Unseen'
2011
HD projections at ShangriLa, Honolulu
Courtesy of Pilar Corrias Gallery

# Shahzia Sikander

Shahzia Sikander's referential leitmotif is the Indo-Persian tradition of miniature painting, in which she trained at the Lahore Academy of Arts. Sikander's drawings and paintings, which can be as small as a sheet of paper or fill an entire wall, represent worlds of exquisite detail, where jewel-toned figures mix and mingle with the calligraphic written word. Sikander updates the miniature tradition both formally, by citing its imagery and textual symbolism in animations and video works, and thematically, by focusing on contemporary issues and themes. The latter is most evident in *Bending the Barrels* (2009), a video that raises the spectres of local and geopolitical conflict by linking the miniature tradition to military pageantry in the artist's native Pakistan. VSR

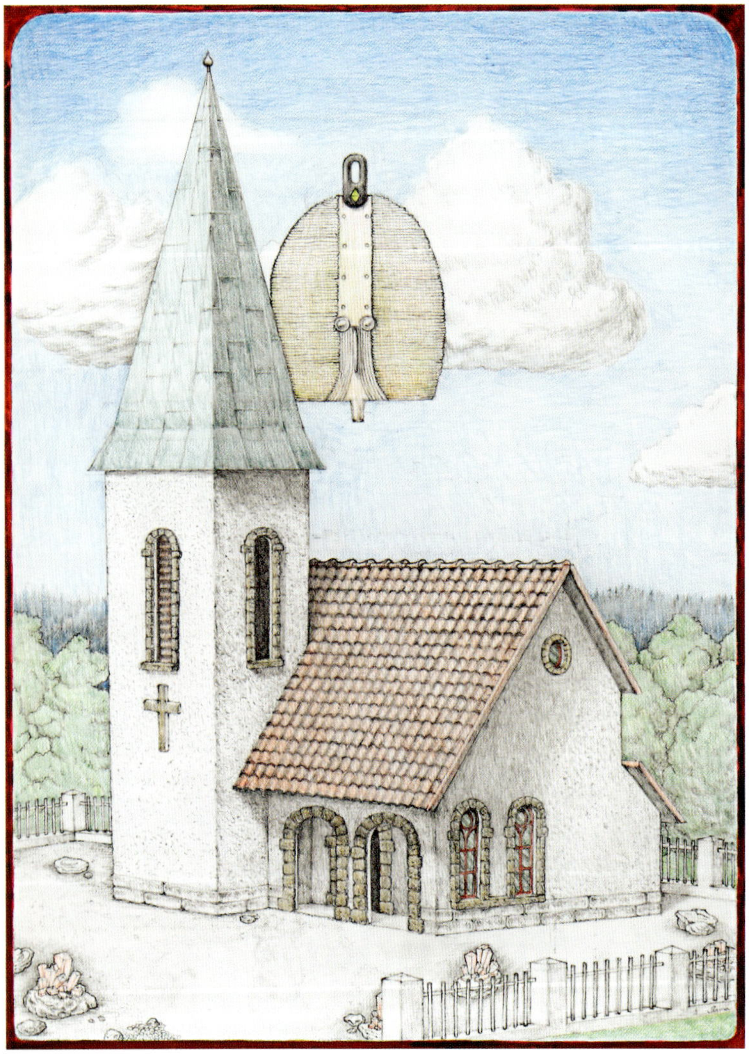

1

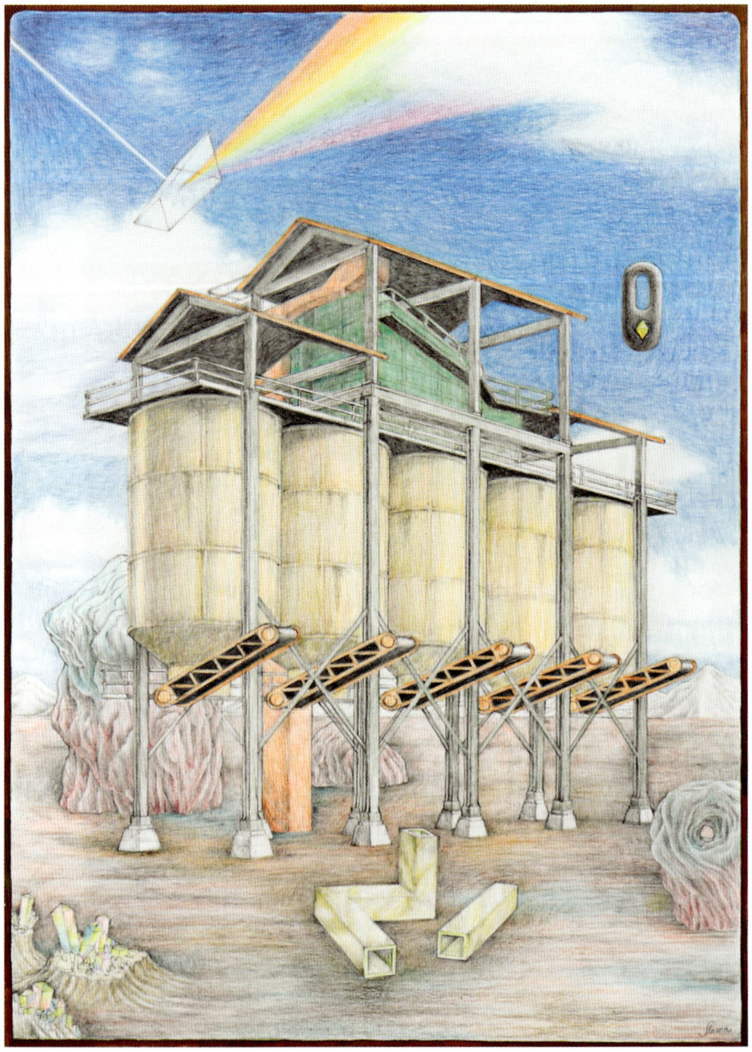

2

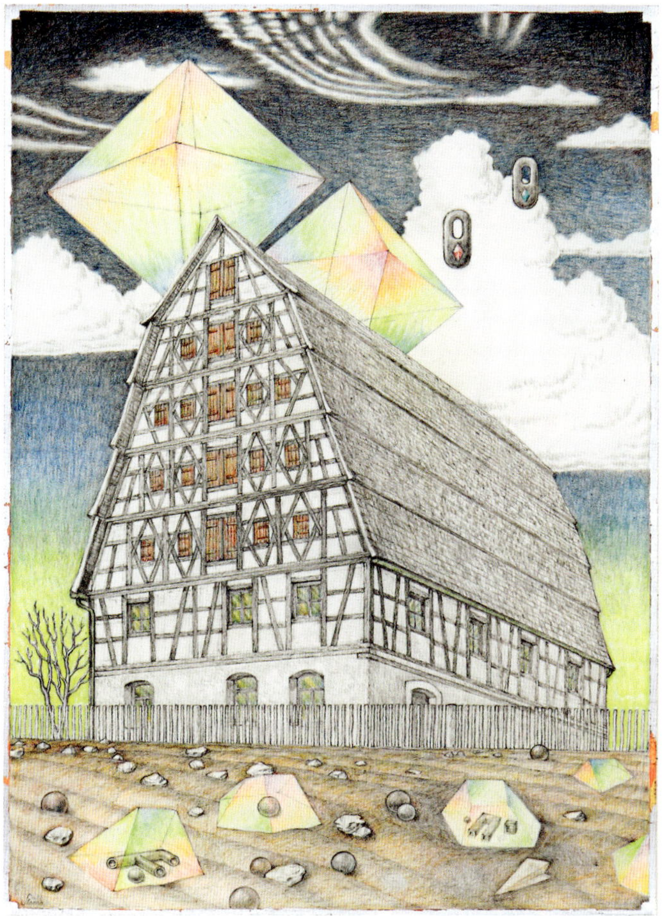

3

**Shown by**
Hotel F5
Kimmerich S17

**Biography**
Born 1967

German-based Austrian-born Slama has presented solo exhibitions recently at galleries such as Kimmerich, New York (2012), Gallery Luis Campaña, Berlin (2010), and Museum of Contemporary Art, Houston (2009). Group shows include 'Private Future', Marc Jancou Contemporary, New York (2011), 'KölnSkulptur 5: Reality Check', Skulpturenpark, Cologne (2009), and 'The Present Order is the Disorder of the Future', Museum de Hallen, Haarlem (2007). His work is part of collections such as MoMA, New York.

1
*Eufrican House of Worship*
2012
Pencil and coloured pencil on paper
42 × 30 cm
Courtesy of Kimmerich

2
*Gravel Preparation Unit with Gold Plated Ultharian Square Tubing Sculpture in the Foreground*
2012
Pencil and coloured pencil on paper
42 × 30 cm
Courtesy of Kimmerich

3
*Schwabach Storehouse for Light Goods (Spalt, Bezirksamt Schwabach)*
2012
Pencil and coloured pencil on paper
42 × 30 cm
Courtesy of Kimmerich

# Focus
# Torsten Slama

A group of coloured-pencil drawings from Torsten Slama's 2012 exhibition 'New Directions in Space Planning (With a Free Gift from the Schessmanweil Powers)' at New York gallery Kimmerich depicted the various Germanic buildings—including a church, sinister half-timbered houses and a silo—supposedly situated on a planet orbiting the star in the Cassiopeia constellation discovered by the Danish nobleman–astronomer Tycho Brahe in 1572. Although the cloudy skies and forested landscapes of this alien world seemed uncannily Earth-like, no humanoid life forms seemed to inhabit them. Instead pill forms, amulets, crystals and rainbow-beam rays floated around this architectural purgatory as if malevolent Wall-E-like robots. Slama has explained: 'in my mind, they are technological placentas, feeding the uteral housings, while the various metal objects are mere drops of sperm.' MA

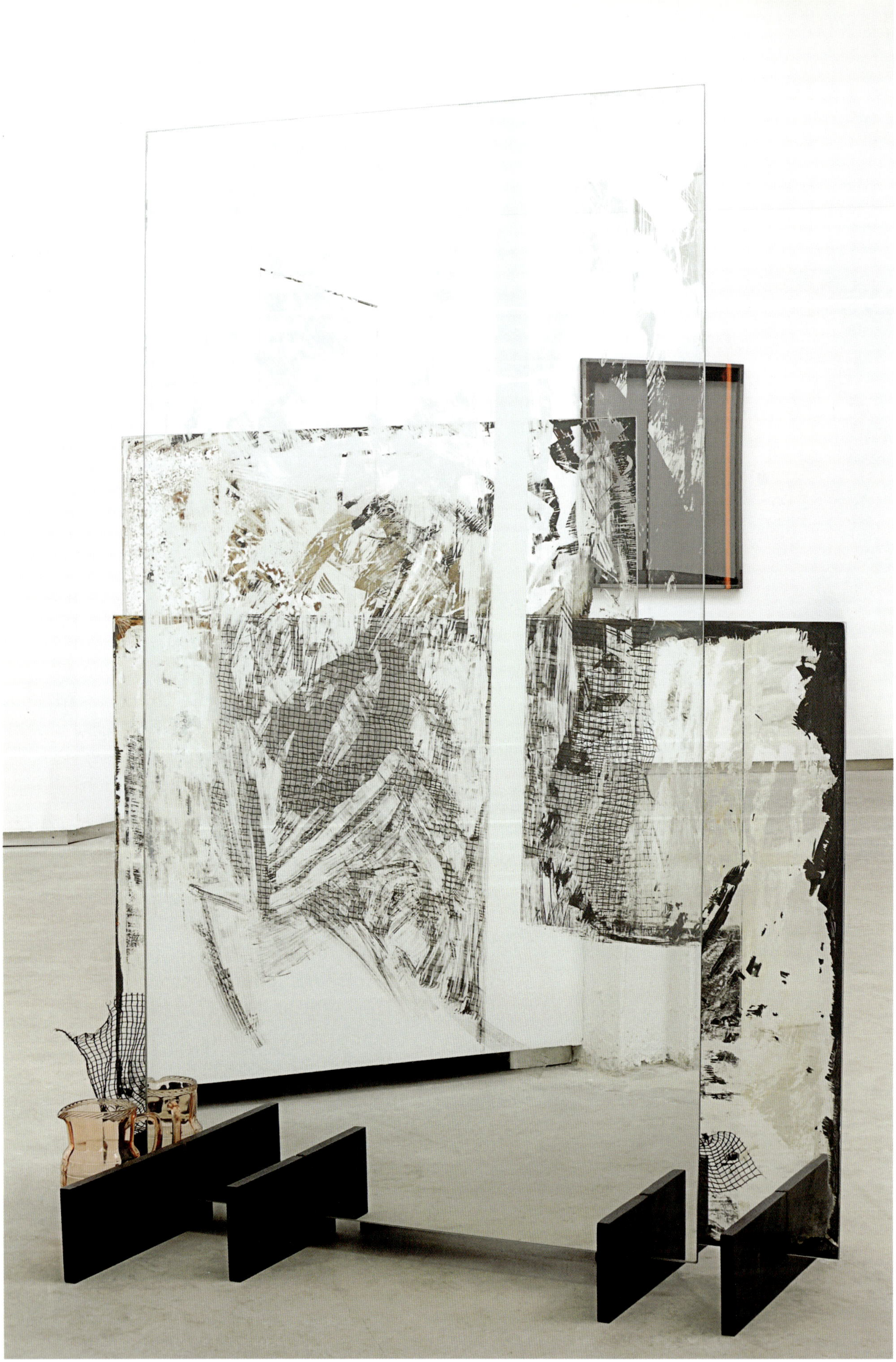

1

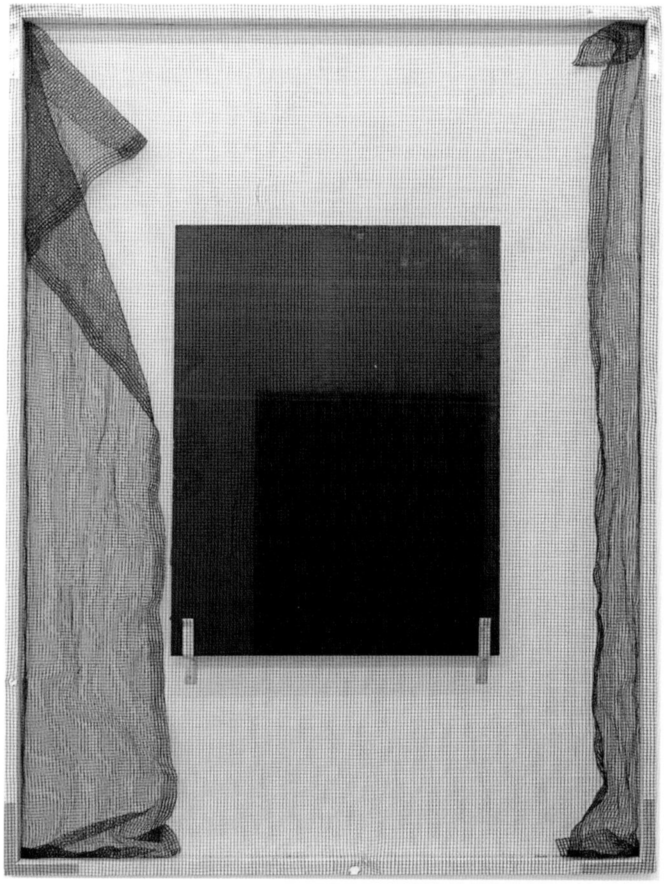

2

**Shown by**
Galerie Catherine Bastide G2

**Biography**
Born 1980
Lives in New York

American artist Snobeck has been the subject of solo shows recently at venues including Thomas Duncan Gallery, Los Angeles (2012), Galerie Catherine Bastide, Brussels (2011), and the University of Delaware, Newark (2011). In 2011 she was a finalist for Prix Sciences Po Pour L'Art Contemporain, Paris. Her work has been included in group shows such as 'Tax Day News & Smoke', Emily Harvey Foundation, New York (2011), and 'Vide-Poche' (Empty Pocket), Sculpture Center, New York (2011).

1
*Shared Territory*
2011
Mixed media
173 × 126 × 71 cm
Courtesy of Galerie Catherine Bastide

2
*Continually*
2011
Mixed media
244 × 183 × 4 cm
Courtesy of Galerie Catherine Bastide

# Valerie Snobeck

In her mixed-media practice Valerie Snobeck reworks transparent or translucent materials such as stretched and framed netting tinted in mainly subdued hues, and panes of translucent mirror glass with gossamer smudges of metal still clinging their surfaces. *Shared Territory* (2011), with its glinting glass sheets slotted into horizontal wooden feet, is more assertively sculptural due to its free-standing position in space, while the rectangular tiers of mesh that comprise *Continually* (2011) are hung on the wall like a canvas. Snobeck's planar works assert themselves ambiguously as both sculpture and painting but defy our common perception of them as solid, weighty objects. Instead, she invites us to see them differently, as if through the looking-glass. VSR

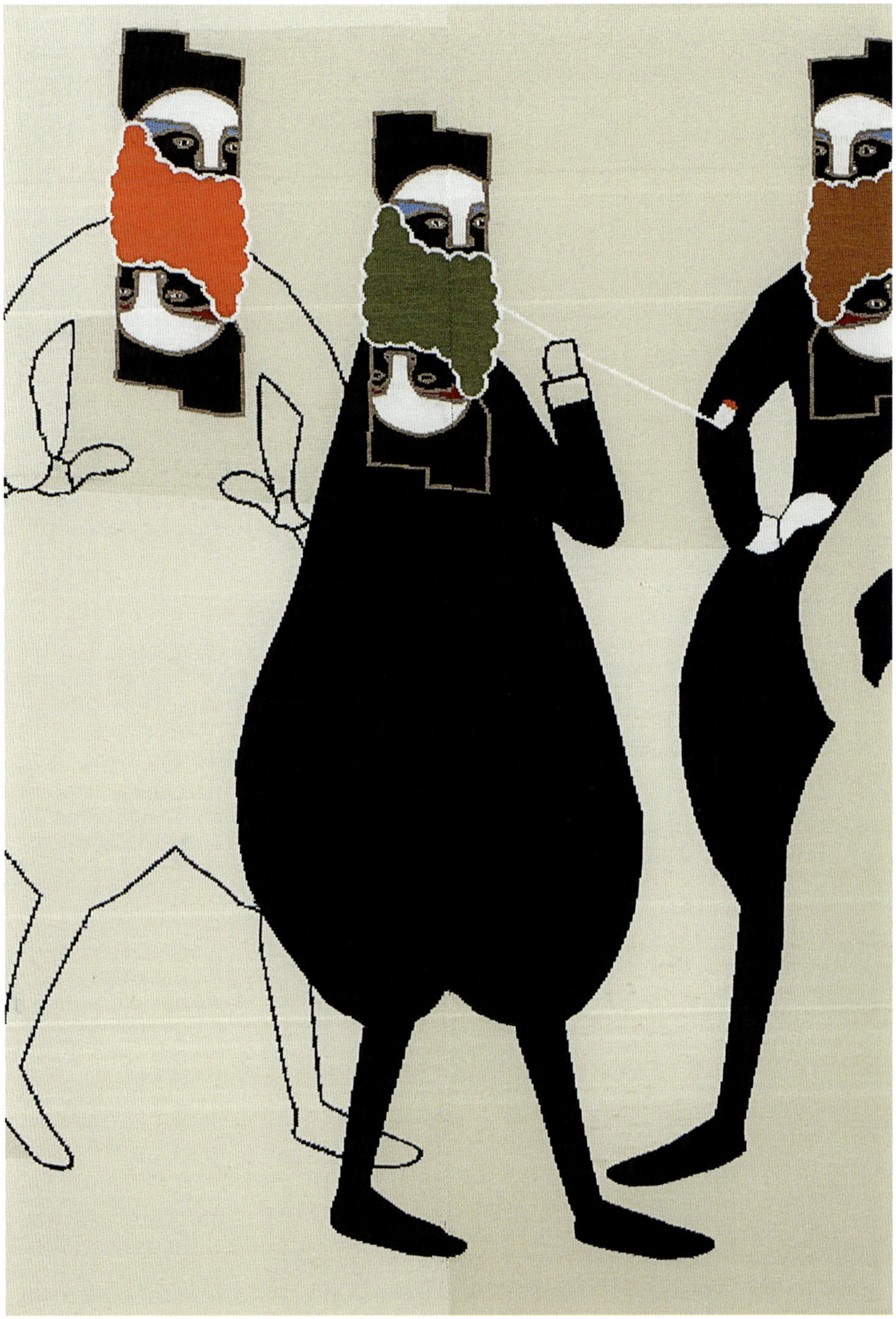

1

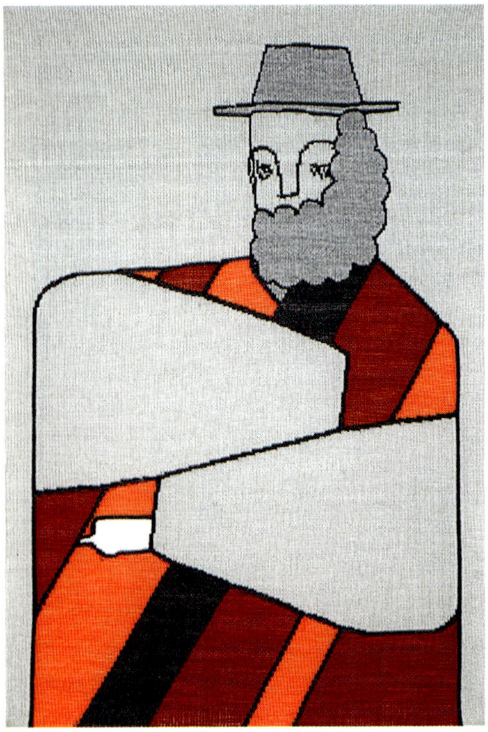

2

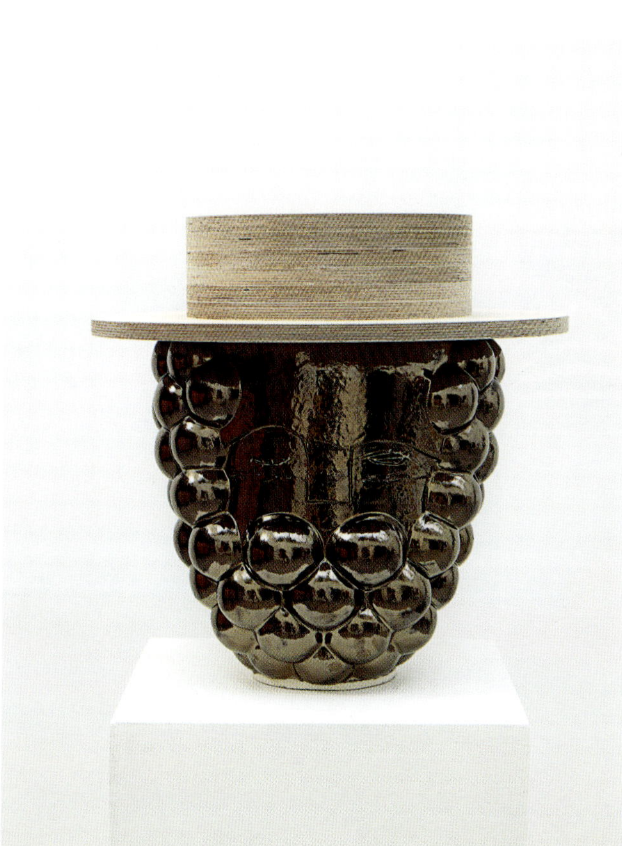



**Shown by**
Kate MacGarry E11

**Biography**
Born 1974
Lives in London

Hong Kong-born So has recently shown solo exhibitions at Kate MacGarry, London (2012 and 2009), Hopkinson Cundy, Auckland (2011), and Uplands Gallery, Melbourne (2010 and 2008). Group exhibitions include 'Newspeak: British Art Now, Part Two', Saatchi Gallery, London (2010), 'Jean-Luc Blanc: Opera Rock', CAPC Musée d'Art Contemporain de Bordeaux (2009), and 'Family Resemblance', Centre for Contemporary Photography, Melbourne (2006).

1
*The Pipe*
2012
Wool and acrylic
184 × 124 cm
Courtesy of Kate MacGarry

2
*Grey Sleeved Man*
2012
Wool and acrylic
93 × 63 cm
Courtesy of Kate MacGarry

3
*Bellarmine X*
2012
Glazed ceramic and birch plywood
47 × 50 × 50 cm
Courtesy of Kate MacGarry

# Renee So

Renee So's gravitation towards ceramics and knitting suggest a craftperson's sensibility, and this is reflected, in some strange distorting mirror, in her imagery too. Bearded, double-headed men in ballooning pantaloons, sporting long-stemmed pipes, hats and canes, resonate with stylistic folk particularities from diverse but eerily related eras, from *Yellow Submarine* to picture playing cards to decadent masked balls to Roman statuary. References to the Bellarmine, a 16th-century drinking cup, bring a bawdy aspect to the work and accentuate So's mischief with forms and materials: a pair of voluminous sleeves or a pipe become graphic devices, while a boater jammed on the head of *Bellarmine X* (2012) weighs heavy in plywood. SOR

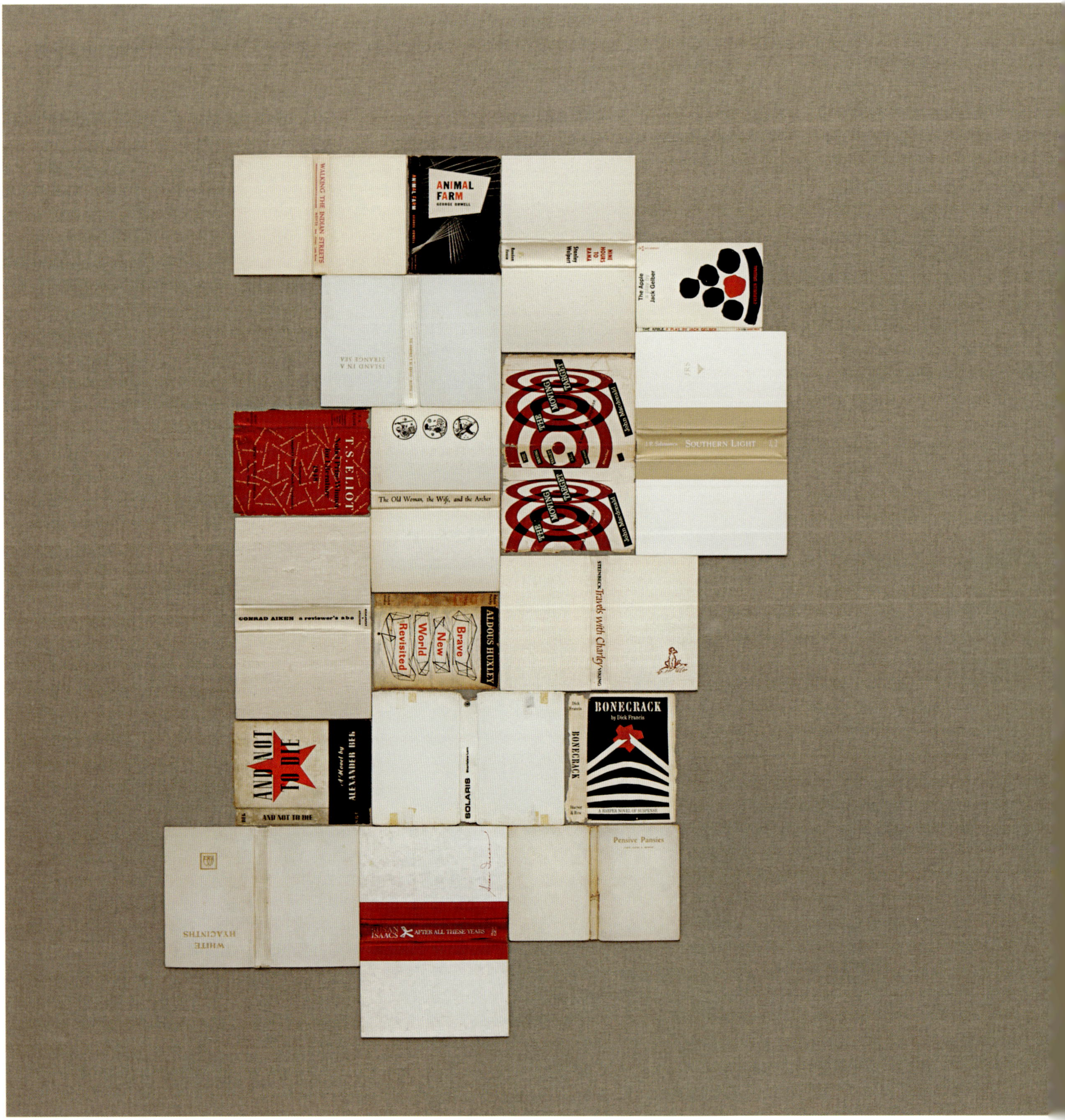
WALKING THE INDIAN STREETS
ANIMAL FARM
GEORGE ORWELL
NINE HOURS TO RAMA
Stanley Wolpert
The Apple
Jack Gelber
ISLAND IN A STRANGE SEA
T. S. ELIOT
THE MOVING TARGET
John Macdonald
SOUTHERN LIGHT
The Old Woman, the Wife, and the Archer
CONRAD AIKEN a reviewer's abc
Brave New World Revisited
ALDOUS HUXLEY
STEINBECK Travels with Charley VIKING
AND NOT TO DIE
A Novel by ALEXANDER BEK
SOLARIS
BONECRACK
by Dick Francis
A HARPER NOVEL OF SUSPENSE
Pensive Pansies
WHITE HYACINTHS
SUSAN ISAACS AFTER ALL THESE YEARS

# Valeska Soares

**Shown by**
Galeria Fortes Vilaça E8

**Biography**
Born 1957
Lives in New York

Born in Belo Horizonte, Brazil, Soares has recently been the subject of solo exhibitions at venues such as Galeria Fortes Vilaça, Sao Paulo (2012), Timothy Taylor Gallery, London (2011), Netherlands Funeral Museum, Amsterdam (2011), and Greenberg Van Doren Gallery, New York (2010). Her work is part of public collections including: the Solomon R. Guggenheim Museum, New York; Hirshhorn Museum and Sculpture Garden, Washington DC; the Tate collection, UK; and MACBA, Barcelona.

*The Moving Target (From Bindings)*
2012
Antique dust-jackets and hardcovers on linen
183 × 259 × 4 cm
Courtesy of Galeria Fortes Vilaça

Like the works of Felix Gonzalez-Torres Valeska Soares' sensitive, sculptural series often take the form of the Minimalist pile or an abstracted horizon of objects, wandering their poetic way across your line of vision. Yet her works mostly have a decidedly literary origin: see her suggestive series 'Bindings' (2012), in which the artist arranges old editions of books in lithe and retro geometric assemblages across linen, painting-like panels. Her interest in the materiality of books can also be discerned in works such as *Timeline I* (2010), which features a long wire hung with the title-pages of various volumes. If her hanging Brazilian cigar boxes writ with tropical *mises-en-scène* (*Horizontes III*, 2009) and parades of light bulbs also take on themes of language and seriality, they are only less literal explorations of her larger narrative concerns. QL

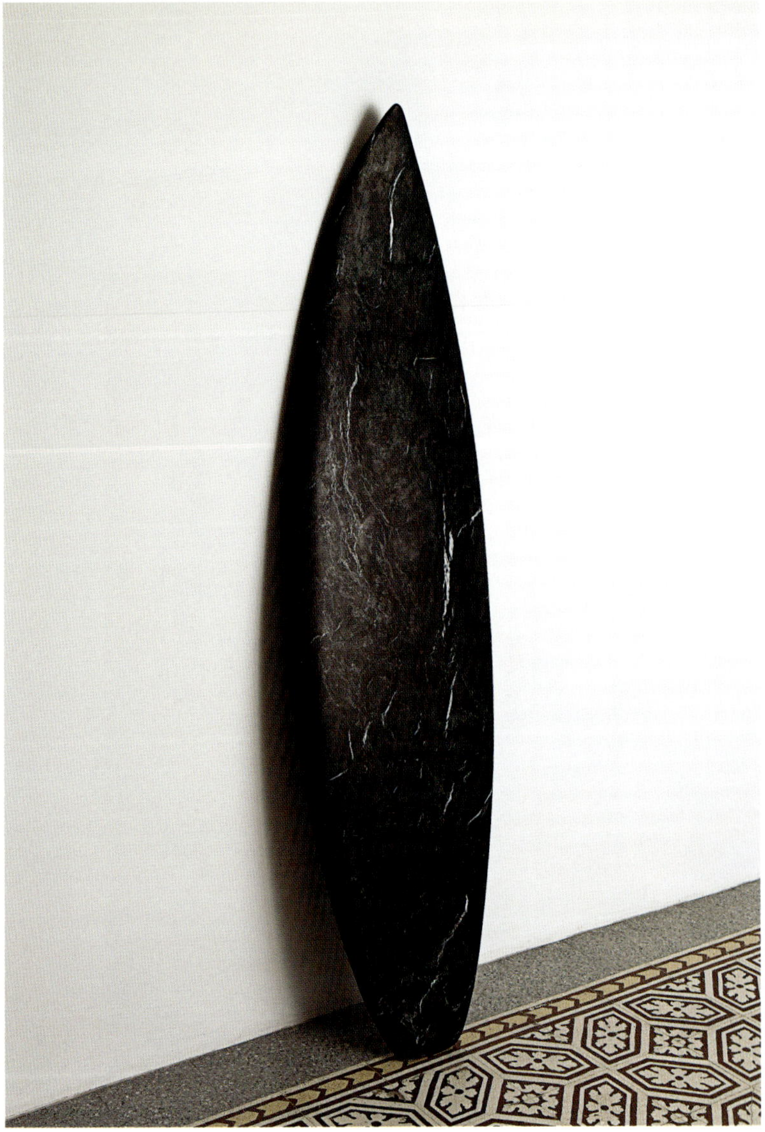

1

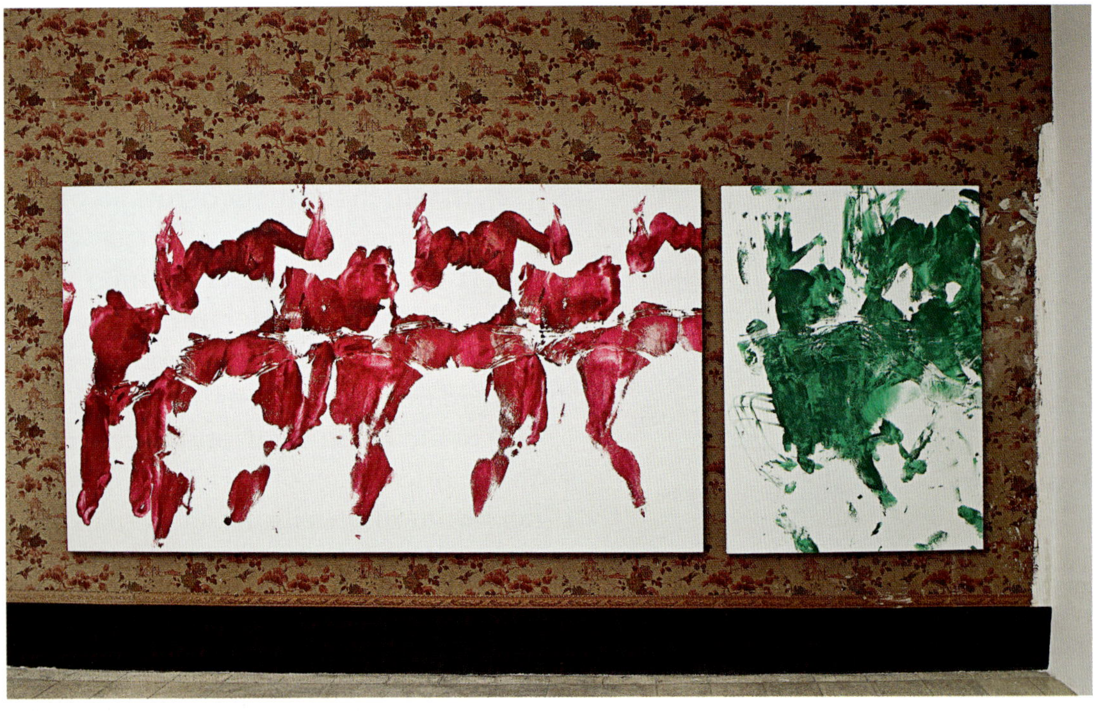

2

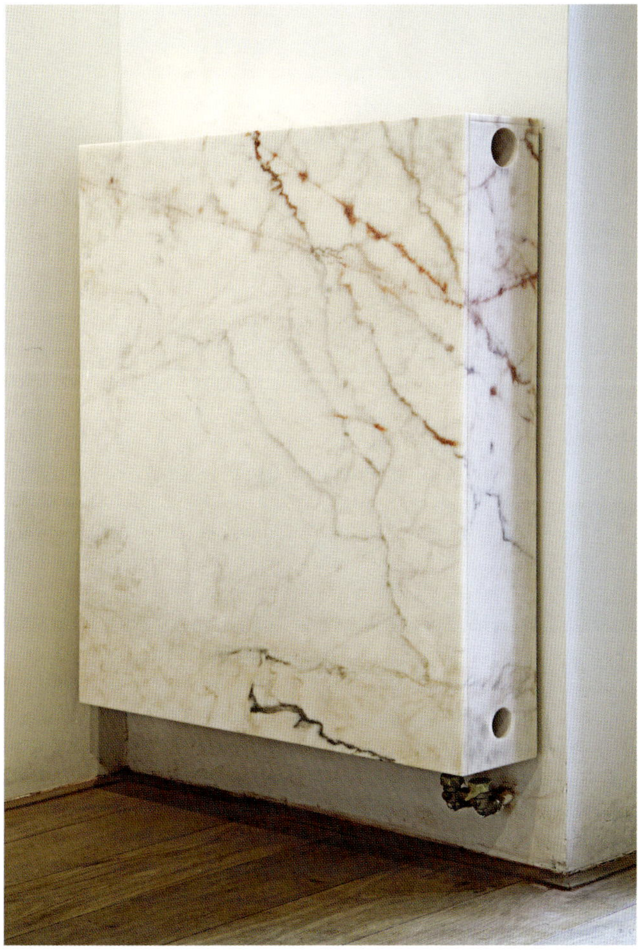

3

**Shown by**
Campoli Presti F5
Galerie Chantal Crousel D11
Galerie Meyer Kainer F2

**Biography**
Founded 2004
Based in New York

New York collective Reena Spaulings developed in 2004 from art gallery Reena Spaulings Fine Art, founded by John Kelsey and Emily Sundblad. Recent solo exhibitions include those at Indipendenza Studio, Rome (2011), Contemporary Art Museum St Louis (2008) and Kunsthalle Zurich (2007). Spaulings' work is part of the public collections of MoMA, New York, and FRAC, Aquitaine.

1
*Mollusk (Verde Nuvolato)*
2011
Verde nuvolato marble
199 × 52 cm
Courtesy of Campoli Presti

2
'More Michael Paintings'
2011–12
Exhibition view at Indipendenza Studio, Rome
Courtesy of Campoli Presti

3
*Radiator 3*
2009
Rosa portagallo marble
90 × 80 × 16 cm
Courtesy of Campoli Presti

# Reena Spaulings

Tracing the art world's economic networks and geographic displacements, the fictional artist Reena Spaulings, an international collective spawned by an actual New York gallery, creates slippery abstractions and narratives from artists, dealers, galleries, money, and even fairs and dinners. The 'Michael Paintings' (2011) resurrect works by Yves Klein, but with a male critic as the human paintbrush. A collector who owns a quarry and marble company collaborated on works including *Mollusk (Verde Nuvolato)* (2011), a mussel-like, Brancusi-esque marble surfboard, and *Radiator 3* (2009), a marble simulacrum of a heating unit removed to make way for art. Forming a ghostly palimpsest, the series 'A Place in the Sun (Shadows)' (2009) combines shadows of palm trees photographed during Art Basel Miami Beach with signatures from a sign-in book. KMJ

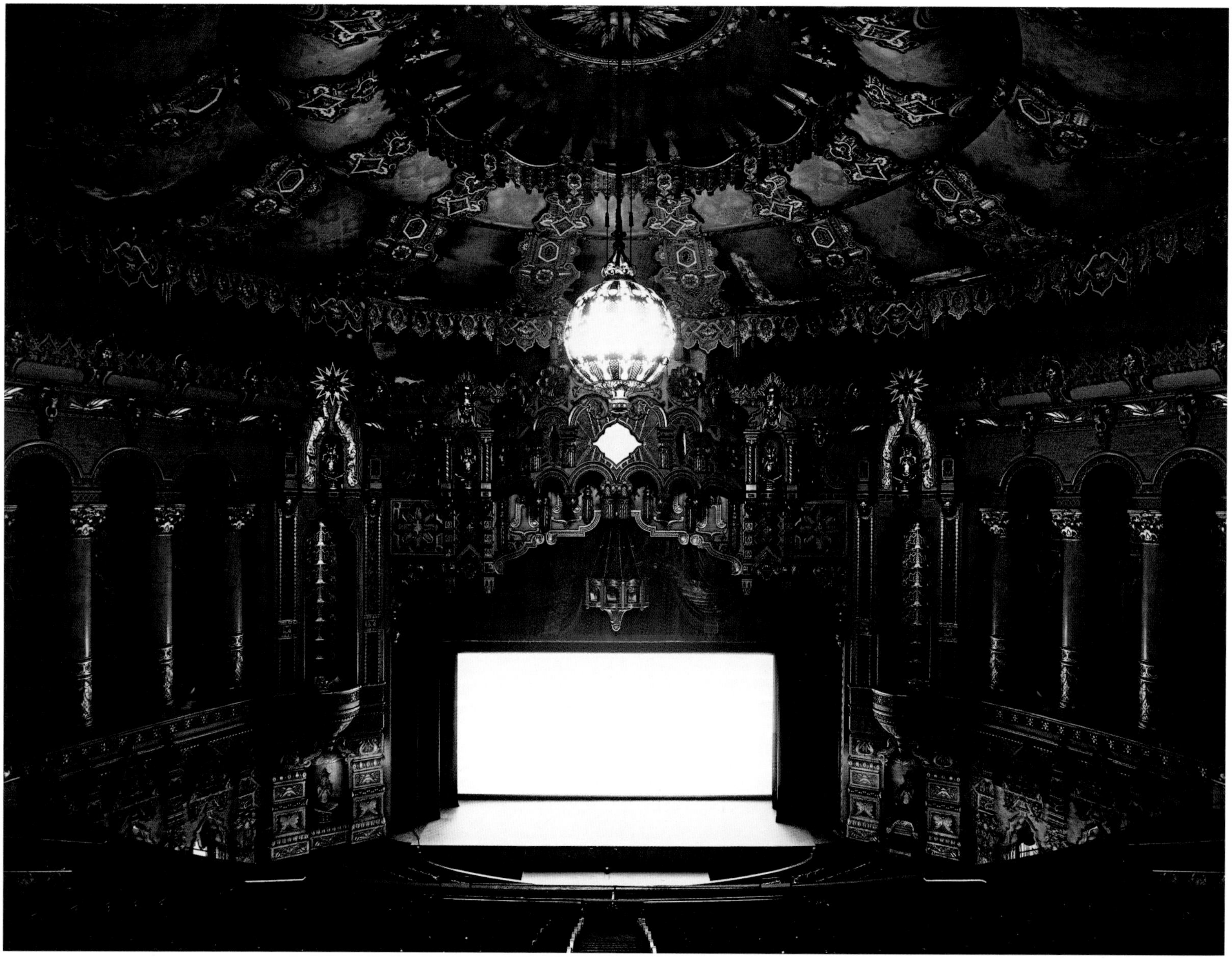

1

# Hiroshi Sugimoto

For Hiroshi Sugimoto photography is both a subject of philosophical speculation and a conceptual tool. While his 'Theatres' series (1978–ongoing), shot in a number of elaborate cinemas, uses long exposures to capture an entire film in a single photographic frame, his recent 'Lighting Fields' series (2008–ongoing) dispenses with the lens altogether. Here he uses a Van de Graaff generator to expose forked bolts of electricity onto photographic plates, in what he has described as an attempt to 'recreate the major discoveries of [...] scientific pioneers in the darkroom and verify them with my own eyes'. In each of these series Sugimoto reduces photography to its essentials—time and light—and demands we rethink the medium anew. TM

**Shown by**
Pace G8

**Biography**
Born 1948
Lives in New York

Tokyo-born Sugimoto has been the subject of solo exhibitions over the last decade at institutions that include the Hara Museum of Contemporary Art, Tokyo (2012), Scottish National Gallery of Modern Art, Edinburgh (2011), Neue Nationalgalerie, Berlin (2008), Arthur M. Sackler Gallery and the Freer Gallery of Art, Smithsonian, Washington DC (2006), and the Serpentine Gallery, London (2003). His work is included in public collections such as: the Metropolitan Museum of Art, New York; The Art Institute of Chicago; and Moderna Museet, Stockholm.

1
*Fox, Michigan*
1980
Silver gelatin print
119 × 149 cm
Courtesy of Pace

2
*Lightning Fields 227*
2009
Silver gelatin print
58 × 47 cm
Courtesy of Pace

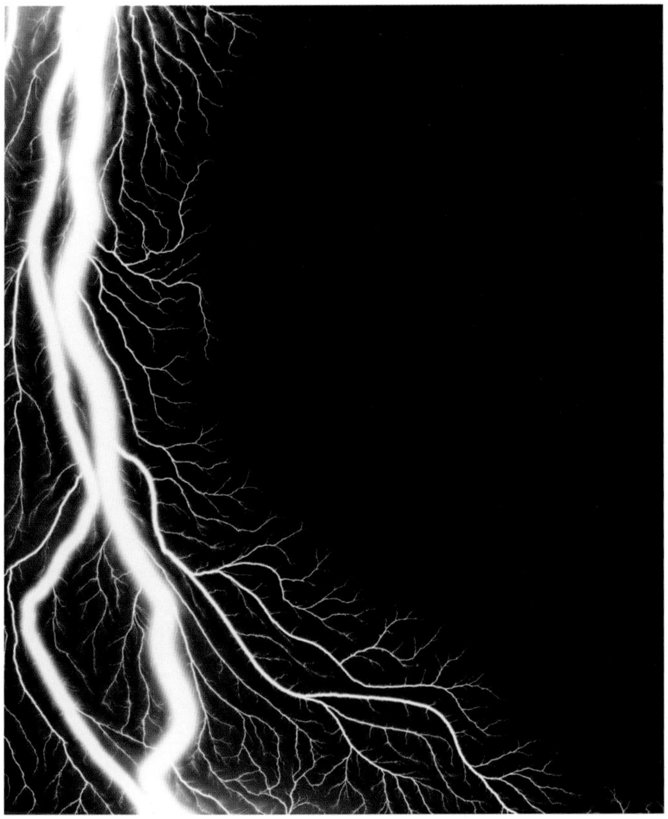

2

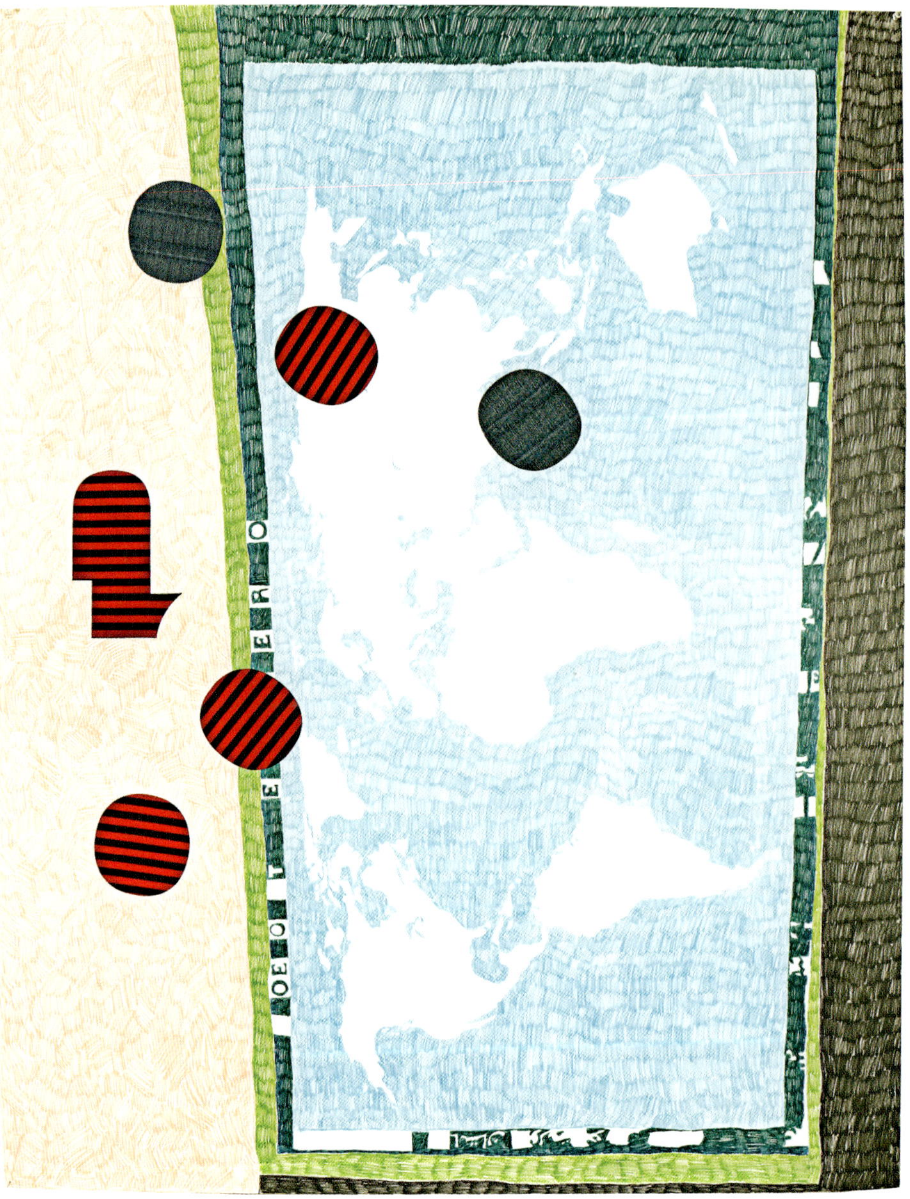

1

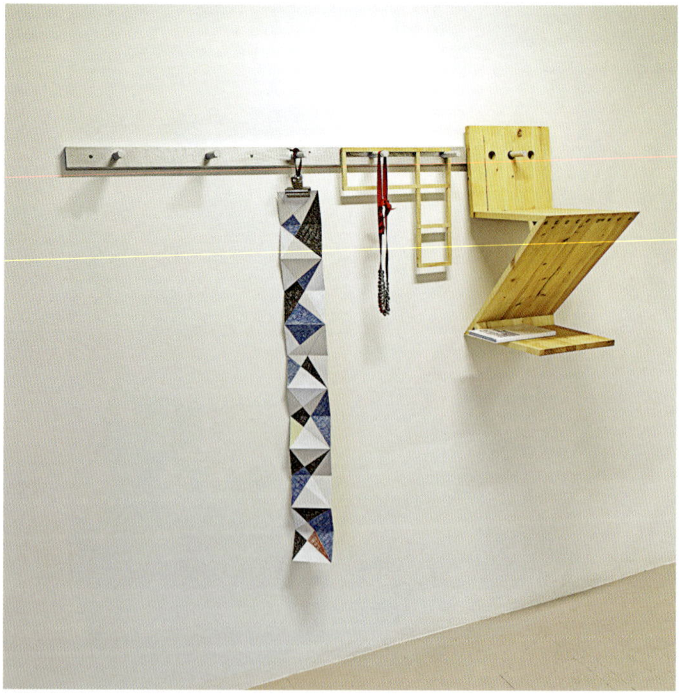

2

# Focus
# Derek Sullivan

The title of Derek Sullivan's 2011 exhibition 'Albatross Omnibus' evoked a compendium of burdensome obligations that can accrue around the act of reading. For Sullivan, the form of the book or habits of reading provoke a larger investigation of how we navigate designated modes of signification. Since 2005, his hand-made 'decoys' of artists' books have raised questions of filiation and affiliation—how we conceive of natural or illegitimate 'genealogical' relations between artists. Elsewhere he has used on-demand printing technologies to pit the artist's real-time alterations against the clock of online commerce. If nearly everything, including a replica of Rietveld's iconic Zig Zag chair, starts to take on the look of a book, it's only because Sullivan makes the book a cipher for so much more. SNS

**Shown by**
Jessica Bradley S4

**Biography**
Born 1976
Lives in Toronto

Canadian artist Sullivan has shown solo exhibitions at galleries such as Galerie Tatjana Pieters, Ghent (2012), Jessica Bradley, Toronto (2011), The Power Plant, Toronto (2011), and University of Waterloo Art Gallery, Ontario (2010). His work has been presented in group shows at venues including the National Gallery of Canada, Ottawa (2012), and the Australian Centre for Contemporary Art, Melbourne (2011). His work was featured in the 7th Biennale de Montréal (2011).

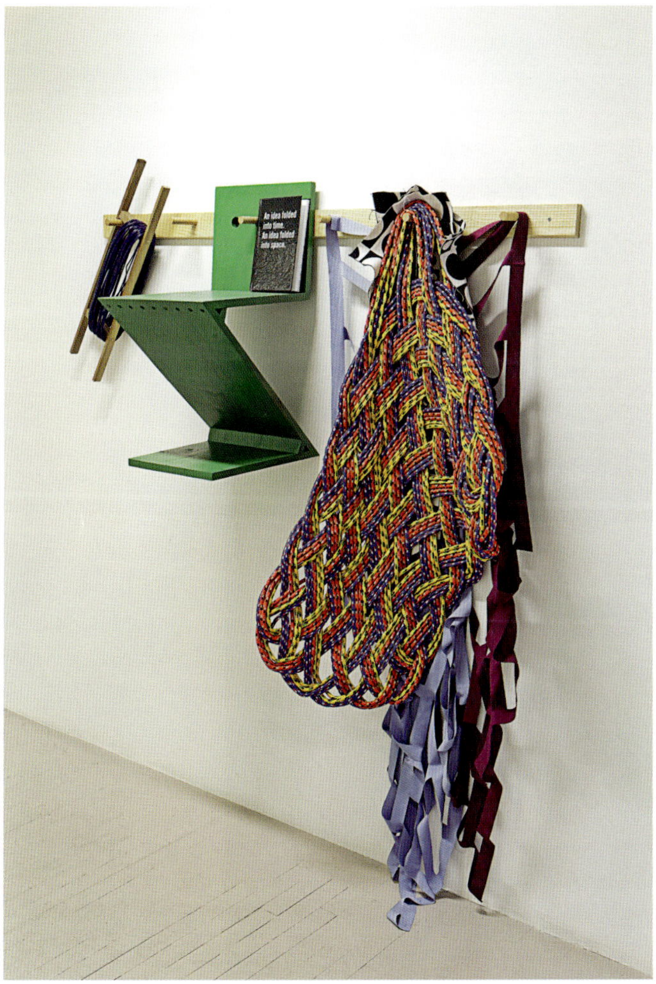

3

1
*#60 Tapestry weaving and television watching*
2010
Coloured pencil on paper
127 × 98 cm
Courtesy of Jessica Bradley

2
*Peg Rail #1 (A turn of 90° is the most that one can change direction without backtracking)*
2011
Mixed media
136 × 155 × 55 cm
Courtesy of Jessica Bradley

3
*Peg Rail #3 (An idea folded into time. An idea folded into space.)*
2011
Mixed media
180 × 153 × 55 cm
Courtesy of Jessica Bradley

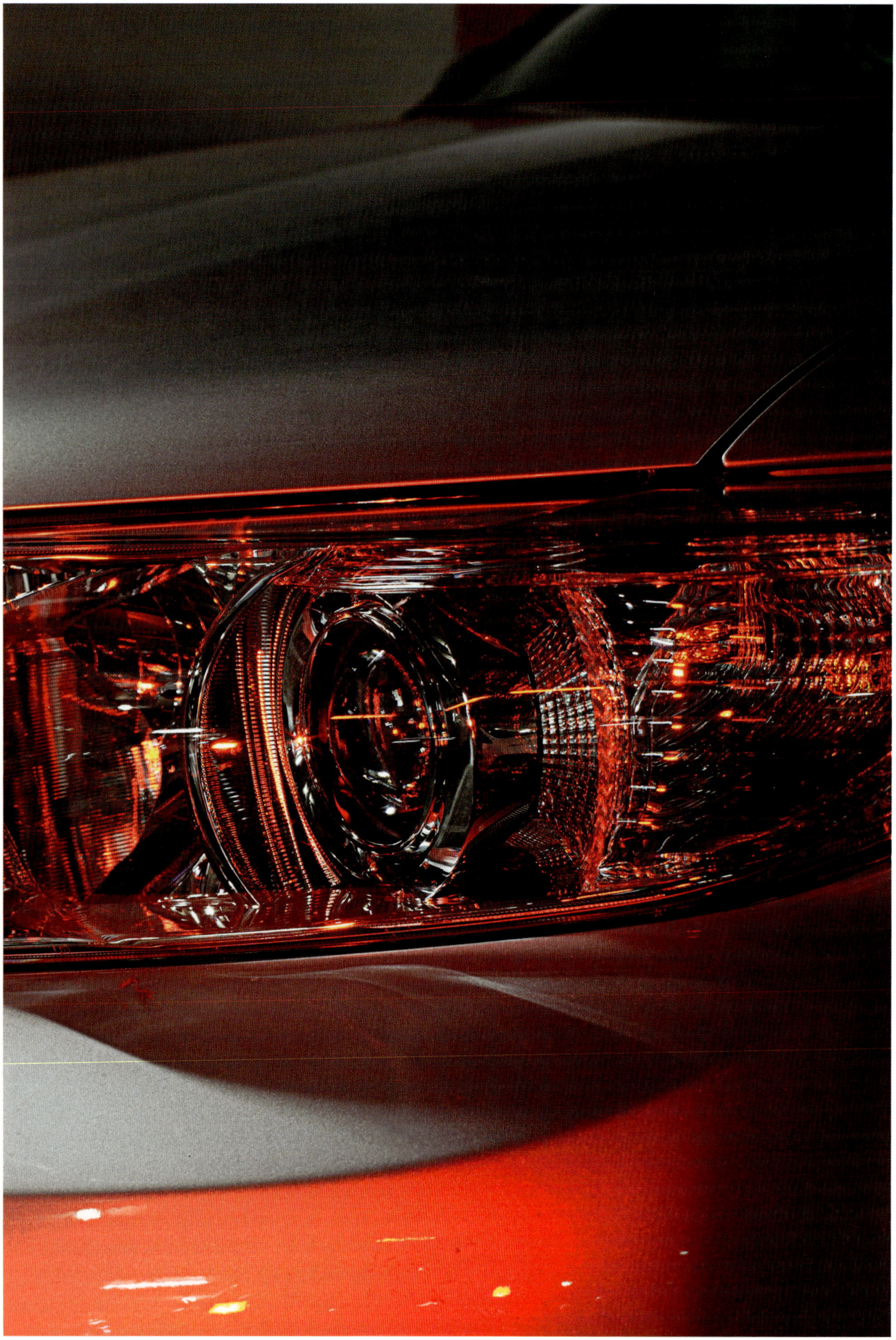

# Wolfgang Tillmans

**Shown by**
Galería Juana de Aizpuru G5
Buchholz C4
Galerie Chantal Crousel D11
Maureen Paley D5
Andrea Rosen Gallery A6
Sommer Contemporary Art E10

**Biography**
Born 1968
Lives in Berlin

German-born Tillmans has presented solo exhibitions at venues that include The Common Guild, Glasgow (2012), Kunsthalle Zurich (2012), Museu de Arte Moderna, Sao Paulo (2012), Zacheta National Gallery of Art, Warsaw (2011), Hirshhorn Museum and Sculpture Garden, Washington DC (2006), MoMA PS1, New York (2006), Tate Britain, London (2003), and Museo Nacional Centro de Arte Reina Sofía, Madrid (1998). His work is part of collections that include: the Solomon R. Guggenheim Museum, New York; Los Angeles County Museum of Art; and Kunstmuseum Basel.

*Headlights (a)*
2012
C-type print
Dimensions variable
Courtesy of Maureen Paley

Wolfgang Tillmans' photography traverses genres, criss-crosses our planet and even looks longingly towards others—as in the saturnine astronomical imagery peppering the placid still lifes and hell-in-a-handcart newspaper clippings of his 2005 installation *Truth Study Centre*. Such diversity is mitigated, though, by Tillmans' tireless revitalising of timeworn modes: jeopardizing authenticity through *faux*-casual portraiture, making an unironed T-shirt redolent of Renaissance drapery—*Faltenwurf (Morgen) II* (Drapery [Morning] II, 2009)—or fashioning celestial-quotidian abstractions from darkroom experiments (e.g., *Freischwimmer 173*, 2011). Whatever unfurling meanings such images have, though, his reshuffling installations seek to unbalance. A successful photograph and how it is presented add up to a storehouse of significations, Tillmans suggests. His practice, equal parts aesthetic and conceptual, is a proliferating primer in how to look for them. MH

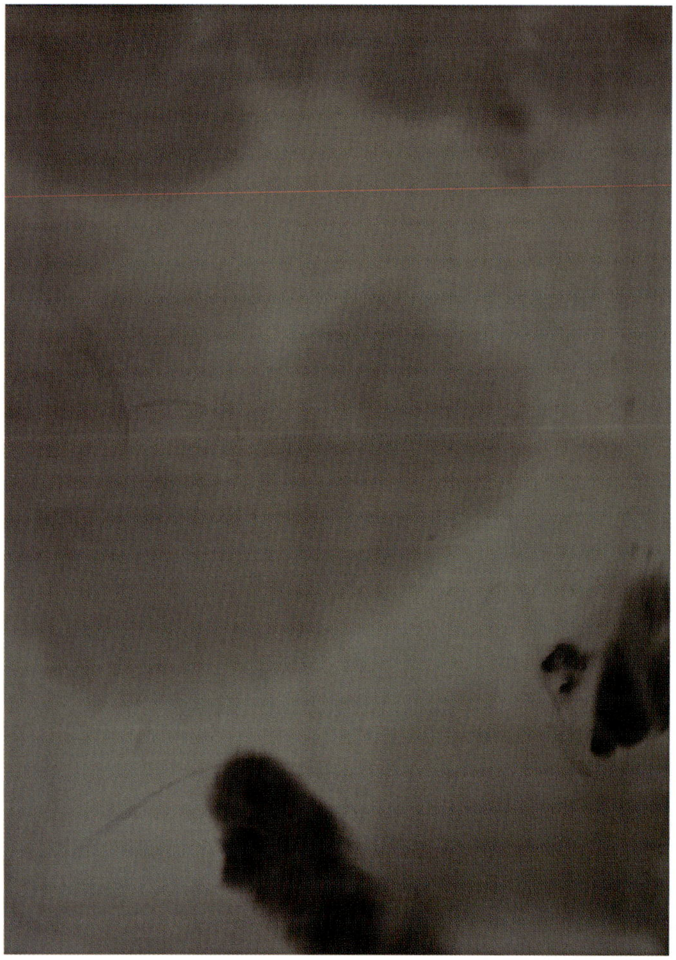

1

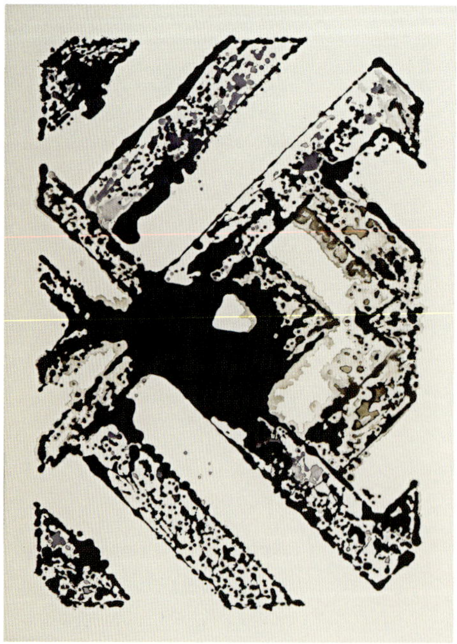

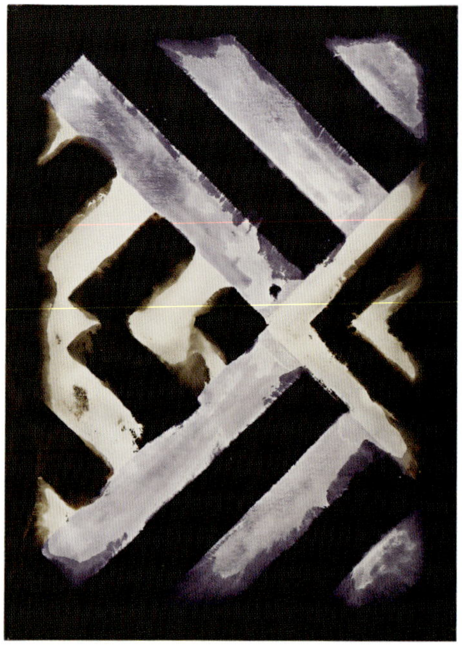

2

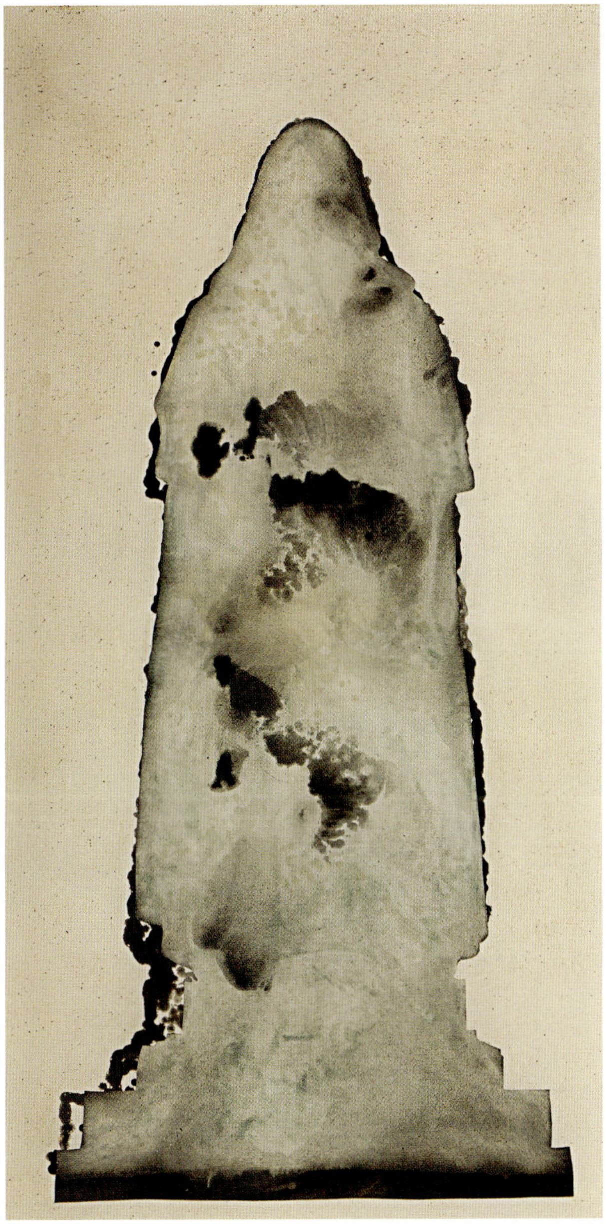

3

**Shown by**
Andrew Kreps Gallery C5
The Modern Institute B12
Galleria Raucci/Santamaria G3

**Biography**
Born 1968
Lives in New York

Northern Irish-born Timoney has been the subject of recent solo exhibitions at Galleria Raucci/Santamaria, Naples (2012 and 2009), The Modern Institute, Glasgow (2012), and Andrew Kreps Gallery, New York (2010). Recent group shows include 'Terminal Convention', Cork International Airport (2011), 'Fade into You', Herald St, London (2010), and 'Frequency', Hugh Lane Gallery, Dublin (2009).

1
*Broken One Way Mirror No. 3*
2009
Rabbit-skin glue and pigments on canvas
196 × 140 cm
Courtesy of Galleria Raucci/Santamaria

2
*Untitled*
2010
Diptych: rabbit-skin glue and sepia ink on canvas
Each 163 × 115 cm
Courtesy of Galleria Raucci/Santamaria

3
*Giordano Bruno No. 2*
2010
Rabbit-skin glue, collage, pigments, ink and dragon's blood on canvas
200 × 100 cm
Courtesy of Galleria Raucci/Santamaria

# Pádraig Timoney

Conceptual painter Pádraig Timoney's work circumvents typical definition—his paintings vary in style and approach from one to the next and appear to be the handiwork of multiple artists. Avoiding any one particular genre, Timoney takes his aesthetic points of reference from the canon of 20th-century painting, yet remains rooted in the present with his evasive methods and eclectic idiosyncrasies. Works such as *Bombed Coral* (2010) are devoid of pictorial content, instead relying on abstract pattern and tone, while *Giordano Bruno No. 2* (2010) nods towards figurative abstraction, its vertical form based on that of the sculpture in Rome of the eponymous Italian philosopher. Timoney's practice is founded on difference, in which new territory is explored and unrestricted possibilities are realized. SC

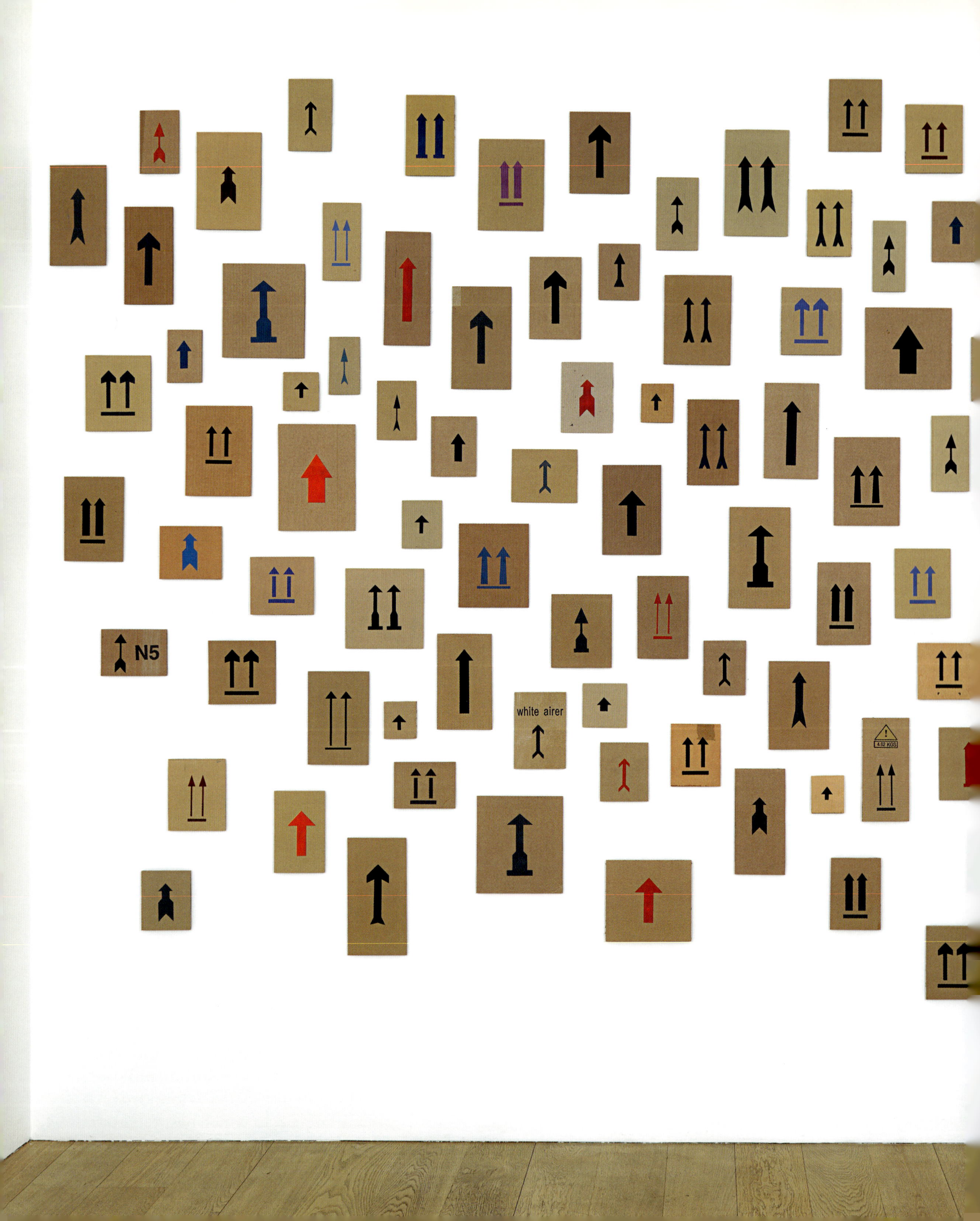
N5
white airer

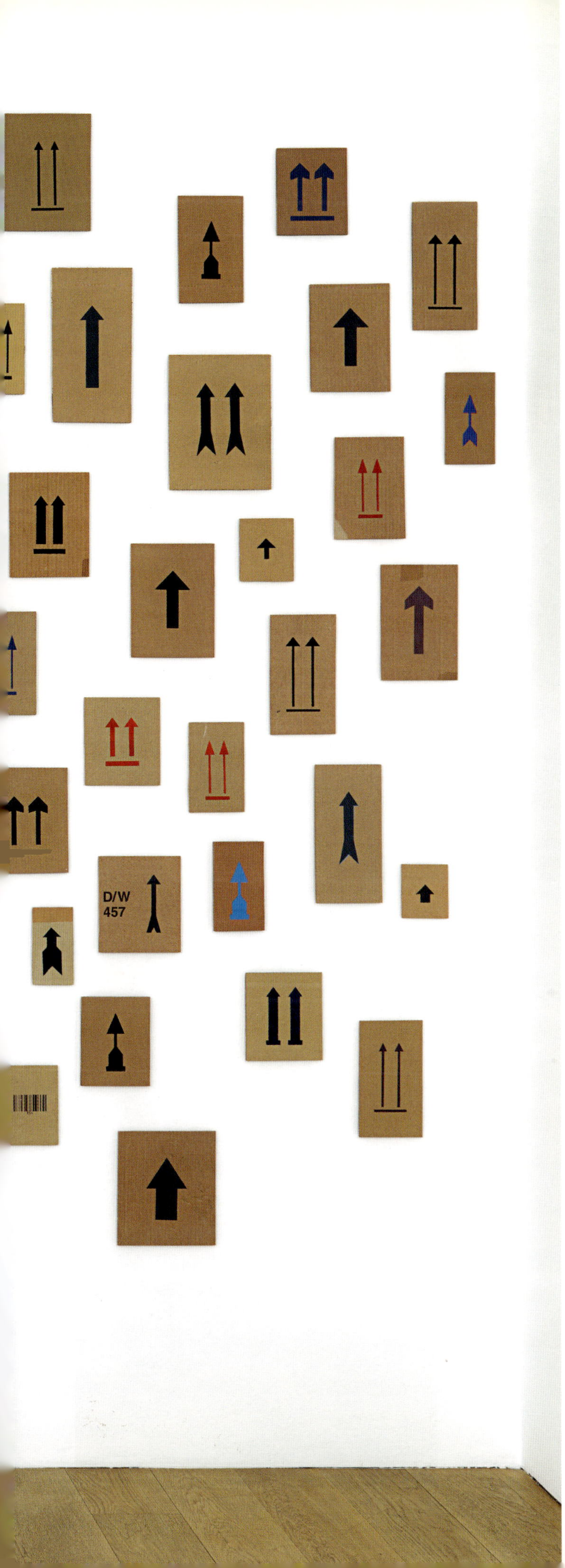


**Shown by**
Anthony Reynolds Gallery F1

**Biography**
Born 1945
Lives in London

Israeli-born Toren has been the subject of solo exhibitions recently at Anthony Reynolds Gallery, London (2012 and 2008), and Noga Gallery, Tel Aviv (2009), and in previous decades Chisenhale Gallery, London (1991), Ikon Gallery, Birmingham (1990), and the Serpentine Gallery, London (1976). In 2012 he participated in the the 4th Guangzhou Triennial and 'The London Open', Whitechapel Gallery, London.

*Moving in the Right Direction II*
2011–12
Ink and gouache on carboard (part ready-made, part ready-faked)
Dimensions variable
Courtesy of Anthony Reynolds Gallery

# Amikam Toren

The conceptually grounded sculptures, paintings and video works of Amikam Toren attest to a career analysing questions of form and representation, often using art-historical tropes as a starting-point. If earlier works such as *Neither a Painting nor a Chair* (1979–80) referenced Joseph Kosuth's thought experiment into the problems of naming and necessity in his *One and Three Chairs* (1965), more recent works such as *Moving in the Right Direction II* (2011–12), an assemblage of small pieces of cardboard each bearing the upward-pointing arrows commonly seen on the side of packing boxes, take just as common an image to reprise the question of which is the original and which the myriad forms of its representation. PT

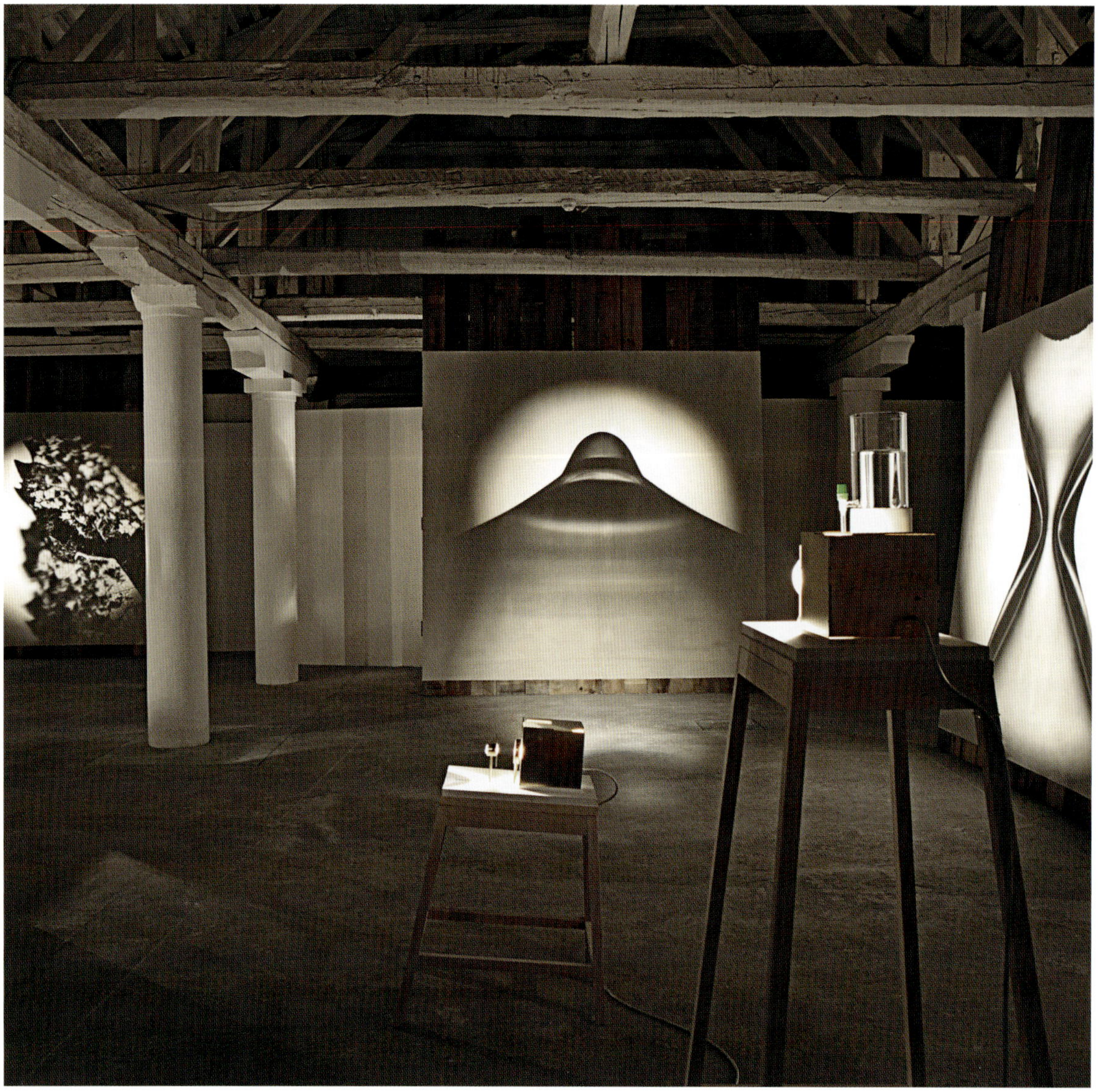

1

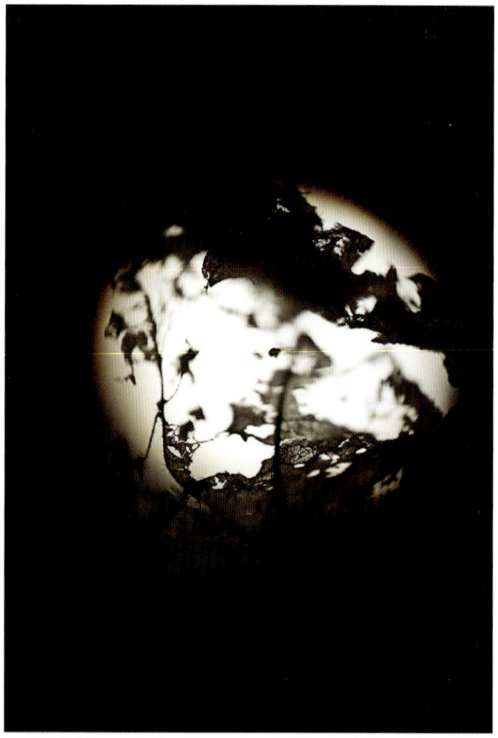

2

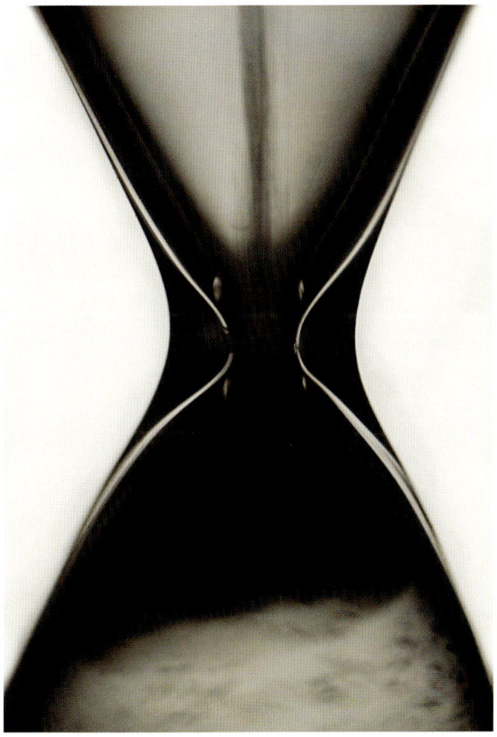

3

**Shown by**
Galerija Gregor Podnar
H3

**Biography**
Born 1968
Lives in Lisbon

Portuguese artist Tropa has presented solo exhibitions at venues such as Fundação Serralves, Porto (2010), and Fundação Calouste Gulbenkian (2003), Lisbon. Tropa represented his country in the 54th Venice Biennale (2011) and participated in the 12th Istanbul Biennial (2011). Recent group exhibitions include 'Locus Solus: Impressions of Raymond Roussel', Museo Nacional Centro de Arte Reina Sofía, Madrid (2012).

1
*Scenario*
2011
Light projections and mixed media
Dimensions variable
Installation view at Portuguese Pavilion, 54th Venice Biennale
Courtesy of Galerija Gregor Podnar

2, 3
*Scenario*
(details)
2011
Light projections and mixed media
Dimensions variable
Installation view at Portuguese Pavilion, 54th Venice Biennial
Courtesy of Galerija Gregor Podnar

# Francisco Tropa

Francisco Tropa's exhibition for the Portuguese Pavilion at the 2011 Venice Biennale filled a former warehouse on the Grand Canal with a series of sculptural projection devices, enchanting magic lanterns which threw images onto the walls of the tiny objects and dramas beheld by their lenses: a dead fly, a leaf skeleton, drops of water dripping from a thread. Seemingly untethering a visual culture of optical perspective, scientific observation and the empirical experiment from the representational reign of the photograph or the film, Tropa corralled an undisguised and live analysis of seeing and perceiving. As curator Sérgio Mah proposed, Tropa's *Scenario* possessed 'a heuristic quality, seeking a sensitive and subjective understanding of the nature of things'. MA

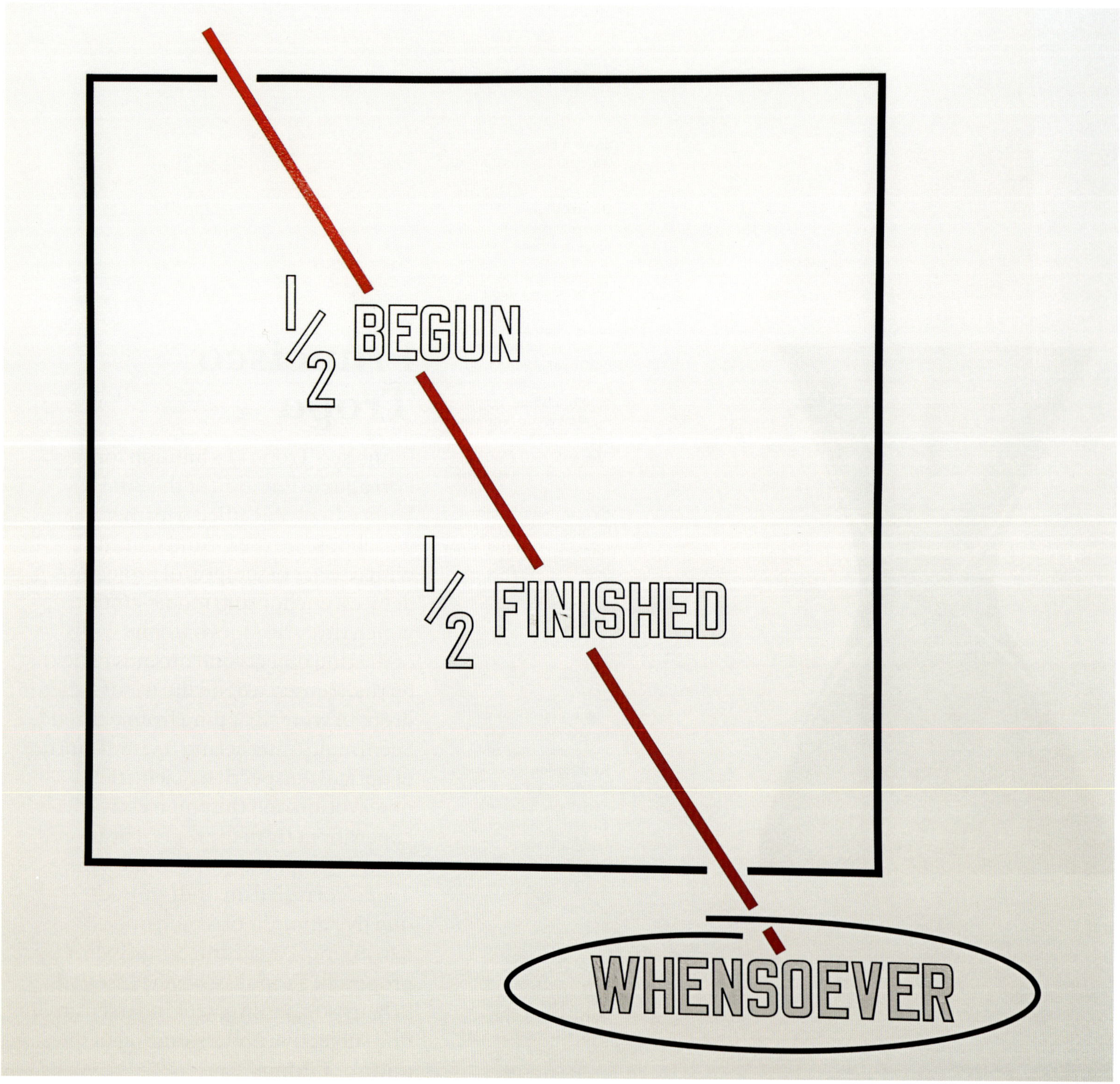
1/2 BEGUN
1/2 FINISHED
WHENSOEVER

**Shown by**
Konrad Fischer Galerie C6
Yvon Lambert C2
Lisson Gallery B9
Mai 36 Galerie D9
Galerie Thaddaeus Ropac F4
Galerie Micheline Szwajcer B3

**Biography**
Born 1942
Lives in New York

Bronx-born Weiner has presented solo exhibitions at institutions such as the Whitney Museum of American Art, New York (2007), Van Abbemuseum, Eindhoven (2006), Kunstmuseum Wolfsburg (2000), Museum Ludwig, Cologne (1995), Walker Art Center, Minneapolis (1994), and the Hirshhorn Museum and Sculpture Garden, Washington DC (1990). His work is featured in collections such as MoMA, New York, and the Solomon R. Guggenheim Museum, New York.

*1/2 BEGUN 1/2 FINISHED WHENSOEVER CAT. #992*
2008
Language and the materials referred to
Dimensions variable
Courtesy of Yvon Lambert

# Lawrence Weiner

Perhaps no artist has contributed more to the philosophical distillation of art than Lawrence Weiner. Since the late 1960s Weiner has constructed art from what he always lists as 'language + the materials referred to'. Sometimes, as with *ONE PINT GLOSS WHITE LAQUER POURED DIRECTLY UPON THE FLOOR AND ALLOWED TO DRY* (1968), the title was the art and the instructions for making it rolled into one. In other instances he would transfer words directly onto the wall. Hence, the stencilled blue words *WATER UNDER A BRIDGE* (1986) are, in Weiner's eyes, as sculptural as their material manifestation could ever be. Other pieces, such as *1/2 BEGUN 1/2 FINISHED WHENSOEVER CAT. #992* (2008), remain materially irresolute, referring, perhaps, only to themselves. JG

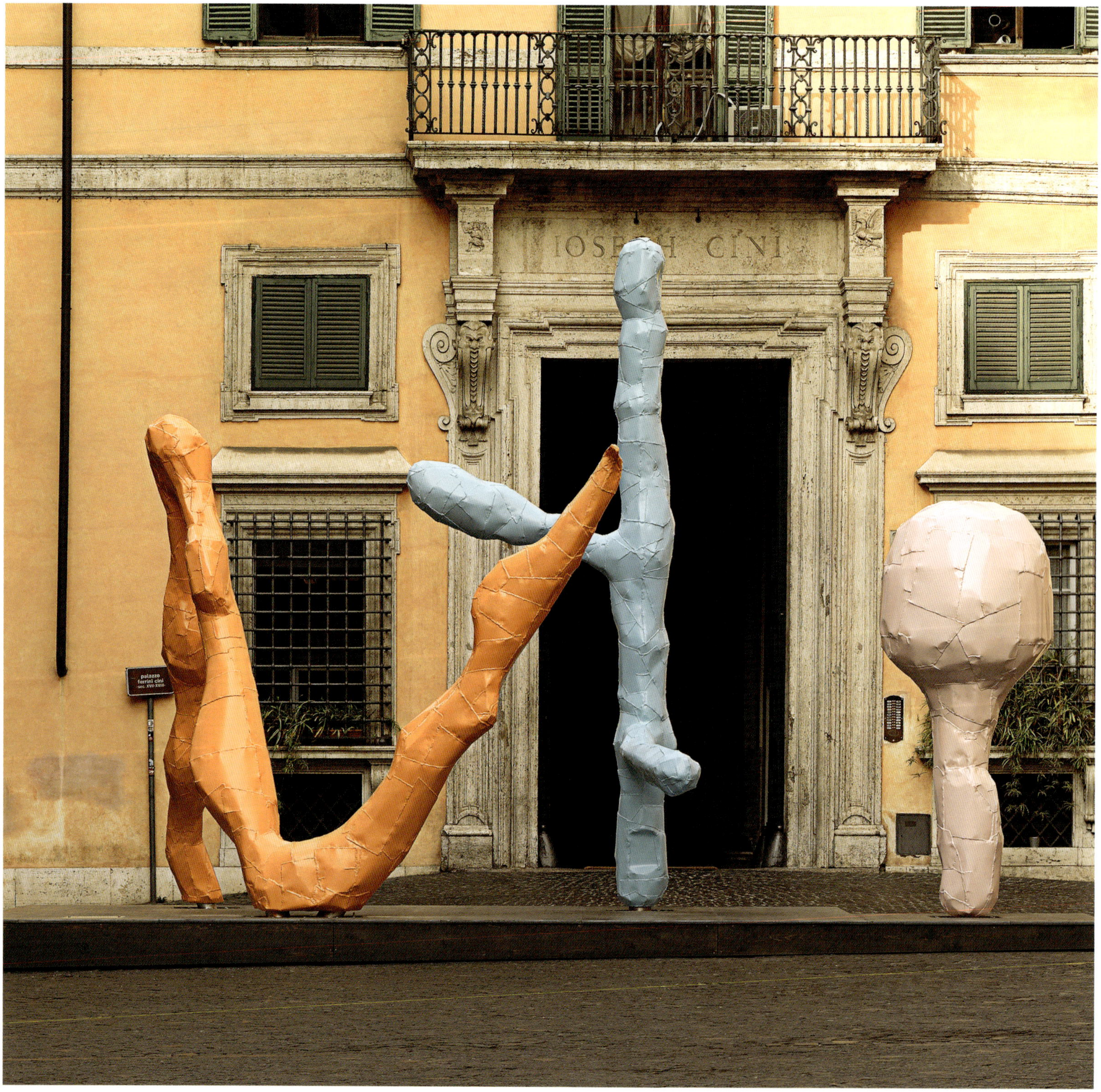


1

# Franz West

'It doesn't matter what art looks like but how it's used.' This comment by Franz West was a guiding principle for all of his work, from his anti-monumental public sculptures to his furniture and portable works (which he called 'Adaptives' or 'Fitting Pieces'). Initially made in response to the blood-spattered performances of the Viennese Actionists, his sculptural works for 40 years encouraged a convivial kind of participation from viewers, incorporating benches or sometimes springs to keep his objects on the cusp of motion. West's brightly coloured forms often appeared to have been sutured into being from plaster, papier mâché or aluminium, always bringing with them unexpected humour. ST

**Shown by**
Galería Juana de Aizpuru G5
Galerie Gisela Capitain C10
Gagosian Gallery D7
Galerie Meyer Kainer F2
Galerie Eva Presenhuber C3
Almine Rech Gallery D18

**Biography**
Born 1947
Died 2012

Austrian artist West was the subject of a retrospective at Museum Ludwig, Cologne, in 2010, which travelled that year to MADRE, Naples, and Kunsthaus Graz. West presented solo exhibitions at other public institutions that include Fondation Beyeler, Basel (2009), the Los Angeles County Museum of Art (2009), MAK, Vienna (2008), Vancouver Art Gallery (2005), Whitechapel Gallery, London (2003), Museo Centro de Arte Reina Sofía, Madrid (2001), and MoMA, New York (1997).

1
*Room in Rome*
2009–10
Aluminium and lacquer work in 3 parts
Dimensions variable
Installation view in Piazza di Pietra, Rome
Courtesy of Gagosian Gallery

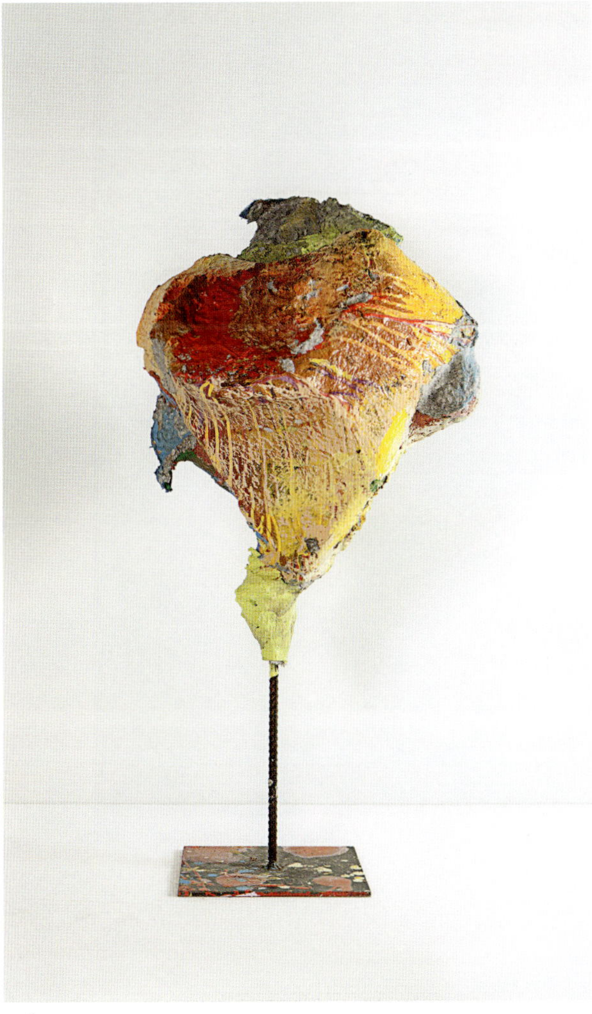

2
*Untitled*
2011
Papier mâché, Styrofoam, acrylic lacquer and steel
115 × 63 × 50 cm
Courtesy of Gagosian Gallery

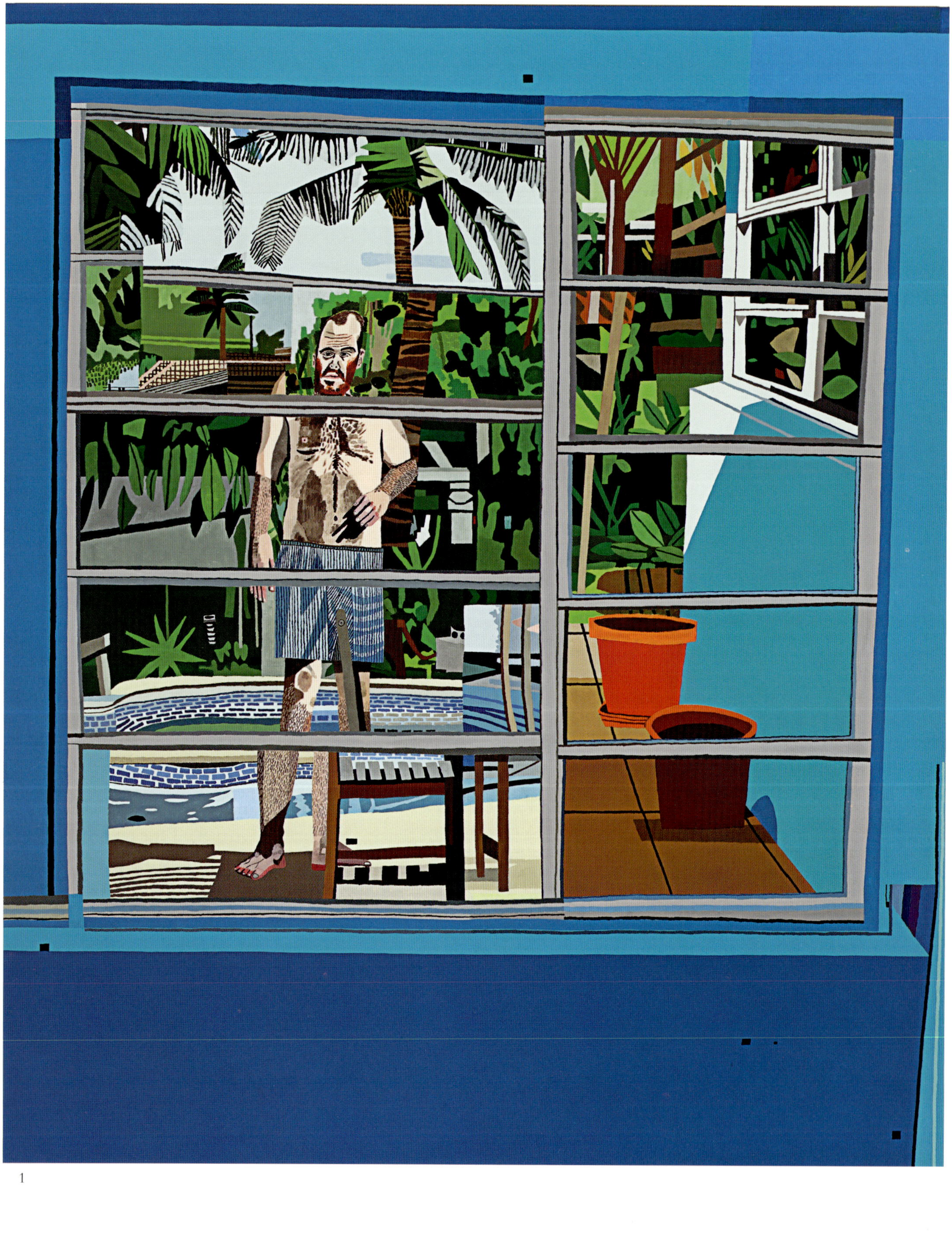

1

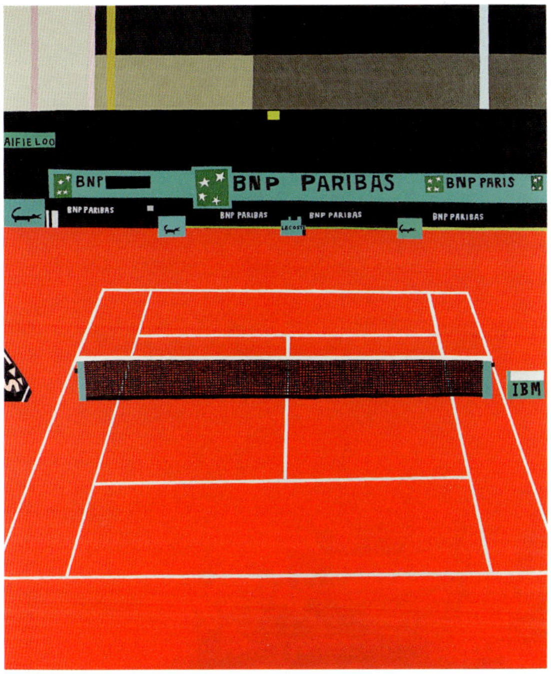


3

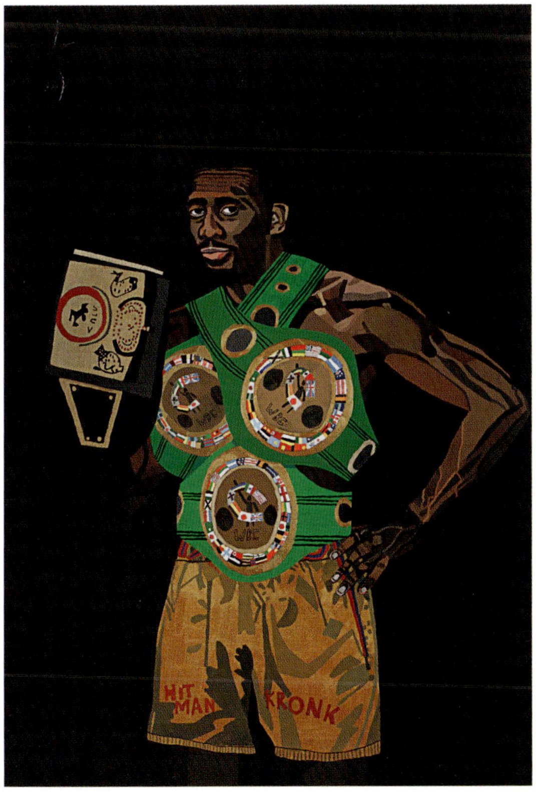


2

**Shown by**
Anton Kern Gallery A4
David Kordansky Gallery C14

**Biography**
Born 1977
Lives in Los Angeles

Boston-born Wood has presented solo shows and projects at galleries such as David Kordansky Gallery, Los Angeles (2012), Anton Kern Gallery, New York (2011), and Hammer Museum, Los Angeles (2010). Recent group exhibitions include 'Greater LA', 483 Broadway, New York (2011), 'Mixed Signals: Artists Consider Masculinity in Sports', Wexner Center for the Arts, Columbus (2010), and 'Abstract America', Saatchi Gallery, London (2009).

1
*Calais Drive*
2012
Oil and acrylic on canvas
264 × 213 cm
Courtesy of David Kordansky Gallery

2
*Hit Man*
2012
Oil and acrylic on linen
183 × 122 cm
Courtesy of David Kordansky Gallery

3
*French Open 2*
2011
Oil and acrylic on linen
218 × 178 cm
Courtesy of David Kordansky Gallery

# Jonas Wood

Jonas Wood's striking paintings live at once in the present moment—reproducing the spaces, clutter and images that surround the artist daily—and in the imperfectly remembered past of art history. Wood inflects the outward naivety of his bold, graphic style with sophisticated homages to painters such as Henri Matisse, Elizabeth Neel, David Hockney and Stuart Davis. The pictorial flatness of Wood's *French Open 2* (2011) recalls Matisse's *The Dessert (Harmony in Red)* (1908) while reproducing a scene from televised tennis. Sport (an under-represented subject in art, but a favourite of Wood's) recurs in *Hit Man* (2012), a strident portrait of a boxer that contrasts revealingly with the fractured, reflected self-portrait in *Calais Drive* (2012). JG

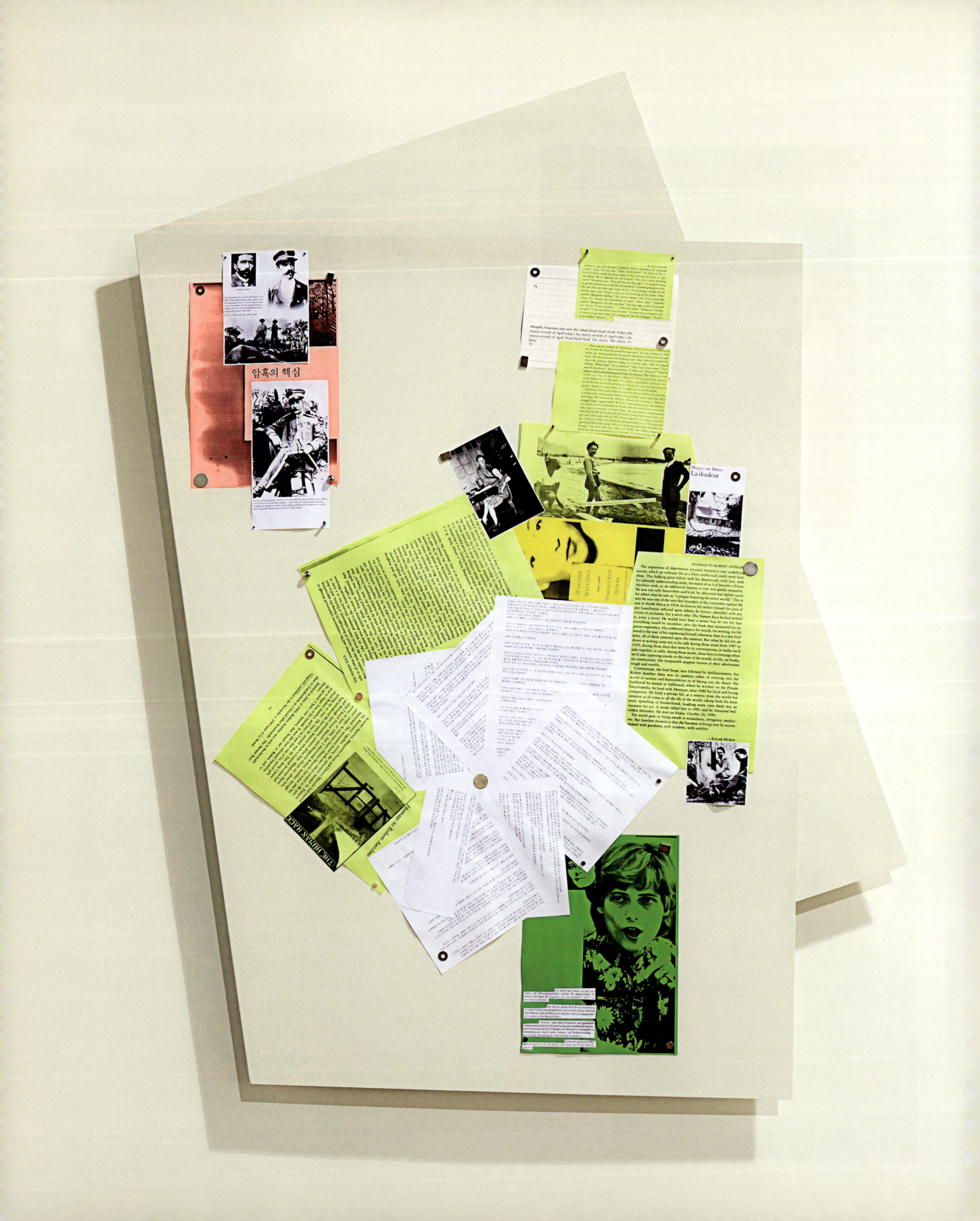

암흑의 핵심
Marguerite Duras
La douleur
HOMAGE TO ROBERT ANTELME
THE HUMAN RACE

**Shown by**
Galerie Chantal Crousel D11
dépendance S11
Greene Naftali B10
Kukje Gallery C13
Wien Lukatsch F16

**Biography**
Born 1971
Lives in Berlin and Seoul

Seoul-born Yang has recently presented solo shows and projects at venues that include Overbeck-Gesellschaft, Lubeck, Germany (2012), Modern Art Oxford (2011), New Museum, New York (2010), Walker Art Center, Minneapolis (2009), Portikus, Frankfurt (2008), and Cubitt Gallery, London (2008). She represented South Korea at the 53rd Venice Biennale (2009) and her work features in collections such as: Hamburger Kunsthalle, Hamburg; the Solomon R. Guggenheim Museum, New York; and the Los Angeles County Museum of Art.

*Rotating Notes*
(detail)
2010
5 wall-mounted sculptures: powder-coated steel, bearings, magnets and notes
Each 140 × 100 cm
Courtesy of Galerie Wien Lukatsch

# Haegue Yang

Haegue Yang's diverse practice ranges from photography and video to multi-sensory, atmospheric installations featuring coloured lights, microphones, infra-red heaters, venetian blinds and scent emitters. Such stimuli conjure individual memory, but also create a common experience to be shared among viewers. Yang fuses this interest in subjectivity and community with a poetic formal language. Her *Rotating Notes* (2010) is a series of steel noticeboards to which texts, images and photographs have been affixed with magnets. Although they reference subjects such as German activist Petra Kelly, the French writer Marguerite Duras, the Black Panthers and the Belgian Congo, the sculptures are meant to be rotated, making their status as formal objects all the more apparent. ND

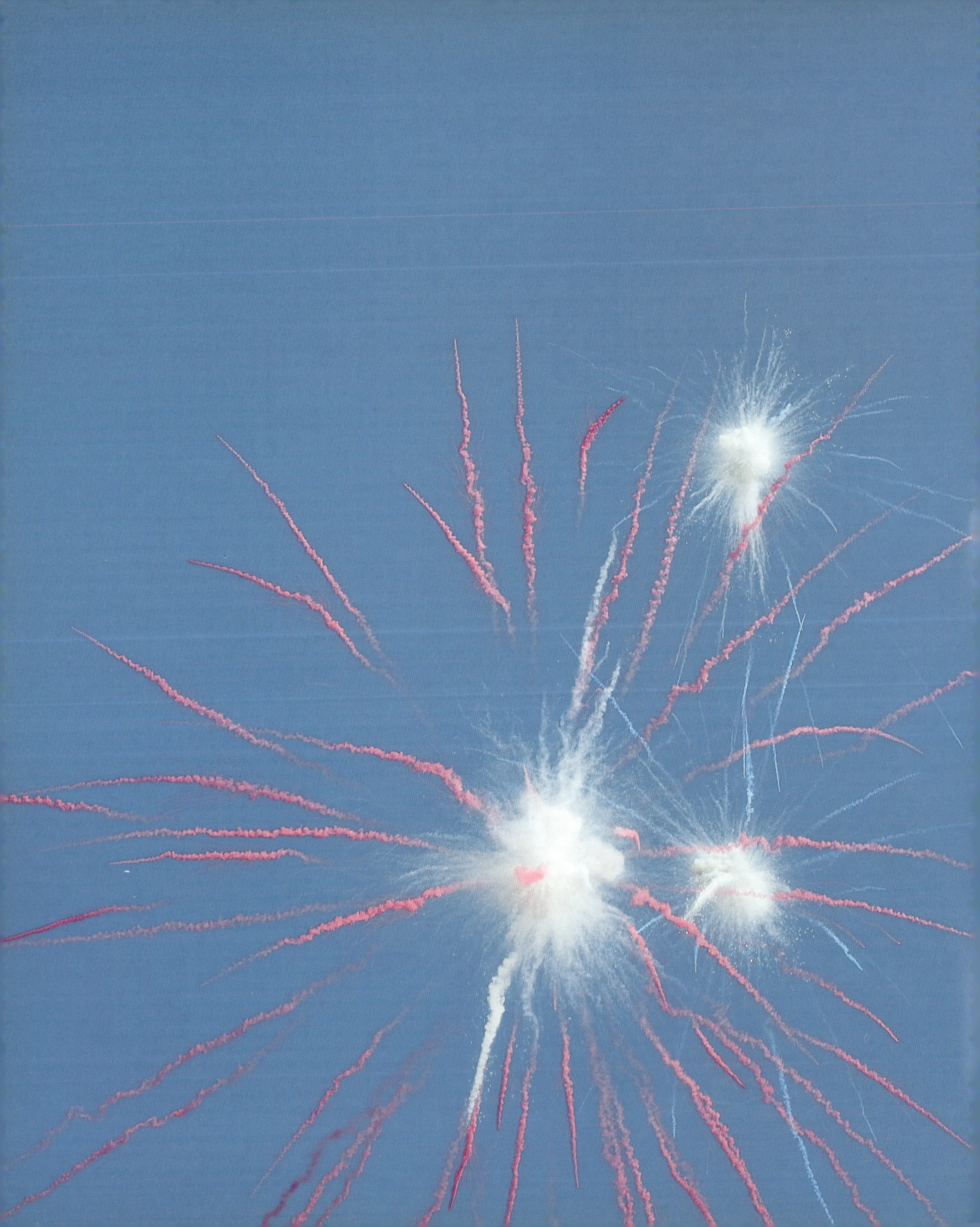

# Frame Artists

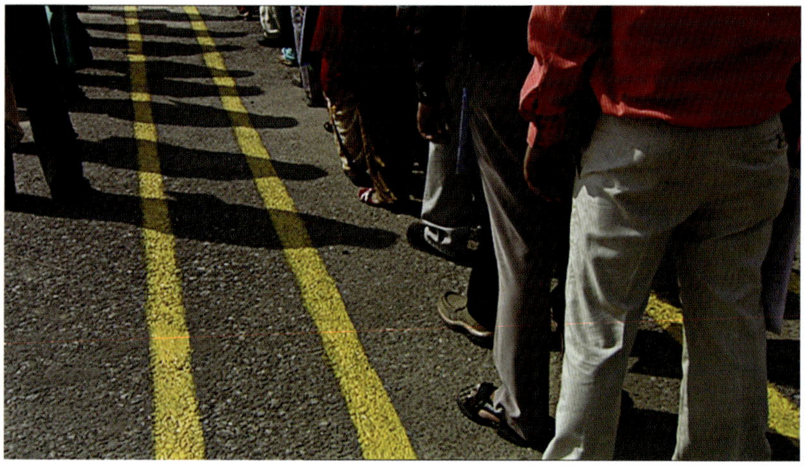

1

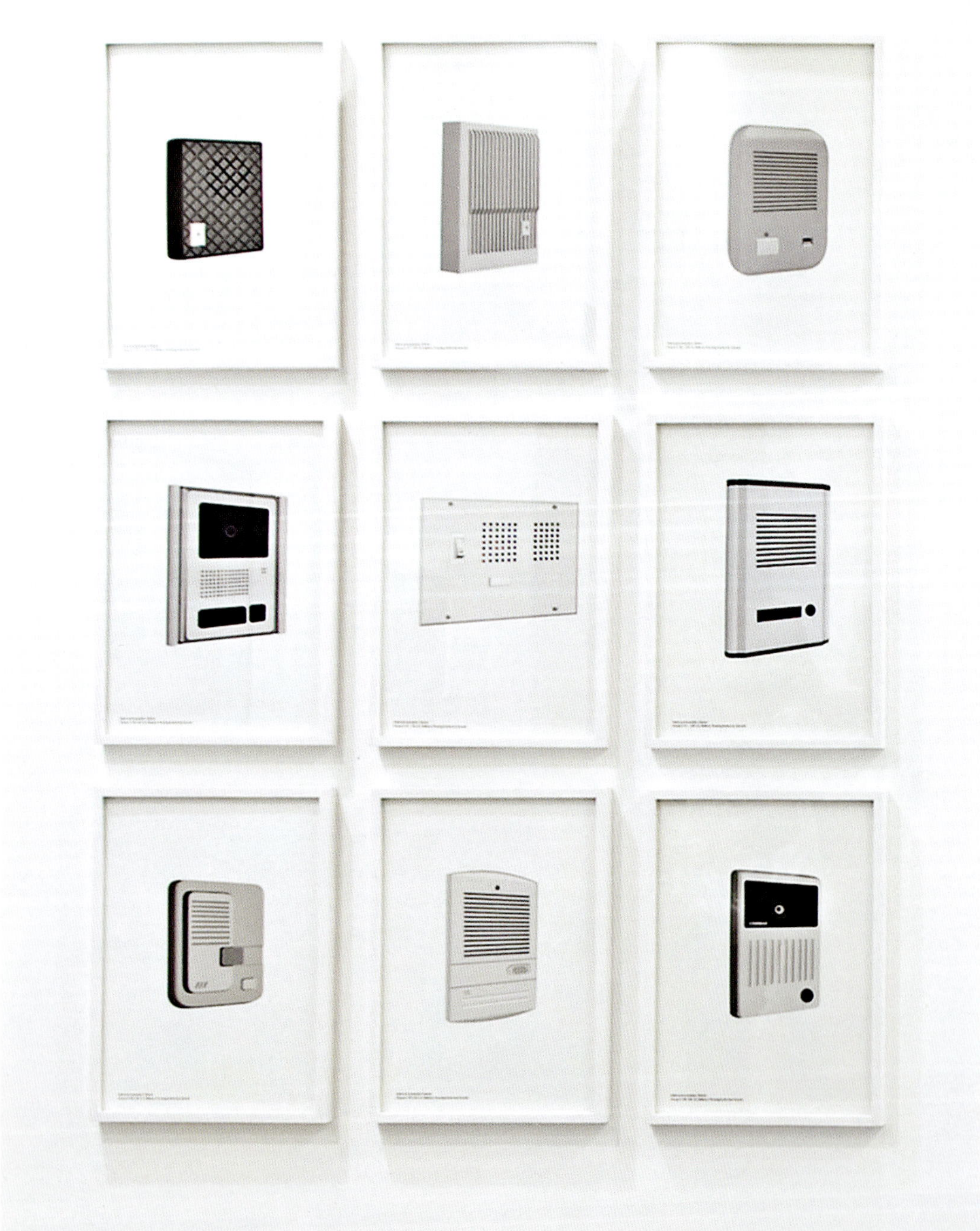

2

# Frame
# Bani Abidi

**Shown by**
Experimenter R5

**Biography**
Born 1971
Lives in Berlin, New Delhi and Karachi

Karachi-born artist Abidi participated in Documenta 13, Kassel (2012), and has presented solo exhibitions at galleries such as Baltic, Gateshead (2011), Project 88, Mumbai (2010), and Green Cardamom, London (2010). Abidi took part in the DAAD Artists-in-Residence Programme, Berlin in 2011. Group exhibitions include 'Making Normative Orders', Frankfurter Kunstverein (2012), and 'Where Three Dreams Cross' at Whitechapel Gallery, London, and Fotomuseum, Winterthur (both 2010).

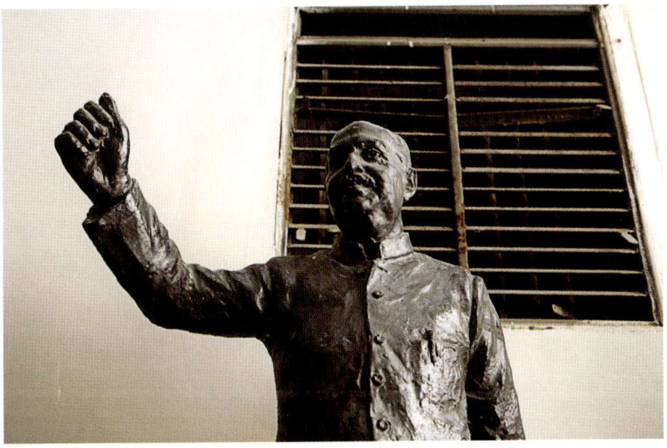
3

1
*The Distance from Here*
2010
Double-channel HD video
12 min.
Courtesy of Experimenter

2
*Intercommunication Devices*
2008
9 archival prints
Each 43 × 23 cm
Courtesy of Experimenter

3
*Proposal for a Man in the Sea*
(detail)
2012
26 archival prints in an assemblage of new and used frames
Dimensions variable
Courtesy of Experimenter

Structures of power, Bani Abidi suggests, are maintained more by habit than anything else. Her videos, drawings and installations explore bureaucracy and the orchestration of authority on a mundane level, from her drawings of street security barriers to her documentary-style video *The Distance from Here* (2010), in which people queue for a staged immigration screening in an empty lot. *Death at a 30 Degree Angle* (2012) is a video detailing a fictitious politician's attempt to increase his influence by commissioning a large public monument to himself; Abidi strums on the unease of us finding her fiction not all that far from real situations. CFW

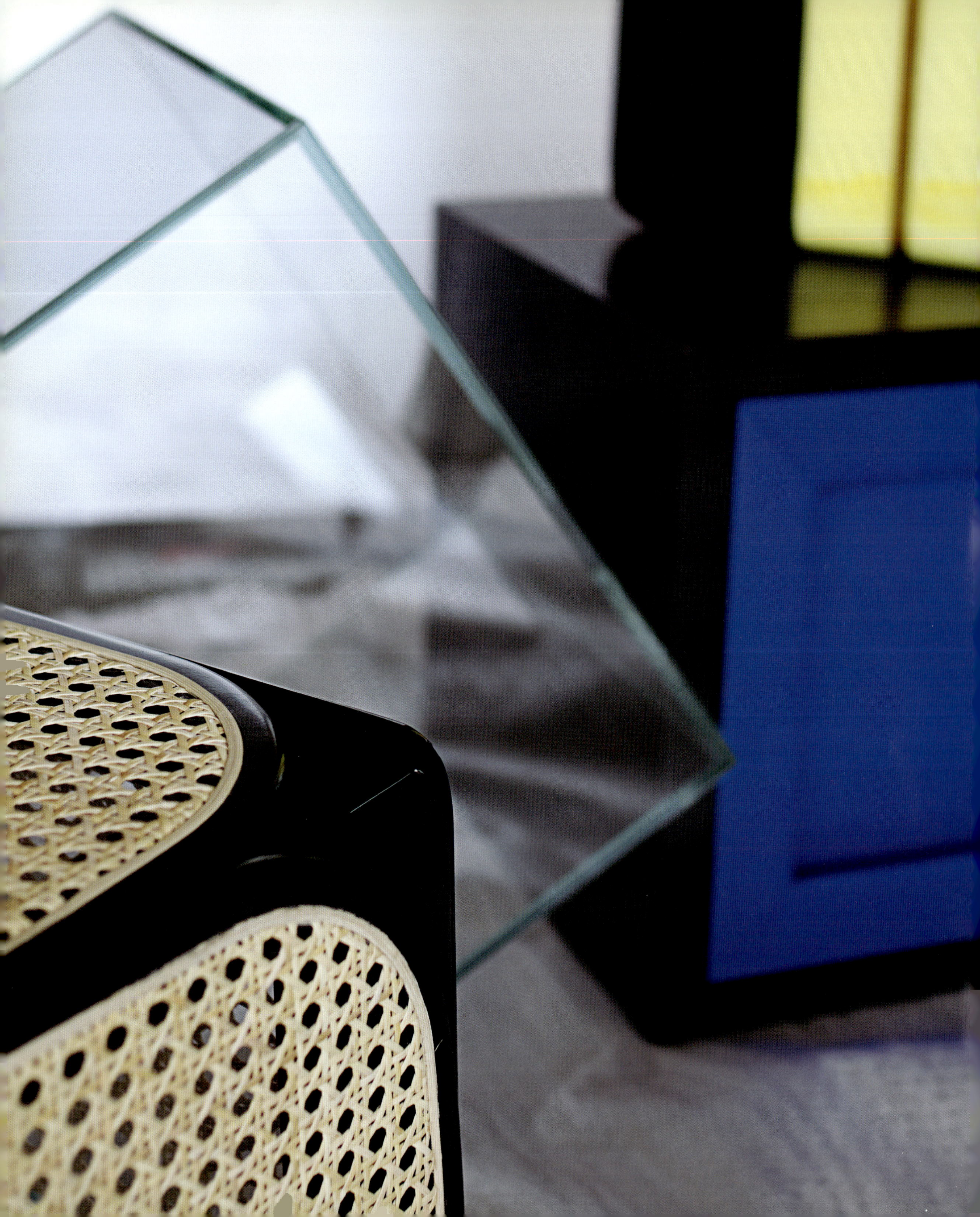

# Frame
# Xavier Antin

**Shown by**
Galerie Crèvecoeur R13

**Biography**
Born 1981
Lives in Paris

French artist Antin presents his first solo exhibition at Galerie Crèvecoeur, Paris, in November 2012. A graduate from London's Royal College of Art in 2010, Antin has participated in recent group exhibitions that include 'Impressed', Galerie ARKO, Nevers (2012), 'Riding The Frothing Thread: Notes from Paris', Jaus Art Gallery, Los Angeles (2011), and 'O'Clock', Triennale Design Museum, Milan (2011).

*Five Conversations*
(detail)
2012
5 cubes in mixed media
Each 38 × 38 × 38 cm
Courtesy of Galerie Crèvecoeur

Trained as a graphic designer, Xavier Antin is fascinated with how things get made. His installation *Just in Time, or a Short History of Production* (2010), involved a row of four different printers—from vintage to hi-tech desktop versions, each with its own specific production history and qualities—that printed out the pages of 100 books with archive images of assembly lines. *Five Conversations* (2012), his work for Frame at Frieze Art Fair, is equally concerned with industrial production and reproduction. Antin has commissioned five different French and German companies—from a surfboard manufacturer to a car-tuning company—to fabricate a 38cm cube. The final objects, and the interviews Antin conducted with his collaborators, foreground various modes, materials and processes of making, as well as the companies' individual histories. VSR

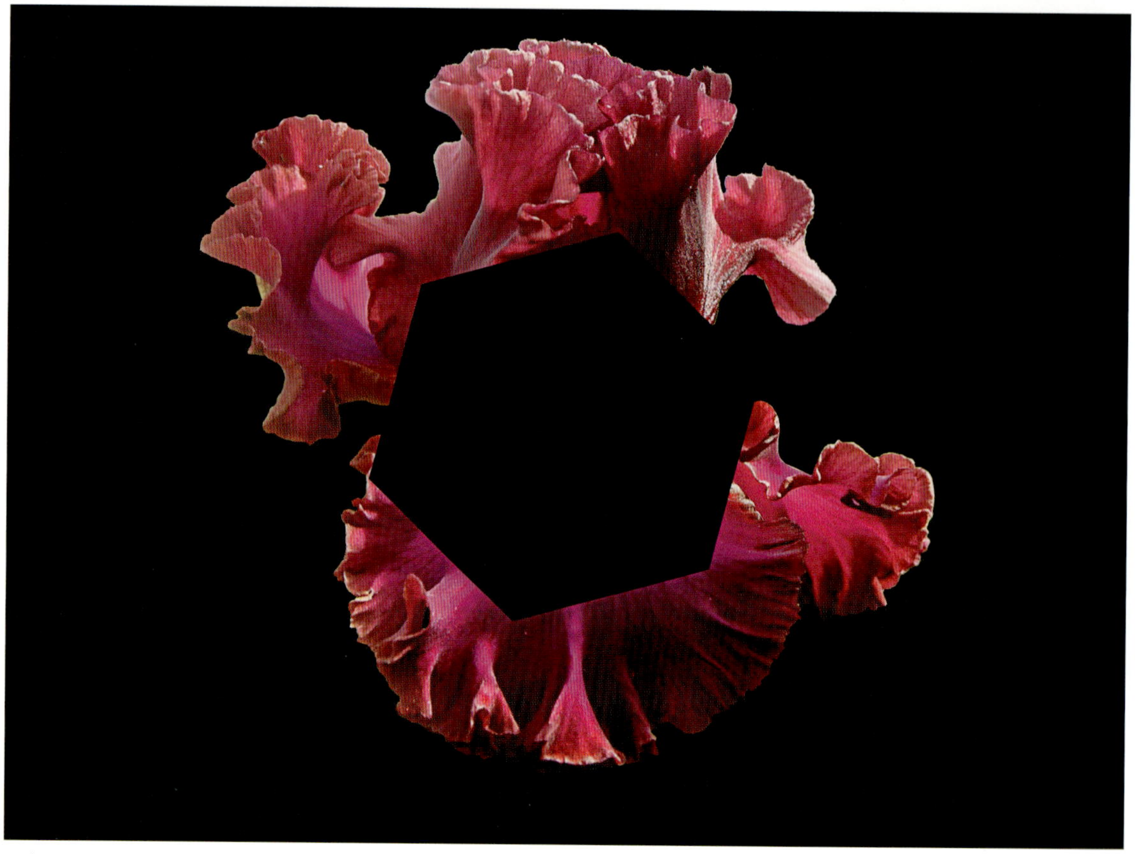

1

2

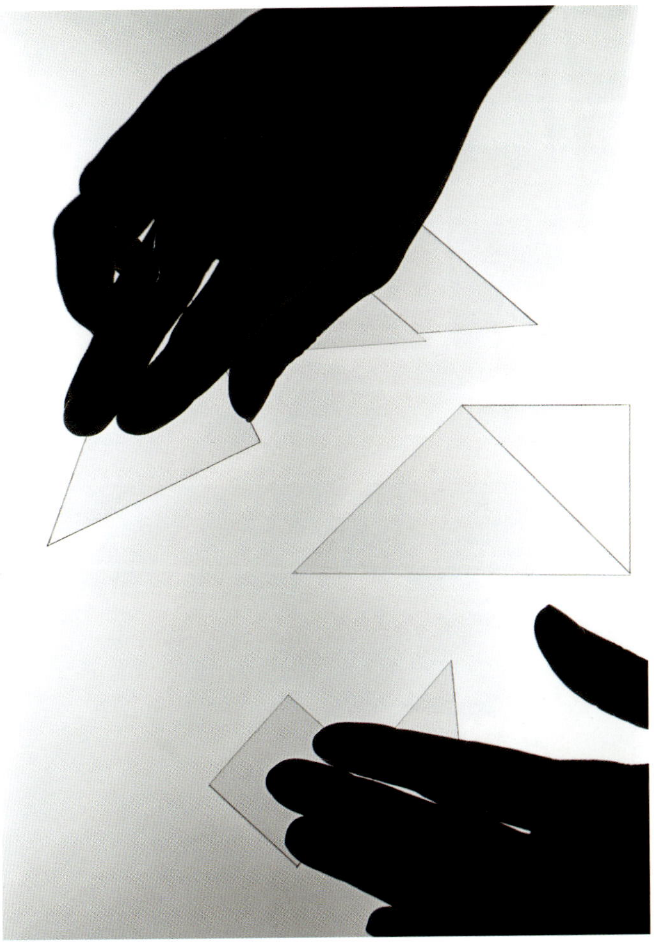

3

**Shown by**
Arcade R2

**Biography**
Born 1974
Lives in London

Recent one- and two-person shows by British artist Barham include those at CCA, Glasgow (2012), and International Project Space, Birmingham (2010). In 2012 she was commissioned by Art on the Underground to produce a new work for White City underground station, London. She has featured in group exhibitions in 2012 at: Studio International, Leipzig; The Drawing Room, London; and Baltic 39, Newcastle upon Tyne. She is currently participating in the group show 'Revolver' at Matt's Gallery, London, until October 2012.

1
*Iris*
2011
Digital projection
58 sec.
Courtesy of Arcade

2
*White City*
(detail)
2012
Poster series and online videos for Art on the Underground
Dimensions variable
Courtesy of Arcade and London Underground Ltd

3
*Magenta, Emerald, Lapis*
2009
Digital projection
30 min.
Courtesy of Arcade

# Frame
# Anna Barham

The city of Leptis Magna, whose extensive remains are still to be seen in present-day Libya, was founded by the Phoenicians, who elaborated one of the first workable alphabets. The ruined city is at the enigmatic heart of a project begun in 2007 by Anna Barham, *Return to Leptis Magna*, which generated texts, drawings, sculptures and performances. At its most emblematic, Barham's is an anagrammatic practice—she frequently produces actual anagrams, such as those of the city's name: 'magenta lips', 'elating amps', 'pliant games'. But her whole approach is similarly ludic and transformative: in 2012 she contrived *White City* for London's Art on the Underground programme, using QR codes on station walls to send commuters into a visual and textual labyrinth. BD

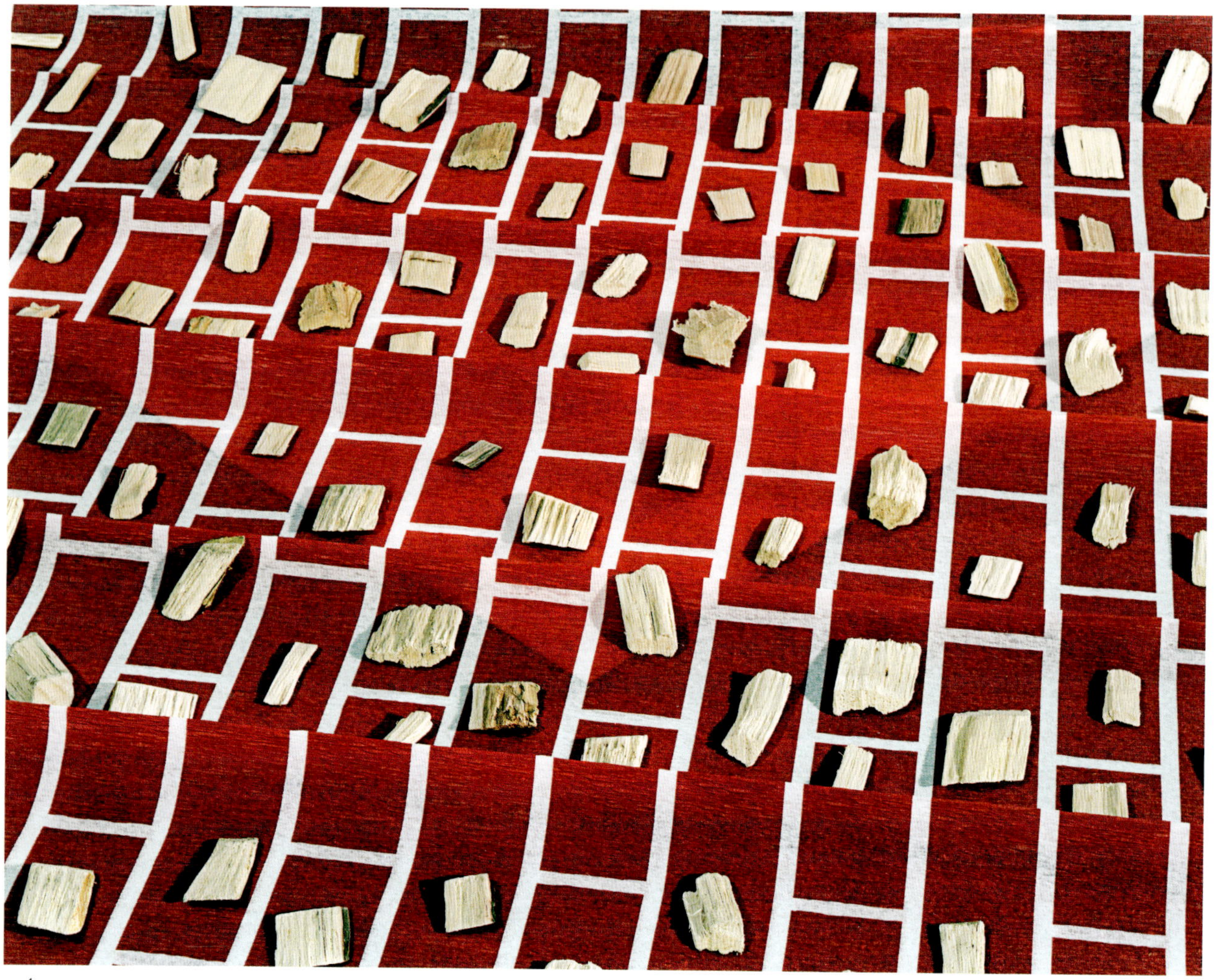
1

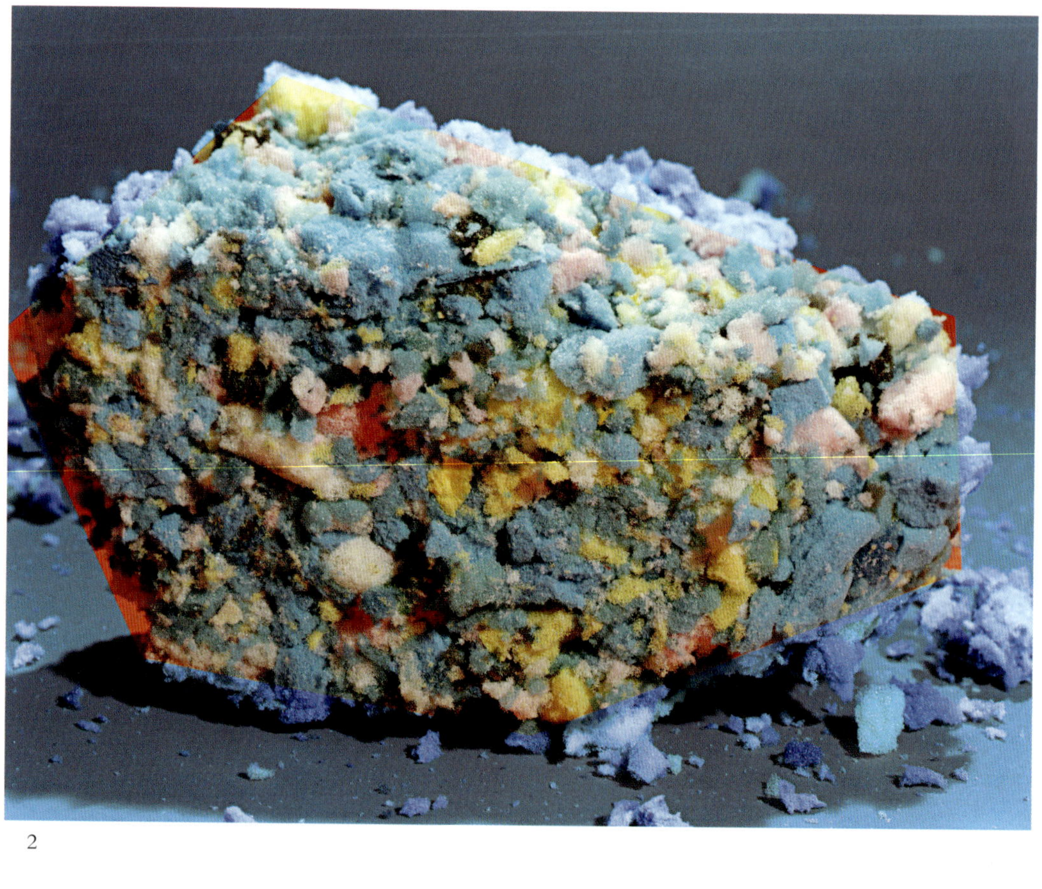
2

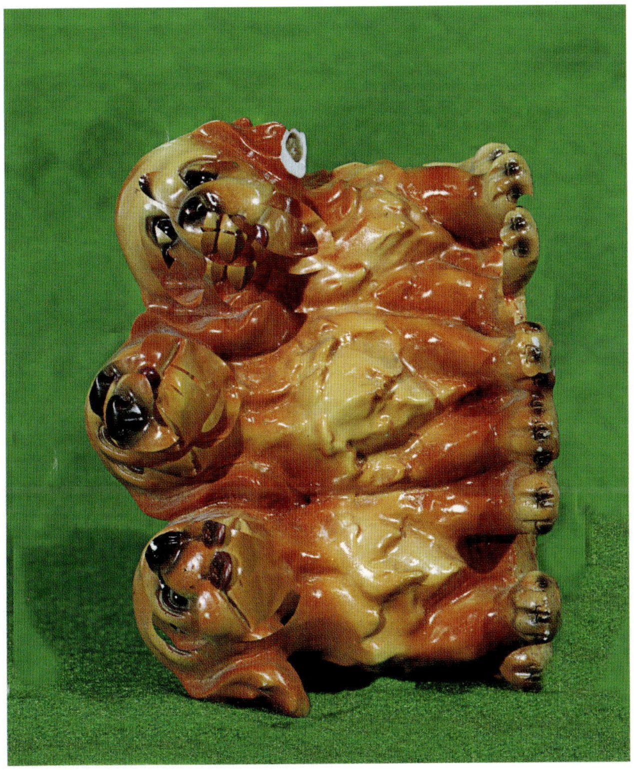

3

**Shown by**
Ramiken Crucible R4

**Biography**
Born 1978
Lives in Los Angeles

American artist Blalock presented the solo exhibition 'xyz' at Ramiken, New York, in 2011, and until April 2013 is featured in the group show 'Second Nature: Abstract Photography Then and Now', deCordova Sculpture Park and Museum, Lincoln, Massachusetts. Other group exhibitions include 'Towards a Warm Math', On Stella Rays, New York (2012), 'Talent', FOAM, Amsterdam (2011), and 'Face, Head and Shoulders', Ny Tap, Copenhagen (2011).

1
*Building Materials*
2011
Chromogenic print
51 × 64 cm
Courtesy of Ramiken Crucible

2
*Foam*
2011
Chromogenic print
58 × 73 cm
Courtesy of Ramiken Crucible

3
*Still Life with Three Puppies*
2012
Chromogenic print
102 × 84 cm
Courtesy of Ramiken Crucible

# Frame
# Lucas Blalock

Lucas Blalock's photographic practice details an expansion of photography into sculptural and painting concerns through its post-production and digital manipulation. Working on photographs in Photoshop, the added crops, rotations, blurrings and deletions highlight the precarious gap between the photograph as real-world documentation and readily mutable digital image. Blalock's recomposed still-life images elide from the physical to the digital surface: the multicoloured *Foam* (2011) could be a simple still-life photograph if not for the rhombus magenta colour field, the edges of which are easily missed at first glance. A similar question of veracity is posed by *Building Materials* (2011), in which a seemingly concertina-ed brick-patterned wallpaper holding pieces of wood forces the viewer to examine the production of an image that one might normally take for granted. PT

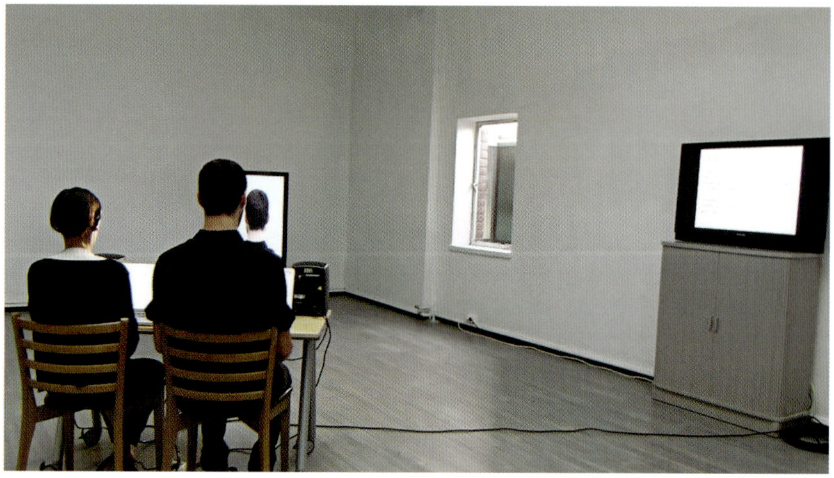
1

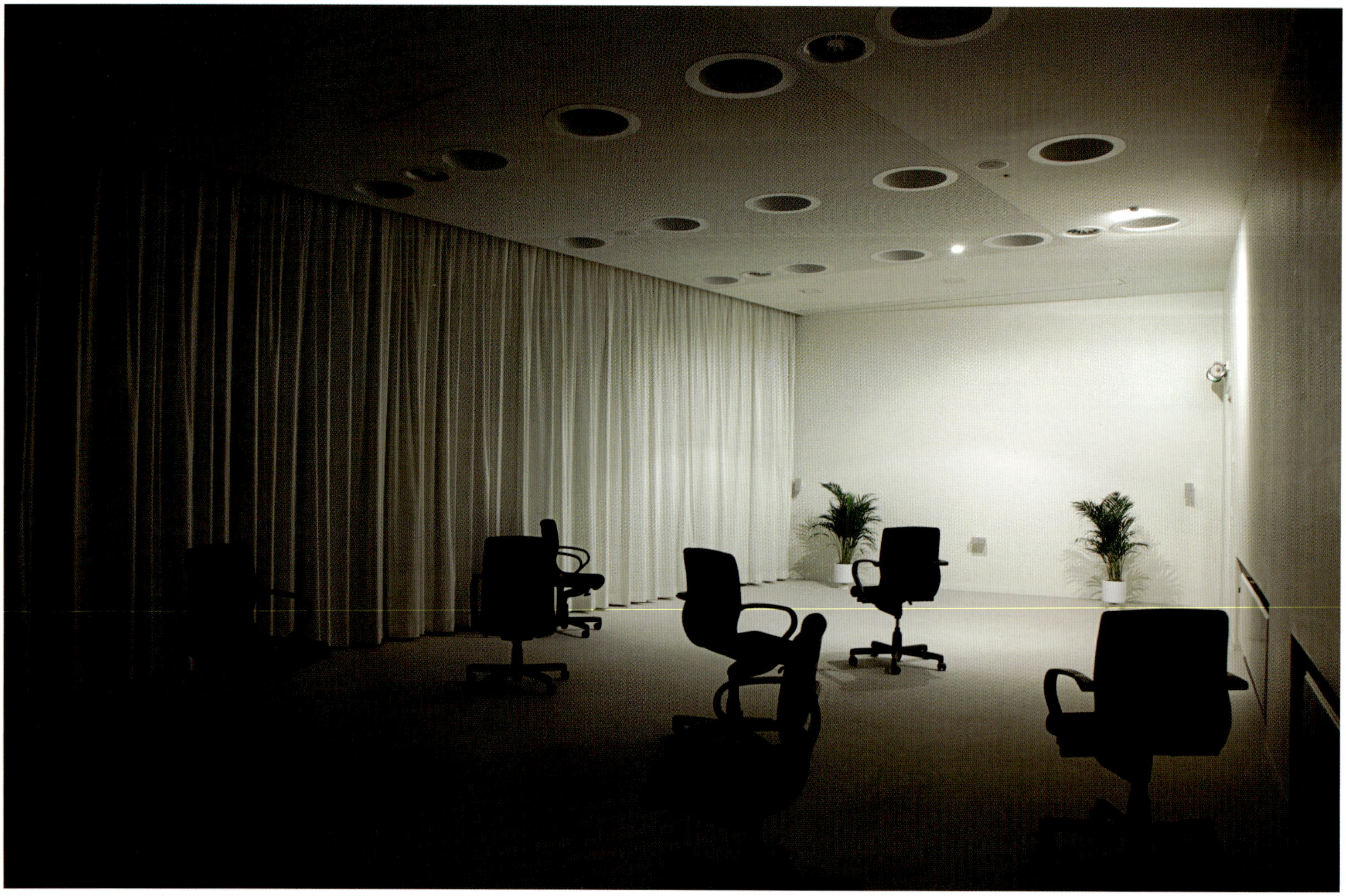
2

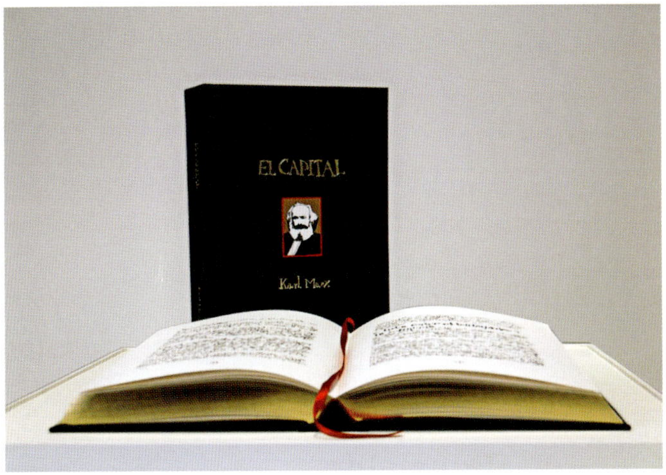


3

**Shown by**
Galerie Mor Charpentier
R10

**Biography**
Born 1975
Lives in Amsterdam

Colombian-born artist Bonilla presented solo exhibitions in 2012 at Centro Colombo Americano, Bogota, and SKMU Sørlandets Kunstmuseum, Kristiansand. Group exhibitions include 'The Idea of Latin America', Centro Andaluz de Arte Contemporáneo, Seville (2012), the 12th Istanbul Biennial (2011) and 'Morality Act VI: Remember Humanity', Witte de With, Rotterdam (2010). Bonilla's work is part of collections such as: the Arco Foundation, Madrid; the Zabludowicz Collection, London; and the Daros Latinamerica Collection, Zurich.

1
*The Destruction of One Someone*
2011–12
Performance in collaboration with Pedro Gómez Egaña
Courtesy of Galerie Mor Charpentier

2
*A Report to an Academy*
2010
Mixed media
Dimensions variable
Courtesy of Galerie Mor Charpentier

3
*Capital/Sinister Manuscript (Luxury Version)*
2007–9
Gilt-edged book and slipcase
23 × 8 × 35 cm
Courtesy of Galerie Mor Charpentier

# Frame
# Milena Bonilla

Milena Bonilla engages with historical narrative, isolating key texts and monuments, and highlighting the structures by which authority enters everyday life and society. Networks of distribution and colonization are of interest to Bonilla, who uses everything from the transit system in Bogota (*Transitory Map*, 2002–4) to book distribution (*Capital/Sinister Manuscript [Luxury Version]*, 2007–9) to explore the landscape of the city. Bonilla does more than simply subvert the original meaning of authority's tools; instead, she examines the ways in which they have acquired their significance. For her project in Frame, she documents monuments of animals across Europe and adds narration ranging from fairy tales to films, capturing the multiple sources of our historical imagination. KK

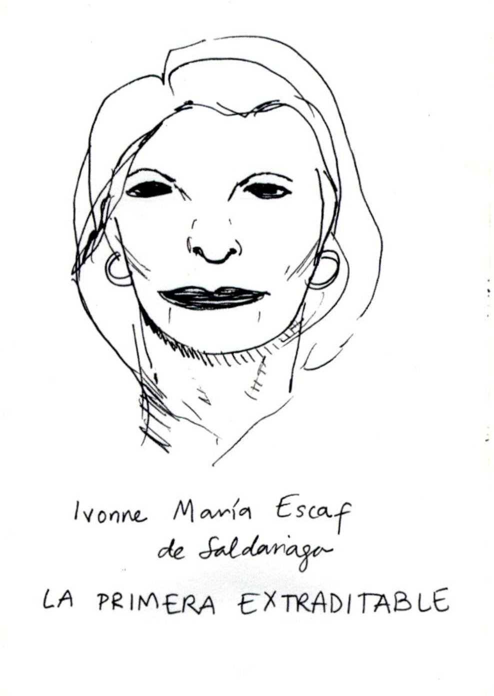
Ivonne María Escaf
de Saldarriaga
LA PRIMERA EXTRADITABLE

3

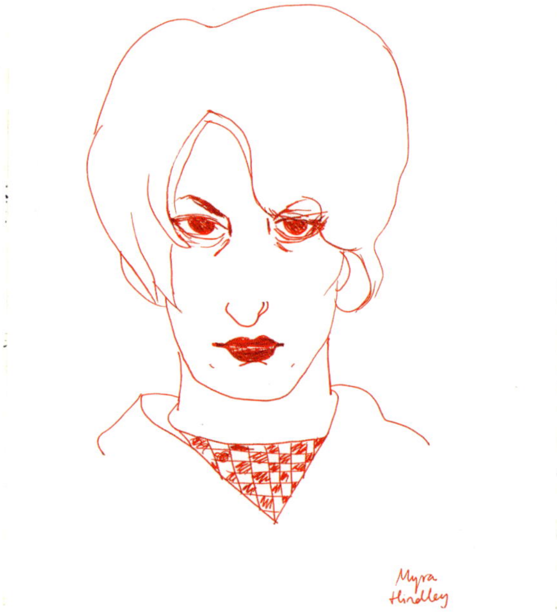
Myra
Hindley

2

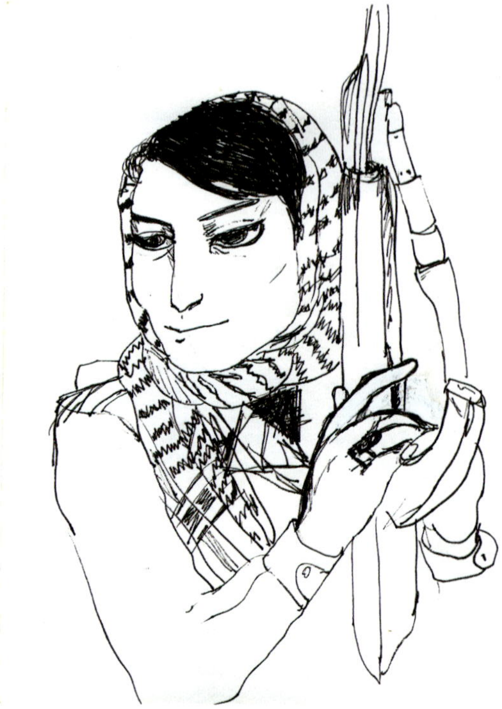

1

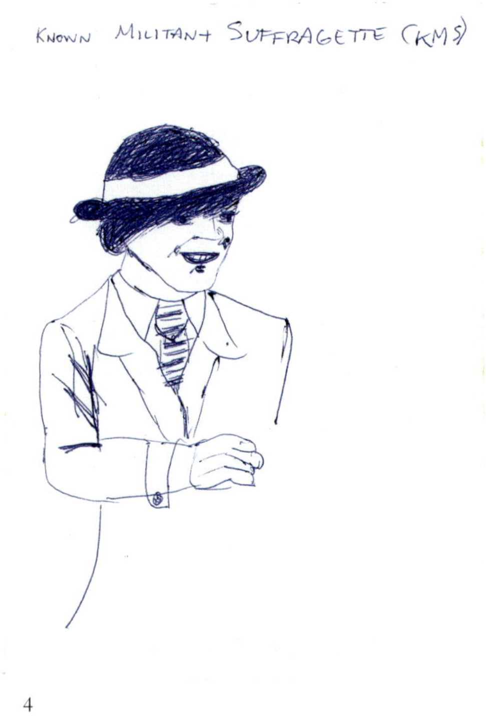
KNOWN MILITANT SUFFRAGETTE (KMS)

4

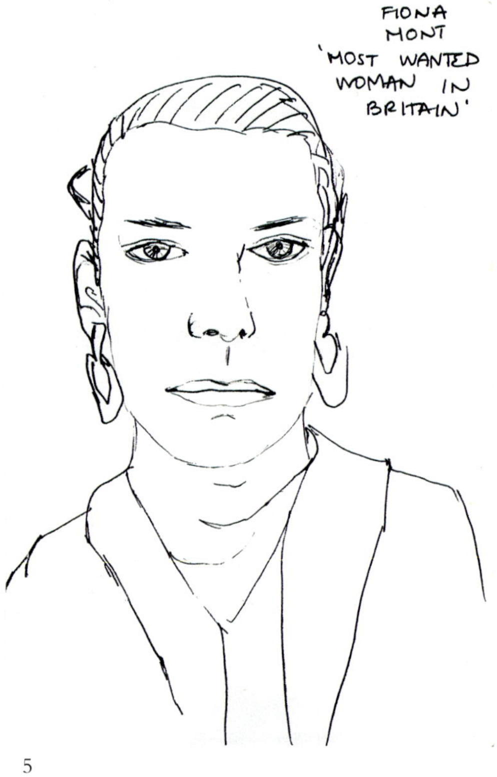
FIONA
MONT
'MOST WANTED
WOMAN IN
BRITAIN'

5

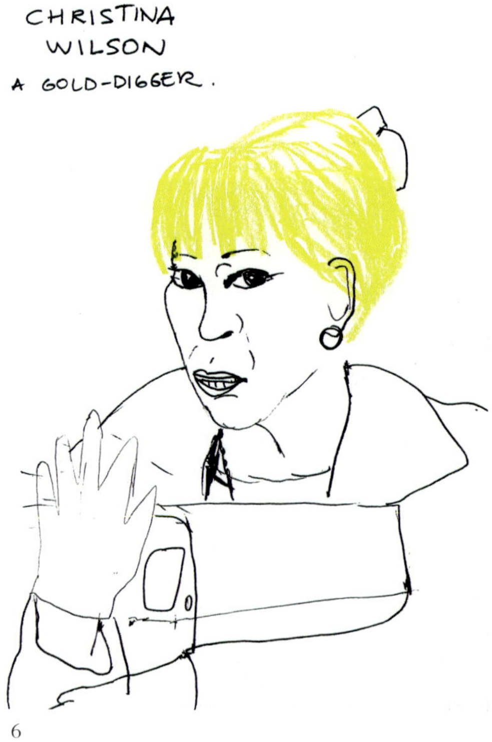
CHRISTINA
WILSON
A GOLD-DIGGER.

6

**Shown by**
La Central R11

**Biography**
Born 1978
Lives in Bogota, Los Angeles and Berlin

London-born Caycedo has presented solo exhibitions and projects at galleries that include La Central, Bogata (2012), ARCO, Madrid (2010), and Black and White Gallery, New York (2007). In 2012 she has taken part in the DAAD Artists-in-Residence Programme, Berlin, and featured in group exhibitions at Hordaland Kunstsenter, Bergen, and Palais de Tokyo, Paris. Caycedo has participated in biennials such as the 10th Havana Biennial (2009), 50th Venice Biennale (2003) and 7th Istanbul Biennial (2001).

*Leila Kahled* (1), *Myra Hindley* (2), *Ivonne Escaf* (3), *KMS* (4), *Fiona Mont* (5), *Christina Wilson* (6)
All from the series 'Criminal Women'
2001–11
Ink on paper
Each 29 × 21 cm
Courtesy of La Central

# Frame
# Carolina Caycedo

Circulation and exchange have been central to Carolina Caycedo's interventionist work in the public spheres of the street, the market and the demonstration. For Frieze Projects in 2009, Caycedo organized *Impossible Exchange*, a daily bartering of personal goods and services and the culmination of her *Day to Day* project (2002–9). Shifting her attention to the media circulation and exchange of images, Caycedo's long-term series 'Criminal Women' (2001–ongoing) comprises 50 drawings, based on print and Internet media portrayals of women accused or convicted of crimes ranging from the political to the passionate: a chilling depiction of female power that is at once, and paradoxically, underestimated and sensationalized. VSR

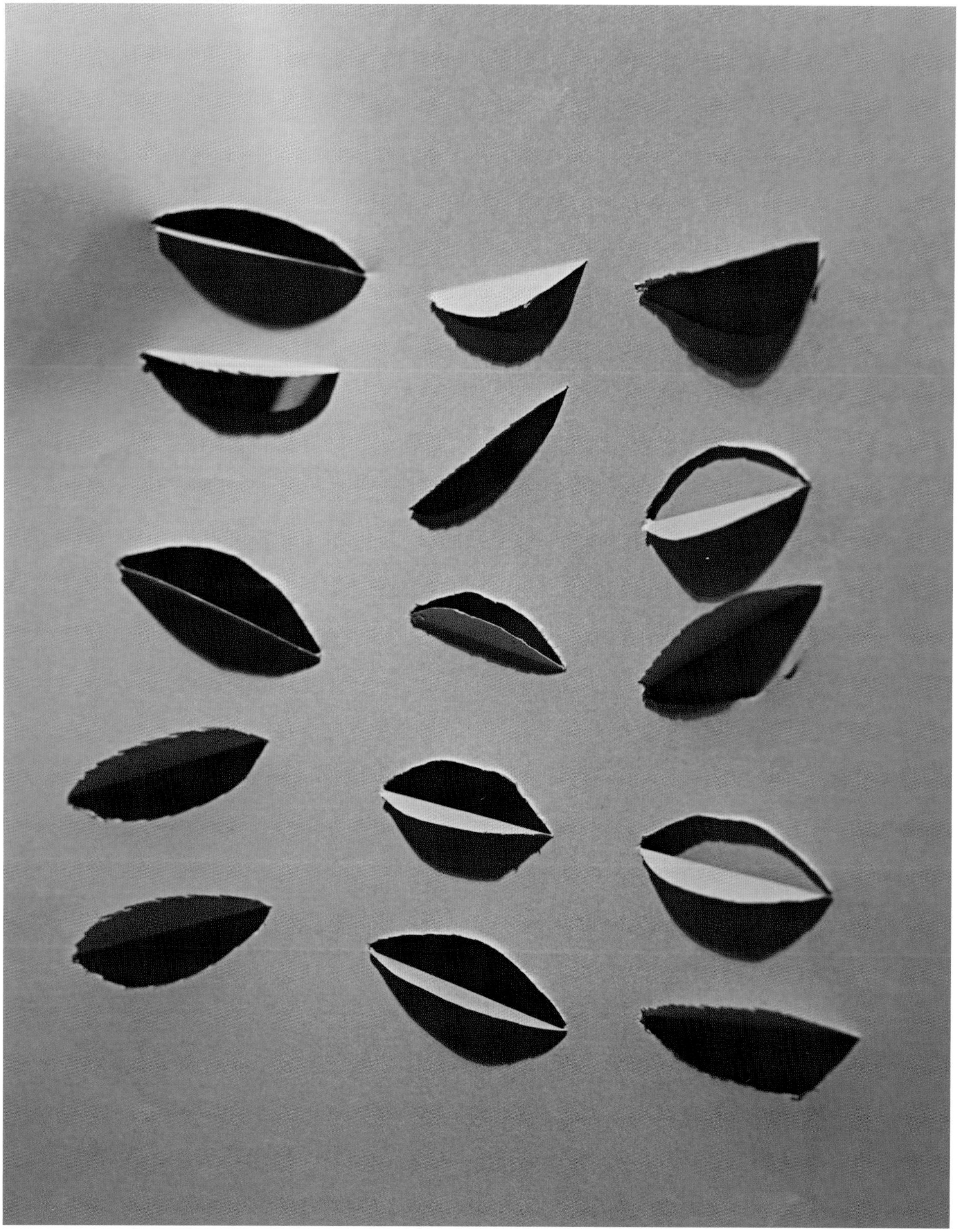

1

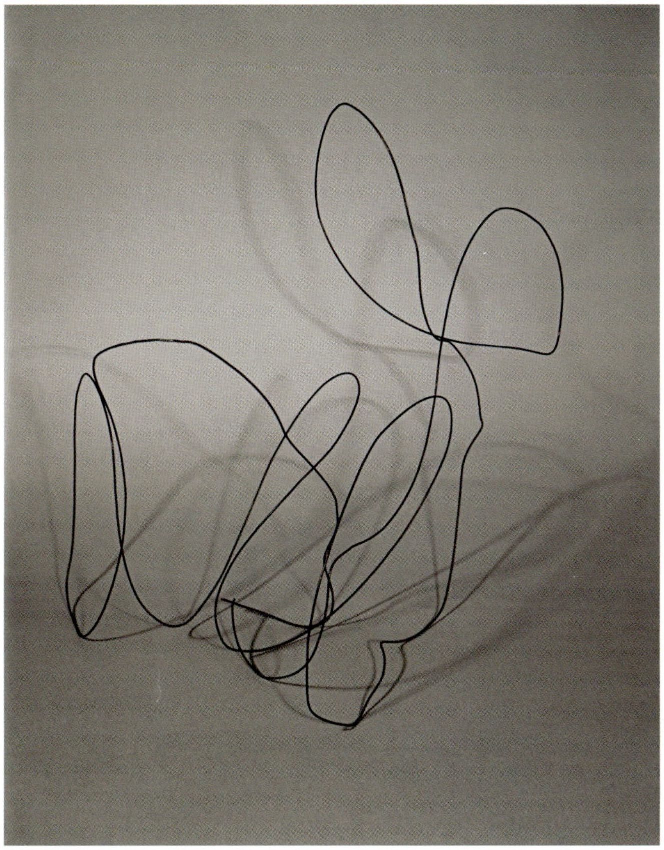

3

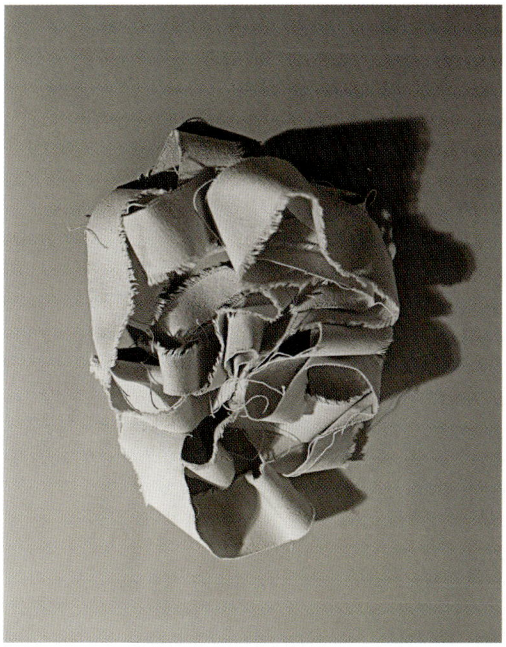

2

**Shown by**
The Box R19

**Biography**
Born 1972
Lives in Los Angeles

American artist Conaway has featured in one- and two-person exhibitions at galleries including The Box, Los Angeles (2011), Iceberg Projects, Chicago (2010), Gallery Diet, Miami (2010), and Bellwether Gallery, New York (2008). Her work has been included in group shows such as 'Made in LA', Hammer Museum, Los Angeles (2012), 'Plurielles', Gallery 64bis, Paris (2009), and 'Post Rose: Artists In and Out of Hazard Park Complex', Galerie Christian Nagel, Berlin (2007).

1
*III*
2011
Chromogenic print
56 × 43 cm
Courtesy of The Box

2
*V*
2011
Chromogenic print
56 × 43 cm
Courtesy of The Box

3
*IV*
2011
Chromogenic print
56 × 43 cm
Courtesy of The Box

# Frame
# Sarah Conaway

In the photographs of artist Sarah Conaway ordinary objects are transformed into sculptural entities. A frayed end of ribbon is transformed into a blossom (*V*, 2011); cuts in a sheet of paper become disembodied mouths (*III*, 2011). Referencing both Surrealism and Modernism, Conaway's photographs might make you think of Dalí or Man Ray, but the emphasis on materiality means that the works remain rooted in the quotidian, as does the easy humour that pervades these images. The life of objects is the sly subject of Conaway's work, and her humour adds another layer to, rather than undercutting, the poetic aspirations of her work. KK

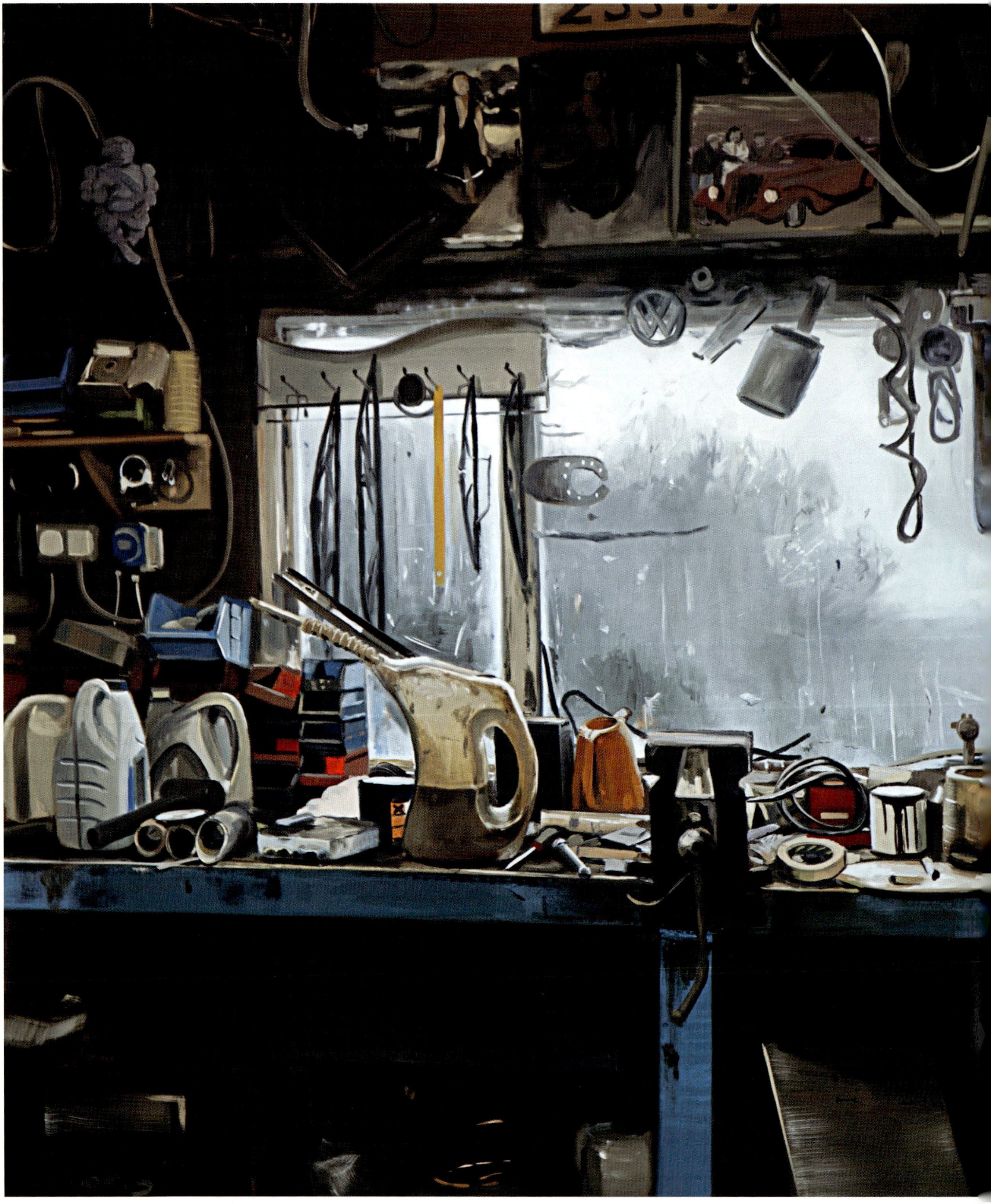

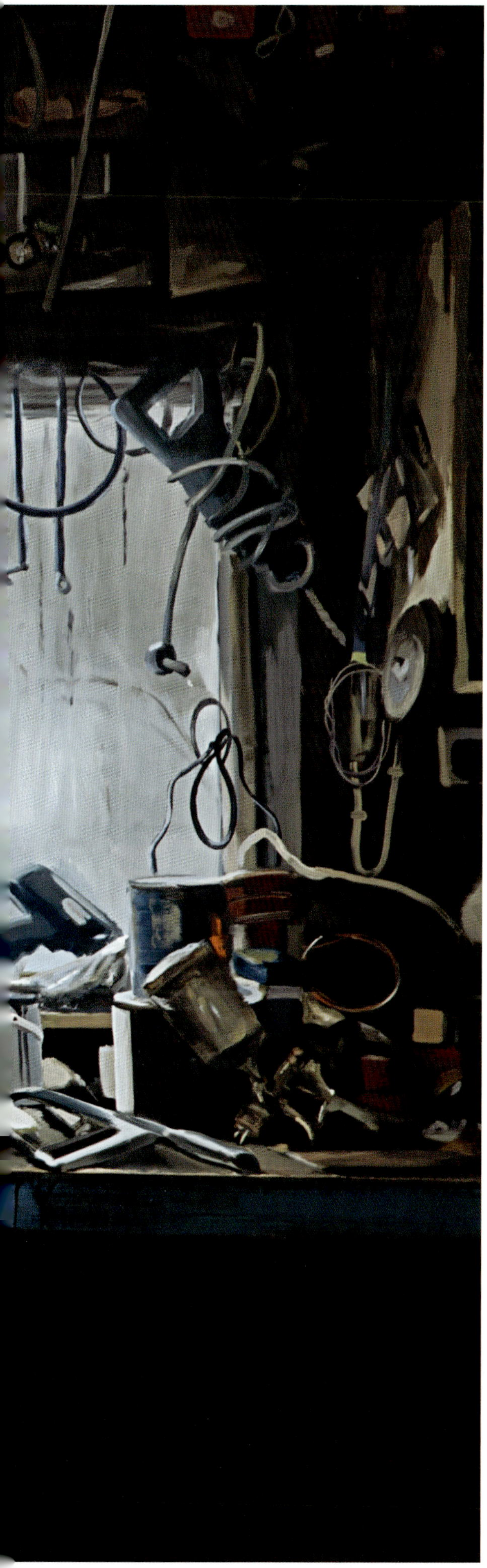

**Shown by**
mother's tankstation R15

**Biography**
Born 1984
Lives in Dublin

Irish-born painter Cosgrove has presented solo exhibitions at mother's tankstation, Dublin (2011 and 2008), and Lena Brüning Gallery, Berlin (2010). His work has been featured recently in group exhibitions that include 'Last', Douglas Hyde Gallery, Dublin (2012), 'Monkey Wrench', Ormoston House, Limerick (2011), and the UK touring exhibition 'Jerwood Contemporary Painters' (2010).

*Workshop (with Blue Bench)*
2011
Oil on linen
120 × 140 cm
Courtesy of mother's tankstation and AmC Collezione Coppola

# Frame
# Kevin Cosgrove

Wrenches, wires, sawdust, grit and oil stains: there's an almost obsessive attention to detail in Kevin Cosgrove's Photorealistic paintings of messy garages, cluttered work benches and immaculate workshops. His continued depiction of the workshop, that traditional male sanctuary, as always empty and unpopulated gives his large works on linen a meditative tone. This is both a steady, precise intent that reflects the characters who inhabit such spaces and also a hint at an elegy for a disappearing way of life. In *Workshop (with Blue Bench)* (2011) the grey light from a dirtied window just barely illuminates a jumbled still life of jugs of oil, tins of paint, tape and tools waiting to be put back to use. CFW

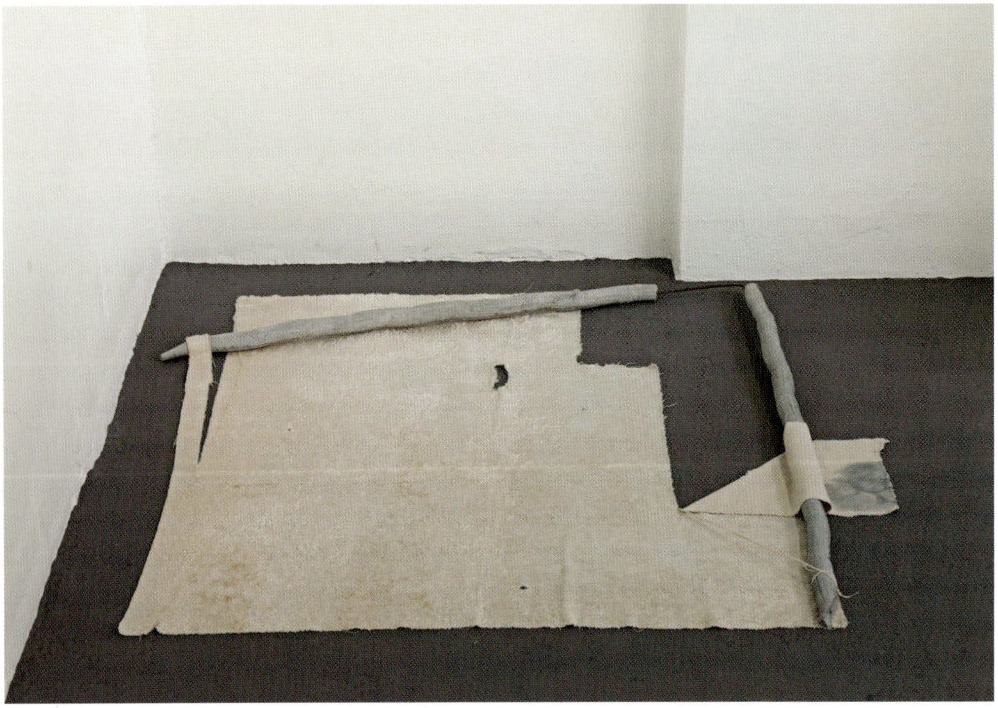

1

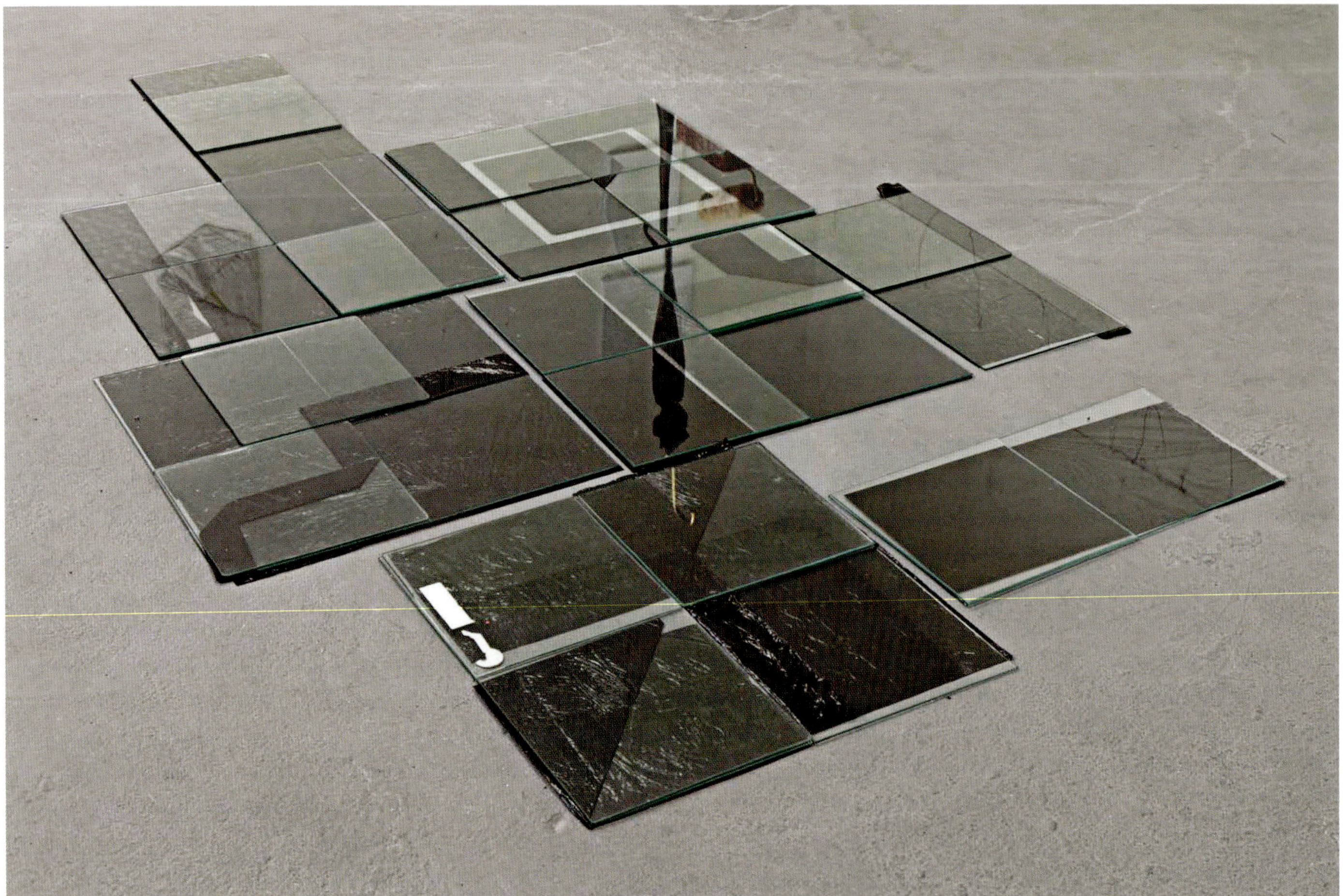

2

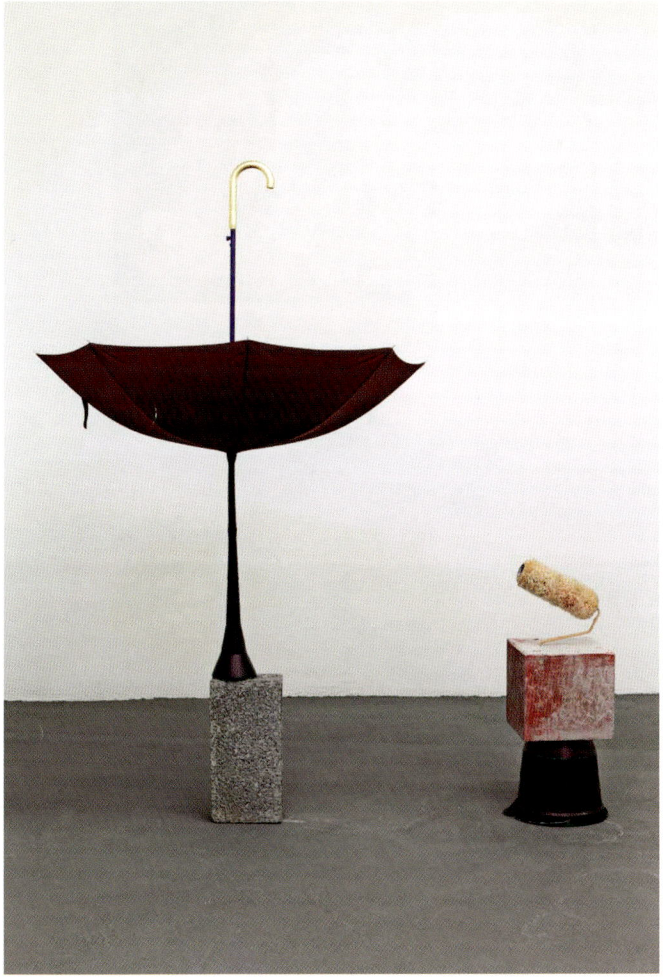

3

**Shown by**
Mendes Wood R17

**Biography**
Born 1975
Lives in Sao Paulo

Brazilian artist Costa has been the subject of solo shows at galleries in Sao Paulo that include Mendes Wood (2012), Centro Cultural Sao Paulo (2010) and Galeria Polinésia (2009). His work has featured as part of group exhibitions such as 'Abre Alas 8', A Gentil Carioca, Rio de Janeiro (2012), 'Mythologies', Cité Internationale des Arts, Paris (2011), and 'Tropical Punk', Whitechapel Gallery, London (2007).

1
*O quadrado campo*
(The Square Field)
2012
Cloth, steel and concrete
110 × 92 cm
Courtesy of Mendes Wood

2
*Os bananas da terra*
(The Plantains)
2012
Glass and plastic bags
190 × 312 cm
Courtesy of Mendes Wood

3
*Untitled*
2012
Umbrella, plastic horn and cement, paint roller, cement and bucket
Dimensions variable
Courtesy of Mendes Wood

# Frame
# Adriano Costa

Adriano Costa uses audaciously sparse materials and found objects to create works that are barely sculptural and seem to dispute the normative opposition between the animate and the inanimate, the organic and the man-made. Almost accidental in appearance, *O quadrado campo* (The Square Field, 2012) comprised a square of cloth alongside concrete casts of sugar cane. *Tapetes* (Carpets, 2010) was formed by scraps of textiles, rugs, T-shirts, raw cotton and flag fragments that had been laid out directly on the gallery floor. Discarded fabric wedges were docked as if a ragged geometry pie chart, for example, and strips of bath towels were gathered like origami. Many of these textiles brought 'a kind of emotional issue', in the artist's words: they were pilfered from friends' houses or bars. MA

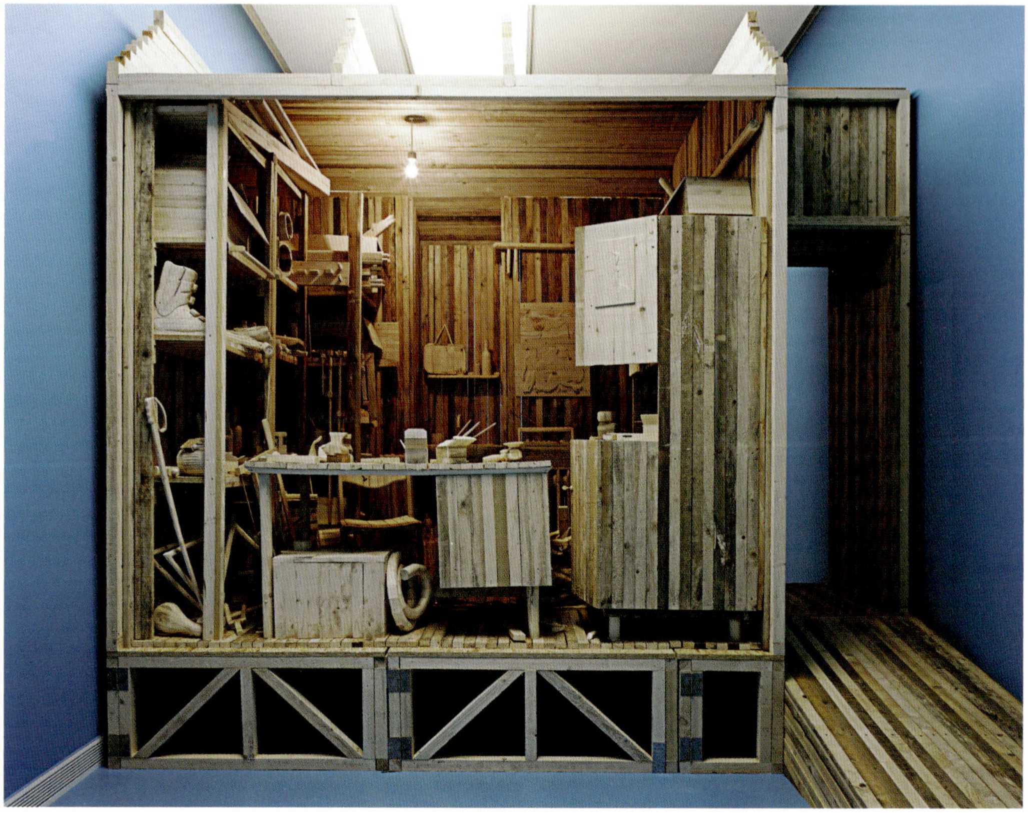

1

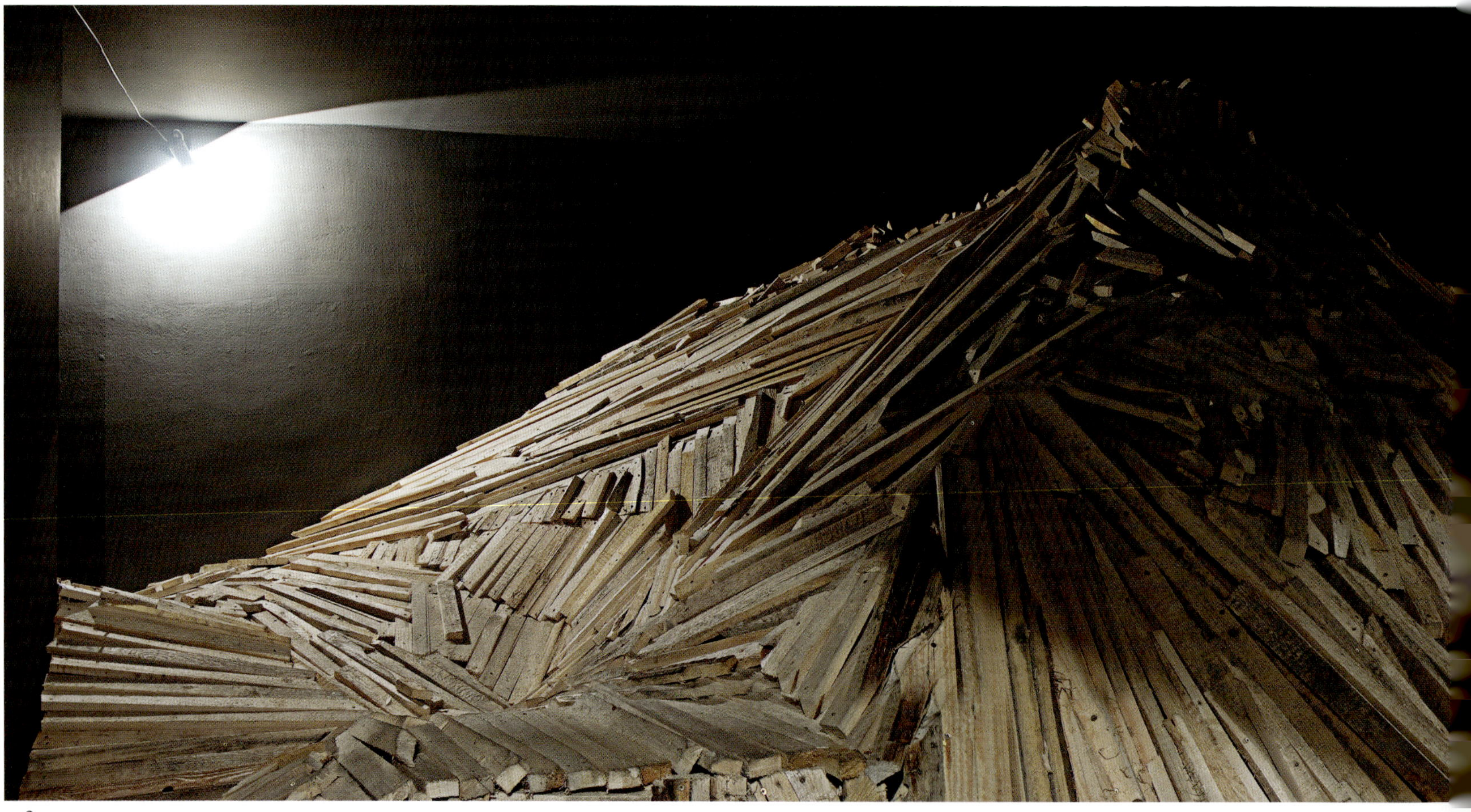

2

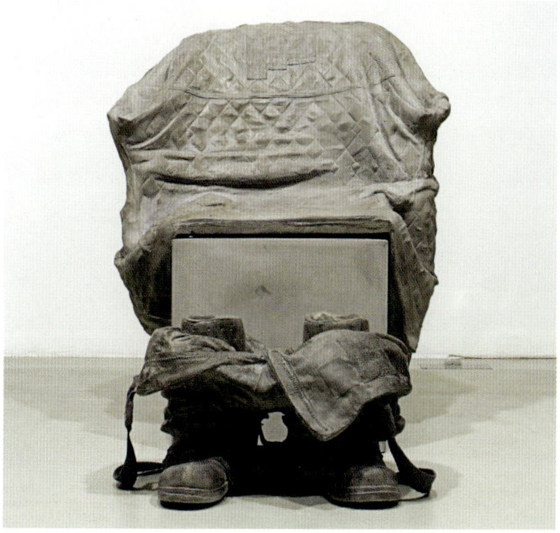

3

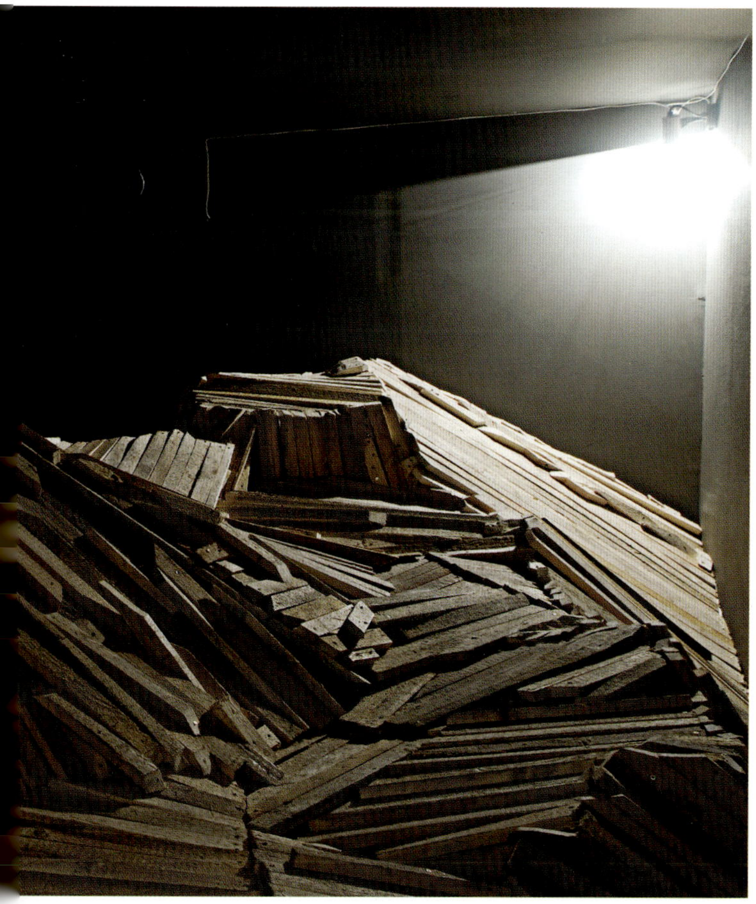

**Shown by**
Kisterem R16

**Biography**
Born 1978
Lives in Budapest

Romanian-born artist Csákány recently participated in Documenta 13, Kassel (2012). In 2010 he was the winner of a public art competition in the city of Pécs in memory of Marcel Breuer. Csákány's work has been featured in group exhibitions at venues such as Ernst Museum, Budapest (2011), and Ludwig Museum of Contemporary Art, Budapest (2010), and is part of collections including MUDAM, Luxembourg. His solo exhibition at the Polish Institute, Budapest, opens in October 2012.

1
*Bernsteinzimmer*
2010
Wood and light bulb
3 × 3 × 4 m
Courtesy of Kisterem

2
*The Choreography of the Mountain*
2008
Wood
4 × 5.5 × 8 m
Courtesy of Kisterem

3
*The Worker of Tomorrow*
2009
Concrete
78 × 130 × 114 cm
Courtesy of Kisterem

# Frame
# István Csákány

The body, and its physical, social and political relationship to the built environment, lies at the heart of István Csákány's practice. His sculptures and installations suggest historical narratives and spaces occupied or inhabited. *The Worker of Tomorrow* (2009), which consists of a cast-concrete pedestal, boots and outerwear, simultaneously awaits a worker inhabitant and memorializes the person who once wore them. In contrast, the immersive installation *The Choreography of the Mountain* (2008) was constructed from thousands of wooden battens and formed a mountain in the gallery that visitors were invited to climb—reaching its highest point, the visitor became the work's subject. Csákány puts the viewer at the centre of his art in an empathetic dialogue with his materials. SC

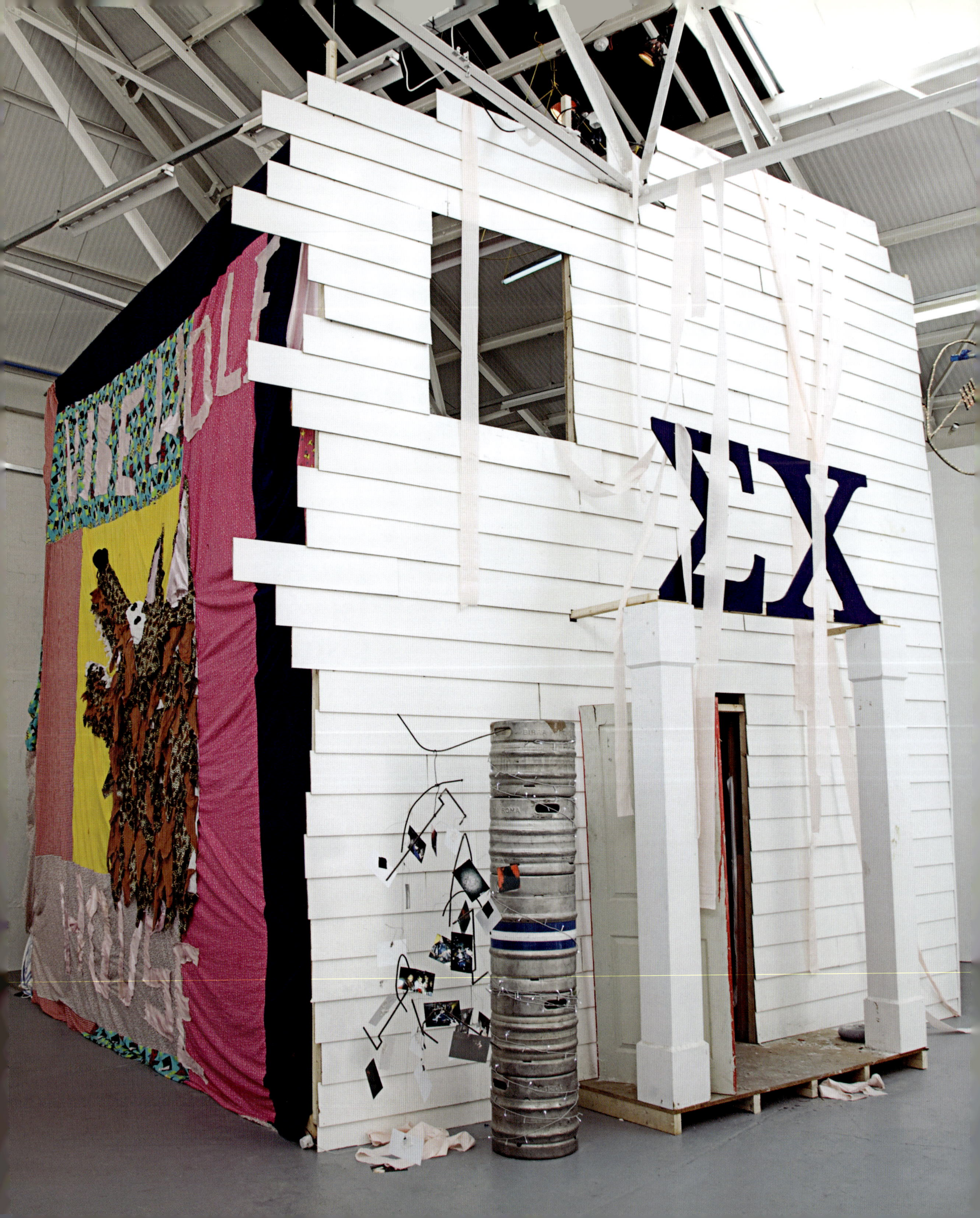
ΣΧ

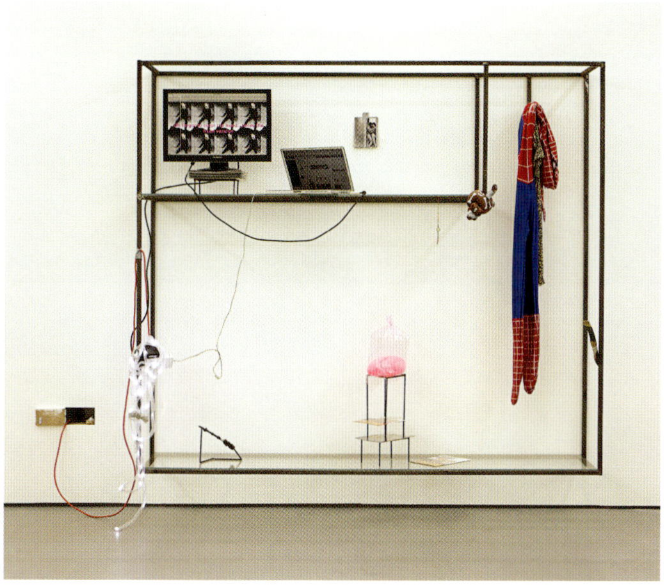

3

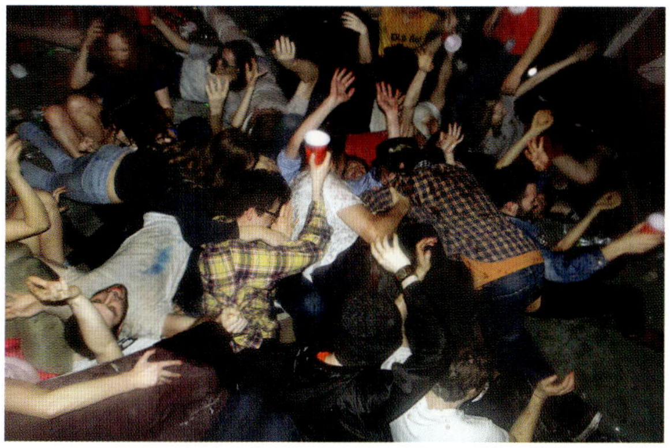

2

**Shown by**
Carlos/Ishikawa R7

**Biography**
Born 1983
Lives in London

British-born Fornieles' solo presentations include 'The Hangover Part II', Carlos/Ishikawa, London (2012), and 'Animal House', Guest Projects, London (2011), as well as a project for the Serpentine Gallery's 'Park Nights' programme (2012). Fornieles has featured in group exhibitions such as 'Technicolor Yawn' at Import Projects, Berlin (2011), and his performances have been presented at venues such as Barbican Art Gallery, London (2011 and 2010).

1
*Animal House 2: Revenge of the Nerdz*
2011
Mixed media
Installation view at the Royal College of Art, London
5 × 4.5 × 5 m
Courtesy of Carlos/Ishikawa

2
*Animal House*
2011
Performance
Courtesy of Carlos/Ishikawa

3
*Adventureland*
2011
Mixed media
202 × 231 × 54 cm
Courtesy of Carlos/Ishikawa

# Frame
# Ed Fornieles

The superficial outputs of popular culture lie at the root of Ed Fornieles' practice. His recent sculptures and installations incorporated the ready-made artefacts of Western youth in amplified or caricatured parodies. *Adventureland* (2011), a wall-based sculpture that incorporates a number of items commonly associated with US-style student living, isolates the items in a museum-esque display, while *Dorm Daze* (2011), Fornieles' 'Facebook sitcom', sees a fictitious narrative played out online. The participants in the live event *Animal House* (2011) engaged in a self-styled frat party, and in the later installation *Animal House 2: Revenge of the Nerdz* (2011) a makeshift fraternity house—complete with bed, iMac and US flag—filled the gallery with imposing brashness. SC

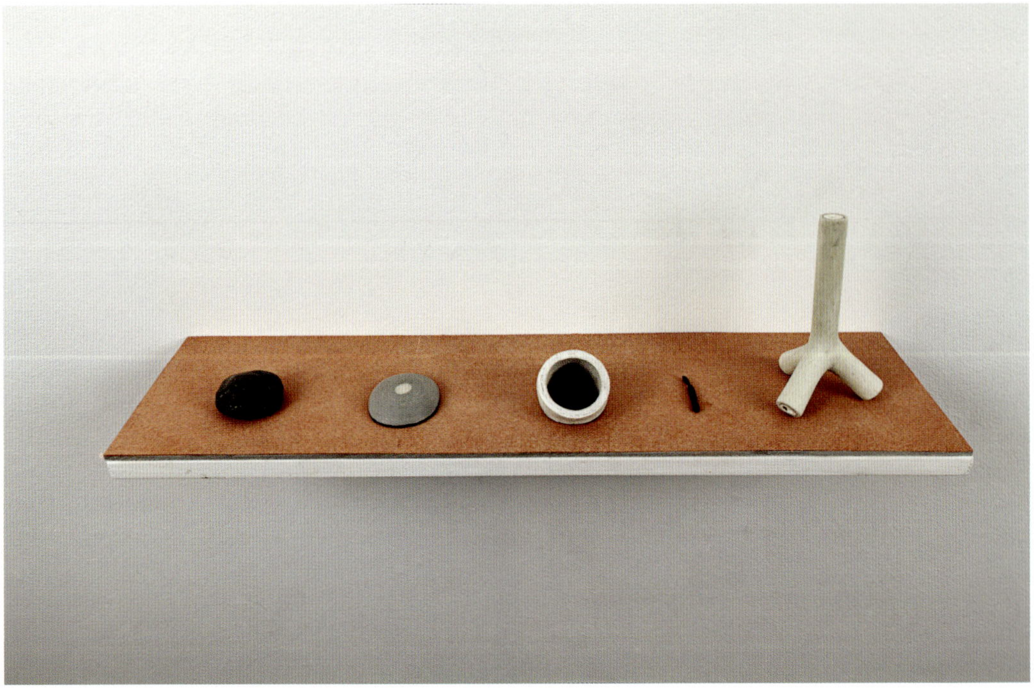

1

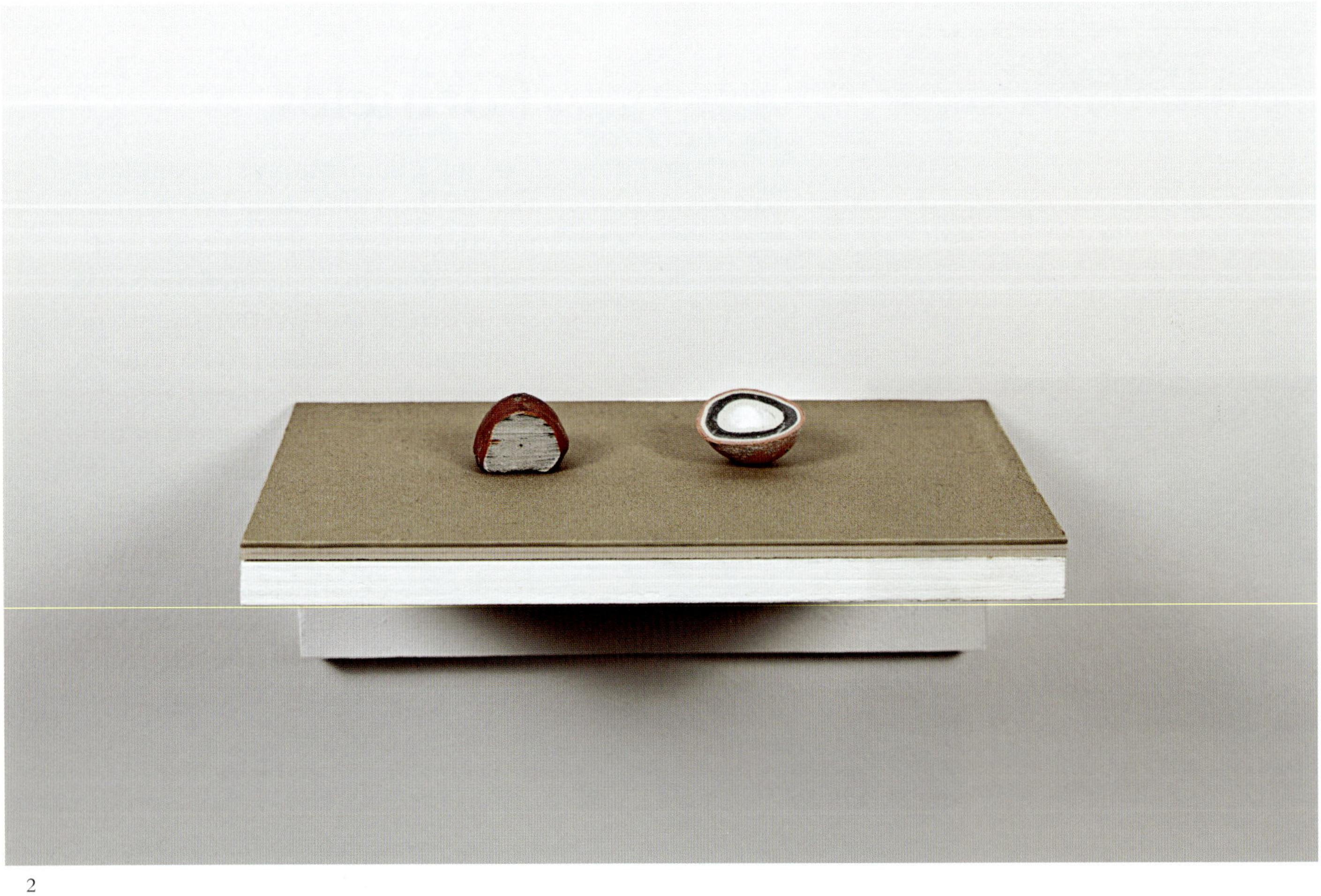

2

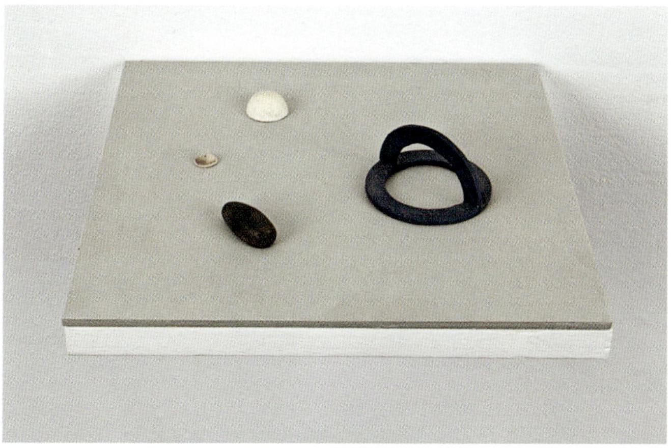

3

**Shown by**
Bureau R12

**Biography**
Born 1975
Lives in New York

American artist Hoyt has presented solo exhibitions at Bureau, New York (2012), and Marquise Dance Hall, New York (2005), and was the subject of a two-person show with Mark Van Yetter, 'Escalator to Common Art', at Dispatch, New York (2008). In 2012 he featured in the Whitney Biennial, Whitney Museum of American Art, New York. Previous group exhibitions include 'Inglorious Days', Coco Kunstverein, Vienna (2011), and 'Greater New York', MoMA PS1, New York (2010).

1
*Untitled (Group 28)*
2006–11
Mixed media
12 × 46 × 13 cm
Courtesy of the Speyer Family Collection

2
*Untitled (Group 60)*
2008–11
Mixed media
3 × 22 × 14 cm
Courtesy of Bureau

3
*Untitled (Group 20)*
2011
Mixed media
3 × 18 × 18 cm
Courtesy of the Speyer Family Collection

# Frame
# Matt Hoyt

Matt Hoyt creates sets of small sculpture, which are carefully arranged for the viewer's contemplation. Apparently simple objects reveal themselves to be complex and mysterious; abstract forms possess multiple textures and materials, and are evocative of both organic and man-made shapes. *Untitled (Group 60)* (2008–11) features two rock-like formations, graphically split in half. These objects invoke a series of possible narratives (excavations, nature expeditions, childhood exploration). But it is in the orchestration of objects on a single plane that Hoyt most excels, each sculptural arrangement taking on an almost architectural significance. KK

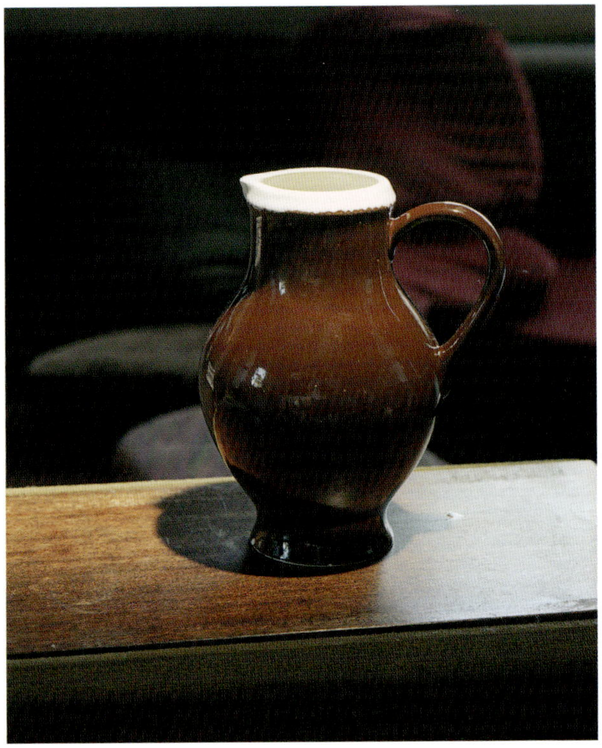

1

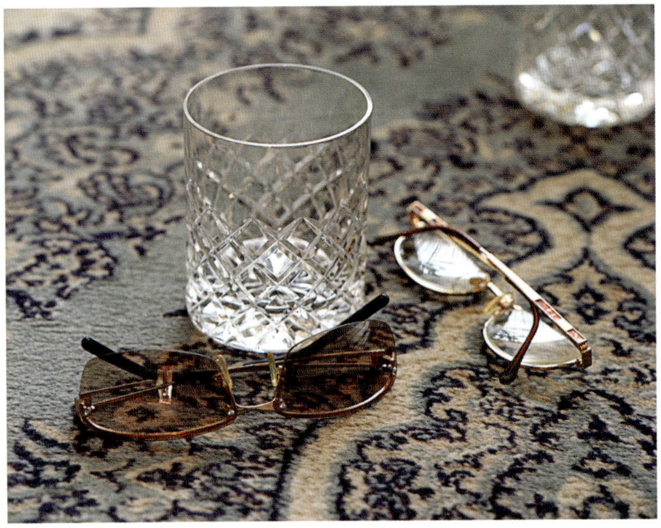

2

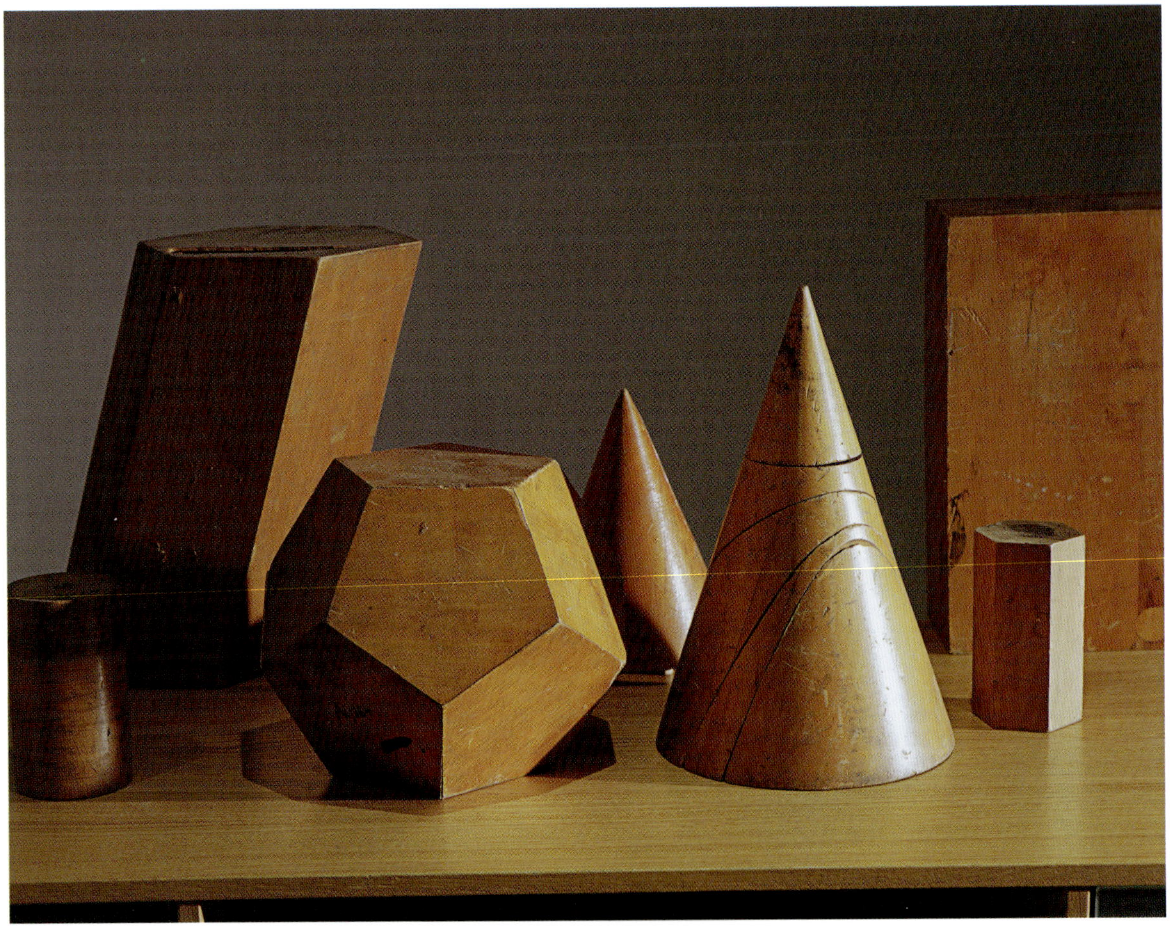

3

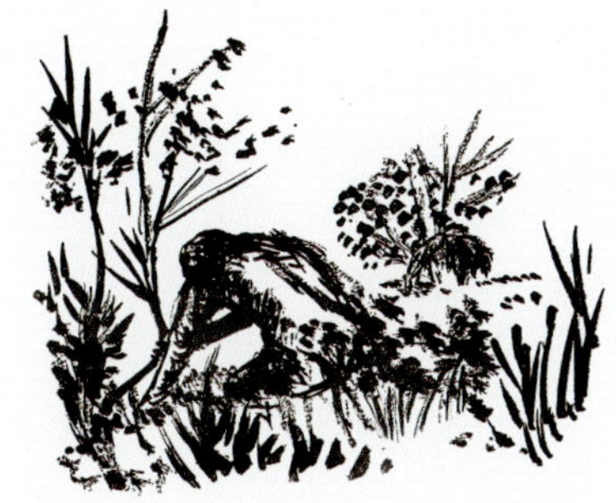

6

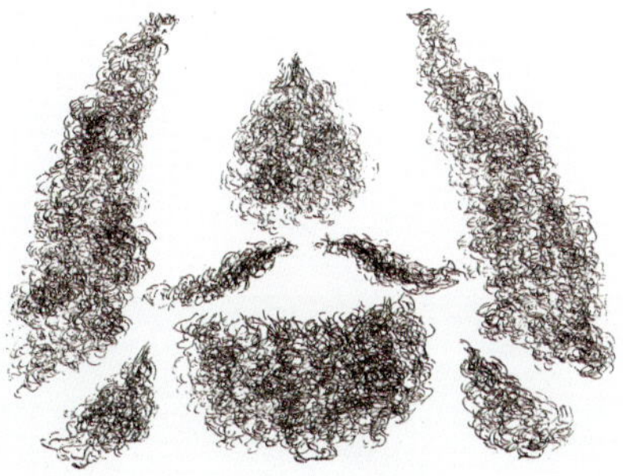

5

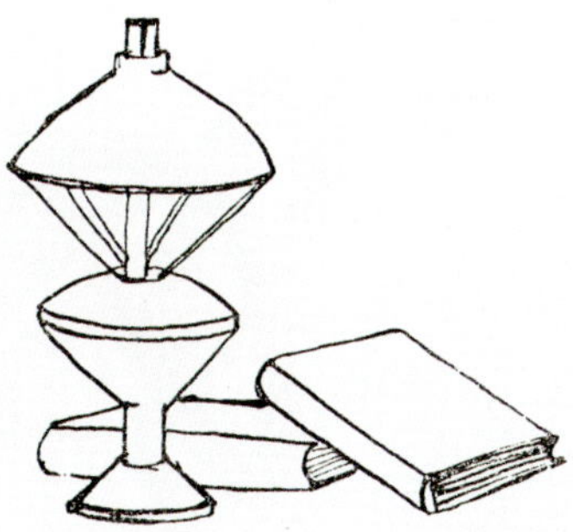

4

**Shown by**
SVIT R9

**Biography**
Born 1965/1966
Live in Prague

Jasanský and Polák, both born in Prague, have presented their work in solo exhibitions in venues that include the Ostrava House of Arts, Ostrava (2011), Ferdinand Baumann Gallery, Prague (2011), Jelení Gallery, Prague (2010), and Wannieck Gallery, Brno (2009). Their work was included in the group show 'The Islands of Resistance: Between the First and Second Modernity, 1985–2012', National Gallery, Prague (2012). JRP-Ringier publishes a book of their work in autumn 2012.

1
*Untitled*
From the series 'Colour Photography'
2010–11
Lambda print
126 × 100 cm
Courtesy of SVIT

2
*Untitled*
From the series 'Colour Photography'
2010–11
Lambda print
40 × 50 cm
Courtesy of SVIT

3
*Untitled*
From the series 'Colour Photography'
2010–11
Lambda print
100 × 126 cm
Courtesy of SVIT

4, 5, 6
*Untitled*
Each from the series 'Drawings'
1988
Silver gelatin prints
Each 50 × 60 cm
Courtesy of SVIT

## Frame
# Lukáš Jasanský & Martin Polák

Lukáš Jasanský and Martin Polák's early work proceeded from a resistance to the subjectivity then dominating Czech fine art photography, in for instance their photo series 'Abstraction' (1994–5), which posed the photographic medium as a bridge between the representational and the abstract, or their later monochrome 'County Photography' (1998–2000), which documented changes occurring in the physical landscape of the former Czechoslovakia during the transition from Communism to capitalism. Their more recent series 'Colour Photography' (2010–12) shares the deadpan quality of their earlier work and, like their previous projects, presents views of odd details (such as an empty whisky glass with two pairs of spectacles) as sly mediations on reality and the nature of truth. SL

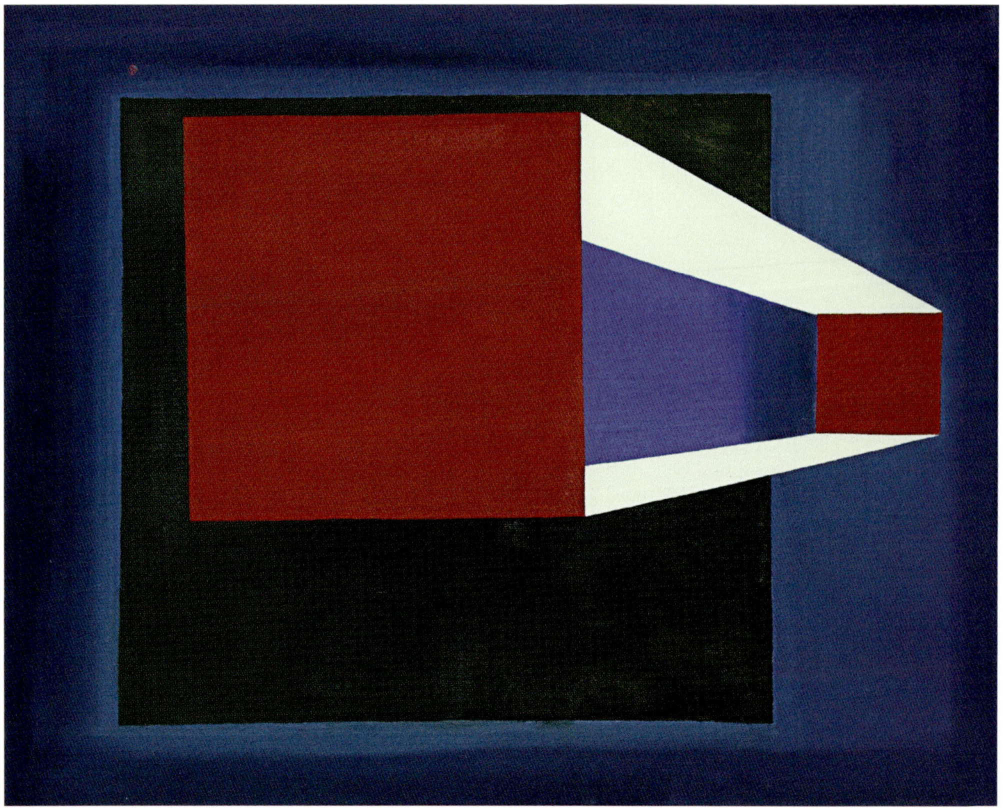

1

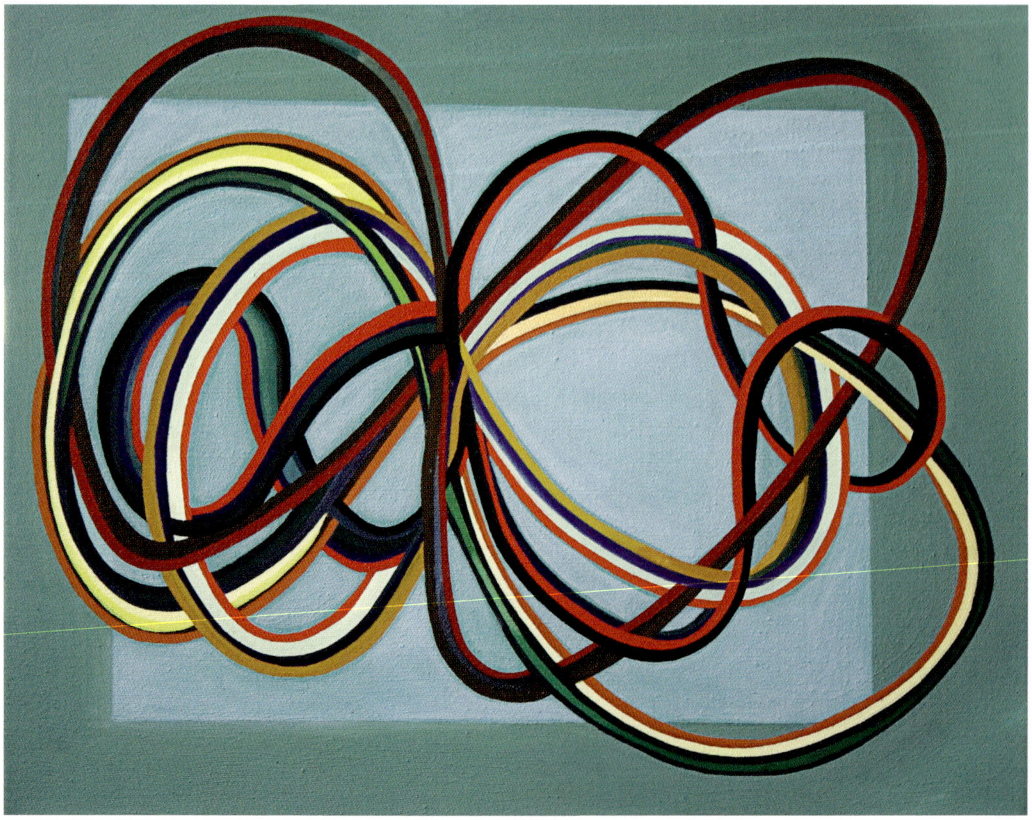

2

# Frame
# Magdalena Jitrik

**Shown by**
Ignacio Liprandi Arte Contemporáneo R18
Galeria Luisa Strina F6

**Biography**
Born 1966
Lives in Buenos Aires

Buenos Aires-born Jitrik has presented solo shows at Galería Luisa Strina, Sao Paulo (2010), Galería Dabbah Torrejón, Buenos Aires (2010), and Museo de Bellas Artes, Bahia Blanca (2009). She participated in Manifesta 9, Genk (2012), and the 12th Istanbul Biennial (2011), and has featured in group exhibitions at galleries such as Fundación OSDE, Buenos Aires (2012), and Centro de Arte Dos de Mayo, Madrid (2010).

1
*Untitled*
2011
Oil on canvas
40 × 60 cm
Courtesy of Ignacio Liprandi Arte Contemporáneo

2
*Untitled*
2011
Oil on canvas
40 × 65 cm
Courtesy of Ignacio Liprandi Arte Contemporáneo

3
*Untitled*
2011
Watercolour on paper
25 × 32 cm
Courtesy of Ignacio Liprandi Arte Contemporáneo

Painting, for Magdalena Jitrik, is a character in a broader epic drama, a player whose importance in the story has yet to be realized. Where previous series of her work have drawn directly from political struggles and slogans, casting abstract painting as an expressly activist personality, the painting of her more recent work is a wandering itinerant. *Untitled* (2011) has a red and white rectangle floating over fields of green and blue, its vibrant colours a sort of Californian take on Constructivism. Presented alongside preparatory drawings of the painting and photos of it in different outdoor settings, it becomes a global tourist, its apparent innocence in the situation altered only by our own views of a burgeoning internationalism. CFW

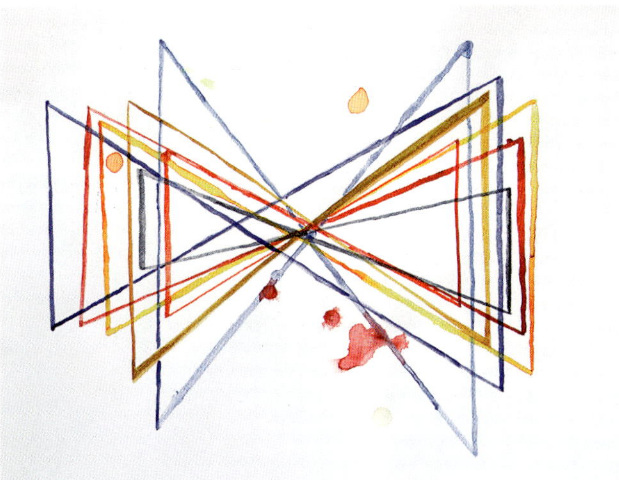

3

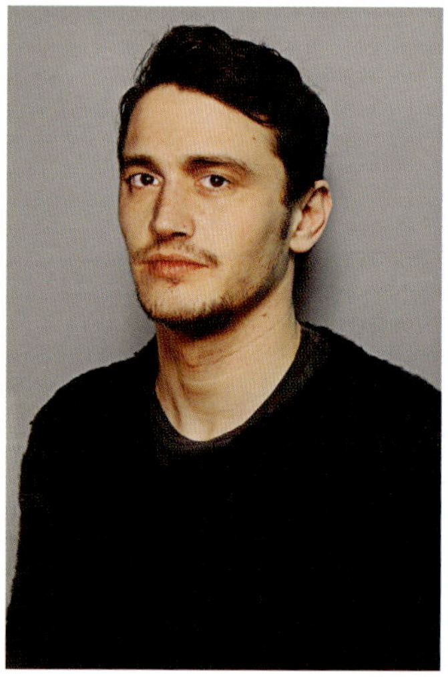

2

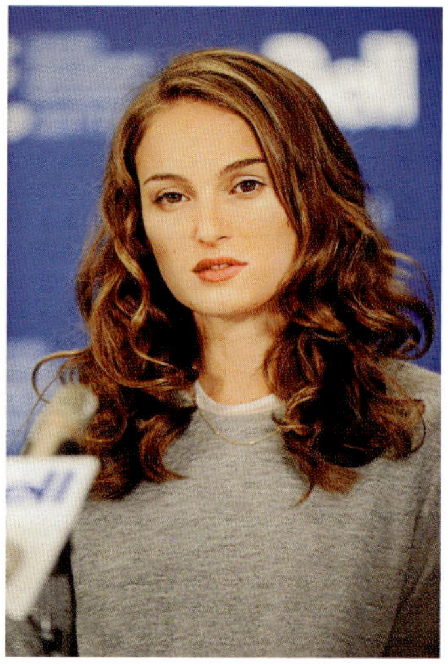

1

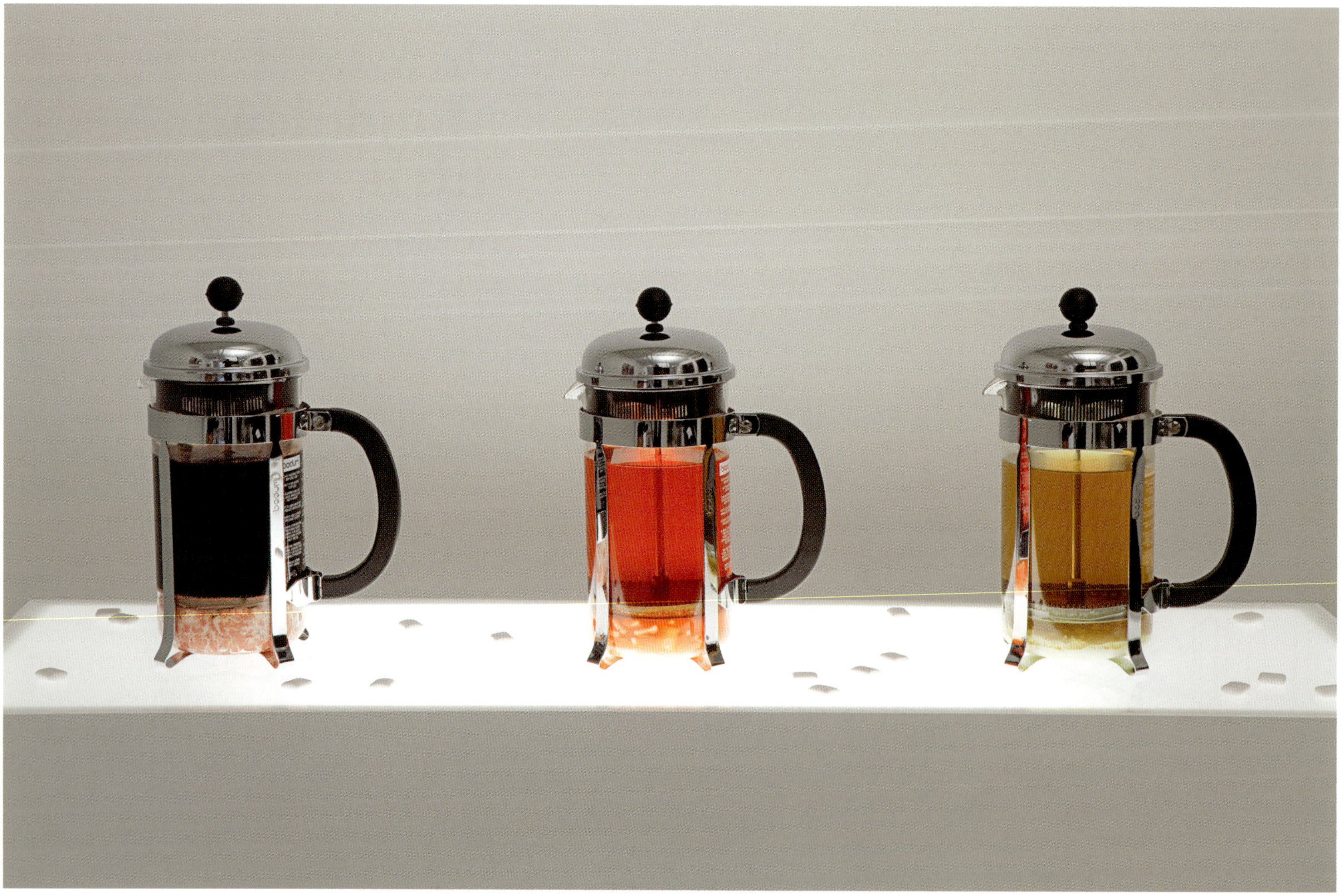

3

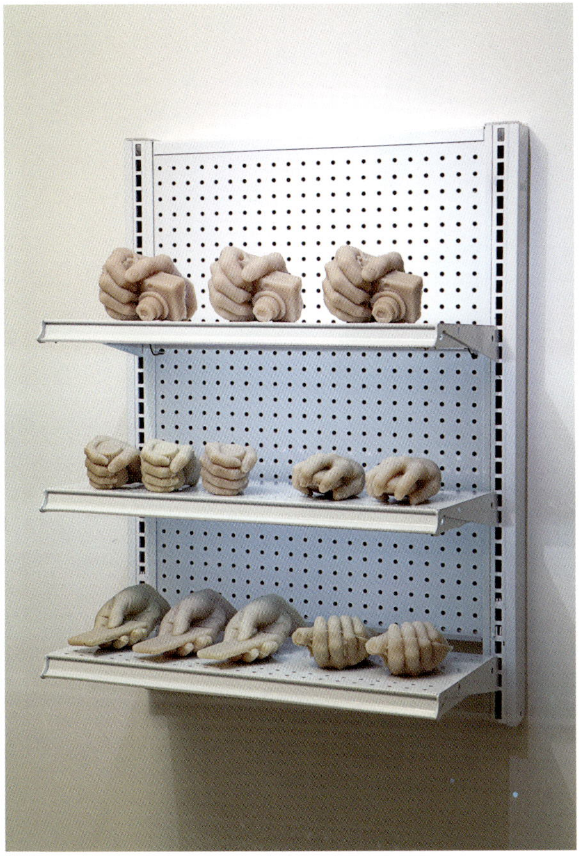

4

**Shown by**
47 Canal R6

**Biography**
Born 1979
Lives in New York

Philadelphia-born Kline presented the solo show 'Dignity and Self Respect' at 47 Canal, New York (2011), and featured together with Anicka Yi in exhibition 'Loveless Marriages', 179 Canal, New York (2010). Group exhibitions include 'Looking Back/The 6th White Columns Annual', White Columns, New York (2011), as well as shows at galleries such as West, The Hague (2011), IMO, Copenhagen (2011), and Galerie Christine Mayer, Munich (2009).

1
*Actress/Shoplifter/Psychology Major*
2011
Photograph
76 × 51 cm
Courtesy 47 Canal

2
*Dress Jeans*
2011
Photograph
76 × 51 cm
Courtesy of 47 Canal

3
*Sleep is for the Weak*
2011
Mixed media
102 × 91 × 31 cm
Courtesy of 47 Canal

4
*Creative Hands*
2011
13 pigmented silicone hands, Madix shelving and LED lights
93 × 67 × 40 cm
Courtesy of 47 Canal

# Frame
# Josh Kline

Envisioning an anxious, post-human existence in which bodies fuse with media images and aspirational tools, Josh Kline has videotaped interviews with real-life internship applicants on a stage set, boiled spring water bottles in the water they contained and refilled them with the plastic-tainted liquid, and subtly Photoshopped celebrity portraits. He sometimes uses cool LED lighting inspired by that of a New York drugstore chain to display his unsettling relics. Coffee presses in *Sleep is for the Weak* (2011) contain jewel-like energizing, numbing and focus-enhancing liquids that resemble bodily fluids, such as Vivarin-infused Red Bull. And in *Creative Hands* (2011), 13 silicone fists—displayed like products on functional shelving—grasp poignantly flesh-coloured accessories of contemporary creative work, including digital cameras and iPhones. KMJ

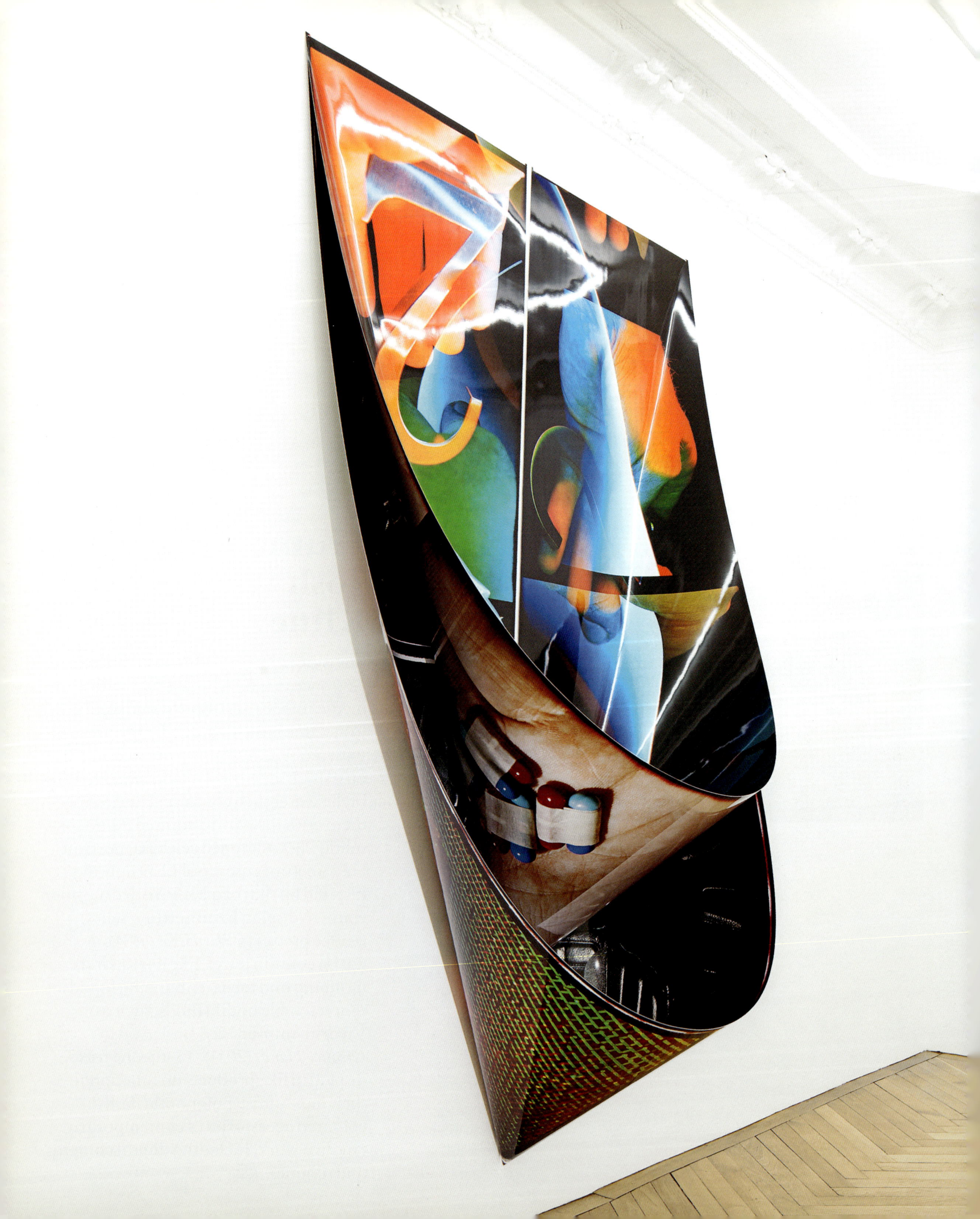

**Shown by**
Société R8

**Biography**
Born 1984
Lives in New York

Brooklyn-based artist Kolbo graduated in 2007 from the Pratt Institute's School of Art and Design, New York, and has since held solo exhibitions at galleries including Société, Berlin (2012), Tony Wight Gallery, Chicago (2011), and Max Hans Daniel, Berlin and London (2010). He had also participated in a range of group shows including 'Schach Matt', Märkischen Museum, Witten (2012), 'Monochrome', Salts, Basel (2012), 'NY: New Perspectives', Brand New Gallery, Milan (2011), and 'Re: Empire', Team Gallery, New York (2011).

*Untitled*
2012
C-type print
356 × 206 × 81 cm
Courtesy of Société

# Frame
# Josh Kolbo

American artist Josh Kolbo explores the sculptural potential of photography. Using large-scale, double-sided colour photographs, he drapes, hangs and layers his images, often obfuscating their 'photographic' legibility in order to create new meaning through three-dimensionality. The combination of gloss and the repurposed makes one think of John Chamberlain's sculptures. But it's clear Kolbo locates himself in a photographic tradition that is rapidly changing; *Untitled* (2012), for example, contains four separate images, each of which is only partially visible, but which together capture the visual multiplicity of contemporary digital culture. KK

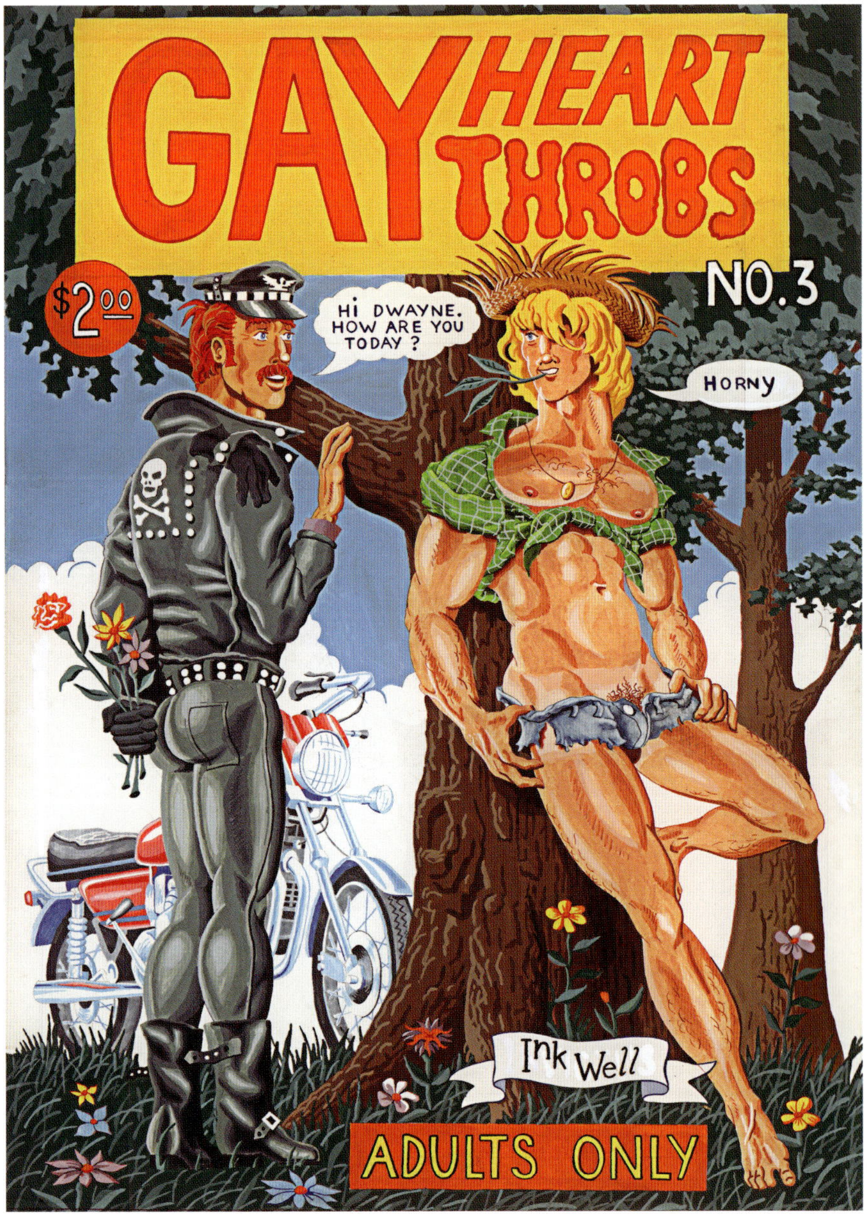
GAY HEART THROBS
NO.3
$2.00
HI DWAYNE. HOW ARE YOU TODAY ?
HORNY
Ink Well
ADULTS ONLY

1

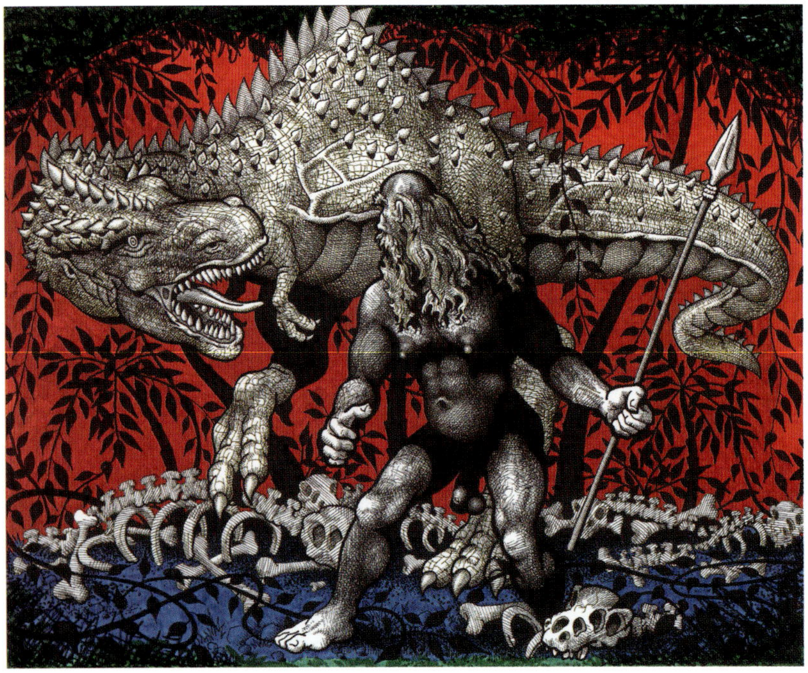

2

# Frame
# Mike Kuchar

In collaboration with his twin brother George Kuchar, Mike Kuchar was a pioneer of the burgeoning underground film scene in New York in the 1960s and '70s. From his early low-budget films using sexual subversion, comedy and bad taste as a testing ground for cinematic and narrative experimentation to his more recent fantastical and erotic illustrations that playfully explore a queer alternative mythological and biblical history, his work examines the aesthetics of camp with a lightness of touch. His work on paper *Adam and Steve* (1985) shows two muscle-bound men in the Garden of Eden demurely eating apples and approached by a long, coiling, serpent-like animal—which turns out to be a harmless brontosaurus. PT

**Shown by**
François Ghebaly
Gallery R21

**Biography**
Born 1942
Lives in San Francisco

New York-born Mike Kuchar received the Vanguard Director Award at the CineVegas Film Festival 2009 and the Frameline Award at the San Francisco International LGBT Film Festival 2009, together with his brother and collaborator George Kuchar. He has taught filmmaking at the San Francisco Art Institute since the 1970s, and his recent exhibitions include group shows 'Material Underground' at François Ghebaly Gallery, Los Angeles (2012), and 'Something Anything' at Matthew Marks Gallery, New York (2002).

1
*Gay Heart Throbs No. 3*
1979
Acrylic on posterboard
71 × 50 cm
Courtesy of François Ghebaly Gallery and 2nd Floor Projects

2
*Man and Monster*
1985
Pen, felt-tip pens, ink and watercolour on paper
40 × 50 cm
Courtesy of François Ghebaly Gallery and 2nd Floor Projects

3
*Adam and Steve*
1985
Pen, felt-tip pens, ink and watercolour on paper
61 × 46 cm
Courtesy of François Ghebaly Gallery and 2nd Floor Projects

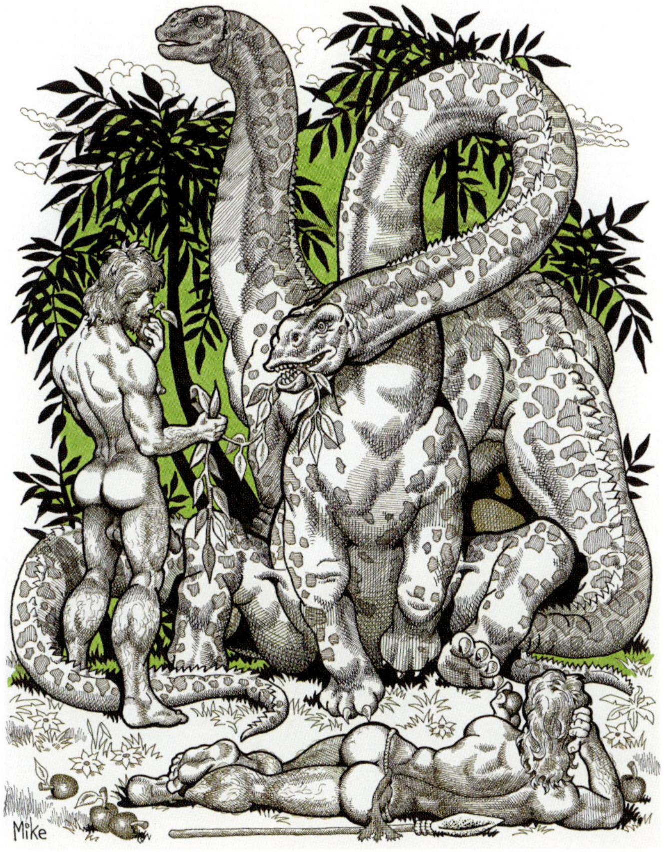


3

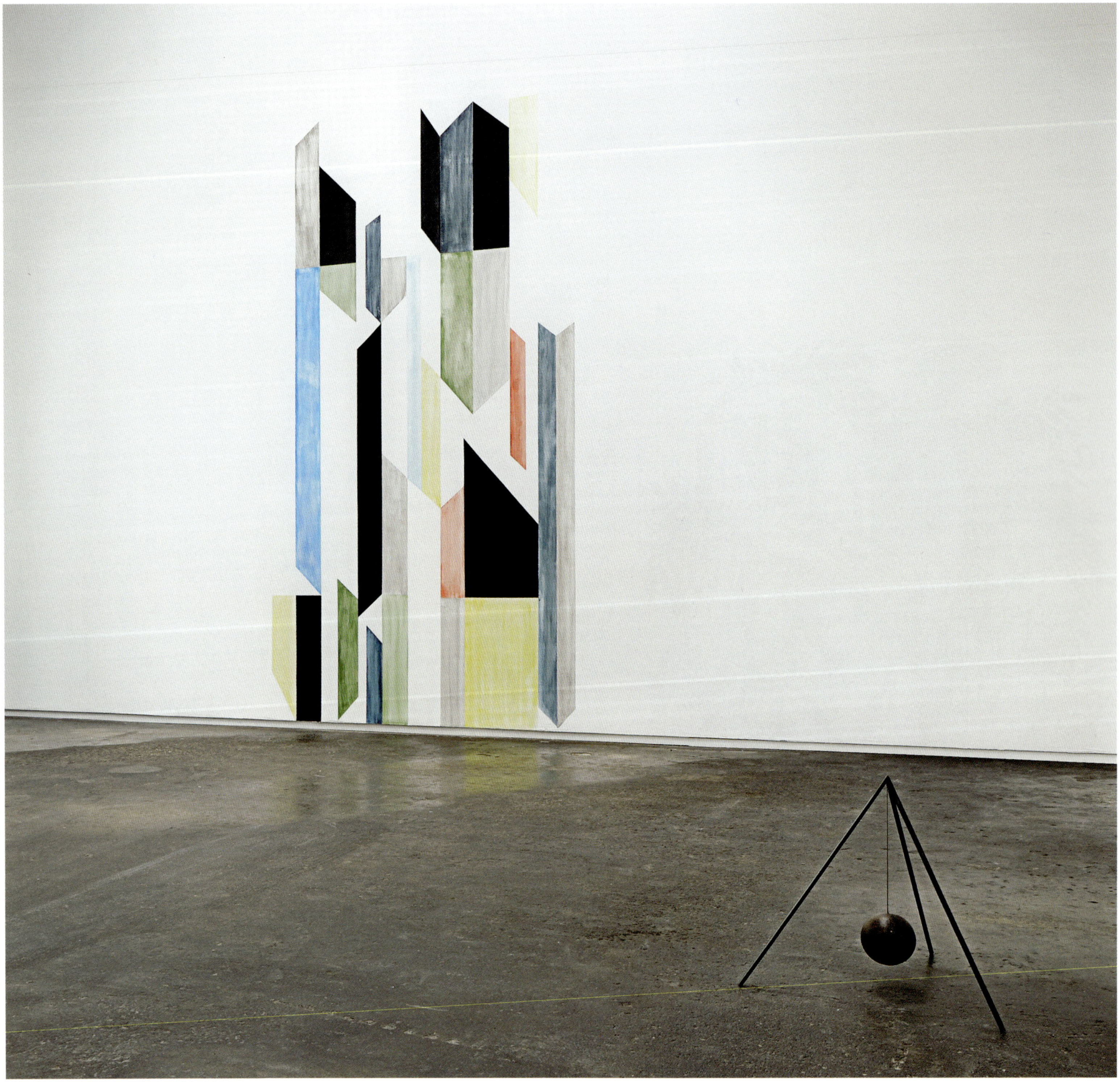

1

**Shown by**
Maisterravalbuena R14

**Biography**
Born 1979
Lives in Paris and New York

Polish artist Loboda has shown solo exhibitions at galleries across Europe including Maisterravalbuena, Madrid (2011), Krome Gallery, Berlin (2010), and Bielefelder Kunstverein, Bielefeld (2010). She has also participated in numerous group shows including 'Soundworks', ICA, London (2012), '(entre) ouverture', Palais de Tokyo, Paris (2012), and 'The Long Dark', Kettle's Yard, Cambridge (2009). In 2012 she presented work as part of Documenta 13, Kassel.

1
*Walldrawing (Cyanide, Arsenic, Mercury, Lead)*
2010
Pigments containing toxins on wall
Installation view
Dimensions variable
Courtesy of Maisterravalbuena and Schleicher+Lange

2
*Curious and Cold Epicurean Young Ladies*
2011
Platinum-plated silver flask, hydrogen, oxygen and metal chain
13 × 11 × 1 cm on variable chain
Courtesy of Maisterravalbuena and Schleicher+Lange

# Frame
# Maria Loboda

Put simply, Maria Loboda is interested in the relationship between language and objects. What complicates things is that this relationship is not at all straightforward. Ciphers, codes, magic spells and translations use encryption and decryption to hide, mask, conjure and transform language. What happens when those tools are imported into an art work? The results can be explosive, as in *Curious and Cold Epicurean Young Ladies* (2011), a platinum-plated flask filled with hydrogen, which would burst if opened and exposed to oxygen. Loboda's project for Frame at Frieze Art Fair, *A Sentence in its Temporary Form as Fabrics and Crystal Ashtrays* (2012), relies on a cipher based on a bilateral alphabet, developed by the philosopher Francis Bacon, and uses objects, such as crystal ashtrays and fabric, to delineate a cryptic field full of hidden meanings. VSR

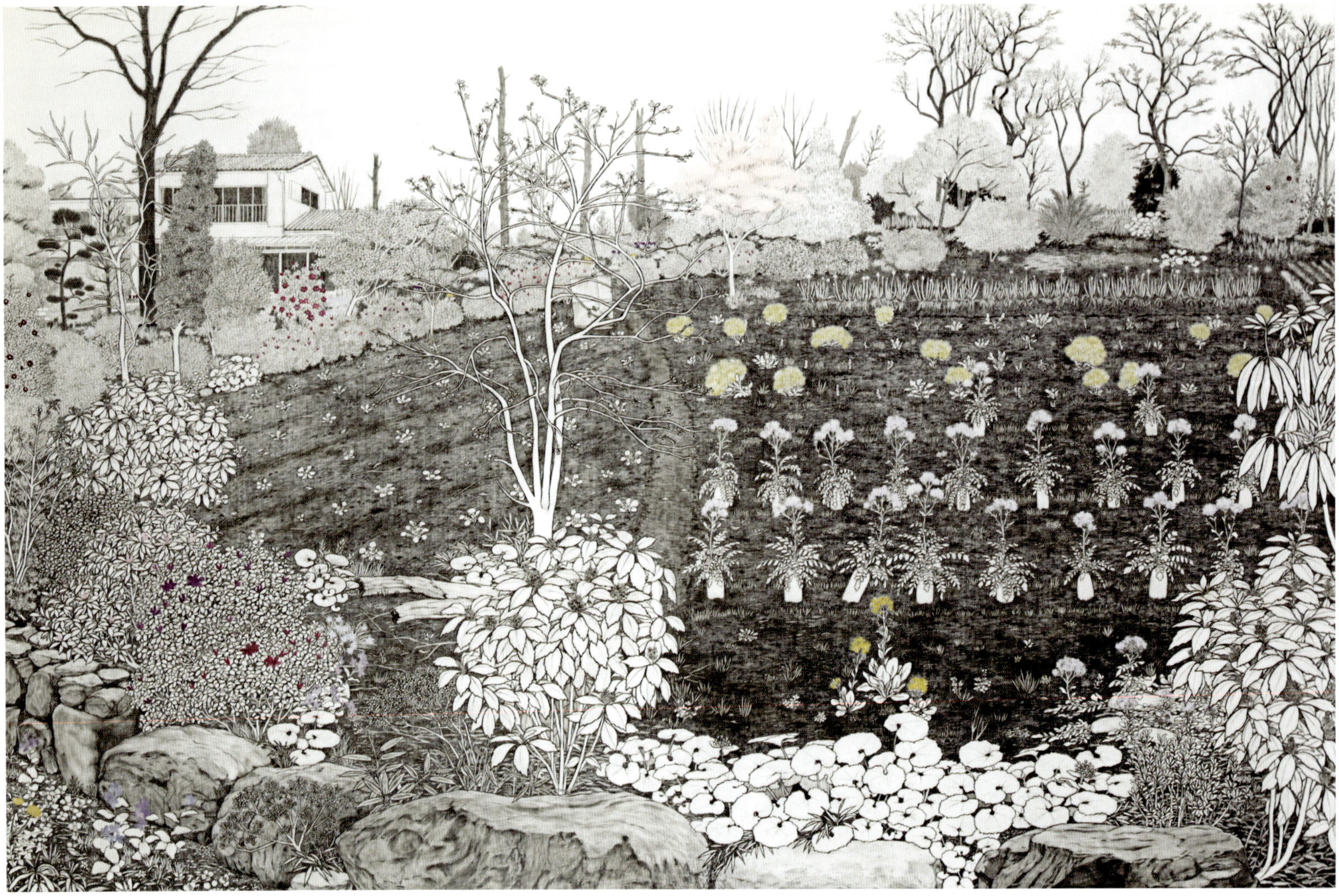

1

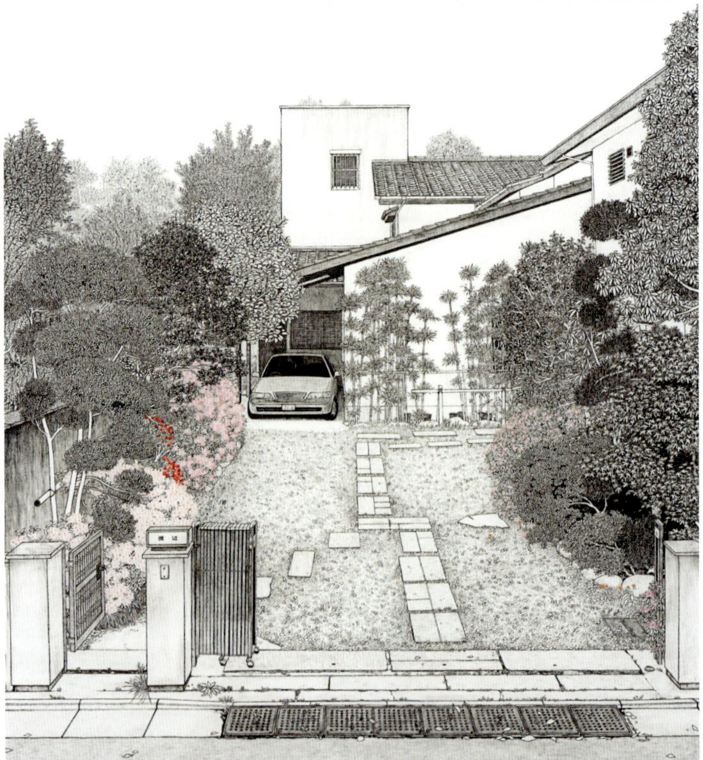

2

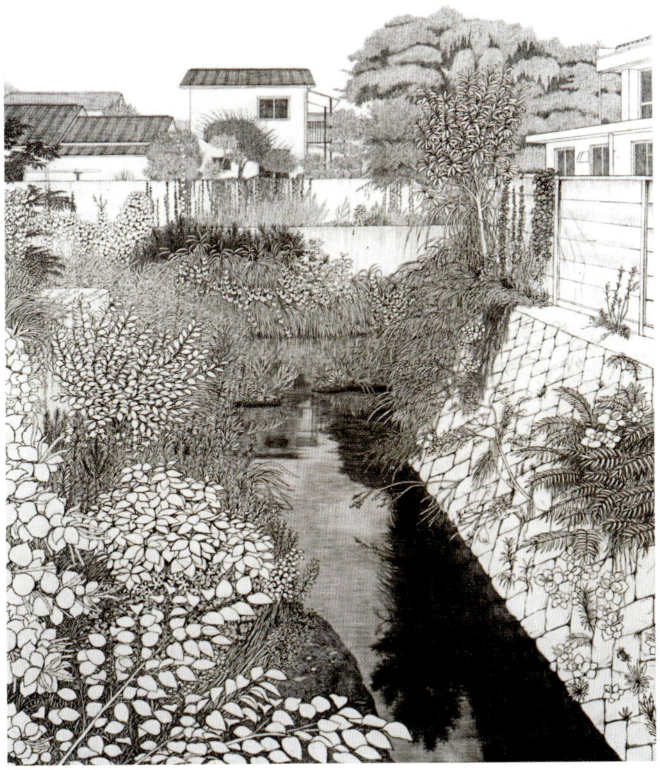

3

**Shown by**
Take Ninagawa R20

**Biography**
Born 1978
Lives in Kanagawa

Japanese artist Suto has presented solo exhibitions at Tokyo venues such as Take Ninagawa (2012, 2010 and 2008), Tokyo Opera City Art Gallery (2007) and Tokyo Wonder Wall, Metropolitan Government Building (2006). Her work has featured in group exhibitions in the city including 'Meguro Address', Meguro Museum of Art (2012), and 'VOCA: The Vision of Contemporary Art', Ueno Royal Museum (2008).

1
*Field in Sengawa – Slope*
2010
Oil, pencil and plaster on canvas mounted on panel
131 × 194 cm
Courtesy of Take Ninagawa

2
*W House – Entrance Side*
2012
Oil, pencil and plaster on canvas mounted on panel
140 × 120 cm
Courtesy of Take Ninagawa

3
*Namerigawa*
2009
Pencil and plaster on canvas mounted on panel
146 × 112 cm
Courtesy of Take Ninagawa

# Frame
# Yukiko Suto

Yukiko Suto transforms banal vistas of housing units, car parks and gardens into lush, hyper-real landscapes. Revealing the influence of *manga* drawing and *ukiyo-e* woodblock prints, her painstaking linear style highlights a diversity of textures and forms: vegetation, building materials, paving stones, hanging laundry, murky water, satellite dishes. Some become graphic patterns, some are indicated by blank expanses, and some are obsessively rendered in minute detail. Based on photographs the artist takes on extensive walks through the city, these large-scale pencil drawings, such as *Field in Sengawa – Slope* (2010) and *W House – Entrance Side* (2012), are meditations on the co-existence of nature and the built environment—particularly poignant ones in the context of Japan's recent nuclear crisis. ND

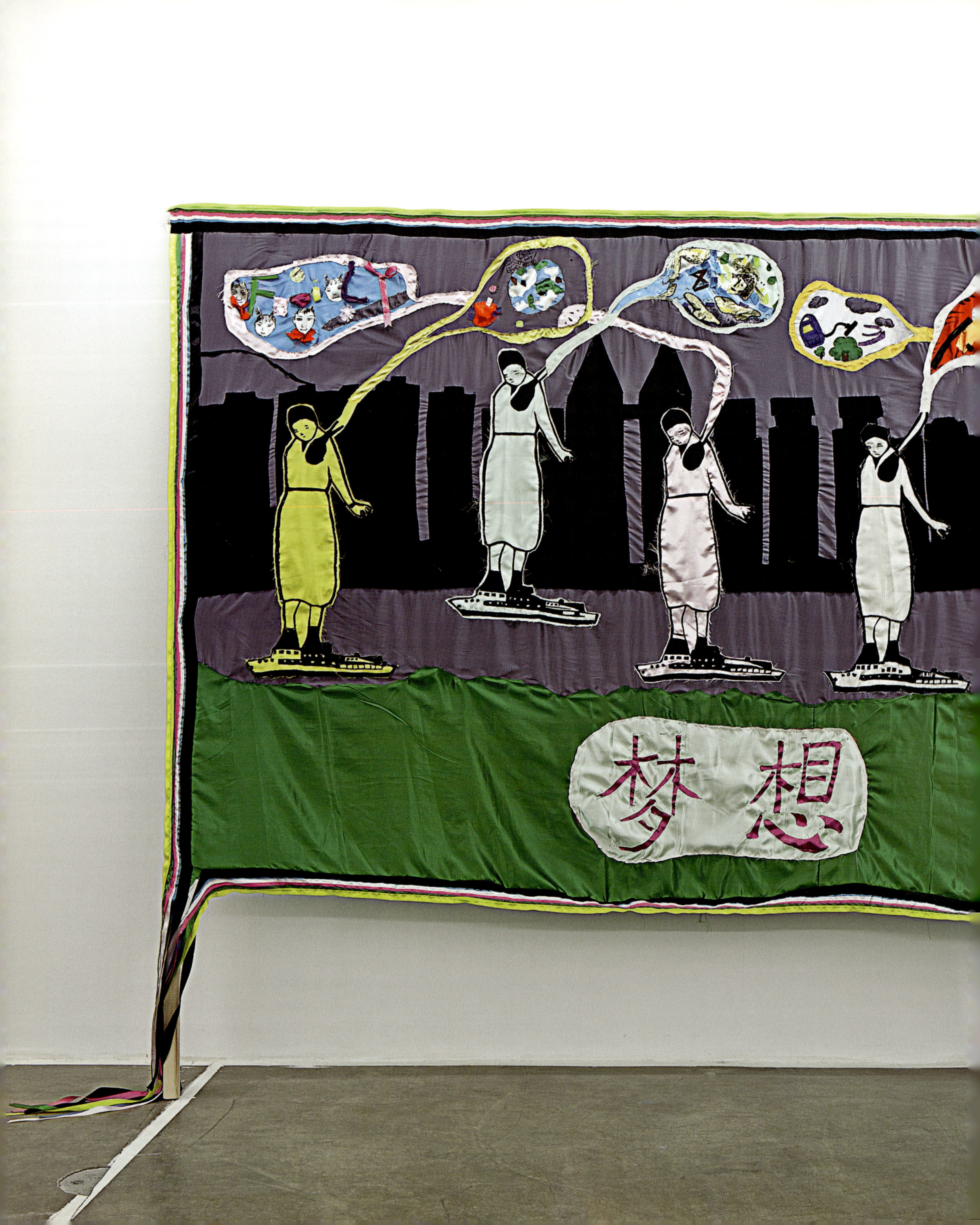
梦想

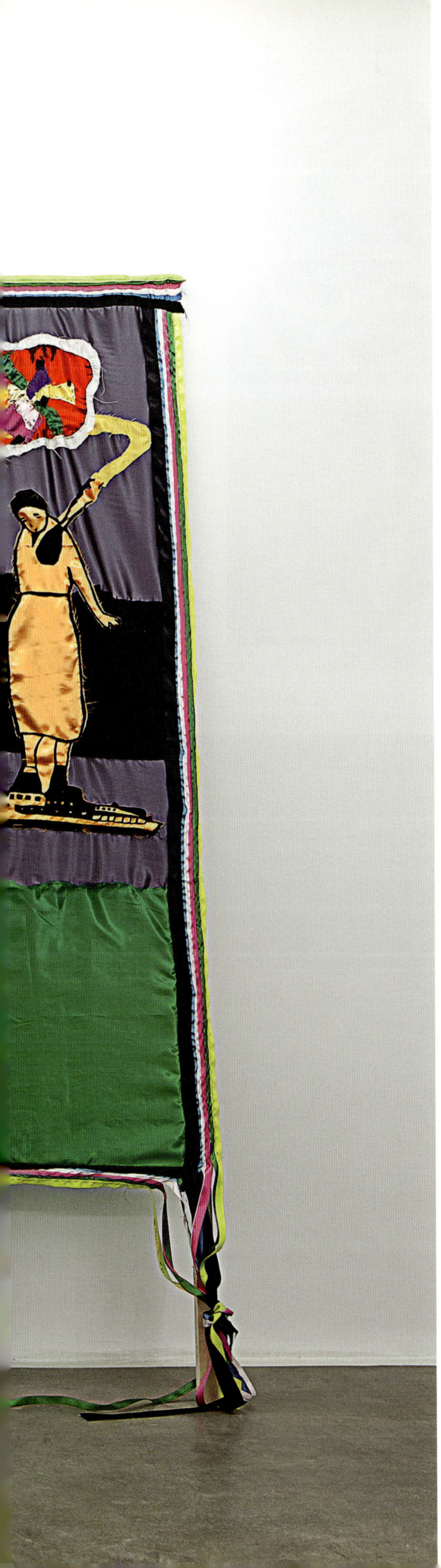

# Frame
# Güneş Terkol

**Shown by**
NON R1

**Biography**
Born 1981
Lives in Istanbul

Ankara-born Terkol has presented solo shows at NON, Istanbul (2012 and 2010), Organhaus Art Space, Chongqing (2011), and Apartment Project, Istanbul (2008). She was artist-in-residence at Organhaus, Chongqing, China, in 2011 and Gasworks, London, in 2010. Her recent group exhibitions include 'Dream and Reality', Istanbul Modern (2011). As part of the collective HA ZA VU ZU she participated in the 10th Biennale de Lyon (2009) and the 10th Istanbul Biennial (2007).

*Dreams on the River*
2011
Sewing on fabric
215 × 286 cm
Courtesy of NON

Although Terkol works across media from video to silkscreen, it is her community-based textile projects that loom largest in her *oeuvre*. *Dreams on the River* (2011) was co-produced at a workshop with women in Chongquing, China: the towering silhouetted females who sail upriver against the city skyline, sprouting illustrated dreams from their hearts, are the not-so-distant kin of the defiant Istanbul women of *Poster for an Afternoon* (2011), who carry banners through the city showing snippets of conversation and internal dialogue. If Terkol summons up rural folk traditions (textiles, popular theatre), she also suggests that such histories are lodged at the heart of even the most 'cosmopolitan' milieux—these banners are fitted with handles, readied for the march of the women who made them. SNS

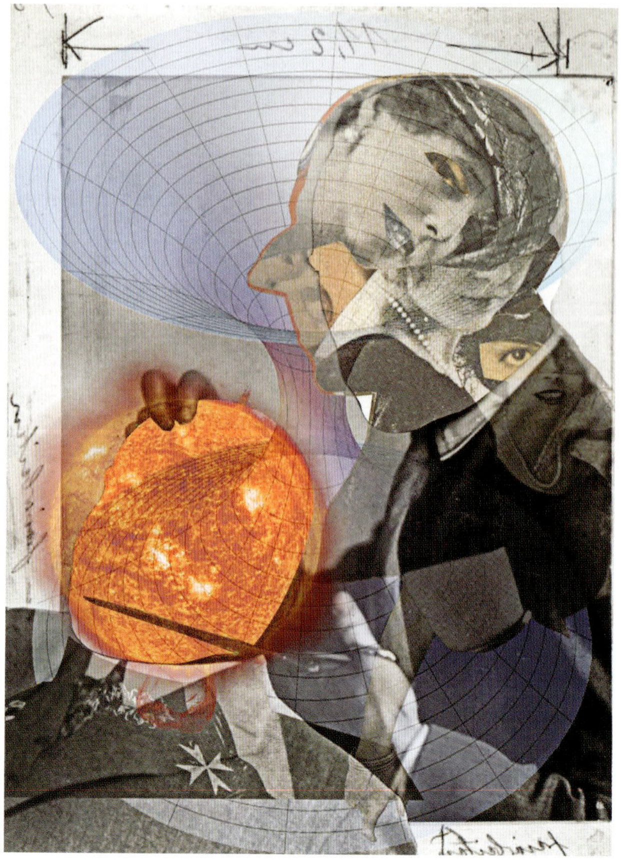

1

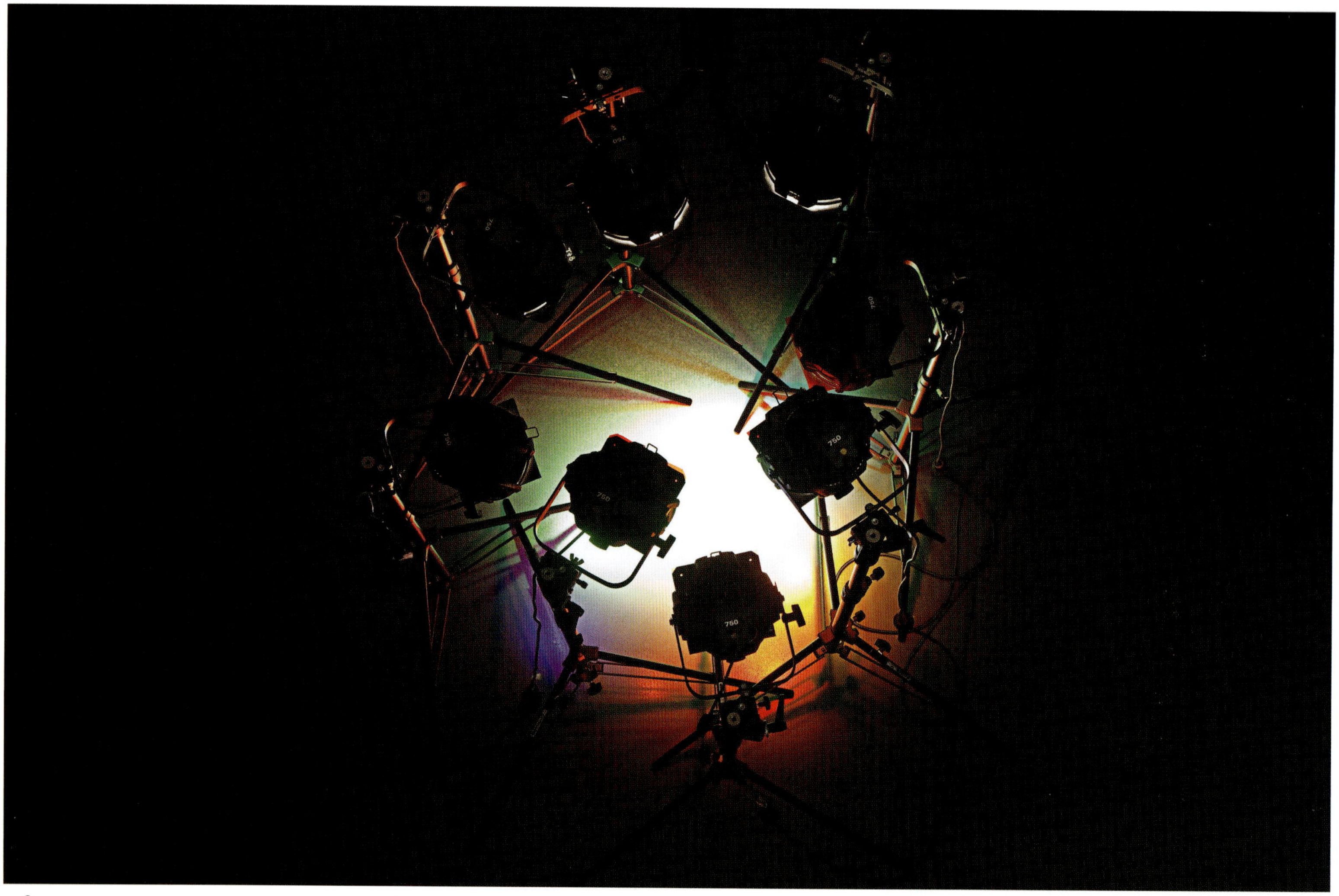

2

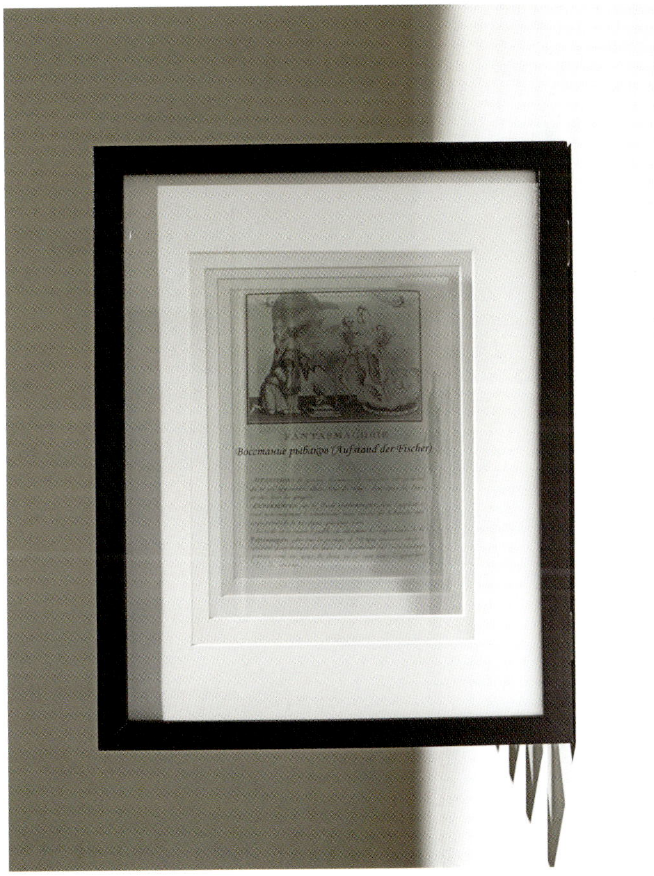


3

**Shown by**
Galerie Cinzia Friedlaender R3

**Biography**
Born 1981
Lives in Frankfurt

German-born Voss has shown solo exhibitions at Galerie Cinzia Friedlaender, Berlin (2011), and Haus Nummer Elf, Frankfurt (2007). He participated in Documenta 13, Kassel (2012), and has featured in group exhibitions that include 'Lecture Performance', on view at Kölnischer Kunstverein, Cologne, and Museum of Contemporary Art, Belgrade (2010), and 'Come in, Friends, the House is Yours!', Künstlerhaus Stuttgart (2009).

1
*Realist Time Wrap*
2012
Mixed media
Dimensions variable
Courtesy of Galerie Cinzia Friedlaender

2
*Untitled (Victory over the Sun)*
2011
Stage projectors and light bulbs
Dimensions variable
Courtesy of Galerie Cinzia Friedlaender

3
*Invitation (Восстание рыбаков)*
2011
6 laser prints on film foil, passepartout and PAR 56 theatre spotlight
Dimensions variable
Courtesy of Galerie Cinzia Friedlaender

## Frame
# Jeronimo Voss

Light, transparency, projection: the ghosts of antiquated spirituality and cinema and political history infuse Jeronimo Voss' illumined and often misleading video installation works. For example, *Aufstand der Fischer (Восстание рыбаков)* (2011) uses the titular 1934 anti-fascist film by Erwin Piscator, based on a novella by Anna Seghers, as the start of an exploration of illusion, disillusion, phantasmagoria and history. Voss' consistent employment of translucent, layered transparencies and overhead projectors (see as well his early installation *Fanfares for Effective Freedom*, 2008) spotlights his chief concerns: the smoke and mirrors both of politics and the artistic and spiritual media in which we describe and channel them. QL

# Contributors

**(MA) Max Andrews** is the co-founder and co-director of Latitudes, Barcelona, and is a regular contributor to *frieze*.

**(SC) Steven Cairns** is a writer and curator based in London, where he is Associate Curator of Artists' Film and Moving Image at the ICA.

**(ND) Natasha Degen** is an art historian and critic based in London.

**(BD) Brian Dillon** is a regular contributor to *frieze* and UK editor of *Cabinet*. He teaches critical writing at the Royal College of Art, London.

**(CFW) Chris Fite-Wassilak** is a writer and curator based in London. He is a regular contributor to *frieze, Art Review*, *Art Monthly*, *Art Papers* and *Monopol*.

**(JG) Jonathan Griffin** is a contributing editor of *frieze*, based in Los Angeles. He writes for various magazines, including *Art Review*, *Texte zur Kunst*, *Tate etc*, *Mousse* and *Flash Art*.

**(KMJ) Kristin M. Jones** is a writer based in New York. She is a regular contributor to *frieze*, *Film Comment* and *The Wall Street Journal*.

**(MH) Martin Herbert** writes regularly for *frieze*, *Artforum* and *Art Monthly*, and is associate editor of *Art Review*. His monograph on artist Mark Wallinger was published in 2011 (Thames & Hudson).

**(KK) Katie Kitamura** is a critic and fiction writer based in New York. Her novels include *The Longshot* (2009, Simon & Schuster) and *Gone to the Forest* (2013, Clerkenwell Press).

**(QL) Quinn Latimer** is an American poet and critic based in Basel. She is a regular contributor to *frieze, Artforum* and various artist monographs and anthologies.

**(SL) Sarah Lowndes** is a writer and curator based in Glasgow, where she is also a lecturer at Glasgow School of Art. Her curatorial projects in the city include the sculpture park Dialogue of Hands (2012).

**(SOR) Sally O'Reilly** is a writer based in London.

**(TM) Tom Morton** is a London-based writer and curator, and is a contributing editor of *frieze*.

**(VSR) Vivian Sky Rehberg** is a contributing editor of *frieze* and Course Director of the Master of Fine Art programme at the Piet Zwart Institute in Rotterdam.

**(SNS) Sarah-Neel Smith** is a writer based in Los Angeles. She writes regularly for *frieze*.

**(PT) Paul Teasdale** is assistant editor of *frieze* and is based in London.

**(ST) Sam Thorne** is associate editor of *frieze* and is based in London. He is a visiting lecturer at the Royal College of Art, London, and is currently researching a project about ethnomusicology.

# Advertisements

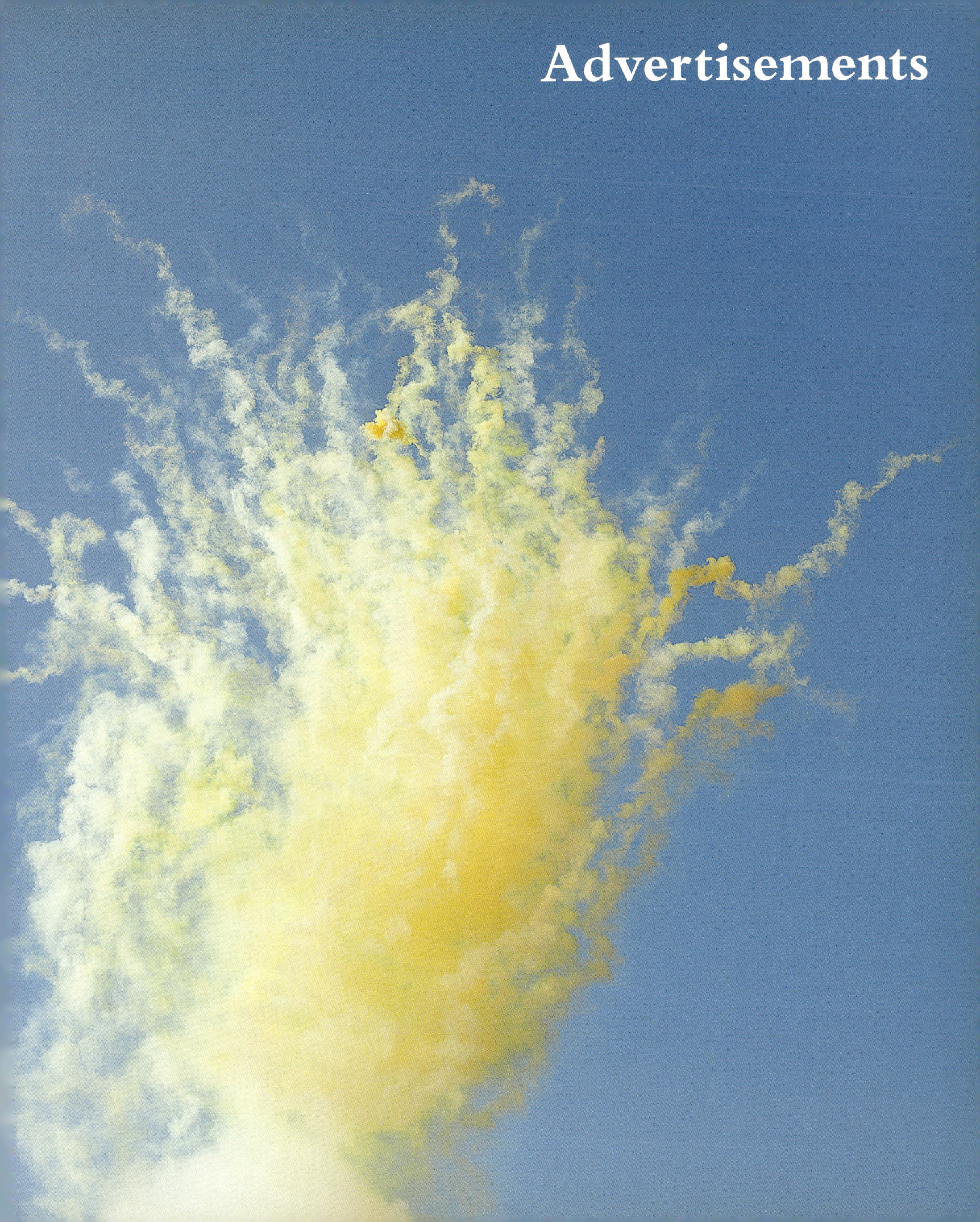

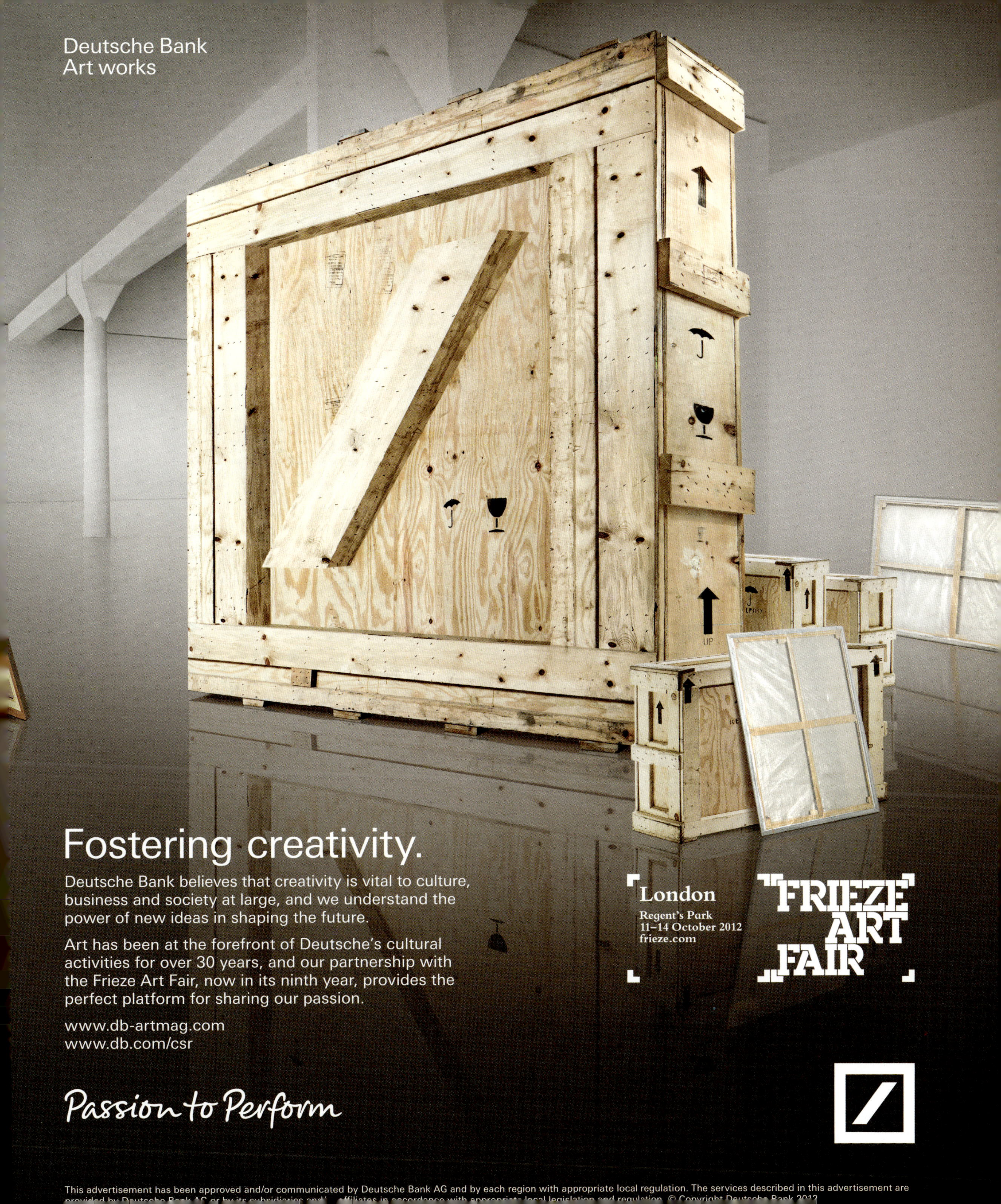

Deutsche Bank
Art works
UP
Fostering creativity.
Deutsche Bank believes that creativity is vital to culture, business and society at large, and we understand the power of new ideas in shaping the future.
Art has been at the forefront of Deutsche's cultural activities for over 30 years, and our partnership with the Frieze Art Fair, now in its ninth year, provides the perfect platform for sharing our passion.
www.db-artmag.com
www.db.com/csr
London
Regent's Park
11–14 October 2012
frieze.com
FRIEZE ART FAIR
Passion to Perform
This advertisement has been approved and/or communicated by Deutsche Bank AG and by each region with appropriate local regulation. The services described in this advertisement are

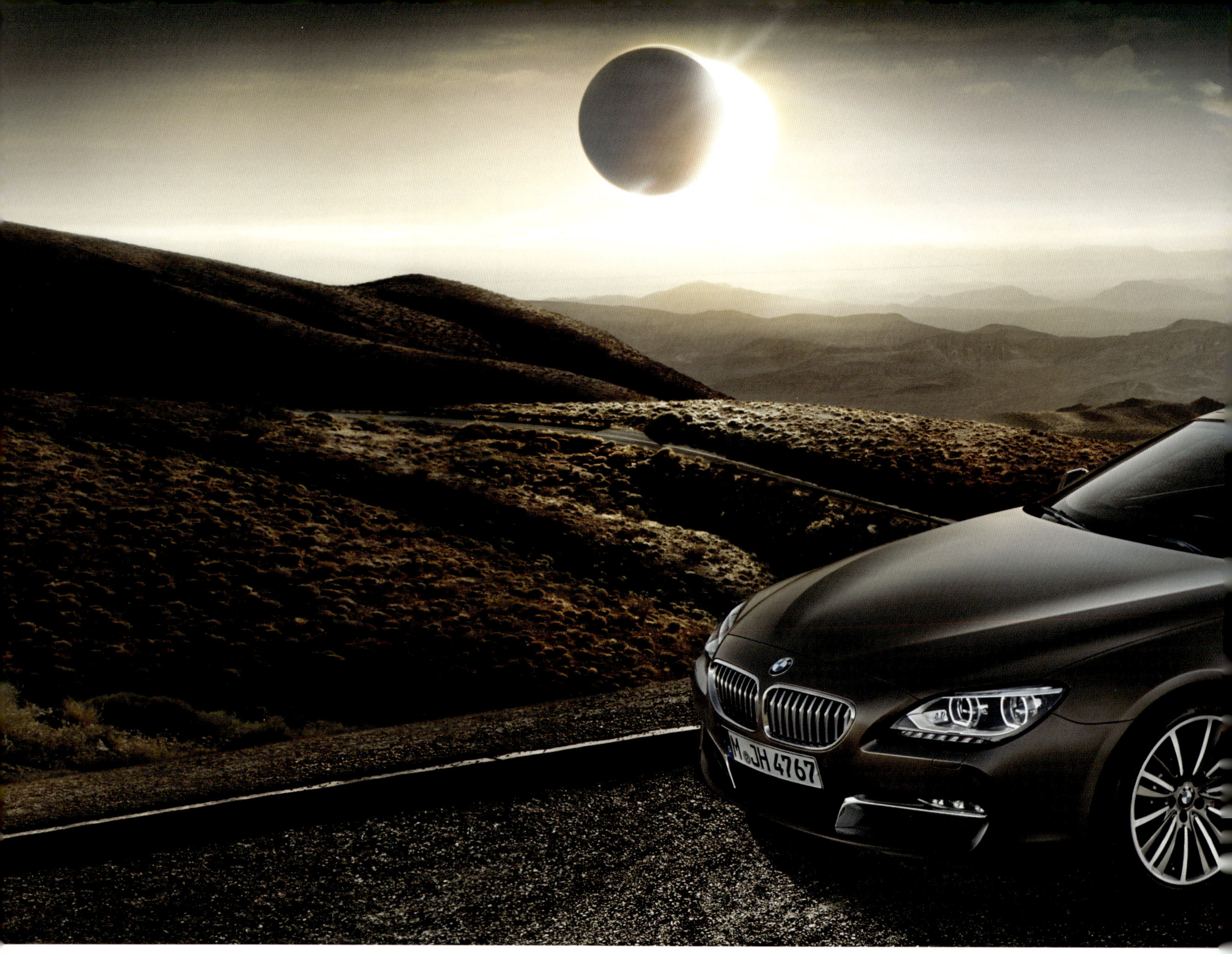

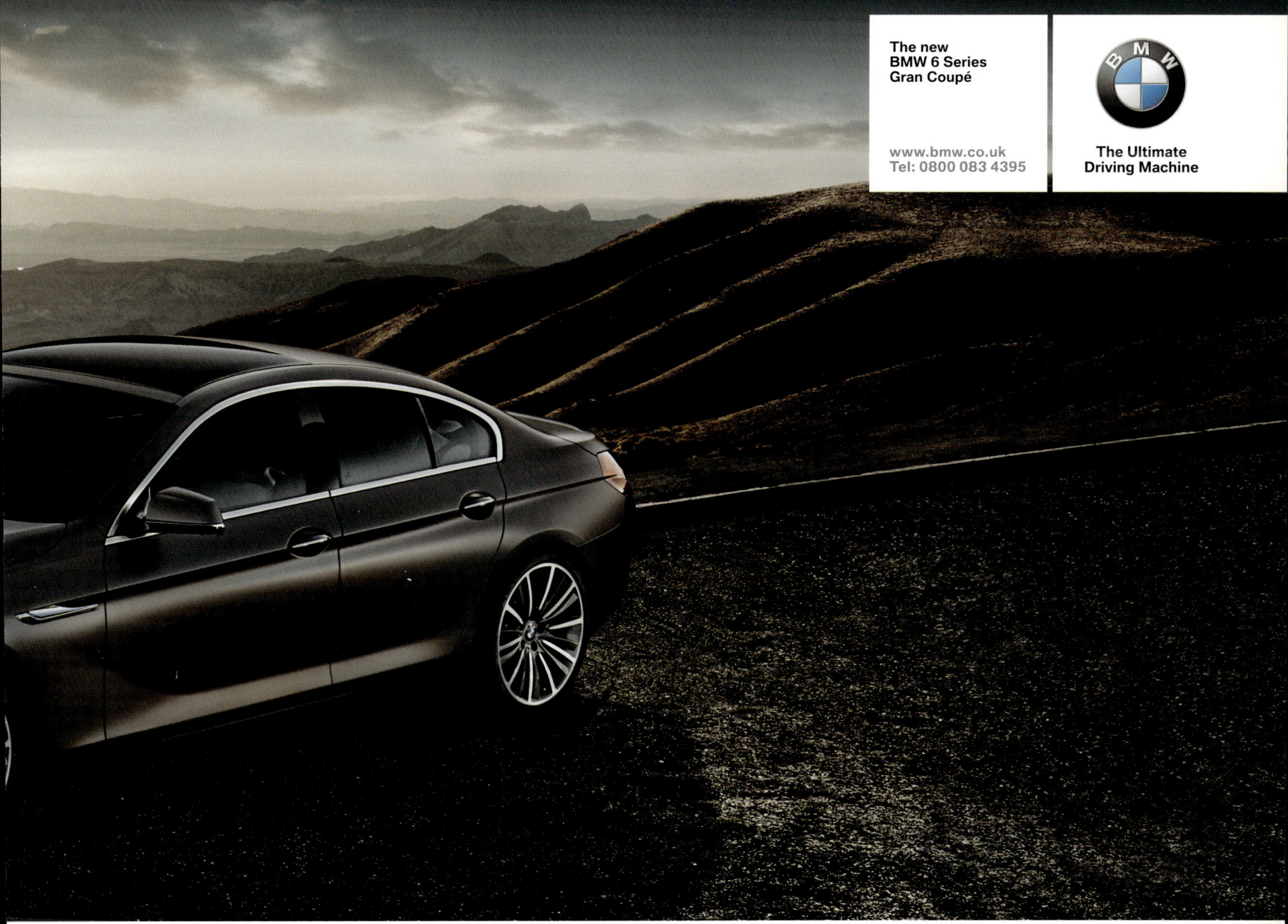
The new
BMW 6 Series
Gran Coupé
www.bmw.co.uk
Tel: 0800 083 4395
The Ultimate
Driving Machine

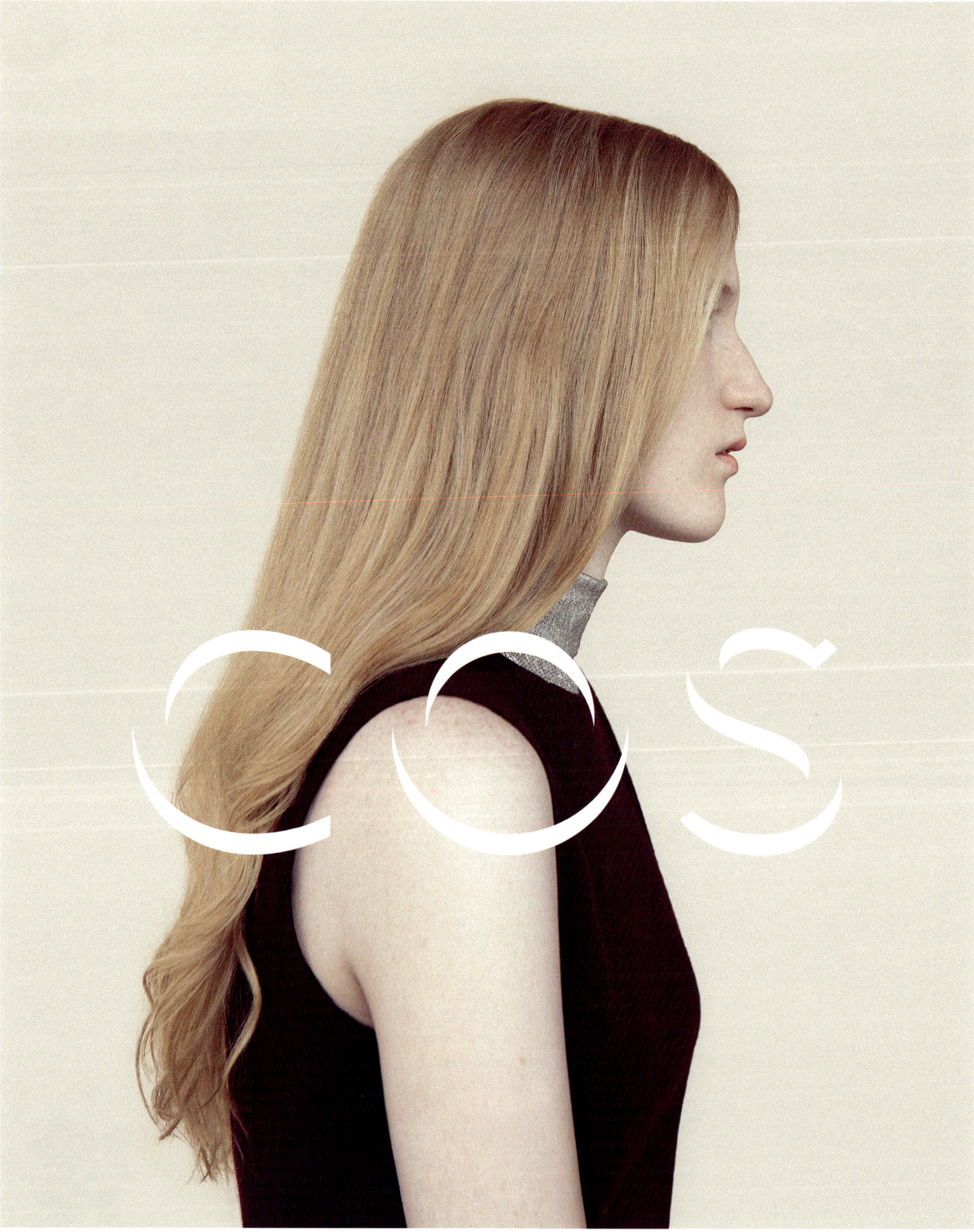


Artist Britta Thie photographed by Benjamin Alexander Huseby

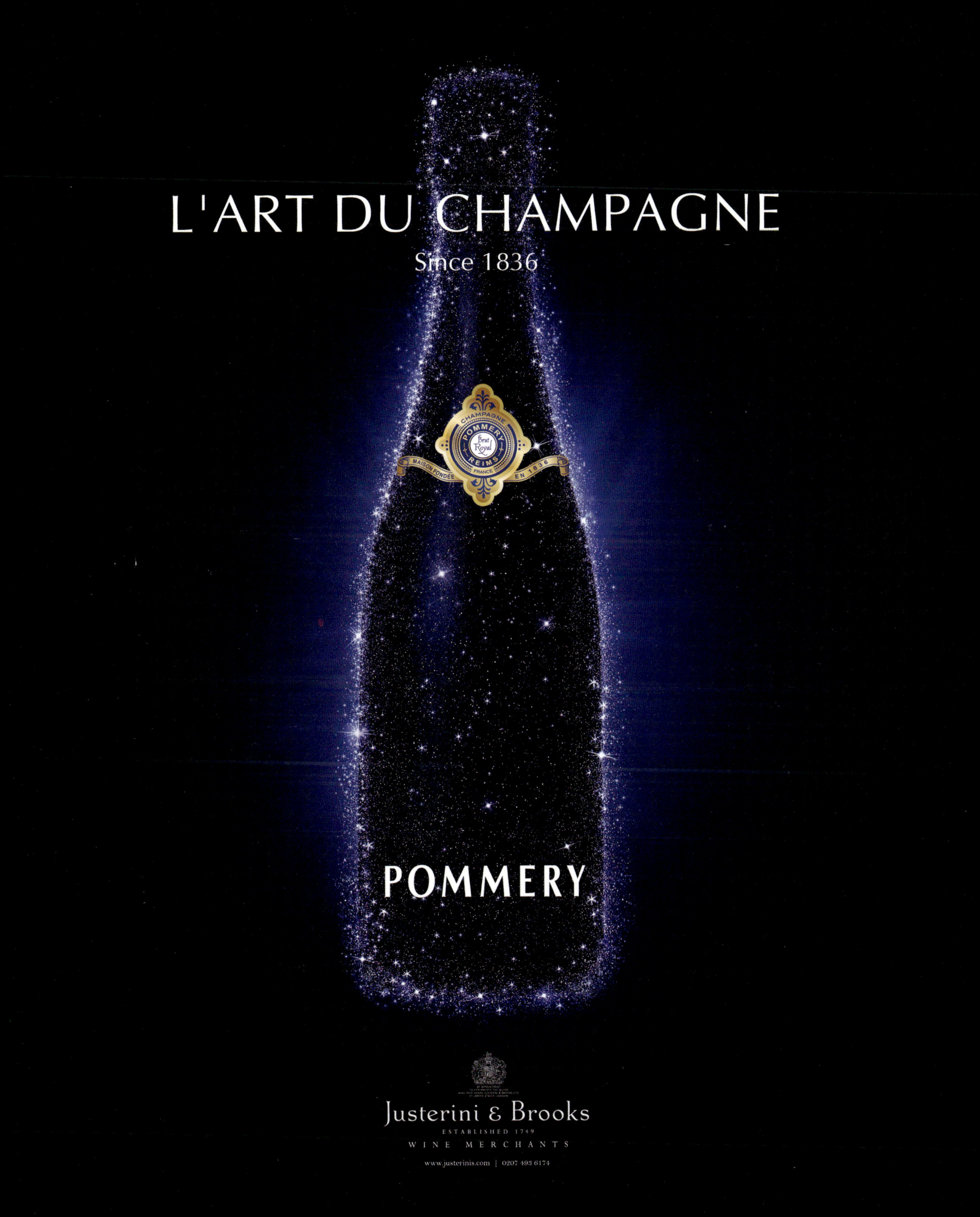
L'ART DU CHAMPAGNE
Since 1836
CHAMPAGNE
POMMERY
Brut Royal
REIMS
FRANCE
MAISON FONDÉE EN 1836
POMMERY
Justerini & Brooks
ESTABLISHED 1749
WINE MERCHANTS
www.justerinis.com | 0207 493 6174

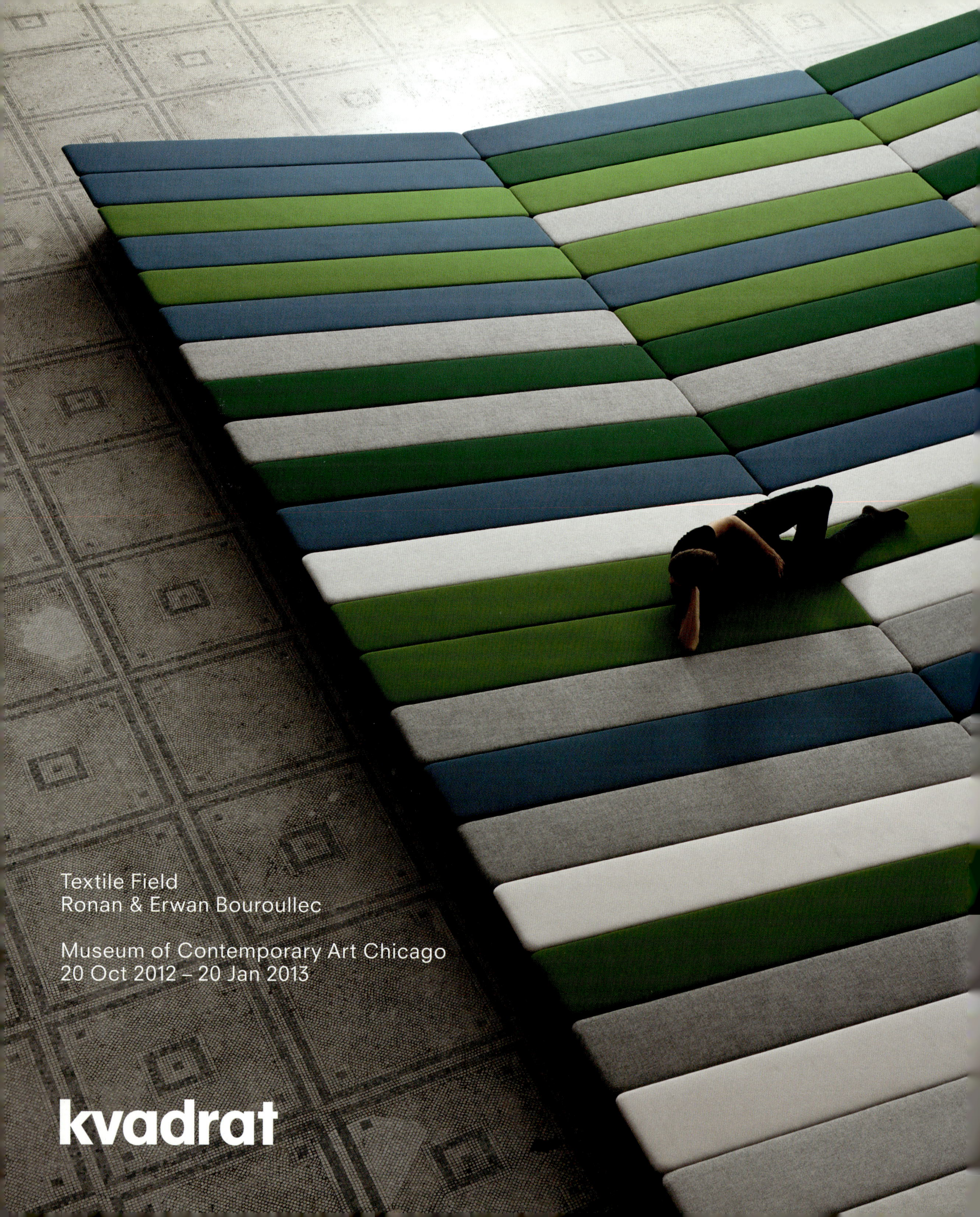
Textile Field
Ronan & Erwan Bouroullec
Museum of Contemporary Art Chicago
20 Oct 2012 – 20 Jan 2013
kvadrat

# outset.

**Supporting New Art**

## CORPORATE PARTNERS

Le Méridien
Leviev Extraordinary Diamonds
Northern Trust
Pentagram
Sotheby's

## PRODUCTION FUND PARTNERS

Victoria Bennett
Micaela & Christopher Boas
Pamela & David Crystal
Bilge & Haro Cumbusyan
Wendy Fisher
Isabelle Georgeaux & Patrick Healy
Candida & Zak Gertler
Elena & Steven Heinz
Isabelle & Marc Hotimsky
Leili Huth
Nonna Materkova
Maria Mattsson-Louguinets
Alexandra Mollof
Averill Ogden & Winston Ginsberg
Sybil & Matthew Orr
Jacqueline & Anthony Orsatelli
Katy & Maurice Ostro
Yana & Stephen Peel
Catherine & Franck Petitgas
Barrie & Emmanuel Roman
Karen Ruimy
Lisa Schiff
Tsukanova Family
Inna & Boris Vainshtock
Catia von Huetz & Rattan Chadha
Mercedes Zobel

## PATRONS

Bodil & Harry Blain
Dafna & Charles Bonas
Silvia Bruttini
Susan Burns
Beverley & Howard Calvert
Helen Chung-Halpern & Abel Halpern
Sadie Coles HQ
Alastair Cookson
Sir Thomas & Lady Croft
Martine d'Anglejan-Chatillon
Blake & Michael Daffey
Miel de Botton
Lisa Dennis
Denise Esfandi
Dietlinde & Carl-Peter Forster
Laure Ghouila-Houri
Samuel Hayek
Brette Kameny & Gordon Holmes
Roumana & Mohammed Khamisa
Oksana Kolomenskaya
Fatima Maleki
Laura & Brett Miller
Joyce & Edward Misrahi
Fumiko & Guy Moar
Mary Moore
Maithili Parekh & Shashank Singh
Francine S. Peters
Charlotte Philipps
Susan Rosenberg & John Lazar
Lana Saffrin Betesh & Mike Betesh
Essie & Miriam Sakhai
Helena & Tom Sikorski
Lucinda & Ed Siskind
Tammy Smulders
Carol & Rick Sopher
Patsy & Christophe Tanghe
Petri & Jolana Vainio

## OUTSET ASSOCIATES

## OUTSET FAMILY

(Director: Micaela Boas)

## OUTSET GERMANY

(Directors: Larissa van Look, Ulrike zu Salm)

## OUTSET GREECE

(in alliance with the Demergon-Daskalopoulos Foundation for Culture and Development, Director: Elina Kountouri)

## OUTSET INDIA

(Director: Feroze Gujral)

## OUTSET ISRAEL

(Director: Vered Gadish)

## OUTSET NETHERLANDS

(Director: Gwen Neumann)

## GOLDSMITHS GALLERY PATRONS

The Pace Gallery
Sadie Coles HQ
Sprüth Magers Berlin London

## FRIENDS

Daniel & Becky Brennan
Lydia & Miles d'Arcy Irving
Georgia Byng & Marc Quinn
Rosemary & Jake Chapman
Tiphane de Lussy & Dinos Chapman
Lady Elena & Lord Norman Foster
Katherine Francey
Polly & Jullien Gaer
Penny Govett
David Hesketh
Carsten Höller
Suzanna & Anish Kapoor
Emily King & Matthew Slotover
Sandra Lawson
Georgina Macpherson
Mourad Mazouz
Antonello di Medici
Petra Mühling
Vicken Parson & Antony Gormley
John Rushworth
Freddy & Muriel Salem
Amanda Sharp
Maria & Malek Sukkar
Keith Tyson
Richard Weinberg
Cheyenne Westphal
Anita & Poju Zabludowicz

Barclays Wealth
Laurent-Perrier

And those who wish to remain anonymous.

**www.outset.org.uk**

Registered charity no. 1101476



*Duro Olowu for Outset (c) 2012*

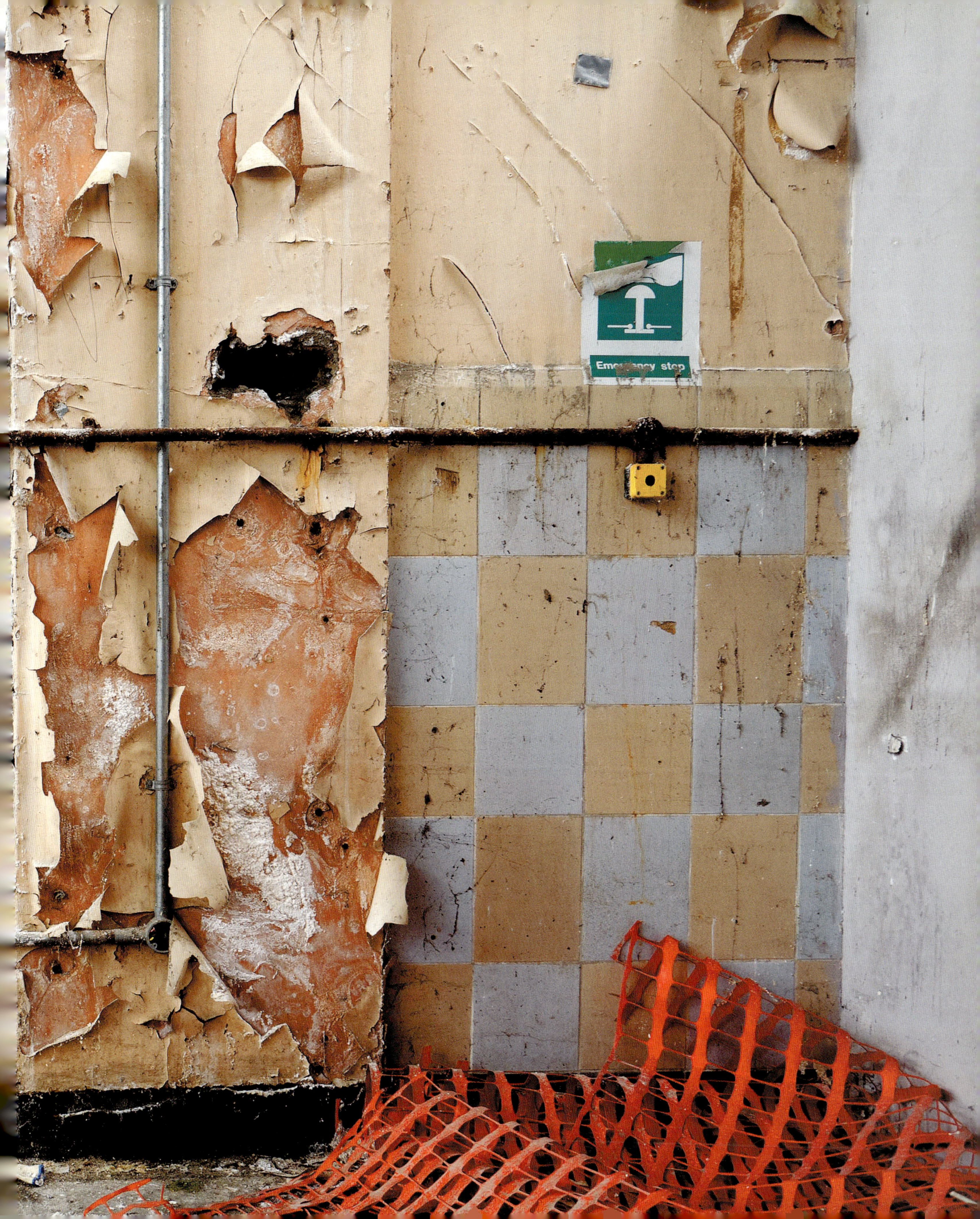
stop

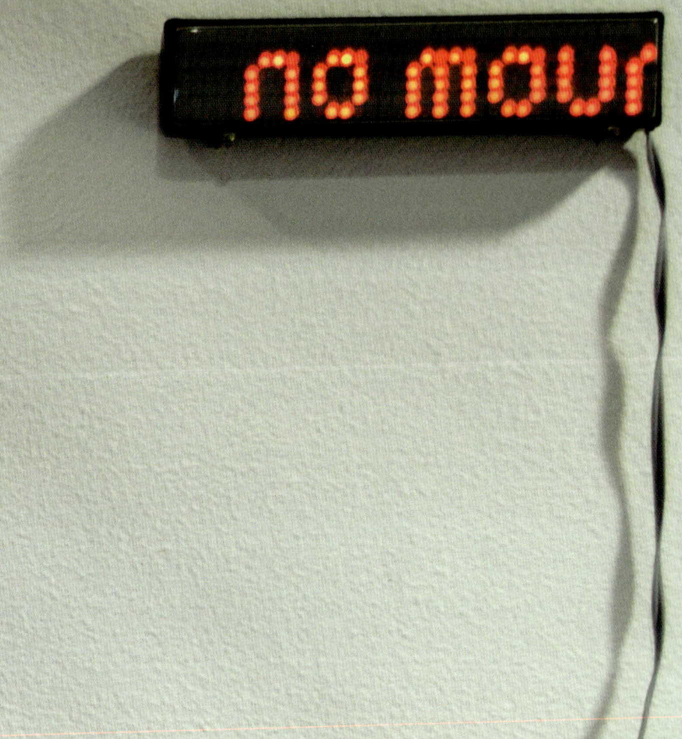


Rose Finn-Kelcey
House Rules, 2001
Miniature circuit board with red LEDs
Simmons & Simmons Collection

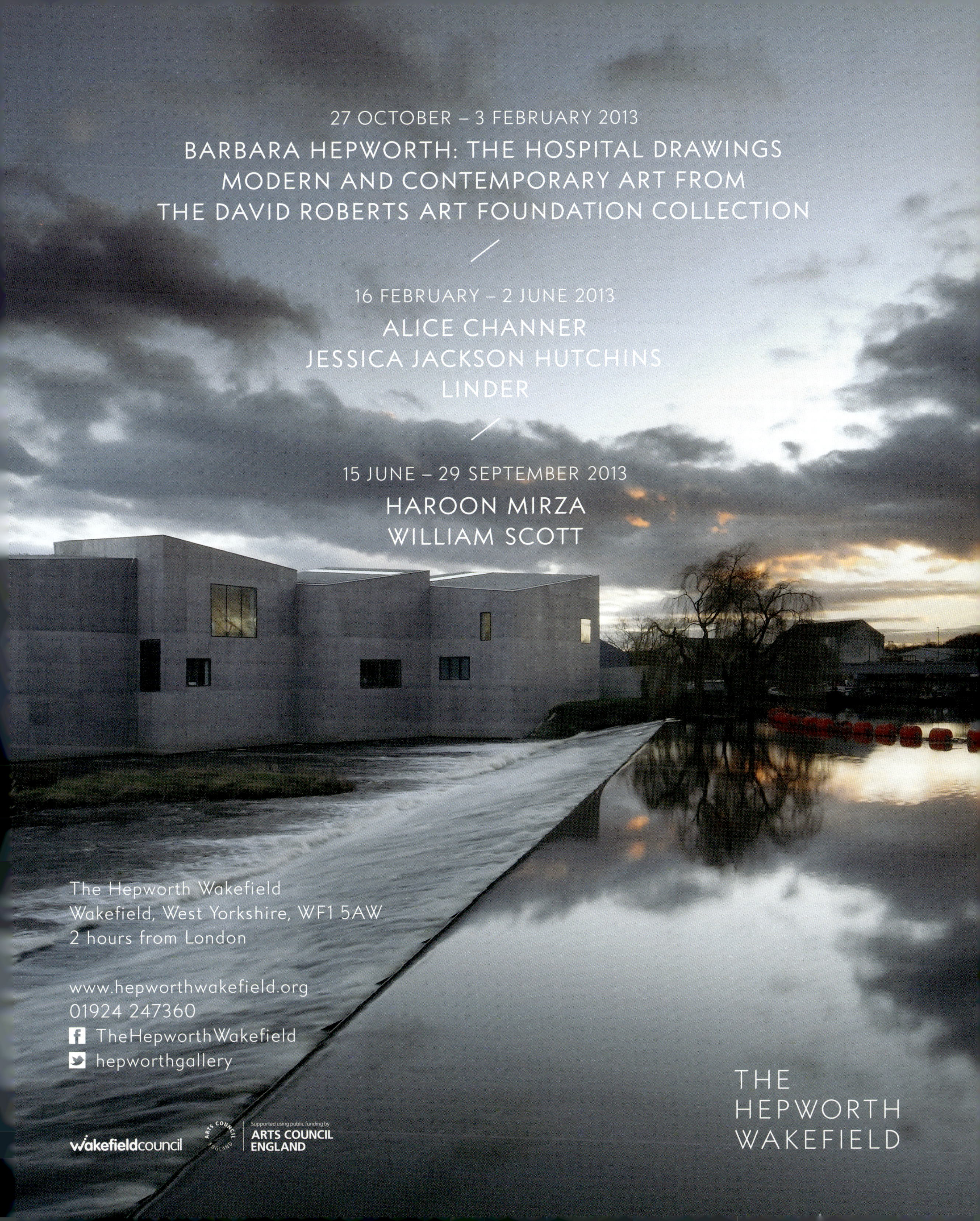
27 OCTOBER – 3 FEBRUARY 2013
BARBARA HEPWORTH: THE HOSPITAL DRAWINGS
MODERN AND CONTEMPORARY ART FROM
THE DAVID ROBERTS ART FOUNDATION COLLECTION
16 FEBRUARY – 2 JUNE 2013
ALICE CHANNER
JESSICA JACKSON HUTCHINS
LINDER
15 JUNE – 29 SEPTEMBER 2013
HAROON MIRZA
WILLIAM SCOTT
The Hepworth Wakefield
Wakefield, West Yorkshire, WF1 5AW
2 hours from London
www.hepworthwakefield.org
01924 247360
TheHepworthWakefield
hepworthgallery
wakefieldcouncil
Supported using public funding by
ARTS COUNCIL ENGLAND
THE HEPWORTH WAKEFIELD

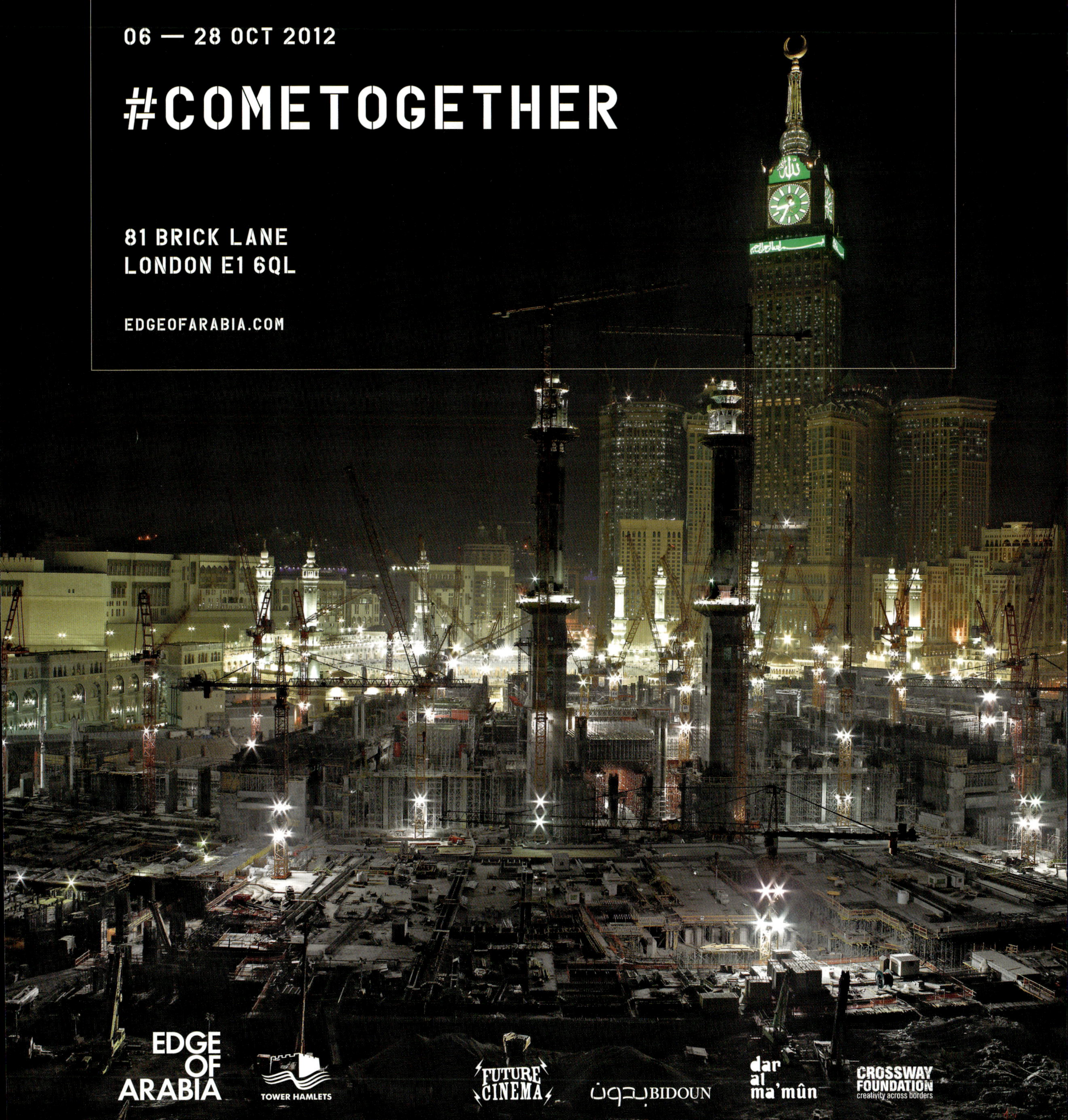
06 — 28 OCT 2012
#COMETOGETHER
81 BRICK LANE
LONDON E1 6QL
EDGEOFARABIA.COM
EDGE OF ARABIA
TOWER HAMLETS
FUTURE CINEMA
بدون BIDOUN
dar al ma'mûn
CROSSWAY FOUNDATION
creativity across borders

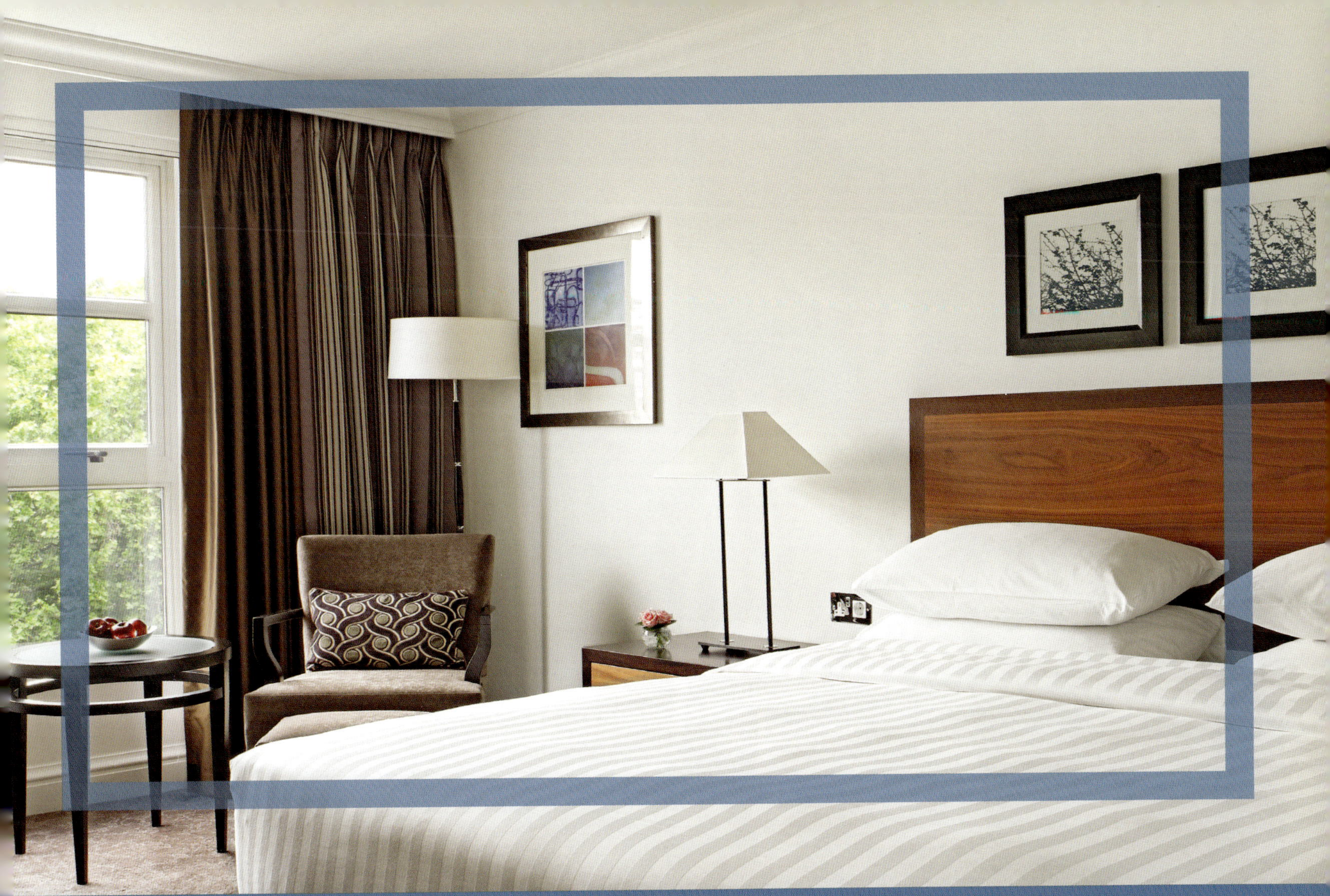

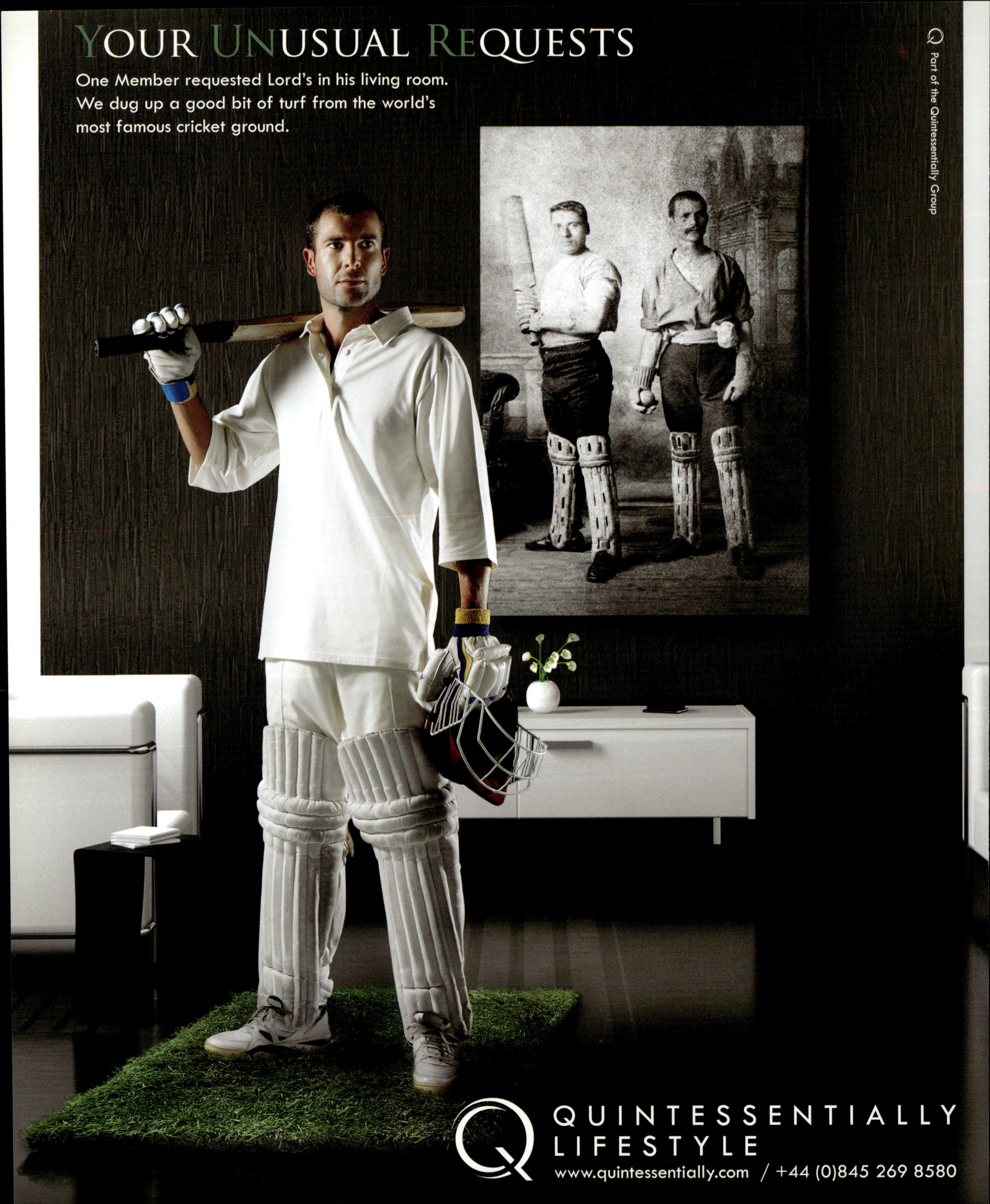

YOUR UNUSUAL REQUESTS
One Member requested Lord's in his living room.
We dug up a good bit of turf from the world's
most famous cricket ground.
Part of the Quintessentially Group
QUINTESSENTIALLY
LIFESTYLE
www.quintessentially.com / +44 (0)845 269 8580

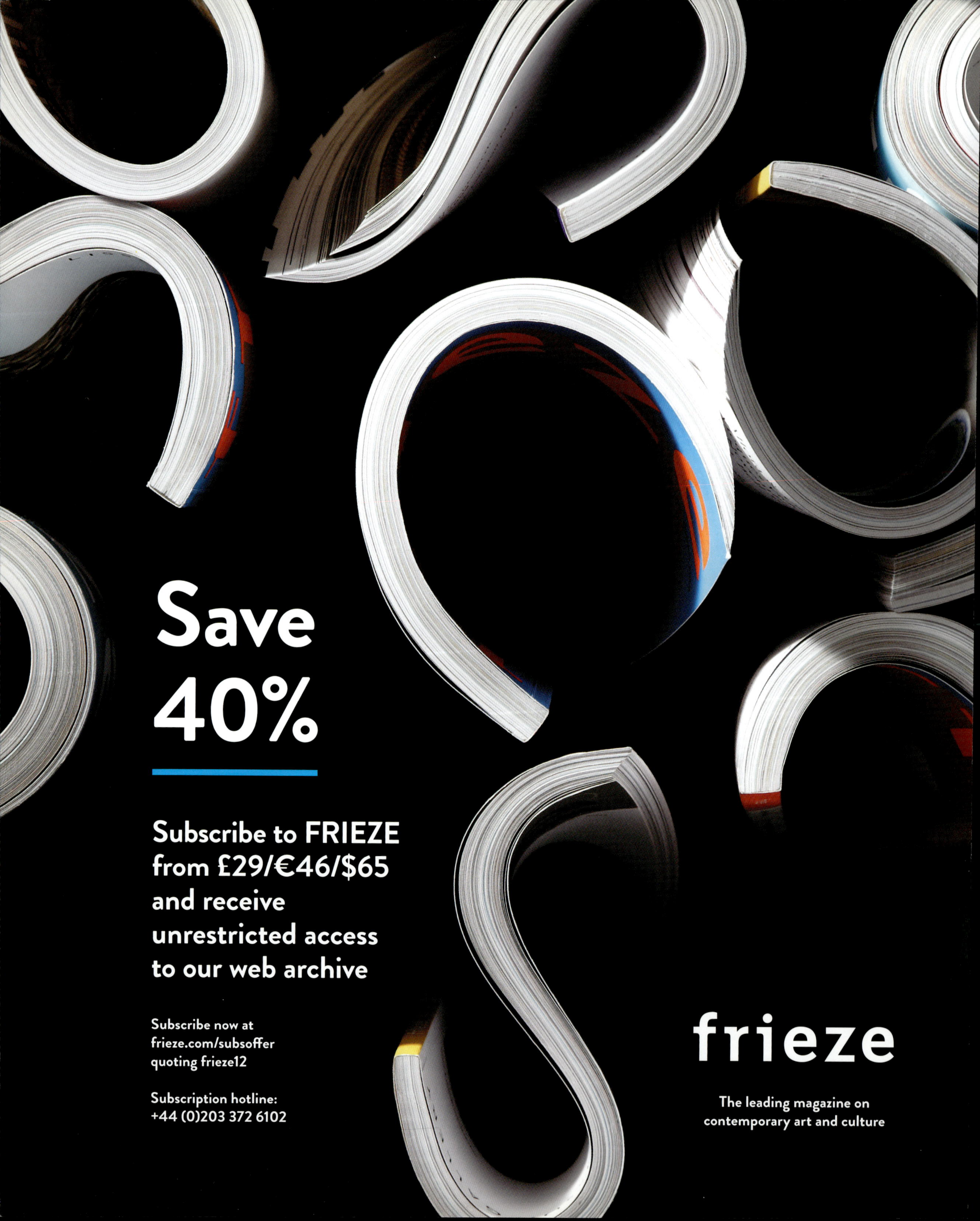
Save
40%
Subscribe to FRIEZE
from £29/€46/$65
and receive
unrestricted access
to our web archive
Subscribe now at
frieze.com/subsoffer
quoting frieze12
Subscription hotline:
+44 (0)203 372 6102
frieze
The leading magazine on
contemporary art and culture

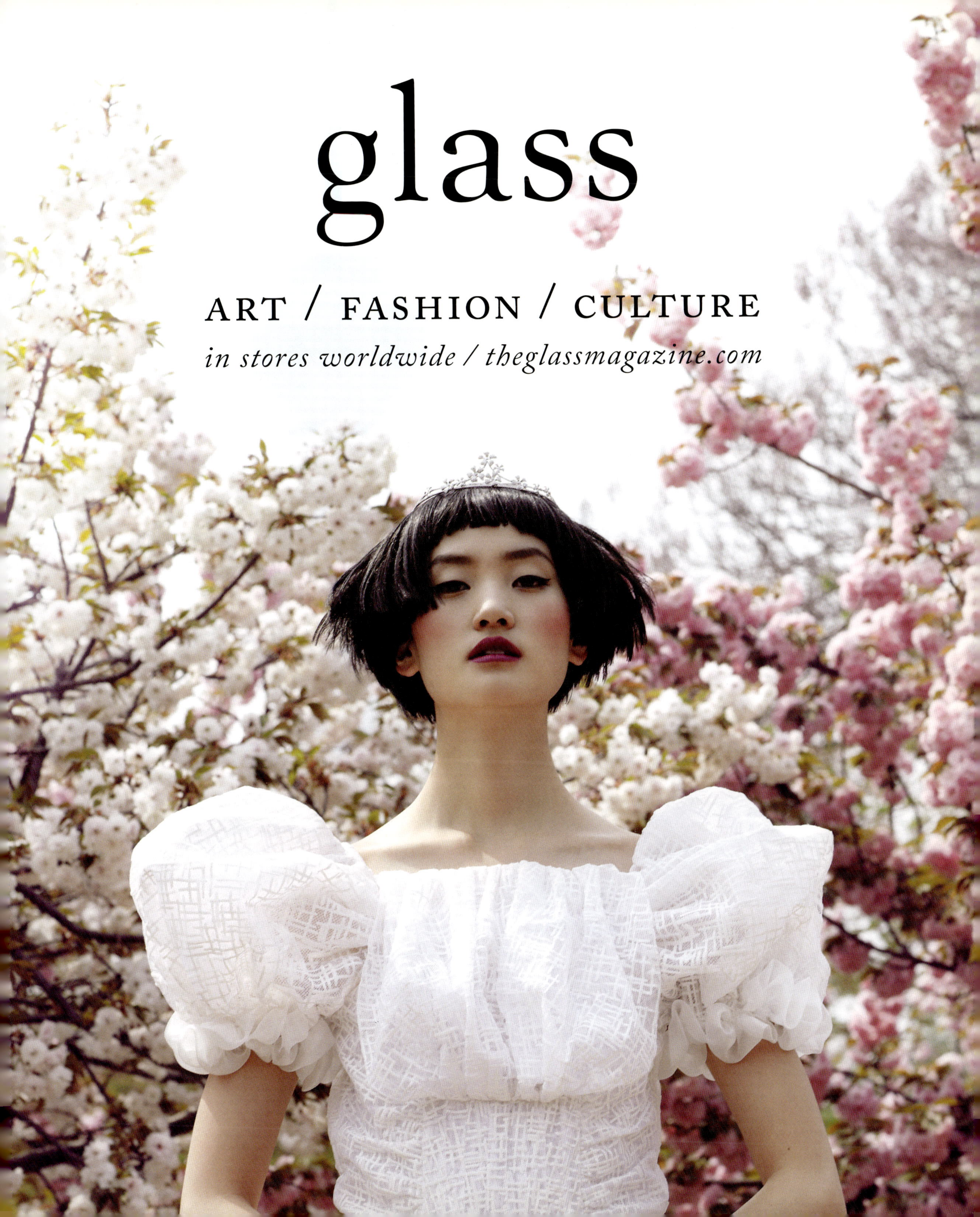
glass
ART / FASHION / CULTURE
in stores worldwide / theglassmagazine.com

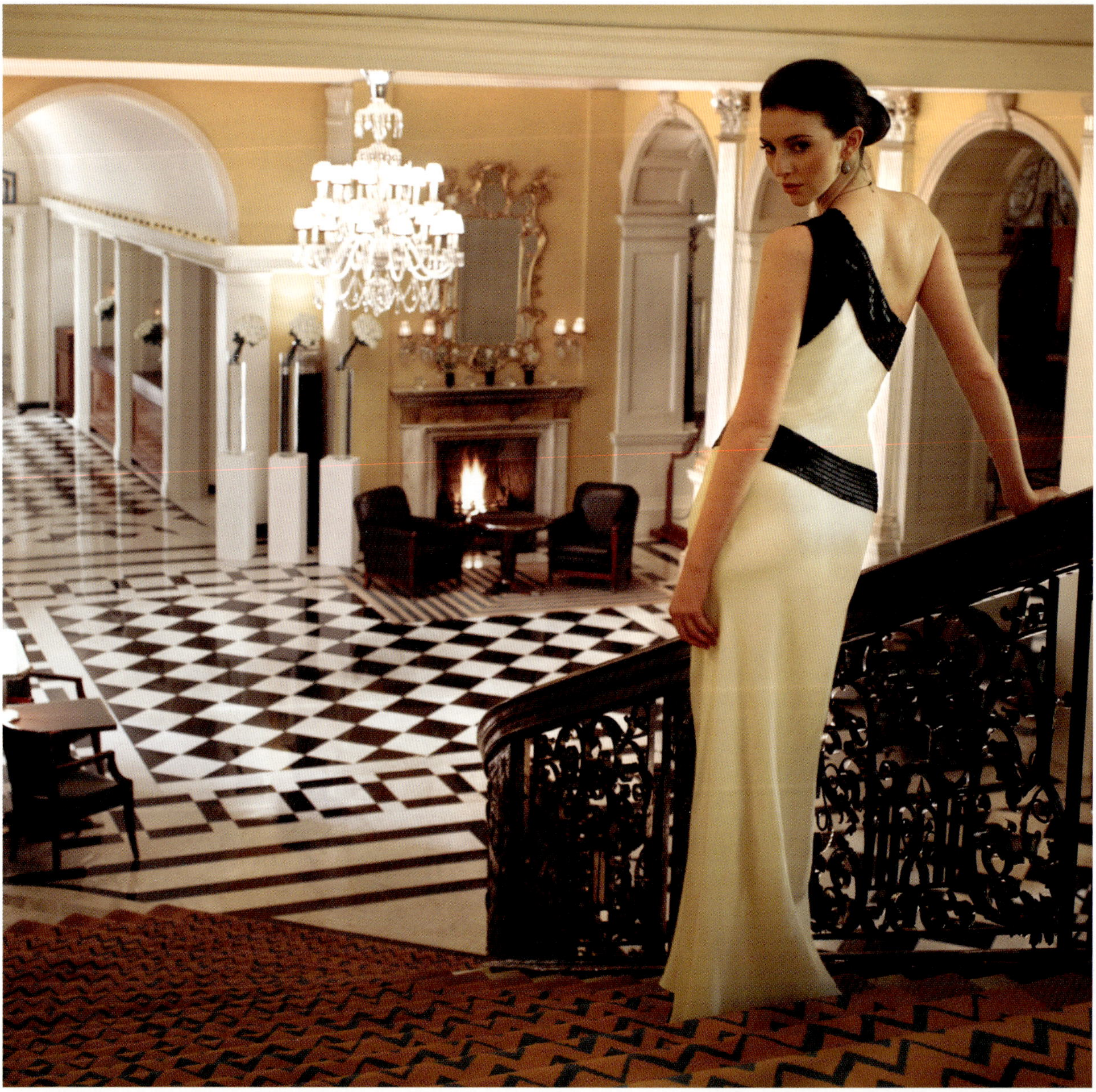

# ARTUPDATE

BERLIN LONDON NEW YORK VENICE

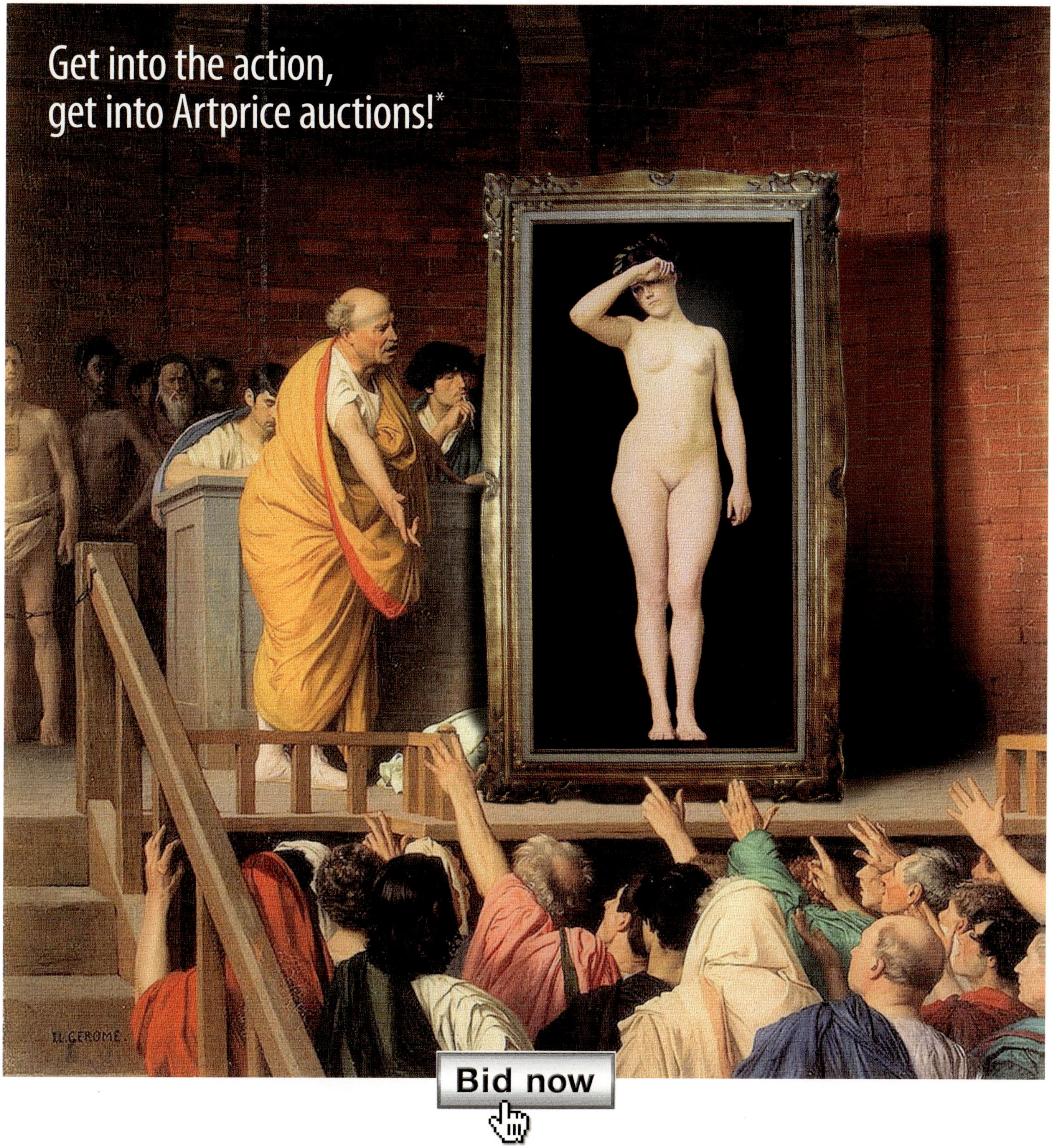
Get into the action,
get into Artprice auctions!*
Bid now

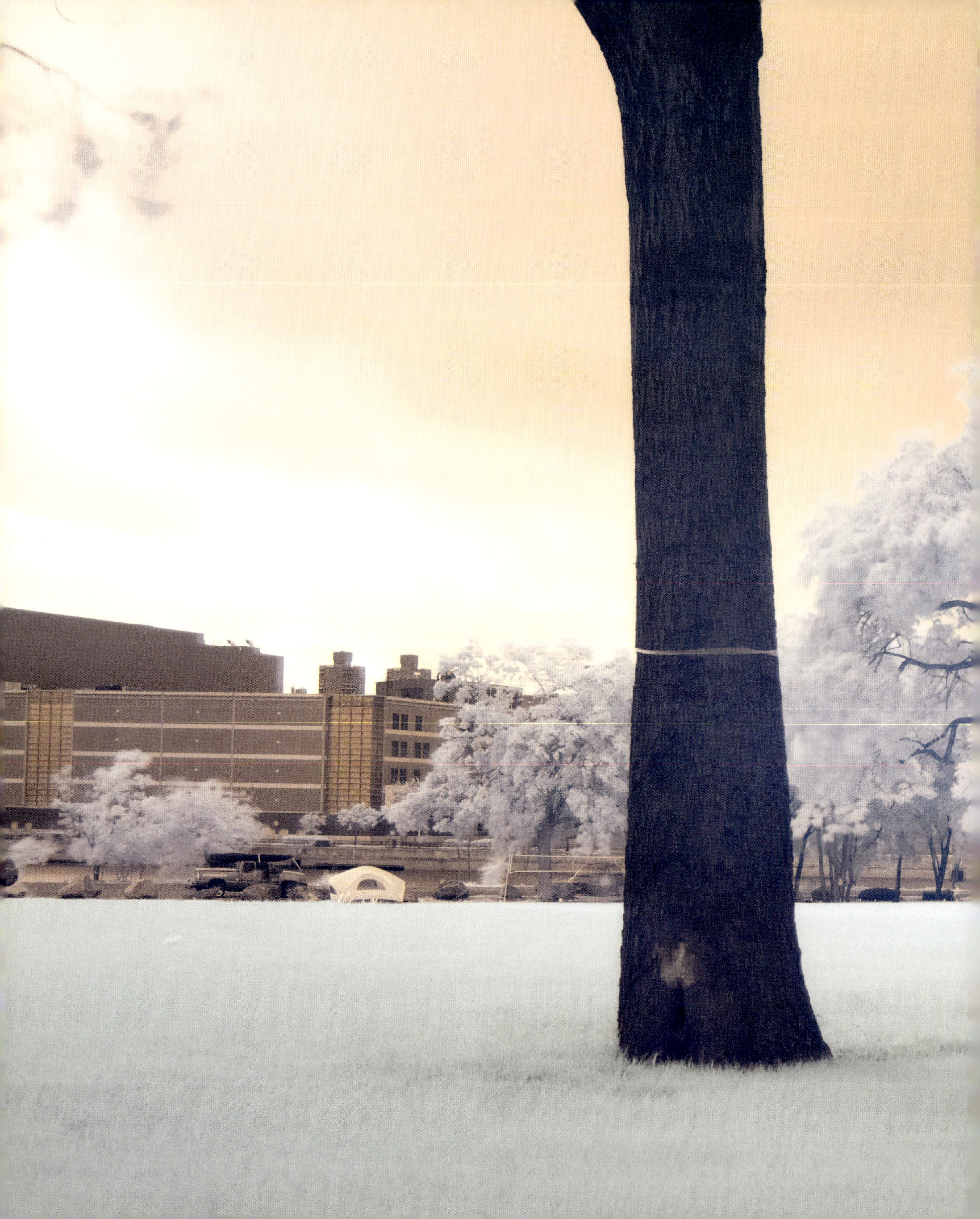

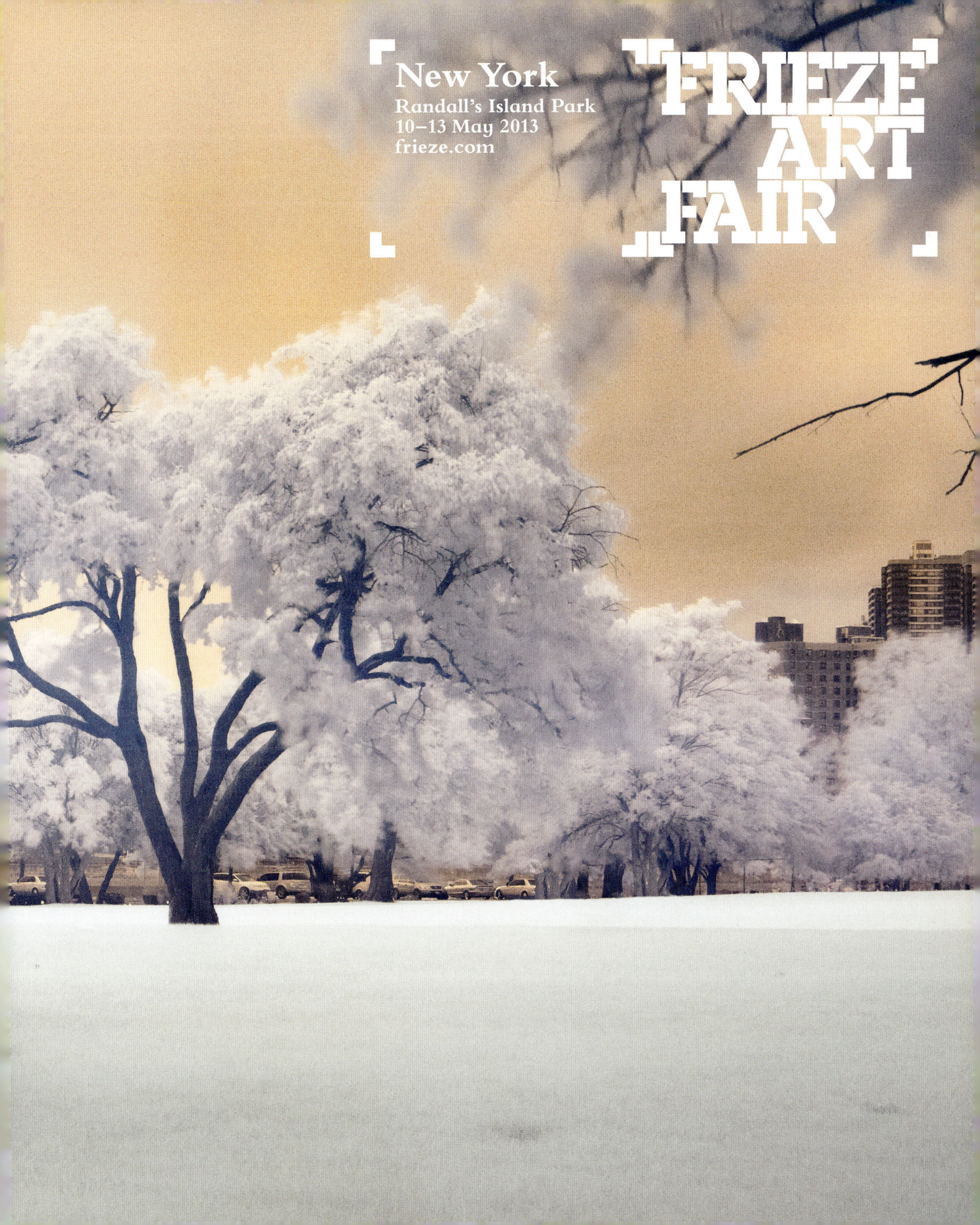
New York
Randall's Island Park
10–13 May 2013
frieze.com
FRIEZE
ART
FAIR

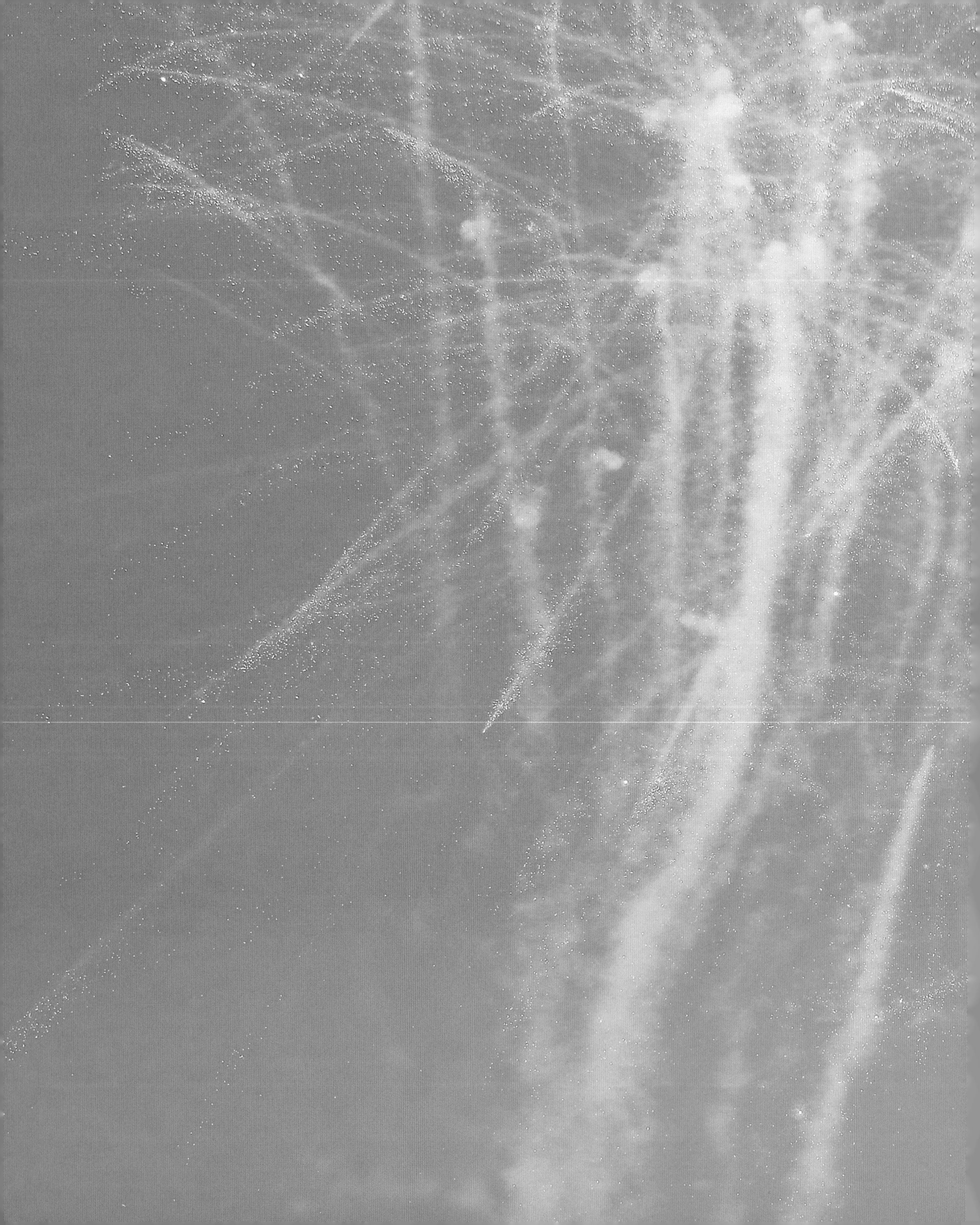

# Index

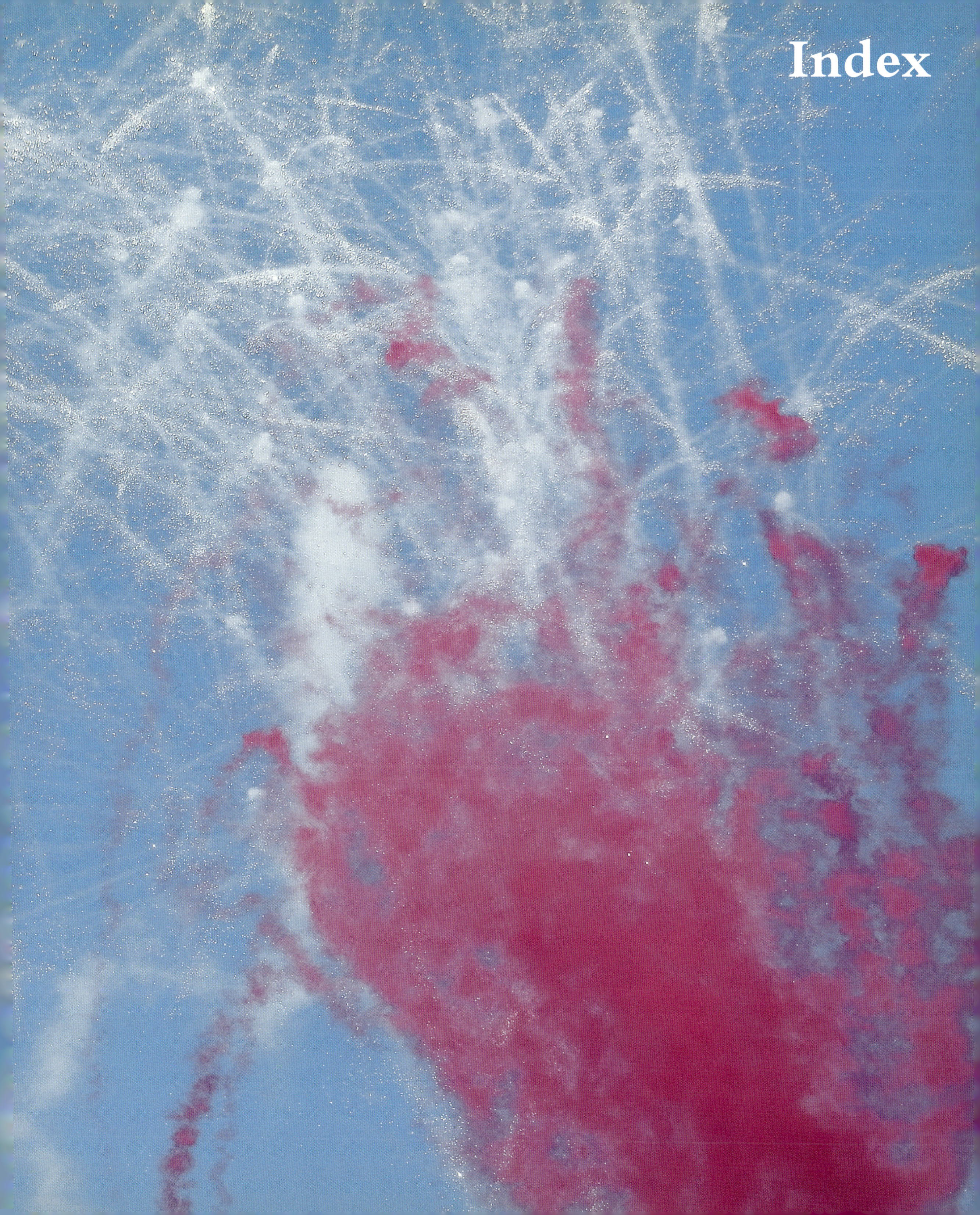

# Gallery Index

## 303 Gallery

**Stand Number C9**
Tel +1 212 255 1121

547 West 21st Street
New York NY 10011
United States
Tel +1 212 255 1121
Fax +1 212 255 5563
info@303gallery.com
www.303gallery.com

**Contact**
Lisa Spellman
Barbara Corti
Cristian Alexa
Mari Spirito

**Artists**
Doug Aitken
Valentin Carron
Anne Chu
Hans-Peter Feldmann
Ceal Floyer
Karel Funk
Maureen Gallace
Tim Gardner
Dominique Gonzalez-Foerster
Rodney Graham
Mary Heilmann
Jeppe Hein
Larry Johnson
Matt Johnson
Karen Kilimnik
Florian Maier-Aichen
Nick Mauss
Mike Nelson
Kristin Oppenheim
Eva Rothschild
Collier Schorr
Stephen Shore
Sue Williams
Jane & Louise Wilson

## 47 Canal

**Stand Number R6**
Tel +1 646 415 7712

47 Canal Street 2nd Floor
New York NY 10002
United States
Tel +1 646 415 7712
info@47canalstreet.com
www.47canalstreet.com

**Contact**
Margaret Lee
Oliver Newton

**Frame Artist**
Josh Kline

**Artists**
Michele Abeles
Alisa Baremboym
Antoine Catala
Gregory Edwards
Amy Lien & Enzo Camacho
Trevor Shimizu
Nolan Simon
Stewart Uoo
Anicka Yi

## Galería Juana de Aizpuru

**Stand Number G5**
Tel +44 7527 403 069

Barquillo 44
Madrid 28004
Spain
Tel +34 91 310 5561
Fax +34 91 319 5286
aizpuru@juanadeaizpuru.es
www.juanadeaizpuru.es

**Contact**
Juana de Aizpuru

**Artists**
Miroslaw Balka
Eric Baudelaire
Tania Bruguera
Jordi Colomer
Jonas Dahlberg
Sandra Gamarra
Carmela García
Dora García
Alberto García Alix
Cristina García Rodero
Pierre Gonnord
Georg Herold
Federico Herrero
Joseph Kosuth
Rogelio López Cuenca
Cristina Lucas
Yasumasa Morimura
Albert Oehlen
Markus Oehlen
Tim Parchikov
Fernando Sánchez Castillo
Andres Serrano
Montserrat Soto
Wolfgang Tillmans
Franz West
Heimo Zobernig

## Algus Greenspon

**Stand Number S20**
Tel +1 212 255 7872

71 Morton Street
New York NY 10014
United States
Tel +1 212 255 7872
gallery@algusgreenspon.com
www.algusgreenspon.com

**Contact**
Mitchell Algus
Amy Greenspon

**Focus Artists**
Gene Beery
Mathew Cerletty
Emily Sundblad

**Artists**
Christopher D'Arcangelo
Ull Hohn
E'wao Kagoshima
Adriana Lara

## Altman Siegel

**Stand Number S9**
Tel +1 415 576 9300

49 Geary Street, 4th Floor
San Francisco CA 94108
United States
Tel +1 415 576 9300
Fax +1 415 373 4471
info@altmansiegel.com
www.altmansiegel.com

**Contact**
Claudia Altman-Siegel
Daelyn Short Farnham
McIntyre Parker

**Focus Artists**
Matt Keegan
Devin Leonardi
Trevor Paglen

**Artists**
Nate Boyce
Shannon Ebner
Liam Everett
Fran Herndon
Chris Johanson
Shinpei Kusanagi
Will Rogan
Sara VanDerBeek
Emily Wardill
Garth Weiser

## Galería Helga de Alvear

**Stand Number A7**
Tel +34 60 676 1169

Doctor Fourquet 12
Madrid 28012
Spain
Tel +34 91 468 0506
Fax +34 91 467 5134
galeria@helgadealvear.com
www.helgadealvear.com

**Contact**
Helga de Alvear

**Artists**
Helena Almeida
Slater Bradley
Angela Bulloch
José Pedro Croft
Ángela de la Cruz
Michael Elmgreen & Ingar Dragset
Jorge Galindo
Katharina Grosse
Axel Hütte
Prudencio Irazabal
Isaac Julien
Jürgen Klauke
Imi Knoebel
Dan Perjovschi
Jorge Queiroz
Thomas Ruff
Santiago Sierra
D.J. Simpson
Jane & Louise Wilson

## Ancient & Modern

**Stand Number S10**
Tel +44 20 7253 4550

201 Whitecross Street
London EC1Y 8QP
United Kingdom
Tel +44 20 7253 4550
Fax +44 20 7253 4550
mail@ancientandmodern.org
www.ancientandmodern.org

**Contact**
Bruce Haines
Emily LaBarge
Hannah Patching

**Focus Artists**
Eva Berendes
Matthias Dornfeld
Rudolf Polanszky

**Artists**
Ketuta Alexi-Meskhishvili
Volker Eichelmann
Jane England
Melissa Gordon
Luke Gottelier
Raphael Hefti
Des Hughes
Paul Johnson
Alan Kane
Norbert Prangenberg
Audrey Reynolds

## Andersen's Contemporary

**Stand Number H4**
Tel + 45 32 95 92 35

Amager Strandvej 50B
Copenhagen S 2300
Denmark
Tel + 45 32 95 92 35
info@andersen-s.dk
www.andersen-s.dk

**Contact**
Claus Andersen
Scot W. Surdez
Jeanette Lindholdt Madsen

**Artists**
Peter Bonde
Jay Chung & Q Takeki
Maeda
Jason Dodge
Simon Dybbroe Møller
Olafur Eliasson
FOS
Gaeudjiparl
Thilo Heinzmann
Ulrik Heltoft
Daniel Lergon
Albert Mertz
Henrik Olesen
Anselm Reyle
Thiago Rocha Pitta
Pia Rönicke
Tomás Saraceno
Anja Schwörer
Katja Strunz
Anna Fro Vodder
Thomas Zipp

## The Approach

**Stand Number E21**
Tel +44 20 8983 3878

1st Floor
47 Approach Road
London E2 9LY
United Kingdom
Tel +44 20 8983 3878
Fax +44 20 8983 3919
info@theapproach.co.uk
www.theapproach.co.uk

**Contact**
Jake Miller
Emma Robertson
Mary Cork
Mike Allen

**Artists**
Phillip Allen
Helene Appel
Cris Brodahl
Alice Channer
Stuart Cumberland
Peter Davies
Patrick Hill
Evan Holloway
Germaine Kruip
Rezi van Lankveld
Jack Lavender
Edward Lipski
Dave Muller
Lisa Oppenheim
Magali Reus
Amanda Ross-Ho
John Stezaker
Evren Tekinoktay
Sara VanDerBeek
Gary Webb
Martin Westwood
Sam Windett

## Arcade

**Stand Number R2**
Tel +44 20 7608 0428

87 Lever Street
London EC1V 3RA
United Kingdom
Tel +44 20 7608 0428
info@arcadefinearts.com
www.arcadefinearts.com

**Contact**
Christian Mooney

**Frame Artist**
Anna Barham

**Artists**
Caroline Achaintre
Can Altay
Luca Bertolo
Ib Braase
Kit Craig
Jeremiah Day
John Finneran
Nick Laessing
John Wallbank
Maria Zahle

## Laura Bartlett Gallery

**Stand Number G14**
Tel +44 20 7404 9251

10 Northington Street
London WC1N 2JG
United Kingdom
Tel +44 20 7404 9251
Fax +44 20 7430 1731
mail@laurabartlettgallery.com
www.laurabartlettgallery.com

**Contact**
Laura Bartlett
Madeleine Martin

**Artists**
Becky Beasley
Nina Beier
John Divola
Simon Dybbroe Møller
Harrell Fletcher
Cyprien Gaillard
Lydia Gifford
Ian Law
Marie Lund
Elizabeth McAlpine
Alex Olson
Martin Skauen

## Galerie Catherine Bastide

**Stand Number G2**
Tel +32 2 646 29 71

Rue Vandenbrandenstraat 1
Brussels 1000
Belgium
Tel +32 2 646 29 71
Fax +32 2 538 61 67
info@catherinebastide.com
www.catherinebastide.com

**Contact**
Catherine Bastide

**Artists**
Jacques André
David Colosi
Sarah Crowner
Sebastian Diaz Morales
Jean-Pascal Flavien
Monique van Genderen
Geert Goiris
Tom Holmes
T. Kelly Mason
Marianne Mueller
William Pope.L
Ola Rindal
Josh Smith
Valerie Snobeck
Catherine Sullivan
Janaina Tschäpe
Kelley Walker

## Galerie Guido W. Baudach

**Stand Number A10**
Tel +49 30 2804 7727

Oudenarder Strasse 16-20
Berlin 13347
Germany
Tel +49 30 2804 7727
Fax +49 30 4502 4481
galerie@guidowbaudach.com
www.guidowbaudach.com

Carmerstrasse 11
Berlin 10623
Germany
Tel +49 030 3199 8101
Fax +49 030 3199 8103

**Contact**
Guido W. Baudach
Berit Homburg

**Artists**
André Butzer
Björn Dahlem
Thilo Heinzmann
Thomas Helbig
Andy Hope 1930
Rashid Johnson
Jürgen Klauke
Erwin Kneihsl
Bjarne Melgaard
Aïda Ruilova
Markus Selg
Thomas Zipp

## Marianne Boesky Gallery

**Stand Number E5**
Tel +44 845 873 7985

509 West 24th Street
New York NY 10011
United States
Tel +1 212 680 9889
Fax +1 212 680 9897
info@marianneboeskygallery.com
www.marianneboeskygallery.com

118 East 64th Street
New York NY 10065
United States
Tel +1 212 680 9889

**Contact**
Marianne Boesky
Adrian Turner
Serra Pradhan
Brad Waywell

**Artists**
Diana Al-Hadid
Andisheh Avini
Hannah van Bart
Sue de Beer
Pier Paolo Calzolari
Jesse Chapman
Robert Elfgen
Rachel Feinstein
Barnaby Furnas
Melissa Gordon
Jay Heikes
Adam Helms
Yuichi Higashionna
Donald Moffett
William O'Brien
Jacco Olivier
Hans Op de Beeck
Anthony Pearson
Salvatore Scarpitta
Mindy Shapero
Kon Trubkovich
John Waters
Claudia Wieser

## Tanya Bonakdar Gallery

**Stand Number A5**
Tel +1 212 414 4144

521 West 21st Street
New York NY 10011
United States
Tel +1 212 414 4144
Fax +1 212 414 1535
mail@tanyabonakdargallery.com
www.tanyabonakdargallery.com

**Contact**
Tanya Bonakdar
Ethan Sklar
Claire Pauley
Renee Coppola

**Artists**
Uta Barth
Martin Boyce
Sandra Cinto
Phil Collins
Mat Collishaw
Mark Dion
Olafur Eliasson
Siobhán Hapaska
Sabine Hornig
Teresa Hubbard & Alexander Birchler
Ian Kiaer
Carla Klein
Liz Larner
Atelier van Lieshout
Charles Long
Rita Lundqvist
Mark Manders
Jason Meadows
Ernesto Neto
Rivane Neuenschwander
Susan Philipsz
Peggy Preheim
Analia Saban
Tomás Saraceno
Thomas Scheibitz
Hannah Starkey
Haim Steinbach
Dirk Stewen
Jack Strange
Sarah Sze
Neal Tait
Jeffrey Vallance
Gillian Wearing
Nicole Wermers

## Bortolami

**Stand Number F11**
Tel +1 212 727 2050

520 West 20th Street
New York NY 10011
United States
Tel +1 212 727 2050
Fax +1 212 727 2060
info@bortolamigallery.com
www.bortolamigallery.com

**Contact**
Stefania Bortolami
Christine Messineo
Charles Libeert
Nicole Will

**Artists**
Richard Aldrich
Avner Ben-Gal
Daniel Buren
Tom Burr
Shane Campbell
Morgan Fisher
Michel François
Piero Golia
Thilo Heinzmann
Patrick Hill
Piotr Janas
Scott King
Jonathan Meese
Luigi Ontani
Anna Ostoya
Peter Peri
Ben Schumacher
Gary Webb
Eric Wesley
Aaron Young

## The Box

**Stand Number R19**
Tel +1 626 463 8144

805 Traction Avenue
Los Angeles CA 90013
United States
Tel +1 213 625 1747
Fax +1 213 625 5747
info@theboxla.com
www.theboxla.com

**Contact**
Mara McCarthy
Jason Underhill
Camille Weiner
LeRoy Stevens III

**Frame Artist**
Sarah Conaway

**Artists**
John Altoon
Judith Bernstein
Julien Bismuth
Mike Bouchet
Simone Forti
Wally Hedrick
Rachel Khedoori
Elke Silvia Krystufek
Leigh Ledare
Los Angeles Free Music Society (LAFMS)
Los Angeles Poverty Department (LAPD)
Robert Mallary
Damon McCarthy
Paul McCarthy
Jennifer Nelson
Spandau Parks
Kiersten Puusemp
Melinda Ring
Barbara T. Smith
Stan VanDerBeek
Lisa Williamson

## BQ

**Stand Number G11**
Tel +49 172 787 9551

Weydingerstrasse 10
Berlin 10178
Germany
Tel +49 30 2345 7316
Fax +49 30 2345 7325
info@bqberlin.de
www.bqberlin.de

**Contact**
Joern Boetnagel
Yvonne Quirmbach

**Artists**
Dirk Bell
Alexandra Bircken
Carina Brandes
Matti Braun
Owen Gump
Andrew Kerr
Kriwet
Friedrich Kunath
Bojan Sarcevic
David Shrigley
Marcus Steinweg
Reinhard Voigt
Richard Wright

## Jessica Bradley

**Stand Number S4**
Tel +1 416 832 6846

1450 Dundas Street West
Toronto M6J 1Y6
Canada
Tel +1 416 537 3125
info@jessicabradleyart projects.com
www.jessicabradleyart projects.com

74 Miller Street
Toronto M6N 2Z8

**Contact**
Jessica Bradley
Leah Turner

**Focus Artists**
Sara MacKillop
Derek Sullivan
Zin Taylor

**Artists**
Daniel Barrow
Shary Boyle
Michel de Broin
Paul Butler
Sarah Cale
Julia Dault
Hadley + Maxwell
Marla Hlady
Kristan Horton
Jed Lind
Jason McLean
David Merritt
Sasha Pierce
Ben Reeves
Jon Sasaki

## The Breeder

**Stand Number F14**
Tel +30 694 464 6800

Iasonos 45
Athens 10436
Greece
Tel +30 210 331 7527
Fax +30 210 331 7527
gallery@thebreedersystem.com
www.thebreedersystem.com

**Contact**
George Vamvakidis
Stathis Panagoulis

**Artists**
Markus Amm
Marc Bijl
Vlassis Caniaris
Matt Connors
Antonis Donef
Iris van Dongen
Stelios Faitakis
Uwe Henneken
Hope
Kalup Linzy
Andreas Lolis
Ryan McGinley
Irini Miga
Scott Myles
Angelos Papadimitriou
Jennifer Rubell
Shirana Shahbazi
Mindy Shapero
Daniel Sinsel
Gert & Uwe Tobias
Scott Treleaven
Alexandros Tzannis
Jannis Varelas
Gabriel Vormstein
Tao Xue

## Broadway 1602

**Stand Number E14**
Tel +1 212 481 0362

1181 Broadway 3rd Floor
New York NY 10001
United States
Tel +1 212 481 0362
Fax +1 212 481 1699
gallery@broadway1602.com
www.broadway1602.com

**Contact**
Anke Kempkes
Aniko Erdosi

**Artists**
Evelyne Axell
Anders Clausen
Margarete Jakschik
Edward Krasinski & Eustachy Kossakowski
Nicola L.
Devin Leonardi
Babette Mangolte
Anna Molska
Zofia Rydet
Xanti Schawinsky
Penny Slinger
Marjorie Strider
Alina Szapocznikow

## Gavin Brown's enterprise

**Stand Number B11**
Tel +44 7958 536 764

620 Greenwich Street
New York NY 10014
United States
Tel +1 212 627 5258
gallery@gavinbrown.biz
www.gavinbrown.biz

**Contact**
Gavin Brown
Lucy Chadwick
Corinna Durland
Bridget Donahue
Laura Mitterrand

**Artists**
Franz Ackermann
James Angus
Uri Aran
Thomas Bayrle
Dirk Bell
Jennifer Bornstein
Joe Bradley
Kerstin Brätsch
Martin Creed
Verne Dawson
Jeremy Deller
Peter Doig
Urs Fischer
Dara Friedman
Mark Handforth
Jonathan Horowitz
Alex Katz
Christopher Knowles
Udomsak Krisanamis
Mark Leckey
Silke Otto-Knapp
Laura Owens
Oliver Payne
Elizabeth Peyton
Steven Pippin
Rob Pruitt
Nick Relph
Steven Shearer
Frances Stark
Katja Strunz
Sturtevant
Spencer Sweeney
Rirkrit Tiravanija

## Buchholz

**Stand Number C4**
Tel +49 221 257 4946

Neven-DuMont-Strasse 17
Cologne 50667
Germany
Tel +49 221 257 4946
Fax +49 221 253 351
post@galeriebuchholz.de
www.galeriebuchholz.de

Fasanenstrasse 30
Berlin 10719
Germany
Tel +49 30 8862 4056
Fax +49 30 8862 4057

**Contact**
Daniel Buchholz
Christopher Müller

**Artists**
Tomma Abts
Nairy Baghramian
Cosima von Bonin
Tony Conrad
Simon Denny
Lukas Duwenhögger
Thomas Eggerer
Vincent Fecteau
Morgan Fisher
Isa Genzken
Jack Goldstein
Julian Göthe
Richard Hawkins
Jochen Klein
Jutta Koether
Michael Krebber
Mark Leckey
Sam Lewitt
Lucy McKenzie
Henrik Olesen
Paulina Olowska
Silke Otto-Knapp
Mathias Poledna
Florian Pumhösl
R.H. Quaytman
Jeroen de Rijke & Willem de Rooij
Willem de Rooij
Frances Stark
Josef Strau
Stefan Thater
Cheyney Thompson
Wolfgang Tillmans
Danh Vo
Martin Wong
Katharina Wulff
Cerith Wyn Evans

## Bureau

**Stand Number R12**
Tel +1 917 861 9300

127 Henry Street
New York NY 10002
United States
Tel +1 917 861 9300
office@bureau-inc.com
www.bureau-inc.com

**Contact**
Gabrielle Giattino

**Frame Artist**
Matt Hoyt

**Artists**
Erica Baum
Ellie Ga
Tom Holmes
Viktor Kopp
Justin Matherly
Lionel Maunz
Julia Rommel

## Cabinet

**Stand Number E3**
Tel +44 7711 066 936

49-59 Old Street
London EC1V 9HX
United Kingdom
Tel +44 20 7251 6114
Fax +44 20 7608 2414
art@cabinetltd.demon.co.uk
www.cabinet.uk.com

**Contact**
Martin McGeown
Andrew Wheatley

**Artists**
Tariq Alvi
Atelier
Ed Atkins
Lutz Bacher
Bernadette Corporation
Bonnie Camplin
Gillian Carnegie
Marc Camille Chaimowicz
Jay Chung & Q Takeki Maeda
Lukas Duwenhögger
Cosey Fanni Tutti
Julian Göthe
Mark Leckey
Danny McDonald
Lucy McKenzie
Henrik Olesen
Lily van der Stokker
Anthony Symonds
Simon Thompson
Tris Vonna-Michell
JD Williams
David Wojnarowicz

## Campoli Presti

**Stand Number F5**
Tel +44 20 7739 4632

223 Cambridge Heath Road
London E2 0EL
United Kingdom
Tel +44 20 7739 4632
info@campolipresti.com
www.campolipresti.com

6 rue de Braque
Paris 75003
France
Tel +33 1 40 29 08 92

**Contact**
Gil Presti
Emanuela Campoli
Cora Muennich

**Artists**
Liz Deschenes
Roe Ethridge
Jutta Koether
Daniel Lefcourt
Scott Lyall
John Miller
Olivier Mosset
Sean Paul
Pavel Pepperstein
Eileen Quinlan
Blake Rayne
Clément Rodzielski
Christoph Ruckhäberle
Nora Schultz
Reena Spaulings
Joanne Tatham & Tom O'Sullivan
Cheyney Thompson

## Canada

**Stand Number G15**
Tel +1 212 925 4631

333 Broome Street
New York NY 10002
United States
Tel +1 212 925 4631
gallery@canadanewyork.com
www.canadanewyork.com

**Contact**
Suzanne Butler
Sarah Braman
Phil Grauer
Wallace Whitney

**Artists**
David Askevold
Katherine Bernhardt
Joe Bradley
Sarah Braman
Matt Connors
Xylor Jane
Lily Ludlow
Michael Mahalchick
Joanna Malinowska
Carrie Moyer
Luke Murphy
Elena Pankova
Robin Peck
Anke Weyer
Wallace Whitney
Michael Williams

## Galerie Gisela Capitain

**Stand Number C10**
Tel +49 221 3557 0100

St Apern Strasse 26
Cologne 50667
Germany
Tel +49 221 3557 0100
Fax +49 221 3557 0129
info@galeriecapitain.de
www.galeriecapitain.de

**Contact**
Gisela Capitain
Regina Fiorito
Dorothee Sorge

**Artists**
Karla Black
Barbara Bloom
Maria Brunner
Gillian Carnegie
Günther Förg
Luke Fowler
Anna Gaskell
Wade Guyton
Uwe Henneken
Charline von Heyl
Margarete Jakschik
Rachel Khedoori
Martin Kippenberger
Zoe Leonard
Meuser
Marcel Odenbach
Albert Oehlen
Laura Owens
Jorge Pardo
Ascan Pinckernelle
Seth Price
Stephen Prina
Sam Samore
Elfie Semotan
Monika Sosnowska
John Stezaker
Kelley Walker
Franz West
Christopher Williams
Johannes Wohnseifer
Christopher Wool

## Carlos/ Ishikawa

**Stand Number R7**
Tel +44 20 7001 1744

Unit 4, 88 Mile End Road
London E1 4UN
United Kingdom
Tel +44 20 7001 1744
gallery@carlosishikawa.com
www.carlosishikawa.com

**Contact**
Vanessa Carlos
Nara Ishikawa

**Frame Artist**
Ed Fornieles

**Artists**
Mary Hurrell
Lloyd Corporation
Oscar Murillo

## Casas Riegner

**Stand Number S16**
Tel +571 249 9194

Calle 70A No. 7-41
Bogota
Colombia
Tel +57 1 249 9194
Fax +57 1 212 4116
info@casasriegner.com
www.casasriegner.com

**Contact**
Catalina Casas
Paula Bossa
Claudia Ramirez
Marta Matiz
Cesar Gonzalez

**Focus Artists**
Bernardo Ortiz
Mateo López
Gabriel Sierra

**Artists**
Johanna Calle
Leyla Cárdenas
Maria Fernanda Cardoso
Antonio Caro
Rosario López Parra
Maria Fernanda Plata
Miguel Angel Rojas
Luis Roldán
Liliana Sánchez
Rosemberg Sandoval
Wilger Sotelo
José Antonio Suárez Londoño
Angélica Teuta
Icaro Zorbar

## La Central

**Stand Number R11**
Tel +57 1 757 4410

Carrera 12A No. 77A-72
Bogota
Colombia 110221
Tel +57 1 757 4410
info@lacentral.com.co
www.lacentral.com.co

**Contact**
Katy Hernandez
Beatriz Lopez

**Frame Artist**
Carolina Caycedo

**Artists**
Felipe Arturo
Otto Berchem
Pia Camil
Nicolas Consuegra
Matthieu Laurette
Alberto Lezaca
Miltos Manetas
Ana Roldán
Manuela Viera Gallo

## Chatterjee & Lal

**Stand Number S1**
Tel +91 22 2202 3787

01/18 Kamal Mansion Floor
1 Arthur Bunder Road
Colaba
Mumbai 400005
India
Tel +91 22 2202 3787
Fax +91 22 2283 0100
info@chatterjeeandlal.com
www.chatterjeeandlal.com

**Contact**
Mortimer Chatterjee
Tara Lal

**Focus Artists**
Nikhil Chopra
Hetain Patel

**Artists**
Minam Apang
Ashish Avikunthak
Michael Bühler-Rose
Kabir Mohanty
Kaushik Mukhopadhyay
Aditya Pande
Rashid Rana
Kiran Subbaiah
Nityan Unnikrishnan

## Chert

**Stand Number S7**
Tel +49 171 205 6452

Skalitzerstrasse 68
Berlin 10997
Germany
Tel +49 30 7544 2118
Fax +49 30 7544 2120
post@chert-berlin.com
www.chert-berlin.com

**Contact**
Jennifer Chert

**Focus Artists**
Kasia Fudakowski
Petrit Halilaj
Erik van der Weijde

**Artists**
Alejandro Almanza Pereda
Lucy Coggle
Carla Scott Fullerton
Jérémie Gindre
Hannah James
Heike Kabisch
Andrea Kvas
Vanessa Safavi

## Sadie Coles HQ

**Stand Number C11**
Tel +44 20 7493 8611

69 South Audley Street
London W1K 2QZ
United Kingdom
Tel +44 20 7493 8611
Fax +44 20 7499 4878
info@sadiecoles.com
www.sadiecoles.com

4 New Burlington Place
London W1S 2HS
United Kingdom
Tel +44 20 7493 8611
Fax +44 20 7499 4878

**Contact**
Sadie Coles
Pauline Daly

**Artists**
Carl Andre
Matthew Barney
Dirk Bell
Avner Ben-Gal
Frank Benson
John Bock
Don Brown
Spartacus Chetwynd
Steven Claydon
John Currin
Sam Durant
Shannon Ebner
Angus Fairhurst
Urs Fischer
Florian Hecker
Georg Herold
Jonathan Horowitz
David Korty
Gabriel Kuri
Jim Lambie
Hilary Lloyd
Sarah Lucas
Helen Marten
Victoria Morton
J.P. Munro
Laura Owens
Simon Periton
Raymond Pettibon
Elizabeth Peyton
Richard Prince
Ugo Rondinone
Wilhelm Sasnal
Gregor Schneider
Daniel Sinsel
Andreas Slominski
Christiana Soulou
Rudolf Stingel
Nicola Tyson
Paloma Varga Weisz
T.J. Wilcox
Andrea Zittel

## Contemporary Fine Arts

**Stand Number C12**
Tel +49 175 526 3499

Am Kupfergraben 10
Berlin 10117
Germany
Tel +49 30 288 7870
Fax +49 30 2887 8726
gallery@cfa-berlin.de
www.cfa-berlin.de

**Contact**
Bruno Brunnet
Nicole Hackert
Philipp Haverkampf

**Artists**
Georg Baselitz
Peter Böhnisch
Marc Brandenburg
Cecily Brown
Zhivago Duncan
Marcel Eichner
Max Frisinger
Georg Herold
Thomas Kiesewetter
Michael Kunze
Jonathan Meese
Chris Ofili
Raymond Pettibon
Tal R
Anselm Reyle
Daniel Richter
Julian Schnabel
Dana Schutz
Norbert Schwontkowski
Dash Snow
Katja Strunz
Gert & Uwe Tobias
Ralf Ziervogel

## Pilar Corrias Gallery

**Stand Number H5**
Tel +44 20 7323 7000

54 Eastcastle Street
London W1W 8EF
United Kingdom
Tel +44 20 7323 7000
Fax +44 20 7323 6400
sales@pilarcorrias.com
www.pilarcorrias.com

**Contact**
Pilar Corrias

**Artists**
Charles Avery
Ulla von Brandenburg
Keren Cytter
Koo Jeong-A
Leigh Ledare
Tala Madani
Elizabeth Neel
Philippe Parreno
Mary Ramsden
Tobias Rehberger
Mary Reid Kelley
Julião Sarmento
Shahzia Sikander
Rirkrit Tiravanija
Tunga
Patrick Tuttofuoco

## Corvi-Mora

**Stand Number E7**
Tel +44 20 7840 9111

1a Kempsford Road
London SE11 4NU
United Kingdom
Tel +44 20 7840 9111
Fax +44 20 7840 9112
tcm@corvi-mora.com
www.corvi-mora.com

**Contact**
Tommaso Corvi-Mora
Tabitha Langton-Lockton
Clare Holden

**Artists**
Richard Aldrich
Abel Auer
Brian Calvin
Pierpaolo Campanini
Anne Collier
Andy Collins
Rachel Feinstein
Dee Ferris
Dominique Gonzalez-Foerster
Richard Hawkins
Roger Hiorns
Jim Isermann
Colter Jacobsen
Dorota Jurczak
Aisha Khalid
Armin Krämer
David Lieske
Eva Marisaldi
Jason Meadows
Monique Prieto
Imran Qureshi
Andrea Salvino
Glenn Sorensen
Tomoaki Suzuki
Naoyuki Tsuji
Lynette Yiadom-Boakye

## Galerie Crèvecoeur

**Stand Number R13**
Tel +33 9 54 57 31 26

4 rue Jouye Rouve
Paris 75020
France
Tel +33 9 54 57 31 26
info@galeriecrevecoeur.com
www.galeriecrevecoeur.com

**Contact**
Axel Dibie
Alix Dionot-Morani

**Frame Artist**
Xavier Antin

**Artists**
Laetitia Benat
Julien Carreyn
Jochen Dehn
André Guedes
Antoine Marquis
Jorge Pedro Nuñez
Mick Peter
Florian & Michaël Quistrebert

## Galerie Chantal Crousel

**Stand Number D11**
Tel +33 1 42 77 38 87

10 rue Charlot
Paris 75003
France
Tel +33 1 42 77 38 87
Fax +33 1 42 77 59 00
galerie@crousel.com
www.crousel.com

11f rue Léon Jouhaux
Paris 75010
France
Tel +33 1 42 01 64 97
Fax +33 1 42 77 59 00

**Contact**
Chantal Crousel
Niklas Svennung

**Artists**
Jennifer Allora & Guillermo Calzadilla
Fikret Atay
Abraham Cruzvillegas
Claire Fontaine
Isa Genzken
Wade Guyton
Fabrice Gygi
Mona Hatoum
Thomas Hirschhorn
Hassan Khan
Michael Krebber
Jean-Luc Moulène
Moshe Ninio
Melik Ohanian
Gabriel Orozco
Seth Price
Clément Rodzielski
Willem de Rooij
Anri Sala
Alain Séchas
José Maria Sicilia
Sean Snyder
Reena Spaulings
Wolfgang Tillmans
Rirkrit Tiravanija
Danh Vo
Wang Bing
Haegue Yang
Heimo Zobernig

## Thomas Dane Gallery

**Stand Number F13**
Tel +44 20 7925 2505

11 Duke Street, St James's
London SW1Y 6BN
United Kingdom
Tel +44 20 7925 2505
info@thomasdane.com
www.thomasdane.com

3 Duke Street, St James's
London SW1Y 6BJ
United Kingdom

**Contact**
Thomas Dane
Martine d'Anglejan-Chatillon
François Chantala

**Artists**
Hurvin Anderson
Kutlug Ataman
Lynda Benglis
Walead Beshty
Abraham Cruzvillegas
Alexandre da Cunha
José Damasceno
Michel François
Anya Gallaccio
John Gerrard
Arturo Herrera
Luisa Lambri
Michael Landy
Glenn Ligon
Steve McQueen
Jean-Luc Moulène
Paul Pfeiffer
Lari Pittman
Jorge Queiroz
Caragh Thuring
Kelley Walker

## Massimo De Carlo

**Stand Number D8**
Tel +39 2 7000 3987

Via Giovanni Ventura 5
Milan 20134
Italy
Tel +39 2 7000 3987
Fax +39 2 749 2135
info@massimodecarlo.it
www.massimodecarlo.it

55 South Audley Street
London W1K 2QH
United Kingdom
Tel +44 20 7287 2005
info@carlsongallery.co.uk
www.carlsongallery.co.uk

6 Heddon Street
London W1B 4BT
United Kingdom

**Contact**
Massimo De Carlo
Oda Albera
Ludovica Barbieri
Roberto Moiraghi
Laura Ravelli

**Artists**
John Armleder
Massimo Bartolini
Maurizio Cattelan
Spartacus Chetwynd
Steven Claydon
Dan Colen
George Condo
Roberto Cuoghi
Michael Elmgreen & Ingar Dragset
Roland Flexner
Gelitin
Carsten Höller
Christian Holstad
Rashid Johnson
Elad Lassry
Sol LeWitt
Nate Lowman
Matthew Monahan
Olivier Mosset
Matt Mullican
Steven Parrino
Diego Perrone
Paola Pivi
Rob Pruitt
Jim Shaw
Josh Smith
Rudolf Stingel
Piotr Uklański
Kaari Upson
Kelley Walker
Yan Pei-Ming
Aaron Young
Andrea Zittel

## Elizabeth Dee

**Stand Number E22**
Tel +1 212 924 7545

545 West 20th Street
New York NY 10011
United States
Tel +1 212 924 7545
Fax +1 212 924 7671
info@elizabethdeegallery.com
www.elizabethdee.com

**Contact**
Elizabeth Dee
Jayne Drost Johnson
Kevin Tobin
Jennifer Brennan
Daniel Pillis

**Artists**
Mac Adams
Mark Barrow
Eric Baudelaire
Miriam Cahn
Philippe Decrauzat
Harry Dodge & Stanya Kahn
Leo Gabin
Jeff Keen
Miranda Lichtenstein
Virgil Marti
Ryan McNamara
Carl Ostendarp
Adrian Piper
Renaud Regnery
Meredyth Sparks

## dépendance

**Stand Number S11**
Tel +32 4 7374 4779

Rue du Marché aux Porcs 4
Brussels BE-1000
Belgium
Tel +32 2 217 7401
Fax +32 2 217 7401
dependance@skynet.be
www.dependance.be

**Contact**
Michael Callies
Ayelet Yanai

**Focus Artists**
Henrik Olesen
Nora Schultz
Josef Strau

**Artists**
Richard Aldrich
Thomas Bayrle
Merlin Carpenter
Michaela Eichwald
Jana Euler
Olivier Foulon
Manuel Gnam
Thilo Heinzmann
Karl Holmqvist
Sergej Jensen
Michael Krebber
Linder
Michaela Meise
Michael Riedel
Benjamin Saurer
Hanna Schwarz
Andreas Slominski
Lucie Stahl
Oscar Tuazon
Haegue Yang

## Allied Editions

A consortium of six public galleries
c/o Whitechapel Gallery
77-82 Whitechapel High Street
London E1 7QX
Tel +44 20 7522 7882
Fax +44 20 7522 7887
info@alliededitions.org

**Participating Galleries and Contacts**
Camden Arts Centre
(Jacqueline Jeffries)
Chisenhale Gallery
(Soraya Rodriguez)
Institute of Contemporary Arts
(Vicky Steer)
Serpentine Gallery
(Tom Harrisson)
Studio Voltaire
(Tamsin Clark)
Whitechapel Gallery
(Johanna Melvin)

**Artists**
Richard Aldrich
Cory Arcangel
Ed Atkins
Phyllida Barlow
Mel Bochner
Pablo Bronstein
Rachael Champion
Alice Channer
Jeremy Deller
Roe Ethridge
Herzog & de Meuron and Ai Weiwei
Simon Martin
Bjarne Melgaard
Oscar Murillo
Yoko Ono
Amalia Pica
Guiseppe Penone
Thomas Schütte
Gillian Wearing
Rachel Whiteread

## Galerie Eigen + Art

**Stand Number G4**
Tel +49 30 280 6605

Auguststrasse 26
Berlin 10117
Germany
Tel +49 30 280 6605
Fax +49 30 280 6616
berlin@eigen-art.com
www.eigen-art.com

Auguststrasse 11-13
Berlin 10117
Germany
Tel +49 246 2840
lab@eigen-art.com

Spinnereistrasse 7 Halle 5
Leipzig 04179
Germany
Tel +49 341 960 7886
Fax +49 341 225 4214
leipzig@eigen-art.com

**Contact**
Gerd Harry Lybke

**Artists**
Akos Birkas
Birgit Brenner
Martin Eder
Tim Eitel
Nina Fischer & Maroan el Sani
Stella Hamberg
Jörg Herold
Christine Hill
Uwe Kowski
Rémy Markowitsch
Maix Mayer
Ryan Mosley
Carsten Nicolai
Olaf Nicolai
Neo Rauch
Ricarda Roggan
Yehudit Sasportas
David Schnell
Annelies Štrba
Matthias Weischer

## Elastic Gallery

**Stand Number S5**
Tel +46 70 656 4319

Monbijougatan 17G
Malmo 211 53
Sweden
Tel +46 40 611 4319
Fax +46 40 611 4319
info@elasticgallery.com
www.elasticgallery.com

**Contact**
Ola Gustafsson

**Focus Artists**
Dave Allen
Camilla Løw

**Artists**
Catrin Andersson
Ditte Ejlerskov
Luca Frei
Maria Hedlund
Knut Henrik Henriksen
Jone Kvie
Runo Lagomarsino
Anna Ling
Per Mårtensson
Kristina Matousch
Anna Nordquist Andersson
Anders Sletvold Moe
Astrid Svangren
Magnus Thierfelder
Magnus Wallin

## galerie frank elbaz

**Stand Number H8**
Tel +33 6 03 33 85 85

66 rue de Turenne
Paris 75003
France
Tel +33 1 48 87 50 04
info@galeriefrankelbaz.com
www.galeriefrankelbaz.com

**Contact**
Frank Elbaz
Daphné Kossmann

**Artists**
Davide Balula
Jesus Alberto Benitez
Wallace Berman
Susan Collis
Julije Knifer
Justine Kurland
Rainier Lericolais
Ari Marcopoulos
Kaz Oshiro
Gyan Panchal
Bernard Piffaretti
Meredyth Sparks
Blair Thurman
Josip Vanista

## Experimenter

**Stand Number R5**
Tel +91 98 3001 5854

2/1 Hindusthan Road
Kolkata 700029
India
Tel +91 33 2463 0465
info@experimenter.in
www.experimenter.in

**Contact**
Prateek & Priyanka Raja

**Frame Artist**
Bani Abidi

**Artists**
Rathin Barman
Natasha de Betak
CAMP
Adip Dutta
Sanchayan Ghosh
Nadia Kaabi-Linke
Naeem Mohaiemen
Mehreen Murtaza
The Otolith Group
Raqs Media Collective
Hajra Waheed

## Konrad Fischer Galerie

**Stand Number C6**
Tel +49 177 356 1826

Platanenstrasse 7
Dusseldorf 40233
Germany
Tel +49 211 685 908
Fax +49 211 689 780
office@konradfischergalerie.de
www.konradfischergalerie.de

Lindenstrasse 35
Berlin 10969
Germany
Tel +49 30 5059 6820
Fax +49 30 5059 6821
berlin-office@konradfischergalerie.de

**Contact**
Dorothee Fischer
Daniel Marzona
Thomas Rieger
Ulla Wiegand
Claudia Pasko

**Artists**
Carl Andre
Giovanni Anselmo
Bernd & Hilla Becher
Guy Ben-Ner
Stanley Brouwn
Matthew Buckingham
Peter Buggenhout
Daniel Buren
Nina Canell
Alan Charlton
Tony Cragg
Hanne Darboven
Jan Dibbets
Hans-Peter Feldmann
Gilbert & George
Sophia Hultén
Cristina Iglesias
Zon Ito
On Kawara
Harald Klingelhöller
Jannis Kounellis
Melissa Kretschmer
Wolfgang Laib
Jim Lambie
Sol LeWitt
Richard Long
Robert Mangold
Rita McBride
Mario Merz
Bruce Nauman
Claes Oldenburg
Giuseppe Penone
Manfred Pernice
Magnus Plessen
Wolfgang Plöger

Charlotte Posenenske
Thomas Ruff
Robert Ryman
Gregor Schneider
Thomas Schütte
Juergen Staack
Yuji Takeoka
Tatjana Valsang
Paloma Varga Weisz
Johannes Wald
Lawrence Weiner
Petra Wunderlich
Jerry Zeniuk

## Foksal Gallery Foundation

**Stand Number E9**
Tel +48 504 268 910

Gorskiego 1A
Warsaw 00-033
Poland
Tel +48 22 826 5081
Fax +48 22 826 5081
mail@fgf.com.pl
www.fgf.com.pl

**Contact**
Andrzej Przywara

**Artists**
Pawel Althamer
Cezary Bodzianowski
Piotr Janas
Katarzyna Jozefowicz
Edward Krasinski
Robert Kúsmirowski
Anna Molska
Anna Niesterowicz
Paulina Olowska
Wilhelm Sasnal
Monika Sosnowska
Jakub Julian Ziolkowski
Artur Zmijewski

## Fonti

**Stand Number S6**
Tel +34 88 210 513

Via Chiaia 229
Naples 80132
Italy
Tel +39 81 411 409
Fax +39 81 411 409
info@galleriafonti.it
www.galleriafonti.it

**Contact**
Giangi Fonti

**Focus Artists**
Daniel Knorr
Fabian Marti
Giulia Piscitelli

**Artists**
Michel Auder
Marc Camille Chaimowicz
Marieta Chirulescu
Peter Coffin
Christian Flamm
Nicola Gobbetto
Piero Golia
Delia Gonzalez
Delia Gonzalez & Gavin Russom
Kiluanji Kia Henda
Birgit Megerle
Seb Patane
Manfred Pernice
Giulia Piscitelli
Gavin Russom
Lorenzo Scotto di Luzio
Eric Wesley

## Galeria Fortes Vilaça

**Stand Number E8**
Tel +55 11 8629 9328

Rua Fradique Coutinho 1500
Sao Paulo 05416-001
Brazil
Tel +55 11 3032 7066
Fax +55 11 3097 0384
galeria@fortesvilaca.com.br
www.fortesvilaca.com.br

Rua James Holland 71
Sao Paulo 01138-000
Brazil
Tel +55 11 3392 3942

**Contact**
Marcia Fortes
Alessandra d'Aloia
Alexandre Gabriel

**Artists**
Franz Ackermann
Efrain Almeida
Armando Andrade Tudela
Barrão
Carlos Bevilacqua
Tiago Carneiro da Cunha
Los Carpinteros
Leda Catunda
José Damasceno
Iran do Espírito Santo
Cerith Wyn Evans
Simon Evans
Tamar Guimarães
João Maria Gusmão and Pedro Paiva
Marine Hugonnier
Sergej Jensen
Lucia Laguna
Jac Leirner
Rodrigo Matheus
Beatriz Milhazes
Gerben Mulder
Ernesto Neto
Rivane Neuenschwander
Damián Ortega
osgemeos
Sara Ramo
Nuno Ramos
Mauro Restiffe
Marina Rheingantz
Michael Sailstorfer
Julião Sarmento
Valeska Soares
Janaina Tschäpe
Adriana Varejão
Erika Verzutti
Luiz Zerbini

## Marc Foxx

**Stand Number B8**
Tel +1 323 857 5571

6150 Wilshire Boulevard
Los Angeles CA 90048
United States
Tel +1 323 857 5571
gallery@marcfoxx.com
www.marcfoxx.com

**Contact**
Marc Foxx
Rodney Hill
Lia Trinka-Browner
Vanesa Zendejas

**Artists**
Leonor Antunes
Cris Brodahl
Anne Collier
Andy Collins
William Daniels
Stef Driesen
Brian Fahlstrom
Sophie von Hellermann
Roger Hiorns
Sanya Kantarovsky
Annette Kelm
Makiko Kudo
Luisa Lambri
Kris Martin
Jason Meadows
Carter Mull
David Musgrave
Michael van Ofen
Alessandro Pessoli
Amalia Pica
Matthew Ronay
Maaike Schoorel
Frances Stark
Hiroshi Sugito
Ricky Swallow
Mateo Tannatt
Guido van der Werve
Jennifer West
Sam Windett

## Carl Freedman Gallery

**Stand Number A8**
Tel +44 20 7684 8890

29 Charlotte Road
London EC2A 3PB
United Kingdom
Tel +44 20 7684 8890
Fax +44 20 7684 8889
info@carlfreedman.com
www.carlfreedman.com

**Contact**
Carl Freedman
Robert Diament

**Artists**
Armando Andrade Tudela
Jess Flood-Paddock
Michael Fullerton
Thilo Heinzmann
John McAllister
Ivan Seal
David Brian Smith
Fergal Stapleton
Catherine Story
Pieter Vermeersch

## Galerie Cinzia Friedlaender

**Stand Number R3**
Tel +49 30 2639 3956

Potsdamer Strasse 105
Berlin 10785
Germany
Tel +49 30 2639 3956
Fax +49 30 2639 3958
mail@galeriefriedlaender.de
www.galeriefriedlaender.de

**Contact**
Cinzia Friedlaender

**Frame Artist**
Jeronimo Voss

**Artists**
Bonnie Camplin
Sunah Choi
Justus Köhncke
Dirk von Lowtzow
Anna Möller
Jutta Pohlmann
Sabine Reitmaier
Matthias Schaufler
Maria Volk
Vincent Vulsma
JD Williams

## Stephen Friedman Gallery

**Stand Number D4**
Tel +44 845 873 7984

25-28 Old Burlington Street
London W1S 3AN
United Kingdom
Tel +44 20 7494 1434
Fax +44 20 7494 1431
info@stephenfriedman.com
www.stephenfriedman.com

11 Old Burlington Street
London W1S 3AQ
United Kingdom
Tel +44 20 7494 1434

**Contact**
Stephen Friedman
David Hubbard
Ticiana Correa

**Artists**
Mamma Andersson
Tonico Lemos Auad
Stephan Balkenhol
Claire Barclay
Huma Bhabha
Robert Buck
Andreas Eriksson
Tom Friedman
Kendell Geers
Wayne Gonzales
Daniel Guzmán
Thomas Hirschhorn
Jim Hodges
Li Tianbing
Paul McDevitt
Beatriz Milhazes
Yoshitomo Nara
Rivane Neuenschwander
Thomas Nozkowski
Catherine Opie
Cornelius Quabeck
Ged Quinn
Jennifer Rubell
Lucas Samaras
Mira Schendel
Yinka Shonibare
David Shrigley
Anne Truitt

## Frith Street Gallery

**Stand Number C1**
Tel +44 20 7494 1550

17-18 Golden Square
London W1F 9JJ
United Kingdom
Tel +44 20 7494 1550
info@frithstreetgallery.com
www.frithstreetgallery.com

**Contact**
Jane Hamlyn

**Artists**
Chantal Akerman
Polly Apfelbaum
Fiona Banner
Anna Barriball
Massimo Bartolini
Ingrid Calame
Dorothy Cross
Tacita Dean
Marlene Dumas
Callum Innes
Jaki Irvine
Cornelia Parker
Raqs Media Collective
John Riddy
Thomas Schütte
Dayanita Singh
Bridget Smith
Fiona Tan
Juan Uslé
Daphne Wright

## Gagosian Gallery

**Stand Number D7**
Tel +44 20 7841 9960

6-24 Britannia Street
London WC1X 9JD
United Kingdom
Tel +44 20 7841 9960
Fax +44 20 7841 9961
london@gagosian.com
www.gagosian.com

17-19 Davies Street
London W1K 3DE
United Kingdom
Tel +44 20 7493 3020
Fax +44 20 7493 3025

**Contact**
Larry Gagosian
Millicent Wilner
Stefan Ratibor

**Artists**
Diane Arbus
Richard Artschwager
Richard Avedon
Georg Baselitz
Dike Blair
Cecily Brown
Glenn Brown
Chris Burden
Alexander Calder
John Chamberlain
Dan Colen
Michael Craig-Martin
Gregory Crewdson
John Currin
Dexter Dalwood
Victoire de Castellane
Walter De Maria
William Eggleston
Roe Ethridge
Alberto Di Fabio
Urs Fischer
Ellen Gallagher
Alberto Giacometti
Piero Golia
Douglas Gordon
Arshile Gorky
Mark Grotjahn
Andreas Gursky
Damien Hirst
Howard Hodgkin
Carsten Höller
Neil Jenney
Y.Z. Kami
Mike Kelley
Anselm Kiefer
Martin Kippenberger
Jeff Koons
Yayoi Kusama
Roy Lichtenstein
Vera Lutter
Florian Maier-Aichen

Sally Mann
Piero Manzoni
Adam McEwen
Joel Morrison
Takashi Murakami
Marc Newson
Paul Noble
Albert Oehlen
Steven Parrino
Richard Phillips
Pablo Picasso
Richard Prince
Robert Rauschenberg
Anselm Reyle
Nancy Rubins
Thomas Ruff
Ed Ruscha
Jenny Saville
Richard Serra
Elisa Sighicelli
Taryn Simon
David Smith
Rudolf Stingel
Hiroshi Sugimoto
Philip Taaffe
Mark Tansey
Robert Therrien
Tatiana Trouvé
James Turrell
Cy Twombly
Piotr Uklański
Francesco Vezzoli
Andy Warhol
Franz West
Rachel Whiteread
Christopher Wool
Richard Wright
Zeng Fanzhi

## Annet Gelink Gallery

**Stand Number H7**
Tel +31 20 330 2066

Laurierstraat 187-189
Amsterdam 1016 PL
The Netherlands
Tel +31 20 330 2066
Fax +31 20 330 2065
info@annetgelink.com
www.annetgelink.com

**Contact**
Annet Gelink
Floor Wullems
Carolien Sijberden
Macarena Dupouy

**Artists**
Yael Bartana
Ed van der Elsken
Alicia Framis
Anya Gallaccio
Ryan Gander
Roger Hiorns
Carla Klein
Meiro Koizumi
Kiki Lamers
Erik van Lieshout
David Maljkovic
Dan McCarthy
Wilfredo Prieto
Muzi Quawson
Sarah van Sonsbeeck
Glenn Sorensen
Barbara Visser
Marijke van Warmerdam
Erik Wesselo

## A Gentil Carioca

**Stand Number G17**
Tel +55 21 2222 1651

Rua Gonçalves Lêdo 17
Rio de Janeiro 20060-020
Brazil
Tel +55 21 2222 1651
Fax +55 21 2222 1651
correio@agentilcarioca.com.br
www.agentilcarioca.com.br

Avenida Epitássio Pessoa
1674/401 Lagoa
Rio de Janeiro 22411-071
Brazil
Tel +55 21 2523 1157

**Contact**
Marcio Botner
Laura Lima
Ernesto Neto

**Artists**
Ricardo Basbaum
José Bento
Marcio Botner & Pedro Agilson
Cabelo
Carlos Contente
Guga Ferraz
Fabiano Gonper
Maria Laet
Laura Lima
Jarbas Lopes
Renata Lucas
Simone Michelin
João Modé
Paulo Nenflidio
Maria Nepomuceno
Bernardo Ramalho
Thiago Rocha Pitta
Rodrigo Torres
Pedro Varela
Alexandre Vogler

## Gerhardsen Gerner

**Stand Number F20**
Tel +49 172 155 4667

Holzmarktstrasse 15-18
S-Bahnbogen 46
Berlin 10179
Germany
Tel +49 30 6951 8341
Fax +49 30 6951 8342
office@gerhardsengerner.com
www.gerhardsengerner.com

Fru Kroghs brygge 4
Oslo 0252
Norway
Tel +47 219 10 191

**Contact**
Atle Gerhardsen
Nicolai Gerner-Mathisen
Marina Gerner-Mathisen
Dominique Wenzel

**Artists**
Amy Adler
Edgar Bryan
Jan Christensen
Carroll Dunham
Lothar Hempel
David Korty
Jim Lambie
Shintaro Miyake
Markus Oehlen
Julian Opie
Lari Pittman
Tal R
Ingegerd Råman
Matthew Ritchie
David Salle
Dirk Stewen
Annika Ström
James White
Andrea Winkler
Ronnie Yarisal & Katja Kublitz

## François Ghebaly Gallery

**Stand Number R21**
Tel +1 310 280 0777

2600 South La Cienega Boulevard
Los Angeles
California 90034
United States
Tel +1 310 280 0777
info@ghebaly.com
www.ghebaly.com

**Contact**
François Ghebaly
Karisa Morante

**Frame Artist**
Mike Kuchar

**Artists**
Dan Bayles
Neïl Beloufa
Marius Bercea
Channa Horwitz
Patrick Jackson
Joel Kyack
Anthony Lepore
David Levine
Candice Lin
Michael Müller
Gina Osterloh
Robert Russell

## Greene Naftali

**Stand Number B10**
Tel +1 212 463 7770

508 West 26th Street 8th Floor
New York NY 10001
United States
Tel +1 212 463 7770
Fax +1 212 463 0890
info@greenenaftaligallery.com
www.greenenaftaligallery.com

**Contact**
Carol Greene
Alexandra Tuttle
Vera Alemani
Jeffrey Rowledge

**Artists**
Trisha Baga
Julie Becker
Bernadette Corporation
Paul Chan
Guy de Cointet
Tony Conrad
Jim Drain
Ida Ekblad
Harun Farocki
Günther Förg
Michael Fullerton
Gelitin
Daan van Golden
Lucy Gunning
Guyton\Walker
Rachel Harrison
Richard Hawkins
Sophie von Hellermann
Jacqueline Humphries
John Knight
Joachim Koester
Michael Krebber
William Leavitt
Michaela Meise
Bjarne Melgaard
Daniel Pflumm
Daniela Rossell
Allen Ruppersberg
Paul Sharits
Gedi Sibony
Josef Strau
Katharina Wulff
Haegue Yang

## greengrassi

**Stand Number D17**
Tel +44 20 7840 9101

1a Kempsford Road
London SE11 4NU
United Kingdom
Tel +44 20 7840 9101
Fax +44 20 7840 9102
info@greengrassi.com
www.greengrassi.com

**Contact**
Cornelia Grassi
Charlaine Brandy
Edwige Cochois
Davide Minuti
Christian Baert

**Artists**
Tomma Abts
Stefano Arienti
Jennifer Bornstein
Moyra Davey
Roe Ethridge
Gretchen Faust
Vincent Fecteau
Giuseppe Gabellone
Joanne Greenbaum
Ellen Gronemeyer
Janice Kerbel
Shio Kusaka
Sean Landers
Simon Ling
Margherita Manzelli
David Musgrave
Kristen Oppenheim
Silke Otto-Knapp
Jennifer Pastor
Alessandro Pessoli
Karin Ruggaber
Allen Ruppersberg
Anne Ryan
Frances Stark
Jennifer Steinkamp
Pae White
Lisa Yuskavage

## Galerie Karin Guenther

**Stand Number H6**
Tel +49 170 556 6994

Admiralitätstrasse 71
Hamburg 20459
Germany
Tel +49 40 3750 3450
info@galerie-karin-guenther.de
www.galerie-karin-guenther.de

**Contact**
Karin Guenther
Harald Popp

**Artists**
Markus Amm
Michael Bauch
Henning Bohl
Wolfgang Breuer
Friederike Clever
Edith Dekyndt
Jeanne Faust
Berta Fischer
Ellen Gronemeyer
Michael Hakimi
Alexander Heim
Kerstin Kartscher
Janice Kerbel
Stefan Kern
Nina Könnemann
Michaela Melián
Claudia & Julia Müller
Silke Otto-Knapp
Gunter Reski
Allen Ruppersberg
Dirk Stewen
Stefan Thater

## Jack Hanley Gallery

**Stand Number A9**
Tel +1 646 918 6824

136 Watts Street
New York NY 10013
United States
Tel +1 646 918 6824
mail@jackhanley.com
www.jackhanley.com

**Contact**
Jack Hanley
Kara Kazanoff
Brandy Carstens

**Artists**
Tauba Auerbach
Ajit Chauhan
Bjorn Copeland
Thomas Dozol
Bernhard Fuchs
Folke Koebberling & Martin Kaltwasser
Margaret Lee
Marie Lorenz
Alicia McCarthy
Aris Moore
Eleanor Moreton
Shaun Odell
Jeff Olsson
Emily Prince
Maeghan Reid
Andrei Roiter
Alex Schweder
Erwin Wurm

## Hauser & Wirth

**Stand Number C8**
Tel +44 20 7287 2300

196A Piccadilly
London W1J 9DY
United Kingdom

23 Savile Row
London W1S 2ET
United Kingdom
Tel +44 20 7287 2300
Fax +44 20 7287 6600
london@hauserwirth.com
www.hauserwirth.com

32 East 69th Street
New York NY 10021
United States
Tel +1 212 794 4970
Fax +1 212 794 4971
newyork@hauserwirth.com

Limmatstrasse 270
Zurich 8005
Switzerland
Tel +41 44 446 8050
Fax +41 44 446 8055
zurich@hauserwirth.com

**Artists**
Rita Ackermann
Ida Applebroog
Phyllida Barlow
Louise Bourgeois
Christoph Büchel
David Claerbout
Martin Creed
Berlinde De Bruyckere
Martin Eder
Ellen Gallagher
Isa Genzken
Dan Graham
Rodney Graham
Subodh Gupta
Mary Heilmann
The Estate of Eva Hesse
Andy Hope 1930
Roni Horn
Thomas Houseago
Matthew Day Jackson
Richard Jackson
Rashid Johnson
Josephsohn
Allan Kaprow Estate
Rachel Khedoori
Bharti Kher
Guillermo Kuitca
Maria Lassnig
The Estate of Lee Lozano
Paul McCarthy
Joan Mitchell
Henry Moore Family Collection

Ron Mueck
Caro Niederer
Christopher Orr
Djordje Ozbolt
Michael Raedecker
The Estate of Jason Rhoades
Pipilotti Rist
Dieter Roth Estate
Anri Sala
Wilhelm Sasnal
Christoph Schlingensief
Roman Signer
Anj Smith
Monika Sosnowska
Diana Thater
André Thomkins
Ian Wallace
Zhang Enli
David Zink Yi
Jakub Julian Ziolkowski

## Herald St

**Stand Number D10**
Tel +44 20 7168 2566

2 Herald Street
London E2 6JT
United Kingdom
Tel +44 20 7168 2566
Fax +44 20 7613 0009
mail@heraldst.com
www.heraldst.com

**Contact**
Nicky Verber
Ash L'ange
Samara Aster

**Artists**
Markus Amm
Alexandra Bircken
Josh Brand
Pablo Bronstein
Peter Coffin
Matthew Darbyshire
Michael Dean
Ida Ekblad
Annette Kelm
Scott King
Cary Kwok
Christina Mackie
Djordje Ozbolt
Oliver Payne
Oliver Payne & Nick Relph
Amalia Pica
Nick Relph
Tony Swain
Donald Urquhart
Klaus Weber
Nicole Wermers

## Hollybush Gardens

**Stand Number S15**
Tel +44 20 7739 9651

Unit 2 B.J. House
10-14 Hollybush Gardens
London E2 9QP
United Kingdom
Tel +44 20 7739 9651
office@hollybushgardens.co.uk
www.hollybushgardens.co.uk

**Contact**
Lisa Panting
Malin Ståhl

**Focus Artists**
Eline McGeorge
Karl Holmqvist

**Artists**
Johanna Billing
Andrea Büttner
Knut Henrik Henriksen
Claire Hooper
Anja Kirschner & David Panos
Benoît Maire
Bruno Pacheco
Falke Pisano
Ruth Proctor

## Hotel

**Stand Number F5**
Tel +44 20 7729 3122

4 Herald Street
London E2 6JT
United Kingdom
Tel +44 20 7729 3122
email@generalhotel.org
www.generalhotel.org

**Contact**
Darren Flook
Christabel Stewart
Emma Fernberger

**Artists**
Mike Bouchet
Carol Bove
Wolfgang Breuer
Agnieszka Brzezanska
Duncan Campbell
Anders Clausen
Keith Farquhar
Alistair Frost
Judith Hopf
Richard Kern
Alan Michael
Joyce Pensato
Torsten Slama
Alexis Marguerite Teplin
Stefan Thater
Mark van Yetter

## Ingleby Gallery

**Stand Number G19**
Tel +44 131 556 4441

15 Calton Road
Edinburgh EH8 8DL
United Kingdom
Tel +44 131 556 4441
info@inglebygallery.com
www.inglebygallery.com

**Contact**
Richard Ingleby
Florence Ingleby

**Artists**
Roger Ackling
David Austen
David Batchelor
Thomas Joshua Cooper
Ian Davenport
Susan Derges
Iran do Espírito Santo
Ian Hamilton Finlay
Richard Forster
Tommy Grace
Howard Hodgkin
James Hugonin
Callum Innes
Peter Liversidge
Jeremy Millar
Andrew Miller
Garry Fabian Miller
Harland Miller
Craig Murray-Orr
Jonathan Owen
Katie Paterson
Winston Roeth
Kay Rosen
Sean Scully
Alison Watt

## International Art Objects Galleries

**Stand Number G16**
Tel +1 323 965 2264

6086 Comey Avenue
Los Angeles CA 90034
United States
Tel +1 323 965 2264
info@international.la
www.international.la

**Contact**
Steve Hanson

**Artists**
Sarah Braman
Paul Cherwick
Mason Cooley
Bjorn Copeland
Sam Falls
Kim Fisher
Morgan Fisher
Mark Hagen
Thomas Helbig
David Korty
Sean Landers
J.P. Munro
Andy Ouchi
Seb Patane
Jonathan Pylypchuk
Jon Rafman
Eric Wesley
Pae White
T.J. Wilcox
Thomas Zipp

## Taka Ishii Gallery

**Stand Number B5**
Tel +81 3 5646 6050

1-3-2 5f Kiyosumi
Koto-ku
Tokyo 135-0024
Japan
Tel +81 3 5646 6050
Fax +81 3 3642 3067
tig@takaishiigallery.com
www.takaishiigallery.com

6-6-9 Roppongi 2f
Minato-ku
Tokyo 106-0032
Japan
Tel +81 3 6447 1035
Fax +81 3 6447 1036

**Contact**
Takayuki Ishii
Elisa Uematsu
Jeffrey Ian Rosen
Nahoko Yamaguchi
Junko Yasumaru

**Artists**
Amy Adler
Ei Arakawa
Nobuyoshi Araki
Thomas Demand
Michael Elmgreen & Ingar Dragset
Mario Garcia Torres
Tomoo Gokita
Dan Graham
Naoya Hatakeyama
Nobuya Hoki
Takashi Ishida
Zon Ito
Naoto Kawahara
Annette Kelm
Yuki Kimura
Sean Landers
Lisa Lapinski
Yukinori Maeda
Helen Mirra
Daido Moriyama
Kyoko Murase
Silke Otto-Knapp
Sterling Ruby
Hiroe Saeki
Taro Shinoda
Kei Takemura
Marijke van Warmerdam
Christopher Wool
Cerith Wyn Evans

## Alison Jacques Gallery

**Stand Number D15**
Tel +44 20 7631 4720

16-18 Berners Street
London W1T 3LN
United Kingdom
Tel +44 20 7631 4720
info@alisonjacquesgallery.com
www.alisonjacquesgallery.com

**Contact**
Alison Jacques
Roger Tatley

**Artists**
Haluk Akakçe
Michael Bauer
Lygia Clark
Tomory Dodge
Dan Fischer
Saul Fletcher
Matt Johnson
Ian Kiaer
Klara Kristalova
Graham Little
Robert Mapplethorpe
Ryan McGinley
Ana Mendieta
Paul Morrison
Ryan Mosley
Michael van Ofen
Hélio Oiticica
Alessandro Raho
Bernd Ribbeck
Dorothea Tanning
Mathew Weir
Hannah Wilke
Catherine Yass
Thomas Zipp

## Galerie Martin Janda

**Stand Number G10**
Tel +43 664 233 5429

Eschenbachgasse 11
Vienna 1010
Austria
Tel +43 1 585 7371
galerie@martinjanda.at
www.martinjanda.at

**Contact**
Martin Janda
Elisabeth Konrath

**Artists**
Martin Arnold
Alessandro Balteo Yazbeck
Benjamin Butler
Adriana Czernin
Svenja Deininger
Milena Dragicevic
Werner Feiersinger
Giuseppe Gabellone
Christine & Irene Hohenbüchler
Christian Hutzinger
Raoul De Keyser
Jakob Kolding
Július Koller
Jan Merta
Roman Ondák
Peter Pommerer
Allen Ruppersberg
Joe Scanlan
Ene-Liis Semper
Gabriel Sierra
Roman Signer
Adrien Tirtiaux
Johannes Vogl
Maja Vukoje
Corinne Wasmuht
Donelle Woolford
Sharon Ya'ari
Jun Yang
Jakub Julian Ziolkowski

## Johnen Galerie

**Stand Number D1**
Tel +49 171 218 2360

Marienstrasse 10
Berlin 10117
Germany
Tel +49 30 2758 3030
mail@johnengalerie.de
www.johnengalerie.de

**Contact**
Jörg Johnen
Cornelia Tischmacher
Manuel Miseur

**Artists**
Jānis Avotiņš
Stephan Balkenhol
Roger Ballen
Stefan Bertalan
Martin Boyce
Michał Budny
Rafał Bujnowski
David Claerbout
James Coleman
Martin Creed
Slawomir Elsner
Elger Esser
Hans-Peter Feldmann
Ryan Gander
Francesco Gennari
Dan Graham
Rodney Graham
Andrew Grassie
David Hahlbrock
Candida Höfer
Olaf Holzapfel
Martin Honert
Raimer Jochims
Robert Kúsmirowski
Tim Lee
Liu Ye
Victor Man
Jan Merta
The Estate of Florin Mitroi
Yoshitomo Nara
Michael van Ofen
Roman Ondák
Pietro Roccasalva
Thomas Ruff
Anri Sala
Wilhelm Sasnal
Tino Sehgal
Helmut Stallaerts
Jeff Wall

## Annely Juda Fine Art

**Stand Number F9**
Tel +44 7802 461 576

23 Dering Street
London W1S 1AW
United Kingdom
Tel +44 20 7629 7578
Fax +44 20 7491 2139
ajfa@annelyjudafineart.co.uk
www.annelyjudafineart.co.uk

**Contact**
David Juda

**Artists**
Roger Ackling
Anthony Caro
Alan Charlton
Eduardo Chillida
Christo
Prunella Clough
Duan Jianyu
Lesley Foxcroft
Gloria Friedmann
Katsura Funakoshi
Philipp Goldbach
Alan Green
Nigel Hall
Werner Haypeter
David Hockney
Sigrid Holmwood
Peter Kalkhof
Tadashi Kawamata
Leon Kossoff
Darren Lago
Edwina Leapman
The Estate of Kenneth and Mary Martin
Michael Michaeledes
David Nash
Sarah Oppenheimer
Alan Reynolds
Kazuo Shiraga
Yuko Shiraishi
Suzanne Treister
Graham Williams

## Casey Kaplan

**Stand Number B4**
Tel +1 212 645 7335

525 West 21st Street
New York NY 10011
United States
Tel +1 212 645 7335
Fax +1 212 645 7835
info@caseykaplangallery.com
www.caseykaplangallery.com

**Contact**
Casey Kaplan
Loring Randolph
Alice Conconi

**Artists**
Henning Bohl
Matthew Brannon
Jeff Burton
Nathan Carter
Jason Dodge
Trisha Donnelly
Geoffrey Farmer
Liam Gillick
Giorgio Griffa
Annika von Hausswolff
Brian Jungen
Jonathan Monk
Marlo Pascual
Diego Perrone
Pietro Roccasalva
Julia Schmidt
Simon Starling
David Thorpe
Gabriel Vormstein
Garth Weiser
Johannes Wohnseifer

## Georg Kargl Fine Arts

**Stand Number D16**
Tel +43 1 585 4199

Schleifmühlgasse 5
Vienna 1040
Austria
Tel +43 1 585 4199
Fax +43 1 5854 1999
office@georgkargl.com
www.georgkargl.com

**Contact**
Georg Kargl
Fiona Liewehr

**Artists**
Richard Artschwager
Carter
Clegg & Guttmann
Martin Dammann
Koenraad Dedobbeleer
Mark Dion
Marcel van Eeden
Andreas Fogarasi
Michael Gumhold
Jitka Hanzlová
Herbert Hinteregger
Chris Johanson
Herwig Kempinger
Bernhard Leitner
Thomas Locher
Inés Lombardi
David Maljkovic
Christian Phillip Müller
Matt Mullican
Muntean/Rosenblum
Max Peintner
Gerwald Rockenschaub
Markus Schinwald
Nedko Solakov
Erwin Thorn
Gabi Trinkaus
Rosemarie Trockel
Nadim Vardag
Costa Vece
Ina Weber
Cerith Wyn Evans

## Galleri Magnus Karlsson

**Stand Number E1**
Tel +46 70 810 6906

Fredsgatan 12
Stockholm 11152
Sweden
Tel +46 8 660 4353
info@gallerimagnuskarlsson.com
www.gallerimagnuskarlsson.com

**Contact**
Magnus Karlsson
Inka Lindergård

**Artists**
Mamma Andersson
Roger Andersson
Lars Arrhenius
Amy Bennett
Mette Björnberg
Thomas Broomé
Amy Cutler
Marcel Dzama
Niklas Eneblom
Sara-Vide Ericson
Jens Fänge
Carl Hammoud
Tommy Hilding
Kent Iwemyr
Richard Johansson
Susanne Johansson (ex-Simonson)
Lisa Jonasson
Johanna Karlsson
Bruno Knutman
Peter Köhler
Klara Kristalova
Hans Lannér
Petra Lindholm
Ulf Lundin
Anne-Marie Nordin
Maria Nordin
Jockum Nordström
Johannes Nyholm
Jeff Olsson
Charlie Roberts

## Karma International

**Stand Number S14**
Tel +41 76 327 22 78

Hönggerstrasse 40
Zurich 8037
Switzerland
Tel +41 43 535 8591
info@karmainternational.org
www.karmainternational.org

**Contact**
Marina Leuenberger
Karolina Dankow

**Focus Artists**
Thomas Julier
Tobias Madison
Thomas Sauter

**Artists**
Kim Seob Boninsegni
Agnieszka Brzezanska
Ida Ekblad
David Hominal
Carissa Rodriguez
Pamela Rosenkranz
Emanuel Rossetti
Martin Soto Climent

## Paul Kasmin Gallery

**Stand Number F10**
Tel +1 212 563 4474

293 10th Avenue
New York NY 10001
United States
Tel +1 212 563 4474
Fax +1 212 563 4494
info@paulkasmingallery.com
www.paulkasmingallery.com

515 West 27th Street
New York NY 10001
United States
Tel +1 212 563 4474

**Contact**
Paul Kasmin
Hayden Dunbar
Clara Ha
Nicholas Olney
Bethanie Brady

**Artists**
Mattia Bonetti
Saint Clair Cemin
William N. Copley
Ian Davenport
Barry Flanagan
Walton Ford
Simon Hantaï
Nir Hod
Robert Indiana
Deborah Kass
David LaChapelle
Claude & François-Xavier Lalanne
Morris Louis
Nyoman Masriadi
Santi Moix
James Nares
Iván Navarro
Erik Parker
Elliott Puckette
Nancy Rubins
Mark Ryden
Will Ryman
Makoto Saito
Kenny Scharf
Andy Warhol

## Kerlin Gallery

**Stand Number E17**
Tel +353 1 670 9093

Anne's Lane
South Anne Street
Dublin D2
Ireland
Tel +353 1 670 9093
Fax +353 1 670 9096
gallery@kerlin.ie
www.kerlin.ie

**Contact**
David Fitzgerald
Darragh Hogan
John Kennedy

**Artists**
Philip Allen
Phil Collins
Dorothy Cross
Willie Doherty
Mark Francis
Maureen Gallace
Mark Garry
Liam Gillick
David Godbold
Siobhán Hapaska
Callum Innes
Jaki Irvine
Merlin James
Sam Keogh
Elizabeth Magill
Eoin Mc Hugh
Stephen McKenna
William McKeown
Isabel Nolan
Kathy Prendergast
Norbert Schwontkowski
Sean Scully
Paul Seawright
Seán Shanahan
Paul Winstanley

## Anton Kern Gallery

**Stand Number A4**
Tel +1 212 367 9663

532 West 20th Street
New York NY 10011
United States
Tel +1 212 367 9663
Fax +1 212 367 8135
info@antonkerngallery.com
www.antonkerngallery.com

**Contact**
Anton Kern
Christoph Gerozissis

**Artists**
Nobuyoshi Araki
Ellen Berkenblit
John Bock
Brian Calvin
Anne Collier
Saul Fletcher
Mark Grotjahn
Bendix Harms
Eberhard Havekost
Lothar Hempel
Richard Hughes
Sergej Jensen
Sarah Jones
Edward Krasinski
Shio Kusaka
Jim Lambie
Marepe
Dan McCarthy
Matthew Monahan
Marcel Odenbach
Manfred Pernice
Alessandro Pessoli
Wilhelm Sasnal
Lara Schnitger
David Shrigley
Andy Warhol
Jonas Wood

## Galerie Peter Kilchmann

**Stand Number E2**
Tel +41 44 278 1010

Zahnradstrasse 21
Zurich 8005
Switzerland
Tel +41 44 278 1010
Fax +41 44 278 1011
info@peterkilchmann.com
www.peterkilchmann.com

**Contact**
Peter Kilchmann
Annemarie Reichen

**Artists**
Francis Alÿs
Maja Bajević
Hernan Bas
Michael Bauer
Armin Boehm
Los Carpinteros
Willie Doherty
Valérie Favre
Bruno Jakob
Raffi Kalenderian
Zilla Leutenegger
Jorge Macchi
Teresa Margolles
Fabian Marti
Claudia & Julia Müller
Adrian Paci
Bernd Ribbeck
Melanie Smith
Javier Téllez
Tercerunquinto
Erika Verzutti
Artur Żmijewski

## Tina Kim Gallery

**Stand Number C13**
Tel +1 917 376 2481

545 West 25th Street
New York NY 10001
United States
Tel +1 212 716 1100
Fax +1 212 716 1250
info@tinakimgallery.com
www.tinakimgallery.com

**Contact**
Eliza Coleman

**Artists**
Ghada Amer & Reza Farkhondeh
Gimhongsok
Kyung Jeon
Yeondoo Jung
Eemyun Kang
Marc André Robinson
Joanna M. Wezyk

## Kimmerich

**Stand Number S17**
Tel +1 212 226 0070

50 White Street
New York NY 10013
United States
Tel +1 212 226 0070
Fax +1 212 226 0079
info@kimmerich.com
www.kimmerich.com

**Contact**
Dennis Kimmerich

**Focus Artists**
Alexandra Bircken
Ellen Gronemeyer
Torsten Slama

**Artists**
Steven Claydon
David Korty
Margherita Manzelli
Ivan Morley

## Kisterem

**Stand Number R16**
Tel +36 30 960 1015

Képíró utca 5
Budapest 1053
Hungary
Tel +36 1 267 0522
Fax +36 1 267 0522
kisterem@kisterem.hu
www.kisterem.hu

**Contact**
Margit Valko

**Frame Artist**
István Csákány

**Artists**
Miklós Erdély
János Fodor
György Jovánovics
Katalin Káldi
Johanna Kandl
Tamás Kaszás
Ádám Kokesch
Tamás Körösényi
Antal Lakner
Little Warsaw
János Sugár
Kamilla Szíj
Júlia Vécsei
Gitte Villesen
Anna B. Wiesendanger

## David Kordansky Gallery

**Stand Number C14**
Tel +1 917 859 7747

3143 South La Cienega
Boulevard Unit A
Los Angeles CA 90016
United States
Tel +1 310 558 3030
Fax +1 310 558 3060
info@
davidkordanskygallery.com
www.
davidkordanskygallery.com

**Contact**
David Kordansky
Mike Homer
Stuart Krimko

**Artists**
Markus Amm
Kathryn Andrews
Amy Bessone
Matthew Brannon
Valentin Carron
Steven Claydon
Heather Cook
Aaron Curry
Will Fowler
Patrick Hill
Richard Jackson
Larry Johnson
Rashid Johnson
William E. Jones
Elad Lassry
Thomas Lawson
Alan Michael
Ruby Neri
David Noonan
Anthony Pearson
Mai-Thu Perret
Jon Pestoni
Pietro Roccasalva
Lesley Vance
John Wesley
Jonas Wood

## Tomio Koyama Gallery

**Stand Number B1**
Tel +81 3 3642 4090

1-3-2-7F Kiyosumi
Koto-ku
Tokyo 135-0024
Japan
Tel +81 3 3642 4090
Fax +81 3 3642 4091
info@tomiokoyamagallery.
com
www.tomiokoyamagallery.
com

483 Nishigawa-cho
Shimogyo-ku
Kyoto 600-8325
Japan
Tel +81 75 353 9992
Fax +81 75 353 9993
kyoto@
tomiokoyamagallery.com

47 Malan Road
1-26 Gillman Barracks
Singapore 109444
singapore@
tomiokoyamagallery.com

**Contact**
Tomio Koyama
Yuko Nagase
Daisuke Watanabe

**Artists**
Franz Ackermann
Masako Ando
Ryota Aoki
Naomi Ashida
Stephan Balkenhol
Benjamin Butler
Varda Caivano
Jeremy Dickinson
Tom Friedman
Atsushi Fukui
Nobuhiro Fukui
Daisuke Fukunaga
Nana Funo
Gelitin
Rieko Hidaka
Satoshi Hirose
Tamami Hitsuda
Dennis Hollingsworth
Aya Ito
Yuka Kashihara
Mika Kato
Hideaki Kawashima
Naoki Koide
Makiko Kudo
Masahiko Kuwahara
Toru Kuwakubo
Takuro Kuwata
Yoshino Masui
Shintaro Miyake
Satoko Nachi
Tomoko Nagai
Yoshitomo Nara
Ernesto Neto
Mika Ninagawa
Tam Ochiai
Satoshi Ohno
Yuko Okazaki
Yoko Ono
Rieko Otake
Jonathan Pylypchuk
Tal R
David Ratcliff
Mark Ryden
Tom Sachs
Makoto Saito
Adam Silverman
Laurie Simmons
Diego Singh
Yuko Someya
Kishio Suga
Hiroshi Sugito
Vibeke Tandberg
Jason Teraoka
Gert & Uwe Tobias
Kumie Tsuda
Naoyuki Tsuji
Mamoru Tsukada
Richard Tuttle
Yutaka Watanabe
Terry Winters
Erwin Wurm
Wang Yahui
Keisuke Yamamoto
Masaya Yoshimura

## Andrew Kreps Gallery

**Stand Number C5**
Tel +1 212 741 8849

525 West 22nd Street
New York NY 10011
United States
Tel +1 212 741 8849
Fax +1 212 741 5163
info@andrewkreps.com
www.andrewkreps.com

**Contact**
Andrew Kreps

**Artists**
Ricci Albenda
Darren Bader
Martin Barré
Frank Benson
Andrea Bowers
Daniel Bozhkov
Roe Ethridge
Uwe Henneken
Jamie Isenstein
Annette Kelm
Goshka Macuga
Ján Mančuška
Robert Melee
Robert Overby
Peter Piller
Ruth Root
Cheyney Thompson
Pádraig Timoney
Hayley Tompkins
Klaus Weber

## Galerie Krinzinger

**Stand Number D13**
Tel +43 676 324 8385

Seilerstätte 16
Vienna 1010
Austria
Tel +43 1 513 3006
Fax +43 1 513 300 633
galeriekrinzinger@chello.at
www.galerie-krinzinger.at

**Contact**
Ursula Krinzinger
Thomas Krinzinger
Michael Rienzner

**Artists**
Marina Abramović
Nader Ahriman
Kader Attia
Günter Brus
Chris Burden
Angela de la Cruz
Vladimir Dubossarsky & Alexander Vinogradov
Sakshi Gupta
Jonathan Hernández
Secundino Hernández
Zenita Komad
Valerie Koshlyakov
Angelika Krinzinger
Oleg Kulik
Ulrike Lienbacher
Atelier van Lieshout
Erik van Lieshout
Jonathan Meese
Bjarne Melgaard
Shintaro Miyake
Otto Muehl
Hermann Nitsch
Hans Op de Beeck
Meret Oppenheim
Werner Reiterer
Eva Schlegel
Erik Schmidt
Rudolf Schwarzkogler
Christian Schwarzwald
Sudarshan Shetty
Eliezer Sonnenschein
Frank Thiel
Gavin Turk
Jannis Varelas
Martin Walde
Mark Wallinger
Ding Zhang
Thomas Zipp

## Kukje Gallery

**Stand Number C13**
Tel +1 917 376 2481

54 Samcheong-ro
Jongno-gu
Seoul 110-200
Korea
Tel +82 2735 8449
Fax +82 2733 4879
kukje@kukjegallery.com
www.kukjegallery.com

**Contact**
Eliza Coleman

**Artists**
Ghada Amer
Joseph Beuys
Louise Bourgeois
Alexander Calder
Anthony Caro
Jae-Eun Choi
Sen Chung
Gimhongsok
Kyung-ah Ham
Eva Hesse
Candida Höfer
Jenny Holzer
Roni Horn
Kyung Jeon
Michael Joo
Yeondoo Jung
Eemyun Kang
Anish Kapoor
Hideaki Kawashima
Anselm Kiefer
Hong-Joo Kim
Kira Kim
Sora Kim
Kimsooja
Bohnchang Koo
Hye-Rim Lee
Kwang-Ho Lee
Richard Long
Joan Mitchell
Sungsic Moon
David Nash
Hein-Kuhn Oh
Julian Opie
MeeNa Park
Seo-Bo Park
Kibong Rhee
Choong-Hyun Roh
SaSa [44]
Meekyoung Shin
U Sunok
Lin Tianmiao
Lee Ufan
Bill Viola
Haegue Yang

## kurimanzutto

**Stand Number D3**
Tel +521 55 3433 3344

Gob. Rafael Rebollar 94
Mexico City 11850
Mexico
Tel +52 55 5256 2408
Fax +52 55 5256 2408
info@kurimanzutto.com
www.kurimanzutto.com

**Contact**
Jose Kuri
Monica Manzutto
Daniela Zárate

**Artists**
Eduardo Abaroa
Jeniffer Allora & Guillermo Calzadilla
Carlos Amorales
Miguel Calderón
Abraham Cruzvillegas
Minerva Cuevas
Jimmie Durham
Daniel Guzmán
Jonathan Hernández
Gabriel Kuri
Dr. Lakra
Roman Ondák
Gabriel Orozco
Damián Ortega
Fernando Ortega
Anri Sala
Gabriel Sierra
Monika Sosnowska
Sofía Táboas
Rirkrit Tiravanija
Adrián Villar Rojas
Apichatpong Weerasethakul

# Yvon Lambert

**Stand Number C2**
Tel +33 1 42 71 09 33

108 rue Vieille du Temple
Paris 75003
France
Tel +33 1 42 71 09 33
Fax +33 1 42 71 87 47
paris@yvon-lambert.com
www.yvon-lambert.com

**Contact**
Yvon Lambert
Oliver Bélot
Nicolas Nahab
Mélanie Meffrer-Rondeau
Eléonore Lambertie

**Artists**
Carlos Amorales
Carl Andre
Robert Barry
Stefan Brüggemann
Mircea Cantor
David Claerbout
Jason Dodge
Gardar Eide Einarsson
Spencer Finch
Vincent Ganivet
Anna Gaskell
Kendell Geers
Nan Goldin
Douglas Gordon
Loris Gréaud
Shilpa Gupta
Karl Haendel
Candida Höfer
Jenny Holzer
Koo Jeong-A
Joan Jonas
On Kawara
Zilvinas Kempinas
Idris Khan
Anselm Kiefer
Barbara Kruger
Bertrand Lavier
Louise Lawler
Sol LeWitt
Jill Magid
Jonathan Monk
Roman Opalka
Giulio Paolini
Diogo Pimentao
Charles Sandison
Markus Schinwald
Ariel Schlesinger
Andres Serrano
David Shrigley
Shinique Smith
Mario Testino
Niele Toroni
Salla Tykkä
Nick van Woert
Francesco Vezzoli
Ian Wallace
Lawrence Weiner
Cerith Wyn Evans

# Lehmann Maupin Gallery

**Stand Number F12**
Tel +1 212 255 2923

540 West 26th Street
New York NY 10001
United States
Tel +1 212 255 2923
Fax +1 212 255 2924
info@lehmannmaupin.com
www.lehmannmaupin.com

201 Chrystie Street
New York NY 10002
United States
Tel +1 212 254 0054
Fax +1 212 254 0055

**Contact**
Rachel Lehmann
David Maupin
Carla Camacho
Katelijne de Backer
Courtney Plummer
Stephanie Smith

**Artists**
Stefano Arienti
Hernan Bas
Ashley Bickerton
Ross Bleckner
Billy Childish
Mary Corse
Tracey Emin
Teresita Fernández
Anya Gallaccio
Gilbert & George
Shirazeh Houshiary
Klara Kristalova
Lee Bul
Liu Wei
Mr.
Jun Nguyen-Hatsushiba
Angel Otero
Tony Oursler
Robin Rhode
Tim Rollins & K.O.S.
Rei Sato
Jennifer Steinkamp
Do Ho Suh
Juergen Teller
Mickalene Thomas
Adriana Varejão
Suling Wang
Nari Ward
Erwin Wurm
Mario Ybarra Jr.

# Ignacio Liprandi Arte Contemporáneo

**Stand Number R18**
Tel +54 9 11 6666 3386

Avenida de Mayo 1480
3rd Floor Izquierdo
Buenos Aires 1085
Argentina
Tel +54 11 4381 0679
info@ignacioliprandi.com
www.ignacioliprandi.com

**Contact**
Ignacio Liprandi
Silvina Geddes
Daniela Riva Rossi

**Frame Artist**
Magdalena Jitrik

**Artists**
Pablo Accinelli
Fabián Bercic
Adriana Bustos
Alejandro Cesarco
Tomás Espina
Claudia Fontes
Ana Gallardo
David Lamelas
Mauricio Lupini
Mathieu Mercier
Eduardo Navarro
Jorge Pedro Nuñez
Vijai Patchineelam
Cristina Piffer
José Alejandro Restrepo
Leandro Tartaglia

# Lisson Gallery

**Stand Number B9**
Tel +44 20 7724 2739

29 & 52-54 Bell Street
London NW1 5DA
UK
Tel +44 20 7724 2739
Fax +44 20 7724 7124
contact@lissongallery.com
www.lissongallery.com

Via Zenale 3
Milan 20123
Italy
Tel +39 02 8905 0608

**Contact**
Nicholas Logsdail
Alex Logsdail
Greg Hilty
Annette Hoffman
Jeannie Freilich
Joanna Thornberry

**Artists**
Marina Abramović
Ai Weiwei
Jennifer Allora & Guillermo Calzadilla
Cory Arcangel
Art & Language
Daniel Buren
Gerard Byrne
James Casebere
Tony Cragg
Angela de le Cruz
Richard Deacon
Spencer Finch
Ceal Floyer
Ryan Gander
Dan Graham
Rodney Graham
Carmen Herrera
Shirazeh Houshiary
Christian Jankowski
Peter Joseph
Anish Kapoor
John Latham
Tim Lee
Sol LeWitt
Liu Xiaodong
Robert Mangold
Jason Martin
Haroon Mirza
Tatsuo Miyajima
Jonathan Monk
Julian Opie
Tony Oursler
Florian Pumhösl
Rashid Rana
Santiago Sierra
Sean Snyder
Lee Ufan
Lawrence Weiner
Richard Wentworth

## Long March Space

**Stand Number B7**
Tel +86 1 34 6638 7334

798 Art Zone
4 Jiuxianqiao Road
Chaoyang District
Beijing 100015
China
Tel +86 10 5978 9768
Fax +86 10 5978 9764
lm@longmarchspace.com
www.longmarchspace.com

**Contact**
Lu Jie
David Tung
Li Danqing
Theresa Liang

**Artists**
Chen Chieh-Jen
Guo Fengyi
Hu Xiangqian
Ran Huang
Li Tianbing
Liu Wei
MadeIn Company
Wang Jianwei
Wang Sishun
Wu Shanzhuan
Wu Shanzhuan & Inga
Svala Thorsdottir
Xu Zhen
Yang Shaobin
Yu Hong
Zhan Wang
Zhang Hui
Zhou Xiaohu
Zhu Yu

## Kate MacGarry

**Stand Number E11**
Tel +44 20 7613 0515

27 Old Nichol Street
London E2 7HR
United Kingdom
Tel +44 20 7613 0515
mail@katemacgarry.com
www.katemacgarry.com

**Contact**
Kate MacGarry

**Artists**
Josh Blackwell
Matt Bryans
Tiago Carneiro da Cunha
Chicks on Speed
Marcus Coates
Iain Forsyth & Jane Pollard
Dr. Lakra
Goshka Macuga
Peter McDonald
Florian Meisenberg
Ben Rivers
Luke Rudolf
Renee So
Francis Upritchard

## Mai 36 Galerie

**Stand Number D9**
Tel +41 76 322 5024

Rämistrasse 37
Zurich 8001
Switzerland
Tel +41 44 261 6880
Fax +41 44 261 6881
mail@mai36.com
www.mai36.com

**Contact**
Victor Gisler

**Artists**
Franz Ackermann
Ian Anüll
John Baldessari
Stephan Balkenhol
Matthew Benedict
Troy Brauntuch
Pedro Cabrita Reis
Ernst Caramelle
Koenraad Dedobbeleer
Jürgen Drescher
Roe Ethridge
Pia Fries
General Idea
Luigi Ghirri
Daan van Golden
Jitka Hanzlová
Robert Mapplethorpe
Rita McBride
Harald F. Müller
Matt Mullican
Manfred Pernice
Magnus Plessen
Glen Rubsamen
Thomas Ruff
Christoph Rütimann
Paul Thek
Stefan Thiel
Lawrence Weiner
Rémy Zaugg
Matthias Zinn

## Maisterravalbuena

**Stand Number R14**
Tel +34 66 441 4296

Doctor Fourquet 6
Madrid 28012
Spain
Tel +34 91 530 7889
galeria@maisterravalbuena.com
www.maisterravalbuena.com

**Contact**
Pedro Maisterra
Belén Valbuena

**Frame Artist**
Maria Loboda

**Artists**
A Kassen
Antonio Ballester Moreno
Karmelo Bermejo
Ana Cardoso
Kate Gilmore
Claire Harvey
Erlea Maneros Zabala
Regina de Miguel
Néstor Sanmiguel Diest
Hiraki Sawa
Katerina Sedá
Cristián Silva

## Giò Marconi

**Stand Number E4**
Tel +39 02 2940 4373

Via Tadino 15
Milan 20124
Italy
Tel +39 02 2940 4373
info@giomarconi.com
www.giomarconi.com

**Contact**
Giò Marconi
Esther Quiroga
Teresa Bovi

**Artists**
Franz Ackermann
Rosa Barba
Will Benedict
John Bock
Kerstin Brätsch
Matthew Brannon
André Butzer
Nathalie Djurberg
Simon Fujiwara
Nikolas Gambaroff
Wade Guyton
Richard Hamilton
Lothar Hempel
Annette Kelm
Atelier van Lieshout
Sharon Lockhart
David Noonan
Jorge Pardo
Tobias Rehberger
Markus Schinwald
Dasha Shishkin
Catherine Sullivan
Vibeke Tandberg
Grazia Toderi
Francesco Vezzoli

## Matthew Marks Gallery

**Stand Number C7**
Tel +1 212 243 0200

502, 522 & 526 West 22nd Street
New York NY 10011
United States
Tel +1 212 243 0200
Fax +1 212 243 0047
info@matthewmarks.com
www.matthewmarks.com

1062 North Orange Grove
Los Angeles CA 90046
United States
Tel +1 323 654 1830

**Contact**
Stephanie Dorsey
Jeffrey Peabody
Adrian Rosenfeld
Jacqueline Tran

**Artists**
Robert Adams
Darren Almond
Nayland Blake
Peter Cain
Thomas Demand
Vincent Fecteau
Peter Fischli & David Weiss
Lucian Freud
Katharina Fritsch
Luigi Ghirri
Robert Gober
Nan Goldin
Martin Honert
Peter Hujar
Gary Hume
Jasper Johns
Ellsworth Kelly
Brice Marden
Ken Price
Charles Ray
Paul Sietsema
Tony Smith
Anne Truitt
Rebecca Warren
Terry Winters

## Mary Mary

**Stand Number F19**
Tel +44 141 226 2257

Suite 2/1
6 Dixon Street
Glasgow G1 4AX
United Kingdom
Tel +44 141 226 2257
Fax +44 141 226 2257
info@marymarygallery.co.uk
www.marymarygallery.co.uk

**Contact**
Hannah Robinson

**Artists**
Sara Barker
Ernst Caramelle
Aleana Egan
Nick Evans
Alistair Frost
Lotte Gertz
Torsten Lauschmann
Lorna Macintyre
Alan Reid
Lili Reynaud-Dewar
Gerda Scheepers
Alexis Marguerite Teplin
Maximilian Zentz
Zlomovitz

## Mendes Wood

**Stand Number R17**
Tel +55 11 3081 1735

Rua da Consolação 3358
Sao Paulo 01416001
Brazil
Tel +55 11 3081 1735
info@mendeswood.com
www.mendeswood.com

**Contact**
Pedro Mendes
Matthew Wood
Felipe Dmab

**Frame Artist**
Adriano Costa

**Artists**
Lucas Arruda
Ana Dias Batista
Theo Craveiro
Jen DeNike
Kota Ezawa
Deyson Gilbert
Kevin Francis Gray
Thiago Martins de Melo
Paulo Nazareth
Leticia Ramos
Marina Simao
Diego Singh
Daniel Steegmann
Tunga

## Galerie Meyer Kainer

**Stand Number F2**
Tel +43 67 6517 3116

Eschenbachgasse 9
Vienna 1010
Austria
Tel +43 1 585 7277
Fax +43 1 585 727 788
contact@meyerkainer.com
www.meyerkainer.com

**Contact**
Renate Kainer
Christian Meyer

**Artists**
Ei Arakawa
Will Benedict
John Bock
Wolfgang Breuer
Olaf Breuning
Bernadette Corporation
Verena Dengler
Peter Friedl
Nikolas Gambaroff
Gelitin
Liam Gillick
Dan Graham
Rachel Harrison
Mary Heilmann
Siggi Hofer
Christian Jankowski
Annette Kelm
Elke Silvia Krystufek
Anita Leisz
Marcin Maciejowski
Michaela Meise
Sarah Morris
Yoshitomo Nara
Jorge Pardo
Raymond Pettibon
Mathias Poledna
Stefan Sandner
Isa Schmidlehner
Gedi Sibony
Reena Spaulings
Lucie Stahl
Martina Steckholzer
Franz West
T.J. Wilcox
Heimo Zobernig

## Meyer Riegger

**Stand Number D14**
Tel +49 721 821 292

Klauprechtstrasse 22
Karlsruhe 76137
Germany
Tel +49 721 821 292
info@meyer-riegger.de
www.meyer-riegger.de

Friedrichstrasse 235
Berlin 10969
Germany
Tel +49 30 3156 6580

**Contact**
Jochen Meyer
Thomas Riegger

**Artists**
Franz Ackermann
Katinka Bock
Armin Boehm
Björn Braun
Miriam Cahn
Henrik Håkansson
Sebastian Hammwöhner
Uwe Henneken
Anna Lea Hucht
Jamie Isenstein
Andree Korpys and Markus Löffler
Eva Kotatkova
Kalin Lindena
Ján Mančuška
Meuser
John Miller
Helen Mirra
Jonathan Monk
Melvin Moti
Scott Myles
Daniel Roth
Silke Schatz
Julia Schmidt
David Thorpe
Gabriel Vormstein
Waldemar Zimbelmann

## Andreiana Mihail Gallery

**Stand Number S3**
Tel +40 722 650 221

Strada Vasile Alecsandri 16
Storck Museum
Bucharest 010639
Romania
Tel +40 722 650 221
info@andreianamihail.com
www.andreianamihail.com

**Contact**
Andreiana Mihail

**Focus Artists**
Ion Grigorescu
Ciprian Mureşan
Cristi Pogăcean

**Artists**
Matei Bejenaru
Razvan Botis
Pavel Braila
Tom Chamberlain
Eduard Constantin
Alexandra Croitoru
Katerina Drzkova
Mihai Iepure Gorski
Philip Patkowitsch
Kerim Seiler
Florin Tudor
Mona Vatamanu & Florin Tudor

## Victoria Miro

**Stand Number D2**
Tel +44 20 7336 8109

16 Wharf Road
London N1 7RW
United Kingdom
Tel +44 20 7336 8109
Fax +44 20 7251 5596
info@victoria-miro.com
www.victoria-miro.com

**Contact**
Victoria Miro
W.P. Miro
Glenn Scott Wright

**Artists**
Doug Aitken
Hernan Bas
Jules de Balincourt
Varda Caivano
Verne Dawson
Peter Doig
Stan Douglas
William Eggleston
Michael Elmgreen & Ingar Dragset
Inka Essenhigh
Ian Hamilton Finlay
Barnaby Furnas
David Harrison
N.S. Harsha
Alex Hartley
Christian Holstad
Chantal Joffe
Isaac Julien
Idris Khan
John Kørner
Udomsak Krisanamis
Yayoi Kusama
Wangechi Mutu
Alice Neel
Maria Nepomuceno
Chris Ofili
Jacco Olivier
Grayson Perry
Tal R
Conrad Shawcross
Sarah Sze
Adriana Varejão
Suling Wang
Stephen Willats
Francesca Woodman

## Stuart Shave/ Modern Art

**Stand Number D12**
Tel +44 20 7299 7950

23-25 Eastcastle Street
London W1W 8DF
United Kingdom
Tel +44 20 7299 7950
Fax +44 20 7299 7951
info@modernart.net
www.modernart.net

**Contact**
Stuart Shave
Jimi Lee
Ryan Moore
Kirk McInroy

**Artists**
David Altmejd
Karla Black
Tom Burr
Nigel Cooke
Tim Gardner
Lothar Hempel
Jacqueline Humphries
Ansel Krut
Phillip Lai
Paul Lee
Linder
Barry McGee
Jonathan Meese
Matthew Monahan
Katy Moran
Oscar Murillo
David Noonan
Eva Rothschild
Bojan Sarcevic
Lara Schnitger
Collier Schorr
Steven Shearer
Ricky Swallow
Richard Tuttle
Clare Woods

## The Modern Institute

**Stand Number B12**
Tel +44 141 248 3711

14-20 Osborne St
Glasgow G1 5QN
United Kingdom
Tel +44 141 248 3711
Fax +44 141 552 5988
mail@themoderninstitute.com
www.themoderninstitute.com

**Contact**
Toby Webster
Andrew Hamilton

**Artists**
Dirk Bell
Martin Boyce
Jeremy Deller
Alex Dordoy
Urs Fischer
Kim Fisher
Luke Fowler
Henrik Håkansson
Mark Handforth
Thomas Houseago
Richard Hughes
Chris Johanson
Andrew Kerr
Jim Lambie
Victoria Morton
Scott Myles
Nicolas Party
Toby Paterson
Simon Periton
Manfred Pernice
Mary Redmond
Anselm Reyle
Eva Rothschild
Monika Sosnowska
Simon Starling
Katja Strunz
Tony Swain
Spencer Sweeney
Joanne Tatham & Tom O'Sullivan
Pádraig Timoney
Hayley Tompkins
Sue Tompkins
Cathy Wilkes
Michael Wilkinson
Gregor Wright
Richard Wright

## Galerie Mor Charpentier

**Stand Number R10**
Tel +33 1 44 54 01 58

8 rue Saint-Claude
Paris 75003
France
Tel +33 1 44 54 01 58
contact@mor-charpentier.com
www.mor-charpentier.com

**Contact**
Alex Mor
Philippe Charpentier

**Frame Artist**
Milena Bonilla

**Artists**
Volvspa Jarpa
Oscar Muñoz
Mohamed Namou
Yoshua Okón
Charwei Tsai

## MOT International

**Stand Number S2**
Tel +44 20 7491 7208

1st Floor
72 New Bond Street
London W1S 1RR
United Kingdom
Tel +44 20 7491 7208
info@motinternational.com
www.motinternational.com

Rue Vandenbrandenstraat 1
Brussels 1000
Belgium
Tel +32 2 511 16 52

**Contact**
Christopher Hammond
Aly Afshar

**Focus Artist**
Elizabeth Price

**Artists**
Shahin Afrassiabi
Simon Bedwell
Alan Brooks
Tom Ellis
Simon Mathers
Helmut Middendorf
Beatriz Olabarrieta
Laure Prouvost
Clunie Reid
Florian Roithmayr
John Russell
Cally Spooner
Ulrich Strothjohann

## mother's tankstation

**Stand Number R15**
Tel +353 1 671 7654

41-43 Watling Street
Usher's Island
Dublin 8
Ireland
Tel +353 1 671 7654
gallery@
motherstankstation.com
www.motherstankstation.
com

**Contact**
Finola Jones
Anne Lynott

**Frame Artist**
Kevin Cosgrove

**Artists**
Uri Aran
Ian Burns
Nina Canell
Brendan Earley
Atsushi Kaga
Shane McCarthy
Locky Morris
Mairead O'hEocha
Matt Sheridan Smith
David Sherry

## Murray Guy

**Stand Number F18**
Tel +1 212 463 7372

453 West 17th Street
New York NY 10011
United States
Tel +1 212 463 7372
Fax +1 212 463 7319
info@murrayguy.com
www.murrayguy.com

**Contact**
Janice Guy
Margaret Murray
Jacob King

**Artists**
Matthew Buckingham
Francis Cape
Alejandro Cesarco
Moyra Davey
Patricia Esquivias
Kota Ezawa
Noriko Furunishi
Matthew Higgs
An-My Lê
Zoe Leonard
Ann Lislegaard
Nashashibi / Skaer
Barbara Probst
Lucy Skaer
Beat Streuli

## Take Ninagawa

**Stand Number R20**
Tel +81 90 9870 5594

2-12-4 Higashi Azabu
Minatoku
Tokyo 106-0044
Japan
Tel +81 3 5571 5844
Fax +81 3 5571 5844
info@takeninagawa.com
www.takeninagawa.com

**Contact**
Atsuko Ninagawa

**Frame Artist**
Yukiko Suto

**Artists**
Ryoko Aoki
Dale Berning
Aki Goto
Shinpei Kageshima
Misaki Kawai
Yoriko Kita
Chikara Matsumoto
Yuuki Matsumura
Shinro Ohtake
Aki Sasamoto
Soju Tao

## Galleria Franco Noero

**Stand Number A2**
Tel +39 36 69 57 93 77

Via Giulia di Barolo 16D
Turin 10124
Italy
Tel +39 011 88 22 08
Fax +39 011 19 83 74 08
info@franconoero.com
www.franconoero.com

**Contact**
Franco Noero
Pierpaolo Falone
Matteo Consonni

**Artists**
Darren Bader
Pablo Bronstein
Tom Burr
Jeff Burton
Neil Campbell
Andrew Dadson
Jason Dodge
Lara Favaretto
Martino Gamper
Henrik Håkansson
Arturo Herrera
Gabriel Kuri
Phillip Lai
Jim Lambie
Robert Mapplethorpe
Mike Nelson
Henrik Olesen
João Onofre
Kirsten Pieroth
Steven Shearer
Simon Starling
Costa Vece
Francesco Vezzoli

## NON

**Stand Number R1**
Tel +9 212 249 8774

İstiklal Caddesi
Mısır Apartmani 163/4
Istanbul 34430
Turkey
Tel +9 212 249 8774
info@galerinon.com
www.galerinon.com

**Contact**
Derya Demir

**Frame Artist**
Güneş Terkol

**Artists**
Gökçen Cabadan
Asli Çavuşoğlu
Erdem Ergaz
Annika Eriksson
Extrastruggle
Sefer Memişoğlu
Karen Mirza & Brad Butler
Güneş Terkol

## Office Baroque Gallery

**Stand Number S8**
Tel +32 484 599 228

Lange Kievitstraat 48
Antwerp 2018
Belgium
Tel +32 484 599 228
info@officebaroque.com
www.officebaroque.com

**Contact**
Marie Denkens
Wim Peeters
Louis-Philippe Van Eeckhoutte

**Focus Artists**
Michel Auder
Aaron Bobrow
Mathew Cerletty

**Artists**
Matthew Brannon
Neil Campbell
David Diao
Tamar Halpern
Owen Land
Leigh Ledare
Kirsten Pieroth
Davis Rhodes
Margaret Salmon
Daniel Sinsel

## Galleria Lorcan O'Neill

**Stand Number G13**
Tel +39 06 68 89 29 80

Via Orti d'Alibert 1E
Rome 00165
Italy
Tel +39 06 6889 2980
Fax +39 06 683 8832
mail@lorcanoneill.com
www.lorcanoneill.com

**Contact**
Lorcan O'Neill
Laura Chiari
Serena Basso
Yuri Oliveira
Maria Orlandi

**Artists**
Manfredi Beninati
Don Brown
Juliana Cerqueira-Leite
Francesco Clemente
Martin Creed
Michael Dean
Tracey Emin
Gary Hume
Anselm Kiefer
Matvey Levenstein
Richard Long
Masbedo (Nicolò Massazza & Jacopo Bedogni)
Carsten Nicolai
Luigi Ontani
Eddie Peake
Simon Popper
Emilio Prini
Pietro Ruffo
Kiki Smith
Sam Taylor-Wood
Jeff Wall
Rachel Whiteread
Cerith Wyn Evans
Carlo Zanni

## One And J. Gallery

**Stand Number S13**
Tel +82 2 745 1644

130-1 Gahoe Dong
Jongro Gu
Seoul 110-260
Korea
Tel +82 2 745 1644
Fax +82 2 745 1642
info@oneandj.com
www.oneandj.com

**Contact**
Won Jae Park
Patrick Lee

**Focus Artists**
Yunho Kim
Seung Yul Oh
Jina Park

**Artists**
Minseung Jang
Honggoo Kang
Jongku Kim
Suyoung Kim
Kyunghwan Kwon
Jung Lee
Nikki S. Lee
Dongwook Suh
Joongho Yum

## Pace

**Stand Number G8**
Tel +44 7795 607 639

6 Burlington Gardens
London W1S 3ES
United Kingdom
Tel +44 020 7437 1050
london@thepacegallery.com
www.pacegallery.com

32 East 57th Street 4th Floor
New York NY 10022
United States
Tel +1 212 421 3292

**Contact**
Marc Glimcher
Mollie Dent-Brocklehurst
Leng Lin

**Artists**
Josef Albers
Coosje van Bruggen
Alexander Calder
Chuck Close
Jim Dine
Jean Dubuffet
Tim Eitel
Tony Feher
Adrian Ghenie
Adolph Gottlieb
Paul Graham
Loris Greaud
Tim Hawkins
Barbara Hepworth
David Hockney
Robert Irwin
Alfred Jensen
Donald Judd
Ilya & Emilia Kabakov
Willem de Kooning
Sol Lewitt
Maya Lin
Robert Mangold
Agnes Martin
Roberto Matta
Elizabeth Murray
Louise Nevelson
Carsten Nicolai
Isamu Noguchi
Thomas Nozkowski
Claes Oldenburg
Adam Pendleton
Pablo Picasso
Fiona Rae
Robert Rauschenberg
Ad Reinhardt
Bridget Riley
Mark Rothko
Michal Rovner
Robert Ryman
Lucas Samaras
Julian Schnabel
Joel Shapiro
Raqib Shaw

James Siena
Kiki Smith
Li Songsong
Keith Sonnier
Saul Steinberg
Hiroshi Sugimoto
Antoni Tàpies
Donovan Tara
James Turrell
Richard Tuttle
Keith Tyson
Corban Walker
Robert Whitman
Fred Wilson
Zhang Huan
Zhang Xiaogang

## Maureen Paley

**Stand Number D5**
Tel +44 20 7729 4112

21 Herald Street
London E2 6JT
United Kingdom
Tel +44 20 7729 4112
Fax +44 20 7729 4113
info@maureenpaley.com
www.maureenpaley.com

**Contact**
Maureen Paley
Susanna Chisholm
Oliver Evans

**Artists**
Keith Arnatt
Kaye Donachie
Thomas Eggerer
Gardar Eide Einarsson
Hamish Fulton
Maureen Gallace
Liam Gillick
Andrew Grassie
Anne Hardy
Sarah Jones
Michael Krebber
Lars Laumann
Daria Martin
Saskia Olde Wolbers
Paul P.
Stephen Prina
James Pyman
Tim Rollins & K.O.S
David Salle
Maaike Schoorel
Hannah Starkey
Dirk Stewen
David Thorpe
Wolfgang Tillmans
Gert & Uwe Tobias
Donald Urquhart
Banks Violette
Rebecca Warren
Gillian Wearing
James Welling

## Galerie Perrotin

**Stand Number F3**
Tel +33 1 42 16 79 79

76 rue de Turenne &
10 Impasse St Claude
Paris 75003
France
Tel +33 1 42 16 79 79
Fax +33 1 42 16 79 74
info@perrotin.com
www.perrotin.com

50 Connaught Road Central
17th Floor
Hong Kong
Tel +852 3758 2180
Fax +852 3758 2186
hongkong@perrotin.com

**Contact**
Emmanuel Perrotin
Peggy Leboeuf
Emmanuelle Orenga de Gaffory
Philippe Joppin
Julie Morhange

**Artists**
Chiho Aoshima
Ivan Argote
Daniel Arsham
Hernan Bas
Sophie Calle
Maurizio Cattelan
Johan Creten
Wim Delvoye
Michael Elmgreen & Ingar Dragset
Lionel Estève
Daniel Firman
Bernard Frize
Giuseppe Gabellone
Gelitin
Duane Hanson
JR
Jesper Just
KAWS
Bharti Kher
Kolkoz
Klara Kristalova
Guy Limone
Jin Meyerson
Farhad Moshiri
Mr.
Takashi Murakami
Kaz Oshiro
Jean-Michel Othoniel
Paola Pivi
Claude Rutault
Michael Sailstorfer
Aya Takano
Tatiana Trouvé
Piotr Uklański
Xavier Veilhan
Peter Zimmermann

## Galerie Francesca Pia

**Stand Number G1**
Tel +41 44 271 2444

Limmatstrasse 275
Zurich 8005
Switzerland
Tel +41 44 271 2444
Fax +41 44 271 2445
info@francescapia.com
www.francescapia.com

**Contact**
Francesca Pia

**Artists**
Thomas Bayrle
Isabelle Cornaro
Stéphane Dafflon
Philippe Decrauzat
Hans-Peter Feldmann
Vidya Gastaldon
Aloïs Godinat
Joseph Grigely
Wade Guyton
Fabrice Gygi
Jutta Koether
Elad Lassry
Kaspar Müller
Mai-Thu Perret
Marta Riniker-Radich
Bruno Serralongue
David Shrigley
Josef Strau
Joanne Tatham & Tom O'Sullivan
John Tremblay

## Galeria Plan B

**Stand Number S12**
Tel +49 172 3 210 711

Strada Henri Barbusse
59-61
Cluj 400616
Romania
Tel +40 740 658 555
contact@plan-b.ro
www.plan-b.ro

Potsdamer Strasse 77-87
Gebäude G, 2 HH
Berlin 10785
Germany
Tel +49 172 321 0711

**Contact**
Mihai Pop
Mihaela Lutea

**Focus Artists**
Rudolf Bone
Adrian Ghenie
Navid Nuur

**Artists**
Alexandra Croitoru
István László
Victor Man
Ciprian Mureşan
Miklos Onucsan
Cristi Pogăcean
Cristian Rusu
Şerban Savu
Gabriela Vanga

## Galerija Gregor Podnar

**Stand Number H3**
Tel +49 30 2593 4651

Lindenstrasse 35
Berlin 10969
Germany
Tel +49 30 2593 4651
Fax +49 30 2593 4652
berlin@gregorpodnar.com
www.gregorpodnar.com

Kolodvorska 6
Ljubljana 1000
Slovenia
Tel +386 1 430 4929
Fax +386 1 430 4928

**Contact**
Gregor Podnar
Marie Graftieaux

**Artists**
Attila Csörgő
Vadim Fiškin
Ion Grigorescu
Alexander Gutke
Irwin
Yuri Leiderman
Anne Neukamp
Marzena Nowak
Dan Perjovschi
Goran Petercol
Tobias Putrih
Ariel Schlesinger
Goran Trbuljak
Francisco Tropa
B. Wurtz

## Galerie Eva Presenhuber

**Stand Number C3**
Tel +41 43 444 5070

Diagonal Building
Zahnradstrasse 21
Zurich 8040
Switzerland
Tel +41 43 444 5070
Fax +41 43 444 7060
info@presenhuber.com
www.presenhuber.com

**Contact**
Eva Presenhuber

**Artists**
Doug Aitken
Emmanuelle Antille
Martin Boyce
Joe Bradley
Angela Bulloch
Valentin Carron
Verne Dawson
Trisha Donnelly
Maria Eichhorn
Matias Faldbakken
Urs Fischer
Peter Fischli & David Weiss
Sylvie Fleury
Liam Gillick
Douglas Gordon
Amy Granat
Mark Handforth
Candida Höfer
Alex Hubbard
Karen Kilimnik
Andrew Lord
Richard Prince
Gerwald Rockenschaub
Tim Rollins & K.O.S.
Ugo Rondinone
Dieter Roth
Eva Rothschild
Jean-Frédéric Schnyder
Steven Shearer
Josh Smith
Beat Streuli
Oscar Tuazon
Franz West
Sue Williams

## Project 88

**Stand Number F15**
Tel +44 7772 246 549

Ground Floor
BMP Building
N A Sawant Road
Colaba
Mumbai 400 005
India
Tel +91 22 2281 0066
Fax +91 22 2281 0099
contact@project88.in
www.project88.in

**Contact**
Sree Goswami

**Artists**
Mahesh Baliga
Sarnath Banerjee
Hemali Bhuta
Chirodeep Chaudhuri
Neha Choksi
Baptist Coelho
Rohini Devasher
Shreyas Karle
Monali Meher
Sandeep Mukherjee
Huma Mulji
Asma Mundrawala
The Otolith Group
Raqs Media Collective
Tejal Shah

## Raeber vonStenglin

**Stand Number S18**
Tel +41 43 818 2100

Pfingstweidstrasse 23
Zurich 8005
Switzerland
Tel +41 43 818 2100
Fax +41 43 818 2101
info@raebervonstenglin.
com
www.raebervonstenglin.
com

**Contact**
Beat Raeber
Matthias von Stenglin

**Focus Artists**
Sofia Hultén
Susanne Kriemann

**Artists**
Saâdane Afif
Karsten Födinger
David Keating
Robert Kinmont
Manuela Leinhoss
Taiyo Onorato & Nico
Krebs
Kilian Rüthemann
Ivan Seal
Alexander Wagner

## Ramiken Crucible

**Stand Number R4**
Tel +1 917 434 4245

389 Grand Street
New York NY 10002
United States
Tel +1 917 434 4245
ramiken@ramikencrucible.
com
www.ramikencrucible.com

**Contact**
Mike Ursuta
Blaize Lehane

**Frame Artist**
Lucas Blalock

**Artists**
Elaine Cameron-Weir
Borden Capalino
Nolan Hendrickson
Gavin Kenyon
Andra Ursuta

## Rampa

**Stand Number E18**
Tel +90 530 783 6056

Sair Nedim Caddesi 21A
Akaretler Besiktas
Istanbul 34357
Turkey
Tel +90 212 327 0800
Fax +90 212 327 0801
info@rampaistanbul.com
www.rampaistanbul.com

**Contact**
Leyla Tara Suyabatmaz
Özkan Cangüven
Mehtap Öztürk

**Artists**
Nevin Aladağ
Hüseyin Bahri Alptekin
Vahap Avşar
Ergin Çavuşoğlu
Cengiz Çekil
İnci Furni
Leyla Gediz
Selma Gürbüz
Nilbar Güreş
Hatice Güleryüz
Servet Koçyiğit
Ahmet Oran
Ebru Özseçen
Güçlü Öztekin
Erinç Seymen

## Raster

**Stand Number S19**
Tel +48 22 245 1239

Wspólna 63
Warsaw 00-687
Poland
Tel +48 22 245 1239
Fax +48 78 458 8854
info@rastergallery.com
www.rastergallery.com

**Contact**
Lukasz Gorczyca
Michal Kaczynski

**Focus Artist**
Michał Budny

**Artists**
Azorro
Agata Bogacka
Rafal Bujnowski
Oskar Dawicki
Slawomir Elsner
Aneta Grzeszykowska
KwieKulik
Zbigniew Libera
Marcin Maciejowski
Przemek Matecki
Bartek Materka
Zbigniew Rogalski
Wilhelm Sasnal
Janek Simon
Slavs & Tatars

## Galleria Raucci/ Santamaria

**Stand Number G3**
Tel +39 081 744 3645

Corso Amedeo di Savoia 190
Naples 80136
Italy
Tel +39 081 744 3645
Fax +39 081 744 2407
info@raucciesantamaria.com
www.raucciesantamaria.com

**Contact**
Umberto Raucci
Carlo Santamaria

**Artists**
Hany Armanious
Mat Collishaw
Danilo Correale
Karl Haendel
Georg Herold
Evan Holloway
Hervè Ingrand
David Robbins
Tim Rollins & K.O.S.
Ugo Rondinone
Norbert Schwontkowski
Glenn Sorensen
Cheyney Thompson
Pádraig Timoney
Torbjörn Vejvi
Cathy Wilkes
James Yamada

## Almine Rech Gallery

**Stand Number D18**
Tel +32 2 648 5684

20 rue de l'Abbaye/
Abdijstraat
Brussels 1050
Belgium
Tel +32 2 648 5684
Fax +32 2 648 4484
contact.brussels@alminerech.com
www.alminerech.com

19 rue de Saintonge
Paris 75003
France
Tel +33 1 45 83 71 90
Fax +33 1 45 70 91 30

**Contact**
Anna Fisher
Carlos Cardenas
Amélie Reisinger
Jason Cori

**Artists**
Ziad Antar
Matthias Bitzer
Joe Bradley
Don Brown
Tom Burr
Beatrice Caracciolo
Johan Creten
Aaron Curry
Philip-Lorca diCorcia
Teresita Fernández
Sylvie Fleury
John Giorno
Mark Hagen
Mark Handforth
Gregor Hildebrandt
Patrick Hill
Alex Israël
Xylor Jane
Isaac Julien
Barbara Kasten
Thomas Kiesewetter
Jeff Koons
Joseph Kosuth
Ange Leccia
Daniel Lergon
Erik Lindman
Liu Wei
Curtis Mann
John McCracken
Andrei Molodkin
Joel Morrison
Peter Peri
Richard Prince
Anselm Reyle
Zbigniew Rogalski
Ugo Rondinone
Matthieu Ronsse
Taryn Simon
Hedi Slimane
Katja Strunz
Tatiana Trouvé
Gavin Turk
James Turrell
Ida Tursic & Wilfried Mille
Angel Vergara
Not Vital
Gabriel Vormstein
Franz West
Tsuruko Yamazaki
Yeesookyung
Aaron Young

## Regina Gallery

**Stand Number E12**
Tel +44 77 6733 1219

1, 4th Syromyatnichesky Pereulok
Moscow 105120
Russia
Tel +7 495 228 1330
moscow@reginagallery.com
www.reginagallery.com

22 Eastcastle Street
London W1W 8DE
United Kingdom
Tel +44 20 7636 7768

**Contact**
Vladimir Ovcharenko
Mike Ovcharenko
Nadia Totskaya
Romilly Eveleigh

**Artists**
Victor Alimpiev
Evgeniy Antufiev
Nikolay Bakharev
Sergey Bratkov
Ivan Chuikov
Semyon Faibisovich
Claire Fontaine
Oleg Golosiy
Inspection Medical Hermeneutics
Tigran Khachatryan
Egor Koshelev
Olya Kroytor
Eli Kuka
Oleg Kulik
Vlad Kulkov
Vladimir Logutov
Jonathan Meese
Slava Mogutin
Andrei Monastyrski
Pavel Pepperstein
Jack Pierson
Kerim Ragimov
Daniel Richter
Andrei Roiter
Maria Serebriakova
Natasha Struchkova
Jorinde Voigt
Stas Volyazlovsky
Erwin Wurm
Rose Wylie
Sergey Zarva
Arseniy Zhilyaev
Constantin Zvezdochotov

## Anthony Reynolds Gallery

**Stand Number F1**
Tel +44 20 7439 2201

60 Great Marlborough Street
London W1F 7BG
United Kingdom
Tel +44 20 7439 2201
Fax +44 20 7439 1869
tristram@anthonyreynolds.com
www.anthonyreynolds.com

**Contact**
Anthony Reynolds
Tristram Pye

**Artists**
David Austen
Richard Billingham
Ian Breakwell
Erik Dietman
Peter Gallo
Leon Golub
Paul Graham
Lucy Harvey
Emily Jacir
Kai Kaljo
Andrew Mansfield
Asier Mendizabal
Lucia Nogueira
Walid Raad/The Atlas Group
Georgia Sagri
Nancy Spero
Sturtevant
Jon Thompson
Amikam Toren
Nobuko Tsuchiya
Mark Wallinger

## Galerie Thaddaeus Ropac

**Stand Number F4**
Tel +33 01 42 72 99 00

7 rue Debelleyme
Paris 75003
France
Tel +33 1 42 72 99 00
Fax +33 1 42 72 61 66
galerie@ropac.net
www.ropac.net

Mirabellplatz 2
Salzburg 5020
Austria
Tel +43 662 881 393
Fax +43 662 881 3939

**Contact**
Thaddaeus Ropac

**Artists**
Cory Arcangel
Mahmoud Bakhshi
Jules de Balincourt
Stephan Balkenhol
Ali Banisadr
Georg Baselitz
Marc Brandenburg
Jean-Marc Bustamante
Francesco Clemente
Tony Cragg
Richard Deacon
Elger Esser
Harun Farocki
Sylvie Fleury
Gilbert & George
Antony Gormley
Ilya & Emilia Kabakov
Alex Katz
Anselm Kiefer
Imi Knoebel
Terence Koh
Wolfgang Laib
Jonathan Lasker
Lee Bul
Robert Longo
Liza Lou
Robert Mapplethorpe
Bernhard Martin
Jason Martin
Farhad Moshiri
Not Vital
Nick Oberthaler
Jack Pierson
Rona Pondick
Marc Quinn
Gerwald Rockenschaub
Tom Sachs
David Salle
Raqib Shaw
Andreas Slominski
Sturtevant
Lee Ufan
Sandra Vásquez de la Horra
Banks Violette
Andy Warhol
Lawrence Weiner
Erwin Wurm

## Andrea Rosen Gallery

**Stand Number A6**
Tel +1 646 528 3044

525 West 24th Street
New York NY 10011
United States
Tel +1 212 627 6000
Fax +1 212 627 5450
andrea@rosengallery.com
www.andrearosengallery.com

**Contact**
Andrea Rosen
Branwen Jones
Andrea Cashman

**Artists**
David Altmejd
Gillian Carnegie
Nigel Cooke
Walker Evans
Lizzie Fitch/Ryan Trecartin
Felix Gonzalez-Torres
Al Hansen
Elliott Hundley
Tetsumi Kudo
Friedrich Kunath
José Lerma
Josiah McElheny
Josephine Meckseper
László Moholy-Nagy
Katy Moran
Dan Peterman
Michael Raedecker
Matthew Ritchie
Matthew Ronay
Mika Rottenberg
Wolfgang Tillmans
Ryan Trecartin
Andrea Zittel

## Salon 94

**Stand Number B14**
Tel +1 212 979 0001

243 Bowery
New York NY 10002
United States
Tel +1 212 979 0001
Fax +1 212 979 0004
info@salon94.com
www.salon94.com

12 East 94th Street
New York NY 10128
United States
Tel +1 646 672 9212
Fax +1 646 672 9217

**Contact**
Jeanne Greenberg Rohatyn
Alissa Friedman
Fabienne Stephan

**Artists**
Jules de Balincourt
Amy Bessone
Huma Bhabha
Carter
Liz Cohen
Gerald Davis
Francesca DiMattio
Dzine Dzine
Sylvie Fleury
Katy Grannan
Kara Hamilton
Jon Kessler
Laleh Khorramian
Matthias Merkel Hess
Marilyn Minter
Carlo Mollino
Takeshi Murata
Aïda Ruilova
David Benjamin Sherry
Laurie Simmons
Lorna Simpson
Lucien Smith
Francis Upritchard
Betty Woodman

## Aurel Scheibler

**Stand Number H1**
Tel +49 30 2593 8607

Schoeneberger Ufer 71
Berlin 10785
Germany
Tel +49 30 2593 8607
Fax +49 30 2593 8608
office@aurelscheibler.com
www.aurelscheibler.com

**Contact**
Aurel Scheibler

**Artists**
Michel Auder
Wolfgang Betke
Jonathan Bragdon
Tom Chamberlain
Öyvind Fahlström
Neil Gall
Anthony Goicolea
Ray Johnson
Stefan Löffelhardt
Ernst Wilhelm Nay
Alice Neel
Jack Pierson
Thomas Rentmeister
Bridget Riley
David Schutter
Gavin Turk
Alessandro Twombly
Christoph Wedding
Erwin Wurm
Michael Wutz

## Esther Schipper

**Stand Number A3**
Tel +49 30 374 433 133

Schöneberger Ufer 65
Berlin 10785
Germany
Tel +49 30 374 433 133
Fax +49 30 374 433 134
office@estherschipper.com
www.estherschipper.com

**Contact**
Esther Schipper
Christophe Wiesner
Florian Luedde
Florian Wojnar
Stefanie Lockwood

**Artists**
Matti Braun
AA Bronson
Angela Bulloch
Nathan Carter
Thomas Demand
Ceal Floyer
The Estate of General Idea
Liam Gillick
Dominique Gonzalez-Foerster
Grönlund-Nisunen
Pierre Huyghe
Ann Veronica Janssens
Christoph Keller
Gabriel Kuri
Isa Melsheimer
Philippe Parreno
Ugo Rondinone
Christopher Roth
Karin Sander
Julia Scher

## Galerie Rüdiger Schöttle

**Stand Number H2**
Tel +49 89 333 686

Amalienstrasse 41
Munich 80799
Germany
Tel +49 89 333 686
Fax +49 89 342 296
info@galerie-schoettle.de
www.galerie-ruediger-schoettle.de

**Contact**
Rüdiger Schöttle
Ingrid Lohaus
Sarah Gilder
Sabine Heuser
Susanne Stettner

**Artists**
Jānis Avotiņš
Stephan Balkenhol
Maria Bartuszova
Armin Boehm
Martin Boyce
Chen Wei
David Claerbout
Steven Claydon
Martin Creed
Slawomir Elsner
Elger Esser
Liam Gillick
Dan Graham
Rodney Graham
Thomas Helbig
Candida Höfer
John Knight
Bela Kolarova
Goshka Macuga
Jan Merta
Alex Mirutziu
Thomas Ruff
Anri Sala
Thomas Schütte
Agathe Snow
Thomas Struth
Florian Süssmayr
Jeff Wall
Anicka Yi
Thomas Zipp

## Micky Schubert

**Stand Number E19**
Tel +49 30 4980 8487

Bartningallee 2-4
Berlin D-10557
Germany
Tel +49 30 4980 8487
info@mickyschubert.de
www.mickyschubert.de

**Contact**
Micky Schubert

**Artists**
Marieta Chirulescu
Thea Djordjadze
Graham Fagen
Lydia Gifford
Manuela Leinhoss
Carolin Leszczinski
Barry Macgregor Johnston
Alan Michael
Gerda Scheepers
Daniel Sinsel
Stephen Sutcliffe
Sue Tompkins
Mark van Yetter
Maximilian Zentz
Zlomovitz

## Sfeir-Semler

**Stand Number G7**
Tel +49 172 420 9668

Tannous Building 4th Floor
Street 56 Jisr Sector 77
Beirut 2077 7209
Lebanon
Tel +961 1 566 550
Fax +961 1 566 551
beirut@sfeir-semler.com

Admiralitätstrasse 71
Hamburg 20459
Germany
Tel +49 40 3751 9940
Fax +49 40 3751 9637
galerie@sfeir-semler.com
www.sfeir-semler.com

**Contact**
Andree Sfeir-Semler
Rana Nasser Eddin
Ulrike Heidelbach

**Artists**
Etel Adnan
Mounira Al Solh
Moritz Altmann
Yto Barrada
Robert Barry
Taysir Batniji
Balthasar Burkhard
Elger Esser
Ian Hamilton Finlay
Hans Haacke
Günter Haese
Marwan Kassab Bachi
Hiroyuki Masuyama
Rabih Mroué
Timo Nasseri
Michelangelo Pistoletto
Walid Raad/The Atlas Group
Khalil Rabah
Marwan Rechmaoui
Hassan Sharif
Wael Shawky
Christine Streuli
Rayyane Tabet
Hoda Tawakol
Akram Zaatari

## Sies + Höke

**Stand Number F21**
Tel +49 177 773 0289

Poststrasse 2&3
Dusseldorf 40213
Germany
Tel +49 21 1301 4360
Fax +49 21 113 5668
post@sieshoeke.com
www.sieshoeke.com

**Contact**
Nina Höke
Alexander Sies

**Artists**
Etienne Chambaud
Talia Chetrit
Björn Dahlem
Marcel Dzama
João Maria Gusmão and Pedro Paiva
Federico Herrero
Thomas Kiesewetter
Kris Martin
Jonathan Meese
Michael van Ofen
Fabrice Samyn
Florian Slotawa
Neal Tait
Claudia Wieser
Sam Windett

## Galeria Filomena Soares

**Stand Number H9**
Tel +351 96 237 3956
Rua da Manutenção 80
Lisbon 1900-321
Portugal
Tel +351 21 862 4122
Fax +351 21 862 4124
gfilomenasoares@mail.telepac.pt
www.gfilomenasoares.com

**Contact**
Filomena Soares
Manuel Santos

**Artists**
Pilar Albarracín
Helena Almeida
Ghada Amer
Julieta Aranda
Vasco Araújo
Pedro Barateiro
Inês Botelho
Herbert Brandl
Carlos Bunga
Jean-Marc Bustamante
Pedro Casqueiro
Jan de Cock
José Pedro Croft
Mauricio Dias & Walter Riedweg
Didier Faustino
Ângela Ferreira
Rui Ferreira
Günther Förg
Susy Gómez
Imi Knoebel
Tracey Moffatt
Carlos Motta
Shirin Neshat
António Olaio
Rodrigo Oliveira
Bruno Pacheco
João Penalva
Júlia Ventura
Peter Zimmermann

## Société

**Stand Number R8**
Tel +49 173 694 0624

Genthiner Strasse 36
Berlin 10785
Germany
Tel +49 30 8161 8962
contact@societeberlin.com
www.societeberlin.com

**Contact**
Daniel Wichelhaus
Hans Bülow

**Frame Artist**
Josh Kolbo

**Artists**
Trisha Baga
Samantha Moyer
Sean Raspet
Matthew Schlanger
Timur Si-Qin
Ned Vena

## Sommer Contemporary Art

**Stand Number E10**
Tel +972 3 516 6400

13 Rothschild Boulevard
Tel Aviv 66881
Israel
Tel +972 3 516 6400
Fax +972 3 516 8677
info@sommergallery.com
www.sommergallery.com

**Contact**
Irit Fine Sommer

**Artists**
Saâdane Afif
Darren Almond
Yael Bartana
Boyan
Tom Burr
Rineke Dijkstra
Ofir Dor
Karl Haendel
Alona Harpaz
Tamar Harpaz
Michal Helfman
Gregor Hildebrandt
Itzik Livneh
Muntean/Rosenblum
Adi Nes
Tal R
Ugo Rondinone
Christoph Ruckhäberle
Wilhelm Sasnal
Yehudit Sasportas
Netally Schlosser
Efrat Shvily
Doron Solomons
Eliezer Sonnenschein
Wolfgang Tillmans
Paloma Varga Weisz
Sharon Ya'ari
Rona Yefman
Guy Zagursky
Thomas Zipp

## Reena Spaulings Fine Art

**Stand Number B6**
Tel +1 212 477 5006

165 East Broadway
2nd Floor
New York NY 10002
United States
Tel +1 212 477 5006
reena@reenaspaulings.com
www.reenaspaulings.com

**Contact**
Emily Sundblad
John Kelsey
Carissa Rodriguez

**Artists**
Ei Arakawa
Merlin Carpenter
Stephan Dillemuth
Michaela Eichwald
Loretta Fahrenholz
Matias Faldbakken
Kim Gordon
Shadi Habib Allah
K8 Hardy
Alex Israel
Jutta Koether
Klara Liden
Henrik Olesen
Seth Price
Josephine Pryde
Nora Schultz
Stephen Willats
Lee Williams

## Sprüth Magers Berlin London

**Stand Number D6**
Tel +44 20 7408 1613

Oranienburger Strasse 18
Berlin 10178
Germany
Tel +49 30 2888 4030
Fax +49 30 2884 0352
info@spruethmagers.com
www.spruethmagers.com

7A Grafton Street
London W1S 4EJ
United Kingdom
Tel +44 20 7408 1613
Fax +44 20 7499 4531

**Contact**
Monika Sprüth
Philomene Magers
Andreas Gegner
Franziska von Hasselbach
Patricia Pratas
Iris Scheffler
Andrew Silewicz

**Artists**
Siegfried Anzinger
Richard Artschwager
John Baldessari
Alighiero Boetti
George Condo
Walter Dahn
Thomas Demand
Philip-Lorca diCorcia
Thea Djordjadze
Marcel van Eeden
Robert Elfgen
Peter Fischli & David Weiss
Sylvie Fleury
Cyprien Gaillard
Andreas Gursky
Jenny Holzer
Gary Hume
Donald Judd
Axel Kasseböhmer
Karen Kilimnik
Astrid Klein
Joseph Kosuth
Kraftwerk
Barbara Kruger
David Lamelas
Louise Lawler
David Maljkovic
Anthony McCall
Robert Morris
Jean-Luc Mylayne
Michail Pirgelis
Nina Pohl
Richard Prince
Sterling Ruby
Ed Ruscha
Gerda Scheepers
Thomas Scheibitz
Frances Scholz
Andreas Schulze
Cindy Sherman
Stephen Shore
Alexandre Singh
Robert Therrien
Rosemarie Trockel
Andrea Zittel

## Standard (Oslo)

**Stand Number B15**
Tél +47 91 707 429

Waldemar Thranes gate 86C
Oslo N-0175
Norway
Tel +47 22 601 310
Fax +47 22 601 311
info@standardoslo.no
www.standardoslo.no

Hegdehaugsveien 3
Oslo N-0352
Norway

**Contact**
Eivind Furnesvik

**Artists**
Tauba Auerbach
Nina Beier
Johanna Billing
Gardar Eide Einarsson
Marius Engh
Matias Faldbakken
Ane Graff
Kim Hiorthøy
Ann Cathrin November Høibo
Alex Hubbard
Michaela Meise
Anders Nordby
Chadwick Rantanen
Nick Relph
Torbjørn Rødland
Josh Smith
Oscar Tuazon
Fredrik Værslev
Emily Wardill

## Stevenson

**Stand Number F17**
Tel +27 72 361 1362

Buchanan Building
160 Sir Lowry Road
Cape Town 7925
South Africa
Tel +27 21 462 1500
Fax +27 21 462 1501
info@stevenson.info
www.stevenson.info

62 Juta Street
Johannesburg 2001
South Africa
Tel +27 11 326 0034
Fax +27 86 275 1918

**Contact**
Federica Angelucci
Joost Bosland
David Brodie
Andrew da Conceicao
Sophie Perryer

**Artists**
Zander Blom
Dineo Seshee Bopape
Conrad Botes
Wim Botha
Steven Cohen
Paul Edmunds
Ângela Ferreira
Frohawk Two Feathers
Meschac Gaba
Simon Gush
Nicholas Hlobo
Pieter Hugo
Anton Kannemeyer
Michael MacGarry
Sabelo Mlangeni
Nandipha Mntambo
The Estate of Billy Monk
Zanele Muholi
Daniel Naudé
Serge Alain Nitegeka
Odili Donald Odita
Deborah Poynton
Jo Ractliffe
Viviane Sassen
Claudette Schreuders
Berni Searle
Penny Siopis
Guy Tillim

## Galeria Luisa Strina

**Stand Number F6**
Tel +55 11 8111 0233

Rua Padre João Manuel 755
Sao Paulo 01411001
Brazil
Tel +55 11 3088 2471
Fax +55 11 3064 6391
info@galerialuisastrina.com.br
www.galerialuisastrina.com.br

**Contact**
Luisa Malzoni Strina
Marli Matsumoto
Maria Quiroga
Ada Hennel

**Artists**
Pablo Accinelli
Caetano de Almeida
Juan Araujo
Alessandro Balteo Yazbeck
Laura Belém
Erick Beltrán
Alexandre da Cunha
Matias Duville
Marcius Galan
Carlos Garaicoa
Fernanda Gomes
Brian Griffiths
David Haines
Federico Herrero
Magdalena Jitrik
Marcellvs L.
Luisa Lambri
Tonico Lemos Auad
Laura Lima
Armin Linke
Jarbas Lopes
Jazmin Lopez
Mateo López
Renata Lucas
Jorge Macchi
Marepe
Gilberto Mariotti
Cildo Meireles
Pedro Motta
Muntadas
Lygia Pape
Nicolás Paris
Pedro Reyes
Marina Saleme
Gabriel Sierra
Edgard de Souza
Adrian Villar Rojas

## SVIT

**Stand Number R9**
Tel +420 608 422 425

Štefánikova 43A
Prague 5 150 00
Czech Republic
Tel +420 608 422 425
info@svitpraha.org
www.svitpraha.org

**Contact**
Zuzana Blochová
Michal Mánek

**Frame Artists**
Lukáš Jasanský & Martin Polák

**Artists**
Vasil Artamonov & Alexey Klyuykov
Habima Fuchs
Andrew Gilbert
Lukáš Jasanský & Martin Polák
Marek Meduna
Markus Selg

## Galerie Micheline Szwajcer

**Stand Number B3**
Tel +32 47 544 1127

Verlatstraat 14
Antwerp 2000
Belgium
Tel +32 3 237 1127
Fax +32 3 238 9819
contact@gms.be
www.gms.be

**Contact**
Micheline Tob-Szwajcer
Caroline Dumalin

**Artists**
Giovanni Anselmo
Stanley Brouwn
Angela Bulloch
David Claerbout
James Coleman
François Curlet
Koenraad Dedobbeleer
Luciano Fabro
Hans-Peter Feldmann
Bernard Frize
Liam Gillick
Daan van Golden
Dan Graham
Jos de Gruyter & Harald Thys
Carsten Höller
Ann Veronica Janssens
On Kawara
Mark Luyten
Guy Mees
Matt Mullican
Manfred Pernice
Tobias Rehberger
Allen Ruppersberg
Lee Ufan
Lawrence Weiner
Marthe Wéry
Christopher Wool
Heimo Zobernig

## T293

**Stand Number E16**
Tel +39 34 70 83 65 09

Via Crescimbeni 11
Rome 00184
Italy
info@t293.it
www.t293.it

Via Tribunali 293
Naples 80138
Italy
Tel +39 8129 5882
Fax +39 81 214 2210

**Contact**
Paola Guadagnino
Marco Altavilla
Monica De Sario

**Artists**
Sonia Almeida
Pennacchio Argentato
James Beckett
Simon Denny
Patrizio Di Massimo
Gregory Fong
Claire Fontaine
John Henderson
Henrik Olai Kaarstein
Keller/Kosmas (Aids-3d)
Helen Marten
Dan Rees
Martin Soto Climent
Alberto Tadiello
Tris Vonna-Michell
Jordan Wolfson

## Timothy Taylor Gallery

**Stand Number B13**
Tel +44 20 7409 3344

15 Carlos Place
London W1K 2EX
United Kingdom
Tel +44 20 7409 3344
Fax +44 20 7409 1316
mail@timothytaylorgallery.com
www.timothytaylorgallery.com

**Contact**
Timothy Taylor
Laurence Tuhey
Emma Dexter
Terry Danziger-Miles

**Artists**
Craigie Aitchison
Ron Arad
Diane Arbus
Jean-Marc Bustamante
Armen Eloyan
Lee Friedlander
Adam Fuss
Ewan Gibbs
Philip Guston
Hans Hartung
Susan Hiller
Volker Hueller
Jessica Jackson Hutchins
Alex Katz
Jonathan Lasker
Agnes Martin
Josephine Meckseper
Richard Patterson
Mai-Thu Perret
Fiona Rae
Bridget Riley
Sean Scully
Kiki Smith
Andy Warhol
Lucy Williams

## Team Gallery

**Stand Number E15**
Tel +1 212 279 9219

83 Grand Street
New York NY 10013
United States
Tel +1 212 279 9219
Fax +1 212 279 9220
office@teamgal.com
www.teamgal.com

47 Wooster Street
New York NY 10013
United States
Tel +1 212 279 9219
Fax +1 212 279 9220

**Contact**
José Freire
Miriam Katzeff

**Artists**
Cory Arcangel
Alex Bag
Pierre Bismuth
Vlassis Caniaris
Brice Dellsperger
Maria Eichhorn
Gardar Eide Einarsson
Massimo Grimaldi
Marc Hundley
Ross Knight
Jakob Kolding
Ryan McGinley
Dawn Mellor
Muntean/Rosenblum
Tam Ochiai
David Ratcliff
Davis Rhodes
Sam Samore
Andreas Schulze
Santiago Sierra
Gert & Uwe Tobias
Chris Vasell
Banks Violette
Stanley Whitney

## The Third Line

**Stand Number H10**
Tel +971 4 341 1367

Al Quoz 3
Dubai 72036
United Arab Emirates
Tel +971 4 341 1367
Fax +971 4 341 1369
artfair@thethirdline.com
www.thethirdline.com

**Contact**
Claudia Cellini
Sunny Rahbar
Laila Binbrek

**Artists**
Ebtisam Abdulaziz
Abbas Akhavan
Tarek Al-Ghoussein
Shirin Aliabadi
Rana Begum
Ala Ebtekar
Fouad Elkoury
Amir H. Fallah
Monir Shahroudy Farmanfarmaian
Golnaz Fathi
Lamya Gargash
Babak Golkar
Sherin Guirguis
Joana Hadjithomas & Khalil Joreige
Hassan Hajjaj
Susan Hefuna
Pouran Jinchi
Hayv Kahraman
Laleh Khorramian
Huda Lutfi
Farhad Moshiri
Youssef Nabil
Slavs & Tatars

## Vermelho

**Stand Number H3**
Tel +44 7700 047 657

Rua Minas Gerais 350
Sao Paulo 01244-010
Brazil
Tel +55 11 3138 1520
Fax +55 11 3138 1529
info@galeriavermelho.com.br
www.galeriavermelho.com.br

**Contact**
Akio Aoki
Eliana Finkelstein
Eduardo Brandao
Jan Fjeld

**Artists**
Gabriela Albergaria
Jonathas de Andrade
Claudia Andujar
Rafael Assef
Nicolás Bacal
Chiara Banfi
Rodrigo Braga
Leya Mira Brander
Cadu
Lia Chaia
Marcelo Cidade
Marilá Dardot
Detanico Lain
Mauricio Dias & Walter Riedweg
Chelpa Ferro
Cia de Foto
Carmela Gross
Maurício Ianês
André Komatsu
Dora Longo Bahia
João Loureiro
Cinthia Marcelle
Odires Mlázsho
Fabio Morais
Gisela Motta & Leandro Lima
Guilherme Peters
Rosângela Rennó
Nicolás Robbio
Marco Paulo Rolla
Daniel Senise
Ana Maria Tavares
Carla Zaccagnini
Marcelo Zocchio

## Vilma Gold

**Stand Number B2**
Tel +44 20 7729 9888

6 Minerva Street
London E2 9EH
United Kingdom
Tel +44 20 7729 9888
mail@vilmagold.com
www.vilmagold.com

**Contact**
Rachel Williams
Laura Lord
Martin Rasmussen

**Artists**
Charles Atlas
Trisha Baga
KP Brehmer
Nicholas Byrne
William Daniels
Vladimir Dubossarsky & Alexander Vinogradov
Michaela Eichwald
Felix Gmelin
Brian Griffiths
Sophie von Hellermann
Hobbypopmuseum
Thomas Hylander
Andrew Mania
Karthik Pandian
R.H. Quaytman
Stephen G. Rhodes
Hannah Sawtell
Markus Selg
Josef Strau
Mark Titchner
Julia Wachtel
Jennifer West

## Vitamin Creative Space

**Stand Number E6**
Tel +86 10 5826 3440

Room 301, 29 Hao
Heng Yi Jie
Guangzhou 510300
China
Tel +86 10 5826 3440
Fax +86 10 5826 3140
mail@vitamincreativespace.com
www.vitamincreativespace.com

2503B Building 2
Northern District
Pingod Community
Beijing 100022
China
Tel +86 10 5826 3440
Fax +86 10 5826 3140

**Contact**
Zhang Weiwei

**Artists**
Cao Fei
Heman Chong
Chu Yun
Duan Jianyu
Kit Lee
Pak Sheung-Chuen
Koki Tanaka
Wong Ming
Xu Tan
Yang Jun
Yangjiang Group
Zheng Guogu
Zhou Tao

## Waddington Custot Galleries

**Stand Number G12**
Tel +44 7824 772 028

11 Cork Street
London W1S 3LT
United Kingdom
Tel +44 20 7851 2200
Fax +44 20 7734 4146
mail@waddingtoncustot.com
www.waddingtoncustot.com

**Contact**
Leslie Waddington
Stephane Custot

**Artists**
Craigie Aitchison
Josef Albers
Carl Andre
Milton Avery
Peter Blake
Patrick Caulfield
John Chamberlain
Ian Davenport
Jean Dubuffet
Barry Flanagan
Dan Flavin
Julio González
Peter Halley
Patrick Heron
Axel Hütte
Robert Indiana
Donald Judd
Fernand Léger
Sol LeWitt
Agnes Martin
Henri Matisse
Fausto Melotti
Henry Moore
Ben Nicholson
Claes Oldenburg & Coosje van Bruggen
Mimmo Paladino
Francis Picabia
Pablo Picasso
Robert Rauschenberg
Susan Rothenberg
Haim Steinbach
Frank StellaAntoni Tàpies
Joe Tilson
William Turnbull
Andy Warhol
John Wesley
Bill Woodrow

## Wallspace

**Stand Number E19**
Tel +1 212 594 9478

619 West 27th Street
New York NY 10001
United States
Tel +1 212 594 9478
Fax +1 212 594 9805
info@wallspacegallery.com
www.wallspacegallery.com

**Contact**
Janine Foeller
Jane Hait
Nichole Caruso

**Artists**
Ron Amstutz
Walead Beshty
Kate Costello
John Divola
Harry Dodge
Shannon Ebner
Martha Friedman
Gaylen Gerber
Daniel Gordon
Jiří Kovanda
Laura Riboli
Helen Verhoeven
Donelle Woolford
Mark Wyse

## Galerie Barbara Weiss

**Stand Number G1**
Tel +49 30 262 4284

Kohlfurter Strasse 41-43
Berlin 10999
Germany
Tel +49 30 262 4284
Fax +49 30 265 1652
mail@galeriebarbaraweiss.de
www.galeriebarbaraweiss.de

**Contact**
Barbara Weiss

**Artists**
Monika Baer
Heike Baranowsky
Thomas Bayrle
Geta Brătescu
Janet Cardiff & George Bures Miller
Maria Eichhorn
Nicole Eisenman
Ayşe Erkmen
Harun Farocki
Friederike Feldmann
Berta Fischer
Mary Heilmann
Christine & Irene Hohenbüchler
Laura Horelli
Jonathan Horowitz
Raoul De Keyser
Boris Mikhailov
John Miller
Rebecca Morris
Deimantas Narkevičius
Susanne Paesler
Mai-Thu Perret
Collier Schorr
Andreas Siekmann
Roman Signer
Niele Toroni
Suse Weber

## Fons Welters

**Stand Number G18**
Tel + 31 20 423 3046

Bloemstraat 140
Amsterdam 1016 LJ
Netherlands
Tel + 31 20 423 3046
Fax + 31 20 423 3047
mail@fonswelters.nl
www.fonswelters.nl

**Contact**
Fons Welters
Laurie Cluitmans
Rosa Streekstra

**Artists**
Eylem Aladogan
Tom Claassen
Jan De Cock
Claire Harvey
David Jablonowski
Folkert de Jong
Job Koelewijn
Sven Kroner
Michael Kunze
Zilvinas Landzbergas
Gabriel Lester
Pere Llobera
Renzo Martens
Matthew Monahan
Paulien Oltheten
Magali Reus
Maria Roosen
Daniel Roth
Berend Strik
Jennifer Tee

## Michael Werner

**Stand Number F8**
Tel +44 20 7495 6855

4 East 77th Street
New York NY 10075
United States
Tel +1 212 988 1623
Fax +1 212 988 1774
info@michaelwerner.com
www.michaelwerner.com

22 Upper Brook Street
London W1K 7PZ
United Kingdom
Tel +44 20 7495 6855

**Contact**
Gordon VeneKlasen
Justine Birbil
Birte Kleemann
Kadee Robbins
Harry Scrymgeour

**Artists**
Hurvin Anderson
Georg Baselitz
Marcel Broodthaers
James Lee Byars
Aaron Curry
Enrico David
Peter Doig
Jörg Immendorff
Per Kirkeby
Eugène Leroy
Markus Lüpertz
Ernst Wilhelm Nay
A.R. Penck
Sigmar Polke
Don Van Vliet

## White Cube

**Stand Number F7**
Tel +44 20 7930 5373

144-152 Bermondsey Street
London SE1 3TQ
United Kingdom
Tel +44 20 7930 5373
Fax +44 20 7749 7480
enquiries@whitecube.com
www.whitecube.com

50 Connaught Road Central
Hong Kong
Tel +852 2592 200048

Hoxton Square
London N1 6PB
United Kingdom

25-26 Mason's Yard
London SW1Y 6BU
United Kingdom

**Contact**
Jay Jopling
Daniela Gareh
Tim Marlow
Susan May
Andrea Schlieker

**Artists**
Franz Ackermann
Darren Almond
Ellen Altfest
Miroslaw Balka
Georg Baselitz
Ashley Bickerton
Mark Bradford
Candice Breitz
Ernesto Caivano
Jake & Dinos Chapman
Chuck Close
Gregory Crewdson
Tracey Emin
Katharina Fritsch
Theaster Gates
Gilbert & George
Antony Gormley
Andreas Gursky
Marcus Harvey
Mona Hatoum
Eberhard Havekost
Damien Hirst
Gary Hume
Robert Irwin
Runa Islam
Sergej Jensen
Anselm Kiefer
Rachel Kneebone
Friedrich Kunath
Elad Lassry
Liza Lou
Christian Marclay
Kris Martin
Josiah McElheny
Julie Mehretu
Harland Miller
Sarah Morris
Gabriel Orozco
Damián Ortega
Richard Phillips
Magnus Plessen
Marc Quinn
Jessica Rankin
Robin Rhode
Doris Salcedo
Raqib Shaw
Haim Steinbach
Neal Tait
Sam Taylor-Wood
Fred Tomaselli
Jeff Wall
Cerith Wyn Evans
Zhang Huan

## Wien Lukatsch

**Stand Number F16**
Tel +49 173 615 6996

Schöneberger Ufer 65
3rd Floor
Berlin 10785
Germany
Tel +49 30 2838 5352
Fax +49 30 2838 5350
info@barbarawien.de
www.wienlukatsch.de

**Contact**
Barbara Wien
Wilma Lukatsch

**Artists**
Nina Canell
Abraham Cruzvillegas
Mariana Castillo Deball
Jimmie Durham
Hans-Peter Feldmann
Robert Filliou
Ludwig Gosewitz
Arthur Köpcke
Dave McKenzie
Elisabeth Neudörfl
Peter Piller
Eva von Platen
Thomas Ravens
Dieter Roth
Tomas Schmit
Ingrid Wiener
Haegue Yang

## Max Wigram Gallery

**Stand Number E13**
Tel +44 20 7495 4960

106 New Bond Street
London W1S 1DN
United Kingdom
Tel +44 20 7495 4960
Fax +44 20 7495 4930
info@maxwigram.com
www.maxwigram.com

**Contact**
Max Wigram

**Artists**
Athanasios Argianas
Slater Bradley
Pavel Büchler
Edwin Burdis
Jose Dávila
FOS
Ximena Garrido-Lecca
Christian Hidaka
Barnaby Hosking
Marine Hugonnier
Mustafa Hulusi
Julian Rosefeldt
Richard Wathen
James White
Luiz Zerbini

## Wilkinson

**Stand Number G6**
Tel +44 20 8980 2662

50-58 Vyner Street
London E2 9DQ
United Kingdom
Tel +44 20 8980 2662
info@wilkinsongallery.com
www.wilkinsongallery.com

**Contact**
Amanda Wilkinson
Anthony Wilkinson

**Artists**
Mark Alexander
Kevin Appel
Tilo Baumgärtel
Dara Birnbaum
Juliette Bonneviot
Matt Calderwood
Heman Chong
Clegg & Guttmann
The Estate of Jimmy De Sana
A.K. Dolven
Harm van den Dorpel
Matthew Higgs
Joan Jonas
Tillman Kaiser
Sung Hwan Kim
Thoralf Knobloch
Makiko Kudo
Marcin Maciejowski
Elizabeth Magill
Renzo Martens
Ciprian Mureşan
Robert Orchardson
Anna Parkina
Barbara Probst
Silke Schatz
George Shaw
Shimabuku
Laurie Simmons
Martina Steckholzer
Phoebe Unwin

## Alex Zachary Peter Currie

**Stand Number E20**
Tel +1 212 628 0189

16 East 77th Street
New York NY 10075
United States
Tel +1 212 628 0189
front@azpcgallery.com
www.azpcgallery.com

**Contact**
Alex Zachary
Peter Currie

**Artists**
Lutz Bacher
Rainer Ganahl
Karl Holmqvist
Judith Hopf
Ken Okiishi
Jordan Wolfson
Amelie von Wulffen
Mark van Yetter

## Zeno X Gallery

**Stand Number A1**
Tel +32 3 216 3888

Leopold De Waelplaats 16
Antwerp 2000
Belgium
Tel +32 3 216 3888
Fax +32 3 216 0992
info@zeno-x.com
www.zeno-x.com

Appelstraat 37
Borgerhout
Antwerp 2140
Belgium
Tel +32 3 216 3888

**Contact**
Frank Demaegd
Benedicte Goesaert
Jelle Breynaert
Koen Van den Brande

**Artists**
Michaël Borremans
Dirk Braeckman
Patrick Van Caeckenbergh
Stan Douglas
Marlene Dumas
Kees Goudzwaard
Noritoshi Hirakawa
Yun-Fei Ji
Kim Jones
Johannes Kahrs
Naoto Kawahara
Anne-Mie van Kerckhoven
Raoul De Keyser
John Körmeling
Jan de Maesschalck
Mark Manders
Jockum Nordström
Jenny Scobel
Maria Serebriakova
Bart Stolle
Luc Tuymans
Jack Whitten
Cristof Yvoré

## David Zwirner

**Stand Number G9**
Tel +1 212 727 2070

525 West 19th Street
New York NY 10011
United States
Tel +1 212 727 2070
Fax +1 212 727 2072
information@davidzwirner.com
www.davidzwirner.com

24 Grafton Street
London W1S 4EZ
United Kingdom

**Contact**
David Zwirner
Kristine Bell
Angela Choon
Justine Durrett
Bellatrix Hubert
Greg Lulay
Ales Ortuzar
Hanna Schouwink

**Artists**
Adel Abdessemed
Tomma Abts
Francis Alÿs
Mamma Andersson
Michaël Borremans
Carol Bove
R. Crumb
Philip-Lorca diCorcia
Stan Douglas
Marlene Dumas
Marcel Dzama
Dan Flavin
Suzan Frecon
Isa Genzken
Donald Judd
On Kawara
Raoul De Keyser
Toba Khedoori
Gordon Matta-Clark
John McCracken
Alice Neel
Jockum Nordström
Chris Ofili
Raymond Pettibon
Neo Rauch
Jason Rhoades
Daniel Richter
Michael Riedel
Thomas Ruff
Fred Sandback
Katy Schimert
Yutaka Sone
Al Taylor
Diana Thater
Luc Tuymans
James Welling
Doug Wheeler
Christopher Williams
Yan Pei-Ming
Lisa Yuskavage

# Magazine Index

## Afterall
**Stand M3**
Central Saint Martins
College of Art and Design
University of the Arts
London
Granary Building
1 Granary Square
London N1C 4AA
United Kingdom
Tel +44 20 7514 8173
contact@afterall.org
www.afterall.org

## Art in America
**Stand M10**
2nd Floor
110 Greene Street
New York NY 10012
United States
Tel +1 212 941 2800
Fax +1 212 941 2870
aiaeditor@brantpub.com
www.artinamerica
magazine.com

## Art Monthly
**Stand M23**
4th Floor
28 Charing Cross Road
London WC2H 0DB
United Kingdom
Tel +44 20 7240 0389
Fax +44 20 7497 0726
info@artmonthly.co.uk
www.artmonthly.co.uk

## The Art Newspaper
**Stand M1**
70 South Lambeth Road
London SW8 1RL
United Kingdom
Tel +44 20 3416 3486
Fax +44 20 7735 3322
subscribe@theartnewspaper.
com
www.theartnewspaper.com

## art press
**Stand M25**
8 rue François Fillon
Paris 75015
France
Tel +33 1 53 68 65 65
Fax +33 1 53 68 65 77
servicelecteurs@artpress.fr
www.artpress.com

## ArtAsiaPacific
**Stand M24**
GPO Box 10084
Hong Kong
Tel +852 2553 5586
Fax +852 2553 1199
info@aapmag.com
www.artasiapacific.com

## Artforum International
**Stand M17**
19th Floor
350 Seventh Avenue
New York NY 10001
United States
Tel +1 212 475 4000
Fax +1 212 529 1257
generalinfo@artforum.com
www.artforum.com

## ArtMag
**Stand M20**
Deutsche Bank AG
CC Art
Taunusanlage 12
Frankfurt 60325
Germany
Tel +49 69 9103 5960
Fax +49 69 9103 3188
mailbox.kunst@db.com
www.db-artmag.com

## ArtReview
**Stand M11**
1 Sekforde Street
London EC1R 0BE
United Kingdom
Tel +44 20 7107 2760
Fax +44 20 7107 2761
office@artreview.com
www.artreview.com

## Bidoun Projects
**Stand M4**
Ground Floor
47 Orchard Street
New York NY 10002
United States
Tel +1 212 475 0123
info@bidoun.org
www.bidoun.org

## Cabinet
**Stand M5**
181 Wyckoff Street
New York NY 11217
United States
Tel +1 718 222 8434
Fax +1 718 222 3700
info@cabinetmagazine.org
www.cabinetmagazine.org

## Camera Austria International
**Stand M14**
Lendkai 1
Graz 8020
Austria
Tel +43 316 81555 00
Fax +43 316 81555 09
editors@camera-austria.at
www.camera-austria.at

## Canvas
**Stand M9**
G-07, Loft 1C
Dubai Media City
PO Box 500487
Dubai
United Arab Emirates
Tel +971 4 367 1693
Fax +971 4 367 2645
info@mixed-media.com
www.canvasonline.com

## Elephant
**Stand M22**
Magma c/o Elephant
117-119 Clerkenwell Road
London EC1R 5BY
United Kingdom
Tel +44 20 7242 9503
Fax +44 20 7242 9504
ana@frameweb.com
www.frameweb.com

## Financial Times
**Stand M15**
Number One
Southwark Bridge
London SE1 9HL
United Kingdom
Tel +44 20 7873 3000
www.FT.com

## Flash Art International
**Stand M13**
Giancarlo Politi Editore
Via Carlo Farini 68
Milan 20159
Italy
Tel +39 02 688 7341
Fax +39 02 6680 1290
info@flashartonline.com
www.flashartonline.com

## frieze
**Stand M19**
1 Montclare Street
London E2 7EU
United Kingdom
Tel +44 20 3372 6111
Fax +44 20 3372 6115
info@frieze.com
www.frieze.com

## frieze d/e
**Stand M19**
Zehdenicker Strasse 28
Berlin 10119
Germany
Tel +49 30 2362 6506
Fax +49 30 2362 6505
berlin@frieze.de
www.frieze-magazin.de

## Frieze Masters
**Stand M19**
1 Montclare Street
London E2 7EU
United Kingdom
Tel +44 20 3372 6111
Fax +44 20 3372 6115
info@frieze.com
www.frieze.com

## Kaleidoscope
**Stand M7**
Galleria Buenos Aires 10
Milan 20124
Italy
Tel +39 02 3653 5563
magazine@kaleidoscope-press.com
www.kaleidoscope-press.com

## Leap
**Stand M21**
5F, Tower 1
China View Building
No. A2, Gongti East Road
Chaoyang District
Beijing 100027
China
Tel +86 10 6561 5550
Fax +86 10 6561 0819
leap@modernmedia.com.cn
www.leapleapleap.com

## Modern Painters
**Stand M6**
Suite 410
601 West 26th Street
New York NY 10001
United States
Tel +1 212 447 9555
Fax +1 212 627 4165
kmurphy@artinfo.com
www.artinfo.com

## Mousse
**Stand M2**
Via De Amicis 53
Milan 20123
Italy
Tel +39 02 835 6631
Fax +39 02 4953 1400
info@moussemagazine.it
www.moussemagazine.it

## Parkett
**Stand M18**
Quellenstrasse 27
Zurich 8031
Switzerland
Tel +41 44 271 8140
Fax +41 44 272 4301
info@parkettart.com
www.parkettart.com

Parkett Publishers
145 Avenue of the Americas
New York NY 10013
United States
Tel +1 212 673 2660
Fax +1 212 271 0704
info@parkettart.com
www.parkettart.com

## springerin
**Stand M12**
Museumplatz 1
Vienna 1070
Austria
Tel +43 15 229 124
Fax +43 15 229 125
springerin@springerin.at
www.springerin.at

## Texte zur Kunst
**Stand M16**
Strausberger Platz 19
Berlin 10243
Germany
Tel +49 30 301 045 345
Fax +49 30 301 045 344
verlag@textezurkunst.de
www.textezurkunst.de

## Yishu
**Stand M8**
200–1311 Howe Street
Vancouver V6Z 2P3
Canada
Tel +1 604 649 8187
Fax +1 604 591 6392
office@yishujournal.com
www.yishu-online.com

# Artist Index

# Artist Index

# Artist Index

# Artist Index

Zeno X Gallery A1
David Zwirner G9
**Dozol, Thomas**
Jack Hanley Gallery A9
**Dragicevic, Milena**
Galerie Martin Janda G10
**Drain, Jim**
Greene Naftali B10
**Drescher, Jürgen**
Mai 36 Galerie D9
**Driesen, Stef**
Marc Foxx B8
**Drzkova, Katerina**
Andreiana Mihail Gallery S3
**Duan, Jianyu**
Annely Juda Fine Art F9
Vitamin Creative Space E6
**Dubossarsky & Vinogradov**
Galerie Krinzinger D13
Vilma Gold B2
**Dubuffet, Jean**
Pace G8
Waddington Custot Galleries G12
**Dumas, Marlene**
Frith Street Gallery C1
Zeno X Gallery A1
David Zwirner G9
**Duncan, Zhivago**
Contemporary Fine Arts C12
**Dunham, Carroll**
Gerhardsen Gerner F20
**Durant, Sam**
Sadie Coles HQ C11
**Durham, Jimmie**
kurimanzutto D3
Wien Lukatsch F16
**Dutta, Adip**
Experimenter R5
**Duville, Matias**
Galeria Luisa Strina F6
**Duwenhögger, Lukas**
Buchholz C4
Cabinet E3
**Dybbroe Møller, Simon**
Andersen's Contemporary H4
Laura Bartlett Gallery G14
**Dzama, Marcel**
Galleri Magnus Karlsson E1
Sies + Höke F21
David Zwirner G9
**Dzine**
Salon 94 B14
**Earley, Brendan**
mother's tankstation R15
**Ebner, Shannon**
Altman Siegel S9
Sadie Coles HQ C11
Wallspace E19
**Ebtekar, Ala**
The Third Line H10
**Eder, Martin**
Galerie Eigen + Art G4
Hauser & Wirth C8
**Edmunds, Paul**
Stevenson F17
**Edwards, Gregory**
47 Canal R6
**van Eeden, Marcel**
Georg Kargl Fine Arts D16
Sprüth Magers Berlin London D6
**Egan, Aleana**
Mary Mary F19
**Eggerer, Thomas**
Buchholz C4
Maureen Paley D5
**Eggleston, William**
Gagosian Gallery D7
Victoria Miro D2
**Eichelmann, Volker**
Ancient & Modern S10
**Eichhorn, Maria**
Galerie Eva Presenhuber C3
Team Gallery E15
Galerie Barbara Weiss G1
**Eichner, Marcel**
Contemporary Fine Arts C12
**Eichwald, Michaela**
dépendance S11
Reena Spaulings Fine Art B6
Vilma Gold B2
**Einarsson, Gardar Eide**
Yvon Lambert C2
Maureen Paley D5
Standard (Oslo) B15
Team Gallery E15
**Eisenman, Nicole**
Galerie Barbara Weiss G1
**Eitel, Tim**
Galerie Eigen + Art G4
Pace G8
**Ejlerskov, Ditte**
Elastic Gallery S5
**Ekblad, Ida**
Greene Naftali B10
Herald St D10
Karma International S14
**Elfgen, Robert**
Marianne Boesky Gallery E5
Sprüth Magers Berlin London D6
**Eliasson, Olafur**
Andersen's Contemporary H4
Tanya Bonakdar Gallery A5
**Elkoury, Fouad**
The Third Line H10
**Ellis, Tom**
MOT International S2
**Elmgreen & Dragset**
Galería Helga de Alvear A7
Massimo De Carlo D8
Taka Ishii Gallery B5
Victoria Miro D2
Galerie Perrotin F3
**Eloyan, Armen**
Timothy Taylor Gallery B13
**van der Elsken, Ed**
Annet Gelink Gallery H7
**Elsner, Slawomir**
Johnen Galerie D1
Raster S19
Galerie Rüdiger Schöttle H2
**Emin, Tracey**
Lehmann Maupin Gallery F12
Galleria Lorcan O'Neill G13
White Cube F7
**Eneblom, Niklas**
Galleri Magnus Karlsson E1
**Engh, Marius**
Standard (Oslo) B15
**England, Jane**
Ancient & Modern S10
**Erdély, Miklós**
Kisterem R16
**Ergaz, Erdem**
NON R1
**Ericson, Sara-Vide**
Galleri Magnus Karlsson E1
**Eriksson, Andreas**
Stephen Friedman Gallery D4
**Eriksson, Annika**
NON R1
**Erkmen, Ayşe**
Galerie Barbara Weiss G1
**Espina, Tomás**
Ignacio Liprandi Arte
Contemporáneo R18
**do Espírito Santo, Iran**
Galeria Fortes Vilaça E8
Ingleby Gallery G19
**Esquivias, Patricia**
Murray Guy F18
**Essenhigh, Inka**
Victoria Miro D2
**Esser, Elger**
Johnen Galerie D1
Galerie Thaddaeus Ropac F4
Galerie Rüdiger Schöttle H2
Sfeir-Semler G7
**Estève, Lionel**
Galerie Perrotin F3
**Ethridge, Roe**
Campoli Presti F5
Allied Editions
Gagosian Gallery D7
greengrassi D17
Andrew Kreps Gallery C5
Mai 36 Galerie D9
**Euler, Jana**
dépendance S11
**Evans, Nick**
Mary Mary F19
**Evans, Simon**
Galeria Fortes Vilaça E8
**Evans, Walker**
Andrea Rosen Gallery A6
**Everett, Liam**
Altman Siegel S9
**Extrastruggle**
NON R1
**Ezawa, Kota**
Mendes Wood R17
Murray Guy F18
**di Fabio, Alberto**
Gagosian Gallery D7
**Fabro, Luciano**
Galerie Micheline Szwajcer B3
**Fagen, Graham**
Micky Schubert E19
**Fahlstrom, Brian**
Marc Foxx B8
**Fahlström, Öyvind**
Aurel Scheibler H1
**Fahrenholz, Loretta**
Reena Spaulings Fine Art B6
**Faibisovich, Semyon**
Regina Gallery E12
**Fairhurst, Angus**
Sadie Coles HQ C11
**Faitakis, Stelios**
The Breeder F14
**Faldbakken, Matias**
Galerie Eva Presenhuber C3
Reena Spaulings Fine Art B6
Standard (Oslo) B15
**Fallah, Amir H.**
The Third Line H10
**Falls, Sam**
International Art Objects Galleries G16
**Fänge, Jens**
Galleri Magnus Karlsson E1
**Fanni Tutti, Cosey**
Cabinet E3
**Fanzhi, Zeng**
Gagosian Gallery D7
**Farmanfarmaian, Monir Shahroudy**
The Third Line H10
**Farmer, Geoffrey**
Casey Kaplan B4
**Farocki, Harun**
Greene Naftali B10
Galerie Thaddaeus Ropac F4
Galerie Barbara Weiss G1
**Farquhar, Keith**
Hotel E12
**Fathi, Golnaz**
The Third Line H10
**Faust, Gretchen**
greengrassi D17
**Faust, Jeanne**
Galerie Karin Guenther H6
**Faustino, Didier**
Galeria Filomena Soares H9
**Favaretto, Lara**
Galleria Franco Noero A2
**Favre, Valérie**
Galerie Peter Kilchmann E2
**Fecteau, Vincent**
Buchholz C4
greengrassi D17
Matthew Marks Gallery C7
**Feher, Tony**

# Artist Index

# Artist Index

## Artist Index

## Artist Index

## Artist Index

## Artist Index

## Artist Index

## Artist Index

## Artist Index

## Artist Index

Published in 2012 by Frieze
1 Montclare Street
London E2 7EU
United Kingdom
Tel +44 20 3372 6111
Email info@friezeartfair.com
www.friezeartfair.com

Frieze is an imprint of Frieze Events Ltd,
registered in England number 4429032

Frieze London Catalogue 2012


ISBN 978-0-9553201-9-4

A catalogue record of this book is available from the British Library

Publisher: Anna Starling
Editor: Sam Phillips
Catalogue Co-ordinators: Madeleine Hodge and Amy Sherlock
Copy-editor: Matthew Taylor
Advertising Sales: Mareike Dittmer, Melissa Goldberg and Adair Lentini
Advertising Production: Sarah Hillier

Art Direction and Design: Graphic Thought Facility, London
Layout: Asuka Sawa
Cover and Divider Page Photography: Angela Moore and Graphic Thought Facility
Printed by: Graphicom, Vicenza, Italy

Distributed outside North America by
Thames & Hudson Distributors Ltd
181a High Holborn
London WC1V 7QX
UK
Tel +44 20 7845 5000
Fax +44 20 7845 5050
Email customerservices@thameshudson.co.uk

Distributed in North America by
DAP
155 Sixth Avenue, 2nd Floor
New York, NY 10013
USA
Tel +1 212 627 1999
Fax +1 212 627 9484
Email orders@dapinc.com